45.00

Fantastic Cinema

Fantastic Cinema Subject Guide

A Topical Index to 2500 Horror, Science Fiction, and Fantasy Films

by

Bryan Senn

and

John Johnson

McFarland & Company, Inc., Publishers
Jefferson, North Carolina, and London

British Library Cataloguing-in-Publication data are available

Library of Congress Cataloguing-in-Publication Data

Senn, Bryan, 1962–
    Fantastic cinema subject guide : a topical index to 2500 horror,
science fiction, and fantasy films / by Bryan Senn and John Johnson.
        p.   cm.
    ISBN 0-89950-681-X (lib. bdg. : 50# alk. paper) ∞
    1. Fantastic films — Catalogs.   2. Horror films — Catalogs.
3. Science fiction films — Catalogs.   4. Fantasy — Film catalogs.
5. Horror — Film catalogs.   6. Science fiction — Film catalogs.
I. Johnson, John.   II. Title.
PN1995.9.F36S46   1992
016.79143′615 — dc20   91-51230
                                                            CIP

Manufactured in the United States of America

McFarland & Company, Inc., Publishers
  Box 611, Jefferson, North Carolina 28640

To Gina Beretta and Pam Casteel,
without whose patience, support and tolerance
this book could not have been written.

Acknowledgments

Quite simply, this book could not have been completed without the help of both Terry Senn and Brad Senn, whose computer knowledge made the impossible possible. Also, the interest, encouragement, and feedback given by McFarland was of immense value. Finally, we'd like to express our appreciation to the filmmakers themselves, whose talent, imagination, and hard work have given us films that are sometimes thought-provoking, often startling, and always entertaining.

Our thanks goes to Paul M. Jensen as well, for his excellent late-hour editorial suggestions.

Bryan Senn
John Johnson

Table of Contents

Introduction

(Or, How to Use This Book)

How many times have you wrestled through stacks of magazines, books, or separate articles to find a complete listing of films on a particular subject or subgenre? The *Fantastic Cinema Subject Guide* is designed to alleviate this problem and fill a long-standing void felt by fans and researchers delving into the fascinating, overlapping genres of horror, science fiction, and fantasy.

This comprehensive guide offers an alphabetized listing of 81 subjects. Under each is a thorough listing of genre films dealing with that particular subject, from the silent era into the nineties.

Following a brief introduction defining the subject and its various particulars — origins, highlights, "lowlights," and trends (keep in mind that often the films define the genre instead of the genre defining the films) — you will find the following:

Title of film and basic data: Specifically, its American release title, along with the year of release, distributor, and country of origin (if not U.S.).

Alternate titles: Other titles that the film may have been released under (including renamings for theatrical reissue, television, and video). For reader convenience, all alternate titles will appear in the Index at the back of the book, along with a "see" reference to the film's main title and entry.

Production credits: The name or names of the director (D); producer (P); screenwriter (S); and cinematographer (director of photography) (C). Some of the film entries may lack one or more of these credits (because of the difficulty of tracking down reliable credits for obscure films), though every effort has been made to make each entry as complete as possible.

Cast: A listing of principal cast members.

A short synopsis of the plot with emphasis on the specific element that ties the film to its subject.

Quotes: Many entries will include a quote directly from the film or an unusual ad line or promotional slogan, introduced by the ¶ symbol. (We believe a quote from a movie often speaks volumes about the film.)

Interesting information (set off by bullets "•") about the film—its production, unique nature, behind the scenes details. (A word of caution—the information listed here cannot always be completely reliable primarily because not everything reported about a film, even by its own production team, is necessarily true. Nevertheless, only the information about which we are reasonably certain is included.)

This is a *reference work* and objectivity has been a primary goal from the start. We generally avoid critical analyses, leaving it up to the reader to decide if a film is a classic or a turkey (though in some cases we have made a comment).

In the Index at the back of the book we have included a rating, on a scale from 1 to 10, on each film. Not only does this allow us to voice our personal opinions on the films in a brief and quantitative fashion, but it also allows the reader to put each film into critical perspective within its own subject by seeing how it stacks up against its fellows.

Also included are three appendices—Blaxploitation, 3-D, and Westerns—which offer the reader lists of films which share a common characteristic other than their subject. Each appendix is a straightforward listing of all the horror, science fiction, or fantasy films (along with their respective years) which fit these categories.

Many films cross the boundaries of more than one subject or topic, featuring subplots or aspects which belong to another subgenre. Extensive cross-referencing accommodates these multisubject movies. These cross-referenced titles are, in their secondary locations, listed simply by title, year, and relevant element (revealing the picture's link to that particular subject). The subject under which the film's main entry is located is listed in parentheses after the title. For example, *Frankenstein Unbound* (1990) has its main entry under the FRANKENSTEIN'S MONSTER topic. There are listed the cast, credits, and most of the pertinent information. However, *Frankenstein Unbound* also appears under the TIME TRAVEL topic, as well as FUTURES ON EARTH—UTOPIAS AND DYSTOPIAS. There you will see:

Frankenstein Unbound (1990) (see FRANKENSTEIN'S MONSTER—FURTHER FRANKENSTEINS). The film begins in "New Los Angeles" in the future of 2031, where scientist John Hurt is experimenting with implosion. He accidentally creates a "time slip," which hurls him back to the shores of Lake Geneva in 1817, where he encounters not only Mary Shelley, soon-to-be author of *Frankenstein,* but also the real Dr. Victor Frankenstein (Raul Julia) and his hideous

creature. In the end, Hurt manages to send
himelf, Frankenstein, and his creation into
the barren uncertainty of the far distant
future.

If the reader desires details on an individual film (rather than an entire subject), the Index at the back of the book indicates the page number of that movie's main entry (listed first) as well as any subsidiary entry in related subjects.

This book covers all feature-length horror, science fiction, and fantasy films released before May, 1991. Excluded are shorts, animated features, and foreign films which have not been translated into English (either subtitled or dubbed). Also, we generally did not include films made for television. Each of these film types deserves a volume of their own. Of course, exceptions were made if the film has some historical significance or popular interest. For example, George Méliès' 1902 film, *A Trip to the Moon*: though only 21 minutes long, it was the first true science fiction movie ever produced—and for the time, 21 minutes was an epic in any case.

The subjects, or topics, chosen represent various offshoots of not one, but three major fields of cinema—science fiction, horror, and fantasy. While it would be foolish to claim that this is a complete source (creating a 100 percent complete source is an impossible task, especially with the seemingly endless direct-to-video product being churned out today), we have been as thorough as possible.

Though we've tried to be complete, it is in the nature of the task that we must fail. We welcome any additions, corrections, or suggestions from readers. Please send all information and comments to us in care of McFarland & Company, Inc., Publishers.

The realm of science fiction, horror, and fantasy features will never go away. That is certain. As long as people continue to use their imaginations, the Cinema of the Fantastic will flourish.

The Abominable Snowman

The Abominable Snowman, or Yeti, can still be classified as a mythical monster since no real proof of its existence has ever been uncovered. Sherpa natives making their home in the Himalayas have long since maintained that the Yeti exists, and legends involving the elusive beast are prominent in their culture. Expeditions have been formed, but only strange snow prints and bits of hair have been found. The few sightings that have been reported lack credibility; the prints can be attributed to falling lumps of snow or mountain bears, and the various Yeti hair put forth as evidence has been traced to yaks, bears, or other animals indigenous to the area. Tibetan lamas had even preserved a Yeti "scalp" in their temple for years, until it was discovered to be only a piece of skin from the back of a mountain antelope called the *serow*.

Unlike the Loch Ness monster, whom many in the field of scientific research believe to have some basis in fact (as evidenced by the ongoing investigations), the Snowman has recently fallen on hard times as far as scientific believability goes. The low output of films on the subject reflects this skepticism (not to mention the fact that the Yeti lives on the other side of the globe, far away from most exploitative filmmakers). The only real good film about Yetis is the British-made *The Abominable Snowman of the Himalayas* (1957), which features an intelligent, sensitive storyline and a solid cast led by Peter Cushing and Forrest Tucker. The film's sense of the Tibetan culture and mysticism involving the legend of the Yeti is used cleverly to persuade the audience of the believability of this hairy tale. Although the monster is seen only briefly, its appearance is more human than animal, thus perpetuating the missing link supposition. Screenwriter Nigel Kneale made the Snowman out to be a wise and gentle creature, desiring only to be left alone. He also carefully played with our natural inclination to doubt such a story by having the film's protagonist agree to keep the secret of these creatures' existence and state that *there are no Yetis* (despite his knowledge to the contrary). This gives our sympathies an unconscious push toward the direction of belief in the existence of the Yeti by teasing us with a mysterious coverup. It is unlikely that another serious Snowman movie will ever pop up in theaters until something more concrete or fantastic is turned up (or made up) by the media.

The Abominable Snowman of the Himalayas (1957; 20th Century–Fox; U.K.; also *The Abominable Snowman*) D: Val Guest. P: Aubrey Baring. S: Nigel Kneale. C: Arthur Grant. Cast: Peter Cushing, Forrest Tucker, Robert Brown, Maureen Connell, Richard Wattis, Michael Brill, Wolfe Morris, Arnold Marle. Peter Cushing joins an expedition in search of the elusive Yeti. Members of the team, apparently influenced by the hypnotic ability of the snow creatures, begin dying one by one, apparently by their own hand, until only Cushing remains. ¶ "McNee died from an accident. Shelley

1

One of the shaggy-haired Snowmen from Man Beast *(1956) pops up through the ice.*

died of his own fear. It isn't what's outside that's dangerous, as much as what's in us. • We only see a distorted glimpse of the Yeti at the very end of the picture. Their facial features are gaunt and sharp and lend the impression that the snow people are very old and very wise. They also possess some kind of thought transference ability. • The picture was adapted from a Nigel Kneale TV play called "The Creature."

Half Human (1958; Toho/DCA; Japan) D: Inoshiro Honda. P: Tomoyuki Tanaka. S: Takeo Murata. C: Tadashi Imura. Cast: Akira Takarada, Kenji Sahara, Momoko Kochi, John Carradine, Morris Ankrum, Robert Karnes. Japanese students climbing high in the mountains come upon a big hairy "snowman" and a lost tribe of mountain people. When the Yeti's son is killed by another interested climber who intends to use the creatures as circus exhibits, the Yeti goes on a violent rampage. ¶ "On this occasion it took considerable force and violence to answer but a few questions . . . and there are thousands more still to answer." • The half human beast, revealed to be an evolutionary missing link, is finally killed when it

falls into a volcano. • There are two versions of this film—the original Japanese version, and the American one which contains a running narrative by John Carradine.

Man Beast (1956; Favorite Films) D/P: Jerry Warren. S: B. Arthur Cassidy. C: Victor Fisher. Cast: Tom Maruzzi, Virginia Maynor, George Skaff, George Wells Lewis, Lloyd Nelson, Rock Madison. An expedition in search of a Yeti encounters a group of Abominable Snowmen. One of the team's trackers happens to be a hybrid of the species, and plans to kill off the men and use the girl to "breed out the Yeti strain." ¶ "I've kept this secret for centuries. No man has ever seen us and lived. No man will, until we're ready." • The Yeti tracker, named Vargas, is actually a fifth generation snowman. He falls to his death at the climax when attempting to scale a cliff by rope.

Night of the Howling Beast (1975) (see WEREWOLVES—SPAIN'S "WALDEMAR DANINSKI" SERIES). In this entry, the popular Werewolf character, played by Paul Naschy, encounters a Yeti on a mountain trek in Tibet. ¶ "The full red moon will soon shine in the sky. The demons will come out of their hiding places and their howls will be heard in the night, announcing death." • The Yeti doesn't appear until the very end of the film, when it shows up to grab the heroine and battle the wolfman. The werewolf wins when he rips out the snowman's throat.

The Seven Faces of Dr. Lao (1964) (see MAGICIANS). A Chinese magician (Tony Randall) comes to town with his traveling circus. One aspect of his incredible powers is the ability to transform himself into different beings (ergo the seven faces). One of those beings is an Abominable Snowman.

Shriek of the Mutilated (1974) (see CANNIBALS) (also *The Mutilated*). A college professor and his students are lured to an island by cannibalistic natives with the ruse of finding a Yeti. The snowman is only a cannibal in disguise. ¶ "It walks. It stalks. It tears the shriek right out of your throat" — ad line.

The Snow Creature (1954; United Artists) D/P: W. Lee Wilder. S: Myles Wilder. C: Floyd Crosby. Cast: Paul Langton, Leslie Denison, Teru Shimada, Rollin Moriyama, Robert Kino, Bill Phipps. An Abominable Snowman is captured in the Himalayas and brought back to Los Angeles where it escapes. The beast is finally killed in the tunneled sewer system under the city. ¶ "If there's one yeti, there must be a whole civilization, or a whole tribe."

Snowbeast (1977; TV movie) D: Herb Wallerstein. P: Wilford Lloyd Baumes. S: Joseph Stefano. C: Frank Stanley. Cast: Bo Svenson, Yvette Mimieux, Robert Logan, Clint Walker, Sylvia Sidney, Michael J. London. A ski resort in the Rocky Mountains gets a visit from the Abominable Snowman during their winter carnival. • Filmed on location in Gunnison County, Colorado. • Screenwriter Joseph Stephano was creative genius (with Leslie Stevens) behind "The Outer Limits" television series.

The Yeti (1977; Italy) D: Frank Kramer. P: Mario Di Nardo, Gianfranco Parolini. S: Mario De Nardo. A lost boy encounters a friendly Yeti. • Though an Italian production, the film was shot in Canada and was never released theatrically in the U.S.

Aliens

It has been said that the cinema is a reflection of our cultural, historical, and technological background. This proposition couldn't be more true when it comes to the science fiction subgenre known as the "alien" film. Just as the invention of the atomic bomb brought forth every kind of radioactive terror imaginable, so did the modern space age bring to the fore the concept of life in outer space.

Due to the tremendous scope of this particular branch of science fiction film, we have broken up the subject into three separate subdivisions: INVADERS ON EARTH; ENCOUNTERS IN OUTER SPACE; and BENEVOLENT ALIENS. The largest of the three, INVADERS ON EARTH, has been further subdivided according to the decades in which the films were made—the founding 50s, the 60s and 70s and finally, the 80s and beyond. The films in each of these three subsections have a distinctive style and identity all their own. In all cases though, the aliens depicted are of the "hostile" variety, and are perpetrating their nefarious deeds on our home planet Earth, hence the term *Invaders*.

Alien invasion films have their roots in two human tendencies. First, we are afraid of the unknown. And second, we are usually fearful of those who are different. It goes without saying that aliens are both unknown and different, and most alien pictures do little to dispel our anxieties (indeed, they often play up to our shortsightedness).

One underlying theme pumping through the heart of many of these pictures is the idea that these alien invasions are a deserved punishment for our advancements in technology. That is, these battles for dominion of the Earth may be a direct result of man's technological zeal and bold expansionistic escapades into outer space. In many cases the alien attacks are viewed as them hitting us before we hit them (*Earth vs. the Flying Saucers,* 1956; *Cape Canaveral Monsters,* 1960; etc.).

The granddaddy of all alien films, and the father of the alien invasion cycle of the 1950s, is Howard Hawks' *The Thing from Another World,* released in 1951. *The Thing* was a technically superior sci-fi film in all departments, script, direction, cinematography, and acting. The film's immortal final warning, "Keep watching the skies!" proved to be the battle cry of the 50s, with both audiences and filmmakers alike taking it to heart. There followed an invasion of invasion films, from classics like *War of the Worlds* (1953) and *Invasion of the Body Snatchers* (1956), to cult favorites such as *Invaders from Mars* (1953) and *Invasion of the Saucermen* (1957), to the inferior *Killers from Space* (1954) and *The Beast with a Million Eyes* (1955). Whether good, bad, or merely ugly, they all contributed to making the 1950s one of the most imaginative periods of science fiction cinema.

While the 50s became known as the golden era of the alien invasion film, the 60s and 70s helped solidify the "invader" scenario as a legitimate subgenre. Like the Western, it became a proven avenue to success, and Hollywood's penchant for imitation caused many a low-budget producer to jump on the alien bandwagon. Predictably, the next two decades gave us more and more of the same, only in cheaper and cheaper packages (which seems almost impossible considering the legion of cost-cutting quickies churned out in the 1950s). Throughout the 60s and 70s, we saw all types of alien life, from foam blobs to love drones. These invaders were after everything under the sun, including Frankenstein's Monster, The Three Stooges, and even Santa Claus. Schlock directors like Larry Buchanan even gave us cheaper imitations of already thrifty 50s movies like *It Conquered the World* (1956 — made again as *Zontar, the Thing from Venus* in 1966) and *Invasion of the Saucermen* (1956 — which Buchanan remade as *The Eye Creatures* in 1965). There were, of course, some very good films sprinkled in, but the group as a whole was not able to capture the same level of magnetic charm that the 50s achieved.

Each new generation of filmmakers has been able to apply their decade's own unique cultural flavor to the genre. Today, the alien invader films are action-packed, special effects–heavy, and often violent, and are just as popular and prolific as ever.

Not all hostile aliens are met on Earth. Along with alien encounters that occur while traveling through space, the ENCOUNTERS IN OUTER SPACE subsection also covers contact with extraterrestrials on other worlds. If this contact takes place on the Moon, Mars, or Venus, the main entry for that film will be found in those respective subject listings, which we felt were large enough to demand their own individual chapters. ENCOUNTERS IN OUTER SPACE contains some of the most popular alien films ever, including *Forbidden Planet* (1956) and *This Island Earth* (1955), not to mention several cult favorites like *It! The Terror from Beyond Space* (1958) and *Planet of the Vampires* (1965), both of which served as inspiration for the 1979 blockbuster, *Alien* (arguably the best alien-encounter-in-space picture to date). One of the most popular film series of ENCOUNTERS in recent years has been the *Star Trek* movies. Captain Kirk and his crew always seem to be entertaining life on other planets, and their moviegoing fans are loyal and legion. Another string of films that are included in this section are the *Star Wars* adventures and their imitators. These movies do not directly involve humans per se, but rather life forms and adventures in other galaxies. This type of film allows the writer and director freedom to create weird new cultures, often mixing deep space with a mystical sword-and-sorcery world in a sci-fi/fantasy hybrid.

Not every alien that has landed on Earth or been met in outer space harbors ill will against humans. The BENEVOLENT ALIENS section deals with friendly alien encounters either on Earth or in space. Two of the earliest and best benevolent alien movies are *The Day the Earth Stood Still* (1951) and *It Came from Outer Space* (1953). Both pictures highlight some disarming truths about human perception and behavior. The fear of the unknown, which hampers our search for truth and enlightenment, proves to be a near-fatal phobia in dealing with alien lifeforms. These films demonstrated that the human race is far from "self-actualization," depicting people as being filled with self-doubt and uncertainty, quick to react with violence. Perhaps it is just as well that aliens have been encountered only on the silver screen after all (tabloids and "UFOlogists" notwithstanding). On the other hand, many of the pictures featured in this final alien category hold forth hope for a peaceful meeting someday. *Close Encounters of the Third Kind* (1977), *Cocoon* (1985; along with its 1988 sequel), and the tension-packed underwater encounter in *The Abyss* (1989) certainly add a touch of optimism for humankind meeting extraterrestrial visitors with an open hand, rather than a closed fist.

Invaders on Earth: The 50s

The Astounding She Monster (1958) (see BENEVOLENT ALIENS). Prior to the climactic twist which reveals her benevolent intentions, the She Monster is seen as an invading menace by the people she continually stalks.

The Atomic Submarine (1959; Allied Artists) D: Spencer Gordon Bennet. P: Alex Gordon. S: Orville H. Hampton. C: Gilbert Warrenton. Cast: Arthur Franz, Brett Halsey, Dick Foran, Tom Conway, Paul Dubov, Victor Varconi. Dick Foran and Arthur Frranz battle a cyclopean alien in the undersea regions of the North Pole with their nuclear submarine, the *Tiger Shark*. ¶ "Your mission of the *Tiger Shark* is to hunt down and identify the cause of these Arctic disasters. If humanly possible, you will remove it." • Dick Foran, the son of a U.S. Senator, began his career as a radio and band singer. He changed his name from John Nicholas Foran to Nick Foran, then finally settled on Dick before moving to Warner Bros. where he appeared with Bette Davis and Humphrey Bogart in *The Petrified Forest* (1936).

Attack of the 50 Foot Woman (1958) (see HUMAN GIANTS). A spaceship lands and its giant alien occupant manages to cause earthling Allison Hayes to grow to a height of 50 feet. • This crazy cult classic features a scene in which the alien giant turns his back and reveals the sequined shape of a bull on his "alien jacket."

The Beast with a Million Eyes (1955; American Releasing Corp.) D/P: David Kramarsky. S: Tom Filer. C: Everett Baker. Cast: Paul Birch, Lorna Thayer, Dona Cole, Richard Sargent, Leonard Tarver, Bruce Whitmore, Chester Conklin. A spaceship lands in the desert and an alien presence menaces a small family by inhabiting the bodies of animals. ¶ "That thing in the crater, it controls minds but its power is limited." • *The Beast with a Million Eyes* actually had just two eyes on the alien puppet designed by Paul Blaisdell. The million eyes mentioned so prominently in the ads refer to its capacity to control millions of things at once. • The Alabama born actor Paul Birch, who played the father-hero, was also seen in TV's "The Fugitive." • According to Mark McGee in his book, *Fast and Furious*, distributors from Boston who saw a screening of the film loved the advertising but hated the picture. "Jim Nicholson believed it could still be salvaged. He took the last reel into the editing room and with a pair of scissors scratched the emulsion on the scenes of the spaceship. He filled in the jagged white scratches with ink from his fountain pen. Projected again, the tank now looked as if it were discharging dangerous rays." The tank he referred to was the kettle-shaped spaceship which housed the alien puppet. • According to executive producer Sam Arkoff, it was actually Roger Corman rather than David Kramarsky who produced and directed the film. Apparently,

Corman was not pleased with it and requested his name be removed, and production assistant Kramarsky was given the screen credit. Arkoff spoke of the movie's genesis, "I told Roger he had only $30,000 to make the picture. Roger took off for Palm Springs with the cast and crew, followed closely by protesting union officials. After two weeks of ducking and running, Roger was back with the footage. The picture wasn't bad for $30,000, but the monster, supposedly an outer space head, was terrible!"

The Blob (1958) (see BLOBS). A meteor lands on Earth, breaks open, and releases the classic titular teen terror. ¶ "You mean this little pebble's been hot roddin' around the universe?"

The Brain from Planet Arous (1958; Howco International) D: Nathan Hertz (Nathan Juran) P/C: Jacques Marquette. S: Ray Buffum. Cast: John Agar, Joyce Meadows, Thomas Henry Browne, Robert Fuller, Tim Graham. Two aliens (resembling oversized disembodied brains) from the planet Arous arrive on Earth. The evil brain, Gor, takes over John Agar's body and delights in human lust and power. ¶ "I can't be destroyed, and any attempt by any means to do so will bring forth reprisals that will shock the world!" • The evil brain's name is "Gor," and later, another brain from the same planet arrives to take the scoundrel back. "Vol" (the good brain) inhabits the family dog, and helps to direct the heroine and her father on what to do. In the final confrontation, Agar, who is momentarily freed from its power, makes head cheese out of Gor with an axe. The sight of this all-powerful transparent alien turning into a pathetic squealing balloon is hysterical. Agar commented on the brain prop in Tom Weaver's book, *Interviews with B Science Fiction and Horror Movie Makers:* "Oh, I thought it was terrible—just awful! They really could have done a heck of a lot better than that—it looked like a balloon with a face painted on it." • The good brain's name—"Vol," was borrowed for the "Star Trek" episode called "The Apple," and used for the god-idol the planet's natives made sacrifices to. • One of the alien brain's chief weapons while he's inhabiting a human body is a power ray that emanates from the eyes, which turn black (actually silver). In one scene he zaps an airplane. Afterwards you can still see a piece of the destroyed model dangling on the screen like a pendulum. Agar related his painful experience with the silvery eye effect: "When that alien

being took over my body, they inserted these full contact lenses in my eyes. They'd painted 'em silver and they forgot that that doggone paint would chip off. Every time I blinked, some of that silver would come off the lens and it was like having sand in my eyes."

The Crawling Eye (1958; Distributors Corporation of America; U.K.; also *The Trollenberg Terror)* D: Quentin Lawrence. P: Robert S. Baker, Monty Berman. S: Jimmy Sangster. C: Monty Berman. Cast: Forrest Tucker, Laurence Payne, Janet Munro, Warren Mitchell, Jennifer Jayne. Huge alien eyeballs, who decapitate people with their large tentacles, wreak havoc in the Swiss mountain village of Trollenberg. ¶ "Didn't you see—his head, it was torn off." • *The Crawling Eye* features some stylish camera work by Desmond Davis who went on to shoot big-budget features like *A Taste of Honey* (1961) and *Tom Jones* (1963). • *The Crawling Eye* was released on a double bill with another Forrest Tucker project, *The Cosmic Monster.* • It is interesting to note that though the film is supposed to be set in the Swiss highlands, the production is curiously studio-bound. Actors are seen standing in front of back screen images of painted landscapes and snow capped peaks, and it features plenty of corner-cutting stock climbing footage. • The unique eyeball aliens were designed by Les Bowie, who began his career as a matte painter for the Rank Organization, and later became associated with the wonderful Hammer studios. His first for Hammer was *The Creeping Unknown.* • The effect of the moving clouds, whose appearance signaled the coming of the alien eyeballs, was accomplished by photographing a piece of cotton tacked onto a photograph(!) of a mountain.

The Creeping Unknown (1956) (see BLOBS). An astronaut returns from space and slowly transforms into a gigantic tentacled blob.

Devil Girl from Mars (1954; Spartan; U.K.) D: David MacDonald. P: Edward J. and Harry Lee Danziger. S: John C. Mather, James Eastwood. C: Lionel Linden. Cast: Hazel Court, Patricia Laffan, Hugh McDermott, Adrienne Corri, Peter Reynolds, Joseph Tomelty, John Laurie, Sophie Stewart, Anthony Richmond. A spaceship lands by mistake in a backwoods area of Britain, disgorging a sexy female alien and her robot. This "Devil Girl's" intentions are far from honorable—she wants to collect males for breeding and conquer the world. ¶ "After the war of the sexes, women became the rulers of Mars, but now the male has fallen into a decline." • Under that black leather widows-peaked space cap was British actress Patricia Laffan, who began her career performing at the Oxford Playhouse Repertory before moving on to the London Stage. She is also an accomplished writer with several published short stories. • Actress Hazel Court's horror career later blossomed in the 1960s working for Roger Corman on his Poe pictures, *Premature Burial* (1962), *The Raven* (1963), and *The Masque of the Red Death* (1964). • Actor Hugh McDermott was an accomplished golfer, winning 27 cups and competitions before leaving school, and then turning pro for a couple of years.

Earth vs. the Flying Saucers (1956; Columbia) D: Fred Sears. P: Charles H. Schneer. S: George Worthington Yates, Bernard Gordon. C: Fred Jackman, Jr. Cast: Hugh Marlowe, Joan Taylor, Donald Curtis, Morris Ankrum, Thomas Browne Henry. Flying saucers, piloted by robot-suited aliens, begin a full scale planetary invasion. ¶ "If they land in our nation's capital uninvited, we won't meet them with tea and cookies!" • High frequency sound beams were used to destroy the Ray Harryhausen-created menaces from space. Some famous Washington, D.C., landmarks (Union Station, Supreme Court building, and Washington Monument) were destroyed by the crashing saucers. • "We are the survivors of a disintegrated solar system . . . at this moment the remainder of our fleet is circling your globe," warned the distorted alien voice of narrator Paul Frees. • Stop-motion animation genius Ray Harryhausen discussed some of the problems concerning this film's animated effects in his book, *Film Fantasy Scrapbook:* "One of the most difficult tasks of this particular project lay in the animation of the destruction of the falling buildings. They had to be photographed in the process of disintegration by a death ray, frame by frame — each falling brick being suspended by invisible wires. It would have been far more effective to photograph them in high-speed photography but the cost of this process was prohibitive."

Enemy from Space (1957; Hammer/ United Artists; UK; also *Quatermass 2*) D: Val Guest. P: Anthony Hinds. S: Nigel Kneale, Val Guest. C: Gerald Gibbs. Cast: Brian Donlevy, John Longden, William Franklyn, Tom Chatto, Percy Herbert, Sidney James, Charles Lloyd Pack, Michael Ripper, Bryan Forbes, Vera Day. A government project to make synthetic food is actually a front for invading alien parasites which are out to control the world. People entering the facility leave under the influence of the aliens, their minds controlled by this alien force. ¶ "Could you call an emergency action on a large scale? An action if I told you that what is really being carried out in Wynnerton Flats is the mass destruction of men's minds." • According to Bill Warren in his book, *Keep Watching the Skies!,* "[Brian Donlevy] had allegedly come to have such a problem with drinking as to render some scenes almost completely unintelligible. Donlevy reportedly memorized the dialogue only moments before the camera rolled, and was, it was said, at times so drunk that he had to be grabbed as scenes ended to keep him from walking into walls, off curbs, etc."

The Giant Claw (1957; Columbia) D: Fred Sears. P: Sam Katzman. S: Samuel Newman, Paul Gangelin. C: Benjamin H. Kline. Cast: Jeff Morrow, Mara Corday, Morris Ankrum, Louis D. Merrill, Edgar Barrier, Robert Shayne, Morgan Jones. A gigantic flying alien buzzard-monster arrives from space to lay an egg of a film for Columbia Pictures. ¶ "Now I don't care if that bird came from outer space or Upasida River, New Jersey. It's still made of flesh and blood of some sort and vulnerable to bullets and bombs." • Producer Sam Katzman was introduced to the movie business at the age of 13, when he worked as a prop boy. His finest science fiction accomplishment is often considered to be *Earth vs. the Flying Saucers* (1956). • Stock footage from the films, *Earth vs. the Flying Saucers* (1956), *It Came from Beneath the Sea* (1955), and *War of the Worlds* (1953), was used in this picture. • The "giant claw" bird is actually a puppet held up by wires.

I Married a Monster from Outerspace (1958; Paramount) D/P: Gene Fowler, Jr. S: Louis Vittes. C: Haskell Boggs. Cast: Gloria Talbott, Tom Tryon, Alan Dexter, Robert Ivers, Chuck Wassill, Valerie Allen, Peter Baldwin, Ty Hungerford. Every bride's worst nightmare is explored as an invading alien inhabits the body of her husband in an attempt to repopulate their dying race. ¶ "I'm telling you, I'm learning what love is." • The shooting schedule for this film lasted approximately three weeks, and according to Gloria Talbott in Tom Weaver's book, *Interviews with B Science Fiction and Horror Movie Makers,* Louis Vittes, the writer, lay on the floor underneath the camera and muttered the lines while the actors were being filmed (a considerable

Midget actress Luce Potter plays the chief alien behind the Invaders from Mars *(1953).*

distraction, which was quickly rectified). Talbott described her co-star Tom Tryon as "very introspective, very into himself, but always professional, always gave 100%." Apparently, Tryon, who was under contract at Paramount, didn't really want to do the picture, but was threatened with a suspension if he failed to perform his assignment. • Director Gene Fowler was quoted in *Filmfax* #10 as saying, "I never liked that title, and neither did my partner, Lou Vittes. But we were making the movie for one specific reason, and that was exploitation. I don't know whether Paramount would have made it if it hadn't had that title." • According to Fowler, the dogs, who in the film destroy the aliens, were at first very frightened of the suited actors. After they had an opportunity to play around a bit together though, it was difficult to make the attack scenes look vicious. The actors had to guide the heads to their bodies to make it look as if they were being bitten.

Invaders from Mars (1953; 20th Century–Fox) D: William Cameron Menzies. P: Edward L. Alperson. S: John Tucker Battle, William Cameron Menzies, Richard Blake. C: John F. Sietz. Cast: Jimmy Hunt, Helena Carter, Arthur Franz, Leif Erickson, Hillary Brooke, Morris Ankrum, Robert Shayne, Bill Phipps, Max Wagner, Douglas Kennedy. A young boy sees alien invaders land secretly in a small town and take control over the minds of key town personnel as well as the boy's parents. At the end, the boy wakes up to find it's all been a dream ... but is that a spaceship landing just over the hill? ¶ "Could you disprove, for example, that the Martians have bred a race of synthetic humans to save themselves from extinction?" • This film, the first alien invasion movie to be shot in color, was hyped with ad lines like: "Weird, fantastic beings of a super intelligence, ruling a race of synthetic humans and pitting them against mankind's dream to conquer the universe." • William Cameron Menzies was one of the most celebrated art directors in all of cinema before graduating to director. He won Oscars for his art direction on *The Dove* and *The Tempest* in 1928, and also *Gone with the Wind* in 1939. As director he

Kevin McCarthy examines an alien pod found in the back trunk of his car during the Invasion of the Body Snatchers *(1956).*

helmed the acclaimed futuristic feature, *Things to Come,* in 1936. Menzies worked on only one other film (*Around the World in 80 Days,* 1956 — in strictly a design capacity) before his death in 1957. • Menzies' pre-production sketches and storyboard drawings were all stolen shortly before this film got underway, making the production much more difficult to organize. • Two separate versions of this movie were made. In the European release, the sequence showing the boy waking up from his nightmare is edited out, making all the alien events real and not just imagined. • Originally, *Invaders from Mars* was planned to be shot in 3-D but the idea was scrapped. If this had occurred, *Invaders* would have beaten out *It Came from Outer Space* (1953) as the first sci-fi picture filmed in 3-D.

Invasion of the Body Snatchers (1956; Allied Artists) D: Don Siegel. P: Walter Wanger. S: Daniel Mainwaring, Sam Peckinpah. C: Ellsworth Fredericks. Cast: Kevin McCarthy, Dana Wynter, King Donovan, Carolyn Jones, Larry Gates, Ralph Dumke, Jean Willes, Virginia Christine, Tom Fadden,

Whit Bissell, Richard Deacon. A doctor arrives back in his home town only to discover that most of its citizens have been replicated by invading seed pods from outer space who possess a collective, unemotional intelligence. ¶ "Suddenly, while you're asleep, they'll absorb your minds, your memories, and you'll be reborn into an untroubled world." • The working titles for the film were *Sleep No More* and *I Am a Pod.* • Kevin McCarthy (playing hero Dr. Miles Bennell) realized that Becky Driscoll had been "taken over" by the pods by the way she responded when he kissed her. • Writer Sam Peckinpah, who assisted Don Siegel in this film, made a brief appearance as a meter-reader in Becky Driscoll's basement. • In an interview with Stuart Kaminsky (appearing in Thomas R. Atkins' book, *Science Fiction Films*), director Don Siegel discussed the controversial prologue and climax which was added to the original concept. "I wanted to end it with McCarthy on the highway turning to the camera and saying, "You're next!" Then, boom, the lights go up. In the final version, however, we go

One of the cabbage-headed aliens strangles Lyn Osborn in this publicity shot from Invasion of the Saucermen *(1957).*

back to the hospital . . . and that's after the fact. Many people do cut that frame, those sequences, when they show it. Every few days the picture is run somewhere, some underground theater. And the tacked-on opening and closing are removed." According to Siegel, "to be a pod means that you have no passion, no anger, the spark has left you. . . . People without being vegetables are becoming vegetables. I don't know what the answer is except an awareness of it. That's what makes a picture like *Invasion of the Body Snatchers* important."

Invasion of the Saucermen (1957; AIP) D: Ed Cahn. P: James H. Nicholson, Robert Gurney, Jr. S: Al Martin, Robert Gurney,

Jr. C: Frederick E. West. Cast: Steve Terrell, Lyn Osborn, Gloria Castillo, Frank Gorshin, Raymond Hatton, Douglas Henderson, Sam Buffington, Russ Bender, Ed Nelson. A flying saucer, complete with little green men (midgets wearing space suits and bulbous heads), lands near lovers lane, and the local teen population must find a way to stop these pesky aliens in this popular comedy/horror/teen film. ¶ "Yes I know, you saw little green men.... Oh sure, they're from another planet.... Well if you see them again give 'em my love and send 'em home, huh." • The saucermen heads were actually made of fiberglass and Paul Blaisdell (their designer) was ordered to make them smaller at the last minute. Blaisdell chopped a chunk out the back and pushed the ends together for the narrower version you see in the film. • Blaisdell and his friend/assistant Bob Burns were oftentimes modeling the saucermen heads in various scenes. In the sequence where Larkin's bull gouges out one of the saucermen's eyes, Burns squeezed chocolate syrup out of a grease gun (from behind the alien's styrofoam eye) to represent blood gushing from the wound. • Alcohol was the substance injected into the aliens' victims through the needles in their fingers. Frank Gorshin, comedian/impersonator extraordinaire, refused to allow them to used the needled fingers on his face in one scene, so Bob Burns had to stand in for him. Gorshin of course went on to become Batman's arch rival, "the Riddler," in the popular TV series, "Batman." • The little green men (the first ones ever alluded to in movie history) were frightened of strong light, and met their demise via teenage hot rod car lights. • Lyn "Cadet Happy" Osborn of TV's "Space Patrol," who starred as Art and narrated the film, died soon after the picture's release. His other 50s appearances include *The Amazing Colossal Man* (1957) and *The Cosmic Man* (1958). • *Invasion of the Saucermen* was released on a double bill with *I Was a Teenage Werewolf.*

The Invisible Invaders (1959; United Artists) D: Ed Cahn. P: Robert E. Kent. S: Samuel Newman. C: Maury Gertsman. Cast: Philip Tonge, John Agar, Jean Byron, Robert Hutton, John Carradine, Paul Langton. Invisible aliens from the moon inhabit dead bodies to create an army of zombies to conquer the Earth. ¶ "The invasion of Earth has started. Within three days the dead will destroy all the living and we will rule the Earth." • Scientist Karol Noyman (John Carradine), the first resurrection vic-

tim of *The Invisible Invaders,* was a character created by Edgar Barrier two years earlier in *The Giant Claw.* Also in *The Giant Claw* is a character with the last name of Penner, which was also the name of the scientist played by Philip Tonge in this film. • These seemingly unkillable alien invaders are finally stopped by the discovery of their susceptibility to high frequency sound.

It Conquered the World (1956; AIP) D/P: Roger Corman. S: Charles B. Griffith, Lou Rusoff. C: Frederick West. Cast: Lee Van Cleef, Peter Graves, Beverly Garland, Sally Fraser, Russ Bender, Jonathan Haze, Dick Miller. A Venusian alien enlists the aid of a misguided scientist (Lee Van Cleef) to help it conquer the small town of Beachwood, with the intention of moving on to conquer the whole world next. Flying bat-like parasites help the creature control the minds of key people. Van Cleef's scientist eventually comes around and kills the invader with a blow torch. ¶ "Every man its prisoner.... Every woman its slave!"—ad line. • This is the only Roger Corman sci-fi film in which Beverly Garland (a Corman regular) was killed by an alien. Bev plays Van Cleef's wife who takes on *It* with a shotgun. • Mark McGee tells in his book, *Fast and Furious,* how Garland "sauntered up to *It* the first day and said, 'That conquered the world?' She kicked it. It fell over. She burst out laughing." • Paul Blaisdell's alien creation, whom hero Peter Graves describes in the film—"He doesn't like. He doesn't dislike. He merely reasons, concludes, and uses," was affectionately called "Beulah" by the cast and crew. • Though shot in black and white, the actual color of the "cucumber monster" from *It Conquered the World* was green. • Mark McGee (in his book *Fast and Furious*) also told of a near-fatal accident involving Paul Blaisdell. "Paul was inside Beulah, duck-walking, the afternoon Jonathan Haze stabbed Beulah between the eyes with a bayonet. Jonathan played a soldier. Lucky for Paul he had borrowed a G.I. helmet from Danny Knight, one of the soldiers. Jonathan's blade ripped right through the foam rubber and the plywood frame and scraped the top of Paul's helmet. Paul kept quiet about it until Roger yelled 'Cut!'" • It's interesting to note that when Blaisdell constructed Beulah inside his house, he realized upon completion that he wasn't able to get it out the door. So, sheepishly, he was forced to disassemble it then rebuild it again outside. • The film's star, Peter Graves, is the brother of James Arness (*The Thing,* 1951; *Them,* 1954). •

Three of the pop-eyed Killers from Space *(1954).*

The movie's prolific composer, Ronald Stein, wrote five musical scores for Roger Corman during the 1950s and a total of ten for the decade.

Killers from Space (1954; RKO) D/P: W. Lee Wilder. S: Bill Raynor. C: William H. Clothier. Cast: Peter Graves, James Seay, Steve Pendleton, Barbara Bestar, Frank Gerstle, John Merrick. Peter Graves battles bug-eyed aliens who plan to conquer the Earth with the aid of giant reptiles and insects. ¶ "Yours is the only planet in this solar system capable of sustaining our civilization." • For this no-budget feature, makeup man Harry Thomas fashioned the crazy-looking alien eyeballs from a white plastic egg tray. The circular pockets which held the eggs were cut out and then painted to resemble dark irises.

Kronos (1957; 20th Century–Fox) D/P: Kurt Neumann. S: Lawrence Louis Goldman. S: Karl Struss. Cast: Jeff Morrow, Barbara Lawrence, John Emery, George O'Hanlon, Morris Ankrum, Robert Shayne. Jeff Morrow battles a gigantic energy-eating machine from space which is controlled by an invading alien that has inhabited the body of a powerful Earth scientist. ¶ "Will it wait for us, scientific expeditions to get underway six months, a year from now, or will it make a move of its own?" • Kronos, named after the gigantic evil monster of ancient mythology, meets its end when Morrow devises a method to reverse the machine's electric polarity. The resulting effect creates an internal chain reaction which destroys Kronos with its own storage of energy.

The Man from Planet X (1951; United Artists) D: Edgar G. Ulmer. P/S: Aubrey Wisberg, Jack Pollexfen. C: John L. Russell. Cast: Robert Clarke, Margaret Field, William Schallert, Raymond Bond, Roy Engel. A reporter recounts his weird experience with the space-suited alien from Planet X who uses a ray gun to control and enslave captured locals on the Scottish Isle of Bury. ¶ "A ghastly caricature, like something distorted by pressure." – description of *The Man from Planet X*. • William Schallert (*The Monolith Monsters; The Incredible Shrinking Man,* both 1957) plays the power-mad Dr. Mears, who tortures the captured alien by shutting off his gas supply. He is killed in military crossfire at the climax, which eventually destroys the ship and its occupant as it attempts to escape. • Margaret Field, known later in her career as Maggie Mahoney (the wife of Jock Mahoney of *The Land Unknown,* 1957, fame) is the mother of the popular Oscar-winning actress, Sally Field. • The picture was filmed in one week on the "fog-laden" sets used for the 1948 film, *Joan of Arc* at Hal Roach Studios, on a very low budget (less than $50,000).

Missile Monsters (1958; Republic) D: Fred C. Bannon. P: Franklin Adreon. S: Ronald Davidson. C: Walter Strenge. Cast: Walter Reed, Lois Collier, Gregory Gay, James Craven, Harry Lauter, Richard Irving. A scientist who designs airplanes agrees to help an alien take over the Earth in exchange for advanced nuclear technology. Their war against our planet is thwarted when Walter Reed manages to set off an atomic bomb within their volcanic center of operations. • This film is a condensed theatrical version of the 1951 serial, *Flying Disk Man from Mars.* It was released on a double-bill with another condensed serial feature film, *Satan's Satellites.*

The Mysterians (1959; Toho/MGM; Japan) D: Inoshiro Honda. P: Tomoyuki Tanaka. S: Takeshi Kimura, Shigeru Kayama. C: Hajime Koizumi. Cast: Kenji Sahara, Yumi Shirakawa, Momoko Kochi, Akihiko Hirata, Takashi Shimura. Alien humanoids hiding behind the Moon unleash a gigantic bird-like robot upon Japan. They come to Earth and establish a domed base where they plan to mate with our women. Eventually their dome is cracked by a ray machine developed by the U.S. • Characters from *The Mysterians* showed up again in a Japanese sequel (of sorts) — *Battle in Outer Space* (1960).

Night of the Blood Beast (1958; AIP) D: Bernard L. Kowalski. P: Gene Corman. S: Martin Varno. C: John Nickolaus, Jr. Cast: Michael Emmett, Ed Nelson, John Baer, Angela Greene, Georgianna Carter, Tyler McVey. The first manned satellite crash-lands in an isolated canyon with its astronaut (Michael Emmett) carrying the spawn of an invading alien occupant. The alien "Beast," which lives on blood, is finally destroyed at the climax by an act of self-sacrifice from the astronaut. ¶ "Why are we always so quick to kill. It's an alien. It's the first of its kind to come to the Earth." • Ross Sturlin wore the Blood Beast costume which

was utilized again for the Roger Corman film, *Teenage Caveman* (1958). • The film's shooting schedule was only seven days and the outside shots were photographed in and around the Bronson Canyon area. The picture cost roughly $70,000 to make. • According to Director Bernard L. Kowalski in Tom Weaver's book, *Interviews with B Science Fiction and Horror Movie Makers,* Roger Corman "was involved creatively and financially" with the production of *Blood Beast.* He was "standing back and just guiding [his brother] Gene and myself." • The "Blood Beast's" last words before dying was the warning, "In your quest for self-destruction you will send up more satellites . . . we will come again!"

Not of This Earth (1956; Allied Artists) D/P: Roger Corman. S: Charles B. Griffith, Mark Hanna. C: John Mescall. Cast: Paul Birch, Beverly Garland, Jonathan Haze, William Roerick, Morgan Jones. An alien (Paul Birch) is sent to Earth to test the compatibility of human blood. Their race is dying out due to a blood disease (the result of prolonged nuclear warfare on their home planet), and they need a fresh supply to survive. This alien looks human, except for his stark white eyes, which he hides behind dark glasses. When he removes the glasses, his eyes cook the brains of anyone who looks at them. He also employs the aid of a rather strange little blood-sucking umbrella-creature to help carry out his dastardly plot. ¶ "Do not run from me Nadine, I'm going to dispatch you." • Corman regular, Dick Miller, turns up in a comedic scene as a vacuum cleaner salesman making a fatal "hard sell" to the alien. • The white eyeball effect was achieved with the use of false lenses. John Agar employed the same technique (though his lenses were black) for *The Brain from Planet Arous* a year later. • Star Paul Birch actually walked off the picture before the film was completed, but fortunately Corman had amassed enough footage to finish his project. Birch was apparently unhappy with the uncomfortable contact lenses he was forced to wear and with Corman in general. A stand-in was used for some of the last shots, including the scene at the climax in which another alien walks up to the tombstone which reads, "Here lies a man who was Not of this Earth."

Phantom from Space (1953; United Artists) D/P: W. Lee Wilder. S: Bill Raynor, Myles Wilder. C: William Clothier. Cast: Ted Cooper, Rudolph Anders, Noreen Nash, James Seay, Harry Landers, Jack

The alien from Night of the Blood Beast *(1958) wrestles with Michael Emmet at the mouth of its lair during the fateful climax. Ross Sturlin is the man inside the Blood Beast costume which coincidentally was salvaged for use in the Roger Corman film,* Teenage Caveman, *that same year.*

Daly, Dick Sands, Michael Mark. An invisible alien is responsible for numerous killings after its flying saucer crash lands. After exposure to infra-red light at a nearby observatory, the alien becomes visible. ¶ "Has it occurred to you that our X-man has no apparent motivation for his act, and might therefore not be an intentional criminal at all?"

Plan Nine from Outer Space (1959: Distributors Corporation of America) D/P/S: Edward D. Wood. C: William C. Thompson. Cast: Gregory Walcott, Mona McKinnon, Dudley Manlove, Tom Keene, Duke Moore, Tor Johnson, Bela Lugosi, Maila Nurmi (Vampira), Lyle Talbot, Paul Marco. Aliens revive corpses for the purpose of conquering the Earth. ¶ "Inspector Clay is dead—murdered—and someone's responsible!" • Ed Wood used footage of Bela Lugosi from an uncompleted film called *Tomb of the Vampire*. Lugosi died just a

few days after shooting began on the film, and the small portions of footage were filed away by Wood, who later found a way to incorporate them into his new film, *Plan Nine from Outer Space*. Since the Lugosi footage consisted of only a few shots of the actor entering and leaving a house, Wood used a double to stretch out the characterization (employing his wife's chiropractor for the job). Bela's widow, Hope Lininger, appeared on-stage during the film's premier along with the gigantic wrestler-turned-actor, Tor Johnson. • Criswell (Jeron King Criswell) served as the narrator. He wrote all of his own lines, because a slight speech impediment made it difficult for him to pronounce certain words and syllables. • Ed Wood's much publicized fetish with wearing women's clothing was discussed by actor Paul Marco in the Tom Weaver book, *Interviews with B Science Fiction and Horror Movie Makers:* "No, [Wood] wasn't flaming around, like I've heard stories of, wearing this and that and using a megaphone and acting like an idiot.... He never pranced around on the street in high heels and a wig, he did it in his own home, and he was never embarrassed about it." • The picture was originally titled *Grave Robbers from Outer Space* but was later changed by the Baptist Church (which had financed the film and who apparently didn't like the words "Grave Robbers"). One of the conditions the Baptists set for financing the picture was that all the people involved with the project had to be baptized, including Ed Wood and Tor Johnson. Two church members played gravediggers in the film.

Robot Monster (1953; Astor Pictures) D/P: Phil Tucker. S: Wyott Ordung. C: Jack Greenhalgh. Cast: George Barrows, Gregory Moffett, George Nader, Claudia Barrett, John Mylong, Selena Royle, Pamela Paulson. An alien named "Ro-man" is sent by his race to conquer the Earth, which he quickly does, leaving only a handful of survivors to consider their position. ¶ "You look like a pooped-out pinwheel!" • Ro-man was played by George Barrows and his cheap costume consisted of an ape suit topped with a diving helmet and antennae. • Director Phil Tucker used stock footage from *Flight to Mars* (1951) and several dinosaur sequences from *One Million B.C.* (1940) to depict the carnage let loose by Ro-man's powers. Tucker apparently had a falling out with the film's backers and he wasn't allowed to see his finished product until it was released. Soon afterwards, Tucker attempted suicide, but survived, and continued on with his career. (One can only speculate that his suicide attempt had anything to do with this film.) • It is interesting to note that popular composer Elmer Bernstein (*The Magnificent Seven,* 1960; and *To Kill a Mockingbird,* 1963) created the musical score for this no-budget movie as well as another low-budget turkey, *Cat Women of the Moon,* made the same year. • The picture purportedly cost less than $16,000 to make, and was shot in a rather unsatisfactory 3-D process.

Satan's Satellites (1958; Republic) D: Fred C. Bannon. P: Franklin Adreon. S: Ronald Davidson. C: John MacBurnie. Cast: Judd Holdren, Aline Towne, Wilson Wood, Lane Bradford, Stanley Waxman, John Crawford, Tom Steele, Roy Engel, Leonard Nimoy. This pared-down feature culled from the 12-chapter serial, *Zombies of the Stratosphere* (1952), concerns a Martian plot to improve their own planetary climate by knocking the Earth out of its orbit with a hydrogen bomb. • *Satan's Satellites* is a spinoff of sorts from the 1945 serial, *The Purple Monster Strikes,* which was also co-directed by Fred C. Bannon.

Space Master X-7 (1958) (see BLOBS). A space probe arrives on Earth carrying a deadly blob-like alien fungus.

Target Earth (1954; Allied Artists) D: Sherman A. Rose. P: Herman Cohen. S: William Raynor. C: Guy Roe. Cast: Richard Denning, Kathleen Crowley, Richard Reeves, Virginia Grey, Robert Roark, Arthur Space, Whit Bissell. A woman awakens to a deserted city besieged by killer robots from Venus. Scientists, led by Richard Denning, destroy the death-ray shooting menaces with the use of ultrasonic waves which crack their hard exteriors. ¶ "Nobody's ever been able to get that close to one without being annihilated." • *Target Earth* is based upon the Paul W. Fairman short story, "Deadly City," and was shot in seven days for approximately $75,000.

Teenagers from Outer Space (1959; Warner Bros.) D/P/S/C: Tom Graeff. Cast: David Love (Tom Graeff), Dawn Anderson, Harvey B. Dunn, Bryan Grant, Tom Lockyear, Robert King Moody. A teenage alien is sent to Earth to breed gigantic monsters (called "Gargans") but he falls for a human girl and double-crosses his race by directing their spaceships to crash against a mountainside. The depressed teen alien dies with them. ¶ "We live like parts of a machine, we don't know our fathers or mothers. We're raised in cubicles." • Tom Graeff not only produced, directed, wrote, and photographed the film, he also did the special effects, sound editing, and even starred as the young alien.

The Thing (1951; Winchester Pictures/ RKO) D: Christian Nyby, Howard Hawks. P: Howard Hawks. S: Charles Lederer. C: Russel Harlan. Cast: Kenneth Tobey, Margaret Sheridan, Douglas Spencer, Robert Cornthwaite, Dewey Martin, James Young, Robert Nichols, John Dierkes, James Arness, Eduard Franz. A group of scientists and Air Force personnel battle a bloodsucking alien at a polar research station. The vicious alien vegetable (which is humanoid in appearance) was recovered from a flying saucer that was discovered buried in the ice near their station. ¶ "There are no enemies in science, only phenomena to study." • This film marked the baptismal beginning of the alien invasion cycle. Credit for the picture's direction was given to Hawks' friend and editor, Christian Nyby. Though many people contend that this was simply a production credit favor, and Hawks was the film's actual director, author Pat Luciano *(Them or Us)* was told by actor Robert Cornthwaite (who played Professor Carrington in the film) that both Nyby and Hawks conferred on every shot and detail, and shared the directorial chores equally. • Actor Dewey Martin described *The Thing*'s appearance in the film by saying, "It's got crazy hands and no hair. And the eyes, well, they're open and they look like they can see." This "intellectual carrot" was played by the tall "Gunsmoke" actor, James Arness. Story has it that the green makeup was so embarrassing that he wouldn't eat lunch with the rest of the cast. • In the Ted Newson article appearing in *Filmfax* #15, star Ken Tobey talked about his director: "Howard Hawks was as good a director as I've ever worked with, because he listened. If an actor had a problem with a line, he'd ask, 'What would you say here?' A secretary would jot down the line and it'd flow much better. We made a lot of that up as we went along." • The spontaneous overlapping dialogue, realistically imbued with fragmented sentences and interruptions (brilliantly timed by the cast) added a great deal of realism to Charles Lederer's acclaimed script. • "So few people can boast that they've lost a flying saucer and a man from Mars all in the same day," commented Scotty (Douglas Spencer) after the saucer is accidentally destroyed by a thermite bomb, and its occupant escapes from a block of ice. • "What do you do with a vegetable? — boil it, stew it bake it. . . . Maybe Dr. Carrington will ask it to crawl into a double boiler." In reality, the Thing was cooked with electricity between the leads of two poles. • Actor Robert Nichols (Lt. MacPherson) made mention of another Howard Hawks feature during the film when he asked if he had any experience firing a very pistol. His reply: "I saw *Sergeant York*" (an Oscar-nominated Hawks film made in 1941). • *When Worlds Collide* (1951) and *War of the Worlds* (1953) both included narration by one of the finest science fiction voices of the 1950s, Paul Frees. Frees gave an outstanding supporting performance in this film as the concerned scientist, Dr. Voorhees. • Several stand-ins of various sizes were made up to resemble the Thing to simulate the climactic melting/shrinking effect of the alien. • The film is loosely based on the short story "Who Goes There?" by John W. Campbell. • Russian-born Dimitri Tiomkin provided the memorable musical score for *The Thing*. This

Oscar-winning composer worked with people like Frank Capra (*It's a Wonderful Life,* 1946) and Alfred Hitchcock (*Strangers on a Train,* 1951) as well as turning in beautiful scores for the Westerns, *High Noon* (1952), *Gunfight at the OK Corral* (1957), *Rio Bravo* (1959), and Hawks' own Western masterpiece, *Red River* (1948).

Twenty Million Miles to Earth (1957; Columbia) D: Nathan Juran. P: Charles Schneer. S: Bob Williams, Christopher Knopf. C: Irving Lippman, Carlos Ventigmilia. Cast: William Hopper, Joan Taylor, Frank Puglia, Thomas Browne Henry, Tito Vuolo, Bart Bradley, Arthur Space. A space rocket, carrying the capsuled egg of an alien creature, returning from the planet Venus, crashes in the waters off the coast of Sicily. The creature escapes and grows to enormous proportions before battling an elephant in the streets of Rome, where it eventually falls to its death from the top of the Roman Coliseum. ¶ "Why is it always so costly for Man to move from the present to the future?" • Special Effects man Ray Harryhausen benefited from the use of a new kind of film stock during the production of this picture. The new Kodak grain was finer, which made the portion of the film where the original negative left off and the duplicate negative began much less noticeable. Harryhausen also appeared in the picture as the man feeding peanuts to the elephants. • The Venusian monster, named by Harryhausen the "Ymir," never actually attacked anyone unless it was provoked. Also, this alien creature did not eat meat — it fed on sulfur.

The 27th Day (1957; Columbia) D: William Asher. P: Helen Ainsworth. S: John Mantley. C: Henry Freulich. Cast: Gene Barry, Valerie French, George Voskovec, Arnold Moss, Azenath Janti, Marie Tsien, Stefan Schnabel, Frederick Ledebur, Paul Birch, Tom Daly. Five different people are given a capsule by an alien. Inside each capsule is the power to destroy all life on an entire continent. The aliens, who wish to take over the planet but must adhere to a policy of non-violence, are gambling that the humans will eventually use their respective capsules and destroy themselves, leaving the Earth open for their invasion. ¶ "One more question, please, do we have your solemn word that if we succeed in keeping the peace for 27 days Earth will be free of invasion?" • The flying saucer sequence in *The 27th Day* was footage borrowed from a previous outer space invasion film, the 1956 Ray Harryhausen movie, *Earth vs. the Flying Saucers*

Ray Harryhausen's Venusian Ymir comes Twenty Million Miles to Earth *(1957) to break a lamp post with one hand while holding a model figure in the other.*

• Actor Gene Barry enjoyed a prestigious stage career in addition to his silver screen performances. He also starred as the popular TV hero, "Bat Masterson." His son Michael has gone on to become a film director.

The Twonky (1953) (see MACHINES). A wife surprises her husband with an unwanted television set. This TV, however, is inhabited by an alien force which first helps, then controls the people around it.

War of the Worlds (1953; Paramount) D: Byron Haskin. P: George Pal. S: Barre Lyndon. C: George Barnes. Cast: Gene Barry, Ann Robinson, Les Tremayne, Lewis Martin, Robert Cornthwaite, Bill Phipps, Paul Birch, Vernon Rich, Carolyn Jones, Paul Frees (radio narration also). Martian ships disguised as meteors land on Earth. Up from these meteors rise a horde of unstoppable killing machines, armed with heat and death rays, which systematically set about destroying all life on the planet. ¶ "From the blackness of outer space we were being scrutinized and studied." • The Martians (one of which was played by Charles Gemora) had three eyes and pinkish toned skin. Neither guns, tanks, nor an atomic bomb dropped by the "Flying Wing" could stop their war machines. It eventually took simply the germs in our own air "which God in his wisdom created for the Earth" to destroy the invading Martians. • Distinguished British actor Sir Cedric Hardwicke provided the brilliant narration for the *War of the Worlds*. Paul Frees performed the prenarrative introduction, the radio announcing, and played the part of a newscaster. • George Pal, the film's producer and creative genius, appeared in the film as a derelict listening to the ominous radio warning. • One of the Pacific Tech scientists out camping with Dr. Forrester (Gene Barry) was played by 50s "scientist" actor, Robert Cornthwaite, fresh from *The Thing* (1951).

Invaders on Earth: The 60s and 70s

Alien Dead (1979) (see ZOMBIE FLESH EATERS) (also *It Fell from the Sky*). An alien force rides to Earth on a meteorite and transforms the locals into hungry walking corpses.

The Alien Factor (1979) D: Don Dohler. Cast: Don Leifert, Tom Griffin. An alien spaceship crash-lands on Earth, then disgorges three different looking space creatures — a furry, long-legged "Zagatile," the clawing "Inferbyce," and the reptilian "Leemoid."

Assignment Terror (1970; AIP-TV; Spain/ W. Germany/Italy) D: Tullio Demichelli, Peter Riethof (English version). P: Jaime Prades. S: Jacinto Molina Alvarez. C: Godofredo Pacheco. Cast: Michael Rennie, Karin Dor, Craig Hill, Patty Sheppard, Angel del Pozo, Paul Naschy. Michael Rennie plays an alien planning to conquer the Earth by reviving all of the classic monsters (Dracula, the Frankenstein Monster, the Mummy, and the Wolfman). ¶ "Remember, success of the mission depends on exploiting to the full the superstitions prevalent among the Earth creatures."

The Body Stealers (1969; Tigon; U.K.) D: Gerry Levy. P: Tony Tenser. S: Mike St. Clair. C: Johnny Coquillon. Cast: George Sanders, Maurice Evans, Patrick Allen, Neil Connery, Lorna Wilde. An alien kidnaps parachutists passing through a red mist, substituting duplicates in their place.

Cape Canaveral Monsters (1960; CCM) D/S: Phil Tucker. P: Richard Greer. C: Merle Connell. Cast: Scott Peters, Linda Connell, Jason Johnson, Katherine Victor, Gary Travis. Two aliens land on earth and inhabit dead bodies in a plot to interfere with the U.S. space program. ¶ "We need more Earthlings for our experiments, especially females." • Director Phil Tucker, who helmed the classic turkey, *Robot Monster* (1953), reportedly chose to write the script himself for *Cape Canaveral Monsters* because of his dissatisfaction with Wyatt Ordung's writing on *Robot Monster*. • Cinematographer Merle Connell had the pleasure of filming his own daughter, who starred in this film.

Children of the Damned (1963; MGM; U.K.) D: Anton M. Leader. P: Ben Arbeid. S: John Briley. C: David Boulton. Cast: Ian Hendry, Alan Badel, Barbara Ferris, Alfred Burke, Sheila Allen. This sequel to *Village of the Damned* (1960) features six children born in different parts of the world who are brought together because of their alien mental powers and seemingly collective intelligence. The debate as to whether they should live or die is settled at the climax when they are accidentally destroyed by the military. ¶ "Anything one of them sees, hears, or reads, they all know." • The eyes of the six children glow when they exercise their alien powers.

The Creeping Terror (1964) (see BLOBS). An alien blob-like creature crashes on Earth and sets out looking for people to consume.

Daleks: Invasion Earth 2150 A.D. (1966; Amicus/Continental; U.K.) D: Gordon Flemying. P: Max J. Rosenberg, Milton Subotsky. S: Milton Subotsky. C: John Wilcox. Cast: Peter Cushing, Bernard Cribbins, Ray Brooks, Andrew Keir, Jill Curzon, Roberta Tovey. A London bobby mistakenly transports a group of Englanders, including the famous Dr. Who (Peter Cushing), forward into the Earth's future. When they arrive, they learn that the alien Daleks have conquered the Earth and are planning to use a bomb to rip apart the planet's inner core. Their nefarious plan is thwarted when Dr. Who and rebel forces create a magnetic force field, diverting the bomb and sucking the aliens deep inside the Earth. • The invading Daleks intend to use the Earth as an enormous spaceship by tearing out the central core with a bomb. The picture is a sequel to the 1965 film, *Dr. Who and the Daleks,* which was made with primarily the same production team.

The Dark (1979; Film Ventures International) D: John "Bud" Cardos. P: Dick Clark, Edward L. Montoro. S: Stanford Whitmore. C: John Morrill. Cast: William Devane, Cathy Lee Crosby, Richard Jaeckel, Keenan Wynn, Warren Kemmerling, Biff Elliot, Casey Kasem, Vivian Blaine. An author and a TV broadcaster discover that a terrible crime wave is being perpetrated by a seven-foot alien armed with a laser. ¶ "On our planet, hundreds of species of animal, plant, and insect life protect themselves by using their ability to change their color or shape, to blend into their surroundings. Many other species are capable of killing their prey by use of electric shocks, acids, or poisons. Of the millions of planets capable of supporting life in the universe, it is a certainty that hundreds of thousands have developed species of life with characteristics similar, and possibly more dangerous, than those found on our own planet Earth. It is also a certainty that not all alien encounters will be friendly!"

The Day Mars Invaded the Earth (1963; 20th Century–Fox) D/P: Maury Dexter. S: Harry Spalding. C: John Nickolaus, Jr. Cast: Kent Taylor, Marie Windsor, William Mims, Betty Beall, Lowell Brown. Martians plot to secretly replace an Earth scientist and his family with exact alien duplicates in a plan to disable Earth's space program. ¶ "There is life on Mars, Dr. Fielding. Oh, not as you know it here, your organisms couldn't exist in our environment. Instead we have intelligence, in the abstract, much like your electricity here. You can't play it or see it, but it can manifest itself just as you see me here manifested before you." • The film's dark climax depicts the alien scheme as a success, with the new Dr. Fielding and his alien family driving back home. Perhaps we will never reach Mars?

Destination Inner Space (1966; Magna Pictures) D: Francis D. Lyon. P: Earle Lyon. S: Arthur C. Pierce. C: Brick Marquard. Cast: Scott Brady, Sheree North, Gary Merrill, Mike Road, Wende Wagner, John Howard. An alien saucer is discovered near an underwater sea lab. Divers explore the ship and bring back a cylindrical giob from which a gill-man creature grows. The humpbacked amphibean wreaks havoc above and below the ocean until its ship is destroyed by a bomb. ¶ "Those five men pounding and clawing at that door, trying desperately to get out of that flooding compartment ... they were just kids Wayne, and you were on the other side of that door, you didn't make a move to help them!" • Actor Mike Road is the familiar voice of "Race Bannon" from the "Johnny Quest" TV cartoon.

The End of the World (1977; Irwin Yablans Co.) D: John Hayes. P: Charles Band. S: Frank Ray Perilli. C: John Huneck. Cast: Christopher Lee, Sue Lyon, Dean Jagger, Kirk Scott, Lew Ayres, MacDonald Carey. Aliens from the planet "Utopia" masquerade as a priest and nuns in an alien plan to destroy the polluted planet Earth. The kicker ending has the human heroes forsaking Earth and returning with the aliens to their home planet. • Christopher Lee plays the alien named "Zandi," disguised as a priest. • MacDonald Carey was a stage and radio performer before he began his screen career in 1942. He is also known for his work in the TV daytime soap, "Days of Our Lives."

The Eye Creatures (1965; Azalea) D/P: Larry Buchanan. S: Robert Gurney, Jr., Al Martin. C: Ralph K. Johnson. Cast: John Ashley, Cynthia Hull, Warren Hammack, Chet Davis. Multi-eyed invading aliens are thwarted by a group of over-aged teenagers. ¶ "I'm just thinking how Carl will feel when I put him on exhibition as the world's first victim of a spaceman." • *The Eye Creatures* is an ultra-cheap (less than $50,000) uncredited remake of the 1957 low budget cult classic, *Invasion of the Saucermen*. It was filmed at Gordon (*The Killer Shrews,* 1959) McClendon's ranch outside Dallas, Texas. • John Ashley commented on the film in Tom Weaver's book, *Interviews with B Science Fiction and Horror Movie Makers:* "There was a guy named Larry Buchanan that came up with a formula of taking some of the early movies that AIP had done and remaking them, shooting them in 16mm, with essentially just one supposedly recognizable name.... *The Eye Creatures* probably ranks right up with some of the all-time worst horror films ever made."

Five Million Years to Earth (1967; Hammer/Seven Arts; U.K.) (also *Quatermass and the Pit*). D: Roy Ward Baker. P: Anthony Nelson Keys. S: Nigel Kneale. C: Arthur Grant. Cast: Andrew Keir, Barbara Shelley, James Donald, Julian Glover, Duncan Lamont, Bryan Marshall. London subway construction unearths an ancient spaceship from Mars containing the remains of insect-like aliens. Although the Martians have long been dead, their spacecraft still emits strange powers. Scientists discover that the human evolutionary process was speeded up by the aliens, apparently by taking apes and systematically altering them, then returning them back to our planet with new, increased intelligence. ¶ "You realize what you're implying. That we owe our human condition here to the intervention of insects." • This is the third chapter in the Quatermass film series, the first being *The Creeping Unknown* (1955) and the second, *The Enemy from Space* (1957). The first two featured Brian Donlevy as Professor Quatermass, but in this entry Andrew Keir took over the role. • Director Roy Ward Baker commented about the film and its stars in John Brosnan's book, *The Horror People:* "I got into horror films by accident. Hammer rang me out of a clear blue sky and asked me if I would like to do a science fiction picture ... so I read the script and of course it was a damned good one.... We also had a very good cast—James Donald, Andrew Keir, and Barbara Shelley—she is very good, and one of the loves of my life."

Frankenstein Meets the Space Monster (1965; Futurama) (also *Duel of the Space Monsters; Mars Invades Puerto Rico*). D: Robert Gaffney. P: Robert McCarty. S: George Garret. C: Saul Midwall. Cast: Jim Karen, Marilyn Hanold, Lou Cutell, Robert Reilly, Nancy Marshall, David Kerman. Bald-headed alien invaders are after "good breeding stock" (women) on Earth, but their mission is foiled by a short circuited half-man, half-robot, who emerges from a crashed U.S. rocket. ¶ Alien stooge: "We continue to hear a modulated hydrogen frequency signal of 21 centimeters, Princess."

Alien princess: "What does that mean?" Alien stooge: "We're not quite sure, Princess." • The film was shot on location in Puerto Rico on a budget of $67,000. • The tremendous battle which is promised by the film's title and advertising is seen only at the climax and takes up less than 40 seconds of screen time. This "mandroid" is not named "Frankenstein," but his first name *is* Frank. Half of his face is completely chewed up after the crash explosion. His foe is a hairy mutant alien creature with huge claws that the Martians use to do their dirty work. Neither wins the fight, but Frank manages to blow the spaceship up in mid flight while they attempt to escape military bombardment. • The film takes great pains to feature the unusual song, "To Have and to Hold" by the Distant Cousins, with profound alien lines like: "We'll do everything that lovers do, two by two-oooooohhhh," and "Oh, oh, oh. Oh, oh, oh." • *Frankenstein Meets the Space Monsters* carried a shooting title of *Operation San Juan.*

Goke: Body Snatcher from Hell (1968; Shochiku; Japan) D: Hajime Sato. P: Takashi Inomata. S: Susumu Takaku, Kyuzo Kobayashi. C: Shizuo Hirase. Cast: Hideo Ko, Teruo Yoshida, Tomomi Sato, Eizo Kitamura, Masaya Takahashi. *Goke* is actually an alien organism which transforms people into vampiric creatures.

Horror Express (1972; Granada/Benmar; Spain/U.K.) D: Gene Martin. P: Bernard Gordon. S: Arnaud d'Usseau, Julian Halvey. C: Alejandro Ulloa. Cast: Christopher Lee, Peter Cushing, Telly Savalas, Silvia Tortosa, Alberto de Mendoza. This period film, set mostly on a train, features an alien who awakens from its fossilized state to boil the brains of whomever it looks at, absorbing their intelligence and turning them into automated zombies. ¶ "It hasn't eaten in two million years." • The creature was unearthed by scientist Christopher Lee, who believed it to be the missing link between man and the apes. Unfortunately for the train passengers, the being turns out to be an alien with mind controlling powers that must kill to learn. • Telly Savalas, later the TV detective "Kojak," played a coarse Cossack in the film.

The Human Duplicators (1965; Independenti Regionali; Italy/U.S.) D: Hugo Grimaldi. P: Hugo Grimaldi, Arthur C. Pierce. S: Arthur C. Pierce. C: Monroe Askins. Cast: George Nader, Barbara Nichols, George Macready, Richard Kiel, Dolores Faith, Richard Arlen, Hugh Beaumont. A seven-foot tall alien named Kolos (Richard Kiel) uses a scientist's lab to create android doubles of people in high places in a plot to control the world. The invasion scheme is stopped when George Nader and Barbara Nichols destroy Kolos with a laser beam. ¶ "I was sent here to prepare your planet for invasion by the Masters of the Galaxy."

The Incredible Invasion (1971; Azteca/Columbia; Mexico) (also *Sinister Invasion; Alien Terror* [video title]). D: Juan Ibañez, Jack Hill. P: Enrique Vergara. S: Karl Schanzer, Enrique Vergara. C: Raul Dominguez, Austin McKinney. Cast: Boris Karloff, Enrique Guzman, Christa Linder, Maura Monti, Yerye Beirute. A mind-controlling alien inhabits the body of a killer to stop a scientist (Boris Karloff) from developing a new power source which could defend the Earth from invasion. ¶ Yes my little friend, I learned a great deal from you since you invaded my body. Did you really think I'd sit quietly in a corner of my brain, while you did exactly what you liked?" • This is one of four films Boris Karloff starred in for Mexican producer Juan Ibañez. These were the last four pictures Karloff made before he died.

Invasion (1966; Allied Artists; U.K.) D: Alan Bridges. P: Jack Greenwood. S: Roger Marshall. C: James Wilson. Cast: Edward Judd, Valerie Gearon, Lyndon Brook, Yoko Tani, Tsai Chin, Barrie Ingham. Alien invaders, looking like beautiful Asian women, place an invisible force field around a remote British hospital. They are searching for an escaped alien prisoner. ¶ "I think I prefer the idea of space being peopled by three-eyed monsters, at least it was nice and remote. Now we've got them killing each other just like us."

Invasion of the Animal People (1962; A.D.P. Productions; Sweden/U.S.) (also *Terror in the Midnight Sun*). D: Virgel W. Vogel. P: Bertil Jernberg. S: Arthur C. Pierce. C: Hilding Bladh. Cast: Barbara Wilson, Robert Burton, Stan Gester, Bengt Blomgren, John Carradine. A giant hairy creature from outer space terrorizes the snow-bound countryside until it is torched by villagers and falls from a cliff. ¶ "Our quest for comprehension is perhaps most complicated by the failure to discover reality in ourselves." • This Swedish/American co-production was filmed on location in Lapland for $40,000 (half from American investors and half from Swedish backers). • The man in the monster suit was a newspaperman who put up part of the Swedish money. • Genre vet John Carradine was the on-screen narrator for the tacked-on footage in the American version of the film.

Invasion of the Body Snatchers (1978; United Artists) D: Philip Kaufman. P: Robert H. Solo. S: W. D. Richter. C: Michael Chapman. Cast: Donald Sutherland, Brooke Adams, Leonard Nimoy, Veronica Cartwright, Jeff Goldblum. This is a modern remake of the 1956 classic about pods from outer space replacing humans with emotionless alien counterparts. ¶ "People are changing, they're becoming less human." • Kevin McCarthy (star of the original) has a brief appearance in this remake as a man on the streets warning of the pod invasion (just as he did at the end of the original 1956 version).

Invasion of the Love Drones (1975) D/P/C: Jerome Hamlin. S: Jerome Hamlin, Conrad Baunz, Michael Gury. Cast: Eric Edwards, Viveca Ash, Bree Anthony, Tony Blue, Sarah Nicholson. Viveca Ash is an alien named Dr. Femme, who plots to start an orgy on Earth in order to fuel her spaceship (which runs on sexual energy) in this obscure adults-only sci-fi feature.

Invasion of the Star Creatures (1962; AIP) D: Bruno Ve Sota. P: Berj Hagopian. S: Jonathan Haze. C: Basil Bradbury. Cast: Robert Ball, Frankie Ray, Dolores Reed, Gloria Victor, Bruno Ve Sota. Two female aliens intend to invade Earth with the use of their vegetable creatures, but are sidetracked from their plan when they fall for a couple of goofy soldiers. ¶ "That's the first time a salad ever tossed me." • The alien monsters were made by Burt Schoenberg out of burlap bags dyed green. • Screenwriter Jonathan Haze was a regular member of the Corman acting troupe during the 50s and 60s. He appeared in *It Conquered the World* (1956), *Not of This Earth* (1957), and *The Viking Women and the Sea Serpent* (1958), to name just a few. He originally intended to call the film *Monsters from Nicholson Mesa* in reference to another Corman regular, his friend Jack Nicholson.

Island of the Burning Doomed (1967; Planet company; U.K.) (also *The Night of the Big Heat; Island of the Burning Damned*). D: Terence Fisher. P: Tom Blakeley. S: Ronald Liles, Pip and Jane Baker. C: Reg Wyer. Cast: Christopher Lee, Peter Cushing, Jane Merrow, Patrick Allen, Sarah Lawson, William Lucas. Blob-like aliens create a heat wave on the British island of Fara, which bakes the locals until the invading creatures are destroyed by rain. • Star Christopher Lee was less than impressed with the appearance of these aliens.

"They were supposed to represent pieces of protoplasm," he told authors Pohle and Hart for their book, *The Films of Christopher Lee*. "To me, they looked like badly fried eggs." • The story is based on John Lymington's novel, *Night of the Big Heat*.

Laserblast (1978; Selected Pictures) D: Michael Rae. P: Charles Band. S: Franne Schact, Frank Ray Perilli. Cast: Kim Milford, Cheryl Smith, Keenan Wynn, Roddy McDowall. A young boy finds a laser gun left by aliens, which changes him into an ugly green-skinned brute. He then proceeds to blast his antagonists, using the gun.

Mars Needs Women (1966) (see BENEVOLENT ALIENS, this chapter). Tommy Kirk plays a generally peaceful Martian who is looking for suitable mates to take back with him. The military views the idea as an invasion. ¶ "They're kidnapping our women!"

The Night Caller (1965; Armitage; U.K.) (also *Night Caller from Outer Space*). D: John Gilling. P: Ronald Liles. S: Jim O'Connolly. C: Stephen Dade. Cast: John Saxon, Maurice Denham, Patricia Haines, Alfred Burke, John Carson, Jack Watson. An alien from the planet "Ganymede" is sent to Earth to obtain women for breeding.

Santa Claus Conquers the Martians (1964; Embassy) D: Nick Webster. P: Paul Jacobson. S: Glenville Mareth. C: David Quaid. Cast: John Call, Leonard Hicks, Vincent Back, Victor Stiles, Donna Conforti, Bill McCutcheon. Santa is captured by Martians in a misguided attempt to spread a little good will to their own listless children. ¶ "Something is wrong with our children, they eat not, they sleep not, they're only interested in watching meaningless Earth programs on the video."

Starship Invasions (1977; Hal Roach International; Canada) (also *Alien Encounter*). D/S: Ed Hunt. P: Ed Hunt, Norman Glick, Ken Cord. C: Mark Irwin. Cast: Robert Vaughn, Christopher Lee, Daniel Pilon, Tiiu Leek, Helen Shaver. Christopher Lee is a hostile alien named Captain Ramses who's come to Earth to claim it for his dying planet. He is opposed by the dome-headed good-guy aliens who run a secret undersea base. ¶ "It's just that UFO's are such bizarre things, and you're so attracted to them." • The peaceful aliens who work for the "Intergalactic League of Races" only want to monitor and study the Earthlings, whereas Ramses and his henchman want to destroy the people of Earth via a ray which induces the humans to commit suicide. • Robert Vaughn plays a UFO specialist who ends up aiding the "good" aliens. Vaughn, of course, is the famous spy from the TV series "Man from U.N.C.L.E." Vaughn's participation in this film apparently convinced Christopher Lee to join the cast. Lee was quoted as saying, "I went to do this picture because if Robert Vaughn was prepared to do it, I had no objection." • Maureen Sweeney was one of the makeup artists spending nine weeks designing and sculpting the molds for the bald-headed aliens to wear. She joked, "Knowing full well only one out of three would bake properly. For this my mother taught me how to cook?" Maureen described the makeup applications saying, "First Tiiu's head was covered with a stocking, then the mold fit over it like a cap. Next I tore away bits of rubber around the eyes for a good eye-socket fit. After that came the tedious work of sticking the edges of the mold to the head with spirit gum.... The makeup consisted of a pinkish flesh tone base made by mixing castor oil and pancake. Then baby powder was generously applied. Black contact lenses gave the alien effect of eyes without pupils."

They Came from Beyond Space (1967) (see BENEVOLENT ALIENS, this chapter). Aliens inhabit the bodies of humans in an attempt to repair their stranded ships.

The Three Stooges in Orbit (1962; Columbia) D: Edward Bernds. P: Norman Maurer. S: Elwood Ullman. C: William F. Whitley. Cast: Moe Howard, Larry Fine, Joe De Rita, Carol Christensen, Emil Sitka, Edson Stroll, George Neise, Rayforn Barnes. Larry, Moe, and Curly Joe navigate a submarine-like flying machine to thwart the plans of the two Martian invaders, Og and Zog. ¶ "Those brainless AstroNuts meet the martians!" — ad line.

Unearthly Stranger (1963; Independent Artists/AIP; U.K.) D: John Krish. P: Albert Fennell. S: Rex Carlton. C: Reg Wyer. Cast: John Neville, Gabriella Licudi, Philip Stone, Patrick Newell, Jean Marsh, Warren Mitchell. John Neville discovers that his wife is an alien, and that her comrades plan to invade Earth. She falls in love with him, however, and is killed for her weakness. ¶ "In a little while I expect to die. To be killed by something you and I know is here, visible, yet moving unseen amongst us all each moment of the day and night. There were times when you thought I was insane, but listen to this tape I beg you, so you could know what it is you have to fight, or is it too late? Even if I'd known what I know now, could I, or anyone, have held back the terror?" • Neville's wife sleeps with her eyes open, tipping him off as to her alien status.

At the climax, she cries and the tears burn marks down her face like acid.

Village of the Damned (1960; MGM; U.K.) D: Wolf Rilla. P: Ronald Kinnoch. S: Wolf Rilla, Stirling Silliphant, George Barclay. C: Geoffrey Faithfull. Cast: George Sanders, Barbara Shelley, Martin Stephens, Michael Gwynne, Laurence Naismith. An entire town is put to sleep and every capable female is impregnated by some mysterious alien force. The alien children born of this phenomenon possess incredible power and a collective, malignant intelligence. At the climax, George Sanders (who at first believes the children should be allowed to live, but later changes his mind) has to focus his thoughts on a brick wall in order to prevent the alien children from reading his mind and discovering the time bomb he has planted to destroy them. ¶ "They're not kids. Have you ever seen them laugh, run, play? No, my God, but you've seen them kill!"

War of the Planets (1965; Mercury/Southern Cross; Italy/Spain) D: Antonio Margheriti. P: Antonio Margheriti, Joseph Fryd, Walter Manley. S: Ivan Reiner, Renato Moretti. C: Riccardo Pallottino. Cast: Tony Russell, Lisa Gastoni, Carlo Giustini, Massimo Serato, Michel Lemoine, Franco Nero. Alien "Diaphanoids" plan to invade Earth, disabling the planetary satellite defense system by secretly inhabiting key human beings.

The Warlords of Atlantis (1978) (see ATLANTIS). Doug McClure and his allies from Atlantis are descendants of an invading Martian race.

The X from Outerpsace (1967; Shochiku; Japan) D: Kazui Nihonmatsu. P: Akihiko Shimada. S: Kazui Nihonmatsu, Hidemi Motomochi, Moriyoshi Ishida. C: Shizuo Hirase. Cast: Eiji Okada, Toshiya Wazaki, Peggy Neal, Itoko Harada, Shinichi Yanagisawa. A strange cell-like substance is brought back to Earth during a space mission, which grows into a gigantic alien monster. • The monster is stopped by showering it with anti-matter collected from space.

Yog, Monster from Outer Space (1970; Toho/AIP; Japan) D: Inoshiro Honda. P: Tomoyuki Tanaka, Fumio Tanaka. S: El Ogawa. C: Taiichi Kankura. Cast: Akira Kubo, Atsuko Takahashi, Toshio Tsuchiya, Kenji Sahara, Noritake Saito. A mysterious mist brought to a Pacific island by an alien spaceship creates giant monsters from turtles, crabs, and squibs. The aliens inhabit one of the islanders to check on matters, then a volcano erupts, destroying the whole works.

Zeta One (1969; Tigon; U.K.) (also *Alien Women*). D: Michael Cort. P: George Maynard. S: Michael Cort, Alastair McKenzie. C: Jack Atchelor. Cast: Robin Hawdon, Yutte Stensgaard, James Robertson Justice, Charles Hawtrey, Dawn Addams. This adults-only tongue-in-cheek feature is about an invasion of alien superwomen which is thwarted by a secret agent. • Yutte Stensgaard, of *Lust for a Vampire* (1971) fame, plays one of the sexy aliens in various modes of undress.

Zontar, the Thing from Venus (1966; Azalea/AIP) D/P: Larry Buchanan. S: Larry Buchanan, H. Taylor. C: Robert B. Alcott. Cast: John Agar, Susan Bjorman, Anthony Houston, Patricia DeLaney, Warren Hammack. A Venusian invader enlists the aid of a disgruntled scientist in its plan to take over the world by turning people into automated, emotionless drones. ¶ "Zontar, you're slimy, horrible! I hate your guts for what you've done to my husband and my world!" • This uncredited remake of the 1956 Roger Corman film, *It Conquered the World,* was filmed at a Dallas area park. • John Agar, frequent 50s sci-fi actor, playing the lead in this pitifully cheap film, later said of director Larry Buchanan, "Larry, God bless him, is a nice guy but he really was not a director."

Invaders on Earth: The 80s and Beyond

The Adventures of Buckaroo Banzai Across the Eighth Dimension (1984; Sherwood Productions) D: W. D. Richter. P: Neil Clanton, W. D. Richter. S: Earl Mac Rauch. C: Fred J. Koenekamp. Cast: Peter Weller, John Lithgow, Ellen Barkin, Jeff Goldblum, Christopher Lloyd, Lewis Smith, Rosalind Cash, Robert Ito. A heroic rocket scientist who manages to break through the Eighth Dimension in his speeding jet car becomes of paramount importance to a coalition of aliens from that dimension. The civilized aliens threaten to push Earth into war unless Buckaroo can somehow stop one of their evil members who has taken over the body of a crazed Earth scientist (John Lithgow). ¶ "Don't be mean. We don't have to be mean because, remember, no matter where you go, there you are." • Peter *(Robocop)* Weller stars as "Buckaroo Banzai, born to an American mother and a Japanese Father"—a martial arts expert, doctor, and rock star. • Buckaroo's comrades in action are known as the Hong Kong Cavaliers, the names of which include Perfect Tommy, New Jersey, Rawhide, Pinky, and Reno Nevada. The feminine interest in the story, a girl named Penny Pretty, is played by Ellen Barkin.

Alien Contamination (1981; Cannon; Italy) D/S: Lewis Coates. P: Claudio Mancini. C: Giuseppe Pinori. Cast: Ian McCulloch, Louise Monroe, Siegfried Rauch, Marino Mase, Lisa Hahn. A cyclopean alien from Mars spreads its eggs throughout the U.S. with the help of an astronaut under its control. • According to star Ian McCulloch, "The producers originally wanted to call it *Alien 2,* but 20th Century–Fox had words to say about that idea" *(Fangoria* #52).

Alien from L.A. (1988) (see ATLANTIS). A California "valley girl" ends up in the underground world of Atlantis. *She* is the "alien" of the title.

Alien High (1987; Gold Gems Entertainment; Canada) D: Eugenie Joseph. P: Pierre Grise. C: Christian Racine. Cast: Roy Thinnes, Skip Lackey, Lee Tergesen, David Kener, Miranda De Pencier, Bill Curry, Robert Dubac. A strict principal brings in a behavioral psychologist to help him rid his high school of insubordinate behavior and rock and roll music. The scientist, however, turns out to be an alien who uses an experimental thought control device, sending subliminal messages to the kids which alters their behavior. A couple of the teens catch on to the scheme and break the alien's control over the staff and students with a helpful jolt of rock 'n' roll. In the end, the thwarted alien, who wanted to control the youth of the world, makes a half-hearted apology saying, "It was never our intent to harm you," and insists they will meet again. ¶ "I want no more of that sexually provocative tribal music. Why do you think they're so promiscuous to begin with?"

Alien Predator (1987; Trans World) D/S: Deran Sarafian. P: Deran Sarafian, Carlos Aured. C: Tote Trenas. Cast: Dennis Christopher, Martin Hewitt, Lynn Holly-Johnson, Luis Prendes, J. O. Bosso. Three American youths on a trip to Europe uncover an alien invasion within a Spanish town. The local inhabitants are being possessed by an alien microbe (à la *Invasion of the Body Snatchers*). • The alien microbe, which drives people mad, came down to Earth attached to a chunk of Skylab spacecraft. People are infected when they contact the contaminated blood. Eventually an alien monster is formed, breaking through the chest (shades of *Alien*) of a gas station attendant. • The picture was filmed in Spain in 1984 and shelved after its initial distributor, Film Ventures International, broke up.

Alien Seed (1989; AIP Distribution, Inc.) D: Bob James. P: Mark Paglia. S: Bob James, Douglas K. Grimm. C: Ken Carmack. Cast: Erik Estrada, Heidi Paine. An 18-year-old girl inexplicably impregnated by an alien messiah is murdered. Her sister vows to uncover the truth, but she soon becomes the new target of the alien seed. Other interested parties include Erik Estrada as a man who wants the mysterious alien spawn to die and a governmental UFO agency who wants the child for research.

Alien Warrior (1985: Goodluck Productions) D: Edward Hunt. P: Yakov Bentsvi, Edward Hunt. S: Edward Hunt, Rueben Gordon, Steve Schoenberg, Barry Pearson. Cast: Brett Clark, Pamela Saunders, Reggie DeMorton. An alien warrior and defender of justice is sent to our planet to clean out the violent city streets.

Bad Taste (1989; WingNut Films; New Zealand) D/P/S: Peter Jackson. Cast: Terry Potter, Pete O'Herne, Craig Smith, Mike Minett, Peter Jackson, Doug Wren. A band of invading aliens take on the form of humans and wipe out an entire rural New Zealand town with the intention of bringing the body parts back as samples for an intended intergalactic fast-food chain. Four commandos (of sorts) from a special government agency do battle with the aliens with guns, knives, and even a chainsaw in order to foil their plans of using Earthlings as cattle. ¶ "Why can't aliens be friendly? There's no glowy fingers on these bastards. We've got a bunch of extraterrestrial psychopaths on our hands." • As well as producing, directing, and writing this over-the-top import, Peter Jackson also did the numerous special effects and even acted in it as well (when one of his actors left to get married). • *Bad Taste* was filmed for $400,000 over a four-year period. It took so long because Jackson and his actors usually worked at their regular jobs six days a week and so could only film on Sundays. • Originally titled *Giles' Big Day,* it acquired its current moniker during production.

Big Meat Eater (1982; BCD Entertainment Corp.; Canada) D/S: Chris Windsor. P/S: Laurence Keane. S: Phil Savath. C: Doug McKay. Cast: George Dawson, Big Miller, Andrew Gillies, Stephen Dimopoulos, Georgina Hededos, Ida Carnevali,

Howard Taylor, Sharon Wahl. Aliens revive a corpse for the purpose of building a device which will collect radioactive baloneum. They are thwarted when a scientist uses the baloneum to build a makeshift rocket from which he shoots down the aliens' saucer.

Biohazard (1984; 21st Century) D/P/S: Fred Olen Ray. C: Paul Elliott, John McCoy. Cast: Aldo Ray, Angelique Pettyjohn, William Fair, Frank McDonald, David Pearson, Christopher Ray. A top-secret experiment in matter transference causes the appearance of a nasty four foot tall lizard-like alien from another dimension. When he kills, this alien injects his victims with a toxic substance which causes the recipient to foam at the mouth and die. ¶ "I'm sorry, it's just that there's this creature out there that can kill an able-bodied man in just a matter of seconds—it's really more than we can handle." • *Biohazard* was filmed on the minuscule budget of $250,000. • The Kenneth Hall–designed monster suit was worn by director Fred Olen Ray's five-year-old son, Chris Ray.

Bloodbath at the House of Death (1983) (see WITCHES, WARLOCKS, AND CULTS). A group of scientists investigating the strange occurrences at Headstone Manor are gruesomely killed off by a group of devil-worshiping monks. It is hinted that the monks are actually aliens, and at the film's end they all enter the house and blast off in what appears to be a spaceship.

Bloodsuckers from Outer Space (1987; Reel Movies International) D/S: Glen Coburn. P: Garl Boyd Latham. C: Chad D. Smith. Cast: Thom Meyers, Laura Ellis, Dennis Letts, Chris Heldman, Robert Bradeen. This comedy/horror story features an alien virus that infects a Texas farm town, turning the citizens into blood-sucking zombies. The military decides to drop a bomb on the town but misses by 60 miles, killing off thousands of innocent Texans down the road.

Breeders (1987; Wizard Video) D/S: Tim Kincaid. P: Cynthia DePaula. C: Thomas Murphy. Cast: Theresa Farley, Lance Lewman, Francis Raines, Natalie O'Connell, Amy Brentano. A cop and a physician attempt to track down a serial attacker of women, whose assaulted victims invariably heal overnight and then disappear from the hospital. Eventually they find a blobbish nest of impregnated women below the city and the monstrous alien creature responsible for the mayhem. • Ed French, who provided the film's makeup FX, also appears in the movie as a doctor who's possessed by the aliens. • Tim Kincaid shot *Breeders* back to back with *Mutant Hunt,* each on a ten-day schedule. • This direct-to-video feature was filmed in the same underground tunnel locations (underneath the Brooklyn Bridge) featured in *Chud* (1984).

Critters (1986; New Line Cinema) D: Stephen Herek. P: Rupert Harvey. S: Dominic Muir, Stephen Herek. C: Tim Suhrstedt. Cast: Dee Wallace Stone, M. Emmet Walsh, Scott Grimes, Billy Green Bush, Don Opper, Terrence Mann, Nadine Van Der Velde. Small, furry alien criminal monsters called "Krites" escape from a passing prison ship and land on Earth near a small Kansas town. These vicious aliens roll themselves up into a ball to chase and eat people. • The flesh-eating critters are disposed of with the help of two bounty hunters from outer space.

Critters 2: The Main Course (1988; New Line Cinema) D: Mick Garris. P: Barry Opper. S: Mick Garris, D. T. Twohyi. C: Russell Carpenter. Cast: Scott Grimes, Liane Curtis, Don Opper, Barry Corbin, Terrence Mann. Two years later, an overlooked batch of "Krite" eggs are hatching hairy critters once again, which then go on a flesh-eating rampage until three alien bounty hunters arrive via spaceship to come wipe them out. • One of the shape-changing alien bounty hunters takes on the form of a "Playboy" centerfold he sees in a magazine he finds — complete with a staple in the navel.

The Deadly Spawn (1983; Filmline Communications) D/S: Douglas McKeown. P: Ted Bohus. C: Harvey Birnhaum. Cast: Charles George Hildebrandt, Tom De Franco, Richard Lee Porter, Jean Tafler. A monster movie buff battles hungry alien invaders that come to Earth during a meteor shower.

Hanger 18 (1980; Taft International) D: James L. Conway. P: Charles E. Sellier, Jr. S: Steven Thornley. C: Paul Hipp. Cast: Darren McGavin, Robert Vaughn, Gary Collins, James Hampton, Joseph Campanella. Darren McGavin plays a NASA snooper trying to crack a UFO conspiracy involving a mid-air collision with an alien craft.

The Hidden (1987; New Line Cinema/ Heron Communications) D: Jack Sholder. P: Robert Shaye, Gerald T. Olson, Michael Meltzer. S: Bob Hunt. C: Jacques Haitkin. Cast: Michael Nouri, Kyle MacLachlan, Ed O'Ross, Clu Gulager, Claudia Christian. An alien (Kyle MacLachlan), posing as an FBI agent, is sent to Earth to track down a renegade killer from his planet. The aliens have the power to inhabit bodies of humans (or any larger life form), and then move on to another when that body has been used up or damaged. • The planet they come from is named "Altair" — an homage to the 1956 sci-fi classic, *Forbidden Planet.* • This entertaining film was made on the relative low budget of $4.5 million.

Hyperspace (1987; Regency) D: Tod Durham. P: Earl Owensby. Cast: Alan Marx, Paula Poundstone, Chris Elliot. An evil Darth Vader clone comes to Earth where he mistakes a group of North Carolina locals for the leaders of a space rebellion, and attempts to zap them into oblivion. • *Hyperspace* was filmed in 3-D.

I Come in Peace (1990; Vision International) D: Craig R. Baxley. P: Jeff Young. S: Jonathan Tydor, Leonard Maas, Jr. Cast: Dolph Lundgren, Brian Benben, Betsy Brantley. A policeman uncovers an alien's plot to use human bodies to manufacture intergalactic narcotics. If his scheme is successful, the alien plans to order a full-scale invasion.

Invaders from Mars (1986; Cannon) D: Tobe Hooper. P: Menahem Golam, Yoram Globus. S: Dan O'Bannon, Don Jakoby. C: Daniel Pearl. Cast: Karen Black, Hunter Carson, Timothy Bottoms, Laraine Newman, James Karen, Bud Cort, Louise Fletcher. This is a contemporary remake of the 1953 cult classic about a young boy who uncovers a scheme by alien invaders to abduct and control humans. ¶ "Don't worry boy, marines have no qualms about killing Martians!" • John Dykstra (*Star Wars,* 1977) provided the film's special visual effects, while Stan Winston, who supervised the creature work in *Aliens* (1986), created the Martian invaders. • Edward L. Alperson is listed as one of the associate producers here. He was also the producer for the original 1953 film. • Tobe Hooper used over 200 *actual* Marines as extras to play the Marines in the film.

Killer Klowns from Outer Space (1988; TWE) D: Stephen Chiodo. P: Edward Chiodo, Stephen Chiodo, Charles Chiodo. S: Charles Chiodo, Stephen Chiodo. C: Alfred Taylor. Cast: Grant Cramer, Suzanne Snyder, John Allen Nelson, Royal Dano, John Vernon, Peter Ligassi, Michael Siegel. A group of teens face an invasion of aliens who look like demonic clowns. These alien clowns are no laughing matter, however, when they begin kidnaping the locals in order to store them in cotton candy cocoons and drink their blood. ¶ "Look Mike, c'mon —

cocoons, popcorn guns, monster shadows — oooooo, what do you think we are, we're not as stupid as we look." • This low ($1.85 million) budget oddity was a family affair from square one. FX team Stephen, Charles, and Edward Chiodo turned director/producer/screenwriters for this feature. • Director Stephen Chiodo explained the origin of this rather unique (not to mention bizarre) concept in a *Fangoria* magazine interview (#69): "All of us have an inherent fear of clowns. For instance, I'll never forget an incident that happened to my brother and I about five years ago. We were waiting for a red light when a clown pulled up next to us in a car, and slowly looked in our direction. What a horrible Sight! That's when we got the idea for *Killer Klowns.*"

Lifeforce (1985; U.K.) D: Tobe Hooper. P: Menahem Golan, Yoram Globus. S: Dan O'Bannon, Don Jakoby. C: Alan Hume. Cast: Steve Railsback, Peter Firth, Frank Finlay, Mathilda May, Michael Gothard. Three humanoid aliens in some form of suspended animation are found in a spacecraft by astronauts investigating Halley's Comet. The bodies are brought back to Earth for study, only to revive and wreak havoc in London. The aliens are a form of "space vampire" who suck the life force from humans, leaving them a dried-up husk. Two hours later the lifeless victim rises up as a homicidal zombie. • *Lifeforce* generally garnered negative reactions from both the critics and the movie-going public. Tobe Hooper blames the film's failure on tampering by the distributor. "If 27 minutes had not been cut, and had it remained *Space Vampires* [its shooting title], you would have seen the movie in a whole different light," Hooper claimed in a *Fangoria* interview (#55). "With those pieces removed, without the story points, it was ruined."

Monster in the Closet (1987; Troma) D/S: Bob Dahlin. P: David Levy and Peter L. Bergquist. Cast: Donald Grant, Denise DuBarry, Henry Gibson, Claude Akins, Stella Stevens, Howard Duff, Paul Dooley, John Carradine, Jesse White, Paul Walker. This sci-fi parody, full of homages to such alien classics as *The Thing* (1951), *Close Encounters of the Third Kind* (1977), and *Alien* (1979), follows a sensitive, put-upon reporter named Mr. *Clark* (played by Christopher Reeve look-alike Donald Grant, complete with Clark Kent glasses) sent to a small town to investigate a recent rash of "closet murders." The person responsible turns out to be a large, ugly, indestructible being from outer space who for some inexplicable

reason likes to inhabit closets. ¶ "Oh no, it wasn't the closet . . . it was beauty killed the beast!" • *Monster in the Closet* was originally filmed as *The Incredible Closet Monster.* • 7'2" Kevin Peter Hall was the man in the alien suit. He played a big-budget invader in *Predator* the same year.

Night of the Creeps (1986) (see ZOMBIES). Alien slugs from outer space (the escaped result of an experiment conducted by aliens traveling past Earth at the time) land in a small college town and burrow into a person's brain, turning them into walking zombies. ¶ "They get in through your mouth and they lay eggs in your brain and you walk around while they incubate; you walk around even if you're dead."

Not of This Earth (1988; Pacific Trust) D: Jim Wynorski. P: Jim Wynorski, Murray Miller. S: Jim Wynorski, R. J. Robertson. C: Zoran Hochstatter. Cast: Traci Lords, Arthur Roberts, Lenny Juliano, Roger Lodge, Ace Mask, Rebecca Perle. This is an updated remake (complete with ample expletives and nudity) of the Roger Corman 1956 cult film about an alien invader who needs human blood for his dying planet. ¶ "I will be dining . . . out." • Roger Corman, who produced and directed the original *Not of This Earth* (1956), served as executive producer for this remake. • The film began as a bet between director Jim Wynorski and Roger Corman. Wynorski bet that he could remake Corman's sci-fi flick in the same amount of days and for the same amount of money as Corman did way back in 1956. Of course, since over 30 years had gone by, the idea was a little difficult to execute, and the budget ended up "under $250,000," according to Wynorski. Happily, Wynorski did win the bet (though what the stakes were, he wouldn't divulge). • Former underage porn queen Traci Lords makes her legitimate acting debut in this film. • Arthur Roberts, who plays the lead alien, Mr. Johnson, disliked the original version, calling it "slow" and "cliched" (*Fangoria* #73).

Peacemaker (1990; Fries Distribution Co.) D/S: Kevin S. Tenney. P: Andrew Lane, Wayne Crawford. C: Thomas Jewett. Cast: Robert Forster, Lance Edwards, Hilary Shepard, Bert Remsen, Robert Davi. Two human-looking aliens land on Earth. One is an extraterrestrial version of a vicious serial killer, and the other is an intergalactic police officer sent to track him down. It is up to the confused heroine to figure out who is who and help the right one. ¶ "I am a 'peacemaker,' what you call a police officer."

Predator (1987; 20th Century–Fox) D:

John McTiernan. P: Lawrence Gordon, Joel Silver, John Davis. S: Jim Thomas, John Thomas. C: Donald McAlpine. Cast: Arnold Schwarzenegger, Carl Weathers, Elpidia Carrillo, Bill Duke, Jesse Ventura. A mercenary sent by the CIA to rescue hostages in Central America encounters an alien creature who has come to Earth to do a little hunting . . . the hunting of humans. ¶ "If it bleeds we can kill it." • *Predator* was filmed on location in the jungles of Mexico in eight weeks. • Richard Edlund, of Boss Films, was hired to build the first Predator monster. When it arrived in Mexico City, director John McTiernan was less than pleased. "I turned to my assistant," McTiernan told *Fangoria* #65, "and said, 'Now we're in trouble.'" So production was temporarily shut down (they had already shot all the non-monster scenes) while they searched for a new creature-creator. Stan Winston (an Oscar winner for *Aliens*) ended up creating one of the decade's most memorable alien invaders. • 7'2" Kevin Peter Hall plays the huge alien, and one of Schwarzenegger's cohorts, Sgt. Blain, is played by professional wrestler Jesse Ventura.

Predator 2 (1990; 20th Century–Fox) D: Stephen Hopkins. P: Lawrence Gordon, Joel Silver. S: Jim Thomas, John Thomas. C: Peter Levy. Cast: Danny Glover, Gary Busey, Ruben Blades, Maria Conchita Alonso, Bill Paxton, Kevin Peter Hall, Robert Davi, Adam Baldwin, Kent McCord, Morton Downey, Jr., Clavin Lockhart. In 1997, another alien comes to Earth to hunt humans for sport, this time choosing the concrete jungle of Los Angeles and targeting the members engaged in a drug war, including the police. Danny Glover plays a detective who must stop the alien hunter. ¶ "He's in town with a few days to kill." — ad slogan. • The "trophy case" in the Predator's ship is filled with alien skulls, including one belonging to the *Alien* (1979).

The Revenge of the Teenage Vixens from Outer Space (1985; Malamute) D/C: Jeff Ferrell. P/S: Jeff Ferrell, Michelle Lichter. Cast: Lisa Schwedop, Howard Scott, Amy Chrumpacker, Sterling Ramberg, Julian Schembri, Peter Guss, Anne Lilly. In this rather innocent no-budget sci-fi comedy, a group of female alien invaders come to Earth looking for a few good men, and end up turning their zap guns on the local male teen population when the youths prove inadequate for their needs. • This one-step-up-from-amateur production was shot over the course of four years, and the predominantly teenage cast visibly ages in the film.

Shadowzone (1989; Full Moon Productions) D/S: J. S. Cardone. P: Carol Kottenbrook. C: Karen Grossman. Cast: David Beecroft, James Hong, Shawn Weatherly, Louise Fletcher, Frederick Flynn, Miguel Nuñez, Lu Leonard, Maureen Flaherty, Robbie Rives. A scientist (James Hong) conducts dangerous sleep experiments for the "Shadowzone" project in an underground complex. When he pushes a subject too far, it opens a doorway to another dimension which allows a vicious shapeshifting alien to enter the complex, where it traps and stalks them one by one. ¶ "This thing doesn't only change its molecular structure, it can assume the physical nature of human thought." • Anti-climactically, after killing off most of the humans (apparently just for the fun of it), the creature finally decides it just wants to go home, and leaves.

Spaced Invaders (1990) (see BENEVOLENT ALIENS, this section). A bumbling group of little green men from Mars lands on Earth with the mistaken idea that their spacefleet has invaded (when they hear a re-broadcasting of Orson Welles' "War of the Worlds"). They soon realize their error, and it's up to a little girl and her sheriff father to aid the aliens in avoiding the clutches of the riled townsfolk and blast off back into space. ¶ "Prepare to die, Earthscum!"

Strange Invaders (1983; Orion) D: Michael Laughlin. P: Walter Coblenz. S: Michael Laughlin, William Condon. C: Louis Horvath. Cast: Paul Le Mat, Nancy Allen, Diana Scarwid, Michael Lerner, Louise Fletcher, Wallace Shawn. Aliens come to New York in search of a few companions who stayed behind on Earth during a previous visit. Paul Le Mat plays a professor who gets involved in the whole affair along with a nosey tabloid reporter. ¶ "It was in Illinois, Centerville. It was standing on the side of the road. I drove right past it, ah, it looked just like this, it had these smooth obsidian eyes. . . ." • Actress Louise Fletcher is a former Oscar winner (for her role of Nurse Ratchett in *One Flew Over the Cuckoo's Nest,* 1975).

Strangest Dreams: Invasion of the Space Preachers (1990; Troma Team) D/S: Daniel Boyd. P: David Wohl, Daniel Boyd, A. U. Gallagher. C: Bill Hogan. Cast: Jim Wolfe, Guy Nelson, Eliska Hahn, Gary Brown, Jesse Johnson, John Riggs, John Marshall. Two men come across a wrecked spaceship and its injured alien passenger. The alien, which can transform itself into a beautiful blonde, is on Earth to bring back fugitive

This terrifying manifestation of The Thing *(1982) is an alien duplication of an Antarctic scientist's head that has separated from its body. Moments later, this ghastly, constantly-changing lifeform sprouts spider-like legs and scuttles out of the room.*

aliens posing as preachers. The evil space preachers are attempting to use broadcast frequencies to control the minds of the community and perhaps, the world. ¶ "Lighten up preacher, have a brew."

Superman 2 (1980) (see COMIC BOOK FANTASY HEROES). Three alien prisoners from the planet Krypton escape their confines and plan to set themselves up as rulers of the Earth.

They Live (1988; Universal) D: John Carpenter. P: Larry Franco. S: Frank Armitage. C: Gary B. Kibbe. Cast: Roddy Piper, Keith David, Meg Foster. Aliens are found to be living amongst humans undetected. They are here to exploit the planet's wealth by controlling everything and everyone with subliminal commands. They can only be seen in their true hideous form with the aid of special lenses. ¶ "I came here to kick ass and chew bubblegum ... and I'm all out of bubblegum." • Director John

Carpenter described the film's premise as, "Aliens from another world exploiting the middle class. Sort of free enterprisers from another galaxy." • The words, "This is your God" were subliminally written on Earth's money, while the prophetic words, "They live, we sleep" are scrawled across a wall. • Star Roddy Piper is a former big time Pro Wrestling star. • The 1957 sci-fi film *The Monolith Monsters* can be seen playing on a shanty town TV during the movie. • *They Live* is based on a short story by F. Ray Nelson written in the early 60s called "Eight O'clock in the Morning." Carpenter noticed Nelson's story when it was adapted for a comic book by Eclipse Comics.

The Thing (1982; Universal) D: John Carpenter. P: Davis Foster, Lawrence Turman. S: Bill Lancaster. C: Dean Cundey. Cast: Kurt Russell, Wilford Brimley, T. K. Carter, David Clennon, Keith David, Richard Dysart, Charles Hallahan. This reworking of the 1951 classic sees team members of an Antarctic research station fall victim one by one to an ancient alien who absorbs, assimilates, and then impersonates them. ¶ "This thing doesn't want to show itself, it wants to hide inside an imitation. It'll fight if it has to, but it's vulnerable out in the open. If it takes us over, then it has no more enemies, nobody left to kill it. Then it's won." • Hailed for its groundbreaking effects work spearheaded by Albert Whitlock, the amazing effects include a head that detaches itself from its body, then sprouts spindly spider-legs and antennae, and goes scuttling down a corridor. • Richard Dysart, the head lawyer on TV's "L.A. Law," plays one of the men battling *The Thing.* • The original 1951 film excluded the alien's ability to imitate other life forms and change shape through absorption. This point makes the remake much closer to its literary source (a short story called "Who Goes There," by John W. Campbell) than the original film version.

The Tripods (1984; BBC-TV; U.K.) D: Graham Theakston, Christopher Barry. P: Richard Bates. Cast: John Shackley, Jim Baker, Ceri Seel, Roderick Horn, Jeremy Young, Richard Wordsworth. Alien machines called Tripods control the minds of earthlings by forcing them to wear silver caps. One young man escapes the capping procedure and joins some other rebel youths who hope to free mankind from their subjugated slavery.

Without Warning (1980; Filmways) D/P: Greydon Clark. S: Lyn Freeman, Daniel Grodnik, Ben Nett, Steve Mathis. C: Dean Cundy. Cast: Jack Palance, Martin Landau, Tarah Nutter, Christopher S. Nelson, Cameron Mitchell, Neville Brand. A fierce alien terrorizes campers in the woods by chucking blood sucking parasites at them.

Xtro (1982; Amalgamated; U.K.) D: Harry Bromley Davenport. P: Mark Forstater. S: Iain Cassie, Robert Smith. C: John Metcalfe. Cast: Bernice Stegers, Philip Sayer, Simon Nash, Danny Brainin. A man whose mother was raped by an alien begins to transform into one himself.

Encounters in Outer Space

Abbott and Costello Go to Mars (1953) (see VENUS). A scheduled flight to Mars goes awry and the boys eventually crash land on the female-inhabited planet Venus.

Aelita (1924) (see MARS). Martians are seen in a dream.

The Airship (1917) (see MARS). On a trip to Mars we encounter a peace-loving race.

Alien (1979; 20th Century–Fox; U.K.) D: Ridley Scott. P: Gordon Carroll, David Giler, Walter Hill. S: Dan O'Bannon. C: Derek Vanlint, Denys Ayling. Cast: Sigourney Weaver, Tom Skerritt, Veronica Cartwright, Harry Dean Stanton, Yaphet Kotto, Ian Holm, John Hurt. After exploring an alien vessel on a remote planet, a spaceship crew is threatened when one of their members is taken back onboard with a creature attached to his face. The alien creature then tears through his chest, quickly grows to full size, and goes on a killing spree, leaving only Sigourney Weaver left to face it at the end. ¶ "In space, no one can hear you scream."— ad line. • Originally, writer Dan O'Bannon had planned on *Alien* being a $500,000 low budget sci-fi thriller, but when director Ridley Scott was assigned to the film, the project continued to get more and more financing. • The commercial towing vehicle named the Nostromo is the primary setting for most of the film's action.

Aliens (1986; 20th Century–Fox) D/S: James Cameron. P: Gale Anne Hurd. Cast: Sigourney Weaver, Michael Biehn, Carrie Henn, Paul Reiser, Lance Henriksen, Jenette Goldstein. Set 50 years after the first *Alien,* Sigourney Weaver, the sole survivor from the original, is found and revived from suspended animation. She leads a group of space-marines to the *Alien* home planet to try and locate any survivors from the colony that was recently established there. It seems the numerous *Alien* eggs have hatched, and Sigourney and her cohorts must battle not just one, but dozens of the nearly unstoppable creatures. • The alien creature effects were supervised by Stan Winston, and, like the original, the impressive monsters were actually men in suits. The actors were given a lot more freedom of movement due to the base suit underneath, made of four-way stretch cloth. Around the actors are a variety of mechanically controlled appendages. In addition to the "men-monsters," there were also several eight-foot-tall mechanical puppets, and a gigantic Queen attached to a crane, built to house two men.

The Angry Red Planet (1960) (see MARS). Astronauts journey to the planet Mars where they encounter a variety of creatures, including a three-eyed Martian and a giant bat-rat-spider monster.

Battle Beyond the Stars (1980; New World) D: Jimmy T. Murakami. P: Ed Carlin. S: John Sayles. C: George D. Dodge, Dennis Skotak, Daniel Lacambre. Cast: Richard Thomas, Robert Vaughn, John Saxon, George Peppard, Sybil Danning. Richard Thomas sets out to recruit the galaxy's finest fighters for the defense of his peaceful planet under siege by an evil alien overlord (John Saxon). • At the time of its release, this five million dollar film was the most expensive movie Corman had ever been associated with. He served as the picture's executive producer. • Richard Thomas is best remembered as John-Boy Walton from the long-running TV family series, "The Waltons." • Actor Robert Vaughn (playing a weary, doomed space-fighter) basically reprises his role from the epic western, *The Magnificent Seven* (1960).

Battle in Outer Space (1960; Toho/Columbia; Japan) D: Inoshiro Honda. P: Tomoyuki Tanaka. S: Shinichi Sekizawa. C: Hajime Koizumi. Cast: Ryo Ikebe, Kyoko Anzai, Minoru Takada, Harold Conway, Koreya Senda, Len Stanford. A series of catastrophic events are only a prelude to the impending war waged by the alien "Natalians" in the stratospheres of Earth and the Moon with laser-like high-tech weaponry. ¶ "See! The Moon recaptured by Earth's space commandos! See! Invaders attacking from space crumble before your eyes!"—excited ad lines. • Several characters that appeared in an earlier Japanese sci-fi film, *The Mysterians* (1957), turn up in this sequel of sorts. • The spectacular optical effects, colorful miniatures, and high speed photography were supervised by Eiji Tsuburaya. In all, over 50 saucers and spaceships were built for the three massive battle sequences in the film.

Battlestar Galactica (1978; Universal) D: Richard A. Colla. P: John Dykstra. S: Glen A. Larson. C: Ben Colman. Cast: Lorne Greene, Richard Hatch, Dirk Benedict, Jane Seymour, Ray Milland, Lew Ayres. A wagon train of spaceships encounters some deadly aliens called Cylons. • This film was made into a short-lived, special effects–heavy television series.

Buck Rogers in the 25th Century (1979) (see COMIC BOOK FANTASY HEROES). Buck Rogers meets up with the power mad evil Princess Ardela in space.

Creature (1985; Universal) (also *Titan Find*). D: William Malone. P: William Dunn, William Malone. S: Alan Reed, William Malone. C: Harry Mathias. Cast: Klaus

Kinski, Stan Ivar, Wendy Schaal, Lyman Ward, Robert Jaffe, Annette McCarthy, Diane Salinger. While on an expedition to Titan, one of the moons of Saturn, a space crew encounters a flesh-eating creature who uses organic devices to control humans.

The Creature Wasn't Nice (1981; Creature Feature Productions) (also *Spaceship*). D/S: Bruce Kimmel. P: Mark Haggard. C: Denny Lavil. Cast: Cindy Williams, Bruce Kimmel, Leslie Nielsen, Gerit Graham, Patrick MacNee, Ron Kurowski. This alien spoof centers around an encounter with a being which can change into a monster. • When hooked up to a computer, the creature performs the song, "I Want to Eat Your Face."

Conquest of the Earth (1980; Universal) D: Sidney Havers, Sigmund Neufeld, Jr., Barry Crane. P: Jeff Freilich, Frank Lupo, Gary B. Winters. S: Glen A. Larson. C: Frank P. Beascochea, Mario DiLeo, Ben Colman. Cast: Kent McCord, Barry Van Dyke, Robyn Douglass, Lorne Greene, Pat Stuart. This is the third part of the *Battlestar Galactica* series, with Lorne Greene establishing contact with Earth to warn them of an alien attack by the Cyclons.

Dark Star (1974) (see SPACE TRAVEL). The space-weary crew of the *Dark Star,* on a prolonged mission to find and destroy unstable planets, adopts an alien as a pet (looking like a beachball with feet). This mischievous creature leads one of the crew members (screenwriter Dan O'Bannon) on a merry chase through the ship, ending in near disaster in an elevator shaft.

Dr. Who and the Daleks (1965; Amicus/Continental; UK) D: Gordon Flemying. P: Milton Subotsky, Max J. Rosenberg. S: Milton Subotsky. C: John Wilcox. Cast: Peter Cushing, Roy Castle, Jennie Linden, Roberta Tovey, Geoffrey Toone, Michael Coles. Dr. Who and friends are transported in time to a futuristic planet called Skaro where they save a friendly alien race called the Thals from destruction by the terrible robot-like Daleks. ¶ "Those who survived and remain on this planet are horrible mutations, monsters!" • This feature film sprang forth from a popular British teleseries created by Terry Nation. The "Dr. Who" adventures have also been chronicled on radio and in books as well as TV.

Dune (1984; Universal) D/S: David Lynch. P: Raffaella De Laurentiis. C: Freddie Francis. Cast: Francesca Annis, Leonardo Cimino, Jose Ferrer, Kyle MacLachlan, Sting, Max Von Sydow, Dean Stockwell. Kyle MacLachlan and his family are run off into the outer desert of the planet Dune by an evil Baron. The hero unites with other unfortunates and together they wrestle back their rightful shares. • The main export of the planet *Dune* is a spice called "melange." The desert planet is besieged with gigantic sandworms. The names of the two warring factions are the Atreides (the good guys) and the Harkonnens.

The Empire Strikes Back (1980; 20th Century–Fox) D: Irvin Kirshner. P: Gary Kurtz. S: Leigh Brackett, Lawrence Kasdan. C: Peter Suschitzky. Cast: Mark Hamill, Harrison Ford, Carrie Fisher, Billy Dee Williams, Anthony Daniels, James Earl Jones, David Prowse, Frank Oz, Kenny Baker, Alec Guinness, Peter Mayhew. After Han Solo rescues Luke Skywalker from certain death on the ice planet Hoth, Luke journeys to the planet Dagaba where he is further instructed in the ways of the Force by his new mentor, Yoda (who had previously trained Obi Wan). There he learns the skills necessary to face Darth Vader. In the climactic battle, Vader hacks off Luke's hand with a light sabre, and Solo is freeze dried by unfriendlies, leaving it all unresolved until *Return of the Jedi* (1983). ¶ "Only a fully trained Jedi Knight with the Force as his ally will conquer Vader and his emperor. If you end your training now, if you choose the quick and easy path, as Vader did, you will become an agent of evil." • This film was nominated for numerous technical awards including Set and Art Direction, and Best Original Score. *Empire* won Oscars for Sound and Visual Effects that year. • Actress Carrie Fisher is the daughter of entertainer Debbie Reynolds.

Enemy Mine (1985; 20th Century–Fox) D: Wolfgang Petersen. P: Stephen Friedman. S: Edward Khmara. C: Tony Imi. Cast: Dennis Quaid, Louis Gossett, Jr., Brion James, Richard Marcus, Carolyn McCormick, Lance Kerwin, Henry Stolow, Bumper Robinson, Jim Mapp. This big-budget space picture tells how two sworn enemies marooned on a hostile planet give way to peaceful coexistence during their mutual struggle to survive. Dennis Quaid and Louis Gosset, Jr., eventually become close friends, and after Gossett's death, Quaid raises and protects his friend's alien offspring like his own. ¶ "Do you understand any English, toad face?" • "Zamese" was the name of the lizard-like alien baby looked after by Dennis Quaid.

Escape from Galaxy 3 (1986; Film Enterprises) D: Ben Norman. P: G. K. Production. S: John Thomas. Cast: Cheryl Bu-

chanan, James Milton, Don Powell. A pair of lovers on a distant planet attempt to escape their tyrannical ruler.

The Ewok Adventure (1984; Lucasfilms) D/C: John Korty. P: Thomas G. Smith. S: Bob Carrou. Cast: Eric Walker, Warwick Davis, Aubree Miller, Fionnula Flanagan, Guy Boyd. Burl Ives narrates this fuzzy spin-off from the *Star Wars* trilogy centering on some new characters who battle a giant with the help of cuddly little Ewoks.

Ewoks, the Battle for Endor (1985; Lucasfilms) D/S: Jim Wheat, Ken Wheat. P: Thomas G. Smith. Cast: Wilford Brimley, Warwick Davis, Aubree Miller, Sian Phillips, Paul Gleason. The little fuzz balls are back again to take on the giant King Terak and his witch companion.

Explorers (1985) (see BENEVOLENT ALIENS, this chapter). Three boys construct a makeshift spaceship in order to visit friendly aliens in space.

Fantastic Planet (1973). This is an animated feature about a race of miniature people revolting against their giant-sized alien-looking counterparts on a distant world called "Ygam." • *Fantastic Planet* was the winner of several film awards including the Special Grand Prix at the Cannes Film Festival, the Gold Medal in Atlanta, and the International Jury Prize in an Italian Fantasy Film Festival. • The names of the two struggling life forms are the Draags and the Oms. • The 39-foot-tall blue Draags adopt Oms (tiny humans) as pets. One of the Oms, named Terr, steals a teaching device and takes it to other discontented Oms, who finally manage to kill a Draag. Their goal is to build a spaceship and escape the planet. They travel to the fantastic planet of meditation where they learn to disrupt the sacred rites and spread confusion. Eventually the Draags decide to negotiate, finally realizing the Oms are an intelligent race. A new satellite is created in the skies of Ygam, and the Oms begin a new civilization there.

Fire Maidens from Outer Space (1956; Topaz) D/S: Cy Roth. P: George Fowler. C: Ian Struthers. Cast: Anthony Dexter, Harry Fowler, Owen Barry, Susan Shaw, Paul Carpenter, Sydney Tafler, Rodney Diak, Jacqueline Curtiss. Astronauts encounter Owen Barry and the female descendants of the lost continent of Atlantis while exploring the thirteenth moon of Jupiter. They rid the community of its snarling monster nemesis at the fiery climax. ¶ "The creature — the man with a head of a beast —

it must be destroyed. Yet it is indestructible." • The classical music of Borodin's "Stranger in Paradise" is used for the film's background score. • Actor Paul Carpenter was a former hockey star who participated in several Olympic matches. He was also a member of the BBC announcing staff. • The picture was filmed at the British studios located in Hertfordshire and at the Mill Hill Observatory, a suburb of London, with the cooperation of Her Majesty's Royal Astronomical Society. • The dark humanoid alien monster is dispatched at the climax when it falls into a fiery altar.

Flash Gordon (1980) (see COMIC BOOK FANTASY HEROES). Most of this adventure takes place in the galaxy of planets run by Emperor Ming, an alien ruler bent on destroying the Earth when it suits him.

Flesh Gordon (1972) (see COMIC BOOK FANTASY HEROES). This R-rated, soft-core sex version of the Flash Gordon adventure sees "Flesh" travel to the planet "Porno" to stop the evil alien emperor "Wang" from using his "sex ray" on the Earth.

Flight to Mars (1951) (see MARS). Astronauts travel through space and land on Mars where they discover a race of humanoid aliens.

Forbidden Planet (1956; MGM) D: Fred Wilcox. P: Nicholas Nayfack. S: Cyril Hume. C: George Folsey. Cast: Leslie Nielsen, Walter Pidgeon, Anne Francis, Warren Stevens, Jack Kelly, Richard Anderson, Earl Holliman, Morgan Jones, James Best. The ruins of the ancient alien civilization known as the "Krel" are discovered by Earthmen on "Altair 4." The astronauts also encounter Dr. Morbius, who has used devices left over from the Krel to expand his knowledge. In doing so, he has created an invisible alien monster which killed off the initial expedition members, leaving himself, his beautiful daughter, and their robot alone and isolated within their protective compound on the planet. ¶ "And yet, always in my mind I seem to feel the creature is lurking somewhere close at hand. Sly and irresistible, and only waiting to be reinvoked for murder." • The monster menace from the *Forbidden Planet* was conceived from Morbius' id. • The special effects team of A. Arnold Gillespie, Irving Ries, and Wesley C. Miller received an Oscar nomination for their work on *Forbidden Planet*. The spaceship landing over Morbius' planet was devised with the aid of a full-sized set and three model ships of differing sizes, the largest being six feet in diameter. In the sequence where Morbius

shows the Earth crew an interplanetary tunnel-generator, Gillespie crafted a miniature set nearly 150 feet long with a mirror at the end. *Forbidden Planet* lost that year's Special Effects Oscar to *The Ten Commandments*. • The original screen treatment was co-written by special effects ace, Irving Block, who loved the William Shakespeare play, "The Tempest," and borrowed its theme for his film treatment. • The Robby the Robot costume (designed by Bob Kinoshita) weighed over 100 pounds and contained over 2500 feet of electrical wires to operate the various lights and moving parts in his head. The narrative voice of Robby was Marvin Miller, a frequent sci-fi narrator.

Forbidden World (1982; New World) (also *Mutant*). D: Allan Holzman. P: Roger Corman. S: Tim Curnen. C: Tim Suhrstedt. Cast: Jesse Vint, June Chadwick, Dawn Dunlap, Linden Chiles, Fox Harris, Ray Oliver. Research scientists on a remote planet are killed off one by one by a vicious carnivorous creature. They destroy the monster by feeding it the cancerous liver of a dying scientist.

Galaxina (1980) (see ROBOTS). Set in the year 3008, a space cruiser travels to the planet "Altair 1" to find the Blue Star. On board the ship, which is navigated by the robotic Galaxina, is an alien monster prisoner called a "Rockeater." ¶ "Rockeaters eat rocks, that's how we get our rocks off, asshole!"

Galaxy of Terror (1981; New World) (also *Mindwarp: An Infinity of Terror*). D: B. D. Clark. P: Roger Corman. S: Marc Siegler, B. D. Clark. C: Jacques Haitkin. Cast: Edward Albert, Erin Moran, Ray Walston, Bernard Behrens, Zalman King, Robert Englund, Taaffe O'Connell, Sid Haig, Grace Zabriskie, Jack Blessing, Mary Ellen O'Neill. A rescue mission is sent to a remote alien planet. When they arrive, the various crew members come face to face with their worst nightmares. ¶ "Doubt is brother demon to despair. The demon's tale, doubt, withers those who do not dare." • Actress Erin Moran left "Happy Days" to enter the *Galaxy of Terror,* which pulls no punches by featuring such sights as a nightmarish rape sequence with a giant worm. • Ray Walston is well known for his TV role of "My Favorite Martian." • Actor Robert Englund has now graduated from alien encounters to dream-killing as the popular 80s maniac, Freddy Krueger, of the *Nightmare on Elm Street* film series.

The Green Slime (1969; MGM; Japan/

U.S.) D: Kinji Fukasaku. P: Walter Manley, Ivan Reiner. S: Charles Sinclair, William Finger, Tom Rowe. C: Yoshikazu Yamasawa. Cast: Robert Horton, Richard Jaeckel, Luciana Paluzzi, Bud Widom, Ted Gunther, David Yurstun, Robert Dunham. A trouble-shooting specialist is called in to join a space station team for the purpose of destroying an asteroid on a collision course with Earth. Although their mission is successful, they accidentally bring back on board a green substance which grows into one-eyed walking slime monsters. ¶ "These creatures could be developing on any part of the station where a drop of this substance can reach any form of energy." • This picture is the first Japanese/American co-production, with a predominantly Japanese production team, and a predominantly American cast. The film's 60-ish sounding theme song, "The Green Slime," and its high-tech musical score were co-produced by Charles Fox and Toshiaki Tsushima. • The special effects department relied heavily on the extensive use of miniature models, including the asteroid, space station, and a futuristic Earth city. The cyclopean creatures with tumorous skins and tentacles were played by men in monter suits.

The Humanoid (1979; Merope; Italy) D: George B. Lewis. P: Georgio Venturini. S: Adriano Bolzoni, Aldo Lado. C: Silvano Ippoliti. Cast: Richard Kiel, Corinne Cléry, Leonard Mann, Barbara Bach, Arthur Kennedy. In yet another Italian *Star Wars* clone, towering actor Richard Kiel plays "Golob," a space jockey out to foil the universe-conquering plans of mad scientist Arthur Kennedy. Golob falls into the scientist's clutches and is transformed into the powerful being known as The Humanoid, though he is finally able to rebel against his master and destroy the madman.

Ice Pirates (1984; MGM) D: Stewart Raffill. P: John Foreman. S: Stewart Raffill, Stanford Sherman. C: Mathew F. Leonetti. Cast: Robert Urich, Mary Crosby, Anjelica Huston, John Matuszak, Michael D. Roberts, Ron Perlman, Bruce Vilanch, John Carradine. This film follows the life and times of space pilots called "ice pirates" who are constantly badgering the ruling Templar race that controls the output of water in the galaxy. ¶ "Long after the great interplanetary wars, the Galaxy has gone dry. Water has become the only thing left of value. Evil Templars from the planet Mithra have gained control of this life-giving resource. Their power is now absolute except for a few

rebel pirates who survive by stealing ice from the great Templar fleet." — prologue. • Angelica Huston is the daughter of famous film director John Huston (*The Maltese Falcon, Treasure of the Sierra Madre, African Queen,* and *Prizzi's Honor* to name a few). • John Matuszak is a former Pro football defensive lineman.

Inseminoid (1980; Jupiter Film Productions; U.K.) (also *Horror Planet*). D: Norman J. Warren. P: Richard Gordon, David Speechley. S: Nick Maley, Gloria Maley. C: Cast: Robin Clarke, Jennifer Ashley, Stephanie Beacham, Judy Geeson, Steve Grimes, Barry Houghton, Victoria Tennant. Exploring an alien planet, a woman archeologist is raped by a hideous creature and gives birth to a pair of vicious mutant babies. During her pregnancy, she attacks and drains the blood of other research station members to satisfy the blood lust of her unborn fetuses. • Screenwriter Nick Maley also provided the bloody special effects for this film.

It! The Terror from Beyond Space (1958; United Artists) D: Edward L. Cahn. P: Robert E. Kent. S: Jerome Bixby. C: Kenneth Peach, Sr. Cast: Marshall Thompson, Shawn Smith, Kim Spalding, Dabbs Greer, Paul Langton, Ann Doran, Robert Bice, Richard Hervey, Richard Benedict. A rescue ship is sent to Mars to investigate the mysterious deaths of a previous expedition and its lone survivor. The murderous alien responsible for their disappearance then stows away on board the new ship to wreak havoc on its return to Earth. • Lurid publicity lines for the picture read: "Bone was its food, blood was its drink, all the Earth was its prey," and ". . . Howling for all the flesh and blood on Earth." In addition, United Artists made the unlikely publicity ploy of offering to pay $50,000 (backed by a "world renowned insurance company") to anyone who could prove that *It* was not on Mars right now. Don't get your hopes up, the offer expired on January 1, 1960. • Well-known stunt man/actor, Ray "Crash" Corrigan, wore the monster suit created by prolific 50s effects artist, Paul Blaisdell. Blaisdell wasn't able to make a sculpture of Corrigan's head size before he made the headpiece, so when it came time to wear the Martian mask, it didn't fit properly — Corrigan's chin could be seen protruding from the mouth of the monster. To disguise this gaff, they just painted his chin green (the same color as the monster suit) and went on with the shooting. *It! The Terror* was the last picture to feature a Blaisdell monster suit. • The alien killer was finally destroyed by asphyxiation when the spaceship doors were opened, sucking all the air out of the ship. The 1979 blockbuster film, *Alien,* patterned its own climactic death sequence via air lock after this 50s cult favorite.

Journey to the Seventh Planet (1962; AIP) D/P: Sidney Pink. S: Ib Melchior. C: Age Wiltrup. Cast: John Agar, Carl Ottosen, Barry O'Neill, Louis Miehe Renard, Peter Monch, Greta Thyssen, Ove Sprogoe, Ann Smyrner, Mimi Heinrich. An exploratory expedition to Uranus encounters an evil disembodied alien brain which can conjure up images from the astronauts' own thoughts to use against them. The alien creature is intent of journeying to Earth to conquer the planet. ¶ "Yes, your planet is rich, warm, filled with life. I shall go there in one of your bodies. Man is weak, I shall make the terrors that dwell in his own mind destroy him, and I shall bring a new race into being." • Star John Agar, a former husband of Shirley Temple, encountered another alien brain four years before in *The Brain from Planet Arous* (1958). • *Journey* was made in Denmark and utilized most of the cast from *Reptilicus,* another Sid Pink Danish venture. • The insipid *Journey to the Seventh Planet* theme song: "Come to me, let your dreams become reality. I wait for you, somewhere on the seventh planet out in space. . . ."

King Dinosaur (1955) (see DINOSAURS— LOST WORLDS). A space expedition to the prehistoric planet "Nova" encounters alien dinosaurs.

Krull (1983) (see SWORD AND SORCERY). A planet in the far reaches of the galaxy is the home of a sword and sorcery–like civilization of alien beings.

The Last Starfighter (1984; Universal) D: Nick Castle. P: Gary Adelson, Edward O. Denault. S: Jonathan Betuel. Cast: Lance Guest, Dan O'Herlihy, Robert Preston, Catherine Mary Stewart, Barbara Bosson, Norman Snow. A humanoid alien (Robert Preston) enlists the aid of a video game wiz (Lance Guest) to help defend his outer space empire from a gang of space villains. ¶ "I was wondering if you wouldn't be willing to stay on, and rebuild the Starfighter Legion." • While Guest is whisked away by Preston, a robot double is left on Earth to act as his replacement. • Young actor Wil Wheaton, star of the "Star Trek: The Next Generation" TV series, appeared in a bit part in this film.

Lorca and the Outlaws (1985; U.K.) D: Roger Christian. P: Michael Guest. S: Roger Christian, Mathew Jacobs. C: John Metcalfe. Cast: John Tarrant, Donogh Rees, Deep Roy, Cassandra Webb. Rebellion occurs on the militaristic planet called Ordessa. • Director Roger Christian worked as a set designer on *Star Wars* (1977) and *Alien* (1979). The film boasts music by Tony Banks, former member of the rock group, Genesis.

Message from Space (1978; Toei/United Artists; Japan) D: Kinki Fukasaku. P: Banjiro Vemura, Yoshinoru Watanabe, Tan Takaiwa, Ryo Hirayama, Yusuke Okada, Simon Tse, Naoyuki Sugimoto, Akiro Ito. S: Hiro Matsuda. C: Toro Nakajima. Cast: Vic Morrow, Shinichi Chiba, Phily Casnoff, Peggy Lee Brennan, Sue Shiomi, Tetsuro Tamba. This is a Japanese *Star Wars* of sorts, with an evil empire thwarted by a band of rebels. • Vic Morrow was given star billing in the American version, though he appeared in only a few scenes. • The name of the beleaguered planet which the evil Gavanas Empire is ganging up on is called "Jilluca."

Metalstorm: The Destruction of Jared-Syn (1983; Universal) D: Charles Band. P: Charles Band, Alan J. Adler. S: Alan J. Adler. C: Mac Ahlberg. Cast: Jeffrey Byron, Tim Thomerson, Kelly Preston, Mike Preston, Richard Moll. This 3-D film is about a tough peace officer from the future who is sent to the planet Lemuria to take care of the desert warriors and their leader, Jared-Syn.

Mission Galactica: The Cylon Attack (1979; Universal) D: Vince Edwards, Christian Nyby II. P: David J. O'Connell. S: Glen A. Larson, Jim Carlson, Terrence McDonnell. C: Frank Thackery, H. John Penner. Cast: Richard Hatch, Dirk Benedict, Lorne Greene, Lloyd Bridges, Herbert Jefferson, Jr. This second entry in the Battlestar Galactica trilogy sports more space war dramatics directed against the evil alien empire of the Cylons. • Co-director Christian Nyby II is the son of Howard Hawks' favorite editor, Christian Nyby, the man who co-directed *The Thing* (1951).

Mission Mars (1968) (see MARS). Astronauts find Russian corpses and an alien energy creature on Mars.

Mission Stardust (1968) (see THE MOON). An expedition to the Moon encounters a superhuman race from another galaxy looking for a cure for their fatal blood disease.

Nightfall (1988; Concorde) D/S: Paul Mayersberg. P: Julie Corman. Cast: David Birney, Alexis Kanner, Sarah Douglas, Andra Millian. In a far off galaxy, three suns are setting in a primitive world of perpetual night. The divided community sees the phenomena differently. The religious cultists see nothing but doomsday, while the scientists confront the fanatics' fear and attempt to infuse reason over panic.

Nightflyers (1987; New Century Vista) D: T. C. Blake (Robert Collector). P/S: Robert Jaffe. C: Shelly Johnson. Cast: Catherine Mary Stewart, Michael Praed, John Standing, Michael Des Barres, Lisa Blount, Glenn Withrow, James Avery, Helene Udy. A scientist and crew aboard a space freighter *(Nightflyer)* encounter a mystical evil presence of unknown origin out in space. • The original director of the film, Fritz Kiersch, quit during production and was substituted with Robert Collector. Collector eventually left the film himself after the producers didn't like his work. He insisted that his name appear only in pseudonym, thus T. C. Blake was born. Producer/screenwriter Robert Jaffe then finished the reshooting and editing of the film.

The Phantom Planet (1961; AIP) D: William Marshall. P: Fred Gebhardt. S: William Telaak, Fred De Gorter, Fred Gebhardt. C: Elwood J. Nicholson. Cast: Dean Fredericks, Dolores Faith, Coleen Gray, Anthony Dexter, Francis X. Bushman, Richard Weber. An astronaut crashlands on an asteroid and shrinks down to six inches (the same size as the alien inhabitants) when he breathes the atmosphere. ¶ "What is Earth in relation to the inconceivable number of other worlds? Is his speed truly the fastest, his achievements the greatest, or is he a mere unimportant piece of driftwood floating in the vast ocean of the universe?" • Towering actor Richard Kiel, later a foe of James Bond, played the Solarite monster menace on *The Phantom Planet*.

Planet of the Vampires (1965; AIP; Italy/Spain) D/S: Mario Bava. P: Fulvio Lucisano. S: Catillo Cosulich, Antonio Roman, Alberto Bevilacqua, Rafael J. Salvia. C: Antonio Rinaldi. Cast: Barry Sullivan, Norma Bengell, Angel Aranda, Evi Morandi, Fernando Villena. Aliens from the planet Aura conspire to take over the bodies of a space team and return to Earth in their ship. ¶ "It's three times the size of us, and judging by the deterioration of the calcium it must have been here a long time, probably belonging to an ancient civilization." • The film's fatalistic ending depicts Sullivan and the rest of his surviving crew heading back to Earth, inhabited by the parasitic creatures of Aura.

Prisoners of the Lost Universe (1983;

United Media Finance; U.K.) D: Terry Marcel. P: Harry Robertson. S: Terry Marcel, Harry Robertson. C: Derek Browne. Cast: Richard Hatch, Kay Lenz, John Saxon, Peter O'Farrell. A journalist teams up with a martial arts expert to save the planet "Vonya" from a villainous ruler (John Saxon).

Queen of Blood (1966; AIP) D/S: Curtis Harrington. P: George Edwards. C: Vilis Lapenieks. Cast: John Saxon, Basil Rathbone, Dennis Hopper, Florence Marley, Judi Meredith, Forrest J Ackerman. A spaceship rescues an alien who's crashlanded on the planet Mars. The greenskinned female alien turns out to be a bloodsucking vampire-like killer. • Renowned film fan and editor of *Famous Monsters of Filmland,* Forrest J Ackerman, has a bit part in this film. • "Roger Corman had acquired some spectacular Russian footage of spaceships. I saw the footage and wrote a screenplay around it. We shot the film in seven and a half days at a cost of $65,000," said Curtis Harrington, the film's director/screenwriter. Corman served as the film's executive producer. • The alien vamp was played by Florence Marley, a multi-lingual actress who died of a heart ailment in 1978. She wrote, produced, and starred in a short feature called *Spaceboy: A Cosmic Love Affair,* which won an award at the Cannes film festival in 1973.

The Queen of Outer Space (1958) (see VENUS). Eric Fleming and crew land on Venus and are captured by female aliens led by a man-hating disfigured Queen wearing a mask.

Return of the Jedi (1983; 20th Century–Fox) D: Richard Marquand. P: Howard Kazanjian. S: Lawrence Kasdan, George Lucas. C: Alan Hume. Cast: Mark Hamill, Harrison Ford, Carrie Fisher, Billy Dee Williams, Anthony Daniels, Frank Oz, Ian McDiarmid, James Earl Jones, David Prowse, Peter Mayhew, Alec Guinness. Luke rescues Leia and Han from the clutches of the vile gangster, Jabba the Hut, and then must confront Darth Vader and the evil Emperor while his friends knock out the Empire's defense system on the forested moon of Endor with the help of the furry little Ewoks. ¶ "Your thoughts betray you father, I feel the good in you, the conflict.... You couldn't bring yourself to kill me before, and I don't believe you'll destroy me now." • *Return* was nominated for Academy Awards in Art Direction/Set Decoration, Sound, Sound Editing, and Original Score. • The film was originally to be

Luke Skywalker (Mark Hamill) and Chewbacca (Peter Mayhew) are captured on the Moon of Endor and bound to poles by the Ewoks, who later become their allies in Return of the Jedi *(1983).*

titled *Revenge of the Jedi,* and many pre-production posters were run off with the *Revenge* title on them. • In this third and final episode to date, two amazing secrets are revealed. First, Darth Vader turns out to be Luke's father, Anakin Skywalker, who was seduced to the dark side of the force by the Emperor. Second, Leia is revealed to be Luke's twin sister, who was separated from him after birth to give them a better chance of survival against the evil Empire. This was revealed to Luke in Yoda's last dying words: "There is another Skywalker." • The Emperor is finally dispatched at the climax by his own pupil, Darth Vader (Anakin Skywalker), when Vader finally realizes he can't destroy his only son. When the "Darth Vader" mask is taken off in the end, the actor playing Anakin is Sebastian Shaw, not David Prowse, who played Vader in all the other scenes. • Although Obi Wan Kenobi, Yoda, and Anakin Skywalker are all dead, they reappear in spirit form at the end of *Return.* • The teddy bear–like Ewoks helped Luke and Han because they believed C3PO to be one of their gods.

Robinson Crusoe on Mars (1964) (see MARS). An astronaut and his pet monkey,

stranded on Mars, encounter alien space-ships looking for slaves.

Slaughterhouse 5 (1972) (see TIME TRAVEL). A man caught in a time continuum becomes the specimen living under a glass dome of an unseen alien race on the planet Tralfama-dor.

Solaris (1972; Mosfilm; U.S.S.R) D: An-drei Tarkovsky. S: Friedrich Gorenstein. C: Vadim Jusov. Cast: Natalya Bondarchuk, Donatas Banionis, Nikolai Grinko, Yuri Jarvet, Vladislav Dvoretsky. A space psy-chologist travels to the outpost on Solaris and discovers that the station is being haunted by images created by the planet's ocean-like alien intelligence. The psycholo-gist is caught up with a phantom of his own—that of his deceased wife.

Space Monster (1965; AIP-TV) D/S: Leonard Katzman. P: Burt Topper. C: Robert Tobey. Cast: Russ Bender, Francine York, James B. Brown, Baynes Barron. In an unnamed future, a rocket carrying three men and one woman blasts off from Earth to find a new planet suitable for coloniza-tion. On the way, they encounter an alien spaceship inhabited by an ugly humanoid alien with an exposed brain and a tongue that inexplicably keeps popping in and out of his mouth. After dispatching the insulting alien, they crash land in the ocean of an unidentified planet and encounter giant sea crabs and a single native gill-man left over from *War Gods of the Deep* (1965). ¶ "By the way Colonel, I think I know where some of those billions of dollars went—to build a special helmet for that *fat* head of yours!" • The giant sea crabs are actually just tiny sand crabs in a fish tank.

Space Raiders (1983; New World) D/S: Howard R. Cohen. P: Roger Corman. C: Alec Hirschfeld. Cast: Vince Edwards, David Mendenhall, Thom Christopher, Patsy Pease, Dick Miller, Drew Snyder. A young castaway is taken in by a wild gang of space raiders who battle the villainous Command Empire. • The film took advantage of its New World company resources by using plenty of space footage from the 1980 extravaganza, *Battle Beyond the Stars.* This Roger Corman space vehicle was designed to cash in on the *Star Wars* phenomena.

Spaceballs (1987; MGM/United Artists) D/P: Mel Brooks. S: Mel Brooks, Thomas Meehan, Ronny Graham. C: Nick McLean. Cast: Mel Brooks, John Candy, Rick Moranis, Bill Pullman, Daphne Zuniga, Dick Van Patten. This Mel Brooks parody on *Star Wars, Alien,* and countless other space epics concerns a villainous plot to steal the atmosphere from the peaceful planet of Druidia. ¶ "My God, it's not just a spaceship, it's a transformer!" • The $22 million film features an endless string of character parodies, including a villain named "Dark Helmet" and a brief appearance from John Hurt comically reprising his landmark "chest-bursting" scene in *Alien.* Rotund comedian John Candy plays "Barf," the half-man, half-dog sidekick, and Joan Rivers does the voice of "Dot Matrix" (a C3PO parody). Dom DeLuise also gets in on the act, providing the voice for "Pizza the Hut," a spoofing of the Star Wars villain, Jabba the Hut.

Spacehunter: Adventures in the Forbidden Zone (1983; Columbia) D: Lamont Johnson. P: Don Carmody, Andre Link, John Dunning. S: David Preston, Dan Goldbert, Edith Rey, Len Blum. C: Frank Tidy. Cast: Peter Strauss, Molly Ringwald, Ernie Hudson, Michael Ironside, Andrea Marcovicci. This 3-D space adventure involves Peter Strauss fighting a variety of baddies and mutants on the planet Terra Eleven.

Star Crash (1979; Columbia/AIP) D: Lewis Coates (Luigi Cozzi). P: Nat Wachsberger, Patrick Wachsberger. S: Lewis Coates, Nat Wachsberger. C: Paul Beeson, Robert D'Ettorre. Cast: Marjoe Gortner, Caroline Munro, Christopher Plummer, Joe Spinnell, David Hasselhoff, Robert Tessier. In this low-budget space opera, Caroline Munro fights space age villains with the help of Marjoe Gortner and her trusty robot. • The robot was played by Caroline Munro's real-life husband, Judd Hamilton.

Star Crystal (1985; New World) D/S: Lance Lindsay. P: Eric Woster. Cast: C. Jutson Campbell, Faye Bolt, John W. Smith. Set in outer space in the year 2035, two astronauts bring back to their ship a rock which contains a murderous life form called Gor. The alien's Star Crystal force enables it to grow both in size and intelligence as it kills. Finally it taps into the ship's computer system to wreak some serious havoc.

Star Trek: The Motion Picture (1979; Paramount) D: Robert Wise. P: Gene Roddenberry. S: Harold Livingstone. C: Richard H. Kline, Mathew Yuricich, Richard Yuricich. Cast: William Shatner, Leonard Nimoy, DeForest Kelley, Persis Khambatta, Stephen Collins, James Doohan, George Takei, Walter Koenig, Nichelle Nichols, Majel Barrett, Grace Lee Whitney, Mark Lenard. The crew of the *Enterprise* encounters a powerful doomsday menace known as "V'ger." ¶ "The possibilities of our returning from this mission in one piece may have just doubled." • V'ger turns out to be a deadly set of space probes (with the *Voyager* space probe at its heart) that has malfunctioned, attained artificial intelligence and is now searching for its creator. • Shocking most "Star Trek" fans, Dr. McCoy sported a beard when he beamed onboard the *Enterprise.* • Stephen Collins plays the son of Matt Decker, a character from the "Star Trek" TV episode, "The Doomsday Machine." At the film's climax, he and the baldheaded Deltan helmswoman, Lt. Ilea, who has been inhabited by V'ger, must mate to gratify the machine's need for love and fulfillment. This merging of the intellect and human emotion is also taken to heart by Mr. Spock, who realizes for the first time in his life that being able to feel friendship is what's most important.

Star Trek II: The Wrath of Khan (1982; Paramount) D: Nicholas Meyer. P: Robert Sallin. S: Jack B. Sowards. C: Gayne Rescher. Cast: William Shatner, Leonard Nimoy, DeForest Kelley, Ricardo Montalban, Kirstie Alley, Bibi Besch, James Doohan,

George Takei, Walter Koenig, Nichelle Nichols, Paul Winfield. Kirk and company meet up with an old adversary, Khan, who is out to steal the life-generating phenomenon known as the Genesis Project. ¶ "The needs of the many outweigh the needs of the few, or the one." • Ricardo Montalban portrayed Khan in *both* this film and in the original TV episode, "The Space Seed," from which this picture takes its background. In the TV episode, Kirk decides to leave the genetic superman "Khan" alone on a remote planet to curb his zest for galactic domination. We discover in this film that astronomical phenomena have left his world paradise a barren wasteland, and his followers half-destroyed by parasitic creatures. Later, he utilizes these little beasties to control Chekov and a starship captain. Khan's compulsive penchant for quoting *Moby Dick* is simply an outgrowth of his avenging wrath. • Spock's farewell words before dying to save the ship are: "I have been and always shall be your friend. Live long and prosper." Kirk expresses his sentiments toward Spock at his funeral saying, "Of all the souls I have encountered in my travels, his was the most human." • The beautiful Vulcan who piloted the refurbished *Enterprise* out of space dock for the first time was Kirstie Alley, later of TV's "Cheers." • Dr. Carol Marcus was in charge of the secret project known as Genesis. Her associate and son is actually the illegitimate offspring of Captain Kirk, though he doesn't learn this until later in the film. Judging from the original TV series, the virile Captain has probably got one in every space port.

Star Trek III: The Search for Spock (1984; Paramount) D: Leonard Nimoy. P: Harve Bennett. S: John Hickridge. C: Charles Correll. Cast: Leonard Nimoy, William Shatner, DeForest Kelley, Christopher Lloyd, Walter Koenig, Robin Curtis, James Doohan, Nichelle Nichols, George Takei, James B. Sikking, Mark Lenard, Dame Judith Anderson. Spock isn't truly dead after all, since his body ended up on the planet undergoing regeneration by the "Genesis" project at the close of *Star Trek II*. And his mind is now sharing the skull of Dr. McCoy (the result of Spock's mind-meld just before dying in Part 2). The Captain and company must steal a ship and return for Spock's regenerated body so that body and soul can be reunited. Along the way they run afoul of a group of Klingons as well. ¶ "That green-blooded son of a bitch, it's his revenge for all those arguments he lost." • Spock's "living spirit" (called a "cotra") was cleverly transmitted to McCoy just prior to his death in the previous film, *Star Trek II.* • Maltz, one of the Klingons, is played by actor/comedian John Larroquette from "Night Court." • Spock was played by five different actors, representing the various stages of growth he endured on the planet regenerated by the Genesis Project. • In this chapter of the Star Trek film saga we actually lose the original starship *Enterprise.* After spending so many years trying to keep it intact, Kirk is forced to destroy it in what McCoy calls a chance "to turn death into a fighting chance for life." • In a poor casting move, Kirstie Alley's Vulcan character, Lt. Saavik from *Star Trek II,* is played by the bland actress Robin Curtis. • Trekkies will no doubt recall the return of another TV series character, "T'Pau," the high Vulcan priestess (played this time by actress Dame Judith Anderson). In this film she assists Spock in getting back his cotra.

Star Trek IV: The Voyage Home (1986; Paramount) D: Leonard Nimoy. P: Harve Bennett. S: Steve Meerson, Peter Krikes, Harve Bennett, Nicholas Meyer. C: Don Peterman. Cast: William Shatner, Leonard Nimoy, DeForest Kelley, James Doohan, George Takei, Walter Koenig, Nichelle Nichols, Catherine Hicks, Mark Lenard, Jane Wyatt, Majel Barrett, Robert Ellenstein, Robin Curtis. The Star Trek crew travels back in time to twentieth century San Francisco to find two humpback whales which hold the key to stopping an alien space probe's unintentional devastation of Earth. ¶ "Your use of language has altered since our arrival. It is currently laced with, shall I say, more colorful metaphors—'double dumbass on you,' and so forth." • A written prologue to the film reads: "The cast and crew of Star Trek wish to dedicate this film to the men and women of the spaceship *Challenger* whose courageous spirit shall live to the twenty-third century and beyond." • "Admiral, there be whales here," shouted Scotty, as George and Gracie were beamed aboard their starship. The whales were named after the comedic duo of George Burns and Gracie Allen. • Kirk was reduced in rank from Admiral to Captain and assigned a starship to command at the close of the film as his "punishment" for breaking Starfleet regulations (in Part 3).

Star Trek V: The Last Frontier (1989; Paramount) D: William Shatner. P: Harve Bennett. S: David Loughery. Cast: William Shatner, Leonard Nimoy, DeForest Kelley, James Doohan, Walter Koenig, Nichelle Nichols, George Takei, David Warner,

Mark Hamill, Carrie Fisher, and one of their two droids, R2D2, watch as the Millennium Falcon *takes off into outer space in* Star Wars *(1977).*

Laurence Luckinbill. In this episode, a being called Sybok hijacks the Enterprise and its crew and takes them on a journey to the center of the galaxy to find the Vulcan equivalent of Eden, and meet God. ¶ "You never cease to amaze me." • Kirk nearly falls to his death in this feature while climbing a mountain in Yosemite National Park on shore leave. • The place they arrive at in the center of the galaxy is called "The Planet of Galactic Peace."

Star Wars (1977; 20th Century–Fox) D/S: George Lucas. P: Gary Kurtz. C: Gilbert Taylor. Cast: Mark Hamill, Harrison Ford, Carrie Fisher, Alec Guinness, Peter Cushing, Anthony Daniels, James Earl Jones, David Prowse, Peter Mayhew, Kenny Baker. A young man (Mark Hamill) is forced to leave his home planet when his step-parents are killed. He and his two robots then join up with an old Jedi-knight and a mercenary pilot named Han Solo to rescue Princess Leia from the evil Empire which has the galaxy under siege with its ultimate weapon, the moon-sized space station called the

"Death Star." ¶ "May the Force be with you." • *Star Wars* garnered 11 Oscar nominations in all, two more than its sci-fi rival that year, *Close Encounters of the Third Kind*. • The principle antagonistic character of Darth Vader, with his long black cloak and Nazi-like helmet, was played by two actors—the 6' 7" David Prowse, who wore the costume, and James Earl Jones, who gave Vader that strong, menacing, deep voice. • Director George Lucas originally intended to remake *Flash Gordon,* but failed to obtain the legal rights for filming. He then wrote his own space opera which incorporated various elements from many films in different genres. Several action sequences, including the many space dogfights, were patterned after the war films, *The Dam Busters* (1954) and *633 Squadron* (1964). • "The Force is the energy field created by all living things. It binds the galaxy together." It is also what gives Obi Wan, Darth Vader, and eventually Luke Skywalker the strength and mystical mental ability to triumph over evil. • The hairy character known as

"Chewbacca" belongs to a species called "Wookie." The actor playing "Chewy," Peter Mayhew, was a former London hospital porter. • The desert planet of "Tatooine," Luke's home planet, was actually Tunisia, in North Africa. • R2D2 was actually two robots. One was a radio controlled model, while the other was a metallic costume worn by the diminutive 3'8" Kenny Baker. • Effects man John Dykstra, who produced over 350 different effects shots in just eight months, was one of the first people to computerize his special effects camera, enabling the camera to move along with the action, providing spectacular results. • Over 75 model spaceships were used in the film. The Death Star landscape covered over 1600 square feet, while the Death Star model used in long shots was only four feet in diameter.

Starship (1986; Cinema Group Venture) D: Roger Christian. P: Michael Guest. S: Roger Christian, Mathew Jacobs. C: John Metcalfe. Cast: John Tarrant, Deep Roy, Donough Rees, Cassandra Webb, Ralph Cotterill. Lorca and his droid incite the rebel workers at a desert mining colony on the remote planet of Ordessa to fight the tyranical Jowitt and his storm trooper army before they kill off the work force.

Terrornauts (1967; Amicus; U.K.) D: Montgomery Tully. P: Max J. Rosenberg. S: John Brunner. C: Geoffrey Faithfull. Cast: Simon Oates, Charles Hawtrey, Zena Marshall, Patricia Hayes, Stanley Meadows, Max Adrian, Frank Barry. Scientists are taken by a robot in an alien spaceship to an uninhabited asteroid. They learn that the robot is the last survivor of a civilization destroyed by an enemy planet, and are taken to yet another planet inhabited by green-skinned humanoids to warn them against the Earth's possible fate. ¶ "The virgin sacrifice to the gods of a ghastly galaxy!"—subtle ad line. • The film is based upon Murray Leinster's novel, *The Wailing Asteroid*. At the time the film was made, Leinster had more of his stories anthologized than any other living science fiction writer. • Art director Bill Constable said of his experience, "We regard a film like this as a challenge to our artistic skills and integrity as well as draftsmanship. Besides, it was fun to do and we could really let our imaginations run wild!" • Actress Zena Marshall is nicknamed "Oily" because of her favorite hobby, oil painting. Star Simon Oates said of Zena's hobby, "If it's her way of blowing off steam, I'd love to see some of her work after a tough day in space on this movie!" • Director Montgomery Tully has worn a lucky charm around his neck in every film he's made that no one's ever been able to explain. "I was in Africa, and I found this curious die with every number but one, so I asked around trying to discover what it could mean.... I used to think it might be some sort of voodoo, but now I regard it as a lucky charm."

This Island Earth (1955; Universal) D: Joseph Newman. P: William Alland. S: Franklin Coen, Edward G. O'Callaghan. C: Clifford Stine. Cast: Rex Reason, Jeff Morrow, Faith Domergue, Russell Johnson, Robert Nichols, Lance Fuller, Douglas Spencer. Aliens from the planet Metaluna engage the services of Earth scientists for repairs on their home planetary defense shield. ¶ "Use a machine to control a man's brain, you destroy his initiative, you destroy his power to help us as we need help." • In the film, scientist/hero Cal Meacham (Rex Reason) is saved by a mysterious green-tinted alien ray when his test plane develops engine trouble. He also has to pass the alien's aptitude test by assembling an "Interoceter." At first he is whisked away to a Georgia mansion to work, then later is taken with Faith Domergue to the planet Metaluna. The opposing alien army attacking Metaluna are called the Zahgons. Only their missile firing spaceships are seen in the film. • The Metaluna mutant, a half-man, half-insect monster, was played by stuntmen Eddie Parker and Regis Parton, and the costume cost approximately $24,000 to create. • Famous 50s director Jack Arnold took over the helm from Joseph Newman near the end of production when Newman fell ill. • The story is based on the Raymond F. Jones novel of the same name. • Jeff Morrow, who played the alien named Exeter with the prominent forehead, was teamed up again with Rex Reason in *The Creature Walks Among Us* in 1956. • *This Island Earth* featured a tremendous Metaluna planet set possessing a striking landscape which stretched over 100 feet in length. • The musical score was prepared by Herman Stine and supervised by Joseph Gershenson, who worked on over 17 fantasy films during the decade.

A Trip to Mars (1910) (see MARS). A professor, working with a substance that can alter the power of gravity, is propelled to Mars where he encounters a gigantic Martian.

Vampire Men of the Lost Planet (1970; Independent International) (also *Horror of the Blood Monsters*). D/P: Al Adamson. S: Sue McNair. C: William (Vilmos) Zsigmond,

The $24,000 "Metaluna Mutant" struggles to its feet prior to menacing alien Jeff Morrow (far left), and humans Rex Reason and Faith Domergue on their way back to This Island Earth *(1955).*

William G. Troiano. Cast: John Carradine, Robert Dix, Vicki Volante, Joey Benson, Jennifer Bishop, Bruce Powers. An exploratory expedition is sent to another planet where they encounter a primitive tribe of vampire-people. • No-budget schlockmeister Al Adamson took black and white footage from an old Filipino vampire film and then color-tinted these scenes in an unconvincing attempt to match the new color footage he shot with American actors.

Voyage to the Planet of Prehistoric Women (1966) (see DINOSAURS — LOST WORLDS). Astronauts on Venus discover beautiful girls, lizard men, and dinosaurs.

War of the Robots (1987) (see ROBOTS). Ships from Earth travel to Anthor to take on the planet's robot army.

War of the Satellites (1958; Allied Artists) D/P: Roger Corman. S: Lawrence Louis Goldman. C: Floyd Crosby. Cast: Dick Miller, Susan Cabot, Richard Devon, Eric Sinclair, Michael Fox, Robert Shayne, Bruno Ve Sota, Beach Dickerson. A race of aliens, possessing the power to duplicate themselves indefinitely, wreak havoc on a space station. ¶ "The whole universe is our new frontier." • Roger Corman hastily pieced together this film in eight days, designed to take advantage of the renewed interest in the U.S. space program after the Soviets launched their Sputnik satellite. The script was written in less than two weeks, and the film was in theaters a mere two months after the Sputnik launching. Corman himself appears in the film as a ground controller.

Wild Wild Planet (1965; MGM; Italy) D: Anthony Dawson (Antonio Margheriti). P: Joseph Fryd, Anthony (Antonio) Margheriti. S: Ivan Reiner. C: Richard Pallton (Pallottini). Cast: Tony Russell, Lisa Gastoni, Massimo Serato, Charles Justin, Franco Nero, Enzo Fiermonte. This futuristic space opera involves a mad scientist who miniaturizes planetary leaders with the aid of his female army. • This picture is a semi-sequel of sorts to *War of the Planets,* made earlier the same year.

Women of the Prehistoric Planet (1965;

Realart) D/S: Arthur C. Pierce. P: George Gilbert. C: Archie Dalzell. Cast: Wendell Corey, Keith Larsen, John Agar, Irene Tsu, Paul Gilbert, Stuart Margolin, Merry Anders, Lyle Waggoner. Astronauts land on a planet inhabited by Asian-looking aliens, giant reptiles, spiders, and a carnivorous plant. They decide to name the planet Earth. •

Many fans remember Lyle Waggoner as one of Carol Burnett's cronies on her popular comedy show.

World Without End (1956) (see TIME TRAVEL). A space expedition lands on a planet occupied by a mutant race. The strange planet turns out to be Earth in the future.

Benevolent Aliens

The Abyss (1989; 20th Century–Fox) D/S: James Cameron. P: Gale Anne Hurd. C: Mikael Salomon. Cast: Ed Harris, Mary Elizabeth Mastrantonio, Michael Biehn, Leo Burmester, Todd Graff, John Bedford Lloyd, J. C. Quinn, Kimberly Scott. Friendly aliens from the deep come to the aid of a team of underwater oil drillers. Ed Harris, his wife (Mary Elizabeth Mastrantonio), and their crew are all trapped within a deep sea rig along with a crazy Navy S.E.A.L. during a rescue mission involving a nuclear submarine. ¶ "Have some new friends down here. Keep pantyhose on, you're gonna love this." • In one of the screen's most dramatic sequences, Harris is forced to hold his wife as she drowns to death when their small underwater craft begins to fill up with water. Because they have only one suit, Mastrantonio decides that their best shot at making it back to the main rig alive is for her to die and then be revived minutes later, since her husband is able to swim much faster than she.

Alien Nation (1988; 20th Century–Fox) D: Graham Baker. P: Gale Anne Hurd, Richard Kobritz. S: Rockne S. O'Bannon. C: Adam Greenberg. Cast: James Caan, Mandy Patinkin, Terence Stamp, Kevin Major Howard, Leslie Bevis, Peter Jason. In the future of 1991 Los Angeles, aliens and humans co-exist. Police detective James Caan and his alien partner investigate a brutal murder involving the recently arrived aliens' dark secret — a super-addictive drug which eventually drives them insane before killing them. ¶ "We were genetically engineered as slave labor. It was our only means of pleasure allowed. The harder you worked the more you got. The more you got the harder you worked. Thousands of my people died! I lost my best friend. It is a nightmare. I will not let it happen again." • The film features Mandy Patinkin as an alien police detective named Sam Francisco. The aliens, who are called "Newcomers," are similar to humans but they react quite differently to some Earth liquids. For instance,

salt water acts like battery acid to the aliens and drinking sour milk produces the same effect on them as alcohol does on humans. • Former "Twilight Zone" story editor Rockne S. O'Bannon wrote the film's screenplay. James Cameron (a writer/director on films like *Aliens* [1986], and husband of co-producer Gale Anne Hurd) supposedly rewrote the script. A Writer's Guild arbitration, however, awarded O'Bannon sole screenplay credit. • It took a team of 30 makeup artists to transform the numerous actors and extras into the alien "Newcomers." • Terence Stamp, who played the lead alien bad guy, refused to don the elaborate transformation makeup required for the film's climactic confrontation, claiming his skin was "hurting." Those scenes were filmed using Stamp's stunt double lip-synching his dialogue.

The Astounding She Monster (1958; AIP) D/P: Ronnie Ashcroft. S: Frank Hall. C: William C. Thompson. Cast: Robert Clarke, Kenne Duncan, Shirley Kilpatrick, Marilyn Harvey, Jeanne Tatum, Ewing Brown. A beautiful alien, who seemingly stalks a small group of people throughout the film, is revealed at the climax to be an emissary of peace, only attempting to deliver a message to the people of Earth welcoming them into the intergalactic brotherhood. ¶ "There is our stage, our characters, unrelated, as apart from one another as the stars from the Earth." — opening narration. • Star Robert Clarke commented in Tom Weaver's book, *Interviews with B Science Fiction and Horror Movie Makers,* "I remember that the director, Ron Ashcroft, planned to make that feature in a week's time and I think we ended up making it in five days. *That* was the "astounding" part of that picture!" • The film's promotion spoke of "The woman whose warmth consumes." Part of the She-Monster's red hot appeal was due to a skin tight metallic-looking suit. According to Clarke, the costume split on actress Shirley Kilpatrick early on during filming, so Ashcroft was forced to show his alien only from

A smiling Mandy Patinkin and James Caan star as police detectives from different worlds who proudly display their wounds after stopping a murderer and exposing an alien drug ring in Alien Nation *(1988).*

the front, and had to have her back away from the camera while retreating so as not to reveal her split backside.

Aurora Encounter (1985; New World) D/P: Jim McCullough, Sr. S: Jim McCullough, Jr. Cast: Jack Elam, Peter Brown, Dottie West, Carol Bagdasarian. A widow meets a friendly alien with advanced mental powers.

Batteries Not Included (1987; Universal) D: Mathew Robbins. P: Ronald L. Schwary. S: Brad Bird, Mathew Robbins, Brent Maddock, S. S. Wilson. C: John McPherson. Cast: Hume Cronyn, Jessica Tandy, Frank

McRae, Elizabeth Pena, Michael Carmine. Friendly little aliens come to the aid of five tenants who are about to be evicted from their homes by a greedy real estate developer. The tiny aliens have a variety of magical powers at their disposal. • The film project was originally to have been made as a 30-minute segment in Steven Spielberg's TV series, "Amazing Stories," but was never completed. The script was then turned over to Mathew Robbins who worked it into a feature length film. • Film advertising tried to capitalize on the numerous free film screenings, boasting that over 400,000

The most astounding thing about The Astounding She Monster *(1958) is its enticing poster art.*

people had already seen and loved the film.
• George Lucas' Industrial Light and Magic special effects company was used extensively for this picture, cutting deeply into the film's $20 million budget. • Co-stars Hume Cronyn and Jessica Tandy are married in real life.

The Brain from Planet Arous (1958) (see INVADERS ON EARTH: THE 50s, this chapter). Two giant disembodied alien brains from the planet Arous arrive on Earth. The evil brain, Gor, takes over John Agar's body and delights in human lust and power. The good brain, Vol (a sort of intergalactic policeman), aids Agar's fiancée in freeing him from Gor's evil influence.

The Brother from Another Planet (1984; A-Train Films) D/S: John Sayles. P: Peggy Rajski, Maggie Renzi. C: Ernest R. Dickerson. Cast: Joe Morton, Tom Wright, Caroline Aaron, Herbert Newsome, Dee Dee Bridgewater. An alien comes to New York as a black man and gets a taste of ghetto culture. He eventually decides to stay. • Director John Sayles plays a bounty hunter assigned to kill the alien (Joe Morton).

The Cat from Outer Space (1978; Walt Disney) D/P: Norman Tokar. P: Ron Miller. S: Ted Key. C: Charles F. Wheeler. Cast: Ken Berry, Sandy Duncan, Harry Morgan, Roddy McDowall, McLean Stevenson. An extraterrestrial feline called Jake is forced to land on Earth. Ken Berry tries to raise enough gold to help the cat repair its ship while antagonist Roddy McDowall attempts to steal the kitty's special power-collar. • The cat's full alien name is "Zunar 15/90 Doric 4-7," and in real life he is called "Rumpler."

Close Encounters of the Third Kind (1977; Columbia/EMI) D/S: Steven Spielberg. P: Julia Phillips, Michael Phillips. C: Vilmos Zsigmond, William A. Franker, Douglas Slocombe. Cast: Richard Dreyfuss, Melinda Dillon, François Truffaut, Teri Garr, Bob Balaban, J. Patrick McNamara. Aliens set up a meeting with scientists and selected individuals for the purpose of a cultural exchange. ¶ "I just want to know that it's really happening." • The desert formation called "The Devil's Tower," located in Wyoming, was the selected rendezvous between Earth scientists and the aliens. • In a November 1977 issue of *Newsweek,* director Steven Spielberg said, "Making movies is an illusion, a technical illusion that people fall for, and my job is to take that technique and hide it so well that never once are you taken out of your chair and reminded where you are." • In *Famous Monsters of Filmland*

#141, Spielberg was quoted as saying, "In 30 years of UFO reportings, the encounters have been very benevolent. No sci-fi death rays, no radiation poisonings. Eighty-five percent of the reports indicate that visitors have been totally rational and benevolent . . . that's the attitude I take in this picture." • The term "close encounter of the third kind" refers to some form of physical contact, or in which the occupants are actually seen. An "encounter of the first kind" is close range sighting (less than 100 feet), while an "encounter of the second kind" is a sighting marked by physical evidence. • Legendary French director François Truffaut (*The 400 Blows,* 1959; *Fahrenheit 451,* 1966; and *Small Change,* 1976) played the supporting role of Lacombe, the chief scientist investigating UFO phenomena. Sadly, Truffaut died during the prime of his career on October 21, 1984. • Douglas Trumbull and his talented special effects team were nominated for an Academy Award. The optical effects cost three and a half million dollars to produce, and the picture's total budget was approximately $20 million. Douglas Trumbull has said he turned down an offer to work on *Star Wars* (released the same year) because it was too similar to other films he had done, such as *2001: A Space Odyssey* (1969). • The production team needed the use of two aircraft hangars for three months to utilize as sound stages. • The giant mothership that lands on Devil's tower at the film's climax was a model six feet wide and weighing 400 pounds. • The aliens used in the film were designed by Carlo Rambaldi, who went on to create another benevolent alien for *E.T. the Extra Terrestrial* in 1982. The tall one was a mechanical dummy operated by remote control, while the smaller ones were merely children in costumes. • *Close Encounters* was nominated for nine Academy Awards, and the film won for Best Cinematography and Best Sound Effects Editing.

Cocoon (1985; 20th Century–Fox) D: Ron Howard. P: Richard D. Zanuck, David Brown, Lili Zanuck. S: Tom Benedek. C: Don Peterman. Cast: Steven Guttenberg, Don Ameche, Wilford Brimley, Hume Cronyn, Brian Dennehy, Jessica Tandy, Tahnee Welch, Maureen Stapleton, Gwen Verdon. Friendly aliens on a mission to retrive others of their kind left behind from a previous visit enlist the aid of a young skipper and a group of senior citizens. The rest-home patrons assisting them become rejuvenated after swimming in a secret pool which houses the cocooned aliens. ¶ "Nature dealt us our hands of cards and we played them. Now at the end of the game, suddenly you're looking to reshuffle the deck." • Veteran actor Don Ameche won an Oscar for his role as the break dancing oldtimer who learns how to live again with the help of the rejuvenative powers of the aliens.

Cocoon 2: The Return (1988; 20th Century–Fox) D: Daniel Petrie. P: Richard D. Zanuck, David Brown, Lili Fini Zanuck. S: Stephen McPherson. C: Tak Fujimoto. Cast: Steve Guttenberg, Don Ameche, Wilford Brimley, Hume Cronyn, Brian Dennehy, Jessica Tandy, Tahnee Welch, Maureen Stapleton, Jack Gilford, Gwen Verdon. The Anterians arrive back on Earth with their senior citizen friends to retrieve an alien who is being subjected to scientific experiments by government researchers. ¶ "For all the snowflakes, and sunsets, and rainbows he won't see—think of what he will have. Think of what he'll gain. A world with no illness, no poverty, no wars. Besides, if we stay here, our child might not be born. We'd never live long enough to see him grow up."

Communion (1989; New Line Cinema) D: Philippe Mora. P: Philippe Mora, Dan Allingham, Whitley Strieber. S: Whitley Strieber. C: Louis Irving. Cast: Christopher Walken, Lindsay Crouse, Frances Sternhagen, Andreas Katsulas, Terri Hanauer. A man has a dream-like encounter with alien visitors. • The story is based on a supposedly actual occurrence. Author Whitley Strieber adapted the initial film script from his own book. • Rock star Eric Clapton wrote the film's theme song.

The Cosmic Man (1959; Allied Artists) D: Herbert Greene. P: Robert A. Terry. S: Arthur C. Pierce. C: John F. Warren. Cast: Bruce Bennett, John Carradine, Angela Greene, Paul Langton, Scotty Morrow, Lyn Osborn. An extraterrestrial sphere arrives at Rock Canyon and its curious occupant ventures out at night to study the planet. The cosmic man (John Carradine), who is seen in "negative" projection form, eventually cures a crippled boy, thus revealing his benevolent intentions. ¶ "There are two kinds of power, constructive and destructive. You say knowledge of the workings of this object would be a great military power. In my opinion, that's the wrong thinking."

Cosmic Monsters (1958) (see BUG GIANTS). Mr. Smith, who turns out to be a friendly alien, helps Earth rid itself of a big bug attack.

The Day the Earth Stood Still (1951; 20th Century–Fox) D: Robert Wise. P: Julian Blaustein. S: Edmund H. North. C: Leo Tover. Cast: Michael Rennie, Patricia Neal, Billy Gray, Hugh Marlowe, Sam Jaffe, Lock Martin. An alien and his all-powerful robot named Gort arrive in Washington, D.C., via flying saucer. Their mission is one of peace but they're met with violence. ¶ "I came here to give you these facts, but if you threaten to extend your violence, this Earth of yours will be reduced to a burned-out cinder." • In an article written by Al Taylor and Doug Finch appearing in *Filmfax* #17, director Robert Wise discussed his film: "It was a picture that would hold an audience and fascinate them while at the same time get a point over about our world and where we were going with it." • The movie is based on Harry Bates' short story, "Farewell to the Master." The film cost approximately $1,200,000 to make and Bates, the story's originator, received only $500 for the movie rights. • Michael Rennie wasn't the only choice considered for the part of Klaatu. Spencer Tracy and Claude Rains were mentioned as possibilities. In the case of Rains, 20th Century–Fox went after the actor, but the 61-year-old Rains was enjoying a huge success on Broadway in *Darkness at Noon* and was unavailable due to his theater commitment. • The popular robot, Gort, was played by giant actor Lock Martin (formerly a doorman at the old Grauman Chinese Theatre). His suit (or suits—there were actually two suits constructed, one having a zipper in the front, the other with the zipper in the back) consisted of foam rubber sprayed with metallic silver paint, and the helmet was fashioned from sheet metal. • In addition to the miniature saucer featured in landing scenes, a life-size ship (24 feet tall, 100 feet wide) was constructed for the sum of $100,000.

The Day Time Ended (1978) (see TIME TRAVEL). Tiny friendly aliens arrive on Earth to warn a family of the dangers of a space-time continuum that has enveloped their ranch.

Dr. Alien (1989) D: Dave DeCoteau. P: Dave DeCoteau, John Schouweiler. S: Kenneth J. Hall. C: Nicholas Von Sternberg. Cast: Billy Jacoby, Olivia Barash, Stuart Fratkin, Troy Donahue, Arlene Golonka, Judy Landers. A sexy biology professor is really an alien scientist experimenting on the campus nerds. One of the boys ends up being a "Buddy Love" (The Nutty Professor) type character no one can resist.

Doin' Time on Planet Earth (1990; Cannon International) Cast: Nichols Strouse, Hugh Gillin, Gloria Henry, Hugh O'Brien,

Adam West, Maureen Stapleton, Roddy Mc-Dowall. Ryan Richmond is looking for a date on a computer dating service. When the test is over, the computer tells him he is actually an alien. A few days later, a whacky couple from outer space come to visit him, believing that he is their leader. Richmond learns that he has a DNA packet in his brain, and when it implodes, he finds out that he's supposed to return to the planet B-52. Richmond doesn't want to leave his new girlfriend though, and after the climax at his father's revolving restaurant (which the alien couple believes is a spaceship) he runs off with his new gal. ¶ "Welcome home extraterrestrial Ryan Richmond." • Clips from the movies, *Plan Nine from Outer Space* (1959) and *Santa Claus Conquers the Martians* (1964) are seen in the picture.

Earth Girls Are Easy (1989; Vestron Pictures) D: Julien Temple. P: Tony Garnett. S: Julie Brown, Charlie Coffey, Terrence E. McNally. C: Oliver Stapleton. Cast: Geena Davis, Jim Carey, Damon Wayans, Jeff Goldblum, Julie Brown. A trio of fun-loving furry aliens crash-lands in Geena Davis' swimming pool. When shaved of their multi-colored fur, they appear as normal humans and set about having some fun in the California sun. Davis and the alien Captain, however, begin to fall in love. ¶ "Fly a spaceship, see the universe. I must be nuts!" — disgruntled alien. • Stars Jeff Goldblum and Geena Davis are husband and wife in real life. They first appeared together onscreen in the David Cronenberg remake of *The Fly* (1986). Comedienne Julie Brown co-wrote as well as co-starred in this film, which appropriately featured scenes from the Ray Harryhausen sci-fi movie, *Earth vs. the Flying Saucers* (1956).

Enemy Mine (1985) (see ENCOUNTERS IN OUTER SPACE, this chapter). Hatred between a lizard-like alien and his human enemy gives way to friendship when they're forced to work together in order to survive on a hostile planet.

Escape to Witch Mountain (1974; Walt Disney) D: John Hough. P: Jerome Courtland. S: Robert Malcolm. C: Frank Phillips. Cast: Eddie Albert, Ray Milland, Donald Pleasence, Kim Richards, Ike Eisenmann, Denver Pyle. Teenagers from outer space are captured by a ruthless human intent on exploiting their super abilities. The alien kids eventually escape to Witch Mountain in a camper they use like a spaceship.

E.T. the Extra Terrestrial (1982; Universal) D/P: Steven Spielberg. P: Kathleen Kennedy. S: Melissa Mathison. C: Allen Daviau. Cast: Dee Wallace, Peter Coyote, Drew Barrymore, Henry Thomas, Robert MacNaughton, K. C. Martel, Sean Frye, Tom Howell. A cute little alien left behind by its spaceship is befriended by a little boy and his family. After the alien is captured by scientists, it grows ill, then miraculously revives to make its scheduled rendezvous with the help of the children. ¶ "E.T. phone home." • In the film, Elliot helps the frogs used in scientific experiments at school to escape because they remind him of E.T. • Little Drew Barrymore is a recent addition to the acting clan of Barrymores which include John, Lionel, and Ethel. • E.T. garnered nine Academy Award nominations that year. John Williams, perhaps the greatest contemporary music composer in cinema, won the Oscar for his contribution. • The E.T. creation which preyed upon the sentiments of young and old alike was created by Carlo Rambaldi. The voice of E.T. was provided, surprisingly, by actress Debra Winger.

Explorers (1985; Industrial Light and Magic) D: Joe Dante. P: Edward S. Feldman. S: Eric Luke. C: John Hora. Cast: River Phoenix, Jason Presson, Amanda Peterson, Dick Miller, Robert Picardo. Three boys build a makeshift spaceship and head for space to meet up with friendly aliens named Wak and Neek.

The Glitterball (1977; Childrens Film Foundation; U.K.) D: Harley Cockliss. P: Mark Forstater. S: Howard Thompson. C: Alan Hall. Cast: Ben Buckton, Keith Jayne, Ron Pember, Marjorie Yates, Barry Jackson. This British forerunner of *E.T.* features a friendly glitterball alien who is aided by a group of boys in its rescue by the mother ship.

Howard the Duck (1986) (see COMIC BOOK FANTASY HEROES). A friendly but cynical extraterrestrial duck is unexpectedly catapulted to Earth from his home planet.

I Married a Monster from Outer Space (1958) (see INVADERS ON EARTH: THE 50s). The aliens in this film are generally non-hostile, only wishing to breed with human females for the survival of their species. Events do get out of hand, however, as they pose more and more of a threat to humanity when they capture and impersonate humans.

Invasion (1965) (see INVADERS ON EARTH: THE 60s AND 70s). Edward Judd attempts to grant asylum of sorts to a friendly alien attempting to escape from the aliens pursuing him.

It Came from Outer Space (1953; Universal) D: Jack Arnold. P: William Alland. S:

Harry Essex, Ray Bradbury. C: Clifford Stine. Cast: Richard Carlson, Barbara Rush, Charles Drake, Russell Johnson, Joseph Sawyer. A spacecraft crash-lands near a small desert town and the aliens are forced to assume the shapes of Earthmen in order to obtain the supplies needed in order to repair their ship in secrecy. ¶ "Where are you? What do you look like? What am I supposed to be looking for? I know you're out there, hiding in the desert!" • The film is based on Ray Bradbury's short story, "The Meteor." Bradbury also contributed to the film's screenplay. • The cyclopean alien, termed a "Xenomorph," pleaded with Carlson to "give us time. Time, or terrible things will happen." The alien's design is credited to Millicent Patrick and was dubbed by set insiders as "the fried egg." • *It Came from Outer Space* is the first science fiction film shot in 3-D. • This feature made genre stars out of both Richard Carlson and the disquieting desert locale, which proved to be one of the favorite settings for 50s science fiction films. • Screenwriter Harry Essex also wrote the screenplay for Arnold's second sci-fi masterpiece, *The Creature from the Black Lagoon* (1954) and contributed to other genre pictures as diverse as *Man Made Monster* (1941) and *What Ever Happened to Baby Jane?* (1962). In Tom Weaver's book, *Interviews with B Science Fiction and Horror Movie Makers*, Essex said of co-author Ray Bradbury: "Yeah, he tried to write a screenplay, and it was just no good. He's not a screenplay writer." • Actor Richard Carlson, who was one of the most popular leading men of 50s sci-fi, was also known as a very heavy drinker, which contributed to his early death in 1977 at the age of 65.

Lords of the Deep (1989; Concorde) D: Mary Ann Fisher. P: Roger Corman. S: Howard R. Cohen, Daryl Haney. C: Austin McKinney. Cast: Bradford Dillman, Priscilla Barnes, Daryl Haney, Melody Ryane, Eb Lottimer. This underwater sci-fi movie, arriving in the wake of films like *Deep Star Six, Leviathan,* and *The Abyss* (all 1989), centers around a group of benign aliens living at the bottom of the ocean who come into contact with a group of humans working down there. The aliens eventually save the humans from an impending earthquake. • Producer Roger Corman has a cameo role in the picture as the Martel Corporation bigwig behind all the dirty dealings.

The Man Who Fell to Earth (1976; British Lion; U.K.) D: Nicolas Roeg. P: Michael Deeley, Barry Spikings. S: Paul Mayersberg. C: Anthony Richmond. Cast: David Bowie, Rip Torn, Candy Clark, Buck Henry, Bernie Casey, Jackson D. Kane. An alien comes to Earth and builds a financial empire with the intent of contructing a spaceship to rescue the inhabitants of his dying planet.

Mars Needs Women (1966; Azalea) D/P/S: Larry Buchanan. C: Robert C. Jessup. Cast: Tommy Kirk, Yvonne Craig, Byron Lord, Roger Ready, Warren Hammack. Tommy Kirk plays a harmless Martian looking for women on Earth to take back and repopulate his planet. The military views the situation as an invasion, and sees to it that the Martians leave empty handed. ¶ "It's very presumptuous of us to expect that Martians are any different than we are." • Tommy Kirk began his career as the young star of numerous Disney ventures, including *Old Yeller* (1957) and *Swiss Family Robinson* (1960). Yvonne Craig is more popularly known as TV's "Batgirl."

A Martian in Paris (1961; Les Films Univers; France) D/S: Jean-Daniel Daninos. P/S: Jacques Vilfrid. C: Marcel Combes. Cast: Darry-Cowl, Nicole Mirel, Henri Vilbert, Gisèle Segur, Michèle Verez. The Martians send one of their members down to Earth to study the emotion of love, which they consider a disease.

Martians Go Home (1990; Taurus Entertainment Group) D: David Odell. P: Michael Pariser. S: Charles Haas. C: Peter Deming. Cast: Randy Quaid, Margaret Colin, Barry Sobel, Vic Dunlop, John Philbin, Anita Morris. Green Martians with an overzealous sense of humor are lured to Earth by a musician where they drive everyone crazy with their constant joke-telling.

A Message from Mars (1913; United Kingdom Films) D/S: J. Wallett Walker. P: Nicholson Ormsby-Scott. Cast: Charles Hawtrey, E. Holman Clark, Chrissie Bell, Frank Hector, Hubert Willis. A Martian reforms a sinner. • The Martian views the Earth from a crystal ball. • The film was remade in 1921.

A Message from Mars (1921; Metro) D/P: Maxwell Karger. S: Arthur Zellner, Arthur Maude. C: Arthur Martinelli. Cast: Bert Lytell, Raye Dean, Gordon Ash, Maud Milton, Alphonz Ethier, Leonard Mudie. This science fiction–styled "A Christmas Carol" features an alien who reforms a sinner by showing him the error of his ways.

Mission Stardust (1968) (see THE MOON). Earth astronauts meet technically advanced but friendly aliens near the Moon. They return to Earth to try and find a cure for a blood ailment that may destroy their alien race.

The Monitors (1968; Second City Productions) D: Jack Shea. P: Bernard Sahlins. S: Myron J. Gold. C: Vilmos Zsigmond. Cast: Guy Stockwell, Susan Oliver, Avery Schreiber, Sherry Jackson, Keenan Wynn. Well-intentioned aliens promoting love and peace unfortunately fail in the end. • Cinematographer Vilmos Zsigmond went on to photograph the popular 1977 benevolent alien classic, *Close Encounters of the Third Kind,* for which he won an Oscar.

Moon Pilot (1962; Walt Disney) D: James Neilson. P: Walt Disney. S: Maurice Tombragel. C: William Snyder. Cast: Tom Tryon, Brian Keith, Edmond O'Brien, Dany Saval, Bob Sweeney, Kent Smith. Tom Tryon plays an astronaut warned by a sexy female alien not to travel into outer space. • Star Tom Tryon had appeared in a previous alien film, *I Married a Monster from Outer Space* (1958).

Morons from Outer Space (1985; Thorn EMI: U.K.) D: Mike Hodges. P: Barry Hanson. S: Griff Rhys Jones, Mel Smith. C: Phil Meheaux. Cast: Mel Smith, Griff Rhys Jones, Paul Brown, Joanne Pearce, Jimmy Nail, Dinsdale Landen, James B. Sikking. Just as the title suggests, four dim-witted but friendly aliens come to Earth in this British science fiction parody. • James B. Sikking is more popularly known for his role of Howard Hunter, S.W.A.T. commander extraordinaire on the TV series, "Hill Street Blues."

Munchies (1987; MGM/United Artists) D: Bettina Hirsch. P: Roger Corman, Ginny Nugent. S: Lance Smith. C: Jonathan West. Cast: Harvey Korman, Charles Stratton, Nadine Van Der Velde, Alix Elias, Charlie Phillips. This *Gremlin* imitation involves a little space alien (called a "Munchie" by anthropologist Harvey Korman), who splits into more diminutive havoc-wreakers when chopped up by Korman's evil twin brother. The creatures are eventually subdued with electricity, which turns them to stone. • The original Munchie was named Arnold Ziffel, after the family pig on the "Green Acres" TV series. The Munchies were actually puppets, with Frank Welker doing the voices.

My Stepmother Is an Alien (1989; Weintraub Entertainment Group) D: Richard Benjamin. P: Ronald Parker, Franklin R. Levy. S: Jerico Weingrod, Herschel Weingrod, Timothy Harris, Jonathan Reynolds. C: Richard H. Kline. Cast: Dan Ackroyd, Kim Basinger, Jon Lovitz, Joseph Maher, Seth Green, Ann Prentiss, Alyson Hannigan. A lonely scientist sending signals outside the solar system contacts a beautiful alien who is sent to Earth to induce him to continue the transmissions. The two fall in love and eventually marry. ¶ "Boy, talk about being married to your work. I spend my whole career trying to prove there's life on other planets and when I finally find it, I *marry* it!"

Omicron (1963; Lux/Ultra/Vides; Italy) D/S: Ugo Gregoretti. P: Franco Cristaldi. C: Carlo Di Palma. Cast: Renato Salvatori, Rosemary Dexter. An alien creature reanimates the dead body of an Italian worker and falls in love during his stay on Earth.

Peacemaker (1990) (see INVADERS ON EARTH: THE 80S AND BEYOND, this chapter). A human-looking alien version of a police officer lands on Earth in search of a vicious extraterrestrial serial killer. The problem is, the heroine who becomes involved in their deadly chase doesn't know who is who and must decide which one to believe.

Phantom from Space (1953) (see INVADERS ON EARTH: THE 50s). An invisible alien kills several people during its stay on our planet. At the climax, however, the alien is judged to have been friendly, and the so-called murders only accidents or misunderstandings.

Popdown (1968; Fremar Productions; U.K.) D/P/S: Fred Marshall. C: Oliver Wood. Cast: Diane Keen, Zoot Money, Jane Bates, Carol Rachell, Debbie Slater, Bill Aaron. Two aliens observing Earth fall for pop music. • Musical groups featured in the film include Dantalion's Chariot, Brian Auger and the Trinity, and Blossom Toes.

Red Planet Mars (1952; United Artists) D: Harry Horner. P: Anthony Veiller, Donald Hyde. S: John L. Balderston, Anthony Veiller. C: Joseph Biroc. Cast: Peter Graves, Andrea King, Herbert Berghof, Walter Sande, Marvin Miller, Morris Ankrum, Lewis Martin, Orley Lendren, Bayard Veiller. A scientist receives messages of peace from the planet Mars which bring about wide sweeping changes across the country when the media are informed. It is revealed, however, that the messages had been sent by the machine's original inventor in a plot to destroy the world's economy. At the climax, a last final message is received from Mars, sent by an unknown source that sounds very much like our own God. ¶ "You'll be the next to advance science, and maybe us, right into oblivion!" • The story's premise is based upon a similar scientific endeavor which occurred prior to the film's making. Scientists apparently tried bouncing a series of radio signals off the moon with the hope that someone or something would respond.

The Rocket Man (1954; 20th Century-

Fox) D: Oscar Rudolph. P: Leonard Gold-stein. S: Lenny Bruce, Jack Henley. C: John Seitz. Cast: George Winslow, Spring Byington, Charles Coburn, Anne Francis, John Agar, Beverly Garland. A friendly alien lends his ray gun to an orphaned boy. When fired, it has the ability to make people tell the truth. The local Justice of the Peace takes in the boy and they use the wondrous spacegun to keep the community honest. ¶ "Times sure have changed. I'll bet when your mom or pop were little like us they used to dream about cowboys and Indians. Only now the cowboys and Indians have turned into men from outer space, and the horses into flying saucers." • The friendly alien showed up wearing Klaatu's spacesuit from *The Day the Earth Stood Still* (1951). • Comedian Lenny Bruce, whose biting social satire and frequent use of expletives made him an underground star, co-scripted this feature. • George Winslow (who plays the orphan) was a popular child actor during the 1950s. His nickname was "Foghorn" because of his unusually deep voice.

The Rocky Horror Picture Show (1975; 20th Century-Fox; U.K.) D/S: Jim Sharman. P: Michael White. S: Richard O'Brien. C: Peter Suschitzky. Cast: Tim Curry, Susan Sarandon, Barry Bostwick, Richard O'Brien, Jonathan Adams, Nell Campbell. This campy sci-fi musical features Brad Majors and Janet Weiss encountering sexually deviant but generally non-hostile aliens from the planet "Transsexual." • British actor/rock singer Tim Curry played the part of Dr. Frank-N-Furter, "a sweet transvestite from Transsexual, Transylvania." At the film's end, Rocky (Frank-N-Furter's creation) climbs a replica of the famous RKO tower used as that studio's logo. • The popular theme song ("The Time Warp"), the crazy costuming, and its combination of provocative and parodic characters has turned this picture into a cult event. *Rocky Horror* remains to this day one of the strongest midnight movie attractions. A tremendous fan following often comes to the theaters dressed up as the characters, and it's not unusual to be sprayed with water, rice, toast, or toilet paper at various moments during the film. Sometimes whole audiences will be singing along with the songs, repeating the lines, or acting out scenes in the aisles while the picture is being played. The film's popularity has become such a cult phenomenon that many theaters constantly show the film every weekend for months, even years, at a time.

Solarbabies (1986) (see FUTURES ON EARTH—UTOPIAS AND DISTOPIAS). In the totalitarian future, young children are rounded up to live in oppressive orphanages and brainwashed to serve the evil system. A visitor from another planet arrives to try and change the world for the better.

The Space Children (1958; Paramount) D: Jack Arnold. P: William Alland. S: Bernard C. Schoenfeld. C: Ernest Laszlo. Cast: Michel Ray, Johnny Crawford, Adam Williams, Peggy Webber, Jackie Coogan, Sandy Descher, Richard Shannon, Russell Johnson. A giant alien brain hides out in a coastal cave and influences the children living at the nearby military site to sabotage the launching of the ultimate missile, called "The Thunderer." The aim of this benign alien is to give the world a second chance at peace. ¶ "Why are you siding with it against us, we're your parents, we love you!" • The space brain was built by Ivyl Burks from a plastic gelatin. Inside the mass were more than $3300 worth of neon lights to make it glow. Solenoids, needle valves, and manifolds were also built into it to enable the creature to pulsate. The large brain version (it grew throughout the film) was over five feet high, ten feet long, and weighed roughly 1,000 pounds. It was covered with strips of lucite and lemurith and welded together with acids. • "The Addams Family" star Jackie Coogan, better known as Uncle Fester, plays a pro-military U.S. space program technician in this film. • One of the "space children," Eadie, is played by Sandy Descher, who appeared as the lost little catatonic girl in *Them* (1954). • Director Jack Arnold always seemed to use his settings as effective atmospheric tools. He told Bill Kelley in *Cinefantastique* Vol. 4, #2, that he used the "beaches and the ocean the way I used the desert in *It Came from Outer Space.*" • The final words showing on the screen were from the Bible, Matthew 18:3 — "Verily, I say unto you . . . except ye become as little children, ye shall not enter into the kingdom of heaven."

Spaced Invaders (1990; Touchstone Pictures) D: Patrick Read Johnson. P: Luigi Cingolani. S: Patrick Read Johnson, Scott Lawrence Alexander. C: James L. Carter. Cast: Douglas Barr, Royal Dano, Ariana Richards, Gregg Berger, Fred Applegate, Wayne Alexander, J. J. Anderson, Patrika Darbo, Tonya Lee Williams. Some wild and crazy little green aliens from Mars land in the Midwest town of Big Bean on Halloween night with the mistaken idea that their spacefleet has invaded (from listening to a re-broadcast of Orson Welles' "War of the

Worlds"). Once they realize their error, it's up to a little girl, her sheriff father, and an old farmer to help the harmless aliens avoid the cluthes of the riled townspeople and escape back to their own planet. ¶ "They're not really bad, they're just — stupid." • This two million dollar production earned $15 million at the box office. • Steven Spielberg was instrumental in getting Touchstone Pictures to pick up and distribute the film. • *Spaced Invaders* was shot under the title *Martians!!*

Starman (1984; Columbia) D: John Carpenter. P: Larry J. Franco. S: Bruce A. Evans, Raynold Gideon. Cast: Jeff Bridges, Karen Allen, Charles Martin Smith, Richard Jaeckel, Robert Phalen. A friendly alien comes to Earth to learn more about human culture, but is hunted down by government agencies after assuming the physical appearance of Karen Allen's dead husband. The two eventually fall in love during their trek to Arizona and he impregnates her just prior to leaving. • Karen Allen plays the distraught wife, who at first is terrified to see the form of her once-dead husband borrowed by the Starman. Later, she decides to help him escape the dragnet established by the antagonistic government agent played by Richard Jaeckel. It was essential for the Starman to reach his rendezvous site in time to be picked up or he would die. Fortunately he made it. Karen Allen was also seen opposite Harrison Ford in *Raiders of the Lost Ark* (1981). • The objects with unlimited power that the Starman brought with him resemble silver marbles. He uses one of these objects to bring a dead deer back to life.

Stranded (1987; New Line Cinema) D: Tex Fuller. P: Scott Rosenfelt, Mark Levinson. S: Alan Castle. C: Jeff Jur. Cast: Ione Skye, Maureen O'Sullivan, Joe Morton, Cameron Dye, Brendan Hughes. Aliens who manage to escape their own world find more terror than they bargained for on our Earth. • The picture's makeup artist, Michael Burke, won an Oscar for his apemen in *Quest for Fire* (1981). *Stranded* was made on the relatively low budget of three million dollars.

Stranger from Venus (1955; Princess Pictures; U.K.) (also *Immediate Disaster*). D/P: Burt Balaban. P: Gene Martel. S: Hans Jacoby. C: Kenneth Talbot. Cast: Helmut Dantine, Patricia Neal, Derek Bond, Cyril Luckham, Willoughby Gray. Much along the lines of *The Day the Earth Stood Still,* this British film follows a mysterious stranger from Venus who visits Earth and falls for Patricia Neal. The Venusian then sacrifices himself to save the Earth when his ships plan to fire their weaponry if a planned military trap is sprung on them. All of these problems arise when Neal's jealous fiancé (Derek Bond) steals a communication device used by the stranger. ¶ "My friend, you have no pulse. There are only two possibilities, I am drunk or you are dead." • Actress Patricia Neal also starred in the most popular benevolent alien classic, *The Day the Earth Stood Still* (1951), directed by Robert Wise. Two years after winning an Academy Award for her role in *Hud* (1963), Neal suffered several massive strokes. Her great determination and courage while recovering culminated in 1968 with another Oscar nomination for *The Subject Was Roses,* and a special award presentation (Heart of the Year) by then–President Johnson. Neal was no stranger to tragedy; one of her five children died of measles at the age of 13, while another, a boy, was struck by a car as a baby, but survived.

Strangest Dreams: Invasion of the Space Preachers (1990) (see ALIEN INVADERS: THE 80S AND BEYOND). A friendly alien who transforms into a blonde bombshell aids an out-of-the-way rural community in getting rid of pesky mind-controlling preachers from outer space.

Supergirl (1984) (see COMIC BOOK FANTASY HEROES). The friendly alien known as Supergirl comes to Earth to retrieve a Kryptonite power source which has fallen into the wrong hands.

Superman: The Movie (1978) (see COMIC BOOK FANTASY HEROES). The friendly alien known as the "Man of Steel" ends up on Earth where he fights for truth, justic, and the American way. • Superman's given Kryptonian name is Kal-El (the son of Jor-El, played by Marlon Brando).

Superman II (1980) (see COMIC BOOK FANTASY HEROES). This time Superman must defeat three arch villains from his own planet, who, along with Lex Luthor, plot the rule the world.

Superman III (1983) (see COMIC BOOK FANTASY HEROES). Richard Pryor is added for comedy relief to this story of Superman's duel nature being exploited when infected with synthetic Kryptonite, orchestrated by a power-mad corporate criminal.

Superman IV: The Quest for Peace (1987) (see COMIC BOOK FANTASY HEROES). After Superman disposes of all the world's nuclear weaponry, Lex Luthor stirs up more trouble by cloning one of the hairs on his head and creating a replicant named Nuclear Man.

They Came from Beyond Space (1967; Embassy; U.K.) D: Freddie Francis. P: Milton Subotsky, Max J. Rosenberg. S: Milton Subotsky. C: Norman Warwick. Cast: Robert Hutton, Jennifer Jayne, Zia Mohyeddin, Bernard Kay, Michael Gough. Stranded aliens inhabit the bodies of Cornwall residents and a terrible plague results. Robert Hutton and Jennifer Jayne eventually learn that the aliens need the Earth bodies to help them repair their crippled ship on the Moon. They finally strike a friendly deal with the aliens that is beneficial to all. • The film is based on Joseph Millard's story, "The Gods Hate Kansas."

This Island Earth (1955) (see ENCOUNTERS IN OUTER SPACE, this chapter). This sci-fi classic features a friendly alien named Exeter (Jeff Morrow) who doesn't wish any harm to befall the two scientists who have been whisked away to their planet to help develop their defense system.

Time Walker (1982; New World) D: Tom Kennedy. P: Dimitri Villard, Jason Williams. S: Karen Levitt, Tom Friedman. C: Robbie Greenberg. Cast: Ben Murphy, Nina Axelrod, Kevin Brophy, Austin Stoker, James Karen. A benign alien, posing as a mummy, is revived when his sarcophagus is x-rayed. The mummy/alien spends the rest of the film running around trying to retrieve his stolen crystals that will allow him to change back into his true alien self and "phone home."

Visit to a Small Planet (1960; Paramount) D: Norman Taurog. P: Hal B. Wallis. S: Edmund Beloin, Henry Garson. C: Loyal Griggs. Cast: Jerry Lewis, Joan Blackman, Fred Clark, John Williams, Jerome Cowan, Lee Patrick, Gale Gordon, Ellen Corby. An alien named Kreton, played by comedic star Jerry Lewis, comes to Earth for laughs and chuckles. Precious few are provided. ¶ "Man, this cat talks off the top, he's tuned in. Tell me, double hipness, what floor do you get out of when you split from the clouds?" • Supporting performers Jerome Cowan and Lee Patrick were no strangers to each other, having been paired together

back in 1941 on the classic Bogart feature, *The Maltese Falcon.*

The Watcher in the Woods (1980; Walt Disney) D: John Hough. P: Ron Miller. S: Brian Clemens, Harry Spalding, Rosemary Anne Sisson. C: Alan Hume. Cast: Bette Davis, David McCallum, Carroll Baker, Lynn-Holly Johnson, Kim Richards, Ian Bannen. A family moves into an old house and the two daughters are seemingly haunted by a strange presence in the woods while one seems to be possessed by the spirit of a young girl who disappeared years earlier during a solar eclipse. Finally it is revealed that the presence is not the ghost of the girl, but an alien from another dimension who had accidentally switched places with the missing girl. The alien is benign and simply wants to return home again, which it does with the help of the sisters during another eclipse. ¶ "I've been trapped on your planet, Karen, in my dimension. We exchanged places by mistake. Magnetic pull of the eclipse transferred our positions." • The only glimpse we get of the other-dimensional alien is of a bright blue light.

Wavelength (1982; New World) D/S: Mike Gray. P: James M. Rosenfield. Cast: Robert Carradine, Cherie Currie, Keenan Wynn. Robert Carradine is a rock star investigating an Air Force facility along with an eccentric prospector after hearing strange voices. They discover a group of aliens, retrieved from a UFO crash site and being held prisoner, and help them escape from government officials who plan to cover up the incident.

Zone Troopers (1985; Altar Productions) D: Danny Bilson. P: Paul Demeo. S: Danny Bilson, Paul Demeo. C: Mac Ahlberg. Cast: Tim Thomerson, Timothy Van Patten, Art Lafleur, Biff Manard. Soldiers trapped behind enemy lines during World War II encounter a wrecked spaceship and its stranded alien pilot. The Zone Troopers are the alien's comrades which are sent to rescue him amidst the turmoil of war. ¶ "We will not help you kill your own kind."

Alligators and Crocodiles

For such a ferocious species, one would think that the monster cinema would have utilized these creatures more often than it has. The alligator is probably the closest living relative of the dinosaur, making it all the more fascinating and

Hook-handed villain Lon Chaney, Jr., battles the misunderstood hero-turned-reptile in The Alligator People *(1959).*

frightening. These fearsome aquatic reptiles often strike from under the water, so you don't always see them coming. They are primitive and terrifying in appearance, are powerful swimmers, and possess a mouth full of jagged teeth. Though alligator attacks on humans are few, they do occur. Still, it wasn't until 1959 (with *The Alligator People*) that these carnivores were fully featured as monster meances. In that particular entry, Beverly Garland's husband suffers from an acute form of "alligatoritis," which transforms his skin into a scaly reptilian tissue. Further scientific treatment only worsened the situation by turning him into an improbable zipper-suited alligator-man. Aside from the infrequent alligator menace movies like *Crocodile* (1979) and *Alligator* (1981; the *Jaws* of the 'gator world and arguably the best alligator film to date), 'gators have usually been used as a prop by mad scientists or despicable villains for destroying evidence of their victims (as in *I Was a Teenage Frankenstein,* 1958; and *Murders in the Zoo,* 1933). The definitive alligator movie is still out there waiting to be made, waiting for someone with the right reptilian sensibilities to prove that alligator movies are not just a crock.

Alligator (1981; Group 1) D: Lewis Teague. P: Brandon Chase. S: John Sayles. C: Joseph Mangine. Cast: Robert Forster, Robin Riker, Michael Gazzo, Dean Jagger, Henry Silva, Bart Braverman. An alligator grows to huge proportions in the sewers under a large city and occasionally ventures forth to snack on the populace. • The carcasses of experimental dogs dumped into the sewer by an irresponsible scientific laboratory and then eaten by the creature is what causes the normal-sized alligator to grow to such a gigantic size. • Writer John Sayles (*Piranha,* 1979; *Battle Beyond the Stars,*

1980) is best known for his personal project, *The Return of the Secaucus Seven* (1979).

The Alligator People (1959; 20th Century–Fox) D: Roy Del Ruth. P: Jack Leewood. S: Orville H. Hampton. C: Karl Struss. Cast: Beverly Garland, George Macready, Lon Chaney, Jr., Richard Crane, Frieda Inescort, Bruce Bennett, Douglas Kennedy. Newlywed Beverly Garland's husband has mysteriously vanished. He has been in an accident and scientists in the Louisiana swamps attempt to use the curative powers of alligator glands to renew her husband's terrible disfigurement. The experiment backfires, giving him reptilian skin and eventually transforming him into a creature with the body of a man and the head of an alligator. ¶ "I injected this substance into the veins of volunteers—horribly injured, hopelessly mangled accident victims on the point of death. It was miraculous, Mrs. Webster. Not only did those dying men and women live, but in an incredibly short time they were completely whole—mangled limbs as good as new—as though they were never injured." • The alligator-headed man was played by Boyd Stockman, and the makeup, which took over two and a half months to finalize, was created by makeup legends Ben Nye and Dick Smith. Nye said of the job, "We really had our hands full with that one, and just like the case of *The Fly,* we had to start from scratch.... The final alligator suit fit snugly over Richard Crane's body and was cemented at the seams, hence the actor was literally sealed in the outfit. We stippled the seams with makeup rubber and colored the entire thing with a special rubber-base oil paint so that the costume would remain flexible. You should have seen the molds! We slush-cast them with latex rubber and it took several men to lift them each time we ran the rubber through!" • In Tom Weaver's book, *Interviews with B Science Fiction and Horror Movie Makers,* Beverly Garland tells of her difficulties with filming: "The hardest thing in that movie was to keep a straight face. I was all right from the beginning of the film up until I found my husband in the sanitarium, and then I just fell apart. That was the end of me! ... I had to say to him, 'I'll love you no matter what,' which I think took me a good half day to say."

Blood Salvage (1990) (see MADMEN — THE SLICE 'N' DICE WAVE). A psychotic backwoods family arranges road "accidents" and then keeps the victims alive on homemade life support systems in order to periodically remove their organs to sell to an illegal organ broker. They keep a full-grown alligator in their salvage yard as an alternative to the usual "junkyard dog." At one point the heroine must outrun the galloping gator and lure it into a compacting machine.

Crocodile (1979; Cobra Media; Hong Kong) D: Sompote Sands. P: Dick Randall, Robert Chan. Cast: Tany Tim. A giant crocodile (the result of exposure to radiation) goes on a village-destroying rampage. • *Crocodile* was filmed in Korea and Thailand, and was presented in the U.S. by Herman Cohen (of *Konga,* 1961, fame).

Death Curse of Tartu (1967) (see WITCHES, WARLOCKS, AND CULTS). In the Florida Everglades, a Seminole witch-doctor's spirit materializes as various reptiles, including an alligator, wreak vengeance upon those who disturbed his resting place.

Dr. Cyclops (1940) (see SHRINKAGE). At one point, the six-inch-tall cast must defend themselves against a hungry alligator.

Eaten Alive (1976) (see MADMEN — EARLY PSYCHOS) (also *Death Trap; Horror Hotel Massacre, Starlight Slaughter*). Neville Brand, the proprietor of a run-down backwoods Louisiana hotel, runs amok by killing his guests with a scythe and or feeding them to a huge crocodile.

The Great Alligator (1980; Italy) D/S: Sergio Martino. P: Lawrence Martin. Cast: Mel Ferrer, Barbara Bach, Richard Johnson. African resort owner Mel Ferrer loses business when a large alligator begins devouring tourists. • *The Great Alligator* is an Italian-produced film which was sold directly to American television without a theatrical release. • This is actor Mel Ferrer's second encounter with an alligator. He had similar troubles in 1976's *Eaten Alive.*

I Was a Teenage Frankenstein (1958) (see FRANKENSTEIN'S MONSTER — FURTHER FRANKENSTEINS). Dr. Frankenstein (Whit Bissell) utilizes a secret basement room filled with alligators to dispose of unwanted body parts (and witnesses).

Murders in the Zoo (1933) (see MADMEN — EARLY MADMEN). Insanely jealous Lionel Atwill employs the crocodile pit at the zoo to settle his domestic conflicts (he feeds his wife to the crocodiles).

Wild Women of Wongo (1959) (see CAVEPEOPLE). On the alligator-infested island of Wongo two lovers from different tribes meet. The Wongans have beautiful women but ugly men. Another tribe, the Goonans have handsome men but ugly women. So they get together and swap. They also worship an alligator (who demands a great deal of sacrificing) as a God.

Androids *see* **Robots**

Animal Giants

In this section you will find a plethora of creatures from the animal kingdom that have grown to enormous size due to scientific mishap, genetic breeding, witchcraft, or simply some aberration of nature. Because some species of giant animal life have evolved into subgenres unto themselves, films about "Ape Giants," "Bug Giants," "Human Giants," "Sea Monsters," and "Japanese (Giant) Monsters" will be listed separately.

Of the four causal factors for the existence of gigantic animals, the "naturally" occurring kind are far and away the most rare. With the notable exception of *The Giant Gila Monster* (1959), most every other animal that has been "enlarged," even the rampaging rabbits from *Night of the Lepus* (1972), are the result of some form of scientific "advancement." The nuclear age, with all its radiation and contaminated waste, has left its mark on the environment—and upon the "gigantic" cinema as well. The gargantuan snake that nearly strangled—*The Cyclops* (1957), the genetically mutated *Killer Shrews* (1959), and the rats that consumed the *Food of the Gods* (1976) were all dramatically affected by the pitfalls of radioactivity. One can only wonder what was written in Captain Nemo's genetic blueprints for all the gigantic fauna inhabiting the *Mysterious Island* (1961). Because nuclear energy and all its byproducts remain such a mystery to us, it will continue to be a frequent scapegoat for every manner of mutant or monster, be it vegetable, mineral—or animal.

Alligator (1981) (see ALLIGATORS AND CROCODILES). A thirty-foot alligator living in the sewer comes topside for human snacks.

Burn, Witch, Burn (1962) (see VOODOO) (also *Night of the Eagle*). A stone statue is brought to life as a giant hawk to terrorize the hero of this British voodoo tale.

Conan the Barbarian (1982) (see SWORD AND SORCERY). Conan does battle with a giant snake that guards a treasure. He also must face James Earl Jones, the high priest of a snake cult who has the ability to transform himself into an oversized python.

Crocodile (1979) (see ALLIGATORS). A crocodile is exposed to radiation and grows to enormous proportions. The rear-projection reptile goes on a village-destroying rampage.

The Cyclops (1957) (see HUMAN GIANTS). Due to radiation, a remote valley in Mexico is home to gigantic wildlife, including a giant falcon, lizard, and snake. • Nineteen years later, producer/director/screenwriter Bert I. Gordon brought us more giant animals in *Food of the Gods* (1976).

Deadly Eyes (1982) (see RATS). Giant mutant rats grow to the size of dogs and begin feasting on humans.

Digby, the Biggest Dog in the World (1973) (see DOGS). A dog is fed an experimental chemical by mistake and grows to gigantic proportions in this British comedy.

Food of the Gods (1976; AIP) D/P/S: Bert I Gordon. C: Reginald Morris. Cast: Marjoe Gortner, Pamela Franklin, Ralph Meeker, Ida Lupino, John Cypher, Belinda Balaski. A mysterious substance bubbling from out of the ground turns animals and insects into giants. Marjoe Gortner and friends must battle giant mosquitoes, chickens, and rats. ¶ "My father used to say, 'Morgan, one of these days the Earth will get even with man for messing her up with his garbage. Just let man continue to pollute the Earth the way he is and nature will rebel. And its going to be one hell of a rebellion.'" • This was the second film Bert I. Gordon made based on the H. G. Wells novel, *Food of the Gods*. The first was *Village of the Giants* (1965).

Food of the Gods Part 2 (1989) (see RATS). An experimental growth hormone causes rats to grow to an enormous size and hunt people for food. Differing from the first *Food of the Gods,* this entry features only rats (whereas the original showed us several different species of animal giants).

The Giant Claw (1957) (see ALIENS— INVADERS ON EARTH: THE 50s). An ugly gigantic bird the size of an aircraft carrier flies in from outer space to invade the Earth, wreak havoc, and lay an egg.

The Giant Gila Monster (1959; McLendon Radio Pictures) D: Ray Kellogg. P: Ken Curtis. S: Jay Sims, Ray Kellogg. C: Wilfred Cline. Cast: Don Sullivan, Lisa Simone, Shug Fisher, Jerry Cortwright, Fred Graham, Beverly Thurman. In a small desert community, a giant gila monster inexplicably turns up to menace the hot rodding, be-bopping overaged teens in the cast. ¶ "It is in these lonely areas of impenetrable forests and dark shadows that the gila monster lives. How large the dreaded gila monster grows, no one can say." • Producer Ken Curtis is best remembered as Festus on TV's "Gunsmoke." • *The Giant Gila Monster* was released on a double bill with another Gordon McLendon production, *The Killer Shrews.* • According to the film's pressbook, *The Giant Gila Monster* might not be that far from reality: "Zoologists have confirmed that reports of ordinary reptiles growing to freakish proportions are not uncommon in the present-day world of science. This, perhaps, is a prime reason that McLendon Radio Pictures terms the production an 'action-adventure' film rather than the far-fetched, improbable 'horror' variety." Right.

Graveyard Shift (1990) (see RATS). A sub-basement of a rat-infested woolen mill is discovered and a clean-up crew is sent down there by the sadistic foreman. The workers are trapped and killed off (and eaten) one by one by a giant rat-bat mutant creature who has made his lair in the nearby graveyard, and tunnels under the mill looking for fresh prey.

The Killer Shrews (1959; McLendon Radio Pictures) D: Ray Kellogg. P: Ken Curtis. S: Jay Sims. C: Wilfred Cline. Cast: James Best, Ingrid Goude, Ken Curtis, Baruch Lumet, Gordon McLendon. Scientists experimenting with genetics create a carnivorous pack of dog-sized shrews on an isolated island. ¶ "They are mutants! In controlling the size factor we seem to have crossed some of the other characteristics." • The last survivors on the island escape their compound surrounded by the deadly rodents by duck-walking to the beach inside empty oil drums, with the giant shrews snapping all around them. • Not only can the shrews devour you in minutes but their bites cause immediate death by poisoning. • Actor Gordon McLendon, who also served as executive producer, shot the film at his own ranch. • McLendon also narrates the descriptive prelude, which states: "The most vicious of all animals is the tiny shrew. The shrew feeds only in the dark of the moon. He must eat his own body weight every few hours or starve. And the shrew devours everything—flesh, marrow, everything. In March, first in Alaska and then invading steadily southward, there were reports of a new species—the giant *Killer Shrews!*" • Baruch Lumet, the actor playing the accidental creator of *The Killer Shrews,* is the father of famous contemporary director, Sidney Lumet.

King Kong (1933) (see APE GIANTS). The mighty ape defeats a giant snake-creature on his island home.

King Kong (1976) (see APE GIANTS). The mighty man-in-an-ape-suit defeats a giant boa constrictor on his island home.

Lair of the White Worm (1988) (see SNAKES). Vampiric snake-people worship and offer up human sacrifices to a legendary giant snake-creature known as the "Dampton Worm" living in a cave in northern England.

The Maze (1953; Allied Artists) D: William Cameron Menzies. P: Richard Heermance. S: Dan Ullman. C: Harry Neumann. Cast: Richard Carlson, Veronica Hurst, Michael Pate, Hillary Brooke, Lillian Bond, Robin Hughes. Richard Carlson inherits a Scottish castle and title, along with the 200-year-old relative inhabiting the castle—the real lord of the castle—who had the misfortune to be born as a giant frog. ¶ "For over two centuries he endured the torment of knowing he was a monster and feeling he was a man." • Carlson gives this explanation for this bizarre anomaly: "The human embryo passes through all stages of evolution, from the invertebrate to the mammal. At one point, the embryo is an amphibian. Sir Roger never developed beyond that point physically, but he grew and developed mentally." • Though a preposterous premise—a man who looks like a giant frog—director Menzies exhibits some sensitivity in his handling of the story and creates some genuine sympathy for the unfortunate man-frog. • *The Maze* was filmed in 3D. • Director William Cameron Menzies is best known to sci-fi fans as the director of *Things to Come* (1936) and *Invaders from Mars* (1953). Menzies also served as his own art director on this film. • Leading man Richard Carlson appeared in many genre films, including two others released this same year — *It Came from Outer Space* and *Magnetic Monster*.

Mysterious Island (1960) (see SEA MONSTERS). A gigantic dodo-like bird (the result of experimentation by none other than Captain Nemo) menaces a few cast members on the Mysterious Island.

Neon Maniacs (1986) (see DEMONS AND DEVILS). A group of assorted monsters live under the Golden Gate Bridge and come out at night to kill unwary citizens. One of the demonic creatures resembles a giant lizard that walks like a man.

Night of the Lepus (1972; MGM) D: William F. Claxton. P: A. C. Lyles. S: Don Holliday, Gene R. Kearney. C: Ted Voightlander. Cast: Stuart Whitman, Janet Leigh, Rory Calhoun, DeForest Kelley, Paul Fix, Melanie Fullerton. A test rabbit, injected with an experimental serum, escapes into the Arizona desert and breeds with the local wild bunny population, resulting in "a scuttling, shambling horde of creatures destroying all in their path" (as the poster so luridly put it) — actually a group of carnivorous rabbits the size of wolves. ¶ "There's a herd of killer rabbits heading this way." • Janet Leigh is a little more successful in fending

off a herd of giant killer bunnies than she was a single *Psycho* in 1960. • After "boldly going where no man has gone before" on TV's "Star Trek," DeForest Kelley (Dr. McCoy) had to fight these oversized wascally wabbits during the *Night of the Lepus*. • Director Claxton is better known for helming low-budget westerns.

Nightmares (1983) (see ANTHOLOGIES). In the "Night of the Rat" segment, a family must defend themselves against a giant demon rat who's bigger than a Saint Bernard. ¶ "That, madame, was not done by your average rodent. I've never seen that kind of destruction."

The Seventh Voyage of Sinbad (1958) (see SINBAD). Among his adventes, Sinbad encounters a giant two-headed bird (the mythological beast known as a "Roc").

Son of Kong (1933) (see APE GIANTS). The first beast to do battle with the titular titan was a giant bear.

Valley of the Dragons (1961) (see DINOSAURS — LOST WORLDS). Two 19th century men are swept up onto a comet where time has stood still for millions of years. They see (amongst the dinosaurs and cave-people) a giant bear cub battling a snake and a herd of giant armadillos(!) mixing in with mastodons, and must flee for their lives from one of the raging mammoths.

Anthologies

The anthology film has frequently been a favored format of the "fantastique" filmmaker because it doesn't restrict a picture to just one specific plot or guideline. Its multi-storied structure allows the movie makers to explore numerous diverse themes and ideas, all within the framework of one picture. This flexible diversity offers anthology artists an opportunity to pull almost every viewer into the film at some point in the 90-minute program. Of course the danger in an anthology film, and the trap into which most every one falls, is that the quality of the various segments is often uneven, featuring one or two strong stories hampered by another two or three weak ones. This frequently makes for an unsatisfying film overall.

In the early 1940s, two critically acclaimed anthology fantasies, *Flesh and Fantasy* (1943) and *Dead of Night* (1945), hit the screens, setting a stylish standard for this species of cinema to follow. *Flesh and Fantasy* was the singular vision of one brilliant French director, Julien Duvivier (*The Golem,* 1937), while *Dead of Night* was directed by four different men and pieced together with the precision of a fine musical composition. These were not the first features to contain multiple segments, however, as master German filmmaker Paul Leni served up a silent expressionistic trilogy entitled *Waxworks* in 1924.

The most prolific and prestigious horror anthology film producers have been the team of Max J. Rosenberg and Milton Subotsky. They have made the term "anthology" almost synonymous with the British film company Amicus. Titles like *Dr. Terror's House of Horrors* (1965), *The House That Dripped Blood* (1971), and *Tales from the Crypt* (1972), to mention just a few, have made this kind of feature an extremely popular subgenre that continues to endure with recent features like *Grim Prairie Tales* and *Tales from the Darkside: The Movie* (both 1990).

Most of these pictures utilize three, four, or five different segments that revolve around, or relate to, an introductory sequence called the "framing" or "wraparound" story. This connecting device is so named because the characters in them lead you into the various episodes, and often conclude them as well — usually with a twist or "kicker" ending added for good measure. While most anthology films use widely different episodes for reasons of entertainment diversity, some multi-storied movies adhere to one topical subject. Films of this nature will be included here with only a relevant element and a cross-referenced listing of where that particular film's main entry can be found. Two examples would be the Japanese ghost anthology *Kwaidan* (1964), whose main entry is in the GHOST chapter, and the 1962 Edgar Alan Poe film, *Tales of Terror,* found in the POE FILMS — THE CORMAN CYCLE section.

After Midnight (1989) (see MADMEN — THE SLICE 'N' DICE WAVE). A bizarre psychology professor gathers some select students at his house to learn the "psychology of fear" by sharing three terror tales of psychos and murder. The first involves a scary practical joke that horribly backfires. In the second, some teenage girls must face a psychotic streetperson and his killer dogs. The third story is about a woman working at an all-night answering service who is plagued by a maniacal phone-caller. • The wraparound story, which ends up in a confusing, surrealistic nightmare, is lifted directly from one of the first and best horror anthologies, *Dead of Night* (1945).

Asylum (1972; Amicus; U.K.) (also *House of Crazies*). D: Roy Ward Baker. P: Max J. Rosenberg, Milton Subotsky. S: Robert Bloch. C: Denys Coop. Cast: Patrick Magee, Robert Powell, Geoffrey Bayldon, Barbara Parkins, Sylvia Syms, Richard Todd, Peter Cushing, Carry Morse, Anna Firbank, Britt Ekland, Charlotte Rampling, James Villiers, Megs Jenkins, Herbert Lom. The story begins when a doctor (Robert Powell) arrives at an asylum and is told by one of the staff (Patrick Magee) that a former colleague has gone mad and is now a patient. He challenges Powell to interview the patients to see if he can find out which one of them is the former doctor. The discussions lead into four separate tales. The first, "Frozen Fear," details the weird account of a wife's dismembered corpse coming to life to attack her unfaithful, murdering husband. The next episode, "The Weird Tailor," is about a magical suit which can restore life to the dead. The third segment, "Lucy Comes to Stay," is a dual personality story which leads to murder. The final story, "Mannikins of Horror," involves miniature killer robot-dolls created by Herbert Lom. The final twist at the climax comes when one of the "Mannikins of Horror" shows up just as Powell declines the job to stab Patrick Magee. Lom then is strangled by the real mad doctor Powell was looking for in the first place. ¶ Amusing poster ad-lines: "Look at the leg that creeps — but there's no body," and "It's not easy breathing in a paper bag.... Especially if you're only a head." • Barbara Parkins, who starred in the "Frozen Fear" episode, said in *Famous Monsters* #97, "I had reservations about appearing in a horror picture, but the people who made *Asylum* have such a track record with past terror pictures that I couldn't resist. I went to the theater one evening to see Sir Ralph Richardson in a new play and I went backstage afterward to congratulate him on his performance and we talked awhile. I told him I was considering the part ... and he urged me to do it. He had just finished starring in *Tales from the Crypt* [another Amicus anthology film] and said he hadn't had so much fun in years." • In the same article, Peter Cushing, who appeared in "The Weird Tailor" episode, joked about his horror longevity, "The fact is I am beginning on my second generation. I am starting to terrorize the children of the people who went to see my pictures when they were young."

Black Sabbath (1964; AIP; Italy) D: Mario Bava. P: Paolo Mercuri. S: Mario Bava, Marcello Fondato, Alberto Bevilacqua. C: Ubaldo Terzano. Cast: Boris Karloff,

Mark Damon, Susy Andersen, Jacqueline Sassard, Michèle Mercier, Lydia Alfonsi, Gustavo De Nardo. In the first story, entitled "The Drop of Water," a ring is taken from the corpse of an old woman by her nurse (Jacqueline Sassard). Later she is haunted by the continual sound of dripping water and the ghost of the old woman which literally scares her to death. In the next segment, "The Telephone," a woman is terrorized by a phantom phone caller. The last and strongest episode features Boris Karloff as a Russian vampire known as "The Wurdulak" who drinks the blood of those he loves most. ¶ "As you will see from one of our tales, vampires — Wurdulaks — abound everywhere. Is that one sitting behind you now?! You can't be too careful you know." — Boris Karloff in one of the rather silly "Thriller"-like introductions. • Karloff's performance as the Wurdulak is the only time in his 60-year film career that he played a vampire.

Blood Bath (1975; Trans Orient Entertainment) D/S: Joel M. Reed. P: Anthony Fingleton. C: Robert M. Baldwin, Jr. Cast: Harve Presnell, Jack Somack, Curt Dawson, Doris Roberts, Jerry Lacy. An arrogant horror film director discusses a series of occult vignettes with his actors in this low-budget New York anthology film. The stories include a bomb assassin who's dealt a strange twist of fate; a magic coin that transports a man into the past; a miser who's confronted by a ghost; a karate champion who learns the dreaded "Tenth Secret of Martial Arts"; and the concluding wrap-around segment about a monster kept in a locked room by the director. ¶ "It only proves that *everyone* believes in the occult, except me."

Cat's Eye (1985; D.E.G.) (also *Stephen King's Cat's Eye*). D: Lewis Teague. P: Martha Schumacher. S: Stephen King. C: Jack Cardiff. Cast: Drew Barrymore, James Woods, Alan King, Kenneth McMillan, Robert Hays, Candy Clark, James Naughton. This Stephen King anthology film runs the gamut from black humor ("Quitters Inc.") to harrowing suspense ("The Ledge") to "cutesie" terror ("The Troll"). "Quitters Inc." employs drastic measures to insure James Woods quits smoking. Robert Hays must walk around "The Ledge" in order to win a bet and gain his freedom and lover back. In the third segment, "The Troll," Drew Barrymore is terrorized by a tiny troll-creature who's out to steal her breath. She's protected by her intelligent cat, General. • The first two are adaptations of Stephen King stories from his book, *Nightshift*. The third tale was written directly for the screen by King. • According to screenwriter Stephen King, on the first day of shooting [executive producer] Dino De Laurentiis "held up production for the first six hours. *Cat's Eye* was the first picture in his new studio and he had to get a priest to bless the studio before any footage could be shot." King added, "You know how much good it did. The place went right down the toilet" (*Cinefantastique,* Feb. 1991). • The Song, "Every Breath You Take" by the rock group, The Police, is played in the "Quitter's Inc." segment, appropriately enough just after Alan King tells James Woods, "We'll be watching you." • There are several references to previous Stephen King movies made throughout the film. In the beginning of *Cat's Eye,* the well known monster car, *Christine,* nearly runs over the fleeing feline. We also see the tiny tabby being chased by *Cujo,* and in the "Quitter's Inc." episode, James Woods watches *The Dead Zone* on TV.

Creepshow (1982; Warner Bros.) D: George Romero. P: Richard Rubinstein. S: Stephen King. C: Michael Gornick. Cast: ("Father's Day") — Viveca Lindfors, Carrie Nye, Ed Harris, Bonnie Bedelia; ("The Lonesome Death of Jory Verrill") — Stephen King; ("Something to Tide You Over") — Ted Danson, Leslie Nielsen; ("The Crate") — Hal Holbrook, Adrienne Barbeau, Fritz Weaver; ("They're Creeping Up on You") — E. G. Marshall. This film tribute to E. C. horror comics opens with a framing story about a small boy who is catching a lot of flack from his dad over his horror comics. When a page from the book is turned, the comic book picture transforms into a film story. The first segment, "Father's Day" relates how a corpse rises from the grave to look for his cake, murdering every relative he meets along the way. The second story stars Stephen King as a hapless backwoods farmer infected by a meteorite chunk, transforming into a living fungus. "Something to Tide You Over" involves a couple who are buried up to their necks in the sand just before high tide by a vindictive husband (Leslie Nielsen). The tide is turned when they return from the dead to administer poetic justice. The fourth episode, "The Crate," answers the question of what to do with your nagging wife. In this tale, Hal Holbrook uses a ferocious Tasmanian devil-like beast found by his colleague inside an old crate to make a meal out of his bitchy wife. The final segment, "They're Creeping Up on You," stars E. G. Marshall as a shrewd tycoon who literally gets his belly full of menacing cockroaches. ¶ "There's a chance you can get out of this. The tide might set you free. Depends on how long you can keep your cool, how long you hold your breath." • Writer Stephen King stated that he wrote the screenplay in one week and that it went through very little revision. • Adrienne Barbeau, who played the role of Hal Holbrook's harpish wife in "The Crate" episode, is married to filmmaker John Carpenter.

Creepshow 2 (1987; Laurel) D: Michael Gornick. P: David Ball. S: George A. Romero. C: Dick Hart, Tom Hurwitz. Cast: Lois Chiles, George Kennedy, Dorothy Lamour, Tom Savini, Domenick John, Frank S. Salsedo, Holt McCallany, David Holbrook, Don Harvey, Paul Satterfield. Three tales of terror—"Old Chief Wood'n-head," "The Raft," "The Hitchhiker"—are featured in this sequel to the original *Creepshow*. They deal with a cigar store wooden Indian come to life to exact tribal vengeance, a mysterious floating mass which absorbs human flesh, and a hitchhiker that is killed but keeps coming back for more. ¶ "Thanks for the ride, lady!" • *Creepshow 2* was originally to feature five segments, but two were dropped for budgetary reasons. • All three segments are based on stories by Stephen King (two of them unpublished). King has a cameo as a truck driver in the final story. • Barbara Eden was originally set to star in "The Hitchhiker" episode, but left during production due to the death of her mother. • Michael Gornick was the cinematographer on the first *Creepshow* and makes his directorial debut on this sequel. Gornick got his start photographing George Romero's zombie movie, *Dawn of the Dead*, in 1979. • Makeup wizard and sometimes actor Tom Savini appears in the wraparound segment as "The Creep." • *Creepshow 2* made less than half the money at the domestic box office of the original ($4,900,000 vs. $10,000,000, according to *Variety*).

Dead of Night (1945; Ealing/Universal; U.K.) D: Alberto Cavalcanti, Charles Crichton, Basil Dearden, Robert Hamer. P: Michael Balcon. S: John Baines, Angus MacPhail, T. E. B. Clarke. C: Stan Pavey, Douglas Slocombe. Cast: Mervyn Johns, Michael Redgrave, Frederick Valk, Basil Radford, Naunton Wayne, Ralph Michael, Googie Withers, Esme Percy, Sally Ann Howes, Miles Malleson, Hartley Power, Elizabeth Welch, Peggy Bryan, Roland Culver, Antony Baird. An architect (Mervyn Johns) experiences a recurring dream wherein he enters a cottage in the country full of people he has met before in a previous nightmare. While they gather round to discuss his predicament, each one relates a weird supernatural occurrence in his own life. The first story tells of a racedriver who, recovering from an accident, is saved from a fatal bus crash by the forewarning presence of a man representing death. The second tale involves a girl who encounters the ghost of a child while playing hide and seek at a Christmas party. The next story is about a man becoming obsessed with a mirror whose former owner once strangled a woman and is now drawing Ralph Michael into the same scenario. The fourth segment is a comedic joke about a pair of zany golfers who play a match for the hand of a girl they both love. The loser drowns himself in a pond then comes back to hauntingly nag his buddy into confessing that he cheated. The last story, told by a skeptical psychiatrist, relates how a ventriloquist loses his own identity after shooting a potential rival and becomes possessed by his own dummy, Hugo. After the telling of the final story, the architect literally lives out the nightmarish conclusion of his dream by murdering the psychiatrist and escaping into a horrific montage of the tales he has just heard. The film's final kicker reveals that what we have just witnessed is only another episode of Mervyn Johns' recurring dream. ¶ "Hamlet was right Doctor, there are more things in heaven and Earth than are dreamed of in your philosophy. My recurring dream isn't just a meaningless trick of the mind. It was sent to me as a warning. A warning against the terror that's waiting for me in this house!" • Michael Redgrave, who drew rave reviews by critics for his supporting role as the mad ventriloquist, was knighted by his country in 1959. Aside from his Oscar nomination for a role in *Mourning Becomes Electra* (1947), Redgrave is the father of two popular actresses, Lynn and Vanessa Redgrave. • Alberto Cavalcanti, who directed the ghost child segment and the chillling ventriloquist episode, taught film at U.C.L.A. in 1968, and wrote the influential book, *Film and Reality*. Cavalcanti's distinguished directing career was temporarily halted when in 1949 he was suspected of Communist activities and fired from a Brazilian film company. • Director Robert Hamer, who was responsible for the haunted mirror segment, began his film career as a clapper boy. *Dead of Night* was his first job as feature film director. His promising film career was cut short due

Mervyn Johns (far right) meets Hugo the living ventriloquist dummy during the nightmarish montage sequence at the climax of Dead of Night *(1945).*

to a long battle with alcoholism in the late 1950s. He died in 1963. • Charles Crichton, who directed the humorous golfing episode, was one of the editors on the classic *The Thief of Bagdad* (1940). He is *not* related to Michael Crichton, who worked on *The Andromeda Strain* (1971) and *Westworld* (1973). • This anthology classic, which opens and closes with exactly the same scene (that of a man receiving a phone call and driving to an English cottage), was the first big "scare" film to be released in Britain after the World War II ban on horror films was lifted.

Deadtime Stories (1987; Bedford Entertainment) D: Jeffrey Delman. P: Bill Paul. S: Jeffrey Delman, Charles F. Shelton. C: Daniel B. Canton. Cast: Michael Mesmer, Brian DePersia, Scott Valentine, Phyllis Craig, Anne Redfern, Kathy Fleg, Casper Roos, Barbara Seldon, Leigh Kirlton. This low-budget independent features three grotesque fairy tales—"Peter and Witches," "Little Red Runninghood," and "Goldi Lox and the Three Baers"—about witches, a werewolf, and a group of psychos. ¶ "I have a meat cleaver and I know how to use it." •

Deadtime Stories was shot over the course of four years in upstate New York and Connecticut.

Destination Nightmare (1958; Medallion TV) D: Paul Landres. P: Ben Fox. S: Ellis Marcus. C: Howard Schwartz. (*Note:* It is suspected that the credits listed on the film prints are only those for the final episode of the feature.) Cast: Boris Karloff, Denise Alexander, Whit Bissell, Olive Blakeney, Frances O'Farrell, Shirley Mitchell, Iphigenle Castiglioni, George Hamilton, Julius Johnson, Tod Andrews, Eve Brent. This is one of the three features culled from the unsold half-hour TV series titled "The Veil" hosted by and often starring Boris Karloff (two years later he launched his similar but successful hour-long series, "Thriller"). The other two features are *Jack the Ripper* and *The Veil.* ¶ "The story you are about to see will be startling, but it's based upon a true experience, something unexplainable from behind the veil.—Karloff's opening narration.

Devil's Messenger (1962; Herts-Lion) D: Herbert L. Strock, Curt Siodmak. P: Kenneth

A young Donald Sutherland carries his "vampire" bride (Jennifer Jayne) over the threshold in the anthology classic, Dr. Terror's House of Horrors *(1965).*

Herts. S: Leo Guild. C: William Troiano. Cast: Lon Chaney, Jr., John Crawford, Karen Kandler, Michael Hinn, Gunnell Brostrom, Tammy Newmara. A proposed TV series known as *13 Demon Street* made in Sweden was edited into a terror trilogy involving a suicide victim who is promised a second chance by the Devil (Lon Chaney, Jr.). The price she must pay is to return to Earth to commit various acts of mayhem on behalf of the netherworld king.

Dr. Terror's Gallery of Horrors (1967; American General) (also *Return from the Past*). D: David L. Hewitt. P: David L. Hewitt, Ray Dorn. S: David Prentiss, Gary Heacock, Russ Jones. C: Austin McKinney. Cast: Lon Chaney, Jr., John Carradine, Rochelle Hudson, Roger Gentry, Vic McGee, Ron Doyle, Mitch Evans, Russ Jones, Karen Joy. This monster-laden no-budget anthology film is not a sequel to the earlier *Dr. Terror's House of Horrors,* despite the title similarity. The five stories included here involve a magical clock ("The Witch's Clock"); a vampire loose in London ("King Vampire"); the walking dead ("Monster

Raid"); an electrical zap which revives the dead ("The Spark of Life"); and a monstrous duel to the death between Dracula and a werewolf ("Count Alucard").

Dr. Terror's House of Horrors (1965; Amicus/Paramount; U.K.) D: Freddie Francis. P: Milton Subotsky, Max J. Rosenberg. S: Milton Subotsky. C: Alan Hume. Cast: Peter Cushing, Christopher Lee, Roy Castle, Neil McCallum, Donald Sutherland, Alan Freeman, Michael Gough, Max Adrian, Tubby Hayes, Isla Blair, Irene Richmond, Katy Wild. A mysterious fortune teller named Dr. Schreck (Peter Cushing) uses tarot cards to reveal the supernatural destinies of five men on a train. The first segment involves a werewolf supposedly sealed up in the basement of an old house. The second story features a creeping vine that engulfs a house. The third episode involves a trumpet player who ignores a warning and steals the musical composition of a voodoo ritual for his jazz band. The fourth segment features Christopher Lee as an art critic who is stalked by the crawling hand of an artist he has run over. The story of the fifth passenger tells how he comes to realize that his bride is a vampire. In the finale, the framing story ends when the five passengers learn that the final tarot card turned over by Dr. Terror is the "death" card. When the train eventually stops, they wander out into the dark station and pick up a newspaper which relates how they were all killed in a train wreck. ¶ "There is within each of us a twin destiny, the natural and the supernatural. The [tarot] cards are attracted to the supernatural part of that destiny, as one pole of a magnet attracts the opposite pole.... The strange, the weird, the unknown, the terrifying, the mysterious! At one time or another during our lives we may any one of us encounter it. This deck can forewarn us. I call it my 'house of horrors.'"

Encounter with the Unknown (1973; Centronics International) D: Harry Thomason. P: Joe Glass. Cast: Rosie Holotik, Gene Ross. This trilogy of supernatural stories narrated by Rod Serling involves a death prophecy, a subterranean creature, and a man's date with a dead woman.

Escapes (1987; Prism Entertainment; U.K.) D/S: David Steensland. P: David Steensland, Angela Sanders. C: Gary Tomsic. Cast: Vincent Price, Todd Fulton, Jerry Grishaw, Michael Pattonhall, John Mitchum, Ken Thorley, Jeff Boudov, Shirley O'Key, Robert Elson, Gil Reade, Rocky Capella. Vincent Price narrates five tales involving beasts, aliens, and magic.

Flesh and Fantasy (1943; Universal) D: Julien Duvivier. P: Charles Boyer, Julien Duvivier. S: Ernest Pascal, Samuel Hoffenstein, Ellis St. Joseph. C: Paul Ivano, Stanley Cortez. Cast: Edward G. Robinson, Robert Benchley, Barbara Stanwyck, Charles Boyer, Betty Field, Robert Cummings, Thomas Mitchell, C. Aubrey Smith, Dame May Whitty, Edgar Barrier, David Hoffman. A man suffering from a terrible nightmare is told three stories of the supernatural. The first one concerns a plain-looking seamstress (Betty Field) who attains physical beauty after falling in love with Robert Cummings. The second story tells of a tightrope artist who is haunted by the vision of Barbara Stanwyck. The final segment features Edward G. Robinson as a man driven to murder by the predictions of a palm reader. • Stars Edward G. Robinson and Barbara Stanwyck were paid $50,000 apiece for their brief appearances. Charles Boyer was given the sum of $125,000 for coproducing and acting in the film. • *Flesh and Fantasy* was filmed on-again off-again over the course of a full year. There were originally four stories planned for the film, but the last one, involving a blind girl's nightmare, was deleted and eventually made into a feature-length film entitled *Destiny* (1944). • The three stories in this supernatural trilogy are introduced by Robert Benchley, the grandfather of *Jaws* novelist Peter Benchley.

From Beyond the Grave (1973; Amicus; U.K.) D: Kevin Connor. P: Max J. Rosenberg, Milton Subotsky. S: Robin Clarke, Raymond Christodoulou. C: Alan Hume. Cast: Peter Cushing, David Warner, Donald Pleasence, Rosalind Ayres, Ian Bannen, Diana Dors, Margaret Leighton, Ian Carmichael, Ian Ogilvy, Lesley Anne Down, Nyree Dawn Porter, Jack Watson. Peter Cushing stars as an antique-shop proprietor relating four stories of the macabre. The first episode stars David Warner, who's possessed by a sinister mirror. The second tale involves an ex-military officer mixed up with black magic. The third episode features an invisible demon harassing a wealthy couple. The fourth story showcases a magical oak door which opens up into the past.

Grim Prairie Tales (1990; East West Film Partners) D/S: Wayne Coe. P: Richard Hahn. C: Janusz Kaminski. Cast: James Earl Jones, Brad Dourif, William Atherton, Lisa Eichhorn, Marc McClure, Scott Paulin, Will Hare, Michelle Joyner, Wendy Cooke. City slicker Brad Dourif, camping alone at night on the prairie, is joined by the formidable wild west native James Earl Jones. The two pass the night and form an uneasy understanding by telling each other "horror stories." Four stories are told, involving Indian revenge taken on a white man who defiled their burial ground; a woman succubus demon; a family coming to frightening terms with unreasoning violence; and a gunfighter who's haunted by his conscience. ¶ "I'm gonna tell you a story that'll stick to you like an eyeball to a cactus needle." • With a subtitle of *Hit the Trail ... to Terror,* it is obvious that this is not your run of the mill horror anthology. It is in fact the screen's very first horror anthology *Western.*

The House That Dripped Blood (1971; Amicus; U.K.) D: Peter Duffell. P: Max J. Rosenberg, Milton Subotsky. S: Robert Bloch. C: Ray Parslow. Cast: Denholm Elliott, Peter Cushing, Christopher Lee, Jon Pertwee, Ingrid Pitt, John Bennett, Joanna Dunham, Joss Ackland, Nyree Dawn Porter, Chloe Franks, Geoffrey Bayldon. Robert Bloch wrote and adapted these four tales of the supernatural which all take place inside the titular mansion. The first story, "Method for Murder," stars Denholm Elliott as a writer who runs up against a strangler and a plot by his wife to drive him insane. The second episode, "Waxworks," features Peter Cushing as a man who literally loses his head over a wax figure. The third tale, "Sweets to the Sweet," involves a matter of family witchcraft that is needling Christopher Lee. The fourth segment, "The Cloak," is a comical vignette about vampirism caused by wearing a special cloak. In the final wraparound story, the man who is interested in living in this troubled house realizes these weren't just made-up stories after all when he encounters the vampires featured in "The Cloak." ¶ "Perhaps you understand the secret of this house now. It reflects the personality of whoever lives in it, and treats him accordingly. I hope it finds a proper tenant soon, perhaps you would like it? There's nothing to be afraid of, if you're the right sort of person. Think it over." • This well-thought-of anthology entry was director Peter Duffell's feature film debut.

The Illustrated Man (1969; Warner Bros.) D: Jack Smight. P: Howard B. Kreitsek, Ted Mann. S: Howard B. Kreitsek. C: Philip Lathrop. Cast: Rod Steiger, Claire Bloom, Robert Drivas, Don Dubbins, Jason Evers, Tim Weldon, Christie Matchett. This Ray Bradbury–inspired anthology film features Rod Steiger as an "illustrated" man whose tattoos relate three separate stories. The first tale, "The Veldt," tells of a future family that owns a machine that creates a three-dimensional African setting. The two children become obsessed with their new toy to the point of trapping their parents (Steiger and Claire Bloom) inside it. While trying to figure a way out they are suddenly attacked and devoured by "real" lions. The second tattoo tale, "Long Rains," takes place on Venus where an unrelenting rainstorm drenches a crash-landed rocket crew, and drives their leader to murder. The third episode, "The Last Night of the World," concerns a false prediction of global disaster in the future that prompts a father to poison his children unnecessarily. In the final framing story, a man named Willie musters enough courage to look upon a blank spot on Rod Steiger which supposedly foretells the destiny of the onlooker. He sees Steiger strangling him, and then initiates a confrontation that brings about that very result. • Claire Bloom, who played the mysterious tattoo artist of the illustrated man, was at the time married to her co-star, Rod Steiger (an Oscar winner for *In the Heat of the*

Night, 1967). Both were featured in all three episodes plus the wraparound. Bloom divorced Steiger shortly after the film was released and married Hilliard Elkins, a stage producer, later on.

Immoral Tales (1974; Argos; France) D/S: Walerian Borowczyk. P: Anatole Dauman. C: Bernard Daillencourt, Guy Durban, Michel Zolat, Noel Very. Cast: Lise Danvers, Charlotte Alexandra, Paloma Picasso, Florence Bellamy. This well-named erotic anthology entry from France features four tales, one of which involves Elizabeth Bathory, the infamous countess who bathed in the blood of virgins (the only "horror" tale in the film).

Jack the Ripper (1958; Medallion TV) D: David MacDonald. P: Hal Roach, Jr. S: Michael Plant. C: Stephen Dade. (*Note:* It is suspected that the credits listed on the film prints are only those for the final episode of the feature.) Cast: Boris Karloff, Harry Bartell, Paul Bryar, Gretchen Thomas, Robert Griffin, Ray Montgomery, Gene Collins, Thomas Henry, Kay Stewart, Tudor Owen, Russ Bender, Eleanor Lucky, Niall MacGinnis. In another of the three features made by combining episodes from Boris Karloff's unsold TV series "The Veil," (*Destination Nightmare* and *The Veil* being the other two) this one features four stories of clairvoyance, vengeful ghosts, and of course Jack the Ripper. ¶ "Down through the ages man has continually struggled to pierce The Veil, behind which lies the unbelievable."—Karloff's opening narration.

Kwaidan (1964) (see GHOSTS). This beautifully photographed Japanese anthology contains four segments adapted from traditional Japanese ghost stories. A Samurai returns home to his wife only to find after a night of passion that he holds a corpse in his arms. Another Samurai is haunted by a spirit manifesting itself in a cup of tea. A blind musician must play for a ghostly gathering of slain warriors, and the spectre of a woman lures men to an icy death.

Master of Horror (1960) (see POE FILMS— MODERN POE). This Argentinian omnibus features adaptations of two Poe tales—"The Facts in the Case of M. Valdemar" and "The Cask of Amontillado" (two stories also featured in Corman's Poe anthology, *Tales of Terror,* the following year). The connecting link is provided by a maid who picks up a book of Poe on a dark and stormy night and scares herself by reading the two stories.

The Monster Club (1980; Chips Productions; U.K.) D: Roy Ward Baker. P: Milton

Subotsky. S: Edward Abraham, Valerie Abraham. C: Peter Jessop. Cast: Vincent Price, John Carradine, Simon Ward, Anthony Steel, Barbara Kellerman, Donald Pleasence, Stuart Whitman, Britt Ekland, Patrick Magee, James Laurenson, Richard Johnson. This British anthology has a vampiric Vincent Price initiating John Carradine into the title nightclub — a disco catering solely to monsters. The first tale involves a creature called a "Shadmock," who possesses a deadly whistle which can turn its victim inside out. The second story concerns a vampire; and the third segment deals with a filmmaker's encounter with ghouls. • This film marks the only time to date that horror star Vincent Price has played a vampire.

Night Gallery (1969; Universal-TV) D: Boris Sagal (segment 1), Steven Spielberg (segment 2), Barry Shear (segment 3). S: Rod Serling. C: Richard Batcheller, William Margulies. Cast: Joan Crawford, Roddy McDowall, Ossie Davis, Richard Kiley, Barry Sullivan, Tom Bosley, George Macready, Sam Jaffe, Barry Atwater. Rod Serling hosts this terror trilogy from within an art gallery in the dead of night. Each story relates to a painting. The first stars Roddy McDowall as a spoiled inheritor of an old man's fortune. He is frightened into a fall when a staircase painting begins to change gradually, depicting the old man rising from his grave in order to kill McDowall. The second episode features Joan Crawford as a wealthy but wicked blind woman who pays a large sum of money for a desperate donor's eyes. The plot twist has her temporarily regain her eyesight just as a blackout occurs in the city. The third story concerns a Nazi war criminal who longs to enter into a peaceful fisherman painting. At the climax he gets his wish, but ironically is transposed into the wrong painting — one in which a man writhes eternally in pain, crucified on a cross. ¶ "A portrait. Its subject, Miss Claudia Mendlow, a blind queen who reigns in a carpeted penthouse on Fifth Avenue. An imperious, predatory dowager who will soon find a darkness blacker than blindness." • This feature was the pilot film for the popular "Night Gallery" TV series.

Nightmares (1983; Universal) D: Joseph Sargent. P: Christopher Crowe. S: Christopher Crowe, Jeffrey Bloom. C: Gerald Perry Finnerman, Mario DiLeo. Cast: Emilio Estevez, Christina Raines, Lance Henriksen, Richard Masur, Veronica Cartwright. The first of these four nightmarish episodes, "Terror in Topanga," involves a slashing knife murderer after a housewife.

The second story, "The Bishop of Battle," stars Emilio Estevez (Martin Sheen's son) as a video game wiz who takes on the ultimate war game with three-dimensional graphics. The third segment, "The Benediction," concerns a fallen priest who regains his faith during a battle with a possessed pickup truck. The final story, "Night of the Rat," involves a huge demonic rat which terrorizes a quarreling married couple. • *Nightmares* was conceived as a TV movie but was released theatrically by Universal.

The Offspring (1987; TMS) (also *From a Whisper to a Scream*). D: Jeff Burr. P: Darin Scott, William Burr. S: Courtney Joyner, Darin Scott. C: Craig Greene. Cast: Vincent Price, Clu Gulager, Terry Kiser, Harry Caesar, Rosalind Cash, Cameron Mitchell, Susan Tyrrell, Martine Beswick, Angelo Rossitto, Ron Brooke, Didi Lanier. A reporter travels to the small town of Oldfield, home of a recently executed murderess, and hears four tales of evil from the local librarian (Vincent Price). The stories involve a monster baby, the secret of longevity, a voodoo priestess running a carnival, and a band of vengeful civil war children. ¶ "The history of this town is written in blood on pages of human skin." — Vincent Price in the wraparound segment. • This $1.1 million film, shot in 28 days, ran out of money after the four stories were shot. Director Jeff Burr then spent eight months finding the financing to finish the film and shoot the connecting story (with Vincent Price). • Vincent Price, who worked for only two days on the film, has made it clear that this will be his *last* horror movie. • In an homage to one of the macabre's great writers, the carnival in the third segment is called "Lovecraft's Travelling Amusements." • Veteran midget actor Angelo Rossitto has been in films for almost 60 years. He appeared in Tod Browning's *Freaks* back in 1932.

Once Upon a Midnight Scary (1979; TV movie) (also *Vincent Price's Once Upon a Midnight Scary*). D: Nell Cox. P: Diane Asselin, Paul Asselin. S: Kimmer Ringwald. Cast: Vincent Price, René Auberjonois, Severn Darden, Micheal Brick, Christian Berrigan, Mary Betten. This aimed-at-children TV anthology features Vincent Price introducing a series of children's fantasy stories, including "The Ghost Belonged to Me," about an apparition warning a boy of danger; a comical retelling of "The Legend of Sleepy Hollow," and "The House with the Clock in Its Walls," about a young boy who must aid his wizard uncle in finding a clock that could destroy the world. ¶ "My name is – oh but my name is unimportant really. After all, you didn't come here to learn my name, did you. You came here because I am an expert, an expert on the terrors of the night." – host Vincent Price.

Screams of a Winter Night (1979; Full Moon) D: James L. Wilson. P: James L. Wilson, Richard H. Wadsack. S: Richard H. Wadsack. C: Robert E. Rogers. Cast: Gil Glasgow, Marry Cox, Patrick Byers, Robin Bradley, Matt Borel, Beverly Allen, Ray Gaspard, Brandy Barrett, Charles Rucker, Jan Norton. A group of teenagers share four spooky stories around a campfire at night. The bogey tales involve a bigfoot creature that likes to hang its victims from the branches of trees, a haunted overnight party, a murderous "child-woman," and a wind demon of Indian legend.

Screamtime (1983; Manson International) D/P: Al Beresford. S: Michael Armstrong. C: Don Lord, Alan Pudney, Mike Spera. Cast: Robin Bailey, Ann Lynn, Jan Saynor, Yvonne Nicholson, David Van Day, Dora Bryan, Jean Anderson. This British anthology features a trio of horror stories, involving a puppeteer who uses his Punch and Judy dolls to take revenge on those who've wronged him; a woman haunted by prophetic visions; and a pair of thieves who run afoul of the supernatural guardians at an old mansion.

Spirits of the Dead (1968) (see POE FILMS – MODERN POE). Three tales of Poe are presented by three European directors. In an adaptation of Poe's story "Metzengerstein" (directed by Roger Vadim), a dead lover's spirit returns in the form of a huge black stallion. "William Wilson" (directed by Louis Malle) follows a man whose sadism is challenged by a mysterious double – his other self. Finally, in "Never Bet the Devil Your Head" (directed by Federico Fellini), a troubled film star is haunted by the vision of a mysterious child leading to his decapitation in a car accident.

Tales from the Crypt (1972; Amicus; U.K.) D: Freddie Francis. P: Milton Subotsky, Max J. Rosenberg. S: Milton Subotsky. C: Norman Warwick, John Harris. Cast: Ralph Richardson, Joan Collins, Peter Cushing, Nigel Patrick, Patrick Magee, Richard Greene, Barbara Murray, Ian Hendry, Robin Phillips, Martin Boddey, David Markham, Roy Dotrice, Robert Hutton, Susan Denny, Angie Grant, Chloe Franks, Geoffrey Bayldon, Oliver MacGreevey, Harry Locks. Ralph Richardson confronts a group of people with their dire fates while in a crypt-like cave that turns out to be a gateway to Hell. The first visionary reflection, "All Through the Night," stars Joan Collins as a woman who kills her husband only to be terrorized by a psycho Santa on Christmas Eve. The second story, "Reflection of Death," concerns a man who is almost killed in a car crash, then makes his way home to find he's really a walking corpse. The third episode, "Poetic Justice," sees Peter Cushing as a kindly old man, who is driven to suicide by some nasty neighbors. He then comes back from the grave to rip out his antagonist's heart for a Valentine gift. The fourth segment, "Wish You Were Here," follows the Monkey's Paw theme when a wife wishes back to life the body of her dead husband, who unbeknownst to her has been embalmed. The final story involves the oppressed patrons of a dilapidated home for the blind, who exact a razor sharp revenge upon their callous administrator. ¶ "You see, I wasn't warning you, but telling you why you are here, for all eternity. And now, who's next? Perhaps you?" • Ralph Richardson, who played the character known as "The Crypt Keeper," was a knighted actor of the British stage and screen. Some of his other fantastique film credits include *The Ghoul* (1933), *Things to Come* (1936), *The Wrong Box* (1966), *Who Slew Auntie Roo?* (1971) and *Rollerball* (1975). He died in 1983, two years after the release of *Dragonslayer* (1981), his last genre effort.

Tales from the Darkside: The Movie (1990; Paramount) D: John Harrison. P: Richard P. Rubinstein, Michael Galin. S: Michael McDowell, George A. Romero. Cast: Deborah Harry, Christian Slater, David Johansen, William Hickey, James Remar, Rae Dawn Chong. Much like *Twilight Zone: The Movie,* this big screen version of a popular TV series features three tales of terror, which are read by a young boy who's being held in a cage for cannibal Deborah Harry's dinner. The first, "Lot 249," is the story of a mummy come to life; the second, "Cat from Hell," deals with a demonically possessed housecat; and the last, "Lover's Vow," features a gargoyle-like demon.

Tales of Terror (1962) (see POE FILMS – THE CORMAN CYCLE). This anthology features three tales culled from four Poe stories – "Morella," "The Black Cat" and "The Cask of Amontillado" (combined in the second segment), and "The Facts in the Case of M. Valdemar." Vincent Price stars in all three tales (as different characters).

Tales That Witness Madness (1973; World Film Services; U.K.) D: Freddie Francis. P: Norman Priggen. S: Jay Fairbank (Jennifer Jayne). C: Ronnie Taylor. Cast: Kim Novak, Georgia Brown, Joan Collins, Jack Hawkins, Donald Houston, Donald Pleasence, Suzy Kendell, Peter McEnery, Michael Jayston, Michael Petrovich, Beth Morris, Zohra Segal, Mary Tamm, Frank Forsyth. In an anthology theme similar to the one used in *Asylum* (1972), the case histories of mental patients are explored in four segments. The first one, "Mr. Tiger," is about a boy who unleashes an invisible tiger on his parents. The second story, "Penny Farthing," tells of a bicycle wheel that propels a man into the past. The third episode, "Mel," concerns a living malevolent tree which Joan Collins has to vie with for her husband's affection. The fourth segment, "Luau," details how an author sacrifices his daughter to revive his own mother from death. The story climaxes with a cannibalistic feast. • The "Luau" segment was to have starred Rita Hayworth as a literary agent, but she was replaced just before filming by Kim Novak *(Vertigo).* • This anthology film features the final performance of Jack Hawkins, who died later that year following an operation for cancer of the larynx. The voice of Charles Gray was dubbed in over Hawkins' faint vocalizing. Hawkins also worked in *Theatre of Blood* that same year. His first wife was Oscar-winning actress Jessica Tandy, and he is perhaps best known for his roles in *The Bridge on the River Kwai* (1957) and *Zulu* (1964).

Three Cases of Murder (1955; Associated Artists; U.K.) D: George More O'Farrall, Wendy Toye, David Eady. P: Ian Dalrymple, Alexander Paal, Hugh Percival. S: Ian Dalrymple, Donald Wilson, Sidney Carroll. C: Georges Perinal. Cast: Alan Badel, Hugh Pryse, Leueen MacGrath, Eddie Byrne, Orson Welles, Andre Morell, Helen Cherry, Elisabeth Sellars, John Gregson. This British trilogy features two tales with fantastic themes. "In the Picture" concerns a man who is able to enter his painting and make improvements. On one such excursion he encounters a taxidermist who's bent on murder. The final tale, "Lord Mountdrago" (from a Somerset Maugham story), tells of two men who are able to hex each other in their dream life.

Torture Garden (1967; Amicus/Columbia; U.K.) D: Freddie Francis. P: Max J. Rosenberg, Milton Subotsky. S: Robert Bloch. C: Norman Warwick. Cast: Burgess Meredith, Jack Palance, Peter Cushing, Michael Bryant, Maurice Denham, Robert Hutton, Beverly Adams, Barbara Ewing, Niall McGinnis, John Standing, Michael Ripper. A carnival showman reveals to a group of people their hidden desires and possible futures. The first revelation, "Enoch," tells of a demonized cat that likes to eat the heads of its victims. The second account, "Terror over Hollywood," follows an actress who learns that the stars she idolizes are really androids. The third segment, "Mr. Steinway," features a grand piano which comes to life and attacks Barbara Ewing. The last (and best) story, "The Man Who Collected Poe," stars Jack Palance as an avid "Poe" collector who gets the opportunity to visit Peter Cushing's home which houses some of the rarest books and collectibles ever assembled, not to mention the man himself—the resurrected Edgar Allan Poe. ¶ "My grandfather was more than a graverobber, he was a student of the occult. Did you know that there are ways to raise the dead?" • Burgess Meredith, who played the "Penguin"—arch enemy to TV's "Batman," plays Dr. Diablo, the devil masquerading as a sideshow host.

Trilogy (1969; Allied Artists) D/P: Frank Perry. S: Truman Capote, Eleanor Perry. C: Joseph Brun, Harry Sunby. Cast: Mildred Natwick, Susan Dunfee, Carol Gustafson, Robin Ponteiro, Beverly Ballard. Only one of the film's three stories can be classified as "fantasy." "Miriam" tells of an elderly nanny who is haunted by the likeness of herself as a child.

Trilogy of Terror (1975; TV movie) D/P: Dan Curtis. S: William F. Nolan, Richard Matheson. Cast: Karen Black, Robert Burton, John Karlen, George Gaynes, James Storm, Gregory Harrison, Kathryn Reynolds. Karen Black stars in three tales of terror in this strong made-for-TV anthology. The first, "Julie," deals with a sexually troubled teacher and her witchcraft-practicing student that is blackmailing her. In the second story, "Millicent and Therese," Black plays twin sisters—one normal, and the other psychotic. The third, and best episode, "Amelia" (based on Richard Matheson's short story, "Prey"), has Black purchase a Zuñi fetish doll which comes to life and terrorizes her.

Twice Told Tales (1963; United Artists) D: Sidney Salkow. P/S: Robert E. Kent. C: Ellis W. Carter. Cast: Vincent Price, Sebastian Cabot, Mari Blanchard, Joyce Taylor, Brett Halsey, Beverly Garland, Jacqueline DeWit, Richard Denning, Gene Roth. This trilogy of terrors is based upon two stories

Jack Palance and Peter Cushing as two avid Poe collectors vying for the ultimate prize in "The Man Who Collected Poe" segment from Torture Garden *(1967).*

and a novel written by Nathaniel Hawthorne. The first tale, "Dr. Heidegger's Experiment," involves a potion which can restore youth to anyone, including a corpse. The next story, "Rappaccini's Daughter," tells of a father who injects his daughter with a special poison which makes her touch lethal. The third segment, "House of the Seven Gables," features Vincent Price looking for a hidden fortune in a haunted house with an unusual curse upon it. When Price is strangled in the finale by the skeletal hand, the curse is lifted and the house destroys itself. ¶ "Thus did the House of the Seven Gables come to its end. Destroyed by the decay of greed and hate that had corroded its very foundation." • The film's title, *Twice Told Tales,* is named after a compilation of stories by Hawthorne which includes the first segment, "Dr. Heidegger's Experiment."

Twilight Zone: The Movie (1983; Warner Bros.) D: John Landis (prologue, segment 1), Steven Spielberg (segment 2), Joe Dante (segment 3), George Miller (segment 4). P: John Landis, Steven Spielberg. S: Richard

Matheson (segments 3, 4, co-2), John Landis (prologue, segment 1), George Clayton Johnson (co-2), Josh Rogan (co-2). C: Stevan Larner (prologue, segment 1), Allen Daviau (segments 2, 4), John Hora (segment 3). Cast: Dan Aykroyd, Albert Brooks, Scatman Crothers, John Lithgow, Vic Morrow, Kathleen Quinlan, Kevin McCarthy, William Schallert, Billy Mumy, Dick Miller, Eduard Franz, Murray Matheson, Bill Quinn, Helen Shaw. A humorous wraparound starring Dan Aykroyd as a driver who likes to show people "something really scary" is the light-hearted prologue for four fantastical stories, three of which were adapted from the original "Twilight Zone" TV series. The first segment involves a bigot (Vic Morrow) who gets a dose of his own medicine when he's caught in a Twilight Zone continuum that turns him into a Jew being hunted by Nazis, a black man being chased by Ku Klux Klan members, and a Vietnamese soldier being shot at by Americans. The second story features Scatman Crothers as a rest home visitor with the ability to make patrons feel and look young again by playing a game of "kick the can." The third segment involves a pretty teacher who visits the home of a young boy who can will anything to happen. She discovers that the spoiled kid's family and relatives are trapped in a cartoon-nightmare existence, forever having to cater to the boy's slightest whims for fear of death, or worse. The final episode stars John Lithgow as a man whose fear of flying only worsens when he spies a gargoyle-like demon outside on the plane's wing, ripping at the engine. ¶ "You unlock this door with the key of imagination. Behind it is another dimension, a dimension of sound, a dimension of sight, a dimension of mind. You're moving into a land of both shadow and substance, of things and ideas, you've just crossed into The Twilight Zone!" • Vic Morrow, who starred as the bigot in the first episode, met a tragic death (along with two child actors) when he was decapitated in a freak accident involving a helicopter. John Landis, the director on that particular segment, was charged with negligence over the incident (he was eventually cleared). • Burgess Meredith provided the familiar "Twilight Zone" opening narrative that used to be read by Rod Serling in the TV series. At the end of the film, a recording of Serling's voice concluded the proceedings. Serling died in 1975 during open heart surgery. • Rob Bottin, who in 1990 created many of the special makeup effects in *Total Recall,* worked on the cartoon animation creatures in the third episode. • The fourth story, directed by Australian filmmaker George Miller, was based on the popular "Nightmare at 30,000 Feet" "Twilight Zone" episode which featured William (Captain Kirk) Shatner as the fearful flyer (played by John Lithgow in the film).

The Uncanny (1977) (see CATS). This terror trilogy begins when Peter Cushing brings a manuscript to a publisher (Ray Milland) that details a plot of how cats are going to take over the world. The first story involves a pair of would-be heirs who conspire to destroy the large household of pet cats whom an eccentric old woman had left her fortune to. The next segment deals with a supernatural cat who aids a young girl in killing her cousin. The third episode relates how two lovers are killed by a cat after murdering the man's wife. In the final wraparound story, Cushing is killed by a group of the feline fiends while his publisher is hypnotized by his own pet cat and ordered to burn the manuscript, thus covering up the kitty conspiracy.

The Vault of Horror (1973; Amicus; U.K.) (also *Further Tales from the Crypt*). D: Roy Ward Baker. P: Milton Subotsky, Max J. Rosenberg. S: Milton Subotsky. C: Denys Coop. Cast: Daniel Massey, Anna Massey, Michael Craig, Curt Jurgens, Dawn Addams, Terry-Thomas, Glynis Johns, Tom Baker, Denholm Elliott, Edward Judd, Erik Chitty, Robin Nedwell, Geoffrey Davies, Jasmina Hilton, John Forbes-Robertson. Five people trapped in a basement room each tell about a recurring dream they've had. The first one, "Midnight Mess," is about a man who kills his sister and then unknowingly goes to a restaurant run by vampires where he becomes the main course. The second tale, "The Neat Job," tells about a wife driven mad, who cuts her hubby up into bits and stores them in neat little pickling jars. The third episode, "This Trick'll Kill You," involves a traveling magician and his wife who steal an Indian rope trick only to fall prey to the supernatural rope itself. In the "Bargain in Death" story, Michael Craig plans an insurance scam by faking death, but gets doublecrossed by a gravedigger. The final segment, "Drawn and Quartered," involves an artist dabbling with voodoo in his paintings. When he alters portraits of those he dislikes, the results appear to happen in real life. In the finale, the five storytellers all realize that they are not merely trapped in a basement, but are serving their judgment in Hell in a cemetery vault. ¶ "Do you think that our fears could be a sort of warning? A warning of what may happen?" • Daniel Massey, son of Raymond *(Things to Come)* Massey, plays opposite his own sister, Anna Massey, in the "Midnight Mess" segment. • Curt Jurgens, who appeared in the "This Trick'll Kill You" episode, said in *Famous Monsters* #104, "It was my first horror film and I must say I was thrilled when I read the script. Previously there was nothing in between the usual monster flick and the kind of psychological thriller that Hitchcock would direct." • Michael *(Mysterious Island)* Craig, who starred in the "Bargain in Death" episode, revealed to *Famous Monsters* readers: "My youngest son is 11 and he is wedded to horror. In fact one of the reasons I act in horror films is because it gives me enormous prestige with my family!" • This was Amicus' sixth omnibus film based on the Al Feldstein, William Gaines horror comics. It was intended as a follow-up to their successful *Tales from the Crypt* (1972).

The Veil (1958; Medallion TV) D: Herbert L. Strock. P: Sidney Morse. S: Fred Schiller. C: Howard Schwartz. (*Note:* It is suspected that the credits given are only those for the final episode of the feature.) Cast: Boris Karloff, Booth Coleman, Roxanne Berard, Leonard Penn, Albert Carrier, Tony Travis, Argentina Brunetti, Elvira Curei, Paul Bryar, Gretchen Thomas, Robert Griffin, Ray Montgomery, Gene Collins, Vici Raaf, Connie Van, Robert Hardy, Patrick MacNee. This is yet another anthology of the "strange and unbelievable" created by combining several episodes of Boris Karloff's unsold "Twilight Zone"–like TV series, "The Veil." Two other features were made, *Destination Nightmare* and *Jack the Ripper.*

Waxworks (1924) (see WAX MUSEUMS) (also *Three Wax Men*). A poet writes about three notorious figures in history after visiting a wax museum. The film then breaks off into expressionistic segments about Harun al-Rashid, Ivan the Terrible, and Jack the Ripper.

The Willies (1990; Filmtown International) D/S: Brian Peck. P: Gary Depew, Brad Southwick. C: Tom Ingalls. Cast: Sean Astin, Michael Bower, Ralph Drischell, Kathleen Freeman, Ian Fried, James Karen, Jeremy Miller, Clu Gulager. Three boys camping out in their backyard tell each other gross and scary stories in order to give each other "the willies." Several pre-credit vignettes are featured (including "Haunted Estate," about an all-too-realistic amusement park ride; and "Poodle Souffle," about an elderly lady who tries to dry off her poodle in a microwave), followed by two longer stories. "Bad Apples," features a kindly elementary school janitor who turns into a demon-monster to give the school bullies their just deserts. "Flyboy" is about a mean kid obsessed with pulling the wings off flies who gets his comeuppance from the insect world. ¶ "Be warned, this story is guaranteed to give you the willies."

The Wonderful World of the Brothers Grimm (1962; MGM) D: Henry Levin, George Pal. P: George Pal. S: David P. Harmon, Charles Beaumont, William Roberts. C: Paul C. Vogel. Cast: Laurence Harvey, Karl Boehm, Claire Bloom, Barbara Eden, Walter Slezak, Oscar Homolka, Russ Tamblyn, Yvette Mimieux, Martita Hunt, Jim Backus, Buddy Hackett, Otto Kruger, Beulah Bondi, Terry-Thomas. A biographical trilogy of fairy tales written by Jacob and Wilhelm Grimm are depicted in this George Pal family anthology. The first story, "The Dancing Princess," concerns a woodsman (Russ Tamblyn) who wins the hand of a princess (Yvette Mimieux), then learns the mysterious secret of her worn slippers when he wears a cloak of invisibility. "The Cobbler and the Elves" tells a story of a frantic cobbler (Laurence Harvey) who falls asleep while working, only to discover upon waking that elves have finished the job for him. The final story, "The Singing Bone," concerns the squire (Buddy Hackett) of a cowardly knight (Terry-Thomas) who slays a dragon, and then is killed by his master who takes credit for the deed. The treacherous knight fashions a flute from the young squire's bones, but when it is played, the song exposes the truth. • The film utilized the wide screen "Cinerama" process and earned its cinematographer, Paul Vogel, an Academy Award nomination. • The dragon in "The Singing Bone" story was brought to life by stop-motion animator Jim Danforth.

Ape Giants

(*See also* Apes and Monkeys)

It seems as if everyone is familiar with the father of this subgenre — "The Eighth Wonder of the World" — *King Kong* (1933). *King Kong* was more than just a *Star Wars*-of-its-time smash hit, with moviegoers standing in long lines and going back again and again to see this early movie magic. It proved to be a prototype that helped mold what we now know as the monster movie.

Although the dinosaur-filled *The Lost World* (1925) preceded this epic by eight years, *King Kong* proved that big monsters (and big apes in particular), accompanied by a little dose of sympathy, was not only a palatable public product, but a financial boon. There was just one hitch however — no one but the film's driving force, Willis O'Brien, could perform the wondrous magic of *King Kong*. Because of the great technical strains associated with stop-motion animation (and O'Brien's reluctance to spread the wealth of his knowledge and expertise), nobody dared to touch the subject except O'Brien.

Later that same year, in self-consuming fashion, O'Brien managed to quickly capitalize on Kong's success with the follow-up film, *Son of Kong*. Unfortunately for O'Brien and RKO, the film's hasty production (in a race to get the film out to theaters that same year) showed, and the picture was a moderate disappointment at the box office. More's the pity since *Son of Kong,* while nothing near its giant predecessor, is still a good little film in its own right and doesn't deserve its relative obscurity.

Not until 1949 did O'Brien manage to get another project off the ground. *Mighty Joe Young,* aimed at the younger audience, was a hit and it garnered for O'Brien a well-deserved Oscar for special effects. Another significant event tied to this film was the emergence of Willis O'Brien's eventual successor, Ray Harryhausen, who worked as O'Brien's assistant. A new animator was born, and with Harryhausen's solo effort four years later (*The Beast from 20,000 Fathoms,* 1953), the giant monster movie was back in business. Along with giant animals of every shape and kind, it was only a matter of time before the *Kong* imitators (such as AIP's dismal *Konga,* 1961), came along. *Kong* himself was resurrected by the Japanese in the juvenile *King Kong vs. Godzilla* (1962) and its follow-ups. Then, in 1976, the Italian movie mogul Dino De Laurentiis (with his "money is never having to say you're sorry" approach to filmmaking) managed to sour the *Kong* mystique for giant ape fans everywhere. As long as there remains a print of the original for fans to watch, however, the magic of *King Kong* will live on.

A*P*E (1976; Worldwide; Korea/U.S.) D: Paul Leder. P: K. M. Yeung, Paul Leder. S: Paul Leder, Ruben Leder. Cast: Rod Arrants, Joanna De Varona, Alex Nicol. A 36-foot-tall giant ape is found on a remote Pacific island and ends up in Korea where it wreaks the usual havoc in this King Kong clone. ¶ "Ten Tons of Animal Fury Leaps from the Screen!"—poster ad line. • Jack H. Harris (producer of *The Blob,* 1958; *The 4-D Man,* 1959; and *Dinosaurus!* 1960, among others) distributed this film in the U.S. • *A*P*E* was filmed in 3-D. • In a screen first, this particular giant ape battles a giant shark (*A*P*E* vs. *J*A*W*S?*)

Goliathon (1977; Shaw Brothers; Hong Kong) (also *The Mighty Peking Man*). D: Homer Gaugh (Ho Meng-Hwa). P: Runme Shaw. S: I Kuang. C: Tsao Hui-chi, Wu Cho-Hua. Cast: Evelyne Craft, Li Hsiu-Hsien, Ku Feng, Lin Wei-Tu, Hsu Shao-Chiang, Wu Hang-Sheng, Ted Thomas, Steve Nicholson, Hsiao Yao. In a Female-Tarzan-Meets-King-Kong plot, a Chinese hunter finds a giant ape and its blonde jungle-woman friend and takes them back to Hong Kong for show, with the expected disastrous results. • Throughout the film the giant ape is referred to as "The Peking

Man," though it is obviously more ape than man, and no explanation is ever given for its tremendous size (a height of ten stories).

King Kong (1933; RKO) D/P: Merian C. Cooper, Ernest B. Shoedsack. S: James Creelman, Ruth Rose. C: Edward Lindon, Vernon L. Walker, J. O. Taylor. Cast: Fay Wray, Robert Armstrong, Bruce Cabot, Frank Reicher, Sam Hardy, Noble Johnson, Steve Clemento, James Flavin, Victor Wong. In one of the greatest stories ever told, the mighty Kong, who was "a king and a god in his world" is captured and brought to New York, only to fall victim to his impossible love for a human "beauty." ¶ "It wasn't the airplanes, it was beauty killed the beast." • *King Kong* was originally planned as a semi-documentary travelogue. • The makers of *King Kong* originally intended to use an actual live gorilla enlarged by trick photography to play Kong. • The model of Kong used in the animation sequences was actually only 18 inches tall, and brought to realistic life by stop-motion animation pioneer Willis O'Brien. • Three body parts of *King Kong* were built to full scale size for the film—a hand (to grab Fay Wray), the head (for close-up reaction shots and for eating natives), and a foot (used to crush natives). • The full-size bust of Kong was covered in bear skins. • The roars heard from the monsters on Skull Island were actually the sounds of a lion recorded at half speed and printed in reverse. • The 1939 classic, *Gone with the Wind,* featured the burning of the giant wall set from *King Kong.* • The jungle sets from *King Kong* are the same ones that appear in *The Most Dangerous Game* (1932). • *King Kong,* one of the most successful films of all time, single-handedly saved RKO from bankruptcy during the depression. • *King Kong* had three alternative titles during production—*Creation; The 8th Wonder;* and *The 8th Wonder of the World.* While it was being shot, they used the title *Jamboree* to maintain some semblance of secrecy concerning the plot. • Willis O'Brien, who was very secretive concerning his effects processes, had intended to make another Kong film, *King Kong vs. Prometheus,* before his death on November 8, 1962.

King Kong (1976; Paramount) D: John Guillermin. P: Dino De Laurentiis. S: Lorenzo Semple, Jr. Cast: Jeff Bridges, Jessica Lange, Charles Grodin, John Randolph, John Agar, Ed Lauter. In this expensive but lackluster remake, a team out looking for oil discovers Kong on his island and brings him back to New York. ¶ "Put me down you male chauvinist ape!" • Instead of toppling off the Empire State Building, Kong takes a header off the World Trade Center this time. • Jessica Lange made her film debut by taking over Fay Wray's role in this 1976 remake. She was a model before turning to acting. • Actor John Agar, a staple of 50s sci-fi (*Tarantula, Revenge of the Creature, Brain from Planet Arous,* others) plays the mayor of New York City. • No brilliant stop-motion animation here, just Rick Baker in an (admittedly realistic) monkey suit he designed, along with a 45-foot-tall electronically controlled model which took a big bite out of the $24 million budget.

King Kong Escapes (1968; Toho/Universal; Japan) (also *King Kong vs. Mecha-Kong*). D: Inoshiro Honda, Arthur Rankin, Jr. (English version). P: Tomoyuki Tanaka, Arthur Rankin, Jr. (English version). S: Kaoru Mabuchi, William K. Keenan (English version). C: Hajime Koizumi. Cast: Rhodes Reason, Linda Miller, Mie Hama, Akira Takarada, Eisei Amamoto. In this second outing for Kong in Japan (following his bout with Godzilla in *King Kong vs. Godzilla,* 1962) Kong is pitted against some evil industrial miners who've built a giant

Kong robot. ¶ From the ads: "Only King Kong can save the world from the forces of evil!" • Not only does King Kong fight his robot counterpart, "Mecha-Kong," but he also battles a giant octopus and one of Godzilla's poor relations. • J. Arthur Rank directed new scenes for the American version featuring Rhodes Reason and Linda Miller. • Female lead Mie Hama returns from *King Kong vs. Godzilla* to face the big ape again here. Ms. Hama had also been in the James Bond film, *You Only Live Twice* (1967).

King Kong Lives (1986; De Laurentiis Entertainment Group) D: John Guillermin. P: Martha Schumacher. S: Ronald Shusett, Steven Pressfield. Cast: Brian Kerwin, Linda Hamilton, John Ashton, Peter Michael Goetz. This sequel to the 1976 version of *King Kong* picks up with Kong needing a heart transplant after his fall from the World Trade Center in the previous film. The story also involves the discovery and capture of a "lady Kong" to keep the big King company. • Linda Hamilton plays the sympathetic doctor who operates on Kong. She later fell in love with her own "beast" in the appropriately titled cult favorite TV show, "Beauty and the Beast." The actress didn't take *King Kong Lives* too seriously, telling *Fangoria* #60, "It's a movie about two giant monkeys. How convincing or exact can you be?" • Kong not only gets a girlfriend in this film, he also sires a son (which, ridiculously enough, is played by a man in a normal-sized ape suit).

King Kong vs. Godzilla (1962; Toho/Universal; Japan) D: Inoshiro Honda, Thomas Montgomery (English version). P: John Beck. S: Shinichi Sekizawa, Paul Mason, Bruce Howard. C: Hajime Koizumi. Cast: Michael Keith, James Yagi, Mie Hama, Kenji Sahara, Akihiko Hirata. Kong is captured and taken to Japan. Godzilla awakens from a frozen iceberg. They meet, throw boulders at one another, and practice their wrestling moves. ¶ Ad slogan: "An all-mighty new motion picture brings them together in the colossal clash of all-time!" • This was the first film to feature Godzilla in color (and the first to show King Kong in color, for that matter). • Two different endings were filmed. For the American audience, *King Kong* was the victor. In the Japanese version, *Godzilla* came out on top.

Konga (1961; AIP) D: John Lemont. P: Herman Cohen. S: Aben Kandel, Herman Cohen. C: Desmond Dickinson. Cast: Michael Gough, Margo Johns, Jess Conrad, Claire Gordon, Austin Trevor, Jack Wat-

King Kong *(1933), "The Eighth Wonder of the World" grapples with a Pterodactyl while Fay Wray looks on in terror.*

son, George Pastell, Leonard Sachs. Michael Gough plays a mad botanist who develops a growth serum which he uses on a chimpanzee, training it to kill for him. But things eventually get out of hand (or more precisely, Gough gets *into* Konga's hand!) when the monkey grows to a height of several stories. ¶ "Fantastic, there's a huge monster gorilla that's constantly growing to outlandish proportions loose in the streets." • Konga started out as a normal sized chimpanzee, then inexplicably changed its species when it grew into a gigantic *gorilla.* • *Konga* was originally intended to be called *I Was a Teenage Gorilla* (obviously clearer heads prevailed in the end). • One reviewer summed up the merits of this imitation by writing: "It's about as good as you would expect a Herman Cohen version of *King Kong* to be." • The final night of shooting required the firing of guns and bazookas in the streets of London. Many citizens actually thought the city was under attack, and Scotland Yard was deluged with phone calls.

The Mighty Gorga (1969; American General Pictures) D: David L. Hewitt. P:

Robert O'Neil, David Hewitt. S: David Prentiss, Jean Hewitt C: Gary Graver. Cast: Anthony Eisley, Megan Timothy, Scott Brady, Kent Taylor, Gary Kent, Graydon Clark, Sheldon Lee, Lee Parish. Anthony Eisley is the owner of a down-and-out circus who journeys to Africa in search of a legendary 50-foot gorilla. ¶ "Mighty Gorga, I know that your thirst for the blood of young virgins is great but leave our village in peace." • Star Anthony Eisley later commented on how low the budget was for this *King Kong* rip off": "I think we were just out in some field that he [director Hewitt] rigged up to look like a jungle somehow, and I remember he got some animal shots by having me walk around a zoo!" • This may be veteran actors Scott Brady's (*Destination Inner Space,* 1966; *Castle of Evil,* 1968, etc.) and Kent Taylor's (*Day Mars Invaded Earth,* 1963; *The Crawling Hand,* 1963; etc.) worst film (and it's facing some stiff competition).

Mighty Joe Young (1949; RKO) D: Ernest B. Schoedsack. P: Merian C. Cooper. S: Ruth Rose. C: J. Roy Hunt. Cast: Terry

Kong reels in hero Bruce Cabot and heroine Fay Wray just before they drop to the river below and make their escape in the 1933 classic, King Kong.

Moore, Ben Johnson, Robert Armstrong, Frank McHugh, Douglas Fowley, Dennis Green, Paul Guilfoyle, Nestor Paiva, Regis Toomey, Primo Carnera. In Africa, a nightclub owner and adventurer finds a 12-foot tall gorilla named "Joe" and the human girl who is his friend. He takes them back to New York, but Joe is mistreated and runs amok in the nightclub. Ordered by the courts to be put to death, Joe is spirited away by his friends and ends up saving a group of children at a burning orphanage. All is well when Joe and his friends return to Africa. ¶ "Goodbye Joe, I should have left you in Africa where you belong." • *Mighty Joe Young* was originally titled *The Great*

Joe Young, and was to be co-produced by John Ford (whose name appears on much of the film's publicity). Ford ultimately dropped out, however, and the title was changed to its final one. • Director Shoedsack and producer Cooper are the same men that brought us *King Kong* and *Son of Kong* in 1933. These two filmmakers hold the record for most (and best) giant ape films. • Robert Armstrong, who plays the crass showman who first captures but later aids the ape, is basically reprising the role he played in both *King Kong* and *Son of Kong.* • Famous wrestlers and strong-men of the 1940s— Henry "Bomber" Kulky, Primo Carnera, and the Swedish Angel, battle Joe in a tug-of-war during one of the nightclub scenes. • Willis O'Brien (the genius animator who brought *King Kong* to life) won an Oscar for this film's special effects. • For this production, O'Brien improved his stop-motion animation technique by filming at 24 frames per second rather than at 6 frames per second as he did on *King Kong* and *Son of Kong.* This gives *Mighty Joe Young* a more natural and fluid motion than its predecessors. • *Mighty Joe Young* was one of the first films for stop-motion animation genius Ray Harryhausen, who worked here as an assistant to Willis O'Brien. These two foremost stop-motion animators, O'Brien and Harryhausen, worked together only once more in their careers—on *Animal World* (1955).

Son of Kong (1933; RKO) D: Ernest B. Shoedsack. P: Merian C. Cooper. S: Ruth Rose. C: Edward Linden, Vernon Walker, J. O. Taylor. Cast: Robert Armstrong, Helen Mack, Frank Reicher, Noble Johnson, Victor Wong, John Marston. Taking up immediately after the end of *King Kong,* Carl Denham (Robert Armstrong) is forced to hastily leave New York after the King Kong debacle, and sets sail with Captain Englehorn for parts unknown. They end up back on Skull Island where they find a "little Kong" which befriends them and helps them locate the island treasure as well as defending them against various giant predators. ¶ "Good boy little Kong. Say, can he scrap, just like his old man!" • All of these actors from *King Kong* returned for *Son of Kong*— Robert Armstrong, Noble Johnson, Frank Reicher, and Victor Wong. • The popular press of the time labeled the son of Kong "Kiko." This ape is played more for laughs and cuteness than for terror and pathos as the original Kong was. • The son of Kong was 12 feet tall (ony about a quarter the height of his papa). • Over the course of the film "Little Kong" fights a giant cave bear and a brontosaurus-type dragon. • At the climax, little Kong saves Carl Denham's life by holding him above the waterline as the island sinks into the sea under him. This is rather ironic since it was Denham who had been responsible for papa Kong's woes in the first film. The son of Kong sacrifices his own life to save the man responsible for his father's death. • Nils Helstrom (who is mentioned but never seen in *King Kong* as the man who had sold Carl Denham the map to Skull Island) is featured as a prominent character in *Son of Kong.* • A horrible tragedy occurred in stop-motion animator Willis O'Brien's life near the finish of *Son of Kong.* His wife was stricken with cancer and tuberculosis at the time, and the drugs she was receiving altered her mind. On October 7, 1933, she shot both of O'Brien's sons and herself. Both of the boys died, but she survived for a full year. • Audiences responded poorly to this hastily rushed out sequel and it scored only moderately at the box office, quelling any further sequel plans.

Apes and Monkeys

(*See also* Ape Giants; Planet of the Apes)

Our evolutionary ancestor, the ape, is a much maligned animal in cinema. Usually the unwitting strong arm of mad scientists, apes and monkeys are goaded into committing terrible atrocities and, more often than not, end up with a bullet-ridden carcass for their trouble. In addition to the straight jungle ape or monkey employed in acts of mayhem, cinema science has often found ways to link the mind of a human with the body of a gorilla (or vice versa). *Captive Wild Woman* (1943) and its two sequels are prime examples of this offshoot of the monkey movie.

With very few exceptions, apes in monster movies have been played by men

A sheepish Mighty Joe Young *(1949) offers the rope to Terry Moore after having defeated a group of the "strongest men in the world" in a tug-of-war match.*

in costumes. One of the busiest "ape-men" was George Barrows, who invested $800 to make his own gorilla suit, which he then wore in over 300 films and television shows. The acting of suited "apes" has always left something to be desired, but it was next to impossible to try to film with a live gorilla. Early audiences generally suspended their disbelief in a most generous manner and accepted this unsatisfactory simian situation. As makeup techniques improved, people like John Chambers (*Planet of the Apes,* 1968) were able to devise some incredibly life-like ape suits and monkey makeovers in more recent years. Today, however, most audiences are too sophisticated to enjoy an "ape" monster movie. For more simian shudders see PLANET OF THE APES SERIES, and APE GIANTS.

The Ape (1940; Monogram) D: William Nigh. P: Scott R. Dunlap. S: Kurt Siodmak, Richard Carroll. C: Harry Neumann. Cast: Boris Karloff, Maris Wrixson, Gene O'Donnell, Dorothy Vaughan, Gertrude W. Hoffman, Henry Hall, Selmer Jackson. Boris Karloff (as Dr. Adrian) is obsessed with finding a cure for polio. For this he needs human spinal fluid, and resorts to murder to obtain it. He dons the skin of an escaped circus gorilla he had previously killed and murders the local undesirables for their spinal fluid, making it appear as if the ape were responsible. ¶ "You gotta give that ape credit — he only picks out the ornery cusses." • *The Ape* is based (very loosely) on the play by Adam Hull Shirk. This is the second adaptation of Shirk's play, the first being *House of Mystery* (1934), which was also directed by William Nigh. • This film fulfilled Boris Karloff's contract with Monogram (he had previously done five films for this studio in the Chinese detective, "Mr. Wong," series). Karloff, unlike the unfortunate Bela Lugosi, never returned to this poverty-row studio.

The Ape Man (1943; Monogram) (also *Lock Your Doors*). D: William Beaudine. P: Sam Katzman, Jack Dietz. S: Barney Sarecky. C: Mack Stengler. Cast: Bela Lugosi, Wallace Ford, Louise Currie, Jack Mulhall, Wheeler Oakman, Henry Hall, Minerva Urecal, Ralph Littlefield, J. Farrell MacDonald. Scientist Bela Lugosi has been experimenting on himself using gorilla spinal fluid and finds he must obtain *human* spinal fluid periodically or revert to a half-man, half-ape creature. He also keeps a large killer gorilla on hand in the lab, which he puts to murderous use in obtaining his precious fluid. ¶ "Me? I'm the author of the story. Screwy idea wasn't it?" — This final line is delivered by a strange man who pops up periodically throughout the film to check on what the characters are doing. Screwy idea wasn't it? • *The Ape Man* is based on the story, "They Creep in the Dark," by Karl Brown. • This film carried a shooting title of *The Gorilla Strikes.* • The makeup for Lugosi is very similar to what he wore in *Island of Lost Souls* (1933) — more of an impoverished "wolfman" look than that of an "ape-man." • Actress Minerva Urecal, here playing Lugosi's sister/assistant, had also assisted Lugosi the year before in *The Corpse Vanishes* (1942). • Director William "One Shot" Beaudine received his nickname because of his reputation for shooting fast and with few retakes (so fast in fact that he directed over 150 movies over the course of his career!).

The Beast That Killed Women (1965; Barry Mahon) P/D/S: Barry Mahon. A gorilla runs amok in a nudist camp in this adults-only obscurity.

Bela Lugosi Meets a Brooklyn Gorilla(1952; Jack Broder Productions/Realart) (also *The Boys from Brooklyn; The Monster Meets the Girl*). D: William Beaudine. P: Maurice Duke. S: Tim Ryan. C: Charles Van Enger. Cast: Bela Lugosi, Duke Mitchell, Sammy Petrillo, Charlita, Muriel Landers, Al Kikume. As Dr. Zabor, Bela Lugosi has discovered a serum which can turn people into gorillas, which he does to one-half of a comedy team stranded on his tropical island. ¶ From the promotional trailer: "Duke Mitchell and Sammy Petrillo turn an island paradise into the zaniest madhouse in the seventh sea." • Once again, director William "One Shot" Beaudine enters ape territory (as he did in 1943 with *The Ape Man,* also starring Bela Lugosi). • The two male leads, Duke Mitchell and Sammy Petrillo, were a pair of Dean Martin and Jerry Lewis imitators (and effective ones at that, for they were threatened with a lawsuit by Martin and Lewis' manager, Hal Wallis). • Reminiscing, Petrillo (the Jerry Lewis half of the team) recalled: "I was fascinated to work with Lugosi, who I discovered to be a heck of a nice guy and a gentleman, but he could never get my name right. He always called me 'Jerry'" (from *The Films of Bela Lugosi* by Richard Bojarski). • Petrillo went on to add: "the only sour note on this film was Ramona the chimp, who grew to dislike me as filming progressed, and bit me whenever her trainer wasn't looking." • This was Lugosi's last movie before his infamous Ed Wood, Jr., films (*Glen or Glenda?,* 1953; *Bride of the Monster,* 1955; *Plan 9 from Outer Sapce,* 1959).

The Black Zoo (1963) (see CATS). Michael Gough runs a private zoo, from which he sends out his animals to murder his enemies. The savage beasts include a lion, tiger — and a gorilla. • The gorilla suit seen here is the same one used in the giant ape film, *Konga* (1961).

The Bride and the Beast (1958; Allied Artists) D/P: Adrian Weiss. S: Edward E. Wood, Jr. C: Roland Price. Cast: Charlotte Austin, Lance Fuller, Johnny Roth, Steve Calvert, William Justine. The wife of a big game hunter accompanies her husband on safari, only to discover that she is the reincarnation of an ape. She is kidnapped by a gorilla and decides to settle down and play "jungle house" with the ape rather than return to her human husband. ¶ "I don't want to go to the water. I'm so frightened of the water. I see my reflection. I ... I'm a gorilla!" • This bizarre no-budget entry in the monkey business field was scripted by none other than the notorious Ed Wood, Jr., maker of *Glen or Glenda?* (1953) and *Plan 9 from Outer Space* (1959), among others. Wood liked to dress in women's clothing and reportedly had a penchant for angora sweaters, thus explaining a rather curious reference to angora which appears as a non sequitur in this film. • Star Charlotte Austin faced a few other terrors in her brief career, including *The Man Who Turned to Stone* (1957), and *Frankenstein 1970* (1958).

Bride of the Gorilla (1951; Jack Broder Productions/Realart) D/S: Curt Siodmak. P: Jack Broder. C: Charles Van Enger. Cast: Lon Chaney, Jr., Barbara Payton, Raymond Burr, Tom Conway, Paul Cavanagh. Raymond Burr plays the manager of a rubber plantation who kills his boss and marries his widow. A faithful servant places a curse upon Burr, causing him to act like (and possibly even turn into) a gorilla. (The question of whether his transformation is physical or merely mental is unanswered.) ¶ "I heard something, something strange and beautiful—a voice, calling me. I couldn't resist going out there. I couldn't resist getting closer and closer. Next thing I knew, I was in a trap." • Herman Cohen, who brought us the big ape movie, *Konga* (1961), as well as related films, *The Black Zoo* (1963) and *Trog* (1970), may have gotten his apish inspiration while working as assistant producer on this early film. • Producer Jack Broder brought us more simian mayhem when his production company released *Bela Lugosi Meets a Brooklyn Gorilla* the following year.

Captive Wild Woman (1943; Universal) D: Edward Dmytryk. P: Ben Pivar. S: Henry Sucher, Griffin Jay. C: George Robinson. Cast: John Carradine, Evelyn Ankers, Acquanetta, Milburn Stone, Lloyd Corrigan, Fay Helm, Paul Fix. Through gland transplants, scientist John Carradine turns an ape into a beautiful woman (who, when aroused, occasionally reverts back to bestial form and wreaks havoc). ¶ "And suppose your experiment is successful. What will you have? A human form with animal instincts." • The hero, Milburn Stone, is best known to modern audiences as "Doc" on TV's long-running series, "Gunsmoke." • The stock footage of a lion tamer in action, sprinkled liberally throughout the picture, is from *The Big Cage* (1933) with Clyde Beatty. • *Captive Wild Woman* was so successful that it spawned two sequels— *Jungle Woman* and *Jungle Captive* (both released in 1944).

Crazy Knights (1944; Monogram) (also *Ghost Crazy*). D: William Beaudine. P: Sam Katzman, Jack Dietz. S: Tim Ryan. C: Marcel le Picard. Cast: Billy Gilbert, Maxie Rosenbloom, Shemp Howard, Jayne Hazard, Minerva Urecal, Tim Ryan, Art Miles. A carnival act stops at a "haunted house." The carnival's gorilla plays a prominent role in this tepid haunted house comedy. • Costar Shemp Howard later went on to become one of the "Three Stooges." • Screenwriter Tim Ryan acted in this movie as a straight man for the comedy trio of Gilbert, Rosenbloom, and Howard.

Dr. Renault's Secret (1942; 20th Century–Fox) (also *Buried Alive*). D: Harry Lachman. P: Sol M. Wurtzel. S: William Bruckner, Robert F. Metzler. C: Virgil Miller. Cast: J. Carrol Naish, George Zucco, John

Shepperd, Mike Mazurki, Jack Norton, Bert Roach, Eugene Borden. Scientist George Zucco transforms an ape into a man (of sorts). • This was director Harry Lachman's last film, after which he turned to painting (or perhaps was driven to it). • Art direction for this film was provided by Nathan Juran, who later graduated to director on *20 Million Miles to Earth* (1957), *The Deadly Mantis* (1957), and *Attack of the 50 Foot Woman* (1958), among others.

The Gorilla (1927; First National) D/P: Alfred Santell. S: Al Cohn, Henry Mc-Carty. C: Arthur Edeson. Cast: Charlie Murray, Fred Kelsey, Alice Day, Gaston Glass, Walter Pidgeon, Tully Marshall. A man poses as a gorilla to commit murder in this silent old dark house spoof. • Walter Pidgeon, who went on to achieve genre fame as Dr. Morbius in *Forbidden Planet* (1956), is revealed to be the murderer who disguises himself as a gorilla. • The film is based on a successful Broadway play by Ralph Spence.

The Gorilla (1930; First National) D: Bryan Foy. S: B. Harrison Orkow, Herman Ruby. C: Sid Hickox. Cast: Joe Frisco, Harry Gribbon, Lila Lee, Walter Pidgeon, Purnell Prat. This is the first sound remake of Ralph Spence's Broadway play about a man wearing a gorilla suit to commit murder. • Walter Pidgeon returns from the 1927 silent version, but in a different role— he is the hero this time.

The Gorilla (1939; Fox) D: Alan Dwan. P: Darryl F. Zanuck. S: Rian James, Sid Silvers. C: Edward Cronjager. Cast: Ritz Brothers, Patsy Kelly, Lionel Atwill, Anita Louise, Bela Lugosi, Joseph Calleia. This is yet another version of Ralph Spence's play about a man impersonating a gorilla to murder those standing in his way. • This time the Ritz Brothers play the bumbling detectives, and Lionel Atwill and Bela Lugosi are on hand to lend their sinister support. • Peter Lorre was originally set to costar but was ultimately replaced by Bela Lugosi. • Director Alan Dwan had this to say about Lugosi: "As far as Bela Lugosi was concerned, we all knew he was exploited for billing purposes. The role did not do justice to his enormous talents." • The elaborate ape suit was constructed at a cost of $2800 (in 1939!) and took 18 months to make.

Gorilla at Large (1954; Panoramic Productions) D: Harmon Jones. P: Robert L. Jacks. S: Leonard Praskins, Barney Slater. C: Lloyd Ahern. Cast: Cameron Mitchell, Anne Bancroft, Lee J. Cobb, Raymond

Detective Garrision (Lee J. Cobb) grills Kovack (Peter Whitney) for information about his caged gorilla, Goliath, with Raymond Burr and Anne Bancroft standing off in the background in Gorilla at Large *(1954).*

Burr, Charlotte Austin, Lee Marvin. *Gorilla at Large* is a carnival murder-mystery centering on murders apparently committed by a gorilla. ¶ "A huge gorilla at the Garden of Evil is the world's most terrifying creature. It seems to those viewing the act, that the one thing he wants to do is kill, kill, kill." • The monstrous ape in question was named "Goliath," and the man in the suit was George Barrows, star of *Robot Monster* (1953). • Surprisingly enough, the murderer turns out to be Anne Bancroft (the gorilla never actually kills anyone but is shot nevertheless at the climax—a very unlucky red herring). • Ms. Bancroft later married comedian/filmmaker Mel Brooks. According to star Cameron Mitchell, *Gorilla at Large* is Mel Brooks' favorite film. • Both Raymond Burr and Charlotte Austin were lucky enough to appear in two gorilla films, this one and *Bride of the Gorilla* for Burr, and *Bride of the Beast* for Austin. • Lee Marvin appears as a simpleton cop in one of his earlier screen performances.

House of Mystery (1934; Monogram) D:
William Nigh. P: Paul Malvern. S: Albert deMond. C: Archie Stout. Cast: Ed Lowry, Verna Hillie, John Sheehan, Clay Clement, Brandon Hurst, Gabby Hayes. This early old dark house mystery features a supposed ghostly killer ape that is finally revealed to be a human cast member. • This story was remade in 1940 as *The Ape* (though with drastic plot differences), and was directed once again by William Nigh.

In the Shadow of Kilimanjaro (1986; Intermedia Productions) D: Raju Patel. P: Gautam Das, Jeffrey M. Sneller. S: Jeffrey M. Sneller, T. Michael Harry. C: Jesus Elizondo. Cast: John Rhys-Davies, Timothy Bottoms, Michele Carey, Irene Miracle, Calvin Jung, Don Blakely, Patty Foley. A terrible drought in Africa causes 90,000 baboons to seek whatever food they can find, including humans. They eventually invade a rural village and lay siege to the town hotel. ¶ "Do you have any idea how many baboons are out there looking for dinner?"

Jungle Captive (1944; Universal) (also *Wild Jungle Captive*). D: Harold Young. P:

Morgan B. Cox. S: M. Coates Wester, Dwight V. Babcock. C: Maury Gertsman. Cast: Otto Kruger, Amelita Ward, Phil Brown, Jerome Cowan, Eddie Acuff, Rondo Hatton, Vicki Lane. A scientist resurrects the body of "Paula the Ape Woman" in this second sequel to *Captive Wild Woman*. • Rondo Hatton (who in real life suffered from the feature-distorting disease, acromegaly) played the monstrous assistant "Moloch." • Vicki Lane takes over the role from Acquanetta as Paula the Ape Woman. • Economy was the watchword of the day on *Jungle Captive*, including using a good deal of stock footage from previous pictures. The hand transformation scenes were lifted from the original *Captive Wild Woman* (1943), and the scene of the morgue truck crashing over the cliff in flames is actually Dr. Kemp's crashing car from *The Invisible Man* (1933).

Jungle Woman (1944; Universal) D: Reginald Le Borg. P: Will Cowan. S: Henry Sucher, Edward Dein, Bernard Schubert. C: Jack McKenzie. Cast: Evelyn Ankers, J. Carrol Naish, Lois Collier, Samuel S. Hinds, Douglas Dumbrille, Acquanetta, Milburn Stone, Alec Craig, Pierre Watkin, Heinie Conklin. In this first sequel to *Captive Wild Woman* (1943), mad scientist J. Carrol Naish brings "Paula the Ape Woman" back to life. ¶ "She's no ordinary girl! She's a horrible creature!" • When Universal first announced a sequel to *Captive Wild Woman,* they called it *Jungle Queen*. It was then changed to *Jungle Girl* during preproduction and finally became *Jungle Woman* when the cameras began rolling. • Acquanetta, Milburn Stone, and Evelyn Ankers all return from the first film, and so does much of the film itself (a lot of stock footage from *Captive Wild Woman* was used to pad out this sequel's already brief 54-minute running time. • J. Carrol Naish, who played an apeman created by a mad scientist in *Dr. Renault's Secret* (1942), gets to play the mad scientist role this time. Respected character actor Naish was marking time on this potboiler between Oscar nominations—for *Sahara* in 1943 and *A Medal for Benny* in 1945. • Director Reginald Le Borg was less than thrilled with this particular assignment. In an interview with Tom Weaver from *Interviews with B Science Fiction and Horror Movie Makers,* Le Borg stated: "It was an atrocious script, and a silly idea anyway. But, again, I was under contract. If I had refused it, I would have been suspended without pay, and I wouldn't have gotten assignments anymore. You had to play ball

with the front office." • Nor was Le Borg very happy with Acquanetta: "She was a nice-looking girl, but she had a squeaky, high-pitched voice. A lower-class Marie Montez."

Link (1986; Cannon Films) D: Richard Franklin. P: Richard Franklin, Rick McCallum. S: Everett DeRoche. Cast: Elisabeth Shue, Terence Stamp. A woman is employed by a scientist to look after his three experimental chimpanzees. The roles are reversed, however, when the savage chimps revolt and start looking after *her.* ¶ "For thousands of years man has enslaved the ape. Now the tables are about to turn"—ad line.

Monkey Shines, an Experiment in Fear (1988; Orion) D/S: George A. Romero. P: Charles Evans. C: James A. Contner. Cast: Jason Beghe, John Pankow, Kate McNeil, Joyce Van Patten. A man becomes a quadriplegic and his scientist friend gives him an experimental monkey as a "helper." Only this monkey is super-intelligent and posseses an often-murderous will of its own. ¶ Advertising jingle: "Once there was a man whose prison was a chair/ The man had a monkey, they made the strangest pair/ The monkey ruled the man, it climbed inside his head/ And now as fate would have it, one of them is dead." • The little malevolent monkey was named Ella in the film. • At the climax, the paralyzed hero finally kills the murderous monkey by grabbing it by the neck with his teeth and biting it to death. • Director George Romero is best known for *Night of the Living Dead* (1968) and its sequels.

The Monster and the Girl (1941; Paramount) D: Stuart Heisler. P: Jack Moss. S: Stuart Anthony. C: Victor Milner. Cast: Ellen Drew, Robert Paige, Paul Lukas, Onslow Stevens, George Zucco, Rod Cameron, Marc Lawrence, Philip Terry, Gerald Mohr, Joseph Calleia. An innocent man is executed, and a scientist (George Zucco) puts his brain into the body of a gorilla. Said gorilla then goes after those responsible for framing him and selling his sister into prostitution. • This is the second time Zucco experimented with gorillas (in 1942's *Dr. Renault's Secret* he went even further and turned a gorilla into a man).

The Monster Walks (1932; Mayfair) D: Frank Strayer. P: Cliff Broughton. S: Robert Ellis. C: Jules Cronjager. Cast: Rex Lease, Vera Reynolds, Mischa Auer, Sheldon Lewis, Martha Mattox, Sleep 'n' Eat (Willie Best). Murders are committed in a strange household that keeps a gibbering ape in the basement. • This was Willie Best's

The simian monster with the brain of a wrongly-executed man contemplates his predicament in The Monster and the Girl *(1941).*

third film, here playing for the first of many times the role of cowardly black servant. In the racist Hollywood of 1932, Best was billed simply as "Sleep 'n' Eat." • Director Frank Strayer went on to bigger and definitely better things with *The Vampire Bat* (1933).

Murders in the Rue Morgue (1932) (see POE FILMS — EARLY POE). Following Edgar Allan Poe's classic tale in name only, this story revolves around a mad scientist attempting to mate humans with apes. ¶ "I'm in the prine of my strength, and I'm lonely."

Murders in the Rue Morgue (1971) (see POE FILMS — MODERN POE). This is a modern revenge story centering on a theater performing Poe's story on stage.

Murders in the Rue Morgue (1986) (see POE FILMS — MODERN POE). This TV movie, about a series of murders committed by an escaped orangutan, is the most faithful treatment of Poe's classic to date.

Night of the Bloody Apes (1968; Cinematografica Calderón/Jerand; Mexico) D: Rene Cardona. P: G. Calderón Stell. S: Rene Cardona, Rene Cardona, Jr., C: Raul Solares. Cast: Armando Silvestre (Armand Silva), Norman Lazareno (Norma LaZar), José Elias Moreno. A scientist places the heart of a gorilla into the body of his dying son, with the result of him changing into an ape-man periodically (though he looks more like a Neanderthal caveman than an ape). ¶ From the trailer: "Half man, half beast, all horror!" • This particular ape man didn't limit himself to just murder, he also liked to rape his female victims, thus allowing for plenty of exploitable nudity. As the promo trailer put it: "The lust of a man in the body of a beast!" • For the surgery scenes, the filmmakers inserted real footage of actual open heart surgery. • The promotional department suggested theaters give fans the opportunity of picking out their own free miniature rubber organs in the lobby.

Phantom of the Rue Morgue (1954) (see POE FILMS — MODERN POE). Karl Malden (Mr. American Express himself) uses an ape to commit murder. He gives a necklace of bells to the intended victims, and this attracts the killer gorilla. • Charles Gemora, who wore the ape suit here, was no stranger to this particular simian role (he had previously played the ape in the 1932 version of Poe's story, *Murders in the Rue Morgue*, as well).

Return of the Ape Man (1944) (see CAVE-PEOPLE). Despite the name, this is not actually a sequel to *The Ape Man* (1943), but a story of a mad scientist finding the preserved body of a prehistoric caveman and giving it a new brain to make it live again. No real apes appear.

Rock 'n' Roll Wrestling Women vs. the Aztec Ape (1962/86) (see BRAINS—BRAIN TRANSPLANTS). A mad scientist transplants the brain of a gorilla into the body of a man and dubs the brute "Gomar." A pair of wrestling women heroines must stop the nefarious plans of the mad doctor in this 1962 Mexican movie which was recut and had a new soundtrack added by Rhino video. ¶ "You, Gomar, you that are part human and half beast and I created you!"

Schlock (1972; Gazotskie/Jack H. Harris) D/S: John Landis. P: James O'Rourke. C: Bob Collins. Cast: John Landis, Saul Kahan, Joseph Piantadosi, Eliza Garrett, Eric Allison, Enrica Blankey, Charles Villiers, John Chambers, Forrest J Ackerman. In this monkey business spoof, a primitive ape-man (more ape than man) thaws out and goes on the rampage, leaving a trail of empty banana skins at the scenes of the crime. • This was director/screenwriter John Landis' (*Animal House,* 1978; *An American Werewolf in London,* 1981; *Twilight Zone: The Movie,* 1983; etc.) debut feature. • It was Landis himself wearing the ape suit. • At one pint, the "schlockthropus" enters a theater showing *The Blob,* but goes berserk because he doesn't like the film's ending.

Secret Witness (1931; Columbia) (also *Terror by Night*). D: Thornton Freeland. P: J. G. Buchman. S: Samuel Spewack. C: Robert Planck. Cast: Una Merkel, William Collier, Jr., ZaSu Pitts, Purnell Pratt, Clyde Cooke, Ralf Harolde, Paul Hurst, Nat Pendleton, Rita LeRoy. A trained gorilla commits murder for its master.

Sinbad and the Eye of the Tiger (1977) (see SINBAD). Sinbad must brave monsters and black magic on a journey to a forbidden land in order to restore his friend, Prince Kassim, who's been turned into a baboon by an evil sorceress. ¶ "He's not really a baboon, he is the prince Kassim."

Son of Ingagi (1940; Sack Amusement) D/P: Richard C. Kahn. S: Spencer Williams, Jr. Cast: Zack Williams, Laura Bowman, Alfred Grant, Daisy Bufford, Arthur Ray, Spencer Williams, Jr. A lonely ape-man steals a bride and keeps her in a basement laboratory in this early all-black horror obscurity. • *Son of Ingagi* "borrowed" its name from *Ingagi* (1930), a faked African "documentary" popular on the roadhouse circuit. Other than sharing the name, the two films are not related (there's not even any "Ingagi" in this film—the ape-man is named "Ingeena"). • Screenwriter/actor Spencer Williams later became famous as the second half of "Amos 'n' Andy."

The Strange Case of Dr. Rx (1942) (see MADMEN—EARLY MADMEN). A mysterious madman calling himself "Dr. Rx" goes on a killing spree, becoming a "self appointed angel of vengeance" who murders crooks that have been acquitted of their crime. He also keeps an ape (named "Bongo") on hand in a bizarre-looking laboratory, using the beast to frighten off all those investigating the case. He straps the hero/detective down and threatens to transplant his brain into Bongo's skull. Of course this was all a bluff and he never intended to do more than terrify the man (since "Dr. Rx" is not really a doctor after all). ¶ "You see in Bongo—he is very stupid, but he will be very smart. And you will be, well, not-so-smart." • Once again, that is Ray "Crash" Corrigan wearing the gorilla suit.

Tanya's Island (1980; Fred Baker Films; Canada) D: Alfred Sole. P/S: Pierre Brousseau. Cast: D. D. Winters. As Tanya, D. D. Winters is stranded on a tropical island where she meets a gentle ape with blue eyes who then fights for Tanya with her jealous boyfriend. • Rick Baker and Rob Bottin designed the realistic ape suit. • D. D. Winters later changed her stage name to "Vanity." • Tanya's island was actually Puerto Rico, where it was filmed. • Clips from another (giant) ape movie, *Mighty Joe Young* (1949), are seen in the film.

The White Gorilla (1947; Special Attractions Film Exchange) D: Harry L. Fraser. P: Adrian Weiss. S: Monro Talbot. S: Bob Cline. Cast: Ray Corrigan, Lorraine Miller. A gorilla is ostracized from his tribe for being the wrong color, and develops a hatred for all upright animals. • Producer Adrian Weiss took footage from a 1927 silent film titled *Perils of the Jungle,* and shot some new footage to make a feature—this feature. • The title character was played by Ray "Crash" Corrigan—stuntman, actor, and gorilla suit owner.

White Pongo (1945; Sigmund Neufeld Productions/PRC) D: Sam Newfield: P:

Sigmund Neufeld. S: Raymond L. Schrock. C: Jack Greenhalgh. Cast: Richard Fraser, Maris Wrixon, Lionel Royce, Al Eben, Gordon Richards, Egon Brecher. An expedition encounters the legendary great white ape.

The Wizard (1927; Fox) D: Richard Rosson. P: William Fox. S: Harry O. Hoyt, Andrew Bennison. Cast: Edmund Lowe, Leila Hyams, Gustav von Seyffertitz, E. H. Calvert, Barry Norton, Oscar Smith, Perle Marshall, Norman Trevor, George Kotsonaros. A scientist grafts a human face onto an ape and uses the creature to carry out this vengeful bidding.

Atlantis

This legendary island in the Atlantic Ocean (about which Plato wrote extensively) has teetered between myth and reality in the minds of people for many years. Lands have sunk into the sea before, so it isn't totally outside the realm of possibility that some kind of ancient civilization may have existed.

The cinematic world, however, has only served to further obscure the plausibility of its reality with the various wild adventures that have been seen on the silver screen. According to the general rules of cinema, Atlantis has often been ruled by evil queens, dinosaurs are frequently seen upon the island, and there may even be scientists who use hypnotism to turn slaves into beast-men. The continent has been linked to the Mediterranean area in general and Greece in particular, but its location has changed from time to time. As well as being "discovered" underwater (*Warlords of Atlantic,* 1978), Atlantis has also been found underground (*Journey Beneath the Desert,* 1961; *Alien from L.A.,* 1988). Descendants of Atlantis often pop up in out of the way places, even so far away as on one of Jupiter's moons (*Fire Maidens from Outer Space,* 1956).

Probably the most comprehensive film ever made on the subject was produced in 1961 by George Pal. *Atlantis, the Lost Continent* attempted to blend common suppositions about the legend with some fantastical elements borrowed from *Island of Lost Souls* (1933). Though it would seem that Pal would be just the man for the task of bringing this myth to cinematic life, the result has generally been regarded as a black mark on his impressive list of accomplishments. Perhaps the definitive film about Atlantis will be made in the years ahead as a remake of Pal's version. Period fantasy films of this type, however, are becoming more and more scarce as popular entertainment looks more toward science fiction than fantasy.

Alien from L.A. (1988; Cannon) D: Albert Pyun. P: Menahem Golan, Yoram Globus. S: Debra Ricci, Regina Davis, Albert Pyun. C: Tom Fraser. Cast: Kathy Ireland, Thom Matthews, Don Michael Paul, Linda Kerridge, Janie du Plessus, Russel Savadier, Simon Poland, Richard Haines, William R. Moses. A California "valley girl" sets out to find her missing father and ends up in the secret underground world of the lost city of Atlantis, who's planning a war against the surface. ¶ "It's dangerous for strangers in Atlantis these days."

L'Atlantide (1922; Metro; France) D/S: Jacques Feyder. C: Georges Specht, Victor Morin. Cast: Stacia Napierkovska, Jean Angelo, Marie-Louise Iribe, Georges Melchior. Two men discover Atlantis and fall under the spell of its evil Queen.

L'Atlantide (1932; International Road Shows; Germany) D: G. W. Pabst. P: Seymour Nebenzal. C: Eugen Schufftan. Cast: Brigitte Helm, Gustav Diessl, Heinz Klingenberg, Tela Tschai, Vladimir Sokoloff. This film, told in flashback, tells the story of Antinea, the cruel queen of Atlantis.

Atlantis, the Lost Continent (1961; MGM) D/P: George Pal. S: Daniel Mainwaring. C: Harold E. Wellman. Cast: Anthony Hall, Joyce Taylor, John Dall, Edward Platt, Jay Novello, Wolfe Barzell, Frank DeKova, Nestor Paiva. A Greek sailor named Demetrios returns the Princess of Atlantis to

her lost island home, then is thrown into the slave mines where scientists experiment on people, changing them into "manimals" (à la *Island of Lost Souls,* 1933). After regaining his freedom by winning the "ordeal of fire and water," Demetrios conspires to foil the ruler's plans to conquer the rest of the world with a powerful crystal-ray device. ¶ "In the days when Atlantis was a just and noble land I was well versed in the sciences. But I hid my eyes when she began to use her great knowledge for evil, and fashioned Gods after her own scientific achievements. For this we will die. The true God will destroy Atlantis."
• In *The Films of George Pal,* by Gail Morgan Hickman, George Pal explained that, "The MGM executives realized while we were shooting that the script wasn't good enough, and they tried to doctor it. But you can't doctor this type of film during production. They came in with suggested pages that were worse than what we had." This is not surprising since the film was rushed into production during a writers' strike—without the finished script. • George Pal used "flying men" in the initial film version but preview audiences were said to have scoffed at the scenes, thinking they looked too much like the puppets they were, rather than real men. All the sequences depicting the flying men were quickly excised from the final prints.

Beyond Atlantis (1973; Dimension Pictures; Philippines) D: Eddie Romero. P: Eddie Romero, John Ashley. S: Charles Johnson. Cast: John Ashley, Patrick Wayne, Lenore Stevens, Sid Haig, George Nader, Leigh Christian. Here Atlantis is found in the Pacific Ocean instead of the Atlantic. The story involves a plot to steal sacred pearls from the island by a mixed group of good guys and gangsters. The native king is scheming too, hoping to perpetuate his race by mating the island beauty named Syrene with one of the newcomers.

Fire Maidens from Outer Space (1956) (see ALIENS—ENCOUNTERS IN OUTER SPACE). Descendents of the lost continent of Atlantis are discovered on the thirteenth moon of Jupiter.

Hercules and the Captive Women (1963) (see MYTHOLOGY) (also *Hercules and the Haunted Women*). Hercules travels to Atlantis and topples the Temple of Uranus, which causes the continent to sink.

Journey Beneath the Desert (1961; France/Italy) (also *L'Atlantide*). Edgar G. Ulmer, Giuseppe Masini. S: Ugo Liberatore, Remigio Del Grosso, André Tabet, Amedeo Nazzari. C: Enzo Serafin. Cast: Haya Harareet, Jean-Louis Trintignat, Amedeo Nazzari, Giulia Rubini. Three helicopter pilots enter the lost world of Atlantis through a desert pathway. • The film is based on the Pierre Benoit novel, *Queen of Atlantis.*

Journey to the Center of the Earth (1959) (see UNDERGROUND WORLDS). The Lindenbrook expedition discovers the remains of the lost city of Atlantis deep below Earth's crust. They escape disaster by riding up through a volcanic shaft in an Atlantean pagan altar stone. ¶ "Now we descend into oblivion *or* we enter the great book of history."

Journey to the Center of the Earth (1989; Cannon International) D: Rusty Lemorande. P: Karen Koch. S: Debra Ricci, Regina Davis, Kitty Chalmers. C: Tom Fraser, David Watkin. Cast: Nicola Cowper, Paul Carafotes, Ilan Mitchell-Smith. A nanny and two teenaged brothers are trapped within a volcano and trek downward until they reach the lost city of Atlantis. After discovering some weird creatures and meeting the bizarre inhabitants of the city they uncover an Atlantean plot to invade the upper world.

Mysterious Island (1961) (see SEA MONSTERS). In the underwater climax, remnants of the lost city of Atlantis are seen in the form of a ruined coliseum-like structure.

Santo Contra Blue Demon en la Atlantida (1968) D: Jesus Sotomayor Martinez. P: Hector Dávila Guajardo. C: Rafael Garcia Travesi. Cast: Jorge Rado, Rafael Baquells, Agustin Martinez Solares, Silvia Pasquel, Magda Giner. Two Mexican wrestlers take on a Nazi scientist who has discovered the secret of eternal youth and plans to conquer the world from his base in Atlantis. His plan involves the use of mind control and brainwashing techniques, and his primary goal for Atlantis is to transform it into the Greek-like world of the past.

Screamers (1979) (see FISH-PEOPLE). On a remote island, an unscrupulous man uses fish-creatures created by a mad doctor to plunder the sunken Atlantean "Temple of the Sun God."

Siren of Atlantis (1949; United Artists) (also *Atlantis; Queen of Atlantis*). D: Gregg Tallas. P: Seymour Nebenzal. S: Roland Leigh, Robert Lax. C: Karl Struss. Cast: Maria Montez, Jean-Pierre Aumont, Dennis O'Keefe, Henry Daniel. Two foreign legionaires discover a desert pathway to Atlantis, and find the lost city ruled by Maria Montez.

Warlords of Atlantis (1978); Amicus/Columbia; Great Britain) D: Kevin Connor. P: John Dark. S: Brian Hayles. C: Alan Hume. Cast: Doug McClure, Peter Gil-

more, Shane Rimmer, Cyd Charisse, Lea Brodie, Daniel Massey. Two Victorian explorers travel to the underwater civilization of Atlantis and battle mutant prehistoric beasts, an octopus, and a dictator who's plotting to conquer the world above the sea.
• In this story, the descendants of Atlantis are actually Martians.

The Atomic Bomb *see* Futures on Earth

Automobiles *see* Cars and Vehicular Villains

Elizabeth Bathory: The Bloody Countess

Unlike many of the more famous characters in fantasy films, such as Lawrence Talbot (the Wolf Man), Dr. Jekyll, and Dracula, Elizabeth Bathory was a real person — a Hungarian Countess who lived in the sixteenth century — and her story is based on historical fact. Many crimes are attributed to "The Bloody Countess" (as history has come to call her), including torture, murder, and that crime for which she has become most infamous and which has inspired filmmakers to sit up and take notice — the bathing in the blood of young virgins. Legend states that she summarily killed over 600 young girls to bathe in their blood because she believed the liquid would keep her young. Historical court records bear out that she did indeed torture and murder upwards of 650 people, usually servants and peasant girls, but no evidence of blood-bathing was ever uncovered. No matter, it still makes for a great story and there have been several filmmakers who have successfully exploited the possibilities.

Curiously, Hollywood never braved the torrid tale, and all cinematic versions of her sanguinary story have originated in Europe.

Bathory films seem to be a phenomenon of the 1970s, with the definitive version being Hammer's handsome and well-acted *Countess Dracula* (1970). The early exception is Riccardo Freda's seminal *I Vampiri* (titled *The Devil's Commandment* for American release) made in 1956, the first appearance of the Bloody Countess. The 1970s, led by Britain's Hammer Films, became the decade that gave horror audiences nudity mixed in with their (now ample) blood, and this new freedom (particularly in Europe) opened up distinct advantages for stories involving women bathing in the blood of virgins.

Those interested in an in-depth history of Elizabeth Bathory's life and crimes should seek out the well-researched (but horribly named) chronicle, *Dracula Was a Woman,* by Raymond T. McNally (1983, McGraw-Hill).

Countess Dracula (1970; Hammer/Fox; U.K.) D: Peter Sasdy. P: Alexander Paal. S: Jeremy Paul. C: Kenneth Talbot. Cast: Ingrid Pitt, Nigel Green, Sandor Eles, Maurice Denham, Patience Collier, Peter Jeffrey, Lesley-Anne Down, Leon Lissek, Nike Arrighi, Charles Farrell. Despite the title, *Countess Dracula* features no Draculas and no vampires. It is the story of Countess Elizabeth Bathory, an evil aging noblewoman who discovers the secret of rejuvenation—bathing in the blood of virgins. With her renewed youth she imprisons and impersonates her own daughter before she is exposed and her true age catches up with her. • Director Peter Sasdy also helmed the bloody tale, *Taste the Blood of Dracula* (1970), again for Hammer Studios. • Ingrid Pitt, who stars as Countess Bathory, went on to portray a *real* vampire in two other features, *The Vampire Lovers* (1970) and the anthology film *The House That Dripped Blood* (1971).

Daughters of Darkness (1971; Gemini; Belgium/France/W. Germany) D: Harry Kumel. P: Paul Collet, Alain Guillaume. S: Harry Kumel, Pierre Drouot. C: Eddy van der Enden. Cast: Delphine Seyrig, John Karlen, Danièle Ouimet, Andrea Rau, Paul Esser, Georges Jamin, Joris Collet, Fons Rademakers. Elizabeth Bathory arrives at a deserted seaside hotel and seduces a newlywed couple into her life of blood and perversion. • Actor John Karlen, who plays the sadistic, sexually-troubled husband, is most remembered by TV horror fans as "Willie," the victim/servant of vampire Barnabas Collins on the daytime horror soap opera "Dark Shadows" from the late 1960s.

The Devil's Commandment (1956; RCIP; Italy) (also *Lust of the Vampires*). D: Riccardo Freda. P: Ermanno Donati, Luigi Carpentieri. S: Piero Regnoli, Riccardo Freda. C: Mario Bava. Cast: Gianna Maria Canale, Antoine Balpêtre, Paul Müller, Carlo D'Angelo, Dario Michaelis. A mad doctor in Paris drains the blood of young virgins to keep his beloved Countess eternally young in this update of the Elizabeth Bathory legend. • Director Riccardo Freda walked off this production due to "artistic differences" after ten days of shooting, allowing cinematographer Mario Bava to make his directing debut by finishing the film in two additional days. • Cinematographer Mario Bava later turned full-time director, and has developed somewhat of a cult following. His *Black Sunday* (1960), *Black Sabbath* (1964), and *Planet of the Vampires* (1965) all contain vampiric themes.

The Devil's Wedding Night (1973; Dimension; Italy) D: Paul Solvay (Luigi Batzella). P: Ralph Zucker (Massimo Pupillo). S: Ralph Zucker, Alan M. Harris (Walter Bigari). C: Aristide Massaccesi. Cast: Sara Bay, Mark Damon, Frances Davis, Miriam Barrios, Stan Papps, Sergio Pislar, Stefano Oppedisano. Using the legendary Ring of the Nibelungen, the evil Countess de Vries hypnotically attracts the local virgin girls in order to bathe in their blood and maintain her eternal beauty. Twin brothers come to investigate; one is vampirized and the other vanquishes the unholy creature. • While firmly based in the Bathory legend, *The Devil's Wedding Night* features some traditional vampire trappings as well. The countess has a fanged vampire servant, and the countess herself appears to turn into a giant bat while making love. • Leading man Mark Damon, who plays both twin brothers, is better known to American audiences as the hero of Roger Corman's *House of Usher* (1960). Damon encountered another sort of foreign vampire in Mario Bava's Italian anthology, *Black Sabbath*. • Sara Bay, here playing the Bloody Countess, had earlier raised up Frankenstein's Monster while in the title role of *Lady Frankenstein* (1972).

The Female Butcher (1972; Film Ventures; Italy/Spain) (also *The Legend of Blood Castle; Blood Ceremony*). D: Jorge Grau. P: José Maria Gonzalez Sinde. S: Juan Tabar, Sandro Continenza. C: Fernando Arribas. Cast: Lucia Bosé, Ewa Aulin, Espartaco Santoni, Ana Farra, Franca Grey, Lola Gaos. Count Bathory, husband of Elizabeth Bathory, commits suicide and returns to life as a vampire. He then goes about supplying victims for his wife so she can bathe in their blood to remain eternally young. ¶ From the ad—"Schooled in carnage and blood, she butchered 610 nubile young virgins." • Director Jorge Grau made another, better-known horror film in 1974 titled *Breakfast at the Manchester Morgue,* a *Night of the Living Dead*–inspired zombie movie. • Actress Lucia Bosé was a former Italian beauty queen of 1947.

Immoral Tales (1975; New Line Cinema; France) D/S: Walerian Borowczyk. P: Anatole Dauman. C: Bernard Daillencourt. Cast: Paloma Picasso, Pascale Christophe. In this erotic anthology, only one segment is in the realm of horror. It tells the story of Countess Erszebet Bathory, who gathers young girls in her castle, murders them, and then bathes in their blood to stay eternally young.

Mama Dracula (1980; UGC; France/Belgium) D/P: Boris Szulzinger. S: Boris Szulzinger, Pierre Stenckx, Marc Henri Wajnberg. C: Willy Kurant. Cast: Louise Fletcher, Maria Schneider, Marc Henri Wajnberg, Alexandre Wajnberg, Jimmy Shuman, Jess Hahn, Michel Israel. In this European farce, "Countess Dracula," who

Hammer starlet Ingrid Pitt appearing as Countess Dracula *(1970) (actually Countess Elizabeth Bathory), here taunting her former lover Nigel Green with her new-found beauty.*

bathes in the blood of virgins to stay young (in the same manner as Elizabeth Bathory), is having trouble finding virgins in these modern times. She enlists the aid of a slightly mad scientist to come up with a synthetic blood substitute. Ms. Dracula also has twin sons who sport traditional fangs and drink blood. ¶ "I am experiencing a terrible shortage of 'virgin' blood." • Louise Fletcher (Countess Dracula) is often remembered for her sinister role in *One Flew Over the Cuckoo's Nest* (1975), and Maria Schneider (heroine) for her role in *Last Tango in Paris* (1972). • This is the first and only (to date) humorous treatment of the Countess Bathory legend. Lines such as, "You're dead Countess Dracula, dead as a doornail," abound.

The Return of the Wolfman (1980) (see WEREWOLVES — SPAIN'S 'WALDEMAR DANINSKY' SERIES) (also *The Craving*). This ninth film in the Waldemar Daninsky werewolf series also features the evil Countess Elizabeth Bathory, here depicted as a traditional vampire. The Countess and her werewolf servant are executed in the sixteenth century. Graverobbers remove the silver cross embedded in Waldemar's heart, and the countess is revived by three students searching for the hidden tomb. The two creatures go at each other, and the werewolf is victorious when he rips out the throat of the vampiress. ¶ "Religious bastards! I'll return again. I'll rise from my ashes and convert your godfearing world into an inferno of death and blood!" — Countess Elizabeth Bathory. • Rather than tapping into the legend of Elizabeth Bathory, the filmmakers simply borrow her name and turn her into a more traditional vampire and satanist. No mention is made of bathing in the blood of virgins.

Bats

The bat has gained its monster reputation by way of the vampire legend. In a great many vampire films, the lead bloodsucker is seen transforming himself (or herself) into a bat. This chapter, however, focuses only on those films in which a bat is truly a bat, not a vampire. Therefore the films listed here include only bats of natural, not supernatural, origin. The one exception is *Kiss of the Vampire* (1963), which has a cross-reference listing in this chapter due to its climax in which a legion of bats are called forth by the heroes to attack a castle full of vampires (turning the tables, so to speak, on their supernatural relations). Bats, as this section can attest, can stand on their own as menaces. Hordes of killer bats have been used to great effect in *The Abominable Dr. Phibes* (1971), *Chosen Survivors* (1974), and *Nightwing* (1979). This section also includes mutated forms of bats such as the scientifically enlarged brute known as *The Devil Bat* (1941) which Bela Lugosi trains to do his murderous bidding, and the half-bat, half-human creatures featured in *The Bat People* (1974) and *The Twilight People* (1972; a Dr. Moreau–like story which features a flying bat-person).

The Abominable Dr. Phibes (1971) (see MADMEN — EARLY PSYCHOS). The mad Dr. Phibes employs the ten biblical curses from the Old Testament, including bats, to dispatch those he feels wronged him.

The Bat People (1974; AIP) D: Jerry Jameson. P/S: Lou Shaw. Cast: John Beck, Marianne McAndrew, Michael Pataki, Stuart Moss, Arthur Space, Paul Carr, Pat Delaney. A biologist is bitten by a bat and mutates into a bat-creature (the real "Batman"?).

Chosen Survivors (1974; Columbia) D: Sutton Roley. P: Charles Fries, Leon Benson. S: H. B. Cross, Joe Reb Moffly. Cast: Jackie Cooper, Bradford Dillman, Richard Jaeckel, Alex Cord, Diana Muldaur. Eleven people take refuge in a deep underground bomb shelter to escape what they think is a nuclear attack (it is only a test). Killer vampire bats invade the shelter and begin to feed off the cast members. • *Chosen Survivors,* though an American production, was shot in Mexico (where filming is cheap).

The Devil Bat (1941; PRC) (also *Killer Bats*). D: Jean Yarbrough. P: Jack Gallagher. S: John Thomas Neville. C: Arthur Martinelli. Cast: Bela Lugosi, Suzanne Kaaren, Dave O'Brien, Hal Price, Donald Kerr, Guy Usher. As Dr. Carruthers, Bela Lugosi plays a scientist working for a perfume manufacturer and raising enlarged killer bats in his off hours. These bats he sends out to murder those who've wronged him. The bats attack all those wearing a special shaving lotion which Lugosi gives to his intended victims. ¶ "You hate this strange oriental fragrance, even when you sleep, as you did before I made you big and strong. Now, if you detect the fragrance in the night, when you're awake, you will strike!"—Lugosi talking to his pet devil bat.

• *The Devil Bat* was the first horror film to be made by PRC (Producers Releasing Corporation), an independent company that churned out many a low-budget potboiler in the 1940s. PRC reached their zenith with the effective, moody ghost story, *Strangler of the Swamp,* in 1946. • In 1946, PRC reworked this same basic plot into *The Flying Serpent* (with George Zucco in the Lugosi role), but instead of a giant killer bat we have a giant killer reptile/bird. • Also in 1946, PRC released a sequel, *Devil Bat's Daughter,* but no devil bats appear (except in one flashback sequence), and it is a straight mystery-thriller focusing on the late Dr. Carruthers' daughter. Incredibly enough, Lugosi's character — so evil in the original film — is totally exonerated in the sequel, which complete negates all the events of the original *The Devil Bat!* • This was somewhat of a turning point in Lugosi's career, as his film roles continued to go downhill from here, with increasingly more frequent appearances in films for poverty-row studios like Monogram (for which he made nine features from 1941 to 1944).

Kiss of the Vampire (1963) (see VAMPIRES — HAMMER'S UNDEAD) (also *Kiss of Evil*). At the climax, a horde of bats are conjured up by the Van Helsing–like professor to attack the castle of Ravenna and kill the vampires residing therein.

Nightwing (1979; Columbia) D: Arthur Hiller. P: Martin Ransohoff. S: Steve Shagan, Bud Shrake, Martin Cruz Smith. C: Charles Rosher. Cast: Nick Mancuso, Kathryn Harrold, David Warner, Strother Martin, Steven Macht, Ben Piazza, George Clutesi. In the Arizona desert, a huge colony of rabid vampire bats terrorize the local community. ¶ As the film closes, a factual blurb appears on the screen stating, "In recent years, vampire bats were discovered and destroyed in a cave in Val Verde County near Del Rio, Texas." • Carlo Rambaldi, the creator of E.T., provided the special visual effects for this film, including a large number of flying bat models. • American Indian actor George Clutesi went from vampire bats to mutant bears when he played a similar role this same year in *Prophecy* (1979). • Director Arthur Hiller didn't imbue his killer bats with nearly as much sensitivity as he did with his actors in *Love Story* (1970).

Twilight People (1972) (see MAD SCIENTISTS). In this low-budget remake of *Island of Lost Souls* (1933), a mad scientist creates animal-people, including a panther-woman, a wolf woman ... and a flying bat-man.

Bears

Up until 1976's *Grizzly,* bears have generally been given benign treatment in the movies and on television (with the likes of Baloo, Br'er Bear, Gentle Ben, and Yogi). Naturalists will say that bears are more of a nuisance than a monster — they'll leave you alone if you do likewise. Now that's not to say that upon occasion one won't go on a rampage. The occasional Grisly Grizzly story involving an attack on hikers attests to this. Although bears are quite humane and loving with their own significant others, you certainly wouldn't run up to one in the wilderness and give it a hug, but you might admire it from a distance.

In this particular subspecies of films, you'll see bears depicted as strong-willed monsters (and smarter than the average bear). These pictures are an offshoot of the nature-strikes-back formula, where for one reason or another the animal kingdom rebels against humankind for disrupting its environment. *Day of the Animals* (1977) and *Prophecy* (1979) are two prime examples of the pollution angle. Then there are the basic killer-bear movies (*Grizzly,* 1976; *Claws,* 1977), hairy clones of the popular killer shark classic, *Jaws* (1975).

Killer bears seem to have run their course, enjoying a brief heyday in the late 1970s, and admittedly, their passing has "bear"ly been noticed. Their distant relatives from the nature-strikes-back order can be found in the following sections: BATS, BIRDS, BUGS, CATS, CRABS AND CRUSTACEANS, DOGS, RATS, and SNAKES.

Claws (1977) (also *Devil Bear*). D: Richard Banslach, Robert E. Pierson. P: Chuck D. Keen. S: Chuck D. Keen, Brian Russell. C: Chuck D. Keen. Cast: Jason Evers, Leon Ames, Myron Healey, Anthony Caruso, Carla Layton, Glenn Sipes. *Claws* is another killer-bear movie in the vein of the previous year's *Grizzly* (1976). ¶ "A few well-placed slugs will turn him into a rug." • The lead actor, Jason Evers, is best remembered by horror fans as the man so in love with his fiancée that he kept her decapitated head alive on a table (though not above taping her mouth shut when annoyed by her nagging tone) in *The Brain That Wouldn't Die* (1959).

Day of the Animals (1977; Film Ventures International) (*Something Is Out There*). D: William Girdler. P: Edward L. Montoro. S: William Norton, Eleanor E. Norton. C: Bop Sorrentino. Cast: Christopher George, Leslie Nielsen, Lynda Day George, Richard Jaeckel, Ruth Roman, Michael Ansara, Paul Mantee. A contaminated ozone layer causes various woodland animals to turn on a group of backpackers hiking in the mountains, including one particularly ferocious bear. ¶ "For centuries they were hunted for bounty, fun and food ... *Now It's Their Turn!*" — poster ad line. • Both Christopher George and Richard Jaeckel faced the *Grizzly* (1976) the year before (you'd think that after the first one they'd have learned enough to stay out of the woods). • Male lead Christopher George and female lead Lynda Day George were husband and wife. • Director William Girdler had earlier directed *Abby* (1974), a take-off on *The Exorcist,* and *Grizzly* (1976), an offshoot of *Jaws.* Perhaps *Day of the Animals* is his answer to *The Birds* (1963)? • Girdler suffered a premature death in 1978 while scouting locations for a new movie in the Philippines.

Grizzly (1976; Film Ventures) (also *Killer Grizzly*). D: William Girdler. P/S: David Sheldon, Harvey Flaxman. C: William Asman. Cast: Christopher George, Richard Jaeckel, Andrew Prine, Joan McCall, Joe Dorsey, Charles Kissinger. A huge killer bear is loose in a national park forest in this blatant attempt to ride in on the big money wake left by *Jaws,* made the previous year. The parallels are striking. There's the unscrupulous park overseer who refuses to close the forest to campers; a trio of mismatched characters going alone into the woods only to have the tables turned to where the hunters become the hunted; a bear-hunting expert brought in (to fill Robert Shaw's moist shoes from *Jaws*); and a killer bear story told around a campfire, reminiscent of Shaw's "Indianapolis" shark attack tale; not to mention the big blow-out of a climax. ¶ "You know that the average grizzly, he's about, uh, seven feet tall. This one here is at least 15 feet." • Though billed as "18 feet of gut-crunching man-eating ter-

ror," *Grizzly* only measured up to a somewhat shorter 15 feet. • Actor Richard Jaeckel was buried alive by the titular terror in true-to-life Grizzly fashion in which the bears buries its prey and later returns to eat it. • Director William Girdler later found himself again giving direction to a thespian bear in *Day of the Animals* (1977). • Producer/writer Harvey Flaxman played the part of a reporter in the film. • It took a bazooka to finally bring down the title titan.

Prophecy (1979; Paramount) D: John Frankenheimer. P: Robert L. Rosen. S: David Seltzer. C: Harry Stradling, Jr. Cast: Talia Shire, Robert Foxworth, Armand Assante, Richard Dysart, Victoria Racimo, George Clutesi. Robert Foxworth plays an environmentalist caught between lumber mill industrialists, local Indians, and a huge mutant killer bear (the result of careless polluting). • Mercury ("the only liquid that isn't wet"), dumped into the river, was the cause of the grisly (or is that "grizzly"?) mutations. • Screenwriter David Seltzer also penned the screenplay for the 1976 megahit *The Omen.* • Lead actress Talia Shire is the younger sister of famed director Francis Ford Coppola. • 7'2" tall Kevin Peter Hall made his Hollywood debut as the monster mutant bear. Hall went on to make a career out of man-in-monster-suit roles like *Predator* (1987) and *Harry and the Hendersons* (1987).

Son of Kong (1933) (see APE GIANTS). The first beast to do battle with the title titan is a giant bear.

Big Bugs *see* Bug Giants

Bigfoot

Here we have the American Northwest's version of the Abominable Snowman. When a series of "sightings" made in the early 1970s generated nationwide interest, the cinema market demanded a flurry of furry adventures about the Bigfoot or "Sasquatch." Of all the many myths and monster legends, the Bigfoot is one of the more documented oddities, as even live (though ultimately unconvincing) footage of the supposed creature has turned up, shot by Roger Patterson. Many of the subsequent Bigfoot films were documentary-like in style, playing up the authenticity angle desired by audiences of the time. Occasionally these docu-dramas would step outside of these parameters of pseudo-reality (*Bigfoot,* 1971; etc.), but generally they tried to maintain a sense of realism. Numerous sightings have been reported and many scientists have agreed that speculation on their existence may be justified.

Still, no one has ever caught one alive, and there remains no real proof, only circumstantial evidence of the existence of Bigfoot. The Bigfoot is primarily a modern screen phenomenon of the 1970s and early 80s and its interest and respectability quickly waned. Most of these films were made by the lower-budget outfits, and a definitive movie on the subject still remains to be seen.

Big Foot — Man or Beast? (1975) D: Lawrence Crowley. This documentary-styled account of the Bigfoot legend features some (supposedly) actual footage of the Northwest "Sasquatch."

Bigfoot (1971; Univeral Entertainment) D: Robert F. Slatzer. P: Anthony Cardoza. S: Robert F. Slatzer, James Gordon White. Cast: Christopher Mitchum, John Carradine, Lindsay Crosby, Joi Lansing, Judy Jordan. The legendary "Bigfoot" captures women for breeding purposes in the Pacific Northwest. ¶ "It was beauty that did him in." • James Stellar played the title creature.

Boggy Creek 2 (1985) (also *Barbaric Beast of Boggy Creek Part 2*). D/P: Charles B. Pierce. Cast: Cindy Butler, Serene Hedin, Chuck Pierce. An anthropologist leads an expedition into the wilds of bayou country where an old hermit has captured one of Bigfoot's offspring in this sequel to *The Legend of Boggy Creek* (1973). • Producer/director Charles B. Pierce also produced, directed, and wrote the original *Legend of Boggy Creek* (1973).

The Capture of Bigfoot (1979; Studio Film Corporation) D/P: Bill Rebane. S: Ingrid Neumeyer, Bill Rebane. C: Bela St. John, Ito. Cast: Stafford Morgan, Katherine Hopkins, Richard Kennedy, Otis Young, John Goff, Wally Flaherty, John Eimerman, Randolph Scott, George Buck Flower. In this outing, Bigfoot runs amok in the city.

Creature from Black Lake (1976; Howco International) D: Joy Houck, Jr. P: Jim McCullough. S: Jim McCullough, Jr. C: Dean Cundey. Cast: Dub Taylor, Jack Elam, Jim McCullough, Jr. A pair of young anthropologists travel to the Louisiana bayous in search of a bigfoot-like creature that lives at Black Lake. • Cinematographer Dean Cundey went on to bigger and better things, photographing John Carpenter's *The Fog* (1980) and *The Thing* (1982).

The Curse of Bigfoot (1972; Universal Entertainment) D: Don Fields. S: J. T. Fields. Cast: William Simonsen, Robert Clymire, Ruth Ann Mannella. A lecturer at a high school recounts an encounter with Bigfoot. ¶ "The story of five students who will never be the same!" — ad line. • Universal Entertainment took an unreleased students-on-field-trip-encounter-hairy-monster film from the 1960s and spliced in new wraparound footage to create this "new" feature.

Harry and the Hendersons (1987; Universal) D: William Dear. P: William Dear, Richard Vane. S: William Dear, William E. Martin, Ezra D. Rappaport. C: Allen Daviau. Cast: John Lithgow, Melissa Dillon, Margaret Langrick, Joshua Rudoy, Kevin Peter Hall, David Suchet, Don Ameche. This first (and only) Bigfoot comedy is a Spielbergesque story about a middle class family who takes in a huge smelly Bigfoot. • The film is based on a story by comedian Brad Garrett that was written as a pilot for an intended 30-minute comedy sitcom. Now, long after the film's release, the TV series has gotten the green light (though it remains to be seen if it will truly materialize). • The creature's makeup was designed by Rick Baker, and worn by 7'2" Kevin Peter Hall.

In Search of Bigfoot (1975; Bostonia Film Production) D/P: Lawrence P. Crowley, William F. Miller, J. H. Moss. C: Lawrence P. Crowley. Narrator: Phil Tonkin. This documentary chronicles an expedition through Washington led by Robert Morgan, a man who claims he saw the Bigfoot as a child, and has dedicated his life to search out the elusive creature.

The Legend of Boggy Creek (1973; Howco International) D/P/C: Charles B. Pierce. S: Earl E. Smith. Cast: Willie E. Smith, John P. Hixon, John W. Oates, Jeff Crabtree, Buddy Crabtree. This docu-drama features a Sasquatch-like beast in the Boggy Creek regions.

Night of the Demon (1980) D: Jim Wasson. S: Paul Cassey. Cast: Mike Cutt, Joy Allen, Richard Fields. Students encounter a Bigfoot and its baby while searching for the legendary missing link.

Return to Boggy Creek (1978; Bayou Productions) D: Tom Moore. P: Bob Gates. S: Robert Bethard. Cast: Dawn Wells, Dana Plato. Three kids are helped by Bigfoot during a storm. • Despite this title, the film is not a sequel to *The Legend of Boggy Creek* (1973). • Actress Dawn Wells is best remembered as the sweet brunette Mary Ann from TV's "Gilligan's Island" and Dana Plato as Kimberly on "Different Strokes."

Screams of a Winter Night (1979) (see ANTHOLOGIES). One campfire story told by the kiddies features the legendary bigfoot.

Birds

A bird is defined as a "warm-blooded vertebrate distinguished by having the body more or less completely covered with feathers and the forelimbs modified as wings" (Webster's). There are 8,500 different species of birds in the world. These wondrous creatures are often used as symbols. For instance, owls are associated with wisdom, the dove stands for peace, the vulture is a symbol of death, and the bald eagle represents freedom. Birds are of great value to humans in several ways — by consuming carrion, eating harmful insects, and providing us with meat and eggs. But ... what if they turned against us? This question was asked and definitively answered by Alfred Hitchcock in the ultimate nature-strikes-back terror film, *The Birds* (1963). Several imitations and variations (including one oddity called *The Vulture*, 1966, which featured a creature with the body of a buzzard and the head of Akim Tamiroff) tried to ride in on its tailfeathers, but most were simply turkeys. For the height of avian terror, one must fly with *The Birds*.

Beaks: The Movie (1987; Ascot Entertainment Corporation) (also *Birds of Prey*). D/P/S: Rene Cardona, Jr. Cast: Christopher Atkins, Michelle Johnson, Sonia Infante, Salvador Pineda, Carol Connery, Gabriele Tinti. Not a spoof as the title suggests, but a deadly serious (and far inferior) clone of *The Birds* (1963) in which our ornithological friends strike back due to man's careless treatment of the environment. ¶ "You don't have a wing of a prayer" — ad line.

The Beast with a Million Eyes (1955) (see ALIENS — INVADERS ON EARTH: THE 50S). An alien possesses the minds of various animals, even turning a flock of innocent birds into bloodthirsty attackers.

The Beastmaster (1982) (see SWORD AND SORCERY). The musclebound hero is able to telepathically communicate with a variety of animals, including a hawk. He can see through its eyes and get a birds-eye-view of the bad guys.

The Birds (1963; Universal) D/P: Alfred Hitchcock. S: Evan Hunter. C: Robert Burks. Cast: Tippi Hedren, Rod Taylor, Jessica Tandy, Suzanne Pleshette, Ethel Griffies, Veronica Cartwright, Charles McGraw, Ruth McDevitt. For a reason never explained, various types of birds conduct an all-out assault on the sleepy town of Bodega Bay in this ornithologist's worst nightmare. ¶ "I have never known birds of a different species to flock together. The very concept is unimaginable. Why, if that happened, we wouldn't have a chance. How could we possibly hope to fight them?!" • *The Birds* was three years in preparation before its final release. • It is based on a short story by Daphne du Maurier (which in turn is supposedly based on factual incidents). • It took a full week to film the one scene in which Tippi Hedren is trapped in a room with the attacking birds, a scene which lasts a mere two minutes onscreen. • Rather than the usual melodic soundtrack, the film's "music" is made up of electronic duplications of bird noises (bird calls, wing flapping, etc.). • Tippi Hedren, who played the blonde beauty Melanie Daniels, retired from filmmaking and now runs a big cat park/reserve with her husband in California. • Rod Taylor, who played Mitch Brenner (the hero), is no stranger to horror and sci-fi. One of his earliest roles was in *World Without End* (1956), and one of his best was as the time traveler in *The Time Machine* (1960). • The final scene, in which thousands of birds sit covering the landscape as far as the eye can see, took thirty-two separate pieces of film to create.

Blood Freak (1972) (also *Blood Freaks*). D/P: Steve Hawkes, Brad Grinter. C: Ron Sill. Cast: Steve Hawkes, Dana Cullivan, Heather Hughes, Tera Anderson, Bob Currier, Anne Shearin. A young drifter named Herschell meets a pair of sisters — one spouts bible quotes and the other is into the "far out" drug scene. He tries some form of super-marijuana, which turns him into an instant drug addict. After getting a job at a poultry farm, Herschell eats some experimental turkey meat which transforms him into a capon-monster with the body of a man and the head of a giant, drug-addicted, mutant turkey. He goes about making gobbling noises and killing female drug addicts to drink their tainted blood. In the end,

This two-minute sequence in which Tippi Hedren is trapped in a closed room with The Birds *(1963) took director Alfred Hitchcock a full week to film.*

Herschell realizes it's all been a drug-induced hallucination and seeks redemption from his wild ways in the bosom of the Lord (which the onscreen narrator drives the moral home for us high-risk viewers: "This has been a story based partly on fact, partly on probability"). ¶ "Gosh Herschell, you sure are ugly." • The editor for this obscure, amateurish turkey (ouch), Gil Ward, also provided the film's insipid musical score.

Burn, Witch, Burn (1962) (see VOODOO) (also *Night of the Eagle*). In this frightening tale of voodoo magic at an English college, the stone statue of a giant hawk is brought to life to terrorize the hero.

The Cyclops (1957) (see HUMAN GIANTS).

A bold ad extolling the merits of the invading anti-matter giant alien buzzard known as The Giant Claw *(1957).*

Due to radiation, a remote valley in Mexico is home to gigantic wildlife, including an oversized falcon.

The Flying Serpent (1946; PRC) D: Sherman Scott. P: Sigmund Neufeld. S: John T. Neville. C: Jack Greenhalgh. Cast: George Zucco, Ralph Lewis, Hope Kramer, Eddie Acuff, Wheaton Chambers, James Metcalfe, Henry Hall. George Zucco plays a professor who's found the fabled treasure of Montezuma, *and* the legendary reptilian bird (known to the Aztecs as "Quetzalcoatl") which it guards. After using the six-foot flying creature to murder a few locals, the case turns into a media farce when a handsome radio crime-solver arrives on the scene. Zucco then falls into the predictable pattern of covering up killings until he himself falls victim to his nasty killer bird. ¶ "The head appeared dragon-like, the wings feathered, a long reptilian tail trailing behind it as it flew through the sky. It is my opinion that only three people have seen this monstrous creature and lived."

Food of the Gods (1976) (see ANIMAL GIANTS). In the Northwest backwoods, a group of people must battle giant animals (the result of eating some mysterious substance bubbling up from the ground) including a roost of giant chickens(!)—a screen first.

The Giant Claw (1957) (see ALIENS—INVADERS ON EARTH: THE 50s). A giant bird (resembling a mangy buzzard) flies in from some other "antimatter galaxy" to invade the Earth and wreak havoc in a fowl fit of feathered fury.

Hex (1973) (see WITCHES, WARLOCKS, AND CULTS). In 1919, an early version of a motorcycle gang runs afoul of two young sisters on an isolated farm, the half-breed daughters of an Indian shaman. When one of the bikers attacks her sister, the eldest daughter uses her powers of Indian magic to call down a large owl which attacks and kills the offending gang member.

Ladyhawke (1985) (see SWORD AND SORCERY). An evil sorcerer's curse causes a beautiful young girl to become a hawk by night, while her valiant lover becomes a wolf by day—thus they can never be together in human form.

Mysterious Island (1960) (see SEA MONSTERS). A comical gigantic dodo-like bird menaces a few survivors on the Mysterious Island before young Michael Callan jumps onto its back and knifes it. Later, we see the party eating the world's biggest drumstick. ¶ "I wonder how many minutes it would take to cook in a slow oven." • The bird's actual cause of death is a bullet fired from the gun of Captain Nemo.

Plucked (1967; Summa Cinemat. and Cine Azimut/Les Films Corona; Italy/France) (also *A Curious Way to Love; Death Has Laid an Egg*). D: Giulio Questi. P: Franco Marras. S: G. Questi, Franco Arcalli. C: Dario Di Palma. Cast: Gina Lollobrigida, Ewa Aulin, Jean-Louis Trintignant, Jean Sobieski, Renato Romano, Giulio Donnini. A chicken farmer hatches a plan to kill his wife but he puts all his eggs in one basket and his plot doesn't fly. During the proceedings, radioactivity creates live headless mutant chickens, and a man is turned into chicken food. • Famous Italian actress and glamour girl Gina Lollobrigida made one foray into the realm of the fantastic when she played Esmeralda opposite Anthony Quinn's Quasimodo in the 1957 version of *The Hunchback of Notre Dame.*

The Raven (1963) (see POE FILMS—THE CORMAN CYCLE). In this broad comedy about a group of wizards, Peter Lorre (as a bumbling, totally incompetent magician) spends much of the film in the form of a talking raven (the result of irritating the high wizard).

The Seventh Voyage of Sinbad (1958) (see SINBAD). Among his adventures, Sinbad encounters a giant two-headed bird (the mythological beast known as a "Roc").

The Vulture (1966; Paramount; Britain/U.S./Canada) (also *Manutara*). D/P/S: Lawrence Huntington. C: Stephen Dade. Cast: Robert Hutton, Akim Tamiroff, Broderick Crawford, Diane Clare, Philip Friend. A scientist uses his matter transmitter on the dead bodies of a man and vulture. The resulting monstrosity menaces a local family, sweeping down to fetch up its intended victims. Only its bird legs and claws are seen until the climax when the creature is fully revealed to be a man-sized vulture with the head and arms of Akim Tamiroff. ¶ "Big black bird like a vulture with a human face—and what was even more horrible, a pair of human hands."

Zombie 3 (1983) (see ZOMBIE FLESH EATERS). Towards the beginning of this Italian zombie gut-muncher, a busload of girls is attacked by a flock of chemically contaminated birds (à la Alfred Hitchcock).

Blobs

Although the common term "blob" didn't really take shape (if you'll pardon the expression) until the 1958 cult classic *The Blob* was released, blobbish substances were featured earlier in the decade by British filmmakers (in *The Creeping Unknown* and *X the Unknown,* both 1956; and *Enemy from Space,* 1957). With all manner of creatures imaginable filling the drive-in screens, it was only a matter of time until filmmakers, always searching for a new angle, thought up a monster without any tangible shape—one that was merely a monstrous menacing mass. The Blob was a totally unique type of creature, with no popular precedent in films or folklore. The idea of being dissolved alive is truly frightening, particularly by an amorphous mass that can slime in through the tiniest crack under a door, slither up through a drainpipe, or squeeze through the smallest grating. This quality of nowhere-to-hide terror is what made the original *The Blob* (1958) such fun and inspired numerous reworkings and even an out-and-out remake in 1988. The originator of *The Blob* was actually a consultant to the Boy Scouts of America named Irvine Millgate, who said, "What I want to think up is a movie monster that is not a guy dressed up in a suit, not a puppet, but some kind of a form that's never been done before. I want it to do things that will undo mankind as we know it if it's not arrested or destroyed. But I want the destruction to be something that Grandma could cook up on her stove on an experimental Sunday afternoon." And so *The Blob* oozed onto the screens and into the nightmares of America.

The Angry Red Planet (1960) (see MARS). One of the alien creatures encountered by a group of astronauts landing on Mars is a gigantic blob which envelops one of the crew members.

The Blob (1958; Paramount) D: Irvin S. Yeaworth, Jr. P: Jack H. Harris. S: Theodore Simonson, Kate Phillips. C: Thomas Spalding. Cast: Steve McQueen, Anita Corseaut, Earl Rowe, Olin Howlin, Steve Chase, John Benson. A blob, carried to Earth in a meteorite, oozes through a sleepy town. Young Steve McQueen, the world's oldest teenager, attempts to warn citizens of the danger, with little result, until it rampages through a midnight spook show. In the finale, the Blob is air lifted to the Arctic to be kept in cold storage. ¶ "There's a man here with some sort of parasite on his arm. It's assimilating his flesh at a frightening speed. I may have to get ahead of it and amputate ... I don't know what it is or where it came from." • Director Irvin S. Yeaworth, Jr., was a Methodist minister who was talked into making the picture by Jack H. Harris (who also co-produced the 1988 remake). Harris convinced Yeaworth that the money made from the films could be used to help spread the word of God. Screenwriter Theodore Simonson was also a minister. • *The Blob* was shot in 31 days (in the state of Pennsylvania), but the special effects took an additional nine months to complete. Producer Jack H. Harris estimated that this cult classic has raked in well over $40 million. • Jack H. Harris had originally planned to use Tony Franciosa or Ben Gazarra for the lead until Steve McQueen (the understudy) took over the role. Harris referred to McQueen as a "dirty jerk, an opinionated pain in the ass." Despite his feelings however, Harris did think his work in the picture was superb. He had thought about casting him in his next two films — *The 4D Man* (1959), and *Dinosaurus!* (1960), but he just couldn't take working with McQueen anymore after *The Blob*. • The Blob monster was made out of silicone and tinted with vegetable coloring. A slime-covered barrage balloon was used in some sequences, pulled by fishing line.

The Blob (1988; Tri-Star Pictures) D: Chuck Russell. P: Jack H. Harris, Elliott Kastner. S: Chuck Russell, Frank Darabont. C: Mark Irwin. Cast: Kevin Dillon, Shawnee Smith, Donovan Leitch, Jeffrey DeMunn, Candy Clark, Joe Seneca, Del Close. This updated version of the original features a far more resourceful (and violent) Blob. Instead of landing on Earth in a meteorite, this Blob was created as a biological weapon by military science. ¶ "Our little experimental virus seems to have grown up into a plasmic lifeform that hunts its prey." • The organism is destroyed by a machine gun–toting girl who blows it into ice crystals after it's been frozen ... all, that is, except a small chunk which a religious revivalist keeps in a glass jar. • "Terror has no shape," proclaimed the posters. The extensive special effects showed us such wonders as a six-foot man getting sucked head first down a four-inch drain pipe.

Caltiki the Immortal Monster (1959; Allied Artists) D: Robert Hampton, Mario Bava. P: Bruno Vailati. S: Philip Just. C: Mario Bava. Cast: John Merivale, Didi Sullivan, Gerard Herter, Daniela Rocca, Giacomo Rossi-Stuart, Gay Pearl, Daiele Pitani. Archeologists encounter a huge blob inside a cave under a Mayan temple in Mexico. After initially killing the substance, fragments of Caltiki take shape again later in the film until it grows big enough to envelop a house. The blob is then dispatched by tanks and flame throwers at the climax. ¶ "Caltiki is the one, the only, immortal God. When her mate appears in the sky, the power of Caltiki will destroy the world." • Early ads on the film carried the slightly altered title, *Caltiki the Undying Monster*. • The movie is based upon an ancient Mexican legend. The film's pressbook reported that the studio put on a worldwide search for a subterranean lake in a cave large enough for a camera crew to maneuver in.

The Creeping Terror (1964; Crown International) D/P: Argyle Nelson. S: Robert Silliphant, Alan Silliphant. C: Maury Gertsman. Cast: Vic Savage, Argyle Nelson, Shannon O'Neil. A blob-like creature creeps out of a wrecked spaceship and terrorizes the countryside. ¶ "Despite Brett's inquiries about what Martin had seen in the spacecraft, he avoided specific details for fear of disturbing her more than she was. If the truth were known, Martin was more than a little disturbed himself." • This infamous no-budget blob film features an alien monster constructed of foam that needed five prop men inside to make it move.

The Creeping Unknown (1956; Hammer/ United Artists; U.K.) (also *The Quatermass Xperiment*). D: Val Guest. P: Anthony Hinds. S: Richard Landau. C: Walter Harvey. Cast: Brian Donlevy, Margia Dean, Richard Wordsworth, Lionel Jeffries, Jack Warner, Thora Hird, Gordon Jackson. An astronaut returns from space and then

Perched upon scaffolding within Westminster Abbey is the blob from The Creeping Unknown *(1956), which is electrocuted at the climax by Professor Quatermass.*

mutates into a giant, tentacled blob. ¶ "What manner or shape of thing do we look for now?" • This feature film really began as a six-part British TV serial called "The Quatermass Experiment." • Richard Wordsworth (who played the doomed astronaut) was quoted in a "Radio Times" interview as saying, "That film has been with me ever since.... The cactus bit was great fun. My face was covered with rubber solution and I had spikes growing out of my arm. Jane Asher played the little girl the monster meets. I had to lurch at her and knock the head off her doll. As soon as the scene was finished there she was crying. Naturally I knelt down to say, 'There, there,' and everybody started yelling at me, 'Get back, you fool!' Of course I was terrifying her. I'd quite forgotten what I looked like." • Executive producer Michael Carreras talked about the title in *Famous Monsters of Filmland* #123: "At home we called our film *The Quatermass Xperiment,* emphasizing its X quality with the eye-catching spelling. "X" in England at that time simply meant that a picture was not children's fare, today

it's for adults only." • Brian Donlevy returned as Professor Quatermass in this film's sequel, *Enemy from Space* (1957).

Enemy from Space (1957) (see ALIENS—INVADERS ON EARTH: THE 50s). (also *Quatermass 2*). Individual alien life-forms bind together inside a pressure dome at Wynnerton Flats to form another gigantic blob-like creature. ¶ "That pipe's been full of human pulp!"

The Flame Barrier (1958; United Artists) D: Paul Landres. P: Arthur Gardner, Jules V. Levy. S: George Worthington Yates, Pat Fielder. C: Jack MacKenzie. Cast: Arthur Franz, Kathleen Crowley, Robert Brown, Vincent Padula, Rodd Redwing. A Mexican jungle expedition finds a missing satellite in a cave with a blobbish substance oozing from it. ¶ "Something deep in the jungle has made the gods angry, the animals die for no reason."

The H-Man (1959; Toho/Columbia; Japan) D: Inoshiro Honda. P: Tomoyuki Tanaka. S: Takeshi Kimura. C: Hajime Koizumi. Cast: Yumi Shirakawa, Kenji Sahara, Ahihiko Hirata, Mitsuru Sato,

Arthur Franz and Robert Brown take on the ever growing mass of alien protoplasm which encircles a satellite and the dead husband of Carol Dahlmann (Kathleen Crowley) in The Flame Barrier *(1958).*

Koreya Senda. Cops and robbers mix with a radioactive liquid blob (created from H-bomb tests) that dissolves people into putrid puddles. ¶ "If man perishes from the face of the Earth due to the effects of hydrogen bombing, it is possible that the next ruler of our planet may be *The H-Man*." • Eiji Tsuburaya, Japan's foremost special effects man, used life-size dolls made of rubber balloons for the melting sequences. He let the air out of them and filmed it in high speed. Then when he projected the scenes at normal speed the dolls appeared to wilt gradually. • When Tsuburaya was young, he began by building his own camera. He then went on to become a cameraman before branching out into special effects.

Son of Blob (1971; Jack H. Harris Enterprises) (also *Beware the Blob*). D: Larry Hagman. P: Anthony Harris. S: Jack Woods, Anthony Harris. C: Al Hamm. Cast: Robert Walker, Gwynne Gilford, Godfrey Cambridge, Carol Lynley, Shelley Berman, Burgess Meredith, Cindy Williams. Geologist Godfrey Cambridge re-turns to the North Pole and brings back a chunk of the Blob. After thawing out, the Blob is back in business, menacing a midwestern town and another pair of teen lovers. • In this sequel, the Blob's first victim is watching TV when the gooey creature attacks. What is he watching? — why, the original 1958 film, *The Blob,* of course. • Actor Burgess Meredith, who played arch criminal "Penguin" on TV's "Batman," appeared in the film as a favor to his friend, director Larry Hagman. Hagman himself plays the part of a hobo who gets devoured by the Blob. • The Blob is finally stopped when it is frozen at an ice rink. • Executive producer Jack H. Harris (who also produced the original) did not consider this film a worthy sequel. "It was too funny and not scary enough," was his assessment (*Fangoria* #53).

Spacemaster X-7 (1958; 20th Century-Fox) D: Edward Bernds. P: Bernard Glasser. S: George Worthington Yates, Daniel Mainwaring. C: Brydon Baker. Cast: Bill Williams, Robert Ellis, Lyn Thomas, Paul

Frees, Thomas Browne Henry, Joan Barry. A space probe returns to Earth covered in a mysterious carnivorous fungus. ¶ "One human contact, one unwitting person who spreads this thing, can carry contagion all over the country, all over the world!" • This picture is notable in that it features the first solo appearance of Moe Howard, one of "The Three Stooges." He appears in a small role as a cab driver.

The Stuff (1985; New World) D/S: Larry Cohen. P: Paul Kurta. C: Paul Glickman. Cast: Michael Moriarty, Paul Sorvino, Andrea Marcovicci, Garrett Morris, Danny Aiello, Scott Bloom. From inside the Earth oozes an addictive yogurt-like food that is actually alive and eats people. ¶ "It moves around all by itself. It moves! I saw it move in the refrigerator." • "Saturday Night Live" alumnus Garrett Morris plays a person who gets eaten from the inside out by the stuff.

The Unknown Terror (1957) (see PLANTS). A woman searching for her brother comes across the legendary "Cave of the Dead" which houses bubbling blobs of deadly fungus. The resident mad doctor creates fungus monsters out of the local natives.

X the Unknown (1956; RKO Radio Pictures; U.K.) D: Leslie Norman. P: Anthony Hinds. S: Jimmy Sangster. C: Gerald Gibbs. Cast: Dean Jagger, Edward Chapman, Leo McKern, William Lucas, John Harvey, Michael Ripper. A radioactive blob-like creature, formed from the Earth's molten core, wreaks havoc along the Scottish moors. The slithering slime released by an earthquake is eventually killed with a lethal dose of radioactivity. ¶ "As long as this thing feeds it will live. And the more it lives the more it will grow." • Poster ads referred to X as an indestructible force: "Machine gun bullets! Dynamite! Flame throwers! Nothing can stop it!" • Executive producer Michael Carreras said of his writer Jimmy Sangster: "We gave Jimmy Sangster his first big film break, entrusting the original screenplay to him, and he came through for us in a big way, eventually becoming one of our [Hammer's] principal creative talents, a triple threat man, as you say, in his capacity as writer, producer, and director." • Anthony Newley, famous London singer/composer and former husband of actress Joan Collins, played Private "Spider" Webb.

Brains

BRAINS is divided up into four categories—DISEMBODIED BRAINS, which refers to films depicting brains outside their usual cranial environment; LIVING HEADS, which refers to severed heads that can sustain life through some kind of scientific or spiritual means; BRAIN SUCKERS, which involves the appetite of someone or something for gray matter; and finally, BRAIN TRANSPLANTS, which features movies about the transferring of a brain into another body, be it human or animal.

The DISEMBODIED BRAIN films began with Curt Siodmak's novel, *Donovan's Brain,* in which the brain of a powerful industrialist (who was killed in a plane crash) is secretly kept alive by an experimenting scientist. Three adaptations of this story have been filmed, the first (and best) being the Erich von Stroheim vehicle, *The Lady and the Monster* (1944). Interestingly enough, Siodmak (a frequent screenwriter) was never asked to adapt his own book into film form, and was even excluded from the one version bearing the original title—the 1953 film, *Donovan's Brain,* starring Nancy Davis (later to become Nancy Reagan).

The Thing That Couldn't Die was a severed head in search of its sixteenth century body—the first of the "Living Head" pictures. This LIVING HEAD subset of films gave us one of the most enjoyably cheesy and outlandish movies in cinema history—*The Brain That Wouldn't Die* (1962). The sight of a makeup-wearing disembodied female head sitting upright in a developer's tray and puffing on a cigarette tells volumes about this low-budget wonder, which in unedited form looks very much like a Herschell Gordon Lewis gore flick (with some style, flair, and wit added). The idea of a living head was not simply an isolated American aberration, it was an international phenomenon. In 1959, no less than four films on the subject were produced by four different countries — *The Head* (W. Germany), *The Living Head* (Mexico), *Man Without a Body* (U.K.), and, of course, the ultimate head-on-a-table movie, *The Brain That Wouldn't Die* (U.S.; though not released until 1962, it was produced three years earlier).

As far as BRAIN SUCKERS go, Mexico gave us a front row seat in the theater of the absurd with Abel Salazar as *The Brainiac* (1961). This brain-eating picture featured a warlock who resembles some sort of paper-maché devil dwarf. With a bulbous head that inflates and deflates for horrific emphasis, a long pointed nose, an even longer 12-inch forked tongue, and lobster pincers for hands, *The Brainiac* is one of the most ludicrously fun monsters to ever suck brains.

While one might think that films about the possibility of brain transplants would be of a more somber nature, transplanted brains were ending up in everything from apes (*Monster and the Girl*, 1941) to robots (*Colossus of New York*, 1958) to gangsters (*Black Friday*, 1940). Of course, the Frankenstein films were the true pioneers of the BRAIN TRANSPLANT movies. Those Frankenstein movies which feature brain transplants will only be cross-referenced here, however, with their main entry located in the FRANKENSTEIN'S MONSTER chapter.

Disembodied Brains

Blood Diner (1987) (see CANNIBALS). Two brothers dig up the corpse of their uncle and remove his brain. The brain (brought to life by cult incantations and stored in a jar) then tells them to set up a cannibalistic blood banquet so they can bring an ancient Goddess back to life in a new body.

The Brain (1962; Governor; U.K./W. Germany) (also *Vengeance*). D: Freddie Francis. P: Raymond Stross. S: Robert Stewart, Phil Mackie. C: Bob Huke. Cast: Peter Van Eyck, Anne Heywood, Cecil Parker, Bernard Lee, Frank Forsyth. In this overly-talky version of the *Donovan's Brain* story, the name is not Donovan but Max Holt, who's disembodied brain periodically takes over the mind of Dr. Corry, using him to play detective in revealing those persons responsible for Max's "death." ¶ "I hope for your sake, Max, that Dr. Corry cooperates. Otherwise I shall have to fulfill my oldest ambition — to beat out your brains." • This is the third adaptation of Curt Siodmak's novel *Donovan's Brain,* the first two being *The Lady and the Monster* (1944) and *Donovan's Brain* (1953). • Actor Bernard Lee is better known as "M," James Bond's boss. • At the climax, the brain is not destroyed as in the other two versions, and the film ends on a note that indicates the brain will continue to exert its will through Dr. Corry.

The Brain (1988; Brightstar Films) D: Edward Hunt. P: Anthony Kramreither. S:

Barry Pearson. C: Gilles Corbeil. Cast: Tom Breznahan, Cyndy Preston, David Gale, George Buza, Brett Pearson. A brain that grows in size and strength after devouring people is in league with the evil scientist Dr. Blake, host of the popular television show called "Independent Thinking." Blake's program causes its viewers to commit suicide and various acts of murder in a subtly clever scheme to control mankind.

The Brain from Planet Arous (1958) (see ALIENS — INVADERS ON EARTH: THE 50s). An evil oversized alien brain takes over the body and mind of a nuclear scientist, lusts after his girlfriend, and attempts to conquer the world with a show of force.

Donovan's Brain (1953; United Artists) D/S: Felix Feist. P: Tom Gries. S: Hugh Brooks. C: Joseph Biroc. Cast: Lew Ayres, Gene Evans, Nancy Davis, Steve Brodie, Lisa K. Howard, Michael Colgan. When a powerful tycoon dies in an accident, a surgeon decides to try an experimental technique which will keep the disembodied brain alive. The experiment succeeds, but the doctor soon becomes a pawn of the living brain, as the gray matter mass manages to periodically take over his mind and force the doctor to carry out its nefarious schemes. ¶ "But this brain contains all the knowledge and experience of Warren Donovan's entire life. In other words, all his thoughts. The impulses of these thoughts must still be alive." • Leading lady Nancy Davis later married Ronald Reagan and became the first lady, Nancy Reagan.

Fiend Without a Face (1958) (see BRAIN SUCKERS, this section). A scientist inadvertently creates invisible mind-monsters that look like flying brains (when they finally become visible at the film's climax).

Frankenhooker (1990) (see FRANKENSTEIN'S MONSTER — FURTHER FRANKENSTEINS). Jeffrey Franken, a young bioelectrical technician and almost-doctor, assembles a new body for his dead fiancée (killed in a tragic lawnmower accident), using the body parts of New York hookers. He also keeps a living brain with a single eyeball stuck into it alive in a fishtank — an early experiment. ¶ Mother (eyeing the brain): "Oh Jeffrey, what is it?" Jeffrey (puzzled): "I'm not sure."

Frankenstein Island (1981) (see FRANKENSTEIN'S MONSTER — FURTHER FRANKENSTEINS). Before he died, Dr. Frankenstein perfected a very startling theory which utilizes an intermediary — a disembodied human brain — as a connecting link for transmission from beyond the grave.

Journey to the 7th Planet (1962) (see ALIENS — ENCOUNTERS IN OUTER SPACE). An international space team lands on Uranus and does battle with a giant alien brain.

The Lady and the Monster (1944; Republic) D/P: George Sherman. S: Dane Lussier, Frederick Kohner. C: John Alton. Cast: Erich von Stroheim, Vera Hruba Ralston, Richard Arlen, Mary Nash, Sidney Blackmer, Lane Chandler. Set in the Arizona desert, a scientist comes across a plane crash victim whose brain he removes and then experiments on. As the brain begins to develop, it starts to send telepathic messages to a lab assistant, until the disembodied brain is finally able to direct the controlled assistant to do its bidding. ¶ "When you try to solve the mysteries of nature it doesn't matter whether you experiment with guinea pigs or human beings. • This film is the first to be based upon the extraordinary Curt Siodmak novel, *Donovan's Brain*. A top screenwriter in his own right, Siodmak was *not* offered a chance to adapt his own work for

the film. • Richard Arlen's real name is Richard Van Mattimore.

The Man with Two Brains (1983) D/S: Carl Reiner. P: David V. Picker. S: Steve Martin, George Gipe. C: Michael Chapman. Cast: Steve Martin, Kathleen Turner, David Warner, Paul Benedict, Richard Brestoff. In this parody of mad doctor films in general and *Donovan's Brain* in particular, Steve Martin plays the world's foremost brain surgeon who has developed the "Screw Top Method of Skull Removal." David Warner is the mad scientist who keeps disembodied brains alive. Martin falls in love with one of the bodyless brains and plans to put the brain he loves into the beautiful body of his evil, scheming wife.

Mind Killer (1987; Flash Features) D: Michael Krueger. P: Sarah H. Liles. S: Michael Krueger, Dave Sipos, Curtis Hannum. C: Jim Kelley. Cast: Joe McDonald, Christopher Wade, Shirley Ross, Kevin Hart, Tom Henry, Diana Calhoun, George Flynn. This shot-on-video cheapie ("filmed entirely in Denver, Colorado") is about a nerdish loser who uncovers a 30-year-old manuscript on "total mind control." From reading the paper he develops mental abilities which eventually culminate with his brain literally popping from his head and taking on a life of its own.

Slime City (1989) (see WITCHES, WARLOCKS, AND CULTS). At the climax, when the heroine is dismembering her possessed boyfriend (now a slime-monster), she hacks off his head. But it's still alive and it directs its body to keep coming after her. Finally, she stabs a knife through the disembodied head, causing it to split open and allow the brain to crawl out. The brain crawls across the floor until she hacks it up into little bits with a cleaver.

The Space Children (1958) (see ALIENS — BENEVOLENT ALIENS). A small brain from space arrives on Earth to put an end to the nuclear arms race. It resides in a coastal cave and gets larger and larger throughout the picture.

Living Heads

Beast of Blood (1970; Hemisphere; Philippines/U.S.) (also *Beast of the Dead*). D/P/S: Eddie Romero. C: Justo Paulino. Cast: John Ashley, Celeste Yarnall, Eddie Garcia, Liza Belmonte, Alfonso Carvajal. This follow-up film to *The Mad Doctor of Blood Island* (1969) has the evil Dr. Lorca keeping

the living head of the "chlorophyll monster" alive on a table.

The Brain That Wouldn't Die (1959/62; AIP) D/S: Joseph Green. P: Rex Carlton. S: Doris Brent. C: Stephen Hajnal. Cast: Herb Evers, Virginia Leith, Leslie Daniel, Eddie Carmel, Adele Lamont. A young brain

Young British actor Michael Ray points at the glowing alien brain which controls
The Space Children *(1958).*

surgeon experimenting at his country estate attempts to keep the head of his fiancée alive after she's been decapitated in an auto accident. He sets out to find the perfect body to go with his lover's head. A terribly deformed monstrosity (the result of earlier failed experiments) gets out from behind a locked room at the climax and tears up everything, including the arm off an assistant's shoulder. ¶ "Like all quantities, horror has its ultimate — and I'm that." • Television and initial video prints were missing some of the goriest scenes in the film. Those scenes include an arm being torn from its socket, and the poor victim's death throes as he leaves bloody smears all over the lab. Another edited segment showed the monster biting a chunk out of the surgeon's neck. The piece of flesh that was being chewed and finally thrown to the floor was actually a hunk of liver. • There was also a proposed scene involving a rat drinking the blood from the tubes that kept the head alive (and then going after the helpless head) but this idea was scrapped when the rat refused to take direction. • Producer Rex Carlton's first suggested title for the film was *I Was a Teenage Brain Surgeon*. It was then changed to *The Head That Wouldn't Die* before finally settling on *The Brain That Wouldn't Die*. The script was written in about three days, and the budget came in around $60,000. • The picture was completed in the fall of 1959, but didn't find its way into theaters until 1962. American International, the company which finally decided to distribute the film, was responsible for cutting the gore (as well as some tame titillation) scenes, shortening the film by about ten minutes.

Bride of Re-Animator (1990) (see ZOMBIES). The disembodied living head of Dr. Hill is back from the first film and re-animated once more. With its powers of mind control, it lets loose a group of re-animated corpses left over from the first movie and forces a weak-willed doctor to graft a pair of bat wings onto its disembodied head, enabling the head to fly about. ¶ "Look at you now, you're nothing but a dead-head, a no-*body*."

Day of the Dead (1985) (see ZOMBIE FLESH EATERS). In one scene from this George Romero zombie gore-fest, one of the protagonists is menaced by the still-living head of a zombie he had just decapitated.

Dr. Hackenstein (1988) (see FRANKENSTEIN'S MONSTER — FURTHER FRANKENSTEINS). Dr. Elliot Hackenstein is intent upon building a new body for his dead wife (who is now only a head). While his wife's head isn't really *alive* per se (its lips don't move when it speaks), it does manage to communicate with the doctor and goad him on in his search for female parts. ¶ "No wonder I have a headache, I'm only a head!"

The Frozen Dead (1966; Seven Arts/Warner Bros; U.K./U.S.) D/P/S: Herbert J. Leder. C: David Boulton. Cast: Dana Andrews, Anna Palk, Philip Gilbert, Karel Stepanek, Kathleen Breck. A Nazi sympathizer attempts to revive the bodies of Hitler's henchmen. Their bodies have been partially dismembered and their brains have been removed. A woman is killed and her disembodied head, kept alive in a box on the table, warns others of his nefarious scheme via mental telepathy.

The Head (1959; Trans-Lux; W. Germany) D/S: Victor Trivas. P: Wolfgang Hartwig. C: Otto Reinwald, Kurt Rendel. Cast: Horst Frank, Michel Simon, Karin Kernke, Christiane Maybach, Paul Dahlke, Helmuth Schmid. A psychopathic doctor uses "Serum Z" to keep its inventor's head alive while he sets about finding a beautiful new body to transplant onto the head of the deformed woman he loves. ¶ "Your brain made you great, the rest doesn't count." • Kindly Professor Abel initially proves the success of his "Serum Z" by keeping the disembodied head of a dog alive. • This picture features art direction by Hermann Warm, who worked on the 1919 version of *The Cabinet of Dr. Caligari* as a set designer. • Ad lines from this film leaned towards camp: "Meet the scientist with the completely detached point of view." • The distributor's publicity department suggested employing such gimmicks as getting local barbers and hairdressers to participate in giving "the works" and "head jobs" to lucky contest winners.

Horror Rises from the Tomb (1972) (see WITCHES, WARLOCKS, AND CULTS). Taking a page out of *The Thing That Couldn't Die* (1958), this gory Spanish import features Paul Naschy as an evil nobleman beheaded for witchcraft in 1454. When his modern-day descendant returns to his ancestral home, the still-living head is uncovered and it uses its hypnotic powers to control people and ultimately rejoin its body. ¶ "There is no repose for me while my severed head continues to be separated from my body." • The disembodied head bit is only a small portion of the film (unlike *The Thing That Couldn't Die*), with most of the bloody deeds and diabolical mayhem taking place after the warlock is whole again and has regained his power.

The Living Head (1959; Azteca; Mexico) D: Chano Urueta. P: Abel Salazar. S: Frederick Curiel, A. Lopez Portillo. C: Joseph Ortiz Ramos. Cast: Abel Salazar, Ana Luisa Peluffo, Maurice Garces, German Robles, Antonio Raxel. A living Aztec head casts a spell over the archeologist who uncovers it. ¶ "Alive for centuries without a body! See and talk to the living head in person!" — ad line.

Man Without a Body (1959; Filmplays; U.K.) D: W. Lee Wilder, Charles Saunders. P: Guido Coen. S: William Grote. C: Brandon Stafford. Cast: George Coulouris, Robert Hutton, Michael Golden, Julia Arnall, Nadja Regin, Sheldon Lawrence. A wealthy industrialist, dying from a brain tumor, robs the grave of Nostradamus and takes the head to a brilliant research doctor with the aim of having his diseased brain supplanted by that of Nostradamus. The disembodied head of Nostradamus is revived and exerts its hypnotic power to carry out its own plans. ¶ "You know it's remarkable, this head mounted on your assistant's body. That was quick thinking on your part, doctor." • Actress Nadja Regin was once a guerrilla fighter who endured days without food and drink to escape the Iron Curtain.

Re-Animator (1985) (see ZOMBIES). Medical student Herbert West creates a formula that will reanimate the dead. At one point, he tries it out on the freshly decapitated head of the unscrupulous Dr. Hill. West learns to regret this action when Dr. Hill's living head commands his headless body to brain West and create further headless mayhem. ¶ "Who's going to believe a talking head? Get a job in a sideshow." • This film contains what has to be the ultimate living head scene: Dr. Hill's body holds his disembodied head in his hands and orally assaults the bound heroine. (This scene can only be found in the unrated version — it was edited out of the R-rated release).

Return of the Living Dead Part 2 (1987) (see ZOMBIE FLESH EATERS). This zombie sequel features a disembodied zombie head which continues to pop up at inopportune moments throughout the film.

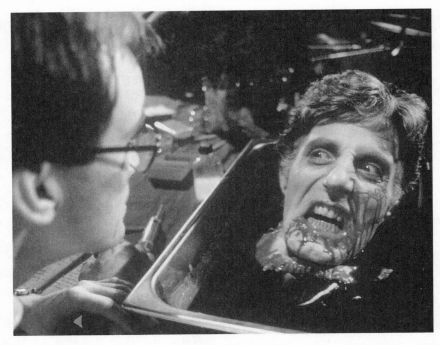

Herbert West (Jeffrey Combs) reanimates the decapitated head of the villainous Dr. Hill (David Gale) in Re-Animator *(1985).*

They Saved Hitler's Brain (1964; Crown International) (also *Madmen of Mandoras*). D: David Bradley. P: Carl Edwards. S: Richard Miles, Steve Bennett. C: Stanley Cortez. Cast: Walter Stocker, Audrey Caire, Carlos Rivas, Nestor Paiva, Scott Peters. The daughter of a neurobiologist and her husband journey to the Caribbean islands to search for her father. There they discover a group of Nazis taking orders from the living head of Adolph Hitler, plotting to take over the world using a deadly nerve gas.

The Thing That Couldn't Die (1958; Universal) D/P: Will Cowan. S: David Duncan. C: Russell Metty. Cast: William Reynolds, Andra Martin, Carolyn Kearney, Jeffrey Stone, Robin Hughes. A young girl with a divining rod uncovers a chest containing the disembodied living head of a warlock. Once it is removed, the head uses its hypnotic powers in an attempt to retrieve a second chest which contains the rest of its body.

The Thing with Two Heads (1972) (see TWO-HEADED CREATURES). The head of a racist doctor is transplanted onto the body of a black convict. At the climax, the extra head is severed from the body ... and miraculously survives.

Zombie 3 (1988) (see ZOMBIE FLESH EATERS). In one particularly gruesome scene from this Italian zombie gut-cruncher, a man opens a refrigerator door only to have a disembodied zombie head leap out at him and rip out his throat.

Brain Suckers

Attack of the Crab Monsters (1957) (see CRABS AND CRUSTACEANS). These giant island crabs absorb their victim's brains into one collective entity. ¶ "That means that the crab can eat his victim's brain, absorbing his mind intact and working." (This results

The living head of a fifteenth century devil worshipper uses his hypnotic powers to make slaves out of a pair of country locals in The Thing That Couldn't Die *(1958).*

in their being able to speak with the voices of their victims.)

Brain Damage (1988; Paramount) D/S: Frank Henenlotter. P: Edgar Levins. C: Bruce Torbet. Cast: Rich Herbst, Gordon MacDonald, Jennifer Lowry, Theo Barnes, Lucille Saint-Peter. Elmer is a talking parasitic creature that likes to eat brains, then excrete an addictive hallucinogenic substance into its host, a young man named Brian. ¶ "Let's get us some hooker. Boy oh boy, I could eat a million of 'em tonight, heh, heh." — Elmer, the brain-sucking talking parasite.

The Brain Eaters (1958; AIP) D: Bruno Ve Sota. P: Ed Nelson. S: Gordon Urquhart. C: Larry Raimond. Cast: Ed Nelson, Alan Frost, Jack Hill, Joanna Lee, Jody Fair, David Hughes. Tiny parasitic creatures emerge from a cone-shaped craft that has come up from the center of the Earth to take over a town. By latching onto the necks of citizens, the Brain Eaters are able to control people's minds. When the furry parasites are removed, the person dies, his mind gone. ¶ "Our social order is pure, innocent." • Leonard Nimoy plays the old man discovered inside the spaceship. He, of course, went on to become the popular Vulcan, Spock, in the "Star Trek" TV series and films. • As well as producing and starring in the film, Ed Nelson also created the title monsters. • *The Brain Eaters* is an uncredited adaptation of Robert Heinlein's novel, *The Puppet Masters*. Heinlein eventually sued American International for copyright infringement. • The film was shot in six days for $26,000. • Director Bruno Ve Sota is probably best remembered as an actor. His credits include *The Giant Leeches* (1959), and *The Wasp Woman* (1959).

The Brainiac (1961; Cinematografica ABSA; Mexico) D: Chano Urueta, Paul Nagle (English version). P: Abel Salazar, K. Gordon Murray (English version). S: Adolpho Lopez Portillo, Frederick Curiel. C: José O. Ramos. Cast: Abel Salazar, Ariadne Welter, David Silva, German Robles, Louis Aragon. The supernatural Baron Vitelius returns to Earth to take vengeance upon the descendants of the inquisitors who had sentenced him to be burned to death in

1661. He possesses the ability to make himself look human, but in his true monstrous persona he sucks the brains out of his victims with a ridiculous 12-inch pronged rubber tongue. This Brainiac also keeps a bowl of brains locked in a cupboard for a tasty between-meal snack. ¶ "I wish they'd find some way to control the subject of Man's studies. A maniac with a lot of knowledge is a threat."

Dead Pit (1989) (see ZOMBIE FLESH EATERS). A zombified mad doctor is transforming patients and staff at the "State Institution for the Mentally Ill" into brain-hungry zombies.

Fiend Without a Face (1958; MGM) D: Arthur Crabtree. P: John Croydon. S: Herbert J. Leder. C: Lionel Barnes. Cast: Marshall Thompson, Kim Parker, Kynaston Reeves, Peter Madden, Stanley Maxted. A scientist's thought transference machine accidentally creates invisible thought monsters that later materialize in the form of leaping brains with spinal tails and antennae. These fiends without faces suck the brains out of humans. ¶ "The brain is gone, sucked out like an egg through the two holes in the neck." • The film is based on the short story, "The Thought Monster," by Amelia Reynolds Long, which was published in *Weird Tales* in 1930. The famous editor of *Famous Monsters of Filmland,* Forrest J Ackerman, was Long's agent and is the man responsible for perking Richard Gordon's (the film's executive producer) interest in the project.

The Incredible Torture Show (1976) (see CANNIBALS). A mad showman stages grotesque cannibalistic acts which includes a woman's brains being sucked out through a straw.

Return of the Living Dead (1985) (see ZOMBIE FLESH EATERS). The flesh-eating zombies in this semi-comic semi-sequel to *Night of the Living Dead* (1968) don't eat just any old flesh, they want only human *brains.* (Apparently, eating brains makes "the pain of being dead" go away.)

Return of the Living Dead Part 2 (1987) (see ZOMBIE FLESH EATERS). Once again a sleepy suburban community is overrun by brain-eating zombies. It is left to a 12-year-old boy, his sister, his sister's would-be boyfriend, and an eccentric doddering doctor to find a way to stop the hungry living dead onslaught in this zombie sequel.

Brain Transplants

Abbott and Costello Meet Frankenstein (1948) (see FRANKENSTEIN'S MONSTER — UNIVERSAL SERIES). Count Dracula and his female assistant plot to transplant the "soft, pliable" brain of Lou Costello into the skull of the Frankenstein mosnter. ¶ "What we need today is young blood — and brains."

The Atomic Brain (1963; Emerson Films) (also *Monstrosity*). D: Joseph V. Mascelli. P: Jack Pollexfen, Dean Dillman, Jr. S: Vi Russell, Sue Dwiggens, Dean Dillman, Jr. Cast: Erika Peters. A widow hires a mad scientist to transplant her brain into a young girl's body. The scientist has some rather odd plans of his own, however, including giving a woman the brain of a cat.

Black Friday (1940; Universal) D: Arthur Lubin. P: Burt Kelly. S: Curt Siodmak, Eric Taylor. C: Elwood Bredell. Cast: Boris Karloff, Bela Lugosi, Stanley Ridges, Anne Nagel, Anne Gwynne, James Craig. A doctor awaiting the electric chair recounts his story of how he transplanted the brain of a gangster into the body of an English professor. The professor then begins to carry out the vengeful plans of the gangster. Seeing the harm he's done, Karloff decides to shoot the professor, which of course, puts him into his present predicament. ¶ "The only possible way to save George Kingsley's life is by a brain transplantation, an operation I performed successfully on animals. This is a dangerous and illegal operation, but a chance to make a great scientific discovery, and perhaps save my friend's life." • When filming began, Boris Karloff was originally scheduled to play the dual role of the professor/gangster and Bela Lugosi was set to play the surgeon. Arthur Lubin, the film's director, decided after viewing film rehearsals, that Karloff wouldn't be believable enough in playing the gangster half of the role so he switched him over to Lugosi's part, then moved Bela down to a supporting role and brought in Stanley Ridges to play the professor. This resulted in a "cheat" to Karloff and Lugosi fans, since in their new roles the two "Titans of Terror" never meet! • A lot of publicity centered around the film's bizarre promotional gimmick of having Lugosi hypnotized by a professional hypnotist named Manley Hall before his big death scene. "Bela Lugosi first to act while in hypnotic trance," claimed the ads. The idea was to give the scene in which Lugosi suffocates to death in a locked closet that added touch of realism. • The aforementioned Manley P. Hall was a friend of Lugosi's and even performed the wedding ceremony for Bela and his wife Hope. • Actress Anne Gwynne was nicknamed the "half-a-murder girl" by the people at Universal after this film. She got the tag when Lubin described his picture as the movie with ten and a half murders, the half being when Gwynne was almost killed. • The significance of "Friday" in the film's title pertains to Friday the 13th, the day Karloff's good friend, Professor Kingsley, was run over by a gangster-driven car.

The Bowery Boys Meet the Monsters (1954) (see MAD SCIENTISTS). A crazy scientist in an old dark house plots to put the brain of one of the Boys into the body of a gorilla.

Brain of Blood (1971; Hemisphere) (also *The Creature's Revenge*). D: Al Adamson. P: Al Adamson, Sam Sherman. S: Joe Van Rodgers, Kane W. Lynn. Cast: Kent Taylor, Regina Carrol, Grant Williams, John Bloom, Reed Hadley, Vicki Volante, Angelo Rossitto, Zandor Vorkov. Kent Taylor plays a mad scientist who transplants the brain of the dying leader of a third world country into the oversized body of a retarded handyman. He then attempts to control his creature and send him out on missions of murder.

Change of Mind (1969; Sagittarius) D: Robert Stevens. P/S: Seeleg Lester, Richard Wesson. C: Arthur J. Ornitz. Cast: Raymond St. Jacques, Susan Oliver, Janet MacLachlan, Leslie Nielsen, Donnelly Rhodes, David Bailey. The brain of a white DA is transplanted into the body of a dead black man. ¶ "Black body—white brain"—ad line.

The Colossus of New York (1958) (see ROBOTS). A father decides to transplant the brain of his genius son into the body of a robot creation so that the son may continue with his valuable research. The young scientist is angered and depressed over being a metallic monster, however, and, unhinged, goes on a killing rampage.

Dr. Butcher M.D. (1979) (see ZOMBIES) (also *Queen of the Cannibals*). Four Americans investigating a tribe of cannibals on a remote island in Indonesia run foul of a mad doctor who's transforming the natives into zombies. He accomplishes this by transplanting the brain of a living person into a lifeless cadaver. ¶ "I must give you an injection that will keep you wide awake so that you will feel as much pain as possible."

Doctor of Doom (1962; K. Gordon Murray; Mexico) D: Rene Cardona. P: William

Calderón Stell, K. Gordon Murray (English version). S: Alfred Salazar. Cast: Elizabeth Campbell, Lorena Vasquez. This first entry in the Mexican wrestling women series features the lady wrestlers thwarting the plans of a mad scientist whose nefarious scheme involves transplanting the brain of an ape into the body of a man. • This was the first of a series of films starring the popular wrestling women. Other features include *Wrestling Women vs. the Aztec Mummy* (1965) and *Rock 'n' Roll Wrestling Women vs. the Aztec Ape* (1962/86).

Frankenstein (1931) (see FRANKENSTEIN'S MONSTER—UNIVERSAL SERIES). Colin Clive unknowingly transplants an abnormal brain into a body he created out of parts of cadavers. ¶ "The brain that was stolen from my laboratory was a criminal brain!"

Frankenstein and the Monster from Hell (1973) (see FRANKENSTEIN'S MONSTER—HAMMER FRANKENSTEINS). Set inside an insane asylum, Baron Frankenstein transplants the brain of an artistic and intelligent person into the grotesque body of an insane killer, with the expected disastrous results.

Ghost of Frankenstein (1942) (see FRANKENSTEIN'S MONSTER—UNIVERSAL SERIES). The brain of Ygor (Bela Lugosi) is transplanted into the body of the Frankenstein monster. ¶ "I have the strength of a hundred men! I, Ygor, will live forever!"

Jesse James Meets Frankenstein's Daughter (1966) (see FRANKENSTEIN'S MONSTER—FURTHER FRANKENSTEINS). Dr. Frankenstein's granddaughter places the brain of a monster into the body of Jesse's bodybuilding buddy. • After the operation she calls the new creation (played by Cal Bolder) "Igor."

The Man Who Lived Again (1936; Gaumont; U.K.) (also *The Man Who Changed His Mind*). D: Robert Stevenson. P: Michael Balcon. S: Sidney Gilliat, John L. Balderston. C: Jack Cox. Cast: Boris Karloff, Anna Lee, John Loder, Frank Cellier, Lyn Harding, Cecil Parker, Donald Calthrop. Boris Karloff plays a scientist who perfects a machine that can transfer brains between bodies (more of a brain *transference* than a transplant). His first experiment places the brain of his elderly assistant into the younger body of a financial wizard. Karloff then decides to place his own brain into the body of the fiancé of his beautiful assistant (Anna Lee). The exchange is made, but before her fiancé dies in Karloff's body, Lee persuades Karloff to reverse the experiment. In a final repenting speech, Karloff asks that his work die with him. ¶ "I shall show you strange things about the mind of

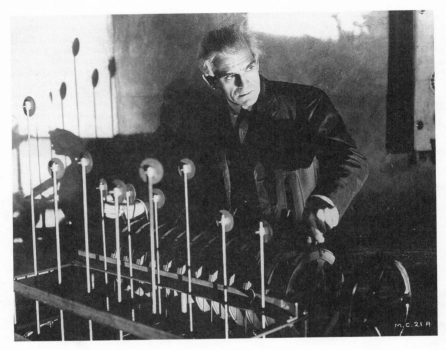

Boris Karloff works his mind transference device in The Man Who Lived Again *(1936).*

man." • For all practical purposes this was really Boris Karloff's first role as a mad scientist and it proved to be such a successful character match that Columbia Pictures went on to produce a string of mad scientist movies for Karloff, beginning with *The Man They Could Not Hang* in 1939. • Anna Lee, born Joanna Winnifrith, was once married to the director of this picture, Robert Stevenson. Some of her other genre outings include *Bedlam* (1946), *Jack the Giant Killer* (1962) and *Picture Mommy Dead* (1966). • This was director Robert Stevenson's only venture into the horror genre, and in 1956 he turned exclusively to family entertainment with Walt Disney Studios.

Man with the Synthetic Brain (1971; Hemisphere) (also *Blood of Ghastly Horror; Fiend with the Electronic Brain; Psycho a Go-Go*). D/P: Al Adamson. S: Dick Poston, Chris Martino. C: Vilmos Szigmund. Cast: John Carradine, Regina Carrol, Kent Taylor, Tommy Kirk. Jewel thieves use a man implanted with an elec-tronically-controlled brain to kill. The scientist who performed the operation is played by John Carradine. • This picture has undergone some remarkable editing in its cinema history. It debuted as *Psycho a Go-Go* in 1965. Then in 1969, additional footage was added and it was released as *Fiend with the Electronic Brain*. Finally in 1971, Al Adamson put more scenes into the picture and released it as it appears today. • The mad scientist's daughter is played by Regina Carrol, who is married to the film's director, Al Adamson.

The Man with Two Brains (1983) (see DISEMBODIED BRAINS, this section). Steve Martin plays a brain surgeon who intends to perform a brain transplant that would create the girl of his dreams.

The Monster and the Girl (1941) (see APES AND MONKEYS). George Zucco transplants the brain of a man framed for murder into the body of an ape. The ape then goes after the gangsters responsible for the murder.

Return of the Ape Man (1944) (see CAVE-PEOPLE). Bela Lugosi plays a deranged scientist who kills his colleague (John Carradine) and transplants his brain into the body of a prehistoric ape-man. The caveman with Carradine's brain has the ability to play the piano, and eventually kills Lugosi.

The Revenge of Frankenstein (1958) (see FRANKENSTEIN'S MONSTER — HAMMER FRANKENSTEINS). Doctor Victor Stein (Peter Cushing) and his assistant transplant the brain of a deformed man into a new body. His new creation turns out to be a cannibalistic murderer. In this story, Cushing himself is attacked and injured by his patients, and has his own brain transferred into another body by his able assistant at the film's end.

Rock 'n' Roll Wrestling Women vs. the Aztec Ape (1962/86; Young American Productions/Rhino; Mexico) D: Rene Cardona, Manuel San Fernando (English version). P: William Calderón Stell, K. Gordon Murray (English version). S: Alfred (Abel) Salazar. C: Henry Wallace. Cast: Lorena Velazquez, Armand Silvestre, Elizabeth Campbell, Robert Canedo, Sonia Infante, Chucho Salinas. A hooded mad scientist transplants a gorilla's brain into a man's body, dubbing him "Gomar." He sends Gomar out to commit various murders until the wrestling women track him down and destroy his lab. For revenge he transplants Gomar's brain into the body of another female wrestler, calling her "Vendetta," and instructs her to kill the heroines during a wrestling match. ¶ "I've done what no one else has been able to do. I've transplanted a gorilla's brain into a living human being." • The Rhino Video company took a 1962 Mexican wrestling women film (*Doctor of Doom*), recut it and added a new soundtrack to produce this "new" feature in 1986.

Bug Giants

(*See also* Bug-People; Bugs)

The "Big Bug" subgenre was born in the midst of the nuclear age decade — the 1950s. It began in 1954, when an intelligently scripted, handsomely produced, and well acted sci-fi thriller unleashed the first (and the best) giant insect menace upon the cinema. *Them* was one of the earliest attempts at injecting nuclear paranoia into a cause and effect formula to create a terrible new kind of plague upon mankind (giant ants). Most insects have extraordinary abilities which allow them to survive in a world much larger than they can hope to cope with. Their wondrous adaptability and resiliency have placed insects in the majority as far as life on Earth goes. Imagine how imposing they'd be if even a small number of them were to grow in size. Ants in particular are incredibly strong, organized, and fiercely savage when they need to be. All the frightening possibilities inherent in this terrifying scenario were explored (to the audiences' delight) in *Them* (1954).

Not only did *Them* garner critical raves, and an Oscar for special effects, it managed to sire an army of insectile offspring. Giant spiders (*Tarantula,* 1955; *Earth vs. the Spider,* 1958), oversized wasps (*The Monster from Green Hell,* 1957), gigantic locusts (*Beginning of the End,* 1957), and even a *Deadly Mantis* (1957) followed suit. *Note:* Though spiders are not truly insects (since they possess eight legs rather than six) the rather loose term of "bug" is usually applied to arachnids, and so they are included here. The 1950s managed to thoroughly saturate the cinema with every manner of big bug imaginable, thanks to directors like Bert I. Gordon (Mr. B.I.G. himself — *Beginning of the End,* 1957; *The Cyclops,* 1957; *Earth vs. the Spider,* 1958). So completely did filmmakers exhaust the subject, that, aside from an occasional lower-berth rehash like *The Giant Spider Invasion* (1975) or *Empire of the Ants* (1977; again from the redoubtable Bert I. Gordon), the big bug movie has gone the way of the dinosaur film (and the dinosaur itself). The one notable exception was a misguided effort carrying the awful moniker of *Blue Monkey.* This 1987 misfire made so little impact that a big bug revival wasn't even considered by

A giant grasshopper from the Bert I. Gordon film, Beginning of the End *(1957), wanders through Chicago before taking on a machine-gun–toting Peter Graves.*

the imitative powers that be in Hollywood. This is unfortunate, though predictable, since modern filmmakers are more than busy with their special effects makeup goop which is best suited to zombie, occult, and alien adventures. Still, the big bug movie may yet make a comeback if some talented director with a brave backer decides to take a risk by jumping into the subgenre once again. Perhaps *Arachnophobia* (1990), a smaller bug variation, may light the torch and lead the way back to its big bug brethren?

See also BUGS for their normal-sized relations, and BUG-PEOPLE for insect hybrids.

Ator, the Fighting Eagle (1982) (see SWORD AND SORCERY). Ator, amongst his many adventures, meets and slays a giant spider.

Beginning of the End (1957; Republic) D/P: Bert I. Gordon. S: Fred Freiberger, Lester Gorn. C: Jack Marta. Cast: Peter Graves, Peggy Castle, Morris Ankrum, Than Wyenn, Thomas B. Henry, James Seay. After eating radioactive vegetables, grasshoppers grow to gigantic proportions and invade Chicago. ¶ "We may be witnessing the beginning of an era that will mean the complete annihilation of man." • A square-jawed Peter Graves said, "Get that equipment on the lake in a boat and I'll be

your 'pied piper,'" as he lured these big bugs to their drowning death in Lake Michigan by duplicating their own mating call. • Bert Gordon began shooting with 200 live grasshoppers and towards the end of production was down to only 12 survivors due to their cannibalistic nature. He said of the experience, "Toward the end of the production we had 188 dead hoppers on our hands and only a dozen live ones! Have you ever tried to invade Chicago with only 12 sickly grasshoppers?" • One of the most audacious cheap effects of all time is Gordon's use of a still photograph to repesent a giant grasshopper-infested building. The result is sometimes hilarious as the little bugs are filmed in slow motion sliding down the two-dimensional photograph.

The Black Scorpion (1957; Warner Bros.) D: Edward Ludwig. P: Frank Melford, Jack Dietz. S: David Duncan, Robert Blees. C: Lionel Lindon. Cast: Richard Denning, Mara Corday, Carlos Rivas, Mario Navarro, Carlos Muzquiz. Volcanic eruptions in Mexico release giant scorpions that ravage the countryside. ¶ "That's how they kill each other, that weak spot on their throat." • Beautiful actress Mara Corday was also seen as the leading lady in another popular big bug film of the 1950s, *Tarantula* (1955). • The amazing special effects were achieved by stop-motion animators Willis O'Brien and Pete Peterson. O'Brien was the genius behind the monsters of *The Lost World* (1925), *King Kong* (1933), and *Mighty Joe Young* (1949). • Cinematographer Lionel Linden *(Destination Moon, The Ten Commandments, The Blue Dahlia)* received Oscar nominations for *I Want to Live* and *Around the World in 80 Days* (for which he won). One of his best segments in this film — the derailing of a train by a giant scorpion — utilized over 60 pieces of film, 15 camera set-ups, and lasted only two minutes and 40 seconds.

Blue Monkey (1987; Canada) D: William Fruet. P: Martin Walters. S: George Goldsmith. C: Brenton Spencer. Cast: Steve Railsback, Gwynyth Walsh, John Vernon, Joe Flaherty, Robin Duke, Susan Anspach. A strange insect gets into a hospital lab and ingests a growth chemical which turns it into a giant bug-monster stalking the hospital corridors. • This unsuccessful film didn't do much to enhance star Steve Railsback's career, who was fresh from another sci-fi flop, 1985's *Lifeforce*. • Creature creator Mark Masters built a giant insect pastiche for this big bug movie. "This insect is as close to a real insect as you could get," claimed Masters in *Fangoria* #69. "We made a nine-foot bug, but each piece of the creature is based on a real insect. The head is from a wasp, the eyes are from a dragonfly, the stomach is from a scorpion, the back parts are from various beetles and it has these arched praying mantis arms."

Cat Women of the Moon (1953 (see THE MOON) (also *Rocket to the Moon*). A man-sized spider inside a moon cave menaces the space crew.

Clash of the Titans (1981) (see MYTHOLOGY). In this mythological fantasy, the young hero battles a number of fantastical creatures, including three scorpions magically grown to the size of a rhinoceros.

Cosmic Monsters (1958; Artists Alliance; U.K.) (also *The Strange World of Planet X*). D: Gilbert Gunn. P: George Maynard. S: Paul Ryder, Joe Ambor. C: Joe Ambor. Cast: Forrest Tucker, Gaby Andre, Martin Benson, Alec Mango, Hugh Latimer, Windham Goldie. A scientist's experiment blows a hole in the Earth's ionosphere with incredible results, the most startling of which is giant insects. A benevolent alien calling himself "Mr. Smith" intervenes to save the Earth. ¶ "*Man* is the cosmic monster." • *Cosmic Monsters* was released on a double bill with *The Crawling Eye*, which also starred "F-Troop" actor, Forrest Tucker. • Martin Benson, who plays the friendly alien, Mr. Smith, was also seen in *The Three Worlds of Gulliver* (1962), *Gorgo* (1962), *Battle Beneath the Earth* (1967), and *The Omen* (1976).

Curse of the Black Widow (1977; TV movie) (also *Love Trap*). D: Dan Curtis. P: Steven North. S: Robert Blees, Earl Wallace. C: Paul Lohmann, Steven Larner. Cast: Tony Franciosa, Donna Mills, Patty Duke Astin, June Lockhart, June Allyson, Jeff Corey, Roz Kelley, Sid Caesar, Vic Morrow. A giant spider-monster menaces a group of near-stars and TV actors. • Director Dan Curtis is best known as the creator of the cult favorite daytime horror soap opera "Dark Shadows" in the 1960s.

The Cyclops (1957) (see HUMAN GIANTS). A group of people discover a valley in which radiation in the soil turns ordinary creatures into giants. At one point they have a brief (and harmless) run-in with a giant spider (of the rear-screen projection variety). • Director Bert I. Gordon did the abysmal special effects himself.

Damnation Alley (1977) (see FUTURES ON EARTH — AFTER THE BOMB). Post-war survivors battle giant scorpions and cockroaches.

The Deadly Mantis (1957; Universal) D: Nathan Juran. P: William Alland. S: Martin Berkeley. C: Ellis Carter. Cast: Craig Stevens, William Hopper, Alix Talton, Don Randolph, Florenz Ames, Phil Harvey. Nuclear testing unleashes a giant praying mantis frozen at the North Pole which then terrorizes various Eskimos, aircraft, and our nation's capital. ¶ "In all the kingdom of the living, there is no more deadly or voracious creature than the praying mantis." • *Deadly Mantis* hero Craig Stevens is more popularly known as the star of TV's "Peter Gunn," and his counterpart, William Hopper, played detective Paul Drake in the long-running "Perry Mason" TV series. • Some of the interesting landmarks the man-

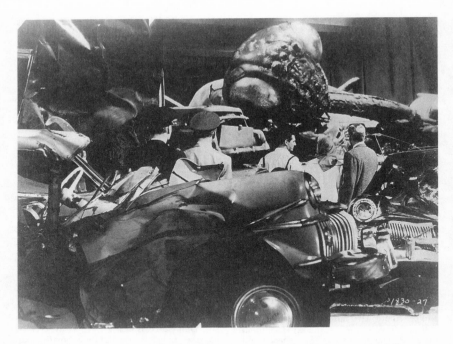

Craig Stevens, Alix Talton, and William Hopper (right side) inspect the fallen mantis lying atop a pile of cars inside the Lincoln tunnel in The Deadly Mantis *(1957).*

tis tours (and destroys) during its stay in Washington D.C. include the Capitol building and the Washington Monument.

Destroy All Monsters (1968) (see JAPANESE GIANT MONSTERS — GODZILLA) (also *Operation Monsterland*). In this ninth Godzilla feature, aliens (known as Kilaaks) intend to let loose all the gigantic beasts on "Monster Island" to decimate the Earth. One of those said beasts is the gigantic caterpillar/moth known as "Mothra."

Earth vs. the Spider (1958; AIP) (also *The Spider* [which, oddly enough, is the title featured on all ads and posters]). D/P: Bert I. Gordon. S: Laszlo Gorog, George Worthington Yates. C: Jack Marta. Cast: Ed Kemmer, June Kenny, Gene Persson, Gene Roth, Hal Torey, Sally Fraser. A huge cave-dwelling spider emerges to menace the citizens of River Falls. ¶ "Do you realize how easy it would be for them to overcome us? Then instead of being the hunters, we'd become the hunted. They'd be our masters, they'd live *on us!*" • Carlsbad Caverns was the location used for the filming inside the spider's lair. • A previous Bert I. Gordon picture, *Attack of the Puppet People* (1958), was shown at the drive-in during this film. • "For shocking, skin-crawling excitement meet face to face 50 creeping tons of black horror," reads the film's publicity. • The spider's asthmatic howling sound effects were later borrowed for the 1959 film, *Beast from Haunted Cave*.

Empire of the Ants (1977; AIP) D/P: Bert I. Gordon. S: Bert I. Gordon, Robert Downey. C: Reginald Morris. Cast: Joan Collins, Robert Lansing, John David Carson, Albert Salmi, Jacqueline Scott, Robert Pine. A group of would-be real estate developers are besieged by superintelligent giant ants. ¶ "Oh my God, they're herding us like cattle!" • Star Robert Lansing is best known to fans as *The 4-D Man* (1959). Lansing later graduated from ants to killer cockroaches (of normal size) in *The Nest* (1988). • One-man moviemaker Bert I. Gordon may be the king of giant bugs with *Beginning of the End* (1957), *The Cyclops* (1957), and *Earth vs. the Spider* (1958), as well as this film to his credit ("credit" being used loosely here).

Food of the Gods (1976) (see ANIMAL GIANTS). Giant mosquitos are seen stinging and sucking a man to death, causing his body to swell to grotesque proportions.

Galaxy of Terror (1981) (see ALIENS—ENCOUNTERS IN OUTER SPACE) (also *Mindwarp: An Infinity of Terror*). On a planet where one's worst fears are realized, a woman astronaut who happens to loathe worms is raped(!) and killed by a giant worm.

Ghidrah, the Three Headed Monster (1965) (see JAPANESE GIANT MONSTERS—GODZILLA). In this fifth Godzilla feature, Godzilla, Rodan and Mothra (the world's first [and only] giant caterpillar/moth) must battle a three-headed, two-tailed flying monster from outer space. Mothra ends up spinning Ghidrah into a cocoon which Rodan and Godzilla knock off into the sea.

The Giant Spider Invasion (1975; Group 1) D: Bill Rebane. P: William W. Gillette. S: Richard Huff, Robert Easton, Bill Rebane. C: Jack Willoughby. Cast: Steve Brodie, Barbara Hale, Leslie Parrish, Alan Hale, Robert Easton, Kevin Brodie. Radiation again is the culprit in this 1950ish spider movie filled with arachnids of differing sizes. ¶ "Bullets don't hurt [the giant spider]. The only thing I've got to stop him here is a traffic light." • This low-budget big bug film featured giant spiders resembling stripped-down Volkswagens with oversized pipe-cleaners stuck on for legs. • Actor Alan Hale finally got off "Gilligan's Island" only to encounter *The Giant Spider Invasion*. • The farmer who discovers the giant spider eggs is actually co-writer Robert Easton. • Heroine Barbara Hale is better known as "Perry Mason" secretary, Della Street.

Godzilla vs. Megalon (1973) (see JAPANESE GIANT MONSTERS—GODZILLA). Godzilla and his cyborg ally, Jet Jaguar, run up against a pair of evil monsters from the alien race known as the Seatopians. One of the "bad guys" is Megalon, a giant death-ray-shooting killer cockroach with drill-like arms.

Godzilla vs. the Thing (1964) (see JAPANESE GIANT MONSTERS—GODZILLA) (also *Godzilla vs. Mothra* [video title]). Once again, one of Mothra's eggs (Mothra, of course, is a giant caterpillar/moth) is taken and exploited by carnival promoters. Meanwhile, Godzilla turns up to tear apart Japan. Mothra, the "good" monster, attempts to stop Godzilla but is killed for its troubles. Not to worry though, because the moth's giant caterpillar-like offspring manage to trap Godzilla in a silky web and topple him off a cliff.

Honey, I Shrunk the Kids (1988) (see SHRINKAGE). Some children are shrunk down to insect size and encounter various gigantic insects (to them anyway), including a giant bee, a terrifying scorpion, and a cute little baby ant the size of a draft horse.

The Horrors of Spider Island (1959; Pacemaker; W. Germany/Yugoslavia) (also *It's Hot in Paradise*). D: Jamie Nolan (Fritz Bottger). P: Gaston Hakim. Cast: Alex D'Arcy. Huge spiders are discovered on a remote island; their bite turns people into big hairy monsters.

The Incredible Shrinking Man (1957) (see SHRINKAGE). As he dwindles away to nothingness, the title character must battle a now-giant spider in order to survive in his vast cellar-world. ¶ "With these weapons I was a man again. I would not die like a helpless insect in the jaws of the spider monster."

Journey to the Seventh Planet (1962) (see ALIENS—ENCOUNTERS IN OUTER SPACE). An alien brain on the planet Uranus tricks a group of astral explorers with a giant spider hallucination. • This particular giant arachnid was actually just tinted footage from the black and white 1958 Bert I. Gordon film, *Earth vs. the Spider*.

Killers from Space (1954) (see ALIENS—INVADERS ON EARTH: THE 50s). Peter Graves discovers gigantic crickets, beetles, and grasshoppers inside the subterranean lair of alien invaders. • Three years later, Peter Graves encountered more giant grasshoppers in *Beginning of the End*. Mr. Graves earns the distinction of being the only actor to star in both of the screen's giant grasshopper films.

The Lost Continent (1968) (see CRABS AND CRUSTACEANS). An ocean liner and its passengers are trapped in the Sargasso Sea where they encounter a lost civilization of Spanish conquistadores and a species of giant hermit crab. The crab is found on an island, and it nearly pinches the head off a man before battling an equally gigantic scorpion.

The Lost World (1960) (see DINOSAURS—LOST WORLDS). An expedition discovers a prehistoric world populated by dinosaurs. The group observes a giant rear-projection spider inhabiting a cave.

Missile to the Moon (1958) (see THE MOON). In this cheap remake of *Cat Women of the Moon* (1953; itself a cheap film), astronauts encounter a giant spider inside a moon cave (along with the titular cat women).

The Monster from Green Hell (1958;

Filmservice Distributing Corp.) D: Kenneth G. Crane. P: Al Zimbalist. S: Louis Vittes, Endre Bohen. C: Ray Flin. Cast: Jim Davis, Robert E. Griffin, Barbara Turner, Eduardo Ciannelli, Vladimir Sokoloff. Two scientists head for the Congo to recover a radioactive rocket which has unleashed giant wasps. ¶ "What happens to life in the airless void above Earth's atmosphere? Will life remain untouched, unharmed by flight through space or will it change into . . . what?" • The gigantic wasps are eventually destroyed by volcanic lava (of the rather poorly superimposed variety). • Extensive safari footage from the 1939 film *Stanley and Livingstone* was used to pad out this film's running time. • The visual effects were created by prolific special effects men Jack Rabin, Louis DeWitt, and Irving Block. Gene Warren produced the stop-motion animation, and it is believed that 50s monster-maker extraordinaire, Paul Blaisdell, designed the cumbersome giant swiveling wasp head whose pincers open and shut while its wings flutter. • Numerous African natives from the Masai, Watusi, Bahuti, Wakumba, and Wareu tribes were used as extras in the film. A suggestion to use the aggressive Karamajo tribesmen of Northern Uganda was vetoed because their attire amounted to something slightly less than a g-string. • *The Monster from Green Hell* was released on a double bill with *Half Human*.

Monster on the Campus (1958) (see CAVE-PEOPLE). The blood of a primitive fish (a coelocanth) causes whatever ingests it to revert to a prehistoric state, including a dog, a man, and a dragonfly, which grows to the size of a hawk after sipping some Coelocanth solution and stiffly buzzes around before being impaled on a table with a knife.

Mothra (1962) (see JAPANESE GIANT MONSTERS—OTHER GIANT JAPANESE MONSTERS). Mothra is a giant caterpillar who, you guessed it, metamorphizes into a giant moth.

Mysterious Island (1960) (see SEA MONSTERS). Captain Nemo has developed a food additive which causes things to grow to enormous proportions, including a gigantic bee, courtesy of the great stop-motion animation wizard, Ray Harryhausen.

Popcorn (1991) (see MADMEN—THE SLICE 'N' DICE WAVE). A college film class stages an old-time horror marathon at a rundown theater, complete with 50s-style gimmicks and hype. During the show, however, the students are killed off by a twisted maniac with a grudge against the heroine. One of the supposed oldie moldie movies shown is called *Mosquito*. Aptly named, it's about mosquitoes grown to the size of cars due to radiation. We get to see quite a bit of footage of this bogus fifties film as these creatures buzz bombers and assault automobiles.

Queen of Outer Space (1958) (see VENUS). A gigantic spider is just one of the menaces found on Venus (apart from Zsa Zsa Gabor and her fellow Venusians).

Rodan (1957) (see JAPANESE GIANT MONSTERS—OTHER GIANT JAPANESE MONSTERS). Giant caterpillar-insects are discovered in a mine, along with two huge eggs. When the eggs hatch, two monstrous pterodactyl-like bird creatures (called Rodans) emerge and level Japan. The giant insects (which Rodan likes to eat) wreak their own form of insectile havoc among the local villagers as well.

Sinbad and the Eye of the Tiger (1977) (see SINBAD). Enlarged through sorcery, a foot-long wasp tries to put the sting on Sinbad and his companions.

Son of Godzilla (1968) (see JAPANESE GIANT MONSTERS—GODZILLA). In this eighth entry in the Godzilla series, the big guy and his son (Minya) must defeat a pair of giant mantises and a deadly giant spider named Spigon.

Tarantula (1955; Universal) D: Jack Arnold. P: William Alland. S: Robert Fresco, Martin Berkeley. C: George Robinson. Cast: John Agar, Mara Corday, Leo G. Carroll, Nestor Paiva, Ross Elliott. A scientist's nutrient formula produces an ever-growing tarantula which escapes and terrorizes the Arizona countryside. ¶ "But what if circumstances were to magnify one of them in size and strength, took it out of its primitive world and turned it loose in ours?" • Clint Eastwood (in one of his first bit parts) drops a lethal dose of napalm on the house-sized tarantula at the climax. • Professor Deemer was played by the man known to TV viewers as Mr. Waverly, the boss of "The Man from U.N.C.L.E.," Leo G. Carroll. • The special effects were created by the talented team of Clifford Stine and David Horsley. Makeup for the meltdown effects of Deemer was provided by Bud Westmore and Millicent Patrick, among others. • Star John Agar, who was once given a premature obituary by Forrest J Ackerman, the popular editor of *Famous Monsters of Filmland* magazine, said of his monster roles, "I think all actors should play opposite monsters at least once!" • The story is based upon a "Science Fiction Theatre" episode, "No Food for Thought," by co-scripter Robert Fresco. • Famous composer Henry Mancini wrote the film's sinister musical score.

James Whitmore is unable to climb out of the Los Angeles storm drains in time to avoid being crushed by the pincer-like jaws of one of Them! *(1954).*

The Thief of Bagdad (1924) (see SWORD AND SORCERY). A thief (Douglas Fairbanks), in love with a Caliph's daughter, tackles a series of terrible foes in order to secure the rights to marry the girl — including battling a giant spider. • The spider creation, made of metal, wood, and wire, reportedly used over 840 leverage principles to give it the illusion of movement.

The Thief of Bagdad (1940) (see GENIES). As the titular thief, Sabu must battle a giant spider to retrieve a magic jewel, the "All-Seeing Eye."

Them! (1954; Warner Bros.) D: Gordon Douglas. P: David Weisbart. S: Ted Sherdeman. C: Sid Hickox. Cast: James Whitmore, Edmund Gwenn, James Arness, Joan Weldon, Onslow Stevens. Nuclear testing in the desert produces 12-foot-long man-eating ants, some of which escape gassing by Department of Agriculture scientists and end up in storm drains beneath Los Angeles. ¶ "When man entered the atomic age, he opened a door into a new world. What we eventually find in that new world, nobody can predict." • *Them!* the very first entry in

the "Big Bug" 50s craze, perked the interest of would-be imitators with gloomy lines like, "Man as the dominant species of life on Earth will probably be extinct within a year." • *Them!* features a variety of interesting supporting players, including Edmund Gwenn, who is best known for his role of Santa Claus in *Miracle on 34th Street* (1947); "Daniel Boone" actor Fess Parker, who portrays a pilot admitted to a mental hospital after seeing the flying ants; and Olin Howlin, who gets a juicy role as the daffy drunkard in the detox ward who rants, "Make me a sergeant in charge of the booze . . . make me a sergeant, give me the booze." Veteran actor Dub Taylor, Leonard "Spock" Nimoy, and 50s regular William Schallert have small parts as well. • Although the nature of the menace was kept as hush-hush as possible during production, the film's poster described *Them!* as "A horror horde of crawl-and-crush giants clawing out of the Earth from mile-deep catacombs!" • Director Gordon Douglas had this to say about the Oscar-nominated ants created by Ralph Ayers: "I asked the editor, 'How does it look?' And he said, 'Fine.' I said, 'Does it look honest?' He said, 'As honest as 12-foot ants can look.'"

The Willies (1990) (see ANTHOLOGIES). The final story, "Flyboy," is about a mean little kid who is obsessed with pulling the wings off flies and making little displays for his "trophies." He steals Old Man Spivey's experimental "Miracle Manure," which he uses to attract and catch the flies. This magical manure causes a batch of flies to grow to gigantic proportions (as big as a man) and these now-giant insects deal out some poetic justice to avenge their fly brethren.

World Without End (1956) (see TIME TRAVEL). A group of astronauts inadvertently travel into a war-ravaged future, and encounter the pitiful remnants of the human race, some ugly-faced mutants, and gigantic spiders.

Bug-People

(*See also* Bug Giants; Bugs)

A popular theme in monster movies has been the scientific melding of human beings with members of the insect world. Perhaps the best rendition of this motif was seen in the now classic 1958 bug-man film, *The Fly,* starring David Hedison. *The Fly*'s success spawned two sequels, followed in 1986 by an excellent remake and its own (inferior) sequel, *The Fly 2* (1989).

Both versions of *The Fly* managed to capture the imagination of the public, producing a monstrous situation that was both repellent and affecting, playing upon audience sympathy. *The Fly* (1958) wasn't the first insect-human seen in cinema, however. *Mesa of Lost Women* used the idea in 1952, with a story about a mad scientist experimenting with spiders and people. His female spider-women were beautiful rather than monstrous, but deadly nonetheless.

Flies aren't the only insects that have been spliced together with mankind. Wasps, beetles, a cockroach, bees, and a moth have also blended with human beings in films. For more listings of insect-related topics see the BUGS and BUG GIANTS sections.

The Beast Within (1982; MGM/UA) D: Philippe Mora. P: Harvey Bernhard, Gabriel Katzka. S: Tom Holland. C: Jack L. Richards. Cast: Ronny Cox, Bib Besch, Paul Clemens, Kitty Moffat, Don Gordon, Ramsay King. A woman is raped by a mysterious creature down South and years later her son begins to transform into a carnivorous bug-monster. • Young actor Paul Clemens transforms into a giant, flesh-eating insect, shedding his skin "just like cicada."

The Blood Beast Terror (1967; Tigon; U.K.) (also *The Vampire Beast Craves Blood*). D: Vernon Sewell. P: Tony Tensor. S: Peter Bryan. C: Stanley Long. Cast: Peter Cushing, Robert Flemyng, Wanda Ventham, Vanessa Howard, David Griffin. A scientist seeks to create a giant moth in order to curtail the bloodlust of his moth-monster daughter, a girl who occasionally transforms into a giant deaths-head moth. ¶ "It was a horrible creature sir — with huge eyes, sir — the wings, the wings, sir!" • Basil Rathbone was signed to play the father of *The Blood Beast Terror* in 1967 but died before filming began (Robert Flemyng inherited the role). • *The Blood Beast Terror* has the dubious distinction of being thought of by star Peter Cushing as his worst film.

Curse of the Fly (1965) (see MAD SCIENTISTS). In this third and final film in the original "Fly" series, there is actually no fly-monster, just further experiments in teleportation resulting in a group of mutants, including a half-man, half-hamster(!) creature. • *Curse of the Fly* is a sequel in name only, for the only connection to the first two "Fly" movies (*The Fly* and *Return of the Fly*) is the use of the Delambre family name and a matter transmission device.

Evil Spawn (1987; American Independent Pictures) D/S: Kenneth J. Hall. P: Anthony Brewster, Frank Bresee. C: Christopher Condon. Cast: Bobbie Bresee, Drew Godderis, John Terrence, Donna Shock, Jerry

Fox, John Carradine. In this no-budget reworking of *The Wasp Woman* (1959), Bobbie Bresee plays an aging actress who ill-advisedly uses a mysterious serum to successfully reverse the aging process. Unfortunately, the serum also has the rather serious side effect of periodically turning her into a nasty bug-monster. • Actress Bobbie Bresee's B-movie career began with her appearance on the cover of the very first issue of *Famous Monsters of Filmland* over 30 years ago. • Former editor of *Famous Monsters* and fright-film fan supreme, Forrest J Ackerman, has a cameo as a pool cleaner. • This direct-to-video feature was shot in 16mm.

The Fly (1958; 20th Century-Fox) D/P: Kurt Neumann. S: James Clavell. C: Karl Struss. Cast: Al Hedison, Patricia Owens, Vincent Price, Herbert Marshall, Charles Herbert. Well-intentioned scientist Andre Delambre (Al Hedison) develops a matter transmitter device and accidentally melds his body with that of a fly. ¶ "As God is my witness I saw the thing. It's unbelievable. I shall never forget that scream as long as I live," declared a shaken Inspector Charas after witnessing the small fly with Andre's head crying "help meeeee!" • Horror actor Vincent Price, who played Hedison's brother, reprised his role in the sequel, *The Return of the Fly,* this time helping the son a bit more successfully than the father. • Screenwriter James Clavell went on to become one of the world's most renowned authors (*King Rat, Shogun, Noble House,* others). • Lead actor Al Hedison later changed his name to David and starred in TV's "Voyage to the Bottom of the Sea." • The story is set in Canada, the birthplace of co-star Patricia Owens. • Noted makeup men Ben Nye and Dick Smith, the creators of the effective Fly head mask worn by Hedison, were teamed again in 1959 for yet another man-monster movie, *The Alligator People.* The Fly mask weighed over 20 pounds despite its formula latex foam compound consistency, and the final bill amounted to $4,500, a great deal in those days. • Nye discussed the Fly makeup in a Verne Langdon article appearing in *Famous Monsters of Filmland* #50: "We began with many sketches of the Fly creature. The story didn't give us much to go on so we had to dream up the physical appearance ourselves. There were so many changes during the actual production that it was difficult keeping up with the pace! We had inserted the eyes into the foam rubber appliance and luckily there was a little way space at the bottom of each eye so at least

Hedison could look down at the floor and see his way clear. The heat from the studio lights doesn't help either, and I think Al lost a couple of pounds during filming. We glued it to a base rubber form of Al Hedison's head, then added a specially made lace hair wig [of] turkey feathers, dyed black for the filament around the eyes, and zipped the whole thing up the back."

The Fly (1986; Brooksfilms/20th Century-Fox) D/P: David Cronenberg. S: Charles Edward Pogue. C: Mark Irwin. Cast: Jeff Goldblum, Geena Davis, John Getz. This graphic remake of the 1958 classic features sympathetic performances and a drawn-out fly transformation culminating in a completely new genetic monstrosity instead of the half-man, half-fly creation of the original. ¶ "I am an insect who dreamt he was a man." • Though he chose to remake the 1958 film, director David Cronenberg stated that he never liked the original version of *The Fly.* • Special effects man Chris Walas won an Oscar for his amazing metamorphical makeover work on Jeff Goldblum.

The Fly 2 (1989; Brooksfilms/20th Century-Fox) D: Chris Walas. P: Steven Charles Jaffe. S: Mick Garris, Jim Wheat, Ken Wheat, Frank Darabont. C: Robin Vidgeon. Cast: Eric Stoltz, Daphne Zuniga, Lee Richardson, Harley Cross, John Getz. This sequel has Martin Brundle follow in his father's insect-like footsteps. He's inherited the fly gene from his father, causing rapid development and eventual mutation into another fly-monster. ¶ "He stole my girl and caused her death. He dissolved my hand and my foot with fly vomit. I have no love for the man. He *bugged* me." • "Like father, like son," read the poster for this 1989 sequel. • In an interesting parallel with the first "Fly" series, the "son" is not killed at film's end and is, in fact, totally cured — just as in *The Return of the Fly,* made 30 years earlier (the sequel to the original *The Fly*). • Chris Walas, the Oscar-winning special effects wizard behind the 1986 remake of *The Fly,* made his directorial debut on this sequel.

Invasion of the Bee Girls (1973; Centaur) D: Denis Sanders. P: Sequoia Pictures. S: Nicholas Meyer. Cast: William Smith, Anita Ford, Victoria Vetri, Rene Bond. This stinging R-rated sci-fi film features William Smith uncovering a nest of buzzy bee-women who are literally loving men to death. ¶ "They'll love the very lives out of your body!" — ad slogan. • Heroine Victoria Vetri is best known as the prehistoric beauty

Special effects man Chris Walas won an Oscar for his makeup work on The Fly *(1986). This photo shows Brundel in the grotesque final stage of his insectile metamorphosis.*

with the pet dinosaur in *When Dinosaurs Ruled the Earth* (1970). • Screenwriter Nicholas Meyer went on to direct the wonderful 1979 Jack the Ripper/H. G. Wells movie, *Time After Time* (1979).

Mesa of Lost Women (1953; Howco) D: Herbert Tevos, Ron Ormand. P: Melvin Gordon, William Perkins. S: Herbert Tevos. C: Gil Warrenton, Karl Struss. Cast: Jackie Coogan, Richard Travis, Allan Nixon, Mary Hill, Robert Knapp, Tandra Quinn (as the sultry spider-woman "Tarantella"). A crazed scientist living on a Mexican mesa produces giant spiders and a formula which

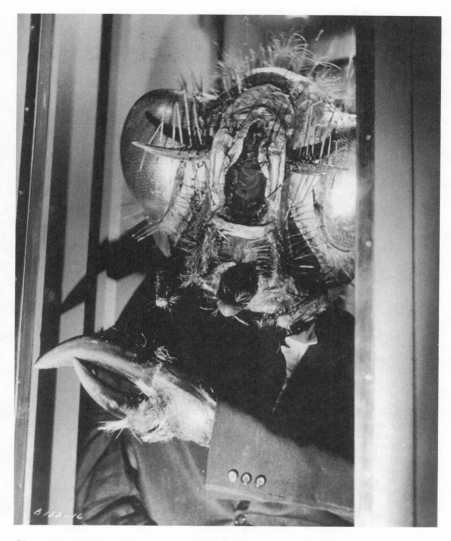

Giant actor Ed Wolff dons the bulb-headed fly head and hairy claw costume in the 1959 "Fly" sequel, Return of the Fly.

gives women a ferocious spider-like persona, but turns men into subservient dwarves. ¶ "Look at this girl, I call her Tarantella . . . if we're successful, I shall have a super female spider!" • Jackie Coogan's mad scientist character "Araña," is Spanish for spider. Most people remember Coogan as Uncle Fester on the TV series "The Addams Family." • George Barrows, the man underneath the ridiculous space-helmeted ape in *Robot Monster* (1953), plays a male nurse named George in this feature. • The 6′3″ actor Allan Nixon first attained prominence as a boxer and then a professional wrestler. • Cinematographer Karl Struss took a giant step backwards in this production after working on classic films like *Island of Lost Souls* (1932), *The Great Dictator* (1940), and *The Fly* (1958).

Metamorphosis (1975; Svenska Filminstitutet; Sweden) D: Ivo Dvorak. P: Bengt Forslund. S: Ivo Dvorak, Lars Foressell. C: Jiri Tirl, Lasse Karlsson, Roland Steiner. Cast: Peter Schildt, Ernst Guenther, Gunn Wallgren, Per Oscarsson, Ingalill Karlsson, Jan Blomberg. A man wakes up to find himself transformed into a giant beetle, alienated from all those around him. • This is the first (and only) full-length film adaptation of Franz Kafka's famous story "Metamorphosis." • Director Ivo Dvorak fled his native Czechoslovakia to seek asylum in Sweden.

A Nightmare on Elm Street 4: The Dream Master (1988) (see DREAMKILLERS). In one particularly revolting scene, Freddy Krueger enters the dreams of a teenage girl and painfully transforms her into a cockroach. He then, of course, squashes her like a bug.

Return of the Fly (1959; 20th Century–Fox) D/S: Edward L. Bernds. P: Bernard Glasser. C: Brydon Baker. Cast: Vincent Price, Brett Halsey, David Frankham, Danielle de Metz, John Sutton. The original Fly's son, Philippe (Brett Halsey), nobly follows in his father's matter-transforming footsteps. He is double-crossed by an assistant, however, and turned into another fly-monster. ¶ "When this same ghastly thing happened to my brother, he still had a human mind and a human conscience. What if Philippe doesn't have the mind of a human, but the murderous brain of a fly?" • Philippe the fly-man was not played by Brett Halsey. The man inside the suit was former circus giant, Ed Wolff. • Ben Nye and Dick Smith, creators of the fly makeup mask for the original, were substituted in this film by Hal Lierley, whose version of the giant fly-head is much bigger (and less

effective). • Director/screenwriter Edward Bernds desperately wanted Herbert Marshall to repeat his role as Inspector Charas but was told Marshall's health at the time prevented him from taking on the role. Bernds' original shooting script contained Charas' name instead of what appears in the final film — Inspector "Beacham." • In Tom Weaver's book, *Interviews with B Science Fiction and Horror Movie Makers,* Bernds describes Vincent Price as, "A delight, no less. Thoroughly professional, always prepared, giving his best to every scene ... his star status and the strength he brought to his performance lifted it out of the B category it might have fallen into."

The Wasp Woman (1959; Allied Artists) D/P: Roger Corman. S: Leo Gordon. C: Harry C. Newman. Cast: Susan Cabot, Anthony Eisley, Michael Mark, Barboura Morris, William Roerick, Bruno Ve Sota. A cosmetic formula made from wasp enzymes makes Susan Cabot look younger but it also periodically turns her into a blood-hungry wasp-monster. ¶ "Miss Starlin is not a human being any longer. She'd kill Mary, as any wasp will kill its enemy, and devour the remains." • Susan Cabot once described how she did all her own stunts, including instances of spitting out chocolate syrup upon the necks of her victims as she pretended to bite them. Concerning her ferocious attacks, Cabot said, "The only way I felt I could convincingly down a bigger person was through swiftness — by coming at them so fast, like a bolt of lightning." • Cabot described how physically demanding the role of a wasp woman could be. At the climax she was stunned when a heavy breakaway bottle hit her in the head, then was nearly asphyxiated by the liquid smoke the prop man threw on her. When she finally tore off her wasp mask so she could breathe, some of her skin came off with it as well.

Bugs

(*See also* Bug Giants; Bug-People)

Of the million-plus species of animals on the Earth, more than 800,000 of them are insects. Every year new species are being discovered. They are an extraordinarily adaptable animal in that they are virtually found everywhere on the Earth, from the polar regions to deserts and jungles. We are usually at war with these multilegged creatures as they continually eat crops and damage property, though they do help pollinate flowers, provide honey, and are food for fish and other animals which are vital to the ecosystem. Life as we know it would cease to exist if all insects were to disappear from the face of the Earth. Bugs come in all shapes and sizes, and many species have been plundered by genre filmmakers. To most humans, bugs are hideous, frightening, and totally alien. For instance, some insects taste with their feet, have ears on their legs or sides, and smell with their antennae. Some have no eyes and some have many. They have enormous strength and are relatively organized. If we had the strength of a flea we could jump 700 feet, or if we were as strong as an ant we could lift four tons. Spiders, centipedes, mites, and ticks are not actually insects (since they have more than six legs), though we generally categorize them in with the loose-termed "Bugs" (and so are included here).

The Abominable Dr. Phibes (1971) (see MADMEN — EARLY PSYCHOS). Phibes employs the ten biblical curses to take vengeance upon his enemies. In this case he employs locusts. • Ingeniously, Phibes lures the locusts to his intended victim by drugging her and covering her while she sleeps with a special brussels sprout sauce.

Arachnophobia (1990; Amblin Entertainment) D: Frank Marshall. P: Kathleen Kennedy, Richard Vane. S: Don Jakoby, Wesley Strick. C: Mikael Saloman. Cast: Jeff Daniels, Julian Sands, Harley Jane Kozak, John Goodman, Brian McNamara, James Handy. A large aggressive lethal spider from a Venezuelan sink-hole stows away in a victim's coffin to invade and infest a small town in America. ¶ "Hey, perk up Lloyd. If we find the spider that did this, you can arrest him." — Hero Jeff Daniels to the piqued sheriff. • "Eight legs, two fangs, and an attitude." — read the comedy-flavored ad slogan. Though there is a comedic figure in the form of John Goodman (from TV's "Roseanne") as the local "Bugs-Be-Gone" exterminator, this film is *not* a "horror/comedy," but a straight horror film with an occasional comedic element. • The initial scenes of the film were shot on location in the jungles of Venezuela. • This is Frank Marshall's directorial debut, but he's no stranger to filmmaking since he produced the "Indiana Jones" trilogy as well as *Who Framed Roger Rabbit* and the *Back to the Future* series. • Steven Spielberg served as co-executive producer along with director Frank Marshall. • The large eight-legged star of the movie was affectionately named "Big Bob" by the production crew. • Five distinct species of spider were employed for the creepy-crawly menaces.

The Bees (1978; New World) D/P/S: Alfredo Zacharias. C: Leon Sanchez. Cast: John Saxon, Angel Tompkins, John Carradine, Claudio Brook, Alicia Encinias. A big corporation captures killer bees from South America to produce honey, but they escape and assault America. ¶ "They prey

on *human flesh!*" — the ad lines promised. • Of historical note, then–President Ford was seen in the film via Rose Bowl Parade footage.

The Believers (1987) (see VOODOO). One scene in this modern tale of voodoo magic has actress Helen Shaver develop an ugly growth on her cheek which bursts to unleash a horde of spindly-legged spiders — the result of a voodoo hex. • "I didn't know how much I was acting when the spiders were walking around on my face," Shaver told *Fangoria* #67. "That was kind of an improved form of acting, like, 'Oh God, can I stay still while they're doing this?!' It took *six* hours of close-ups."

Bug (1975; Paramount) D: Jeannot Szwarc. P/S: William Castle. C: Michel Hugo. Cast: Bradford Dillman, Joanna Miles, Richard Gilliland, Jamie Smith Jackson. Fire-making insects are crossed with cockroaches to create flesh-eating killer bugs. • Producer William Castle, the "Master of Gimmicks" himself (*House on Haunted Hill,* 1959; *The Tingler,* 1959; *13 Ghosts,* 1960; etc.), intended to continue his showmanship with this entry. Castle described the gimmick he'd planned for *Bug:* "During the screening of the picture the roaches will seem to get loose in the theater..." (thankfully it was never tried). • *Bug* was based on the novel, *The Hephaestus Plague,* and was Castle's final production.

Creepers (1985; Dacfilm-Rome; Italy) (also *Phenomena*). D: Dario Argento. S: Dario Argento, Franco Ferrini. Cast: Donald Pleasence, Jennifer Connelly, Dario Nicolodi, Dalila Di Lazzaro. A young girl has the power to control insects in this convoluted thriller involving a maniacal killer.

Creepshow (1982) (see ANTHOLOGIES). In the episode titled "They're Creeping Up on You," E. G. Marshall is besieged by vindictive cockroaches and comes to a messy end. ¶ "I'm going to clear up this damn cockroach problem once and for all."

The Deadly Bees (1967; Amicus; U.K.) D: Freddie Francis. P: Max J. Rosenberg,

Milton Subotsky. S: Robert Bloch, Anthony Marriott. C: John Wilcox. Cast: Suzanna Leigh, Frank Finlay, Guy Doleman, John Harvey, Catharine Finn, Michael Ripper. A buggy bookkeeper creates a deadly bee breed which will attack all those wearing a special scent. • This is the very *first* "killer bee" movie. • *The Deadly Bees* is an adaptation of the novel, *A Taste of Honey,* by H. F. Heard.

Deadly Blessing (1981) (see DEMONS AND DEVILS). During a vivid dream sequence, a spider falls into a girl's open mouth.

Dr. Phibes Rises Again (1972) (see MADMEN — EARLY PSYCHOS). Phibes is up to his old tricks again in this amusing sequel. He devises all manner of clever ways to murder his enemies, including trapping a man in a special "scorpion chair" and then releasing a horde of aggressive scorpions to do their stuff.

Frogs (1972) (see SEA MONSTERS). Ray Milland and family are menaced by assorted nasty reptiles and spiders (who make the first on-screen kill). These creatures are seemingly led by the ferocious frogs in their rebellion against the thoughtlessly polluting humans.

The Giant Spider Invasion (1975) (see BUG GIANTS). Numerous spiders, many of the normal size variety, attack a small town.

Halloween 3: Season of the Witch (1982) (see WITCHES, WARLOCKS, AND CULTS). Not a slasher sequel as the name suggests, but a story about modern members of a Druid cult who manufacture Halloween masks containing microchips from Stonehenge. When a special signal is broadcast over TV, the heads of the tiny tot viewers wearing these diabolical masks explode in a disgusting puddle of crawling bugs and slimy goo.

It Happened at Lakewood Manor (1977; TV movie) (also *Ants; Picnic at Lakewood Manor*). D: Robert Scheerer. P: Peter Nelson. S: Guerdon S. Trueblood. C: Bernie Abramson. Cast: Suzanne Somers, Robert Foxworth, Myrna Loy, Lynda Day George, Gerald Gordon, Bernie Casey. Swarms of killer ants attack a destination resort in this made-for-TV movie. • The same production company also made *Tarantulas, the Deadly Cargo,* which aired the same month. • *It Happened at Lakewood Manor* was released theatrically in Europe.

Kingdom of the Spiders (1977; Dimension Pictures) D: John Cardos. P: Igo Kantor, Jeffrey M. Sneller. S: Richard Robinson, Alan Caillou. C: John Morrill. In this nature-takes-revenge film, some 5,000 tarantulas lay siege to a small desert town. • The veterinarian hero is played by none other

than "Captain Kirk" himself (William Shatner). • Director John Cardos was no stranger to handling non-human actors, having been a "bird wrangler" on Alfred Hitchcock's *The Birds* (1963). • Cardos had no complaints about his arachnid actors, saying, "The tarantulas in *Kingdom of the Spiders* didn't really bother me. Most people don't know anything about them and are very scared of them. While filming, we didn't have any problems — not one person was bitten." (from a 1984 interview in *Cinefantastique*.)

Kiss of the Tarantula (1976; Omni) (also *Shudder*). D: Chris Munger. P: Daniel B. Cady. S: Warren Hamilton, Jr. C: Henning Schellerup. Cast: Suzanne Ling, Eric Mason, Herman Wallner, Patricia Landon, Beverly Eddins. This film follows the life and times of a disturbed young girl who repeatedly uses her pet spiders to carry out acts of vengeance. • The young girl is played by two actresses. Beverly Eddins plays the girl at a young age when she frightens her mother to death with tarantulas. Suzanne Ling then completes the role as the spider-loving girl grown older.

The Legend of Spider Forest (1971; Cupid/Action Plus; U.K.) (also *Venom*). D: Peter Sykes. P: Michael Pearson, Kenneth Rowles. S: Donald and Derek Ford. C: Peter Jessop. Cast: Simon Brent, Neda Arneric, Derek Newark, Sheila Allen, Gerard Heinz. While touring Bavaria, Simon Brent falls for a beautiful "Spider Goddess," whose Nazi father has concocted a nerve drug from spider venom. • At the climax the "Spider Goddess" voluntarily kills herself by joining her father in the burning flames set by the angry locals.

The Naked Jungle (1954; Paramount) D: Byron Haskin. P: George Pal. S: Philip Yordan, Ranald MacDougall. C: Ernest Laszlo. Cast: Charlton Heston, Eleanor Parker, William Conrad, Abraham Sofaer, John Dierkes, Douglas Fowley. A South American cocoa planter marries a wife by proxy and has her brought to the plantation to live with him. After nearly driving each other mad, their existence is threatened by a destructive mass of soldier ants sweeping through the African jungles. Despite tremendous odds, they decide to stay and fight it out with the ants till the bitter end. ¶ "You're up against a monster 20 miles long and two miles wide — 40 square miles of agonizing death. You can't stop it! They're organized, they're a trained army. They're not individuals, they have generals and they think. That's the worst part of these ants — they actually think." • Producer George Pal admitted that most of the ants were made of rubber, "But, for the closeup, where the ant headed straight for the victim's eyes, we had to hunt out a genuine desert ant. We protected the actor with a transparent shield." • The sound of the swarming ants was achieved by recording the fizzing sound produced when ice is put into a glass of coke. That sound was then amplified many times.

The Nest (1987; Concorde) D: Terence H. Winkless. P: Julie Corman. S: Robert King. Cast: Robert Lansing, Lisa Langlois, Franc Luz, Terry Treas. An experimental form of cockroach escapes from a corporate genetics lab and terrorizes a small town. The killer cockroaches also have the nasty habit of mutating into whatever it is they collectively eat, taking the old axiom "you are what you eat" to its ultimate literal conclusion. • First-time director Terence Winkless was an actor and screenwriter before trying his hand at directing on this film. He got his acting start (of sorts) playing one of "The Banana Splits" (the gorilla) on that popular children's TV show. His best-known cinematic credit is co-screenwriter of *The Howling* (1980). • Producer Julie Corman is the wife of low-budget movie mogul Roger Corman (whose film company, Concorde, financed *The Nest*). • *The Nest* is based on the novel by Eli Cantor.

976-Evil (1989) (see DEMONS AND DEVILS). A nerdish high school student dials this number, which turns out to be a hotline to hell. He is possessed by demonic forces, and in one scene uses his newfound evil power to cause a horde of poisonous spiders to emerge from a TV dinner and swarm over and kill a young girl.

Phase 4 (1974; Paramount; U.K.) D: Saul Bass. P: Paul B. Radin. S: Mayo Simon. C: Dick Bush. Cast: Nigel Davenport, Lynne Frederick, Michael Murphy, Alan Gifford, Helen Horton, Robert Henderson. In another revenge-of-nature film, Michael Murphy and friends must wage war against millions of super-intelligent ants in the Arizona desert. • In the most metaphysical ending ever to conclude a nature-strikes-back movie, the hero and heroine are somehow transformed by the seemingly omnipotent ants into a new species (à la *2001: A Space Odyssey*)—neither man nor insect, but a combination of both. • Ken Middleton, who filmed the excellent macro-footage of the ants, also worked on *Bug* (1975). • Director Saul Bass is best known in Hollywood as a film title designer. • *Phase 4* won the Grand Prix at the 1975 Trieste Festival of Science Fiction Films.

Prince of Darkness (1988) (see DEMONS AND DEVILS). The "Essence of Satan" is unleashed and terrible things happen, including one man being eaten from the inside out by a disgusting array of bugs.

The Savage Bees (1976; TV movie) D/P: Bruce Geller. S: Guerdon Trueblood. C: Richard C. Glouner. Cast: Ben Johnson, Michael Parks, Paul Hecht, Gretchen Corbett, Horst Buchholz. African killer bees invade New Orleans during Mardi Gras. • Director/Producer Bruce Geller is best known as the creator of the TV series "Mission Impossible." • Screenwriter Guerdon Trueblood co-wrote this movie's 1978 sequel as well *(Terror Out of the Sky)*. • Don Kirshner (of "Rock Concert" fame) co-produced.

Something Wicked This Way Comes (1982) (see WITCHES, WARLOCKS, AND CULTS). At one point in the film, the satanic carnival master, Mr. Dark, unleashes a throng of deadly spiders to carry out his acts of vengeance.

Spider Baby (1968; American General) (see CANNIBALS) (also *The Liver Eaters; Cannibal Orgy or the Maddest Story Ever Told*). Lon Chaney, Jr., is the caretaker for a crazy family of eccentric cannibals. One of the adolescent girls is fascinated with spiders and likes to tie people up and pretend she's got a "big fat juicy spider" stuck in her web, then "sting" the unfortunate with a pair of carving knives. She also keeps pet tarantulas around the house; they get loose and menace the hero.

The Spider Woman (1944; Universal) (also *Sherlock Holmes and the Spider Woman*). D/P: Roy William Neill. S: Bertram Millhauser. C: Charles Van Enger. Cast: Basil Rathbone, Nigel Bruce, Gale Sondergaard, Dennis Hoey, Vernon Downing, Alec Craig. The great detective matches wits with a murderess who collects life insurance policies from her victims then kills them using a highly poisonous spider.

The Spider Woman Strikes Back (1946) (see PLANTS). Despite the misleading title, the focus of the story is on killer plants, not spiders. • Universal used the name and the same actress, Gale Sondergaard, to capitalize on the success of *Sherlock Holmes and the Spider Woman* (1944). There is no real relation to the Holmes film, however.

Squirm (1976; AIP) D/S: Jeff Lieberman. P: George Manasse. C: Joseph Mangine. Cast: John Scardino, Patricia Pearcy, R. A. Dow, Peter MacLean, Fran Higgins, Jean Sullivan. A farmhouse out in the sticks is beset by thousands of carnivorous worms on a killing frenzy, the result of electricity being pumped into the ground by a downed power line. ¶ "An avalanche of killer worms! Writhing across the land in a tidal wave of terror!"—ad line.

The Swarm (1978; Warner Bros.) D/P: Irwin Allen. S: Stirling Silliphant. C: Fred J. Koenekamp. Cast: Michael Caine, Katherine Ross, Richard Widmark, Richard Chamberlain, Ben Johnson, Olivia de Havilland. A star-studded cast gathered by Irwin "Mr. Disaster" Allen is the main attraction of this African-killer-bees-arriving-in-America movie. • Multi-Oscar winning actress Olivia de Havilland made a cameo appearance here—a far cry from starring roles in films such as *Gone with the Wind, To Each His Own,* and *The Snake Pit.* Ms. de Havilland also appeared in the 1965 genre film, *Hush ... Hush, Sweet Charlotte.*

Tarantulas, the Deadly Cargo (1977; TV Movie) D: Stuart Hagmann. P: Paul Freeman. S: Guerdon Trueblood, John Groves. C: Robert L. Morrison. Cast: Claude Akins, Charles Frank, Deborah Winters, Sandy McPeak, Bert Remsen, Pat Hingle, Tom Atkins, Howard Hesseman. A cargo plane crashes and disgorges a load of aggressive South American spiders who terrorize a southwestern town. • Co-screenwriter Guerdon Trueblood also wrote or co-wrote three other made-for-TV killer insect

movies—*The Savage Bees* (1976); *It Happened at Lakewood Manor* (killer ants this time), the same year; and *Terror Out of the Sky* (1978) with killer bees.

Terror Out of the Sky (1978; TV movie) D: Lee Katzin. P: Peter Nelson. S: Guerdon Trueblood, Doris Silverton. C: Michel Hugo. Cast: Efrem Zimbalist, Jr., Dan Haggerty, Tovah Feldshuh, Lonny Chapman, Ike Eisenmann, Steve Franken. A swarm of vicious South American killer bees make its way to North America and invades a small California town. ¶ "The bees are back ... and this time they're really mad"—ad line. • This is a sequel to the 1976 TV movie, *The Savage Bees.*

The Vineyard (1989) (see WITCHES, WARLOCKS, AND CULTS). Through the use of black magic, a modern-day sorcerer causes a torrent of live spiders to disgorge from a young girl's mouth—an arachniphobe's worst nightmare.

The Worm Eaters (1977; New American) D/S: Herb Robins. P: T. V. Mikels. Cast: Herb Robins. Director/Screenwriter Herb Robins also stars in this low-budget wrigglefest about a worm-farmer who talks to worms, eats worms, and turns people into worm-monsters. • At the Las Vegas premiere a worm-eating contest was staged (truth in advertising carried to the extreme?).

Cannibals

With two notable exceptions, cannibalism didn't become a prominent film subject until the late 1960s and early 1970s, when the relaxing of screen censorship and the advent of gore movies (heralded by Herschell Gordon Lewis' ultra-cheap, ultra-bloody exploitation films) brought about just the right atmosphere to get the most out of scenes of people eating one another up on the silver screen.

The earliest film dealing with cannibalism is *Dr. X* (1932), a mad doctor movie about a scientist using synthetic flesh to turn himself into the "moon killer." This killer not only murdered, he also devoured parts of his victims. The theme of cannibalism, however, was touched on merely in passing in this mad scientist film. The only other early cinematic cannibal was *The Demon Barber of Fleet Street* (1936), a.k.a. Sweeney Todd (played by that madman of melodramatics, Tod Slaughter), a barber who turns his murder victims into meat pies to be sold at the bakery next door.

After a few fledgling efforts in the 1960s, such as Herschell Gordon Lewis' impossibly cheap and incredibly gory *Blood Feast* (1963) and the offbeat one-of-a-kind *Spider Baby* (1968), cannibals came into their own in the 1970s. The year of the cannibal turned out to be 1972, when no less than four flesh-eater pictures were unleashed: Two cannibal comedies—*Cannibal Girls* and *The Folks at Red Wolf Inn;*

plus *The Mad Butcher,* with Victor Buono taking over for Tod Slaughter, and Britain's *Raw Meat.*

Cannibalism has also been at the root of more than a few black comedies, best typified by the subtle, satirical, and darkly funny *Motel Hell* (1980), which is arguably the best (and certainly most entertaining) cannibal movie ever made.

Excluded from this section are all of the cannibal zombie pictures (found in the ZOMBIE FLESH EATERS section) begun by *Night of the Living Dead* (1968), in which the dead come back to eat the living. Neither are any other monster or supernatural flesh-eaters included, such as the man-made monster cannibal from *The Revenge of Frankenstein* (1958) or the centuries-old warlock with a penchant for fresh human hearts in *Horror Rises from the Tomb* (1972). Those types of films don't feature "true" cannibals, which are defined as "human beings who eat human flesh" (Webster). Also not included are the many jungle-cannibal films, in which primitive natives are typically shown eating their enemies. Since cannibalism in these instances is not an aberration but a culturally accepted act, we felt that these "mondo" or "exposé" movies (such as *Cannibal Holocaust*) didn't belong here, being a subgenre unto themselves. Bon appétit!

The Beast's Carnival (1980; Dalmata Films/Hori Kikaku Company; Spain/Japan) D/P/S: Jacinto Molina. C: Alejandro Ulloa. Cast: Paul Naschy (Jacinto Molina), Eiko Nagashima, Lautaro Murua, Silvia Aguilar, Azucena Hernandez, Julia Saly, Kogi Maritugu, Mieko Gustanave. Paul Naschy is a thief who steals a load of diamonds. He hides out in a house which turns out to be inhabited by cannibals. • Director/producer/screenwriter Jacinto Molina is actually Spanish horror star Paul Naschy using his real name for his behind-the-camera credits.

Blood Diner (1987; Vestron) D: Jackie Kong. P: Jimmy Maslon, Jackie Kong. S: Michael Sonye. C: Jurg Walther. Cast: Rick Burks, Carl Crew, Rogert Dauer, LaNette La France, Lisa Guggenheim, Max Morris, Roxanne Cybelle. Two brothers kill and dismember nubile young women with the aim of constructing a "perfect body" for Sheetar, an ancient goddess, to inhabit. They serve the leftover body parts at their health food store and acquire a dedicated clientele for their particular type of cuisine. At the climax, they host a "Blood Banquet" which causes the guests to go on a cannibalistic rampage. • Filmmaker Jackie Kong admitted to watching most of Herschell Gordon Lewis' gore films before making this, and that Lewis' *Blood Feast* (1963) was a major inspiration for this effort. • Kong, one of the few women directors in horror, has often been criticized for making these low-budget exploitation pictures "without any female sensibility." In response, she delivered this message in *Fangoria* #70 to "the ladies out there": "I've shown *Blood Diner* to the executive in

charge, who's female; I'm female; and I've shown it to women who are executives at major companies, and we all love it. Any girl with a good sense of humor will love this."

Blood Feast (1963; Box Office Spectaculars) D/C: Herschell Gordon Lewis. P: David F. Friedman. S: Allison Louise Downe. Cast: Connie Mason, Thomas Wood, Mal Arnold, Lyn Bolton, Scott H. Hall, Toni Calvert. In Miami, Egyptian caterer Faud Ramses murders young women for their body parts to be used in his "Egyptian feast," which he intends to feed to guests at a dinner party and thus fulfill a ritual which he thinks will resurrect the ancient goddess he worships. ¶ From the poster: "Nothing so appalling in the annals of horror! You'll recoil and shudder as you witness the slaughter and mutilation of nubile young girls—in a weird and horrendous ancient rite! (An admonition: if you are the Parent or Guardian of an impressionable adolescent *Do Not Bring Him or Permit Him to See This Motion Picture.*) More grisly than ever in *Blood Color!*" • This is the very first gore film. As filmmaker Herschell Gordon Lewis (the "Godfather of Gore") himself told Todd McCarthy in *King of the Bs*: "*Blood Feast* I've often referred to as a Walt Whitman poem—it's no good, but it's the first of its type and therefore it deserves a certain position." • In an interview for a 1988 TV show called "The Incredibly Strange Film Show," Lewis explained how the idea for *Blood Feast* came about. He was staying at the Suez Motel in Florida which had an Egyptian motif, including a large plaster sphinx at the front of the building. "I turned to go back into the motel to start putting some notes together," recounted Lewis, "and there confronting me was this fake sphinx. The sphinx and I exchanged a meaningful glance and *Blood Feast* was born."

Bloodthirsty Butchers (1970; Constitution) D/S/C: Andy Milligan. P: William Miskin. Cast: John Miranda, Annabella Wood, Berwick Kaller. This no-budget (shot in 16mm) retelling of the Sweeney Todd story has a deranged killer turning people into meat pies.

Cannibal Girls (1972; AIP; Canada) D: Ivan Reitman. P: I. Reitman, Daniel Goldberg. S: Ivan Reitman, Daniel Goldberg, Robert Sandler. C: Robert Saad. Cast: Eugene Levy, Andrea Martin, Ronald Ulrich, Randall Carpenter, Bonnie Neilson. A group of young people wind up in a bizarre restaurant where they're not only patrons, they're the blue plate special. ¶ "They do *exactly* what you think they do!" — ad line. • With tongue planted firmly in cheek, this film comes complete with a warning bell which sounds just before the gore scenes (for those sensitive members of the audience). As the ads put it: "The picture with the *warning bell!* When it rings — close your eyes if you're squeamish!" Director Ivan Reitman was a little disappointed with the results of this gimmick, telling *Take One* magazine that, "I thought it was a good idea, but they handled it really badly. And the bell afterwards — to tell you you can open your eyes again — sounded like the Avon Lady." • Reitman later struck it big in comedy with *Meatballs* (1979), *Stripes* (1981) and *Ghostbusters* (1984).

Cannibal Hookers (1987; Lettuce Entertain You Inc.) D/S: Donald Farmer. P: Donald Farmer, Gary J. Levinson. C: Tony Fasian, Richard Kashanski, Glenn Kral. Cast: Marya Grant, Diana Cruz, Annette Munro, Datina Garner, Tommy Carrano, Donald Trimborn, Amy Waddell, Sheila Best, Gary Levinson. A group of prostitutes who've developed a taste for human flesh give their "johns" more than they bargained for in this amateur-level shot-on-video gore film. ¶ "We're gonna have a *killer* weekend."

Cannibal Women in the Avocado Jungle of Death (1988; Guacamole Films) D/S: J. D. Athens. P: Garry W. Goldstein. C: Robert G. Knous. Cast: Shannon Tweed, Adrienne Barbeau, Karen Mistal, Brett Stimely, Barry Primus, Bill Maher. A party in search of a missing scientist penetrates deep into the dreaded "Avocado Belt" hidden in the wilds of Southern California and

lorded over by the cannibalistic "Piranha Women." ¶ "Like a black widow spider, they have sex with their men and then kill them. Then they tear them into strips like beef jerky and eat them with guacamole." • This is actress Karen Mistal's second journey into the land of horror spoofs; she played the tomato-girl heroine in *Return of the Killer Tomatoes* the same year.

Cannibals in the Streets (1982; Almi Films; Italy) (also *Invasion of the Flesh Hunters*). D: Anthony M. Dawson (Antonio Margheriti). P: Maurizio Amati, Sandro Amati. S: Jimmy Gould, Anthony Dawson (Antonio Margheriti). C: Fernando Arribas. Cast: John Saxon, Elizabeth Turner, John Morghen, Cindy Hamilton, Tony King, Wallace Wilkinson, Ray Williams, John Geroson. A group of ex–Green Berets, infected with a cannibal virus in Vietnam, go on a cannibalistic rampage back in the States. • One of the cannibals is named Charles Buchinsky, the real name of Charles Bronson.

C.H.U.D. (1984; Media) D: Douglas Cheek. P: Andrew Bonime. S: Parnell Hall. Cast: John Heard, Daniel Stern, Christopher Curry. A clandestine operation called "Contamination Hazard Urban Disposal" (C.H.U.D.) dumps radioactive toxic waste into the city's sewers, which turns derelicts into flesh-eating mutants dubbed "Cannibalistic Humanoid Underground Dwellers" (C.H.U.D.'s again). • Though this was a socially relevant, serious (and effective) monster movie, a comic sequel (C.H.U.D. II: Bud the Chud) was released in 1989, but instead of mutated cannibals it featured comical zombies.

The Demon Barber of Fleet Street (1936; Select; U.K.) (also *Sweeney Todd, the Demon Barber of Fleet Street*). D/P: George King. S: H. F. Maltby. C: Jack Parker. Cast: Tod Slaughter, Stella Rho, Johnny Singer, Eve Lister, Bruce Seton, D. J. Williams, Davina Craig, Jerry Verno. Tod Slaughter, the "Horror Man of Europe," plays Sweeney Todd, the barber who sends his customers through a trap door into the basement to be made into meat pies for the bakery next door. ¶ "Not only the closest shave, but I promise to polish you off quicker than any other barber in London." • Though it is obvious where those tasty meat pies originate, the film "minces" around their gruesome nature and it is never explicitly discussed.

Dr. Butcher M.D. (1979) (see ZOMBIES) (also *Queen of the Cannibals*). A rash of cannibalism in the hospitals and environs of New York City prompts four American investigators to journey to a remote island in the "Malottos Archipelago." There they encounter a tribe of cannibals and a mad doctor who's transforming the natives into zombies via brain transplants. ¶ "This island's hiding something, something even *worse* than those cannibals."

Dr. Caligari (1989) (see MAD SCIENTISTS). The granddaughter of the original Dr. Caligari is performing mad experiments on her charges at the "Caligari Asylum" in this bizarre day-glow art film. One of her patients, Mr. Pratt, is a raving cannibal. She transfers some of his "glandular extract" into another patient, causing this second inmate to "mesquite grill" her husband in a flesh-eating frenzy. ¶ "Soft supple American girl-patty — slice it thick, Ma!"

Dr. X (1932) (see MAD SCIENTISTS). The sinister "moon killer" is on the prowl. He not only murders his victims, but he eats part of them as well.

Eating Raoul (1982; Bartel Film) D: Paul Bartel. P: Anne Kimmel. S: Richard Blackburn, Paul Bartel. C: Gary Thieltges. Cast: Paul Bartel, Mary Woronov, Robert Beltran, Susan Saiger, Buck Henry, Dick Blackburn, Edie McClurg, Ed Begley, Jr., John Paragon, Hamilton Camp. This delicious black comedy stars Paul Bartel (who also directed) and Mary Woronov as the Blands, a quiet couple who find that they can lure perverts to their apartment, rob them, kill them (usually by braining them with a frying pan), and then cook them up for dinner. ¶ "Will you buy me a new frying pan? I don't feel good about cooking in the one we're using to kill people."

Flesh-Eating Mothers (1989; Panorama Entertainment) D: James Aviles Martin. P: Miljan Peter Ilich, James Aviles Martin. S: James Aviles Martin, Zev Shlasinger. C: Harry Eisenstein. Cast: Robert Lee Oliver, Valorie Hubbard, Donatella Hecht, Neal Rosen, Terry Hayes, Grace Pettijohn. A new strain of VD transforms a group of dissatisfied housewives into raving cannibals. The mothers' kids, with the aid of a police doctor, must find a way to stop these "flesh-eating mothers" without killing them in this amateurish tongue-in-cheek independent. ¶ Girl: "My mother ate my baby brother." Boy: "Yeah, and we're fed up with it too."

The Folks at Red Wolf Inn (1972; Scope 3) (also *Terror at Red Wolf Inn; Terror House*). D: Bud Townsend. P: Michael Macready. S: Allen J. Actor. C: John McNichol. Cast: Linda Gillin, John Neilson, Mary Jackson, Arthur Space. In yet another cannibal comedy, a traveling student stays at an inn run by a nice elderly couple and their mentally deficient grandson, who all happen to be cannibals.

Frightmare (1974; Miracle; U.K.) (also *Frightmare 2* [video title]). D/P: Peter Walker. S: David McGillvray. C: Peter Jessop. Cast: Rupert Davies, Sheila Keith, Deborah Fairfax, Paul Greenwood, Kim Butcher, Fiona Curzon, John Yule, Tricia Mortimer, Pamela Farbrother, David McGillivray. After their release from an asylum, a pair of cannibals live on an isolated farm where they rip up their victims with an electric drill before devouring the raw flesh in this gory British import. • For its video release the film was retitled *Frightmare 2* to distinguish it from another, unrelated, *Frightmare*.

The Ghoul (1975; Tyburn; U.K.) D: Freddie Francis. P: Kevin Francis. S: John Elder. C: John Wilcox. Cast: Peter Cushing, Alexandra Bastedo, John Hurt, Gwen Watford, Veronica Carlson, Don Henderson. Set in the 1920s, Peter Cushing plays an English gentleman who lives on a remote estate and keeps a horrible secret locked in an upstairs room — his mad cannibalistic son. • Producer Kevin Francis is the son of director Freddie Francis.

Goremet, Zombie Chef from Hell (1986; Swanfilms) D/P: Don Swan. S: Don Swan, Jeff Baughn, William Highsmith. C: Don Swan. Cast: Theo Depusy, Kelley Kunicki, C. W. Casey, Alan Marx, Michael O'Neill, Joy Merchant, Jeff Pilars, Jeff Baughn, Chuck Clubb, Billy Scott, Arnold William, John Rodgers. In 1386, a fallen priest named Goza is cursed with eternal life by the "Righteous Brotherhood" — he must continually consume human flesh or his body will decay. In the present, Goza runs "Goza's Deli and Beach Club," where he murders the patrons and serves them up in his daily specials. The evil cannibal is finally undone when the reincarnation of the Brotherhood's high priestess shows up and super-glues his mouth shut(!). ¶ "This potion will decompose your body to a state of that of the living dead. In order to restore and maintain it at its present condition, you will be required to consume flesh each day. This will be your eternal curse. You will lust for flesh when you do not have it, and despise it when you do!" • This tongue-in-cheek no-budget gore fest was filmed primarily at Smokey Joe's Cafe ("Try the Slimey Slider").

The Grim Reaper (1981; Film Ventures; Italy) (also *Anthropophagus*). D: Joe

D'Amato (Aristide Massaccesi). P: Oscar Santaniello. S: Lewis Montefiore, Joe D'Amato. C: Enrico Biribicchi. Cast: Tisa Farrow, Saverio Vallone, George Eastman, Vanessa Steiger, Mark Bodin, Margaret Donelly, Bob Larson, Rubina Rey, Zora Kerova. A Greek island is the home of a degenerate cannibal, a man shipwrecked there and forced to eat his wife and son in order to survive. Tisa Farrow (Mia's sister) and companions end up on the island and must fight off the ravenous cannibal.

The Hills Have Eyes (1977; Vanguard) D/S: Wes Craven. P: Peter Locke. C: Eric Saarinen. Cast: Russ Grieve, Virginia Vincent, Susan Lanier, Dee Wallace, Robert Houston, Martin Speer, John Steadman, Janus Blythe, Arthur King, James Whitworth, Michael Berryman. A typical middle-class American family, traveling through the desert on their way to a vacation in California, are stranded when their car breaks down. There they meet a very atypical American family—a group of wild cannibals living in the hills, led by a scarred patriarch named "Jupiter." The grown "kids" are called Mars, Mercury, and Pluto, and they pick off the family members one by one and kidnap the family's baby (a delicacy), until the all-American kids answer the cannibals' brutality with their own. ¶ From the film's trailer: "The story of an American family who lost everything except the will to survive—murdered, raped, burned, but not beaten. The story of one family's refusal to die." • Wes Craven got the idea for the film when he read about a fifteenth century Scottish family called Beane—a wild, feral family who for two generations waylaid and ate passersby. • Craven made a belated (and totally unnecessary) sequel in 1984.

The Hills Have Eyes Part 2 (1984; New Realm/VTC) D/S: Wes Craven. P: Barry Cahn, Peter Locke. C: David Lewis. Cast: Michael Berryman, Kevin Blair, John Bloom, Janus Blythe, Peter Frechette, Robert Houston, Penny Johnson, John Laughlin, Willard Pugh, Colleen Riley, Tamara Stafford. Members of a teenage moto-cross racing team get stranded in the desert at the same spot at which the grisly proceedings from the first film occurred. As expected, they are picked off one by one by the lone surviving cannibal from the original, "Pluto," who is aided by a new one, "Reaper," his animal-like uncle. ¶ "You never shoulda got off the road; I ain't the only crazy out here." • Three actors returned to reprise their characters from the original: Michael Berryman

(Pluto), Janus Blythe (Ruby—the little sister of the cannibals who turned on her kin and ended up helping the normal family), and Robert Houston (Bobby, one of the two survivors from the first, and now the boyfriend of the reformed Ruby, who calls herself "Rachael"). • Wes Craven used extensive footage from his original *The Hills Have Eyes* for (money-saving) flashback sequences. So much of the original was shown that he even gave screen credit to several actors from the first film who did not even appear in the new footage for the sequel.

The Incredible Torture Show (1976) (see MADMEN — EARLY PSYCHOS) (also *Blood Sucking Freaks*). In one scene, a demented dentist drills a hole in the top of a woman's skull and sucks out her brains with a straw. There's also a group of naked women kept in cages in the basement who have turned into mad cannibals.

Leatherface: The Texas Chainsaw Massacre 3 (1990; New Line Cinema) (also *The Texas Chainsaw Massacre 3*). D: Jeff Burr. P: Robert Engelman. S: David Schow. C: James L. Carter. Cast: Kate Hodge, William Butler, Ken Foree, Tom Hudson, Viggo Mortensen, Joe Unger, R. A. Mihailoff. Without explanation, the maniac butcher/cannibal "Leatherface" is back (with saw in hand), though he seems to have acquired a new family, including a prepubescent sister who carries around a mummified baby corpse as her doll. The demented family kidnaps travelers and takes them back to their house to be butchered, dressed out, and eaten. ¶ "There's road kill all over Texas. I like liver, and onions, and pain, and pain, and pain!" • The over-sized custom-built silver chain saw given to Leatherface as a present by his "family" set the film's budget back by $3,000.

Lucky Stiff (1988; New Line Cinema) D: Anthony Perkins. P: Gerald T. Olson. S: Pat Proft. C: Jacques Haitkin. Cast: Donna Dixon, Jeff Kober, Joe Alaskey, Elizabeth Arlen, Charles Frank, Barbara Howard, Leigh McCloskey, Bill Quinn, Fran Ryan, Morgan Sheppard, Joe Unger, Andy Wood. This amusing black comedy features a rather corpulent hero lured to the Mitchell family's backwoods farm by their beautiful daughter—to be the main course at their family's Christmas dinner; the Mitchells are your typical down-home cannibal clan. ¶ "I'm not a guest, I'm the *buffet!*" • Actor Anthony Perkins (Norman Bates himself from *Psycho,* 1960) stepped behind the camera to direct. • *Lucky Stiff* carried a shooting title of *Mr. Christmas Dinner*.

Farmer Vincent and his sister Ida from Motel Hell *(1980) cultivate their human victims — the prime ingredient needed to make their popular "Farmer Vincent Fritters."*

The Mad Butcher (1972; Ellman; Italy) (also *Meat Is Meat; Strangler of Vienna*). D: John Zuru (Guido Zurli). P: Harry Hope, Eugenio Corso. S: Charles Ross, Enzo Gicca. C: Enrico Betti. Cast: Victor Buono, Karin Field, Brad Harris, John Ireland, Franca Polcelli, Hannsi Linder, Sybil Martin, Arthur Mann, Carl Stearns, Michael Turner. In Vienna, Otto (Victor Buono) creates his succulent sausages by straining his female victims through a meat grinder. ¶ "Sausage lovers, don't see this movie!" — warned the ads for this cannibal comedy.

Microwave Massacre (1979; Reel Life) D: Wayne Berwick. P/S: Thomas Singer, Craig Muckler. C: Karen Grossman. Cast: Jackie Vernon, Loren Schein, Al Troupe, Claire Ginsberg, Lou Ann Webber, Anna Marlo, Sarah Alt, Cindy Gant, Karen Marshall, Marla Simon. Jackie Vernon plays a construction worker whose nagging wife loves her new microwave more than she does him. He kills her in a rage, chops her body up and stores it in the freezer. Mis-

taking a piece of her corpse for a steak, he develops a taste for human flesh, and now resupplies his dwindling freezer with local hookers. ¶ "I'm so hungry I could eat a whore." • In this cannibal opus, the comedy carries over even into the credits, which are titled: "Le Menu (in order of consumption)"; followed by, "The producers wish to express their thanks to *microwave ovens,* without which this movie would have taken much longer"; and one final shot: "Remember, dismember a friend for lunch." • In the end, the jovial cannibal is done in by his own microwave — he has a pacemaker.

Motel Hell (1980; United Artists) D: Kevin Connor. P/S: Steven Charles Jaffe, Robert Jaffe. C: Thomas Del Ruth. Cast: Rory Calhoun, Paul Linke, Nancy Parsons, Nina Axelrod, Wolfman Jack. In this subtle black comedy, Rory Calhoun plays likable Farmer Vincent, whose famous spicy meats contain a secret ingredient — human flesh. He stages road accidents, then plant the victims up to their necks in the ground, slits their vocal cords, and fattens them up in his secret garden until ready for the meat grinder. Basically a good man, his philosophy is: "There's too many people in the world and not enough food. Now this takes care of both problems at once." ¶ "It takes all kinds of critters to make 'Farmer Vincent's Fritters'."

The Offspring (1987) (see ANTHOLOGIES) (also *From a Whisper to a Scream*). In the film's final tale, set at the close of the civil war, a group of children whose parents have been slaughtered by the war make a pact to punish all adults for the evil that they've caused. They torture, kill, and finally eat three Union soldiers who stumble upon their bizarre little community.

Parents (1988; Vestron) D: Bob Balaban. P: Bonnie Palef. S: Christopher Hawthorne. C: Ernest Day, Robin Vidgeon. Cast: Randy Quaid, Mary Beth Hurt, Sandy Dennis, Bryan Madorsky, Juno Mills-Cockell, Kathryn Groody, Deborah Rush, Graham Jarvis. Set in 1950's suburbia, a young boy makes a startling and gruesome discovery—his meat-loving parents are actually cannibals. ¶ "I'm sure you'll acquire a taste for it; your mother did." • Director Bob Balaban likened his film to "a cross between 'The Donna Reed Show' and *Psycho*."

Rabid (1977; New World; Canada) (also *Rage*). D/S: David Cronenberg. P: John Dunning. C: Rene Verzier. Cast: Marilyn Chambers, Frank Moore, Joe Silver, Howard Ryshpan, Patricia Gage, Susan Roman. The victim of a motorcycle accident (Marilyn Chambers) is given an experimental skin graft treatment which results in the development of a new organ under her armpit. With this new organ she punctures a person's skin and draws out their blood for nourishment. This has the nasty side effect of causing the victim to go mad, rabid with a lust for human flesh, and soon an epidemic of violence and cannibalism is sweeping the city of Montreal. • Star Marilyn Chambers, former porn queen, made her legitimate screen debut in this film.

Raw Meat (1972; AIP; U.K.) (also *Death Line*). D: Gary Sherman. P: Paul Maslansky. S: Ceri Jones. C: Alex Thomson. Cast: Donald Pleasence, Norman Rossington, David Ladd, Sharon Gurney, Hugh Armstrong, Christopher Lee. Descendants of people trapped in a cave-in during London's underground subway construction in 1892 have turned into plague-ridden cannibals who prey on the occasional subway rider. ¶ "Mind the doors!"—the only words the near-mindless cannibal knows.

Shriek of the Mutilated (1974; AM Films) (also *The Mutilated*). D: Michael Findlay. P: Ed Adlum. S: Ed Adlum, Ed Kelleher. C: Roberta Findlay. Cast: Alan Brock, Jennifer Stock, Tawm (Tawn) Ellis, Darcy Brown, Michael Harris, Morton Jacobs. Four college students journey with their professor to a remote island in search of the elusive Yeti. A huge white hairy beast kills several of the students before they learn that the creature is actually the professor, who is the leader of a cannibal cult, donning the fake Yeti suit to put food on the table, so to speak. ¶ From the ads: "A frenzied hunt for a hideous beast uncovers an evil cannibal cult and death is the devil's blessing." • Producer/co-screenwriter Ed Adlum is the man in the Yeti suit, which was sewn together by Adlum's wife. Cinematographer Roberta Findlay had some difficulty in constantly having to shoot around the huge zipper running up the back of the suit. • Roberta Findlay is the wife of director Michael Findlay.

Silence of the Lambs (1991) (see MADMEN—THE SLICE 'N' DICE WAVE). An F.B.I. trainee (Jodie Foster) agrees to interview a "real life" cannibal, the infamous Dr. Hannibal Lecter (a former psychiatrist) in a maximum security institution with the hope of attaining some new insight on a present serial killer case. Lecter provides the needed clues, then escapes after being transferred to a new holding facility. ¶ "I'm having an old friend for dinner." • *Silence of the Lambs* was written by Thomas Harris. Two of his other books were also made into movies, including a story called *Red Dragon* (made into the film *Manhunter*). *Red Dragon* introduced the character of Hannibal Lecter, a demented psychiatrist with a gourmet's taste in human flesh, whom Harris again featured in *Silence of the Lambs*.

Slaughterhouse Rock (1987) (see GHOSTS). A group of college students are terrorized at the abandoned prison on Alcatraz Island by the ghost of a sadistic cavalry officer. The Colonel was the Commandant of the island when it was an Army outpost—and he was a vicious cannibal, indulging his lust to consume human flesh first on prostitutes and then on the local Indian women before being caught and burned alive by the natives. ¶ "They thought they were coming to dinner but they didn't know they were going to be the main course."

Soylent Green (1973) (see FUTURES ON EARTH—UTOPIAS AND DYSTOPIAS). Charlton Heston plays a New York City police detective in an overpopulated 2022, who during the course of an investigation, stumbles upon the "great secret" — that "Soylent Green," the synthetic food which the government has been feeding the populace, is actually small squares of dead people. ¶ "You gotta tell them . . . they're making our food out of *people!*"

Spider Baby (1968; American General) *(The Liver Eaters; Cannibal Orgy or the Maddest Story Ever Told).* D/S: Jack Hill. P: Paul Monka, Gil Laskey. C: Alfred Taylor. Cast: Lon Chaney, Jr., Carol Ohmart, Quinn Redeker, Beverly Washburn, Jill Banner. Lon Chaney, Jr., is the caretaker for the crazy "Merrye" family who suffer from the "Merrye Syndrome," a strange disease which causes their mental age to regress and turns them into mindless cannibals. ¶ From the film's theme song called "The Monster's Holiday": "Frankenstein, Dracula and even the Mummy/ Are sure to wind up in somebody's tummy." • Though filmed in 1964, it was not released until 1968. • The title is derived from one of the adolescent girls (still in the beginning stages of the disease) who is fascinated with spiders and likes to tie people up and pretend she's got a "big fat juicy spider" stuck in her web, then "sting" the unfortunate with a pair of carving knives. • Carol Ohmart is best remembered by horror fans for her role in *House on Haunted Hill* (1958) as Vincent Price's sexy scheming wife. • This production features music by prolific 50s sci-fi composer Ronald Stein (*It Conquered the World,* 1956; *Invasion of the Saucermen,* 1957; etc.). • Lon Chaney, Jr., himself sings the film's theme song.

Tales from the Darkside: The Movie (1990) (see ANTHOLOGIES). The wraparound sequence of this anthology film features Deborah Harry as a cannibal woman who's captured a ten-year-old boy for her dinner. She gives him a book to read while she makes her preparations and this is where the three stories originate.

Tales That Witness Madness (1973) (see ANTHOLOGIES). In the final episode, the guests at a luau-style party unwittingly consume human flesh as part of a diabolical sacrifice. • Kim Novak replaced Rita Hayworth in this "Luau" episode shortly after the production began.

The Texas Chainsaw Massacre (1974; Bryanston) D/P: Tobe Hooper. S: Kim Henken, Tobe Hooper. C: Daniel Pearl. Cast: Marilyn Burns, Allen Danziger, Paul A. Partain, William Vail, Teri McMinn, Edwin Neal, Jim Siedow, Gunnar Hansen, John Dugan. In rural Texas, five young people end up at the isolated house of a family of cannibals, which include the infamous "Leatherface" — a burly mute maniac who wears a mask of human skin and wields a nasty looking chain saw. ¶ "The film which you are about to see is an account of the tragedy which befell a group of five youths. . . . It is all the more tragic in that they were very young. But had they lived very, very long lives, they could not have expected nor would they have wished to see as much of the mad and macabre as they were to see that day. The events of that day were to lead to the discovery of one of the most bizarre crimes in the annals of American history, The Texas Chainsaw Massacre" — opening narration. • *The Texas Chainsaw Massacre* was inspired by real-life grave robber/murderer Ed Gein, the "Wisconsin Ghoul" (though spreading out the mayhem among three crazy central characters instead of one for this film). • Director/producer Tobe Hooper once said that this unrelenting low-budget horror landmark is about "crazy retarded people going beyond the line between animal and human." • Despite its reputation as the ultimate splatter film, there is very little bloodshed shown on-screen — the gore is *implied;* and only one person is killed by chain saw. • John Larroquette provides the film's opening narration. He later achieved TV stardom on TV's "Night Court." • Two sequels have been filmed to date (with the first one again being helmed by Tobe Hooper).

The Texas Chainsaw Massacre 2 (1987; Cannon) D: Tobe Hooper. P: Menahem Golan, Yoram Globus, Tobe Hooper. S: L. M. Kit Carson. C: Richard Kooris. Cast: Dennis Hopper, Caroline Williams, Jim Siedow, Bill Moseley, Bill Johnson. The bizarre cannibal family is back from the original, living in an abandoned Texas amusement park and selling their prize-winning barbecue meat supplied by "Leatherface" and his active chain saw. This time the hulking, grunting Leatherface falls in love with a local female DJ, which complicates matters for the crazy cannibal clan. ¶ "I got one too; a *bonus body!* Look at that beef!" • This direct sequel picks up 13 years after the original with this opening narration: "But during the last 13 years, over and over again reports of bizarre, grisly chain saw mass-murders have persisted all across the state of Texas. The Texas Chainsaw Massacre has not stopped. It haunts Texas. It seems to have no end." • Tobe Hooper also produced/directed the original "Massacre." He co-wrote this sequel's musical score as well. • The pivotal role of the

Gunnar Hansen stars as "Leatherface," a cannibal killer who dons the facial skins of his victims in the Tobe Hooper cult classic, The Texas Chainsaw Massacre *(1974). Leatherface and his family of cannibals was loosely patterned after real-life grave robber/murderer Ed Gein—"the Wisconsin Ghoul."*

mask-wearing, chain saw–waving "Leatherface" was actually played by two actors— Bill Johnson, who played him in the "acting" scenes, and stuntman Bob Elmore, who did all the chain saw–wielding and chase scenes.

Three on a Meathook (1973; Studio One) D/S: William Girdler. P: John Asman, Lee Jones. Cast: Charles Kissinger, James Pickett. This gory semi-comedy shot in Louisville, Kentucky, follows the exploits of a cannibal maniac who murders and eats young girls, with his innocent son taking the blame for the heinous crimes. ¶ "I ain't havin' no trash in your Ma's home.... You know what happens to you when you get around women!" • Like *Psycho* (1960), *Deranged* (1974), and *The Texas Chainsaw Massacre* (1974), this film is supposedly based on real-life grave robber/killer Ed Gein, though this movie and *Texas Chainsaw* are the only ones to deal with cannibalism (though sus-

pected, there was never any *conclusive* evidence that Gein was indeed a cannibal).

Two Thousand Maniacs (1964) (see GHOSTS). This early gore film features a whole southern town reappearing 100 years after being slaughtered during the Civil War in order to take its revenge on a group of traveling Northerners. At one point, some of the ghostly townsfolk slowly roast a victim's arm over an open fire and then eat it.

The Undertaker and His Pals (1967; Howco) D/P: David C. Graham. S: T. L. P. Swicegood. C: Andrew Janczak. Cast: Ray Dennis, Robert Lowery, Warrene Ott, Marty Friedman, Sally Frei, Tiffany Shannon O'Hara, Charles Fox. This low-budget gory black comedy features two motorcycle-riding maniacs who kill women to drum up business for their "pal" the undertaker (who offers trading stamps with his funerals). The victims then end up as specials of the day at the adjoining diner (as in "Leg of Lamb" taken from a Miss Lamb). ¶ From the ads: "A macabre story of 2 motorcycle-riding, knife-wielding, shiv-shoving, eye-gouging, arm-twisting, chain-lashing, scalpel-flashing, acid-throwing, bone-breaking, pathological nuts and their pal the *undertaker*."

The Vampire's Night Orgy (1973) (see VAMPIRES — OTHER VAMPIRES) (also *Orgy of the Vampires*). A busload of tourists are stranded in a small village which (unbeknownst to them) is populated by vampires. The hospitable vampiric villagers provide food and lodging for their guests, but since there is no meat in the village (vampires don't eat food), they resort to feeding their visitors human flesh while they pick them off one by one.

Warlock Moon (1973; CW Film Co.) D/P: William Herbert. S: John Sykes. C: Larry Secrist. Cast: Laurie Walters, Joe Spano, Edna Macafee, Richard Vieille, Ray Goman, Steve Solinsky, Michael Herbert, Larry Bauer, Joan Zerrien, Charles Raino. A young reporter and his girlfriend end up at the old Soda Springs Spa, abandoned since 1930 when a horrible incident of cannibalism shocked the area. The pair run into the outwardly kind Mrs. Abacrombe, who turns out to be the leader of a group of cannibals who've chosen the young woman to be their special sacrificial victim. ¶ "After everybody had finished eating, a couple of the guests went out to the kitchen to congratulate the cook on the wonderful dinner. We found that the cook had killed the girl, and cooked her, and then fed her to the guests." • This no-budget, slow-moving

cannibal tale was shot in the San Francisco Bay area, with a deserted Army tuberculosis clinic standing in for the "Soda Springs Spa."

Welcome to Arrow Beach (1973; Brut Productions) (also *Tender Flesh*). D: Laurence Harvey. P: Jack Cushingham, Steven North. S: Wallace C. Bennett. C: Gerald Perry Finnerman. Cast: Laurence Harvey, Joanna Pettet, Stuart Whitman, John Ireland, Meg Foster, Dody Heath, Gloria LeRoy, David Macklin. A Santa Barbara man living with his sister near Arrow Beach is actually a cannibal. He developed a taste for human flesh when he was forced to eat three Korean War comrades in order to survive being stranded on a deserted Pacific island. ¶ "He killed more than he could eat" — ad line. • Warner Bros. was originally set to distribute the film, but backed out after a nearly non-existent original run, leaving it to sit on the shelf for three years before finally releasing it on the exploitation circuit in 1976 in a cut version under the title *Tender Flesh*. • Director Laurence Harvey also stars as the lead cannibal.

World Gone Wild (1988) (see FUTURES ON EARTH — UTOPIAS AND DYSTOPIAS). In the post-apocalyptic world of 2087, water is the most precious commodity. A group of warriors is contracted by the small peaceful community of "Lost Wells" to protect it from a band of sadistic fanatics. On the way there, the men encounter a band of cannibals, and one of the flesh-eaters decides to reform and join their group. ¶ First warrior: "We can't take him, he's a cannibal." Second warrior: "Nobody's perfect."

Cars and Vehicular Villains

This upspring of films is a by-product of our increasing technological dependency in the modern age. Beginning with the popular made-for-TV thriller, *Duel* (1971), the vehicular monster movie was born. Cars were big in the 1940s, but cinema had a lot more on its mind back then. In the 1950s, the movie moguls were preoccupied with space aliens and nuclear atrocities. The 60s practically exhausted every means of terror imaginable, so when the 70s came along, horror film producers and writers had to find something new to exploit. And so our new best friend and trusted ally — the car — turned out to be our worst nightmare. Although car manufacturers were already trying to sell vehicles as separate entities, giving them their own unique names for instance, it took a few years until our mode of transportation began to control us. As the highways and byways became increasingly congested at the beginning of the 1970s, one only had to drive on the freeways in and around L.A. or try motoring across town in New York City to realize that those metallic demons on wheels with headlights for eyes were out for blood. You lose your identity when you get inside a car. Driving down the crowded roadways, you look upon other motorists not as human individuals, but rather as obstacles in your path who are the epitome of self-centered greed. The films in this section exploit these feelings and fears to the nth degree, turning the cars themselves into the villains of the road. Besides automobiles, this section covers a few variations on vehicular villains as well, such as the possessed title terror in *Killdozer* (1974) and the murderous sea-vessel known as the *Death Ship* (1980).

Brotherhood of Satan (1971) (see WITCHES, WARLOCKS, AND CULTS). At the film's opening, a child's toy tank is transformed into a life-sized raging monster of metal which crushes a station wagon and the terrified family within it.

The Car (1977; Universal) D: Elliot Silverstein. P: Marvin Birdt, Elliot Silverstein. S: Dennis Shryack, Michael Butler, Lane Slate. C: Gerald Hirschfeld. Cast: James Brolin, Kathleen Lloyd, R. G. Armstrong, John Marley, John Rubinstein, Kim Richards. A mysterious black car that can't be hit by bullets, has no driver, and has no door handles, rolls into James Brolin's town and begins killing everyone it can get its fenders on. • The car is finally buried under 100 tons of earth, causing a spout of flame to shoot into the air containing some indistinct demon form.

Christine (1982; Columbia) D: John Carpenter. P: Richard Kobritz. S: Bill Phillips. C: Donal M. Morgan. Cast: Keith Gordon, John Stockwell, Alexandra Paul, Robert Prosky, Harry Dean Stanton. A 1958 Plymouth with a murderous mind of its own and the ability to magically repair itself becomes the obsession of a misguided teen. ¶ "No shitter ever came between me and Christine!" • Producer Richard Kobritz bought the movie rights to Stephen King's novel, *Christine,* for $500,000 even *before* the book had been printed (when it was still in galley form). Production on the film began four days before the book was officially published. • Director John Carpenter explained why *Christine* failed to generate big box office (only $9 million in domestic theatrical rentals): "The problem with *Christine* was simple—it wasn't scary. I made a big mistake by taking out Roland LeBay's rotting corpse (a gruesome, ghostly character that was central to the book). I was just tired of rotting corpses at the time, and I tried to do it all with the car. I failed" (*Cinefantastique,* Feb. 1991).

Death Race 2000 (1975) (see FUTURES ON EARTH—UTOPIAS AND DYSTOPIAS). A transcontinental death race has become the most popular sporting event of the future. In this "Death Race," the more people you run over the more points you score. Its top driver, known simply as "Frankenstein," must win the race in order to get close enough to the corrupt President to kill him, thereby putting an end to the sanctioned violence. • While the cars do not take on a life of their own (like in the other films featured in this section), these machines are designed for only two things—speed and dealing death.

Death Ship (1980; Canada) D: Alvin Rakoff. P: Derek Gibson, Harold Greenberg. S: John Robins. C: Rene Verzier. Cast: George Kennedy, Richard Crenna, Nick Mancuso, Sally Ann Howes, Kate Reid. A deserted Nazi interrogation ship with a mind of its own roams the seven seas looking for victims. It rams a cruise liner, rescues a handful of passengers, and then proceeds to do away with them one by one. ¶ "No one leaves *my* ship!" • Instead of diesel fuel, this Death Ship is propelled by blood.

Duel (1971; TV movie) D: Steven Spielberg. P: George Eckstein. S: Richard Matheson. C: Jack Marta. Cast: Dennis Weaver, Tim Herbert, Charles Seel, Eddie Firestone, Shirley O'Hara. Dennis Weaver plays a middle-class businessman who finds himself inexplicably locked in a deadly cat and mouse game with a ten-ton diesel truck on a lonely stretch of highway. The driver of this truck is never seen, and more and more it seems as if the truck itself has taken on some malevolent life of its own. ¶ "I gave you the road, why don't you take it?" • *Duel* was released as a theatrical feature outside the United States with some additional footage added. • Cinematographer Jack Marta earned an Emmy nomination for his fine camera work.

Equinox (1967/71) (see DEMONS AND DEVILS). After the lone survivor of a battle with the Devil himself escapes the Evil One's clutches and makes it back to the highway, he is run down by a driverless, possessed Volkswagen.

The Hearse (1980; Crown International) D: George Bowers. P: Mark Tenser, Charles

Russel. S: Bill Bleich. C: Mori Kawa. Cast: Trish Van Devere, Joseph Cotten, David Gautreaux, Donald Hotton, Med Flory, Perry Lang. A 1953 Packard hearse is on the prowl, menacing Trish Van Devere who's inherited an old mansion full of dark secrets.

Killdozer (1974; TV movie) D: Jerry London. P: Herbert F. Solow. S: Theodore Sturgeon, Ed MacKillop. C: Terry K. Meade. Cast: Clint Walker, Carl Betz, Neville Brand, James Wainwright, James A. Watson, Jr., Robert Urich. A bulldozer possessed by an invisible force decides to go after a construction crew working on an isolated island in the Pacific. • Theodore Sturgeon adapted his own novel for this teleplay.

Look What's Happened to Rosemary's Baby (1976) (see DEMONS AND DEVILS) (also *Rosemary's Baby 2*). The now-grown Son of Satan owns a black sports car which occasionally starts up by itself to run down his enemies in this tepid TV follow-up to the chilling *Rosemary's Baby* (1968).

Maximum Overdrive (1986; De Laurentiis Entertainment Group) D/S: Stephen King. P: Martha Shumacher. Cast: Emilio Estevez, Pat Hingle, Laura Harrington, Christopher Murney. A comet circling the Earth wreaks havoc with machines and turns the "Dixie Boy" truck stop into an automotive nightmare lorded over by driverless trucks with murder on their mechanical minds. • *Maximum Overdrive* was universally panned by critics and audiences alike. Author-turned–first time director Stephen King was his own worst critic. "I didn't do a very good job of directing it," admitted King in *Cinefantastique* (Feb. 1991). "It was a crash course in film school. What some guys take six years to learn, I learned in about ten weeks. The result was a picture that was just terrible." He went on to explain, "When I went in to do *Maximum Overdrive,* I didn't even know about shooting a master and then shooting cutaways. That's how totally ignorant I was about the filmmaking process. I learned *while I was there.*" • Director Stephen King makes a cameo appearance in the film as a man insulted by a rogue cash machine(!). • The rock musical score was provided by the group AC/DC.

Nightmares (1983) (see ANTHOLOGIES). The third segment of this anthology, entitled "The Benediction," features a sinister pickup truck who challenges the faith of a religious man (Lance Henriksen).

Wheels of Terror (1990; TV movie) D: Christopher Cain. P: Richard Learman. S: Alan B. McElroy. C: Richard Bowen. Cast: Joanna Cassidy, Marcie Leeds, Carlos Cervantes, Arlen Dean Snyder. A mysterious black sedan comes to a sleepy small town where it kidnaps and kills children. It sets its sights (or headlights as the case may be) on a single mother and her school-age daughter, who must engage in an automotive battle to the death using a small school bus. ¶ "It was there the day that Kimberly disappeared. I saw it! I heard it during the night, it was outside my house. I'm not having just some whacko nightmare here! It's real!" • The driver of the car is never seen and it is intimated that there is some sinister supernatural force "driving" the car to its diabolical actions.

Cat-People

(*See also* Cats)

According to cinematic legend, cat-people are supposed to be a race of humans who transform into cats (usually leopards) when they are emotionally or sexually aroused. The first and most effective depiction of this mythic motif is found in the Val Lewton film, *Cat People* (1942). *Cat People* is generally regarded as a horror classic due to its brilliantly subtle use of suggestive terror rather than the direct, hit-you-over-the-head approach employed by its 1982 remake (again called *Cat People*), which starred Nastassia Kinski.

Other pictures which run along the same lines include *The Catman of Paris* (1946) and *The Cat Girl* (1957). However, "Cat-People" isn't wholly devoted to this specific brand of monster manifestation. Films more akin to *The Fly* (1958), which depict scientifically-created creatures (part man/part cat), are included in this chapter as well. *Terror Is a Man* (1959) is one such example, as are the many

"Moreau" monsters of science. On the lighter side of this subgenre would be the unintentionally hilarious alien film, *Cat Women of the Moon* (1953), which paraded beautiful girls in black tights, long fingernails, tails, and cat-like mannerisms in front of unsuspecting astronauts.

In most cases, man-monsters of the animal variety are usually listed within their own subject species, but like the BUG-PEOPLE subgenre, the CAT-PEOPLE movies seem to have struck their own vein of cinematic ore. For more films in which felines play a significant role, see the CATS section.

The Cat Girl (1957; Insignia Films/AIP; U.K.) (also *The Cat Woman*). D: Alfred Shaughnessy. P: Herbert Smith. S: Lou Russof. C: Peter Hennessey. Cast: Barbara Shelley, Robert Ayres, Kay Callard, Paddy Webster, Ernest Milton, Lilly Kann. In this obscure British entry in the *Cat People* vein, a family curse allows a young woman (Barbara Shelley) to unleash a phantom leopard on her unsuspecting victims. At the climax the big cat is hit by a car and transforms back into a woman. ¶ "To be condemned to live a life of horror and anguish, to have the form and intellect of a man, yet the cunning savagery and bloodlust of one of those creatures." • This was actress Barbara Shelley's first appearance in a long line of horror films. She later encountered more feline trouble in *The Shadow of the Cat* (1960). • Screenwriter Lou Russof penned many a screenplay for AIP, including *Day the World Ended* and *The She-Creature* (both 1956). • *The Cat Girl* was originally released in America as the second feature on a double bill with *The Amazing Colossal Man* (a rather odd combination to say the least).

Cat People (1942; RKO) D: Jacques Tourneur. P: Val Lewton. S: Dewitt Bodeen. C: Nicholas Musuraca. Cast: Simone Simon, Kent Smith, Tom Conway, Jane Randolph, Jack Holt, Alan Napier. A young woman, descended from a race of cat-people, changes into a black panther when amorous feelings are aroused. ¶ "She· was marked by the curse of those who slink and court and kill by night" — poster ad line. • This was the first film in producer Val Lewton's series of low-budgeted but sensitive and intelligent horror pictures he made for RKO. *Cat People* was made for $134,000 and grossed over $4 million (helping to save a financially troubled RKO from bankruptcy). • In the famous swimming pool sequence, the shadow of the stalking panther was actually cast by the fist of director Jacques Tourneur. The scene was inspired by Tourneur's own experience of nearly drowning while swimming alone at

night. • Tourneur directed two others films (both in 1943) for Lewton's RKO unit — *I Walked with a Zombie* and *The Leopard Man* (a story about a maniacal killer, *not* a man who changes into a leopard). • Ironically, Val Lewton suffered from gatophobia — the fear of cats. • Val Lewton produced a sequel in 1944 when he was handed the lurid title *The Curse of the Cat People* by the front office. *Curse. . .* is a sequel in name only, for it involves no cat-people, merely the ghost of Irena from the original (with no reference to her previous feline condition) and the fantasies of a little girl (the daughter of Irena's former husband). Screenwriter Dewitt Bodeen also penned this sequel.

Cat People (1982; Universal) D: Paul Schrader. P: Charles Fries. S: Alan Ormsby. C: John Barley, Paul Vom Brack. Cast: Nastassia Kinski, Malcolm McDowell, John Heard, Annette O'Toole, Ruby Dee, Ed Begley, Jr. In this graphic remake, there are two cat-people this time (Malcolm McDowell and Nastassia Kinski), who transform into panthers whenever they have sex with someone outside their own race. ¶ "We are an incestuous race. We can only make love with our own, otherwise we transform, and before we can become human again — we must kill." • This version repeats the classic swimming pool scene from the original *Cat People* in which the heroine is stalked by a shadowy panther while swimming alone in a dimly-lit pool. This time though, since this is a "modern" movie, the heroine is swimming topless. • Screenwriter Alan Ormsby is best remembered as the screenwriter/makeup man/star of *Children Shouldn't Play with Dead Things* (1972). Ormsby also appears in *Cat People* as an interested bystander. • David Bowie wrote and performed the theme song.

Cat Women of the Moon (1953) (see THE MOON). Women in black tights and tails are discovered living on the dark side of the Moon.

The Catman of Paris (1946; Republic) D: Lesley Selander. P: Marek M. Libkov. S: Sherman L. Lowe. Cast: Carl Esmond, Le-

The dead phantom leopard invoked by Barbara Shelley lays across the bumper of Robert Ayres' car at the climax of The Cat Girl *(1957).*

nore Aubert, Adele Mara, Douglass Dumbrille, Gerald Mohr, John Dehner, Anthony Caruso, Fritz Feld, Robert J. Wilke. A man periodically changes into a cat-man or "werecat" and commits gruesome murders. ¶ "Death has been denied me, until I've fulfilled the cycle of my destiny." • Leading lady Lenore Aubert is best remembered by horror fans as the beautiful but sinister Dr. Sandra Mornay, who wanted to put Lou Costello's brain into the skull of the monster in *Abbott and Costello Meet Frankenstein* (1948).

The Creeper (1948; 20th Century–Fox) D: Jean Yarbrough. P: Bernard Small. S: Maurice Tombragel. C: George Robinson. Cast: Eduardo Ciannelli, Onslow Stevens, June Vincent, Ralph Morgan, Janis Wilson, John Baragrey, Richard Lane, Philip Ahn, Lotte Stein, Ralph Peters, David Hoffman. A scientist, experimenting with a special breed of West Indian cats, has developed a serum which he injects into himself to transform his hands into vicious cat-like paws which he uses to murder his enemies. ¶ "I see it all too clearly. It is big, too big. We

can't control it. We'd be releasing energies that would result only in mutations, monstrosities, and death. We can't benefit mankind, we can only do immeasurable harm. That's why I beg you, Jim, leave well enough alone." • According to the film's pressbook, top-billed Eduardo Ciannelli earned an M.D. degree, had a career as an opera singer in his native Italy, and authored several plays. • Aside from *Abbott and Costello Meet Frankenstein,* which was a horror comedy, *The Creeper* was the only straight horror film released in the lean year of 1948.

The Curse of the Cat People (1944) (see GHOSTS). In this sequel-that-is-not-a-sequel, the husband from *Cat People* (1942) has remarried and has a daughter. The lonely little girl creates a fantasy world for herself and conjures up the ghost of Irena (the original "cat-person") to be her friend. Irena is entirely friendly and nothing of her former feline nature is ever mentioned. This is basically a charming, sensitive fantasy with a few chilling moments and absolutely *no* cat-people.

The Island of Dr. Moreau (1977) (see MAD SCIENTISTS). In this pale update of the classic *Island of Lost Souls* (1933), Dr. Moreau intends to mate his nearly-perfect "panther woman" with a man shipwrecked on his island. The panther woman was made by Dr. Moreau via extensive surgery on a panther.

Island of Lost Souls (1933) (see MAD SCIENTISTS). *Island of Lost Souls* is the definitive classic adaptation of H. G. Wells' book, *The Island of Dr. Moreau.* Dr. Moreau creates "Lota," a panther transformed through surgery into a sensuous woman, whom the mad doctor intends to mate with the hero.

Terror Is a Man (1959; Valiant; U.S./ Philippines) (also *The Blood Creature*). D: Gerry De Leon. P: Kane W. Lynn, Edgar F. Romero. S: Harry Paul Harber. C: Emanuel I. Rojas. Cast: Francis Lederer, Greta Thyssen, Richard Derr, Oscar Keesee, Lilia Duran, Peyton Keesee. In a small-scale (uncredited) reworking of *The Island of Dr. Moreau,* a scientist transforms a leopard into a cat-man. Unlike the other (credited) versions of H. G. Wells' story, this leopard-man is the only "humanimal" created by the mad doctor. ¶ "He's entering another life. Can you imagine what he feels?" • Filmed during the height of the "gimmick" craze, this cheap (but well done) horror import featured a buzzer which warned audiences of upcoming shots of gruesome surgery. • Star Francis Lederer was born in Prague and was fluent in six different languages.

Twilight People (1972) (see MAD SCIENTISTS). In yet another version of *The Island of Dr. Moreau,* a mad scientist creates animal-people, including the obligatory panther-woman. This version is the least effective of the lot.

Cats

(*See also* Cat-People)

Cats and all their feline relatives have been a "natural" in horror movies. Their mysterious character and natural propensity to be loners has made them a suspicious breed of animal in the minds of humans. What's really going on behind those cold, unblinking eyes ... what are they really thinking? Is there more to a cat than soft fur and a penchant for milk? Filmmakers have generally thought so, and frequently featured the smaller version (often of the dreaded black variety) as creatures possessing supernatural knowledge of events and hidden mysteries. In *The Black Cat* (1941) and *The Cat Creeps* (1946) (both films borrowing titles — and not much else — from earlier classics), the cat has become an integral part in some type of murder mystery set in a spooky old house. This idea of cats possessing forbidden knowledge is not a new concept. Certain aspects of Egyptian culture and religion have thought of cats as gods, and of course cats have frequently played an important role in tales of witchcraft. The black cat itself, even today, is still commonly thought of as a superstitious symbol of impending doom ("don't let a black cat cross your path").

Aside from the predominant mystery vein inherent in this subgenre, there are also many films included here which feature a larger species of felines such as the leopard and tiger. No one can dispute the terror they instill in people's hearts whenever these huge, deadly, and ferocious animals are encountered anyplace outside a zoo, game park, or circus. For other cat-related horrors, see CAT-PEOPLE.

The Beastmaster (1982) (see SWORD AND SORCERY). In this sword and sorcery fantasy, the hero is able to communicate with and control various animals, including a ferocious tiger.

The Black Cat (1934) (see POE FILMS — EARLY POE). Despite the title and its nominal basis in Edgar Allan Poe, this Golden Age classic has virtually nothing to do with Poe's story, except that one character (played by

Bela Lugosi) has an overpowering fear of cats. ¶ "You must be indulgent of Dr. Werdegast's weakness. . . . He has an intense and all-consuming horror—of cats."

The Black Cat (1941; Universal) D: Albert S. Rogell. P: Burt Kelly. S: Robert Lees, Fred Rinaldo, Eric Taylor, Robert Neville. C: Stanley Cortez. Cast: Basil Rathbone, Hugh Herbert, Broderick Crawford, Bela Lugosi, Anne Gwynne, Gladys Cooper, Gale Sondergaard. This tepid horror-mystery involves an elderly philanthropist, her house full of cats, and the greedy relatives waiting for their inheritance. The titular feline causes the death of the villainess, who ends up being burned alive. ¶ "Everything around here is for the cats, that's why this place is going to the dogs." • Bela Lugosi, star of the 1934 version of *The Black Cat,* is wasted here in a red herring role.

The Black Cat (1966) (see POE FILMS—MODERN POE). This updating of Edgar Allan Poe's story follows a disturbed man who becomes morbidly obsessed with the black cat given him by his wife, first gouging out its eye and eventually killing it. It (or another cat) comes back and is instrumental in exposing the man's hideous crimes.

The Black Cat (1981; Selenia Cinematografica; Italy) D: Lucio Fulci. P: Giulio Sbarigia. S: Lucio Fulci, Biagio Proietti. C: Sergio Salvati. Cast: Mimsy Farmer, Patrick Magee, David Warbeck, Dagmar Lassander, Daniela Doro, Al Cliver, Bruno Corazzari, Geoffrey Copleston. A mysterious black cat is at the root of a series of vicious murders. • Italian director Lucio Fulci is best known for his prolific output of blood and guts zombie films such as *Zombie* (1979), *The Gates of Hell* (1980), and *The House by the Cemetery* (1981).

The Black Zoo (1963; Allied Artists) D: Robert Gordon. P: Herman Cohen. S: Aben Kandel, Herman Cohen. C: Floyd Crosby. Cast: Michael Gough, Jeanne Cooper, Rod Lauren, Virginia Grey, Elisha Cook, Jr., Jerome Cowan, Edward Platt. Private zoo owner Michael Gough sends his big cats (lions and tigers) out to dispatch his enemies. ¶ "This zoo, it isn't exactly the Garden of Eden." • Producer Herman Cohen had teamed up twice before with star Michael Gough, in *Horrors of the Black Museum* (1959) and *Konga* (1961). • A photo/comic book of *The Black Zoo* was put out by *Horror Monsters* magazine.

The Cat Creature (1973; TV movie) D: Curtis Harrington. P: Douglas S. Cramer. S: Robert Bloch. C: Charles Rosher. Cast: Meredith Baxter (Birney), David Hedison,

Gale Sondergaard, John Carradine, Stuart Whitman, Renne Jarrett, Keye Luke, Kent Smith, John Abbott, Peter Lorre, Jr. Gale Sondergaard plays a cat-goddess possessing victims while searching for a golden amulet; many cat in-jokes and cat motifs are featured. • This was Gale Sondergaard's first movie since 1949 (largely due to the Communist blacklist episode in Hollywood). • Actor Kent Smith was the male lead in both *Cat People* (1942), and its "sequel," *Curse of the Cat People* (1944; though *no* cat-people, or even ordinary cats, appeared). • Peter Lorre, Jr., turns up as a victim. His real name is Eugene Weingand and he is unrelated to Peter Lorre. The real Lorre once took him to court for illegal use of his name.

The Cat Creeps (1946; Universal) D: Erle C. Kenton. P: Will Cowan. S: Edward Dein, Jerry Warner. C: George Robinson. Cast: Fred Brady, Noah Beery, Jr., Lois Collier, Paul Kelly, Douglass Dumbrille, Rose Hobart. A sharp-witted reporter and his sidekick photographer have a field day cracking one-liners in an old dark house full of murder suspects and a mysterious black cat. ¶ "There's two hundred thousand dollars hidden around here, that oughta cure any pain in the neck."

The Cat from Outer Space (1978) (see ALIENS—BENEVOLENT ALIENS). An extraterrestrial that looks like an Abyssinian housecat is stranded on Earth.

The Cat Girl (1957) (see CAT-PEOPLE). A phantom leopard is sent to kill undesirables.

Cat's Eye (1985) (see ANTHOLOGIES). In this Stephen King–scripted anthology film, a resourceful tabby named "General" is the thread holding the three stories together. The cat is featured prominently in the final episode in which General must battle a tiny evil troll trying to steal the breath from little Drew Barrymore. • At times the six-inch troll was played by a man in full suit shot on a huge oversized set (containing the largest furniture ever built for a film production), and at other times the troll was an inanimate figure brought to life via the wonders of stop-motion animation.

The Corpse Grinders (1971; Gemini) D/P: Ted V. Mikels. S: Arch Hall, Joseph L. Cranston. C: Bill Anneman. Cast: Sean Kenney, Monika Kelly, Sanford Mitchell, J. Byron Foster, Warren Ball. Cat food producers grind human beings into their special recipe which turns their feline consumers into man-eating savages. ¶ "I know the answer is in that pet food factory and I'm going down there"—famous last words. • No-budget filmmaker Ted V. Mikels also did the music and editing as well as producing/directing the film.

Dr. Cyclops (1940) (see SHRINKAGE). A scientist develops a shrinking ray and turns it on a group of people who must then deal not only with the mad doctor but with various giant-sized animals, including the doctor's hungry housecat.

Eye of the Cat (1969; Universal) D: David Lowell Rich. P: Bernard Schwartz, Philip Hazelton. S: Joseph Stefano. C: Russell Metty, Ellsworth Fredricks. Cast: Michael Sarrazin, Gayle Hunnicutt, Eleanor Parker, Tim Henry, Laurence Naismith. In a murder-the-aunt-for-her-money plot, the aunt's cats eventually avenge their mistress' death, led by the spirit of one of their deceased brethren. • *Eye of the Cat* was written by Joseph Stefano, the same man who scripted *Psycho* (1960). • The frisky felines were trained by Ray Berwick, who also trained *The Birds* for Alfred Hitchcock in 1963.

The Illustrated Man (1969) (see ANTHOLOGIES). In the segment titled "The Veldt," a futuristic machine which is capable of simulating whole environments makes an African landscape all too real for the parents of two lonely children when the veldt's carnivorous wildlife proves to be more than just an illusion.

The Incredible Shrinking Man (1957) (see SHRINKAGE). The two-inch title character is almost eaten by his own housecat.

The Magic Sword (1962) (see SWORD AND SORCERY). In this early low-budget sword and sorcery film, Estelle Winwood plays a good witch who transforms herself into a panther at film's end to kill the evil wizard Lodac (Basil Rathbone).

Murders in the Zoo (1933) (see MADMEN — EARLY MADMEN). A maniacally jealous Lionel Atwill uses various zoo animals to dispose of his wife's actual and suspected paramours. At the climax, all the cages in the big cat house are opened, and the resultant feline free-for-all indirectly leads to Atwill's death.

Night of a Thousand Cats (1972; Ellman Enterprises; Mexico) D: Rene Cardona, Jr. P: Mario Z. Zacaria. S: Mario Marzac, Rene Cardona, Jr. C: Alex Phillips, Jr. Cast: Hugo Stiglitz, Gerardo Cepeda, Anjanette Comer, Zulma Faiad, Christa Linder, Tereza Velasquez, Barbara Angel. A wealthy sicko uses his helicopter to pick up women, take them to his castle retreat, cut their heads off, and feed their bodies to his pit full of flesh-eating cats ... until, of course, he receives his just desserts (or more aptly, the cats do). ¶ "Alone, only a harmless pet ... one thousand strong, they become a man-eating machine!" — poster ad line.

Persecution (1973; Tyburn; U.K.) (also *The Terror of Sheba; The Graveyard* [video title]). D: Don Chaffey. P: Kevin Francis. S: Robert B. Hutton, Rosemary Wooten, Frederick Warner. C: Kenneth Talbot. Cast: Lana Turner, Ralph Bates, Olga Georges-Picot, Trevor Howard, Patrick Allen, Suzanne Farmer, Mark Weavers. Lana Turner is a crippled, sadistic matriarch whose household is closely tied to her pet cats. Said felines are linked to a number of mysterious murders. • Screenwriter (and actor) Robert Hutton explained to *Fangoria* #87 how he came up with the film's concept: "I don't like cats, and I came up with this idea about a cat that could destroy a family. Our original title was *I Hate You, Cat,* which I thought was a much better title than *Persecution*." • This was Lana Turner's first feature since 1969, and Ms. Turner did not think too highly of her come-back vehicle, referring to it as "a bomb." • Producer Kevin Francis is the son of Freddie Francis, a respected cinematographer (*The Innocents,* 1961) and sometimes director (*The Evil of Frankenstein,* 1964; *Dracula Has Risen from the Grave,* 1968).

Pet Sematary (1989) (see ZOMBIES). A little girl's dead housecat is buried in an ancient Indian burial ground, and comes back inhabited by an evil spirit.

Shadow of the Cat (1961; BHP/Universal; U.K.) D: John Gilling. P: Jon Pennington. S: George Baxt. C: Arthur Grant. Cast: William Lucas, Barbara Shelley, Andre Morell, Conrad Phillips, Alan Wheatley, Vanda Godsell, Richard Warner, Feda Jackson, Andrew Crawford, Catherine Lacey. A wealthy woman is murdered and her cat, the only witness, acts as a vengeful presence, leading to the deaths of the guilty. • John Gilling wrote and or directed many films for Britain's Hammer Studios, including *Plague of the Zombies,* and *The Reptile* (both 1966). Gilling also wrote and directed the finest version of the "Burke and Hare" story to date — *Mania* (1960).

Tales from the Darkside: The Movie (1990) (see ANTHOLOGIES). In the "Cat from Hell" segment, a demonic housecat causes problems for a rich old man and the hitman he's hired to "terminate" the possessed pussy. • This segment is from a Stephen King story, adapted by filmmaker George A. Romero (*Night of the Living Dead,* 1968 and sequels).

Tales of Terror (1962) (see POE FILMS — THE

CORMAN CYCLE). In this Edgar Allan Poe anthology, the second story combines two of Poe's tales — "The Cask of Amontillado" and "The Black Cat." A jealous husband walls up his unfaithful wife and her lover in a wine cellar only to have his crime revealed by his wife's yowling housecat which he had inadvertently walled up with them. • The vociferous feline (a *black* cat of course) is aptly named "Pluto" in the story (Pluto being the Roman god of the underworld — the Lord of Death).

Tales that Witness Madness (1973) (see ANTHOLOGIES). In the "Mr. Tiger" segment, a young boy has an invisible tiger for an imaginary playmate, only it turns out to be not-so-imaginary when he uses it to dispose of his hostile parents.

The Tomb of Ligea (1964) (see POE FILMS — THE CORMAN CYCLE). The spirit of Vincent Price's dead wife possesses her black cat, which terrorizes his new wife and leads to Price's ultimate destruction.

Torture Garden (1967) (see ANTHOLOGIES). In the first story, "Enoch," a man kills his rich uncle and then finds himself driven by the dead man's cat to commit further murders so that the felonious feline can eat human heads(!). • Robert Bloch, author of the novel *Psycho,* adapted his own short story for the screenplay.

The Uncanny (1977; Cinevideo/TOR Productions; Canada/U.K.) D: Denis Heroux. P: Claude Heroux, Rene Dupont. S: Michael Parry. C: Harry Waxman, James Bawden. Cast: Peter Cushing, Ray Milland, Susan Penhaligon, Simon Williams, Joan Greenwood, Alexandra Stewart, Samantha Eggar, John Vernon, Donald Pleasence. This anthology features a trio of tales revolving around cats and their own feline brand of justice. The first story involves a pair of would-be heirs who conspire to destroy the large number of cats whom an eccentric old woman had willed her fortune to. The second vignette deals with a supernatural cat who aids a young girl in killing her cousin. The final episode relates how two lovers are killed by a cat after murdering the man's wife.

Uninvited (1987; Heritage Entertainment) D/P/S: Greydon Clark. C: Nicholas Von Sternberg. Cast: George Kennedy, Alex Cord, Clu Gulager, Toni Hudson, Eric Larson. Onboard a luxury yacht, a group of people must content with a killer mutant housecat. ¶ "You'll never look at a cat the same way again!" — ad slogan.

Cavepeople

Virtually every scrap of scientific evidence that has been compiled over the last century and a half can be discarded when it comes to the CAVEPEOPLE cinema subgenre. Of course, authenticity has never really coincided with box office success. It should not come as any surprise, then, that the two most successful caveman epics — *One Million B.C.* (1940), and its superior remake, *One Million Years B.C.* (1966) — managed to earn huge profits despite their historically inaccurate mixing of cavepeople and dinosaurs. Many scholars even think it unlikely that the stone age Neanderthals shared the Earth with warm-blooded woolly mammoths and saber-toothed tigers, who appeared millions of years *after* the last dinosaur had died out. Let's face it, cavepeople are much more interesting to the movie-going public when surrounded by those huge "thunder lizards." Occasionally however, a reasonable attempt at anthropological accuracy is made in cinema — *Quest for Fire* (1981), for example. Still, for all this film's honest aspirations and critical acclaim, *Quest for Fire* failed to spark the public's interest.

This section is devoted specifically to prehistoric people — that is, those who lived before we learned to write and record history — approximately 5000 years ago. The "Cavepeople" films usually follow one of four formats — films depicting tribal life set in prehistoric times (*One Million B.C.,* 1940; *Clan of the Cave Bear,* 1985); films about prehistoric individuals encountered within a contemporary setting (*Trog,* 1970; *Iceman,* 1984); features that show cavepeople living in a prehistoric lost world somewhere in modern times (*The Last Dinosaur*, 1977); or films in which contemporary scientists find a way to transform themselves or their experimental subjects into primitive beings (*The Neanderthal Man*, 1953; *Monster on the Campus*, 1958; *Altered States*, 1980).

Many of the films about cavepeople also feature a variety of prehistoric animals. Movies with a strong emphasis on dinosaurs will have their main entries listed in the DINOSAURS section, with only a Relevant Element featured here. To get the full prehistoric picture, we suggest you also look into the DINOSAURS section.

Altered States (1980; Warner Bros.) D: Ken Russell. P: Howard Gottfried. S: Sidney Aaron (Paddy Chayevsky). C: Jordan Cronenweth. Cast: William Hurt, Blair Brown, Bob Balaban, Charles Haid, Miguel Godreau. A progressive anthropologist experiments with hallucinogens and a sensory deprivation tank, and regresses back into some kind of prehistoric simian caveman. ¶ "I don't think we're dealing with genetics, we're beyond mass and matter here, beyond even energy — what we're back to is the first thought." • Charles Haid went on to star in the TV series "Hill Street Blues" as officer Andy Renko. William Hurt went on to become one of Hollywood's best actors of the decade, garnering multiple Academy Award nominations and Oscars.

Cavegirl (1985; Crown International) D/P/C: David Oliver. S: Phil Groves, David Oliver. Cast: Daniel Roebuck, Cindy Ann Thompson, Darren Young, Saba Moor, Jeff Chayette, Charles Mitchell, Bill Adams. A nerdish student is propelled back into the past during a time continuum test to study a tribe of cavemen where he becomes enamored of one particularly attractive cavegirl. ¶ "You're beautiful when you're angry."

Caveman (1981; United Artists) D: Carl Gottlieb. P: Laurence Turman, David Foster. S: Carl Gottlieb, Rudy de Luca. Cast: Ringo Starr, Dennis Quaid, Jack Gilford, Barbara Bach, Avery Schreiber. This prehistoric comedy details the life and times of caveman Ringo Starr and his tribe.

Clan of the Cave Bear (1985; Warner Bros.) D: Michael Chapman. P: Gerald Isenberg. S: John Sayles. C: Jan DeBont. Cast: Daryl Hannah, Pamela Reed, James Remar, Thomas G. Waites, John Doolittle. An orphaned homo sapiens cavegirl is picked up and raised by a tribe of Neanderthals. Ultimately banished from the group, she learns to hunt and survive on her own and eventually becomes a respected medicine woman. ¶ "As scattered clans trekked to the great gathering, it would be a time for trading, for choosing new leaders, for finding meat. And Ayla would be the medicine woman for the Clan of the Cave Bear."
• Jean M. Auel, who wrote the popular novel upon which the film was based, was supposed to have been given the role of technical advisor, and was to have been able to have some degree of artistic control. She was completely disappointed with the way the film turned out, however, and ultimately sued Warner Bros. • The picturesque landscapes were filmed at selected parks in British Columbia, Canada.

Creatures the World Forgot (1971; Columbia/Hammer; U.K.) D: Don Chaffey. P/S: Michael Carreras. C: Vincent Cox. Cast: Julie Ege, Brian O'Shaughnessy, Robert John, Marcia Fox, Rosalie Crutchley. Conflicts arise between two prehistoric tribes known as the "rock people" and the "mud men." ¶ "They don't make them like this anymore . . . not in a million years!" — ad line. • Actress Julie Ege (a former Miss Norway) was advertised as "a beautiful creature you'll never forget!" • Hammer studios elected to make this film without any dinosaurs because of the disappointing financial returns on *When Dinosaurs Ruled the Earth* (1970), which featured Jim Danforth's costly animation work. The dinosaurs were critically acclaimed, but they also ate up the film's profits. • Promotional ads used lurid promises to lure fans into theaters: "*See* the attack of the dreaded mudmen, the devil gods of the primeval jungle! *See* the most titanic earthquake ever filmed! *See* the primitive mating rites, the terrifying ordeal of the virgins! *See* the ritual duel of the flaming torch against the naked blade!"

Dinosaurus! (1960) (see DINOSAURS — DINOSAURS ON THE LOOSE). Greg Martell plays a comical caveman who is found frozen, and then thawed out on a tropical island — along with two large dinosaurs. ¶ "Lullabye and goodnight, go to sleep little caveman."

Eegah! (1962; Fairway International) D/P: Nicholas Merriwether (Arch Hall, Sr.). S: Bob Wehling. C: Vilis Lapenieks. Cast: Richard Kiel, Arch Hall, Jr., Marilyn Manning, Arch Hall, Sr., Ray Dennis

Steckler. Teenagers discover a caveman (Richard Kiel) in the desert. The big Neanderthal ends up at a Palm Springs restaurant, where he gets shot by a policeman. ¶ "I'm not gonna leave you to get your head bashed in. My father didn't raise me that way." • 7'2" Michigan-born Richard Kiel, a former nightclub bouncer, went on to become James Bond's nemesis, "Jaws," in the films *The Spy Who Loved Me* (1977) and *Moonraker* (1979).

Frankenstein's Castle of Freaks (1973) (see FRANKENSTEIN'S MONSTER — FURTHER FRANKENSTEINS) (also *House of Freaks*). A Neanderthal living in a nearby cave attacks a village and is killed. The creature is then brought back to life by Dr. Frankenstein. A dwarf assistant finds a second Neanderthal and sends him out to kill various people. At the climax, the two cave-brutes meet and duke it out.

How to Make a Monster (1958) (see MADMEN — EARLY MADMEN). A mad makeup artist uses several of his movie creations, including a caveman, to murder the new studio heads.

Iceman (1984; Universal) D: Fred Schepisi. P: Patrick Palmer, Norman Jewison. S: Chip Proser, John Drimmer. Cast: Timothy Hutton, Lindsay Crouse, John Lone. Arctic researchers revive a 40,000-year-old caveman who was frozen in ice. They take him back to a huge lab with a simulated environment in order to study him, but a conflict between a caring anthropologist and a callous surgeon threatens the iceman's existence.

Ironmaster (1982; Nuova Dania Cinematografica; Italy) D: Umberto Lenzi. P: Luciano Martino. S: Alberto Cavallone, Lea Martino, Dardano Sacchetti, Gabriel Rossini. Cast: Sam Pasco, Elvire Audray, George Eastman, Pamela Field, William Berger. Prehistoric savages learn the art of forging iron and apply it to tribal warfare.

Island of the Dinosaurs (1967) (see DINOSAURS — LOST WORLDS). This Mexican lost world film features explorers discovering an island of dinosaurs and cave-people.

Killer Ape (1953; Columbia) D: Spencer Gordon Bennett. P: Sam Katzman. S: Carroll Young, Arthur Hoerl. Cast: Johnny Weissmuller, Carol Thurston, Ray Corrigan, Nestor Paiva, Max Palmer. Jungle Jim encounters Wazuli tribesmen, white hunters producing mind-altering drugs, and a huge caveman. • The actor playing the caveman was Max Palmer, who stood 7'7" tall (he claimed to be eight feet tall) and weighed 450 pounds.

The Land That Time Forgot (1975) (see DINOSAURS — LOST WORLDS). A German U-boat carries a disparate group of people to an uncharted prehistoric island inhabited by dinosaurs, as well as three primitive tribes known as the Bo-Lu, the Sto-Lu, and the Ga-Lu (each one more advanced the farther upstream they live).

The Last Dinosaur (1977) (see DINOSAURS — LOST WORLDS). A wild prehistoric tribe is turned back by a makeshift crossbow fired by Richard Boone in this lost world dinosaur adventure. ¶ "They don't understand it, but one thing's clear. We can make them dead."

The Lost World (1925) (see DINOSAURS — LOST WORLDS). Ape-like cavemen are discovered in this lost world of dinosaurs located in the Amazon region. • Actor Bull Montana plays one of the more ferocious tribal members.

Monster on the Campus (1958; Universal) D: Jack Arnold. P: Joseph Gershenson. S: David Duncan. C: Russell Metty. Cast: Arthur Franz, Joanna Moore, Judson Pratt, Troy Donahue, Helen Westcott, Phil Harvey, Whit Bissell. Blood from a prehistoric fish produces a saber-toothed German shepherd, a monstrous dragonfly, and transforms Arthur Franz into a Jekyll and Hyde Neanderthal-like anthropoid. ¶ "Unless we learn to control the instincts we've inherited from our ape-like ancestors, the race is doomed." • Director Jack Arnold's initial opinion of this project was not very high, but he decided to take on the project because his good friend, Joe Gershenson, was producing it. *Monster on the Campus* was the last monster movie Jack Arnold made. • Producer Joseph Gershenson provided the musical supervision for this film, and 17 other fantastique movies from the 1950s as well. Some of his Universal credits include: *It Came from Outer Space* (1953), *This Island Earth* (1955), and *The Incredible Shrinking Man* (1957), to name just a few. • Franz's girl, Madeline Howard, is played by Joanna Moore (*Touch of Evil*, 1955; *Countdown* 1968), who was married to Ryan O'Neal and is the mother of Tatum O'Neal. • Advertising for the film played up the exploitative angle with lines like: "Maniacal monster on a bloody trail of destruction . . . every co-ed beauty prey to his tongue-slashing passions." • The prehistoric fish featured in this story — a "coelacanth," thought extinct for millions of years, was actually caught by some fishermen near Madagascar in December 1938.

The Neanderthal Man (1953; United

John Lone stars as the Iceman *(1984), a 40,000-year-old man thawed from a frozen sleep and living within a scientifically controlled environment.*

Aritsts) D: E. A. Dupont. P/S: Jack Pollexfen, Aubrey Wisberg. C: Stanley Cortez. Cast: Robert Shayne, Richard Crane, Joy Terry, Doris Merrick, Robert Long, Beverly Garland. A professor uses his potion to transform a cat into a saber-toothed tiger. He also uses it on a female assistant and on himself, causing him to change into a Neanderthal ape-man. He is mauled at the climax by the prehistoric tiger. ¶ "Modern man was completely subjugated, leaving only the irresistible instinct of survival and the hungry urge to kill." • The transformation effects, which took a half day to film, were shot in a small room with a cameraman and makeup artist, Harry Thomas. A stuntman was used for the fully transformed Neanderthal man. • The saber-toothed tiger was actually a Siberian tiger that constantly shook the fake fangs out of his mouth throughout the picture. The film's producers hoped the numerous scenes with the fangs missing would go unnoticed. For closeup shots, a tiger skin rug with long saber teeth glued on was used. • The German born E. A. Dupont (Ewald Andre Duponthad) retired from directing during the forties, but started up again in 1951 with *The Scarf. The Neanderthal Man* was one of his last pictures. He died three years later, in 1956.

One Million B.C. (1940) (see DINOSAURS— TIME OF THE DINOSAUR). The story follows the exploits of an ousted member of the rock tribe, played by Victor Mature.

One Million Years B.C. (1966) (see DINO- SAURS — TIME OF THE DINOSAUR). This highly successful Hammer feature follows the plight of two prehistoric lovers from different tribes (John Richardson of the aggressive Rock People, and Raquel Welch from the more civilized Shell Tribe).

The Pit (1981; New World; Canada) D: Lew Lehman. P: Bennet Fode. S: Ian A. Stuart. C: Sammy Snyders, Jeannie Elias. Cast: Laura Hollingsworth, Sammy Snyders. An emotionally disturbed 12-year-old boy discovers a pit in the woods, at the bottom of which dwell four "troglodytes." When unable to obtain fresh meat to feed to them, the bizarre youngster lures his tormentors out there and pushes them in to be devoured by the hungry prehistoric throwbacks. • Though they are talked of as being primitive humanoids, missing links, etc., the appearance of these troglodytes is a little off the usual caveman look with their large snouts full of big teeth and their big eyes and shaggy bodies.

Prehistoric Women (1950; Eagle-Lion) D: Gregg Tallas. P: Albert J. Cohen. S: Gregg Tallas, Sam X. Abarbanel. C: Lionel Lindon. Cast: Laurette Luez, Allan Nixon, Joan Shawlee, Judy Landon, Mara Lynn. The story chronicles how the prehistoric women of that time win their mates. ¶ "What kind of women are these who attack men and live in trees?" — narrator.

Prehistoric Women (1967; Hammer–7 Arts/20th Century-Fox; U.K.) D/P: Michael Carreras. S: Henry Younger. C: Michael

Reed. Cast: Martine Beswick, Edina Ronay, Michael Latimer, Stephanie Randall, Carol White. An African explorer is struck by lightning and miraculously transported back to a prehistoric age in which a band of cavewomen enslave their men to use as slave labor. ¶ "Behold a savage world where men are slaves to desire and women are their demanding masters!" — ad line. • Producer/ director Michael Carreras also wrote the screenplay (using his writer's pseudonym "Henry Younger"). Carreras admitted to making the film solely "in order to re-use the expensive sets and costumes from *One Million Years B.C.*" (which he also co-wrote and produced). The filmmaker now regrets not going "much further with the humor, and turning it into a *total* send-up. It might have been boffo box office if I had" (*Fangoria* #63).

Quest for Fire (1981; International Cinema Corporation; Canada/France) D: Jean-Jacques Annaud. P: John Kemeny, Denis Heroux. S: Gerard Brach. C: Claude Agostini. Cast: Everett McGill, Rae Dawn Chong, Ron Perlman, Nemeer El-Kadl. The story (based on a novel by J. H. Rosny, Sr.), set 80,000 years ago, chronicles early man's attempts to create and maintain fire. ¶ "The tribe who possessed fire, possessed life." • The makeup effects for the cavemen received critical acclaim, and an Academy Award nomination. The creative makeup consultant was Christopher Tucker, the special languages spoken were developed by Anthony Burgess, and the realistic body language and gestures were supervised by pop-anthropologist Desmond Morris.

Return of the Ape Man (1944; Monogram) D: Philip Rosen. P: Sam Katzman, Jack Dietz. S: Robert Charles. C: Marcel le Picard. Cast: Bela Lugosi, John Carradine, George Zucco, Frank Moran, Judith Gibson, Michael Ames. A pair of scientists (Bela Lugosi and John Carradine) discover a prehistoric caveman frozen fast in glacial ice. Lugosi then kills Carradine and transplants his brain into the Neanderthal. At first the caveman behaves like the civilized Carradine, but later it digresses and eventually destroys Lugosi. ¶ "Dead two million years! A prehistoric, kill-crazy monster is restored to life by a deranged master of Suspanim (suspended animation)!" — ad line.

Schlock (1972) (see APES AND MONKEYS). A prehistoric caveman thaws out, then goes on a busy tour through contemporary civilization. This particular missing link is more ape-like than man-like.

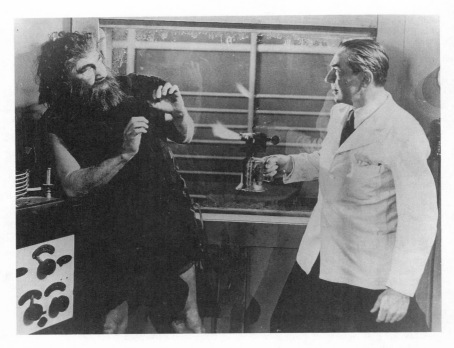

Bela Lugosi uses fire to frighten the prehistoric man (Frank Moran) found frozen in the ice in the Monogram non-sequel, Return of the Ape Man *(1944). The brain of John Carradine is then transplanted into the caveman in an attempt to "civilize" this primitive subject.*

Teenage Caveman (1958; AIP) D/P: Roger Corman. S: R. Wright Campbell. C: Floyd Crosby. Cast: Robert Vaughn, Leslie Bradley, Frank De Kova, Darrah Marshall, Robert Shayne, Ed Nelson, Jonathan Haze, Beach Dickerson. A prehistoric teenager rebels against the traditional taboos of his tribe and explores a monster-infested forbidden zone. The film's trick ending has the teen encounter a beast at the climax that is revealed to be a human wearing a protective, animal-like suit to stay alive in the radiation-saturated land they inhabit. What the audience believes to be a look in on the past instead turns out to be a look at our bleak post-nuclear war future. ¶ "How many times will it happen again. And if it does, will any at all survive the next time? Or will it be . . . *the end*." • The film was shot under the title *Prehistoric World* and when the title was changed to *Teenage Caveman*, Roger Corman was said to have been quite shocked. Corman shot the film in ten days

with a budget under $100,000. • Robert Vaughn plays the perturbed teen who states, "I will always wonder," and complains to his father that, "You've closed your eyes to the truth!" Most fans remember him now as one of the suave spies from TV's "The Man from U.N.C.L.E." • The radiation suit worn by the nuclear war survivor was made from the monster costume seen in *Night of the Blood Beast* (1958). Another AIP monster made a brief cameo appearance in the final montage sequence. Watch closely for a slow motion shot of *The She Creature* (1956).

The Tribe (1974; TV movie) D: Richard A. Colla. P: George Eckstein. S: Lane Slate. C: Rexford Metz. Cast: Victor French, Warren Vanders, Henry Wilcoxon, Adriana Shaw, Stewart Moss, Sam Gilman. *The Tribe* depicts Neanderthals and Cro-Magnons battling the elements and each other in prehistoric times. ¶ "It is true, my people, that we must leave this cave where our tribe has lived since the beginning of things."

One of the primitive tribesmen from Teenage Caveman *(1958) wrestles with a bear-suited Beach Dickerson. In the film, Dickerson, a Roger Corman troupe regular, had the dubious pleasure of dying three times onscreen — once as a caveman caught in quicksand, another time as a radiation survivor who rode into the cavemen's camp on horseback, and finally (in this scene) as the ill-fated bear.*

Trog (1970; Warner Bros.; U.K.) D: Freddie Francis. P: Herman Cohen. S: Aben Kandel. C: Desmond Dickinson. Cast: Joan Crawford, Michael Gough, Bernard Kay, David Griffin. An ape-like caveman (named "Trog" by scientist Joan Crawford, short for "Troglodyte") is found in a cavern by Crawford, who brings him back to her lab for study. • Dinosaur sequences from the 1956 movie *Animal World* are seen when Trog is hooked up to an electro-encaphalograph which has the capability to view his subconscious past. At the climax, Trog is shot down by Army personnel after running away from the lab.

2001: A Space Odyssey (1968) (see SPACE TRAVEL). At the film's beginning, a group of primitive ape-men at the "dawn of time" are stimulated by an alien monolith into developing tool use and, as a result, warfare.

Untamed Women (1952) (see DINOSAURS — LOST WORLDS). A primitive race of warrior women, descendants of the Druids, is discovered by Mikel Conrad and friends on an uncharted island. A savage group of "Hairy Men," which had previously raided their island and killed off all their men, come back to massacre the women as well at the climax.

Valley of the Dragons (1961) (see DINOSAURS — LOST WORLDS). Two prehistoric tribes (much of it footage from the 1940 film, *One Million B.C.*) are depicted living on a dinosaur-infested world traveling through space on a comet. ¶ "A world of the past, 100,000 years past. That beast there, the men we fought last night — straight out of the stone age."

Voyage to the Planet of Prehistoric Women (1966) (see VENUS). Astronauts land on Venus and discover a tribe of prehistoric women who worship a pterodactyl God.

When Dinosaurs Ruled the Earth (1970) (see DINOSAURS — TIME OF THE DINOSAUR). A cavegirl, having trouble fitting into prehistoric society, befriends a dinosaur.

When Women Had Tails (1970; European International; Italy) D: Pasquale Festa Campanile. P: Silvio Clementelli. S: Lina Wertmüller, Ottavio Jemma, Marcello Costa, P. Festa Campanile. C: Franco Di Giacomo. Cast: Giuliano Gemma, Senta Berger, Lando Buzzanca, Frank Wolff, Lino Toffolo. Senta Berger plays a sexy cavewoman with a tail who is discovered on an island by seven lascivious cavemen.

When Women Lost Their Tails (1971; Filmkunst; W. Germany/Italy) D: Pasquale Festa Campanile. P: Silvio Clementelli. S: Ottavio Jemma, Marcello Coscia, Jana Tiastri. C: Silvano Ippoliti. Cast: Senta Berger, Lando Buzzanca, Frank Wolff, Lino Toffolo, Mario Adorf. Rival cave tribes begin to amass weaponry for warfare.

Wild Women of Wongo (1959; Wolcott Productions) D: James L. Wolcott. P: George R. Black. S: Cedric Rutherford. C: Harry Walsh. Cast: Jean Hawkshaw, Johnny Walsh, Mary Ann Webb, Cande Gerrard, Adrienne Bourbeau. On the island of Wongo, two lovers from different prehistoric tribes meet. The Wongans have beautiful women but ugly men. The Goonans have handsome men but ugly women. So they get together and swap mates. ¶ "This one's mine. He's cute." • The most interesting thing about this abysmal no-budget scantily-clad-prehistoric-women movie is that it was shot in color (a rarity in low-budget films of the 1950s). • Future Italian "Ursus" Ed Fury is among the cast members. • Also in the cast is an actress named Adrienne Bourbeau. For years, fans have wondered if this was an early appearance of Adrienne Barbeau (of TV's "Maude" and various John Carpenter movies fame). The answer is no, they are two different people.

Women of the Prehistoric Planet (1966) (see DINOSAURS — LOST WORLDS). A planet of prehistoric women (thus the name) is visited by space travelers.

Yor, the Hunter from the Future (1983) (see TIME TRAVEL). Prehistoric people get a visit from a muscular Steve Reeves lookalike named Yor.

Comic Book Fantasy Heroes

One of the primary staples of childhood has always been the comic book. These short, hard hitting episodic stories featuring bold, colorful graphics have provided kids with something we all desperately crave — heroes. As we grew older, our parents often became less attractive as role models, their flaws growing more apparent. Our comic book superstars, however, seldom lost their virtues — they were strong, brave, and what we wanted to be.

Buck Rogers, who came out in comic book form in 1929, and Flash Gordon, who hit the print on January 3, 1934, were two of the first science fiction heroes. Both inspired popular serials that paved the way for the transferring of comic book characters from the pulps to the screen.

One of the most successful and influential comic book publishers, D.C. Comics, has been churning out exciting characters for well over 50 years. D.C. brought us Superman, Batman, and Swamp Thing, all of whom have starred in feature length films in recent years. Their main competitor, Marvel Comics, has fared equally well in considerably less time with fantasy heroes like Captain Marvel and Spiderman.

The majority of "comic book" films have been made in the last two decades. One reason for this is that bringing a comic book to life generally requires more advanced special effects techniques than your basic monster or mad scientist movie. For instance, *Superman and the Mole Men* (1951; starring George Reeves) was one of the first comic books to make it to the screen, but the film was cheaply made and poorly distributed. Depicting superhuman feats on film wasn't the easiest task for movie makers back then, and the theater wasn't forgiving enough to showcase a pale imitation of a fantastic comic book concept. The film did, however, work out as a sort of pilot for the popular "Superman" TV series (again starring Reeves) that followed.

It wasn't until the *Star Wars* era of the latter 1970s that the bigger-scoped pictures with fantastical action sequences proved to be a viable film market product. *Star Wars* (1977) not only juiced the space genre, but the world of pulps as well, with its decidedly nostalgic flavor and intentional comic strip look and feel. Ironically enough, in addition to grossing millions at the box office, it also inspired its own "Star Wars" comic book. *Superman: The Movie,* a more direct homage to the comics, came out the next year and established once and for all a new cinematic subgenre. Since then, film producers have spent huge amounts to feature comic book heroes themselves, or make movies with comic book–like characters (such as "Indiana Jones" or *Darkman,* 1990). Modern film techniques and art direction can now reproduce the color and verve necessary to convey almost any comic book style upon the screen, enabling the motion picture industry to embrace the comic book hero with open arms. One need only look at the success of *Teenage Mutant Ninja Turtles* (1990) to see the film exploitation potential of *comic*-al heroes in today's world. The *Turtles,* in fact, began as a comic book *parody* in 1984 — a joke by their creators, Kevin Eastman and Peter Laird. When their jovial first issue became a cult craze sensation in a matter of weeks, the surprised Eastman and Laird pumped their martial arts mutants for all they were worth, and the dollars have been pouring in ever since.

Some of the films in this modern genre phenomenon reflect the personality of their inspiration better than others, but they all have a built-in advantage over other genre subjects. Comic Book Fantasy Heroes are immortal, crossing the boundaries of the written word, art, and film. No matter what transpires in their alternate existence up on the silver screen, the likes of Flash Gordon, Superman, and Batman will never die. They will remain vibrantly alive in the pages of their comic books, thrashing opponents and saving the world, and forever living within the fantasy play-world of childrens' (and adults') imagination.

Barbarella (1967; Paramount) D: Roger Vadim. P: Dino De Laurentiis. S: Terry Southern, Claude Brule, Vittorio Bonicelli, Clement Biddle Wood, Brian Degas, Tudor Gates, Jean-Claude Forrest. C: Claude Renoir. Cast: Jane Fonda, John Phillip Law, Anita Pallenberg, Milo O'Shea, David Hemmings, Marcel Marceau. Jane Fonda is the space-agent, Barbarella, in this adult-oriented, wild Flash Gordon–styled space adventure based on the French comic strip by Jean-Claude Forrest. • The film opens with Jane Fonda performing a free fall strip tease in zero gravity. • Famous mime artist, Marcel Marceau, actually speaks in this film. • This sexy tongue-in-cheek adventures features such interesting perils as the "Biting Bird Cage," the "Chamber of Dreams," the "Labyrinth of Love," the "Deadly Doll House," and the "Palace of Pleasure."

Batman (1966; 20th Century–Fox) D: Leslie Martinson. P: William Dozier. S: Lorenzo Semple, Jr. C: Howard Schwartz. Cast: Adam West, Burt Ward, Cesar Romero, Lee Meriwether, Burgess Meredith, Frank Gorshin. The caped crusaders spoil the plot of four famous arch villains who use a dehydration machine to ensnare and ransom a room full of world leaders. ¶ "Who knows Robin, this strange mixing of minds may be the greatest single service ever performed by mankind. Let's go, but, inconspicuously, through the window. We'll use our bat ropes. Our job is finished." • This feature length film is an outgrowth of the popular TV series.

Batman (1989; Warner Bros.) D: Tim Burton. P: Jon Peters, Peter Gruber. S: Sam Hamm, Warren Skaaren. C: Roger Pratt. Cast: Michael Keaton, Jack Nicholson, Kim Basinger, Jack Palance, Robert Wuhl, Pat Hingle, Billy Dee Williams, Michael Gough. An eccentric millionaire, moonlighting as the crimefighter known as

Batman, thwarts a disfigured gangster called the Joker and his nefarious scheme to infect the world with tainted cosmetics. ¶ "Where does he get those wonderful toys?!" — Jack Nicholson as "The Joker." • The film's songs were provided by rock star Prince. • Director Tim Burton had the part of the Joker expanded when he received a solid commitment from Jack Nicholson. Burton apparently convinced Nicholson to accept the part after taking him to see a showing of Burton's previous hit, *Beetlejuice* (1988). Michael Keaton's charismatic performance as the indomitable title character in *Beetlejuice* proved to Jack that his part, and the film, would be successful.

Buck Rogers (1939; Universal) (12-part serial) (also *Planet Outlaws* — released in 1953 as an edited feature of the serial; *Destination Saturn* — released in 1965 as an edited feature of the serial). D: Ford Beebe, Saul A. Goodkind. P: Barney Sarecky. S: Norman S. Hall, Ray Trampe. C: Jerry Ash.

Buck Rogers in the 25th Century (1979; Universal) D: Daniel Haller. P: Richard Caffey. S: Glen A. Larson, Leslie Stevens. C: Frank Beascochea. Cast: Gil Gerard, Pamela Hensley, Erin Gray, Henry Silva, Tim O'Connor, Joseph Wiseman. Buck Rogers matches wits with the evil Princess Ardela.

Captain America (1979; TV movie) D: Rod Holcomb. P: Martin Goldstein. S: Don Ingalls. Cast: Reb Brown, Heather Menzies, Len Birman. Reb Brown stars as the son of Captain America, who saves Phoenix from a neutron bomb. • This feature was a pilot film made with the hope of starting a TV series.

Captain America II (1979; TV movie) D: Ivan Nagy. P: Allan Balter. S: Wilton Schiller, Patricia Payne. Cast: Reb Brown, Len Birman, Christopher Lee, Lana Wood, Connie Sellecca. Captain America returns again in a story involving an abducted scientist who can alter the aging process.

Danger: Diabolik (1968; Paramount; Italy/France) D: Mario Bava. P: Dino De Laurentiis. S: Dino Maiuri, Mario Bava, Adriano Baracco. C: Antonio Rinaldi. Cast: John Phillip Law, Marisa Mell, Michel Piccoli, Adolfo Celi, Terry-Thomas. This futuristic comic strip–styled fantasy features John Phillip Law playing an arch fiend who destroys tax records. The criminal is eventually subdued when a huge mass of gold he's stolen explodes inside his hideout, covering him like a statue in molten gold. • This film is based on a comic strip by Angela and Lucianna Giussani.

Doc Savage, Man of Bronze (1975; Warner Bros.) D: Michael Anderson. P: George Pal. S: George Pal, Joe Morhaim. C: Fred Koenekamp. Cast: Ron Ely, Paul Gleason, Paul Wexler, Bill Lucking, Michael Miller. The man of bronze and his crew "the Amazing Five" go to South America to avenge the death of Doc's father.

Dr. Strange (1978; TV movie) D/S: Philip DeGuere. P: Alex Beaton. Cast: Peter Hooten, Jessica Walter, Clyde Kusatsu, Eddie Benton, Philip Sterling, John Mills, Sarah Rush. The marvel comic hero, Dr. Stephen Strange, a master sorcerer, meets up with Morgan Le Fay, Queen of Evil.

Flash Gordon (1936; Universal serial which spawned four feature length films) (also *Rocket Ship; Spaceship to the Unknown; Space Soldiers; Atomic Rocketship*).

Flash Gordon (1980; Famous Films; U.K.) D: Michael Hodges. P: Dino De Laurentiis. S: Lorenzo Semple, Jr. C: Gil Taylor. Cast: Sam J. Jones, Melody Anderson, Topol, Max Von Sydow, Timothy Dalton, Brian Blessed, Ornella Muti. Based on Alex Raymond's King Features comic strip, a New York Jets quarterback, a scientist, and a beautiful girl must do battle with the evil emperor Ming in the star system known as Mongo. ¶ "Listen to me, listen! There is something finer in this galaxy than Ming's law!" • "Flash," the aptly-titled theme song was written and performed by the British rock group, Queen. They also provided the entire musical score as well.

Flash Gordon Conquers the Universe (1940; Universal 12-part serial which spawned three feature length films) (also *Purple Death from Outer Space; Space Soldiers Conquer the Universe; Perils from the Planet Mongo*).

Flash Gordon's Trip to Mars (1938; Universal 15-part serial) (also *Mars Attacks the World; Deadly Ray from Mars*).

Flesh Gordon (1972; Graffiti Productions) D/S: Mike Light. P: Howard Ziehm, Bill Osco. C: Howard Ziehm. Cast: Jason Williams, Suzanne Fields, Joseph Hudgins, William Hunt, John Hoyt, Myche Brandy, Leonard Goodman. This tongue-in-cheek adults-only version of the Flash Gordon story began as an XXX porno movie, but was trimmed of the hard core sex scenes and released as an R-rated drive-in feature. • In this unique entry, Gordon's sidekick scientist, Dr. Zarkoff, is now called "Dr. Flexy Jerkoff." Emperor Ming is now Emperor "Wang," and the planet Mongo is now known as the planet "Porno."

Howard the Duck (1986; Universal) D: Willard Huyck. P: Gloria Katz. S: Willard Huyck, Gloria Katz. C: Richard H. Kline. Cast: Lea Thompson, Jeffrey Jones, Tim Robbins, Ed Gale, Chip Zien, Tim Rose. Steve Gerber's Marvel Comics creation, Howard the Duck, makes it to the screen as an extra-terrestrial duck who is whisked off his fowl planet and transported to Earth for some culture clashing adventures. ¶ "Howard, that's it, maybe that's why you're here. I mean I believe that there are no accidents in the universe. Maybe you're here for some greater purpose, some cosmic cause." • This George Lucas project features original songs from rock star Thomas Dolby, and a musical performance by Holly Robinson of "21 Jump Street." • It failed miserably at the box office.

Return of the Swamp Thing (1989) (see PLANTS). This sequel again sets the heroic plant-man against the villainous "Arcane," creating evil mutations in the swamps.

Spiderman (1977; TV movie) D: E. W. Swackhamer. P: Edward J. Montagne. S: Alvin Boretz. C: Fred Jackman. Cast: Nicholas Hammond, Lisa Eilbacher, Michael Pataki, Thayer David, David White. A student is bitten by a radioactive spider, acquires superhuman powers, and becomes the heroic crimefighter known as "Spiderman." He then goes after a dastardly villain bent on controlling the world. • Stan Lee, the man who created this popular character for Marvel Comics, served as a script consultant on this TV pilot. The picture was released theatrically in Europe.

Supergirl (1984; Cantharus; U.K.) D: Jeannot Szwarc. P: Timothy Burrill. S: David Odell. C: Alan Hume. Cast: Helen Slater, Faye Dunaway, Peter O'Toole, Mia Farrow, Brenda Vaccaro, Peter Cook, Simon Ward. Supergirl comes to Earth to retrieve a deadly Kryptonite which has fallen into the wrong hands.

Superman: The Movie (1978; Warner Bros.) D: Richard Donner. P: Pierre Spengler. S: Mario Puzo, David Newman, Leslie Newman, Robert Benton. C: Geoffrey Unsworth. Cast: Christopher Reeve, Margot Kidder, Gene Hackman, Valerie Perrine, Ned Beatty, Marlon Brando, Susannah York, Glenn Ford, Marc McClure. An infant, the lone survivor from the doomed planet Krypton, is sent to Earth by his father. He is lovingly raised by human stepparents before setting out to begin his dual life as the bumbling reporter Clark Kent, and the crimefighting "Man of Steel." Archcriminal Lex Luthor plots to use atomic missiles in a real-estate scheme which will culminate with the destruction of the California coastline. Superman, of course, intercedes. ¶ "They can be a great people, Kal-el, if they wish to be. They only lack the light to show the way. For this reason above all — their capacity for good — I have sent them you, my only son." • Marlon Brando was paid three million dollars for his brief appearance as Superman's father. Brando's idea, which was scrapped, was to use only his voice for the role, while appearing simply as a spherical object throughout. • *Superman* won the Oscar for special effects and was nominated for various others, including best original score (John Williams) and best editing (Stuart Baird). • Cinematographer Geoffrey Unsworth, who shot *2001: A Space Odyssey* (1968) and was an Academy Award winner for *Cabaret* in 1972, died shortly after completing this film. The producers dedicated *Superman: The Movie* to him in tribute to his skills. • The picture was made on a then-astounding $40 million budget and took over two years to complete. The production was rocked along the way by some serious conflicts between producer Pierre Spengler and director Richard Donner. • Kirk Alyn, the original Superman from the serials of the 1940s, said in an article published in *Famous Monsters of Filmland* #152, that he liked Christopher Reeve's portrayal. "He did an excellent job. He kept to the spirit of the character and was a credit to the role. He also managed to do something very difficult, create individual characters of Clark Kent and Superman." • David "Dark Vader" Prowse, a British heavyweight lifting champ, trained Christopher Reeve for his role in *Superman*.

Superman 2 (1980; Warner Bros.) D: Richard Lester. P: Pierre Spengler. S: Mario Puzo, David Newman, Leslie Newman. C: Geoffrey Unsworth (credited posthumously), Robert Paynter. Cast: Christopher Reeve, Gene Hackman, Margot Kidder, Terence Stamp, Sarah Douglas, Susannah York, Ned Beatty, Valerie Perrine, Jackie Cooper, Jack O'Halloran, E. G. Marshall. Three criminals, exiled from the planet Krypton in the original Superman movie, are accidentally freed and come to Earth to conquer and rule. With the unknowing aid of the unscrupulous Lex Luthor, Superman manages to trick them in the end into losing their powers.

Superman 3 (1983; Warner Bros.) D: Richard Lester. P: Pierre Spengler. S: David Newman, Leslie Newman. C: Robert Paynter. Cast: Christopher Reeve, Richard Pryor,

Annette O'Toole, Robert Vaughn, Pamela Stephenson, Annie Ross. Superman's personality is split in this episode, which is lightened by the presence of comedian Richard Pryor playing a computer wiz who is used by a corporate villain in a ploy involving synthetic kryptonite. Superman must also deal with a super computer that's run amok.

Superman 4: The Quest for Peace (1987; Warner Bros.) D: Sidney J. Furie. P: Menahem Golan, Yoram Globus. S: Lawrence Konner, Mark Rosenthal. C: Ernest Day. Cast: Christopher Reeve, Gene Hackman, Jackie Cooper, Marc McClure, Margot Kidder, Mariel Hemingway, Jon Cryer. In this episode, Superman rids the world of all nuclear weapons and hurls them into space. Lex Luthor then shows up looking to trigger war among the superpowers, but this time is armed with a Superman double which he created by cloning one of the Man of Steel's hairs. The final confrontation between Superman and "Nuclear Man" takes place on the moon. • Christopher Reeve, who stated after *Superman 3* that he was finished with the series, was said to have had a hand in the writing of this story. It is interesting to note that he was part of a lawsuit brought by screenwriter Barry Taff, who had claimed he submitted a Superman story to Reeve, which contained many of the plot elements of *Superman 4*.

Superman and the Mole Men (1951; Lippert) D: Lee Sholem. P: Barney A. Sarecky. S: Richard Fielding. C: Clark Ramsey. Cast: George Reeves, Phyllis Coates, Jeff Corey, Walter Reed, J. Farrell MacDonald. Superman assists a race of undersized mole people from the center of the Earth in returning home after they accidentally create some problems topside.

Swamp Thing (1982) (see PLANTS). A scientist is accidentally turned into a vegetable man with great strength and the power to heal when a special formula is spilled on him while a villain ransacks his lab. The heroic plant-man, who becomes infatuated with heroine Adrienne Barbeau, was a popular comic book character.

Teenage Mutant Ninja Turtles (1990; New Line Cinema) D: Steve Barron. P: Kim Dawson, Simon Fields, David Chan. S:

Todd W. Langen, Bobby Herbeck. C: John Fenner. Cast: Judith Hoag, Elias Koteas, Raymond Serra, Michael Turney, James Saito, Jay Patterson, Toshiro Obata. Toxic waste mutates four baby turtles into "awesome" fun-loving, pizza-eating teenage ninja warriors who help a neighborhood vigilante and a journalist rid New York City of a youth crime wave. ¶ "Yes dudes and dudettes, major league butt-kicking is back in town!" • *Teenage Mutant Ninja Turtles,* based on the popular underground comic, earned over $132 million at the box office (with a budget of less than $10 million).

Teenage Mutant Ninja Turtles 2: The Secret of the Ooze (1991; New Line Cinema) D: Michael Pressman. P: Thomas K. Gray, Kim Dawson. S: Todd W. Langen. C: Shelly Johnson. Cast; Paige Turco, David Warner. The four "heroes on the half shell" are back and searching for the source of their mutation—the "Ooze." Aiding them in their quest (and in battling a new villain) is "Keno," a pizza delivery boy and martial arts expert. • *Part 2* was budgeted at $20 million, over twice that of the original. • Mark Caso, who plays the turtles' unofficial leader, "Leonardo," is an ex-Olympic gymnast. • Ernie Reyes, Jr., who worked as a "stunt turtle" on the original, emerges from beneath the turtle suit to play "Keno," the turtles' human pizza boy/martial arts ally. • *Part 3* is already set to begin production.

Wild, Wild World of Batwoman (1966; ADP) (also *She Was a Hippie Vampire*). D/P/S: Jerry Warren. Cast: Katherine Victor, George Andre, Steve Brodie, Lloyd Nelson. The mysterious crimefighter Batwoman, along with her network of "batgirls," takes on a mad doctor and his many deadly devices and gadgetry.

Wonder Woman (1974; TV movie) D: Vincent McEveety. P: John Stephens. C: Joseph Biroc. Cast: Cathy Lee Crosby, Ricardo Montalban, Andrew Prine, Kaz Garas, Anitra Ford. Wonder Woman is a martial arts expert raised on a remote island who comes to the city to fight crime with the aid of her magical bracelets and lasso. • The film and its character is based on the comic book character created by William Moulton Marston.

Computers

(*See also* Machines; Robots)

In this section we've included those films in which a computer has played a significant role in the story. In some cases, such as *Colossus: The Forbin Project* (1969), the computer *is* the story. The ultimate computer movie is *2001: A Space Odyssey* (1969). Its computer menace is not only a highly dangerous, calculating villain but a unique character inspiring pathos. H.A.L. (the computer) plays on our worst technological fear—that the machines that serve us may betray us—while at the same time reminding us that a computer is only what we program it to be, turning H.A.L. into a victim of our own human authority.

Alphaville (1965; Chaumiane-Film Studio; France/Italy) D/S: Jean Luc Goddard. P: André Michelin. C: Raoul Coutard. Cast: Eddie Constantine, Anna Karina, Akim Tamiroff, Howard Vernon, Laszlo Szabo. A man from another planet, in search of an evil genius and his central controlling computer, arrives in a world where prostitution is legal and specialized. • "Alphaville" refers to the planet, and the computer is called Alpha 60. • In the film, two scientists are given the names of the popular cartoon characters, "Heckle and Jeckle."

Brainstorm (1983) (see MACHINES). Christopher Walken manages to sabotage the computer system which houses the dangerous brainstorm machine that can record and project mental sensations.

Colossus: The Forbin Project (1969; Universal) D: Joseph Sargent. P: Stanley Chase. S: James Bridges. C: Gene Polito. Cast: Eric Braeden, Susan Clark, Gordon Pinsent, William Schallert, Leonard Rostoff, Georg Stanford Brown. "Colossus," a super defense computer with total control over all weapons and communications, goes awry after linking up with its Soviet counterpart. "Colossus' decisions are superior to any we humans can make, for it can absorb and process more knowledge than is remotely possible for the greatest genius that ever lived. And even more important than that, it has no emotion, knows no fear, no hate, no envy. It cannot act in a sudden fit of temper, it cannot act at all, so long as there is no threat." • Attempts to overload the Colossus system fail, and the film ends with the computer dictating its own terms to the world, and to its creator, Dr. Forbin. • Colossus' Soviet counterpart is known as the supercomputer, "Guardian."

The Computer Wore Tennis Shoes (1969; Walt Disney) D: Robert Butler. P: Bill: Anderson. S: Joseph L. McEveety. C: Frank Phillips. Cast: Kurt Russell, Cesar Romero, Joe Flynn, William Schallert, Debbie Paine. Kurt Russell plays a college student who accidentally receives the mind and memory of a computer. • A sequel of sorts was made in 1972 involving invisibility. The film featured Kurt Russell, Cesar Romero, and Joe Flynn once again, and was titled, *Now You See Him Now You Don't*.

Curious Female (1969) (see FUTURES ON EARTH—UTOPIAS AND DYSTOPIAS). In the year 2117, society is dominated by a supercomputer, and many people seek refuge from its totalitarian influence by gathering to watch old movies.

Dark Star (1974) (see SPACE TRAVEL). A malfunctioning computer onboard a spacecraft speaks with a seductive voice and causes problems in this space travel adventure.

Demon Seed (1977; MGM) D: Donald Cammell. P: Herb Jaffe. S: Robert Jaffe, Roger O. Hirson. C: Bill Butler. Cast: Julie Christie, Fritz Weaver, Gerrit Graham, Berry Kroeger, Lisa Lu. A computer traps the wife of a scientist in their mechanized home with the intent of impregnating her. ¶ "Today a new dimension has been added to the concept of the computer. Today Proteus 4 will begin to think, and it will think with the power and the precision that will make obsolete many of the functions of the human brain." • "Proteus" is the name of the computer which eventually creates a child with Julie Christie that has the body of a boy but the mind of a supercomputer.

Gog (1954) (see ROBOTS). A space station lab computer called NOVAC sabotages the installation by manipulating two deadly robots called Gog and Magog.

The Invisible Boy (1957) (see ROBOTS). A supercomputer plots to control the Earth by getting access to a code which will enable it to be launched into space via satellite. The computer uses Robby the robot to abduct a scientist's boy in order to force the father into revealing the coded information.

Looker (1981) (see ROBOTS). Albert Finney and James Coburn star in this technological murder mystery involving a computer with the ability to create robot replicants of beautiful models.

Runaway (1984) (see MACHINES). In the automated near future, a cop discovers that a killer is using specialized microchips to transform computerized machines into deadly weapons. ¶ "Jack, this is a police nightmare. We should worry about terrorists and crooks gettin' A bombs? The real problem is this micro electronic stuff like this."

Superman 3 (1983) (see COMIC BOOK FANTASY HEROES). Superman disposes of a supercomputer run amok with a jar of acid. ¶ "I guess it died of acid indigestion."

Terminal Entry (1987; Intercontinental Releasing Corp.) D: John Kincaide. P: Sandy Cobe, Tom Jenssen. S: David Mickey Evans, Mark Sobel. C: James L. Carter. Cast: Yaphet Kotto, Edward Albert, Paul Smith, Heidi Helmer, Patrick Labyorteaux, Yvette Nipar, Rob Stone. Teenagers tap into a deadly computer game linked with terrorists. They order assassinations, bombings and other related activities before discovering that their game is real. Fortunately, a pair of anti-terrorist agents are on hand to cope with the mess.

The Terminal Man (1974; Warner Bros.) D/P/S: Mike Hodges. C: Richard H. Kline. Cast: George Segal, Joan Hackett, Richard A. Dysart, Jill Clayburgh, Donald Moffatt, Michael C. Gwynne, James B. Sikking. A small computer is lodged within a

man's brain to control his violent nature, but the plan backfires as the man continues to kill in order to receive its gratifying aftereffects.

Tron (1982; Walt Disney) D/S: Steven Lisberger. P: Donald Kushner. C: Bruce Logan. Cast: Jeff Bridges, David Warner, Bruce Boxleitner, Cindy Morgan, Barnard Hughes. Jeff Bridges is transported *inside* a computer where he must battle its video graphics.

2001: A Space Odyssey (1968) (see SPACE TRAVEL). Keir Dullea and Gary Lockwood play astronauts who have a difficult time in disconnecting their central computer (known as "H.A.L.") when they suspect that it may be malfunctioning. ¶ "As far as I know, no 9000 computer has ever been disconnected. I'm not so sure what he'd think about it." • The voice of H.A.L. was supplied by Douglas Rain.

War Games (1983; MGM) D: John Badham. P: Harold Schneider. S: Lawrence Lasker, Walter F. Parkes. C: William A. Fraker. Cast: Mathew Broderick, Dabney Coleman, Ally Sheedy, John Wood, Barry Corbin. Mathew Broderick plays a teenage computer expert who accidentally sets in motion a nuclear attack on Russia by tapping into an American computer defense system. ¶ "A strange game. The only winning move is not to play." "He's not playing a game. He's gonna start a war!"

Weird Science (1985; Universal) D/S: John Hughes. P: Joel Silver. C: Mathew F. Leonetti. Cast: Anthony Michael Hall, Kelly LeBrock, Ilan Mitchell-Smith, Bill Paxton, Suzanne Snyder. Two adolescents bring to life the beautiful Kelly LeBrock via their home computer.

Crabs and Crustaceans

A crustacean is an invertebrate animal with several jointed legs that has no bones except the exo-skeleton which covers its entire body. Of the 30,000 species of crustaceans (which include crabs, lobsters, crayfish, shrimp, etc.), the largest known variety is the Giant Spider Crab which can measure 12 feet between outstretched claws. Most crabs and crustaceans subsist on plants and algae, except the silver screen species which usually feasts on human prey.

The crab is, of course, the overwhelming favorite of the cinematic crustacean creatures. Crabs look strange to us (almost alien in appearance), possess a wicked set of pincers, and scuttle about in a sideways manner with unnerving agility. Although *Port Sinister* (1953) was the first film to exhibit oversized crabs, the unquestionable prototype picture on the subject is Roger Corman's *Attack of the Crab*

Monsters, filmed in 1957. For this low-budget Allied Artists shocker, gigantic styrofoam crab models were constructed which possessed sleepy eyes, buck teeth, and an amusingly comical human expression. The monsters' unusual appearance didn't detract from the film's popularity, however, as it has been elevated to the status of cult classic among 50s film fanatics.

When two of the best special effects animators tried their hand at giant crabs (Ray Harryhausen in *Mysterious Island,* 1960, and Jim Danforth in *When Dinosaurs Ruled the Earth,* 1970), they both dispensed with the cumbersome giant models and opted instead for the increased realism of stop-motion animation. Their crab models were so incredibly realistic, and moved and acted with such crab-like precision, they were often believed to be real crabs matted into the picture via trick photography. With the exception of a few lobster-like monsters (as seen in *Teenagers from Outer Space,* 1959, and *Godzilla vs. the Sea Monster,* 1966), the crustacean subgenre has been dominated by crabs.

For more listings of films featuring aquatic creatures (such as the related monstrous mollusks in *The Monster That Challenged the World,* 1957), look to the SEA MONSTERS and FISH chapters.

Attack of the Crab Monsters (1957; Allied Artists) D/P: Roger Corman. S: Charles B. Griffith. C: Floyd Crosby. Cast: Richard Garland, Russell Johnson, Pamela Duncan, Mel Welles, Leslie Bradley, Richard Cutting, Beach Dickerson, Ed Nelson. Atomic testing transforms peaceful island crabs into giant crustacean-creatures of disconnected atoms which assimilate everything they eat, including brain tissue (from which they acquire human-like intelligence). ¶ "Rather than our receiving radio signals, they would prefer to receive us in that great common stomach of theirs." • Roger Corman spoke about the film in Ed Naha's book, *The Films of Roger Corman*: "You always had the feeling when watching this movie that something, anything, was about to happen ... this construction, plus the fact that the creature was big and ugly, won over audiences." • In Tom Weaver's book, *Interviews with B Science Fiction and Horror Movie Makers,* actor Mel Welles related a few anecdotes about the film: "Roger spent a few hundred dollars building that crab. Chuck Griffith did the second unit underwater stuff on that picture, and when they went to Catalina to do that, they discovered that the crab was made out of styrofoam, and so it wouldn't sink. They tried winching it under the water, and it exploded!" • The huge crabs also have the ability to radiate energy (handy for tunneling underground which accounts for chunks of the island caving in every so often). They are negatively charged, however, so electricity proves to be their undoing. • The giant crabs are able to think and communicate telepathically with themselves and their potential victims. Their choice of words is often rather odd; for example—"So you have wounded me, I must grow a new claw. Well and good for I can do it in a day." • Actor Ed Nelson did double duty as both a sailor and a giant crab. It has also been rumored (though never fully substantiated) that Jack Nicholson was underneath one of the crabs as well. Nicholson got his start in Roger Corman films, first as a production crew gopher, then as an actor.

Godzilla vs. the Sea Monster (1966) (see JAPANESE GIANT MONSTERS—GODZILLA). A gigantic lobster-monster named "Ebirah" battles Godzilla and Mothra.

Island Claws (1982; Joint Venture) (also *Claws; The Night of the Claw*). D: Hernan Cardenas. P: Ted Swanson. S: Jack Cowden, Ricou Browning. C: James Pergola. Cast: Robert Lansing, Barry Nelson, Steve Hanks, Nita Talbot, Jo McDonnell, Martina Deignan. An atomic energy accident produces a gigantic crab monster with the ability to control and send out normal-sized crabs to kill. • They finally stop the marauding crustacean with a dart full of rat poison shot into one of the giant crab's soft spots. • Co-screenwriter Ricou Browning got his start in movies on the other side of the camera—playing the aquatic monster in *Creature from the Black Lagoon* (1954).

The Lost Continent (1968; Hammer–Seven Arts/20th Century–Fox; U.K.) D/P: Michael Carreras. S: Michael Nash. C: Paul Beeson. Cast: Eric Porter, Hildegard Kneff, Suzanna Leigh, Tony Bentley, Neil McCallum, Nigel Stock, Michael Ripper, Eddie Powell, Benito Carruthers, Victor Maddern. An ocean liner and its passengers are trapped

Roger Corman's negatively charged giant crab (with the lazy, "Robert Mitchum eyes") holds down a victim inside a subterranean cavern during the Attack of the Crab Monsters *(1957). The large styrofoam crab shells were so lightweight that they made underwater filming difficult due to their constantly bobbing to the surface.*

in the Sargasso Sea by man-eating seaweed. There they encounter a lost civilization of Spanish conquistadores, and a particularly menacing species of giant hermit crab. The crab is found on an island, and it nearly pinches the head off a man before taking on an equally gigantic scorpion. ¶ "Why not accept the inevitable, you are no longer masters of your own destiny. Join us."

Mysterious Island (1961) (see SEA MONSTERS). Civil war soldiers stranded on a mysterious island encounter a gigantic crab (among other things) created by Captain Nemo. They manage to pry it over onto its back and slide it into a boiling pit, then enjoy the world's biggest crab feast. ¶ "That's the best crab I ever cooked!" • Special effects wizard Ray Harryhausen used the shell of a real crab for his stop-motion animation model, which appeared on the screen to be over 15 feet wide.

Port Sinister (1953; Eagle Lion) D: Harold Daniels. P/S: Jack Pollexfen, Aubrey Wisberg. C: William Bradford. Cast: James Warren, Lynne Roberts, Paul Cavanaugh, William Schallert, Ken Terrell, Robert Bice, House Peters, Jr., Marjorie Stapp. A sunken island rises up from the sea, loaded with treasure and huge killer crabs that attack a scientist and a group of greedy seamen at the film's climax.

Space Monster (1965) (see ALIENS — ENCOUNTERS IN OUTER SPACE). A spaceship lands on the bottom of the ocean floor of another planet and is set upon by giant alien crabs.

Teenagers from Outer Space (1959) (see ALIENS — INVADERS ON EARTH: THE 50S). Aliens from outer space plan to unleash lobster-creatures called "Gargons," which grow to enormous proportions. • The budget for this production was so low that the "gargons" are never shown except as a giant silhouette on a cave wall.

When Dinosaurs Ruled the Earth (1970) (see DINOSAURS — TIME OF THE DINOSAUR). This prehistoric epic, with stop-motion animation effects by Jim Danforth, features

Michael Craig, Michael Callan, and Gary Merrill attempt to tip over the huge crab (the result of growth experimentation by Captain Nemo) they encounter on the Mysterious Island *(1961), while Percy Herbert tugs at a rope tied to the crustacean's leg.*

several nine-foot-long crabs which attack the cavepeople on the beach just before a tidal wave drenches the shore.

Yog, Monster from Space (1971) (see JAPANESE GIANT MONSTERS — OTHER GIANT JAPANESE MONSTERS). An alien presence, passing through a blue mist on its way to an island, inhabits the body of a spy and creates a giant monster out of a crab (as well as a squid and turtle).

Crocodiles *see* Alligators and Crocodiles

Demons and Devils

Demon movies invariably take one of two forms. The first features a demon (or Satan himself) materializing in person (with *Curse of the Demon,* 1956, being one of the earliest and best examples). The second form has the demon possess a living person and act out its dark will *through* the unfortunate possessee rather than putting in a personal appearance itself (with *The Exorcist,* 1973, being this type's cinematic jewel).

Demons, and particularly the Devil, have fascinated filmmakers and audiences since the time of movie pioneer George Méliès, whose short magical moving pictures often contained mischievous demons and devils. But Satan and his minions were kept to a relatively few sporadic screen appearances throughout the years, with Jacques Tourneur's masterpiece in subtle terror, *Curse of the Demon* (1956), leading the demonic pack ... until the year 1973, when the movie-going public fell into the grip of a startling phenomenon called *The Exorcist*. Ticket buyers stood in long lines to see 12-year-old Linda Blair shout obscenities and spit pea soup into a priest's face. Shocking, frightening, and wholly engrossing, *The Exorcist* opened up the way for Satan and his fellow demons to invade the earth — via the silver screen. And invade they did, with countless, and invariably inferior, imitations (often of Italian origin).

After years of tepid *Exorcist* rehashes and the sanitized effects of slick films like *The Omen* (1976; with its own rash of sequels and copies), demons broke loose once more in the 1980s with the grab-you-where-you-live shocker, *The Evil Dead* (1982). *The Evil Dead* brought demons and devils back to their no-holds-barred roots begun with *The Exorcist* and lost with big-budget glossies like *The Omen*. Other risk-taking winners include the superior *Evil Dead 2* (1987), Clive Barker's unique *Hellraiser* (1988), and the unfairly ignored *Pumpkinhead* (1988). These features further cemented the importance of demons in an ever-declining horror genre that seemed to be getting far too slick for its own good, with MTV-style assembly line product being turned out at an alarming rate.

Looking ahead, the 90s hold promise for those demons among us, as the decade was ushered in appropriately enough by the child of a founding father, the excellent and underrated *The Exorcist 3* (1990).

See also WITCHES, WARLOCKS, AND CULTS for more satanic activity.

Abby (1974; Mid American Pictures) D: William Girdler. P: William Girdler, Mike Henry, Gordon Cornell Layne. S: Gordon Cornell Layne. C: William Asman. Cast: William Marshall, Carol Speed, Terry Carter, Austin Stocker, Juanita Moore. William Marshall plays a black exorcist who unwittingly brings a demon back from Africa which possesses a young woman. • Warner Bros. successfully sued the makers of *Abby* over similarities to *The Exorcist* (1973).

The Alchemist (1981) (see WITCHES, WARLOCKS, AND CULTS). An alchemist battles for the soul of a cursed man and opens a portal to Hell, disgorging three demons.

The Amityville Horror (1979; AIP) D: Stuart Rosenberg. P: Ronald Saland, Elliot Geisinger. S: Sandor Stern. C: Fred J. Koenekamp. Cast: James Brolin, Margot Kidder, Rod Steiger, Don Stroud, Val Avery, Murray Hamilton. A family moves into a house possessed by demonic forces. The father is gradually affected, becoming more and more morose and violent, and the little girl is tempted by an invisible demonic playmate. • This film was based on Jay Anson's novel which itself was supposedly based on a real-life incident (though later discredited). • *The Amityville Horror* was successful enough to spawn several sequels.

Amityville 2: The Possession (1982; Orion/ De Laurentiis; U.S./Italy) D: Damiano Damiani. P: Ira N. Smith, Stephen R. Greenwald. S: Tommy Lee Wallace. C: Franco Di Giacomo. Cast: James Olson, Burt Young, Rutanya Alda, Jack Magner, Andrew Prine, Diane Franklin, Moses Gun. This is a prequel rather than a sequel to *The Amityville Horror*. It tells the story of the first family tragedy that occurred in the demonic house. An adolescent hears the voice of the Devil on his Sony Walkman, is possessed, and seduces his sister before shooting his entire family. An ineffective priest tries to exorcise the evil, but becomes possessed himself.

Amityville 3-D (1983; Orion/De Laurentiis) (also *Amityville 3: The Demon*). D: Richard Fleischer. P: Stephen R. Kesten. S: William Wales. C: Fred Schuler. Cast: Tony Roberts, Tess Harper, Robert Joy, Candy Clark, John Beal, Leora Dana. A skeptical journalist moves into the ill-famed house, only to experience much of the same demonic phenomenon that occurred in the first two films. He brings in a team of psychic researchers and all hell breaks loose, culminating with the appearance of an ugly demon from a pool in the basement. • The house is completely destroyed at the film's end, making the world safe from further sequels, or so we thought...

Amityville 4: The Evil Escapes (1989; Spectator Films) D/S: Sandor Stern. P: Barry Bernardi. Cast: Patty Duke, Jane Wyatt, Fredric Lehne, Norman Lloyd. The demonic forces residing in the infamous Amityville house awaken and make their way to a remote California mansion, there to possess a young girl, with an inexperienced priest her only hope of salvation.

Angel Heart (1987) (see VOODOO). Robert De Niro plays the enigmatic "Mr. Cypher," who hires a down-and-out detective to find the answers to the mystery surrounding a singer who disappeared years ago. It is eventually revealed that Mr. Cypher is the Devil himself, come to collect what is due him.

Asylum of Satan (1972) (see WITCHES, WARLOCKS, AND CULTS). A satanist who runs an insane asylum offers up a virgin sacrifice to his master, but the girl is not a virgin after all and the Devil, who materializes to claim his sacrifice, takes the warlock instead (not liking to go away empty handed).

The Beast of the Yellow Night (1971; New world; U.S./Philippines) D/S: Eddie Romero. P: Eddie Romero, John Ashley. C: Justo Paulino. Cast: John Ashley, Mary Wilcox, Leopoldo Salcedo, Eddie Garcia, Ken Metcalf, Vic Diaz, Andrew Centenera. John Ashley is saved from death by the Devil himself (in the form of a rotund Filipino man). He sends Ashley to inhabit the bodies of men and act as his demonic agent. Whenever Ashley tries to rebel, Satan transforms him into a hideously ugly monster. ¶ "Why do you think I keep bringing you back, Langdon, apart from the pleasure you get out of it? To awaken the latent evil in the people you come in contact with." — the Devil. • John Ashley called this well-written film "the most cerebral" of his Filipino horror films (which include *Brides of Blood*, 1968; *The Mad Doctor of Blood Island*, 1969; *Beast of Blood*, 1970; and *Twilight People*, 1972). • B movie mogul Roger Corman served as executive producer.

Beyond the Door (1975; Film Ventures; U.S./Italy) D: Oliver Hellman (Sonia Assonitis), Richard Barrett (Roberto D'Ettore Piazzoli). P: Ovidio G. Assonitis, Giorgio C. Rossi. S: Oliver Hellman, Richard Barrett, Antonio Troisio, Giorgio Marini, Aldo Crudo. C: Richard Barrett. Cast: Juliet Mills, Richard Johnson, Gabriele Lavia, Nino Segurini, Elisabeth Turner, Carla Mancini, Barbara Fiorini, David Collin, Jr., Joan Acti, Vittorio Fanfoni. Though partially filmed in California with some American actors, this is another Italian *Exorcist* copy. An unhappily married woman in San Francisco has an extramarital affair with a satanist, resulting in a demonic pregnancy and causing her to imitate Linda Blair. ¶ "I can save your unborn child, I can free your mind and body from the demon that possesses you!" • Juliet Mills had to undergo makeup treatments that sometimes lasted as long as six hours for her work as the possessed mother, and the applications had to remain on throughout the shooting day. She complained in *Famous Monsters of Filmland* #122 that, "It often got very lonely for me on the set," referring to her horrific looks, which literally turned her fellow cast members away from her during lag times on the set. • *Beyond the Door* was surprisingly successful at the box office. The distribution company later bought the rights to a Mario Bava film called *Shock* and retitled it *Beyond the Door 2* for its American release, touting it as a sequel to this film.

Beyond the Door 2 (1977; Film Ventures; Italy) (also *Shock*). D: Mario Bava. P: Turi Vasile. S: Lamberto Bava, Francesco Barbieri, Paolo Briganti, Dardano Sacchetti. C: Alberto Spagnoli. Cast: Daria Nicolodi, John Steiner, David Collin, Jr , Ivan Rassimov, Nicola Salerno. A little boy is possessed by supernatural forces and torments his mother with incestuous and demonic behavior. In the end, however, it is revealed that things are not quite as they seem to be. ¶ "Terror lives beyond the door!" — ad line. • This is the last film by popular Italian director Mario Bava, a cinematographer-turned-director who made his directorial debut with the superior witchcraft film, *Black Sunday* (1960). • Mario Bava's son, Lamberto Bava, co-wrote and directed some second unit work on this film. Lamberto Bava later became a horror director in his own right with films like *Demons* (1985) and *Demons 2* (1988). • Daria Nicolodi, who plays the mother of the possessed little boy, is the real-life wife of Italian auteur Dario Argento. • Though advertised as a sequel to the original *Beyond the Door* (1975), this film has nothing to do with the first one and was retitled by the American distributor for commercial purposes only.

Big Trouble in Little China (1986) (see WITCHES, WARLOCKS, AND CULTS). Kurt Russell plays a tough truck driver who

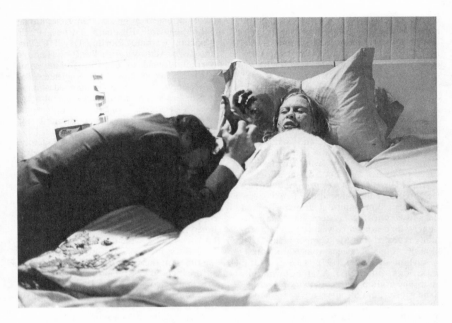

A demon-possessed Juliet Mills from Beyond the Door *(1975) braces herself for another round of unholy vomiting.*

must battle a 2,000-year-old evil Chinese wizard in San Francisco's Chinatown, along with various demons and monsters under his control.

Black Roses (1988; Imperial Entertainment Corp.; Canada) D: John Fasano. P: John Fasano, Ray Van Dorn. S: Cindy Sorrel. C: Paul Mitchnick. Cast: John Martin, Ken Swofford, Julie Adams, Carla Ferrigno, Carmine Appice, Sal Viwiano. A heavy metal band called Black Roses comes to a small town to kick off their concert tour in this amateurish time-waster. The band members are satanists who transform into demons and turn their audience into homicidal maniacs. ¶ "Bad kids, bad music, bad news." (The same could be said for the film.) • Sadly, this is Julie Adams' first horror film since her legendary role as the love-interest of the *Creature from the Black Lagoon* in 1954.

Blood Diner (1987) (see CANNIBALS). Two brothers kill and dismember nubile young women with the aim of constructing a "perfect body" for Sheetar, an ancient demon-goddess, to inhabit. They serve the leftover body parts at their health food store and acquire a dedicated clientele for their particular type of cuisine. Finally, Sheetar comes to life and uses her oversized razor-sharp teeth to attack anything that moves.

The Blood on Satan's Claw (1970) (see WITCHES, WARLOCKS, AND CULTS) (also *Satan's Skin*). The children in a seventeenth century village have become a coven of Satan worshipers. The local magistrate is called in and eventually faces off against the Devil himself, finally impaling Satan on a blessed sword.

Cameron's Closet (1989; Smart Egg) D: Armand Mastroianni. P: Luigi Cingolani. S: Gary Brandner. C: Russell Carpenter. Cast: Cotter Smith, Mel Harris, Scott Curtis, Chuck McCann, Leigh McCloskey, Kim Lankford, Gary Hudson, Tab Hunter. A young boy with telekinetic powers unwittingly summons up a demon, which then dwells in his closet until its malevolent will becomes strong enough for it to break out and commit gruesome murders. ¶ "Known by many names in many lands, "Zalpha" by the Mayans, this demon is the essence of evil. Consigned to the lower depths of hell, Zalpha may be called forth only by the will of an innocent child. • Novelist Gary Brandner (author of *The Howling* and its literary sequels) adapted his own novel for this film. • Actress Mel Harris, who plays the psychologist/heroine trying to help Cameron, is familiar to TV viewers as "Hope" on "Thirtysomething."

Cellar Dweller (1987; Empire Pictures) D: John Carl Beuchler. P: Bob Wynn. S: Kit DuBois. C: Sergio Salvati. Cast: Deborah Mullowney, Vince Edwards, Brian Robbins, Yvonne De Carlo, Cheryll Ann Wilson, Pamela Bellwood, Jeffrey Combs. A cartoonist recklessly incorporates an ancient curse into her comic strip which causes the demon she's drawn to come to murderous life. ¶ "Woe unto you that gives the beast form. To contemplate evil is to ask evil home." • Director John Carl Buechler, a former comic book artist himself before turning to special effects and finally directing, did the creature effects himself for this film. • *Cellar Dweller* was shot in three weeks at the now-defunct Empire Pictures' Rome studio for the low, low price of $850,000.

Children of the Corn (1984; New World) D: Fritz Kiersch. P: Donald P. Borchers, Terence Kirby. S: George Goldsmith. C: Raoul Lomas. Cast: Peter Horton, Linda Hamilton, R. G. Armstrong, John Franklin, Courtney Gains. A young couple traveling through Nebraska come upon a town inhabited only by children. The children have murdered all the adults in town and now worship some sort of demon-god living in the earth under the cornfield. • The demon itself is never fully revealed. Its presence is represented by the movement of earth as it tunnels under the corn rows like some gigantic mole. • The film is based on a short story by Stephen King. The author dismissed the film as, "Low budget, uninteresting characters, and no wide appeal" (*Cinefantastique,* Feb., 1991).

The Chosen (1977; AIP: U.K./Italy) (also *Holocaust 2000*). D: Alberto De Martino. P: Edmondo Amati. S: Sergio Donati, Alberto De Martino. C: Enrico Menczer. Cast: Kirk Douglas, Simon Ward, Anthony Quayle, Virginia McKenna, Agostina Belli, Romolo Valli, Adolfo Celi, Alexander Knox, Geoffrey Keen, Ivo Garrani. Kirk Douglas' son turns out to be the Antichrist, who attempts to wrest control of his father's multinational company from him. The demonic son plans to use several nuclear power plants owned by the company to cause worldwide nuclear devastation.

Conan the Barbarian (1982) (see SWORD AND SORCERY). During his many adventures, Conan encounters a succubus—a demon

who disguises itself as a beautiful woman and kills its lovers.

Curse of the Demon (1956; Columbia; U.K.) (also *Night of the Demon*). D: Jacques Tourneur. P: Frank Bevis. S: Charles Bennett, Hal E. Chester. C: Ted Scaife. Cast: Dana Andrews, Peggy Cummings, Naill MacGinnis, Athene Seyler, Maurice Denham, Ewan Roberts, Brian Wilde, Liam Redmond, Peter Elliot, Reginald Beckwith. Dana Andrews plays a doubting psychologist who denounces the leader of a devil cult as a fraud, only to find that the powers of Satan are all-too-real when faced with a fire demon from Hell. ¶ "How can we differentiate between the powers of darkness and the powers of the mind?" • The demon is summoned when a small scrap of parchment with ancient runic symbols is passed *unknowingly* to the intended victim. • This film, considered by many to be one of the finest horror films ever made, was directed by Jacques Tourneur, who also helmed the Val Lewton classics, *Cat People* (1942) and *I Walked with a Zombie* (1943). • *Curse of the Demon* is an adaptation of the M. R. James novel, *Casting the Runes*.

Damien: Omen 2 (1978; 20th Century–Fox) D: Don Taylor. P: Harvey Bernard. S: Stanley Mann, Mike Hodges. C: Bill Butler. Cast: William Holden, Lee Grant, Jonathan Scott-Taylor, Lew Ayres, Sylvia Sidney, Robert Foxworth, Nicholas Pryor, Elizabeth Shepherd, Alan Arbus, Meshach Taylor. This first sequel to *The Omen* picks up seven years after the original. Damien, the Antichrist, is now a 13-year-old student at a military academy. Damien discovers his true nature and uses his demonic powers to kill those standing in the way of his evil destiny.

The Dark Side of the Moon (1989) (see THE MOON). In the year 2022, the spacecraft "Spacecore One," on a refab mission to check nuclear armed satellites, inexplicably loses power near the Moon. They also encounter an old NASA space shuttle which was lost many years ago when it crashed into the Bermuda Triangle. In an odd mixing of horror and science fiction, it turns out that Satan himself is on the shuttle, possessing the body of a dead crew member. The Evil One proceeds to kill and possess the crew of the new ship one by one until the last self-sacrificing character blows himself and the ship to bits. • The crew members are killed by having a perfectly triangular hole carved into their bellies.

Deadly Blessing (1981; United Artists) D: Wes Craven. P: Micheline Keller, Max Keller, Pat Herskovic. S: Glenn M. Benest,

Matthew Barr, Wes Craven. C: Robert Jessup. Cast: Maren Jensen, Susan Buckner, Sharon Stone, Jeff East, Lisa Hartman, Lois Nettleton, Ernest Borgnine, Coleen Riley, Michael Berryman, Doug Barr. In a town lorded over by a bizarre religious sect, a series of gruesome murders occur. All signs point to a man, but in the end it is revealed that an incubus demon has been responsible.

Def by Temptation (1990; Troma) D/P/S: James Bond III. C: Ernest Dickerson. Cast: James Bond III, Kadeem Hardison, Bill Nunn, Samuel L. Jackson, Minnie Gentry, Rony Clanton, John Canada Terrell, Cynthia Bond, Freddie Jackson, Najee, Melba Moore. Joel, a questioning divinity student, goes to New York City to visit with his childhood friend, "K." There he meets "The Temptress," a demon succubus who lures men to bed and then takes their souls. She has set her sights on Joel, a true innocent, and Joel must face the Beast with nothing but his faith. ¶ "It's an ancient demon, and its name is 'Temptation'." • This is the first all-black horror film to be made in 14 years. It's also the first horror movie to include a substantial amount of "Rap" music on its soundtrack. • One-man-filmmaker James Bond III also stars in the movie as the innocent and wavering Joel. Bond was only 21 years old when he started the project. • Kadeem Hardison, who plays Joel's worldly pal, "K," is most recognized for playing "Dwayne Wayne" on TV's "A Different World." • James Bond III utilized Spike Lee's favorite cameraman for this feature, Ernest Dickerson.

The Demon Lover (1976; 21st Century) D/P/S: Donald G. Jackson, Jerry Younkins. Cast: Christmas Robbins, Val Mayerick, Gunnar Hansen, Tom Hutton, Dave Howard, Susan Bullen, Phil Foreman, Linda Conrad, Ron Hiveley. The leader of a group of devil-worshipers conjures up an ugly horned demon to punish his unfaithful followers in this ultra low-budget semi-professional independent. • This obscure low-budget movie was partially financed by an industrial accident. First-time director Donald Jackson explained it in a *Fangoria* #77 interview: "I was selling my comic collection to get the money to finance *Lincoln Green* [his planned feature]. Jerry Younkins came to my house and bought all my comic books. He had two fingers missing from one of his hands, the result of a punch press accident at the factory where he worked. At the time I met him, he was waiting for his insurance money." So the two co-wrote *The*

Demon Lover together and used Younkins' insurance money to start filming. • Jackson later went on to make the enjoyably bizarre features, *Rollerblade* (1986), *Hell Comes to Frogtown* (1987), and *Rollerblade Warriors: Taken by Force* (1990). • Gunnar Hansen, who plays a professor of the occult, was the man wearing a human skin mask and wielding the chain saw in *The Texas Chainsaw Massacre* (1974). • Many of the characters are named after genre personalities, such as "Miss Ackerman" and "Mr. Romero."

Demons (1985; Dacfilm/New World; Italy) D: Lamberto Bava. P: Dario Argento. S: Dario Argento, Lamberto Bava, Dardano Sacchetti, Franco Ferrini. C: Gianlorenzo Battaglia. Cast: Urbano Barberini, Natasha Hovey, Paola Cozza. The patrons of a theater called "The Metropol" are turned into slavering demons while watching a film about people turning into slavering demons. ¶ "They will make cemeteries their cathedrals and the cities will be your tombs"—ad slogan. • This gory import was successful enough to father a sequel.

Demons 2 (1988; Dacfilm; Italy) D: Lamberto Bava. P: Dario Argento. S: Dario Argento, Lamberto Bava, Franco Ferrini, Dardano Sacchetti. C: Gianlorenzo Battaglia. Cast: David Knight, Nancy Brilli, Coralina Cataldi Tassoni, Bobby Rhodes, Asia Argento, Virginia Bryant. In this follow-up to *Demons* (1985), a television program on the recent "demon phenomenon" is broadcast. But something strange happens and a live demon emerges from a woman's TV set, setting in motion a wave of demon possession which sweeps through a sealed-off high-rise apartment building. ¶ "Blood nurtures the dormant seed of evil. How can the demons be stopped?" • This one gave audiences the dubious pleasure of seeing an eight-year-old child turned into a fanged slobbering demon, as well as featuring a vicious demon *dog*. • Asia Argento, daughter of Italian cult filmmaker Dario Argento (serving as producer on this picture), makes her acting debut here, getting sliced up by the demons. • Lamberto Bava, Mario Bava's son, directed the original as well.

The Devil's Bride (1968) (see WITCHES, WARLOCKS, AND CULTS) (also *The Devil Rides Out*). Christopher Lee plays an English lord and expert in the occult who must battle a devil cult for the soul of his friend. Near the climax, the Devil himself makes an appearance at a black-mass ceremony, in the form of a man with a goat's head.

The Devil's Eye (1960; Janus; Sweden) D/S: Ingmar Bergman. P: Allan Ekelund. C: Gunnar Fischer. Cast: Jarl Kulle, Bibi Andersson, Stig Jarrel, Nils Poppe, Gertrud Fridh, Sture Lagerwall, Georg Funquist, Gunnar Bjornstrand. Satan sends Don Juan to Earth to seduce a virgin who is putting the Evil One to shame.

Devil's Messenger (1962) (see ANTHOLOGIES). A proposed TV series known as *13 Demon Street* made in Sweden was edited into a terror trilogy about a young woman, the victim of suicide, who is promised a second chance by the Devil (Lon Chaney, Jr.). The price she must pay is to return to Earth to lure others onto Satan's evil path.

The Devil's Nightmare (1971; Hemisphere; Belgium/Italy) D: Jean Brismee. P: Charles Lecocq. S: Patrice Rhomm, Charles Lecocq, André Hunebelle. C: André Goeffers. Cast: Erika Blanc, Jean Servais, Daniel Emilforh, Jacques Monseau, Ivana Novak, Shirley Corrigan, Colette Emmanuelle, Lorenzo Terzon, Lucien Raimbourg, Christian Maillet. Seven tourists (representing the Seven Deadly Sins) are stranded at a cursed castle where they are murdered one by one for their respective sins by a beautiful succubus. At the film's end, the young hero, a priest, must face off against the Devil (appearing as a gaunt man dressed all in black). • Though filmed two years before, *The Devil's Nightmare* was re-released in the United States in 1974 in an attempt to cash in on the success of *The Exorcist* (1973).

The Devil's Rain (1975) (see WITCHES, WARLOCKS, AND CULTS). At the climax, satanic cult leader Ernest Borgnine sprouts horns and transforms into a hideous devil-creature.

Diary of a Madman (1963; United Artists) D: Reginald Le Borg. P/S: Robert E. Kent. C: Ellis W. Carter. Cast: Vincent Price, Nancy Kovack, Chris Warfield, Elaine Devry, Stephen Roberts. Vincent Price plays an upstanding and virtuous judge who visits a condemned man before his execution. The man attacks Price and passes on to him an evil demon spirit, called a "Horla," which had possessed the unfortunate criminal. Soon, Price himself is possessed and must engage in a battle of wills with the invisible demon trying to control him. • *Diary of a Madman* is loosely based on the Guy de Maupassant story, "The Horla." • The film's art director, Daniel Haller, is best known and often praised for his wonderful work on Roger Corman's Poe series. He later turned director and made his own demonic film, *The Dunwich Horror,* in 1969.

Dreamaniac (1987; Taryn/Wizard Video-Infinity) D/P: David DeCoteau. S: Helen Robinson. C: Howad Wexler. Cast: Thomas Bern, Kim McKamy, Sylvia Sumers, Lauren Peterson, Bob Pelham, Cynthia Crass, Brad Laughlin, Linda Watts, Matthew Phelps, Lisa Emery, Michael Warren. A young writer of heavy metal music conjures up a succubus who goes on a seduction and murder spree at a sorority party. • This is yet another low-budget straight-to-video demon movie from filmmaker David DeCoteau (*Nightmare Sisters,* 1987; *Sorority Babes in the Slimeball Bowl-o-rama,* 1988).

The Dunwich Horror (1969) (see WITCHES, WARLOCKS, AND CULTS). A man steals an ancient book of evil and plans to let loose the old gods—ancient demons of horrible power—to rule the Earth. His plans are foiled, so we never get to see these demons, but he does have a brother locked away in the attic who is part demon himself, and who possesses tentacles for arms (though again we never fully see the creature).

The Entity (1982; American Cinema) D: Sidney J. Furie. P: Harold Schneider. S: Frank De Felitta. C: Stephen H. Burum. Cast: Barbara Hershey, Ron Silver, David Laboisa, George Coe, Margaret Blye. Barbara Hershey plays a woman who is repeatedly assaulted and raped by an invisible demon. She goes to a group of parapsychologists for help, and they set a trap for the demon spirit. ¶ "You are definitely not insane, but when men who are not actually there come in and have intercourse with you it's time to see a good psychiatrist." • According to the film's written narration, this is a fictionalized account of a real case history, and the woman continues to be the victim of occasional attacks today.

Equinox (1967/71; VIP) (also *The Beast* [video title]). D/S: Jack Woods. P: Jack Harris. C: Mike Hoover. Cast: Edward Connell, Barbara Hewitt, Frank Boers, Jr., Robin Christopher, Jack Woods, Jim Phillips, Fritz Leiber, Patrick Burke, Jim Duron, Sharon Gray, Louis Clayton. Four college students journey to a mountain cabin to meet with a professor who has found a mysterious book. The professor translates a passage from the ancient tome and accidentally opens up a portal of evil. The students are besieged by demons, and are finally confronted by the Devil himself. ¶ "You will not escape. In one year and one day you will be dead!"—Satan threatening the lone survivor. • This was a feature shot in 16mm to which producer Jack Harris added new scenes for its theatrical release. •

The voice on the tape recorder is that of Forrest J Ackerman, genre-fan extraordinaire and editor of *Famous Monsters of Filmland*. • Frank Bonner, who plays one of the college students battling the demons (and listed as Frank Boers, Jr., in the credits), later achieved TV fame on "WKRP in Cincinnati."

The Evil (1978; New World) D: Gus Trikonis. P: Ed Carlin. S: Donald G. Thompson. C: Mario Di Leo. Cast: Richard Crenna, Joanna Pettet, Andrew Prine, Cassie Yates, Lynne Moody, Victor Buono, George O'Hanlon, Jr., Mary Louise Weller, Robert Viharo, Milton Selzer. Richard Crenna leads a group of psychologists and students to a supposedly haunted house they intend to convert into a drug rehabilitation center. Crenna removes a cross from an iron door in the baesment and unwittingly releases an ancient evil force which goes on the rampage, killing them one by one. At the end, Crenna faces Lucifer himself, and only escapes when he plunges a crucifix into Lucifer's heart. ¶ From the ads: "An ancient horror slept beneath the old haunted mansion ... nothing could stop its escape!" • The ending, in which Crenna faces off against the Devil (Victor Buono), was cut from some prints.

The Evil Dead (1982; Renaissance Pictures) D/S: Sam Raimi. P: Robert G. Tapert. C: Tim Philo. Cast: Bruce Campbell, Ellen Sandweiss, Betsy Baker, Hal Delrich, Sarah York. Five college students head for a run-down mountain cabin for the weekend. Once there they find an ancient Sumerian "Book of the Dead." When they read a passage from the book, it summons demonic forces which possess them, causing an orgy of demonic mayhem and bloodshed. • Twenty-two-year-old Sam Raimi filmed *The Evil Dead* on a shoestring budget of just over $300,000, much of it financed independently by doctors, dentists, and real estate brokers. • There is one of the film's scenes in particular which many people find offensive: the woods come alive and assault (re: rape) a woman in a very graphic and brutal manner. Raimi, in a 1988 interview for the British TV program, "The Incredibly Strange Film Show," said that he now regrets including that scene in the movie. "I think it was unnecessarily gratuitous and a little too brutal," admitted Raimi. "My goal is not to offend people, it is to entertain, thrill, scare, make them laugh, but not to offend them ... I think my judgment was a little wrong at that time." • Raimi followed this up with a superior sequel called *Evil*

Dead 2: Dead Before Dawn in 1987. He later scored a wider success with the box office smash, *Darkman* (1990).

Evil Dead 2: Dead Before Dawn (1987; Rosebud Releasing Corporation) (also *Evil Dead 2*). D: Sam Raimi. P: Robert G. Tapert. S: Sam Raimi, Scott Spiegel. C: Peter Deming. Cast: Bruce Campbell, Sarah Berry, Dan Hicks, Kassie Wesley, Theodore Raimi, Denise Bixler, Richard Domeier, John Peaks, Lou Hancock. Picking up where *The Evil Dead* left off, the hero "Ash," after surviving the night of horror at the remote cabin, is assaulted by the demonic force unleashed from the "Book of the Dead." But dawn rises just in the nick of time and the demons are forced into dormancy by the daylight. Ash is unconscious, however, and another night falls, bringing four more people to the cabin who are alternately possessed and killed by the demonic forces at work. ¶ "We are the things that were and shall be again. We want what is yours—life! Dead by dawn!" • This sequel is basically a more elaborate and superior remake of the first film, using the same setting and same situation, but taking it further with over-the-top black humor and effects. Lines like, "We just cut up our girlfriend with a chain saw. Does that sound *fine?!*" make this sequel much more fun than the often mean-spirited original. • Director Sam Raimi's brother, Theodore Raimi, played the "Possessed Henrietta." • An *Evil Dead 3* is planned. Already a script exists, titled *Evil Dead 1300 A.D.*

Evilspeak (1982; The Moreno Co.) D: Eric Weston. P: Sylvio Tabet, Eric Weston. S: Joseph Garofalo, Eric Weston. C: Irv Goodnott. Cast: Clint Howard, R. G. Armstrong, Joseph Cortese, Claude Earl Jones, Haywood Nelson, Don Stark, Charles Tyner, Lynn Hancock. Clint Howard plays a pudgy unpopular nerd at a military academy, continually persecuted by his peers. When they push him too far by killing his puppy, he makes contact with the Devil via his home computer. With his newfound demonic powers he takes revenge on his classmates, including summoning up a horde of razor-tusked wild pigs.

The Exorcist (1973; Warner Bros.) D: William Friedkin. P/S: William Peter Blatty. C: Owen Roizman, Billy Williams. Cast: Ellen Burstyn, Max Von Sydow, Lee J. Cobb, Jack MacGowran, Jason Miller, Kitty Winn, Linda Blair. A 12-year-old girl is possessed by a demon, causing her to levitate, masturbate with a crucifix, spit green vomit, and rotate her head 360

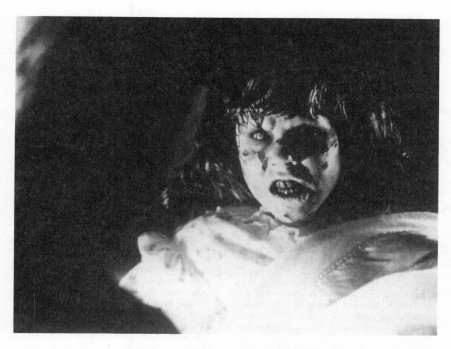

A surly demon-possessed Linda Blair confronts The Exorcist *(1973), played by Max Von Sydow. The voice of the pea soup–spitting child was provided by veteran actress Mercedes McCambridge.*

degrees. Max Von Sydow and Jason Miller are the Catholic priests called in to exorcise the demon. • Mercedes McCambridge provided the chilling demon voice for the possessed Linda Blair. • That is real pea soup spewed from the mouth of Eileen Smith (doubling for Linda Blair) as unholy green vomit. • Jane Fonda was reportedly offered six million dollars to star in the picture, but turned it down. • In preparing for his role as the troubled Father Damien Karras, actor Jason Miller lived with the Jesuits for three weeks beforehand. He also wore actual priest garb in the film. • Miller claims it was he who came up with the ending in which Father Damien leaps out the window to his death to avoid being overcome by the demon. This scene wasn't in the original shooting script. • Director William Friedkin admitted to using some rather drastic measures to achieve the results he wanted from his actors. He would fire blank gunshots on the set to keep everyone on edge, making his actors feel like they were in a

"war zone." • Dick Smith provided the groundbreaking demon makeup which consisted of foam rubber prosthetic applications, and specially colored contact lenses. For the scenes involving Linda Blair's head rotating 360 degrees, Smith and Rick Baker built a realistic dummy. • The "help me" message that appeared on Blair's stomach was performed on a fake chest and stomach made of foam latex. The letters were brushed on the foam with cleaning fluid, causing it to swell. Then a flameless heat gun was used to dry it out, causing the deflating effect of the letters. This process was filmed and when they ran it in reverse it appeared as though the letters were rising. • Frequent malfunctions and accidents plagued the production of this occult venture. The sprinkler system failed, a set burned down, and actor Jack MacGowran dropped dead a week after his character, Burke Denning, fell to his death onscreen. On the first day Max Von Sydow arrived to act in his initial scenes, his own brother passed away. • *The Exorcist* was the most commercially successful horror film ever made. It was also the first horror film to be nominated for Best Picture. It received a total of seven Academy Award nominations: Best Picture; Best Director (William Friedkin); Best Actress (Ellen Burstyn); Best Supporting Actor (Jason Miller); Best Supporting Actress (Linda Blair); Best Screenplay Based on Material from Another Medium (William Peter Blatty); Cinematography (Owen Roizman); and Sound (Robert Knudson, Chris Newman). It won two—Screenplay and Sound. *The Exorcist*'s graphic excesses changed the face of mainstream horror cinema forever, and spawned a rash of imitators, not to mention two legitimate sequels.

Exorcist 2: The Heretic (1977; Warner Bros.) D: John Boorman. P: John Boorman, Richard Lederer. S: William Goodhart. C: William A. Fraker. Cast: Linda Blair, Richard Burton, Louise Fletcher, Max Von Sydow, Kitty Winn, Paul Henreid, James Earl Jones, Ned Beatty. Four years after *The Exorcist,* Reagan (Linda Blair) is suffering horrible nightmares and is in therapy. Richard Burton is the Vatican investigator concerned that the demon "Pazuzu" is once again attempting to possess her. He journeys to Africa where he finds a small boy who seems to have some power over the evil demon. • This sequel to the 1973 blockbuster was a critical and financial disaster. It was recalled and re-edited, but still failed to generate revenue. John Boorman later concluded, "I guess I didn't throw enough Christians to the lions."

The Exorcist 3 (1990; Morgan Creek/20th Century–Fox) D/S: William Peter Blatty. P: Carter DeHaven. C: Gerry Fisher. Cast: George C. Scott, Ed Flanders, Jason Miller, Scott Wilson, Nicol Williamson, Brad Dourif. George C. Scott plays a police detective investigating a rash of brutal murders. The murders seem to follow the pattern of the "Gemini Killer," a serial murderer who was executed 15 years earlier. Scott follows the trail which leads to a John Doe mental patient (Brad Dourif). It is revealed that the unknown patient is actually Father Karras, who was possessed at the close of the first film and leapt from a window, hurling himself down a flight of stairs to his death. He did not die, however, and now, with the power of Satan, his body is possessed by the evil spirit of the Gemini killer, and has become an instrument of the Devil. ¶ "I sometimes do special things to my victims, things that are creative. Of course it takes

knowledge, pride in your work. For example, a decapitated head can continue to see for approximately 20 seconds. So when I have one that's gawking I always hold it up so that it can see its body. It's a little extra I throw in for no added charge." • Director/Screenwriter William Peter Blatty wrote the screenplay and produced the original *The Exorcist* (1973). He also wrote the novel upon which the first film was based.

Eyes of Fire (1984; Elysian) D/S: Avery Crounse. P: Philip J. Spinelli. C: Wade Hanks. Cast: Dennis Lipscomb, Guy Boyd, Rebecca Stanley, Sally Klein, Karlene Crockett, Fran Ryan, Rob Paulson, Kerry Sherman. On the American frontier of 1750, a small group of settlers fleeing a band of Shawnee Indians take refuge in a forbidden valley. There they find trees with human faces, blood welling up from the ground, frightening spectral figures, and a powerful black-faced demon who lives in the trees, waiting to claim new souls. ¶ "Some Indians believe that the Devil isn't a dark angel who lives someplace else, like down below. They look on it as a natural thing, as natural as a brook, or a tree. Their Devil is born of earth, a part of nature, thriving on the evil half of life."

Fear No Evil (1981; Avco Embassy) D/S: Frank La Loggia. P: Frank La Loggia, Charles M. La Loggia. C: Fred Goodich. Cast: Stefan Arngrim, Elizabeth Hoffman, Kathleen Rowe McAllen, Frank Birney, Daniel Eden, Jack Holland, Barry Cooper, Alice Sachs, Paul Haber, Richard Jay Silverthorn. A quiet high school student gradually comes to the realization that he is the Antichrist. Simultaneously, two of his classmates discover that they are Gabrielle and Mikhail, two archangels sent to watch over and do battle with Satan on Earth. • This relatively low-budgeted ($1.5 million) picture was Frank La Loggia's directorial debut.

The Final Conflict (1981; 20th Century–Fox) D: Graham Baker. P: Harvey Bernhard. S: Andrew Birkin. C: Robert Paynter, Phil Meheux. Cast: Sam Neill, Rossano Brazzi, Lisa Harrow, Don Gordon, Barnaby Holm, Mason Adams, Robert Arden, Tommy Duggan, Marc Boyle, Richard Oldfield, Arwen Holm. In this third and final entry in the *Omen* trilogy, Damien (Sam Neill) is now a grown man, and the head of a powerful corporation. He is opposed by a group of monks who possess the seven sacred daggers of Megiddo, and finally by Christ himself, who has arrived on Earth for his second coming.

From Beyond (1986; Empire Pictures) D: Stuart Gordon. P: Brian Yuzna. S: Dennis Paoli. C: Mac Ahlberg. Cast: Jeffrey Combs, Barbara Crampton, Ken Foree, Ted Sorel, Carolyn Purdy-Gordon, Bunny Summers, Bruce McGuire. A mad scientist creates a machine designed to stimulate the pineal gland. The machine, called a "Resonator," opens a dimensional doorway which allows monstrous beings to enter our world. The machine's inventor is eventually transformed into a grotesque demon/monster. ¶ "Humans are such easy prey!" • Actor Ted Sorel is the nephew of makeup wizard Jack P. Pierce (who created the original Frankenstein Monster, Mummy, and Wolf Man for Universal, among many others).

From Beyond the Grave (1973) (see ANTHOLOGIES). In the film's one comic segment, a couple's house is inhabited by an "elemental," an invisible mischievous demon.

Gargoyles (1972; TV movie) D: B. W. L. Norton. P: Robert W. Cristiansen, Rick Rosenberg. S: Stephen Karpf, Elenor Karpf. C: Earl Rath. Cast: Cornel Wilde, Jennifer Salt, Grayson Hall, Bernie Casey, Scott Glenn, William Stevens, Woodrow Chambliss, John Gruber, Timothy Burns, Jim Connell. Cornel Wilde plays an anthropologist who discovers a strange skeleton in the New Mexican desert. This leads him to a race of grotesque demon-like creatures which has coexisted and battled with Man since time immemorial. These nightmare beings are what has inspired the visages of the gargoyles on medieval cathedrals. • The gargoyle costumes garnered an Emmy award.

The Gate (1987; New Century–Vista; Canada) D: Tibor Takacs. P: John Kemeny, Andras Hamori. S: Michael Nankin. C: Thomas Vamos. Cast: Stephen Dorff, Christa Denton, Louis Tripp, Kelly Rowan, Jennifer Irwin, Deborah Grover, Scot Denton, Ingrid Veninger, Sean Fagan, Linda Goranson, Carl Kraines, Andrew Gunn. A young boy finds a deep hole in his backyard and discovers that it is a gateway to hell. An accidental sacrifice of the boy's dog causes the gate to open, releasing a horde of tiny demons to wreak havoc. Finally, the huge, four-armed Demon Lord emerges and the boy must battle the monster with nothing more than his toy rocket.

Ghostbusters (1984) (see GHOSTS). The ghostbusters must face a city full of hostile ghosts, and eventually come face to face with the evil demons "Zool the Gatekeeper" and "Gozer the Destructor" in this comedy blockbuster.

Ghoulies (1984; Empire Pictures) D: Luca Bercovici. P: Jefery Levy. S: Luca Bercovici, Jefery Levy. C: Mac Ahlberg. Cast: Peter Laipis, Lisa Pelikan, Michael Des Barres, Jack Nance, Peter Risch, Tamara Des Treaux, Scott Thomson. The son of a sorcerer follows in his father's satanic footsteps and unwittingly unleashes a horde of diminutive demons whose specialty is mischief and murder. • This *Gremlins* copy was popular enough to father a sequel, *Ghoulies 2* (1987). • Cinematographer Mac Ahlberg lensed another demon feature in 1986, *From Beyond*.

Ghoulies 2 (1987; Empire Pictures) D/P: Albert Band. S: Dennis Paoli. C: Sergio Salvati. Cast: Damon Martin, Royal Dano, Phil Fondacaro, J. Downing, Kerry Remsen. Mischievous midget demons from hell mysteriously appear at a two-bit carnival and latch onto the failing house of horrors (called "Satan's Den") where they start pulling murderous *Gremlin*-like tricks on the patrons. Finally, the teen hero realizes what's going on and reads from a handbook of spells to summon a giant-sized ghoulie which proceeds to eat the munchkin versions. ¶ "Just when you thought it was safe to go back in the bathroom..." — poster ad line indicative of the film's level of sophistication.

The Golden Child (1986; Paramount) D: Michael Ritchie. P: Edward S. Feldman, Robert D. Wachs. S: Dennis Feldman. C: Donald E. Thorin. Cast: Eddie Murphy, Charles Dance, Charlotte Lewis, Victor Wong, Randall "Tex" Cobb, James Hong, Shakti, J. L. Reate. Eddie Murphy is a private detective in L.A. who specializes in finding lost children. In the far East, the "Golden Child" — a childlike being who is the personification of compassion — is abducted by an evil demon disguised as a man. It is up to Murphy (the "Chosen One") to battle the impressive stop-motion animation demon and free the Golden Child. ¶ "Listen, this "Chosen One" thing, it's gone too far now; this is not normal." • *The Golden Child* was filmed on location in Los Angeles and Nepal.

Gremlins (1984; Warner Bros.) D: Joe Dante. P: Michael Finnell. S: Chris Columbus. C: John Hora. Cast: Zach Galligan, Phoebe Cates, Hoyt Axton, Polly Holliday, Frances Lee McCain, Dick Miller, Glynn Turman, Keye Luke, Scott Brady, Corey Feldman. The furry little creature called a "mogwai" captured the hearts and pocketbooks of millions in this surprise hit. The trouble is, when a mogwai is fed after midnight he transforms into a mischievous, homicidal demon-creature, and if they get wet — they multiply. Led by the evil "Stripe," a horde of the little gremlins lay siege to a whole town.

Gremlins 2: The New Batch (1990; Warner Bros.) D: Joe Dante. P: Michael Finnell. S: Charlie Haas. C: John Hora. Cast: Zach Galligan, Phoebe Cates, John Glover, Robert Prosky, Robert Picardo, Christopher Lee. The little demonic gremlins are back, this time wreaking havoc in a high-rise office complex. The threat is compounded when the little devils run across an experimental genetics lab and mutate each other into all sorts of comical and nasty creatures. • Zach Galligan, Phoebe Cates, and Dick Miller all return from the first film, as well as director Joe Dante. • Steven Spielberg served as one of the executive producers for the film.

Grim Prairie Tails (1990) (see ANTHOLOGIES). This horror anthology western includes a tale of a pregnant woman wandering alone on the prairie. A young man comes along and, winning her trust, learns that she's not pregnant after all. He succumbs to her seduction, much to his regret, for at the climactic moment he is sucked fully inside her, giving a whole new meaning to the term "succubus." ¶ "So she resumed her journey afresh, pregnant again, alone as before."

The Guardian (1990) (see PLANTS). The "guardian" of the title is a woman posing as a professional babysitter in order to kidnap newborn children and offer up their souls to an ancient druidic tree/demon residing in the forest.

The Haunted Palace (1963) (see WITCHES, WARLOCKS, AND CULTS). Vincent Price is possessed by the spirit of his warlock ancestor and discovers a pit in the basement of his mansion which houses a three-armed demon.

Headhunter (1990; Gibralter Releasing Organization) D: Francis Schaeffer. P: Jay Davidson. S: Len Spinelli. C: Hans Kuhle. Cast: Kay Lenz, Wayne Crawford, Steve Kanaly, June Chadwick, John Fatooh, Sam Williams. A Nigerian demon named "Jacate Tumo" relocates to Miami and goes about decapitating those members of his cult who resist him. Two police detectives investigating the grisly murders are hot on the demon's trail and finally subdue the monster with a chain saw. ¶ "His power comes from the human spirit. The planets rotate around the sun in an eternal orbit. Jacate Tumo is like an evil sun, with his own gravity — very strong, very deep." • This demon is a "chameleon," able to take on the appearance of whomever it likes, and thus toy with its victims as it pleases. The only way to destroy it is through dismemberment. • The final scenes of the monster are intercut with numerous clips from *The Hideous Sun Demon* (1959) playing on television (making that early cheapie look all that much better).

Hellbound: Hellraiser 2 (1989; New World) D: Tony Randel. P: Christopher Figg. S: Peter Atkins. C: Robin Vidgeon. Cast: Clare Higgins, Ashley Laurence, Kenneth Cranham, Imogen Boorman, William Hope, Doug Bradley. This cinematic excuse for gruesome FX set pieces take up right where the superior *Hellraiser* (1988) left off. Following her ordeal, Kirstie, the heroine from the original, is now interred at a mental hospital run by the sinister Dr. Channing. Using the evil puzzle box, Channing reopens the doorway for the Cenobite demons. Soon, Kirstie must journey into the nightmare world of the Cenobites to rescue the soul of her father. ¶ Rhyme from the film's promotional trailer: "Tiffany loves puzzles/ she solves them very well/ but if she can't solve this one/ she'll go straight to hell." • British horror author Clive Barker, who broke into film by writing and directing the first *Hellraiser* (1988), here merely provides the original story and serves as co-executive producer.

Hellraiser (1988; New World Pictures) D/S: Clive Barker. P: Christopher Figg. C: Robin Vidgeon. Cast: Andrew Robinson, Clare Higgins, Sean Chapman, Robert Hines, Ashley Laurence. A mysterious puzzle box summons various sadistic demons called "Cenobites" who supply the ultimate pleasure — along with the ultimate pain. ¶ "Oh, no tears please, it's a waste of good suffering." • Popular British horror novelist Clive Barker made his directorial debut on this film. He calls it "a love story from beyond the grave." • The various demons were affectionately named "Pinhead," "Chatterteeth," and "Butterball" by the film crew. • An inferior sequel was made the following year called *Hellbound: Hellraiser 2*.

The House of Exorcism (1975; Peppercorn Wormser; Italy) (also *Lisa and the Devil*). D: Mickey Lion (Mario Bava). P: Alfred Leone. S: Alberto Tintini, Alfred Leone. C: Cecilio Paniagua. Cast: Elke Sommer, Telly Savalas, Sylva Koscina, Alida Valli, Robert Alda, Alessio Orano, Gabriele Tinti, Eduardo Fajardo, Carmen Silva, Franz Von Treuberg, Espartaco Santoni. Elke Sommer encounters a man who resembles the Devil in a painting and soon becomes trapped in an eerie mansion inhabited by weird characters. Eventually she is possessed and begins spewing toads and bile at exorcist Robert Alda. • The possession scenes were reportedly added later to the original Mario Bava film, in an effort to capitalize on the popularity of *The Exorcist* (1973).

Incubus (1965; Daystar) D/S: Leslie Stevens. P: Anthony M. Taylor. C: Conrad Hall. Cast: William Shatner, Allyson Ames, Eloise Hart, Robert Fortier, Ann Atman, Milos Milos. In this allegorical fantasy, William Shatner plays a man who is tempted by the powers of evil when a demonic succubus is sent to corrupt him. • This is the first (and only) horror film to be filmed in the artificial language of Esperanto. (English subtitles were provided for those unfamiliar with this novel concept.) • Director/screenwriter Leslie Stevens was the creator of the popular TV series, "The Outer Limits." • This was William Shatner's last film before achieving fame as "Captain Kirk" on TV's "Star Trek." He faced more demonic forces in *The Devil's Rain* (1975). • Tragically, Milos Milos (Milos Milosevicz), who plays a demonic incubus sent to seduce and destroy Shatner's sister, later mirrored this plot in real life when he killed his lover, Barbara Rooney (wife of Mickey), and then committed suicide.

Incubus (1982; Film Ventures; Canada) D: John Hough. P: Marc Boyman, Johnny Eckert. S: George Franklin. C: Albert J. Dunk. Cast: John Cassavetes, Kerrie Keane, John Ireland, Duncan McIntosh, Erin Flannery. A demon capable of assuming human form commits a series of sex-murders in a small town. The local sheriff and doctor must track down the demon's identity and destroy the evil. • Director John Hough also directed the horror films, *Twins of Evil* (1971) and *The Legend of Hell House* (1973).

The Keep (1983; Paramount) D/S: Michael Mann. P: Gene Kirkwood, Howard W. Koch, Jr. C: Alex Thomson. Cast: Scott Glenn, Alberta Watson, Jurgen Prochnow, Robert Prosky, Gabriel Byrne, Ian McKellen. In World War II Romania, a small force of Nazi soldiers arrives to guard an obscure mountain pass and its ancient fortress, where they come into conflict not only with the local villagers but with a monstrous demon whose prison is The Keep. ¶ "It's constructed backwards. This place was not designed to keep something . . . out." • *The Keep* is based on the novel by F. Paul Wilson. • The film's haunting electronic musical score is by Tangerine Dream.

Look What's Happened to Rosemary's Baby (1976; TV movie) (also *Rosemary's Baby 2*). D: Sam O'Steen. P/S: Anthony Wilson. C: John A. Alonzo. Cast: Stephen McHattie, Patty Duke Astin, Broderick Crawford, Ruth Gordon, Lloyd Haynes, David Huffman, Tina Louise, George Maharis, Ray Milland, Donna Mills. This made-for-TV sequel to the critically acclaimed blockbuster, *Rosemary's Baby* (1968), follows the demonic awakenings of the now-grown son of Satan. • Oscar winner Ruth Gordon reprises her role from the original.

Making Contact (1985) (see PSYCHIC ABILITY). Little Joey must use his telekinetic powers to battle demonic creatures from another dimension.

Mausoleum (1982; Motion Picture Marketing) D: Michael Dugan. P: Robert Barich, Robert Madero. S: Robert Barich, Robert Madero. C: Robert Barich. Cast: Marjoe Gortner, Bobbie Bresee, Norman Burton, La Wanda Page, Maurice Sherbanee, Laura Hippe, Sheri Mann, Julie Christy Murray. A young girl is drawn towards a sinister mausoleum inhabited by an evil demon. Years later, as a grown woman, she is possessed by the demon and slays all those she loves. ¶ "Departing the confines of the outer rimmed area of hell, he was rewarded with the eternal possession of the first female born of the family known as Nomed." • In a screen first, the demon-possessed woman kills her husband when her breasts develop teeth which bite him to death. • Marjoe Gortner, who plays the ill-fated husband mauled by the malicious mammaries, was a child evangelist before turning to a career as an actor.

Meatcleaver Massacre (1977; Group 1) (also *The Hollywood Meatcleaver Massacre*). D: Evan Lee. P: Ray Atherton. S: Ray Atherton, Keith Burns, C: Guerdon Trueblood. Cast: Christopher Lee, Larry Justin, J. Arthur Craig, James Habif, Robert Clark, Doug Senior. When a professor of the occult is beaten and paralyzed, and his family is killed by a group of thugs, he conjures up a demon named "Merake" to avenge him. • Christopher Lee merely performs the prologue narration for the film, and there is some controversy as to whether he was fully informed about the movie he was working on.

Mr. Frost (1990; SVS; France/U.K.) D: Philip Setbon. P: Xavier Gelin. S: Philip Setbon, Brad Lynch. C: Dominique Brenguier. Cast: Jeff Goldblum, Alan Bates, Kathy Baker, Jean-Pierre Cassel, Daniel Gelin, François Negret, Maxime Leroux,

Doug Bradley stars as "Pinhead," the leader of the Cenobite demons from the Clive Barker cult classic, Hellraiser *(1988).*

Vincent Schiavelli, Roland Giraud. Jeff Goldblum plays Mr. Frost, the enigmatic murderer of 24 people—and the Devil incarnate. Incarcerated at a posh European mental institution, he engages in a cat-and-mouse game of faith and belief with a young female psychiatrist there. His aim is to convince her, an atheist, that he is indeed Satan and induce her to kill him (the ultimate validation of her belief). This would prove that his evil power of faith was still stronger than the power of science. ¶ "I must reveal to the world your impotence in the face of The Wild Side."

My Demon Lover (1989; New Line Cinema) D: Charles Loventhal. P: Robert Shaye. S: Leslie Ray. C: Jacques Haitkin. Cast: Scott Valentine, Michelle Little, Arnold Johnson, Robert Trebor, Alan Fudge, Gina Gallego, Calvert DeForest. Scott Valentine plays a man suffering from an ancient Romanian curse which causes him to transform into a horned demon whenever amorously aroused in this low-key horror/comedy. The curse can only be lifted (or more accurately—transferred) if he per-

forms an heroic selfless act. He gets his chance when his path crosses that of "the Mangler," a maniac who's been terrorizing the city. • Screenwriter Leslie Ray appears in a cameo as the "leggy redhead."

Neon Maniacs (1986; Cimmeron Productions) D: Joseph Mangine. P: Steven Mackler, Christopher Arnold. S: Mark Patrick Carducci. C: Oliver Wood, Joseph Mangine. Cast: Allan Hayes, Leilani Sarelle, Dorina Locke, Victor Elliot Brandt, David Muir, Marta Kober, P. R. Paul, Jeff Tyler, Amber Austin. A group of demon-like creatures live under the Golden Gate Bridge in San Francisco and come out at night to kill whomever crosses their path. A group of teens and pre-teens discover their secret hiding place and must do battle with the monsters. ¶ "When the world is ruled by violence and the soul of mankind fades, the children's path shall be darkened by the shadows of the Neon Maniacs." • No explanation is ever given as to the nature or the origin of the various creatures, so it is only assumed that they are some kind of demons. • The creatures can't stand water of any kind, so the kids arm themselves with squirt guns(!) to fight the demons.

Night Angel (1990; Paragon Arts International) D: Dominique Othenin-Girard. P: Joe Augustyn, Jeff Geoffray. S: Joe Augustyn, Walter Josten. C: David Lewis. Cast: Isa Andersen, Linden Ashby, Debra Feuer, Helen Martin, Doug Jones, Sam Hennings, Gary Hudson, Karen Black. A mysterious woman shows up at the glamour magazine *Siren* and begins to exercise an evil hold over the staff. She is Lilith, a demon succubus who was once the first wife of Adam, before Eve, but whose evil and lust caused her to become the demonic thing she is. At the film's climax, her true nature is revealed when she transforms into a hideous winged demon. ¶ "She is Lilith, the temptress, seducer and destroyer, harlot of demons and enemy of love."

Night of the Demons (1988; Paragon) D: Kevin S. Tenney. P/S: Joe Augustin. C: David Lewis. Cast: Alvin Alexis, Allison Barron, Lance Fenton, William Gallo, Hal Havins, Mimi Kinkade, Cathy Podewell, Linnea Quigley, Philip Tanzini, Jill Terashita. On Halloween night, a group of teenagers stage a party at an old abandoned mortuary which was built on unholy ground. They unwittingly unleash the demons which are trapped there, and are possessed and killed by demonic forces. • *Night of the Demons* features the best animated credit sequence since Roman Polanski's horror/comedy, *The Fearless Vampire Killers* (1967). • The film was shot under the title *Halloween Party.*

Nightmare Sisters (1987; Trans World Entertainment) P/S: Dave DeCoteau. S: Kenneth J. Hall. C: Voya Mikulic. Cast: Linnea Quigley, Brinke Stevens, Michelle McClellan, Richard Gabai, William Dristas, Marcus Vaughter, Timothy Kauffman, Matthew Phelps, C. J. Cox, Jim Culver, Sandy Brooke, Dukey Flyswatter. In this tongue-in-cheek no-budget independent, three nerdy sorority sisters are possessed by demonic forces inhabiting a crystal ball and are transformed into sensuous succubi. They seduce their lovers then bite off their sex organs, causing them to disintegrate into a pile of ash. ¶ "I don't know, you start messin' around and *your* head starts doing 360s, don't say I didn't warn ya." • *Nightmare Sisters* was originally announced under the more descriptive title of *Sorority Succubus Sisters.* • David DeCoteau, along with contemporary Fred Olen Ray, has turned out to be the grade-Z horror king of the 1980s, with a string of films which in-

cludes another demon drama, *Sorority Babes in the Slimeball Bowl-a-Rama* (1988). • Actress Michelle McClellan (a.k.a. Michelle Bauer), here playing one of the well-endowed succubi, had a brief career in porno films as "Pia Snow."

976-Evil (1989; Cinetel Films) D: Robert Englund. P: Lisa M. Hansen. C: Paul Elliot. Cast: Stephen Geoffreys, Maria Rubell, Sandy Dennis, Patrick O'Bryan. A nerdish high school student finds that a "horrorscope" phone number is actually a hotline to hell. Through continued use he acquires demonic powers and is finally possessed, taking vengeance on those whom he thinks have wronged him. ¶ "I am the master of the dark, the guide to your destiny." • Director Robert Englund is known to horror fans as Freddy Krueger from the *Nightmare on Elm Street* film series. This, his directorial debut, did not do well either with the critics or at the box office.

Nomads (1986; Atlantic Releasing Corporation) D/S: John McTiernan. P: George Pappas, Cassian Elwes. C: Steven Ramsey. Cast: Lesley-Anne Down, Pierce Brosnan, Anna-Maria Monticelli, Frances Bay, Jennie Elias, Adam Ant, Mary Woronov. A photographer is hounded by a group of leather-jacketed punks, who are not quite what they appear to be. They are the physical incarnation of nomadic demon-spirits who roam the Earth, and now he must pay the price for learning their secret. • Director/screenwriter John McTiernan based his screenplay on Eskimo legends. "I projected the notion of these Eskimo monsters as something happening all over the world," he told *Fangoria* #52. "After I wrote it, I discovered that all nomadic cultures have the same bloody myth, that some of the people out there really *aren't* people."

The Omen (1976; 20th Century–Fox) D: Richard Donner. P: Harvey Bernhard. S: David Seltzer. C: Gilbert Taylor. Cast: Gregory Peck, Lee Remick, Harvey Stephens, David Warner, Billie Whitelaw, Patrick Troughton, Leo McKern, Martin Benson, Robert Rietty, Holly Palance. Gregory Peck plays an American whose wife has lost her baby in childbirth. At the urging of a priest, another child is substituted. As the changeling child grows, strange and horrible things occur, and it is revealed that his "son" is in actuality the Antichrist. ¶ "Good morning. You are one day closer to the end of the world." — ad slogan. • Charlton Heston turned down the role of Damien's stepfather which eventually went to Gregory Peck.

Playroom (1989; Smart Egg Pictures) D: Manny Coto. P: Luigi Cingolani. S: Keaton Jones. C: James L. Carter. Cast: Lisa Aliff, Aron Eisenberg, Chris McDonald, James Purcell, Jamie Rose, Vincent Schiavelli. Legend has it that a sadistic medieval boy prince named Eloch worshiped an ancient demon and was promised eternal life. He developed a set of "toys"—devious torture devices—which he used to while away the hours of eternity by wringing enjoyment from human suffering. An archeologist and his family uncover Eloch's tomb in an abandoned Romanian monastery, and all but the pre-teen boy are murdered. Years later the boy returns to complete his father's work, but is taken over by the influence of Eloch, who had passed himself off as the boy's imaginary playmate years earlier. • *Playroom* was filmed on location in Belgrade, Yugoslavia.

Prime Evil (1988) (see WITCHES, WARLOCKS, AND CULTS). Members of a Satanic cult must sacrifice a blood relation every 13 years in order to retain their eternal youth and power. During the climactic sacrificial ceremony, a fleshless goat/bat-thing appears (presumably some type of demon, though its presence is never explained). When the creature is stabbed, the devil worshipers dissolve into piles of putrid bones.

Prince of Darkness (1987; Universal) D: John Carpenter. P: Larry Franco. S: Martin Quatermass (John Carpenter). C: Gary B. Kibbe. Cast: Donald Pleasence, Jameson Parker, Victor Wong, Lisa Blount, Dennis Dun, Susan Blanchard, Anne Howard, Ann Yen. Donald Pleasence plays a priest who discovers a strange cannister in the basement of a church along with an ancient tome. Calling in his friend, a physics professor, they discover that the pulsing liquid inside the container is the embodiment of Satan's son—pure evil. The liquid leaks out and possesses those around it, who then lay plans for the return of the father—Satan himself. • Director John Carpenter refers to *Prince of Darkness* as "a cross between *Quatermass and the Pit* and *The Exorcist* (*Fangoria* #69). • Carpenter wrote the script using the pseudonym "Martin Quatermass" (in homage to British writer Nigel Kneale, who created the character of Bernard Quatermass on TV and in films, beginning with "The Quatermass Experiment," a BBC TV serial of 1953, later filmed and shown in the United States as *The Creeping Unknown,* 1956). "That's my way of saying the picture was inspired by Nigel Kneale," explained Carpenter.

Pumpkinhead (1988; MGM/UA) D: Stan Winston. P: Howard Smith, Richard C. Weinman. S: Mark Patrick Carducci, Gary Gerani. C: Bojan Bazelli. Cast: Lance Henriksen, Jeff East, John DiAquino, Kimberly Ross, Joel Hoffman, Cynthia Bain, Kerry Remsen. Lance Henriksen plays the owner of a country store whose little boy is accidentally killed by a group of vacationing teens. Consumed with grief, he visits a backwoods crone and asks for vengeance. With her help he summons up a demon called "Pumpkinhead" which fulfills his murderous lust for revenge, and eventually exacts the ultimate price. ¶ "What you're askin's got a powerful price." • At one point during *Pumpkinhead*'s laborious production schedule, its name was changed to *Vengeance: The Demon,* before finally returning to the original moniker of *Pumpkinhead.* • Inside the demon suit (one of the best demon-creatures to ever stalk the screen) was creature designer Tom Woodruff, Jr.

Rabid Grannies (1989; Troma; Belgium/France) D/S: Emmanuel Kervyn. P: James Desert, Jonathan Rambert. C: Hugo Labye. Cast: Elie Lison, Catherine Aymerie, Jacques Mayar, Françoise Moens, Robert Du Bois, Florine Elslande, Guy Van Riet, Françoise Lamoureux. *Demon Aunties* would be a more accurate title for this gory import laced with mean-spirited humor. A dozen greedy relatives gather at the estate of their two aged aunts for their birthday party. One nephew, Christopher, was not invited, however. He is a satanist and is considered the black sheep of the family. He sends a gift anyway, a small box which, when opened, transforms the two nice old ladies into ugly ravenous demons intent upon murdering and devouring all the people in the house. Finally, with only a few folks left alive, someone gets the idea to destroy the box, which returns the ladies back to their normal sweet selves. ¶ "The two of them enjoy a good laugh. They throw guts around like so many slapstick cream pies."

Rawhead Rex (1987; Empire; U.S./Ireland) D: George Pavlou. P: Kevin Attew, Don Hawkins. S: Clive Barker. C: John Metcalfe. Cast: David Dukes, Kelly Piper, Niall Toibin, Ronan Wilmot, Niall O'Brien, Hugh O'Conor, Cora Lunny. In a small Irish village, a farmer topples an ancient Celtic monument which unleashes an age-old demon-monster. The demon enslaves the parish priest and goes about terrorizing the countryside and ripping the heads off its victims. ¶ "He was here before Christ, before civilization, he was *king* here! 'Rawhead,' that's what they called him, *Rawhead*!" • Clive Barker, who's been called "The British Stephen King," adapted his own short story for the screen. Barker reportedly was not too pleased with the final result of the film. • The rubber-suited Rawhead Rex was played by a seven-foottall German actor named Heinrich von Schellendorf. • *Rawhead Rex* was shot entirely on location in southern Ireland.

Repossessed (1990; Seven Arts) D/S: Bob Logan. P: Steve Wizan. C: Michael D. Margulies. Cast: Linda Blair, Ned Beatty, Leslie Nielsen, Anthony Starke, Thom J. Sharp, Lan Schwab. Linda Blair spoofs herself from *The Exorcist* (1973) when she plays a woman who was possessed by a demon as a child. Now the demon is back, and her old exorcist (Leslie Nielsen) is back in action in this *Naked Gun*-meets-*The Exorcist* parody. ¶ "So it happened, victory over the Devil. A *great* day for mankind and a pretty good day for split-pea soup."

Revenge (1986) (see WITCHES, WARLOCKS, AND CULTS). A small Oklahoma town is plagued by a series of gruesome murders perpetrated by members of the cult of Caninis ("the god of death, resurrection, and worldly advancement"). These cult members murder people to take their body parts for a hideous sacrifice ritual, by which they hope to resurrect their demon-god. ¶ "In 16-whatever, a preacher named Martin Bradford founded the cult, claiming that a demon revealed itself to him, a demon that took the form of a dog—the god dog Caninis." • Though no dog-demon appears, one of the cult member's visage is transformed into an ugly demonic face at the film's end.

Rock 'n' Roll Nightmare (1987; Thunder/ Shapiro; Canada) D: John Fasano. P/S: Jon-Mikl Thor. C: Mark MacKay. Cast: Jon-Mikl Thor, Jillian Peri, Frank Dietz, Dave Lane, Teresa Simpson, Clara Pater, Jesse D'Angelo. A heavy-metal band goes to a remote farmhouse to use the converted barn as a recording studio in which to practice their songs for their upcoming tour. The band members begin dying, possessed and killed by a group of diminutive demons. Finally, the band leader's girlfriend reveals herself to be none other than Satan, lord of all demons. But not to worry, the band leader is actually the archangel Triton and they engage in a battle of good against evil.

Rosemary's Baby (1968) (see WITCHES,

WARLOCKS, AND CULTS). A young couple move into an apartment building inhabited by modern-day witches. The wife dreams of being raped by a horned demon and becomes pregnant. Soon it becomes apparent that she has been chosen to bear the child of Lucifer himself.

Satan's Mistress (1978; Manson International) (also *Dark Eyes; Demon Rage; Fury of the Succubus*). D/P: James Polakof. Cast: Lana Wood, Britt Ekland, John Carradine, Kabir Bedi, Tom Hallick. Lana Wood plays a bored housewife who is raped by a demon spirit.

Satan's Mistress (1990; Paramount) D/P: Bert I. Gordon. S: Stephen Katz. C: Thomas F. Denove. Cast: Robert Forster, Lydie Denier, Caren Kaye, Phillip Glasser, M. K. Harris, Ellen Geer, Jack Carter, Henry Brown, Marlena Giovi. An ex-detective searching for a missing girl learns that the beautiful head of a modeling agency is actually a succubus who's "existed for nearly 500 years and killed over 1,000 men." The demon/woman possesses his son and makes his life a living hell until the final fiery showdown. ¶ "Very few guys come back a second time to party with *me*." • This is producer/director Bert I. Gordon's first film in ten years. Gordon is best remembered for his "big" 50s films like *The Amazing Colossal Man* (1957) and *Earth vs. the Spider* (1958).

Scarecrows (1988; Effigy Films) D: William Wesley. P: Cami Winikoff, William Wesley. S: Richard Jefferies, William Wesley. C: Peter Deming. Cast: Ted Vernon, Victoria Christian, Richard Vidan, B. J. Turner, David Campbell, Michael Simms, Kristina Sanborn. A paramilitary unit steals three and one-half million dollars from a military base. They hijack a plane and land near a remote abandoned farm. There they are killed off one by one by three hideous living scarecrows. The backwoods family who had previous lived there dabbled in black magic and were transformed into these demon-scarecrows.

The Sentinel (1977; Universal) D/S: Michael Winner. P: Michael Winner, Jeffrey Konvitz. C: Dick Kratina. Cast: Chris Sarandon, Cristina Raines, Martin Balsam, John Carradine, Arthur Kennedy, Burgess Meredith, Sylvia Miles, Deborah Raffin, Eli Wallach, Christopher Walken. A fashion model moves into a stately old Brooklyn brownstone and discovers that it is built over an entrance to Hell. Eventually the gateway is opened and the demonic denizens of Hell run rampant.

Sorority Babes in the Slimeball Bowl-o-Rama (1988) (see GENIES). A sorority initiation requires the pledges to break into a bowling alley and steal a trophy as proof of the deed. Things go awry when an evil imp, "imp"prisoned inside the bowling trophy, gets out and begins granting wishes. The diminutive demon-genie's evil nature is revealed when the wishes go sour and he possesses several of the girls, sending them out as she-demons to kill the rest. ¶ "Goddamned she-demons, I hate 'em!" • This is the second tongue-in-cheek demonic possession movie made by prolific no-budget filmmaker David DeCoteau. He earlier filmed *Nightmare Sisters* (1987) with many of the same cast members.

The Soul of a Monster (1944; Columbia) D: Will Jason. P: Ted Richmond. S: Edward Dein. C: Burnett Guffey. Cast: Rose Hobart, George Macready, Jim Bannon, Jeanne Bates, Erik Rolf. A noble doctor, a good and kind man, is dying, and his wife makes a desperate plea to any force which can make him live. Her plea is heard by a mysterious, sinister woman—the agent of evil, a demon, perhaps even the devil himself (or herself)—who miraculously cures the doctor, then exercises an evil influence over him. He is changed, however—his soul blackened, and he must engage in a monumental struggle to free himself from this evil. ¶ "The man who walks with evil walks alone." • Columbia imbued this tense supernatural melodrama with a heavy moral message, beginning with this implicit warning in the opening written prologue: "You may have lived or perhaps dreamed the story you are about to see. To many of you it may be grim reality; to others, perhaps just a dream." • According to Rose Hobart (who played the Emissary of Evil), "We shot two different endings for the picture. I was supposed to be the Devil in female form, so when George [Macready] shot me and I went out the window, nothing landed. In the other version, I landed, but a black cat walked out of my body" (*Filmfax* #26). Neither version made it into the final cut.

Spiritism (1961) (see WITCHES, WARLOCKS, AND CULTS). A middle-aged couple become involved with a benevolent group of spiritualists. When their finances fail, the wife calls upon evil forces to help her. Satan himself appears and gives her "Pandora's Box" to open if she chooses. Desperately in need of money, she opens the box, and finds a severed hand which works much like "The Monkey's Paw."

Tales from the Darkside: The Movie (1990) (see ANTHOLOGIES). In the "Lover's Vow" episode, a struggling artist sees a demon—a living gargoyle—who makes him promise on pain of death never to reveal its hideous form. Soon after, he meets a beautiful young woman, they fall in love, and he achieves critical and financial success. His blissful state is shattered, however, when he breaks his promise and learns the awful truth upon the demon's return.

The Tomb (1985; Trans World Entertainment) D: Fred Olen Ray. P: Fred Olen Ray. S: Kenneth J. Hall. C: Paul Elliot. Cast: Cameron Mitchell, John Carradine, Susan Stoky, Richard Alan Hench, Michelle Bauer, Sybil Danning, Kitten Natividad. This low-budget feature is about an ancient but beautiful Egyptian demon named Nefratis, who comes to L.A. seeking vengeance on those who desecrated her tomb and stole her magic amulets. As well as having demonic powers, she sports fangs and doesn't mind the occasional drop of blood. ¶ "Nothing's obvious to me—except that a man's dead, murdered, and somebody's responsible"—director/screenwriter Fred Olen Ray's nod to Ed Wood's *Plan Nine from Outer Space* (1959).

Trick or Treat (1986) (see GHOSTS). High school misfit Eddie Weinbauer idolizes heavy metal superstar Sammi Curr. When Curr dies in a bizarre fire, his satanic spirit returns to help Eddie exact revenge on his teen tormenters. At one point, the evil ghost summons up a gargoyle-like demon (dubbed "Skeezix" by the production crew) to carry out acts of mayhem.

Troll (1986; Empire Pictures) D: John Buechler. P: Albert Band. S: Ed Naha. C: Romano Albani. Cast: Noah Hathaway, Michael Moriarty, Shelley Hack, Jenny Beck, Sonny Bono, Phil Fondacaro, Brad Hall, Anne Lockhart, Julia Louis-Dreyfus, Gary Sandy, June Lockhart. When a family moves into an old apartment building, their daughter is possessed by a troll hiding in the basement. All hell breaks loose as the mischievous creatures transform the various apartments into bizarre and dangerous other-dimensional worlds. Eventually, the girls' brother must enter the land of the trolls and battle a huge winged demon to free his sister. • Effects-man-turned-director John Buechler also designed the numerous creature effects for the film.

Twilight Zone: The Movie (1983) (see ANTHOLOGIES). In the film's strongest segment, John Lithgow plays a man deathly afraid of flying. This stormy flight goes beyond even his fearful imaginings when he sees a flying demon on the wing of the plane tearing at the engine. Though no one believes him, he takes drastic action to stop the hideous fiend from crashing the airplane.

The Undead (1956) (see WITCHES, WARLOCKS, AND CULTS). A woman journeys backwards in time via hypnosis and returns to her former life, where she is accused of witchcraft. There she must face a coven of real witches, led by Satan himself.

The Unholy (1988; Vestron) D: Camilo Vila. P: Mathew Hayden. S: Philip Yordan, Fernando Fonseca. C: Henry Vargas. Cast: Ben Cross, Ned Beatty, William Russ, Jill Carroll, Hal Holbrook, Trevor Howard. In New Orleans, a demon takes on the guise of a beautiful woman to tempt and slay priests. Young Father Michael (Ben Cross) is chosen to take over the vacant parish because the church elders feel he has been spiritually blessed and is "the chosen one" to do battle with the evil demon. ¶ "Evil has never been so irresistible ... or so deadly"—poster ad line. • "I don't consider this a horror film," stated director Camilo Vila in *Fangoria* #74, despite later adding, "of course, we're gonna have a demon and a monster." Vestron, the film's distributor, didn't agree with Vila's not-a-horror-film attitude and contracted makeup FX man Bob Keen (*Hellraiser; Waxwork,* both 1988) to rework the film's ending in a ten-day reshoot. "The ending just needed a little polish," claimed Keen. "It's still the original director's and the original team's film. I'm just doing the ending."

The Unnamable (1989; Yankee Classic Pictures) D: Jean-Paul Ouellette. P: Dean Ramser, Jean-Paul Ouellette. S: Jean-Paul Ouellette. C: Tom Fraser. Cast: Charles King, Mark Kinsey Stephenson, Alexandra Durrell. In the fictional town of Arkhara, four college students visit the local haunted house, which just happens to be the home of an unspeakable demon-spawn from hell, an offspring of the "Old Ones." • *The Unnamable* is based on the H. P. Lovecraft story of the same name.

Warlock (1991) (see WITCHES, WARLOCKS, AND CULTS). A seventeenth century warlock is rescued from a death sentence by the powers of Satan and transported to modern day L.A. to find the "Grand Grimoire," a bible of black magic which could threaten creation itself. Upon arriving, the warlock seeks out a fake "channeler" in order to communicate with his unholy master. Satan speaks through the body of the channeler, and offers up her eyes, which the warlock extracts and carries with him in order to help find the three pieces of the evil book. • To summon Lucifer, the warlock calls upon him by one of his names—"Zamiel."

The Willies (1990) (see ANTHOLOGIES). Three kids tell each other scary stories, one of which deals with a demon-monster inhabiting the boys' bathroom at an elementary school. A young boy named Danny uses it to take care of the bullies tormenting him. It turns out that this creature disguises itself as a friendly janitor who travels from school to school weeding out all the "Bad Apples" (the name of the story).

Witchcraft Through the Ages (1922) (see WITCHES, WARLOCKS, AND CULTS) (also *Haxan*). This early fictionalized documentary-style account of "witchcraft through the ages" features scenes of the witches' sabbath in which they pledge their souls to Satan. The horned Devil appears and requires each witch to prove their loyalty by kissing his posterior. • Satan is played by the film's director/screenwriter, Benjamin Christensen.

The Witches of Eastwick (1987) (see WITCHES, WARLOCKS, AND CULTS). Jack Nicholson plays a debonaire demon who is attracted to the sleepy town of Eastwick by the untapped feminine powers of three women. He seduces them and releases the hidden passions and hidden powers locked inside of each of them (much to his eventual regret). • Among other things, he uses his demonic powers to cause a woman to violently and continually regurgitate cherry pits. • At the film's special-effects heavy climax, the enraged demon grows as big as a house and threatens to kill them all before the women can subdue him with their new-found magical powers.

Dinosaurs

(*See also* Japanese Giant Monsters)

On August 2, 1841, Richard Owen presented a paper to a British scientific association proposing that the large fossil bones recently discovered belonged to creatures he termed "dinosaurs" (Greek for "terrible lizards"). Mr. Owen probably never dreamed of a time in which these prehistoric beasts would be re-created for mass-media viewing by the likes of Willis O'Brien, Ray Harryhausen, and Jim Danforth.

Special effects technician and stop-motion animator Willis O'Brien is truly the pioneer of the dinosaur subgenre. O'Brien began in 1915 with a series of stop-motion silent shorts (often featuring prehistoric beasts), then reached his stride in 1925 with his classic feature epic of Sir Arthur Conan Doyle's brilliant novel, *The Lost World. The Lost World* featured over 50 fantastic dinosaur models, made with the precision crafting and supervision of Marcel Delgado, and brought to life with stop-motion photography and a variety of other means of cinematic trickery. Since then, a legion of dinosaur movies have followed, and many of them, including O'Brien's other classic, *King Kong* (1933), were just as exciting and credible. In recent years, with animation taking a back seat to other forms of graphic special effects work, the dinosaur film (like their subjects) has almost dwindled to extinction. The dinosaur movie, however, will never completely disappear as long as people inspired by the work of Willis O'Brien and Ray Harryhausen continue on in the film industry.

The DINOSAUR subgenre has been split up into three natural formula trends. The TIME OF THE DINOSAUR section features films set in the days when dinosaurs walked the Earth. LOST WORLDS contains movies in which contemporary people discover hidden pockets of dinosaurs — secret lost worlds found underground, on tropical islands, inside volcanoes, even in outer space. DINOSAURS ON THE LOOSE is a term applied to films depicting prehistoric monsters escaping their secret habitat, or being freed from years of sleep by some aspect of human science or exploration, and running amok in our modern society. In this type of film, they usually wreak havoc upon some local community or even venture into modern cities.

Each sub-section has had its own classic film contributions. For instance, the TIME OF THE DINOSAUR section features the two *One Million* classics — the original *One Million B.C.* (1940), starring Victor Mature, and its 1966 (superior) remake, *One Million Years B.C.* The latter features dinosaurs brought to life by Willis O'Brien's pupil and successor, Ray Harryhausen, who went on to become the world's greatest monster animator. The LOST WORLD films are best represented by the aforementioned 1925 epic, *The Lost World;* while the prototype DINOSAURS ON THE LOOSE picture has to be *The Beast from 20,000 Fathoms* (1953) (another Ray Harryhausen project).

See also CAVEMEN, JAPANESE GIANT MONSTERS, and SEA MONSTERS for more prehistoric topics.

Time of the Dinosaur

Animal World (1956; Warner Bros.) D/P/S: Irwin Allen. C: Harold Wellman. Cast: Narration by Theodore von Eltz, John Storm. This is a documentary-style "nature" film about all kinds of animal life forms which includes a segment about the time of the dinosaurs. ¶ "And now the cataclysms that finally come to rip and fire the Earth, and bring an end to the dinosaur." • Ray Harryhausen provided the stop-motion animation and Willis O'Brien designed the dinosaurs as well as the layouts of the glass shots and settings. Several mechanical dinosaur models were constructed to be used in closeup shots. Much of the realistic footage of dinosaurs devouring one another was cut from the film due to a negative response from preview audiences. • Harryhausen said of his work on this film, "I often have to act the role of a dinosaur, or an ape, or even a flying saucer to feel how to move the models in portraying a certain kind of scene. For *Animal World* I studied movements of lizards because the dinosaurs were actually mammoth reptiles. I got considerable inspiration from the famous paintings of dinosaurs by Charles Knight that hang in the Museum of Natural History in New York." • Footage from this film's dinosaur segment turned up in the 1970 caveman film, *Trog,* starring Joan Crawford.

Caveman (1981) (see CAVEPEOPLE). David Allen and Roy Arbogast engineered a few stop-motion dinosaurs for this comedy covering the life of the average caveman.

Journey to the Beginning of Time (1955/ 66; Gottwaldow/New Trends; Czechoslovakia) D: Karel Zeman. P: William Cayton (English version). S: Karel Zeman, William Cayton (English version). C: Vaclav Pazdernik, Antonin Horak. Cast: Vladimir Bejval, Petr Herrman, Zdenek Hustak, Josef Lukas, Victor Betjal, Peter Hermann, Charles Goldsmith. Four boys floating down an underground river are carried backwards in time, passing through the ice age, the dawn of mammals, and finally, the time of the dinosaurs. After witnessing many prehistoric animals, including mammoths, pterodactyls, stegosauruses, etc., they eventually arrive at the ocean where life had originally begun. • The dinosaur sequences were created by the combined use of puppets, stop-motion animation, and live action. • Karel Zeman, Czechoslovakia's answer to Ray Harryhausen, was a window dresser and poster artist in his early days, and he is the originator of the popular Czech cartoon character, "Mr. Prokouk." He also is responsible for *The Fabulous World of Jules Verne* (1957) and *Baron Munchhausen* (1962). • American producer William Cayton bought the film, dubbed it, added some new scenes involving a trip to the Museum of Natural History, and released this new version in 1966.

Journey to the Center of Time (1967) (see TIME TRAVEL). A group of scientists are hurled into the past by a time machine. At one point they must face off against a dinosaur (a photographically enlarged lizard).

One Million B.C. (1940; United Artists) D: Hal Roach, Hal Roach, Jr. P: Hal Roach. S: Mickell Novak, George Baker, Joseph Frickert. C: Norbert Brodine. Cast: Victor Mature, Carol Landis, Lon Chaney, Jr., John Hubbard, Nigel de Brulier, Conrad Nagel. Tourists entering a cave imagine life in the days of the dinosaur. Victor Mature plays a member of the Rock Tribe, turned away from his own people, and forced to wander the dinosaur-infested

landscape until he is taken in by the Shell People and falls for cavegirl Carol Landis. ¶ "His was a cruel tribe. Pity and compassion played little part in the existence of those people, who ate only what they could kill." • The prehistoric animals depicted here are not animated by stop-motion. They were either men in suits (the allosaurus), dressed-up beasts (the shaggy elephant/ mastodon), large models (the baby triceratops Mature wrestles with early on), or photographically enlarged lizards. • Victor Mature, the actor dubbed by studio publicists as "a beautiful hunk of man," enjoyed his first starring role in this film. It also marked the first "monster movie" role for Lon Chaney, Jr. (who played Akoba, leader of the Rock Tribe). Chaney was said to have developed his own makeup for the part until union regulations disallowed it. • The attractive Carol Landis committed suicide eight years later at the age of 29, from an overdose of sleeping pills. The motive for her suicide was said to have stemmed from an affair with actor Rex Harrison, who was married to actress Lilli Palmer at the time. • Werner R. Heymann received an Academy Award nomination for the film's musical score.

One Million Years B.C. (1966; Hammer/ 20th Century–Fox; U.K./U.S.) D: Don Chaffey. P: Michael Carreras. S: Mickell Novak, George Baker, Joseph Frickert, Michael Carreras. C: Wilkie Cooper. Cast: John Richardson, Raquel Welch, Robert Brown, Percy Herbert, Martine Beswick, Jean Wladon. A caveman named Tumak is ousted from his tribe by his ruthless father and chief. After emigrating across dinosaur-infested regions, he is taken in by Raquel Welch and her civilized fair-haired companions. ¶ "A young world, a world early in the morning of time. A hard, unfriendly world"—opening narration. • Special effects wizard Ray Harryhausen discussed the project in Jeff Rovin's book, *From the Land Beyond Beyond:* "I did it because I had the opportunity to utilize an animated process for dinosaurs. I mean, I wouldn't have wanted to go back and do an alligator and an iguana locked in mortal combat." • There was to be a sequence with a brontosaurus attacking Tumak's tribe near the end of the film. The animation, however, was getting too expensive so they decided to change the story and have the two tribes battle each othe instead. The model wasn't discarded altogether though, as Harryhausen used it for a brief instance during Tumak's initial trek across the wilderness. •

A prehistoric tribesman clubs the gigantic flipper of a menacing plesiosaur in the Jim Danforth–animated dinosaur film, When Dinosaurs Ruled the Earth *(1970).*

British special effects man Les Bowie used porridge for the molten lava effect. • The live action portion of the film was shot in the Canary Islands, specifically on the island of Lanzarote. • Producer Michael Carreras also co-wrote the screenplay as well. He once joked, "I may be the only member of the Writers Guild who continues to get royalty checks for a script containing *no dialogue*" (*Fangoria* #63). • 1966 was a great year for the beautiful actress Raquel Welch. She was immediately elevated to stardom for her roles in this picture and *Fantastic Voyage.* Apparently, the up-and-coming Ms. Welch was not easy to work with. "She drove me and everyone else *crazy,*" reported co-star Martine Beswick in a *Fangoria* #55 interview.

When Dinosaurs Ruled the Earth (1970; Hammer; U.K.) D/S: Val Guest. P: Aida Young. C: Dick Bush. Cast: Victoria Vetri, Robin Hawdon, Patrick Allen, Drewe Henley, Sean Caffrey, Magda Konopka, Patrick Holt, Imogen Hassall. Victoria Vetri escapes death at the hands of her own super-stitious people, only to be rescued, then framed by a jealous girl from the neighboring Sand tribe. She then sets out on her own and ends up befriending a motherly dinosaur. ¶ "A time when the color of a woman's hair condemned her — a sacrifice to the sun" — narration. • This follow-up to *One Million Years B.C.* (1966) was supposed to feature stop-motion animation by Ray Harryhausen again, but he was busy with *The Valley of Gwangi* (1969) at the time. The job of dinosaur animator instead went to the very able Jim Danforth (*The Wonderful World of the Brothers Grimm,* 1962). • The location shooting was done on the island of Fuerteventura within the Canary Islands region. The terrain was extremely "prehistoric"-looking, with its craggy mountain cliffs and 90-degree-plus temperature. It took five months to shoot the live action sequences followed by 17 more months of animation work. The results rivaled Harryhausen's work but the film itself was a box office disappointment for the producers.

Lost Worlds

At the Earth's Core (1976) (see UNDER-GROUND WORLDS). A geological expedition journeys to the underground world of "Pellucidar" where they encounter dinosaurs and a race of Pterodactyl-people.

Dinosaur Island (1966; Mexico). A fierce storm near the Bermuda Islands region blows a planeload of explorers to an uncharted island inhabited by ancient tribes and dinosaurs. A girl from the party follows a tribal chief and befriends him. In the end she asks him to leave with them but he refuses. At the climax, a volcano erupts and the plane takes off, leaving the girl and the chief on Dinosaur Island.

Ghost of Slumber Mountain (1919; World Film Corporation) D/S/C: Willis O'Brien. P: Herbert M. Dawley. Cast: Herbert M. Dawley, Willis O'Brien. Author and amateur artist, Jack Holmes, tells a story to children about his trip to Slumber Mountain. He falls asleep at camp and dreams about encountering the spirit of a hermit named "Mad Dick." The hermit gives him a camera-like device with which Holmes views prehistoric creatures down in Dream Valley. An allosaurus, fresh from killing a triceratops, begins to chase him prior to his waking up. ¶ "Horned dinosaurs twice the size of rhinoceroses battled for supremacy." • This early two-reel Willis O'Brien dinosaur film made in 1919 cost $3,000 to film and earned $100,000. • The film's producer, Herbert M. Dawley, took credit from Willis O'Brien for the special effects, which resulted in Willis severing their relationship.

House 2: The Second Story (1987) (see GHOSTS). One of the rooms in this haunted house of evil features a jungle with an array of prehistoric animals.

Island of the Dinosaurs (1967; Azteca; Mexico) D: Rafael Lopez Portillo. P: G. Calderón Stell. S: Alfredo Salazar. Cast: Armando Silvestre, Alma Delia Fuentes, Elsa Cardenas, Jenaro Moreno, Manolo Fabregas. This Mexican lost world adventure features explorers discovering an island full of dinosaurs and cavemen. • The picture uses extensive footage from *One Million B.C.* (1940).

The Jungle (1952; Lippert; U.S./India) D/P: William Berke. S: Carroll Young. C: Clyde DeVinna. Cast: Rod Cameron, Cesar Romero, Marie Windsor, Sulochana, David Abraham, M. N. Namblar. A herd of prehistoric mammoths are discovered in an unexplored region of India. ¶ "I didn't kill

your brother, I just crossed that bridge. The others were on this side when the mammoths charged. I hollered for them to cross over, your brother went first. He took two steps and froze, started screaming for someone to save him." • The picture was shot entirely on location in India, and featured authentic Indian music for the accompanying score. • The mammoths were simply shaggy elephants with long, twisted tusks attached. • At the film's end, the mammoths get caught up in an avalanche, but it is not clear if they are actually destroyed.

Journey to the Center of the Earth (1959) (see UNDERGROUND WORLDS). Professor Oliver Lindenbrook leads an expedition to an underground world featuring prehistoric dimetrodons and a gigantic monitor lizard.

Jungle Manhunt (1951; Columbia) D: Lew Landers. P: Sam Katzman. S: Samuel Newman. C: William Whitley. Cast: Johnny Weissmuller, Bob Waterfield, Sheila Ryan, Rick Vallin, Lyle Talbot. Jungle Jim grapples with human-sized dinosaurs (resembling tyrannosaurs), while searching for a missing football hero in the heart of Africa. • The missing football hero is played by a real life football hero—Bob Waterfield, former Los Angeles Rams star quarterback.

King Dinosaur (1955; Lippert) D/P: Bert I. Gordon. S: Tom Gries. C: Gordon Avil. Cast: Bill Bryant, Wanda Curtis, Douglas Henderson, Patricia Gallagher. A scientific expedition travels to a new planet in our solar system, there to discover a hostile world populated by prehistoric animals. ¶ "Many of the mysteries of this vast ocean of space would soon be found. It would be a race between countries to see which one would be the first—the first to bring our civilization to another planet in space." • The animal life discovered on the planet "Nova" included mastodons, a giant armadillo, some yaks, a strange looking turtle, large snakes, elk, birds, a variety of bears, a crocodile, and a smattering of common lizards (iguanas, baby crocs, etc.), photographically enlarged to represent dinosaurs. • These supposed prehistoric animals are found on an isolated island and are disposed of by an atom bomb. At the film's conclusion, the voyagers reflect, "Yeah, we sure have done it—brought civilization to planet Nova." • Bert I. Gordon is credited for the story and special effects in addition to directing and producing this picture. He said of the film, "It was a cut above

This Tyrannosaurus rex from The Land Unknown *(1957), lumbering after a Navy helicopter, was actually an actor inside a cumbersome 12-foot-tall dinosaur suit with hydraulically operated eyes and mouth.*

the amateur 16mm films I started making when I was given a camera at the age of 13, but now I regard it as a prehistoric production in more ways than one. I've come a long way from that 'caveman' quickie, although I've yet to complete the picture I'm perfectly satisfied with."

King Kong (1933) (see APE GIANTS). Skull Island, the home of the mighty Kong, houses many species of prehistoric creatures, including a stegosaurus, a brontosaurus, a tyrannosaurus, and a pteranodon.

The Land That Time Forgot (1975; Amicus/AIP; U.K.) D: Kevin Conner. P: John Dark. S: James Cawthorn, Michael Moorcock. Cast: Doug McClure, Susan Penhaligon, John McEnery, Keith Barron, Bobby Parr, Anthony Ainley, Declan Mulholland, Ben Howard. Members of a British merchant ship and a German U-boat clash during World War II, then end up fighting for survival on an uncharted prehistoric island inhabited by dinosaurs. ¶ "It's like a geologic exhibit—a world of life outside of

time, yet representing almost all the ages of the Earth." • The varied prehistoric life encountered on the forgotten island known as "Caprona" includes a plesiosaurus, a diplodocus, a triceratops, allosauruses, and pterodactyls. Also existing on Caprona is an evolutionary triad of tribes known as the Bo-Lu, the Sto-Lu, and the Ga-Lu, each one more advanced the farther upstream they live. • Roger Dicken (*2001: A Space Odyssey,* 1968; *When Dinosaurs Ruled the Earth,* 1970) provided the lifesize wire-operated mechanical dinosaurs for the film. • The sound stage used in the picture was originally constructed to hold the huge sets in Alexander Korda's *Things to Come* (1936). *Dr. Strangelove* (1963) also utilized this sound stage. • This Edgar Rice Burroughs story first appeared in *Blue Book* magazine in 1918.

The Land Unknown (1957; Universal) D: Virgil Vogel. P: William Alland. S: Laszlo Gorog. C: Ellis Carter. Cast: Jock Mahoney, Shawn Smith, William Reynolds,

Henry Brandon, Phil Harvey, Douglas R. Kennedy. A group of officers and scientists on a mapping and meteorological operation over Antarctica crash-land inside a volcano and find a hidden world full of prehistoric reptiles dominated by a savage survivor of a previous excursion. ¶ "It's true that you can't live among beasts without becoming one, but it's just as true that you can't live among human beings without becoming affected by their humanity." • Universal's top sci-fi director, Jack Arnold, was the original choice to direct the picture, but Arnold declined after the special effects department used up most of the film's already frugal budget. Initially *The Land Unknown* was to be a big-budgeted "A" production, filmed in color and containing a star-studded cast (with Cary Grant mentioned as a possible lead). Alas, it was not to be. • The dinosaurs, which accounted for most of the film's budget, included a Tyrannosaurus rex, which was actually a 12-foot high hydraulically-operated suit inside which a man was stationed. The sea serpent–like elasmosaurus was approximately 15 feet across and seven feet high, and hydraulically operated by a man onshore. The pterodactyl which flew into the helicopter above the volcano was just a prop on a fishpole. All three monsters were kept in Yvonne De Carlo's former dressing room, one of the largest at Universal. The other "thunderlizards" were simply photographically enlarged monitors. • The (completely studio bound) art direction provided by Richard Riedel and Alexander Golitzen was done on a huge process stage, containing a 300-foot-long pool with railroad-like tracks at the bottom for the elasmosaur to glide in and out of the water on. • The surreal landscape background was actually a 300-foot-long, 75-foot-high canvas with the scenery painted on it. • Star Jock Mahoney was one of Hollywood's top stuntmen before he became a lead actor. The 6'4" actor performed all of his own stunts in this film, including the dive from the hovering helicopter into the lake. He said of his experiences on this movie, "I used to do three or four stunts for a film as a stunt man — now they've got me doing at least five times that many." Known to those in the stunt profession as Jocko, Mahoney became the subject of a Burt Reynolds/Brian Keith movie called *Hooper* in 1978.

The Last Dinosaur (1977; Rankin-Bass; U.S./Japan) D: Alex Grasshof, Tom Kotani. P: Arthur Rankin, Jr., Jules Bass. S: William Overgard. C: Shoshi Ueda. Cast: Richard Boone, Joan Van Ark, Steven Keats. Oil drillers in the polar cap discover a prehistoric lost world with a Tyrannosaurus rex and wild natives. Richard Boone plays a big game hunter who travels to the remote land to hunt this biggest game of all. ¶ "That is its fifth victim and I tell you this, it is the last! I will hunt that thing down and I will kill it!" • The tyrannosaur, like Godzilla, is actually a man in a suit. At the climax, Boone elects to stay in the lost world while his nemesis, the Rex, is still alive. Other dinosaurs are featured as well, including pterodactyls and a triceratops. • Richard Boone (*I Bury the Living*, 1958) has had previous experience with oil drilling outside of this film. When he was younger he worked at the oil fields in Southern California. Before Boone became an actor he was also a boxer. Once while attending Stanford University as a student and boxing team member, he was expelled for campus infractions.

The Lost Continent (1951; Lippert) D: Samuel Newfield. P: Sigmund Neufeld. S: Richard H. Landau. C: Jack Greenhalgh. Cast: Cesar Romero, John Hoyt, Hugh Beaumont, Chick Chandler, Sid Melton, Whit Bissell, Acquanetta. A team of scientists and military flyers track their missing space rocket to an island in the South Seas. The rocket, a large uranium deposit, and prehistoric reptiles are all found atop a steep mountain plateau. ¶ "It's almost as if time forgot this place." • The animation work was spearheaded by Augie Lohman (*The Maze*, 1953; *The Monster That Challenged the World*, 1957), who gives us three authentic dinosaur species — a triceratops, a brontosaurus, and a pterodactyl (plus one photographically enlarged lizard seen in the climbing sequence).

The Lost World (1925; First National Pictures) D: Harry O. Hoyt. P: Earl Hudson, Watterson R. Rothacker. S: Marion Fairfax. C: Arthur Edeson. Cast: Wallace Beery, Lewis Stone, Bessie Love, Lloyd Hughes, Arthur Hoyt, Bull Montana. Professor Challenger leads an expedition to an Amazon jungle plateau where dinosaurs and cavemen still exist. A brontosaurus is brought back to London, then escapes and rampages through the city before finally swimming off into the sunset. ¶ "A brontosaurus — feeding merely on leaves — perfectly harmless, unless it happens to step on us." • Sir Arthur Conan Doyle (the creator of Sherlock Holmes) published his novel, *The Lost World* (upon which this film is based) in 1912. • Each of the dinosaurs created by Willis O'Brien and Marcel Del-

A pair of brontosauruses look on as an allosaurus viciously attacks a trachodon in the stop-motion classic, The Lost World *(1925). The more than 50 dinosaur models were designed and animated by Willis O'Brien, with the help of his 19-year-old model-making assistant, Marcel Delgado.*

gado (the chief model maker) were roughly 12 inches high and 16 to 20 inches long. Delgado was only 19 years old when assigned to the project, which included over 50 models built from sponge and poseable wooden skeletons, and covered with a rubberish, clay-like substance known as dental dam. The authentic appearance of the dinosaurs is greatly indebted to the Charles R. Knight paintings from the American Museum of Natural History, upon which Delgado and O'Brien patterned their beasts. • The models were set in position, then exposed to one frame of film, then moved again a fraction of an inch, and exposed to another frame. Combining this one frame at a time shooting with glass shots, split screen effects, and static and traveling mattes took long hours, patience and great concentration. O'Brien's team was only able to make about 30 *seconds* of animation a day, and the entire stop-motion process took over one year to complete. • Small rubber blad-

ders filled with air that could be inflated or deflated were also installed inside the models to add realism by simulating breathing. Also, a huge life-size dinosaur tail was constructed for the scenes in London where the monster attempts to knock people over. Animator Willis O'Brien used chocolate syrup to represent blood on his dinosaurs (an oft-imitated trick which was used 35 years later by Alfred Hitchcock in *Psycho,* 1960). • O'Brien was born in Oakland, California, in 1886, and at one time was an animal trapper in Oregon. Once he led a group of scientists to Crater Lake in search of prehistoric remnants. No doubt this sparked his imaginative interest in dinosaurs. His first monster movie was a prehistoric comedy called *The Dinosaur and the Missing Link* (1915). This short feature ran five minutes, but took two months to shoot.

The Lost World (1960; 20th Century-Fox) D/P: Irwin Allen. S: Irwin Allen, Charles Bennett. C: Winton Hoch. Cast:

David Hedison, Claude Rains, Michael Rennie, Jill St. John, Fernando Lamas, Richard Haydn, Ray Stricklyn, Jay Novello, Vitina Marcus, Ian Wolfe. This retelling of the Arthur Conan Doyle story features Professor Challenger and a new cast of characters landing atop the prehistoric jungle plateau by helicopter. In this version's finale, however, the film ends before the tyrannosaurus (not a brontosaurus as in the 1925 original) can be brought to London. ¶ "It will live long enough to grow as big as a house and terrify all London." • In this entry, Irwin Allen decided to forego historical authenticity and dress up photographically enlarged lizards to pass off as dinosaurs in order to save money. This cost-cutting technique led to Professor Challenger (played by Claude Rains) calling a live lizard with fins a "brontosaurus" and a baby alligator with horns a "Tyrannosaurus rex." Sad. • The special effects team of L. B. Abbott, James B. Gordon, and Emil Kosa, Jr., were supervised by the master animator of the first *Lost World* film (1925), Willis O'Brien. Unfortunately, O'Brien's animation talents were not utilized, but his name added weight to the production. The money saved by not using stop-motion went into buying the all-star cast, shooting the film in color, and utilizing the cinemascope process. • A sequel involving the tyrannosaurus (seen at the film's climax) being brought back to London was discussed but never made.

The Mighty Gorga (1969) (see APE GIANTS). Treasure hunters in Africa find a lost plateau of dinosaurs lorded over by a big gorilla (sound familiar?).

The People That Time Forgot (1977; Amicus/AIP) D: Kevin Connor. P: John Dark. S: Patrick Tilley. C: Alan Hume. Cast: Patrick Wayne, Thorley Walters, Sarah Douglas, Doug McClure, Dana Gillespie, Shane Rimmer. A search party headed by Patrick Wayne flies to the lost prehistoric continent of Caprona to find Bowen Tyler (Doug McClure), who had previous dropped a bottled message in the ocean at the climax of *The Land That Time Forgot* (1975). ¶ "Pterodactyls are far more interesting than Germans." • After crash-landing on Caprona, the inventive group uses a stegosaurus like a winch to pull their plane out of the mud. • The picture was filmed on location at Santa Cruz de la Palma and at Pinewood studios in England.

Planet of the Dinosaurs (1978; Filmpartners) D/P: James K. Shea. S: Ralph Lucas. C: Henning Schellerup. Cast: James Whitworth, Pamela Bottaro, Louie Lawless, Harvey Shain, Charlotte Speer, Chuck Pennington, Derna Wylde, Michael Thayer, Mary Appleseth. Astronauts sporting mustaches, bell bottom pants, and turtleneck sweaters crashland on a prehistoric planet. Their struggle to survive is complicated by internal bickering and a large menacing tyrannosaurus-like beast. ¶ "We can't risk lives trying to tame dinosaurs; we'll stay here, we're safe!" • An interesting variety of dinosaurs were created by Bill Malone and animated by Douglas Beswick, including a brontosaurus, a stegosaurus, and a "rhedosaurus"-like creature which looks exactly like *The Beast from 20,000 Fathoms* (1953). Celebrated animator Jim Danforth was credited with the matte work on this film.

Son of Kong (1933) (see APE GIANTS). This continuation of the Kong saga has Carl Denham running off to the China Seas with Capt. Englehorn to avoid his clamoring creditors. There he hooks up with a beautiful girl and the ruthless man who originally sold him the map of Skull Island. Together they sail back to Kong's home and encounter his smaller, white-furred son, as well as other prehistoric creatures, including a steracosaur and a dragon-like dinosaur.

Two Lost Worlds (1950; Eagle-Lion Classics) D: Norman Dawn. P: Boris Petroff. S: Tom Hubbard, Phyllis Parker. C: Harry Neumann. Cast: James Arness, Laura Elliott, William Kennedy, Gloria Petroff, John Hubbard, Pierre Watkins. James Arness attempts to save his girl from pirates but gets sidetracked and shipwrecked on an island inhabited by stock "dinosaur" footage from *One Million B.C.* (1940). ¶ "And at long last as the worn and beaten little group lifted their red-rimmed eyes to the dust clouded dawn, the incredible eruption began to subside." • The ceaseless narration, written by Bill Shaw and read by Don Riss, contained literary gems such as: "...greedily they crammed the tasty morsels, grabbing eager handfuls right and left!" • James Arness, who appeared in the science fiction classics, *The Thing* (1951), and *Them* (1954), was listed in the credits here as "Jim Aurness," his right name.

Unknown Island (1948; Film Classics) D: Jack Bernhard. P: Albert Jay Cohen. S: R. T. Shannon, Jack Harvey. C: Fred Jackman, Jr. Cast: Virginia Grey, Barton MacLane, Richard Denning, Philip Reed, Dick Wessell, Dan White. A photography expedition is led to a lost island of dinosaurs by a drunken flyer (Richard Denning) who is the only one to have ever returned from the

A pair of stranded astronauts desperately attempt to ward off one of the prehistoric beasts on the Planet of the Dinosaurs *(1978).*

island alive. Unscrupulous sea captain Barton MacLane gets mangled by a giant sloth(!) in the end, and Denning gets the girl. ¶ "Those flesh eating monsters have been destroying each other for centuries — survival of the fittest. It seems a pity doesn't it?" • Some of the slow-moving monsters featured include a brontosaurus, a dimetrodon, and several tyrannosaurus-like creatures, as well as a huge prehistoric sloth (represented by a man in a reddish ape suit with a long snout and claws). A climactic battle sequence pitting a tyrannosaurus against a giant sloth (both are men in cumbersome suits) results in the sloth winning the big-time wrestling match by throwing the rex out of the ring ... er, off a cliff.

Untamed Women (1952; United Artists) D: W. Merle Connell. P: Richard Kay. S: George W. Sayre. C: Glen Cano. Cast: Mikel Conrad, Doris Merrick, Richard Monahan, Mark Lowell, Morgan Jones, Midge Ware. A pilot is rescued by naval authorities and tells of his lost world adventure on an island inhabited by a tribe of "un-tamed" beauties, savage "hairy men," and dinosaurs. ¶ "Hey, maybe all those broads have is a lot of bounce and no brains?" • The untamed women are actually descendants of druids. Their priestess, Sondra, who speaks with "thees," "thys," and "thous," and uses colorful phrases like, "They fly, but they do not fly," was played by Doris Merrick, who starred in another UA prehistoric-type film, *The Neanderthal Man,* the following year. • Interestingly, every character in the film except Conrad is massacred at the climax, including Brooklyn Benny (with his "dancin' goils, broads and dames" wise-cracks). • The characters and scenery from this film were spliced together with stock footage from *One Million B.C.* (1940). Some of the menaces encountered include woolly mammoths, giant armadillos, dressed-up lizards, and man-eating plants.

The Valley of Gwangi (1969; Warner Bros.) D: James O'Connolly. P: Charles H. Schneer. S: William E. Bast, Julian More. C: Erwin Hillier. Cast: James Franciscus, Gila Golan, Richard Carlson, Laurence

Naismith, Freda Jackson, Gustavo Rojo. A tiny prehistoric horse (an eohippus) turns up at a western sideshow in Mexico and, after being freed, it is tracked back to a forbidden valley of dinosaurs by a band of cowboys. One of the brutes, an allosaur called "Gwangi," is brought back to a city where it escapes, battles an elephant, and goes on the rampage. ¶ "Eohippus, if you are one, what are you doing here over 50 million years after you should be extinct?" • Ray Harryhausen combines stop-motion work with realistic life-size models, like that of the pteranodon which snatches a rider off his horse in one scene. For part of that shot, the actor was actually lifted from his saddle by cable wires attached to a crane. The live-action footage was shot in Spain, and the special effects work took Harryhausen a year and a half to complete. • Harryhausen talked about his Gwangi creation in Jeff Rovin's book, *From the Land Beyond Beyond,* saying, "It had more things to do than an ordinary animated character, so I had to make it much more detailed, keeping in mind what activities are going to be utilized so it can perform them all." • Willis O'Brien's *Valley of the Mist* script was the inspiration for this film. O'Brien had planned to make a film about cowboys and dinosaurs years earlier but the project never went past the planning stages. • *The Valley of Gwangi* was originally to be titled *The Valley Where Time Stood Still.*

Valley of the Dragons (1961; Columbia) D/S: Edward Bernds. P: Byron Roberts. C: Brydon Baker. Cast: Cesare Danova, Sean McClory, Joan Staley, Danielle de Metz, Gregg Martell, Gil Perkins. Two duelists are whisked away to a comet on which a prehistoric world exists. They encounter two primitive tribes—the Cave and River People, weird albino morlock man-beasts, dinosaurs, and an erupting volcano. ¶ "It is in this land, a fragment of the distant past, that we now find ourselves." • The film is based upon the Jules Verne novel, *Off on a Comet,* and the visual action borrows extensive footage from *One Million B.C.* (1940) to tell the story. • Ads promised eager fans they would "*See* fight for survival against brutal, bestial Neanderthals! *See* subterranean mole-men inflicting weird tortures on all captives! *See* Mastodons! Dinosaurs! Flying reptiles! Humankind makes its last stand!"

Voyage to the Planet of Prehistoric Women (1966) (see VENUS). Astronauts land on Venus and discover a tribe of prehistoric women who worship a pterodactyl as a god.

Where Time Began (1977) (see UNDERGROUND WORLDS) (also *Journey to the Center of the Earth*). An exploratory team travels deep underground to find a lost world inhabited by dinosaurs in this low-budget remake of *Journey to the Center of the Earth* (1959).

Women of the Prehistoric Planet (1966; Realart) D/S: Arthur C. Pierce. P: George Gilbert. C: Archie Dalzell. Cast: Wendell Corey, Keith Larsen, John Agar, Irene Tsu, Paul Gilbert, Merry Anders, Stuart Margolin, Stuart Lasswell. Astronauts land on a prehistoric planet with cave people and giant lizards. The world is revealed to be Earth and at the climax one of the women decides to stay behind and live with the cavemen.

Dinosaurs on the Loose

Baby, Secret of the Lost Legend (1985; Walt Disney/Touchstone Films) D: B. W. L. Norton. P: Jonathan T. Taplin. S: Clifford Green, Ellen Green. C: John Alcott. Cast: William Katt, Sean Young, Patrick McGoohan, Julian Fellowes, Kyalo Mativo, Hugh Quarshie, Olu Jacobs. A zealous dinosaur expert (Patrick McGoohan) steals a baby brontosaurus from some friendly scientific researchers and attempts to exploit the beast. ¶ "In the equatorial rain forest of West Africa, rumors persist of a huge reptile-like creature. Said to be larger than an adult elephant, the natives call it Mokele-Mobembe"—prologue.

The Beast from 20,000 Fathoms (1953; Warner Bros.) D: Eugene Lourie. P: Jack Dietz. S: Louis Morheim, Fred Freiberger. Cast: Paul Christian, Paula Raymond, Cecil Kellaway, Kenneth Tobey, Donald Woods, King Donovan, Michael Fox. A prehistoric monster is freed from its Arctic berth by atomic testing, then goes on a whirlwind rampage down the North Atlantic coast. ¶ "The world's been here for millions of years. Man's been walking upright for a comparatively short time. Mentally, we're still crawling." ¶ The Beast, termed "rhedosaurus" in the film, is eventually dispatched by a radioactive isotope, bazooka-fired by Lee Van Cleef at the Coney Island amusement park. A "rhedosaurus" is a purely fictional dinosaur. • The film is loosely based on the Ray Bradbury short story, "The Foghorn" (only one scene from the finished film is actually in any way related to his short story, however). • The affable old Dr. Thurgood Elson was played by Cecil Kellaway, who starred in classics like *The Mummy's Hand* (1940), *Harvey* (1950), and *Guess Who's Coming to Dinner* (1967). He said of his role in *Beast:* "As a scientific professor, I am supposed to register a strange fascination for the monster, a behemoth with a taste for fresh meat and a menacing disposition. Expressing sympathy for an animal like that and still keeping it believable was an acting problem ... and problems are the things that make the job of acting interesting." • The picture only cost $200,000 to make, but enjoyed phenomenal success, and its monster-on-the-loose formula was copied again and again in the years to come. • The construction of the full-sized icebergs for the film's beginning called for 30 tons of plaster, ten tons of salt, 500 pounds of corn flakes and 40 tons of ice, the latter to be sprayed over the structure by a machine which turns the ice in a snowy blanket.

Beast of Hollow Mountain (1956; United Artists; U.S./Mexico) D: Edward Nassour, Ismael Rodriguez. P: William Nassour, Edward Nassour. S: Robert Hill, Ismael Rodriguez, Carlos Orellana. C: Jorge Stahl, Jr. Cast: Guy Madison, Patricia Medina, Eduardo Moriega, Carlos Rivas, Mario Navarro. Missing livestock (and people) prompts rancher Guy Madison to investigate a Mexican valley which just happens to be home to a Tyrannosaurus rex. ¶ "My papa didn't come back from the swamp!" • The dinosaur is lured to its death when Madison swings from a rope on a tree over a quicksand pit. The beast attempts to bite him and follows the moving target into the drowning mud. • Although the storyline for the film was submitted by Willis O'Brien, the (inferior) stop motion work was handled by Jack Rabin and Louis DeWitt. They employed a process called "Regiscope" which supposedly had an electronic type of "memory" for duplicating movement exactly, thus eliminating a lot of jerky motions. Pressbook ads bragged how the process was developed after 18 years of experimentation by Edward Nassour. • One sequence in the film shows an authentic Indian dance, purportedly for the first time ever onscreen. Nassour had to obtain special permission to photograph it. These particular film locales were said to have been infested by ticks, rattlesnakes, and wild boars, and had never been used before in motion pictures.

The Crater Lake Monster (1977; Crown International) D/P: William R. Stromberg. S: William R. Stromberg, Richard Cardella. A criminal, a sheriff, and all the Crater Lake locals encounter a plesiosaurus which emerges from time to time from this deepwater lake to snack on the populace. • This $200,000 production was predominantly financed by inheritance money.

Dinosaurus! (1960; Universal) D: Irvin S. Yeaworth, Jr. P: Jack H. Harris. S: Jean Yeaworth, Dan E. Weisburd. Cast: Ward Ramsey, Gregg Martell, Fred Engelberg, Alan Roberts, Kristina Hanson. Two frozen dinosaurs (a brontosaurus and tyrannosaurus), along with a caveman, are discovered on a Caribbean island after harbor demolition work unearths their preserved bodies. When they are brought to shore, they quickly thaw out, return to life, and liven up the island community with their prehistoric romping. ¶ "It's just not possible! This island is without power and right now two prehistoric monsters are somewhere in that jungle, alive!" • The brontosaurus is wounded by the tyrannosaur and steps into a quicksand pit, while the tyrannosaur is later knocked off a cliff by a right hook from a crane. • The monster models were built by Marcel Delgado, the man who crafted the creations used in Willis O'Brien's *The Lost World* (1925), and *King Kong* (1933). The special effects animation was executed by Wah Chang and Gene Warren.

The Giant Behemoth (1959; Allied Artists; U.K./U.S.) D/S: Eugene Lourie. P: David Diamond. C: Ken Hodges. Cast: Gene Evans, Andre Morell, Jack MacGowran, Maurice Kaufman, Henry Vidon, Leigh Madison, John Turner. Atomic testing off the shores of Great Britain awakens a prehistoric monster, and gives it the added ability to emit a powerful radioactive ray, burning everything in its path. ¶ "Gentlemen, we are witnessing a biological chain reaction, a geometrical progression of deadly menace." • The special effects crew included Willis O'Brien and Pete Peterson, who had teamed up two years earlier on the Warner Bros. big bug classic, *The Black Scorpion* (1957). • Andre Morell, who played James Bickford in this film, was Professor Quatermass in the third 1950s BBC TV production. Morell's fantasy film roles include Dr. Watson in Hammer's version of *Hound of the Baskervilles* (1959), *Plague of the Zombies* (1965), *Shadow of the Cat* (1961), *The Mummy's Shroud* (1967) and many others.

Ray Harryhausen's hungry "Rhedosaurus" strolls through the streets of New York in The Beast from 20,000 Fathoms *(1953).*

Gorgo (1961; MGM; U.K./U.S.) D: Eugene Lourie. P: Wilfred Eades. S: John Loring. C: F. A. Young, Jack Mills. Cast: Bill Travers, William Sylvester, Bruce Seton, Joseph O'Conor, Martin Benson, Vincent Winter. A 50-foot-tall dinosaur, dubbed "Gorgo," is captured off the British coast and transported to London to become the star attraction of the Dorkin circus. Trouble starts when its 200-foot-tall mother comes out of the deep to fetch it back, destroying most of London's monuments along the way. ¶ "The great city overwhelmed, exhausted, lies helpless under the immeasurable power and ferocity of this towering apparition from before the dawn of history." • Gorgo represents the third part of filmmaker Eugene Lourie's trilogy of dinosaur films which began with *The Beast from 20,000 Fathoms* in 1953, followed by *The Giant Behemoth* in 1959. *Gorgo* contains a sensitive seafaring musical score, and features a theme of motherly love, all contributing to make this entry a "kinder and gentler" monster movie.• In design, *Gorgo* is quite a departure from the animated dinosaurs of Lourie's earlier films. *Gorgo* is simply a man in a suit (with cute wiggly ears), and the rampaging effects throughout the city relies more heavily on extensive model work than the previous two pictures. The miniature sets alone cost $75,000 to construct. There was also a small mechanical model used in some shots, and a full-sized head was crafted for the sequence in which Gorgo is toted on a truck through the streets of London. • This MGM monster knocked down Big Ben, Westminster Abbey, *and* London's Tower Bridge, but it was never destroyed. The "gorgosaurus libratus," as it was called, managed to find its offspring and head back home, unaffected by all the weaponry man could throw at it.

The Legend of the Dinosaurs (1983; Toei/King Features; Japan) D: Junji Kurata. P: Keiichi Hashimoto. S: Masaru Igami, Isao Matsumoto, Ichiro Otsu. C: Sakuji Shiomi. Cast: Tsunehiko Watase, Nobiko Sawa, Shotako Hayashi, Tomoko Kiyoshima, Fuyukichi Maki, Akira Moroguchi. A recently-hatched plesiosaur and pterodactyl cause havoc at a resort lake in modern day Japan.

The Lost World (1925) (see LOST WORLDS, this section). Professor Challenger brings back a brontosaurus to London which terrorizes the city before falling off a crumbling bridge. The brute simply swims away at the climax, much like *Gorgo* does 36 years later.

One of Our Dinosaurs Is Missing (1975; Walt Disney) D: Robert Stevenson. P/S: Bill Walsh. C: Paul Beeson. Cast: Peter Ustinov, Helen Hayes, Derek Nimmo, Clive Revill, Joan Simms, Bernard Bresslaw. A Chinese secret, termed Lotus X, causes the bones of a dinosaur to regenerate into a living creature. The monster breaks out and tramples through London.

Reptilicus (1962; Alta Vista/American International; Denmark/U.S.) D/P: Sidney Pink. S: Ib Melchoir, Sid Pink. C: Aage Wiltrup. Cast: Carl Ottosen, Ann Smyrner, Asbjorn Andersen, Bent Mejding, Poul Wildaker, Mimi Heinrich. A serpent-like dinosaur grows a new body from a piece of excavated tail, then runs amok across Denmark, ravaging Copenhagen. ¶ "It's a good thing there's no more like him." • The climax promises a return when the film's final shot shows a shorn-off claw lying on the ocean bottom, waiting to regenerate. (Thankfully) a sequel never came about. • Reptilicus was a wire-propped puppet which was often shown in slow motion photography. In the farmhouse sequence where the monster swallows up a farmer, the character being eaten was Ib Melchoir's son, Dirk. • Members of an athletic club were used for the sequence in which people are seen running off a bridge to avoid being eaten by Reptilicus. Sidney Pink managed to round up all these members by promising to supply needed equipment to their club.

Robot Monster (1953) (see ALIENS—INVADERS ON EARTH: THE 50s). The alien invader, "Robot Monster," sends cosmic lightning bolts down to Earth which initiate natural disasters and revive dinosaurs. • The footage used in the prehistoric segment of this film is taken from the 1940 Hal Roach film, *One Million B.C.* Not all prints of *Robot Monster* contain this footage, however.

The Secret of the Loch (1934) (see SEA MONSTERS). A professor is scoffed at when he claims that there is a recently-hatched aquatic dinosaur living in Loch Ness. This "dinosaur" turns out to be a photographically enlarged iguana(!). No other evidence or confirmation is ever given, apart from this one statement made by the professor, that it truly is a dinosaur. • This beast is only onscreen for a minute or so, and the only mayhem it causes is to eat one diver (who had invaded his underwater cave) and menace the hero at the film's climax.

Sinbad and the Eye of the Tiger (1977) (see SINBAD). Sinbad encounters a giant saber-toothed tiger in this particular adventure. (Though not a dinosaur, it is included here since it is generally considered a "prehistoric" animal.)

Sound of Horror (1964; Zurbano Films; Spain) D: J. A. Nieves Conde. P: Gregorio Siechristian. S: Sam X. Abarbanel, Gregg Tallas, José Antonio Nieves Conde, Gregorio Sacristan. C: Manuel Berenguer. Cast: James Philbrook, Arturo Fernandez, Soledad Miranda, José Bodaló, Ingrid Pitt, Antonio Casas. A group of treasure hunters discover a prehistoric egg which hatches to disgorge an invisible dinosaur. The prehistoric creature then goes on a rampage, slicing up everyone it can get its claws on. ¶ "And are we going to be rewarded for unearthing a prehistoric monster?" • This Spanish oddity features an early appearance by actress Ingrid Pitt, who later achieved a modicum of fame in the Hammer films, *The Vampire Lovers* (1970) and *Countess Dracula* (1972). Ms. Pitt speaks fluent Spanish.

The Valley of Gwangi (1969) (see LOST WORLDS, this section). Gwangi is captured and carted from his prehistoric valley home into the city where it escapes to wreak havoc, including battling an elephant at a stadium. Gwangi is burned to death inside a cathedral at the film's climax.

Dogs

Nothing is sacred in the world of science fiction and horror, not even man's best friend. This section features films about killer canines possessed by demons (*Devil Dog: The Hound of Hell,* 1978), turned into slavering monsters by rabies (*Cujo,* 1983), and even stricken with vampirism (*Dracula's Dog,* 1978).

The fear inspired by a vicious pack of dogs was exploited in *Day of the Animals* and *Dogs* (both 1976), and then the following year the same scent was picked up by *The Pack*. The dog subgenre has been influenced by the rebellious nature-strikes-back theme to some extent, but for the most part dogs in fantastique-oriented pictures have gone their own way. Comedy has made its mark with *The Shaggy Dog* (1959) and *Digby the Biggest Dog in the World* (1973). Mad science transformed a dog into a ghostly killer in *Face of Marble* (1946) and John Agar had a king sized look-see at one in *Attack of the Puppet People* (1958).

Still, no matter how far science, the occult, or even Stephen King may go to try to erode our canine trust, the dog will always be one of our most trusted and faithful friends. If you don't agree, then just ask Don Johnson, who in the futuristic thriller *A Boy and His dog* (1975) settled the dispute over man's best friend by choosing to feed his prospective girlfriend to his lifelong buddy and bosom pal, "Blood" — a dog.

After Midnight (1989) (see MADMEN — THE SLICE 'N' DICE WAVE). An eccentric psychology professor gathers some select students at his house to learn the "psychology of fear" by telling three terror tales of psychos and murder. The middle story is about a group of teenage girls who stumble upon a psychotic street person and his killer dogs. After dispatching the psycho, the girls must flee the three killer canines, who relentlessly pursue them through the back alleys and dirty deserted streets.

Attack of the Puppet People (1958) (see SHRINKAGE). A six-inch-tall John Agar and girlfriend are menaced by a dog, which from their perspective looks gigantic.

The Beast with a Million Eyes (1955) (see ALIENS — INVADERS ON EARTH: THE 50s). An alien lands in the desert and takes control of the minds of animals, even turning the family dog into a ferocious beast.

A Boy and His Dog (1975) (see FUTURES ON EARTH — UTOPIAS AND DYSTOPIAS). In a post-holocaust world, a young Don Johnson is accompanied by his faithful telepathic companion "Blood" — a superintelligent, highly cultured dog.

Cujo (1983; Taft Entertainment Co.) D: Lewis Teague. P: Daniel H. Blatt, Robert Singer. S: Don Carlos Dunaway, Lauren Currier. C: Jan de Bont. Cast: Dee Wallace, Daniel Hugh-Kelly, Danny Pintauro, Christopher Stone, Ed Lauter, Kaiulani Lee, Billy Jacoby, Mills Watson, Sandy Ward, Jerry Hardin. A Saint Bernard is bitten by a rabies-infested bat and becomes a vicious, nearly unstoppable monster, relentlessly laying siege to a woman and her small son. • *Cujo* is based on the best selling novel by Stephen King. Made for only five million dollars, it is one of King's favorite movie adaptations of his work. • Stephen King had written his own screenplay for *Cujo*, but Taft passed it up in favor of one by Don Carlos Dunaway (rewritten from an earlier draft by Barbara Turner, a.k.a. Lauren Currier). • Of all the automobiles Dee Wallace and Danny Pintauro could have sought refuge in to escape the slavering jaws of Cujo, the filmmakers chose a Ford Pinto. • Cujo made an unbilled guest appearance as an in-joke in the 1985 Stephen King anthology *Cat's Eye* (chasing the title tabby through a wraparound sequence).

Day of the Animals (1976) (see BEARS) (also *Something Is Out There*). One of those "marauding mammal" menaces is a pack of killer dogs.

Demons 2 (1988) (see DEMONS AND DEVILS). Demons go on the rampage through a high-rise apartment building, killing everyone they can get their claws on, and turning their victims into demons as well, thereby spreading the contagion. When a woman's pet sheepdog laps up some demon blood, it is transformed into a snarling demon doggie and makes short work of its owner.

Devil Dog: The Hound of Hell (1978; TV movie) D: Curtis Harrington. P: Lou Morheim, Hal Landers. S: Stephen Karpf, Elinor Karpf. C: Gerald Perry Finnerman. Cast: Richard Crenna, Yvette Mimieux, Kim Richards, Ike Eisenmann, Victor Jory, Lou Frizzell, Ken Kercheval, R. G. Armstrong, Martine Beswick. A suburban family's dog is possessed by the devil. • *Devil Dog* made its TV premiere on Halloween (naturally). • Not only did Richard Crenna have to deal with a devilish dog here, but this same year he came face to face with Satan himself (in the form of Victor Buono) in *The Evil* (1978). • Yvette Mimieux is best known as the Time Traveler's love of the future in *The Time Machine* (1960). •

Actress Martine Beswick got her start as a starlet for Britain's Hammer Studios, appearing in *One Million Years B.C.* (1966), *Prehistoric Women* (1967), and *Dr. Jekyll and Sister Hyde* (1972).

Devil's Partner (1958) (see WITCHES, WARLOCKS, AND CULTS). Ed Nelson uses his powers of black magic to transform a rival's family dog into a snarling vicious brute which attacks and disfigures its owner.

Digby, the Biggest Dog in the World (1973; Walter Shenson Films; U.K.) D: Joseph McGrath. P: Walter Shenson. S: Michael Pertwee. C: Harry Waxman. Cast: Jim Dale, Spike Milligan, Angela Douglas, Richard Beaumont, Milo O'Shea, John Bluthal. The title pooch (an English sheepdog, appropriately enough) is fed an experimental chemical by mistake and grows to gigantic proportions in this British comedy.

Dr. Cyclops (1940) (see SHRINKAGE). A mad scientist develops a shrinking ray and turns it on a group of people who must then deal not only with the mad doctor but with a variety of giant-sized animals, including a dog.

Dogs (1976; TV movie) (also *Slaughter*). D: Burt Brinckerhoff. P: Allan F. Bodoh, Bruce Cohn. S: O'Brien Tomalin. C: Bob Steadman. Cast: David McCallum, George Wyner, Eric Server, Linda Grey, Holly Harris, Barry Greenberg, Dean Santoro, Sterling Swanson, Cathy Austin. In a small college town, all the domestic dogs suddenly turn into canine killers and stalk the unsuspecting populace. Taking its cue from Alfred Hitchcock's *The Birds* (1963), no real explanation is ever given for this sudden change in man's best friend. ¶ "And now you want me to tell them they're going to be eaten by their poodles?!" • Star David McCallum is best remembered as superspy "Ilya Kuryakin" of TV's "The Man from U.N.C.L.E." McCallum was once married to actress Jill Ireland. • One scene features a *Psycho*-style shower scene with a dog playing the Anthony Perkins part.

Dogs of Hell (1982) (also *Rottweiler*). D: Worth Keeter. P: Earl Owensby. Cast: Earl Owensby, Bill Gribble, Jerry Rushing. Covert army experiments create the "ultimate killers" — a horde of Rottweilers specially trained for combat who escape and go on a killing rampage. • Producer Earl Owensby is a movie mogul from Texas whose low-budget films (often starring himself) play almost exclusively on the southern drive-in circuit.

Dracula's Dog (1978) (see VAMPIRES —

DRACULA AND FAMILY) (also *Zoltan — Hound of Dracula*). Zoltan, Dracula's vampiric dog, is revived when his tomb is disturbed by modern-day soldiers. Accompanied by a faithful servant of his old master, the pair journey to America in search of a new master, seeking out the last descendant of the Draculas, a normal human living in L.A. They intend to initiate this descendant into the world of the undead. • The film ends on a close-up of a German Shepherd puppy who'd previously been attacked by Zoltan . . . and revealed to us is the screen's very first (and only) vampire puppy.

Face of Marble (1946) (see MAD SCIENTISTS). John Carradine's experiments in bringing the dead back to life backfire on the family's pet Great Dane, turning the dog into a ghost-like creature which can walk through solid objects and has a thirst for blood.

Invasion of the Body Snatchers (1978) (see ALIENS — INVADERS ON EARTH: THE 60S AND 70S). In one scene, the heroine is startled into revealing her human-ness by the bizarre figure of a dog with the head of a man, the result of an error in the space pods' duplication process.

Night of the Creeps (1986) (see ZOMBIES). This amusing tale of slug-like creatures from outer space turning frat boys into walking zombies features a zombie dog who, among other things, causes a fatal bus crash, providing more zombie fodder for the infesting creatures.

The Pack (1977; Warner Bros.) D/S: Robert Clouse. P: Fred Weintraub, Paul Heller. Cast: Joe Don Baker, Hope Alexander-Willis, Richard B. Shull, R. G. Armstrong. On a remote resort island, "starving pets form a rampaging pack" of killer dogs to terrorize the vacationing humans. • *The Pack* is based on the novel by David Fisher. • Director/screenwriter Robert Clouse graduated from normal-sized dogs here to giant mutant rats in *Deadly Eyes* (1982).

The Shaggy Dog (1959; Buena Vista) D: Charles Barton. P: Walt Disney. S: B. Walsh, Lillie Hayward. C: Edward Colman. Cast: Fred MacMurray, Jean Hagen, Tommy Kirk, Annette Funicello, Cecil Kellaway, Alexander Scourby, Tim Considine, Strother Martin. A teenager is turned into a sheepdog by a magic ring and must outwit a band of enemy spies. • Director Charles Barton helmed several of the Abbott and Costello films of the 1940s, including *Abbott and Costello Meet the Killer Boris Karloff* (1949), and the duo's best monster feature — *Abbott and Costello Meet*

A former household pet named Brutus menaces Claudia Drake after being transformed into a phantom canine during John Carradine's experiments to bring the dead back to life in Face of Marble *(1946).*

Frankenstein (1948). • *The Shaggy Dog* is based on the novel *The Hound of Florence,* by Felix Salten.

The Shaggy D.A. (1976) This inferior sequel to *The Shaggy Dog* stars Dean Jones as a district attorney who finds the magic ring which turns him into a sheepdog.

Watchers (1988) (see MAD SCIENTISTS). A precocious teen is befriended by a super-intelligent, genetically mutated golden retriever (which he names "Fur-face"), who's being followed by a genetically bred killing machine dubbed "Oxcon" (the result of experiments gone haywire in a clandestine government lab). • This dog is smart enough to communicate by typing on a computer and also beat the boy at a game of Scrabble.

Watchers 2 (1990) (see MAD SCIENTISTS). The super-intelligent golden retriever returns and teams up with a marine. The dog and his new pal contact an animal psychologist at the original genetics lab, all the time dodging attacks by a hybrid monster sent out after them.

Dolls

This section features dolls that come to life. While one might think that this would be a rather short section, a surprising number of killer doll movies have been made (even generating their own film series, like the recent *Child's Play* and *Puppet-master* films). The first, and perhaps finest, "killer doll" movie was released in 1936 by the famed director of *Dracula* (1930) and *Freaks* (1932) — Tod Browning. Though more accurately a SHRINKAGE picture, *The Devil Doll* was the first to utilize the "living doll" concept. The film starred Lionel Barrymore as a prison escapee who uses the incredible miniaturized people of an eccentric elderly couple for acts of vengeance, controlling these diminutive killers by sheer force of will. Though the tiny figures were not truly "dolls," but actually mindless shrunken people, Barrymore (who disguises himself as an old woman to avoid detection) passed them off as life-like dolls to his customers/intended victims. Browning used live actors for the devil dolls and relied heavily on some brilliant state of the art trick photography and enormous props to create the illusion of their gigantic environment. In 1958, B science fiction filmmaker Bert I. Gordon explored a similar theme in *Attack of the Puppet People,* his no-budget answer to Jack Arnold's *The Incredible Shrinking Man* (1957). Abandoning the use of expensive trick work, director Benito Alazraki found an even cheaper method of bringing dolls to life by simply employing midget performers to play the titular menaces in the Mexican *Curse of the Doll People* (1960).

Aside from dolls or doll-like figures being infused with movement or life (a popular theme today with the release of films like *Dolls,* 1987; *Mannequin,* 1987; and *Child's Play,* 1988), another cinematic "doll" theme concerns mad ventriloquists or puppeteers and their doll-like dummies. Two of the better entries along these lines would be *Dead of the Night* (1945) and *Magic* (1978). Often these pictures played with audience expectations by creating some doubt as to whether the dummies were actually alive, or merely a manifestation of their masters' insanity.

Asylum (1972) (see ANTHOLOGIES). The final segment, entitled "Mannikins of Horror" (written by Robert Bloch), features miniature homicidal dolls created by Herbert Lom.

Attack of the Puppet People (1958) (see SHRINKAGE). A mad dollmaker shrinks anyone he takes a shine to down to doll size to keep as his living playthings. ¶ "I love my dolls and I'm quite sure they'll never leave me."

Babes in Toyland (1961; Walt Disney) D: Jack Donohue. P: Walt Disney. S: Ward Kimball, Joe Rinaldi, Lowell S. Hawley. C: Edward Colman. Cast: Tommy Sands, Annette Funicello, Ray Bolger, Ed Wynn, Tommy Kirk, Ann Jillian, Gene Sheldon, Henry Calvin, Kevin Corcoran. Wooden soldiers come to life in this fantasy remake of the 1934 Laurel and Hardy movie. The picture also features a host of fairy tale characters including Little Boy Blue, Simple Simon, Bo Peep, Mary Contrary, Mother Goose, and Jack B. Nimble. • Annette Funicello began her entertainment career as a Mouseketeer on the "Mickey Mouse Club" TV show. She said in *Filmfax* #24, "People ask me what my favorite film is that I have done, and I have to admit, this is it." • Male

lead Tommy Sands was a close friend of singing stars Elvis Presley and Fabian. He was married to Nancy Sinatra for a short while. Scriptwriter Ward Kimball said of Sands in *Filmfax,* "The trouble was that Tommy was supposed to be a very young kid, and he had this very heavy five o'clock shadow. The makeup people did a heroic job covering it up." • Actress Ann Jillian, who later went on to star in television, said of Walt Disney, "He liked the idea that he was playing a father figure to the children who were working at the studio and to everyone else there too, for that matter. I remember that whenever he came onto the set, everyone would snap to." • George Bruns received an Academy Award nomination for its musical score. He lost to *West Side Story* that year.

Child's Play (1988; United Artists) D: Tom Holland. P: David Kirschner. S: Don Mancini, John Lafia, Tom Holland. C: Bill Butler. Cast: Catherine Hicks, Chris Sarandon, Alex Vincent. A birthday doll (named "Chucky") for a six-year-old boy turns out to be inhabited by the soul of a psychotic killer, not yet ready to die. The murderous doll goes on a killing spree looking for the right person into whom he can transfer his soul so that he doesn't have to spend the rest of his life as a toy. ¶ "Something's moved in with the Barclay family, and so has terror"—ad line. • Star Chris Sarandon said about Chucky: "The whole idea of this lovable figure that turns into a monster is every child's nightmare." • The only way to kill Chucky is to shoot (or otherwise destroy) its heart. The ironic brand name of the possessed killer doll is "Good Guy Doll." • Much bitterness arose over the authorship of *Child's Play*. According to statements made in several interviews, director Tom Holland, who had rewritten the film's final shooting script, apparently tried to claim full credit for the screenplay, calling it an "original screenplay" instead of a rewrite. A Writer's Guilt arbitration awarded Don Mancini and John Lafia co-credit. Bad blood ensued, with Holland barring the two writers, formerly friends of his, from the set.

Child's Play 2 (1990; Universal) D: John Lafia. P: David Kirschner. S: Don Mancini. C: Stefan Czapsky. Cast: Alex Vincent, Jenny Agutter, Gerrit Graham, Christin Elise, Grace Zabriskie. Chucky rises from the ashes when he's reconstructed at a toy factory. The murderous doll with the soul of a killer once again sets out to look for another body to possess. ¶ "Sorry Jack, Chucky's back"—tag line.

Curse of the Doll People (1960; AIP-TV; Mexico) D: Benito Alazraki, Paul Nagle (English version). P: William Calderón Stell, K. Gordon Murray (English version). S: Alfred Salazar. C: Henry Wallace. Cast: Elvira Quintana, Raymond Gay, Robert G. Rivera. A man steals an idol from a voodoo cult and is stalked by a voodoo priest and his army of killer dolls. ¶ "And actually you think this stupid doll has the ability to murder someone—don't be ridiculous!" • The dolls are actually midgets in doll masks and half-pint business suits.

Dead of Night (1945) (see ANTHOLOGIES). A man suffering from a recurring nightmare is told a weird tale of a ventriloquist whose dummy eventually comes to control him. In the deam-like climax we see the dummy come to life in a jail cell.

The Devil Doll (1936) (see SHRINKAGE). An escaped prisoner (Lionel Barrymore) masquerades as an old doll-making woman to escape authorities. Using a scientist's shrinking secret, he sends out his little "doll-people" (who are responsive to mental control) to take revenge on those responsible for his unjust imprisonment. ¶ "You'll never know how happy it makes me to leave one of my dolls in your beautiful home."

The Devil Doll (1963; Galaworld/Gordon Films; U.K./U.S.) D/P: Lindsay Shonteff. S: George Barclay, Lance Z. Hargreaves. C: Gerald Gibbs. Cast: Bryant Halliday, William Sylvester, Yvonne Romain, Francis De Wolff, Sandra Dorne. A ventriloquist manages to infuse his wooden dummy with a human soul. In the table-turning climax, he himself ends up inside the dummy. ¶ Promotional ads posed the questions: "What is the strange, terrifying, evil secret of the dummy? And why is it locked in a cage every night?" • Oakland-born actor William Sylvester was discovered by John Barrymore, who saw him in an amateur play and suggested he develop his talents at the Royal Academy of Dramatic Arts in London. Sylvester later went on to appear in the 1968 sci-fi classic, *2001: A Space Odyssey*.

Dolls (1987; Empire) D: Stuart Gordon. P: Brian Yuzna. S: Ed Naha. C: Mac Ahlberg. Cast: Ian Patrick Williams, Carrie Loraine, Carolyn Purdy-Gordon, Stephen Lee, Guy Rolfe, Hillary Mason. A disparate group of people end up at a gothic mansion during a thunderstorm. The elderly eccentric occupants, the Hartwickes, take great pride and pleasure in showing their guests their numerous handmade dolls. Later that night, the myriad dolls come to life and punish the guilty among them. • Stuart Gordon also directed the H. P. Lovecraft film, *From Beyond* (1986) as well as the modern classic, *Re-Animator* (1985). • The dolls were designed and created by Mechanical and Makeup Imageries, Inc., using up most of the $1.2 million budget.

House of Evil (1968; Columbia/Azteca; U.S./Mexico) D: Juan Ibañez, Jack Hill. P: Luis Enrique Vergara. S: Jack Hill. C: Raul Dominguez, Austin McKinney. Cast: Boris Karloff, Julissa East, Andres Garcia, Angel Espinosa, Beatriz Baz, Quintin Bulnes. Greedy heirs, awaiting their payoff at an old spooky castle, are killed off one by one by various life-sized mechanical dolls. • The dolls are played by actors pretending to be toys. • This is one in a series of four films Boris Karloff did back to back for Mexican producer Vergara in 1968. They were the last movies Karloff made before he died later that same year.

Kiss Me, Kill Me (1973) (see WITCHES, WARLOCKS, AND CULTS). A woman is drawn into the sado-masochistic world of a modern-day witch. The witch owns a doll which can move on its own and transform into a leather-clad dominatrix.

Magic (1978) (see MADMEN—EARLY PSY-

CHOS). A ventriloquist (Anthony Hopkins) appears to have a split personality, which he shares with his stage dummy. It is just possible, however, that this dummy has a life of its own.

Mannequin (1987; 20th Century-Fox) D: Michael Gottlieb. P: Art Levinson. S: Edward Rugoff, Michael Gottlieb. C: Timothy Suhrstedt. Cast: Andrew McCarthy, Kim Catrall, Estelle Getty, James Spader, G. W. Bailey. A young man falls in love with a store mannequin, which, in his eyes, then comes to life. After overcoming many obstacles, they decide to marry, and she becomes real for all to see. ¶ "You've got good hands. I like the way they felt when you were putting me together." • A sequel is scheduled to be released in late 1991.

Poltergeist (1982) (see GHOSTS). This special effects–heavy movie about vengeful ghosts features one shuddery scene involving a little clown doll brought to frightening life by demonic forces.

Puppetmaster (1989; Paramount) D: David Schmoeller. P: Hope Perello. S: Joseph G. Collodi. C: Sergio Salvati. Cast: Paul Le Mat, Irene Miracle, Matt Roe, Kathryn O'Reilly, Marya Small, Jimmie F. Skaggs, Robin Frates, Barbara Crampton, William Hickey. An aged dollmaker imbues his unique creations with life. A group of unscrupulous people at an old mansion are set upon by these killer puppets who punish them for their various sins. • Each deadly doll has its own unique ability. "Tunneler" bores holes into people with his drill-bit head. "Ms. Leech" regurgitates killer leeches. "Pinhead" strangles victims with vice-like hands. "Blade" slashes with a hook and a razor-knife, and "Jester" is the group's dangerous leader. • David Allen did the stop-motion animation effects which brought the dolls to murderous life. • Charles Band, who originally began as producer on the project, stated in a *Fangoria* #83 interview that *Puppetmaster* was inspired by the killer doll episode of the TV movie *Trilogy of Terror* (1975). "It made quite an impression on me and on many other people who saw it."

Puppetmaster 2 (1990; Paramount) D: David Allen. P: David DeCoteau, John Schouweiler. S: David Pabian. C: Thomas F. Denove. Cast: Elizabeth Maclellan, Collin Bernsen, Gregory Webb, Charlie Spradling, Steve Welles, Jeff Weston, Nita Talbot. The murderous puppets from the original *Puppetmaster* are back, using their precious animating fluid to revive their master from the dead. A group of psychic researchers just happen to be at the old abandoned hotel at the time, and the reanimated puppetmaster has his creations murder them one by one in order to obtain the special ingredient necessary to make their life-giving fluid—bits of human brain. The puppetmaster intends to transform himself and the heroine (whom he believes to be the reincarnation of his dead wife) into life-sized animated puppets. ¶ "Of course, you may wither into dry wood, but you've given me back my wife." • All the special puppets from the original are back—"Tunneler," "Pinhead," "Ms. Leech," "Blade," and "Jester,"—as well as one additional killer doll, "Torch," who has a flamethrower for an arm. • David Allen, who provided the stop-motion animation effects for the original, turned director for this sequel. • According to Charles Band's Full Moon Productions, a *Puppetmaster 3* is in the works.

Screamtime (1983) (see ANTHOLOGIES). In this British anthology feature's first (and best) segment, a puppeteer brings his Punch and Judy dolls to life to take revenge on those who've wronged him.

Tourist Trap (1978) (see PSYCHIC ABILITY). Chuck Connors stars as a madman with telekinetic power and a museum full of mannequins which he animates in order to terrorize a group of teenagers.

Trilogy of Terror (1975) (see ANTHOLOGIES). In the third episode of this TV anthology, Karen Black takes home a Zuñi doll that comes to life with boundless homicidal energy.

Dorian Gray *see* Gray, Dorian

Dracula *see* Vampires — Dracula and Family

Dreamkillers

When the term "dreamkiller" pops up, the name of Freddie Krueger immediately comes to mind. While a sadistic child molester wielding a glove with razor-sharp knives for fingers makes for a rather sick hero figure, this perverted maniac (who invades the dreams of teens in order to slice and dice with impunity) struck a cord with moviegoers everywhere. Wes Craven's seminal masterpiece, *A Nightmare on Elm Street* (1984), created a character so frightening yet so compelling that Freddie Krueger became the horror icon of the eighties, even launching his own TV show called "Freddie's Nightmares." While a continuous stream of sequels (all box office successes) and overexposure have dimmed Craven's first frightening achievement, it still stands out as one of the truly innovative horror films of a generally barren decade.

Though a recent phenomenon, the *Nightmare* movies were not the first to deal with the frightening realm of dreamland. William Castle's *The Night Walker* (1964) featured a woman tormented by her dream lover come-to-life, though the cheat ending reveals it to be another drive-the-heiress-mad plot. The first film to truly focus on terrors conjured up from the other side of waking is Oliver Stone's rather muddled feature debut, *Seizure* (1973).

It was the *Elm Street* movies, however, which opened up the floodgates and let the nightmare boogeymen loose in the celluloid dreams of an unsuspecting public.

Bad Dreams (1988; 20th Century–Fox) D: Andrew Fleming. P: Gale Anne Hurd. S: Andrew Fleming, Steven E. de Souza. C: Alexander Gruszynski. Cast: Jennifer Rubin, Bruce Abbott, Richard Lynch, Dean Cameron, Harris Yulin, Susan Barnes, John Scott Clough. The sole survivor of a mass suicide pact at one of the last holdout communes of the 1970s wakes up from a 13-year coma and she's haunted by visions of the Jim Jones–type leader. He is trying to induce her to commit suicide, thereby completing their former group's "oneness." Along the way, he also incidentally kills all of her friends. ¶ "Come to me my lovechild." • Star Jennifer Rubin had nightmares of another dream killer the year before in *A Nightmare on Elm Street 3: Dream Warriors* (1987).

Dreamscape (1984; Zupnik-Curtis Enterprises) D: Joseph Ruben. P: Bruce Cohn Curtis. S: David Loughery, Chuck Russell, Joseph Ruben. C: Brian Tufano. Cast: Dennis Quaid, Max Von Sydow, Christopher Plummer, Eddie Albert, Kate Capshaw, David Patrick Kelly, George Wendt, Larry Gelman. Dennis Quaid plays a young man with telephathic powers who is recruited by scientist Max Von Sydow for his dream research project. Quaid learns to project himself into another person's dream, and thereby help that person overcome the demons of their subconscious. Unfortunately, the project is backed by a sinister government figure, who intends to use it to create a group of dream assassins. He orders a psychotic young telepath to enter the dream of the President of the United States, who is there for treatment of his recurring nightmares of nuclear devastation, and Quaid is the only one who can stop him. ¶ "When you dream, if you die, you die in real life."

I, Madman (1989; Trans World Entertainment) D: Tibor Takaks. P: Rafael Eisenman. S: David Chaskin. C: Brian Englund. Cast: Jenny Wright, Clayton Rohner, Randall William Cook, Steven Memel, Stephanie Hodge, Bruce Wagner, Michelle Jordan, Murray Rubin, Vincent Lucchesi. A young woman becomes obsessed with an obscure pulp horror novel called *I, Madman* and somehow, through her dreams, brings the evil disfigured character to life. • Randall William Cook, who provided the special effects for the film, also stars as the grotesque dreamkiller. Director Tibor Takaks explained to *Fangoria* magazine why an FX man was cast in such a pivotal role: "It was something that Randy always wanted to do. To entice him to work on the low-budget movie, I had to come up with something!" • Screenwriter David Chaskin was an old hand at the dreamkiller

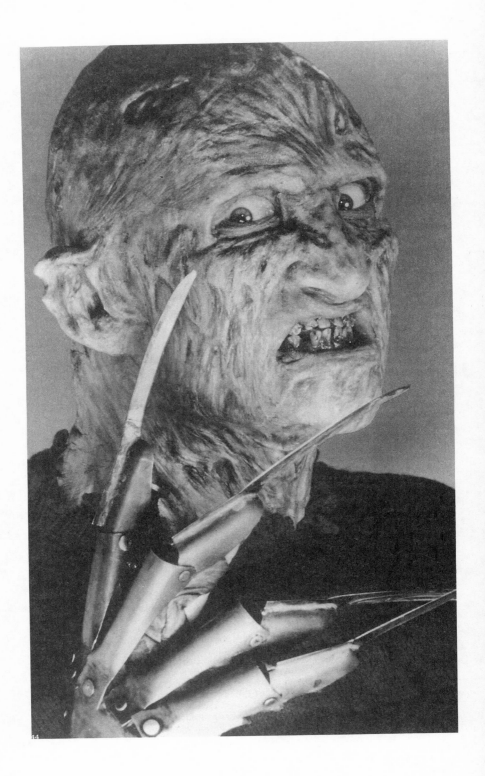

game, having penned Freddy Krueger's second outing, *A Nightmare on Elm Street 2: Freddy's Revenge,* in 1985.

The Night Walker (1964; Universal) D/P: William Castle. S: Robert Bloch. C: Harold Stine. Cast: Barbara Stanwyck, Robert Taylor, Hayden Rorke, Lloyd Bochner, Judith Meredith, Rochelle Hudson, Jess Barker. A woman's dreams are haunted by the specters of her disfigured dead husband and a mysterious dream lover. Nightmare blends with reality when her dream date materializes and escorts her to a bizarre chapel populated with wax figurines. In the end it all turns out to be another drive-the-woman-mad plot.

A Nightmare on Elm Street (1984; New Line Cinema) D/S: Wes Craven. P: Robert Shaye. C: Jacques Haitkin. Cast: John Saxon, Ronee Blakley, Heather Langencamp, Amanda Wyss, Nick Corri, Johnny Depp, Robert Englund. A vicious child-murderer named Freddy Krueger is set free on a technicality and a group of outraged parents band together and burn him alive. Years later, Krueger returns to invade the dreams of their teenage children, killing them in their nightmares and thereby causing their actual gruesome deaths. ¶ "Whatever you do, don't ... fall ... asleep." ▪ This innovative surprise horror hit was successful enough to spawn four sequels (with a fifth on the near horizon) as well as a TV series called "Freddie's Nightmares" (all starring Robert Englund as the wise-cracking, razor-gloved dreamkiller), making Freddy Krueger the most successful monster of the latter 1980s. ▪ Wes Craven came up with the idea for the film after reading a newspaper article detailing three separate incidents in which young Asian men died in their sleep, apparently as a result of an intense nightmare. ▪ According to Craven, he tried to sell the project for three years before New Line Cinema finally funded it to the low-budget tune of $1.8 million.

A Nightmare on Elm Street 2: Freddy's Revenge (1985; Heron) D: Jack Sholder. P: Robert Shaye. S: David Chaskin. Cast: Robert Englund, Mark Patton, Kim Myers, Robert Rusler, Clu Gulager, Hope Lange. A family moves into the old *Nightmare on Elm Street* house, the site of the dreamkillings from the first film. Freddy Krueger soon invades the dreams of their teenage son Jesse and eventually takes physical possession of his body, embarking on another slaughtering rampage through the Elm Street neighborhood teens. ¶ "Animals just don't explode into flames for no reason."

A Nightmare on Elm Street 3: Dream Warriors (1987; New Line Cinema) D: Chuck Russell. P: Robert Shaye, Sara Risher. S: Wes Craven, Bruce Wagner, Chuck Russell, Frank Darabont. C: Roy Wagner. Cast: Robert Englund, Heather Langenkamp, Patricia Arquette, Larry Fishburne, Priscilla Pointer, Craig Wasson, Brooke Bundy, Rodney Eastman, Bradley Gregg, Ira Heiden, Ken Sagoes, Penelope Sudrow, Jennifer Rubin, John Saxon, Dick Cavett, Zsa Zsa Gabor. In this third installment in the ever-popular "Freddy Krueger" series, the dreamkiller invades the dreams of various troubled teens at a psychiatric hospital. The teens had once lived on Elm Street and Krueger wants his "children" back. ¶ "Freddy Krueger—the bastard son of a thousand maniacs!" ▪ Wes Craven, creator of the original *A Nightmare on Elm Street* (1984), co-wrote the script and served as associate producer for this installment (he was not involved in Part 2 at all). ▪ Both Heather Langenkamp and John Saxon return from the original. This time Langenkamp is now a doctor specializing in dream disorders. ▪ Made on the low budget of $4.5 million, it made $8.8 million during its opening weekend alone, going on to take in over $40 million.

A Nightmare on Elm Street 4: The Dream Master (1988; New Line Cinema) D: Renny Harlin. P: Robert Shaye, Rachel Talalay. S: Brian Helgeland, Scott Pierce. C: Steven Fierberg. Cast: Robert Englund, Rodney Eastman, Danny Hassel, Andras Jones, Tuesday Knight, Ken Sagoes, Lisa Wilcox. Freddy Krueger, America's number one dreamkiller, is back and ready to take out the surviving teenage "dream warriors" from the previous entry. ¶ "When deep sleep falleth on men, fear came upon me, and trembling, which made all my bones to shake."—biblical quote used as an introduction.

A Nightmare on Elm Street 5: The Dream Child (1989; New Line Cinema) D: Stephen Hopkins. P: Robert Shaye, Rupert Harvey. S: Leslie Bohem. C: Peter Levy. Cast: Robert Englund, Lisa Wilcox. Alice, survivor of Part 4, is back and pregnant. Freddy sets his demoniacal sights on her unborn baby, invading the dreams of the developing fetus. ▪ Ironically, female lead Lisa Wilcox (returning from Part 4) auditioned for a role in Part 3 but was turned down cold.

Opposite: Freddy Krueger (Robert Englund) shows off his razor-sharp fingers in this publicity pose from the Nightmare on Elm Street *film series.*

Nightwish (1989; Channel Communications/PIV International) D/S: Bruce R. Cook. P: Keith Walley. C: Sean McLin. Cast: Clayton Rohner, Alisha Das, Jack Starrett, Robert Tessier, Elizabeth Kaitan, Artur Cybulski, Tom Dugan, Brian Thompson. The incredibly confused and convoluted storyline of this nearly plotless picture centers around a group of parapsychology students who are involved in dream research, trying to control their dreams and ultimately face their own deaths in their dream world. They go to a supposedly haunted house to conduct their experiments, and experience a barrage of hallucinations and real-life horrors which *could* be dreams or *could* be reality. Included is a psychotic groundskeeper, the demented professor leading the group, plenty of bugs, and some kind of alien ectoplasmic creatures. At the end it is revealed to be only a dream, but even *that* turns out to be a dream as well. ¶ "We are not dealing with the supernatural here. There are aliens living in this mine"—a very confused heroine.

Paperhouse (1988; Vestron Pictures; U.K.) D: Bernard Rose. P: Tim Bevan, Sarah Radclyffe. S: Matthew Jacobs. C: Mike Southon. Cast: Charlotte Burke, Ben Cross, Glenne Headly, Elliott Spiers, Gemma Jones, Jane Bertish, Samantha Cahill, Sarah Newbold, Gary Bleasdale, Steven O'Donnell. A young girl draws a picture of a house on paper, which she visits in her dreams. There she meets a young crippled boy named Mark. The two of them must fight for their lives against a frightening figure which turns out to be the twisted image of her estranged father. Finally the real Mark dies of his illness and the girl leaves her dream world behind, secure in the knowledge that Mark is now all right where he's going. ¶ "I know Mark, I know him from my dreams. I drew a house on paper, he walks there too. It was me who made Mark ill and me who made him get better again. Then we had to escape, and we did." • The film is based on the novel *Marianne Dreams* by Catherine Storr.

Seizure (1973; Cinerama Releasing; Canada) D: Oliver Stone. P: Garrard L. Glenn, Jeffrey D. Kapelman. S: Edward Mann, Oliver Stone. C: Roger Racine. Cast: Jonathan Frid, Martine Beswick, Joe Sirola, Christina Pickles, Anne Meacham, Roger De Koven, Troy Donahue, Mary Woronov, Hervé Villechaize. The largely incoherent story centers around a writer (Jonathan Frid, of "Dark Shadows" fame) who invites a group of friends for a weekend and also inadvertently materializes three nightmare figures from his own imaginative dreams—an evil dwarf (Hervé Villechaize, later of TV's "Fantasy Island"), a black executioner, and the "Queen of Evil" (Martine Beswick), who is at one point characterized as being the goddess Kali(!). ¶ "You will do as you are told, though nothing will make sense." (Unfortunately, the same can be said of his movie.) • *Seizure* was the feature film debut of Oscar-winning writer/director Oliver Stone (*Midnight Express* [which he wrote; Alan Parker directed]; *Platoon*), though since hitting the big time he's dropped this B-film from his resumé. • The film was shot at a supposedly haunted house in Canada, near a lake that reportedly contained dead bodies. "That was the most *extraordinary* experience I've ever had on a movie," exclaimed co-star Martine Beswick in a *Fangoria* #55 interview. "Before I read the script, I had a nightmare about a giant threatening me with a knife. The next day, I discovered it was a scene from the picture."

Slumber Party Massacre 2 (1987; Concorde) D/S: Deborah Brock. P: Deborah Brock, Don Daniel. C: Thomas Callaway. Cast: Crystal Bernard, Jennifer Rhodes, Kimberly McArthur, Patrick Lowe, Juliette Cummins, Heidi Kozak, Cynthia Eilbacher, Atanas Ilitch, Joel Hoffman. One of the surviving sisters from the original *Slumber Party Massacre* (1982) begins having dreams about a homicidal leather-jacketed singer with a drill at the end of his guitar. Her dream comes to life as the rock 'n' roll maniac begins offing her friends one by one. • Carrying on the tradition from the first film, *Slumber Party Massacre 2* holds the rare distinction of being made by a woman.

Edgar Allan Poe *see* Poe Films
ESP *see* Psychic Ability

Fish

(*See also* Fish-People; Sea Monsters)

In 1975, the incredible critical and financial success of Steven Spielberg's terror film, *Jaws,* proved that what lies in wait beneath the water is an exploitable (and bankable) horror. The first significant fish film would be *Moby Dick* — first the 1930 version with John Barrymore as Ahab, then Gregory Peck's 1956 remake. But *Moby Dick* (both versions) focused on melodrama rather than horror, and it took *Creature from the Black Lagoon* (1954; found in the FISH-PEOPLE section) to really bring out the fright potential of underwater horrors. Spielberg took it a step further with *Jaws,* the ultimate shark movie. *Jaws* set the fish world afire, spawning a slew of imitations faster than a salmon hatchery. In this section we only include films that deal with fish — sharks, barracudas, killer whales (though technically not a fish, whales are usually lumped in with the group), etc. — that have become a menace (the ultimate fish story so to speak). Other underwater denizens such as giant squid and octopi will be found in the SEA MONSTERS section (since that is what they are commonly held to be by seamen and monster fans alike).

Barracuda (1978; Republic) D: Harry Kerwin. P: Harry Kerwin, Wayne Crawford. S: Harry Kerwin, Wayne Crawford. Cast: Jason Evers, Bert Freed, Wayne David Crawford. Marine biologists discover that chemicals dumped into the water are responsible for a rash of violent acts in the area, as well as a deadly strain of killer barracudas causing mayhem along the Florida coast. ¶ "A new set of '*Jaws*' with an insatiable appetite" — imitative ad line. • The picture was photographed on location in Florida and the title theme music was performed by the Frankfurt Radio Symphony Orchestra.

The Deep (1977; Columbia) D: Peter Yates. P: Peter Guber. S: Peter Benchley, Tracy Keenan Wynn. C: Christopher Challis, Al Giddings, Stan Waterman. Cast: Nick Nolte, Jacqueline Bisset, Robert Shaw, Lou Gossett, Eli Wallach, Robert Tessier. A vacationing couple on an underwater treasure hunt discovers a sunken shipload of morphine which an island drug dealer wants desperately. Along with the treasure, they also find a huge man-killing moray eel which puts the bite on the villain at the climax. ¶ "Damn thing bit off my entire foot, look at this bloody stump. I almost drowned!" • Screenwriter Peter Benchley helped adapt the script from his own novel.

Devilfish (1984; Italy) D: Lamberto Bava. P: Mino Loy. S: Lewis Coates, Don Lewis, Martin Dolman. Cast: John Garko, William Berger, Iris Peynard, Lawrence Morgant. A prehistoric fish, an evolutionary throwback with the ability of self-regeneration, is discovered off the Florida coast, where it wreaks havoc among (and eats) the local boaters.

Great White (1982; Film Ventures; Italy) D: Enzo G. Castellari. P: Maurizio Amati, Ugo Tucci. S: Mark Princi. C: Alberto Spagnoli. Cast: James Franciscus, Vic Morrow, Joshua Sinclair, Micky Pignatelli, Timothy Brent. This is basically a cheap Italian remake of *Jaws.* • Universal obtained a preliminary injunction from the courts to stop the showing of this film because of its blatant copying of their 1975 blockbuster, *Jaws.*

Hello Down There (1969; Paramount) D: Jack Arnold. P: George Sherman. S: Frank Telford, John McGreevey. C: Cliff Poland. Cast: Tony Randall, Janet Leigh, Jim Backus, Roddy McDowall, Ken Berry, Merv Griffin, Bruce Gordon, Arnold Stang. Tony Randall and family live in an underwater home besieged by sharks. • The film reunites director Jack Arnold with his favorite underwater actor, Ricou *(Creature from the Black Lagoon)* Browning, who helped coordinate the diving sequences.

Jaws (1975; Universal) D: Steven Spielberg. P: Richard D. Zanuck, David Brown. S: Peter Benchley, Carl Gottlieb. C: Bill Butler. Cast: Roy Scheider, Richard Dreyfuss, Robert Shaw, Lorraine Gary, Murray Hamilton. A huge great white shark settles into the waters off Amity Island to dine on swimmers and fishermen. The island's chief of police (who happens to be deathly afraid of the water) decides to enlist the aid of a grizzled mariner named Quint, along with a young researcher, to hunt down the killer behemoth. Once out on the water, however, the tables are turned and the hunters become the hunted. ¶ "Sometimes that shark, he looks right into you, right into your eyes. You know the thing about a shark is he's got lifeless eyes, black eyes like a doll's eyes. When he comes at you he doesn't seem to be living — until he bites you. Those black eyes roll over white, and oh, then you hear that terrible high-pitched screamin'. The ocean turns red. In spite of all the poundin' and the hollerin', they all come in, rip ya to pieces." • There were actually three sharks (all mechanical) used to represent *Jaws* (which the film's crew nicknamed "Bruce"). They were 25 feet long, had the capability to make a short burst from the water, and together cost approximately $250,000 to construct. In the Universal Studios Tour it is possible to see *Jaws* in person. A visitors' tram passes by a tranquil lagoon, and from out of the water pops Bruce, right at you. • *Jaws* won Academy Awards for Sound, Editing, and Original Score, and was nominated for many others, including Best Picture. *Jaws* is also one of the biggest box office grossers of all time. • *Jaws* is based on the Peter Benchley novel, and Benchley himself appears in the film as a beachfront reporter interviewing vacationers. In the original novel, Richard Dreyfuss' character (the researcher) has an affair with Chief Brody's wife, and, unlike in the movie, gets eaten by the shark.

Jaws 2 (1978; Universal) D: Jeannot Szwarc. P: Richard D. Zanuck, David Brown. S: Carl Gottlieb, Howard Sackler. C: Michael Butler. Cast: Roy Scheider, Lorraine Gary, Joseph Mascolo, Jeffrey Kramer, Collin Wilcox, Murray Hamilton. Another killer shark returns to Amity and spoils everyone's good time, especially the teenage boys and girls off on sailing excursions. Chief Brody once again comes to the rescue, dropping an electric cable into the great white's mouth, frying it beyond recognition.

Jaws 3-D (1983; Universal) D: Joe Alves. P: Rupert Hitzig. S: Richard Matheson, Carl Gottlieb. C: James A. Contner. Cast: Dennis Quaid, Bess Armstrong, Simon MacCorkindale, Louis Gosset, Jr., John Putch. A 35-foot mother shark manages to get inside a Florida aquatic park called the "Undersea Kingdom," where it attempts to rescue its captive offspring and eat the entire cast. • This 3-D production features not one but two killer sharks.

Jaws 4: The Revenge (1987; Universal) D/P: Joseph Sargent. S: Michael de Guzman. C: John McPherson. Cast: Lorraine Gary, Lance Guest, Michael Caine, Mario Van Peebles, Karen Young. When the widowed wife of Chief Brody loses one of her sons in a shark attack, she travels to the Bahamas to be with her other marine scientist son. There she falls for Michael Caine, and everything seems to be getting back to normal when the nightmare returns. This time, she personally sets out to get the killer shark who has some kind of personal vendetta against her family. No shark hath seen the fury of a mother scorned. • In this particular outing, the great white shark had such a huge chip on its shoulder (or should that be "tear in his fin"?) that it followed the Brody family all the way to the Bahamas, waters totally alien to its particular species. • Michael Caine was unable to attend the Academy Awards ceremony at which he won an Oscar for his supporting role in Woody Allen's *Hannah and Her Sisters* (1985) because he was away making this $20 million fish-flick.

Killer Fish (1979; Associated Films; Italy/Brazil) D: Anthony Dawson (Antonio Margheriti). P: Alex Ponti. S: Michael Rogers. Cast: Lee Majors, Karen Black, James Franciscus, Margaux Hemingway, Marisa Berenson. Deep sea divers encounter killer piranhas guarding sunken treasure.

Mako, Jaws of Death (1976; Selected) (also *The Jaws of Death*). D/P: William Grefe. Cast: Richard Jaeckel, Jennifer Bishop, Harold Sakata, Luke Halpin, John Davis Chandler, Buffy Dee. Richard Jaeckel plays a lover of sharks who occasionally rents them out to researchers. He also sends them out to kill when he is crossed. • Filmmaker William Grefe went on to work on numerous James Bond films as an assistant director.

Orca (1977; Paramount) D: Michael Anderson. P: Luciano Vincenzoni. S: Sergio Donati, Luciano Vincenzoni. C: Ted Moore. Cast: Richard Harris, Will Sampson, Charlotte Rampling, Bo Derek, Keenan Wynn, Robert Carradine. At a small fishing village, a vindictive killer whale stalks those responsible for the death of its pregnant mate. • Orca drops Bo Derek from a 10 to an 8 by chomping off one of her legs in one of the film's more gruesome scenes.

Piranha (1978; New World) D: Joe Dante. P: Jon Davison, Chako Van Leeuwen. S: John Sayles. C: Jamie Anderson. Cast: Bradford Dillman, Heather Menzies, Kevin McCarthy, Keenan Wynn, Dick Miller, Barbara Steele. Mutant flesh-eating piranha (the result of an abandoned military experi-

The man-eating great white shark from Jaws *(1975) leaps onboard Quint's boat in search of human food. At the climax,* Jaws *is blown apart when a shot fired by Roy Scheider hits a compressed air tank protruding from the side of its gaping mouth.*

ment left over from the Vietnam era) are accidentally let loose upriver from a summer camp and resort. ¶ "I know what to do, we'll pollute them to death!"—hero Bradford Dillman when he forms the plan to release a pipe full of filth into the river in order to choke the deadly fish to death. • Producer Jon Davison: "We're not denying that *Piranha* is a ripoff of *Jaws,* but we'd much rather think of it as a ripoff of *The Creature from the Black Lagoon.*" • Paul Bartel, here taking an acting role as a camp counselor–turned-fish-food, is better known as a director (*Death Race 2000,* 1975; *Eating Raoul,* 1982). • Screenwriter John Sayles later wrote and directed the acclaimed low-budget film *The Return of the Secaucus Seven* (1979). • *Piranha* features a rare appearance by former scream queen Barbara Steele after her semi-retirement from the movies in the late 1960s. • Kevin McCarthy, best known as the man who exposed the *Invasion of the Body Snatchers* in 1956, plays the scientist responsible for letting the killer fish loose on an unsuspecting populace.

Piranha 2: The Spawning (1982; Embassy) D: James Cameron. P: Jeff Schechtman, Chako Van Leeuwen. C: Roberto D'Ettore Piazzoli. Cast: Tracie O'Neil, Steve Marachuk, Lance Henriksen, Ted Richert, Ricky G. Paull. Piranha eggs hatch at an island resort in this sequel to the popular 1978 feature. Due to some imprudent gene-splicing experiments, this new set of killer fish are able to fly up out of the water and attack people on land. • Actor Lance Henriksen (playing the island's police chief) broke his hand during filming (performing a stunt in which he jumped from a helicopter into the ocean) and finished the picture with a broken hand. • Henriksen told *Fangoria* #65 about director Cameron's difficulties with the film's producers: "When they were cutting it in Rome, they locked Jim out of the editing, and he had to crawl through the window at night, re-edit, and hope that they didn't discover his changes."

The Sea Bat (1930; MGM) D: Wesley Ruggles. S: Bess Meredyth, John Howard Lawson. C: Ira H. Morgan. Cast: Raquel Torres, Charles Bickford, Nils Asther, George F. Marion, John Miljan. A monstrous manta ray (dubbed "Sea Bat" by the superstitious natives) menaces divers off a Caribbean island. ¶ "Don't you understand, they went to kill Sea Bat for me. I sent them, maybe they'd still be alive, except for me." • Boris Karloff, before attaining stardom with *Frankenstein* (1931), has a brief role in the picture as a villainous half-breed Corsican.

Shark Kill (1976; TV movie) D: William A. Graham. P: Barry Weitz. S: Sandor Stern. C: Terry K. Meade. Cast: Richard Yniguez, Phillip Clark, Jennifer Warren, Elizabeth Gill, Victor Campos. This television version of *Jaws* again features a man-killing great white shark on the prowl.

She Gods of Shark Reef (1958; AIP) D: Roger Corman. P: Ludwig H. Gerber. S: Robert Hill, Victor Stoloff. C: Floyd Crosby. Cast: Don Durant, Lisa Montell, Bill Cord, Jeanne Gerson, Carol Lindsay. Two brothers, one good (Bill Cord), one bad (Don Durant), end up on a tropical island populated by bathing beauties and surrounded by shark-infested waters. Durant becomes shark-bait when he attempts to abscond with a cache of pearls. ¶ "Beautiful maidens in a Lush Tropical Paradise ruled by a Hideous Stone God!"—ad line. • This picture was shot back to back on Kauai with another lightweight island adventure called *Thunder Over Hawaii*. Roger Corman commented in Ed Naha's book, *The Films of Roger Corman:* "Filming this movie and *She Gods of Shark Reef* was one of the most pleasurable experiences I've ever had.... Visually, these two movies are probably the most beautiful I've ever shot."

Tintorera ... Bloody Waters (1977; United Film Distribution; Mexico/U.K.) D: Rene Cardona, Jr. P: Gerald Green. S: Ramon Bravo. Cast: Susan George, Jennifer Ashley, Fiona Lewis. Two shark hunters, vying for the same girl, go out in search of a terrible great white. ¶ "There's a monstrous killer churning up the sea"—ad slogan.

Up from the Depths (1979; New World; Philippines) D: Charles B. Griffith. P: Cirio H. Santiago. S: Alfred Sweeny, Anne Dyer. Cast: Sam Bottoms, Susanne Reed, Virgil Frye, Kedric Wolfe, Charles Howerton. A huge prehistoric fish is the menace in this exploitation feature sailing in on the wake of *Jaws*. ¶ "Your vacation is about to end!!!" decreed the ads. • Director Charles B. Griffith is better known as the prolific screenwriter of numerous Roger Corman cult classics like *Not of This Earth* (1956), *Attack of the Crab Monsters* (1957), and *The Little Shop of Horrors* (1960).

Zombie (1980) (see ZOMBIE FLESH EATERS). In one of the more inventive sequences in this zombie gut-muncher, a submerged zombie engages in hand-to-fin battle with a shark. (The shark loses.)

Fish-People

(*See also* Fish; Sea Monsters)

It is no great secret who the founding father of this particular subject is. The *Creature from the Black Lagoon* (1954) has risen to stardom in the monster world, and is counted as one of the five classic monsters, rubbing slimy shoulders with the Mummy, the Vampire, the Werewolf, and the Frankenstein Monster.

The *Creature*'s success at the box office was monumental, and singlehandedly started its own subgenre. True, fish-people were seen in the 1929 film, *Mysterious Island,* but the little monsters didn't have the charisma that the Creature possessed. Not only did *Creature from the Black Lagoon* spawn two sequels (both solid efforts), it also inspired a riot of relatives—some of natural origin, and some mutations caused by radiation or mad scientists.

Also in this section you will find the mermaid films, which feature a more classical type of fish-person.

For additional aquatic action, see CRABS AND CRUSTACEANS, FISH, and SEA MONSTERS.

The Amphibian Man (1961; Lenfilm; U.S.S.R.) (also *The Amphibious Man*). D: Guennadi Kazansky, Vladimir Chebotorev. S: Akiba Golburt, Aleksander Ksenofontov, Aleksei Kapler. C: Edouard Rasovski. Cast: Vladimir Korenev, Anastasia Vertinskaya, Nikolai Simonov, Mikhail Kozakov. A marine biologist turns his adopted son into a benevolent fish-man, who falls in love with a girl he saves from drowning.

Bat Woman (1967; Mexico) Cast: Maura Monti, Mario Robles. Hero Mario Robles teams up with the masked heroine Bat Woman to investigate the death of a wrestler. They discover that certain glands are missing from the victim and are being used by a scientist in a plan to create an army of fish-men with which to conquer the world. Like all good monsters, the powerful prototype fishman-monster eventually turns on its creator.

Blood Waters of Dr. Z (1972; Barton) D/P: Don Barton. S: Lee Laren, Ron Kivett. Cast: Marshall Graver, Nancy Lien, Paul Galloway. A mad doctor is turned into an aquaman by his own serum and kidnaps a woman for breeding. • The picture was photographed on location in the Florida swamps.

Bog (1978; Marshall Films) D: Don Keeslar. P: Michelle Marshall. S: Carl N. Kitt. C: Wings. Cast: Gloria De Haven, Aldo Ray, Marshall Thompson, Leo Gordon, Ed Clark, Jeff Schwaab, Robert Fry, Carol Terry, Lou Hunt, Glen Voros. Fishermen disturb the slime creature living at the bottom of Bog Lake. The bloodsucking fishman goes on the rampage and doctors Gloria De Haven and Marshall Thompson must find a way to stop it.

Creature from the Black Lagoon (1954; Universal) D: Jack Arnold. P: William Alland. S: Harry Essex, Arthur Ross. C: William E. Snyder, Charles S. Welbourne (underwater sequences). Cast: Richard Carlson, Julia Adams, Richard Denning, Nestor Paiva, Antonio Moreno, Whit Bissell. An expedition to the forbidden Amazonian "Black Lagoon" encounters the "gillman"—an evolutionary throwback which is half man, half fish. This intelligent fish-man outwits its would-be captors and sets his scaly sights on the beautiful female of the party. ¶ "My boys call it the Black Lagoon. A paradise, only they say no one has ever come back to prove it." • Former Olympic swimming Ricou Browning played the gillman underwater while Ben Chapman played the creature on land. Browning was selected for the part because of his tremendous ability to hold his breath for up to five minutes at a time. According to Browning, the first suit they made for the film was rejected, and the second one, after a month's work, was the one that finally made it to the screen. The suit-building cost the special effects department over $12,000, which was quite a bit at that time. • Most of the underwater sequences were photographed at Silver Springs in Florida. Arnold said of those shots: "I thought there was a mystery and romance to the underwater scenes and also a sense of terror ... those scenes with the girl swimming on the surface and the monster looking up at her from below played upon a basic fear that people have about what might be lurking below the surface of any body of water." • Jack Arnold had a nickname for the Creature. He called it his little "Beastie." • Bud Westmore, who helped design the famous Creature's appearance, came from a family of makeup artists. He and his brother Wally Westmore (*Dr. Jekyll and Mr. Hyde*, 1932; *Island of Lost Souls*, 1933) died within five days of each other. • The sound effects created by Joe Lapis and Leslie I. Carey lent a great deal of support to the film's mood and atmosphere with their use of echoes and offscreen noise. Joe Lapis teamed up with Carey again in numerous films, including another Jack Arnold effort, *Monster on the Campus* (1958). Lapis is by far the most prolific sound man of 1950's horror and science fiction. He provided the sound for over 16 genre films during the decade, almost exclusively for Universal. • *Creature from the Black Lagoon* was released in 3-D. Two sequels were filmed—*Revenge of the Creature* (1955; also in 3-D) and *The Creature Walks Among Us* (1956; filmed flat).

Creature of Destruction (1967; Azalea) D/P: Larry Buchanan. S: Enrique Touceda. C: Robert C. Jessup. Cast: Les Tremayne, Aron Kincaid, Pat Delaney, Neil Fletcher. A hypnotist predicts murders and then makes them happen by putting a woman under a trance and calling forth a reincarnated fish-creature from her past. • *Creature of Destruction* is another one of those uncredited remakes of an AIP monster hit from the 50s which Buchanan redid in the 1960s. This is, or was, *The She-Creature* (1956). • The monster was used again in another Larry Buchanan quickie, *It's Alive*, released the same year.

The Creature Walks Among Us (1956; Universal) D: John Sherwood. P: William Alland. S: Arthur Ross. C: Maury Gertsman. Cast: Rex Reason, Jeff Morrow,

Leigh Snowden, Gregg Palmer, Maurice Manson, Frank Chase. In this third and final entry in the *Creature* series, Rex Reason and Jeff Morrow head an expedition into the Florida Everglades to retrieve the gill-man who got away in *Revenge of the Creature* (1955). After capturing the man-fish once again they perform a humanizing operation on it, changing the creature into a monstrous man. ¶ "Gentlemen, the Creature can be changed, we can make the giant step and bring a new species into existence." • Don Megowan played the hulking Creature after his humanizing operation. Ricou Browning played the creature underwater. The creature's new face was designed primarily by makeup artists Millicent Patrick and Jack Kevan. • The music was provided by contemporary composer Henry Mancini (who later won Oscars for his contributions to *Breakfast at Tiffany's,* 1961; and *Days of Wine and Roses,* 1962). • Actor Jeff Morrow joked about his and Rex Reason's cinematic contribution to the world of science: "So we've resisted the urge of the makeup department to decorate us with beards and bald domes. You can call that our contribution to science, or at least to scientists."

Curse of the Swamp Creature (1966; AIP-TV) D/P: Larry Buchanan. S: Tony Houston. C: Ralph K. Johnson. Cast: John Agar, Francine York, Jeff Alexander, Shirley McLine, Cal Duggan, Charles McLine, Bill McGee, Ted Mitchell, Rodger Ready. A mad doctor creates a reptilian man-fish in the Florida Everglades. He even uses his own wife in one of his experiments. ¶ "You're ready to come off the preserver, and make your debut into the world of humans, my beautiful, indestructible fish-man." • Grade-Z director Larry Buchanan made two other fish-people debacles two years later — *Creature of Destruction,* and *It's Alive* (both 1968).

Demon of Paradise (1987; Concorde) D: Cirio H. Santiago. P: Leonard Hermes. S: Frederick Bailey. C: Ricardo Remias. Cast: Kathryn Witt, William Steis, Laura Banks, Frederick Bailey, Lesley Huntly. A murderous fish-man, called "Akua" by the fearful Hawaiian natives who regard him as a deity, rises up and goes on a rampage after being disturbed by some local drug dealers setting off dynamite in his lagoon. ¶ "With all the pan-fried toxic muck we throw at this planet, you never know what it might throw back at you."

Horror of Party Beach (1964; 20th Century-Fox) D/P: Del Tenney. S/C: Richard L. Hilliard. Cast: John Scott, Alice Lyon,

Allen Laurel, Eulabelle Moore, Marilyn Clark. Radioactive waste in the ocean transforms sunken skeletons into fish-creatures bent on rousting beach parties and murdering teens. ¶ From the promotional trailer: "While teenagers prepare for a secluded slumber party, terror strikes from the bottom of the sea. An invasion of ghoulish atomic beasts who live off human blood."

Humanoids from the Deep (1980; New World) D: Barbara Peeters. P: Martin B. Cohen. S: Frederick James. C: Daniel Lacambre. Cast: Vic Morrow, Doug Mc-Clure, Ann Turkel, Cindy Weintraub. Ugly amphibian monsters emerge from the ocean to disrupt a seaside carnival where they rape and pillage. As a grotesque afterthought at the film's end, one of the girls impregnated by the fishy "humanoids," gives a gruesomely fatal birth to a baby fish-creature.

It's Alive (1968; Azalea) D/P/S: Larry Buchanan. C: Robert Alcott. Cast: Tommy Kirk, Shirley Bonne, Billy Thurman, Corveth Osterhouse, Annabelle Macadams. A backwoods local discovers a prehistoric fish-man which he keeps locked inside a cave, feeding unwary tourists to it from time to time. • Richard Matheson's novel, *Being,* reportedly was the inspiration for this story. • No-budget filmmaker Larry Buchanan is best remembered for his numerous remakes of AIP favorites, which often copied the dialogue word for word from the original (*The Eye Creatures* [1965]; *In the Year 2889* [1966]; *Zontar, the Thing from Venus* [1966]).

Mermaids of Tiburon (1962; Filmgroup) D/P/S: John Lamb. C: John Lamb, Hal McAlpin, Brydon Baker. Cast: George Rowe, Diane Webber, Timothy Carey, José Gonzalez, John Mylong, Gil Baretto. A pearl diver encounters a group of mermaids.

Monster from the Surf (1965; U.S. Films/AIP-TV) (also *The Beach Girls and the Monster*). D: Jon Hall. P: Edward Janis. S: Joan Gardner. C: Dale Davis. Cast: Jon Hall, Sue Casey, Walker Edmiston, Arnold Lessing, Elaine Dupont. A rash of teen murders at the beach are blamed on a sea monster, but it turns out the creature in question is an oceanographer in a monster suit with a grudge against surfers. ¶ "She's dead! Look, she's all clawed up!" • *Monster from the Surf* features bongo music by Frank Sinatra, Jr.

Monster of Piedras Blancas (1959; Filmservice) D: Irvin Berwick. P: Jack Kevan. S: C. Haile Chace. C: Philip Lathrop. Cast: Don Sullivan, Jeanne Carmen, John

The Monster of Piedras Blancas *(1959) stands on the beach admiring one of his severed-head trophies. Stunt actor Pete Dunn wore the green rubber suit constructed by Jack Kevan, but could only stand it for ten minutes at a time due to the intense heat generated inside the costume.*

Harmon, Les Tremayne, Forrest Lewis. A superstitious lighthouse keeper takes to feeding a scaly man-creature with a penchant for blood. The amphibious monster lives in the watery caves below the lighthouse and has the nasty habit of decapitating unwary humans. After terrorizing the coastal village, the monster cartwheels off the top of the lighthouse after receiving a rifle-butt in the chest by teen hero Don Sullivan. ¶ "Does he have a brain that's capable of rational thinking, or is he just a beast? If he can think, we're in real trouble." • Stuntman Pete Dunn played both the monster and a character named Eddie, who gets his head torn off in an earlier scene. Apparently the suit wasn't able to "breathe" much so Dunn could only wear it for ten minutes at a time. • Producer Jack Kevan, a noted makeup artist and monster maker (who helped build the *Creature from the Black Lagoon* suit) utilized some of the molds from the monster suits used in *This*

Island Earth (1955) (the Metaluna mutant) and *The Mole People* (1956) to make his Piedras Blancas creature. • The picture was made on a $29,000 budget and filmed in six (long) days. The lighthouse work was done on the California coast at Point Conception. The movie was released on a double bill with *Okefenokee,* and the poster claimed *Monster of Piedras Blancas* was the winner of the *Famous Monsters of Filmland*'s Shock Award. Forrest J Ackerman, editor of the magazine, wasn't aware they were giving out "Shock Awards." • The little boy named Jimmy (Wayne Berwick), who runs into a funeral service screaming bloody murder, was the son of director Irvin Berwick. • Lead actress Jeanne Carmen was an exceptional golfer. The film's pressbook called her a trick shot artist who could hit a hole-in-one from anywhere within 30 feet of the pin. • Lurid publicity lines described the monster as: "A claw-fingered scaly-skinned half human crustacean, turning a lonely lighthouse village into a frenzied bedlam of blood-curdling horror."

The Monster Squad (1987) (see VAM-PIRES — DRACULA AND FAMILY). One of the classic monsters encountered is a gill-man (a close relation of the *Creature from the Black Lagoon*).

Mysterious Island (1929; MGM) D: Lucien Hubbard, Maurice Tourneur, Benjamin Christensen. P: J. Ernest Williamson. S: Lucien Hubbard. C: Percy Hilburn. Cast: Lionel Barrymore, Jane Daly, Lloyd Hughes, Montagu Love, Harry Gribbon. This early semi-silent epic adventure stars John Barrymore as the creator of a fabulous submarine, who gets double-crossed by his friend and associate. The unfolding drama is highlighted by a breathtaking voyage to an underwater kingdom populated by midget fish-men. ¶ "Suppose, that in all the ages that Man has been developing to his present state, that a distant cousin of his, starting from the same source, has been going through a similar process of evolution under the water." • This troubled production was begun in 1927 as a silent, and completed in 1929 with a few talking sequences and some background music added. It was the first of five adaptations of the Jules Verne novel of the same name (itself a sequel to his book, *20,000 Leagues under the Sea*). • The hundreds of little fish-men appearing in the film were actually midgets in rubber fish-suits. Director Lucien Hubbard told editor Forrest J Ackerman in an article appearing in *Famous Monsters of Filmland* #68: "Every midget in America must have worked in that picture.... We sent out the call to every circus and sideshow and they streamed in from the four corners of the country."

Night Tide (1961; AIP) D/S: Curtis Harrington. P: Aram Kantarian. C: Vilis Lapenieks, Floyd Crosby. Cast: Dennis Hopper, Linda Lawson, Gavin Muir, Luana Anders, Marjorie Eaton. A sailor falls in love with a mermaid-girl while visiting a fairground sideshow, leading to tragedy. • Star Dennis Hopper was an ardent admirer of James Dean, whom he worked with in the films *Rebel Without a Cause* (1955), and *Giant* (1956). *Night Tide* was the first of four movies he did for American International Pictures. • Low-budget film actor and director Bruno VeSota worked as a makeup man on this picture, and he also had a bit part as a rotund man who sucks in his ample gut to let Dennis Hopper pass by on the steps of an apartment building.

Octaman (1971; Filmers Guild) D: Harry Essex. P: Harry Essex, Joel Freeman. S: Leigh Chapman. C: Robert Caramico. Cast: Kerwin Mathews, Pier Angeli, Jeff Morrow, David Essex, Jerome Guardino. A weird octopus-man with four arms and a couple of extra appendages lurks in the caves by the water's edge, coming out to terrorize campers. ¶ "Horror heap from the nuclear trash!" described the poster. • Director/writer Harry Essex commented in Tom Weaver's book, *Interviews with B Science Fiction and Horror Movie Makers,* on the film's conception: "Let's do some kind of a takeoff on the science fiction junk that's around.... Our shooting schedule was probably 16 to 18 days, and the budget was about $250,000. We shot it on the Universal lot and in Griffith Park." • Harry Essex's son, David Essex, plays an Indian in the film.

Revenge of the Creature (1955; Universal) D: Jack Arnold. P: William Alland. S: Martin Berkeley. C: Charles S. Welbourne. Cast: John Agar, Lori Nelson, John Bromfield, Nestor Paiva, Grandon Rhodes, Dave Willock. This, the second film in the *Creature* trilogy, chronicles the capture and transporting of the gill-man to the Florida Oceanarium. There, he is studied by scientists John Agar and Lori Nelson, then escapes to wreak havoc along the Florida Keys. ¶ "This beast exists because it is stronger than this thing you call evolution." • Ricou Browning played the Creature throughout the picture and had a particularly difficult time with a sea turtle while filming inside the oceanarium water tank. The animal kept biting off chunks of his suit. They finally had to have a special prop man in the water nearby just to keep the turtle off him. • Ricou Browning was spelled at times by Tom Hennesy, who donned the Creature suit for some of the land shots (including the impressive scene in which the Creature overturns a car). • It is interesting to note that in all three of the creature films a different batch of scientists studies him each time. Richard Carlson (who originally discovered the gill-man) was replaced by John Agar in this entry, who relinquished the job to Rex Reason for *The Creature Walks Among Us.* Neither of the previous scientists were shown or mentioned in the latter films. Apparently one go-round with the Creature was enough for these guys. • John Agar related an amusing anecdote about the making of *Revenge of the Creature* in Tom Weaver's book, *Interviews with B Science Fiction and Horror Movie Makers:* "We all got kind of carried away on that

The Gillman clears a path to the beach after escaping from the Florida-based Oceanarium in Revenge of the Creature *(1955).*

picture, we started having water gun fights."
• In one humorous lab scene, bit-player Clint Eastwood (in one of his earliest film roles) is trying to locate a missing lab mouse. It turns up in his coat pocket moments later.
• Jack Arnold detailed his experiences in filming the water tank sequences with live sharks and barracudas, etc., in John Brosnan's book, *The Horror People:* "I said if they [the actors and crew] took one look at those sharks in there I would never get them in.... He [cameraman Charles Welbourne] said to me that I'd better go into the tank with him to demonstrate to the actors that it was safe.... I closed my eyes at first. After awhile I opened one eye and there was a damn shark, at least 12 feet long, his mouth open and looking at me. And he was only about a yard away. I didn't know what to do ... so I just shut my eyes again .... Then he brushed by me and I felt his skin, it was just like sandpaper, but he just swam away and ignored me. So I shot to the surface and said, 'come on in—nothing to it!'"

Screamers (1979; New World; Italy/U.S.)

D: Sergio Martino, Dan T. Miller. P: Lawrence Martin. S: Sergio Donati, Cesare Frugoni, Sergio Martino. Cast: Barbara Bach, Richard Johnson, Joseph Cotten, Beryl Cunningham, Cameron Mitchell, Mel Ferrer. On a remote island, a greedy nobleman forces a mad scientist to transform humans into hideous fish-monsters in order to use them to plunder a lost temple of Atlantis he has found sunk beneath the waves off the island. • The original Italian version of the film didn't have the added footage with Cameron Mitchell and Mel Ferrer.

The She-Creature (1956; AIP) D: Edward L. Cahn. P: Alex Gordon. S: Lou Rusoff. C: Frederick E. West. Cast: Chester Morris, Marla English, Tom Conway, Cathy Downs, Lance Fuller. A hypnotist named Lombardi is able to call forth the prehistoric fish-monster buried deep in his beautiful assistant's evolutionary past. He uses this aquatic "She-Creature" to fulfill his predictions of murder which have made him famous. In the end though, the She-Creature turns on the master, but before he dies, Lombardi manages to release his assistant from the deadly trance, and the monster walks back into the sea, never to return. ¶ "My next experiment is a most interesting one, doctor. I shall prove that life is an endless chain, that we are given the gift of it not for one life span, but since the beginning of time." • Popular actors Peter Lorre and Edward Arnold were originally slated for the roles of "the Hypnotist" and "the Businessman" before Chester Morris and Tom Conway got the jobs. • The She-Creature suit was built and worn by monster-maker Paul Blaisdell. The costume was six feet six inches in height and constructed of foam rubber and latex. The suit weighed over 90 pounds. Its affectionate behind-the-scenes nickname was "Cuddles." Although the picture was filmed in black and white, and the movie's advertising showed the monster as lobster red, the creature suit was actually painted bright green. • The She-Creature suit turned up in four other AIP pictures — *Voodoo Woman* (1957), *How to Make a Monster* (1958), *Teenage Caveman* (1958), and *The Ghost of Dragstrip Hollow* (1959). • The film owes its existence to an exhibitor who happened to mention to producer Alex Gordon that *"The She-Creature"* would make a nice title for a movie. One of the popular news items of that time was the Bridey Murphy hypnosis case, and writer Lou Rusoff just melded those two concepts together in his script. The film was budgeted slightly over $100,000.

Space Monster (1965) (see ALIENS — ENCOUNTERS IN SPACE). When a spaceship lands on the ocean floor of another planet, the crew encounters one of the primitive fish-man inhabitants (a left-over suit from *War Gods of the Deep*, 1965).

Spawn of the Slithis (1978; Fabtrak) (also *Slithis*). D/S: Stephan Traxler. P: Stephan Traxler, Paul Fabian. Cast: Alan Blanchard, Judy Motulsky, Dennis Lee Falt. Radioactive organic mud forms into a large, slimy, man-like creature who rises from the contaminated water and starts preying on the inhabitants of Venice, California. ¶ "How are you going to convince people that there's a slime-creature feasting on the residents of Venice?" • *Spawn of the Slithis* was shot in 12 days for $100,000.

Splash (1984) D: Ron Howard. P: Brian Grazer. S: Bruce Jay Friedman, Lowell Ganz, Babaloo Mandel. C: Don Peterman. Cast: Tom Hanks, Daryl Hannah, John Candy, Eugene Levy, Dody Goodman, Shecky Greene. Tom Hanks falls in love with a mermaid he encountered as a young boy. On land she is human, but when she gets wet she transforms into an amphibious beauty. In the end, Hanks, his brother, and a daffy scientist plot to free her from the cold hands of researchers, with Hanks following her to a magical life under the sea. ¶ "What are you looking at? You never saw a guy who slept with a fish before!?" • The film is based on a story written by the film's producer, Brian Grazer.

Sting of Death (1967; Thunderbird International) D: William Grefe. P: Hank Rifkin. S: Richard S. Flink. C: Julio C. Chavez. Cast: Joe Morrison, Valerie Hawkins, John Vella, Jack Nagle, Sandy Lee Kane, Neil Sadaka. A scientist goes crazy and changes himself into a man-fish with poisonous tentacles. • Stuntman Doug Hobart played the creature for actor John Vella. The species of fish in this man-mutant film is the Portuguese man-o-war.

Swamp of the Lost Monster (1964; AIP-TV; Mexico) D: Rafael Baledon. P: Alfred Ripstein, Jr. S: Ramon Obon. C: Raul Martinez Solares. Cast: Gaston Santos, Manola Savedra, Manuel Dondi. The swamplands are being terrorized by what turns out to be a fake fish-creature.

Terror Beneath the Sea (1966; Teleworld; Japan) D: Terence Ford (Hajime Sato). P: Masafumi Soga. S: M. Fukuishima. C: K. Shimomura. Cast: Shinichi Chiba, Peggy Neal, Franz Gruber, Gunther Braun, Andrew Hughes, Mike Daneen. A scientist turns men into water-breathing creatures which only he can control. • Director Hajime Sato used the pseudonym, Terence Ford, for the film's American release. • Shinichi Chiba, who plays the heroic reporter, is known in the martial arts cinema as "Sonny" Chiba.

War Gods of the Deep (1965; AIP; U.K./U.S.) (also *City under the Sea*). D: Jacques Tourneur. P: Daniel Haller. S: Charles Bennett, Louis M. Heyward. C: Stephen Dade. Cast: Vincent Price, Tab Hunter, Susan Hart, David Tomlinson, John LeMesurier. Fish-people kidnap a girl for their ruler, Vincent Price, who believes her to be the reincarnation of his dead wife. Two heroes get caught in a whirlpool and make it down to the undersea kingdom where Price and the inhabitants have been kept ageless for centuries. At the climax, the girl is rescused and the Lyonesse people begin to show their true age. • Vincent Price said of the film: *"War Gods of the Deep* was just a disaster. Nobody knew what it was about. Jacques [Tourneur] was a marvelous director, but he just couldn't get around the script."

Frankenstein's Monster

Weird electrical machines crackle and spark menacingly, lightning pierces the sky overhead, peals of thunder reverberate off the massive dank stone walls of the hidden laboratory, while Colin Clive, his face a mask of insane zeal, shouts hysterically, "It's alive! It's alive! It's alive!" Soon after, backing out from the gloom, a hulking figure is seen. As it turns towards us the camera focuses in tighter and tighter to reveal the hideous yet sadly sympathetic visage of Boris Karloff as ... The Frankenstein Monster. And so Universal, with its 1931 blockbuster, *Frankenstein,* created yet another timeless monster — one that has become another icon of popular culture that rivals even Dracula (who Universal had introduced earlier that same year).

The classic novel, *Frankenstein (or, the Modern Prometheus),* was conceived in 1816 (nearly a century before its first cinematic incarnation) by a 19-year-old woman named Mary Wollstonecraft Shelley, a "free thinker" and (then) mistress of famed British poet Percy Bysshe Shelley. Mary Shelley's creation was first brought to the screen in 1910 by Thomas Edison's pioneering film company as a 16-minute short. In this long-thought-lost recent rediscovery, Dr. Frankenstein creates his monster not by harnessing the "bolts from heaven" using electrical equipment, but by whipping it up in what looks like a gigantic witches' cauldron. Skeletal bones rise up from the depths of the unholy pot and take on a macabre shape through primitive time-lapse photography, until finally there stands a very *Golem*-like figure.

Universal had a hit on their hands with *Frankenstein* (1931), a film to rival *Dracula* in cinema horror, and one that catapulted an unknown 43-year-old bit player named Boris Karloff to stardom. With this, the first of the two great Frankenstein series was born. Director James Whale followed up his monster hit four years later with what many consider to be an even better film (and arguably the greatest horror movie of all time), the macabre masterpiece, *Bride of Frankenstein* (1935). There followed the lesser but still grand *Son of Frankenstein* (1939) (sadly missing James Whale but possessing one of the finest casts in horror history), which is often thought of as the last classic entry in Universal's Frankenstein series. What remained to be made were cheaper but still very entertaining "B" pictures, as the studio decided to wring every box-office dollar it could out of their declining creation. Universal quickly sought to boost the creature's box-office clout by pairing him up with a bevy of their aging monsters until finally finishing him off by introducing Frankenstein's Monster to Abbott and Costello.

The Monster lay dormant for nearly a decade until Britain's Hammer Films took a chance at a time when aliens and giant bugs were king at the drive-ins. While flying saucers zoomed across the skies of America's theaters, Hammer decided to make a gothic horror picture. Unlike their predecessors, however, they forsook the dark expressionistic mood of the Universal series and went for vibrant color and plenty of (for the time) bright red blood. Their choice to launch this gothic revival — Mary Shelley's creation. The stylish *The Curse of Frankenstein* (1957) was immensely successful with the public and equally deplored by the stodgy critics. Its success prompted Hammer to make six more Frankenstein films over the next 15 years. Differing from the Universal series, which had the Monster returning for each film (usually with a new member of the Frankenstein household in charge or even the occasional unrelated third party mad scientist), the thread of continuity in the

Hammer Frankensteins was Baron Frankenstein himself. Peter Cushing played the unflappable Baron in all but one of the entries, creating a new monster for each feature.

Many variations followed, for Frankenstein and his creation still had (and has) box-office draw. Some merely borrowed the name (*Frankenstein Meets the Space Monster,* 1965, and *Frankenstein's Bloody Terror,* 1968, for instance) while others returned to the source in an attempt to faithfully bring Ms. Shelley's creation to life just as she wrote it (*Victor Frankenstein,* 1975). Such a successful subgenre ultimately spawned that deepest form of flattery—the spoof—with the witty and beloved homage, *Young Frankenstein* (1974) creating the last word in horror parodies. Remember, "that's *Fronk-en-steen!*"

Universal Series

Abbott and Costello Meet Frankenstein (1948; Universal) D: Charles T. Barton. P: Robert Arthur. S: Robert Lees, Frederic I. Rinaldo, John Grant. C: Charles Van Enger. Cast: Bud Abbott, Lou Costello, Lon Chaney, Bela Lugosi, Glenn Strange, Lenore Aubert. Count Dracula (played by Bela Lugosi) enlists the aid of a female mad scientist in a plan to transplant Costello's brain into the body of the Frankenstein Monster. ¶ "Frankie, I'm telling ya, it's a bad deal. I've had this brain for 30 years and it hasn't worked right yet!"—Lou Costello upon learning they want his brain for the Monster. • *The Brain of Frankenstein* was the original script title. • Apparently the British took exception to the titling of *Abbott and Costello Meet Frankenstein* and changed it to *Abbott and Costello Meet the Ghosts* for its release in the United Kingdom. • Upon first reading the script, Lou Costello reportedly complained: "You don't think I'll do that crap, do you? My five-year-old daughter can write something better than that!" • Director Charles Barton had this to say about working with the horror actors and with Abbott and Costello: "All three of the 'monsters' were the nicest. The *real* monsters were Abbott and Costello." • Glenn Strange (playing Frankenstein's Monster) broke his foot during the production, and had to complete the film wearing a foot cast. At one point, Lon Chaney (playing the Wolf Man) wore the Frankenstein Monster makeup to fill in for injured Strange. Chaney was an old hand at playing the monster, having done so in *The Ghost of Frankenstein* (1942). Strange said of Chaney and the scene in which the Monster throws the villain through the window: "My pal Lon did me the great favor of getting into the Frankenstein makeup and, when you saw the scene on the screen, it was he who threw the girl through!"

Bride of Frankenstein (1935; Universal) D: James Whale. P: Carl Laemmle, Jr. S: William Hurlbut. C: John Mescall. Cast: Boris Karloff, Colin Clive, Valerie Hobson, Ernest Thesiger, Elsa Lanchester, Gavin Gordon, Douglas Walton, Una O'Connor, E. E. Clive, Lucien Prival, O. P. Heggie, Dwight Frye. This classic first sequel to *Frankenstein* (which many consider to be superior even to that timeless original) takes up where the first film left off. Surviving his fall from the windmill, a recovering Henry Frankenstein (Colin Clive) is simply trying to put all the hellish events of *Frankenstein* behind him. Enter the devilish Dr. Praetorius, intent upon taking up Henry's experiments again. Praetorius has befriended the Monster (who survived the inferno at the windmill by falling into a pond underneath the mill), and uses the creature to blackmail Henry into helping him create a woman—the monster's intended mate. ("Alone, you have created a man. Now, together, we will create his mate," enthuses Praetorius.) ¶ "Made me from dead. I love dead, hate living"—the Monster. • *Bride of Frankenstein* was originally announced as *The Return of Frankenstein.* • Initially, James Whale declined to direct and Kurt Neumann was slated to head the production. Eventually Whale accepted the project. • Brigitte Helm (of *Metropolis,* 1926 fame) was among those considered for the brief but key part of the Monster's mate, which eventually went to Elsa Lanchester. Ms. Lanchester also played the role of "Mary Shelley" in the film's prologue. Though she received credit for playing Mary Shelley, the actress gamely went along with the studio's trick of billing "The Monster's Mate" with a "?" in the opening and closing credits. ¶ Dr. Praetorius was originally to have been played by Claude Rains, but Rains was assigned to the film, *The Mystery of Edwin Drood,* and Whale recruited his old friend Ernest Thesiger for the part. • Thesiger was an expert at needlepoint and even authored a book on the subject entitled *Adventures in Embroidery.* • The small but pivotal role of the hermit who befriends the monster was played by Scottish stage actor O. P. Heggie. Whale wanted Heggie so badly that he held up production for ten days until the actor finished his current assignment and became available. • Director Whale, the "Ace of Universal," earned more than star Boris Karloff ($15,000 vs. $12,500 — both princely sums by the standard of the day). • Dwight Frye, who played Frankenstein's hunchbacked assistant "Fritz" in the original *Frankenstein,* returned for this film as "Karl," Dr. Praetorius' ghoulish henchman. • This is the first Universal film in which the Frankenstein Monster gains the ability to speak. He talks in two other entries in the series, *Ghost of Frankenstein* (1942; after Ygor's brain is put into the body of the monster) and *Abbott and Costello Meet Frankenstein* (1948). Boris Karloff fought against the idea of giving the monster the power of speech, calling it "stupid." • Though top-billed in the original, Colin Clive had to settle for second billing here — the top position going to one of Universal's biggest stars, Boris Karloff. The actor was enjoying so much popularity and prestige at the time that Universal billed him by surname only, simply as *"KARLOFF"* (an honor awarded to only a handful of actors over the years). • Karloff had a special "monster chair" constructed for him on this film, allowing him to rest from the heavy burden of the monster suit while leaning upright in the specially designed chair. • This was definitely an A-budgeted picture. The huge sum of $2,000 was spent on electrical props alone. • Makeup genius Jack Pierce received a mere $450 to create the immortal makeup for Karloff and his "Bride." • A then-unknown John Carradine had a bit part as the hunter who discovers the monster in the hermit's cottage.

Frankenstein (1931; Universal) D: James Whale. P: Carl Laemmle, Jr. S: Garrett Fort, Francis Edwards Faragoh, John Russell (uncredited), Robert Florey (uncredited). C: Arthur Edeson. Cast: Colin Clive, Mae Clarke, John Boles, Boris Karloff, Edward Van Sloan, Frederick Kerr, Dwight Frye, Lionel Belmore, Marilyn Harris, Michael Mark. Arguably the most famous horror film of all time, *Frankenstein* focuses on the brilliant, obsessed Henry Frankenstein (Colin Clive) and his mad dream to create an artificial man out of the dead tissues of corpses and bring the being to life. His noble ideals go awry when a halfwit assistant steals a criminal brain and the creature is born a monster. ¶ It's alive! It's alive! Oh — in the name of god, now I know what it feels like to be God!" — one of Colin Clive's lines originally censored from the film but recently restored. • This, of course, is the film that made Boris Karloff into the screen's foremost bogeyman. Up to this point, the 43-year-old actor had been mostly an extra or bit player in his 12-year screen career, but his brilliantly sensitive portrayal of the Frankenstein Monster catapulted Karloff to an instant and unexpected stardom (Karloff eventually became Universal's highest paid star in the mid 1930s). • Ironically, the then-reigning horror king, Bela Lugosi, was originally going to play the Monster and even did a two-reel screen test for director Robert Florey (the film's original intended director). Dissatisfied with the role (saying, "You don't need an actor for that part, anybody can moan and grunt!"), Lugosi backed out of the project and opened up the way for his biggest rival, resulting in Lugosi playing second fiddle to Karloff in both money and billing for the remainder of their careers. Lugosi created his own monster in Karloff. • Another actor who supposedly was considered for the part of the Monster was the then-unknown John Carradine. According to Carradine himself, he "never played a monster.... I was offered one and turned it down. I turned down Frankenstein." His reason: "I wasn't going to play the monster. I was from the the-a-tuh!" (from the 1974 ABC TV special, "The Horror Hall of Fame"). • Robert Florey was the director initially chosen for the project, and many of his early contributions remained (uncredited) in the script. For instance, it was his idea to have Frankenstein inadvertently place a criminal brain into the body of the Monster. Also, Florey set the climax in the burning windmill (he claims to have gotten the idea from looking out his window and seeing the Van De Kamp Bakery logo — a windmill). The project was taken away from Florey by James Whale, called "the Ace of Universal," who was enjoying carte blanche at the studio at this time. As a consolation prize, Florey was awarded the directorship of *Murders in the Rue Morgue* (1932), starring Bela Lugosi. • Bette Davis was initially considered for the

Dwight Frye (far right, holding coat) had most of his scenes cut (including this one) from the final print of Bride of Frankenstein *(1935).*

female lead in *Frankenstein* in 1931, but was rejected when producer Carl Laemmle, Jr., decided, "She's got as much sex appeal as Slim Summerville." • In an interview appearing in *Famous Monsters of Filmland* #100, Mae Clarke, who won the lead role of Elizabeth, discussed the controversial censored scene in which the Monster throws a little girl into the lake. "They purposely wanted to keep it very simple so that the little girl wouldn't get upset or distracted. They had to work with her, you know, letting her know Boris first, watch the makeup being put on, so she had absolutely no trouble being friendly with him. . . . Through *not* showing how it happened pictorially and what his reactions were, you missed the whole pathos — that this was unintentional." Clarke also described her director: "James Whale was a very sensitive man. He was a true artist through and through who understood the necessity and effect of the finest kind of music or color or smell or when to have tea. He was a joy and a pleasure to know."

Frankenstein Meets the Wolf Man (1943;

Universal) D: Roy William Neill. P: George Waggner. S: Curt Siodmak. C: George Robinson. Cast: Ilona Massey, Patrick Knowles, Lon Chaney, Lionel Atwill, Bela Lugosi, Maria Ouspenskaya, Dennis Hoey. Lawrence Talbot (the Wolf Man) rises from his crypt and journeys to the Frankenstein estate to seek out the doctor's records. There he finds the Monster, whom he befriends while in human form and then battles as the Wolf Man in the spectacular climax. ¶ "I can't destroy Frankenstein's creation! I've got to see it at its full power!" • According to writer Curt Siodmak, this film was born when he jokingly suggested to producer George Waggner: "Why don't you make a picture, *Frankenstein* Wolfs *the* Meat *Man?*" • The original title of *Frankenstein Meets the Wolf Man* was *The Wolf Man Meets Frankenstein.* • In this fifth entry in the series, we learn of the only way to kill the Monster from Dr. Frankenstein's diary: "This, my creation, can never perish unless its energies are drained off artificially — by changing the poles from plus to minus."

This, explains why fire (*Frankenstein* and *Ghost*...), explosions (*Bride*...), and boiling sulfur pits (*Son*...) never worked. • Ironically, 22 years after he has turned down the part for the original *Frankenstein* and spawned his greatest rival—Boris Karloff, Bela Lugosi finally put on the Monster's shoes. The ailing actor was 60 years old at the time and stuntman Eddie Parker had to double for Lugosi through much of the film. • Lugosi's performance as the Monster is often lambasted by critics and fans alike. To be fair, his blind gropings and stumbling footsteps are not entirely the actor's fault. In the script as it was shot, the Monster is partially blind! (the result of the crossing of bloodtypes during the brain transplant at the close of *The Ghost of Frankenstein*). However, all references to this fact were edited out of the final print. This occurred when all the Monster's dialogue was deleted. The Monster actually spoke in this film (appropriately enough, it would have been with Lugosi's voice, since the Monster now had the brain of Ygor). But the effect of Frankenstein's Monster speaking with a Hungarian accent was too much and all his dialogue and several whole scenes were discarded. It seems to have been a wise move, if this sample dialogue exchange is any indication—Larry Talbot: "I change into a wolf at night." The Monster: "Are you kidding?" • Ironically, it was neither of the two monsters (Bela Lugosi and Lon Chaney, Jr.) who was billed first in the film, but the heroine, Ilona Massey, and the milquetoast hero, Patrick Knowles, who received the top two billing spots.

The Ghost of Frankenstein (1942; Universal) D: Erle C. Kenton. P: George Waggner. S: W. Scott Darling. C: Milton Krasner, Woody Bredell. Cast: Sir Cedric Hardwicke, Lon Chaney, Jr., Ralph Bellamy, Lionel Atwill, Bela Lugosi, Evelyn Ankers, Janet Ann Gallow. Following up where *Son of Frankenstein* left off, neither Ygor nor the Monster is dead. Ygor finds the Monster (who lived through being knocked into a boiling sulfur pit in the previous film. As Ygor explains: "My friend, they didn't kill you! You lived through the pit! The sulfur was good for you!"). They travel to the town of Vasaria and the home of another son of Frankenstein (Sir Cedric Hardwicke). This well-intentioned second son plans on giving the monster a new, kindly brain, but is tricked by an evil associate into placing the evil brain of Ygor into the Monster instead. ¶ "Your father was Frankenstein, but your mother was the lightning!" • This is the fourth film in the series, and is generally considered to be the first step in the Monster's downward slide. Karloff abdicated his monster chair, and the creature's boots were filled by Lon Chaney, Jr. To help the continuity, Bela Lugosi returns from *Son of Frankenstein* as the malevolent Ygor. • Chaney had problems with the monster makeup, complaining that his prosthetic forehead piece was painful to wear. One day, after his demands of having it removed were ignored, Chaney angrily ripped it off his forehead, and removed much of his skin with it. Universal was forced to send him home while the gash healed. • There *is* actually a ghost in *The Ghost of Frankenstein*—the ghost of the original Dr. Frankenstein, who appears to his son. • The Monster's strength is renewed at the beginning of *The Ghost of Frankenstein* when he is struck by lightning—the very thing that Ygor claimed *drained* his strength and put him in a coma in *Son of Frankenstein*.

House of Dracula (1945; Universal) D: Erle C. Kenton. P: Paul Malvern. S: Edward T. Lowe. C: George Robinson. Cast: Lon Chaney, Jr., John Carradine, Martha O'Driscoll, Lionel Atwill, Onslow Stevens, Jane Adams, Ludwig Stossel, Glenn Strange. Larry Talbot, a.k.a. the Wolf Man, shows up at the house of renowned scientist Dr. Edelmann, begging for help with his lycanthropic condition. Likewise, Dracula arrives asking the doctor to help *him*. Also, the Frankenstein Monster is found in some caves underneath the doctor's house, carried there by the mud and quicksand he had sunk into at the close of *House of Frankenstein*. Dr. Edelmann is tricked by Dracula and is contaminated by the vampire's blood. This causes a Jekyll and Hyde condition in him, and he sets about reviving the Frankenstein Monster. ¶ From Universal's publicity department—"Universal's Super-Sequel to Record-Wrecking *House of Frankenstein*." • This follow-up to *House of Frankenstein* is the last serious Frankenstein entry in the Universal series. Next was the comical horror of Abbott and Costello. Much as in the previous film, the Monster was reduced to the level of a mobile prop. In this picture he lies strapped to a table throughout most of the film until the last five minutes, when he is revived just in time to expire in the final conflagration. • As an economy measure, director Erle C. Kenton merely inserted the fiery finale from *The Ghost of Frankenstein* for this film's climax. • Lionel Atwill, John Carradine, Lon Chaney, Jr., and Glenn Strange all returned from *House of Frankenstein*.

The Monster (Boris Karloff) makes his shocking first appearance in James Whale's classic landmark horror film, Frankenstein *(1931).*

House of Frankenstein (1944; Universal) D: Erle C. Kenton. P: Paul Malvern. S: Edward T. Lowe. C: George Robinson. Cast: Boris Karloff, Lon Chaney, John Carradine, J. Carrol Naish, Anne Gwynne, Peter Coe, Lionel Atwill, George Zucco, Elena Verdugo. *"Frankenstein's Monster! Wolf Man! Dracula! Hunchback! Mad Doctor!"* screamed

the ads for this plot by Universal to unite as many of their classic monsters as could fit on the screen. Dr. Niemann (Boris Karloff), after making use of and then betraying Dracula, heads to the ruins of Castle Frankenstein where he finds the bodies of the Wolf Man and Frankenstein's Monster and revives them both. The Wolf Man is dispatched first, when he is mercifully shot and killed by the gypsy girl who loves him. Next, the villagers storm the castle and chase the Frankenstein Monster into the swamps, where he sinks into the quicksand with his beloved Dr. Niemann. ¶ "The undying monster, the triumphant climax of Frankenstein's genius." • Director Erle C. Kenton was no newcomer to the Frankenstein series, having directed *The Ghost of Frankenstein* three years earlier. • For this feature, stuntman/cowboy actor Glenn Strange took over the role of the Monster, a role he was to play two more times—in *House of Dracula* (1945) and *Abbott and Costello Meet Frankenstein* (1948). Karloff coached Strange on the set in the art of being the Monster (though unfortunately his tutelage didn't seem to significantly help Strange's performance). • According to Universal's publicity department, J. Carrol Naish studied for his role of Daniel the hunchback by locating a derelict hunchback and spending time with him to learn his mannerisms. • *House of Frankenstein* was shot under the title of *The Devil's Brood*. • Initially, the Mummy was also scheduled to appear in *House of Frankenstein* but was eventually dropped from the roster.

Son of Frankenstein (1939; Universal) D/P: Rowland V. Lee. S: Willis Cooper. C: George Robinson. Cast: Basil Rathbone, Boris Karloff, Bela Lugosi, Lionel Atwill, Josephine Hutchinson, Donnie Dunagan, Emma Dunn, Edgar Norton, Perry Ivins, Lawrence Grant, Lionel Belmore. Wolf Frankenstein, the son of Henry, returns to his ancestral home after growing up abroad. He encounters the unsavory character of Ygor, a thief and body snatcher who had been hanged for his crimes but did not die. Ygor has found the still-living Monster and has befriended him. But the Monster is now in a coma and Ygor entreats Wolf to restore his power. With thoughts of vindicating his father's ignoble name, Wolf revives the Monster, only to have Ygor use the creature for his own murderous acts of vengeance. ¶ "Here he planned a miracle, and saw it come to pass—a miracle that the good people of Frankenstein called a 'monster.'" • Universal played up their horror stars in the advertising for this third film in the series, promising, "The Menace of Basil Rathbone! The

Fright of Boris Karloff! The Horror of Bela Lugosi! The Hate of Lionel Atwill!" • *Son of Frankenstein* was originally to be in color (which would have made it the first full-color horror film), but the idea was scrapped due to the poor effect of the monster makeup in the color tests. • Peter Lorre was originally scheduled to play the *Son of Frankenstein,* before Basil Rathbone was given the part. • In the opinion of director Rowland V. Lee, it was Bela Lugosi who "stole the show" as the broken-necked Ygor in *Son of Frankenstein.* At the time, Lugosi was in financial straits, and Universal planned on taking advantage of this. According to an interview with Lugosi's widow, Lillian Lugosi Donlevy, in Gregory Mank's book, *It's Alive:* "They cut Bela's salary from $1,000 per week to $500. Then they planned to shoot all his scenes in the picture in one week! When Rowland V. Lee heard about this, he said, and I quote, 'Those God-damned sons of bitches! I'll show them. I'm going to keep Bela on this picture from the first day of shooting right up to the last!' And he did." Lee expanded Lugosi's part of Ygor into what became one of the horror screen's most beloved characterizations. • Boris Karloff received top billing in *Bride of Frankenstein* (1935), but had to settle for second billing in this picture (with Basil Rathbone taking top honors). (Ironically, Karloff had ousted Colin Clive from the top spot in *Bride,* only to be bumped himself for *Son.*) This is the third and last time Karloff played the Frankenstein Monster on the silver screen. He later explained his reasons for not continuing with the character in an article from the October 1965 issue of *Shriek:* "There was not much left in the character of the Monster to be developed; we had reached his limits. I saw that from here on, he would become rather an oafish prop, so to speak, in the last act or something like that, without any great stature." And that is exactly what happened. • During the filming of *Son of Frankenstein,* Karloff learned on his fifty-first birthday that he had become a father. • Star Basil Rathbone was not altogether pleased with his involvement in the film, referring to it as a "penny dreadful." • Dwight Frye played a villager in this entry but had all his scenes edited out of the final print.

Hammer Frankensteins

The Curse of Frankenstein (1957; Hammer/Warner Bros; U.K.) D: Terence Fisher.

P: Anthony Hinds. S: Jimmy Sangster. C: Jack Asher. Cast: Peter Cushing, Hazel

Court, Robert Urquhart, Christopher Lee, Valerie Gaunt, Noel Hood, Melvyn Hayes, Paul Hardtmuth. The brilliant but obsessive Baron Victor Frankenstein puts his scientific zeal before his moral judgment and murders a great scientist so that he can place the brilliant brain into the body of the creature he has created. Frankenstein's horrified assistant tries to stop the Baron's hideous plan, and in the ensuing struggle the brain is damaged, so that when the creature is brought to life it is as an inarticulate monster rather than a great intellect. The creature's violent tendencies result in a series of murders (though one is engineered by the Baron himself when his work is threatened) and the Baron, blamed for the murders, goes to the guillotine. ¶ "We hold in the palms of our hands such secrets that have never been dreamed of. While Nature puts up her own barriers to confine the scope of Man, we've broken through those barriers. There's nothing to stop us now." • Hammer's version of the Mary Shelley novel strays just as far from the source as the Universal classic, but in a different direction. Here the focus is on the brilliant, obsessed, unscrupulous Baron Frankenstein himself (superbly played by Peter Cushing), with the Monster in the role of supporting player. This trend continued in each subsequent Hammer entry, with the recurring character being the Baron (with Cushing returning for all but one), who whips up a new monster for each new film (unlike the Universal series, which kept the same monster but changed the mad scientists). • In a *Fangoria* magazine interview, Cushing revealed his personal insight into how he played this recurring character: "Baron Frankenstein is based strongly upon the real-life anatomist Dr. Robert Knox, who closed his one good eye to the way Burke and Hare obtained cadavers for him so he could pursue his research for the ultimate good of mankind." • This was the movie that started the gothic horror revival and set the path that Hammer (and many imitators) would take for two decades to come. It was reviled by critics at the time for its use of (now seemingly tame) gore, and lapped up by audiences who made it a huge commercial success, earning back seven times its initial cost of £80,000. • Christopher Lee made his horror film debut playing the Frankenstein Monster. Due to fear of copyright infringement (Universal had copyrighted their monster makeup) the monster in this version looked very different from Karloff's creature. • Hazel Court (who

played Elizabeth, Frankenstein's innocent fiancée) volunteered her daughter to play Elizabeth as a young child. As Ms. Court told *Fangoria* #91: "They wanted someone who looked like me to play me as a little girl, so I suggested Sally." Apparently, young Sally didn't want to follow in her mom's acting footsteps after all — "She *hated* it, hated being in it!"

The Evil of Frankenstein (1964; Hammer/Universal; U.K.) D: Freddie Francis. P: Anthony Hinds. S: John Elder (Anthony Hinds). C: John Wilcox. Cast: Peter Cushing, Peter Woodthorpe, Duncan Lamont, Sandor Eles, Katy Wild, David Hutcheson, Kiwi Kingston. After a six-year hiatus, Baron Frankenstein is back (last seen in *The Revenge of Frankenstein,* 1958). He finds his creature encased in glacial ice (an earlier creation he thought destroyed), and thaws it out. Unfortunately, the brain has been damaged, and Frankenstein enlists the aid of a mesmerist named Zoltan to fully revive the creature. The evil Zoltan takes control of the Monster through his hypnotic power and uses it to kill his enemies. ¶ "Why is it that when Baron Frankenstein's name is mentioned people react as though I'd asked them about Satan himself?" • This is the only Hammer Frankenstein film in which the creature resembles Universal's Monster (though with a greatly inferior makeup job). • Unlike in the previous entry, the Baron doesn't get away in the end, he perishes in a fire (or so we're led to believe) along with his creation. But Frankenstein is not dead after all, he's back with a new twist in *Frankenstein Created Woman* (1967). ¶

Frankenstein and the Monster from Hell (1973; Hammer/Paramount; U.K.) D: Terence Fisher. P: Roy Skeggs. S: John Elder (Anthony Hinds). C: Brian Probyn. Cast: Peter Cushing, Shane Briant, Madeline Smith, John Stratton, Bernard Lee, Clifford Mollison, Dave Prowse, Patrick Troughton. Peter Cushing is back, playing Baron Frankenstein for the sixth and last time. He now runs an insane asylum and uses body parts from the inmates to complete yet another creature. • This is the seventh and final film in the series. • David Prowse plays the Monster here just as he did in the previous film, *Horror of Frankenstein* (though the two creatures look quite different — here he is a hairy, bald-headed apish creature). • At the film's conclusion, the Monster meets his end when it's ripped to pieces by a mob of asylum inmates.

Frankenstein Created Woman (1967; Hammer–Seven Arts/20th Century–Fox;

Christopher Lee makes his horror debut as Hammer's version of the Frankenstein Monster in The Curse of Frankenstein *(1957). British makeup artist Phil Leakey made his monster significantly different than the previous Universal model due to copyright complications.*

U.K.) D: Terence Fisher. P: Anthony Nelson-Keys. S: John Elder (Anthony Hinds). C: Arthur Grant. Cast: Peter Cushing, Susan Denberg, Thorley Walters, Robert Morris, Duncan Lamont. For this entry, Frankenstein (Peter Cushing, for the fourth time) moves from the physical realm into that of the spiritual. He and an assistant are experimenting with the transferring of souls. When a crippled girl drowns herself over the death of her lover who was wrongly executed for murder, Frankenstein performs

surgery on her corpse and transfers the soul

surgery on her corpse and transfers the soul of her dead lover into the now-perfect, voluptuous body. Consumed with vengeance, the beautiful creature first entices and then murders all those responsible for framing him/her. ¶ Ad line—"Now Frankenstein has created a beautiful woman with the soul of the devil." • *Frankenstein Created Woman* was originally to be called *And Frankenstein Created Woman* to cash in on the notoriety of the Brigitte Bardot sensation, *And God Created Woman*. Screenwriter Anthony Hinds admitted, "We pinched the title, yes. That was my idea" (*Fangoria* #74). • At the end of this fourth film in the series, the unhappy creature commits suicide— again (ironically by drowning herself a second, and final, time). • *Frankenstein Created Woman* was released on a double bill with *The Mummy's Shroud*).

Frankenstein Must Be Destroyed (1969; Hammer/Warner Bros.–Seven Arts; U.K.) D: Terence Fisher. P: Anthony Nelson-Keys. S: Bert Batt. C: Arthur Grant. Cast: Peter Cushing, Veronica Carlson, Simon Ward, Freddie Jones, Thorley Walters, Maxine Audley. Baron Frankenstein blackmails a young surgeon into helping him in his experiments in brain transplantation. He transfers the brain of a dying surgeon into the body of a professor, and the scarred, confused soul, thinking himself the surgeon, goes to visit his wife and home—with disastrous results. In the end, the shattered creature takes revenge on its creator by trapping him in a burning barn. ¶ "Frankenstein! I thought the world had heard the last of you!" (Not likely in this popular series.) • This is the fifth film in the series, with the next being the semi-comic *Horror of Frankenstein* (1970).

Horror of Frankenstein (1970; Hammer/ MGM-EMI; U.K.) D/P: Jimmy Sangster. S: Jeremy Burnham, Jimmy Sangster. C; Moray Grant. Cast: Ralph Bates, Kate O'Mara, Graham James, Veronica Carlson, Bernard Archard, Dennis Price, Joan Rice, David Prowse. Hammer spoofs their own film series in this sixth entry. Basically a semi-comic remake of *The Curse of Frankenstein,* the film follows Ralph Bates as he assembles his muscle-bound creature by numbers and uses it for his own evil ends. • This is the only film in the series without Peter Cushing as the Baron (the young Ralph Bates fills the Baron's shoes). It is also the only entry with a comical bent. • David Prowse (later to play Darth Vader in the *Star Wars* series) plays the monster. Prowse was the monster again (though a new creature) in the next (and final) entry, *Frankenstein and the Monster from Hell* (1973). • Jimmy Sangster wrote the first two films in the series and now tried his hand at directing and producing (as well as shouldering the writing chores) on this sixth entry.

The Revenge of Frankenstein (1958; Hammer/Columbia; U.K.) D: Terence Fisher. P: Anthony Nelson-Keys. S: Jimmy Sangster. C: Jack Asher. Cast: Peter Cushing, Francis Matthews, Eunice Gayson, Michael Gwynn, John Welsh, Lionel Jeffries, Oscar Quitak, Richard Wordsworth. This first sequel to *The Curse of Frankenstein* picks up just where the first film left off—with Baron Frankenstein about to be guillotined. His neck is saved when a few well-placed bribes cause a priest to be substituted in his place, allowing him to escape and continue his work under the alias of "Dr. Stein." He creates another man, this one normal until its brain is damaged in a fight, transforming it into a crazed creature with a taste for human flesh. An enraged mob dispatches the monster and nearly finishes Dr. Stein, until his assistant uses some of Stein's own techniques to save him. The film ends with Stein taking up residence in another town as "Dr. Frank." ¶ "The brain must be a living one. Unlike the limbs, life cannot be restored once life is gone. The brain *is* life, and so a living brain must be used." (Oddly, Frankenstein didn't seem too concerned with this detail in the original film, since he placed the brain of a man already dead into his creature—not a "living brain.") • Next stop, *The Evil of Frankenstein* (1964).

Further Frankensteins

Andy Warhol's Frankenstein (1974; Bryanston; Italy) (also *Flesh for Frankenstein*). D: Paul Morrissey. P: Andrew Braunsberg. S: Paul Morrissey, Antonio Margheriti. C: Luigi Kuveiller. Cast: Udo Kier, Monique Van Vooren, Joe Dallesandro, Carlo Mancini, Arno Juerging. The necrophiliac Baron Frankenstein (Udo Kier) creates two creatures, one male and one female, out of body parts taken from murdered villagers, planning to use them to start his "Serbian master race." ¶ "To know death, Otto, you must fuck life in the gall bladder." • This gory, tongue-in-cheek shocker is the only Frankenstein film to date to be filmed in 3-D. It is also the only X-rated (for excessive gore and violence) version of *Frankenstein*. Forrest J Ackerman, editor of *Famous Monsters of Filmland,* claimed this film "makes *The Exorcist* look like a picture about Pollyanna with a mild case of eczema" (issue #112). • German actor Udo Kier, who plays the perverted and demented Baron Frankenstein, played another famous villain this same year — Dracula in *Andy Warhol's Dracula.*

Assignment Terror (1970) (see ALIENS — INVADERS ON EARTH: THE 60s AND 70s). Michael Rennie plays an alien who plans to dominate the world by preying on human fears of the supernatural. To this end he revives Dracula, the Mummy, the Wolf Man, and of course, the Frankenstein Monster. • The filmmakers attempted to duplicate Universal's classic makeup for the Monster, but failed miserably. The actor, in green face and with eyes half closed, looks more like a fatigued costume party-goer than a hideous creature stitched together from dead bodies.

Blackenstein (1973; Exclusive International) (also *Black Frankenstein*). D: William A. Levey. P/S: Frank R. Saletri. Cast: John Hart, Ivory Stone, Andrea King, Liz Renay, Roosevelt Jackson, Joe de Sue. Dr. Frankenstein grafts on new limbs to a crippled Vietnam vet, but a jealous servant sabotages the operation and transforms the man into a rampaging monster with a big afro. • Amazingly enough, Kenneth Strickfaden performed some of the special effects work for this cheap blaxploitation film. It was Strickfaden who had created the incredible electrical equipment and memorable creation effects for the original Universal Frankenstein series.

The Body Shop (1974) (see MAD SCIENTISTS) (also *Dr. Gore*). Though not a true Frankenstein film, this amateurish gore movie gleans its inspiration from the series, particularly *Bride of Frankenstein* (1935). A mad scientist loses his wife and vows to make himself the perfect mate. With the help of his hunchback assistant (of course), this Frankenstein-wannabe kills various girls for their choicest body parts and assembles his perfect woman. He brings her to life, teaches her only what he wants her to know, but loses her when she discovers there are other men in the world ("I'm a woman and you're a man" is her favorite greeting to strangers she meets). The movie ends with the scientist wasting away in prison while his bikini-clad creation hitches a ride with another stranger. Dr. Praetorius never had troubles like these.

The Bride (1985; Columbia) D: Franc Roddam. P: Victor Drai. S: Lloyd Fonvielle. C: Stephen H. Burum. Cast: Sting, Jennifer Beals, Geraldine Page, Clancy Brown, Anthony Higgins, David Rappaport. Baron Frankenstein is a brilliant renegade scientist who creates a man and then rejects the huge ugly creature. The pitiful, scarred monster escapes and joins up with a kindly dwarf in a traveling circus. Perfecting his craft, Frankenstein again creates a human being, this one a woman and this time it is physically perfect. As he teaches her, he yearns to dominate and possess her, until she defies him and it all comes to a head with the return of his first creation, now seeking a mate. • Rock star–turned-actor Sting, of the popular band "The Police," plays the lustful, power mad Dr. Frankenstein. • In this remake (a critical and financial flop) of the 1935 classic, *Bride of Frankenstein,* the Monster actually *gets* his intended mate (and sails off into the sunset with her) — a first for serious Frankenstein films.

Bride of Re-Animator (1990) (see ZOMBIES). In this gory, tongue-in-cheek sequel to *Re-Animator* (1985), mad doctor Herbert West is back, working at a hospital during the day and experimenting with stolen body parts at night. He decides (à la Dr. Frankenstein) to create a new life — a woman — out of the parts, building on the heart of his assistant's girlfriend (who died in the first film). He succeeds, but when the hideous, pieced-together creature is rejected by West's handsome assistant, she rips the heart from her own chest and offers it to him, as she dissolves in a gory puddle due to tissue rejection. The scene is interrupted by several reanimated zombies left over from the first movie, who've escaped from the psychiatric unit at the hospital, and are led by the reanimated (and annoyed) disembodied head of Dr. Hill.

Dr. Frankenstein on Campus (1970; Medford; Canada) (also *Flick*). D: Gil Taylor. P: Bill Marshall. S: David Cobb, Bill Marshall, Gil Taylor. C: Jackson Samuels. Cast: Robin Ward, Kathleen Sawyer, Austin Willis, Sean Sullivan, Ty Haller. Robin Ward plays a university student named Viktor Frankenstein IV. It turns out he is not a relation to the Frankenstein family after all, but the *creature* itself, created by one of the professors.

Dr. Hackenstein (1988; Vista Street Films) D/S: Richard Clark. P: Reza Mizbani, Megan Barnett. C: Jens Sturup. Cast: David Muir, Stacey Travis, Catherine Davis Cox, Dyanne Dirosario, John Alexis, William Schreiner, Cathy Cahn, Phyllis Diller, Anne Ramsey, Logan Ramsey. In 1909 ("the dawn of modern medical science"), Dr. Elliot Hackenstein is intent upon building a new body for his dead wife (who is now only a head). A trio of lovelies stumble into his house, and the doctor begins "borrowing" parts from them in order to complete his experiment and bring his creature to life. ¶ "I've been dead for three years and all you can find is a flabby arm like this?"—the complaining creature. • This was actress Anne Ramsey's *(Throw Momma from the Train)* last film before she died. It is also the only picture in which she appeared with her real-life husband, Logan Ramsey (they played Mr. and Mrs. Rose, a pair of bumbling grave robbers).

Dracula Against Frankenstein (1972) (see VAMPIRES—DRACULA AND FAMILY) (also *Dracula vs. Dr. Frankenstein; The Screaming Dead* [video title]). In this nonsensical import by prolific Spanish filmmaker Jess Franco, Dr. Frankenstein creates a creature to combat Dracula. • Dr. Frankenstein was played by British actor Dennis Price. The monster is played by Fernando Bilbao.

Dracula vs. Frankenstein (1972; Independent International) P/D: Al Adamson. S: William Pugsley, Samuel M. Sherman. Cast: J. Carrol Naish, Lon Chaney, Regina Carrol, Angelo Rossitto, Zandor Vorkov, Anthony Eisley, Russ Tamblyn, Jim Davis, John Bloom. Dracula takes the dormant body of the Monster to Dr. Frankenstein, currently hiding under the alias Dr. Durea, and convinces him to revive the creature. Dracula hopes to use a blood serum that the doctor has been working on to allow him to endure sunlight. The Monster is employed to procure victims for their experiments, but alas, all does not go as planned and the expected confrontation between Dracula and the Frankenstein Monster occurs at the climax. • As originally shot in 1971, the film was called *The Blood Seekers* and did not feature either Dracula or Frankenstein. When this feature was deemed too short and incomprehensible by Sam Sherman at Independent International, the characters of Dracula and Frankenstein were added, new scenes shot, and a movie was made (more or less). The reason why J. Carrol Naish is called Dr. Durea throughout the film when he's supposed to be Dr. Frankenstein is

because his was a character from the original version, whose name was changed to Frankenstein after the fact. • Forrest J Ackerman, editor of *Famous Monsters of Filmland,* has a cameo as the Monster's first victim. • Sadly, this was J. Carrol Naish's last feature; a pitiful ending for the actor who graced such films as *House of Frankenstein* (1944; in which he played a hunchback servant) and *The Beast with Five Fingers* (1946).

Frankenhooker (1990; S.G.E.) D: Frank Henenlotter. P: Edgar Ievins. S: Robert Martin, Frank Henenlotter. C: Robert M. Baldwin. Cast: James Lorinz, Patty Mullen, Charlotte Helmkamp, Lia Chang, Shirley Stoler, Sandy Colosimo, Vicki Darnell, Jennifer Delora, Gittan Goding, Heather Hunter, Stephanie Ryan, Kimberly Taylor, Louise Lasser. James Lorinz plays Jeffrey Franken, a young "bioelectrical technician" kicked out of three medical schools, who is indirectly responsible for his girlfriend's death by lawn mower. So he preserves her head and assembles a new body for her from parts taken from New York hookers in this outrageous, sleazy horror/comedy. ¶ "It's so simple. If I need female body parts, then I'll *buy* female body parts, and there's a place across the river where there are thousands of women anxious to sell their parts, no questions asked." • Jeffrey Franken's rather rotund fiancée is named "Elizabeth," the same name as Henry Frankenstein's fiancée in the original *Frankenstein* (1931). • Beloved horror host Zacherle makes a brief cameo appearance as a demented weatherman. • Director/co-screenwriter Frank Henenlotter is the man responsible for the midnight favorite, *Basket Case* (1982), and the generally unseen *Basket Case 2* (1990). *Frankenhooker* was shot back to back with *Basket Case 2,* at a budget of two million dollars each. • *Frankenhooker* could not get an "R" rating from the MPAA and so was released unrated.

Frankenstein (1973; TV Movie) D: Glenn Jordan. P: Dan Curtis. S: Sam Hall, Richard Landau. C: Ben Colman. Cast: Robert Foxworth, Susan Strasberg, Bo Svenson, John Karlen, Robert Gentry, Philip Bourneuf, George Morgan, Heidi Vaughn. TV producer Dan Curtis remakes the Frankenstein story starring big Bo Svenson as the monster. Nearly three hours long, it was originally aired over two nights. ¶ "If superhumans are to exist, then it is clearly our duty as scientists to create that life in the laboratory." • In this version, the monster is not invulnerable, since he is shot and killed by ordinary lead bullets at film's end. Here,

the creature is billed simply as "The Giant."
• Dan Curtis produced TV versions of several other great literary horror stories, including *The Strange Case of Dr. Jekyll and Mr. Hyde* (1968), and *Dracula* (1973). Curtis also produced the TV horror soap opera "Dark Shadows," and cast one of that series regulars, John Karlen, in this film.

Frankenstein (1984; TV Movie; U.K.) D: James Ormerod. P: Bill Siegler. S: Victor Gialanella. C: Stuart Hinchliffe. Cast: Robert Powell, Carrie Fisher, David Warner, John Gielgud, Terence Alexander, Susan Wooldridge. Robert Powell is Victor Frankenstein, who creates an articulate creature in the form of David Warner. When Frankenstein spurns his creation, the pitiful, lonely creature vows vengeance, culminating in the death of Frankenstein's fiancée, Elizabeth. ¶ "You, who have no soul, will rest in peace. I am damned forever."—the final words of Victor Frankenstein as he destroys both the creature and himself. • This fairly faithful adapation of Mary Shelley's novel was filmed on location in Yorkshire, England.

Frankenstein Conquers the World (1964) (see HUMAN GIANTS). A young boy eats the heart of the Frankenstein Monster and grows to a huge size, taking on green skin and an ugly raised forehead. Dubbed "Frankenstein" by the Japanese people, he fights a Godzilla-clone named Baragon and saves Japan.

Frankenstein General Hospital (1988; New Star Entertainment) D: Deborah Roberts. P: Dimitri Villard. S: Michael Kelly, Robert Deel. C: Tom Fraser. Cast: Mark Blankfield, Leslie Jordan, Jonathan Farwell, Kathy Shower, Hamilton Mitchell, Lou Cutell, Katie Caple, Dorothy Paterson, Irwin Keyes. Young Dr. Bob Frankenstein (the great-great-grandson of the original) makes use of his secret hospital lab to create his own creature in this horror spoof of the classic Frankenstein story. ¶ "Look at my creation! I gave him life! I am his *mom!*" • At one point, Bob Frankenstein says, "We've done it great-great-grandfather!" and the camera pans to a photograph of Colin Clive (the original Frankenstein from Universal's *Frankenstein,* 1931, and *Bride of Frankenstein,* 1935).

Frankenstein Island (1981; Astral Films) D/P: Jerry Warren. S: Jacques Lacouter. C: Murray De Ately. Cast: Robert Clarke, Steve Brodie, Cameron Mitchell, Robert Christopher, Tian Bodkin, Patrick O'Neil, Andrew Duggan, John Carradine. Four balloonists crash-land on an uncharted island inhabited by a group of bikini-clad bimbos

and Sheila Frankenstein, the great-great-granddaughter of Dr. Frankenstein. Along with her 200-year-old husband (Frankenstein's former assistant), a thought-projecting disembodied brain, a group of zombie-like sailors wearing sweaters and wool hats, and of course the Frankenstein Monster, she conducts esoteric experiments on the girls (the remnants of an alien race who had visited the island years before). Transmitted by the disembodied brain, the giant superimposed image of Dr. Frankenstein himself (John Carradine) pops up occasionally to mutter things like "The power, the power, the power!" ¶ "You know, when I hear you casually mention communicating with Dr. Frankenstein, communicating with a dead man, I don't know quite how to take it." • Sheila Frankenstein's husband (and former assistant to Dr. Frankenstein) is named "Dr. Von Helsing" (in an odd mixing of classic stories—"Van Helsing" was the name of the knowledgeable vampire-killer in *Dracula*). • The Monster doesn't make an appearance until the free-for-all brawl at the finale. According to Von Helsing, since the mind of the Monster had never developed, Dr. Frankenstein and he "had to chain him to the reef, underwater, beneath the grotto" years earlier (where he has been ever since). • John Carradine (or at least his superimposed image) plays Dr. Frankenstein for the first and only time in his long career. He had been in two earlier Frankenstein films—Universal's *House of Frankenstein* (1944) and *House of Dracula* (1945), but played the role of Dracula in both. • This was Grade Z filmmaker Jerry Warren's (*Teenage Zombies,* 1960; *Creature of the Walking Dead,* 1966; etc.) first film in nearly 15 years and his old-style shoestring approach to moviemaking hadn't changed (much to his eventual regret). Warren later admitted to Tom Weaver in his book *Interviews with B Science Fiction and Horror Movie Makers:* "I don't think I'd seen a movie since maybe the mid-60s. I didn't see what was happening, and I assumed that I could still make 'em like I used to. But they had changed an awful lot. I didn't update *Frankenstein Island* enough to really compete with what was out."

Frankenstein Meets the Space Monster (1965) (see ALIENS—INVADERS ON EARTH: THE 60s AND 70s). Having absolutely nothing to do with Mary Shelley's creation, this name-stealing low-budget cheapie is about alien invaders come to Earth to steal women for breeding. In a parallel plot, an android astronaut named Frank Saunders is damaged and goes on a killing spree, finally coming out of it enough to battle the evil aliens in the end. • The *only* tie-in to "Frankenstein" is this credit at the film's end: "And featuring Robert Reilly as L. Frank Saunders and Frankenstein."

Frankenstein 1970 (1958; Allied Artists) D: Howard W. Koch. P: Aubrey Schenck. S: Richard Landau, George Worthington Yates. C: Carl E. Guthrie. Cast: Boris Karloff, Tom Duggan, Jana Lund, Donald Barry, Charlotte Austin, Mike Lane. Boris Karloff plays a present day Baron Frankenstein who has built an ultra-modern laboratory in a secret room under the family crypt in which he plans to make a new, improved version of his family's infamous monster. For this he needs an atomic reactor, and allows a TV crew to use his castle as the background to their show in exchange for the equipment he needs. The Baron brings his monster to life, but without eyes. The rest of the film is taken up with the creature searching for just the right pair of eyes. ¶ "Ah, Schuter, yours is not the brain I would have chosen, but at least you are obedient." • This is the only film in which Boris Karloff played *Doctor* Frankenstein, and not his creation. • The monster is all wrapped in bandages and lumbers about with a box-like contraption over its head for most of the picture. When the bandages finally come off at the very end, it is unsurprising to see that Frankenstein had given his creation the face of a younger version of himself.

Frankenstein '80 (1973; M.G.D. Film; Italy) D: Mario Mancini. P; Benedetto Graziani. S: Mario Mancini, Ferdinando Di Leoni. C: Emilio Varriano. Cast: John Richardson, Renato Remano, Xiro Papas, Dalila Parker, Bob Fiz, Gordon Mitchell, Dada Gallotti, Lemmy Carson, Marco Mariani. A mad scientist steals another doctor's revolutionary anti-rejection serum for organ transplants in order to use it on the man-made creature he has named "Mosaic." Looking like a huge man with ugly scars, Mosaic periodically goes out and kills, either to obtain organs for the doctor to replenish his own rejected ones, or to have violent sex with prostitutes. ¶ "Listen, if you don't behave I shall destroy you the same as I made you."

Frankenstein: The True Story (1974; TV Movie; U.K.) D: Jack Smight. P: Hunt Stromberg, Jr. S: Christopher Isherwood, Don Bachardy. C: Arthur Ibbetson. Cast: James Mason, Leonard Whiting, David McCallum, Jane Seymour, Nicola Paget, Michael Sarrazin. Not really "The True Story" as claimed, but still closer than most to Mary Shelley's novel. For this version, Dr. Frankenstein creates an attractive "perfect" man (Michael Sarrazin) whose flesh gradually deteriorates, turning him into a monstrous creature. The wicked Dr. Polidori uses the creature to force Frankenstein to create a mate for the monster (à la *Bride of Frankenstein*). ¶ "I wronged you I know. I disowned you, I wanted to destroy you. How can I blame you for anything you've done? Poor creature, you're as weary of life as I am. If only I could rid mankind of us both." • This two-part TV movie was condensed and released theatrically in Europe. • At the close of the story, the Monster, unable to die, is buried alive under tons of ice and snow along with its creator.

Frankenstein Unbound (1990; 20th Century–Fox) D: Roger Corman. P: Roger Corman, Thom Mount, Kobi Jaeger. S: Roger Corman, F. X. Feeney. C: Armando Nannuzzi, Michael Scott. Cast: John Hurt, Raul Julia, Bridget Fonda, Chatherine Rabett, Jason Patric, Michael Hutchence, Nick Brimble. John Hurt plays a scientist in the future of 2031 whose research leads to the creation of a "time slip," which hurls him back to the shores of Lake Geneva in 1817 Switzerland. There he meets Mary Shelley, soon-to-be author of *Frankenstein,* and also learns that her novel is not an entirely fictional one. Hurt encounters the real Dr. Victor Frankenstein (Raul Julia) and his hideous creature, and eventually faces off against the brilliant but cruel Frankenstein and his mad plans. ¶ "Scientists have made far greater monsters than yours, Victor." • Though heavily involved in producing and film distribution, this is the first film Roger Corman has directed in 19 years. He also co-wrote the script (an unusual occurrence for Corman) from the novel of the same name by Brian W. Aldiss. • Corman originally felt that height and size were his main considerations in casting the role of the monster: "My thought was to get a basketball player — someone 6-foot-8 or 10 who could move as a basketball player can move — and I would dub the dialogue later.... Then I interviewed Nick Brimble in England. He wasn't quite as tall as my original idea, about 6-foot-4 or 5, but he gave such a good reading that I made a last-minute decision shortly before we began shooting to change my whole concept, go with an actor and give up a few inches of height" (from an interview in *Fangoria* #92). • Corman also talked about his ideas for the monster's appearance: "The concept I started with was that it must not in any way suggest the original Boris Karloff Monster. It has to be new. If Dr. Frankenstein would try to create life, he would try to improve upon it, he would try to do better than God. So the Monster is stronger than a human being, his eyesight is better, his hearing is better, he has six fingers on each hand, including two opposed thumbs, so he can grip better."

Frankenstein's Bloody Terror (1968) (see WEREWOLVES — SPAIN'S "WALDEMAR DANINSKY" SERIES). This first entry in the Waldemar Daninsky Werewolf series, originally called *The Mark of the Wolfman,* features a werewolf who seeks the aid of a pair of occult experts in trying to cure his condition. Unfortunately, the couple turn out to be vampires. The only Frankenstein present is in the film's misleading title.

Frankenstein's Castle of Freaks (1973; Cinerama; Italy) (also *House of Freaks*). D: Robert H. Oliver. P: Robert Randall. S: Mario Francini. Cast: Rossano Brazzi, Michael Dunn, Edmund Purdom, Christiane Royce, Boris Lugosi, Gordon Mitchell, Alan Collins, Xiro Papas, Loren Ewing, Lewis Garfield. Rossano Brazzi (star of *South Pacific,* 1958) plays Count Frankenstein who, with the help of a dwarf, a hunchback, and various misfits of humanity, transplants a brain into a creature named Goliath. When the dwarf has a falling out with the Count, he goes to his friend "Ook the Neanderthal Man" living in a nearby cave. They return and slay everyone. • Ook the Neanderthal Man is played by an actor who bills himself as "Boris Lugosi"(!) — no relation to either of the horror stars.

Frankenstein's Daughter (1958; Astor) D: Richard Cunha. P: Marc Frederick. S: M. E. Barrie. C: Meredith Nicholson. Cast: John Ashley, Sandra Knight, Donald Murphy, Sally Todd, Harold Lloyd, Jr. A descendant of Dr. Frankenstein, calling himself Oliver Frank, works as an assistant to Dr. Carter, who is working on a drug to wipe out destructive cells. Frank (or Frankenstein) is also working in secret on some illicit experiments of his own. He administers a drug which transforms Dr. Carter's innocent niece into an ugly monster. He also creates a creature out of stolen body parts, using the body of a girl he has killed. • Though the hideous creature is supposedly a woman, there is no indication that this is the case from its rather masculine appearance.

Frankenstein's Great Aunt Tillie (1985; Filmier Productions; Mexico) D/P/S: Myron J. Gold. C: Miguel Garzon. Cast: Donald Pleasence, Yvonne Furneaux, June Wilkinson, Rod Colbin, Garnett Smith, Zsa Zsa Gabor. Donald Pleasence as Frankenstein and Yvonne Furneaux as his great aunt Tillie return to the family mansion, only to find it in the midst of being repossessed for back taxes in this Frankenstein farce.

How to Make a Monster (1958) (see MADMEN — EARLY MADMEN). When a studio makeup man is fired, he uses a special makeup base to control the actors wearing his monster makeup. He sends out a caveman, a "teenage werewolf," and of course the "teenage Frankenstein Monster" to kill the studio heads who axed him. • Producer Herman Cohen also made *I Was a Teenage Werewolf* and *I Was a Teenage Frankenstein* (both 1957), and used the same monster makeups from those films for the creatures here.

I Was a Teenage Frankenstein (1957; AIP) D: Herbert L. Strock. P: Herman Cohen. S: Kenneth Langtry. C: Lothrop Worth. Cast: Whit Bissell, Phyllis Coates, Robert Burton, Gary Conway, George Lynn, John Cliff. A modern-day Dr. Frankenstein living in L.A. collects the body parts of teenagers to assemble his teenage creation. ¶ "Speak, you've got a civil tongue in your head. I know you have because I sewed it back myself" — the often (mis)quoted Dr. Frankenstein. • Producer Herman Cohen followed up his incredibly successful *I Was a Teenage Werewolf* (1957) with this exploitation entry. It was released on a double bill with *Blood of Dracula* (which *should* have been called *I Was a Teenage Vampire*). • Screenwriter Kenneth Langtry is a pseudonym for writer Aben Kandel. Kandel also wrote *How to Make a Monster* (1958), again for producer Cohen, and again featuring the same Frankenstein Monster. • Aside from the classic Universal makeup, this is the only Frankenstein Monster makeup to be used in more than one film.

Jesse James Meets Frankenstein's Daughter (1965; Embassy) D: William Beaudine. P: Carroll Case. S: Carl K. Hittleman. C: Lothrop Worth. Cast: John Lupton, Cal Bolder, Narda Onyx, Estelita, Steven Geray, Jim Davis. Despite the title, it is Frankenstein's *grandaughter* who transplants the brain of her ancestor's monster into Jesse James' muscle-bound sidekick and renames the creature "Igor." ¶ "Roaring Guns against Raging Monster!" — ad slogan. • This is the last feature made by prolific B-movie director William "One Shot" Beaudine, whose career spanned over 150 films! • Appropriately enough, this was paired with *Billy the Kid vs. Dracula* (also directed by William

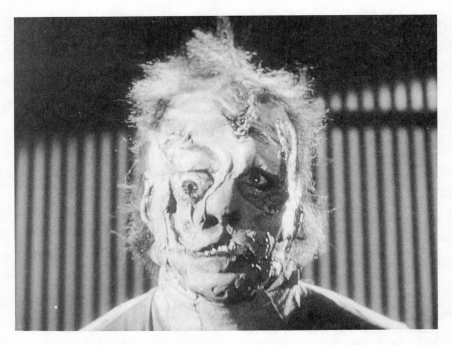

Gary Conway reprises his role (of sorts) from I Was a Teenage Frankenstein *(1957) for the movie monster hodge-podge called* How to Make a Monster *(1958).*

Beaudine) to make the most unique grade Z double feature ever released. • Cinematographer Lothrop Worth also lensed another teen exploitation Frankenstein film, *I Was a Teenage Frankenstein* (1957).

Lady Frankenstein (1972; New World; Italy) D: Mel Welles. P: Harry Cushing. S: Edward Di Lorenzo. C: Richard Pallotin. Cast: Joseph Cotten, Sara Bay, Mickey Hargitay, Paul Mueller, Paul Whiteman, Herbert Fuchs, Renate Kasché, Ada Pometti, Lorenzo Terzon. Joseph Cotten plays Dr. Frankenstein, but dies early in the picture. His daughter, also a surgeon, carries on his work. Two monsters are created— one ugly, who promptly goes on a rampage, and the other handsome, whom the daughter promptly makes love to—before the creature strangles her and perishes in a fire. ¶ "Only the monster she made could satisfy her strange desires!"—exploitative ad line. • Director Mel Welles was an actor before stepping behind the camera. He appeared in Roger Corman's *Attack of the Crab Monsters* (1957), and played Mr. Mushnik, the flower shop owner from *The Little Shop of*

Horrors (1960). Welles liked the exploitative advertising approach taken by Corman's New World Pictures, calling it "a very interesting campaign." • Welles claimed that *Lady Frankenstein* "was the first gothic horror film with an explicit sex scene in it" (*Fangoria* #58). • *Lady Frankenstein* was shot at Depaulus Studio, the oldest studio in Rome. Except for four or five of the smaller parts, all the actors mouthed the dialogue in English and it was dubbed later.

The Monster Squad (1987) (see VAM-PIRES—DRACULA AND FAMILY). The evil Dracula has summoned all the famous classical monsters together (the Creature from the Black Lagoon, the Mummy, the Wolf Man, and Frankenstein's Monster) in an attempt to gain possession of an occult amulet which would let the forces of darkness rule the earth. Their only opposition is a band of young kids and an old man. The Frankenstein Monster, befriended by a little girl, turns against the other monsters and aids the youngsters in their fight against the evil Dracula.

Orlak, the Hell of Frankenstein (1960;

Columbia; Mexico) D/P: Rafael Baledon. S: Alfredo Ruanova, Carlos Enrique Toba-oda. C: Fernando Alvarez Garces. Cast: Joaquin Cordero, Armando Calvo, Andres Soler, Rosa de Castilla, Irma Dorantes, Pedro de Aguillon, David Reynoso, Carlos Incira, Carlos Nieto, Antonio Rabal. A criminal, sharing a cell with Dr. Franken-stein, gains control of his creature and sends him out to kill those who convicted him. Both he and the creature fall in love with the woman Elvira, and the creature finally turns on its master. • The monster has an ugly, scarred face and so wears a metal box over its head for most of the movie. Despite the encumbrance of the metal box, the creature also has the ability to speak.

The Rocky Horror Picture Show (1975) (see ALIENS—BENEVOLENT ALIENTS). The transvestite alien Dr. Frank-N-Furter cre-ates a creature to satisfy his lustful desires in this midnight cult favorite. He names his handsome blond (male) creation "Rocky," and when Rocky throws him over for a woman, Frank-N-Furter kills him with a ray gun in a jealous rage. • At the film's end, Rocky climbs a replica of the famous RKO tower used as that studio's logo.

Spirit of the Beehive (1974; Spain) D: Vic-tor Erice. P: Elia Querejeta. S: Victor Erice, Angel Fernandez. C: Luis Cuadrado. Cast: Fernando Fernan Gomez, Teresa Gimpera, Ana Torrent, Isabel Telleria, Laly Solde-villa, Miguel Picazo, José Villasante, Juan Margallo. Two little girls live in their own fantasy world where they believe they can conjure up the Frankenstein Monster, who is not a terrible monster after all, but a good and kind creature.

Victor Frankenstein (1975; FAW; Sweden/ Ireland) (also *Terror of Frankenstein*). D/P: Calvin Floyd. S: Yvonne Floyd, Calvin Floyd. C: Tony Forsberg, John Wilcox. Cast: Leon Vitali, Per Oscarsson, Nicholas Clay, Stacey Dorning, Jan Ohls-son, Olof Bergstrom, Mathias Henrickson,

Archie O'Sullivan, Harry Brogan. This is the most faithful adaptation of Mary Shel-ley's novel to date. It focuses on the creature's agonizing development and his pain at being rejected by humanity and by his own creator. Following the classic story, the creature punishes Frankenstein for his cruel rejection by killing all those close to him in a plan to force the doctor to create a mate for him. ¶ "When the world was new to me, I would have wept to die. Now death is my only consolation, because in death I cease to be a monster."

Young Frankenstein (1974; 20th Cen-tury-Fox) D: Mel Brooks. P: Michael Gruskoff. S: Gene Wilder, Mel Brooks. C: Gerald Hirschfeld. Cast: Gene Wilder, Peter Boyle, Marty Feldman, Cloris Leach-man, Teri Garr, Kenneth Mars, Madeline Kahn, Gene Hackman. This wonderfully funny parody, which is as much an homage as it is a spoof of the first three Universal Frankenstein classics (*Frankenstein,* 1931; *Bride of Frankenstein,* 1935; and *Son of Frankenstein,* 1939), stars Gene Wilder as Frederick Frankenstein ("That's pronounced Fronk-en-steen!"), the grandson of Baron Victor Frankenstein. He returns to his ancestral estate, discovers his father's secret diary ("How I Did It") and is inspired to create his own creature. ¶ "From what was once an inarticulate mass of lifeless tissues, may I now present a cultured, sophisticated, man about town"—Frankenstein introduc-ing his creation. • True to the originals, *Young Frankenstein* was filmed in black and white. They also used the very same ma-chinery which appeared in the three original Universal features. • Printed on the brain jars from which "Eye-gor" chooses the monster's abnormal brain are the names of Albertus Magnus and Cornelius Agrippa. These two historical figures were real life heroes of Percy Shelley, husband of Mary Shelley, who wrote the original Franken-stein novel.

Freaks

We hate to use the word "freaks" for this subject because it is a degrading term that is openly refuted by many of the films listed in this section (such as *The Elephant Man,* 1980). Basically it comes down to semantics. For lack of a better term that would be familiar to the majority of genre fans, I'm afraid we are stuck with this terrible catchword. What is abnormal to one person is normal to another. However, our own shortsightedness has certainly been reflected by many filmmakers, who have used a particular physical defect as the basis for their twisted horror theme. Circus performers fitting this description have certainly taken their lumps from cinema because of this cruel label placed on them by society. Why these kinds of films remain popular today is simple. Some people are fascinated with deformity. Many of us seem to be drawn to "real life" horrors.

This subgenre contains a plethora of different "abnormalities" (whether of natural origin or as a result of some medical or scientific means) which are alternately explored or exploited, depending upon the sensibilities of the filmmaker. Many of the films of the great Lon Chaney, Sr., have been included in this section, though they are not necessarily true "freak" films. His work has generally been lumped into the horror genre by fans of monster movies, and he has assayed a variety of "twisted" characters — both in their phsyical as well as mental attributes. Also included in this section will be the hunchbacks. There are a number of films that include some minor hunchbacked assistant, but we have only listed those movies in which the hunchback is featured prominently in the story.

Basket Case (1981; Shapiro Glickenhaus Entertainment) D/S: Frank Henenlotter. P: Edgar Ievins. C: Bruce Torbet. Cast: Kevin Van Hentenryck, Terri Susan Smith, Robert Vogel, Beverly Bonner, Diana Brown. A young man keeps his monstrously deformed Siamese twin — severed from him in an awful operation — in a wicker basket. The little creature, named Belial, can communicate telepathically with his big brother, and the pair set out to kill the doctors responsible for the operation. • *Basket Case* was filmed on the incredibly low budget of $35,000. • Though a bonafide cult film and much beloved by its hardy fans, *Basket Case*'s worst critic is its own director/screenwriter, Frank Henenlotter. "I hate *Basket Case*," Henenlotter told *Fangoria* #69, adding, "What a piece of shit." He softened up a bit by going on to say, "It was good for a film shot for $35,000 but that's still no excuse for it."

Basket Case 2 (1990; Shapiro Glickenhaus Entertainment) D/S: Frank Henenlotter. P: Edgar Ievins. C: Robert M. Baldwin. Cast: Kevin Van Hentenryck, Annie Ross, Kathryn Meisle, Heather Rattray, Jason Evers, Ted Sorel. Duane Bradley and his hideous basket buddy are taken in by a family of freaks in this belated (and many claim, unnecessary) sequel. When a tabloid reporter and photographer threaten to rock the boat, Duane decides to defend the freaks' privacy with murder. ¶ "Ripping the faces off people may not be in your best interests." • At the film's climax, Duane stitches his freakish twin brother back onto his body. • A photograph on a newsman's wall pictures the living head featured in *The Brain That Wouldn't Die* (1959).

Beauty and the Beast (1946; Lopert; France) D/S: Jean Cocteau. P: Émile Darbon. C: Henri Alekan. Cast: Josette Day, Jean Marais, Marcel André, Mila Parely, Nane Germon, Michel Auclair. Madame Le Prince de Beaumont's classic fairy tale of a merchant's daughter who falls for a man with the appearance of a bestial lion is told in a beautifully poetic style in this early classic. At the climax, her greedy human paramour is killed while trying to steal the Beast's fortune. When the girl expresses her love for the Beast (lying in a state of near-death), his face magically changes to that of her lover. Together, after a loving embrace, Beauty and the ex–Beast are whisked away into the clouds. ¶ "Do not call me 'My Lord,' call me 'Beast.' I detest compliments." • Director Jean Cocteau worked on location in the Loire Valley for over six months shooting the picture. Cocteau himself applied the makeup, piece by piece, upon actor Jean Marais (who played both the beast and the boyfriend, "Avenant"). Marais was one Cocteau's closest friends, and starred in a number of films for the French director. In addition to his directing and writing talent, Cocteau wrote poems, plays, and was an accomplished painter and set designer. The last picture he directed before dying in 1965 was *The Testament of Orpheus* (1960), which he wrote and also acted in.

Beauty and the Beast (1963; Harvard) D: Edward L. Cahn. P: Robert E. Kent. S: George Bruce, Orville H. Hampton. C: Gilbert Warrenton. Cast: Joyce Taylor, Mark Damon, Eduard Franz, Michael Pate, Merry Anders. In this low-budget rendition of the famed fairy tale, the beast is normal until sunset, at which time he transforms into a werewolf-like beast. • This film is noteworthy in that it was prolific director Edward Cahn's (*Invasion of the Saucermen,* 1957; *It! The Terror from Beyond Space,* 1958; etc.) last picture.

The Being (1982) D/S: Jackie Kong. P: William Osco. C: Robert Ebinger. Cast: Martin Landau, Jose Ferrer, Dorothy Malone, Ruth Buzzi, Marianne Gordon Rogers, Johnny Dark. A genetic freak, partially created by radioactive waste, enjoys decapitating citizens in the small town of Pottsville, Idaho.

A Blind Bargain (1922; Goldwyn) D: Wallace Worsley. P: Sam Goldwyn. S: J. G. Hawks. C: Horbert Brodine. Cast: Lon Chaney, Jacqueline Logan, Raymond McKee, Virginia True Boardman, Fontaine LaRue, Aggie Herring, Virginia Madison. Lon Chaney plays a hunchbacked simian-type character who allows a mad doctor to experiment on him in exchange for a free operation for his dying mother. • This "lost" picture (so far) is based on the Barry Pain novel, *The Octave of Claudius.*

The Brute Man (1946; PRC/Universal) D: Jean Yarbrough. P: Ben Pivar. S: George Brickern, M. Coates Webster. C: Maury Gertsman. Cast: Rondo Hatton, Jane Adams, Tom Neal, Jan Wiley, Donald MacBride. An ex-football star (played by Rondo Hatton) is disfigured in a chemistry accident and then goes on a killing spree. The only person not afraid of this brute-man is a sweet blind girl, whom the "Creeper" (as he is called by the media) adores. Later, when she discovers his identity and turns him in for the murders, the Creeper tries to kill her. • Rondo Hatton, who in real life tragically suffered from the feature-distorting disease of acromegaly, was callously thought of as the monster actor who needed no makeup. This picture turned out to be Hatton's last film, as he died shortly before this film was released, from complications arising from the disease. • Universal was so ashamed of their exploitative product that they sold the distribution rights for *The Brute Man* to poverty-row studio PRC. • Actress Jane Adams, here playing the blind heroine, appeared as a hunchbacked assistant in the 1945 monster mash film, *House of Dracula.*

Dark Intruder (1965) (see WITCHES, WARLOCKS, AND CULTS). A horribly malformed creature (separated from his normal Siamese twin at birth), uses ritualistic murder and black magic in an attempt to transfer his soul from his own misshapen body into the normal body of his twin.

The Darling of Paris (1916; Fox) D: J. Gordon Edwards. S: Adrian Johnson. Cast: Theda Bara, Walter Law, John Webb Dillon, Glen White, Herbert Hayes. This first screen adaptation of the Victor Hugo novel, *Notre Dame de Paris,* stars Glen White as a handsome hunchback named Quasimodo who wins the hand of Esmerelda. • The film was reshot with new scenes in 1919 showing the hunchback killing a priest and Esmerelda being executed at the climax.

Edward Scissorhands (1990; 20th Century-Fox) D: Tim Burton. P: Tim Burton, Denise Dinovi. S: Caroline Thompson. C: Stefan Czapsky. Cast: Johnny Depp, Wynona Ryder, Diane Wiest, Alan Arkin, Anthony Michael Hall, Vincent Price, Kathy Baker. A young boy, created by scientist Vincent Price, possesses scissors for hands (he was unfinished at the time of Price's death). He is found by a visiting Avon lady (Diane Wiest), who welcomes the awkward Edward into her home. At first the gossip-minded neighborhood welcomes the shy, innocent youth, but later they turn against him after he is set up to look like a dangerous thief by Wynona Ryder's scheming boyfriend. At the climax, Edward is chased back to his gloomy castle on the hill, and there spends the rest of his life, alone, presumed dead, cut off from a humanity that won't accept him. • "You see, before he came down here it never snowed, and afterward it always did." • 20th Century-Fox tried to woo Tom Cruise for the title role, but Cruise turned it down reportedly because of the character's lack of masculinity. Several other actors were considered (Tom Hanks and William Hurt among them) before TV heartthrob Johnny Depp secured the role. • Wynona Ryder, who fell in love with Johnny Depp's tragic character in the movie, fell for the actor in real life as well.

The Elephant Man (1980; Paramount) D: David Lynch. P: Stuart Cornfield. S: Christopher de Core, Eric Bergren, David Lynch. C: Freddie Francis. Cast: John Hurt, Anthony Hopkins, John Gielgud, Anne Bancroft, Freddie Jones, Wendy Hiller. *The Elephant Man* is a poignant film about a terribly deformed man, brutally abused and treated like a circus freak, who rises above the callous indifference of society to "gain himself," shaming our ignorance with his kindness, humility and beauty of character. ¶ "I am not an elephant! I am not an animal! I am a human being!" • The picture was nominated for a number of Academy Awards, including Best Film, Screenplay, Editing, Art Direction, and Costume Design. • The film is based upon the true

Olga Baclanova stars as the scheming trapeze artist Cleopatra, who suffers the ironic fate of being carved into a limbless human chicken by the Freaks *(1932) she once ridiculed.*

life experiences of the inspirational John Merrick.

Eraserhead (1976; Libra) D/P/S: David Lynch. C: Frederick Elmes, Herbert Cardwell. Cast: John Nance, Judith Anna Roberts, Laurel Near, Jack Fisk, Jean Lange. This surreal low-budget prenatal picture filmed in black and white centers around a weird baby who possesses a head in the shape of a pencil-top eraser. The father's hold on reality is tenuous at best when at one point he believes he is being attacked by little worm-like parasites, and the next moment, while his head has been pushed off, he is looking at the baby within himself. • *Eraserhead* has become one of the most notable cult films from the 70s decade, often showing up time and time again in midnight movie houses much like *The Rocky Horror Picture Show.*

A Face in the Fog (1936; Victory) D: Robert Hill. P: Sam Katzman. S: Al Martin. C: Bill Hyer. Cast: June Collyer, Lloyd Hughes, Lawrence Gray, Jack Mulhall, Al St. John. A crazed hunchback known as the "Fiend" uses untraceable bullets of frozen poison to terrorize the players of a theater.

Face of Fire (1959; Allied Artists; U.S./Sweden) D: Albert Band. P: Albert Band, Louis Garfinkle. S: Louis Garfinkle. Cast: James Whitmore, Cameron Mitchell, Bettye Ackerman, Royal Dano. A man whose face is horribly burned in a fire while rescuing a boy is perceived as a monster by some local townsfolk. • The film is based on a Stephen Crane story entitled "The Monster."

Frankenstein (1931) (see FRANKENSTEIN'S MONSTER — UNIVERSAL SERIES). Dr. Frankenstein employs the hunchbacked assistant, Fritz, to aid him in his experiment. Unfortunately, Fritz is the one responsible for the Monster having a criminal brain; sent to steal a specific brain from the medical college, Fritz drops the organ and substitutes a criminal brain in its place.

Frankenstein's Castle of Freaks (1973) (see FRANKENSTEIN'S MONSTER — FURTHER FRANKENSTEINS) (also *House of Freaks*). The Count's dwarf assistant (Michael Dunn), along with various other misfits of humanity, aid the doctor in his experiments.

Freaks (1932; MGM) D/P: Tod Browning. S: Willis Goldbeck, Edgar Allen Woolf, Leon Gordon, Al Boasberg. C: Merritt B. Gerstad. Cast: Wallace Ford, Harry Earles, Leila Hyams, Olga Baclanova, Daisy Earles, Henry Victor, Roscoe Ates, Rose Dione. A trapeze artist named Cleopatra and her strongman lover, Hercules, conspire to filch the secret fortune from a circus midget. After repeated attempts to poison the midget become known, the circus freaks initiate their own brand of justice by attacking Hercules and transforming the beautiful Cleopatra into the most hideous of the circus denizens. ¶ "How many times have I told you not to be frightened? Have I not told you God looks after all his children?" • The fate of Cleopatra (Olga Baclanova) is revealed in the final scene when we discover she has been turned into a limbless chicken, forever suffering the sad plight of the freaks she once ridiculed. • Director Tod Browning, who as a teenager ran away from home to join a traveling circus, wanted to relate the tragic experiences of these unique individuals by letting them participate in the telling of their story. Some of the real life circus performers who appear include Johnny Eck (the "half-boy"), Josephine Joseph (half man–half woman), Randion (a man without limbs), Angelo Rossitto (a dwarf), and Zip and Pip (two "pinheads"). • *Freaks,* now hailed as a classic, was reviled by the public and critics alike at the time of its release, almost ruining Browning's career. • MGM tried to soften the criticism initially leveled at what people thought was a distasteful and exploitative picture by adding an opening written narration, ending with this line: "With humility for the many injustices done to such people (they have no power to control their lot), we present the most startling story of the *abnormal* and the *unwanted.*" • *Freaks* was quickly withdrawn from its initial release by an embarrassed MGM, who later tried re-releasing it disguised under the new title of *Nature's Mistakes.* • This controversial tale of revenge within a traveling circus is based on the short story, "Spurs," by Tod Robbins.

House of Dracula (1945) (see VAMPIRES— DRACULA AND FAMILY). Jane Adams plays the hunchbacked female assistant of Dr. Edelmann, who is working on a cure for her unfortunate condition.

House of Frankenstein (1944) (see FRANK-ENSTEIN'S MONSTER — UNIVERSAL SERIES). J. Carrol Naish plays the hunchback servant of Boris Karloff, who is promised a new, unblemished body by Karloff and so does his murderous bidding.

House of Horrors (1946; Universal) D: Jean Yarbrough. P: Ben Pivar. S: George Bricker. C: Maury Gertsman. Cast: Martin Kosleck, Rondo Hatton, Virginia Grey, Alan Napier, Robert Lowery. Rondo Hatton, known as the monstrous killer, "the Creeper," is fished out of a river by a poor sculptor, who then uses his deformed friend to murder the critics who dislike his work. ¶ "A nice harmless little guy like you wouldn't hurt a fly." • *House of Horrors* carried the shooting title of *Murder Mansion.* • Though Universal publicity insisted it was introducing a new character in the form of Rondo Hatton playing "the Creeper," Hatton in fact had played basically the same character in *Pearl of Death* (1944), when he was called "the Hoxton Creeper" and pitted against Sherlock Holmes. • Rondo Hatton had no need of makeup to play his part, as he suffered from the real life disease called acromegaly which enlarges and deforms the extremities like the hands, feet, and facial features. • Kent Taylor was originally set to play the part of the police lieutenant but was replaced at the last minute by Bill Goodwin.

House of the Damned (1963; 20th Century–Fox) D/P: Maury Dexter. S: Harry Spalding. C: John Nickolaus, Jr. Cast: Ronald Foster, Merry Anders, Richard Crane, Erika Peters, Georgia Schmidt. A haunted house, complete with a missing landlord (a former circus showman) and frightened guests, turns out to be inhabited by a group of circus freaks who don't wish to leave, playing upon the house's reputation to frighten people away. In the end, however, they do decide to try it again in the "real" world. • *House of the Damned* "introduced" gigantic actor Richard Kiel (it was his fourth film, at least), later to achieve fame as James Bond's arch-enemy, "Jaws."

The Hunchback of Notre Dame (1923; Universal) D: Wallace Worsley. P: Carl Laemmle. S: Edward T. Lowe. C: Robert Newhard, Tony Korman. Cast: Lon Chaney, Ernest Torrence, Patsy Ruth Miller, Norman Kerry, Kate Lester. Lon Chaney plays the simian-styled hunchback "Quasimodo," whose ill-fated love for a gypsy girl leads him to protect her from the girl's ruthless guardian. • It took Universal a full year to prepare the enormous sets for *Hunchback,* a cast of 3,500 people was employed. The story was plotted on drawing boards for six months before any footage was shot. At the time of its release, this $1,250,000 film was the most expensive movie ever made. • Since the film was shot exclusively at Universal City, an exact replica of the Notre Dame

Cathedral in Paris had to be built. The massive structure stood over 200 feet high and 150 feet wide and stretched over an area of 6,000 square feet. • For the Grand Ball sequence of Louis XI, 2,000 extras were forced to rehearse for 48 hours until director Wallace Worsley was satisfied with the action. Radio amplifiers came in handy in giving special instructions to the multitude of extras. • The hump that Lon Chaney wore on his back weighed 72 pounds. He also wore a light-weight leather harness which joined a breast plate and a back plate in such a manner that it made it impossible to stand erect. The harness was hidden by a rubber suit covered with animal hair. Chaney also wore false teeth and a wig during the production, and was required to wear this painful getup for 12 continuous weeks of shooting.

The Hunchback of Notre Dame (1939; RKO) D: William Dieterle. P: Pandro S. Berman. S: Sonya Levien. C: Joseph H. August. Cast: Charles Laughton, Maureen O'Hara, Edmond O'Brien, Thomas Mitchell, Cedric Hardwicke, George Zucco. A gypsy girl is framed for murder by a Bishop, then rescued by Quasimodo, the hunchback who gives her sanctuary at the Notre Dame Cathedral. When the beggars come to save the girl from hanging, Quasimodo mistakenly takes them for a lynch mob and hurls stones and dumps hot liquid upon them. In the finale, the girls' sentence is pardoned by the King (after learning of the clergyman's treachery), and Quasimodo is left sitting atop Notre Dame with the stone gargoyles. ¶ "Why was I not made of stone like thee?" • Charles Laughton's hunchback makeup consisted of latex compositions covering more than one-fourth of his face. These applications took three hours to put on and one hour to remove. • This film was nominated for Academy Awards in Sound Recording (John Aalberg) and Musical Score (Alfred Newman).

The Hunchback of Notre Dame (1956; Allied Artists; France/Italy) D: Jean Delannoy. P: Robert Hakim, Raymond Hakim. S: Jean Aurenche, Jacques Prévert. C: Michel Kelber. Cast: Anthony Quinn, Gina Lollobrigida, Alain Cuny, Jean Danet, Jean Tissier, Robert Hirsch. The tragic hunchback of Notre Dame protects the girl he loves by pouring molten lead on an angry mob, but in the end dies of grief when he finds her dead body. ¶ "Years later, the skeletons were found locked in an embrace. When an attempt was made to separate them, they crumbled into dust."

The Hunchback of the Morgue (1972; Janus/Eva Films; Spain) (also *The Rue Morgue Massacre*). D/S: Javier Aguirre. P: Francisco Lara Polop. S: Paul Naschy, Alberto S. Insua. C: Raul Perez Cubero. Cast: Paul Naschy, Rossana Yanni, Alberto Dalbes, Maria Perschy, Vic Winner. The hunchbacked employee of a hospital morgue (Paul Naschy) goes after the students who want to dissect the body of a girl that he loves (she died of tuberculosis). • In one sequence inside the underground crypt where Naschy has taken the corpse of the girl, he has to fight off a myriad of hungry rats. The actor was actually bitten several times in the scene. • Paul Naschy (real name of Jacinto Molina) won the Best Acting Award that year at the Paris Convention of Fantastic Cinema for his performance as Gotho, the hunchback.

Iguana (1985; Imperial Entertainment) D: Monte Hellman. S: David M. Zehr, Steven Gaydos. C: José Maria Civit. Cast: Everett McGill, Monte Hellman, Maru Valdivielso, Michael Madsen, Joseph Culp, Tim Ryan. A deformed seaman, oppressed by his shipmates, gets even.

The Incredible Shrinking Man (1957) (see SHRINKAGE). Grant Williams plays the incredible Scott Carey, a man dwindling in size from radioactive exposure. In one sequence, Carey, who has become a media "freak" himself, wanders off into the night and stumbles across a side show carnival featuring other unfortunates. ¶ "I felt puny and absurd. A ludicrous midget. . . . I loathed myself, our home, the caricature my life with Lou had become. I had to get out."

It Lives Again (1978; Warner Bros.) D/P/S: Larry Cohen. C: Fenton Hamilton. Cast: Frederic Forrest, Kathleen Lloyd, John P. Ryan, John Marley, Andrew Duggan. In this first sequel to *It's Alive,* the original father and doctor aid in stopping other mutant baby pregnancies caused by the experimental drug. The story focuses on a new couple, who attempt to save their newborn "mama's little killer." • *It Lives Again* is distinguished as being the last full musical credit received by the famous cinema composer, Bernard Herrmann, who died a few years earlier. His work was pieced together by Laurie Johnson and made into a final finished score for this film.

It's a Small World (1959; Eagle Lion) D: William Castle. P: Peter Scully. S: Otto Schreiber. Cast: Paul Dale, Will Geer, Steve Brodie, Lorraine Miller. A midget struggles to find his way in a world that thinks of him as a freak. • This was one of William Castle's

Quasimodo (Charles Laughton) ponders his wretched existence for a moment in the lavishly produced 1939 version of The Hunchback of Notre Dame.

early efforts and its box office failure prompted him to delve into a more profitable market area—horror exploitation films.

It's Alive (1973; Warner Bros.) D/P/S: Larry Cohen. C: Fenton Hamilton. Cast: John Ryan, Sharon Farrell, Andrew Duggan, Guy Stockwell, James Dixon. A woman taking new drugs during her pregnancy gives birth to a freakish homicidal baby with fangs, who promptly murders all the attending medical personnel in the delivery room and goes on a rampage through Los Angeles. ¶ Ad-line: "Whatever it is, *It's alive!*" • This is the first killer mutant baby film (a dubious distinction), and spawned two sequels—*It Lives Again* (1978) and *It's Alive 3: Island of the Alive* (1987). • When originally released in 1973, Warner Bros.

failed to see the film's potential, according to filmmaker Larry Cohen. They only made 55 prints, so of course the film did not do well. Then in 1977, there was a changeover in Warner's management, and Cohen induced them to re-release it. Eight hundred and fifty prints were struck and the film became a nationwide hit (as well as spawning a quick sequel the following year—which Warners did the same thing to, again).

It's Alive 3: Island of the Alive (1987; Warner Bros.) D/S: Larry Cohen. P: Paul Stader. C: Daniel Pearl. Cast: Michael Moriarty, Karen Black, Laurene Landon, Gerrit Graham, James Dixon, Neal Israel, MacDonald Carey. The killer mutant babies from *It Lives Again* (1978) are now man-sized mutant adolescents who have been transported to a deserted island. Father Michael Moriarty comes to a sympathetic understanding with his hideous offspring and helps them escape the island and persecution. • The now-adult mutant babies all die at the film's end from the common disease of measles. • *It's Alive 3: Island of the Alive* was shot (in four weeks) virtually back to back with another Larry Cohen film, *A Return to Salem's Lot.* • The title island is actually the Hawaiian island of Kauai.

The Kindred (1986; FM Entertainment) D: Stephen Carpenter, Jeffrey Obrow. P: Jeffrey Obrow. S: Stephen Carpenter, Jeffrey Obrow, John Penney, Earl Ghaffari, Joseph Stefano. Cast: David Allen Brooks, Amanda Pays, Talia Balsam, Rod Steiger, Kim Hunter. A molecular biologist accidentally creates a half-human monster from her son's living tissue during a genetic experiment. The genetic freak, which has tentacles and continues to grow larger, is kept in the basement, but has plans for his human brother. Rod Steiger plays a crazy scientist who wants to alter human evolution. • Writer Joseph Stefano is best known for being one of the creative geniuses behind the "Outer Limits" television series, and writing the screenplay for Hitchcock's *Psycho* (1960).

The Man Who Laughs (1928; Universal) D: Paul Leni. P: Carl Laemmle. S: J. Grubb Alexander. C: Gilbert Warrenton. Cast: Conrad Veidt, Mary Philbin, Olga Baclanova, Josephine Crowell, George Siegmann, Brandon Hurst, Cesare Gravina. The son of a Scottish nobleman is disfigured as punishment for the political crimes of his father. With his mouth now fixed in a perpetual hideous grin, he becomes a sideshow freak. Later, however, his rightful title is reinstated, and he finds love with a blind girl. ¶ "What a lucky clown you are—you don't have to rub off your laugh." • During the 1960s, Kirk Douglas planned to film a remake of this picture, but scrapped the idea after finally seeing a copy of the original. • Russian actress Olga Baclanova also starred in the ultimate "freak" film, *Freaks* (1932). • Star Conrad Veidt died at the young age of 50, on a golf course across from 20th Century-Fox studios.

The Maze (1953; Allied Artists) (see ANIMAL GIANTS). Richard Carlson inherits a Scottish castle and title, along with the 200-year-old relative inhabiting the estate—the real lord of the castle—who had the misfortune to be born resembling a giant frog. ¶ "For over two centuries he endured the torment of knowing he was a monster and feeling he was a man."

The Miracle Man (1919; Par Artcraft) D: George Leone Tucker. Cast: Lon Chaney. Lon Chaney, Sr., plays a fake cripple known as "Frog," whose limbs are miraculously cured at the climax. • Director George Leone Tucker had initially wanted a professional contortionist to play the part but couldn't find one who could act to his satisfaction. When Chaney's turn came to test for the role, Lon used an old childhood trick of double crossing his legs to achieve the desired effect of a twisted man. He simply unraveled himself when the time came for the miraculous healing.

Mr. Sardonicus (1961; Columbia) D/P: William Castle. S: Ray Russell. C: Burnett Guffey. Cast: Ronald Lewis, Guy Rolfe, Oscar Homolka, Audrey Dalton, Vladimir Sokoloff, Erika Peters, Lorna Hanson. A young man attempting to retrieve a winning lottery ticket from his dead father's grave is transformed into a perpetually grinning freak by his own guilt and fear. ¶ "His affliction came not from God above nor from the fiend below, but from within his own heart, his own brain, his own soul." • Director William Castle, the king of horror gimmickry, came up with a "thumbs up" or "thumbs down" "Punishment Poll" card with which the audience could decide the fate of Sardonicus. Castle only had one ending filmed, however, and so banked on the viewers' natural inclination to choose the "thumbs down," figuring they would always want the most terrible form of justice for the cruel Sardonicus. The "Punishment Poll" cards were luminous, and glowed rather brightly in the darkened theater. • *Mr. Sardonicus* is based on a Ray Russell story which appeared in *Playboy*'s January 1961 issue. • A review by *Variety* magazine said of the film: "Those who dig the shock for shock's sake approach are apt to feel a little cheated because William Castle has woven the tale of *Mr. Sardonicus* with rather more intelligence than is usually accorded the genre, and the moments aimed at making audiences recoil are well spaced and story integrated with relative plausibility." • Paul Leni's 1928 masterpiece, *The Man Who Laughs,* was the forerunner of this weird grinning fiend, only the character in the original was cast in an entirely sympathetic light.

The Monster Maker (1944; PRC) D: Sam Newfield. P: Sigmund Neufeld. S: Pierre Gendron, Martin Mooney. C: Robert Cline. Cast: J. Carrol Naish, Ralph Morgan, Wanda McKay, Glenn Strange, Tala Birell. A medical scientist (J. Carrol Naish), who has found a cure for the feature-distorting disease of acromegaly, falls in love with the daughter of a concert pianist. When her father orders the lascivious doctor to leave her alone, Naish fiendishly injects the objecting parent with acromegaly. Since Naish is the only one who can cure this hideous disease, he plans on forcing the afflicted man's daughter to marry him. His nefarious scheme is finally foiled by his own assistant, and in the finale, the father's health is restored after villain Naish has been dispatched. ¶ "Doesn't it look as if my fingers were thicker? My feet too, feel enlarged. All my shoes feel tight." • J. Carrol Naish starred as a freak of sorts himself — a hunchback — in *House of Frankenstein* that same year.

Mutations (1972; Columbia; U.K.) (also *Freakmaker*). D: Jack Cardiff. P: Robert Weinbach. S: Garson Raye. C: Paul Beeson. Cast: Donald Pleasence, Michael Dunn, Tom Baker, Julie Ege, Jill Haworth, Brad Harris. A scientist produces animal and plant mutations which include a lizard lady, a frog boy, a human pin cushion, a monkey woman, and a boy pretzel. • Real-life dwarf actor Michael Dunn, who had a recurring role on TV's "Wild, Wild West," died shortly after this film was completed, making this his last screen role. • Tom Baker, who played Dunn's assistant in the film, was television's "Dr. Who." • British-born director Jack Cardiff was a child actor and famous cinematographer. He won an Academy Award for his photography on *Black Narcissus* (1947), and he also shot the classic dance film, *The Red Shoes* (1948).

Nightbreed (1990; Morgan Creek/20th Century-Fox) D/S: Clive Barker. P: Gabriella Martinelli. C: Robin Vidgeon. Cast: Craig Sheffer, Anne Bobby, David Cronenberg, Danny Elfman. A subterranean world called "Midian" is inhabited by a host of freakish creatures which only come out at night. ¶ "Everybody has a secret face." • Respected genre director David Cronenberg (*Scanners,* 1980; *The Fly,* 1986; *Dead Ringers,* 1988; etc.) turned actor for this film, playing the part of a vicious serial killer drawn to Midian.

The Offspring (1987) (see ANTHOLOGIES). In the third segment, a glass eater in a freak show falls in love with a local girl. The carnival's female owner, who is also a Voodoo priestess, casts a spell on him, making everything he's eaten explode from within. The girlfriend is then trapped in the show, taking his place as a human pin cushion.

Ratboy (1987; Warner Bros.) D: Sondra Locke. P: Fritz Manes. S: Rob Thompson. C: Bruce Surtees. Cast: Sondra Locke, Robert Townsend, Christopher Hewett, Larry Hankin, Sydney Lassick, Gerrit Graham. A boy whose face resembles that of a rat is captured and then exploited. ¶ "Mister Ratboy? Are you all right? Hey listen eh, all I want is a quick interview, five, six minutes tops." • Rotund comedian Louie Anderson appears as a cop in this film. • The Ratboy's design was credited to modern makeup master, Rick Baker.

She Freak (1966; Sonney-Friedman) D: Byron Mabe. P/S: David F. Friedman. C: Bill Troiano. Cast: Claire Brennan, Lee Raymond, Lynn Courtney, Bill McKinney, Van Teen, Felix Silla. A conniving woman marries the owner of a freak show, then has him killed and takes it over, only to become the victim of the freaks' revenge (à la *Freaks,* 1932). • The producer, David F. Friedman, was a frequent partner of early goremeister Herschell Gordon Lewis (on films like *Blood Feast,* 1962; and *2000 Maniacs,* 1964).

Sisters (1973; AIP) D: Brian De Palma. P: Edward R. Pressman. S: Brian De Palma, Louisa Rose. C: Gregory Sandor. Cast: Margot Kidder, Charles Durning, Jennifer Salt, Bill Finley, Lisle Wilson, Barnard Hughes. Margot Kidder stars as a surviving Siamese twin who, at times, is dominated by the psychopathic personality of her dead sister. Charles Durning plays a private detective hired to solve a murder committed by Kidder. ¶ "It's all so obvious this girl is protecting someone. But the murderess is someone this girl knows. She was shorter, and had a, a twisted face, and stringy hair and was having a terrible fit of some kind." • Famous New York composer Bernard

Herrmann supplied the musical score for this film. On December 24, 1975,he passed away in his sleep after conducting that very evening. Herrmann was credited with the film score of another "freak" film—the sequel, *It Lives Again* (1978)—three years after his death.

The Spider Woman Strikes Back (1946) (see PLANTS). Gale Sondergaard is the "Spider-woman," who with the help of her malformed assistant (Rondo Hatton, a real-life sufferer from the disease of acromegaly), has women murdered for the blood needed to grow her poisonous flowers.

SSSSSSS (1973) (see SNAKES). Dirk Benedict is transformed into a snake-man by Strother Martin, ending up as an exhibit in a sideshow.

Terror in the Wax Museum (1973) (see WAX MUSEUMS). A deformed hunchback mute who has lived within a wax museum for years gets tossed (by a Jack the Ripper lookalike) into a bubbling vat at the climax, giving a young Scotland Yard inspector just enough time to rescue the girl and solve the murder mystery.

Transmutations (1986; Empire Pictures) (also *Underworld*). D: George Pavlou. P: Kevin Attew, Don Hawkins. S: Clive Barker, James Caplin. C: Sidney Macartney. Cast: Denholm Elliott, Steven Berkoff, Larry Lamb, Miranda Richardson, Art Malik, Nicola Cowper, Irina Brok. A sinister biochemist creates a subhuman species of deformed freaks that take refuge underneath the city. The transmutated freaks, dependent upon drugs made by the evil biochemist, abduct an immune prostitute who may hold the key to an antidote which will free them from their hideous condition. An adventurer comes to rescue the girl and learns the horrible truth.

The Unearthly (1957) (see MAD SCIENTISTS). John Carradine is a mad glandular scientist experimenting on human beings with freakish results. ¶ "You deny you mutilated innocent human beings, you transformed them into creatures so hideous they'd be better off dead?" • The makeup applied to the numerous scientific "freaks" was created by Harry Thomas.

The Unholy Three (1925; MGM) D/P: Tod Browning. S: Waldemar Young. C: David Kesson. Cast: Lon Chaney, Mae Busch, Matt Moore, Victor MacLaglen, Harry Earles. This Lon Chaney vehicle is a silent drama about three circus freaks who become criminals. ¶ "That's all there is to life, just a little laugh, a little tear."

The Unholy Three (1930; MGM) D: Jack Conway. S: J. C. Nugent, Elliot Nugent. C: Percy Hilburn. Cast: Lon Chaney, Lila Lee, Elliott Nugent, Harry Earles, Ivan Linow, John Miljan. Three circus performers—Hercules the strongman, a midget, and a ventriloquist (played by Lon Chaney) turn to crime when the circus they appear in closes down. ¶ "That's us! The unholy three. Understand, from tonight on we fade out, there'll be no Hercules, no Tweedle Dee, no Echo." • This is a remake of the 1925 version, again starring Lon Chaney and midget Harry Earles. • "Thank you doctor, thank you," was the first sentence uttered in speaking films by the great silent horror star, Lon Chaney. This picture proved to be Chaney's first—and last—talkie (he died of throat cancer shortly afterwards). • Chaney was battling the cancer during the filming of this picture, and a month after it was released, Lon Chaney, the legend, was dead. • Just prior to his death, MGM had offered Chaney a five-year star contract at the then-unheard-of sum of $10,000 a week.

The Unknown (1927; MGM) D: Tod Browning. S: Waldemar Young. C: Merritt B. Gerstad. Cast: Lon Chaney, Joan Crawford, Norman Kerry, Nick de Ruiz, John George, Frank Lanning. Lon Chaney, Sr., plays a man who voluntarily has both his arms amputated to win the love of the heroine (because she dislikes being touched). • Chaney wore a tight straitjacket to bind his arms to his side in this film. Unfortunately, this setup contributed to his ever-worsening back condition, and in the November issue of *Photoplay,* 1930, he said, "I can't play these crippled roles anymore. That trouble with my spine is worse every time I do one, and it's beginning to worry me." • Chaney said of his role: "I contrived to make myself look like an armless man, not simply to shock and horrify you, but merely to bring to the screen a dramatic story of an armless man, or rather one who pretended to be so. I play unusual characters not for the sake of applying grotesque makeup but always to advance the drama of a startling plot." • Horror legend Boris Karloff said of Chaney: "A fine actor. I think it is a dead certainty I wouldn't be sitting here now if Chaney had lived and done *Frankenstein.*"

Where East Is East (1929; MGM) D/P: Tod Browning. S: Richard Schayer. C: Henry Sharp. Cast: Lon Chaney, Lupe Velez, Estelle Taylor, Lloyd Hughes, Louis Stern. A man who traps wild animals for a living (Lon Chaney) has become disfigured because of the many maulings he has suffered in his experiences. His unsympathetic wife leaves him, which drives Chaney into a rage, and he sets an ape out after her.

A Woman's Face (1941; MGM) D: George Cukor. P: Victor Saville. S: Donald Ogden Stewart. C: Robert Planck. Cast: Joan Crawford, Melvyn Douglas, Conrad Veidt, Osa Massen, Reginald Owen, Marjorie Main. A horribly disfigured woman turns to crime. • Joan Crawford, born Lucille LeSuer, had previously appeared in another "freak" film — *The Unknown* (1927), starring Lon Chaney.

Young Frankenstein (1974) (see FRANKEN-STEINS — FURTHER FRANKENSTEINS). Marty Feldman plays "I-gor," the bug-eyed hunchbacked assistant of Dr. "Fronk-en-steen."

Futures on Earth

The FUTURES ON EARTH section has been divided up into two separate subsections. The first, AFTER THE BOMB, deals with the explosion of the atomic bomb, its immediate aftereffects, and life in the short term post-nuclear war future. The devastating results of a nuclear holocaust have taken many forms in the cinema. There are the realistic portrayals, such as the big-budgeted *On the Beach* (1959), the smaller-scaled but still effective *Five* (1951) and the hard-hitting *Testament* (1983). Aside from these horrible realities, there is also room for the imaginative fare, such as the three-eyed horned mutant seen menacing some of the Earth's last survivors in the Roger Corman picture, *Day the World Ended* (1956). Though often set in present day, our reasoning for including this particular type of film in the FUTURES ON EARTH section is that there has not yet been a full-scale atomic war. Hence, any depiction of such would necessarily describe some point in the future.

The second subsection, UTOPIAS AND DYSTOPIAS, also features films which depict a future that was directly affected by atomic war. Unlike the movies in AFTER THE BOMB, however, these are set in a far distant future, as opposed to the days and first weeks directly after the blast. UTOPIA AND DYSTOPIA films deal with new future societies and or the long-term coping necessary after some form of world-shattering holocaust. Hopefully genre fans will be able to distinguish the difference and the necessity for this sub-division. In addition, many films in the UTOPIAS AND DYSTOPIAS section deal with futures on Earth that were not brought about by atomic war. Sometimes the future vision is shaped by viral plagues (*Dead Man Walking,* 1988), or naturally occurring sociological phenomena (*1984,* 1984). Whatever the future-shaping event might be, the movies in this latter section have an established setting years or even centuries from today. Whether this world will, in reality, become a peaceful utopia or a nightmarish dystopia remains to be seen. While most cinematic treatments pessimistically predict the latter, one can only hope (and strive for) the former.

After the Bomb

Damnation Alley (1977; 20th Century–Fox) D: Jack Smight. P: Jerome M. Zeitman, Paul Maslansky. S: Alan Sharp, Lukas Heller. C: Harry Stradling, Jr. Cast: Jan-Michael Vincent, George Peppard, Dominique Sanda, Paul Winfield, Jackie Earle Haley, Kip Niven. Four survivors of the nuclear holocaust agree to transport a plague serum across the wasteland infested with giant bugs. • The story is based upon Roger Zelazny's novel of the same name.

Day the World Ended (1956; American Releasing Corporation) D/P: Roger Corman. S: Lou Rusoff. C: Jock Feindel. Cast: Richard Denning, Lori Nelson, Paul Birch, Mike "Touch" Connors, Adele Jergens, Ray-

After the Day the World Ended *(1956), a three-eyed scaly mutant (monster-maker Paul Blaisdell wearing his own suit) stands over Lori Nelson, one of seven uncontaminated survivors hiding out in a canyon geographically shielded from the resultant radioactive fallout.*

mond Hatton, Paul Dobov, Jonathan Haze. This outrageous end of the world story features a group of people hiding out in a sheltered valley after the blast. The radioactive fallout makes mutant monsters out of the unprotected people and animals in the area. One such three-eyed creature stalks the canyon in an attempt to get its claws on heroine Lori Nelson. ¶ "There are two forms of life fighting for survival here in this valley, and only one of them can win. It's got to be us." • Mike Connors, who kills his barfly girlfriend in this picture, is more popularly known as the TV detective, "Mannix." • Adele Jurgens, who utters the immortal lines: "What's my renchon count? Read me daddy!" previously appeared in *Abbott and Costello Meet the Invisible Man* (1951). She married Glenn (*The Amazing Colossal Man*) Langan in 1949. • Monster-maker Paul Blaisdell played the three-eyed mutant in the film. Blaisdell nearly drowned

in his own monster suit (affectionately named "Marty") after shooting the creature's death scene in a rainstorm. Apparently it was so hot in the suit that Paul remained on the ground soaking in the water after the scene was completed in an attempt to cool off. Problem was, he couldn't get up, and feared he might drown as the water began to fill up inside the mutant head. Fortunately he was rescued moments later, but if he hadn't had anyone close by he might have ended up with one of the world's most unusual obituaries.

Dr. Strangelove, or How I Learned to Stop Worrying and Love the Bomb (1964; Columbia; U.K.) D/P: Stanley Kubrick. S: Stanley Kubrick, Terry Southern, Peter George. C: Gilbert Taylor. Cast: Peter Sellers, George C. Scott, Sterling Hayden, Keenan Wynn, Slim Pickens, Peter Bull. A demented Air Force general orders a nuclear attack on the Soviet Union. Attempts to recall all the planes fail—one gets through and touches off World War III. ¶ "Mr. President, I'm not saying we wouldn't get our hair mussed, but I do say no more than ten to 20 million killed, tops! . . . depending on the breaks." • Originally, director/writer Stanley Kubrick intended the film to be a serious dramatization, then changed his mind, utilizing black comedy to drive his message home. In Alexander Walker's book, *Stanley Kubrick Directs,* Kubrick said, "As I tried to build the detail for a scene I found myself tossing away what seemed to me to be very truthful insights because I was afraid the audience would laugh. After a few weeks I realized that these incongruous bits of reality were closer to the truth than anything else I was able to imagine. And it was at this point I decided to treat the story as nightmare comedy." • Peter Sellers received an Academy Award nomination for Best Actor for his trilogy of roles in this film. He played a British Air Force officer, the President, and the title character (a German advisor to the President). *Dr. Strangelove* also received nominations for Best Picture, Best Director, and Best Screenplay. • Slim Pickens plays Major Kong, the redneck Texan who rides his falling H-bomb rodeo style down into Russia. Pickens had much real life experience around rodeos as a clown before moving on to pictures (mostly Westerns) in 1950. His real name was Louis Bert Lindley, Jr.

Doomsday Machine (1967) (see SPACE TRAVEL). (also *Escape from Planet Earth*). The Chinese set off a nuclear "doomsday device" which destroys most of the life on Earth. Two spaceships which escaped the destruction head for Venus, where they encounter a collective intelligence which sends them on to an "even greater journey."

The Final War (1962; Toho; Japan) (also *The Last War*). D: Shue Matsubayashi. P: Tomoyuki Tanaka. S: Toshio Yasumi, Takeshi Kimura. C: Rokuro Nishigaki. Cast: Frankie Sakai, Nobuko Otowa, Akira Takarada, Yuriko Hoshi, Yumi Shirakawa. The final nuclear holocaust between the superpowers erupts when Cold War tensions snap after an aircraft collision.

Five (1951; Columbia) D/P/S: Arch Oboler. C: Sid Lubow, Louis Clyde Stoumen. Cast: William Phipps, Susan Douglas, James Anderson, Charles Lampkin, Earl Lee. Five survivors of a nuclear holocaust deal with racism, radioactive poisoning, and jealousy over the last woman (Susan Douglas). ¶ Catchy promotional slogan: *"One—One girl . . . the last left on Earth! Two—*

Two hours of the most spellbinding entertainment ever filmed! *Three*—A story of the three elemental passions . . . love, hate, fear! *Four*—Four men . . . alone with the knowledge that in all the world there is only one woman! *Five!"* • Director/writer Arch Oboler used to script radio plays in the 1930s before directing his first picture, *Bewitched,* in 1945. He is also the creator of the first 3-D film, *Bwana Devil* (1952). • The entire production was filmed on Arch Oboler's own ranch, high in the Santa Monica Mountains of California. The lodge in which the five survivors live in the film is part of Oboler's own home, designed by Frank Lloyd Wright. • The general idea of *Five* originated way back to the year 1938, when Oboler wrote a radio show for Bette Davis called "The Word." He then expanded the show, which told of a couple alone on Earth, into a feature film script (adding the nuclear element) while he was in Africa making a movie. • According to Sid Pink, who eventually picked up and distributed the film, *Five* bombed on its initial regional release. Then Pink put together a program which would televise the film's "gala premier" in Hollywood. With the aid of the fledgling small-screen medium (and an appearance at the premier by actress Bette Davis) *Five* became a huge success.

In the Year 2889 (1966; Azalea Pictures/ AIP-TV) D/P: Larry Buchanan. S: Harold Hoffman. C: Robert C. Jessup. Cast: Paul Peterson, Quinn O'Hara, Charla Doherty, Neil Fletcher, Billy Thurman. This uncredited remake of Roger Corman's *Day the World Ended* (1956) follows a group of atomic war survivors who hide out in a sheltered valley and face mutant monsters. ¶ "Down through the ages the prophets have forewarned us that in one day thousands of years of accomplishments could be wiped away by the destructive hand of power. Now that day has come." • Actor Paul Peterson is well known for his role as the all-American teen on the "Donna Reed" TV show.

Invasion U.S.A. (1953; Columbia) D: Alfred E. Green. P: Albert Zugsmith, Robert Smith. S: Robert Smith. C: John L. Russell, Jr. Cast: Gerald Mohr, Peggie Castle, Dan O'Herlihy, Robert Bice, Phyllis Coates, Tom Kennedy. Dan O'Herlihy hypnotizes a group of bar patrons into believing the Russians have initiated an atomic assault. • The people who listen begin to commit suicide, and one does so by jumping off a skyscraper. • The pictured used liberal stock footage of World War II for scenes involving the bombing of contemporary cities. • *Invasion U.S.A.* was shot in seven days on a budget of $127,000, and brought in profits amounting to $950,000.

The Last Man (1968; France) D/S: Charles Bitsch. P: Dovidas Annouchka. C: Pierre L'homme. Cast: Sofia Torkeli, Corinne Brill, Jean-Claude Bouillon. A man, his wife, and another woman emerge from a cave expedition to discover the world has been rubbed out by nuclear warfare. He begins to lust after the "other woman," then dies of radiation exposure.

The Last Woman on Earth (1960; Filmgroup/Vistascope) D/P: Roger Corman. S: Robert Towne. C: Jacques Marquette. Cast: Antony Carbone, Betsy Jones-Moreland, Edward Wain (Robert Towne). Three survivors of the nuclear holocaust fight over ideals and possession of the last woman. ¶ "I killed him. Will we never learn?" • This Roger Corman picture features one of Robert Towne's first scripts. He later went on to win an Oscar for his *Chinatown* screenplay (1974). The script for *Last Woman* was unfinished at the time shooting began, so Corman had Towne fly to Puerto Rico (where it was being filmed) in order to finish the script during the shoot. Corman could not afford to fly Towne down solely as a writer, so he also cast him as an actor. Towne plays the pivotal role of "Martin," one of the two males who finally battle for *The Last Woman on Earth*. So Robert Towne acted during the day, and worked on the script at night. • While filming *Last Woman* and *Battle of Blood Island* back-to-back on location in Puerto Rico, Corman decided to make a third film as well. The quickie he came up with was called *The Creature from the Haunted Sea*.

On the Beach (1959; United Artists) D/P: Stanley Kramer. S: John Paxton, James Lee Barrett. C: Giuseppe Rotunno. Cast: Gregory Peck, Ava Gardner, Fred Astaire, Anthony Perkins, Donna Anderson, Guy Doleman. Survivors of a nuclear holocaust await their end on the shores of Australia.

Panic in the Year Zero (1962; AIP) D: Ray Milland. P: Arnold Houghland, Lou Rusoff. S: Jay Simms, John Morton. C: Gilbert Warrenton. Cast: Ray Milland, Frankie Avalon, Jean Hagen, Mary Mitchell, Joan Freeman, Richard Garland. In this interesting cinematic manual for thermonuclear survivalists, a family takes refuge from the crumbling post-war anarchy in an isolated meadow, but encounter a small band of vicious teen thugs. ¶ "When civilization gets civilized again, I'll rejoin." • Direc-

tor/star Ray Milland, who began his screen career under the name of Spike Milland, won an Oscar for his performance as an alcoholic in *The Lost Weekend* (1945).

The People Who Own the Dark (1975; Newcal; Spain) D: Leon Klimovsky. P: Robert Moreno. S: Vincent Aranda, Harry Narunsky. Cast: Maria Perschy, Tony Kendall, Paul Naschy. When a nuclear war begins, everyone in a small country village goes blind except for a small group of hedonistic party-goers living it up in the protected cellar of a beautiful country house at the time. It then becomes a battle between the horde of now-homicidal blind villagers and the handful of unscathed survivors squabbling amongst themselves while the blind lay siege to the house. ¶ "Perhaps one day the world will start to be a different one, a better one."

Radioactive Dreams (1986) P: Albert Pyun, Thomas Karnowski. Cast: Michael Dudikoff, John Stockwell, Lisa Blount, George Kennedy, Don Murray. A pair of missile site workers dig their way up to the post holocaust surface and get hold of the keys that can launch the last remaining missile. They are pursued by a plethora of strange characters with names from famous old detective mystery movies.

Rat (1960; Yugoslavia) (also *War*). D: Velko Bulajic. S: Cesare Zavattini. C: Kresko Grcevic. Cast: Anton Vrdoljak, Eva Krzyzewski, Ita Rina, Janez Vrhovic, Tana Mascarelli. A marriage is interrupted by a nuclear blast, and the sights they see afterwards drive the bride insane.

Testament (1983; CFI) D/P: Lynee Littman. P: Jonathan Bernstein. S: John Sacret Young. C: Steven Poster. Cast: Jane Alexander, William Devane, Ross Harris, Roxana Zal, Lukas Haas. This is a realistic, gripping account of the effects of post war radiation on the people and families of a small town in America. • Jane Alexander received an Academy Award nomination for her performance. • The film is based upon an adaptation of Carol Amen's magazine story, "The Last Testament."

The War Game (1966; BBC-TV; U.K.) D/P/S: Peter Watkins. C: Peter Bartlett. Cast: Narration by Michael Aspel, Dick Graham. This is a feature-length documentary charting the effects of a nuclear attack on the people of Kent, England. • The BBC actually banned the film from television because of its horrific realism (depicting disfigured casualties, radiation poisoning, and police execution squads). • The picture won an Oscar in 1966 for Best Documentary.

The World, the Flesh, and the Devil (1959; MGM) D/S: Ranald MacDougall. P: George Englund. C: Harold J. Marzorati. Cast: Harry Belafonte, Inger Stevens, Mel Ferrer. Three survivors in post-war New York (a black man, a white girl, and a white racist male) wander about the city and get worked up, before working it out. ¶ "Come out! Come out! You're all crazy! Why ya hiding? What are you hiding from me for?

What did I do? I know you're there, you're staring at me. I can feel you all staring at me! Come out!"

Year of the Cannibals (1971; AIP; Italy) D/S: Liliana Cavani. P: Enzo Doria. C: Giulio Albonico. Cast: Britt Ekland, Pierre Clementi, Delia Boccardo, Tomás Milian, Francesco Leonetti. The Italian government fights rebel survivors after World War III takes place.

Utopias and Dystopias

After the Fall of New York (1984; Impex; Italy/France) D/S: Martin Dolman. P: Luciano Martino. S: Julian Berry, Gabriel Rossini. C: Giancarlo Ferrando. Cast: Michael Sopkiw, Valentine Monnier, Roman Geer, George Eastman, Louis Ecclesia. In the world of the future, the "Pan American Confederation" sends a man out to search for the last fertile woman left on the planet.

America 3000 (1986) D/S: David Englebach. Cast: Chuck Wagner, Lawrene Landon, Steve Malovic. Nine hundred years after a nuclear holocaust, a band of warrior women keep men as slaves. • This two million dollar film, though an American production, was filmed in Israel.

Battle for the Planet of the Apes (1973) (SEE PLANET OF THE APES SERIES). More problems on the post-atomic monkey planet: an ape faction wants to create cultural equality between apes and humans—a noble idea—but a band of "Gorilla" forces and mutant humans are against it.

Battletruck (1982; New World) (also *Warlords of the 21st Century*). D/S: Harley Cockliss. P: Lloyd Phillips, Rob Whitehouse. S: Irving Austin, John Beech. C: Chris Menges. Cast: Michael Beck, Annie McEnroe, James Wainwright, John Ratzenberger, Bruno Lawrence. After "oil wars" have left the world in chaos, a biker decides to join a band of people who believe the new world must be rebuilt around alternative energy sources. Like Mad Max, he eventually takes on a ruthless gang and their powerful "battletruck."

Beneath the Planet of the Apes (1969) (see PLANET OF THE APES SERIES). This first sequel to *Planet of the Apes* has astronaut James Franciscus arriving in the post-holocaust Earth of our future (in which apes have become the dominant species) to discover what happened to the previous expedition led by Charlton Heston. He encounters what's left of the intelligent human race—a group of hideously scarred mutants living

in the underground ruins of New York City who worship the last doomsday bomb as a god. ¶ "Glory be to the Bomb and to the holy fallout, as it was in the beginning is now and ever shall be, world without end, Amen."

Beyond the Universe (1981; Gold Key Entertainment) D: Robert Emenegger, Steven Posner, Seth Marshall. P/S: Allan Sandler. Cast: David Ladd, Jacqueline Ray, Henry Darrow, John Dewey-Carter. One hundred years after the nuclear holocaust, scientists of the future experiment with crystals to harness the power of the mind in an attempt to find a solution to the dying planet Earth and the oxygen crises. ¶ "Prepare yourselves for the destruction that is to come, but fear not for we shall be together in the rebirth that is coming."

Blade Runner (1982) (see ROBOTS). This futuristic cop drama has Harrison Ford trying to track down and destroy renegade androids who only wish to live out their lives in peace and freedom.

The Blood of Heroes (1989; New Line Cinema/King's Road Entertainment) D/S: David Peoples. P: Charles Roven. C: David Eggby. Cast: Rutger Hauer, Joan Chen, Vincent Phillip D'Onofrio, Anna Katarina, Delroy Lindo, Hugh Keays-Byrne, Gandhi Macintyre, Max Fairchild, Justin Monjo. In the distant future, man has forgotten the "miraculous technology of the 20th century" and the "cruel wars that followed" and has sunk into another "dark age." Out of this has sprung The Game, in which a team of warriors, called "juggers," battle to place a dog skull on a stake. Rutger Hauer is a jugger ousted from The League in the city for insulting a noble, returned to face the ultimate challenge with his new team. ¶ "I've broken juggers in half, smashed their bones, and left the ground beside me wet with brains. I'll do anything to win, but I never hurt a soul for any reason but to put a dog skull on a stake." • Joan Chen, of the television series "Twin Peaks," plays a tough village girl who joins up with Rutger Hauer's band of juggers.

A Boy and His Dog (1975; Third LQJ Inc./JAF) D/S: L. Q. Jones. P: Alvy Moore. C: John Arthur Morrill. Cast: Don Johnson, Susanne Benton, Jason Robards, Tim McIntire, Alvy Moore. After the nuclear holocaust, Don Johnson and his superintelligent, telepathic dog, Blood, roam the wasteland. • The adage, "a man's best friend is his dog," is taken to extremes in this film. At the climax, Don Johnson must choose between his newfound girlfriend and his starving companion, Blood. He makes the right choice when he feeds the conniving girl to the dog.

Brazil (1985; U.K.) D: Terry Gilliam. P: Arnon Michan. S: Terry Gilliam, Tom Stoppard, Charles McKeown. C: Roger Pratt. Cast: Jonathan Pryce, Robert De Niro, Michael Palin, Kim Greist, Ian Holm, Katherine Helmond, Ian Richardson. A daydreamer gets involved with a rebel superhero and a beautiful woman in the technical nightmare fury where everyone is monitored by an all-powerful government agency that forbids any emotion that can get in the way of efficiency.

Buck Rogers (1939) (see COMIC BOOK FANTASY HEROES). Buster Crabbe wakes up in the year 2500 to face a variety of caped criminals, zombie thugs, and mutants in this condensed film-length version of the 12-part chapter serial.

Buck Rogers in the 25th Century (1979) (see COMIC BOOK FANTASY HEROES). Gil Gerard is Buck Rogers, the space hero battling the evil Princess Ardela who plans to conquer our Earth in the future of the twenty-fifth century.

Captive Women (1952; RKO) D: Stuart Gilmore. P/S: Aubrey Wisberg, Jack Pollexfen. C: Paul Ivano. Cast: Ron Randell, Margaret Field, Stuart Randall, Robert Clarke, William Schallert, Robert Bice. This story, set in the post-atomic war-torn world of the year 3000, details the racial strife between three groups of people in what was once Manhattan—the "Norms," the "Mutates," and the "Up-River People." ¶ "Man was born in brotherhood and in brotherhood must live if he is not to die in chaos." • The film was originally to be titled *3000 A.D.* before RKO executive Howard Hughes changed the title to *Captive Women.* • Margaret Field and William Schallert also starred in Edgar G. Ulmer's *Man from Planet X* a year earlier.

Cherry 2000 (1986; Orion) D: Steve De Jarnatt. P: Edward R. Pressman, Calderot Chubb. S: Michael Almerevda. C: Jacques Haitkin. Cast: Melanie Griffith, David Andrews, Ben Johnson, Tim Thomerson, Brion James, Harry Carey, Jr. Set in the over-mechanized future, a tough female tracker (Melanie Griffith) escorts a man into dangerous gangland regions to find him a robot mate identical to the one he had had and grown to love (a Cherry 2000 model) before it short-circuited. ¶ "She's a Cherry 2000. I want you to go into Zone 7 and get me one just like her." • At the climax, after all the trouble they incur in getting his robot girl, David Andrews decides to leave the machine behind and ride off with the live Melanie instead. • Early in the film, while touring through a storeroom of machine models, Andrews passes by two famous robots from the 1950s—Gort, from *The Day the Earth Stood Still* (1951), and Robby the Robot from *Forbidden Planet* (1956). • Melanie Griffith, a recent Oscar nominee for *Working Girl* (1989) is the daughter of Hitchcock film actress Tippi Hedren (*The Birds,* 1963; *Marnie,* 1964). Her character's name in the film is "E. Johnson." Her tracking mentor, "Six-fingered Jake," is played by western character actor Ben Johnson.

Circuitry Man (1990) D: Stephen Lovy. P: Steven Reich, John Schouweiler. S: Stephen Lovy, Robert Lovy. C: Jamie Thompson. Cast: Lu Leonard, Dennis Christopher, Vernon Wells. In the toxic future where mutant leeches, subterranean cities, poisoned air, and programmable humans are commonplace, Circuitry Man, a girl named Lori, her bodyguard, and an android travel from L.A. to New York smuggling valuable computer chips. Dogging their steps at every corner is the evil "Plughead" (played by Vernon "Wez" Wells, of *Road Warrior* fame).

City Beneath the Sea (1970; Warner Bros.) D/P: Irwin Allen. S: John Meredyth Lucas. C: Kenneth Peach. Cast: Stuart Whitman, Robert Wagner, Rosemary Forsyth, Robert Colbert, Richard Basehart, Joseph Cotten. A futuristic city under the sea is threatened by a planet on collison course with Earth. The planetoid is finally stopped by a missile barrage.

A Clockwork Orange (1971; Warner Bros; U.K.) D/P/S: Stanley Kubrick. C: John Alcott. Cast: Malcolm McDowell, Patrick Magee, Michael Bates, Adrienne Corri, Miriam Karlin, Warren Clarke, John Clive, Carl Duering. In the bleak, anarchistic future, a ruthless young gang leader named Alex is sentenced for murder and volunteers

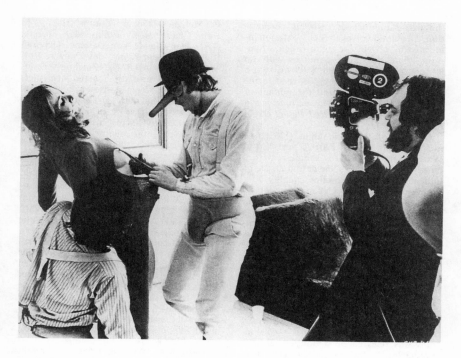

A behind-the-scenes look at the filming of A Clockwork Orange *(1971) with a disguised Malcolm McDowell (in hat and nose) violating the wife of a prominent writer. Director Stanley Kubrick is the man at the right getting a camera eye's view of the scene.*

for a bizarre behavioral shock treatment designed to rid him of his criminal tendencies. The cure's controvesial aftereffects, however, foster strong public pressure opposing such rehabilitation, and Alex undergoes some ironic trials and tribulations which eventually return him to his original (and violent) state of mind. ¶ "The Durango 95 purred away real horrorshow, a nice warm vibratey feeling in your gutty-wuts" — future slang. • Alex's favorite drink is called "Milk Plus," which is milk laced with hallucinogenic drugs. He has a pet boa constrictor, and loves listening to Beethoven's "Ninth Symphony." Unfortunately, after the "Ludovico Technique" rehab treatment, Alex gets incredibly sick whenever he hears the music he once loved. His favorite pastimes include "the old in-out-in-out" (intercourse by rape) and "ultra-violence" (which consists of wino-beating and gang rumbles with his fellow "droogs"). He

is finally sentenced to 14 years in prison for the murder of the "cat-lady," and the brutal beating of Patrick Magee while singing the warm song made famous by Gene Kelly — "Singin' in the Rain." • *A Clockwork Orange* received Academy Award nominations for Best Picture, Best Director, and Film Editing (Bill Butler), but didn't win in any of the categories. The New York Film Critics, however, chose Kubrick as Best Director, and *Clockwork* as the year's best film. • Actor David Prowse, who plays a bodyguard named Julian, was the man behind the Darth Vader costume in *Star Wars* (1977).

Crash and Burn (1990; Paramount) D: Charles Band. P: David DeCoteau, John Schouweiler. S: J. S. Cardone. C: Mac Ahlberg. Cast: Paul Ganus, Megan Ward, Bill Moseley, Eva LaRue, Jack McGee, Ralph Waite. This Orwellian futuristic film is about resistance fighters rebelling against

the world-dominating UNICOM corporation. The plot involves a rebel TV station in-
filtrated by a UNICOM robot called a Synthoid. The resistance counters with an
80-foot robot of their own. ¶ "UNICOM is a
free enterprise democracy dedicated to the
ideals of life, liberty, and the pursuit of
economic stability." • The heroine has a
poster from *The Angry Red Planet* (1960)
hanging over her bed.

Creation of the Humanoids (1962) (see
ROBOTS). This look at Earth's post–World
War III future features rebuilt cities, a
mostly sterile human society, and a race of
humanoid robots demanding equality.

Creepozoids (1988; Urban Classics) D:
David DeCoteau. P: David DeCoteau, John
Schouweiler. S: Burford Hauser. C: Thomas
Callaway. Cast: Linnea Quigley, Ken Abraham, Michael Aranda, Richard Hawkins,
Kim McKamy, Joi Wilson. Set in the post-
holocaust world of 1998, a group of army
deserters takes refuge from the dangerous
acid rain in an abandoned research lab. Unbeknownst to them, the last research project
conducted there turns out to be an out-of-
control genetically mutated monster ...
and it's still there. ¶ "Your flesh will crawl
right off your bones" — ad line. • *Creepozoids* was released on a double bill with
another low-budget effort, *Slavegirls from
Beyond Infinity,* in what was advertised as
"Attack of the Double Feature. The Movies
Your Mother Wouldn't Take You to See."

Crimes of the Future (1970; Emergent
Films; Canada) D/P/S/C: David Cronenberg. Cast: Ronald Mlodzik, Jon Lidolt,
Tania Zolty, Jack Messinger, Paul Mulholland. A cosmetic plague in the future brings
about mutations and the widespread death
of all post-pubertal women.

Crimezone (1989; Concord) D/P: Luis
Llosa. S: Daryl Haney. Cast: David Carradine, Peter Nelson, Sherilyn Fenn, Michael
Shaner. A police state in the future with a
strict stratified society is threatened when a
troubleshooter (David Carradine) decides to
help a couple escape their particular crime
zone and steal a valuable computer chip. ¶
"Beware young traitors, the State knows
who you are."

Curious Female (1969; Fanfare Films)
D/P: Paul Rapp. S: Winston R. Paul. C:
Don Birnkrant. Cast: Angelique Pettyjohn,
Charlotte Jones, Bunny Allister, David
Westberg, Julie Connors. Set in the year
2117, the story centers around a group of
film buffs who live in a future run by a
master computer.

Cyborg (1989; Cannon) D: Albert Pyun.
P: Mehahem Golan, Yoram Globus. S:
Kitty Chalmers. C: Philip Alan Waters.
Cast: Jean-Claude Van Damme, Deborah
Richter, Vincent Klyn, Alex Daniels, Rolf
Muller, Jackson "Rock" Pinckney, Dayle
Haddon. A futuristic martial arts mercenary is hired to make sure a cyborg loaded
with information about a radiation sickness
cure gets through the wasteland, lorded over
by a *Terminator*-like psychopathic leader. ¶
"First there was the collapse of civilization —
anarchy, genocide, starvation. Then when it
seemed things couldn't get any worse, we
got the plague — the living death."

Dead End Drive-in (1986; New World;
Australia) D: Brian Trenchard-Smith. P:
Andrew Williams. S: Peter Smalley. C: Paul
Murphy. Cast: Ned Manning, Peter Whit-
ford, Natalie McCurry, Dave Gibson, Ollie
Hall, Sandie Livingston, Wilbur Wilde. In
the out-of-control near-future, the government traps riotous youths inside drive-ins
and keeps them locked inside these disguised
prison compounds. The youths are kept
manageable by supplying them with all the
junk food, drugs, and bad movies they
could want. ¶ "People can't have a life in
here. All they can have is a heap of shit, and
a gut ball poisonous hamburger! I'll tell you
where bloody life is — out there!"

Dead Man Walking (1988; Metropolis
Pictures) D/P: Gregory Brown. S: John
Weidner, Rick Marx. C: Paul Desatolf.
Cast: Wings Hauser, Brion James, Pamela
Ludwig, Leland Crooke, Sy Richardson,
Joseph d'Angerio, Jeffrey Combs. In the
plague-decimated future, a chauffeur hires a
terminally ill soldier of fortune (called a
"zero man") to help him retrieve the daughter of a corporate big-wig abducted by a
ruthless criminal and taken into the Plague
Zone. ¶ "Infected with a non-contagious yet
fatal strain of the plague, the zero men had
one to two years left to live. With knowledge
of their impending death, their behavior was
sometimes erratic." • *Dead Man Walking*
was filmed on the very low budget of
$340,000. • Actor Brion James played the
psychotic "zero man" Decker with bright
orange hair. "That was my choice," proclaimed the actor in a *Fangoria* #82 interview. "My image of that character was to
play him like a lit match, so I lit him up."

Deadly Harvest (1976; Canada) D: Timothy Bond. Cast: Clint Walker, Nehemiah
Persoff, Roy Davies, Jim Henshaw. A
futuristic world is featured here in which
food has become the most prized resource.

Death Race 2000 (1975; New World) D:
Paul Bartel. P: Roger Corman. S: Robert

David Carradine is the futuristic race car driver known as "Frankenstein" who steps away from his souped-up monster auto during the Death Race 2000 *(1975). Simone Griffeth plays his navigator in this transcontinental road race in which drivers rack up points by running over pedestrians.*

Thom, Charles B. Griffith, Ib Melchior. C: Tak Fujimoto. Cast: David Carradine, Simone Griffeth, Sylvester Stallone, Mary Woronov, Roberta Collins, Martin Kove. A transcontinental death race has become the most popular sporting event of the future. Its top driver, known simply as "Frankenstein," decides to kill the President after the race concludes and put an end to the sanctioned violence. ¶ "In the year 2000, hit and run driving is no longer a felony, it's the national sport!" — ad line. • The enigmatic "Frankenstein" character, presumably disfigured (actually just a perpetuated myth), possessing lightning quick reflexes, was played by David "Kung Fu" Carradine. • In this "Death Race," the more people you run over the more points you score. Age plays a part in point value as well. The picture utilized some common movie stereotypes for the racing entrants, including one car decked out with steer horns, and another driver named "Mathilda the Hun." Frankenstein's chief adversary was called "Ma-chine Gun Joe Viterbo," played by up-and-coming rough and ready star, Sylvester Stallone. • In Ed Naha's book, *The Films of Roger Corman,* editor Joe Dante was quoted as saying, "Roger re-cut it to make it more of an action film. A lot of the humor was excised because Roger felt it would alienate the audience. There are whole scenes in this movie that lead up to jokes that have been cut out of the film."

Deathsport (1978; New World) D: Henry Suso, Allan Arkush. P: Roger Corman. S: Henry Suso, Donald Stewart. C: Gary Graver. Cast: David Carradine, Claudia Jennings, Richard Lynch, William Smithers, David McLean. In the far distant future, David Carradine plays a warrior called a "Range Guide" who is captured by an evil warlord and forced to participate in gladiatorial competition involving deadly jousting on futuristic motorbikes. ¶ "Man is like a candle, he must radiate life by burning himself." • David Carradine, who was also the star of *Death Race 2000,* plays a fearless range guide who is kidnapped and forced to battle a gangland chief's top riders. • Female lead Claudia Jennings is a former *Playboy* Playmate of the Year.

Deluge (1933; RKO) D: Felix Feist. P: Samuel Bischoff. S: John Goodrich, Warren B. Duff. C: Norbert Brodine. Cast: Sidney Blackmer, Peggy Shannon, Lois Wilson, Matt Moore, Fred Kohler. New York City is destroyed in the future by earthquakes and tidal wave following an eclipse of the sun. The male survivors then fight over the last remaining woman. • The tremendous scenes of destruction were borrowed by Republic studios for their film serials and the 1939 feature, *S.O.S. Tidal Wave.*

Endgame (1983; Italy) D: Steven Benson. Cast: Al Cliver, Laura Gemser, George Eastman, Jack Davis. In the post-war future of 2025, surviving warriors play a bloody sport called "Endgame," in which they battle to the death. The best of the wasteland gladiators decides to call a time out and help escort some intelligent mutants across the savage war-torn wilderness.

Equalizer 2000 (1987; Concorde) D: Cirio H. Santiago. P: Leonard Hermes. S: Frederick Bailey. C: Johnny Araojo. Cast: Richard Norton, Corinne Wahl, William Steis, Robert Patrick, Frederick Bailey. In yet another *Road Warrior*-style post-holocaust picture (set in Alaska this time, which is now a desert), a military/industrial compound protects the precious commodity of oil (sound familiar?). One of the guarding group's officers is betrayed so his son takes off for the wasteland. There is he captured by rebels, and eventually leads an assault on the compound where virtually everyone but himself dies in the carnage.

Escape from New York (1981; Avco Embassy) D: John Carpenter. P: Debra Hill, Larry Franco. S: John Carpenter, Nick Castle. C: Dean Cundey, Jim Lucas. Cast: Kurt Russell, Lee Van Cleef, Ernest Borgnine, Adrienne Barbeau, Donald Pleasence, Isaac Hayes, Harry Dean Stanton, Season Hubley. In the year 1997, Manhattan has been turned into a chaotic island prison, housing all of the city's worst criminals. Unfortunately, the President's plane crash lands inside the city and he is taken hostage, prompting Lee Van Cleef to send in a war-hero/felon to retrieve him. ¶ "Amnesty for all prisoners in New York City in exchange for President. 69th Street bridge tomorrow, 12 noon. No bullshit or he's dead." • Kurt Russell plays the eye-patched super stud, Snake Plissken, who is sent in to retrieve the President. This role helped erase Russell's nice

boy Disney image, and inaugurate his new-found status as one of the cinema's most charismatic, hard hitting stars. Donald Pleasence, the popular star of numerous contemporary horror films, plays the President. • Writer/ director John Carpenter provided the musical score, and cast his wife, Adrienne Barbeau, as the film's heroine.

Escape from the Bronx (1985; Fulvia Films; Italy) D: Enzo D. Castellari. P: Fabrizio De Angelis. S: Enzo G. Castellari, Tito Carpi. C: Blasco Giurato. Cast: Mark Gregory, Henry Silva, Valeria D'Obici, Timothy Brent, Thomas Moore. This futuristic tale features a gunfighter who saves the people of the Bronx from a ruthless big-wig who wants the area cleared for new housing developments.

Escape 2000 (1982; New World) (An Australian film known there as *Turkey Shoot.*) D: Brian Trenchard-Smith. P: Anthony Ginnane, William Fayman. S: Jon George, Neill Hicks. Cast: Steve Railsback, Olivia Hussey, Michael Craig, Carmen Duncan, Noel Ferrier. In the year 1995, the world population lives in a strict society devoid of individuality. People who refuse to conform are labeled as "deviates" and are sent to behavioral modification centers and then hunted in jungles for sport.

Exterminators of the Year 3000 (1984; Italy/Spain) D: Jules Harrison. P: Carmillo Teti. S: Elisa Briganti, Dardano Sacchetti, José Truchado Reyes. Cast: Robert Jannucci, Alicia Moro, Alan Collins, Eduardo Fajardo, Luca Venantini, Fred Harris, Beryl Cunningham. Far off in the post-war future, the barren wastelands are teeming with psychos in souped-up cars and motor bikes searching for clean water. A huge tank of the precious H_2O is being guarded by a band of scarred mutants. A macho exterminator, his girl, and a bionic orphan decide to take on the whole works.

Fahrenheit 451 (1966; Universal; U.K.) D/S: François Truffaut. P: Lewis M. Allen. S: Jean-Louis Richard. C: Nicholas Roeg. Cast: Julie Christie, Oskar Werner, Anton Diffring, Cyril Cusak, Jeremy Spenser. A totalitarian society of the future controls its population by strict mass media supervision. This entails the use of "firemen" who start fires (by burning books) instead of putting them out. • The title's significance, "Fahrenheit 451," refers to the temperature at which books burn. At the close of the film, the protagonist (named Montag—German for the word "Monday") uses a flamethrower to stop the firemen who are after him. He then escapes to a rebel faction in the community who wish to continue reading (by choosing a book and committing it to memory). The book he chooses to memorize is one by Edgar Allan Poe. • Julie Christie plays two roles—the vacuous wife of a fireman, and one of the rebel "book people."

Frankenstein Unbound (1990) (see FRANK-ENSTEIN'S MONSTER—FURTHER FRANKEN-STEINS). The film begins in "New Los Angeles" in the future of 2031, where scientist John Hurt is experimenting with implosion. He accidentally creates a "time slip," which hurls him back to the shores of Lake Geneva in 1817 Switzerland, where he encounters not only Mary Shelley, soon-to-be author of *Frankenstein,* but also the real Dr. Victor Frankenstein (Raul Julia) and his hideous creature. In the end, Hurt manages to send himself, Frankenstein, and his creation into the barren uncertainty of the far distant future.

Gassss! (1970; AIP) D/P: Roger Corman. S: George Armitage. C: Ron Dexter. Cast: Robert Corff, Elaine Giftos, Bud Cort, Talia Shire, Ben Vereen, Cindy Williams, Phil Borneo, Alex Wilson. A nerve gas accident causes everyone over 25 to rapidly age and die. Two young lovers, Cole and Cilla (Robert Corff, Elaine Giftos), decide to make a cross country odyssey. After meeting some new friends along the way, they head for a commune and eventually battle a vicious football team. • The final confrontation between the fascist football players and the commune members is broken up by dead world leaders who come to life, including John F. Kennedy, Martin Luther King, and writer Edgar Allan Poe. • Screenwriter George Armitage appears in the film as a modern "Billy the Kid" looter, and singer/dancer/actor Ben Vereen plays Carlos, one of the young pilgrims who joins Cole and Cilla on their trek to the commune. Also appearing in the film is the musical group known as Country Joe and the Fish. • *Gassss!* marks an historic move in Roger Corman's film career. Because of some editorial tampering, Roger decided to leave American International and start up his own company so no one could cut his films without consent. (Apparently, while he was away in Europe, company executives decided to slash parts of the film, including a key character—God, played by Lenny Weinrib.) The new company he formed became New World Pictures which he eventually sold in the mid–1980s before starting up his current film company, Concorde.

Generation (1985) Cast: Richard Beymer,

Hanna Cutrona. In the year 1999, the American way of life centers around a popular *Rollerball*-like sport called "Combat Hockey."

Glen and Randa (1971; UMC Pictures) D/S: Jim McBride. P: Sidney Glazier. S: Rudolph Wurlitzer, Lorenzo Mans. C: Alan Raymond. Cast: Steven Curry, Shelley Plimpton, Woodrow Chambliss, Garry Goodrow, Roy Rox. The exploits of Glen and Randa are depicted as they trek across nuclear-devastated regions in search of the mythical city of Metropolis which they read about in an ancient comic book.

The Handmaid's Tale (1989; Cinacom Entertainment Group) D: Volker Schlondorff. P: Daniel Wilson. C: Igor Luther. Cast: Natasha Richardson, Faye Dunaway, Aidan Quinn, Elizabeth McGovern, Robert Duvall, Victoria Tennant. This horrifying look into the future features a society where a woman's identity is solely determined by her ability to conceive and produce children. In the year 2030, widespread environmental pollution has caused sterility for most of its inhabitants. The film focuses on Offred, a strong-willed "Handmaid" (a fertile woman) who tries desperately to keep her past alive as she struggles to cope with the frightening reality of the present. ¶ "They don't send you to the colony if your ovaries are still jumping." • Female lead Natasha Richardson is the daughter of Vanessa Redgrave. • The film is based on the novel by Margaret Atwood.

Hardware (1990) (see ROBOTS). Set in the radiation-polluted, dehumanized Earth of the near distant future, a man finds the broken pieces of a dangerous android called Mark 13. After taking it home to his girl, the thing reassembles itself and goes on a killing spree.

Hell Comes to Frogtown (1987; New World) D: R. J. Kizer, Donald G. Jackson. P: Donald G. Jackson, Randall Frakes. S: Randall Frakes. Cast: Roddy Piper, Sandahl Bergman, Cec Verrell. In the post-nuclear holocaust future, Rowdy Roddy Piper is coerced into helping a government organization journey into the wasteland and rescue a flock of fertile females. They journey to "Frogtown," a makeshift city populated by talking, man-sized mutant frogs. ¶ "Eat lead, froggies!" • The film's risqué, tongue-in-cheek approach is reflected in its advertising: "Trapped in a nuclear wasteland, surrounded by mutants, Sam Hell has a mission ... to fertilize as many women as possible. It's a tough job but somebody's got to do it."

High Treason (1929; Tiffany; U.K.) D: Maurice Elvey. P/S: L'Estrange Fawcett. Cast: Benita Hume, Basil Gill, Jameson Thomas, James Carew, Humberston Wright. This early futuristic film features London in the year 1940 and a cold war between Europe and America.

In the Aftermath (1987; New World) D: Carl Colpaert. P: Tom Dugan. S: Carl Colpaert, Mamoru Oshii. C: Geza Sinkovics. Cast: Tony Markes, Rainbow Dolan. In the wake of the great world war, a soldier and a young girl fight to survive in the polluted wasteland. A spherical object belonging to the girl may hold the key to the future.

In the Year 2014 (1914; Joker) P: Carl Laemmle. Cast: Max Asher. A look into the possible future from the 1914 perspective. Women now have the right to vote and run the business world.

Just Imagine (1930; 20th Century–Fox) D: David Butler. P/S: Ray Henderson, Lew Brown, B. G. De Sylva. C: Ernest Palmer. Cast: El Brendel, Maureen O'Sullivan, John Garrick, Marjorie White, Frank Albertson. This futuristic musical is set in the wondrous world of New York City of 1980. ¶ *"Just Imagine* the New York of 1980, when everybody has a number instead of a name, and government tells you whom you should marry. *Just Imagine* 1980." • This sci-fi musical, starring Tarzan's most famous Jane (Maureen O'Sullivan), spent $250,000 for the miniature New York City set. Construction employed over 200 engineers and craftsmen for over five months.

Land of Doom (1984; Manson International) D: Peter Marris. P: Peter Marris, Sunny Vest. S: Craid Rand. Cast: Deborah Rennard, Garrick Dowhen, Daniel Radell, Frank Garret, Richard Allen. A warrior couple travels to Blue Lake, a city without war, but first they must get past brutal tribes in the post-war wasteland.

The Last Chase (1980; Argosy Films) D: Martyn Burke. P: Fran Rosati, Martyn Burke. S: C. R. O'Christopher, Roy Moore, Martyn Burke. Cast: Lee Majors, Chris Makepeace, Burgess Meredith. In the barren future, a pair of young rousers trek across the wilderness to join an underground movement which hopes to build a new society. An airforce killer (Meredith) is out to hunt them down in his phantom jet.

The Last Days of Man on Earth (1974; New World; U.K.) (also *The Final Programme*). D/S: Robert Fuest. P: John Goldstone, Sandy Lieberson. C: Norman Warwick. Cast: Jon Finch, Sterling Hayden, Jenny Runacre, Patrick Magee, Graham Crowden, Derrick O'Connor, George Coulouris. These futuristic adventures of Jerry Cornelius chronicle his attempt to save the world, kill his brother, and father the new messiah. • The film is based on Michael Moorcock's novel.

Last Man on Earth (1924; 20th Century–Fox) D/P: John G. Blystone. S: Donald W. Lee. C: Allen Davey. Cast: Earle Foxe, Grace Cunard, Derelys Perdue, Gladys Tennyson, Maryon Aye. An epidemic wipes out all males over the age of 14.

The Last Man on Earth (1964) (see ZOMBIES). The last survivor of a global plague battles the zombie-like victims with garlic and stakes in the heart. Eventually he discovers an isolated group who have avoided the disease by chemicals, but they too want to kill him to avenge his inadvertent murdering of their people.

Logan's Run (1976; MGM) D: Michael Anderson. P: Saul David. S: David Zelag Goodman. C: Ernest Laszlo. Cast: Michael York, Jenny Agutter, Richard Jordan, Peter Ustinov, Roscoe Lee Browne, Farrah Fawcett-Majors. In the twenty-third century, life doesn't begin at 40, it stops at the age of 30. Michael York plays a policeman-like "runner" whose job it is to seek out and kill those who don't wish to voluntarily die when their time is up. He, of course, grows suspicious of the societal laws and sets out to find the truth. Along with Jenny Agutter, they find an old man (Peter Ustinov) living outside the domed civilization, which proves that no one *has* to die at 30. ¶ "No, don't go in there! You don't have to die! No one has to die at 30! You can live, live! Live and grow old. I've seen it!" • The people who live inside the domed city have a radiant crystal implanted in the palm of their hand at birth. As they grow old, the stone changes color from red, to yellow, to green and finally to black (when your time is up). • The bulk of the filming was done at gigantic MGM sound stage on a budget of just under ten million dollars. Most of the money went to L. B. Abbott, who provided the special effects, and Dale Hennesy, who supervised the production design. Hennesy won an Oscar in 1966 on Saul David's film, *Fantastic Voyage*. The domed city was at the time one of the largest model cities ever built for films, taking up over 80 square feet of space. • Producer Saul David (*Fantastic Voyage*, 1966) said in the June, 1976, issue of *American Cinematographer* that, "When you make this kind of film, depending upon your wit or your temperament, you extrapolate from what you've got in the present to what you think may happen in the future ... you take all the tendencies you see around you now—juvenile delinquency, sexual license, you name it, and you project those things to the future, simply exaggerating them."

Mad Max (1979; Mad Max Pty. Ltd.; Australia) D: George Miller. P: Byron Kennedy. S: George Miller, James McCausland. C: David Eggby. Cast: Mel Gibson, Joanne Samuel, Hugh Keays-Byrne, Steve Bisley, Tim Burns, Roger Ward. A cop in the violent chaotic near-future avenges the death of his wife and friend by hunting down the savage motorcycle gang responsible. ¶ "I am the Night Rider! I'm a fuel-injected suicide machine. I am a rocker, I am a roller, I am an out-of-controller!" • This "little" picture enjoyed a cult status among fans, and later, director George Miller expanded the character into two sequels with far greater production values and widely acclaimed success— *The Road Warrior* (1981) and *Mad Max Beyond Thunderdome* (1985).

Mad Max Beyond Thunderdome (1985; Warner Bros; Australia) D: George Miller, George Ogilvie. P: George Miller. S: George Miller, Terry Hayes. C: Dean Semler. Cast: Mel Gibson, Tina Turner, Helen Buday, Frank Thring, Bruce Spence, Robert Grubb, Angelo Rossitto. The continuing adventures of Mad Max in the Australian postwar wastelands: Max comes under a dualistic community called "Bartertown" run by two opposing forces—"Aunt Entity" (Tina Turner), and "Masterblaster." After he puts Masterblaster out of commission for Turner, he is expelled into the desert where he meets and aids a tribe of children. ¶ "And right now I've got two men, two men with a gut full of fear. Ladies and gentlemen, boys and girls, dyin' time's here." • The character known as "Masterblaster" is actually two people in one—a superintelligent dwarf (Master, played by Angelo Rossitto), and his huge warrior counterpart (Blaster, who possesses the mind and face of a child), whom Max bests in a Thunderdome battle. • "Thunderdome" is the name of a gladiatorial caged arena where people go to settle their disputes to the death. "Two men enter, one man leaves" is the motto. Prior to the battle, the Thunderdome emcee introduces the two adversaries—Blaster and Gibson: "He's the ball cracker, death on foot, you know him, you love him, he's Blaster! The challenger, direct from out of the wasteland— he's bad, he's beautiful, he's crazy, it's ... it's the man with no name!" • Bruce Spence, who was sensational as Max's comic side-

kick, the gyro captain, in *Road Warrior,* plays a similar character with a different name (Jedediah the pilot) in this picture. • Tina Turner, who plays Aunt Entity, the queen of Bartertown, is of course more popularly known as a singer/dancer than an actress. She has, however, received rave reviews for her acting prowess in this film, and from her appearance in the 1975 rock opera (featuring the legendary group "The Who") *Tommy,* directed by Ken Russell.

Madrid in the Year 2000 (1925; Madrid Films; Spain) D/S: Manuel Noriega. P: Luis Maurente. C: Agustin Macasoli. Cast: Roberto Rey, Javier Rivera, Amalia Sanz Cruzado, Juan Nada. A futuristic depiction of life in Madrid, where the city has become a waterway for ships.

Metropolis (1926; Paramount/UFA; Germany) D/S: Fritz Lang. P: Erich Pommer. S: Thea von Harbou. C: Karl Freund, Gunther Rittau. Cast: Brigitte Helm, Gustav Froehlich, Alfred Abel, Rudolf Klein-Rogge, Heinrich George. The industrial ruler of Metropolis conspires with an evil scientist to keep the masses in line by replicating a robot in the image of their beloved Maria. His son Freder catches onto the scam and rescues her, but not before the robot Maria incites a rebellion which nearly devastates both the lower city of the workers, and the upper city of the jet set industrialists. In the sentimental climax, Freder brings the union of workers and the administration together for a handshake, representing the act of mediation. ¶ "We have made machines out of men. Now I will make men out of machines, a robot indistinguishable from a real woman." • Fritz Lang (who was an architect, drew cartoons, wrote, and was a World War I veteran) designed movie posters in Berlin during his youth. He married a novelist named Thea von Harbou in 1924, who wrote the screenplay for *Metropolis.* Coincidentally, Thea von Harbou was just recently divorced from actor Rudolf Klein Rogge, the man Lang eventually chose to play the part of Rotwang in this film. • Lang, who was much admired by Hitler for his work on *Metropolis,* was offered to head the Nazi film industry, but he declined and left the country for France. He then emigrated to America. • In 1984, Georgio Moroder pieced together whatever he could find from the original reels and gave the picture a contemporary rock musical score and sound effects. Some of the rock groups featured on the new soundtrack included Pat Benatar, Queen, and Loverboy.

Moon 44 (1990) (see MOON). In the year

2038, greedy multinational corporations wrestle over valuable mining planets necessary for replenishing the Earth's dissipating resources. Michael Pare discovers there's more than just espionage and corruption going on at Moon 44.

Mutant Hunt (1987) (see ROBOTS). Set in New York City of the near future, cyborgs on the drug Euphoron commit murder for pleasure. Their inventor is held hostage by a corporate chairman who manufactures the drug.

984 Prisoner of the Future (1984) (also *Tomorror Man*). D: Tibor Takacs. P: William Macadam. S: Stephen Zoller. Cast: Don Francks, Stephen Markle, Gail Dahms. This futuristic nightmare depicts a world in which a man without a name is incarcerated by an automated electronic society.

1984 (1956; Columbia; U.K.) D: Michael Anderson. P: N. Peter Rathvon. S: William P. Templeton, Ralph Bettinson. C: C. Pennington Richards. Cast: Edmond O'Brien, Jan Sterling, Michael Redgrave, David Kossoff, Mervyn Johns, Donald Pleasence, Michael Ripper. This first film version of George Orwell's novel centers around the plight of two outer party members who carry on a romance despite the monitoring dominion of Big Brother, ruler of the totalitarian future world of Oceania. The couple is betrayed by a high-ranking official named O'Connor who pretends to oppose the regime then turns them in to the Thought Police. In the end they are brainwashed by O'Connor and renounce each other. ¶ "While you were kissing last night . . . 'They' were watching you! Love forbidden! Your sweetheart forced to join the anti-sex league! Here is the most terrifying glimpse into the future ever filmed!"—ad line. • The film *1984* is based upon the novel of the same name by George Orwell, and was released on a double bill with *The Gamma People*. • Edmond O'Brien and Jan Sterling appeared in scenes filmed at the historical "Hatfield House" and at a glade which overlooks the terraces on which Queen Elizabeth I took the Elizabethan version of afternoon tea.

1984 (1984; U.K.) D/S: Michael Radford. P: Simon Perry. C: Roger Deakins. Cast: John Hurt, Richard Burton, Suzanna Hamilton, Cyril Cusak, George Fisher, James Walker. In the year 1984, Winston Smith (John Hurt) hides from Big Brother and the "Thought Police," but is eventually captured and re-educated (brainwashed). • Noted British superstar Richard Burton tortures protagonist Winston Smith with his most deadly fear—rats—by placing

a cage full of them over his head. • The first film version of this story was made in 1956, and starred Edmond O'Brien as Winston Smith.

1990: The Bronx Warriors (1982; Deaf Film International; Italy) D: Enzo G. Castellari. P: Fabrizio De Angelis. S: Enzo G. Castellari, Dardana Sacchetti, Elisa Livia Briganti. C: Sergio Salvati. Cast: Vic Morrow, Mark Gregory, Stefania Girolami, Fred Williamson, Christopher Connelly. In New York of the future, a wealthy woman from the elite Manhattan district gets kidnapped by street gangs in the Bronx criminal community. Tough cop Vic Morrow goes in to clean house and retrieve the girl. Former football star Fred Williamson plays the main Bronx heavy.

No Blade of Grass (1970; MGM; U.K.) D/P: Cornel Wilde. S: Sean Forestal, Jefferson Pascal. C: H. A. R. Thompson. Cast: Nigel Davenport, Jean Wallace, John Hamill, Patrick Holt, George Coulouris, Anthony May. Pollution creates a virus that destroys crops and causes famine and widespread death. One family though is determined to survive as they wander across barren Britain to the Lake District. • The film is based upon the John Christopher novel, *The Death of Grass*.

The Omega Man (1971; Warner Bros.) D: Boris Sagal. P: Walter Seltzer. S: John William Corrington, Joyce H. Corrington. C: Russell Metty. Cast: Charlton Heston, Anthony Zerbe, Rosalind Cash, Paul Koslo, Lincoln Kilpatrick. A plague in Los Angeles decimates the population and turns the survivors into light-shunning mutants led by a man named Mathias. Their heavily armed antagonist, Charlton Heston, plays one of the last normal humans, who barricades himself in his apartment at night, and goes out searching for others like himself by day. ¶ "One creature caught, caught in a place he cannot stir from in the dark, alone, outnumbered hundreds to one. Nothing to live for but his memories. Nothing to live with but his gadgets, his cars, his guns, gimmicks, and yet the whole Family can't bring him out of that . . . that honky paradise." • The Omega Man's favorite movie, one he watches over and over again, is the 1970 documentary film, *Woodstock*. • The picture is based on the Richard Matheson novel, *I Am Legend*, as was the 1964 film starring Vincent Price—*The Last Man on Earth*. Matheson has repeatedly expressed his disappointment with the way both films turned out, especially *The Omega Man*, which Matheson said bore little resemblance to his story.

Osa (1985) D/S: Oleg Egorov. P: Constantin Alexandrov. C: John Drake. Cast: Kelly Lynch, Daniel Grimm, Peter Walker, Phillip Vincent, John Forristal, Étienne Chicot. In the terrible future, corpses litter the land and the only uncontaminated water supply is ruled by an evil man and his dangerous thugs. "Osa" is a young girl who swears to avenge the death of her murdered family by stopping this tyrant.

Parasite (1982; Embassy) D/P: Charles Band. S: Alan J. Adler, Michael Shoob, Frank Levering. C: Mac Ahlberg. Cast: Robert Glaudini, Demi Moore, Luca Bercovici, Cherie Currie. Set in an atomic devastated world, a scientist develops a parasitic creature which chows down on the local surviving humans. • This is an early appearance by actress Demi Moore, whose career has blossomed with roles in the films *About Last Night* (1986) and *Ghost* (1990). • *Parasite* was filmed in 3-D.

Planet of the Apes (1968) (see PLANETS OF THE APES SERIES). A space expedition travels through time to a planet in which the ape is the dominant species and Man is just a mute animal. In one of science fiction's most famous and powerful scenes, astronaut Charlton Heston learns at the climax that this chimpanzee world is actually our planet Earth in the post-nuclear future.

Privilege (1967; Universal; U.K.) D: Peter Watkins. P: John Heyman. S: Norman Bogner. C: Peter Suschitsky. Cast: Paul Jones, Jean Shrimpton, Mark London, Max Bacon, Jeremy Child. Paul Jones plays a rock star who is built up by the establishment to be a religious messiah, so they can use him to manipulate the youth of Britain. His girlfriend (played by Jean Shrimpton) tunes him in to the scam, but when he rebels, his fans massacre him.

Project X (1968; Paramount) D/P: William Castle. S: Edmund Morris. C: Harold Stine. Cast: Christopher George, Greta Baldwin, Henry Jones, Monte Markham, Harold Gould, Phillip E. Pine, Keye Luke, Robert Cleaves. An agent in the year 2118 is given a new identity but is unaware that he's carrying a lethal germ, and vital espionage secrets. • Director/producer William Castle is best known as the master of theatrical gimmicks for films like *House on Haunted Hill* (1958), *The Tingler* (1959), and *13 Ghosts* (1960). • Christopher George (*Day of the Animals,* 1976) plays the agent who knows the secret that will save the West but whose memory has been wiped out (similar to the 1990 mega-hit, *Total Recall*).

Punishment Park (1971; Chartwell/Fran-

çois) D/S: Peter Watkins. P: Susan Martin. C: Joan Churchill. Cast: Carmen Argenziano, Stan Armsted, Jim Bohan, Frederick Franklyn, Gladys Golden. This futuristic account of wartime America features punishment camps for draft dodgers. • To attain amnesty for their political rebellion, the draft dodgers are forced to trek across a dangerous desert gauntlet and reach an American flagpole. The entire event is recorded by television so the country can watch them get blown away by army patrols. • The film was made during the Vietnam War period, and blatantly attempted to attract interest from the youth protest movement.

Quintet (1979; 20th Century–Fox) D/P: Robert Altman. S: Frank Barhydt, Patricia Resnick, Robert Altman. C: Jean Boffety. Cast: Paul Newman, Vittorio Gassman, Fernando Rey, Bibi Andersson, Nina Van Pallandt, Brigitte Fossey. Quintet is the deadly game a group of post-atomic survivors play in their new ice age world.

Rage (1984; Italy) D: Anthony Richmond. Cast: Conrad Nichols, Steve Eliot, Chris Huerta. In the distant post-holocaust future, a superwarrior named Captain Rage is dogged by the evil Sergeant Flash in his attempt to find uranium in "the forbidden land." ¶ "It won't be easy building up a new world, but there's no harm in trying."

Rats: Night of Terror (1983) (see RATS) (also *Rats*). In the post-holocaust year of 2225, a surviving band of humans discover a town with uncontaminated food and water. Unfortunately, this town also houses an army of rats with a taste for human flesh.

The Ravagers (1979; Columbia) D: Richard Compton. P: John W. Hyde. S: Donald Sandford. C: Vincent Saizis. Cast: Richard Harris, Art Carney, Alana Hamilton, Ernest Borgnine, Ann Turkel, Woody Strode. Richard Harris joins forces with Art Carney's cronies in an attempt to avenge his wife's death and rebuild their nuclear-devastated society.

The Road Warrior (1982; Warner Bros.; Australia) (known in Australia as *Mad Max 2*). D: George Miller. P: Byron Kennedy. S: Terry Hayes, George Miller, Brian Hannant. C: Dean Semler. Cast: Mel Gibson, Bruce Spence, Mike Preston, Vernon Wells, Kjell Nilsson, Max Phipps, Emil Minty, Virginia Hey, William Zappa, Arkie Whiteley, Steve Spears, Syd Heylen. This apocalyptic fantasy vision tells the story of Mad Max, a rogue super-cop who, along with his tag-along partner called the Gyro Captain, help a small band of civilians escape a refinery

Mel Gibson stars as Max, better known as The Road Warrior *(1982). Though his character initially appeared in the film* Mad Max *three years earlier, it was Gibson's role in this popular sequel that set this Australian actor on the road to superstardom.*

compound in the Australian outback. The precious gasoline fortress is surrounded by a brutal horde of scavenging psychos led by the articulate Hercules known as "the Humungus," and his human weapon of destruction, the ultra-warrior "Wez." ¶ "Greetings from the Humungus, the Lord Humungus, Warrior of the Wasteland, the Ayatollah of Rock 'n' Rolla!" • This power-packed Australian import launched Mel Gibson into superstardom and eclipsed its predecessor, *Mad Max* (1979), in every way. A sequel, entitled *Mad Max Beyond Thunderdome,* was filmed by George Miller (again three years later) in 1985, co-starring singer Tina Turner. • The violent car chase antics photographed by Dean Semler included some of the longest and most difficult auto stunts ever shot on film. • Vernon Wells, the actor who played the indomitable punk warrior Wez, made a brief appearance in the Anthony Michael Hall film, *Weird Science* (1985), wearing his character's exact getup.

Robocop (1987) (see ROBOTS). A slaughtered cop, rebuilt into a powerful man-machine, is tested in the ever-growing violent inner cities of the near future. • A bevy of comedic news stories detailing future life includes the "Reagan Star Wars Peace Platform," and a medical commercial featuring mechanical hearts which you can pick and choose from.

Robocop 2 (1990) (see ROBOTS). This sequel to *Robocop* depicts a futuristic Detroit with the police on strike, crime and drugs running rampant, and political corruption aplenty. • A powerfully addictive drug called "nuke" becomes the new ultimate opiate for the masses in futuristic Detroit.

Robot Holocaust (1987) (see ROBOTS). In the future, a robot revolt against humanity has left mankind controlled by a mysterious force known as "The Dark One."

Robot Jox (1990) (see ROBOTS). In the war-ravaged world of 2050, there are now only two opposing countries. These two superpowers settle all disputes through the battling

Jonathan E (James Caan), the superstar of the violent futuristic sport of Rollerball *(1975), prepares to defend a goal against an opposing team. This Norman Jewison production celebrates the victory of one man against a corporate society bent on stifling individuality.*

of gigantic transformer-like robots controlled by highly trained fighters called Robot Jox.

Roller Blade (1986; New World) D/P/C: Donald G. Jackson. S: Donald G. Jackson, Randall Frakes. Cast: Suzanne Solari, Jeff Hutchinson, Shaun Michelle, Katina Garner, Sam Mann, Robby Taylor, Christopher Douglas-Olen Ray. A "holy roller" group of warrior women skaters look for a magic crystal in a crazy post-holocaust world of rollerskates and skateboards. ¶ "We must go forth and bring order out of the chaos. It is our holy mission as I have seen in my visions." • This quirky low-budget feature is "the only futuristic rollerskating rebel nun movie," according to filmmaker Donald Jackson (until its sequel, *Rollerblade Warriors: Taken by Force* came out, that is).

Rollerball (1975; United Artists) D/P: Norman Jewison. S: William Harrison. C: Douglas Slocombe. Cast: James Caan, John Houseman, Maud Adams, John Beck,

Moses Gunn, Ralph Richardson, Pamela Hensley, Robert Ito. In the near distant future, "Rollerball" is a violent game created to demonstrate the futility of individual effort, and used to keep the masses in line by the global corporations which have replaced individual nations as the governments of the world. ¶ "You know what those executives dream about out there behind their desks? They dream they're great rollerballers—they dream they're Jonathan—they have muscles, they *bash* in faces." • James Caan plays "Jonathan E," the greatest rollerballer in the history of the sport, surviving ten seasons. The corporations want him out, but he refuses to retire, so they change the rules, making the game a life and death struggle instead of a sport. He wears number 6 and plays for Houston. His best friend, and fellow teammate, Moonpie, is turned into a vegetable by the Tokyo team in the semifinal match of the tournament which is getting more and more violent. • *Rollerball* is based

on a short story by William Harrison. •
Distinguished British actor Ralph Richardson plays the caretaker of a worn-down
computer called "Zero." • Producer/direc-
tor Norman Jewison was born in Toronto,
and began his career with London's BBC
television. He then went on to work for CBS
to produce and direct numerous musical
specials. He directed and produced the
musical classics *Fiddler on the Roof* (1971)
and *Jesus Christ Superstar* (1973) prior to
his work on this science fiction classic.

Rollerblade Warriors: Taken by Force
(1990; Golden Circle) D/C: Donald G.
Jackson. P: Jonathan S. Kaplan. S: Lloyd
Strathern. Cast: Kathleen Kinmont, Jack
Damon, Elizabeth Kaitan, Rory Calhoun,
Norman Alden, Cleve A. Hall, Kathleen
Elizabeth, Sam Mann, Abby Dalton. A
cosmic order of female rollerblade warriors
on skates armed with swords wander through
the apocalyptic wasteland to take on a
monstrous mutant and a pack of death-
dealing males. The rollerblade sisters are on
a mission to transport a young girl, a seer,
safely through the wasteland back to the
safety of their order. ¶ "Now, go forth and
skate the paths of righteousness." • Star
Kathleen Kinmont is the daughter of 60s TV
star Abby Dalton (who also appears in the
film as "Mother Speed," head of the Cosmic
Order of Roller Blade). • Much of the film
was shot at an abandoned Kaiser Steel
Plant.

Runaway (1984) (see MACHINES). In the
micro-electronic future, sophisticated robots, computers, and machines begin to
malfunction, due to some technical chips
that are programmed to go haywire by a
dangerous killer. ¶ "Let me tell you the way
the world is — nothing works right."

The Running Man (1987; Taft Entertainment Pictures) D: Paul Michael Glaser. P:
Tim Zinnemann, George Linder. S: Steven
de Souza. C: Thomas Del Ruth. Cast:
Arnold Schwarzenegger, Maria Conchita
Alonso, Yaphet Kotto, Richard Dawson. In
the year 2019, a gladiatorial-like life and
death TV game show exists where convicts
can compete for pardons by running a
dangerous gauntlet. Arnie takes a chance
and battles four of the game's best killers. ¶
"Come on down!" • The muscular Schwarzenegger goes up against four different killers
with their own distinctive talents. "Subzero"
attacks with a hockey stick, "Buzzsaw" is a
motorcycle-riding slasher, "Dynamo" works
with electric shock devices, and "Fireball"
has a wonderful arsenal of flame throwers.
• The original director of the film, George

Pan Cosmatos, was fired from the project
when he wanted to increase the $10 million
budget to $18 million. Paul Michael Glaser,
who starred in the TV series, "Starsky and
Hutch," ended up at the helm with the final
budget coming in at $28 million (ironically a
full $10 million above the figure Cosmatos
wanted). • Richard Dawson, the real life
game show host of "Family Feud," appeared
as the villainous host of the gladiatorial-like
game show called "The Running Man." •
The film is based upon the Richard Bachman book, *The Running Man*. Bachman is
a pseudonym used by writer Stephen King.
• Singer Mick Fleetwood (from the rock
group Fleetwood Mac) and Dweezil Zappa
(offspring of the infamous Frank Zappa)
make their acting debuts in this picture.

Rush (1984; Italy) D: Anthony Richmond. Cast: Conrad Nichols, Gordon
Mitchell, Sybil Danning. More post-nuclear
war action with a rogue warrior aiding
prisoners of a vicious militarized villain in
the desert.

She (1985) (see SWORD AND SORCERY). A
sword and sorcery-like world exists years
after the nuclear holocaust. *She* is Sandahl
Bergman, the warrior woman who takes on
a race of mutants.

Sins of the Fleshapoids (1965) (see RO-
BOTS). In the far-off future (after the nuclear
holocaust) are a group of people living dull
lives with robot servants called Fleshapoids.

Sleeper (1973; United Artists) D: Woody
Allen. P: Jack Grossberg. S: Woody Allen,
Marshall Brickman. C: David M. Walsh.
Cast: Woody Allen, Diane Keaton, John
Beck, Mary Gregory, Don Keefer. A neurotic
health food store owner awakens from his
frozen state in the twenty-first century. He
masquerades as a robot butler and attempts
to erase the totalitarian society by making
off with a "nose" dictator whose body has
been used for cloning purposes. ¶ "I'm 2,000
months behind on my rent!"

Slipstream (1990) D: Steven M. Lisberger.
P: Gary Kurtz. S: Tom Kayden. Cast: Mark
Hamill, Ben Kingsley, F. Murray Abraham,
Kitty Aldridge, Bob Peck, Bill Paxton,
Eleanor David. A lawman and his female
partner capture a mysterious fugitive in a
futuristic world where nature has gone wild.
They then follow a bounty hunter who steals
their prisoner and takes him through a weird
barrier called "the Slipstream" where the
wind is used as fuel and the ruins of a secret
civilization exist.

Solarbabies (1986; MGM) D: Alan Johnson. P: Irene Walzer, Jack Frost Sanders. S:
Walon Green, Douglas Anthony Metrov. C:

Peter MacDonald. Cast: Richard Jordan, Jami Gertz, Charles Durning, Jason Patric, Lukas Haas, Sarah Douglas. In the far future, young children are rounded up to live in totalitarian orphanages where they are taught to serve the system and its evil protectorate which is hoarding the Earth's water supply. A visitor from another planet arrives to change the world for the better. ¶ "Sometimes in my dreams I see the Earth as it was before, green with flowing rivers and mighty oceans. Can it ever be like that again?" • The main method of transportation in this future of a hard waterless Earth surface is by rollerskating.

Soylent Green (1973; MGM) D: Richard Fleischer. P: Walter Seltzer, Russell Thatcher. S: Stanley R. Greenberg. C: Richard H. Kline. Cast: Charlton Heston, Leigh Taylor-Young, Edward G. Robinson, Chuck Connors, Joseph Cotten, Brock Peters. Charlton Heston is a New York cop in the year 2022 investigating a murder in a hot and overpopulated society. He eventually uncovers a conspiracy behind the making of a synthetic food called Soylent Green, which the down-trodden masses live on almost exclusively. ¶ "They're making our food out of people. Next thing they'll be breeding us like cattle for food. You've got to tell them,you got to tell 'em ... Soylent Green is *People!*" • At the climax, Heston learns that Soylent Green is actually made from dead bodies processed into little squares and passed off as food. • The film is based upon the Harry Harrison novel, *Make Room! Make Room!* In John Brosnan's book, *Future Tense,* Harrison commented on *Soylent Green*: "Overall I think it succeeds as a film ... but it lost a lot of the feeling of the book. Originally it was even worse, but the people who were really involved with the idea — the producers Walter Seltzer and Russ Thatcher, and the star Charlton Heston — managed to improve it some. • This was the last film of Edward G. Robinson, who died prior to the picture's release. Author Harry Harrison claimed he helped clarify the role and explain the character's motivations for Edward G. Robinson. "Very simply, you are me in this story. I'll be your age at the time when all the events of the film are taking place. You are the only living connection with the old world...." • The picture was made on a (then) hefty budget of four million dollars, and originally the studio heads didn't believe that a film about future overpopulation warranted that kind of money. So the cannibalistic subplot was added to give the picture a little more dramatic

punch. • After the first week of shooting, director Richard Fleischer fired the original cameraman and hired Richard H. Kline because he didn't like the visual look up to that point.

Steel Dawn (1987; Silver Lion) D: Lance Hool. P: Lance Hool, Conrad Hool. S: Doug Lefler. C: George Tirl. Cast: Patrick Swayze, Lisa Niemi, Christopher Neame, Brion James, John Fujioka. In the post-nuclear wasteland a warrior known as "The Nomad" is hired to be a town's peacemaker and settle a water rights battle. • Actor Brion James, who played one of the faction's head musclemen, explained the appeal of these types of pictures: "Kids don't watch Westerns anymore. They watch SF and fantasy adventures. So what movie makers do is take Westerns and set them in the future. *Steel Dawn* was *Shane* set 1,000 years from now."

Stryker (1983; HCI International; Philippines) D/P: Cirio H. Santiago. S: Howard R. Cohen. C: Ricardo Remias. Cast: Steve Sandor, Andria Savio, William Ostrander, Michael Lane, Julie Gray. This Filippino post-nuclear drama centers around a dispute over some precious water rights.

Surf Nazis Must Die (1987; Troma) D: Peter George. P: Robert Tinnell. S: Jon Ayre. C: Rolf Kesterman. Cast: Gail Neely, Robert Harden, Barry Brenner, Dawn Wildsmith, Michael Sonye. After the big earthquake of the future, California has been turned into a lawless region where a group of neo–Nazis lord over the beaches on their battle-armed surfboards. Gail Neely plays a mad momma out to avenge the death of her son. ¶ "A wave of crime is sweeping unchecked through the South Bay. One word describes the state of the beaches — anarchy." • The leader of the Surf Nazis is named (appropriately enough) Adolf.

Survival Zone (1983) Cast: Gary Lockwood, Morgan Stevens. Ranchers trying to salvage what is left of the nuclear-devastated land have big-time trouble with savage motorcycle gangs.

Teenage Caveman (1958) (see CAVEPEOPLE). At the film's climax, the prehistoric world that the inquisitive teen explores turns out to be our own future on a nuclear-devastated Earth.

The Tenth Victim (1965; Embassy; Italy/France) D: Elio Petri. P: Carlo Ponti. S: Elio Petri, Ennio Flaiano, Tonino Guerra, Georgio Salvione. C: Gianni Di Venanzo. Cast: Marcello Mastroianni, Ursula Andress, Elsa Martinelli, Massimo Serato, Evi Rigano, Salvo Randone. Marcello Mastroianni and

Ursula Andress are killers in the dehumanized twenty-first century where the government sanctions murder to control population and ease aggressive tendencies towards war. • The film is based upon the Robert Sheckley short story, "The Seventh Victim." • In the film, if a "hunter" has a "ten-kill" score, he or she is given unlimited political and financial privileges. The killers are trained, just like athletes, in a gymnasium.

The Terminator (1984) (see ROBOTS). A man and his robot adversary travel from the machine-controlled future of 2029 to the present to fight for a woman whose son will affect the destiny of their time.

The Terror Within (1988; Concorde) D: Thierry Notz. P: Roger Corman. S: Thomas M. Cleaver. C: Ronn Schmidt. Cast: George Kennedy, Andrew Stevens, Starr Andreeff, Terri Traes, John LaFayette, Tommy Hinchley. In the plague-ravaged future ("with 99 percent of the population gone"), a group of underground scientists rescue a pregnant woman from the mutants on the surface. Unfortunately, the woman has been contaminated and gives violent birth to a mutant baby which grows into a huge vicious creature and runs amok in the underground lab. ¶ "'The accident.' You know, I used to think we'd go out in a ball of fire, not because of some leaky test tube in a lab somewhere."

Things to Come (1936; London Films; U.K.) D: William Cameron Menzies. P: Alexander Korda. S: H. G. Wells, Lajos Biro. C: George Perinal. Cast: Raymond Massey, Edward Chapman, Cedric Hardwicke, Ralph Richardson, Margaretta Scott, Sophie Stewart. This H. G. Wells–inspired epic spans over 100 years of life in the city known as "Everytown." After a terrible war, a group of scientists with vast technical knowledge rebuild the city, and a look into the future demonstrates the advanced technocratic civilization which they have created. ¶ "If we don't end war, war will end us." • Hungarian filmmaker Alexander Korda lived in England during the early 1930s and it was there that he talked H. G. Wells into adapting his own book, *The Shape of Things to Come,* for his proposed film. Wells' screenplay underwent numerous changes and rewriting before making it to the screen. • This modestly-budgeted film (only $350,000), originally titled *One Hundred Years to Come,* was a box office failure. • Star Raymond Massey played two members of the Cabal family from different generations. First he plays the (then) contemporary John, and then in the year 2036, he appears as John's grandson, Oswald.

THX 1138 (1971; American Zoetrope) D/S: George Lucas. P: Lawrence Sturhahn. S: Walter Murch. C: Dave Meyers, Albert Kihn. Cast: Robert Duvall, Donald Pleasence, Don Pedro Colley, Maggie McOmie, Ian Wolfe, Marshall Efron. Robert Duvall attempts to escape from a sterile underground world of the future run by computers and robots. • Johnny Weissmuller, Jr., son of the Tarzan actor, plays a robot in this film. • This sci-fi cult classic was developed from George Lucas' 20-minute UCLA film school project.

The Time Machine (1960) (see TIME TRAVEL). Rod Taylor discovers that in the future mankind will fall prey to nuclear warfare, which will lead to the creation in the far distant future of a dual civilization—one passive, the other mutant cannibals.

Time Trackers (1989) (see TIME TRAVEL). A group of scientists in the near-idyllic world of 2025 must chase one of their evil members back in time first to 1991, then to 1146, to try and prevent him from altering history and wiping them all out of existence. ¶ "1991—five years before the politicians gave up power to the scientists. Bombs, pollution—the scientists fixed it. There's not a problem science can't solve."

The Time Travelers (1964) (see TIME TRAVEL). The survivors of a nuclear war build a spaceship and set off for a new world. They are joined by a group of scientists, who then attempt to travel back in time in order to stop the war before it starts.

Trancers (1984) (see TIME TRAVEL) (also *Future Cop*). Tim Thomerson plays a cop from the future who comes to the present to stop a mad time traveler and his army of Trancers.

The Tripods (1984) (see ALIENS—INVADERS ON EARTH: THE 80s AND BEYOND). In the future, alien machines called Tripods rule mankind and control their thoughts with the mandatory use of silver caps.

Twisted Justice (1990; Arena Home Video) D/P/S: David Heavener. C: David Hue. Cast: David Heavener, Erik Estrada, Jim Brown, Shannon Tweed, James Van Patten, Don Stroud, Karen Black. In the year 2020, a serial killer is murdering women in a violent society where all guns are banned. A renegade cop decides to stop the fiend with an illegal weapon.

2010 (1984) (see SPACE TRAVEL). This space-age sequel to the classic Kubrick masterpiece gives us a brief glimpse of life on Earth in the year 2010.

2020 Texas Gladiators (1985; Italy) D: Kevin Mancusco. S: Alex Carver. Cast: Harrison Miller, Al Cliver, Daniel Stephen, Peter Hooten, Sabrina Siani, Al Yamanouchi. A nuclear holocaust has turned the world into a wasteland infested with barbaric road warriors. The worst of these is a terrible tyrant and his renegade regime, which is after a valuable refinery. Standing in their way are three gladiators who are determined to stop them.

Voyage to the End of the Universe (1964) (see SPACE TRAVEL). Space voyagers in the twenty-fifth century encounter the deadly radioactive hazards of intergalactic travel and end up on Earth, or another parallel planet just like Earth.

War of the Planets (1965) (see ALIENS— INVADERS ON EARTH: THE 60S AND 70S). This Italian effort, set in the twenty-first century, features an Earth which has developed a planetary satellite defense system.

Warlords (1989; American Independent) D: Fred Olen Ray. P: Harel Goldstein, Fred Olen Ray. S: Scott Ressler. C: Laszlo Regos. Cast: David Carradine, Sid Haig, Ross Hagen, Fox Harris, Robert Quarry, Brinke Stevens, Victoria Sellers, Dawn Wildsmith. In a post-apocalyptic future, David Carradine plays a genetically-engineered warrior who must battle an evil warlord to rescue his captive wife. ¶ "I often ask myself how such a wonderful theory like nuclear deterrence was expected to work when the lucky men holding the triggers really couldn't give a damn." • *Warlords* was filmed predominantly in Hollywood's Bronson Canyon.

Warriors of the Apocalypse (1987; Film Concept) (also *Time Raiders*). D/P: Bobby A. Suarez. S: Ken Metcalfe. C: Jun Pereira. Cast: Michael James, Debrah Moore, Franco Guerrero, Ken Metcalfe, Robert Marius. One hundred fifty years in the future, a warrior and an old man trek into the jungle and liberate slaves who work inside a mountain housing a nuclear power plant.

Warriors of the Lost World (1985) D/S: David Worth. P: Roberto Bessi, Frank E. Hildebrand. Cast: Robert Ginty, Persis Khambatta, Donald Pleasence, Fred Williamson, Harrison Muller. Many years after the radiation wars of the future, a warrior known as "The Rider" battles the Omega force on his computerized motorcycle. During his travels, The Rider breaks through the "wall of illusion" and encounters a group of mystics and a young woman named Nastassia. He decides to help the mystics and rescue the girl's father, despite the danger

involving deformed mutants and the Omega force.

Warriors of the Wasteland (1983; New Line Cinema) D: Enzo G. Castellari. P: Fabrizio De Angelis. S: Tito Carpi, Enzo Girolami. Cast: Fred Williamson, Timothy Brent, George Eastman, Anna Kanakis, Thomas Moore. Two mighty warriors intercede between postwar survivors trying to reach a distant land emitting radio signals and a terrible antagonistic society known as the Templars, led by an evil priest. ¶ "There's only one thing that matters— winning!"

Wild in the Streets (1968; AIP) D: Barry Shear. P: James H. Nicholson, Samuel Z. Arkoff. S: Robert Thom. C: Richard Moore. Cast: Christopher Moore, Shelley Winters, Hal Holbrook, Diane Varsi, Millie Perkins, Richard Pryor. In this futuristic political satire about the New America, the voting age is now 14, half the country is under 25, and the old folks are sent to L.S.D. retirement houses when they reach age 35. • Fred Feitshans and Eve Newman were nominated for an Academy Award in Editing for this effort. • This film marks the third screen appearance of comedian/actor Richard Pryor, who went on to become a star in the 1970s. He was nominated as Best Supporting Actor four years later in *Lady Sings the Blues.*

Wild Wild Planet (1965) (see ALIENS— ENCOUNTERS IN OUTER SPACE). This futuristic space opera features robots, fiendish females, space travel, miniaturization, a mad scientist, and a glimpse of life on Earth in the year 2015.

Wired to Kill (1986) D/S: Franky Schaeffer. Cast: Emily Longstreth, Devin Hoelscher, Merrit Butrick, Frank Collision, Tommy Lister, Jr., Kim Milford. A crippled teen uses a tough-minded girl and a primitive robot to take revenge on a despicable gang of perverted thugs in the lawless year of 1998. ¶ "Know what? Life's a bitch. First the New Plague killed my mom along with 120 million other people. Now my dad kicks me out of the house so he can screw around. What is this, the Dark Ages?" • The film was shot under the title *Booby Trap.*

World Gone Wild (1988) D: Lee H. Katzin. Cast: Bruce Dern, Michael Pare, Catherine Mary Stewart, Adam Ant, Anthony James, Rick Podell. In the post-apocalyptic world of 2087, water is the most precious commodity. The small peaceful community of "Lost Wells" is besieged by a band of sadistic fanatics led by Derek (Adam Ant), whose bible is *The Charles Manson Story.* ¶ "Like the man said, nothin' makes sense in a world gone wild." • This futuristic update of *The Magnificent Seven* was filmed in and around Tucson, Arizona.

World Without End (1956) (see TIME TRAVEL). A team of astronauts, headed by Hugh Marlowe, enters a time warp and lands on the nuclear devastated Earth of the future, where ugly mutants roam the surface and anemic survivors live underground.

Zardoz (1973; 20th Century–Fox; U.K.) D/P/S: John Boorman. C: Geoffrey Unsworth. Cast: Sean Connery, Charlotte Rampling, John Alderton, Sara Kestelman, Sally Anne Newton, Niall Buggy. Earth in the year 2293 is divided into two zones by a force field. On one side is the wasteland, inhabited by an uncivilized group of people known as the "Brutals," and on the other side is the Vortex region, where the ruling intellectuals live. Sean Connery plays one of the wasteland exterminators, controlled by the stone god known as Zardoz. • Zardoz is a huge flying stone head, symbol of the god Zardoz. The figurehead provides the weapons used by the exterminators, who force the Brutals to grow food and place it into the statue. Eventually the exterminators grow suspicious of their stone master and one of them (Sean Connery) hides within the head, which takes him inside the Vortex. There he learns that Zardoz is simply a tool used by the Vortex community to keep the outlanders under control. In the end, he makes off with a female intellectual (Charlotte Rampling) after destroying the Tabernacle computer system, bringing an end to the "Immortals" society as other exterminators come in for the kill. • The name Zardoz was a contraction of "Wizard of Oz," conceived by director John Boorman as an in-joke. • Zed, the exterminator, was the character played by Sean Connery, but the role was originally conceived with Burt Reynolds in mind.

Zero Population Growth (1972; Paramount) (also *Z.P.G.*). D: Michael Campus. P: Thomas F. Madigan. S: Max Ehrlich, Frank De Felitta. C: Michael Reed. Cast: Oliver Reed, Geraldine Chaplin, Diane Cilento, Don Gordon, Bill Nagy, Aubrey Woods. The over-populated world of the future decrees that no one may have children for the next 30 years. Reed and Chaplin can't wait that long and decide to go against society's dictates and have a baby.

Gamera *see* Japanese Giant Monsters

Genies

A genie, also known as a *djinn,* or *jinn,* is a specific supernatural creature or spirit capable of assuming human or animal form. They are usually depicted as possessing a wide range of magical powers with which they can influence people or events. The genie comes from Muslim legend (just like the magic carpet) and has been most often seen in conjunction with Arabian Nights–style fantasy features. The most popular, and most filmed motif is of course the story of Aladdin's lamp. In this tale, the genie is imprisoned within an oil lamp and can be called forth to carry out one's bidding. Sometimes a limit is put on the number of times a genie can be used (with three being the most frequent number). In most cases, as with the two most notable films on the subject — *Thief of Bagdad* (1940) and *The Seventh Voyage of Sinbad* (1958) — the bottled genie greatly desires to be set free. Rex Ingram, the actor portraying the genie in *Thief of Bagdad,* set the standard by which most djinns are measured. His power was unlimited and his demeanor charismatic (to say the least). However, he also proved to be of only normal intelligence, as Sabu managed to trick him back into his bottle. Not all films on this subject are set within an Arabian framework. Genie bottles can turn up anywhere today, and filmmakers have often let one loose within a contemporary setting, as in *Where Do We Go from*

Here? (1945), *The Brass Bottle* (1964), and *The Outing* (1987). It is likely we will see a continued mixing of genres involving this supernatural character in the future, as period films become increasingly difficult to make and sell to the public in these modern times.

Aladdin (1986; Cannon; U.S./Italy) D: Bruno Corbucci. P: Menahem Golan, Yoram Globus, Ugo Tucci. S: Mario Amendola, Bruno Corbucci, Marcello Fondato. C: Silvano Ippoliti. Cast: Bud Spencer, Luca Venantini, Janet Agren, Julian Voloshin, Diamy Spencer. In this juvenile fantasy, a 14-year-old boy named Al Haddin(!) finds the famous lamp and its friendly genie. The wise djinn sets about solving his various family problems before Al finally wishes him to become human and they live happily ever after. ¶ "Our magic is for the good of mankind. We feel that power in the hands of only one man, someone like yourself in this case, is asking for trouble" — the genie to a power hungry politician.

Aladdin and His Lamp (1951; Monogram) D: Lew Landers. P: Walter Wanger. S: Howard Dimsdale, Millard Kaufman. C: Gilbert Warrenton. Cast; Patricia Medina, Noreen Nash, John Sands, John Dehner, Billy House. This rendition of the Aladdin's lamp story involves a genie that can change and alter his shape.

Arabian Adventure (1979; Badger Films; U.K.) D: Kevin Connor. P: John Dark. S: Brian Hayles. C: Alan Hume. Cast: Christopher Lee, Oliver Tobias, Mickey Rooney, Milo O'Shea, Peter Cushing. A young prince goes in search of a magic rose to win the hand of an emperor's daughter. Along the way he encounters monsters, magic carpets, and a bottled genie.

Arabian Nights (1942; Universal) D: John Rawlins. P: Walter Wanger. S: Michael Hogan. C: Milton Krasner. Cast: Maria Montez, Jon Hall, Sabu, Billy Gilbert, Shemp Howard, Leif Erickson, Turhan Bey, Acquanetta. Shemp Howard (one of the Three Stooges) plays Aladdin in this tropical version of the famous story.

Born of Fire (1987; IFEX-Vidmark/Film Four International; U.K.) D: Jamil Dehlavi. P: Jamil Dehlavi, Therese Pickard. S: Raficq Abdulla. C: Bruce McGowan. Cast: Peter Firth, Suzan Crowley, Stefan Kalipha, Nabil Shaban, Oh-Tee. A flautist (Peter Firth) and an astronomer who have both heard the same strange music in their heads travel to Turkey to learn about an Islamic djinn-god that is plotting to envelop the world in fire, through music. The entity unexpectedly arrives via the astronomer's stomach, killing her, and then meets Firth in a pied pier showdown at the climax. • The picture was filmed on location in Turkey.

Bowery to Baghdad (1955; Allied Artists) D: Edward Bernds. P: Ben Schwalb. S: Elwood Ullman, Edward Bernds. C: Hary Neumann. Cast: Huntz Hall, Leo Gorcey, Bernard Gorcey, Stanley Clements, Joan Shawlee. Look out, it's the Bowery Boys with Aladdin's lamp and a genie. • Director Ed Bernds told Ted Okuda in an article published in *FilmFax* magazine that this film was his favorite of all the Bowery Boys entries. • Actor Bernard Gorcey is the father of Leo. Ed Bernds said in the Okuda article that Bernard "wasn't treated well by Leo. Oh, there was a rough affection there, but Leo could have been kinder. Leo used to make fun of his father and put him down."

The Boy and the Pirates (1960; United Artists) D/P: Bert I. Gordon. S: Lillie Hayward, Jerry Sackheim. C: Ernest Haller. Cast: Charles Herbert, Susan Gordon, Murvyn Vye, Paul Guilfoyle, Joseph Turkel, Morgan Jones. A genie sends a boy back to the time of Blackbeard the Pirate. • Susan Gordon is director Bert I. Gordon's daughter.

The Brass Bottle (1964; Universal) D: Harry Keller. P: Robert Arthur. S: Oscar Brodney. C: Clifford Stine. Cast: Tony Randall, Burl Ives, Barbara Eden, Edward Andrews, Ann Doran. This contemporary comedy features Burl Ives as a bumbling genie who aids Tony Randall. • The film also features a second genie, played by Kamala Devi.

The Genie (1953; U.K.) D: Lance Comfort. P: Douglas Fairbanks, Jr. S: Doreen Montgomery. C: Brendan Stafford. Cast: Douglas Fairbanks, Jr., Yvonne Furneaux, Martin Miller. Douglas Fairbanks, Jr., plays the djinn of Aladdin's lamp who becomes mortal for a time until he is forced to return to his former occupation when he is pressed into using his magic. • There also exists a 1957 film short titled *The Genie* written by Fritz Leiber (who also plays the genie) and starring the guru of monster fandom, Forrest J Ackerman, editor of the magazine, *Famous Monsters of Filmland.*

I Dream of Jeannie: 15 Years Later (1985; TV Movie) D: William Asher. P: Hugh Benson. S: Irma Kalish. C: Jack Whitman. Cast: Barbara Eden, Wayne Rogers, Bill

Daily, Hayden Rorke, John Bennett Perry, Mackenzie Astin. Fifteen years after the series, Jeannie is happily married to her astronaut and former master. She is upset when he breaks his promise to retire in order to go on one more mission—accompanied by an attractive female colleague. • Mackenzie Astin, son of Patty Duke and John Astin, plays Jeannie's teenage son.

1001 Arabian Nights (1959; Columbia; animated) D: Jack Kinney. P: Stephen Bosustow. S: Czenzi Ormonde. Cast (voices): Jim Backus, Kathryn Grant, Hans Conried, Dwayne Hickman, Herschel Bernardi. This is an animated cartoon adventure about Aladdin finding a lamp and resident genie. • The voice of "Mr. Magoo" (Jim Backus) plays Aladdin's uncle.

The Outing (1987; H.L.T. Films) D: Tom Daley. P/S: Warren Chaney. C: Herbert Raditschnig. Cast: Deborah Winters, James Huston, Andra St. Ivanyi, Scott Bankston, Mark Mitchell. An evil genie possesses a teenage girl, killing all her friends in a variety of nasty ways. At the climax, the genie reveals itself, showing off his 20-foot demonic appearance, only to be killed when the lamp is destroyed. • Writer/producer Warren Chaney is the husabnd of top-billed actress Deborah Winters. • The film was predominantly financed by investors in Kuwait.

Sabu and the Magic Ring (1957; Allied Artists) D: George Blair. P: Maurice Duke. S: Sam Roeca, Benedict Freedman, John Fenton Murray. C: Harry Neuman. Cast: Sabu, Daria Massey, Robert Shafto, Peter Mamakos, William Marshall, Vladimir Sokoloff, Ken Terrell. When Sabu rubs an enchanted ring, a genie (played by William Marshall) appears.

The Seventh Voyage of Sinbad (1958) (see SINBAD). Sinbad uses a boy-genie to help protect himself and his princess bride-to-be from an evil sorcerer and the monstrous cyclops which menaces the island of Colossa. ¶ "The genie of the lamp cannot be used to work harm, but in protection his powers are invincible." • At the climax, the genie, who was granted freedom from his bottle and the ability to live out a normal mortal life, ends up back aboard Sinbad's ship as his willing cabin boy.

Sinbad, Ali Baba, and Aladdin (1963) (see SINBAD). Sinbad and Ali Baba team up with Aladdin and his genie to face a fire-breathing dragon in this amalgam from India.

Sorority Babes in the Slimeball Bowl-o-Rama (1988; Urban Classics) D: David DeCoteau. P: David DeCoteau, John Schouweiler. S: Sergei Hasenecz. C: Stephen Ashley Blake. Cast: Linnea Quigley, Andras Jones, Robin Rochelle, Hal Havins, Brinke Stevens, Michelle McClellan, Kathi Obrecht, Carla Baron, John Stuart Wildman. A group of sorority sisters and pledges break into a bowling alley with the aim of stealing a bowling trophy to complete their initiation. The trophy they choose just happens to contain a two-foot-tall devilish imp who, when released, promises to grant them each a wish. It turns sour, though, when the imp's true evil nature is revealed. He possesses several of the girls and sends them out to kill the rest. ¶ "Hey, you in the front row, you want a wish? Heh, heh, heh." • This tongue-in-cheek film features a *Bride of Frankenstein* homage when one of the sorority sisters–turned-demon (looking very much like Elsa Lanchester's monster) re-enacts the *Bride*'s famous hiss.

The Thief of Bagdad (1940; United Artists; U.K.) D: Ludwig Berger, Michael Powell, Tim Whelan. P: Alexander Korda. S: Miles Malleson, Lajos Biro. C: George Perinal. Cast: Conrad Veidt, Sabu, June Duprez, John Justin, Rex Ingram. A thief named Abu (Sabu) utilizes the powers of a gigantic genie to help find his friend King Ahmad (John Justin) who, like himself, had been shipwrecked by the evil sorcerer Jaffar (Conrad Veidt). After stealing a gem called the "All-Seeing Eye," Abu is reunited with Ahmad, but thoughtlessly uses his genie's last wish to send his friend to Jaffar's palace. After being left in the wilderness by the genie, Abu breaks the gem which catapults him to an imaginative otherworld. There he receives a magic carpet and a silver crossbow, which enables him to return to the palace and shoot down the sorcerer. In the final moments, Ahmad is reunited with his princess lover and his rightful position is reinstated, leaving Abu free to seek other adventures. ¶ "Oh great and merciful master, let me out and I'll grant you three wishes." • Sabu first encounters the genie on a beach. After freeing the vengeful djinn from his bottle prison, he manages to trick him back inside and blackmail the genie into granting him three wishes. Sabu's first wish was for food (his mother's sausages). His second was to be taken to the place where his friend Ahmad is. His third and last wish is wasted by sending his pal back to the palace. • The associate producers on the film were Zoltan Korda, Alexander's brother, and William Cameron Menzies, the man who directed the 1953 cult classic, *Invaders from Mars*. • All three of the movie-making Kordas were involved in the project—Alexander pro-

The Thief of Bagdad *(1940), played by Sabu, is nearly squashed by the gigantic foot of a frustrated genie (Rex Ingram). Sabu, who freed the djinn, manages to stave off his own death and fool his antagonist into granting him three wishes.*

duced the film, Zoltan was associate producer, and Vincent was credited for the production design. • The numerous, impressive special effects were supervised by Lawrence Butler.

The Thief of Bagdad (1978; TV movie) D: Clive Donner. P: Aida Young. S: A. J. Carothers. C: Denis Lewiston. Cast: Roddy McDowall, Kabir Bedi, Frank Finlay, Marina Vlady, Peter Ustinov, Terence Stamp, Paula Ustinov. A down-on-his-luck thief runs head-on into adventures with a sorcerer, magic carpets, and a lamp-encased genie. • Peter Ustinov's daughter, Paula, also appears in the film.

A Thousand and One Nights (1945; Columbia) D: Alfred E. Green. P: Samuel Bischoff. S: Richard English, Jack Henley, W. H. Pettit. C: Ray Rennahan. Cast: Cornel Wilde, Evelyn Keyes, Phil Silvers, Adele Jergens, Dusty Anderson, Philip Van Zandt, Nestor Paiva, Shelley Winters. Cornel Wilde rubs the magic lamp and out pops Evelyn Keyes as the female genie. • Watch for a brief appearance by Rex Ingram, reprising his role as a genie from *The Thief of Bagdad* (1940).

Where Do We Go from Here? (1945; 20th Century–Fox) D: Gregory Ratoff. P: William Perlberg. S: Morrie Ryskind. C: Leon Shamroy. Cast: Fred MacMurray, Joan Leslie, June Haver, Gene Sheldon, Anthony Quinn, Alan Mowbray. Fred MacMurray finds Aladdin's lamp and asks the genie to get him into the army, but the genie sends him into the past by mistake. Fred ends up serving in George Washington's Minutemen brigade. • Co-star Anthony Quinn was born in Chihuahua, Mexico, and married the adopted daughter of Cecil B. DeMille about one year after he entered the movies in 1936. It took a long time before Quinn really became a success (1952 to be exact), winning a supporting Oscar for *Viva Zapata*. He also appeared in the genre pictures *Ulysses* (1954) and *The Hunchback of Notre Dame* (the 1957 French version).

The Wizard of Bagdad (1961; 20th Century–Fox) D: George Sherman. P: Sam Katzman. S: Jesse L. Lasky, Jr., Pat Silvers. C: Ellis Carter. Cast: Dick Shawn, Diane Baker, Barry Coe, John Van Dreelen, Robert F. Simon. Dick Shawn plays a genie who temporarily loses his magical powers when he fails to follow through with a marriage guarantee. All is set right when the couple is married later on, and the genie uses a magical horse and flying carpet to aid him in his attempt to help a prince.

Wonders of Aladdin (1961; MGM; Italy) D: Henry Levin. P: Joseph E. Levine. S: Luther Davis. C: Tonino Delli Colli. Cast: Donald O'Connor, Noelle Adam, Vittorio De Sica, Aldo Fabrizi, Michèle Mercier. Aladdin finds a magical lamp inhabited by a genie who grants him three wishes. • Popular horror director Mario Bava directed most of the second unit action on this film. • One of Italy's foremost filmmakers, Vittorio De Sica, played the genie in this picture. De Sica won four Best Foreign Film Oscars over the course of his career (*Shoeshine* [1946], *The Bicycle Thief* [1948], *Yesterday, Today and Tomorrow* [1963], and *The Garden of the Finzi-Continis* [1971]). His masterpiece of Italian neorealism, *The Bicycle Thief,* is often mentioned by film historians and critics as the best film ever made. Despite his great success as a director, De Sica was far more prolific as an actor (appearing in 154 pictures), which helped in bringing in enough money to finance his directing endeavors. • Director Henry Levin was the man who made the 1959 Jules Verne hit, *Journey to the Center of the Earth.*

Ghosts

Ghost stories are among the oldest tales in history. Nothing sends chills up the spine and sets the hair on edge like a scary story. Everyone likes a good ghost yarn. Psychologically, the appeal of ghost stories can be traced to something much deeper than the delicious chills they induce. A ghost tale can be seen as a way to combat the age-old fear of death. By their very nature, ghosts validate the idea that there is a further existence after death and maybe even a way back to life. While frightening on the surface, ghost stories are also comforting in their reaffirmation of an existence after death.

With one notable exception, ghosts began in the cinema as creatures of comedy, appearing in films like *Topper* (1937) and *The Ghost Breakers* (1940). Producers apparently felt that ghosts lent themselves better to sight gags than fright gags. The early exception is the 1933 Halperin Brothers' misfire, *Supernatural.* This tepid tale, starring Carole Lombard as a woman possessed by the ghost of a murderess, was panned by critics and ignored by moviegoers. (Incidentally, "sophisticated comedies" like *Topper* and its relations will not be found in this book, since due to space limitations only those ghost films with at least some brief element of horror or suspense are included.)

Surprisingly, Hollywood was a little slow in taking advantage of the frightening possibilities of this particular aspect of the occult (though perhaps not so surprisingly if they were using *Supernatural* as a gauge). Audiences had to wait until 1944 for the first well-made serious ghost movie. *The Uninvited,* a truly haunting tale of love and hate from beyond the grave, is the first of what are considered the "big three" ghost films (the other two being *The Innocents,* 1961, and *The Haunting,* 1963). There followed a smattering of spirits, haunted houses, and vengeful specters, led by Britain's first horror film since the beginning of World War II — the classic anthology, *Dead of Night* (1945). Another early highlight came from the surprising direction of poverty row, in the form of the atmospheric *Strangler of the Swamp* (also 1945), PRC's finest achievement. The 1950s saw showman supreme William Castle launch plastic skeletons at unsuspecting audiences during the entertaining *House of Haunted Hill* (1959), and later handing out cardboard "Ghost Viewers" to patrons of his aptly named *13 Ghosts* (1960).

Then, in 1961, filmmaker Jack Clayton took Henry James' classic novel, *The*

Turn of the Screw, and turned it into a terrifying study of repressed hysteria and spectral possession for *The Innocents* (number two in the "big three").

What is perhaps the definitive haunted house film came a mere two years later in the form of Robert Wise's chilling masterpiece in understated terror, *The Haunting* (1963). Though no ghosts are ever shown onscreen, Wise uses sounds, camera movement, and editing to create a supernatural atmosphere ripe with ghostly terror, and in the process delivers several of the most frightening moments in the history of cinema. With *The Innocents, The Haunting,* and nearly two dozen other ghost movies (including no less than five Barbara Steele imports), the 1960s became the decade of the ghost.

The next ten years were relatively lean ones spectrally-speaking, with the ghostly output dropping off to less than half the volume of the 1960s, and with the entertaining but rather hokey *The Legend of Hell House* (1973) being the decade's dubious pinnacle.

Then came the 1980s. Roughly 40 percent of all the ghost movies filmed to date were made betwen 1980 and 1989, proving that ghosts were not dead after all (at least at the box office and video store). The 1980s also saw a revival of the ghost comedy on a large scale, with megahit horror/comedies like *Ghostbusters* (1984) and *Beetlejuice* (1988) rubbing phantom shoulders with the frightening *The Shining* (1980) and the mass-appealing *Poltergeist* trilogy.

Coming into the 90s, ghosts are very much alive and kicking, represented by films like *The First Power* and *The Sleeping Car* (both 1990). And if the number one surprise hit of the summer of 1990 is any indication (the romantic thriller, *Ghost*), ghost movies will undoubtedly go on haunting the screen for many years to come.

An Angel for Satan (1966; Discobolo Cinematografica; Italy) D: Camillo Mastrocinque. P: Liliana Biancini, Giuliano Simonetti. S: Camillo Mastrocinque, Giuseppe Mangione. C: Giuseppe Aquari. Cast: Barbara Steele, Anthony Steffen, Claudio Gora, Ursula Davis, Aldo Berti, Maureen Melrose, Vassili Karamesinis, Betty Delon. An old statue is recovered from a lake, which triggers a ghost to appear and possess the body of a young woman in this gothic-flavored Italian ghost story. • British actress Barbara Steele earned her title as scream queen supreme in roles like this one. She made a spate of Italian horror films in which she played vengeful spirits, including *Castle of Blood* (1964), *The Long Hair of Death* (1964), *Nightmare Castle* (1965), and *The She Beast* (1965).

Back from the Dead (1957; 20th Century–Fox) D: Charles Marquis Warren. P: Robert Stadler. S: Catherine Turney. C: Ernest Haller. Cast: Peggy Castle, Arthur Franz, Marsha Hunt, Marianne Stewart, Evelyn Scott, Otto Reichow. Arthur Franz takes his new wife to a seaside retreat. There she falls under the spell of his deceased first wife, who was a powerful satanist when she was alive. The evil spirit possesses the new bride

with plans to make it a permanent arrangement. • *Back from the Dead* was released on a double bill with *The Unknown Terror,* also directed by Charles Marquis Warren.

Beetlejuice (1988; Geffen Company/Warner Bros.) D: Tim Burton. P: Michael Bender, Larry Wilson, Richard Hashimoto. S: Michael McDowell, Warren Skaaren. C: Thomas Ackerman. Cast: Alec Baldwin, Geena Davis, Michael Keaton, Jeffrey Jones, Catherine O'Hara, Winona Ryder, Sylvia Sidney, Robert Goulet, Dick Cavett, Glenn Shadix, Annie McEnroe. The Maitlands, a likable young couple, are killed in a car accident and become ghosts trapped in their own home, with nothing but the cryptic *Guide to the Newly Deceased* handbook to explain it all. Along comes a rich, abrasive, "avant-garde" New York family who moves into their small-town home. The title character, "Betelgeuse," is a bizarre renegade spirit hired by the Maitlands to scare the annoying living folks out of their house, with disastrously funny results. ¶ "I'm the ghost with the most, babe." • This wildly inventive brainchild from second-time director Tim Burton cost only $13 million to film and grossed over $73 million. Burton went on to direct the mega-hyped megahit, *Batman*

(1989), and the wonderful fantasy, *Edward Scissorhands* (1991).

Beyond Evil (1980; IFI-Scope III) D: Herb Freed. P: David Baughn, Herb Freed. S: Herb Freed, Paul Ross. C: Ken Plotin. Cast: John Saxon, Lynda Day George, Michael Dante, Mario Milano, Anne Marisse, Janice Lynde, David Opatoshu. Lynda Day George is possessed by the spirit of a vengeful witch. With the aid of a local healer, husband John Saxon uses his love to fight off the satanic spirit. ¶ "For over a hundred years her spirit has terrorized the island. To keep her power alive, she needs the sacrifice of innocent victims. Some she simply kills, for others the fate is far worse."

Black Sabbath (1964) (see ANTHOLOGIES). In "The Drop of Water" segment, a nurse steals a valuable ring from the hand of a dead woman, but the woman's ghost seeks revenge.

The Boogeyman (1980; Jerry Gross Organization) D/P/S: Ulli Lommel. C: David Sperling, Jochen Breitenstein. Cast: Suzanna Love, Ron James, John Carradine, Nicholas Love, Raymond Boyden, Felicite Morgan, Bill Rayburn, Llewelyn Thomas, Jay Wright. A woman is haunted by the spirit of her mother's murdered lover. She returns to the house where it happened and sees the spirit in a mirror, which she smashes. But one of the fragments still contains the evil force, and becomes the impetus for further death and destruction.

Boogeyman 2 (1982; New West Films) (also *Revenge of the Boogeyman*). D: Bruce Starr. P: Bruce Starr, Ulli Lommel. S: Ulli Lommel, Suzanna Love. C; Philippe Carr-Foster, David Sperling. Cast: Suzanna Love, Shannah Hall, Ulli Lommel, Shoto Von Douglas, Bob Rosenfarb, Ashley Du-Bay, Rhonda Aldrich, Sarah Jean Watkins, Rock MacKenzie. Suzanna Love returns in this sequel to *The Boogeyman* (1980) as the woman haunted by the spirit inhabiting a broken shard of mirror. It is six months later, and she moves to Los Angeles to stay with a filmmaker friend. The director wants to make a movie out of her experiences, but those experiences become all too real when that possessed shard of glass shows up again, causing another round of gruesome deaths. • In a nice bit of ironic casting, Ulli Lommel plays the director who wants to film the woman's experiences from the previous movie. Lommel actually directed the previous film. • In the interest of economy, a large portion of this film's running time is taken up with flashback sequences lifted from the first movie.

Carnival of Souls (1962; Herts-Lion) D/P: Herk Harvey. S: John Clifford. C: Maurice Prather. Cast: Candace Hillgloss, Frances Fiest, Sidney Berger, Art Ellison, Herk Harvey. A woman is apparently drowned when her car plunges off a bridge into a river. But hours later she reappears on the shore and makes her way to Lawrence, Kansas, to take up a job as a church organist. Troubled, she is haunted by the frightening apparition of a strange, dead-looking man. Drawn to an abandoned amusement park, she sees the specters of the dead dancing in a macabre ballroom dance and is forced to join in the bizarre scene. Later, when her car is finally pulled from the river, we see her dead body in the front seat. • This ultra-low budget ($30,000) oddity filmed in Kansas has become a cult movie favorite and has garnered quite a large critical following as well. Its moody black and white photography and almost surrealistic scenes create an otherworldiness hard to find in most bigger-budgeted films. • This was industrial filmmaker Herk Harvey's only feature film. Due to budgetary restrictions, Harvey himself played the lead specter.

Castle of Blood (1964; Woolner; France/Italy) (also *Castle of Terror*). D: Anthony Dawson (Antonio Margheriti). P: Frank Belty (Marco Vicario), Walter Sarch (Giovanni Addessi). S: Jean Grimaud (Gianni Grimaldi), Gordon Wilson, Jr. (Sergio Corbucci). C: Richard Kramer (Riccardo Pallottini). Cast: Barbara Steele, Georges Rivière, Margaret Robsahn, Sylvia Sorente, Henry Kruger, Montgomery Glenn (Silvano Tranquili), Raoul H. Newman (Umberto Raho). A man is challenged by Edgar Allan Poe and Lord Blackwood to spend a night in a haunted castle of All Soul's Eve. He accepts the challenge and witnesses several ghosts reenact their murders. He also falls in love with Elizabeth Blackwood (Barbara Steele) and discovers she has no heartbeat — she too is a ghost inhabiting the castle. ¶ From the ads: "The living and the dead change places in an orgy of terror." • Director Antonio Margheriti remade his own film as *Web of the Spider* in 1972.

Cathy's Curse (1977; 21st Century; Canada) D: Eddy Matalon. P: Eddy Matalon, Nicole Mathieu Boisvert. S: Myra Clement, Eddy Matalon, Alain Sens-Cazanave. C: Jean-Jacques Tarbes, Richard Cuipka. Cast: Alan Scarfe, Randi Allen, Beverly Murray, Roy Witham, Mary Morer, Dorothy Davis, Linda Koot, Peter McNeil. A young girl dies in a car crash with her father. Thirty years later, her grown brother and his wife and daughter move back to the old family home. Their daughter is possessed by the malignant spirit of the dead girl (her aunt in fact), whose power seems to emanate from a strange old doll.

The Changeling (1980; Associated Film Distribution; Canada) D: Peter Medak. P: Joel B. Michaels, Garth H. Drabinsky. S: William Gray, Diana Maddox. C: John Coquillon. Cast: George C. Scott, Trish Van Devere, Melvyn Douglas, John Colicos, Jean Marsh, Barry Morse, James Douglas, Roberta Maxwell. George C. Scott is a composer who moves into a house inhabited by the spirit of a murdered child. The sickly child was killed and a changeling was substituted in his place, growing up to become a powerful senator. Now the ghost of the cheated child wants vindication, and it is up to Scott to discover the secret. • The film's most frightening moments come when the ghost takes possession of its child's wheelchair and causes it to chase the terrified cast members through the house.

The Curse of the Cat People (1944; RKO) D: Gunther V. Fritsch, Robert Wise. P: Val Lewton. S: DeWitt Bodeen. C: Nicholas Mosuraca. Cast: Simone Simon, Kent Smith, Jane Randolph, Ann Carter, Eve March, Julia Dean, Elizabeth Russell, Erford Gage, Sir Lancelot. This sequel that's not a sequel picks up years after Irena's death in *Cat People* (1942). Her husband (Kent Smith) has remarried and has a young daughter. The daughter is lonely and troubled. She wishes for a friend and the ghost of Irena appears to her as a playmate. The child sinks deeper and deeper into her fantasy world until she is in danger of becoming lost in it, until the ghost of Irena helps her find the way back. ¶ "Do you know why I came to you Amy, why I came to be your friend? Because you called to me. Out of your loneliness you called me and brought me into being. And I came, so that your childhood could be bright and full of friendliness. Now, you must send me away." • Producer Val Lewton made an intelligent, sensitive dark fantasy film rather than the out and out horror sequel expected by the RKO front office. No cat people appear in the film, just the ghost of Irena (and no mention is made of her previous feline troubles). • Robert Wise made his directorial debut on *The Curse of the Cat People*. He had previously been an editor (he'd edited *Citizen Kane* for Orson Welles,) and when director Gunther Fritsch was drafted into the army, Wise was promoted to director

and finished the film. Years later, screenwriter DeWitt Bodeen claimed that Wise took over from Fritsch because Fritsch "was going too slowly and had to be replaced. A satisfactory explanation was made about his removal because he was going into the army anyway." Wise went on to direct three more genre classics — *The Body Snatchers* (1945; also for producer Val Lewton), *The Day the Earth Stood Still* (1951), and *The Haunting* (1963; arguably the greatest ghost film ever made). • Some critics have claimed that producer Val Lewton's influence on his films has been overemphasized. According to DeWitt Bodeen, Lewton's influence was key to all his films. *"Curse of the Cat People,"* stated Bodden in a later interview, "was Val's concept entirely. When he was given the assignment to make the sequel to *Cat People* he groaned because he was told to call it *Curse of the Cat People*. So he said, 'What I'm going to do is make a very delicate story of a child who is on the verge of insanity because she lives in a fantasy world.'" It is also purported that Lewton wrote the ending to *Curse*.

Dark Places (1972; Cinerama; U.K.) D: Don Sharp. P: James Hannah, Jr. S: Ed Brennan, Joseph Van Winkle. C: Ernest Steward. Cast: Christopher Lee, Robert Hardy, Joan Collins, Herbert Lom, Jane Birkin, Carleton Hobbs, Jennifer Thanisch, Michael McVey, Jean Marsh, Linda Gray. Robert Hardy ("Siegfried" from the British TV series "All Creatures Great and Small") is a man searching for a hidden cache of money in an old abandoned manor house. Christopher Lee, Joan Collins, and Herbert Lom try to scare him away, but Hardy is gradually possessed by the spirit of the house's former owner who murdered his own family.

Dead of Night (1945) (see ANTHOLOGIES). Three of this early classic anthology film's stories concern ghosts. In one, a man is possessed by a haunted mirror. In another, a young girl encounters the sad ghost of a young child at a Christmas party. And in the film's comic segment, the ghost of a golfer comes back to haunt his cheating golf partner.

The Demons of Ludlow (1983) D/P: Bill Rebane. S: William Arthur. C: Ito. Cast: Paul Van Hansen, Stephanie Cushna, James R. Robinson, Carol Perry, D. Dave Davis, Debra Dulman, Angailica. The tiny town of Ludlow receives a mysterious gift of an old type of organ called a harmonium for its bicentennial celebration. Soon the townspeople begin dying in horrible ways. The ghost of the founder of Ludlow has re-turned to exact vengeance on the descen-dants of the superstitious villagers who had cut off his hands (they thought he and his harmonium were a source of evil) and banished him. • This amateurish production was filmed entirely in Wisconsin.

The Evil (1978) (see DEMONS AND DEVILS). When psychologist Richard Crenna leads a group of students into an old haunted house they intend to turn into a drug rehabilitation center, a friendly ghost tries to warn them of the demonic force inhabiting the house.

Eyes of Fire (1984) (see DEMONS AND DEVILS). In 1750, a small group of settlers on the American frontier stumble into a haunted valley. There they encounter a black-faced demon who captures souls and stores them in the trees of the valley. These souls become its ghostly slaves, who materialize to serve the demon in its quest for fresh souls. ¶ "She said the people who built the cabin were now captives of the Devil-Witch. She said the Devil-Witch wanted to make *us* captives too."

The Fall of the House of Usher (1983) (see POE FILMS — MODERN POE). Prolific low-budget Spanish filmmaker Jess Franco's ver-sion of Poe's classic story features Howard Vernon as Roderick Usher, who murders his young wife in a fit of unfounded jealousy. She returns as a ghost to torment him and drive him insane until finally her corpse is burnt and Roderick suffers a fatal heart at-tack as the house crumbles around him.

The First Power (1990; Nelson Entertain-ment) D/S: Robert Resnikoff. P: David Madden. C: Theo Van de Sande. Cast: Lou Diamond Phillips, Tracy Griffith, Jeff Kober, Mykel T. Williamson, Elizabeth Arlen, Dennis Lipscomb, Carmen Argenziano. Lou Diamond Phillips is a police detective who catches the vicious serial killer known as the "Pentagram Killer." The murderer goes to the electric chair, but is granted the demonic "First Power" (the power of resur-rection) and returns as a vengeful ghost to possess various people and continue his reign of terror, with only Phillips and a female psychic able to see the killer's true nature. ¶ "All I know is that he's a spirit now, and except for mind games like mak-ing you see things or hear things, a spirit can't really do anything in the physical world without a body. So Channing pos-sesses bodies." • Director/screenwriter Rob-ert Resnikoff drew his inspiration from a real-life serial killer. "Gary Gilmore be-lieved in reincarnation," Resnikoff told *Fangoria* #90. "He told people, while he was

awaiting execution, 'I don't care if you kill me. I'll just come back as somebody else.' I thought, 'Gee, what an interesting idea.'" • *The First Power* was shot under the title of *Transit*.

The Fog (1980; Avco Embassy) D: John Carpenter. P: Debra Hill. S: John Carpenter, Debra Hill. C: Dean Cundey. Cast: Adri-enne Barbeau, Hal Holbrook, Janet Leigh, Jamie Lee Curtis, John Houseman, Tom Atkins. The small town of Antonio Bay is invaded by the ghosts of a band of drowned pirates on the one hundredth anniversary of their deaths. It is discovered that six of the original town founders made a deal with the pirates and then betrayed them by luring them to their deaths on the rocks. The vengeful ghosts arrive under cover of an eerie unnatural fog and their entrance is always preceded by three ominous knocks. ¶ "It is told by the fishermen and their fathers and grandfathers that when the fog returns to Antonio Bay, the men at the bottom of the sea out in the water by Spivey Point will rise up and search for the campfire that led them to their dark, icy death." • Female lead Adrienne Barbeau is the wife of director John Carpenter.

The Forgotten One (1989; Wind River Productions) D/S: Phillip Badger. P: Peter Garrity. C: James Mathers. Cast: Terry O'Quinn, Kristy McNichol, Elisabeth Brooks, Blair Parker. A troubled writer moves into a house haunted by the spirit of a woman murdered by her jealous husband in the nineteenth century. He is first frightened by, then attracted to, and finally obsessed with her ghost until he eventually succumbs to the apparition and joins her in the spirit world. ¶ "This is not normal. This is not healthy. This is about death." • Star Terry O'Quinn is most recognized for his in-credibly disturbing portrayal of *The Step-father* (1987).

The Ghost (1963) (see MADMEN — EARLY PSYCHOS). In this follow-up film to *The Horrible Dr. Hichcock* (1962), Dr. Hich-cock is back as a cripple who's killed by his unfaithful wife (Barbara Steele) and her lover. The doctor is only faking his death, however, and returns to drive his wife in-sane and exact revenge on her lover. Despite the title, no real ghosts appear.

Ghost (1990; Paramount) D: Jerry Zucker. P: Lisa Weinstein. S: Bruce Joel Rubin. C: Adam Greenberg. Cast: Patrick Swayze, Demi Moore, Whoopi Goldberg, Tony Goldwyn, Rick Aviles, Gail Boggs, Armelia McQueen, Vincent Schiavelli. Patrick Swayze and Demi Moore play an upscale couple in

New York. Swayze is murdered and returns as a ghost. Aided by phony medium Whoopi Goldberg, he must prevent Moore from falling prey to the evil machinations of his own killer. • This romantic ghost story became the surprise runaway hit of the summer (earning well over $200 million). • Whoopi Goldberg won the Best Supporting Actress Oscar for her role in this film (becoming only the second black actress to win this award).

The Ghost Breakers (1940; Paramount) D: George Marshall. P: Arthur Hornblow, Jr. S: Walter De Leon. C: Charles Lang, Theodore Sparkuhl. Cast: Bob Hope, Paulette Goddard, Richard Carlson, Paul Lukas, Willie Best, Anthony Quinn, Noble Johnson. Bob Hope and his valet Willie Best go to Cuba to help Paulette Goddard investigate her recently inherited haunted castle. Once there, they run afoul of human villains, a zombie, and a real ghost in this early horror/comedy. ¶ "I'm a ghost-breaker. You've heard of trust-breakers and home-breakers, I'm a ghost-breaker. I take family skeletons out of the closet and dust them off" — Bob Hope. • Paramount made this film to capitalize on their previous success at teaming Bob Hope and Paulette Goddard in the mystery/comedy *The Cat and the Canary* (1939). The publicity department played it up in their advertising: "The stars of *The Cat and the Canary* find love and laughter in a haunted house!"

Ghost Catchers (1944; Universal) D: Eddie Cline. P/S: Edmund L. Hartman. C: Charles Van Enger. Cast: Ole Olsen, Chic Johnson, Gloria Jean, Martha O'Driscoll, Leo Carrillo, Andy Devine, Lon Chaney, Kirby Grant, Walter Catlett, Ella Mae Morse. Former vaudevillian team Olsen and Johnson were a low-class version of Abbott and Costello who starred in a string of low-budget comedies in the 1940s. Here they play nightclub owners who match wits (what little they possess) with a bunch of gangsters holed up in the house next door. They are finally aided by the comical (and lecherous) ghost of the house's deceased owner. • Olsen and Johnson started together in vaudeville in 1914 and, unlike most entertainment partners, remained as a team up until 1962 when Johnson died. • Lon Chaney, Jr., is wasted in a role requiring him to wear a bear suit most of the time. • One of the gangsters is Tor Johnson in an early bit part. Tor later achieved a modicum of notoriety in grade-Z horror and sci-fi films of the 1950s, particularly those of Ed Wood. • Morton Downey, who plays a singer in the film, is the father of TV's loud-mouthed "most obnoxious man on television," Morton Downey, Jr. • Director Eddie Cline got his start in the movies as one of the Keystone Cops. • *Ghost Catchers* was shot under the title *High Spirits*.

Ghost Chasers (1951; Monogram) D: William Beaudine. P: Jan Grippo. S: Bert Lawrence. C: Marcel Le Picard. Cast: Leo Gorcey, Huntz Hall, Lloyd Corrigan, Robert Coogan, Jan Kayne, Bernard Gorcey, George Gorcey, Philip Van Zandt, Billy Benedict. This puerile entry in the Bowery Boys series has the "boys" up against a group of phony spirit mediums, aided by the friendly ghost of a jolly fat pilgrim.

Ghost in the Invisible Bikini (1966; AIP) D: Don Weis. P: James H. Nicholson, Samuel Z. Arkoff. S: Louis M. Heywood, Elwood Ullman. C: Stanley Cortez. Cast: Tommy Kirk, Deborah Walley, Aron Kincaid, Quinn O'Hara, Jesse White, Harvey Lembeck, Nancy Sinatra, Basil Rathbone, Patsy Kelly, Boris Karloff, Susan Hart. Boris Karloff plays the recently deceased Hiram Stokely who is visited by the ghost of his long-dead girlfriend. She tells him he must perform one good deed in the next 24 hours if he wants to get into heaven. He sends her ghost (in the invisible bikini) back to Earth to help his rightful heirs win out over those trying to cheat them. ¶ From the ads — "There's Something *Horrid* for Everyone! ... it's the scandalous lowdown on what every young *ghoul* should know!" • *Ghost in the Invisible Bikini* was the biggest budgeted of AIP's "Beach Pictures," but it failed at the box office and so became the last of the beach movies as well. • Guest star Basil Rathbone, renowned for his Hollywood fencing prowess, reportedly did his own fencing in a swordfight with teen star Tommy Kirk, despite the fact that the actor was 73 years old! • One of Larry Buchanan's *Eye Creatures* (1965) turns up to bedevil the cast.

The Ghost of Dragstrip Hollow (1959; AIP) D: William Hole, Jr. P/S: Lou Rusoff. C: Gilbert Warenton. Cast: Jody Fair, Martin Braddock, Russ Bender, Leon Tyler, Elaine Dupont, Paul Blaisdell. A group of drag-racing teenagers stage a party in a haunted house and are treated to the usual phony spook-fest, though one real ghost puts in a cameo appearance at the film's conclusion. ¶ "Hep cats and hot rodders, they're all alive to the jive" — promotional trailer.

Ghost Ship (1952; Abtcon Pictures; U.K.) D/P/S: Vernon Sewell. C: Stanley Grant. Cast: Dermot Walsh, Hazel Court, Hugh

Burden, John Robinson, Joss Ambler, Joan Carol, Hugh Latimer, Joss Ackland, Mignon O'Doherty. A young couple buy a yacht which turns out to be haunted by the ghost of the boat's previous owner who had murdered his wife and her lover, hiding their bodies onboard. With the aid of a psychic investigator they are able to dispel the malignant spirit and take possession of their new happy home. • Filmmaker Vernon Sewell used his own yacht as a setting for the film. • Leading lady Hazel Court was married to leading man Dermot Walsh at the time.

Ghost Story (1981; Universal) D: John Irvin. P: Burt Weissbourd. S: Lawrence D. Cohen. C: Jack Cardiff. Cast: Fred Astaire, Melvyn Douglas, Douglas Fairbanks, Jr., John Houseman, Craig Wasson, Patricia Neal, Alice Krige. Fred Astaire, Melvyn Douglas, Douglas Fairbanks, Jr., and John Houseman play the elderly members of "The Chowder Society" who are haunted by the vengeful spirit of a beautiful girl they accidentally killed five decades earlier. • The film is based on the popular novel of the same name by Peter Straub.

Ghost Town (1988; Empire Pictures) D: Richard Governor. P: Timothy D. Tennant. S: Duke Sandefur. C: Mac Ahlberg. Cast: Frank Luz, Jimmie F. Skaggs, Catherine Hickland, Bruce Glover, Michael Alldredge. A modern-day sheriff visits the ghost town of "Cruz del Diablo" only to find it populated by ghosts and lorded over by an evil ghostly gunfighter named "Devlin." ¶ "The Good, the Bad, the Satanic"—an apropos ad-line. • At the film's climax, the hero dispatches the specter of the gunfighter by hitting him with an old sheriff's badge right between the eyes.

Ghostbusters (1984; Columbia) D/P: Ivan Reitman. S: Dan Aykroyd, Harold Ramis. C: Laszlo Kovacs, Herb Wagreitch. Cast: Bill Murray, Dan Aykroyd, Sigourney Weaver, Harold Ramis, Rick Moranis, Annie Potts, William Atherton, Ernie Hudson, David Margulies, Steven Tash. Three out-of-work psychic investigators form a ghost exterminator service when New York is plagued by ever-increasing instances of ghostly disturbances. They finally discover the root of this evil—an ancient Sumerian demon who intends to invade and destroy the world. ¶ "We came, we saw, we kicked its ass!" • This blockbuster horror/comedy's theme song, "Ghostbusters," became a hit for Ray Parker, Jr.

Ghostbusters 2 (1989; Columbia) D/P: Ivan Reitman. S: Harold Ramis, Dan Ayk-royd. C: Michael Chapman. Cast: Bill Murray, Dan Aykroyd, Sigourney Weaver, Harold Ramis, Rick Moranis, Ernie Hudson, Annie Potts, Peter MacNichol, Kurt Fuller, David Margulies. Those irrepressible "Ghostbusters" are back, this time battling the spirit of an evil Moldavian prince, who has come back through his own portrait and attempts to possess Sigourney Weaver's baby. There's also a river of slime flowing under New York City ("pure concentrated evil") which causes all manner of ghostly infestations. ¶ "Great, while you're working on it I'm going down in history as the mayor who let New York get sucked down into the tenth level of hell." • This so-so sequel to the 1984 megahit didn't fare well with critics and scored only moderately at the box office.

Ghostriders (1988; Ghost Riders Inc.) D: Alan Stewart. P: Alan Stewart, Thomas L. Callaway, James J. Desmarais. S: Clay McBride, James J. Desmarais. C: Thomas L. Callaway. Cast: Bill Shaw, Mike Ammons, Arland Bishop, Ricky Long, Jim Peters, Cari Powell. In rural Texas, the ghosts of a band of outlaws return 100 years after their deaths to take revenge on the descendants of those who hanged them in this small-scale production filmed on location near Waco, Texas. ¶ "You, you're all dead! You're all dead!" • Though these ghostly outlaws appear to die when shot, they soon turn up again with six-guns blazing. The only way to truly kill them and send their souls back to Hell is to shoot them with an antique shotgun which belonged to the outlaw leader.

Ghosts in Rome (1961; Lux Films/Vides/Galatea; Italy) D: Antonio Pietrangeli. P: Franco Cristaldi. S: Antonio Pietrangeli, Ennio Flaiano, Sergio Amidei, Ettore Scola, Ruggero Maccari. C: Guiseppe Rotunno. Cast: Marcello Mastroianni, Vittorio Gassman, Belinda Lee, Sandra Milo, Eduardo De Filippo. In this Italian ghost comedy, the lord of a manor house is killed when his hot water heater blows up, and he bands together with the other ghosts of the house to prevent the sale of his property. • Director Antonio Pietrangeli was a qualified doctor before turning to a career in film.

Ghosts—Italian Style (1969; MGM; Italy) D: Renato Catellani. P: Jone Tuzi. S: Renato Castellani, Adriano Baracco, Leo Benvenuti, Piero De Bernardi. C: Tonino Delli Colli. Cast: Sophia Loren, Vittorio Gassman, Mario Adorf, Aldo Guiffre, Margaret Lee. Sophia Loren and Vittorio Gassman play poor newlyweds who move into a haunted house in this Italian ghost comedy. • Male lead Vittorio Gassman starred in another supernatural comedy, *Ghosts in Rome,* in 1961.

Ghosts of Hanley House (1968; Victoria Productions) D/S: Louise Sherrill. P: Joseph S. Durkin, Jr. C: Claude Fullerton. Cast: Elsie Baker, Barbra Chase, Wilkie De Martel, Roberta Reeves, Cliff Scott, Leonard Shoemaker. A group of young people decide to spend the night at a notorious haunted house to try and solve the mysterious events that occur there. They are confronted by real ghosts who first frighten them and then aid them in uncovering the horrible secrets behind their hauntings. ¶ "I don't believe in ghosts—and I don't think there's anything wrong with the Hanley place that a good bucket of paint won't fix." • It turns out the malignant spirits wanted nothing more than a decent burial all along: "Bury our bodies and we'll haunt this house no more," they finally tell the protagonists.

The Girl in a Swing (1988; Nordisk; U.K.) D: Gordon Hessler. P: Just Betzer, Benni Korzen. C: Claus Loof. Cast: Meg Tilly, Rupert Frazer, Nicholas le Prevost, Elspet Gray, Lorna Heilbron, Claire Shepherd. An Englishman marries a young woman seemingly haunted by a female specter who knows the woman's secret guilt. • Three versions of this film exist—the full director's cut shown theatrically in Europe, the truncated American theatrical version, and the American video release which consists of the shortened version with a narration added to smooth over some of the missing material. • The film is based on Richard Adams' novel of the same name.

Grave Secrets (1989; Shapiro Glickenhaus Entertainment) D: Donald P. Borchers. P: Michael Alan Shores. S: Jeffery Polman, Lenore Wright. C: Jamie Thompson. Cast: Paul Le Mat, Renee Soutendijk, Lee Ving, Olivia Barash, David Warner, John Crawford. A woman, disturbed by ghostly manifestations at her old house, contacts a psychic investigator. Together they learn the horrific truth about the headless ghost which has attached its evil presence to the terrified woman. ¶ "This demented thing will stop at nothing. It will destroy everything it contacts."

Hatchet for a Honeymoon (1969) (see MADMEN—EARLY PSYCHOS). A psychotic fashion designer axes women in bridal gowns to make up for his impotency with his own wife. When he finally gets around to axing her, she returns as a ghost to haunt him. The only thing is, he is the only one who *cannot* see her! She follows him around and

everyone else assumes she's alive since nobody knows he murdered her. This strange twist on the usual ghostly haunting eventually causes this psycho to become even crazier than he already is.

The Haunting (1963; MGM) D/P: Robert Wise. S: Nelson Gidding. C: David Boulton. Cast: Julie Harris, Claire Bloom, Richard Johnson, Russ Tamblyn, Lois Maxwell, Fay Compton, Rosalie Crutchley, Valentine Dyall, Diane Clare. A group of psychic investigators comes to stay at the legendary Hill House, an evil mansion with a history of murder, suicide, and strange occurrences. Once there they are plagued by frightening noises, supernatural chills, and feelings of dread, seeming to focus in particular on one repressed member of their party (Julie Harris). ¶ "Silence lay steadily against the wood and stone of Hill House, and whatever walked there walked alone." • Though no ghosts are ever shown onscreen, director Robert Wise used sound, camera angles, and suggestion to make a superior ghost film considered by many to be the finest of its type. In a 1988 interview for *Deep Red #3*, respected makeup artist Tom Savini gave this endorsement: "One of the greatest horror movies around had absolutely no makeup effects or monsters—*The Haunting.* That was a scary, scary film. It was all in manipulating the audience and then scaring them with the stuff you planted in their brains early on." • *The Haunting* is based on the Shirley Jackson novel, *The Haunting of Hill House.*

The Haunting of Julia (1977; Discovery; U.K./Canada) D: Richard Loncraine. P: Peter Fetterman, Alfred Pariser. S: Dave Humphries. C: Peter Hannan. Cast: Keir Dullea, Mia Farrow, Tom Conti, Jill Bennett, Cathleen Nesbitt, Robin Gammell, Edward Hardwicke, Mary Morris, Pauline Jameson. Mia Farrow plays a woman who feels repsonsible for the death of her child. She moves into an old house which is haunted by the evil spirit of a little girl who led her playmates in murdering another child. • The film is based on the novel *Julia* by Peter Straub (who also wrote *Ghost Story,* from which the film of the same name was made).

The Headless Ghost (1959; AIP; U.K.) D: Peter G. Scott. P: Herman Cohen. S: Kenneth Langtry. C: John Wiles. Cast: Richard Lyon, Clive Revill, Liliane Sottane, David Rose, Jack Allen, Alexander Archdale, Carl Bernard. This juvenile ghost comedy is about three American teenagers who must help a restless spirit in Ambrose Castle find his missing head. • Herman Cohen rushed *The Headless Ghost* into production strictly because he needed a second feature for his *Horrors of the Black Museum*.

Hello Mary Lou, Prom Night 2 (1987; Samuel Goldwyn Company; Canada) (also *The Haunting of Hamilton High*). D: Bruce Pittman. P: Peter Simpson. S: Ron Oliver. C: John Herzog. Cast: Michael Ironside, Wendy Lyon, Justin Louis, Richard Monette, Lisa Schrage, Terri Hawkes, Beverly Hendry, Brock Simpson, Beth Gondek. The ghost of Mary Lou Maloney, a prom queen accidentally burned to death in 1957, comes back to her high school to wreak supernatural havoc. • This follow-up to *Prom Night* (a straight slasher film) is a sequel in name only. • Mary Lou returns in *Prom Night 3: The Last Kiss*.

High Spirits (1988; Tri-Star Pictures/ Vision P.D.G.) D/S: Neil Jordan. P: Stephen Woolley, David Saunders. C: Alex Thomson. Cast: Daryl Hannah, Peter O'Toole, Steve Guttenberg, Beverly D'Angelo, Jennifer Tilly, Liam Neeson, Peter Gallagher, Ray McAnally, Martin Ferrero, Connie Booth. Peter O'Toole plays the eccentric lord of a Scottish castle who turns his home into a hotel for tourists in order to save the family estate. He concocts a desperate plan to drum up business by advertising it as a haunted castle (providing his own phony ghosts of course). It turns out the castle really *is* haunted, and one American visitor falls in love with a female ghost (Daryl Hannah) who is forced to reenact the night of her murder over and over again. ¶ "If I'm murdered one more time, I'll scream." • Though uncredited, screenwriter Michael McDowell worked with Neil Jordan on the screenplay. McDowell is the author of the most successful ghost comedy of the decade, *Beetlejuice* (1988).

Hillbillys in a Haunted House (1967; Woolner Brothers) D: Jean Yarbrough. P: Bernard Woolner. S: Duke Yelton. Cast: Ferlin Husky, Joi Lansing, Don Bowman, Basil Rathbone, John Carradine, Lon Chaney, Jr., Molly Bee, Merle Haggard, Sonny James, George Barrows. Two country music stars spend a night in a haunted house which is being used as a hideout for a ring of spies seeking an atomic formula in this laughable attempt at a horror comedy. • Sadly, this pitiful affair was Basil Rathbone's last film. The former star was paid $10,000 for two weeks. It was also the last film of director Jean Yarbrough, who got his start in horror with the Bela Lugosi vehicle, *The Devil Bat*, in 1940. • John Carradine later made this comment about the film: "I suppose it was crap but we had to do it." • *Hillbillys in a Haunted House* is a sequel to *Las Vegas Hillbillys* (1966).

The Horror Show (1989; United Artists) D: James Isaac. P: Sean S. Cunningham. S: Alan Smithee, Leslie Bohem. C: Mac Ahlberg. Cast: Lance Henriksen, Brion James, Rita Taggart, Dedee Pfeiffer, Aron Eisenberg, Thom Bray, Matt Clark. Lance Henriksen plays a police detective responsible for the capture of the notorious psychokiller Horace Pinkerton (Brion James). When Pinkerton is put to death in the electric chair he vows to return and take revenge on the detective. During his particularly messy electrocution, Pinkerton's spirit manages to escape into the electrical system and now can travel about as an electrical ghost to wreak his vengeance.

House (1985; New World Pictures) D: Steve Miner. P: Sean S. Cunningham. S: Ethan Wiley. C: Mac Ahlberg. Cast: William Katt, George Wendt, Richard Moll, Kay Lenz, Michael Ensign, Susan French, Mary Stavin. A successful writer, struggling with setting his Vietnam experiences down on paper, inherits a creepy house from his aunt. He moves in and is terrorized by all manner of supernatural happenings. He finally confronts the cause of all this ghostly phenomena—the specter of an old Army buddy who blames him for being tortured at the hands of the enemy. • Despite the grim subject matter, the filmmakers took a decidedly tongue-in-cheek approach. It was a surprise hit and inspired an inferior sequel in 1987.

House on Haunted Hill (1958; Allied Artists) D/P: William Castle. S: Robb White. C: Carl E. Guthrie. Cast: Vincent Price, Carol Ohmart, Richard Long, Alan Marshal, Elisha Cook, Jr., Carolyn Craig. Vincent Price plays eccentric millionaire Frederick Loren, who offers five people $10,000 for a one-night stay at his wife's haunted house party. The guests are besieged by all manner of frightening occurrences, including blood dripping from a ceiling, a severed head, a suicide, an acid vat complete with emerging skeleton, and two particularly frightening encounters with the caretaker's blind wife. It is all revealed to be a homicidal double cross set up by the Lorens, who wish to kill each other while the guests serve as pawns in their deadly game ... or are there really ghosts after all? ¶ "It's a pity you didn't know when you started your game of murder, that I was playing too." • The gimmick christened "Emergo" (a skeleton being run across the theater on a hidden wire) was used to startle (or more likely amuse) audiences. • The angular, modernistic, fortress-like mansion used to represent the sinister haunted house was actually the Ennis-Brown House located in the Hollywood Hills. It was designed by Frank Lloyd Wright and built in 1925. It is also very close to the famed Acker-museum (FJA's house of movie memorabilia). • Ad lines extolled such thrills as: "The 13 Greatest shocks of all time! The ever flowing pool of blood that drips from the ceiling. The crawling rope of Death, human heads without bodies. The murder cellar with 20 doors. Room of the living dead. The spectral hangman who roams at midnight." • In an article written by Tom Weaver and John Brunas appearing in *FilmFax* #18, Robb White talked at length about *House on Haunted Hill*. "I liked the whole thing, and liked it right from the beginning. I liked Carol Ohmart too, and I was the one who insisted on having her. We could have had Vincent Price for $12,000 but Bill said, 'No, we'll give him a piece of the movie.'" White said of the skeletons in the theaters, "We finally got it figured out so they worked all right, but then the kids shot them down! They'd come in with everything up to bazookas, and kill our skeletons! Those things cost us more than the movie!"

House 2: The Second Story (1987; New World Pictures) D/S: Ethan Wiley. P: Sean S. Cunningham. C: Mac Ahlberg. Cast: Ayre Gross, Jonathan Stark, Royal Dano, Bill Maher, John Ratzenberger, Lar Park Lincoln, Amy Yasbeck. A young man moves into his haunted ancestral house only to find that it is the gateway to several ghostly dimensions, including Aztec sacrifices, a prehistoric setting, and the old west. The film focuses around their search for a crystal skull with magical properties. ¶ "Look's like you got some kind of alternate universe in there or somethin'." • First time director Ethan Wiley wrote the first *House* (though this sequel has very little to do with the original). • The original had George Wendt ("Norm" from TV's "Cheers"), and the sequel stuck to tradition by featuring John Ratzenberger, who plays "Cliff" in the same series.

The House Where Evil Dwells (1982; MGM/UA; U.S./Japan) D: Kevin Connor. P: Martin B. Cohen. S: Robert A. Subotsky. C: Jacques Haitkin. Cast: Edward Albert, Susan George, Doug McClure, Amy Barrett, Mako Hattori, Toshiyuki Sasaki, Toshiya Maruyama, Tsuyako Okajima,

Henry Mitowa. An American couple moves into a house in Kyoto, Japan, and are taken over by the ghosts of murder and hara-kiri victims, the results of a 140-year-old love triangle. When possessed, the couple and a family friend are forced to reenact the fateful events. • The film was shot entirely at the Toei studios in Japan. Director Kevin Connor had previously directed the witty, dark-humored *Motel Hell* in 1980. Unfortunately, he was also responsible for the juvenile dinosaur movies, *The Land That Time Forgot* (1975) and *The People That Time Forgot* (1977), both again with Doug McClure as the hero.

The Innocents (1961; 20th Century–Fox; U.K./U.S.) D/P: Jack Clayton. S: Truman Capote, William Archibald. C: Freddie Francis. Cast: Deborah Kerr, Martin Stephens, Pamela Franklin, Megs Jenkins, Michael Redgrave, Peter Wyngarde, Clytie Jessop, Isla Cameron, Eric Woodburn. Based on the Henry James classic ghost novel, *The Turn of the Screw,* the story deals with a young repressed governess arriving to take charge of two young children (Miles and Cora). She gradually comes to believe that the house is haunted by the ghosts of the former governess and her handyman lover, and that her two charges are under the influence of the evil spirits. • Oscar-winning cinematographer Freddie Francis (for *Sons and Lovers,* 1960) went on to become a prolific director in the horror field, and helmed several Hammer features, including *The Evil of Frankenstein* (1964) and *Dracula Has Risen from the Grave* (1968). Recently, he has returned to cinematography for films like *Dune* (1984) and the critically acclaimed *Glory* (1989). • Michael Redgrave, who plays the aloof uncle of *The Innocents,* starred in the most famous segment (about a tormented ventriloquist) of the British ghost anthology, *Dead of Night,* in 1945. • The British child actor Martin Stephens played the leader of the children in *Village of the Damned* in 1960 before becoming one of *The Innocents* (Miles). • Pamela Franklin (little Cora) later grew up to investigate more ghostly goings-on in *The Legend of Hell House* in 1973. • Two years later, actress Deborah Kerr again played a governess (this time in charge of a troubled teenager — expertly played by Hayley Mills) in the Ronald Neame masterpiece of mystery-drama, *The Chalk Garden* (1964).

J.D.'s Revenge (1976; AIP) D/P: Arthur Marks. S: Jaison Starkes. C: Harry May. Cast: Glynn Turman, Joan Pringle, Lou Gossett, Carl Crudup, James Louis Watkins,

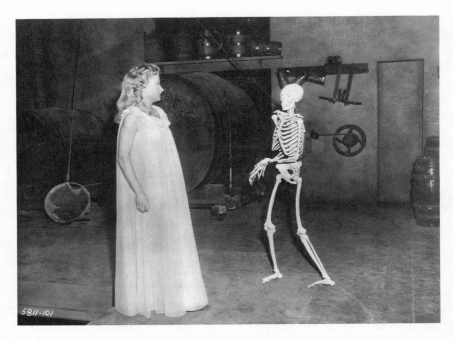

Lovely Carolyn Ohmart is about to be pushed into a vat of acid by the skeleton of Vincent Price in House on Haunted Hill *(1958). In the film, this shocking conclusion is revealed to be a vengeful trick by Price who operates the skeleton with concealed wires.*

Alice Jubert, Stephanie Faulkner, Fred Pinkard, Fuddle Bagley, David McKnight. A young law student in New Orleans gradually becomes possessed by the spirit of a dead 1930s gangster named J. D. Walker, who seeks to avenge an old gangster feud in this all-black horror film. • *J.D.'s Revenge* features an early song, "I Will Never Let You Go," by the then-unknown Prince.

Jack the Ripper (1958) (see ANTHOLOGIES). This omnibus feature, created by combining four episodes of an unsold TV series hosted by Boris Karloff, contains two stories dealing with ghosts. The first is about two spiteful brothers, each with a different version of their dead father's will. The deceased patriarch returns from the grave to help settle matters. The second story has the ghost of a sea captain's murdered wife return to seek revenge.

Kill Baby Kill (1966; Europix; Italy) (also *Curse of the Living Dead*). D: Mario Bava. P: Nando Pisani, Luciano Catenacci. S: Romano Migliorini, Roberto Natale, Mario

Bava. C: Romano Rinaldi. Cast: Erica Blanc, Giacomo Rossi-Stuart, Fabienne Dali, Gianna Vivaldi, Piero Lulli. The ghost of a seven-old girl who died due to the negligence of some villagers returns to exact vengeance. • Under the title *Curse of the Living Dead,* this film was released on the infamous "Orgy of the Living Dead" triple bill along with *Revenge of the Dead* (a.k.a. *The Murder Clinic,* 1966) and *Fangs of the Living Dead* (a.k.a. *Malenka, the Vampire,* 1968).

Kiss of the Beast (1990) (see WEREWOLVES — OTHER LYCANTHROPES) (also *Meridian*). In this "Beauty and the Beast" update, a young woman returns to her ancestral home in Italy and becomes involved with a man who is cursed to transform into a beast whenever he is aroused. The woman is haunted by the ghost of a girl in white, another victim of the curse. The heiress is also aided by her childhood nanny, and only discovers towards the end that her wise, friendly companion had died six months earlier, and she is a ghost.

Kwaidan (1964; Bungei; Japan) D: Masaki Kobayashi. P: Shigeru Wakatsuki. S: Yoko Mizuki. C: Yoshio Miyajima. Cast: Rentaro Mikuni, Michiyo Aratama, Ganemon Nakamura, Noboru Nakaya, Katsuo Nakamura, Takashi Shimura, Tetsuro Tamba. This beautifully photographed Japanese anthology contains four segments adapted from traditional Japanese ghost stories. A Samurai returns home to his wife only to find after a night of passion that he holds a corpse in his arms. Another Samurai is haunted by a spirit manifesting itself in a cup of tea. A blind musician must play for a ghostly gathering of slain warriors; and the specter of a woman lures men to an icy death.

Lady in White (1988; Samuel Goldwyn Co.) D/S: Frank LaLoggia. P: Andrew G. La Marca, Frank LaLoggia. C: Russell Carpenter. Cast: Lucas Haas, Len Cariou, Alex Rocco, Katherine Helmond, Jason Presson, Renata Vanni, Angelo Bertolini. Lucas Haas is a young boy living in the sleepy town of Willowpoint Falls who is stalked by a serial child killer. He is saved, however, by the ghost of a little girl named Melissa (a previous victim of the murderer) and the ghost of her mother (the title character). ¶ "She wants her mother . . . Her mother is the lady in white."

The Legend of Hell House (1973; 20th Century-Fox) D: John Hough. P: Albert Fennell, Norman T. Herman. S: Richard Matheson. C: Alan Hume. Cast: Pamela Franklin, Roddy McDowall, Clive Revill, Gayle Hunnicutt, Roland Culver, Peter Bowles. The ghost of a depraved millionaire is responsible for the evil forces which inhabit the notorious "Hell House." A team of psychic researchers is sent to investigate the mysterious hauntings and succumb to the murderous forces one by one. • British horror star Michael Gough made an unbilled cameo appearance as the corpse behind *The Legend of Hell House.* • *The Legend of Hell House* features a screen first when Pamela Franklin (formerly one of *The Innocents,* 1961) has sexual relations with a ghost. • Richard Matheson adapted his own novel for the screenplay.

The Long Hair of Death (1964; Cinegai; Italy) D: Anthony Dawson (Antonio Margheriti). P: Testa Gay. S: Robert Bohr (Bruno Valeri). C: Richard Thierry (Riccardo Pallottini). Cast: Barbara Steele, Georges Ardisson, Halina Zalewska, Robert Rains, Laureen Nuyen, Jean Rafferty, John Carey, Jeffrey Darcey. In the fifteenth century, a woman is wrongly accused of murder and burned at the stake, witnessed by her daughter (Barbara Steele). Steele is murdered but returns from the dead to torment and finally engineer the death of the real murderer, the son of a powerful nobleman. ¶ "Every time I think of Elizabeth I lose control of my senses. She's the cause of all our troubles. I curse the shrew who brought her into this castle of hell."

Loves of the Living Dead (1986; Cinema City & Films Co./Long Shong Pictures; Hong Kong) D: Peter Mak. S: Raymond Hwang. C: Chris Chen. This little-seen horror/comedy import features the ghosts of a stripper named "Pinkish Red," along with all the patrons who died in the fire that killed her, coming back through a haunted mirror to seek revenge on those responsible for the fire. The ghosts want to find substitutes to take their place so that they can be reborn. ¶ "Actually, a ghost is a cloud of radio waves left by a dead person. So ghosts are afraid of hair dryers because hair dryers can blow away their radio waves." • The four protagonists use magic symbols pasted to their foreheads to make themselves invisible to the ghosts. They also battle the apparitions with hair dryers(!).

The Nesting (1981; Mature Pictures) D/P: Armand Weston. S: Armand Weston, Daria Price. C: João Fernandes. Cast: Robin Groves, Christopher Loomis, Michael David Lally, John Carradine, Gloria Grahame, Bill Rowley, David Tabor, Patrick Farelley. A mystery writer (Robin Groves) suffering from agoraphobia moves into a spooky country mansion which was once a brothel. It is inhabited by the ghosts of a madam and the victims of a massacre which took place there years before. She is gradually drawn into the ghosts' plan to take revenge upon their murderers. • Producer/director/co-writer Armand Weston is a former porno movie maker. • Sadly, this was Gloria Grahame's last role (as the madam).

The Newlydeads (1987; City Lights) D: Joseph Merhi. P: Ronald L. Gilchrist. S: Sean Dash, Joseph Merhi. C: Richard Pepin. Cast: Jim Williams, Jean Levine, Jay Richardson, Roxanna Michaels, Scott Kaske, Rebecca Barrington, Michael Springer, Michelle Smith, Doug Jones, Rene Wade, Ron Preston. The manager of "The Newlywed Lodge" kills a transvestite with an ice pick. Fifteen years later he is getting married and the ghost of the murdered man comes back to haunt him and kill off his guests.

Night of Dark Shadows (1971; MGM) D/P: Dan Curtis. S: Sam Hall. C: Richard Shore. Cast: David Selby, Lara Parker,

Kate Jackson, Grayson Hall, John Karlen, Nancy Barrett, James Storm, Diana Millay, Christopher Pennock, Thayer David. Quentin Collins inherits a large spooky mansion and gradually finds himself taken over by the ghost of his evil ancestor. • This followup to the previous year's *House of Dark Shadows* again features characters taken from the popular daytime horror soap opera, "Dark Shadows," but follows a different storyline than its predecessor (ghosts here instead of vampires in *House*). • Grayson Hall, John Karlen, Nancy Barrett, and Thayer David were all in *House of Dark Shadows* as well, but play different characters in this film.

Nightmare Castle (1965; Allied Artists; Italy) D: Allen Grunewald (Mario Caiano). P: Carlo Caiano. S: Fabio De Agostino, Mario Caiano. C: Enzo Barboni. Cast: Barbara Steele, Paul Müller, Helga Line, Lawrence Clift, John McDouglas, Rik Battaglia. Barbara Steele assays a dual role, first as the adulterous wife (Muriel) of a scientist, who is caught with her lover and tortured and killed by her jealous husband. The man then marries his wife's blonde cousin, "Jenny" (Steele's second role), and the ghost of Muriel periodically possesses Jenny in order to torment him. At the end, the two ghosts materialize and personally take care of the evil doctor. ¶ "Souls living in another world, trying to hide themselves behind Jenny, trying to possess her, to destroy her mind and free will." • This is the third film in which scream queen Barbara Steele plays a ghost, the other two being *Castle of Blood* and *The Long Hair of Death* (both 1964). Her haunting presence continued in *An Angel for Satan* (1966).

Nurse Sherri (1977; Independent International) D: Al Adamson. P: Mark Sherwood. S: Al Adamson, Michael Bockman, Greg Tittinger. C: Roger Michaels. Cast: Geoffrey Land, Jill Jacobson, Marilyn Joi, Mary Kay Pass, Prentiss Moulden, Erwin Fuller, Clayton Foster, Caryl Briscoe, Bill Roy. Jill Jacobson plays a kindly nurse who is possessed by the spirit of a man who died on the operating table, and then goes about killing all those involves with the operation.

Once Upon a Midnight Scary (1979) (see ANTHOLOGIES) (also *Vincent Price's Once Upon a Midnight Scary*). This aimed-at-children TV anthology features Vincent Price introducing a series of children's horror stories, including "The Ghost Belonged to Me," about an apparition warning a boy of danger; and a comical retelling of "The Legend of Sleepy Hollow." ¶ "There have

been so many books written about ghosts. Are they just words on a piece of paper, nothing to be afraid of, or do you find when you read them very late at night that they seem very real?"—host Vincent Price.

The Oracle (1986; Reeltime) D/C: Roberta Findlay. P: Walter E. Sear. S: R. Allen Leider. Cast: Caroline Capers Powers, Roger Neil, Pam LaTesta, Victoria Dryden, Chris Maria DeKoron, Dan Lutzky, Stacey Graves, G. Gordon Cronce. A woman finds an old ouija board and with it conjures up the spirit of a murdered businessman. She learns that his death was not a suicide as the police thought, but that he was murdered by his wife. The woman confronts his wife, who promptly sends her hulking servant out to kill the troublesome meddler.

Pet Sematary (1989) (see ZOMBIES). In this story about an ancient Indian burial ground which brings the dead back to life, the doctor hero is visited by the ghost of a patient he tried to save. The ghost has come to warn the doctor of the dangers of using this evil power.

Poltergeist (1982; MGM/UA) D: Tobe Hooper. P: Steven Spielberg, Frank Marshall. S: Steven Spielberg, Michael Grais, Mark Victor. C: Matthew F. Leonetti. Cast: JoBeth Williams, Craig T. Nelson, Martin Casella, Richard Lawson, Zelda Rubinstein, James Karen. A family moves into a new housing development only to find their lives turned upside down by a barrage of ghostly phenomena, including the disappearance of their young daughter—abducted by "the people in the TV." It finally comes out that the neighborhood was built over the site of an old cemetery, which had been moved *without* the removal of the corpses, and the souls of those buried there don't like it one bit. ¶ "They're heeeeere." • Much controversy arose over who was really responsible for this box office bonanza. Some have claimed that though Tobe Hooper (*The Texas Chainsaw Massacre,* 1974) directed, the man calling the shots was producer Steven Spielberg. • *Poltergeist* was successful enough to father two (inferior) sequels.

Poltergeist 2: The Other Side (1986; MGM) D: Brian Gibson. P/S: Michael Grais, Mark Victor. C: Andrew Laszlo. Cast: JoBeth Williams, Craig T. Nelson, Heather O'Rourke, Oliver Robins, Julian Beck, Zelda Rubinstein, Will Sampson, Geraldine Fitzgerald. The beleaguered family from the first film is back, though they have moved in with their in-laws after the tumultuous happenings four years ago.

They have not fully escaped, however, since the ghost of an evil preacher named Kane has arrived to try and lure Carol Anne "into the light" once more. ¶ "They're baaaaack."

Poltergeist 3 (1988; MGM) D: Gary Sherman. P: Barry Bernard. S: Gary Sherman, Brian Taggert. C: Alex Nepomniaschy. Cast: Tom Sherritt, Nancy Allen, Heather O'Rourke, Lara Flynn Boyle, Richard Fire, Kip Wentz, Nathan Davis, Zelda Rubinstein. Carol Anne is sent to live with her uncle and aunt in a modern Chicago highrise in this third film in the series. However, she has not escaped the ghost of the evil Reverend Kane (whom she faced in *Poltergeist 2*). Kane now materializes and uses his powers of darkness to try once again to get her to cross over to "the other side." • Filmed on location in Chicago, *Poltergeist 3* includes no post-production optical effects. All of the special effects were done on-set at the time of shooting. "There is no blue screen in this film, nor opticals," director Gary Sherman told *Fangoria,* "everything the audience sees in this movie is what we shot. So when they descend the window washing rig in the climax, they *are* descending the rig down one of the tallest buildings in the world."

The Possession of Joel Delany (1972; Paramount) D: Waris Hussein. P: Matin Poll. S: Matt Robinson, Grimes Grice. C: Arthur J. Ornitz. Cast: Shirley MacLaine, Perry King, Michael Hordern, Lovelady Powell, Barbara Trentham, Miriam Colon. The brother of Shirley MacLaine's Puerto Rican maid is possessed by the ghost of a murderer fond of decapitating people, and now Shirley must pay for all the abuse she's heaped on her poor sevant in the past.

Prison (1987; Empire Pictures) D: Renny Harlin. P: Irwin Yablans. S: C. Courtney Joyner. C: Mac Ahlberg. Cast: Lane Smith, Vigo Mortensen, Chelsea Field, Lincoln Kilpatrick, Andre De Shields, Ivan Kane, Arlen Dean Snyder. An abandoned prison is reopened and the vengeful spirit of a man unjustly sent to the electric chair returns to take murderous revenge on prisoners and guards alike, including one instance in which a prison guard is done in by a roll of animated barbed wire. ¶ "There's a 'conna,' a bad spirit trapped in this prison, and it's waitin' to take us out one by one." • *Prison* was shot primarily at an old abandoned Wyoming State Penitentiary near the town of Rawlins. • Director Renny Harlin spent several weeks interviewing real prisoners at the nearby Wyoming State Prison for background research, and ended up giving several of them speaking parts in the film.

Prom Night 3: The Last Kiss (1989; Norstar Entertainment) D: Ron Oliver, Peter Simpson. P: Ray Sager, Peter Simpson. S: Ron Oliver. C: Rhett Morita. Cast: Tim Conlon, Cyndy Preston, David Stratton, Jeremy Ratchford, Dylan Neal, Courtney Taylor. The evil ghost of prom queen Mary Lou Maloney is back (from *Hello Mary Lou, Prom Night 2,* 1987). She sets her spectral sights on Alex, a likable student at Hamilton High, and uses her demonic powers to murder all those standing between her and her new chosen "boyfriend." ¶ "It can't be you, you're dead! I watched you die!"

Retribution (1988; Taurus Entertainment) D/P/S: Guy Magar, Lee Wasserman. C: Gary Thieltges. Cast: Dennis Lipscomb, Leslie Wing, Suzanne Snyder, Jeff Pomerantz, George Murdock, Pamela Dunlap, Susan Peretz, Clare Peck, Chris Caputo, Hoyt Axton. George, a down-and-out middle-aged artist, tries to commit suicide by jumping off a building. At the same time, a man named Vito is tortured and killed by a group of bookies he owes money to. Vito's spirit possesses George and whenever the unlucky artist goes to sleep, Vito's vengeful ghost leaves George's body (but borrows his image) and goes out to take revenge on those who murdered him. ¶ "I don't think he's possessed in a satanic way, but he acts like he's possessed by some other *force*." • Co-director/producer/screenwriter Guy Magar also served as editor as well as acting in the film.

Ruby (1977; Dimension) D: Curtis Harrington, Stephanie Rothman. P: George Edwards. S: George Edwards, Barry Schneider. C: William Mendenhall. Cast: Piper Laurie, Stuart Whitman, Roger Davis, Janet Baldwin, Crystin Sinclaire, Paul Kent, Len Lesser, Jack Perkins, Sal Vecchio, Fred Kohler. A former gangster's moll now owns and operates a drive-in theater, employing a variety of former thugs. Her teenager daughter is possessed by the ghost of a dead hood, intent on taking revenge on those responsible for his death. • The drive-in is playing the 1958 camp classic, *Attack of the 50 Foot Woman.*

Scared Stiff (1953; Paramount) D: George Marshall. P: Hal B. Wallis. S: Herbert Baker, Walter De Leon. C: Ernest Laszlo. Cast: Dean Martin, Jerry Lewis, Lizabeth Scott, Carmen Miranda, George E. Stone, Dorothy Malone, Jack Lambert. This remake of *The Ghost Breakers* (1940) features Martin and Lewis helping out a girl who has just inherited a spooky old castle on a Caribbean island. Once there, they encounter thieves, a zombie, and a real ghost.

Scared Stiff (1988) (see VOODOO). A young family moves back into an old house once owned by a notorious slave-trader named Masterson. A flashback sequence reveals that a voodoo curse was placed on him by his mistreated slaves which transformed him into a hideous monster. Masterson's evil spirit returns from the dead, induces hallucinations in the mom, and possesses her husband.

The Screaming Skull (1958; AIP) D: Alex Nichol. P/S: John Kneubuhl. C: Floyd Crosby. Cast: John Hudson, Peggy Webber, Russ Conway, Tony Johnson, Alex Nicol. A new bride, home recovering from a nervous breakdown, is seemingly haunted by the grinning, screaming skull of her husband's dead first wife. It turns out to be a plot by her husband to drive her insane. The scheming conniver gets his comeuppance at the end, however, when the *real* ghost sends the screaming skull after *him*. ¶ "Free! ... We guarantee to bury you without charge if you die of fright"—gimmicky ad campaign.

The Sender (1982) (see PSYCHIC ABILITY). A young amnesiac with telepathic abilities is able to transmit his nightmares to those around him, wreaking havoc via his horrific hallucinations. The spirit of the young man's mother appears and aids her son in achieving peace.

The She Beast (1965) (see WITCHES, WARLOCKS, AND CULTS). Barbara Steele plays a new bride honeymooning in Transylvania who is possessed by the vengeful spirit of a 200-year-old witch named Vardella. When possessed, she takes on the visage of a hideous old crone and embarks on a murder spree.

The Shining (1980; Warner Bros.) D/P: Stanley Kubrick. S: Stanley Kubrick, Diane Johnson. C: John Alcott. Cast: Jack Nicholson, Shelley Duvall, Danny Lloyd, Scatman Crothers, Barry Nelson, Philip Stone, Joe Turkel, Anne Jackson, Tony Burton. Jack Nicholson plays Jack Torrance, a down-on-his-luck writer who accepts a job as the winter caretaker at the Overlook Hotel. With his wife and young son, he moves into the snowbound resort, only to be driven to the brink of murderous insanity by the evil influence of the sinister ghost-infested hotel. ¶ "All work and no play makes Jack a dull boy." • *The Shining* is based on the successful novel by Stephen King. Filmmaker Stanley Kubrick dismissed the source, saying, "The novel is by no means a serious literary work." Stephen King himself had written a script, but Kubrick never read it. • King responded to the film in a 1983 *Playboy* interview: "It's a film by a man who thinks too much and feels too little.... It never gets you by the throat and hangs on the way real horror should." • Actor Joe Turkel, who plays the spectral bartender "Lloyd," appeared in another ghost film two decades earlier, Bert I. Gordon's *Tormented* (1960).

The Skull (1966; Amicus/Paramount) D: Freddie Francis. P: Max J. Rosenberg, Milton Subotsky. S: Milton Subotsky. C: John Wilcox. Cast: Peter Cushing, Christopher Lee, Patrick Wymark, Anna Palk, Jill Bennett, Nigel Green, April Olrich, Michael Gough, George Coulouris, Patrick Magee. A collector of supernatural antiquities buys the original skull of the Marquis de Sade. The skull is inhabited by the evil spiritual force of the sadistic Marquis, which possesses the collector and forces him to commit murder. ¶ "De Sade said he wasn't mad, and I believe it. He was far worse than mad, he was possessed—possessed by an evil spirit, a spirit which still inhabits the skull." • *The Skull* carried a working title of *The Skull of the Marquis de Sade,* the title of Robert Bloch's original short story. It was released in France under this moniker, but was quickly changed when the Marquis' living descendents vehemently objected.

Slaughterhouse Rock (1987; First American Arista Films) D: Dimitri Logothetis. P: Louis George. S: Ted Landon, Sandra Willard, Nora Goodman. C: Nicholas Von Sternberg. Cast: Nicholas Cellozi, Tom Reilly, Donna Denton, Hope Marie Carlton, Tamara Hyler, Steven Brian Smith, Ty Miller, Toni Basil. A young college student, troubled by horrible nightmares, is drawn to the old prison on Alcatraz Island. There he meets the ghost of a rock singer named Sammi Mitchell who had accidentally released an evil spirit which then possessed and murdered her. The powerful spirit is that of a cannibalistic cavalry commander who was burned alive for his atrocities when the island was an Army outpost. Aided by the singer's benign ghost, the hero sets out to destroy the diabolical spirit before all of his friends fall victim to the evil. ¶ "Stop me if I'm getting this wrong—you're dead and you're *lonely?*" • According to this film, "spirits can't cross over water" (and so are trapped on the island). • This two million dollar feature included a four-day shoot on Alcatraz Island, which presented some

Isolated in the ghost-haunted Overlook Hotel, Jack Nicholson goes mad and, influenced by the Overlook's evil forces, attempts to murder his wife Wendy (Shelly Duvall) in The Shining *(1980).*

problems. "Alcatraz has no electrical power," director Dimitri Logothetis told *Fangoria* #72. "No running water—nothing. . . . We had a skeleton crew of four people with us, and of course, we couldn't bring a dolly along. And so my cinematographer, Nicholas Von Sternberg, put on roller skates and skated along doing dolly shots." • Interiors were shot on the old *Escape from Alcatraz* set in Culver City, California. • The new wave rock group "Devo" provides the music.

The Sleeping Car (1990; Vidmark Entertainment) D: Douglas Curtis. P: Douglas Curtis, Bob Manning. S: Greg O'Neill. C: David Lewis. Cast: David Naughton, Judie Aronson, Jeff Conaway, Dani Minnick, Kevin McCarthy. David Naughton plays a journalism student who moves into an old train compartment converted into an apartment. He is haunted by the ghost of a sadistic ex-train worker who liked to bring women to the sleeping car and brutally murder them. ¶ "One should never make light of the darkness."

Strangler of the Swamp (1945; PRC) D/S: Frank Wisbar. P: Raoul Pagel. C: James S. Brown. Cast: Rosemary La Planche, Robert Barrat, Blake Edwards, Charles Middleton, Effie Parnell, Nolan Leary, Frank Conlan, Theresa Lyon, Virginia Farmer. The vengeful ghosts of a swampland ferryman, a man lynched for a crime he didn't commit, haunts the swamps of a sleepy backwater town, causing the deaths of those responsible for his unjust demise. He will continue to strike down the guilty until one of their number, or one of their descendants, makes the ultimate sacrifice and offers himself or herself up freely to the ghost, breaking the curse and releasing the spirit. ¶ "Give up the fight. Leave vengeance to the Almighty. Make peace with Him." • Although PRC stands for "Producers Releasing Corporation" it could just as easily mean "Poverty Row Cinema." Many consider this atmospheric film (with a record amount of dry ice per square foot) to be the best horror movie made by this prolific low-budget outfit. • Future producer/director/screenwriter Blake

Edwards (*The Pink Panther* series, among others) stars as the young hero (in his only horror film). • Tall, gaunt actor Charles Middleton, who plays the vengeful ghost, is often remembered for his role as "Ming the Merciless" in the *Flash Gordon* serials.

Supernatural (1933; Paramount) D: Victor Halperin. P: Victor Halperin, Edward Halperin. S: Harvey Thew, Brian Marlow. C: Arthur Martinelli. Cast: Carole Lombard, Randolph Scott, Vivienne Osborne, Alan Dinehart, H. B. Warner. A vicious murderess is executed for her crimes and her body is brought to the laboratory of a doctor experimenting in spirit transmigration. Wealthy socialite Carole Lombarde visits the doctor and is inadvertently possessed by the spirit of the murderess. In her new body, the vengeful spirit plans the demise of the man who turned her in. • This generally panned feature was made by the producer/director team of the Halperin Brothers, the same team that filmed the superior *White Zombie* (1932).

Supernatural (1982; Paraguas Films; Spain) D: Eugenio Martin. P: Antonio Cuevas. S: Eugenio Martin, Antoni Cuevas, José de Una, Eduardo Alvarez. C: Antonio Cuevas, Jr. Cast: Maximo Valverde, Cristina Galbo, Candida Losada, Gerardo Malla, Juan Jesus Valverde, Lola Lemos. A skeptical woman is haunted by the spirit of her domineering late husband, and is finally forced to accept the supernatural as reality and employ those same supernatural forces to defeat the evil spirit.

The Supernaturals (1987) (see ZOMBIES). A platoon of new Army recruits on a survival mission in the backwoods of Alabama begin dying mysteriously one by one. It is revealed that they are being killed by the walking dead zombies of murdered Confederate soldiers. The ghost of the mother of one of the Confederate soldiers appears and finally aids the surviving recruits in dispelling the horror.

Superstition (1982) (see WITCHES, WARLOCKS, AND CULTS). In 1774, Elondra Sharack is crucified as a witch. Her satanic soul lurks in nearby Black Pond and 200 years later rises from the depths seeking vengeance.

Tales of Terror (1962) (see POE FILMS — THE CORMAN CYCLE). In the first story, "Morella" is the wife of Vincent Price who dies in childbirth. The griefstricken man sends the child, a daughter, away. She returns 26 years after her mother's death to find that her father is still fixated on his dead wife and keeps her mummified corpse in the house.

The restless spirit of Morella possesses the body of her daughter and takes revenge on Price, who after all was the ultimate cause of her death. ¶ "What happens after death — to someone who does not choose to die — someone like ... Morella?"

The Terror (1963; AIP) D/P: Roger Corman. S: Leo Gordon, Jack Hill. C: John Nicholaus. Cast: Boris Karloff, Jack Nicholson, Sandra Knight, Richard Miller, Dorothy Neuman, Jonathan Haze. Jack Nicholson is miscast early in his career as a French officer in Napoleon's army who stumbles upon an old castle inhabited by the mad nobleman Boris Karloff. Unaware that she is really a ghost, Nicholson falls in love with Karloff's long-dead wife, leading to tragedy. ¶ "With all respect, Baron, for a ghost she's a very active young woman." • The story behind the making of *The Terror* is more interesting than the film itself. Roger Corman explained: "I was going to play tennis and it rained. I was roaming around the house. I started thinking of this immense set we had built for the film [*The Raven*] that was going to be torn down in five days. I thought it was a shame to tear it down after using it only once. 'If I could write a script in one week and get some actors,' I thought, 'I could walk right into that set and shoot another picture for very little money!'" (from *The Films of Roger Corman*, by Ed Naha). • Jack Nicholson called it "the only movie I ever made that didn't have a plot." • Five other directors worked on the film, though only Corman receives credit: Francis Ford Coppola, Monte Hellman, Jack Hill, Dennis Jacob, and even Jack Nicholson.

13 Ghosts (1960; Columbia) D/P: William Castle. S: Robb White. C: Joseph Biroc. Cast: Donald Woods, Charles Herbert, Jo Morrow, Rosemary De Camp, Martin Milner, Margaret Hamilton, John Van Dreelen. A family moves into a haunted house chock full of ghosts, including a flaming skeleton and the ghost of a headless lion tamer and his lion. They can only see the ghosts by using a special ghost-viewing device. A subplot involves a hidden cache of money and a turncoat friend who tries to frighten them out of the house. ¶ "See The Ghosts in Ectoplasmic color!" — ad line. • The film featured another gimmick from showman William Castle. This one utilized something called the "Ghost Viewer," which was handed out to theater patrons. This "Ghost Viewer" was merely a card with two transparent squares to look through — one red (the "ghost viewer") and the other blue (the "ghost remover").

Tomb of Torture (1965) (see MADMEN— EARLY PSYCHOS). A young woman is mysteriously drawn to an abandoned castle where she encounters a giggling madman and the ghost of a murdered countess.

Tormented (1960; Allied Artists) D: Bert I. Gordon. P: Bert I. Gordon, Joe Steinberg. S: George Worthing Yates. C: Ernest Laszlo. Cast: Richard Carlson, Juli Reding, Susan Gordon, Lugene Sanders, Joe Turkel. Richard Carlson plays a jazz pianist engaged to marry a wealthy socialite. His old mistress comes to his beachfront home and threatens to expose his sordid past to his fiancée. When the scheming mistress falls to her death from an abandoned lighthouse (with Carlson refusing to help her), he is secretly pleased, until he is haunted by disembodied hands, ghostly footprints, and a spectral head—the ghost of his mistress. ¶ "Flesh he couldn't feel . . . lips he couldn't touch . . . but a vengeance that haunted him to death!"—poster ad line. • Director Bert I. Gordon's own daughter, Susan Gordon, plays the pre-teen sister of Richard Carlson's fiancée.

Tower of London (1962; United Artists) D: Roger Corman. P: Gene Corman. S: Leo V. Gordon, Amos Powell, James B. Gordon. C: Arch R. Dalzell. Cast: Vincent Price, Michael Pate, Joan Freeman, Robert Brown, Bruce Gordon, Joan Camden, Richard Hale, Sandra Knight, Charles Macaulay. Roger Corman's update of the wonderful 1939 Basil Rathbone/Boris Karloff vehicle relating the tale of England's Richard III and his nefarious crimes to gain the throne eschews the classic historical melodrama of the first film and gives us a tale of murder and ghosts and conscience, this time starring Vincent Price in the role of the power-mad Richard. Price kills off various family members standing in his way to the throne, including his two young nephews, only to be haunted by the ghosts of his victims come back to torment him (though these ghosts may simply be a product of his own guilt-tortured mind). ¶ "He escaped the headsman's block, but he could never escape the ghosts of his conscience." • Roger Corman apparently did not know the film was to be shot in black and white when he signed on, assuming it was a color production like his Edgar Allan Poe series. He later said in *The Films of Roger Corman* by Ed Naha: "To my great surprise, I found that I was supposed to shoot the picture in black and white. Somehow, nobody had bothered to tell me that! I was flabbergasted. This was 1963!" • Interestingly

enough, Vincent Price played the supporting role of the Duke of Clarence, whom Rathbone and Karloff drown in a vat of wine, in the 1939 version. Here, of course, he graduated to the starring role of Richard.

Trick or Treat (1986; De Laurentiis Entertainment Group) D: Charles Martin Smith. P/S: Michael S. Murphey, Joel Soisson. C: Robert Elswit. Cast: Marc Price, Tony Fields, Gene Simmons, Ozzy Osbourne. High school misfit Eddie Weinbauer idolizes heavy metal superstar Sammi Curr. When Curr dies in a bizarre fire, his satanic spirit returns to help Eddie exact revenge on his teen tormentors, until finally Eddie realizes his one-time idol is merely using him for his own vicious form of vengeance. ¶ "What are you afraid of? It's only rock & roll"—ad slogan. • Actor Charles Martin Smith (*Never Cry Wolf, The Untouchables,* etc.) went behind the camera for this, his directorial debut. • Gene Simmons, of the rock group "Kiss," plays a sympathetic D.J., while heavy metal rocker Ozzy Osbourne plays an anti-rock TV evangelist(!).

Turn of the Screw (1974; TV movie) D/P: Dan Curtis. S: William F. Nolan. C: Ben Colman. Cast: Lynn Redgrave, Jasper Jacob, Eva Griffith, Megs Jenkins, John Baron, Anthony Langdon, Benedict Taylor, James Laurenson, Kathryn Leigh Scott. TV producer Dan Curtis turns to Henry James to make another literary horror adaptation for the small screen (he did the same for *Dracula* and *Frankenstein*). The story concerns a new governess coming to care for two young children haunted by the ghosts of their former governess and her corruptive lover. • Megs Jenkins played the same role here (the concerned housekeeper) that she did in the critically acclaimed 1961 version called *The Innocents*.

Twice Dead (1988; Concorde) D: Bert Dragin. P: Guy J. Louthan, Robert McDonnell. S: Bert Dragin, Robert McDonnell. C: Zoran Hochstatter. Cast: Tom Breznahan, Jill Whitlow, Jonathan Chapin, Christopher Bugard, Sam Melville, Brooke Bundy. A family moves into a recently inherited dilapidated old mansion which just happens to be in an area lorded over by a gang of vicious street punks. If that wasn't trouble enough, the house is also haunted by the ghost of a former owner. When the thugs assault the family, the spirit steps in to dispatch the brutal gang members one by one in grisly, gruesome, ghostly fashion. • In an interview for *Gorezone* magazine, director Bert Dragin recounted this real-life ghost story involving his film (swearing it was true): "We rented the house we shot in from the housekeeper of an 80-year-old man named Al Green, who was in the hospital at the time, and during the filming he died. Later on, my production manager came up to me and said, 'Look at these pictures we took for continuity.' I looked through them, and there were two pictures which had a white, ghostlike apparition above the bed in which the old man slept. We traced them back to the day we took them, and it was the day the man died. The lab could absolutely not explain it when we took the pictures back."

Twice Told Tales (1963) (see ANTHOLOGIES). In "The House of the Seven Gables," the third story from this group of Nathaniel Hawthorne tales, Vincent Price plays a man who searches for a fortune hidden in his ancestral home but finds deadly ghosts and his own death instead.

Two Thousand Maniacs (1964; Box Office Spectaculars) D/S/C: Herschell Gordon Lewis. P: David Friedman. Cast: Connie Mason, Thomas Wood, Jeffrey Allen, Ben Moore, Shelby Livingston, Vincent Santo, Gary Bakeman, Mark Douglas, Michael Korb. The small southern town of Pleasant Valley, which was wiped out by the Union Army during the Civil War, reappears 100 years later. The townspeople entice six vacationing Northerners into becoming their guests of honor at their 100-year celebration and then exact their bloody revenge on them. At the end, the town full of ghosts just fades away. ¶ Refrain from the *Two Thousand Maniacs* theme song: "Oooooo-Eeeeee, oh the South's gonna rise again!" • This follow-up gore film by the "Godfather of Gore," Herschell Gordon Lewis, to his *Blood Feast* (1963) is often considered his best film. • One-man production crew Herschell Gordon Lewis (director/screenwriter/cinematographer) wrote the musical score as well.

The Uninvited (1944; Paramount) D: Lewis Allen. P: Charles Brackett. S: Dodie Smith, Frank Partos. C: Charles Lang. Cast: Ray Milland, Ruth Hussey, Gail Russell, Donald Crisp, Cornelia Otis Skinner, Dorothy Stickney, Barbara Everest, Alan Napier, Jessica Newcombe, John Kieran. A brother and sister buy a large old house on the Cornish coast only to find it is haunted by two spirits, one benign and the other malevolent. ¶ "The Story of a Love That is Out of This World"—ad line. • *The Uninvited* is Hollywood's first serious ghost movie, and many consider it to be one of the best (film historian William K. Everson considers it to be *the* best). • In Great Britain,

the British film censors removed all shots of the ghosts (seen as wavering ectoplasmic apparitions in the film), creating a psychological rather than supernatural focus.

Warlock Moon (1973) (see CANNIBALS). A young couple end up at the old abandoned Soda Springs Spa where they are stalked by a group of cannibals. The heroine is visited and seemingly aided by the ghost of the head cannibal's first victim. She had been the guest of honor at a banquet on her wedding day, but she ended up being served as the main course by the psychotic cook, and now haunts the abandoned resort. ¶ "There's people who swear that they've seen the ghost of that bride out here walking around in a white wedding dress, and people have come out here and were never seen again."

Web of the Spider (1972; Cinema Shares; Italy) (also *In the Grip of the Spider*). D: Anthony M. Dawson (Antonio Margheriti). P: Giovanni Addessi. S: Bruno Corbucci. C: Sandro Mancori, Memmo Mancori. Cast: Anthony Franciosa, Michèle Mercier, Peter Carsten, Klaus Kinski, Silvano Tranquilli, Karin Field, Raf Baldassare, Irina Meleva, Paolo Gozlino. In this remake of *Castle of Blood* (1964; also directed by Antonio Margheriti) a man is challeged by Edgar Allan Poe to spend a night in a haunted castle. He accepts the challenge and is beset by ghosts reenacting their own murders, until he too finally falls victim to the evil castle and joins their ranks.

The Witch's Mirror (1960) (see WITCHES, WARLOCKS, and CULTS). A surgeon poisons his wife, who is the goddaughter of his housekeeper. He remarries and the housekeeper, a witch, uses her magic mirror to conjure up the ghost of his first wife, who torments and takes revenge on both the doctor and his new bride.

Witchboard (1986; Cinema Group/Paragon Arts International) D/S: Kevin S. Tenney. P: Gerald Geoffray. C: Roy H. Wagner. Cast: Todd Allen, Tawny Kitaen, Stephen Nichols, Kathleen Wilhoite, Burke Byrnes, James W. Quinn, Rose Marie. Tawny Kitaen plays a woman who accidentally contacts a spirit with a ouija board. Thinking it is the spirit of an unhappy child, she continues to contact him through the witchboard until it becomes an obsession. Finally it is revealed that the spirit is not that of a lonesome child, but the ghost of an evil warlock who uses his powers to possess her. ¶ "When someone uses the ouija alone, she's very susceptible to the spirits she contacts, and the wrong spirit will take advantage of this." • *Witchboard* was quite successful,

Ray Milland and Ruth Hussey are The Uninvited *(1944) brother and sister who buy a haunted house situated along the Cornish coast in England.*

with a $2.3 million investment reaping over eight million dollars at the box office.

Witchtrap (1989; Cinema Plus/G.C.O.) D/S: Kevin S. Tenney. P: Daniel Duncan, Kevin S. Tenney. C: Thomas Jewett. Cast: James W. Quinn, Kathleen Bailey, Judy Tatum, Rod Zapple, Jack W. Thompson, Clyde Talley II, Hal Havins, Linnea Quigley. A group of psychic researchers are hired to investigate a haunted house. Once there, they are terrorized and killed off one by one by the spirit of the house's previous owner, an evil satanist. ¶ Medium: "The police found his body on this very altar, his chest carved open, burning candles everywhere. Neither his killer nor his heart were ever found." Detective: "You know, San Francisco is nearby; maybe he left it there." • This is the second ghost/witchcraft film by Kevin S. Tenney. He wrote and directed *Witchboard* in 1986. When *Witchtrap* was released to video (after a nearly nonexistent theatrical run), the distributors put this disclaimer at the beginning of the picture: "Notice: This motion picture is not a sequel to *Witchboard*."

The Wraith (1986; New Century Entertainment) D/S: Mike Marvin. P: John Kemeny. Cast: Charlie Sheen, Nick Cassa-vetes, Sherilyn Fenn, Randy Quaid, Clint Howard. Soon after a gang of hoodlums and car thieves go too far and murder a young man, a mysterious stranger shows up in the town driving a strange black turbo-charged sportscar. It is implied that the stranger is the manifestation of the murdered youth, sent from above to administer justice to the guilty thugs. • The Wraith's car, a Turbo Interceptor, was designed and built as a prototype by Dodge. It came with its own driver, mechanic, and bodyguard. Six cars (at a cost of $1.5 million) were made—two that could be driven and four that could be blown up. • Nick Cassavetes, who plays the vicious leader of the gang of "road pirates," is the son of actor John Cassavetes (*Rosemary's Baby,* 1968).

Zombie Brigade (1988) (see ZOMBIES). A small town in the Australian Outback is besieged by zombie soldiers who crawl up out of the local Vietnam Veterans monument when the development-hungry mayor blows it up. Nothing is able to stop them until a local Aborigine uses tribal magic to call up the spirits of the town's World War II veterans to do battle with the zombie soldiers. ¶ "He called up the spirits of the tribe and they drove off the soldier guys."

Ghouls *see* **Zombie Flesh Eaters**

Giants *see* **Animal Giants; Ape Giants; Human Giants**

Gill-men *see* **Fish-People**

Godzilla *see* **Japanese Giant Monsters**

Golem *see* **Statues Come to Life**

Grave Robbers

In the early part of the nineteenth century, Irish, English, and Scottish doctors and students of medicine were in desperate need of raw materials for teaching and study. Because of the restrictive laws of the time, they were often forced to deal with grave robbers to obtain their specimens (the only legal source being the infrequently supplied bodies of executed criminals). This repressive legislation forbidding the dissection of human corpses for study created a new profession — the "resurrection man" (much as prohibition created the "bootlegger" in America). Considered a necessary evil by the medical profession of the time, the issue of "body snatching" came to a head in 1828, when the nefarious crimes of a poor Edinburgh lodging house owner named William Hare and his accomplice William Burke were exposed to the world. Burke and Hare had foregone the robbing of graves and gone straight to the source — by murdering street people to sell their bodies to the anatomists, with the respected Dr. Knox as one of their most frequent customers. Sixteen fell victim to their suffocating hands (creating a new verb in the English dictionary: To *burke,* meaning "to suffocate or strangle in order to obtain a body to be sold for dissection" [Webster]). Burke was hanged (and in a bit of ironic justice, sent to the medical college for dissection), while Hare was granted immunity by turning King's Evidence against his former partner. Hare did not escape unscathed, however, for when a group of workmen discovered his identity, they threw him into a vat of lime, which completely destroyed his sight.

It seemed inevitable that such gruesome doings be translated to film, and it is a wonder that it took as long as it did for filmmakers to exploit the grisly subject in an historical horror movie. The first (and best) film to deal primarily with resurrectionists was *The Body Snatcher* (1945), in which Boris Karloff, giving one of the finest performances of his career, played cabman John Gray in the William Burke mold. In a coincidental twist on historical fact, the two lodgers who discover Burke and Hare's latest victim and exposed the murderous pair were named Mr. and Mrs. Gray — sharing the same name with Karloff's character. A handful of films followed, some featuring characters merely patterned after Burke and Hare (*Horror Maniacs,* 1948, and *Corridors of Blood,* 1958) while others featured Burke and Hare themselves (with *Flesh and the Fiends* [1960] being the first, and finest, example). While historical horror has fallen out of vogue in recent times, this particular bit of shameful history still has the power to fascinate, as evidenced by another retelling of the Burke and Hare story as late as 1985 in *The Doctor and the Devils.*

In the screen's finest "Grave Robber" film, Boris Karloff (giving one of his best performances) stars as The Body Snatcher *(1945), a malevolent "resurrection man" who procures the bodies needed by Henry Daniell for medical research.*

The Anatomist (1961; Dola Films/Richard Gordon; U.K.) D: Leonard William. P: Vincent Johnston. Cast: Alastair Sim, George Cole, Jill Bennett, Adrienne Corri, Margaret Gordon, Michael Ripper. This is another British version of the Burke and Hare story about a pair of grave robbers who turn to murder to keep up with the demand of an unscrupulous doctor needing anatomy specimens. • Leading lady Adrienne Corri had previously appeared in another body snatching film, *Corridors of Blood* (1958). • The film is based on James Bridie's historical play of the same name.

The Body Snatcher (1945; RKO) D: Robert Wise. P: Val Lewton. S: Carlos Keith (Val Lewton), Philip MacDonald. C: Robert de Grasse. Cast: Boris Karloff, Bela Lugosi, Henry Daniell, Edith Atwater, Russell Wade, Rita Corday, Sharyn Moffett, Donna Lee. This first and best film to focus on the crime/profession of "body snatching" stars Boris Karloff as John Gray, cabman and "resurrectionist," who sells bodies he has stolen from fresh graves to

haughty Dr. McFarland for his anatomy classes. When McFarland's demand exceeds Gray's supply, the resourceful body snatcher resorts to murder to obtain fresh goods. Gray also has a terrible hold over the prominent Dr. McFarland, having shielded McFarland years earlier from the Burke and Hare scandal (McFarland was a student of Dr. Knox). Gray delights in tormenting the doctor, until finally McFarland retaliates, only to find that there is no escaping one's fate as dictated by conscience. ¶ "I am a small man, a humble man. And being poor, I have had to do much that I did not want to do. But so long as the great Dr. McFarland jumps to my whistle, that long am I a man. And if I have not that, I have nothing. Then I am only a cabman and a grave robber." • While it does not feature those two most famous (or infamous) grave robbers — Burke and Hare — several references are made in the film to the historical pair: McFarland's past is interwoven with their nefarious crimes, and Gray even sings a little ditty about the two villains. • *The Body*

Snatcher, hailed as a subtle classic, was placed on *Time* magazine's "Ten Best" movie list. • The ever-frugal RKO horror unit, headed up by Val Lewton, utilized sets built for *The Hunchback of Notre Dame* (1939) for this film's exteriors, giving it a lavishness and authenticity which could not have been found in its moderate budget otherwise. • The British censors were ruthless to *The Body Snatcher,* cutting over four minutes from the film, including all shots of Gray's body riding in the carriage at the film's climax. This omitted all supernatural and or psychological overtones, making it seem as if McFarland simply had a carriage accident.

Bride of Frankenstein (1935) (see FRANKENSTEIN'S MONSTER — UNIVERSAL SERIES). This sequel to *Frankenstein* (1931) once again has scientists digging up fresh corpses to use in creating life — this time *female* corpses. A pair of grave robbers are employed by the sinister Dr. Praetorius, an unscrupulous scientist who enjoys picnicking in the crypts he violates. • One of the grave robbers, Karl, is played by Dwight Frye, who assayed the role of hunchbacked assistant Fritz in the original *Frankenstein* (and who had helped Dr. Frankenstein rob graves in that earlier film as well).

Burke and Hare (1971; United Artists/ Kenneth Shipman/Armitage; U.K.) (also *Horrors of Burke and Hare*). D: Vernon Sewell. P: Guido Cohen. S: Ernie Bradford. C: Desmond Dickinson. Cast: Harry Andrews, Derren Nesbitt, Glynn Edwards, Yootha Joyce, Dee Shenderey, Françoise Pascal, Alan Tucker, Robin Hawdon. Another British retelling of the Burke and Hare story, this time played by Derren Nesbitt and Glynn Edwards as two drunken Irishmen robbing graves and murdering people to supply specimens for the pioneering medico Dr. Knox. • Swedish beauty Yutte Stensgaard (the lead bloodsucker inspiring *Lust for a Vampire* the previous year) has a small role here as one of their victims.

Comedy of Terrors (1963; AIP) D: Jacques Tourneur. P: James H. Nicholson, Samuel Z. Arkoff. S: Richard Matheson. C: Floyd Crosby. Cast: Vincent Price, Peter Lorre, Boris Karloff, Basil Rathbone, Joe E. Brown, Joyce Jameson, Beverly Hills, Paul Barsolow, Linda Rogers, Luree Holmes, Buddy Mason. Unscrupulous undertaker Waldo Trumbull (Vincent Price) and his bumbling assistant (Peter Lorre) decide to drum up business by murdering prospective clients and then collecting fat burial fees from them. They then go back and dig up the grave — not to steal the corpse but to get back the coffin, which can be reused again for the next funeral. • This was the first (and only) film to team this particular quartet of horror stars — Price, Lorre, Karloff, and Rathbone. It was Peter Lorre's last starring role. • Though an amusing film, *Comedy of Terrors* was a disappointment from director Jacques Tourneur late in his career, who had established his reputation as a first class horror director with classics like *Cat People* (1942), *I Walked with a Zombie* (1943), and *Curse of the Demon* (1958).

Corridors of Blood (1958; MGM; U.K.) (also *Doctor from Seven Dials*). D: Robert Day. P: John Croydon, Charles Vetter, Jr. S: Jean Scott Rogers. C: Geoffrey Faithfull. Cast: Boris Karloff, Betta St. John, Finlay Currie, Francis Matthews, Adrienne Corri, Francis De Wolff, Basil Dignam, Christopher Lee. In 1840, before the discovery of anesthesia, Mr. Bolton (Boris Karloff) is working on developing a drug which can be used as an anesthetic (despite being cited as "Dr." Bolton in other sources, he is referred to throughout the film, as are his medical colleagues, simply as "Mr."). After an initial demonstration goes badly, Bolton is eventually dismissed from the hospital. In the course of his research, Bolton has become addicted to the drugs, and now finds his way to a seedy tavern where the innkeeper and his partner, a grave robber known as "Resurrection Joe" (Christopher Lee), uses the doctor's addiction to blackmail him into signing phony death certificates — for lodgers they have murdered in order to sell their bodies to anatomists. ¶ "These people have disappeared from the Seven Dials, and Mr. Blaunt has practically admitted that he's none too careful of how he gets his bodies for his anatomy classes." • Though not named as such, the innkeeper "Black Ben" and his partner "Resurrection Joe" are obviously Burke and Hare. • Though filmed in England in 1958, *Corridors of Blood* went unreleased in the United States for nearly five years. It was shot back to back with another Karloff film, *The Haunted Strangler,* also directed by Robert Day. • This was the first teaming of horror greats Boris Karloff and Christopher Lee, though Lee had previously appeared in an episode of Karloff's British TV series, "Colonel March of Scotland Yard" (episode title: "At Night All Cats Are Grey").

The Doctor and the Devils (1985; 20th Century-Fox) D: Freddie Francis. P: Jonathan Sanger. S: Ronald Harwood (based on an original screenplay by Dylan Thomas).

C: Gerry Turpin, Norman Warwick. Cast: Timothy Dalton, Jonathan Pryce, Twiggy, Julian Sands, Stephen Rea, Phyllis Logan, Lewis Fiander, Beryl Reid, T. P. McKenna, Patrick Stewart, Sian Phillips. This, the most recent version of the Burke and Hare story, stars Timothy Dalton (the new "James Bond") as Dr. Knox, who needs fresh cadavers for his medical research and who is not too particular as to where they come from. ¶ "The science of anatomy contributes to the great sum of all knowledge, and I believe that all men must work towards that end, and I believe that that end justifies *any* means!" • Rather than Burke and Hare, there are "Fallon" (Jonathan Pryce) and "Broom" (Stephen Rea). Also, instead of it being set in the historically accurate 1820s (when Burke an Hare were "in business"), director Freddie Francis set his film in the 1840s, "not because I wanted to kid people into thinking it wasn't Burke and Hare," he explained, "but purely because I prefer the *costumes*" (*Fangoria* #54). • Comic filmmaker Mel Brooks served as executive producer on this deadly serious film.

Dr. Hackenstein (1988) (see FRANKENSTEIN'S MONSTER — FURTHER FRANKENSTEINS). Dr. Elliott Hackenstein is intent upon building a new body for his dead wife (who is now only a head). To this end he employs the services of two bumbling body snatchers (played by real-life husband and wife Anne and Logan Ramsey). When they bring him a male body instead of a female one, Hackenstein "borrows" what he needs from a trio of lovelies who have had the misfortune of stumbling upon his house. ¶ "All you two ever got me was *one* female, one lousy female body — armless, legless, headless, and it's been in the icebox for months! What in God's name can a man do with something like that?!"

Dr. Jekyll and Sister Hyde (1971) (see JEKYLL, DR. AND FAMILY). In this unusual variation on the Jekyll and Hyde story, Dr. Jekyll uses female hormones in his elixir. This changes not only his personality, but his sex as well, creating the evil *Mrs.* Hyde. To create his elixir, Jekyll needs select female organs, and employs the services of those two infamous body snatchers, Burke and Hare, to obtain his materials.

Flesh and the Fiends (1960; Triad; U.K.) (also *Mania; The Fiendish Ghouls; Psycho-Killers*). D: John Gilling. P: Robert S. Baker, Monty Berman. S: John Gilling, Leon Griffiths. C: Monty Berman. Cast: Peter Cushing, Donald Pleasence, June

Laverick, Dermot Walsh, Renee Houston, George Rose, Billie Whitelaw, John Cairney, Melvyn Hayes. Peter Cushing plays the redoubtable surgeon Dr. Knox, who flies in the face of convention in his quest to teach anatomy ("I am producing surgeons who will fight for humanity, not destroy it, and in the process of that nothing will stand in my way, nothing!"). To obtain subjects for dissection, he must employ the services of two grave robbers, Burke and Hare, who eventually turn to murder to ply their profitable trade. ¶ "Those bits of clay, all lumps of humanity that Burke and Hare brought in — I have to confess to you now, they seemed so small in the scheme of things, but I knew how they died." • This is the first film to feature characters named Burke and Hare, and with its seedy Edinburgh backsteet atmosphere and brilliant portrayal by Peter Cushing, is the best screen version of the infamous story.

Frankenstein (1931) (see FRANKENSTEIN'S MONSTER — UNIVERSAL SERIES). This timeless classic opens with Dr. Frankenstein and his assistant Fritz stealing a body from the graveyard. Later they steal the body of a hanged man from the gallows as well.

Frankenstein Meets the Wolf Man (1943) (see FRANKENSTEIN'S MONSTER — UNIVERSAL SERIES). The film's opening features a pair of grave robbers breaking into the tomb of Larry Talbot — the Wolf Man — and getting a nasty surprise in the bargain.

Horror Maniacs (1948; Hoffberg; U.K.) D: Oswald Mitchell. P: Gilbert Church. S: John Gilling ("from Historic Findings"). C: D. P. Cooper, S. D. Onions. Cast: Tod Slaughter, Aubrey Woods, Henry Oscar, Jenny Lynn, Winifred Melville, Pat Addison, Arnold Bell, Mary Love, Ann Trego, Edward Malin, Hubert Woodward, Denis Wyndham. Tod Slaughter, the self-proclaimed "Horror Man of Europe," and partner Henry Oscar play a pair of Burke and Hare–type grave robbers who make their own subjects via murder when unable to obtain enough bodies from the kirkyards.

The Mad Ghoul (1943) (see ZOMBIES). George Zucco discovers an ancient Mayan gas which causes its victim to transform into a living zombie in need of fresh hearts to survive. Zucco, with eyes for his assistant's fiancée, uses the gas on his assistant and then sends him out to graveyards to dig up fresh corpses for their hearts.

Mr. Sardonicus (1961) (see FREAKS). This gothic yarn from William Castle features a grinning madman, leeches, nightmares and a ghoulish grave robbing sequence. ¶ "A ghoul as I'm sure you know, is a disgusting creature who opens graves and feeds on corpses."

The Oblong Box (1969) (see POE FILMS — MODERN POE). Titled after Poe's story "The Oblong Box" but closer to "The Premature Burial," the plot follows Vincent Price who ends up burying alive his disfigured brother. Two grave robbers dig him up and deliver his coffin to a Dr. Neuhart (Christopher Lee). Shocked at finding a live specimen rather than the expected cadaver, the body snatching doctor is blackmailed into sheltering the disfigured madman while he carries out his plan of revenge against his brother. ¶ "Do you realize the penalty for body snatching is hanging?"

The Premature Burial (1962) (see POE FILMS — THE CORMAN CYCLE). Ray Milland plays a man deathly afraid of being buried alive. Confronted with the fact of his own father's premature interment, he dies of shock. Seeking a fresh corpse, two grave robbers named Sweeny and Mole come to dig up his grave, but they find a corpse that is a bit *too* fresh. Unhinged, Milland seeks vengeance upon those who buried him alive.

The Texas Chainsaw Massacre (1974) (see CANNIBALS). In rural Texas, five young people end up at the isolated house of a family of cannibals. The creepy clan also robs graves to decorate their home with gruesome bits of decayed flesh and bone, including an arm chair made of *real* arms(!). ¶ "Subsequent investigation has revealed at least a dozen empty crypts and it's feared more will turn up as the probe continues. Deputies report that in some instances, only parts of corpses had been removed—the head or in some cases the extremities removed, the remainder of the corpse left intact."

Dorian Gray

Like Robert Louis Stevenson's *Dr. Jekyll and Mr. Hyde,* Oscar Wilde's classic novel, *The Picture of Dorian Gray,* was the subject of numerous short films from around the world in the silent era. Though not as popular as Stevenson's work with sound filmmakers, three full-length theatrical versions and two television adaptations have been made.

While this may be one of the shortest sections in the book (with only five films on the subject), it is by no means an uninteresting one. The idea of achieving immortality by having one's portrait age while the subject stays young forever is a fascinating and very appealing one. When Dorian Gray is given this wonderful gift, he abuses it by indulging his cruel and baser instincts. Of course, outwardly he stays as young and boyishly innocent as ever, but the portrait bears the full hideous weight of his debaucheries and bares the truth about his inner corruption. Finally, Dorian can no longer live with this horrendous evidence of his evil and lashes out at the painting which has become his detached conscience—with the expected tragic result.

The first sound version has turned out to be the definitive one—MGM's lavish classic, *The Picture of Dorian Gray* (1945; starring Hurd Hatfield as Dorian and the screen's premiere cad, George Sanders, as the man who leads Dorian astray). Dorian's portrait lay at rest for nearly three decades until a multi-national co-production updated the story to contemporary 1972 in *Dorian Gray.* The next year, TV horror mogul Dan Curtis created a small-screen version of Wilde's novel, with the excellent Shane Briant in the title role. The final version to date (also a TV movie) came ten years later, adding a few new strokes to the old canvas. For *The Sins of Dorian Gray* (1983), Dorian is a woman, and it is not a painting that holds her soul and takes on her burdens of conscience, but a reel of film—a screen test.

Dorian Gray (1972; AIP: Italy/W. Germany/Liechtenstein/U.S.) (also *The Secret of Dorian Gray*). D: Massimo Dallamano. P: Harry Alan Towers. S: Marcello Coscia, Massimo Dallamano. C: Otello Spila. Cast: Helmut Berger, Richard Todd, Herbert Lom, Marie Liljedahl, Margaret Lee, Maria Rohm. This version (the most explicit to date as far as violence and nudity go) updates the story of Dorian Gray to contemporary times, but follows the same general pattern as the classic 1945 version. ¶ "What does it profit a man to gain the whole world and lose his soul?" • In a unique variation on the classic ending, Dorian takes a knife and stabs *himself* rather than the hideous portrait, as in the other versions. His corpse, of course, is then revealed to be a hideous old man while his untouched portrait is now once again that of a handsome, youthful Dorian.

Dinner with a Vampire (1988) (see VAMPIRES — OTHER VAMPIRES). Four young actors and actresses are chosen from an audition to spend a weekend at the castle of Karl Urich, a "world famous horror director," and 4,000-year-old vampire. The only way to kill this undead fiend is to destroy a film (à la *The Sins of Dorian Gray,* 1983) which was taken when a film crew accidentally released him from his tomb in the 1920s. ¶ "The film ... is like the portrait of Dorian Gray — it represents the soul of Urich. Which means that Urich will die the minute we destroy this film."

The Picture of Dorian Gray (1917; Richard Oswald Films; Germany) D/P/S: Richard Oswald. C: Max Fassbender. Cast: Bernd Aldor, Lupo Pick, Ernst Pittschau, Andreas Van Horn, Lea Lara, Ernst Ludwig. Though Oscar Wilde's story of the duality and corruption of the soul had been filmed as early as 1910 (in a Danish short), with the other short versions coming in 1913, two in 1915 (one American and one Russian), and 1917 (British), this German film *(Das Bildnis Des Dorian Gray)* is the first full-length version of the tale.

The Picture of Dorian Gray (1945; MGM) D/S: Albert Lewin. P: Pandro S. Berman. C: Harry Stradling. Cast: George Sanders, Hurd Hatfield, Donna Reed, Angela Lansbury, Peter Lawford, Lowell Gilmore, Richard Fraser. This second (and best) full-length adaptation of Oscar Wilde's classic story (and the first English-language version), set in 1886 London, follows the innocent Dorian Gray and the moral degradation and corruption of his soul through the influence of the cynical Lord Wootton. A painter friend has just completed a portrait of him, and Dorian makes a fanciful, fateful wish to remain young forever while the portrait grows old in his place. As Dorian sinks ever deeper into sin and depravity, his youthful countenance does not change — but the portrait does — with each vile thought and deed reflected in the now-hideous face in the painting. Finally, Dorian, with his last shred of conscience and humanity, takes a knife to the portrait, with the expected tragic results. ¶ Introductory stanza from "The Verse of Omar Khayyam": "I sent my soul through the invisible/ Some letter of that after-life to spell:/ And by and by my soul returned to me,/ And answered, 'I myself am Heaven and Hell.'" ¶ "There's only one way to get rid of a temptation and that is to yield to it." • Though filmed in black and white, director Albert Lewin chose to show the ever-changing portrait in full color — the only color to be seen in the entire film — to emphasize the importance of the painting. • Cinematographer Harry Stradling won an Oscar for his camerawork. • Angela Lansbury (in her third film) was nominated for Best Actress for her role as the love interest seduced and cast off by Dorian. She did not win, however.

The Picture of Dorian Gray (1973; TV movie) D: Glenn Jordan. P: Dan Curtis. S: John Tomerlin. C: Ben Colman. Cast: Nigel Davenport, Charles Aidman, Shane Briant, Fionnuala Flanagan, Linda Kelsey, Vanessa Howard, John Karlen, Dixie Marquis, Brendan Dillon. TV producer Dan Curtis retains his TV horror crown with this small screen retelling of the classic story starring Shane Briant as Dorian. Curtis has also made TV movie versions of *Dracula, Frankenstein, Dr. Jekyll and Mr. Hyde,* and *Turn of the Screw.* ¶ "Even locked away in this room it haunts me.... It knows what I've done, what I'm doing, and its vile features alter with every sin I commit, every pain I inflict." • Producer Dan Curtis, who created the popular daytime horror soap opera "Dark Shadows" in the late 1960s, recycled much of the music from that successful program for this telefilm, including the well-worn tune called "Quentin's Theme." • Also from "Dark Shadows" is actor John Karlen, who plays Dorian's one-time friend, Alan Campbell.

The Sins of Dorian Gray (1983; TV movie) D: Tony Maylam. P: Jules Bass. S: Ken August, Peter Lawrence. C: Zale Madger. Cast: Anthony Perkins, Belinda Bauer, Olga Karlatos, Joseph Bottoms,

Donna Reed, George Sanders, and Hurd Hatfield gaze at a statue of an ancient Egyptian cat-god (intimated to be at the root of Dorian's strange predicament) in this publicity photo from the 1945 version of The Picture of Dorian Gray.

Michael Ironside, Caroline Yeager, Patsy Rahn. In an 80s update of *The Picture of Dorian Gray,* Dorian is a beautiful, innocent *woman* who wishes for eternal youth and gets it, only to have her soul aged and corrupted by her own weakness and depravity while her body stays young. ¶ "Somehow, God knows how, you've kept your looks. But underneath it all you've changed. You're just an image kiddo, an empty, beautiful, vicious *nothing!*" • Technology, as well as feminism, is well represented in this updated version, for Dorian's soul is not trapped in a painting as in the book and all the previous versions, it is instead held inside a reel of film—a screen test which Dorian had done. • The character of Sybil Vane from the previous versions, who commits suicide on account of Dorian, is now *Stuart* Vane.

Hands

When it comes to cinematic hands, there are two types. The first and more literate of the two is the "Hands of Orlac" camp, with its basis in the Maurice Renard novel, *Les Mains d'Orlac*. Four versions of this story have been filmed — the story of a man who loses his hands, only to have the hands of a murderer grafted onto his arms (with the new members seemingly possessing a lethal will of their own). It was first made in 1925, with silent screen star Conrad Veidt agonizing over his new appendages. Then came the 1935 adaptation carrying the altered title of *Mad Love,* in which cinematographer-turned-director Karl Freund created the definitive version. *Hands of a Stranger* was a weak remake from 1962, and the British *The Hands of Orlac* was a slight improvement in 1965.

The second hand theme can be called "The Beast with Five Fingers" concept. In these films a disembodied hand takes on a life of its own. Not many things are more horrible than dismemberment, but having the chopped-off member take on a malignant life of its own is truly a grisly and terrifying thought. Unfortunately, Hollywood has taken only infrequent advantage of these macabre possibilities. The first, and still the best, is of course *The Beast with Five Fingers* (1947), in which Peter Lorre sees the disembodied hand of his murdered employer crawling out of boxes, playing the piano, scuttling behind bookshelves, etc. While the hand effects are uneven, director Robert Florey (aided by Lorre's intense performance) managed to produce some genuine chills. There followed a handful of hand films, including the unintentionally amusing *The Crawling Hand* (1963) and the Oliver Stone/ Michael Caine misfire, sparingly named *The Hand* (1981). Disembodied hands have been given supporting roles in nearly a dozen other films, from the comical (*Return of the Living Dead,* parts 1 and 2, 1985 and 1987) to the vengeful (*Dr. Terror's House of Horrors,* 1965). While a relatively minor subject area, malignant members have managed to at least lend a helping hand to the continuing horror and science fiction film odyssey.

And Now the Screaming Starts (1973; Amicus/Cinema Releasing; U.K.) D: Roy Ward Baker. P: Milton Subotsky, Max J. Rosenberg. S: Roger Marshall. C: Denys Coop. Cast: Peter Cushing, Ian Ogilvy, Stephanie Beacham, Herbert Lom, Patrick Magee, Guy Rolfe, Geoffrey Whitehead, Rosalie Crutchley, Janet Key, Gillian Lind. A young man and his pregnant wife move into the Fengriffin Manor and are terrorized by the old family curse involving a disembodied hand avenging the rape of a servant by a Fengriffin ancestor. ¶ From the ads: "The dead hand that crawls, kills and lives!"

Asylum (1972) (see ANTHOLOGIES). In the "Frozen Fear" segment, a woman is set upon by the dismembered but still ambulatory corpse of her lover's murdered wife. Out of the freezer crawls the wrapped remains, including a disembodied arm which attempts to strangle her.

The Beast with Five Fingers (1947; Warner Bros.) D: Robert Florey. P: William Jacobs. S: Curt Siodmak. C: Wesley Anderson. Cast: Robert Alda, Peter Lorre, Andrea King, Victor Francen, J. Carrol Naish, Charles Dingle. Francis Ingram, a famous pianist now paralyzed, dies soon after rewriting his will. His close friends who have precariously lived off his fortune for years find the new will contested by Ingram's greedy relatives. Terror unfolds when Ingram's hand is mysteriously severed and creeps away to kill one member of the household and haunt another. The shocks that follow are only a deception though, as Peter Lorre turns out to be the real killer, with the crawling hand being merely an hallucination created by his guilt-ridden insanity. ¶ "I caught it, I locked it up — the horrible hand. It can't escape anymore. It can't get out, it can't!" • Director Robert

Florey was so dissatisfied with the initial script and shooting schedule that he took a three-month studio suspension before finally capitulating and directing the picture. • Besides directing, Robert Florey literally lent a hand during the filming by using his own hand for the live-action shots of the murderous member.

The Crawling Hand (1963; Hansen Enterprises) D: Herbert L. Strock. P: Joseph F. Robertson. S: William Edelson, Herbert L. Strock. C: Willard Vander Veer. Cast: Peter Breck, Kent Taylor, Rod Lauren, Arline Judge, Richard Arlen, Alan Hale. An astronaut in space is taken over by some kind of evil space organism which commands its host to "Kill! Kill! Kill!" So the astronaut, with what remaining will he has left, contacts Mission Control and begs them to detonate the self-destruct button for him, since his possessed arm won't obey. They blow up the rocket, but his arm (the uncooperative one) falls to Earth and is promptly found by a young medical student who takes it home and puts it on a shelf in the basement. That nasty space organism is still inside the arm and now attempts to possess the student (when not crawling about on its own). ¶ "Does a living cell from Earth romance a cosmic ray and give birth to an illegitimate monster?"

Demonoid (1979; American Panorama) (also *Macabra*). D/P: Alfred Zacharias. S: David Lee Fein, Alfred Zacharias. C: Alex Phillips, Jr. Cast: Samantha Eggar, Stuart Whitman, Roy Cameron Jenson, Narcisco Busquets, Erika Carlson, Lew Saunders. A couple working a silver mine uncover an ancient mummified hand which once belonged to a devil-cult. The hand possesses various people and forces them to commit murder and to cut off their own hands.

Dr. Terror's House of Horrors (1965) (see ANTHOLOGIES). In this omnibus' strongest tale, Christopher Lee plays a pompous art critic who is humiliated by an artist he had been denigrating. Lee retaliates by running him down with his car, causing the amputation of the artist's hand. The vengeful hand turns up to torment Lee again and again until engineering the final bit of ironic justice.

Evil Dead 2: Dead Before Dawn (1987) (see DEMONS AND DEVILS). In this tale of ancient demonic forces possessing a group of people in a remote mountain cabin, the hero's own hand becomes possessed and turns against him, breaking plates on his head, hitting him in the face, etc. He finally cuts it off with a chain saw, but that doesn't stop the possessed member. It continues to scuttle about and even ends up killing the heroine by stabbing her in the back with a knife.

Frankenstein: The True Story (1974) (see FRANKENSTEIN'S MONSTER — FURTHER FRANKENSTEINS). One of Dr. Frankenstein's early experiments was to keep a disembodied arm alive. It comes back to haunt him when he hears a knock at the door, opens it, and is startled by the now-decaying arm crawling towards him.

Galaxy of Terror (1981) (see ALIENS — ENCOUNTERS IN OUTER SPACE). On a planet where one's worst fears are brought to life to test one's mettle, a crew member is forced to cut off his own arm, which then springs to life and throws a crystal star at its former owner, killing him.

The Hand (1981; Warner Bros./Orion) D/S: Oliver Stone. P: Edward R. Pressman. C: King Baggot. Cast: Michael Caine, Andrea Marcovicci, Viveca Lindfors, Rosemary Murphy, Bruce McGill. A cartoonist (Michael Caine) loses his drawing hand in a car accident. The hand, which was never found, returns to do his subconscious bidding, scuttling up to murder all those the troubled artist wishes dead.

Hands of a Stranger (1962; Allied Artists) D/S: Newton Arnold. P: Newton Arnold, Michael DuPont. C: Henry Cronjager. Cast: Paul Lukather, Joan Harvey, James Stapleton, Irish McCalla, Ted Otis, Michael DuPont. In yet another adaptation of Maurice Renard's French novel, *The Hands of Orlac*, a pianist has the hands of a murdered man grafted onto his arms after an accident. Unlike in the first sound version, *Mad Love* (1935), the surgeon who performed the operation is not an obsessed madman, but instead is the romantic lead and falls in love with Orlac's sister. Orlac, in the meantime, is driving himself mad because of his new hands' awkwardness at playing the piano. He resolves to kill all those associated with his misfortune.

The Hands of Orlac (1925; Pan Film; Austria) D: Robert Wiene. S: Ludwig Nerz. C: Hans Androschin. Cast: Conrad Veidt, Fritz Kortner, Carmen Cartellieri, Alexandra Sorina, Fritz Strassny, Paul Askonas. In this first adaptation of Maurice Renard's novel, concert pianist Stephen Orlac loses his hands in an accident and has the hands of a murderer transplanted onto his arms, finding that the hands seem to have a will of their own.

The Hands of Orlac (1960; British Lion Films/Britannia Film Distributors; U.K.) D: Edmond T. Greville. P: Steven Pallos,

Donald Taylor. S: John Baines, Edmond T. Greville, Donald Taylor. C: Desmond Dickinson. Cast: Mel Ferrer, Christopher Lee, Dany Carrel, Lucile Saint Simon, Felix Aylmer, Basil Sydney, Peter Reynolds, Campbell Singer, Sir Donald Wolfit, Donald Pleasence. Concert pianist Stephen Orlac has his hands mutilated in a plane crash. His fiancée has him taken to an eminent surgeon, passing along the way the guillotining of a notorious strangler named Louis Vasseur. Stephen gets it in his mind that he now has Vasseur's hands and cannot fully control them. His deteriorating mental state is exacerbated by an opportunistic stage magician named Nero, who preys on Stephen's mind in a scheme to get blackmail money. ¶ "Look at these hands — they're not mine, they belong to someone else. They have their own thoughts, their own will. I can't control them!" • It is never truly established whether or not his hands are those of Louis Vasseur (the doctor who operated has a cerebral hermorrhage and cannot communicate, and the French police refuse to release a copy of Vasseur's fingerprints when asked). It is made clear at the end, however, that Vasseur turned out to be innocent — he was not a strangler after all, so even if Orlac has Vasseur's hands, he has nothing to worry about (as he gratefully explains at film's end: "Louis Vasseur was innocent ... my hands are innocent!") • David Peel, best known as the blond vampire Baron Mienster from *Brides of Dracula* (1960), appears in a small role as an airplane pilot.

Mad Love (1935; MGM) (also *Hands of Orlac*). D: Karl Freund. P: John W. Considine. S: Guy Endore, P. J. Wolfson, John L. Balderston. C: Chester Lyons, Gregg Toland. Cast: Peter Lorre, Frances Drake, Colin Clive, Ted Healy, Sarah Haden, Edward Brophy, Henry Kolker, Keye Luke, May Beatty. ¶ "I, a poor peasant have conquered science; why can't I conquer love?!" In this classic, best-known version of Maurice Renard's novel, *Les Mains d'Orlac (The Hands of Orlac),* concert pianist Stephen Orlac has his hands horribly mutilated in a train wreck. In desperation his wife Yvonne goes to the brilliant surgeon Dr. Gogol (Peter Lorre) for help. Gogol harbors a mad love for Yvonne, a stage actress, and agrees to help. He grafts the hands of an executed murderer — a knife-thrower — onto Stephen's arms. He then sets about driving Stephen insane by tormenting him about his new hands, which have acquired an unwanted skill — knife throwing. Gogol frames him

for murder, but is found out just in time for Stephen to put his new hands' talent to work to save his wife from Gogol's maniacal clutches. • This was Peter Lorre's first American film, and only his second English-speaking role. • This was the second Golden Age horror classic directed by cinematographer-turned-director Karl Freund. He had directed Boris Karloff in *The Mummy* in 1932. Despite these successes, Freund soon returned to cinematography.

Necropolis (1987) (see WITCHES, WARLOCKS, AND CULTS). A 300-year-old witch sets out to complete a ceremonial virgin sacrifice designed to endow her with eternal life. At the climactic confrontation, the witch is burned alive, but not before her charred severed hand wearing her magic ring has crawled away on its own. The hand makes its way to the heroine's apartment and possesses her, turning her into the next incarnation of the witch.

Return of the Living Dead (1985) (see ZOMBIE FLESH EATERS). This ground-breaking comical zombie flesh eater flick features zombies which are basically unstoppable, even when totally dismembered. Several of the protagonists do just that to a medical cadaver which had come to life, and one arm latches onto the leg of a mortician, causing more than a little concern.

Return of the Living Dead Part 2 (1987) (see ZOMBIE FLESH EATERS). At one point in this comical zombie movie, a disembodied hand crawls into a car with our little band of survivors and proceeds to try and choke anyone it can get its zombie fingers on. The hand is finally tossed out of the moving car and defiantly gives them the finger as they speed away.

Spiritism (1961) (see WITCHES, WARLOCKS, AND CULTS). In this Mexican variation on "The Monkey's Paw," a woman calls upon evil forces to aid her, and the Devil himself appears bearing "Pandora's Box." Inside the box is a severed human hand, which, when wished upon, comes alive and crawls about. • In scenes of the hand crawling about on its own, it is obvious that a mechanical mechanism causes the fingers to move. but it is still superior to the phony hand movements in *The Beast with Five Fingers* (1947), *The Crawling Hand* (1963), and *Dr. Terror's House of Horrors* (1965).

The Witch's Mirror (1960) (see WITCHES, WARLOCKS, AND CULTS). A surgeon murders his wife. The housekeeper, a witch, vows vengeance and summons up her ghost. The doctor remarries and the new wife is tormented and finally disfigured by the ghost.

Peter Lorre stars as the mad surgeon Dr. Gogol, obsessed with a Mad Love *(1935), who transplants the hands of a murderer onto the arms of an injured pianist in this definitive film version of* The Hands of Orlac.

With his current wife's hands and face horribly burned, the doctor murders a girl for her hands, which he transplants onto the arms of his wife. The ghost, however, intervenes, and replaces the fresh hands with her own ghostly members. The new wife, with the hands of the old wife, finds she cannot control her new hands, which stab her husband to death. Then the hands drop off her arms and, moving on their own, crawl up the back of the doctor's lab assistant and stab *him*.

Heads *see* Brains—Living Heads

Human Giants

Originating from Greek and Norse mythology, giants were said to be a race of primeval beings who were finally overcome and destroyed by the pantheon of new gods. Brutus was reported to have found giants in Cornwall after the fall of Troy; and even the Bible, specifically in the book of Numbers, told of giants in the land of Canaan.

Folklore is filled with tales of giant people—whether simply oversized humans or terrifying monsters (such as the one-eyed Cyclops of Greek legends). Animal fossils thought to be the bones of giants have helped to perpetuate the myths, and even a few real-life giants, such as the "9 foot, 3 inch" Eddie Carmel, have served to keep our imaginations active on the subject.

European folktales often depicted giants as dim savages, a characteristic that has usually stuck with the human gargantuas represented in the films. Most of the brutes in the Hercules and period-fantasy movies were often bested by brains rather than brawn (à la David and Goliath).

Many of the films listed in this section are related in some way to mythology or folklore, but some of the most fascinating giants were spawned not from legend but from science, radiation, or outer space. Two of the best-known scientific "giant" features were made in the 1950s—Bert I. Gordon's *The Amazing Colossal Man* (1957), and Nathan Juran's camp classic, *Attack of the 50 Foot Woman* (1958). Both films deal with the effects of gigantism on modern everyday people, with sometimes unintentionally amusing results (as in *50 Foot Woman*) but other times with an introspective, sensitive approach (as seen in *Colossal Man*). The latter film's success at the box office was due in part to a reasonably literate script and some thought-provoking dialogue effectively delivered in part by Glenn Langan, who openly discussed his ever growing condition with bitter frustration.

This chapter features films containing a variety of human giants. Though some may be monstrous, all are humanoid in appearance and possess two legs and two arms (though occasionally are missing an eye, or sporting a second head). It is doubtful that this subgenre will ever enjoy a boom decade like the 1950s again (which featured no less than ten "giant" movies), since these "giant" special effects are difficult to make convincing for today's more demanding audiences.

The Amazing Colossal Man (1957; AIP) D/P/S: Bert I. Gordon. C: Joseph Biroc. Cast: Glen Langan, Cathy Downs, William Hudson, James Seay, Larry Thor, Russ Bender, Lyn Osborn. A plutonium bomb blast victim miraculously regenerates new skin, then grows to a height of 60 feet. ¶ "I just don't want to grow anymore!" • Towards the film's end, scientists attempt to subdue the rampaging gargantuan by injecting him with an unforgettable giant six-foot syringe. After taking the shot in the ankle, the enraged colossal man hurls the oversized syringe like a spear through the body of ac-

tor James Seay (*The Day the Earth Stood Still,* 1951; *When Worlds Collide,* 1951) The annoyed giant then lumbers through Las Vegas, and eventually falls off Boulder Dam at the climax. • Mr. *BIG,* producer/director/writer Bert I. Gorton, also created the special effects for the film. Gigantism was a favorite topic of his, and he has made numerous films about giant things over his career. Some featured other giant humanoids—*The Cyclops, War of the Colossal Beast, The Magic Sword,* while others featured giant bugs—*Beginning of the End, Earth vs. the Spider, Empire of the Ants,* and even giant

Glenn Langan, The Amazing Colossal Man *(1957), sits inside a makeshift room filled with miniature props built by special effects man Paul Blaisdell.*

dinosaurs—*King Dinosaur.* • The film's premise is said to have originated from a story called "The Nth Man" by Homer Flint, which Forrest J Ackerman's agency had purchased at that time. Bert Gordon, however, has stated that he thought of the story himself: "I knew nothing of this at the time and independently one evening, on a paper napkin of all things, developed my idea for *The Amazing Colossal Man.* • Prolific effects man and monster-maker Paul Blaisdell designed the various oversized props. • In 1958, Gordon filmed a sequel called *War of the Colossal Beast,* but the actor who played the colossal man in the first film, Glen Langan, was replaced by stuntman/actor Dean Parkin. Very few people noticed the change since the Beast was now disfigured, and not required to demonstrate a high caliber of acting prowess. • Clips from *The Amazing Colossal Man* showed up in another Gordon film, *Attack of the Puppet People* (1958). In one scene, John Agar takes his girl to a drive-in at which *Colossal Man* is playing.

Atlantis the Lost Continent (1961) (see ATLANTIS). A Greek battles an oversized brute in the "ordeal of fire and water." He eventually drowns him, thus winning his freedom in Atlantis.

Atlas Against the Cyclops (1961) (see MYTHOLOGY) (also *Atlas in the Land of the Cyclops, Maciste in the Land of the Cyclops*). The Italian strongman faces a giant cyclops.

Attack of the 50 Foot Woman (1958; Allied Artists) D: Nathan Juran. P: Bernard Woolner. S: Mark Hanna. C: Jacques Marquette. Cast: Allison Hayes, William Hudson, Yvette Vickers, George Douglas, Frank Chase, Ken Terrell, Roy Gordon. A two-timing scoundrel conspires with floozy Yvette Vickers to do away with his mentally unbalanced wife (Allison Hayes). Hayes

Allison Hayes touches a small model electrical structure during her rampage through town in Attack of the 50 Foot Woman *(1958).*

gets her revenge, however, after being touched by an alien giant who lands in a nearby desert in his flying satellite. She grows to a height of 50 feet and breaks the town up looking for her conniving husband. ¶ "It's your wife—she's wrecking the town looking for you." • "There's a small flying satellite and a 30-foot giant a few miles out on 66." The giant mentioned in the quote was wearing a leather jacket with a sequined pattern of a bull on the back. Imagine, aliens who drink malt liquor! • Director Nathan Juran, sometimes known as Nathan Hertz (his middle name), was born in Austria and broke into Hollywood as an art director. He won an Academy Award for his art direction on *How Green Was My Valley* (1941). Juran turned to directing low and medium budget movies in the 1950s.

Some of his genre credits include *20 Million Miles to Earth* (1957), *The Seventh Voyage of Sinbad* (1958), and *First Men in the Moon* (1964). • Actress Allison Hayes was born on the day Lon Chaney died—February 27, 1930. In addition to being a popular B-movie actress, Allison (whose real name is Mary Ann Hayes) earned a law degree and was an accomplished pianist.

The Cyclops (1957; Allied Artists) D/P/S: Bert I. Gordon. C: Ira Morgan. Cast: Gloria Talbott, Lon Chaney, Jr., James Craig, Tom Drake, Duncan Parkin. Gloria Talbott goes to Mexico to search for her missing fiancé, whose plane crashed within a government-restricted zone out in the wilderness. Uranium deposits in the area have caused the animal life to grow, and the expedition encounters a one-eyed giant man, presumably her disfigured fiancé. ¶ "There's something about that giant that makes me terribly sad." • *The Cyclops* was originally to be paired with *Daughter of Dr. Jekyll* on an RKO double-bill, but the film company broke up and subsequently sold each of the movies to new distributors. With films like these, it becomes rather apparent why RKO was in such bad shape before the collapse. • Jack H. Young created the makeup for the cyclops here, as well as for another Bert I. Gordon giant human film— *War of the Colossal Beast* (1958). In both films, the creature's right eye is missing. In *Beast,* there's just an empty socket, while in *Cyclops* there's a putty-like compound covering the eye and right side of his face. At the climax of *The Cyclops,* a flaming spear is thrown into his one good eye. To add a little grotesqueness to the film, Gordon has his cyclops pull the spear out so we can see some gushing blood pour out between his fingers. • Gloria Talbott mentioned in Tom Weaver's book, *Interviews with B Science Fiction and Horror Movie Makers,* that Lon Chaney, Jr., and Tom Drake were "absolutely smashed" in the scene when they were flying the plane into the restricted region. She also said the stuntman who wrestled the python was nearly strangled to death by the snake. Of Flora Gordon, Bert's wife and special effects associate, she said, "His wife was so sweet— she was doing the script supervising, the wardrobe, making cookies, everything."

Food of the Gods Part 2 (1989) (see RATS). An experimental growth hormone is accidentally exposed to a group of rats in a college laboratory, causing them to grow to the size of Saint Bernards. A subplot features an eight-year-old child who is administered the hormone and grows to gigantic proportions.

Frankenstein Conquers the World (1964; Toho/AIP; Japan/U.S.) D: Inoshiro Honda. P: Tomoyuki Tanaka. S: Kaoru Mabuchi. C: Hajime Koizumi. Cast: Tadao Takashima, Nick Adams, Kumi Mizuno, Yoshio Tsuchiya, Takashi Shimura, Kenchiro Kawaji, Seuko Togami. A boy eats the heart of the Frankenstein Monster, grows to enormous height, and fights a resurrected dinosaur. ¶ "How did he escape destruction in the heart of the giant blast?" • Star Nick Adams (born Adamschock), the son of a Pennsylvania coal miner, said of this picture: "I must say I enjoyed it very much … I was the guy in the middle who had to fight the monsters—sort of like the referee in a Liston-Clay dancing lesson.… One of our

technicians is so good with monsters that he is called upon for the monster pièce de resistance in every horror picture.… His wife has left him 20 times because she asked him what he did at the studio that day and he told her."

Giant from the Unknown (1958; Astor Pictures) D/C: Richard E. Cunha. P: Arthur A. Jacobs. S: Frank Hart Taussig, Ralph Brooke. Cast: Ed Kemmer, Sally Fraser, Buddy Baer, Morris Ankrum, Bob Steele. A gigantic conquistador named Vargas is resurrected by a storm and sets off to menace the countryside. The brute kidnaps an archeologist's daughter, and is eventually cornered up in the mountains. Despite a barrage of bullets the giant manages to escape to an old mill, but falls to his death off a dam. ¶ "And during that electrical storm, a bolt of lightning struck near enough to rekindle the spark of life?" • *Giant from the Unknown* was budgeted at $55,000 and was shot in only six days (while avoiding the Unions) at Big Bear, outside Los Angeles. • Harold Banks made the Giant's props—the shields, the armor, the hats—all out of fiberglass. • Actor Buddy Baer, who played the "giant," was only 6'4″ tall in real life. • Sheriff Parker was played by actor Bob Steele, whose most famous role came in the Bogart classic, *The Big Sleep* (1946), as the gunman "Canino."

Jack the Giant Killer (1962) (see SWORD AND SORCERY). A handsome peasant rises to fame by destroying a cloven-hoofed giant named "Cormoran." Later on, he bags another big brute—the two-headed monstrosity known as "Galligantua." ¶ "It's been years since giants were banished, why would they return now?"

The Magic Sword (1962) (see SWORD AND SORCERY). One of the evil wizard Locac's seven deadly curses he sends against the hero includes a huge ugly ogre, which George defeats with the help of his speedy horse.

The Princess Bride (1987) (see SWORD AND SORCERY). This tongue-in-cheek swashbuckler features three villains kidnapping a Princess. One of the villains is a kindly giant who realizes the error of his ways and comes over to the side of good. • Andre the Giant, who of course played the giant (named "Fezzik," not Andre) is a popular big-time professional wrestler.

Sword and the Dragon (1956) (see SWORD AND SORCERY). A warrior named Ilya slays a huge giant, who is carted to a feast on the backs of 1,000 men.

The Thirty Foot Bride of Candy Rock

Six foot four inch Buddy Baer plays the resurrected giant conquistador named "Vargas" in Giant from the Unknown *(1958).*

(1959; Columbia) D: Sidney Miller. P: Lewis J. Rachmil. S: Rowland Barber, Arthur Ross. C: Frank G. Carson. Cast: Lou Costello, Dorothy Provine, Gale Gordon, Jimmy Conlin, Charles Lane. Lou Costello, inventor of an all-purpose talking machine called Max, manages to cause his girlfriend to grow to the height of 30 feet. When the military sends in troops to dispatch what they think is a giant from outer space, Lou uses his machine to regress the soldiers into progressively primitive types of fighting men. In the end, Lou marries the girl and tries to make her normal but only manages to make things worse, first shrinking her to two inches and then back to 30 feet again. • Lou Costello (born Louis Francis Cristillo in New Jersey) died shortly after the making of this picture, his last. Ironically, it was the only picture in which he appeared without his longtime buddy and partner, Bud Abbott. They split up as a team in 1957.

The Three Stooges Meet Hercules (1962) (see MYTHOLOGY). The Stooges and their friend Skyler topple a two-headed Siamese Cyclops with sleeping pills and a slingshot.

The Three Worlds of Gulliver (1959; Columbia) D: Jack Sher. P: Charles H. Schneer. S: Jack Sher, Arthur Russ. C: Wilkie Cooper. Cast: Kerwin Mathews, June Thorburn, Jo Morrow, Lee Patterson, Gregoire Aslan, Charles Lloyd Pack, Basil Sydney, Sherri Alberoni. A disillusioned young English doctor in the year 1699 is shipwrecked on the isle of Lilliput, where the pint-sized inhabitants are at war over trivial affairs. After being driven off by one of the tiny armies, he eventually lands in Brobdingnag, a place where everyone is gigantic, and he is now the tiny one. ¶ "Anyone with any sense knows that you should open your eggs from the little end." • The story is based on the Jonathan Swift satirical novel, *Gulliver's Travels.* • During the filming of the Brobdingnag sequences, cameras had to be set deep down inside holes in the ground to help create the illusion of a gigantic world from Gulliver's perspective. • Special effects wizard Ray Harryhausen chose to shoot the film in England because a color special effects process called "sodium backing" was available there. Unlike blue screen backing, which is tricky and often leaves matting lines between the two pieces of film, sodium backing (a screen lit by a monochromatic yellowish light from sodium vapor lamps) enables the shot to be composed on two similar strips of film with the aid of a special beam-splitter mechanism, saving several steps along the way.

Ulysses (1955) (see MYTHOLOGY). Kirk Douglas manages to get the gigantic cyclopean son of Neptune drunk in order to free himself and his men. ¶ "How do you prefer me, master – roasted, boiled, spiced, raw?"

Village of the Giants (1956; Embassy) D/P: Bert I. Gordon. S: Alan Caillou. C: Paul C. Vogel. Cast: Tommy Kirk, Johnny Crawford, Beara Bridge, Bob Random, Ronny Howard. Teenagers grow to gigantic proportions after eating a special food prepared by an inventor. ¶ From the ads: "See them burst out of their clothes and bust up the town!" • Bert I. Gordon, who claimed the story is based on H. G. Wells' *Food of the Gods,* coined the term "perceptovision" for the photographic effects in this film. • Ads which read, "Teenagers zoom to supersize and terrorize a town ... See ... The wildest, weirdest 'Party Rumble' of 'em all!" featured a shot of a teenage boy hanging onto the bra straps of a gigantic young girl.

War of the Colossal Beast (1958; AIP) D/P: Bert I. Gordon. S: George Worthington Yates. C: Jack Marta. Cast: Sally Fraser, Dean Parkin, Roger Place, Russ Bender, Charles Stewart. This continuation of *The Amazing Colossal Man* story now has Manning residing in Mexico, horribly disfigured after his fall from Hoover Dam. He is captured, then escapes for more routine rampaging. ¶ "I'm afraid the world doesn't think of a 60-foot man the way a sister does." • The picture's promotion promised its fans they would "See a 60-foot giant destroyed ... in color!" The fact is, the sequence they refer to lasts only a few seconds and the color quality is minimal. Instead of being burned to death when he grabs a set of high-tension wires (which is what would happen to a victim of electrocution), the Colossal Beast simply vanishes into thin air. • Although the part played by Dean Parkin involves only snarling (often sounding exactly like a buzzing chain saw), at the climax he does utter one final intelligible world – "Joyce," the name of his sister. • Several flashback scenes from *The Amazing Colossal Man* are used for this film. • Actor Glen Langan, the original Colossal Man, was substituted by Dean Parkin for this picture. Also, Cathy Downs, Glen's fiancée, is not included or mentioned in this sequel. Sally Fraser takes the female lead here – as the Colossal Man's *sister.* It is interesting to note that actor Russ Bender appears in both films, but as different characters. In *Colossal Man,* he plays Richard Kingman, and in *Beast,* he plays Dr. Carmichael.

War of the Gargantuas (1967) (see JAPANESE GIANT MONSTERS – OTHER GIANT JAPANESE MONSTERS). A friendly brown giant and his evil green twin catch a case of sibling rivalry that nearly levels Tokyo. After their battle they are both engulfed by a volcanic eruption.

Hunchbacks *see* Freaks

Hypnotists

Hypnosis is the act of changing a person's conscious awareness through some sort of stimulus or verbal suggestion. A "hypnotized" person may experience a variety of physical phenomena which can include a loss of sensation, paralysis, or rigidity. Alterations in consciousness and or memory may also occur in response to a specific post-hypnotic suggestion. Those performing the hypnotic procedure usually bring about this state of increased suggestibility by continuously repeating monotonous commands while their subject concentrates on a fixed point or a brightly colored object. A person under hypnosis may often appear completely normal, and may even be able to ask questions or move about freely.

Hypnotism is used every day, and is more commonplace now than ever. People use it for things such as weight reduction and the battling of bad habits (smoking, etc.). Even sports figures use it to enhance their performances. Boxer Sugar Ray Leonard is a good example, claiming that hypnosis increases both his confidence and focus in the ring.

Despite its long history (most notably in the psychiatric profession), hypnosis is still a controversial "science." Skepticism surrounds the subject, much of this due to its link with age regression (and reincarnation) and religious rituals. The Cinema of the Fantastic hasn't helped establish any further credibility for hypnosis either. Crazed screen hypnotists like those seen in *The Cabinet of Dr. Caligari* (1919) and *Svengali* (1931) have helped bring a connotation of wild fiction to the subject. Very few serious dramas have been made on hypnotism, leaving it wide open for the exploitational clutches of the science fiction/horror movie maker. Universal's Inner Sanctum mysteries, for example, were quick to utilize hypnotism for their own cinematic ends. Two of these features, 1943's *Calling Dr. Death,* and 1945's *The Frozen Ghost,* featured hypnotists using their skills to ferret out the truth surrounding mysterious murders. Both films utilized this technique to study the unconscious (though these films cast a crude, improbable light on the subject which Freud took so seriously).

Two of the wildest depictions of hypnotism in film can be found in *The She-Creature* (1956) and *The Hypnotic Eye* (1960). In the first, a mesmerist uses hypnosis to conjure up a prehistoric female fish-creature (the past incarnation of a young girl). The latter featured a nightclub hypnotist who utilized the powers of a small, glowing, eye-shaped object to plant post-hypnotic suggestions in the minds of beautiful women, causing them to go out and mutilate themselves. One woman took a burning hot shower, while another dried her hair over an oven burner. Alongside the gruesome plotting, *The Hypnotic Eye* also employed some absurd William Castle–like parlor gimmicks by handing out free "hypnotic eye" balloons, and urging theater audiences to imitate the "hypnotic" tricks demonstrated up on the screen.

The use of hypnotism is also found in other horror subjects like REINCARNATION, VOODOO, and WITCHES, WARLOCKS, AND CULTS. Vampires even have the power to hypnotize individuals (much like snakes transfix their victims with an icy stare before striking). However, hypnotism in these subjects is more of a supernatural power than a scientific/mental phenomenon. The main focus of this chapter is on "true" hypnotists and their nefarious deeds, rather than on supernatural creatures possessing hypnotic powers.

Abbott and Costello Meet the Killer, Boris Karloff (1949; Universal) D: Charles T. Barton. P: Robert Arthur. S: Hugh Wedlock, Jr., Howard Snyder, John Grant. C: George Robinson. Cast: Lou Costello, Bud Abbott, Boris Karloff, Roland Winters, Gar Moore, Lenore Aubert, Alan Mowbray, Percy Helton, Billy Gray. A pair of zany hotel detectives hot on a murder mystery encounter a phony mystic (Boris Karloff), who attempts to hypnotize Lou.

The Bells (1926; Chadwick) D/S: James Young. P: I. E. Chadwick. C: William O'Connell. Cast: Lionel Barrymore, Boris Karloff, Fred Warren, Gustav von Seyffer-titz, Edward Phillips, Lola Todd. Lionel Barrymore plays an innkeeper who kills a rich traveler to clear his own debts. Karloff is a fairground hypnotist who helps bring Barrymore's guilty conscience to the forefront. • Boris Karloff reported his makeup experiences on the film to horror author Robert Bloch: "The first makeup they gave me made me look like a Svengali, and Lionel Barrymore, the picture's star, said 'No, that's no good,' and, since I was supposed to be a sinister mesmerist, he went to work transforming me into a kind of Werner Krauss. A marvelous man, a great man, Lionel; so stimulating to work with."

Black Friday (1940) (see BRAINS — BRAIN TRANSPLANTS). A professor is turned into a gangster after receiving a brain transplant. The doctor who performed the operation wants to find the dead gangster's hidden loot and so periodically uses hypnotism to bring the gangster side of the meek professor's personality to the fore.

Blood of Dracula (1957) (see VAMPIRES — OTHER VAMPIRES). An unscrupulous instructor at a girls' boarding school uses an amulet to hypnotically transform a teenager into a vampire bobby-soxer. ¶ "I can release a destructive power in a human being that would make the split atom seem like a blessing." • Though a vampire film, it is included here because of the prominent role of hypnotism in actually *creating* the vampire-creature.

The Cabinet of Dr. Caligari (1919; Decla Film: Germany) D: Robert Wiene. P: Erich Pommer. S: Carl Mayer, Hans Janowitz. C: Willy Hameister. Cast: Werner Krauss, Conrad Veidt, Lil Dagover, Friedrich Feher, Hans Von Twardowksi, Rudolf Klein-Rogge, Rudolf Lettinger. Dr. Caligari is a carnival mesmerist who uses hypnotism to control a somnambulist named Cesare. The demented Caligari sends Cesare out to murder on his command. In an epilogue, it is revealed that the story is nothing more than the ravings of a lunatic. • Famed director Fritz Lang was approached to direct *The Cabinet of Dr. Caligari* but was unavailable at the time. The picture he was engaged with was *Die Spinnen.* • It is interesting to note that light beams were oftentimes painted on the sets and backdrops because Decla studios (located in Berlin) had already used up much of its portion of electricity for the month. • The prologue and epilogue are reported to have been an addition suggested by the director, which was opposed at first by the film's writers.

Calling Dr. Death (1943; Universal) D: Reginald LeBorg. P: Ben Pivar. S: Edward Dein. C: Virgil Miller. Cast: Lon Chaney, Jr., Patricia Morison, J. Carrol Naish, David Bruce, Ramsay Ames, Fay Helm, Holmes Herbert. A neurologist (Lon Chaney, Jr.), whose wife is murdered, is haunted by his own subconscious until he employs a hypnotist to find out the truth of his innocence or guilt. It turns out that Chaney is innocent, but his female assistant is not, and she engages in some hypnotic trickery of her own. ¶ "Pretty dangerous invading the unknown. You learn strange things, you think of strange things — I understand you even *do* strange things." • This is one of six "Inner Sanctum" features made by Universal and all starring Lon Chaney, Jr. (in different roles). • "This is the Inner Sanctum ... A strange, fantastic world, controlled by a mass of living pulsating flesh ... the mind! It destroys, distorts, creates monsters ... commits murder!" This opening narration is featured at the beginning of most of the "Inner Sanctum" films.

The Climax (1944; Universal) D/P: George Waggner. S: Curt Siodmak, Lynn Starling. C: Hal Mohr, W. Howard Greene. Cast: Boris Karloff, Susanna Foster, Turhan Bey, Gale Sondergaard, June Vincent, Thomas Gomez. Boris Karloff is an opera-house doctor who hypnotizes a young opera singer because he thinks she possesses the voice of his dead lover. ¶ "That voice was never yours. It belongs to Marcellina. It must be silenced forever." • Universal originally panned this film as an expensive sequel to their ultra-successful 1943 version of *Phantom of the Opera,* but finally settled on this version of Edward Locke's stage play, *The Climax.* • This was Boris Karloff's first color film. He was paid $40,000 for his work in *The Climax* (as part of a two-picture deal with Universal for a total of $60,000; *House of Frankenstein* was the second picture). • *The Climax* was nominated for an Academy Award in Art/Set Direction (Alexander Golitzen, John B. Goodman, Russell A. Gausman, and Ira S. Webb receiving the nominations). Though they didn't win the Oscar this time, this same group had won the year previous with *Phantom of the Opera* (1943).

Creature of Destruction (1967) (see FISH-PEOPLE). A hypnotist commits murder by calling forth the ancient sea monster inside a woman under hypnosis. The picture is an (uncredited) remake of the 1956 film, *The She-Creature.*

Curse of the Demon (1956) (see DEMONS AND DEVILS). A man who exposes cults and witchcraft attends a conference in which the local doctor hypnotizes a devil worshiper in a cataleptic state. Under hypnosis, the man (Rand Hobart) recounts his experience with demons and a mysterious parchment, then goes berserk and jumps out of a window to his death. ¶ "Where does imagination end and reality begin ... what is this twilight, this half world of the mind that you profess to know so much about?"

The Evil of Frankenstein (1964) (see FRANKENSTEIN'S MONSTER — HAMMER FRANKENSTEINS). Baron Frankenstein finds his creature encased in glacial ice (an earlier creation), and thaws it out. Unfortunately, the brain has been damaged, and Frankenstein enlists the aid of a hypnotist named Zoltan to fully revive the creature. The evil Zoltan takes control of the monster through his hypnotic power and uses it to kill his enemies. ¶ "I want you to stimulate his brain, start some train of thought, anything to act as a catalyst. Accelerate a reaction in his brain"—Frankenstein to the hypnotist.

The Exorcist (1973) (see DEMONS AND DEVILS). Father Karras attempts to hypnotize the possessed Linda Blair, asking to speak with the various entities within her.

Fear in the Night (1947; Paramount) D/S: Maxwell Shane. P: William H. Pine, William C. Thomas. C: Jack Greenhalgh. Cast: Paul Kelly, DeForrest Kelley, Ann Doran, Kay Scott. DeForrest Kelley ("Star Trek's" Dr. McCoy), suffering from a bizarre nightmare, learns that he has been hypnotized into committing a murder.

Fright (1957 (see REINCARNATION) (also *Spell of the Hypnotist*). A psychiatrist's use of hypnotism accidentally causes a woman to return to a former life.

The Frozen Ghost (1945; Universal) D: Harold Young. P: Will Cowan. S: Bernard L. Schubert, Luci Ward. C: Paul Ivano. Cast: Lon Chaney, Jr., Evelyn Ankers, Milburn Stone, Douglass Dumbrille, Martin Kosleck, Elena Verdugo, Tala Birell, Arthur Hohl. Lon Chaney, Jr., is "Gregor the Great," a stage hypnotist. During his act, he puts a doubting man from the audience under hypnosis. The uncooperative drunk infuriates Gregor and the mesmerist wishes him dead. The man dies, and Gregor, sure that it was his hypnotic power that killed him, withdraws to the wax museum of a friend. Another death occurs, and it is revealed that Gregor's business manager is plotting to drive him mad. Using his powers of hypnosis, Gregor uncovers the truth in time to save yet another victim from death. ¶ "Suddenly, tonight I will a man dead—he dies. Oh, it's very simple inspector, I killed that man." • This is yet another of the "Inner Sanctum" films made by Universal. All six starred Lon Chaney, Jr. (in differing roles). *Calling Dr. Death* (1943) was a previous entry which featured hypnotism.

Hold That Hypnotist (1957) (see REINCARNATION). The Bowery Boys regress back to the seventeenth century with the aid of hypnotism.

Horrors of the Black Museum (1959) (see MADMEN—EARLY MADMEN). A madman, who writes about the murders he is committing, uses hypnosis on his assistant to induce him to carry out his nefarious wishes.

The Hypnotic Eye (1960; Allied Artists) D: George Blair. P: Charles B. Bloch. S: Gitta Woodfield, William Read Woodfield. C: Archie Dalzell. Cast: Jacques Bergerac, Merry Anders, Marcia Henderson, Allison Hayes, Joe Patridge, Fred Demara. A famed hypnotist uses a small hypnotic device resembling an eye to entrance young women into mutilating themselves in various ways. His motivation is slim, in that his beloved assistant (Allison Hayes) is herself disfigured, and wants anyone who is beautiful to be just like her. ¶ "Eleven women, attractive, some even beautiful, each one of them mutilated herself in some crazy way." • The picture's advertising claimed it used the magic of "HypnoVista"—which simply meant that the starring hypnotist used a flashing eyeball to bring audiences under his spell. • The promotional department gave patrons free Hypnotic Eye balloons as gifts.

I Was a Teenage Werewolf (1957) (see WEREWOLVES—OTHER LYCANTHROPES). With the use of a drug named Scapolomine, a doctor hypnotizes a boy into becoming a werewolf. ¶ "Through hypnosis I'm going to regress this boy back, back into the primitive past that lurks within him."

Invasion U.S.A. (1953) (see FUTURES ON EARTH—AFTER THE BOMB). Patrons at a New York bar are hypnotized into believing that Communists have launched an atomic assault and are invading the country.

Let's Do It Again (1975; Warner Bros.) D: Sidney Poitier. P: Melville Tucker, Pembroke J. Herring. S: Richard Wesley. C: Donald M. Morgan. Cast: Sidney Poitier, Bill Cosby, Calvin Lockhart, John Amos, Denise Nicholas, Ossie Davis, Jimmy Walker. A trio of church members devise a scheme to make money by hypnotizing a boxer and winning a big fight.

London After Midnight (1927; MGM) (see VAMPIRES—OTHER VAMPIRES) (also *The Hypnotist*). A Scotland Yard inspector, who doubles as a hypnotist, poses as a vampire to solve a murder. He eventually uses his hypnotic skills on two suspects, exposing the murderer by having them hypnotized at the scene of the crime.

The Magician (1926) (see MAGICIANS). A sorcerer uses hypnotism on his beautiful young victim to make her believe that she is residing in hell.

The Mask of Diijon (1946) (see MAGICIANS). Erich von Stroheim plays a magician who uses hypnosis on his unfaithful wife and commands her to murder her lover.

Master of Horror (1960) (see POE FILMS—MODERN POE). This Argentinian film fea-

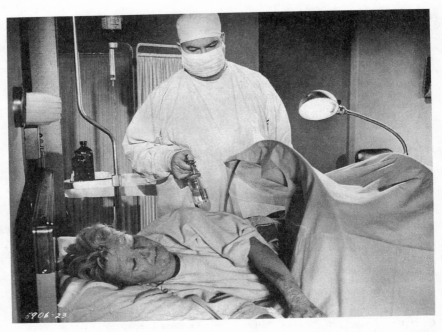

Surgeons are unable to restore this horribly disfigured victim of The Hypnotic Eye *(1960). The makeup was provided by Emile La Vigne, who helped create the grotesque makeovers for the masked* Queen of Outer Space *(1958) as well as the hideous surface mutants from* World Without End *(1956).*

tures two Poe stories, one of which is "The Facts in the Case of M. Valdemar." As an experiment, a hypnotist mesmerizes a man on the brink of death, keeping him suspended between life and death as long as he remains in hypnotic control over the unfortunate subject.

Nightmare (1956; United Artists) D/S: Maxwell Shane. P: William Thomas, Howard Pine. C: Joseph Biroc. Cast: Edward G. Robinson, Kevin McCarthy, Virginia Christine, Connie Russell, Barry Atwater. A musician who believes he is a murderer tries to unravel a mystery which involves hypnosis and a record played at the wrong speed. • This is a remake of the 1947 film, *Fear in the Night,* based on a Cornell Woolrich short story.

On a Clear Day You Can See Forever (1970) (see REINCARNATION). A psychiatrist uses hypnosis to help Barbara Streisand stop smoking, then accidentally learns of her past incarnations while she is in her trance state.

Rasputin, the Mad Monk (1966; Hammer/20th Century-Fox; U.K.) D: Don Sharp. P: Anthony Nelson Keys. S: John Elder (Anthony Hinds). C: Michael Reed. Cast: Christopher Lee, Richard Pasco, Suzan Farmer, Barbara Shelley, Francis Matthews. Christopher Lee plays the evil, scheming monk Rasputin, who uses his hypnotic powers to control the Tsar's court and drive heroine Barbara Shelley to suicide. • Though not wholly accurate, this film is based on historical characters and real events. Star Christopher Lee commented on the scarcity of Rasputin movies for *The Films of Christopher Lee,* by Pohle and Hart: "For many years, no film company was allowed to portray Rasputin's murder and death as described by the man who claimed to have killed him, Prince Yousoupoff. It is a known fact that the Prince brought a lawsuit against MGM in 1935 that resulted in the withdrawal of the Barrymore film. Subsequently, no other film company was prepared to risk the inevitable litigation from the Prince, who lived until quite recently in Paris." • Ironically, Lee met Rasputin's killers as a small boy. "My mother woke me up and brought me down to the drawing room of our house, where I was introduced to two men," related Lee. "She said that in years to come I would remember this meeting. This is certainly true, to this very day. A young boy, destined to portray the Monk in a film far in the future, actually met the two most famous of Rasputin's assassins. They were Prince Yousoupoff and the Grand Duke Dmitri, both friends of my parents." • American patrons received free "Rasputin beards" upon entering the theater.

The She-Creature (1956) (see FISH-PEOPLE). A hypnotist's murderous predictions are engineered when he entrances a young woman and calls forth her monstrous past incarnation from the ocean.

The Sorcerers (1967) (see PSYCHIC ABILITY). An old couple uses a telepathic machine which enables them to hypnotize a young man and feel what he feels. Boris Karloff plays Professor Monserrat, a one-time stage hypnotist.

Svengali (1931; Warner Bros.) D: Archie Mayo. S: J. Grubb Alexander. C: Barney McGill. Cast: John Barrymore, Marian Marsh, Luis Alberni, Lumsden Hare, Donald Crisp, Paul Porcasi. An obsessed Russian hypnotist (John Barrymore) uses his powers of thought control to transform a beautiful but untalented girl into a tremendous singer. • Cinematographer Barney McGill received an Academy Award nomination for his work on this picture. • John Barrymore was a part of the famous family of acting talents which included his brother Lionel (*The Devil Doll,* 1936) and his sister Ethel (*None But the Lonely Heart,* 1944). After an illustrious stage and film career he began to suffer from lapses of memory (no doubt partly due to his legendary drinking excesses). In 1942 he died, two years after his last fantasy film, *The Invisible Woman.*

Tales of Terror (1962) (see POE FILMS — THE CORMAN CYCLE). This collection of Poe stories includes "The Facts in the Case of M. Valdemar," in which Basil Rathbone plays a ruthless mesmerist who hypnotizes the dying Vincent Price at the exact moment of death, thus keeping him in a shadowy state between life and death.

Thirteen Women (1932; RKO) D: George Archainbaud. P: David O. Selznick. S: Bartlett Cormack, Samuel Ornitz. C: Leo Tover. Cast: Irene Dunne, Ricardo Cortez, Jill Esmond, Myrna Loy, Mary Duncan, Kay Johnson, Florence Eldridge, C. Henry Gordon. A woman with strange hypnotic powers terrorizes 12 members of a college sorority who scorned her years ago. She gets her revenge by sending them a horoscope in the name of a notable swami, predicting a dire fate for each, inducing them to fulfill that fate through auto-suggestion. She uses her hypnotic ability to control the swami and one of her victims at the climax. ¶ "You two are stumbling in a dark material world. I am above it ... Death means peace, freedom." • The President of the National Astrological Association, Dr. Henry J. Gordon, visited the set and cast real horoscopes for each of the 13 actresses.

Trog (1970) (see CAVEPEOPLE). After capturing and studying a prehistoric caveman, Joan Crawford uses hypnosis and electrodes to probe the mysteries that lie deep within his subconscious mind. • Dinosaur segments from Irwin Allen's *Animal World* (1956) were used to repesent the memories that popped up on the electronic viewer.

The Undead (1956) (see WITCHES, WARLOCKS, AND CULTS). A woman goes to see a psychiatrist, who uses an experimental hypnotic technique to send her back in time to a former life where she was accused of being a witch.

Vampire at Midnight (1988; Skouras Pictures) D: Gregory McClatchy. P: Jason Williams, Tom Friedman, S: Danny Ross Clements. C: Daniel Yarussi. Cast: Jason Williams, Gustav Vintas, Lesley Milne, Esther Alise, Jeanie Moore, Ted Hamaguchi, Robert Random, Johnny Solomon, Barbara Hammond, Eddie, Jr., Christina Whitaker. A rash of "vampire killings," in which young women are found drained of their blood, holds the city in a grip of fear. Dr. Victor Radkoff is a "hypno-therapist" who works with performing artists to bring out their true potential, using his powers of hypnotism to release their inner talents. He is also the "vampire killer," who hypnotizes his victims and then cuts their throats and drinks their blood. ¶ "He is as a shadow and hath no reflection. At night he penetrates the walls and doors. Abandon all hope ye whom he doth approach." • Throughout the film, the audience is led to believe that Radkoff is a real vampire (he sleeps during the day, he shies away from crosses, and he even sports a set of fangs when he kills). It is revealed, however, that he is a decidedly human killer (with fake fangs), though his powers of hypnotism are very real. • Actor Jason Williams, who plays the tough detective hero, also co-produced the film.

Voodoo Man (1944) (see VOODOO). In this poverty-row quickie, Bela Lugosi plays Dr. Marlowe, who abducts girls in the hope of finding one on the "same mental plane" as his zombiefied wife. To this end he employs a voodoo practitioner and his own powers of hypnotism in an attempt to transfer the life force of these girls into his undead wife.

Whirlpool (1950; TCF) D/P: Otto Preminger. S: Lester Barstow, Andrew Solt. C: Arthur Miller. Cast: Gene Tierney, Jose Ferrer, Richard Conte, Charles Bickford, Barbara O'Neil, Eduard Franz, Fortunio Bonanova. A girl is accused of a murder actually committed by her hypnotist, who, in a state of trance, is able to leave his hospital bed.

The Woman in Green (1945; Universal) D/P: Roy William Neill. S: Bertram Hillhauser. C: Virgil Miller. Cast: Basil Rathbone, Nigel Bruce, Hillary Brooke, Henry Daniell, Mathew Boulton. This Sherlock Holmes murder mystery features a female arch-criminal who blackmails innocent individuals by placing a severed finger from a murder victim upon their person after she has hypnotized them. They wake up next morning uncertain of where they have been and terrified to discover the finger in their possession.

Insects *see* Bug Giants; Bug-People; Bugs

Invisibility

Invisibility as a concept first entered the public consciousness in 1897 with the publication of H. G. Wells' science fiction novella, *The Invisible Man*. Appropriately enough, the first invisibility film was based on this very novel. *The Invisible Man* (1933), James Whale's classic tale of a scientist-turned-dangerous egomaniac by his meddling in "things man must leave alone" brought Wells' story to vibrant life, adding a liberal dose of black humor to spice up the unseen proceedings. The idea of an invisible man or monster is a frightening one (after all, it is what we *cannot* see that we are most afraid of) and Whale took full advantage of this. Claude Rains' chilling voice, along with John P. Fulton's startling invisibility effects, created a classic of the horror cinema yet to be equaled by any further invisibility attempts.

Universal waited seven long years before following up on their original success with *The Invisible Man Returns* (1940), starring Vincent Price. The popularity of this first sequel initiated another Universal series and created an additional "monster" to add to their growing roster which included Dracula, Frankenstein's Monster, the Mummy, and the Wolf Man. *The Invisible Agent* (1942) and *The Invisible Man's Revenge* (1944) followed, as well as an unrelated comedy, *The Invisible Woman* (1940). Universal finished off their creation, like they did so many of their monsters, in a meeting with Abbott and Costello (not once but twice) in *Abbott and Costello Meet Frankenstein* (1948; featuring an unbilled cameo appearance by Vincent Price as the voice of the Invisible Man) and *Abbott and Costello Meet the Invisible Man* (1951).

A number of remakes and variations have been made over the years (including invisible criminals—*The Amazing Transparent Man,* 1960; invisible crimefighters—*Invisible Avenger,* 1958; invisible aliens—*Phantom from Space,* 1953; even an invisible dinosaur(!)—*Sound of Horror,* 1964), but none have achieved the style or popularity of the Universal films.

Abbott and Costello Meet Frankenstein (1948) (see FRANKENSTEIN'S MONSTER — UNIVERSAL SERIES). After all the monsters have been dispatched, Bud and Lou are frightened by the Invisible Man making a comical cameo "appearance" (played by the voice of Vincent Price — lately from *The Invisible Man Returns,* 1940).

Abbott and Costello Meet the Invisible Man (1951; Universal) D: Charles Lamont. P: Howard Christie. S: Robert Lees, Frederic Rinaldo, John Grant. C: George Robinson. Cast: Bud Abbott, Lou Costello, Arthur Franz, Sheldon Leonard, Nancy Guild, Adele Jurgens. Bud and Lou are now graduates of Dugan's School of Detectives. In their first case, they are hired by a young boxer (Arthur Franz) who has been framed for murder. Franz has taken a scientist friend's invisibility potion to hide from the police. Using Lou as a boxing front, he attempts to clear his name.

The Amazing Transparent Man (1960; American International) D: Edgar G. Ulmer. P: Lester D. Guthrie. S: Jack Lewis. C: Meredith M. Nicholson. Cast: Douglas Kennedy, James Griffith, Marguerite Chapman, Ivan Triesault, Red Morgan. A megalomaniac madman with world-conquering designs intends to force a scientist (by holding his daughter hostage) to use his invisibility machine to create an invisible army. An escaped convict stumbles into the weird tableau, turns hero, and throws an invisible monkey wrench into the madman's plans. ¶ At the film's end, a character turns to the audience and asks, "What would *you* do with an invisible ray?" • This movie was made back to back (or as some sources claim, *simultaneously*) with another Edgar Ulmer sci-fi cheapie, *Beyond the Time Barrier.* Both were filmed at the Texas 1936 Centennial Fairgrounds. • Marguerite Chapman, who plays the madman's moll, also appeared in another invisibility movie nearly two decades earlier — *The Body Disappears* (1941).

The Body Disappears (1941: Warner Bros.) D: D. Ross Lederman. P: Brian Foy. S: Erna Lazerus, Scott Darling. C: Allen G. Siegler. Cast: Jeffrey Lynn, Jane Wyman, Edward Everett Horton, Marguerite Chapman, David Bruce, Willie Best. This lighthearted romantic comedy is about an invisibility serum and the trouble it causes for its inventor.

Fiend Without a Face (1958) (see BRAINS — BRAIN SUCKERS). The "mental vampires" featured here (disembodied ambulatory brains with spinal column attached), were created by a scientist attempting to materialize his thoughts with the aid of atomic power. Like thought, the creatures are invisible (until the climax) and go on a feeding binge, sucking out the brains and spinal cords of everyone they meet. ¶ "Like thought itself, it was invisible."

Forbidden Planet (1956) (see ALIENS — ENCOUNTERS IN OUTER SPACE). The monster that stalks this Forbidden Planet is conceived from the Id of Dr. Morbius, and like the subconscious it is invisible.

Gemini Man (1976; TV movie) (also *Code Name: Minus One*). D: Alan J. Levi. P: Robert F. O'Neill. S: Leslie Stevens. C: Enzo A. Martinelli. Cast: Ben Murphy, Katherine Crawford, Richard Dysart, Dana Elcar, Paul Shenar, Quinn Redeker, H. M. Wynant, Len Wayland. This pilot for the unsuccessful TV series "The Invisible Man" stars Ben Murphy as a secret agent who has the ability to become invisible after being exposed to an underwater explosion. His invisibility comes and goes, however, so his undercover missions must be well timed so as not to expose him at the wrong moment.

The Golden Voyage of Sinbad (1973) (see SINBAD). At one point during his "Golden Voyage," Sinbad engages in an exciting battle with an invisible swordsman.

H. G. Wells' The New Invisible Man (1957; Screen Gems; Mexico) (also *The New Invisible Man*). D: Alfredo Crevenna. P: Paul Castelain. S: Julio Alejandandro. C: Raul Martinez Solares. Cast: Arturo de Cordova, Ana Luisa Peluffo, Augusto Benedico, Raul Meraz. A man wrongly convicted of murder is given an invisibility drug by his scientist brother so that he can escape and clear his name. Unfortunately, the drug has a side effect — it causes him to go insane, and the invisible madman threatens to unleash a deadly bacteria into the city's water supply. ¶ "I must wipe out all evil in this world, the Supreme Judge commands me to do so ... and I am His messenger, and that is why He made me invisible!" • There is nothing *new* in this south-of-the-border version of the Invisible Man, which is merely an inferior rehash of the 1940 Universal sequel, *The Invisible Man Returns.* It even goes so far as to steal whole scenes from that earlier film, such as when the Invisible Man, trapped in a house full of smoke and gas by the police, steals a policeman's uniform and gas mask in order to carry a woman out of the house to safety disguised as one of the officers and thereby make his escape.

Invisible Agent (1942; Universal) D: Edwin L. Marin. P: George Waggner. S: Curtis (Kurt) Siodmak. C: Lester White. Cast: Ilona Massey, Jon Hall, Peter Lorre, Sir Cedric Hardwicke, J. Edward Bromberg, Albert Basserman. The grandson of the Invisible Man uses the secret family formula once again to stop the Germans and Japanese during World War II. • John P. Fulton (along with Bernard B. Brown) received an Oscar nomination for his excellent special effects work on this film. This was the third time in the Universal series Fulton had been nominated (the first two being for *The Invisible Man Returns* and *The Invisible Woman,* both 1940). He never won. • Ilona Massey, born Ilona Hajmassy, married Alan Curtis, star of *The Invisible Man's Revenge.* When Ilona died in 1974, she was married to a retired Air Force general.

Invisible Avenger (1958; Republic) (also *Bourbon St. Shadows*). D: James Wong Howe, John Sledge. P: Eric Sayers, Emanuel Demby. S: George Bellack, Betty Jeffries, C: Willis Winford, Joseph Wheeler. Cast: Richard Derr, Mark Daniels, Helen Westcott, Jeanne Neher, Dan Mullin, Lee Edwards, Jack Doner, Steve Dano, Leo Bruno, Sam Page. The Shadow is a crimefighter who, by using "certain ancient techniques of mind," can make himself invisible. While investigating a murder, he becomes embroiled with the plans of an exiled Latin American dictator. ¶ "The mind is capable of transmitting and receiving images. When you become The Shadow, you send a powerful image into the mind of another, and he sees not you, but a shadow." • The film is based on the character "The Shadow" featured in the Street and Smith magazine stories by Maxwell Grant and later on the popular radio series. "Who knows what evil lurks in the hearts of men? Only The Shadow knows." • Co-director James Wong Howe is better known as an Oscar-winning cinematographer (for his work on *The Rose Tattoo* in 1955 and *Hud* in 1963). • *The Invisible Avenger* was filmed on location in New Orleans.

The Invisible Boy (1957) (see ROBOTS). Robby the robot makes a young boy, the son of a renowned scientist, invisible with a chemical potion. ¶ "Take a spoonful twice daily, or whenever you start to reappear."

The Invisible Dr. Mabuse (1962; Thunder Pictures; W. Germany) (also *The Invisible Horror*). D: Harald Reinl. P: Artur Brauner. S: Ladislas Fodor. C: Ernst W. Kalinke. Cast: Lex Barker, Karin Dor, Siegfried Löwitz, Werner Peters, Wolfgang Preiss. A professor is disfigured in a car wreck and creates "Operation X," which will make him invisible in order to hide his ugliness. The evil Dr. Mabuse, with world domination in mind, kidnaps the professor's girlfriend in a plot to obtain the invisibility secret.

The Invisible Ghost (1941) (see MADMEN — EARLY MADMEN). The only invisibility here is in the title.

Invisible Invaders (1959) (see ALIENS — INVADERS ON EARTH: THE 50s). Invisible aliens from the Moon plan to conquer Earth by inhabiting dead bodies. ¶ "We are invisible. Long ago we learned to change the molecular structure of our bodies. You cannot see us."

The Invisible Kid (1988; Taurus Entertainment) D/S: Avery Crounse. P: Philip J. Spinelli. C: Michael Barnard. Cast: Jay Underwood, Wally Ward, Chynna Phillips, Brother Theodore, Karen Black. A nerdish high school student uses an invisibility formula to outwit a group of bullying jocks.

The Invisible Man (1933; Universal) D: James Whale. P: Carl Laemmle, Jr. S: R. C. Sheriff, Philip Wylie. C: Art Edeson. Cast: Claude Rains, Gloria Stewart, William Harrigan, Henry Travers, Una O'Connor, Forrester Harvey, Holmes Herbert, E. E. Clive, Dudley Digges, Harry Stubbs, Donald Stuart, Merle Tottenham. An ambitious young scientist named Jack Griffin (Claude Rains) develops an invisibility drug which he tests on himself. Unable to make himself visible again, he hides away at a remote country inn to try and find the antidote. His brain is adversely affected by the drug and he goes mad for power, murdering and causing destruction throughout the English countryside. ¶ "We'll begin with a reign of terror. A few murders here and there. Murders of great men, murders of little men, just to show we make no distinction." • Originally planned by Universal as a horror vehicle for Boris Karloff, director James Whale had other ideas and did not want the actor and the "horror" label that went with him. Whale chose instead for the part of The Invisible One ("who meddled in things men must leave alone") Claude Rains, a respected stage actor but then unknown in the movies—this was Rains' film debut. During his subsequent career, the illustrious actor received four Oscar nominations (*Mr. Smith Goes to Washington,* 1939; *Casablanca,* 1943; *Mr. Skeffington,* 1944; and *Notorious,* 1946), but never won. • An article in Forrest J Ackerman's fan magazine, *Famous Monsters of Filmland* #101, reported that "[Claude Rains] spent over three years on the Western Front in France. And

The Invisible Man *(1933), played by Claude Rains, shrugs despondently over his notes when he is unable to find a way back to visibility.*

once, when a shell exploded and hurled a herd of sandbags thru the air, they landed on Capt. Rains and almost buried him alive in a trench." Ackerman also published a favorite quote of Rains', which Claude found comforting after the loss of his last wife. It reads, "I wept because I had no shoes—until I saw a man who had no feet." • Some things that the Invisible Man, Jack Griffin, had to look out for were fog, smoke, and rain, which can settle on his head and shoulders and make him shine like a bubble. Dirt, even between his fingernails, was also a problem; and after eating, the food remains visible for one hour until it is digested. Footprints in the snow gave away the Invisible Man's presence at the film's climax, resulting in his being shot by the police. • The fictitious Indian drug that *The Invisible Man* took that made him not only invisible but mad was called "monocaine." • Character actress Una O'Connor (cast here as the screeching innkeeper's wife) played the epitome of the "hysterical old woman" in another Whale film, *Bride of Franken-stein* (1935). • Character actor Henry Trav-ers, who played the part of the heroine's scientist father, is often remembered as Clarence the Angel in Frank Capra's *It's a Wonderful Life* (1946). • Walter Brennan, John Carradine (then called John Peter Richmond), and Dwight Frye all appear in brief walk-on parts. • *The Invisible Man* was a huge financial and critical success, with the *New York Times* placing it at number nine on its 1933 "Ten Best" list.

The Invisible Man (1975; TV movie) D: Robert Michael Lewis. P/S: Steven Bochco. C: Enzo A. Martinelli. Cast: David McCal-lum, Melinda Fee, Jackie Cooper, Henry Darrow, Alex Henteloff, Arch Johnson, John McLiam, Ted Gehring, Paul Kent. A scientist working at a think tank develops the secret of invisibility, but flees with his secret rather than let it fall into the hands of the military. • This was the pilot film for a short-lived TV series which ran for a few brief weeks in 1975.

The Invisible Man Returns (1940; Univer-sal) D: Joe May. P: Ken Goldsmith. S: Lester Cole, Kurt Siodmak. C: Milton Krasner. Cast: Sir Cedric Hardwicke, Vin-cent Price, Nan Grey, John Sutton, Cecil Kellaway, Alan Napier. Geoffrey Radcliffe (Vincent Price) is wrongly accused of mur-dering his brother and sentenced to die. Desperate to escape, he agrees to take the dangerous invisibility drug given him by his friend Frank Griffin (brother of Jack Grif-fin, the original *Invisible Man,* 1933). Now it is a race against time as Geoffrey tries to clear his name by finding the real murderer, while Frank attempts to create an antidote before Geoffrey goes mad from the effects of the drug. ¶ "You know, being invisible has distinct advantages. It gives one a sense of power that's exciting. Power for good if you're so inclined, or should you feel perverse, for evil." • This is the first sequel to *The Invisible Man* (1933). Next in the series is *Invisible Agent* (1942), though Universal made another, unrelated, in-visibility movie in between, the comical *In-visible Woman* (1940). • Director Joe May worked under the handicap of speaking no English. He was German, and star Vincent Price got on quite well with him because of the actor's working knowledge of that language. • John P. Fulton received an Oscar nomination for his wondrous special effects work on *The Invisible Man Returns* (he did not win, however). • For some inex-plicable reason, the name of the invisibility-inducing drug was changed from "mono-

caine," as it was called in the original, to "duocaine" for the sequel.

The Invisible Maniac (1990; Runnymeade House Music) D/S: Rif Coogan. P: An-thony Markes. C: James Bay. Cast: Noel Peters, Shannon Wilsey, Melissa Moore, Robert R. Ross, Rod Sweitzer, Eric Champ-nella, Kalei Shellabarger Gaillyon, Debra Lamb. A brilliant but unstable physics scientist attempts to find the secret of in-visibility. When his colleagues laugh at him during a conference, he goes berserk and kills four of them. He escapes from the "State Hospital for the Criminally Insane," and gets a job teaching summer school physics to a group of high schoolers. The malicious pranks of his students send him over the edge once again. He locks the door to the school and goes on a rampage of ter-ror using his newly perfected invisibility serum, killing them off one by one. ¶ "'Tis I, your friendly neighborhood invisible maniac!"

The Invisible Man's Revenge (1944; Uni-versal) D/P: Ford Beebe. S: Bertram Mill-hauser. C: Milton Krasner. Cast: Jon Hall, Leon Errol, John Carradine, Alan Curtis, Evelyn Ankers, Gale Sondergaard. Jon Hall plays an escaped madman named Robert Griffin who stumbles across eccentric scien-tist Dr. Drury (John Carradine), inventor of an invisibility formula. Carradine has never tested it on a man, so Hall volunteers to be the first. When it works, he eventually kills Carradine and embarks on a plan of revenge against those he feels have wronged him. ¶ "In this house, you've got to believe what you *can't* see!" • Universal originally wanted Claude Rains to play the title role (just as he had 11 years earlier in the original *The Invisi-ble Man*). When they were unable to secure his services, they chose Jon Hall, veteran of *The Invisible Agent* (1943). Running the gamut from good to evil, Hall went from playing an invisible hero in *The Invisible Agent* to playing an invisible criminal psychopath in this film. • This time out—the fourth and last *serious* entry in Universal's Invisible Man series (discounting *Abbott and Costello Meet the Invisible Man,* 1951)— it is not the invisibility drug that slowly drives its user insane as in their other films; *this* invisible man was insane to begin with! • Though the character here shares the same last name as Universal's original *Invisible Man* (1933)—Griffin—no reference to any of the previous Griffins is made, and no ex-planation of a possible familial relationship is given (*The Invisible Man Returns* [1940] featured the original Griffin's brother, and

A marginally visible Virginia Bruce gives her despicable employer Mr. Growley (Charlie Ruggles) a swift kick in this publicity photo from the Universal science fiction comedy, The Invisible Woman *(1940).*

The Invisible Agent [1942] followed the exploits of his grandson).

The Invisible Terror (1963; R & B; W. Germany) D/S: Raphael Nussbaum. S: Wladimir Semitjof. C: Michael Marszalek. Cast: Hanaes Hauser, Ellen Schwiers, Herbert Stass, Hans von Borsody, Hans Schmid-Hauser, Ivan Desny, Ilse Steppat, Harry Fuss, Christiane Nielsen. A thief steals a scientist's experimental invisibility drug.

The Invisible Woman (1940; Universal) D: A. Edward Sutherland. P: Burt Kelly. S: Robert Lees, Fred Rinaldo, Gertrude Purcell. C: Elwood Bredell. Cast: John Barrymore, Virginia Bruce, John Howard, Charlie Ruggles, Oscar Homolka, Maria Montez. A daft scientist creates an invisibility serum, then advertises in the paper for a test subject. Virginia Bruce applies for the job and soon secret agents are after the formula. ¶ "What would you do if you could completely disappear?" • For the second time, John Fulton (along with Johan Hall) received an Academy Award nomination for Special Effects (though again he didn't win).

The Invisible Woman (1983; TV movie) D/P: Alan J. Levi. S: Sherwood Schwartz,

Lloyd J. Schwartz. C: Dean Cundey. Cast: Bob Denver, Jonathan Banks, David Doyle, George Gobel, Anne Haney, Harvey Korman, Alexa Hamilton. Bob Denver plays a biochemist whose reporter niece stumbles into an invisibility chemical at his lab. She uses her invisibility to crack the case of a million-dollar art heist. • This was the pilot to a comedy series that was never made. It was shot on videotape rather than film, and initially contained a laugh track. The series was to have been called "Out of Sight."

Mr. Superinvisible (1969; Peter Carstein; Spain/Italy/W. Germany) (also *The Invincible Invisible Man*). D: Anthony M. Dawson (Antonio Margheriti). S: M. Eller, Luis Marquina. C: Alejandro Ulloa. Cast: Dean Jones, Gastone Moschin, Ingeborg Schoener, Roberto Camardiel. A researcher rescues his girlfriend from the villains using an invisibility filter.

Now You See Him, Now You Don't (1971; Walt Disney) D: Robert Butler. P: Ron Miller. S: Joseph L. McEveety. C: Frank Phillips. Cast: Kurt Russell, Cesar Romero, Joe Flynn, Jim Backus, William Windom. Kurt Russell is the student who uses an invisibility serum to save his college from a gangster.

Orloff and the Invisible Man (1970; Mezquiriz/Celia; Spain/France). D: Pierre Chevalier. S: Pierre Chevalier, Juan Fortuny. C: Juan Fortuny. Cast: Howard Vernon, Isabel del Rio, Francisco Valladares, Brigitte Carva, Fernando Sancho, Evane Hanska. In another sequel to *The Awful Dr. Orloff* (1962), Dr. Orloff is back, but this time he has developed an invisibility drug, which he adminsiters to a man who slowly goes mad from the effects.

The Phantom Creeps (1939) (see MAD SCIENTISTS). In this feature version of a 12-chapter serial, Bela Lugosi plays mad scientist Zorka, who is after world domination, with the use of an eight-foot-tall robot and a "devisualizer belt" which renders the wearer invisible.

Phantom from Space (1953) (see ALIENS—INVADERS ON EARTH: THE 50s). An alien lands on Earth, is involved in several deaths (perhaps accidentally), and is hunted like a fugitive. This alien is a silicon-based life form rather than carbon-based like Earth creatures, and is therefore invisible without his spacesuit on.

Predator (1987) (see ALIENS—INVADERS ON EARTH: THE 80s AND BEYOND). A group of mercenaries sent by the CIA to rescue hostages in Central America encounters an alien creature who begins hunting the men for sport. This intergalactic big-game hunter possesses a device which enables him to blend in with the jungle background, making himself nearly invisible.

Predator 2 (1990) (see ALIENS—INVADERS ON EARTH: THE 80s AND BEYOND). In 1997, another alien hunter comes to Earth to hunt humans for sport, this time landing in the concrete jungle of Los Angeles and targeting the opposing forces of a drug war, including the police. Once again, the alien uses his camouflage device to blend in with his surroundings and become nearly invisible.

Siegfried (1924) (see SWORD AND SORCERY). One of the mystical objects featured in this tragic story of a dragon-slayer caught up in a web of fate and atonement is a wondrous cloak of invisibility.

Sound of Horror (1964) (see DINOSAURS—DINOSAURS ON THE LOOSE). This Spanish oddity features a prehistoric egg which hatches to disgorge a man-sized dinosaur that goes on the rampage, ripping a group of people to shreds. The odd thing is, this dinosaur is invisible. ¶ "Maybe it absorbs the color of its background as protection and becomes invisible immediately."

The Wonderful World of the Brothers Grimm (1962) (see ANTHOLOGIES). The first story of this George Pal anthology, entitled "The Dancing Princess," concerns a woodsman (Russ Tamblyn) who wins the hand of a princess (Yvette Mimieux), then learns the mysterious secret of her worn slippers when he dons a cloak of invisibility.

Jack the Ripper

Without question the most famous serial murderer in history is Jack the Ripper. The image of a caped man prowling through the backstreets of a fog-enshrouded London, looming out of the dimly-lit night to slit the throats of unwary streetwalkers has become an indelible fixture in the public consciousness, entering the realm of popular mythology. But who was this mysterious "Jack the Ripper" who stalked, murdered, and mutilated at least five prostitutes in the seedy Whitechapel district of London in 1888? His horrendous crimes held an entire city in an icy grip of fear until strangely, the murders simply stopped. Jack the Ripper remains a mystery to this day, though countless theories have been put forth by avid "Ripperologists" (everything from "unhinged surgeon" to "itinerant Irishman" to "mad prince," to "royal conspiracy"). This air of mystery, coupled with the gruesome, depraved nature of the crimes, is what makes Jack the Ripper such an intriguing and enduring character even a century after he committed his horrible acts.

Jack the Ripper first appeared in film a mere 38 years after he disappeared in real life. Alfred Hitchcock's 1926 silent thriller, *The Lodger,* was something of a cheat, however, for it turns out that the mysterious "lodger" is not the Ripper after all but an innocent man falsely accused. Maurice Elvey remade Hitchcock's film in 1932, again calling it *The Lodger,* and again proving the suspect innocent. Then in 1944 came the first *real* appearance by the notorious mystery killer, in yet another remake of *The Lodger.* This time the title character really *was* Jack the Ripper. Laird Cregar gave what is arguably the screen's definitive portrayal of the infamous murderer (and secured for himself the dubious typecasting label of "screen villain") with his intense, disturbing performance. In 1950 came an odd little British variation called *Room to Let,* which is set some years after the Ripper murders and has Jack planning to pick up where he left off. In 1953, 20th Century–Fox remade their 1944 version of *The Lodger* as *Man in the Attic,* with Jack Palance filling Laird Cregar's bloody shoes. Several more increasingly exploitative Ripper movies followed, culminating in the tasteless, gory 1976 import, *Jack the Ripper,* with Klaus Kinski in the title role.

In what would seem the ultimate confrontation, Sherlock Holmes crossed paths with Jack the Ripper, not once but twice—in *A Study in Terror* (1965) and *Murder by Decree* (1978). One of the most interesting variations on Ripper movies came in 1979 with *Time After Time,* in which Jack the Ripper encounters H. G. Wells himself and escapes to the present day in the author's own time machine. Though the plot may sound a little farfetched for a Ripper film, David Warner (as Jack) and Malcolm McDowell (as Wells) make this detective story/time travel/ murder mystery work.

There will probably never be a completely satisfactory solution to the Jack the Ripper mystery, and so he will remain in our imagination, continuing to stalk the dark alleys of our cinematic nightmares.

Bridge Across Time (1985; TV movie) (also *Arizona Ripper; Terror at London Bridge*). D: E. W. Swackhamer. P: Jack Michon, Richard Maynard. S: William F. Nolan. C: Gil Hubbs. Cast: David Hasselhoff, Stepfanie Kramer, Randolph Mantooth, Adrienne Barbeau, Clu Gulager, Lindsay Bloom, Ken Swofford, Rose Marie, Lane Smith. In nineteenth century London, police chase Jack the Ripper onto the London Bridge where a stone gives way and he falls to his death in the River Thames. Nearly 100 years later, in the present day, London Bridge has been transported stone by stone to Lake Havasu, Arizona. Now the missing stone has been recovered from the bottom of the Thames and sent to the States to be put in its proper place on the bridge. When a woman cuts herself and drips blood upon the stone, Jack the Ripper is magically resurrected and continues his murder pattern right there in Arizona, with a young police detective trying to solve the mystery and stop the slaughter. ¶ "God help me, there never was a copycat killer. The man who butchered Alice Williamson and Lynn Chandler was the *real* Jack the Ripper."

Dr. Jekyll and Sister Hyde (1971) (see JEKYLL, DR., AND FAMILY). In this unusual variation on the Jekyll and Hyde story, Dr. Jekyll uses female hormones in his elixir. This changes not only his personality, but his sex as well, creating the evil *Mrs.* Hyde. To create his elixir, Jekyll needs select female organs, and eventually resorts to the brutal murder of prostitutes to obtain them. These killings are attributed to Jack the Ripper, and so, in a screen first, Jack the Ripper is revealed to be none other than Jekyll the Ripper.

Hands of the Ripper (1971; Hammer/ Rank/Universal; U.K.) D: Peter Sasdy. P: Aida Young. S: L. W. Davidson. C: Kenneth Talbot. Cast: Eric Porter, Angharad Rees, Jane Merrow, Keith Bell, Derek Godfrey, Dora Bryan, Marjorie Rhodes. As a child, Anna sees her father, who happens to be Jack the Ripper, murder her mother and flee. As a young woman, whenever she is kissed and exposed to bright reflected light, she goes into a trance and follows in her father's bloody footsteps. A psychiatrist tries to help her overcome her murderous tendencies, but eventually falls victim himself.

Jack the Ripper (1958) (see ANTHOLOGIES).

This anthology film culled from episodes of an unsold TV series hosted by Boris Karloff featured one story about a retired doctor gone insane, and all evidence points to his being Jack the Ripper. He is admitted to an insane asylum before the police can charge him with the slayings and find conclusive proof, and so the mystery remains. ¶ Closing narration: "Dr. Willardon was beyond the reach of English law, his guilt or innocence could never be proved. But strangely enough, the slaughter in Whitechapel ended that night. Jack the Ripper never claimed another victim."

Jack the Ripper (1959; Paramount; U.K.) (also *The Return of Jack the Ripper*). D/P/C: Robert S. Baker, Monty Berman. S: Jimmy Sangster. Cast: Lee Patterson, Eddie Byrne, Betty McDowall, Ewen Solon, John LeMesurier. This time Jack the Ripper is a venereal disease–ridden surgeon intent upon cutting the corruption (prostitution) out of the heart of London. An American detective aids Scotland Yard in hunting down the murderous madman. • At the film's climax, the Ripper is crushed to death by an elevator, and the black and white film goes into full color for this final gruesome scene.

Jack the Ripper (1971; International Apollo; Spain/Italy) (also *Jack the Mangler of London*). D/P: José Luis Madrid. S: Jacinto Molina, José Luis Madrid, Sandro Continenza. C: Diego Uberda. Cast: Paul Naschy, Patricia Loran, Rensso Marinano, Andres Resino, Orquidea de Santis, Franco Borelli, Irene Mir, Victor Iregua. In the modern-day Soho district of London, a series of Jack-the-Ripper-style murders is being committed by a madman imitating Jack's old gruesome methods, with the added twist of cutting off body parts to keep as mementos.

Jack the Ripper (1976; Cinemac; W. Germany/Switzerland). D/S: Jesus Franco. P: Erwin C. Dietrich, Max Dara. C: Peter Baumgartner. Cast: Klaus Kinski, Josephine Chaplin, Herbert Fux (Fuchs), Lina Romay, Nikola Weisse, Ursula V. Wiese. This gory version of the infamous Jack the Ripper mystery stars Klaus Kinski as a philanthropic but disturbed doctor who's driven by an insane desire to murder and mutilate prostitutes (in a mad attempt to exorcise the memory of his mother, a street walker). ¶ "With your blood my sins will wash away and you'll be purified." • Heroine Josephine Chaplin is the daughter of Charlie Chaplin.

Jack's Back (1988; Paramount) D/S: Rowdy Herrington. P: Tim Moore, Cassian Elwes. C: Shelly Johnson. Cast: James Spader, Cynthia Gibb, Rod Loomis, Rex Ryon, Robert Picardo, Jim Haynie, Wendell Wright, Chris Mulkey. A psycho-killer is repeating Jack the Ripper's bloody pattern exactly 100 years after the original crimes. It is up to the identical twin of one of the murder victims to unmask the deranged killer.

The Lodger (1926; American Anglo; U.K.) D: Alfred Hitchcock. P: Michael Balcon. S: Alfred Hitchcock, Elliot Stannard. C: Hal Young. Cast: Ivor Novello, Malcolm Keen, Arthur Chesney, June, Marie Ault. This silent drama is about a man falsely thought to be Jack the Ripper. • In 1966 Alfred Hitchcock said of this film: "It was the first time I exercised my style . . . you might say it was my first picture." • This is the first of four films based on the novel by Marie Belloc Lowndes. In the first two (this and the 1932 version), the lodger of the title turns out to be innocent. In the latter two (*The Lodger*, 1944; and *Man in the Attic*, 1953) the lodger truly is Jack the Ripper. • The film's distributors were less than pleased with the finished product and were reluctant to release it. When it finally was released, they were surprised by the public and critical acclaim it garnered.

The Lodger (1932; Olympic; U.K.) (also *The Phantom Fiend*). D: Maurice Elvey. P: Julius Hagan. S: Miles Mander, Paul Rotha. C: Stanley Blythe, Basil Emmott. Cast: Ivor Novello, Elizabeth Allan, Jack Hawkins, W. E. Bascomb, Kynaston Reeves, Barbara Everest. This is a faithful sound remake of the 1926 silent Hitchcock film. • Lead actor Ivor Novello reprised his title role from the first version.

The Lodger (1944; 20th Century-Fox) D: John Brahm. P: Robert Bassler. S: Barre Lyndon. C: Lucien Ballard. Cast: Merle Oberon, George Sanders, Laird Cregar, Sir Cedric Hardwicke, Sara Allgood. Laird Cregar is Mr. Slade, alias Jack the Ripper, who moves into the upstairs rooms of a middle class London household as their reclusive lodger during the height of the Ripper murders. ¶ "Yes, he used his knife pretty extensively; they don't call him 'the Ripper' for nothing." • In this version, the impetus behind Jack the Riper's homicidal madness is the earlier death of his brother ("You corrupt and destroy men, as my brother was destroyed," he tells a potential victim). So he ventures forth to cut out the corruption by killing prostitutes. • At the film's opening at the Roxy Theater in New York City, star

Laird Cregar made a personal appearance on the stage, reenacting a scene from the movie to a standing ovation. The actor was so proud of the reception his performance received, he appeared onstage throughout the entire run of *The Lodger,* enjoying the applause his impromptu live performances won him night after night. • 20th Century-Fox made this film again (with many scenes nearly word for word) in 1953 as *Man in the Attic,* with Jack Palance inheriting the knife from Laird Cregar.

Man in the Attic (1953; 20th Century-Fox) D: Hugo Fregonese. P: Robert L. Jacks. S: Robert Presnell, Jr., Barre Lyndon. C: Leo Tovar. Cast: Jack Palance, Constance Smith, Byron Palmer, Frances Bavier, Rhys Williams, Sean McClory, Leslie Bradley, Tita Phillips, Lester Mathews, Hany Cording, Lisa Daniels. Jack Palance plays the shy, reclusive "Mr. Slade," who becomes the mysterious upstairs lodger of a London family. As a pathologist at the University Hospital he works on blood by day, and as Jack the Ripper goes out to spill it by night, the result of his love/hate relationship with his prostitute mother. ¶ "[You are the] same as my mother, same as all of them—mocking love, living for lust! You are evil! Your beauty must be cut away!" • This inferior remake of *The Lodger* (1944) traces Jack's psychosis back to his mother, a beautiful but wicked woman who eventually took to the streets to earn a living. She was Jack's first victim, which started him on his bloody spree of murdering prostitutes. • Television viewers will recognize Frances Bavier, who plays the suspicious landlady; Bavier played Aunt Bee on "The Andy Griffith Show."

The Monster of London City (1964; PRC; W. Germany) D: Edwin Zbonek. P: Artur Brauner. S: Robert A. Stemmle. C: Siegfried Hold. Cast: Marianne Koch, Hansjorg Felmy, Dietmar Schoenherr, Hans Nielsen, Chariklia Baxevanos, Fritz Tillmann. An actor who plays Jack the Ripper in a successful stage production is plagued with blackouts and is afraid he is responsible for the recent rash of Ripper-style murders plaguing the city. • The film is based on a story by Bryan Edgar Wallace, the son of famous mystery/crime writer Edgar Wallace.

Murder by Decree (1978; Avco-Embassy; U.K./Canada) D: Bob Clark. P: Bob Clark, Rene Dupont. S: John Hopkins. C: Reginald H. Morris. Cast: Christopher Plummer, James Mason, Anthony Quayle, David Hemmings, Susan Clark, John Gielgud, Donald Sutherland, Frank Finlay, Genevieve Bujold. Sherlock Holmes is on the trail of Jack the Ripper, and uncovers a conspiracy involving high-ranking government officials. • This is the second time Holmes crossed cinematic paths with Jack the Ripper, the first being *A Study in Terror* (1965).

The Ripper (1986; United Entertainment) D: Christopher Lewis. P: Linda Lewis. S: Bill Groves. C: Paul MacFarlane. Cast: Tom Schreier, Mon VanPernis, Wade Tower, Tom Savini, Andrea Adams, Randall White, Bennie Lee McGowan. A college professor teaching a course on "Famous Crimes in Film" finds a ring that belonged to Jack the Ripper. Soon a new series of Ripper murders occurs, while at the same time the professor seems to be seeing them in his dreams. In the end it is revealed that the original Jack the Ripper (Tom Savini) has achieved a form of immortality (exactly *how* is never explained) and has possessed the body of the professor. ¶ "You know, it's kinda weird having Jack the Ripper in our town after all these years, killin' people." • This no-budget shot-on-video turkey's main claim to fame is the acting appearance of makeup wizard Tom Savini as the Ripper. Though Savini is given top billing on the posters and is billed fourth in the screen credits, he is only on-screen for a total of four minutes at the film's end.

Room to Let (1950; Exclusive Films) D: Godfrey Grayson. P: Anthony Hinds. S: John Gilling, Godfrey Grayson. C: Cedric Williams. Cast: Jimmy Hanley, Valentine Dyall, Christine Silver, Merle Tottenham, Charles Hawtrey, Constance Smith. Valentine Dyall plays the mysterious Mr. Fell, who rents a room from a London family. It is 1904, 16 years after the Ripper murders, and the family soon comes to suspect that their new lodger is none other than Jack the Ripper, about to start up again. ¶ "In four days time it will be the ninth, and then I shall begin again where I left off. And then everyone will recognize me!" • *Room to Let* was adapted from the BBC feature by Marjorie Allingham.

A Study in Terror (1965; Columbia; England/U.S.) D: James Hill. P: Henry G. Lester. S: Donald Ford, Derek Ford. C: Desmond Dickinson. Cast: John Neville, Donald Houston, John Fraser, Robert Morley, Cecil Parker, Anthony Quayle, Barbara Windsor, Adrienne Corrie, Frank Finlay. Sherlock Holmes investigates the Whitechapel slayings of Jack the Ripper. ¶ From the advertising: "Holy terror! Sherlock Holmes vs. Jack the Ripper!"

Terror in the Wax Museum (1973) (see WAX MUSEUMS). In Victorian London, a wax museum owner is found murdered the night before he was to have sold his exhibits to an American showman, apparently killed by the statue of Jack the Ripper. Soon several other Ripper-like murders occur before the killer is finally unmasked.

Time After Time (1979) (see TIME TRAVEL). Dr. John Stevens, alias Jack the Ripper (David Warner), escapes into the future of modern-day San Francisco via H. G. Wells' time machine, closely pursued by Wells himself. ¶ "The world has caught up with me and *surpassed* me. Ninety years ago I was a freak, today I'm an amateur" — Jack the Ripper.

Waxworks (1924) (see WAX MUSEUMS). A poet dreams of being chased by Jack the Ripper. Werner Krauss plays the Ripper.

Japanese Giant Monsters

The historical origin of the Japanese giant monster movie can best be summed up in two words — Hiroshima and Nagasaki. No other people on Earth have had the singular horror of experiencing the terrible force of nuclear devastation and its deadly aftereffects like the Japanese.

Though Japanese filmmakers were reluctant to reproduce Hiroshima itself for a war-weary nation, they did fully exploit the radioactive panic it produced along with the terrible consequences of bomb blasts on the region's ecosystem. Without getting too close to the pain of their historical reality, Japanese filmmakers turned nuclear science and experimentation into a horror-once-removed (showing not the devastation of nuclear bombings, but the devastation caused by the monstrous offspring of this nuclear technology). The infamous Bikini Island atomic tests led to the creation of Japan's first and foremost nuclear age monster, *Gojira,* better known to the western world as *Godzilla, King of the Monsters* (1954). Godzilla was more than just a purveyor of mayhem aroused from his slumber by a loud bang, he was a symbolic reminder of the destructive potential that the nuclear age had unleashed upon the world. He was an atomic creation that derived its powers (most notably, his radioactive breath of fire) from nuclear sources. *Godzilla* was a smash both in Japan and the rest of the world. Japan's major monster studio, Toho, and its team of sci-fi filmmakers (which included director Inoshiro Honda, producer Tomoyuki Tanaka, and special effects master Eiji Tsuburaya) decided to channel the highly charged interest in Godzilla into long-term profit potential, and a long-lived film series was born. So, like the bad boy professional wrestlers of America (which Godzilla's foot-stomping and monster-wrestling came to emulate), Godzilla's reputation was cleaned up and he was transformed from a vicious island-stomper into a loyal monster-hero. He became a champion, willing to fight off all foreign, domestic, and alien enemies that might challenge his beloved Japan. This startling metamorphosis even went so far as to picture young children writing letters of gratitude to Godzilla for saving their homeland (as in *Godzilla vs. the Smog Monster,* 1972, which even boasted of Godzilla's ability to clean up our polluted environment!).

Although Godzilla was clearly the country's favorite monster, he was not the only giant show in town. Rodan, Mothra, and an affable giant turtle named Gamera caught on with the public as well. Gamera was Godzilla's (and Toho's) biggest competitor, created by the rival Daiei studio as an answer to Godzilla's popularity. After Gamera fans shelled out enough financial support following the release of *Gammera the Invincible* (1966), Daiei parlayed this success into a seven-picture series (an achievement still overshadowed by Godzilla's *17* films to date, however). Both of these popular monsters have their own individual subsections within this chapter. Every other Japanese giant, including Dagora, Varan, Gappa, Gorath, and the indomitable samurai statue known as Majin, will be lumped together in a third subdivision entitled *Other Giant Japanese Monsters.*

Please note that not every Japanese science fiction monster will be found in this section; only the gigantic ones are listed here. For example, the oozing *H-Man* (1959) will be listed in its own subject area — BLOBS, while the Matango mushroom monsters from *Attack of the Mushroom People* (1963) can be found in the PLANTS section.

Godzilla

Destroy All Monsters (1968; Toho/AIP; Japan) (also *Operation Monsterland*). D: Inoshiro Honda. P: Tomoyuki Tanaka. S: Kaoru Mabuchi, Inoshiro Honda. C: Taiichi Kankura. Cast: Akira Kubo, Jun Tazaki, Yoshio Tsuchiya, Kyoko Ai, Kenji Sahara, Andrew Hughes, Yukiko Kobayashi, Itoh sisters. Set in the future, aliens (known as Kilaaks) set up bases on the Moon and under the Earth with the purpose of setting loose all the gigantic beasts on "Monster Island" to decimate the planet. ¶ "Godzilla attacks New York! Rodan devastates Moscow! Manda obliterates London! and Mothra smashes Peking! Is this the warcry that will save the world . . . Destroy All Mosnters!" — ad line. • Toho studios used this giant monster rally to celebrate their twentieth monster movie. This was the ninth appearance of the lizard legend, Godzilla. • Eleven monsters appeared in all: Anzilla (sometimes referred to as Angorus), Baby Godzilla (or Minya), Baragon, Ebirah, Ghidrah, Godzilla, Manda, Mothra, Rodan, Varan, and Wenda. • Special effects star Eiji Tsuburaya teamed up with Sadamasa Arikawa in this picture. Tsuburaya died two years later, in 1970.

Ghidrah, the Three-Headed Monster (1965; Toho/Continental; Japan) D: Inoshiro Honda. P: Tomoyuki Tanaka. S: Shinichi Sekizawa. C: Hajime Koizumi. Cast: Yosuke Natsuki, Yurihiko Hoshi, Hiroshi Koizumi, Emi Itoh, Yumi Itoh, Takashi Shimura, Eiji Okada. A three-headed, two-tailed flying monster from outer space arrives on Earth to battle Godzilla, Rodan, and Mothra. Mothra ends up spinning Ghidrah into a cocoon which Rodan and Godzilla knock off into the sea. ¶ Movie ads excited audiences with announcements like, "See — the world quake before the unleashed fury of the battle of the monsters! See — unimaginable terrors that will never be equaled!" • This is the fifth time Godzilla graced the screen.

Gigantis, the Fire Monster (1955; Toho/Warner Bros.; Japan) (also *Godzilla Raids Again* [video title]). D: Motoyoshi Oda. P; Tomoyuki Tanaka. S: Takeo Murata, Sugeaki Hidaka. C: Seichi Endo. Cast: Hiroshi Koizumi, Setsuko Wakayama, Minoru Chiaki, Takashi Shimura. In this direct sequel to *Godzilla, King of the Monsters* (1954), atomic blasts awaken two monsters — Godzilla (here named Gigantis) and a dog-faced scaly giant called Angurus (also known as Anzilla). Godzilla — or rather Gigantis — wins and marches on to Tokyo until he is buried in an avalanche of snow. ¶ "Born in hell to destroy each other but first they'll destroy the world!" — claimed the ads. • An American version of this film (released in 1959 by Warner Bros.) was produced by Paul Schreibman and directed by Hugo Grimaldi. • Warner Bros., America's distributor, did not own the rights to the name "Godzilla," thus the name change to Gigantis. • Pressbook hype described Gigantis as "raging out of the bowels of the Earth . . . A hundred tons of hell and fire to ravage and destroy!" Angurus was said to be, "Screaming its challenge of mortal combat . . . Shooting 10,000 degree jets of flaming devastation!"

Godzilla, King of the Monsters (1954; Toho/Embassy; Japan) D: Inoshiro Honda, Terry Morse (American scenes). P: Tomoyuki Tanaka. S: Inoshiro Honda, Takeo Murata. C: Masao Tamai. Cast: Raymond Burr (American version), Akira Takarada, Akihiko Hirata, Takashi Shimura, Momoko Kochi, Fuyuki Murakami, Sachio Sakai. The film's American story reconstruction begins with American reporter Raymond Burr lying amid the rubble and misery left in the wake of disaster caused by Godzilla. His account is told in flashback, detailing the mysterious events leading up to the tremendous assault on Japan by the gigantic reptile known as Godzilla. In the end, a Japanese scientist uses his new superweapon to remove all oxygen from the water of Tokyo harbor, leaving Godzilla a lifeless skeleton (though not stopping his return for 16 subsequent features). ¶ "Tokyo, a smouldering memorial to the unknown. An unknown which at this very moment still prevails and could at any time lash out with its terrible destruction anywhere else in the world. There were once many people here who could have told of what they saw, now there are only a few." • Billed as the "Earth-shaking, Screen-shattering King of the Monsters!," Godzilla (known as Gojira in the original Japanese version) stood over 400 feet tall, and spewed forth a lethal radioactive breath ray. • According to longtime producer Alex Gordon, he and Sam Arkoff (soon to form AIP) originally cut a deal to buy *Godzilla*'s American distribution rights for a mere $12,000. "But," said Gordon, "Arkoff and I were double-crossed by the Toho home office and several American entrepreneurs who were able to contact Japan directly and persuade Tokyo headquarters to renege on our deal" (*Fangoria* #72). Joseph E. Levine ended up with *Godzilla* and added the American scenes with Raymond Burr. • Godzilla, who has appeared in 16 other movies (and who knows how many more will be made?), underwent some interesting personality changes throughout the series. He was a screen "heavy" bent on destruction in his first four films and then in *Ghidrah, the Three-Headed Monster* (1965), Godzilla became a national hero for stopping a more terrible menace than himself. Godzilla's principal producer, Tomoyuki Tanaka, then decided to exploit the giant lizard's young audience appeal by making the monster into a more personable clown, giving him more human characteristics and moods. With the addition of *Godzilla 1985*, the monster is once again portrayed as a baddie, and the beat (or make that "beast") goes on. • There were actually three different Godzillas used in the film—a man in a suit, a hand puppet, and a foot-tall mechanical robot model. • Effects man Eiji Tsuburaya discussed how Godzilla got his name: "Actually there was a tough looking fellow working on the Toho lot, with the nickname Gojira. We used his name! It certainly fit well."

Godzilla 1985 (1984; Toho/New World Pictures; Japan) D: Koji Hashimoto, R. J. Kizer. P: Tomoyuki Tanaka, Anthony Randel. Cast: Raymond Burr, Kenju Kobayashi, Ken Tanaka, Tasuko Sawagochi, Shin Takuma, James Hess. After finding a ship's crew horribly mutilated, scientists believe that Godzilla is responsible. Ray-

mond Burr reprises his role as journalist Steve Martin to chronicle the path of destruction by the new "mean" version of Godzilla. ¶ "Nature has a way sometimes, of reminding man just how small he is. She occasionally throws up the terrible offspring of our pride and carelessness to remind us of how puny we really are in the face of a tornado, an earthquake, or a Godzilla."

Godzilla vs. Biollante (1990) Godzilla faces a giant biological threat, cloned from various plant cells as well as those of Godzilla. The creature is larger than Godzilla, and resembles a monstrous flower with weird tentacles that end in snapping mouths. • This sequel to *Godzilla 1985* has yet to be released in an English language version.

Godzilla vs. Gaigan (1972; Toho/Cinema Shares; Japan) (also *Godzilla on Monster Island*). D: Jun Fukuda. P: Tomoyuki Tanaka. S: Shinichi Sekizawa. C: Kiyoshi Hasegawa. Cast: Hiroshi Ichikawa, Yuriko Hishimi, Minoru Takashima, Tomoko Umeda, Kunio Murai, Toshiaki Nishizawa. Alien invaders resembling cockroaches use two monsters—Ghidrah (the three-headed one) and Gaigan (or Gigan—a cyclopean creature with a saw in its stomach) to conquer the Earth. Standing in their way is our tag team heroes Godzilla and his foe from *Gigantis the Fire Monster,* Angorus (sometimes called Anzilla), who is now an ally. After successfully defending the Earth (and their title of monster wrestling champions) the two head back to their home on Monster Island. ¶ "Space monsters war with Godzilla for the Earth!"—ad line. • This is the twelfth entry in the Godzilla series.

Godzilla vs. Mechagodzilla (1974; Toho; Japan) (also *Godzilla vs. the Bionic Monster; Godzilla vs. the Cosmic Monster*). D: Jun Fukuda. P: Tomoyuki Tanaka. S: Jun Fukuda, Hiroyasu Yamamura. C: Yuzuru Aizawa. Cast: Masaki Daimon, Akihiko Hirata, Kazuya Aoyama, Hiroshi Koizumi, Kenji Sahara. Alien invaders send a robot double to battle Godzilla. • Godzilla's fourteenth appearance in the series includes a cameo appearance by Angorus, who teamed up with Godzilla in *Godzilla vs. Gaigan* (1972), and features a dog-like reptilian monster as well.

Godzilla vs. Megalon (1973; Toho/Cinema Shares; Japan). D/S: Jun Fukuda. P: Tomoyuki Tanaka. C: Yuzuru Aizawa. Cast: Katshuhiko Sasaki, Hiroyuki Kawase, Yutaka Hayashi, Kotaro Tomita. Godzilla and his cyborg buddy, Jet Jaguar, run up against two monsters from the alien race known as the Seatopians. The two "bad

The gigantic Japanese menace known as Godzilla, King of the Monsters *(1954) blasts buildings with his radioactive breath during his rampage through Tokyo.*

guys" are Megalon, a death-ray shooting killer cockroach with drill-like arms, and Gigan (or Gaigan), a huge bird-like beast with a buzzsaw belly. ¶ "Shit, Jet Jaguar, what'll we do?" • This is lucky number 13 in the Godzilla saga.

Godzilla vs. the Sea Monster (1966; Toho/Continental; Japan) D: Jun Fukuda. P: Tomoyuki Tanaka. S: Shinichi Sekizawa. C: Kazuo Yamada. Cast: Akira Takarada, Toru Watanabe, Hideo Sunazuka, Jun Tazaki, Kumi Mizuno. Godzilla plays catch with the lobster-like sea monster known as Ebirah. Mothra also makes a friendly guest appearance, along with the tiny twins called the Alilenas. • This is the seventh entry in the Godzilla series.

Godzilla vs. the Smog Monster (1972; Toho/AIP; Japan) D: Yoshimitu Banno, Lee Kresel (English version). P: Tomoyuki Tanaka. S: Kaoru Mabuchi. C: Yoichi Manoda. Cast: Akira Yamauchi, Hiroyuki Kawase, Toshie Kumura, Keiko Mari. In the big guy's eleventh film, Godzilla must battle a monster tadpole made out of living sludge and pollution (dubbed "Hedora") to save mankind from its own environmental folly. ¶ "All I can say is, no Earth creature can survive in the atmosphere Hedora does. In other words, a world of death, pollution, smoke and sludge. Oxygen is the only antidote worth trying." • Electricity (with the aid of Godzilla of course) kills the Smog Monster. The sludge tadpole grows in stages throughout the film—first, it can swim, then it develops four legs and thrives on smoke. In the third stage it begins to fly and emit sulfuric acid mist. In the last stage it becomes a humanoid creature, handy for Godzilla to grapple with. • The theme song, "Save the Earth," was sung by Adryan Russ. • The film features a poem by Ken Yano of Tojo School, class 4B, illustrating Godzilla's new role as defender of the people (and especially small children): "Atomic bombs, hydrogen bombs, and radioactive fallout falls into the sea. Poison gas, man's garbage, everything into the sea, thrown by you and me. Godzilla would rage if he could see, he'd turn the page, and clean it for you and me."

Godzilla vs. the Thing (1964; Toho/AIP;

Japan) (also *Godzilla vs. Mothra* [video title]). D: Inoshiro Honda. P: Tomoyuki Tanaka. S: Shinichi Sekizawa. C: Hajime Koizumi. Cast: Akira Takarada, Yuriko Hoshi, Hiroshi Koizumi, Emi Itoh, Yumi Itoh. Once again, one of Mothra's eggs is taken and exploited by carnival promoters. When the "peanut sisters" (who were kidnapped in the original *Mothra*) come to ask for the egg back, Godzilla turns up to tear apart Japan. The tiny twins then call upon their god, Mothra, to save the country. Godzilla, the brute, kills the friendly Mothra, but the moth's caterpillar-like offspring manage to trap Godzilla in a silky web and topple him off a cliff. • This was Godzilla's fourth appearance, and the last time he was cast as a "bad" monster.

Godzilla's Revenge (1969; Toho/UPA; Japan) D: Inoshiro Honda. P: Tomoyuki Tanaka. S: Shinichi Sekizawa. C: Mototaka Tomioka. Cast: Kenji Sahara, Tomonori Yazaki, Machiko Naka, Sachio Sakai, Yoshibumi Tajima. A young boy dreams about adventures with Godzilla and his son on the fabled "Monster Island." • This comical outing featured Godzilla's son, Minya, who learns to breathe fire (at first exhaling only harmless smoke rings). • This tenth film in the Godzilla series economically utilizes footage from the previous films, *Godzilla vs. the Sea Monster* (1966) and *Son of Godzilla* (1968).

Kong Kong vs. Godzilla (1962) (see APE GIANTS). American subs accidentally free Godzilla from an iceberg, and off he goes to pound Japan into submission. King Kong is then air-lifted in to stop the big reptile. An earthquake settles their dispute. • This particular segment in the series, the third, is thought of as the initiator of the "clown" Godzilla (for instance, he and Kong are seen kicking and tail-whacking a giant boulder back and forth), signaling the beginning of the silliness (and big-time wrestling persona) of Japan's top monster.

Monster Zero (1965; Toho; Japan) (also *Godzilla vs. Monster Zero*). D: Inoshiro Honda. P: Tomoyuki Tanaka. S: Shinichi Sekizawi. C: Hajime Koizumi. Cast: Nick Adams, Akira Takarada, Kumi Mizuno,

Keiko Sawai, Jun Tazaki. A mysterious planet near Jupiter is discovered and the World Space Authority sends a ship to investigate Planet X. When they arrive, they learn that the alien inhabitants are plagued by a monster and would like to return to Earth to transport Japan's Godzilla and Rodan back with them to kill "King Ghidrah" (Monster Zero). The conniving aliens' real plan, however, is to conquer the Earth. ¶ "'Cause if we don't find a solution to this thing, happiness in this world ain't gonna be worth a hill of beans!" • This is the sixth episode in the Godzilla series, and the second time Rodan and Godzilla have had it out for Ghidrah (the first being *Ghidrah, the Three-Headed Monster*, 1965).

Son of Godzilla (1968; Toho; Japan) D: Jun Fukuda. P: Tomoyuki Tanaka. S: Shinichi Sekizawa. C: Kazue Shiba. Cast: Tadao Takashima, Akira Kubo, Beverly Maeda, Akihiko Hirata, Kenji Sahara. Godzilla has a son (hatched from an enormous egg) and now he must teach him the fine art of self-defense. Instead of having a destructive radioactive breath, however, all the baby can muster is a few smoke rings at first. After body-slamming a few giant mantises, and burning a deadly spider named Spigon, the island that they live on is frozen over by scientists observing the entire affair. ¶ "Godzilla and its youngster, the two Mantises, and now Spigon—it's an island of monsters." • This eighth appearance of Godzilla is the first one featuring his son, Minya.

Terror of Mechagodzilla (1975; Toho; Japan) (also *Terror of Godzilla*). D: Inoshiro Honda. P: Tomoyuki Tanaka. S: Yukiko Takayama. C: Motoyoshi Tomioka. Cast: Katsuhiko Sasaki, Tomoko Ai, Akihiko Hirata, Tadao Nakamura, Katsumasu Uchida, Kenji Sahara, Toru Kawane, Kazunari Mori. Godzilla gets some help from a supersonic machine in his defense against those pesky alien Cyborg Women, the terrible Titanosaurus, and of course, the restored Godzilla double, Mechagodzilla. • This was the fifteenth and last Godzilla film until the series was re-vamped with the release of *Godzilla 1985* (1984).

Gamera

Gamera vs. Barugon (1966; Daiei; Japan) (also *War of the Monsters*). D: Shigeo Tanaka. P: Hidemasa Nagata. S: Fumi Takahashi. C: Michio Takahashi. Cast: Kojiro Hondo, Kyoko Enami, Akira Natsuki,

Koji Fujiyama, Ichiro Sugai. The giant flying turtle returns from space when a meteor diverts the rocket he was trapped in (at the end of *Gammera the Invincible*) back to Earth. In this episode, Gamera mends his ways and becomes the good guy, staving off an attack by Barugan, a monster that produces a deadly energy field in the form of a rainbow. • This is the first sequel to the original *Gammera the Invincible* and the only one not directed by Noriyaki Yuasa.

Gamera vs. Guiron (1969; Daiei; Japan) (also *Attack of the Monsters*). D: Noriyaki Yuasa. P: Hidemasa Nagata. S: Fumi Takahashi. C: Akira Kitazaki. Cast: Nobuhiro Kashima, Miyuki Akiyama, Christopher Murphy, Eiji Funakoshi, Yuko Hamada. The friendly turtle travels to a world on the other side of the sun to retrieve two boys from brain-eating female aliens. Unfortunately for Gamera, he must also face a dangerous "knife-headed" beast, but, fortunately for Tokyo, the battle is on another planet. • This is the fifth installment in the Gamera series.

Gamera vs. Gyaos (1967; Daiei/AIP-TV; Japan) (also *Return of the Giant Monsters*). D: Noriyaki Yuasa. P: Hidemasa Nagata. S: Fumi Takahashi. C: Akira Inouye. Cast: Kojiro Hongo, Kichijiro Ueda, Hisayuki Abe, Reiko Kasahara. Gamera, the giant turtle, goes up against the laser beam–spitting flying Gyaos. • *Gamera vs. Gyaos* is the third entry in the Gamera series.

Gamera vs. Monster X (1970; Daiei, Japan) (also *Gamera vs. Jiger*). D: Noriyaki Yuasa. P: Hidemasu Nagata. S: Fumi Takashaski. C: Akiro Kitazaki. Cast: Tsutomu Takakuwa, Kelly Varis, Katherine Murphy, Kon Omura, Junko Yashiro. Monster X, known as Jiger, is an iguana-like beast who wants to wreck Expo '70. In his first encounter with Gamera, Jiger slashes the turtle with his tail, releasing a parasitic offspring which drains Gamera's blood, thus weakening our hero's chances. A couple of kids enter Gamera before the climax in a minisub and affect a cure, then off goes the turtle to save the Expo and dispose of Monster X. • This is the sixth film for Gamera.

Gamera vs. Outer Space Monster Virus (1968; Daiei; Japan) (also *Destroy All Planets; Gamera vs. Viras*). D: Noriaki Yuasa. P: Hidemasa Nagata. S: Fumi Takahashi. C: Akira Kitazaki. Cast: Kojiro Hongo, Toru Takatsuka, Peter Williams, Michiko Yaegaki, Carl Crane. Gamera, the friendly turtle, is discovered by a pair of young boys to be controlled by aliens in spaceships. The kids manage to free Gamera from their evil powers and the turtle resumes his role as protector of the Earth. The "Viras" monster is a tentacled creature with six legs. • This is the fourth entry in the turtle series.

Gamera vs. Zigra (1971; Daiei; Japan) D: Noriyaki Yuasa. P: Yoshihiko Manabe. S: Fumi Takahashi. C: Akira Uehara. Cast: Reiko Kasahara, Koji Fujiyama, Mikiko Tsubouchi, Isamu Saeki, Yasushi Sakagami. Aliens from the polluted planet Zigra come to Earth in a spaceship which has the ability to turn into a giant monster. The Zigra-beast manages to kill Gamera and send the giant turtle to the bottom of the ocean, where it stays until kiddies revive it with electricity. ¶ "*Gamera* is the friend of all children." • This is the seventh and last episode of the Gamera monster series.

Gammera the Invincible (1966; Daiei/World Entertainment Corp; Japan) D: Noriyaki Yuasa. P: Yonejiro Saito. S: Fumi Takahashi. C: Nobuo Munekawa. Cast: Eiji Funakoshi, Harumi Kiritachi, Junichiro Yamashita, Yoshiro Kitahara. A gigantic flying fire-beathing turtle is unleashed from the Arctic ice during atomic bomb blasts. The menacing monster is finally trapped and sent off into outer space via rocket. ¶ "Gammera doesn't scare us. We're not afraid of a *turtle,* are we?" • The American version of this picture starred Brian Donlevy (*The Creeping Unknown,* 1956) and Albert Dekker (*Dr. Cyclops,* 1940), and was scripted by Richard Kraft, who made the Americans the heroes. • For this first Gamera film, the giant turtle's name is spelled with two m's — Gammera. In each succeeding entry, it was shortened to only one m — Gamera.

Other Giant Japanese Monsters

Atragon (1963; Toho/AIP; Japan) D: Inoshiro Honda. P: Tomoyuki Tanaka. S: Shichi Sekizawa. C: Hajime Koizumi. Cast: Tadao Takashima, Hiroshi Koizumi, Jun Tazaki, Yoko Fujiyama, Ken Uehara, Kenji Sahara, Akihiko Hirata. The underwater tyrant "Mu" commands the serpent-god "Wenda," and is threatening the Earth.

A flying supersub named the Atragon is called in to stop the monster and thwart the tyrant's plans.

Dagora the Space Monster (1964; Toho; Japan) D: Inoshiro Honda. P: Tomoyuki Tanaka. S: Shinichi Sekizawa. C: Hajime Koizumi. Cast: Yosuke Natsuki, Yoko Fujiyama, Akiko Wakabayashi, Hiroshi Koizumi. This addition to the Japanese monster cycle features a giant radioactive octopus/jellyfish monster with the ability to fly and a taste for raw materials. The threat of Dagora is stopped when a scientist discovers that wasp venom is fatal to the monster.

Frankenstein Conquers the World (1964) (see HUMAN GIANTS). A young boy is discovered in the remnants of an A-bomb blast, and he then grows to enormous size. Now a giant, he comes up against a flying, floppy-eared reptile (known as Baragon).

Gappa, Triphibian Monster (1967; Nikkatsu; Japan) (also *Monster from a Prehistoric Planet*). D: Haruyasu Noguchi. P: Hideo Koi. S: Iwao Yamazaki, Ryuzo Nakanishi. C: Muneo Keda. Cast: Tamio Kawaji, Yoko Yamamoto, Yuji Okada, Koji Wada, Tatsuya Fuji. This *Gorgo*esque entry in the Japanese Monster arena features a baby monster that is kidnapped from its island home. Its parents, of course, come to the rescue and wipe out most of Tokyo along the way. • Gappa is called the Triphibian monster because of its species' ability to walk, swim, and fly.

Gorath (1963) (see SPACE TRAVEL). A spaceship observing a magnetic meteor (dubbed "Gorath") is nearly drawn into the fiery mass and destroyed. Explosions in the Antarctic, intended to move the Earth off its orbit and out of the way of this oncoming planetoid, accidentally unleash a gigantic walrus-like monster. • Gorath is seen only in the original Japanese version of the film. These sequences were excised from the American release print.

King Kong Escapes (1968) (see APE GIANTS). Kong is a pawn in a mining scheme by a mad scientist, who has made a robot replica of the popular ape. Kong eventually squares off against his metallic relative after a preliminary warmup against a dinosaur.

Majin, Monster of Terror (1966) (see STATUES COME TO LIFE). A Japanese prince and princess are helped to regain their rightful status when a giant idol awakens and lends a hand.

Majin Strikes Again (1966) (see STATUES COME TO LIFE). Earthquakes and floods bring forth the giant statue known as Majin, who stops another tyrant and rescues some children in this third and final Majin entry.

Mothra (1962; Toho/Columbia; Japan) D: Inoshiro Honda. P: Tomoyuki Tanaka. S: Shinichi Sekizawa. C: Hajime Koizumi. Cast: Frankie Sakai, Hiroshi Koizumi, Kyoko Katawa, Emi Itoh, Yumi Itoh, Ken Eehara. When a giant egg and two miniature twin girls are taken from an H-bomb test island, the giant monster known as Mothra (or "Mosura" to the Japanese) comes forth to retrieve them. • *Mothra* appeared in three other films during the decade, all with Godzilla: *Godzilla vs. the Thing* (1964), *Godzilla vs. the Sea Monster* (1966), and the Japanese monster fest, *Destroy All Monsters* (1968).

The Mysterians (1959) (see ALIENS: INVADERS ON EARTH: THE 50s). Caped alien invaders turn a giant metallic bird loose on Earth.

Return of Giant Majin (1966) (see STATUES COME TO LIFE). Majin comes out of a lake in this sequel to *Majin, Monster of Terror* and goes berserk after some unthinking locals deface his sacred effigy.

Rodan (1957; Toho; Japan) D: Inoshiro Honda. P: Takashi Kuronuma. S: Takeshi Kumura, Takeo Murata. C: Isamu Ashida. Cast: Kenji Sawara, Kumi Shirakawa, Akihiko Hirata, Akio Kobori, Yasuko Nakata. Giant caterpillar-insects and two huge eggs are discovered in a mine. When the eggs hatch, two monstrous pterodactyl-like bird creatures (called Rodans) emerge and level Japan with the velocity of their giant wings. The giant insects (which Rodan likes to eat) have a heyday wreaking havoc among villagers as well. ¶ "Because of its size and supersonic flying speed, it generates a shock wave with all the destructive force of a typhoon." • According to the movie, Rodan is a carnivorous prehistoric relative of the pteranodon, with a weight of 100 tons and a wing span over 500 feet. • Billions of years ago, the egg was hermetically sealed inside a volcano with the "germ of life" buried in it. It was found in a mine, but exited from a nearby volcano.

Varan the Unbelievable (1962; Toho/Crown International Pictures; Japan/U.S.) D: Inoshiro Honda. P: Tomoyuki Tanaka, Jerry A. Baerwitz (U.S. version). S: Shinichi Sekizawa, Sid Harris (U.S.). C: Hajime Koizumi, Jacques Marquette (U.S.). Cast: Kozo Nomura, Ayumi Sonoda, Koreya Senda, Akihiko Hirata, Myron Healey (U.S.), Tsuruko Kobayashi (U.S.). A prehistoric monster emerges from a lake following military experimental testing (involving the removal of salt from seawater), then goes on a rampage towards—you guessed it—Tokyo! • The original Japanese version is about 15 minutes longer than the American print, and was released in 1958. In the Japanese version, the monster has the capability of flight, while in the shortened American version, Varan is basically grounded. The American print also includes a Commander Bradley (played by Myron Healey) and his Japanese wife Anna (played by Tsuruko Kobayashi).

War of the Gargantuas (1967; Toho; Japan) D: Inoshiro Honda. P: Tomoyuki Tanaka. S: Inoshiro Honda, Kaoru Mabuchi. C: Hajime Koizumi. Cast: Russ Tamblyn, Kumi Mizuno, Kipp Hamilton, Kenji Sahara, Jun Tazaki. A giant octopus is dispatched by two huge hairy man-beasts called "Gargantuas." One of them is good (the brown one), and the other evil (the green one). When the green Gargantua is nearly killed by the military, his friendly brother nurses him back to health. His reward is treachery, as the evil green giant decides that there isn't enough room in Japan for two monsters. The grappling Gargantuas are put out of their misery by a volcanic eruption. ¶ Ad lines asked the question, "Can a country survive when two Gargantuas battle to the death?" • *War of the Gargantuas* was intended to be a sequel to *Frankenstein Conquers the World* (1964), with the monster being a brother of sorts to the Frankenstein creature. When the Gargantua makeup was designed, its resemblance to the Frankenstein was so slight that the film producers thought it better to bill this as a new creation instead of an offshoot. • The Gargantuas' fur was actually the skins of wild dogs.

The X from Outer Space (1967; Shochiku; Japan) D: Kazui Nihonmatsu. P: Akihiko Shimada. S: Kazui Nihonmatsu, Hidemi Motomochi, Moriyoshi Ishida. C: Shizuo Hirase. Cast: Eiji Okada, Peggy Neal, Toshiya Wazaki, Shinichi Yanagisawa, Itoko Harada, Franz Gruber. An international space expedition brings back a substance to Earth which grows into a giant steel-spitting monster which stomps on Tokyo. • An anti-matter component from space called Guilalalium is used to re-shrink the creature, making him pliable enough to send back into space.

Yog, Monster from Space (1971; Toho/AIP; Japan) D: Inoshiro Honda. P: Tomoyuki Tanaka, Fumio Tanaka. S: El Ogawa. C: Taiichi Kankura, Yasuichi Sunokura. Cast: Akiro Kubo, Atsuko Takahashi, Kenji Sahara, Yoshio Tsuchiya, Noritake Saito, Yukiko Kobayashi. An alien presence, passing through a blue mist on its way to an island, inhabits the body of a spy, and creates giant monsters from a squid, a crab, and a turtle. ¶ Ads proclaimed Yog as: "The mightiest monster ever . . . spewed from intergalactic space to clutch the planet Earth in its terror tentacles!"

Yongari, Monster from the Deep (1967; Toei/AIP-TV; Japan/S. Korea). D: Kiduck Kim. S: Yunsung Suh. C: Kenichi Nakagawa, Inchib Byon. Cast: Yungil Oh, Chungim Nam, Soonjai Lee, Moon Kang, Kwang Ho Lee. Atomic testing causes an earthquake in China which unleashes the Godzilla lookalike, Yongari. After stomping across South Korea and smashing Seoul, the monster succumbs to a chemical ammonia spray called X2.

Dr. Jekyll and Family

Dr. Jekyll (and Mr. Hyde), along with Count Dracula and the Frankenstein Monster, is one of (or more precisely, *two* of) the most frequently appearing characters in the horror cinema. Nothing evokes the idea of the duality of man quite like Dr. Jekyll and Mr. Hyde. The inner struggle of good vs. evil (or in psychological terms, of ego vs. id) has fascinated philosophers for centuries, and the Jekyll/Hyde story captures this eternal conflict perfectly. Robert Louis Stevenson's classic novella, *Dr. Jekyll and Mr. Hyde,* has been filmed numerous times over the years, beginning with a number of silent shorts and two full-length silent versions (one of which caused many of the day's critics to herald John Barrymore, who assayed the dual role, as the screen's greatest living actor). Of course, the most acclaimed and best known version is the classic 1932 *Dr. Jekyll and Mr. Hyde,* which earned Fredric March a Best Actor Oscar—the only one ever given to a performer in a horror film. Next came the lesser but still handsome Spencer Tracy version in 1941. Nearly two dozen versions and variations followed, in which Jekyll/Hyde met Abbott and Costello (*Abbott and Costello Meet Dr. Jekyll and Mr. Hyde,* 1953), cavorted with the Wolf Man (*Dr. Jekyll and the Wolfman,* 1971), and was even transformed into a woman (*Mrs.* Hyde!) in Hammer's *Dr. Jekyll and Sister Hyde* (1971). There followed the inevitable parodies (*Dr. Heckyll and Mr. Hype,* 1980; *Jekyll and Hyde Together Again,* 1982), and even a blaxploitation version (*Dr. Black and Mr. Hyde,* 1975).

The Jekyll and Hyde story is a timeless one, even for filmmakers. Two recent remakes bear this out—*Edge of Sanity* (1989) in which Anthony Perkins' Jekyll transforms into Hyde when he uses a highly addictive drug (a thinly-veiled cocaine); and *Jekyll and Hyde,* a well-done 1990 TV movie featuring big-screen star Michael Caine.

Abbott and Costello Meet Dr. Jekyll and Mr. Hyde (1953; Universal) D: Charles Lamont. P: Howard Christie. S: Leo Loeb, John Grant. C: George Robinson. Cast: Bud Abbott, Lou Costello, Boris Karloff, Craig Stevens, Helen Westcott, Reginald Denny, John Dierkes. Bud and Lou play "Slim" and "Tubby" (it's not difficult to guess which is which), two American detectives in London who become embroiled in the affairs of one "Dr. Jekyll" (Boris Karloff), a thoroughly sinister character who is using his personality-changing formula to commit nefarious crimes as the hideous Mr. Hyde. At the comical finale, Costello is turned into a Mr. Hyde himself and bites a group of bobbies, who are then all transformed into identical Hydes as well. ¶ "Now look, you can't make two persons out of one. If there's a monster, there's a monster. If there's a Dr. Jekyll, there's a Dr. Jekyll. But one can't be the other!" • While Boris Karloff played Dr. Jekyll (for the first and only time in his long career as a screen bogeyman), it was stuntman Eddie Parker who was Mr. Hyde (wearing a rubber "Hyde" mask).

Daughter of Dr. Jekyll (1957; Allied Artists) D: Edgar G. Ulmer. P/S: Jack Pollexfen. C: John F. Warren. Cast: John Agar, Gloria Talbott, Arthur Shields, John Dierkes, Martha Wentworth. Gloria Talbott plays the daughter of the infamous scientist who comes to England to claim her father's estate. Mysterious murders occur and suspicion falls upon her, but the truth comes out that her former guardian (Arthur Shields) has discovered Jekyll's secrets and periodically turns himself into a werewolf-like creature (presumably Mr. Hyde). ¶ "If you love me, you'll kill me." • *Daughter of Dr. Jekyll* was shot not at a soundstage, but in an old mansion on Sixth Street in Hollywood. Though the film is supposedly set at an earlier time, in one scene you can spot through a window contemporary 1956 cars driving by.

Dr. Black and Mr. Hyde (1975; Dimension) D: William Crain. P: Charles Walker. S: Larry LeBron. C: Tak Fujimoto. Cast: Bernie Casey, Rosalind Cash, Marie O'Henry, Ji-Tu Cumbuka, Milt Kogan, Stu Gilliam. More blaxploitation from the director of (the far superior) *Blacula* (1972). This film features a Watts free-clinic doctor named Dr. Pride who develops a serum to regenerate liver tissue. Unfortunately it has a side effect—it turns him into a super strong deranged white man with a grudge against prostitutes. ¶ "You're gonna check out this cock 'n' bull story about a black doctor that turns white at night?!" • Stan Winston, later to become a respected special effects man and director, created the rather unconvincing Hyde makeup. Though several times he's referred to as "white," the pasty-face makeup, frosted hair, and blue contact lenses on Bernie Casey make him look more like a sickly albino than a creepy Caucasian.

Dr. Heckyl and Mr. Hype (1980; Cannon) D/S: Charles B. Griffith. P: Menahem Golam, Yoram Globus. C: Robert Carras. Cast: Oliver Reed, Sunny Johnson, Maia Danziger, Virgil Frye, Mel Welles, Kedric Wolfe, Sharon Compton, Denise Hayes, Jackie Coogan. In this satirical version, Oliver Reed plays a hideously ugly podiatrist who overdoses on an experimental diet formula and is transformed into a handsome but nasty murderer. ¶ "Were I not so far beyond mere ugliness, I might wish to be handsome; handsome guys can get away with murder." • Writer/director Charles B. Griffith got his start as a writer on early Roger Corman horror/satires such as *A Bucket of Blood* (1959) and *The Little Shop of Horrors* (1960). Griffith even cast two actors from *Little Shop* for this film—Dick Miller and Mel Welles.

Dr. Jekyll and Mr. Hyde (1920; Pioneer) P: Louis B. Mayer. Cast: Sheldon Lewis, Alexander Shannon, Dora Mills Adams, Gladys Field, Harold Forshay, Leslie Austin. Made the same year as the better-known

John Barrymore version, this film updates Stevenson's story to a then-contemporary New York. Sheldon Lewis plays Dr. Jekyll, who dreams of the horror created by his experiments in separating the good and evil natures of humans. When he awakens he realizes the danger of his dream is coming true, and decides to discontinue his research. • Reportedly, the unknown director was so dissatisfied with the cheapness of the film that he had his name removed from the credits.

Dr. Jekyll and Mr. Hyde (1920; Paramount) D: John S. Robertson. P: Adolph Zukor. S: Clara S. Beranger. C: Karl Struss, Roy Overbough. Cast: John Barrymore, Martha Mansfield, Nita Naldi, Brandon Hurst, Charles Lane, Louis Wolheim. John Barrymore plays the brilliant Dr. Jekyll who invents a potion which releases the evil side of his nature in the form of Mr. Hyde. The plot also borrows a bit from *The Picture of Dorian Gray* by including the person of Sir George Carew, a cynic who encourages Jekyll in his fateful experiments. ¶ "In each of us, two natures are at war — the good and the evil. All our lives the fight goes on between them, and one of them must conquer. But in our own hands lies the power to choose — what we want most to be, we *are*" — opening written narration. • Numerous short versions of the Dr. Jekyll story were filmed even before this first full-length treatment. They include a 1908 Selig Polyscope production, a 1910 Danish version produced by Ole Olsen, a 1912 film directed by Lucius Henderson, a 1913 Universal feature produced by Carl Laemmle and starring King Baggot, a 1914 Starlight production, another Universal showing in 1915, and a 1920 Arrow Film Corp. picture starring Hank Mann. • Barrymore's wonderful portrayal of the two opposing sides of human nature, and his incredible (for the time) transformation on-screen *without* appreciable makeup, caused many critics of the day to hail him as the screen's greatest actor.

Dr. Jekyll and Mr. Hyde (1932; Paramount) D/P: Rouben Mamoulian. S: Samuel Hoffenstein, Percy Heath. C: Karl Struss. Cast: Fredric March, Miriam Hopkins, Rose Hobart, Holmes Herbert, Edgar Norton. The kind but controversial young Dr. Jekyll manages to split his human nature into two halves — one his normal self, the other a purely evil being which he dubs "Mr. Hyde." At first he revels in his newfound freedom as Hyde, but soon comes to loathe the monster he has become. Unfortunately, he cannot control the transforma-

tions at this point, as the Hyde personality has become too strong. Hyde's involvement with, and eventual murder of, a beautiful saloon singer leads to Jekyll's ultimate demise. ¶ "I saw a light, but I could not see where it was leading. I have gone further than man should go." • The unknown actor Fred Bickel got his start in show business as understudy to matinee idol and soon-to-be horror star Lionel Atwill in the Broadway play "Deburau" in 1920. Fred Bickel later changed his name to Fredric March. • March went home with an Academy Award for Best Actor that year for his fierce dualistic performance, the first and only time a Best Actor Oscar has been awarded to a performer in a horror film. • This version was also nominated for Academy Awards in Writing Adaptation (Samuel Hoffenstein, Percy Heath) and in Cinematography (Karl Struss). • Director Rouben Mamoulian ran up and down stairs recording his own heartbeat to be used on the soundtrack during the film's incredible transformation sequence. The scene itself has long been the subject of much conjecture about how it was achieved. Mamoulian finally revealed that the masterful transformation was accomplished through a series of colored filters being removed from the camera lens, allowing the special makeup on March's face to seemingly appear out of nowhere without the usual overlapping photography. • Cinematographer Karl Struss explained the process to *Famous Monsters of Filmland* #115: "Wally Westmore used a lot of red makeup in the first transformation of Fredric March and by photographing through red gelatin filters about 2 inches square held close to the camera lens, it [the transformation] was indetectable." Struss had used a similar technique for his work in the 1923 version of *The Ten Commandments* while filming the healed lepers. • According to Karl Struss, Irving Pichel (*Dracula's Daughter,* 1936) was originally considered for the role of Dr. Jekyll.

Dr. Jekyll and Mr. Hyde (1941; MGM) D/P: Victor Fleming. S: John Lee Mahin. C: Joseph Ruttenberg. Cast: Spencer Tracy, Ingrid Bergman, Lana Turner, Donald Crisp, Ian Hunter, Barton MacLane, Sara Allgood, Billy Bevan, C. Aubrey Smith. This big-budgeted version of the Jekyll/Hyde story is basically a remake of the classic 1932 film. ¶ "You see what you've done, don't you? You ... you've gone beyond, you've committed the supreme blasphemy!" • This time, Spencer Tracy plays the two parts with only minimal

Fredric March evinces the amazing makeup of Wally Westmore for his dynamic dual role of Dr. Jekyll and Mr. Hyde *(1932).*

makeup as Hyde, reportedly prompting Somerset Maugham to ask while visiting the set, "Which one is he playing now?" Robert Donat (*The Ghost Goes West,* 1935) was originally considered for the role of Dr. Jekyll before the part(s) went to Tracy. • In a casting twist, Lana Turner, who was usually cast as the scheming bad girl, plays Jekyll's innocent fiancée, while Ingrid Bergman, who was usually seen as the essence of purity, here plays Ivy, the tempting barmaid. • Director Victor Fleming is revered as the creator of two of Hollywood's best-loved films, *The Wizard of Oz* and *Gone with the Wind* (both 1939). • Cinematographer Joseph Ruttenberg received an Academy Award nomination for his work on this picture. • The rights were bought by MGM to the earlier (superior) version from Paramount and suppressed the film for many years in order to protect their own version from possible unfavorable comparisons.

Dr. Jekyll and Sister Hyde (1971; Hammer/AIP; U.K.) D: Roy Ward Baker. P: Albert Fennel, Brian Clemens. S: Brian Clemens. C: Norman Warwick. Cast: Ralph Bates, Martine Beswick, Susan Brodrick, Dorothy Alison, Ivor Dean, Philip Madoc, Irene Bradshaw, Niel Wilson, Paul Whitsun-Jones, Tony Calvin, Dan Meaden, Virginia Wetherell. Dr. Jekyll, in searching for an "elixir of life" through the use of female hormones, finds that his elixir has an odd side-effect, it changes the subject's sex as well as its personality. Thus is born Jekyll's seductive, thoroughly evil alter-ego, *Mrs.* Hyde, who poses as Jekyll's sister. Jekyll requires select body parts of women to concoct his elixir and continue his research, and when the local morgue runs dry, the good doctor turns to murder — all in the name of humanity, of course. The story throws in those infamous London grave robbers Burke and Hare, and even ties in Jack the Ripper mystery as the results of Jekyll's handiwork (*Jekyll* the Ripper?). ¶ "I saw it as the first step in an exciting scientific adventure. I could not know then that it was the first step towards the black abyss, towards a myriad of horrors, towards self-destruction." •

The lurid ad campaign: "*Warning!* The sexual transformation of a man into a woman will actually take place before your very eyes!" Thankfully, this turned out to be just more overblown hype, with the transformations being handled much more tastefully than this exploitative statement intimated. • Star Ralph Bates (Dr. Jekyll) met his future wife on this picture, actress Virginia Wetherell. She plays his first victim in the film. • Martine Beswick won the Best Actress award at a Paris fantasy film festival for her half of the title role.

Dr. Jekyll and the Wolfman (1971; International Cinema Films; Spain) D: Leon Klimowsky. P: José Frade. S: Jacinto Molina. C: Francisco Fraile. Cast: Paul Naschy, Shirley Corrigan, Jack Taylor, Mirta Miller, Barta Barri, Luis Induni. In this sixth film in the "Waldemar Daninsky" werewolf series, a descendant of Dr. Jekyll attempts to cure Waldemar of his lycanthropy by using his great grandfather's infamous "personality changing" serum — with the expected disastrous results. Now instead of two personalities, the poor wretch has three to deal with — Waldemar, the Werewolf, and Mr. Hyde. ¶ "I'll inject Waldemar with the formula which will turn him into a Mr. Hyde — that is the evil part of his character, which will be strong and powerful. When the moon is full he'll fight against the mutation, which the same full moon produces on him to turn him into a werewolf."

Dr. Jekyll's Dungeon of Death (1982; Rochelle) D/P: James Wood. S: James Mathers. Cast: James Mathers, John Kearney, Nadine Kalmes, Dawn Carver. In 1958 San Francisco, the great-grandson of Dr. Jekyll, aided by his lobotomized sister and a deformed giant, experiments with a mind-control serum worked on by both his ancestor and Nazi scientists. The serum transforms its user into a martial arts fighter. Mr. Hyde is nowhere to be found in this bastardization of Stevenson's classic story.

Edge of Sanity (1989; Allied Vision) D: Gerard Kikoine. P: Edward Simons, Harry Alan Towers. S: J. P. Filix, Ron Raley. C: Tony Spratling. Cast: Anthony Perkins, Glynis Barber, Sarah Maur-Thorp, David Lodge, Ben Cole, Lisa Davis, Ray Jewers, Jill Melford. In this version, Anthony Perkins plays Dr. Jekyll as a saintly physician who's disturbed alter ego stays buried by day but comes out in his troubled dreams at night. While investigating a drug (obviously cocaine, though never stated outright) for possible uses as an anesthetic, he becomes addicted. Use of the drug (via freebasing) then causes his whole personality to transform into a sadistic, mysoginistic fiend. • This version concentrates not on the physical transformations (which consist of nothing more than a rather pasty complexion, red-rimmed eyes, and disheveled hair) but on the change in personality, or more likely, the *release* of the disturbed side of his personality. • Anthony Perkins was no novice at playing split personalities, having created the most disturbed momma's boy in cinema history — Norman Bates in *Psycho* (1960).

The Head of Janus (1920; Decla Bioscop/ Lipow Film; Germany) D: Friedrich Wilhelm Murnau. S: Hans Janowitz. C: Karl Fruend, Carl Hoffmann. Cast: Conrad Veidt, Margarete Schlegel, Willy Kayser-Heyl, Margarete Kupfer, Gustav Botz, Bela Lugosi, Jaro Fuerth, Manus Stifter, Marga Reuter. Originally titled *Der Januskopf,* this apparently lost German version of Stevenson's story features Conrad Veidt in the dual role of the wealthy Dr. Warren who periodically transforms himself into the evil Mr. O'Connor. • This, much like the German film *Nosferatu* (1921), is an "unofficial," uncredited version of a classic story, with only the names changed to disguise its source. Unlike *Nosferatu,* which went through a lengthy legal battle, no one apparently noticed or cared about the deception pulled off by *The Head of Janus.* • Before he emigrated to America and struck it big with *Dracula* (1931), a then-unknown Bela Lugosi appears in a supporting role as Dr. Warren's butler.

Horror High (1973; Crown International) (also *Twisted Brain*). D: Larry Stouffer. P: Tom Moore. S: Jake Fowler. Cast: Pat Cardi, Austin Stoker, Rosie Holotik, John Niland, Joy Hash, Mike McHenry. For this modern version on Stevenson's theme, a nerdy chemistry student develops a potion that turns him into a monster, allowing him to take murderous revenge on those students and teachers that have persecuted him.

I, Monster (1971; Amicus/Cannon; U.K.) D: Stephen Weeks. P: Max J. Rosenberg, Milton Subotsky. S: Milton Subotsky. C: Moray Grant. Cast: Christopher Lee, Peter Cushing, Mike Raven, Richard Hurndall, George Merritt, Kenneth J. Warren, Susan Jameson, Margie Lawrence, Michael Des Barres. For this British version, the names are changed from Dr. Jekyll and Mr. Hyde to Dr. Marlowe and Mr. Blake. It follows Stevenson's storyline quite closely, but with each transformation making Blake all the more uglier. ¶ "Suppose that what Dr. Marlowe said were true. Suppose that, just for a while, we could let loose the reins, fulfill our desires — without restrictions, without control. I think, I might choose evil." • The film was begun using a new 3-D process, but was abandoned when director Stephen Weeks ran into difficulties with the complicated process, causing long delays. • Christopher Lee, who plays the Jekyll/Hyde character (Marlowe/Blake), has called this one of the best performances of his career.

Jekyll and Hyde (1990; TV movie) D/S: David Wickes. P: Patricia Carr. C: Norman Langley. Cast: Michael Caine, Cheryl Ladd, Joss Ackland, Ronald Pickup, Diane Keen, Kim Thomson, Kevin McNally, David Schofield, Lee Montague, Lionel Jeffries. Michael Caine assays the immortal dual role in this recent TV movie adaptation.

Jekyll and Hyde Together Again (1982; Paramount) D/S: Jerry Belson. P: Lawrence Gordon. S: Monica Johnson, Harvey Miller, Michael Leeson. C: Philip Lathrop. Cast: Mark Blankfield, Bess Armstrong, Krista Errickson, Tim Thomerson, Michael McGuire. Dr. Jekyll, a surgeon, transforms into Hyde and uses his new identity to step out on his girlfriend and date a punk rocker. • Actor Tim Thomerson, a well known stand-up comedian, has a supporting role as a wacky plastic surgeon in the film.

The Man with Two Heads (1972; William Mishkin; U.K./U.S.) D/S/C: Andy Milligan. P: William Mishkin. Cast: Denis DeMarne, Julia Stratton, Gay Feld, Jacqueline Lawrence, Berwick Kaler. In nineteenth century England, Dr. Jekyll is experimenting with controlling the evil side of human nature. This time when the good doctor takes the potion he turns into his evil alter ego known as "Mr. Blood." • Director/screenwriter and jack of all film trades Andy Milligan served as his own cinematographer on this low, low, low-budget independent shot in England.

The Nutty Professor (1963; Paramount) D: Jerry Lewis. P: Ernest D. Glucksman. S: Jerry Lewis, Bill Richmond. C: W. Wallace Kelley. Cast: Jerry Lewis, Stella Stevens, Del Moore, Kathleen Freeman, Howard Morris. A nerdy, buck-toothed professor uses his serum to transform himself into a cool lounge-lizard/ladies' man named "Buddy Love" in this comedy vehicle for Jerry Lewis.

Oversexed (1974) D/S: Joe Sarno. Cast: Veronica Parrish. A woman's touch this time, with Dr. Shirley Jekyll turning into the big-breasted, oversexed Ms. Sherry Hyde in this low-budget sexploitation version of Stevenson's tale.

The Son of Dr. Jekyll (1951; Columbia) D: Seymour Friedman. S: Edward Huebsch. C: Henry Freulich. Cast: Louis Hayward, Jody Lawrence, Alexander Knox, Lester Mathews, Gavin Muir, Paul Cavanagh, Rhys Williams. Picking up where most Jekyll and Hyde movies end, Dr. Jekyll (in the persona of Mr. Hyde) is chased by a mob back to his lab. When the mob sets fire to his house, Jekyll/Hyde falls to his death from the roof. Thirty years later his son, Edward, when told of his heritage, decides to clear his father's name by proving the validity of the experiment. Edward's trustee, Dr. Lanyon, substitutes Jekyll's original notes with a false set. He then tries to drive Edward mad and frames him for murder in order to keep a hold of Edward's estate. But Edward finds him out and Lanyon meets the same fate as Jekyll did 30 years earlier. ¶ "The fiery death of Dr. Lanyon ended the Jekyll-Hyde legend. Both the original manuscript and the fake copy went into Scotland Yard files to go down in history with other tales of bizarre crimes" — closing narration. • Star Louis Hayward goes one up on his fellow Jekyll/Hyde actors since he plays not two but *three* roles — Dr. Jekyll, Mr. Hyde, and the son of Dr. Jekyll. • Hayward uses the same sword-cane in *The Son of Dr. Jekyll* that John Barrymore used in his famous 1920 version of *Dr. Jekyll and Mr. Hyde*.

The Strange Case of Dr. Jekyll and Mr. Hyde (1968; TV movie) D: Charles Jarrott. P: Dan Curtis. S: Ian McClellan Hunter. C: Tom Farquharson. Cast: Jack Palance, Denholm Elliott, Billie Whitelaw, Tessie O'Shea, Torin Thatcher, Oscar Homolka, Leo Genn. This made-for-TV movie is a long, fairly faithful adaptation of Stevenson's novel, with Jack Palance portraying his Hyde with minimal makeup and maximum acting.

The Testament of Dr. Cordelier (1959; RTF/Sofirad/Compagnie Jean Renoir; France) (also *The Doctor's Horrible Experiment*). D/P/S: Jean Renoir. C: Georges Leclerc. Cast: Jean-Louis Barrault, Micheline Gary, Michel Vitold, Teddy Bilis, Jean Topart. French filmmaker Jean Renoir's Jekyll and Hyde version features Jean-Louis Barrault as Dr. Cordelier, who revels in his newfound freedom when he transforms into the bestial, evil Monsieur Opale.

The Two Faces of Dr. Jekyll (1960; Hammer/AIP; U.K.) (also *House of Fright;*

Jekyll's Inferno). D: Terence Fisher. P: Michael Carreras. S: Wolf Mankowitz. C: Jack Asher. Cast: Paul Massie, Dawn Addams, Christopher Lee, David Kossoff, Norma Marla, Francis De Wolff, Joy Webster, Oliver Reed. In this version, the rather dreary Dr. Jekyll is transformed into the handsome but evil Mr. Hyde. As Hyde, he discovers his wife's faithlessness with his good friend and takes murderous revenge on the pair. ¶ "Good—Evil—this moral quibbling is useless. Man as he *is* comprises two beings—one whom I call Man-As-He-*Could*-Be. In his perfection, this inner Man is beyond good and evil. [The other man] too is beyond good and evil: Man-As-He-*Would*-Be, free of all the restrictions society imposes upon us, subject only to his own will." • Christopher Lee, who plays Jekyll's faithless friend, later played the ill-fated doctor himelf (or a renamed version of same) in *I, Monster* (1971), wherein he played Dr. Marlowe and Mr. Blake.

Machines

(*See also* Cars and Vehicular Villains; Computers; Robots)

The industrial revolution gave birth to a new kind of menace—machines. A machine is "any system, usually of rigid bodies, formed and connected to alter, transmit, and direct applied forces to accomplish a specific objective" (*Webster's*). This definition covers a very wide spectrum of devices—from automobiles to computers to robots. Since we already have separate sections for the more specific CARS AND VEHICULAR VILLAINS, COMPUTERS, and ROBOTS, this section is devoted to all those other types of monstrous machines—terrible televisions, evil elevators, vicious video games, or even household gadgets run amok. The key element that makes a machine an object of terror is that these machines take on a life of their own in many cases, and they themseves *become* the menace.

The Andromeda Strain (1971; Universal) D/P: Robert Wise. S: Nelson Gidding. C: Richard H. Kline. Cast: Arthur Hill, David Wayne, James Olson, Kate Reid, Paula Kelly, George Mitchell. A research team attempting to isolate and destroy a mysterious microorganism gets caught within the facility's failsafe defense system. When the organism (called Andromeda) mutates into a passive form, the scientists must battle against time and the complex's dangerous laser protection capabilities in order to shut down the system before it blows everything apart. ¶ "When the bomb goes off there will be a thousand mutations. Andromeda will spread everywhere, they'll never be rid of it!" • In this film, the real menace turns out to be the highly complex mechanized facility whose defense system is built to deadly perfection ("It'll even bury our mistakes.").
Blades (1989; Troma) D: Thomas R. Rondinella. P: John P. Finegan. S: William R. Pace, Thomas R. Rondinella. C: James Hayman. Cast: Robert North, Jeremy Whelan, Victoria Scott, Holly Stevenson, William Towner, Peter Wray, Charlie Quinn.

This *Jaws* formula spoof features a "mauling, munching, marauding" industrial lawnmower which is terrorizing the Tall Grass country club, grinding up any golfer it can get its blades on. This machine menace to the golfing industry is blown apart when a golf ball struck by the club pro hits its motor. He did, in fact, yell "fore." ¶ "What are you gonna do pro, whack it to death with your putter?" • After the closing credits a short segment appears on the screen depicting a hedger turning on by itself. A caption above reads, "*Hedges*—Just when you thought it was safe to trim!"
Brainstorm (1983; MGM/United Artists) D/P: Douglas Trumbull. S: Robert Stitzel, Philip Frank Messina. C: Richard Yuricich. Cast: Christopher Walken, Natalie Wood, Louise Fletcher, Cliff Robertson. A brainstorm machine is developed which can record human sensations then replay them to anyone hooked into the machine. ¶ "Alex turns the whole thing over to some covert operation called the Brainstorm Project. He's taken my work and turned it into something bad." • Natalie Wood tragically

died (of drowning) during the filming of this picture. Instead of scrapping the entire project, the filmmakers decided to restructure the film around Ms. Wood.

The Flying Saucer (1950; Film Classics/Colonial) D/P/S: Mike Conrad. S: Howard Irving Young. C: Philip Tannura. Cast: Mikel Conrad, Pat Garrison, Hantz Von Teuffen, Lester Sharpe, Russel Hicks, Denver Pyle, Roy Engel, Frank Darien. A man is sent to Alaska to investigate the report of a flying saucer. He finds the saucer and its human inventor, as well as a group of communist agents after the incredible machine. ¶ Lobby posters for the film used a quote from *True* magazine saying: "The flying saucers are real! Out of the unknown comes a strange new terror!" • One of the picture's claims to fame was that it was partially financed by bingo winnings.

Kronos (1957) (see ALIENS—INVADERS ON EARTH: THE 50s). A gigantic energy-eating machine from outer space is thwarted by Jeff Morrow, who has a plane drop dust between its antenna terminals causing it to malfunction. The machine then begins to consume itself instead of outside forces.

The Lift (1983; Sigma Films; Netherlands) D/S: Dick Maas. P: Mathijs Van Heijningen. C: Marc Felperlaan. Cast: Huub Stapel, Willeke Van Ammelrooy, Josine van Dalsum, Piet Romer. An elevator, whose control board has been built with experimental biomechanical circuits, takes on a murderous mind of its own and wreaks havoc in an office building. An elevator repairman must go one-on-one with the malicious machine. ¶ "Take the stairs! Take the stairs! For God's sake, take the stairs!"—ad line. • Writer/director Dick Maas provided the film's musical score as well.

The Lost Missile (1958; United Artists) D: William Berke. P: Lee Gordon. S: John McPartland, Jerome Bixby. C: Kenneth Peach. Cast: Robert Loggia, Ellen Parker, Phillip Pine, Larry Kerr, Marilee Earle. Robert Loggia plays a young scientist trying to stop an unidentified missile orbiting the Earth with tremendous destructive powers. At the climax, he develops a counter-rocket which he launches at the malevolent missile (which seemingly has a mind of its own). ¶ "A weird invader ... turning oceans to steam ... melting mountains ... turning men and women white with the awesome, horrible way it *kills!!!*—ad line. • In some theaters, free shock tags were given out to patrons to allow them to be taken home by limousine in case they were stricken with a

temporary loss of consciousness and or power of speech due to shock. • Another unique gimmick involved the handing out of cotton gloves. "If you are a nail-biter ask usher for a pair of gloves to keep your nails covered while you see the thing from outer hell, *The Lost Missile!*"

Maximum Overdrive (1986) (see CARS AND VEHICULAR VILLAINS). A comet causes various machines to malfunction. Video machines flash and beep wildly, electric carving knives turn on their users, and soda machines violently spit out cans with deadly accuracy. The film's setting is a truck stop, where the huge, animated vehicles lay siege to a group of people holed up in the building.

Nightmares (1983) (see ANTHOLOGIES). One segment features a teen battling a video game which has taken on a life of its own and is able to project its violent graphics out into the arcade. ¶ "You are good Earthling, but not good enough. I am the Bishop of Battle, master of all I survey. I have 13 progressively harder levels. Try me if you dare—insert coin."

Pulse (1988) D/S: Paul Golding. P: Patricia Stallone. C: Peter Lyons Collister. Cast: Cliff DeYoung, Roxanne Hart, Joey Lawrence, Matthew Lawrence, Charles Tyner, Myron Healey. When a boy visits his father and stepmother in the summer, he sees the house next door destroyed and a man electrocuted by his own electrical appliances. It turns out that an evil energy force can control various machines such as TVs, microwaves, computers, and other electrical devices, transforming them into deadly weapons.

Runaway (1984; Tri-Star Pictures) D/S: Michael Crichton. P: Michael Rachmil. C: John A. Alonzo. Cast: Tom Selleck, Cynthia Rhodes, Gene Simmons, Stan Shaw, Kirstie Alley, Joey Cramer, G. W. Bailey. Set in the automated near future, a policeman assigned to malfunctioning "runaway" robots and machines discovers that a killer named Luther plans to use special microchips to turn machines into killers. Luther uses a variety of gadgets for murder and mayhem, including heat-seeking bullet missiles, and spider-like machines that inject acid. ¶ "You can't run away Ramsey, I'll find you. My little machines will find you wherever you go."

The Twonky (1953; United Artists) D/P/S: Arch Oboler. C: Joseph Biroc. Cast: Hans Conried, Billy Lynn, Janet Warren, Gloria Blondell, Ed Max, William Phipps. This comedic science fiction entry features a hen-pecked husband whose wife buys him an unwanted television set. This particular TV, however, is inhabited by an alien presence, enabling it to walk about on its wooden legs and to control people's minds. • Director Arch Oboler got his start writing radio dramas. He has authored over 800, which have been performed by such stars as James Cagney, Bette Davis, and Ronald Colman. • According to executive producer Sid Pink, director Arch Oboler surrounded the production with an air of secrecy. "Not one member of the organization saw a complete script until after the picture was made and edited," claimed Pink (in an article he wrote for *Filmfax* #26). Oboler took this secrecy to an extreme. "We discovered later," continued Pink, "that Arch Oboler intended to make it a comedy and felt it would be much more intriguing if his actors didn't know about it. Consequently, all the actors played it literally for horror, *per* the original short story." • *The Twonky* is based on the terrifying short story by Henry Kuttner.

The Video Dead (1987) (see ZOMBIES). An evil television set has the ability to turn itself on and show a film called "Zombie Blood Nightmare." The zombies in the film break out of the TV set and go on a bloody rampage.

Videodrome (1982; Filmplan International; Canada) D/S: David Cronenberg. P: Claude Heroux. C: Mark Irwin. Cast: James Woods, Deborah Harry, Sonja Smits, Peter Dvorsky, Les Carlson. James Woods is the head of a small fringe TV station, which pirates a bizarre program called "Videodrome." "Videodrome" is not some simple sitcom, however — it is a program which shows real-life torture, mutilation, and death. It also causes physical and mental changes in its viewers. Woods, under the spell of Videodrome, eventually develops a grisly new orifice in his stomach, into which living videotapes that program his actions are inserted. • Actress Deborah Harry is popularly known as the rock star, "Blondie."

Mad Scientists

(*See also* Brains; Frankenstein's Monster; Invisibility; [Dr.] Jekyll and Family; Shrinkage)

This section pertains to people of science (whether they be professors, doctors, or inventors) who instigate some fantastic result or effect on themselves, other people, or other things. Although there are virtually thousands of films that contain a scientist or two, we've included only those movies which feature them as an integral element of the plot.

The theme of "Man Meddling in Things He Should Leave Alone" is a popular one — a cinematic backlash against the technological advancements of science. Along with our more comfortable and sophisticated lifestyle provided by scientific and technological breakthroughs, we now live with the possibility of world scale nuclear devastation, various bacteriological horrors, and computers that come close to thinking on their own. These fears have spawned a distrust of science (at least at a subconscious level), which filmmakers have been quick to exploit.

Many of the obsessed scientists featured here began in the service of a noble cause, but their methods were unsound, involving unethical practices like human experimentation and even murder to achieve their results.

Several themes have developed in the mad scientist subgenre. For example, the horrific side effects of an untested serum have often been a juicy plot for filmmakers, leaving the door wide open for whatever means of monster or menace the writers and directors could imagine.

Another trend in the mad scientist subgenre is the medical offshoot in which a doctor's obsession with healing leads to murder, madness, and or mayhem. For instance, a whole slew of films revolve around a mad surgeon's compulsion to restore the face of a disfigured wife, daughter, girlfriend, etc. by means of grafting the skin from an innocent victim onto the scarred visage of his loved one (with the poetic, yet gruesome *Eyes Without a Face* (1959) being one of the earliest and best examples).

Some scientists are popular enough to have their own series and or subgenres. See also BRAINS, FRANKENSTEIN'S MONSTER, INVISIBILITY, [DR.] JEKYLL AND FAMILY, and SHRINKAGE for more featured mad scientists.

The Ape (1940) (see APES AND MONKEYS). Boris Karloff plays the likable but slightly mad Dr. Adrian, who is so obsessed with finding a cure for polio that he resorts to murder to obtain the human spinal fluid he needs (donning the skin of an escaped circus gorilla and killing the local undesirables for their spinal fluid — making it appear as if an ape were responsible).

The Ape Man (1943) (see APES AND MONKEYS). Mad scientist Bela Lugosi has unwisely been experimenting on himself using gorilla spinal fluid and finds he must obtain human spinal fluid periodically or revert to a half-man, half-ape creature.

The Astro-Zombies (1968) (see ZOMBIES) (also *Space Vampires* [video title]). John Carradine plays a mad scientist named Dr. DeMarco, who is trying to build a race of artificial men by creating zombies in his basement lab. The "zombies" look like actors wearing dime store skull masks who run about holding cheap flashlights to their heads in order to recharge themselves.

Atom Age Vampire (1961; Topaz; Italy) D: Anton Giulio Majano, Richard McNamara (English version). P: Mario Bava. S: Anton Giulio Majano, Piero Monviso, Gino de Sanctis, Alberto Bevilacqua, John Hart (English version). C: Aldo Giordano. Cast: Alberto Lupo, Susanne Loret, Sergio Fantoni, Roberto Bertea, Franca Parisi, Andrea Scotti. A mad doctor attempts to restore the scarred face of the woman he loves by killing women and removing their glands. He also makes use of a serum which transforms him into a pasty-faced monster, allowing him to go out and acquire his "materials" without being recognized. Despite the title, no vampires appear. ¶ "You've been impressed by the re-occurring factor in these cases of the wound from the throat to the sternum — the obsession of a vindictive minded man who has been poisoned or disfigured forever by atomic radiation. One might even say, a vampire of the atom age who wants to recover."

The Awful Dr. Orloff (1962; Sigma III Corporation; Spain/France) D/S: Jesus Franco. P: Serge Newman, Leo Lax. C: God-fredo Pacheco. Cast: Howard Vernon, Diana Lorys, Riccardo Vale, Conrado Sanmartin, Perla Cristal. A mad surgeon and his stone-faced assistant stalk and kill young females for the skin needed to restore his disfigured daughter's face. • This seminal European trendsetter spawned four sequels.

Beast of Blood (1970) (see BRAINS — LIVING HEADS) (also *Beast of the Dead*). This sequel to *The Mad Doctor of Blood Island* (1969) features mad scientist Dr. Lorca keeping the living head of the monster alive on a table.

Beast of Yucca Flats (1961; Crown International) D/S: Coleman Francis. P: Anthony Cardoza. C: John Cagle. Cast: Tor Johnson, Douglas Mellor, Barbara Francis, Bing Stafford, Larry Aten, Linda Beilema. A top scientist escapes from behind the Iron Curtain with secret Russian rocket information. Communist agents follow him and run his car off the highway near an H-bomb testing site. A gun battle triggers an explosion which kills the agents and transforms the scientist into the hulking title Beast (Tor Johnson). After some vicious acts of mayhem involving a married couple, the beast is cornered on a plateau and killed by police gunfire. ¶ "A man runs. Somebody shoots at him" — narration. • The film was shot near Yucca Flats, Nevada, with temperatures soaring as high as 126 degrees. Apparently, the cast and crew could only work for short intervals and portable electric power units were brought in to cool off camping trailers during rest periods. • The film's producer, Tony Cardoza, plays a communist agent in the movie.

Before I Hang (1940; Columbia) D: Nick Grinde. P: Wallace McDonald. S: Robert D. Andrews. C: Benjamin Kline. Cast: Boris Karloff, Evelyn Keyes, Bruce Bennett, Edward Van Sloan, Ben Taggart, Pedro de Cordoba, Wright Kramer, Bertram Marburgh, Don Beddoe, Robert Fiske. Boris Karloff plays the kindly scientist Dr. Garth, who is sentenced to die for a "mercy killing." Aided by the prison doctor, he continues his important research in retarding the aging process as he waits to be executed. Perfecting his serum, he injects himself with the blood of a hanged murderer, and it works! Garth is pardoned, but the murderer's blood has contaminated his own and he periodically transforms into a savage killer himself. ¶ "It is true I am a murderer in the eyes of the law, but in my own heart I am innocent." • This is the third in Karloff's "mad doctor" series for Columbia begun with *The Man They Could Not Hang* (1939). Next there was *The Devil Commands* (1941).

Bela Lugosi Meets a Brooklyn Gorilla (1952) (see APES AND MONKEYS) (also *The Boys from Brooklyn; The Monster Meets the Girl*). On a tropical island, the mad Dr. Zabor (Bela Lugosi) uses his serum to turn people into gorillas.

Black Dragons (1942; Monogram) D: William Nigh. P: Sam Katzman, Jack Dietz. S: Harvey Gates. C: Art Reed. Cast: Bela Lugosi, Joan Barclay, Clayton Moore, George Pembroke, Robert Frazer, Stanford Jolley, Bob Fiske, Kenneth Harlan. An evil mad doctor (Bela Lugosi) transforms six Japanese agents into six American industrialists via plastic surgery. • The film's scenario was partly inspired by a real-life murderous Japanese secret society called "Black Dragon." • According to actor Stanford Jolley, who played the leader of the Black Dragons, the atmosphere on the set was less than ideal: "It was less than a two-week shooting schedule. Dialogue was being rewritten daily and it was hectic. I remember Lugosi and I didn't get along well at all, nor did he get along smoothly with any of his co-workers" (from *The Films of Bela Lugosi,* by Richard Bojarski).

The Black Sleep (1956; United Artists) D: Reginald LeBorg. P: Howard W. Koch. S: John C. Higgins. C: Gordon Avil. Cast: Basil Rathbone, Herbert Rudley, Laurie Monroe, Akim Tamiroff, Bela Lugosi, Lon Chaney, Jr., John Carradine, Tor Johnson, Sally Yarnell. A brain surgeon (Basil Rathbone) uses the "black sleep" drug to smuggle out an imprisoned colleague (whom he himself had framed) to help with his experiments that may someday revive his comatose wife. Rathbone's numerous failures on test subjects (which has created a wide variety of malformed individuals locked in his cellar) eventually proves to be his undoing as they break out and take revenge on the mad surgeon. ¶ "I would put my knife into the brains of a hundred men, a thousand, and destroy them all ... if I could restore her to me for only one day." • "Even if a woman's brain is smaller than a man's, I'm sure the area that controls her tongue must be much larger." Lines like these could

only have originated in the 1950s! • Bela Lugosi, in one of the last legitimate roles of his career, was not pleased with his small, non-speaking part. The once-renowned actor complained: "There is Basil Rathbone playing my part. I used to be the big cheese. Now I'm playing just a dumb part." Lugosi and Lon Chaney, Jr., almost came to blows during filming over their bitter rivalry as actors. • The "black sleep" drug was used like an anesthetic and its effect was to make one appear dead.

The Blood Beast Terror (1967) (see BUG-PEOPLE) (also *The Vampire Beast Craves Blood*). A mad scientist seeks to create a giant moth in order to curtail the bloodlust of his moth-monster daughter, a girl who occasionally transforms into a giant deaths-head moth.

The Blood Rose (1969; Allied Artists; France) D: Claude Mulot. P: Edgar Oppenheimer. S: Claude Mulot, Edgar Oppenheimer, Jean Carriaga. Cast: Howard Vernon, Frédéric Lansac, Anny Duperey, Elizabeth Teissier. In another doctor-murders-to-restore-the-face-of-a-disfigured-woman plot (à la *Eyes Without a Face,* 1959), a wealthy painter blackmails a disgraced plastic surgeon into restoring his wife's horribly burned face. To accomplish this, women are needed to "donate" their faces for the procedure.

The Body Shop (1974; Studio 1) (also *Dr. Gore*). D/P/S: J. G. Patterson, Jr. C: W. Martin Hill. Cast: Don Brandon, Jenny Driggers, Roy Mehaffey, Linda Fiele, Jan Benfield, Janine Aber, Candy Furr, Vickie O'Neal. A mad scientist loses his wife and vows to make himself the perfect mate. With the help of his hunchback assistant, this poverty-row Frankenstein kills various girls for their choicest body parts and assembles his perfect woman. He brings her to life, teaches her only what he wants her to know, but loses her when she discovers there are other men in the world ("I'm a woman and you're a man" is her favorite greeting to strangers she meets). This hopelessly amateurish and inept gore movie ends with the scientist wasting away in prison while his bikini-clad creation hitches a ride with another stranger. ¶ Closing theme song sung to the tune of "Sugar and Spice": "With a scientific plan/ an arm or a hand/ may be joined to a beautiful torso/ when sewn all together/ the perfect cadaver/ will be just the right girl only more so." • No-budget filmmaker J. G. (Pat) Patterson died in 1974, soon after completing this film. • *The Body Shop* was filmed in Milwaukee.

The Boogie Man Will Get You (1942; Columbia) D: Lew Landers. P: Colbert Clark. S: Edwin Blum. C: Henry Freulich. Cast: Boris Karloff, Peter Lorre, Maxie Rosenbloom, Larry Parks, (Miss) Jeff Donnell. In the sleepy town of "Jinxville," Boris Karloff plays Professor Billings ("doctor of biochemistry at Century College — before it went under"), who is attempting to aid the war effort by creating a race of supermen in this mad-doctor farce. ¶ "I'm merely toying with a few physiodynamics — shaking the unshakable laws of existence so to speak." • At the time, Karloff was enjoying a huge success on Broadway in "Arsenic and Old Lace," calling it "the happiest role of my life." Columbia had to obtain permission from the play's producers to borrow Karloff, and the studio deliberately fashioned the picture to capitalize on the play's current success. • This mad scientist spoof was Karloff's fifth and final "mad doctor" picture for Columbia, and fulfilled his commitment to that studio.

The Bowery Boys Meet the Monsters (1954; Allied Artists) D: Edward Bernds. P: Ben Schwalb. S: Ellwood Ullman, Edward Bernds. C: Harry Neumann. Cast: Leo Gorcey, Huntz Hall, Lloyd Corrigan, Ellen Corby, John Dehner, Laura Mason, Bernard Gorcey, Paul Wexler. The boys encounter a mad scientist in a spooky old house full of monsters, including a robot, a vampire, a gorilla, and a dangerous plant. Huntz Hall even gets turned into a hairy monster in this madcap monster spoof. • The Bowery Boys were originally known as the Dead End Kids and sometimes the East Side Kids. The director, Edward Bernds, frequently worked with another movie comedy team — The Three Stooges. • Ed Bernds stated in an interview with Ted Okuda, "*Filmfax* #9, that this film "was the best money-maker of them all. Something about the juxtaposition of the Bowery Boys and a bunch of monsters appealed to audiences."

The Boys from Brazil (1978; 20th Century-Fox) D: Franklin J. Schaffer. P: Martin Richards, Stanley O'Toole. S: Heywood Gould. C: Henri Decaë. Cast: Gregory Peck, Laurence Olivier, James Mason, Lilli Palmer, Denholm Elliott, Uta Hagen, Steven Guttenberg, Anne Meara, Michael Gough. A sinister Nazi scientist intends to revive the new Third Reich by cloning numerous young Hitlers throughout the world. Eventually the mad Dr. Mengele is dispatched by one of the young boys' dogs. • Laurence Olivier received an Academy Award nomination for his role as the Jewish Nazi-hunter uncovering the plot. Composer Jerry Goldsmith (*Planet of the Apes,* 1968; *The Omen,* 1976) was also nominated for his musical contribution. • Gregory's Peck's character, Dr. Mengele, is patterned after a real-life Nazi known as "The Angel of Death" at the Auschwitz concentration camp.

Bride of Re-Animator (1990) (see ZOMBIES). In this gory, tongue-in-cheek sequel to *Re-Animator,* mad scientist Herbert West is back, working at a hospital during the day and experimenting with stolen body parts at night, creating all manner of warped, freakish creatures with his reanimation serum. With these parts he decides to create a new life — a woman (à la Dr. Frankenstein) — but is interrupted in his moment of triumph by several reanimated zombies left over from the first movie, who have escaped from the psychiatric unit at the hospital, and are led by the reanimated (and annoyed) disembodied head of Dr. Hill (again from the original film).

Bride of the Monster (1956; Realart) (also *Bride of the Atom*). D/P: Ed Wood, Jr. S: Ed Wood, Jr., Alex Gordon. C: William Thompson. Cast: Bela Lugosi, Tor Johnson, Loretta King, Tony McCoy, Harvey B. Dunn, Paul Marco, Billy Benedict. Bela Lugosi plays a mad scientist who uses a super-ray to turn men into super-beings. ¶ "I was classified a madman, a charlatan, outlawed in the world of science which previously had honored me as a genius. Now, here in this forsaken jungle hell, I have proven that I am alright!" • Paul Marco, actor and friend of Ed Wood, said in a *Filmfax* #6 interview: "There's so much written about Ed Wood ... they have him speaking through a megaphone, they have him dressed up in women's clothes behind the camera. That's all completely false.... He loved *Bride* and really wanted to direct it. In fact, that was his favorite picture because it showed a lot of direction, and it was not piecework like *Plan 9.*" • The little octopus monster that resides in the swamp and eventually kills Lugosi in the finale was actually an old left-over prop from a John Wayne film called *Wake of the Red Witch* (1948). Apparently Wood simply snuck into the studio, found the deflated cephalopod, and walked out with it without asking for permission. • Paul Marco said of Bela Lugosi in Tom Weaver's *Interviews with B Science Fiction and Horror Movie Makers:* "I remember that he had this tremendous speech to deliver to George Becwar, lots of dialogue ... Bela was not sickly, but he was tired, and not 100 percent well. So we put all his dialogue on cue cards.... Then came time to shoot ... Ed was escorting him to the sofa where he was going to play the scene when suddenly Bela came out with, 'Oh, take those cards away. I'm going to do it!' By this time, the picture was running short on time and money, and allowing Bela to try it without benefit of cue cards seemed somewhat risky.... Well, he did it, without even looking at the cards, and the whole crew burst into applause and told him how great it was." • Actor Tor Johnson, whom Bela Lugosi told in the film, "You will be soon as big as a giant ... or, like all the others — dead," was already "big as a giant," weighing in at nearly 350 pounds.

Captive Wild Woman (1943) (see APES AND MONKEYS). Through gland transplants, mad scientist John Carradine turns an ape into a beautiful woman (who, when aroused, occasionally reverts back to bestial form and wreaks havoc). ¶ "I watched a brain that once was fine and brilliant begin to warp, and tamper with things that no man or woman should ever touch."

Castle of the Creeping Flesh (1967; Aquila Film Enterprises; W. Germany) (also *Castle of Bloody Lust; The Castle of Unholy Desires*). D: Percy G. Parker (Adrian Hoven). P: Pier A. Caminneci. S: Percy G. Parker, Eric Martin Schnitzler. C: Jorge Herrero, Franz Hofer. Cast: Janine Reynaud, Howard Vernon, Michael Lemoine, Elvira Berndorff, Claudia Butenuth, Jan Hendricks, Pier A. Caminneci, Vladimir Medar. A small group of hedonistic partygoers, headed by a brutal baron (Michael Lemoine), stumble into the castle of the reclusive Count von Saxon. The Count is trying to revive his dead daughter through some kind of mad medical operation and chooses one of the visiting girls as an unwilling donor. ¶ "Life and death — *they* are alike. But there is also love. Love creates life; love has a right to kill. But he who kills for revenge will be cursed." • This unpleasant import (filled with real shots of actual open-heart surgery) was made by the same man (Adrian Hoven) who brought us the mean-spirited *Mark of the Devil* (1969) and *Mark of the Devil 2* (1972). • Howard Vernon, who plays Count von Saxon, was no stranger to the role of mad medico, having previously played Dr. Orloff, a surgeon trying to restore the face of his disfigured daughter in *The Awful Dr. Orloff* (1962).

Castle of the Living Dead (1964; Woolner; Italy/France) (also *Castles of the Dead; Castle of Horror*). D: Herbert Wise (Lu-

ciano Ricci). P: Paul Maslansky. S: Warren Kiefer, Michael Reeves. C: Aldo Tonti. Cast: Christopher Lee, Gaia Germani, Philippe Leroy, Jacques Stanislawski, Mirko Valentin, Donald Sutherland. A group of traveling performers arrive at the castle of Count Drago (Christopher Lee), a scientist who is experimenting with a drug that turns people into motionless figures (in order to "preserve" their beauty). ¶ "Beware the castle of the living dead, I see all that lies ahead. Some will live and some will die, before tomorrow's sun is high!" • Though direction was credited to Herbert Wise (Luciano Ricci's pseudonym) for quota reasons, the picture was actually directed by co-screenwriter Warren Keifer. Keifer's co-writer, Michael Reeves, also directed some of the film's end scenes. Reeves later went on to direct his own films, including the well-thought-of *The Conqueror Worm* (1968). • Donald Sutherland made his screen debut in this film, not in one role but in two (and of both sexes no less) — as a local gendarme and a witch-like old crone.

Chopper Chicks in Zombie Town (1989) (see ZOMBIE FLESH EATERS). A mad scientist, posing as a small-town moritician, has been killing off the townspeople and turning them into walking zombies to mine radioactive materials. It's up to a gang of all-girl motorcyclists to save the town from the escaped flesh-eating ghouls. ¶ "I didn't do it for science and I didn't do it for glory; I'm just *me!*"

The Corpse Vanishes (1942; Monogram) (also *The Case of the Missing Brides*). D: Wallace Fox. P: Sam Katzman, Jack Dietz. S: Harvey H. Gates. C: Art Reed. Cast: Bela Lugosi, Joan Barclay, Tristram Coffin, Minerva Urecal, Angelo Rossitto, Elizabeth Russell, Luana Walters, Frank Moran. A mad botanist (Bela Lugosi) uses orchids to poison newlywed victims and then abducts them for glandular experiments that will keep his 80-year-old wife looking young. ¶ "Just forget about all that silly nonsense about those brides dropping dead." • Actor Tristram Coffin stated (in *Filmfax* #15), "Bela Lugosi was a very unusual man who kept to himself a great deal ... Lugosi and Elizabeth Russell were required to sleep in caskets instead of beds ... she refused to get in it. She was fearful of it, you know. Eventually they had to use a double."

Corruption (1968; Columbia; U.K.) D: Robert Hartford-Davies. P: Peter Newbrook. S: Donald Ford, Derek Ford. C: Peter Newbrook. Cast: Peter Cushing, Sue Lloyd, Noel Trevarthen, Kate O'Mara,

David Lodge, Anthony Booth. Peter Cushing plays a surgeon who decapitates young women in order to graft their skin onto the disfigured face of his fiancée. Near the end, the laser beam he uses in his experiments goes out of control and kills some unwanted visitors, and then the whole story is fobbed off as a terrible nightmare. • *Corruption* employed the business-generating gimmick of imposing a ban on women without escorts. As the radio promotional spots said: "*Corruption* is not a woman's picture; therefore, no woman will be admitted alone to see this supershocker."

Creator (1985) D: Ivan Passer. P: Stephen Friedman. S: Jeremy Leven. Cast: Peter O'Toole, Mariel Hemingway, Vincent Spano, Virginia Madsen, David Ogden Stiers. A lonely biologist decides to create a being in the form of his dead wife, but falls in love with a sexy assistant instead.

Creature of the Walking Dead (1965) (see ZOMBIES). A mad doctor discovers how to retain his youth by extracting a special fluid from young girls. He is found out, however, and hanged. But many years later his descendant, who happens to look exactly like him, digs him up and brings him back to life. Soon the evil ancestor imprisons his well-meaning descendant and menaces his fiancée.

Creature with the Atom Brain (1955) (see ZOMBIES). A mad scientist uses atomic energy to create robot-like zombies. The gangster who financed the work sends these atom-powered living-dead creatures out to murder his rivals.

The Creeper (1948) (see CAT-PEOPLE). A mad scientist, experimenting with a special breed of West Indian cats, has developed a serum which he injects into himself to transform his hands into vicious cat-like paws, which he uses to murder his enemies. • Eduardo Ciannelli, who plays the role of sinister scientist, actually studied medicine and received an M.D. degree before turning to acting.

Curse of the Fly (1965; 20th Century–Fox) D: Don Sharp. P: Robert L. Lippert, Jack Parsons. S: Harry Spalding. C: Basil Emmott. Cast: Brian Donlevy, George Baker, Carole Gray, Michael Graham, Rachel Kempson, Jeremy Wilkins. A scientist, tampering with a matter-transmission device, creates an assortment of man-mutants, including a man who's been crossed with a guinea pig(!). • This third and final film in the "Fly" series is a sequel in name only, for the only connection to the first two "Fly" movies (*The Fly* and *Return of the Fly*)

is the use of the "Delambre" family name and the idea of matter transmission. • Originally, 20th Century-Fox offered the role of the ill-fated scientist to Claude Rains, but the 75-year-old actor had to turn down the part due to his failing health, and Brian Donlevy (of the "Quatermass" films) won the role.

Curse of the Swamp Creature (1966) (see FISH-PEOPLE). A mad scientist creates fish-monsters in the Florida Everglades. He even uses his wife in one of the experiments. ¶ "You will obey all my commands. I am your master. You will live when I say live, and you will die when I say die."

Darkman (1990; Universal) D: Sam Raimi. P: Robert Tapert. S: Chuck Pfarrer, Sam Raimi, Ivan Raimi, Daniel Goldin, Joshua Goldin. C: Bill Pope. Cast: Liam Neeson, Frances McDormand, Colin Friels, Larry Drake. A scientist is turned into the horribly disfigured, phantom-like creature known as "Darkman" after a group of gangsters cause an "accident." He then sets out to take revenge on those responsible. He uses his scientific knowledge to create new faces and impersonate his enemies. ¶ "Who's the real monster? I'm a man who destroys to build something better whereas you, you destroy for revenge" — the bad guy confronting Darkman. • The grotesque "Darkman" makeup was provided by Tony Gardner and Larry Hamlin.

Day of the Dead (1985) (see ZOMBIE FLESH EATERS). In this third (and last to date) film in Romero's "Living Dead" series, a rather eccentric mad doctor, holed up with some military personnel in an underground complex, conducts experiments in domesticating the flesh-eating ghouls.

Dead Heat (1988) (see ZOMBIES). Two cops run afoul of a mad scientist and his zombie "resurrection machine" in this buddy-cop-zombie-horror-comedy.

Dead Pit (1989) (see ZOMBIE FLESH EATERS). Mad Dr. Colin Ramsey is conducting inhuman experiments on mental patients in a hidden basement laboratory beneath the "State Institution for the Mentally Ill." A colleague discovers his secret and is forced to kill him and seal up the unholy place. Twenty years later, an earthquake opens up the secret lab and the now-zombified doctor is back at work again, turning patients and staff alike into brain-hungry zombies. ¶ Horrified colleague: "My God, you're a doctor. You're supposed to be *saving* lives!" Mad doctor: "I've done life, now I'm doing death."

Death Warmed Up (1984) (see ZOMBIES).

Mad medico Dr. Acher Howell creates a batch of scientific zombies at his remote Trans-Cranial Applications Hospital in this new-wave import from New Zealand. ¶ "Now Man is back on the brink of his immortality. For this to succeed, we have to make a commitment to challenge—to *risk*, and be willing to pay the price of taking those risks by going further than Man has ever dreamt of!"

Deep Space (1986; Trans World Entertainment) D: Fred Olen Ray. P: Alan Amiel, Fred Olen Ray. S: Fred Olen Ray, T. L. Lankford. C: Gary Graver. Cast: Charles Napier, Ann Turkel, Ron Glass, Julie Newmar, Bo Svenson, James Booth, Norman Burton, Anthony Eisley, Michael Forest, Peter Palmer, Elizabeth Brooks. A sinister scientist, presiding over a clandestine military-funded operation searching for the "ultimate weapon," develops a huge vicious *Alien*-like creature that shoots out organic tentacles from its body to drag its screaming victims to its waiting jaws. The killer organism was bred in space, but something went wrong, causing the spacelab to crash in Charles Napier's precinct. Napier plays a tough-guy cop who bucks bureaucracy and the Federal agency bad buys to go one-on-one with the vicious beastie. ¶ "I'm gonna kick some monster ass." • Director Fred Olen Ray told *HorrorFan* #2: "[The producers] actually tried to change the plot of this film after we made it. It was originally a 'monster from space' picture, it had nothing to do with government. It was just a neat little compact story. After it was all shot and edited, they decided they wanted a 'government project' theme. They insisted that we shoot seven more days!"

The Devil Bat (1941) (see BATS) (also *Killer Bats*). Bela Lugosi plays the disgruntled Dr. Carruthers, a mad scientist working for a perfume manufacturer and raising enlarged killer bats in his off hours. He sends his killer friends out to murder all those he feels have wronged him.

The Devil Commands (1941; Columbia) D: Edward Dmytryk. P: Wallace MacDonald. S: Robert D. Andrews, Milton Gunzburg. Cast: Boris Karloff, Amanda Duff, Anne Revere, Richard Fiske, Ralph Penney. Boris Karloff is the unhinged scientist who attempts to contact his dead wife by using corpses hooked up to electrical machinery. ¶ "This is science, Mrs. Walters! There's nothing of the occult about it." • The picture was based on a William Sloane story entitled, "The Edge of Running Water." The film was originally to be called *The Devil Says No.* • *The Devil Commands* was made on a very low budget and was shot almost entirely inside the studio. The opening shot of the scientist's house on the cliff was merely a model.

The Devil's Commandment (1956) (see BATHORY, ELIZABETH: THE BLOODY COUNTESS) (also *Lust of the Vampires*). This Italian update of the Elizabeth Bathory legend features a mad doctor in Paris who drains the blood of young virgins to keep his beloved Countess eternally young.

The Diabolical Dr. Z (1965; France/W. Germany) D: Henri Baum (Jesus Franco). P: Serge Silberman, Michel Safra. S: Jesus Franco, Jean-Claude Carrière. C: Alejandro Ulloa. Cast: Howard Vernon, Mabel Karr, Estella Blain, Guy Mairesse, Fernando Montes, Antonio J. Escribano. Dr. Zimmer has developed a bizarre machine which blends acupuncture and hypnosis to turn people into obedient slaves. He dies after being ridiculed by the medical authorities and his maniacal daughter avenges his humiliation by using his machine to transform an exotic dancer into an angel of death with deadly, curare-tipped fingernails. ¶ "Thanks to me, all the killers, all the abnormal, all the sadists, all the maniacs could be transmuted into wise and good persons"—Dr. Z explaining the benefits of his mind-control machine.

Dr. Blood's Coffin (1961; United Artists; U.K.) D: Sidney J. Furie. P: George Fowler. S: Jerry Juran. C: Stephen Dade. Cast: Kieron Moore, Hazel Court, Ian Hunter, Fred Johnson, Gerald C. Lawson, Kenneth J. Warren, Paul Stockman. Set mainly in the underground mines of Cornwall, a mad biochemist kills the locals for their hearts which he intends to use in experiments to revive the dead. • Much of *Dr. Blood's Coffin* was shot on location in a cave in Cornwall, England.

Dr. Caligari (1989; Steiner Films) D: Stephen Sayadian. P: Joseph F. Robertson. S: Jerry Stahl, Stephen Sayadian. C: Ladi Von Jansky. Cast: Madeleine Reynal, Fox Harris, Jennifer Balgobin, Laura Albert, Gene Zerna, Barry Phillips, David Parry, John Durbin. The granddaughter of the original Dr. Caligari is performing mad experiments (involving the transference of "glandular extracts") on her charges at the "Caligari Asylum" in this bizarre day-glow art film. ¶ "She's no longer a research doctor, she's a flat-out sadist!" • Director Stephen Sayadian *(Cafe Flesh)* commented on this bizarre update of the 1919 classic in the June, 1991, issue of *Cinefantastique*: "I wanted to update it with an S&M dominating woman in charge. The idea was to capture the spirit of the original but not to use a little old man. I wanted an intense female instead." • *Dr. Caligari* was shot in 20 days, using only interiors, for a budget "well under half a million dollars."

Dr. Orloff's Monster (1964; AIP-TV; Spain) D: Jesus Franco. S: Jesus Franco, Nick Frank. Cast José Rubio, Agnes Spaak. This first sequel to *The Awful Dr. Orloff* (1962) features the mad Dr. Orloff utilizing a human robot for murder.

Dr. Renault's Secret (1942) (see APES AND MONKEYS). Obsessed scientist George Zucco transforms an ape into a man (of sorts).

Dr. X (1932; First National Pictures) D: Michael Curtiz. S: Robert Tasker, Earl Baldwin. C: Ray Rennahan, Richard Tower. Cast: Lee Tracy, Lionel Atwill, Fay Wray, Preston Foster, John Wray, Harry Beresford, Arthur Edmund Carewe, Leila Bennett. A cannibalistic fiend who kills during the full moon is suspected to be one of the members of Dr. Xavier's medical college. The culprit turns out to be a mad one-armed professor who makes a new limb out of his experimental synthetic flesh. ¶ "That's what I needed, living flesh from humans for my experiments!" • This film was one of the first horror features to utilize the two-color technicolor process. Its success persuaded Warner Bros. to follow it up with another color horror film, *The Mystery of the Wax Museum*, the next year, again starring Lionel Atwill. • In 1939, a film called *The Return of Dr. X* was made starring Humphrey Bogart, but the storyline has absolutely nothing to do with this picture. • Lionel Atwill was probably the screen's most effective mad doctor, a character type he excelled at throughout the 1930s and 40s. Atwill was born in Croydon, England, in 1885, five miles from where Boris Karloff was born. When he was a teenager he had aspirations of becoming a real-life doctor until he found stage acting too fascinating to give up. *Dr. X* was the first horror film he ever played in, and it was also a horror first for another great genre star, Fay Wray, who was later immortalized by starring alongside *King Kong* (1933).

Electronic Monster (1958; Columbia) (also *Escapement*). D: Montgomery Tully. P: Alec C. Snowden. S: Charles Eric Maine, J. MacLaren-Ross. C: Bert Mason, Teddy Catford. Cast: Rod Cameron, Mary Murphy, Meredith Edwards, Peter Illing, Carl Jaffe. The head of a clinic (and a Nazi sympa-

thizer) uses a doctor's dream machine to control and brainwash patients.

Embryo (1976; Cine Artists) D: Ralph Nelson. P: Anita Doohan, Arnold H. Orgalini. S: Anita Doohan, Jack W. Thomas. C: Fred Koenekamp. Cast: Rock Hudson, Diane Ladd, Barbara Carrera, Roddy McDowall, Ann Schedeen, John Elerick. A scientist (Rock Hudson), looking for the perfect woman, manages to grow Barbara Carrera in his laboratory in four a half weeks. His devoted creation eventually withers and dies at the climax after a fatal injection. • Famous behavioral scientist Dr. Joyce Brothers makes a brief appearance in the film. • Diane Ladd, who plays Rock Hudson's jealous housekeeper, was fresh from an Oscar-nominated supporting performance in *Alice Doesn't Live Here Anymore* (1975). Her first husband was actor Bruce Dern, with whom she co-starred in Roger Corman's Hell's Angels tribute, *The Wild Angels* (1966).

Evil Town (1987; Trans World Entertainment) D: Edward Collins, Peter S. Traynor, Larry Spiegel, Mardi Rustam. P: Peter S. Traynor, William D. Sklar. S: Larry Spiegel, Richard Benson. C: Bill Mann, Bob Ioniccio. Cast: James Keach, Michele Marsh, Doria Cook, Robert Walker, Dean Jagger, Keith Hefner, Greg Finley, Lurene Tuttle, Regis Toomey. Dean Jagger plays a mad scientist trying to find the secret of eternal youth via the pituitary gland. For this he needs frequent human subjects and donors, which are supplied by the inhabitants of the small town he lives in.

Eyes Without a Face (1959; Lopert/ United Artists; France/Italy) (also *Horror Chamber of Dr. Faustus*). D: Georges Franju. P: Jules Borkon. S: Georges Franju, Jean Redon, Claude Sautet, Pierre Boileau, Thomas Narcejac. C: Eugen Shufftan. Cast: Pierre Brasseur, Alida Valli, Edith Scob, François Guerin, Juliette Mayniel, Alexandre Rignault. A mad doctor makes countless attempts to graft the faces of innocent victims upon the disfigured visage of his daughter. All of his experiments fail and, in the end, the daughter, grief-stricken over what her father has done, sets the household dogs upon him and wanders off into the night.

Face of Marble (1946; Monogram) D: William Beaudine. P: Jeffrey Bernard. S: Michael Jacoby. C: Harry Neumann. Cast: John Carradine, Claudia Drake, Robert Shayne, Maris Wrixon, Rosa Rey, Willie Best. John Carradine stars as a scientist attempting to bring the dead back to life. His experiments run askance of their purpose as the subjects (including the pet dog and his wife) become locked in a ghostly existence, able to walk through solid objects and drinking the blood of the living. ¶ "Science is supposed to have an answer for everything, but who can say where fact ends and superstition begins." • This was the last horror outing by that prolific poverty-row studio, Monogram.

Faceless (1988; René Chateau; France/Spain) D: Jesus Franco. P: René Chateau. S: Pierre Ripert, Fred Castle, Jean Nazarin. C: Maurice Fellous. Cast: Helmut Berger, Brigitte Lahaie, Chris Mitchum, Telly Savalas, Stephane Audran, Christiane Jean, Anton Diffring, Caroline Munro, Howard Vernon, Tilda Thamar, Florence Guerin. When the sister of a brilliant plastic surgeon named Dr. Flammond is horribly disfigured by acid, he sends for a Dr. Moser (a former Nazi S.S. doctor who experimented on humans during the war). The mad Dr. Moser has beautiful models and actresses kidnapped and brought to Flammand's clinic to be used as guinea pigs in his face-grafting experiments. ¶ "There are too many corpses in this clinic." • Director Jesus Franco returns to his roots with this film — his career took off with *The Awful Dr. Orloff* (1962), a film about a mad scientist trying to restore the face of his disfigured daughter. Howard Vernon, who played Dr. Orloff in the 1962 film, even makes a cameo appearance in this film as none other than Dr. Orloff himself, whom Dr. Flammond seeks out for a consultation. • *Faceless* was shot at an actual medical clinic which was undergoing renovation at the time. • Co-screenwriter Fred Castle is actually producer René Chateau. • Top-billed actress Brigitte Lahaie is France's reigning porn queen, here in a rare "straight" role. • In an unusual twist for this type of medical horror film, the operation is a success and Flammond's sister is given a new face. It ends with her and the two mad medicos toasting each other while the film's hero and heroine are walled up alive and left to die.

The Fear Chamber (1968; Azteca; U.S./Mexico) D: Juan Ibañez, Jack Hill. P: Louis Enrique Vergara. S: Jack Hill. C: Raul Dominguez, Austin McKinney. Cast: Boris Karloff, Julissa East, Santanon East, Carlos East, Isela Vega, Yerye Beirute, Eva Muller. Boris Karloff puts in a brief appearance as a scientist who uses a fear chamber to terrify young women before extracting their blood. The adrenalin-charged blood then goes to feed a living rock he has discovered (which is slowly trnsforming into a tentacled monster). Karloff's corrupt assistants attempt to use the rock to control the world. • This feature is one of four south-of-the-border films Boris Karloff made for producer Vergara. Karloff's scenes for all four movies were shot back to back in five weeks at a Hollywood soundstage. These features, which include *House of Evil, The Incredible Invasion* and *The Snake People,* were Boris' final film appearances. • A Walt Lee article appearing in *Famous Monsters* #125 quoted Karloff as saying, "This *Fear Chamber* is far out sci-fi. I have mountains of dialogue; my word! is there mountains to memorize! And I haven't the slightest idea what I'm saying."

Flatliners (1990; Stonebridge Entertainment/Columbia Pictures) D: Joel Schumacher. P: Michael Douglas, Rick Bieber. S: Peter Filardi. C: Jan de Bont. Cast: Kiefer Sutherland, Julia Roberts, Kevin Bacon, William Baldwin, Oliver Platt. A group of brilliant young medical students attempt to find out if there's anything after death by conducting experiments in which they simulate death and are brought back to life. Strange things happen to them afterwards, for somehow their deepest guilt has been given life and manifests itself in hallucinations *and* in physical reality. ¶ "We experienced death. Somehow we brought our sins back with us ... and they're pissed." • The film's title comes from the label the students give their death experiences — "flatlining," named for when the EKG reading becomes a flat line, signifying death.

The Flesh Eaters (1964) (see SEA MONSTERS). Martin Kosleck stars as a mad scientist creating flesh-eating bacteria on a remote island.

Flesh Feast (1970; Cine World Corporation; Canada) D: Brad F. Ginter. P: Veronica Lake, Brad F. Ginter. S: Brad F. Ginter, Thomas Casey. C: Thomas Casey. Cast: Veronica Lake, Phil Philbin, Martha Mischon, Heather Hughes, Yanka Mann, Dian Wilhite. This time it is a female scientist fresh from the asylum who aspires to restore youth to the aged. Her treatments involve the use of maggots which feast on faces, and one of her subjects is no less than Adolf Hitler himself. ¶ "Creeping, Crawling, Flesh-Eating Maggots!" — less-than-subtle ad line. • Veronica Lake (born Constance Frances Marie Ockelman) was a beautiful blonde of the 1940s who rocketed to stardom alongside Alan Ladd in the classic 40s films, *This Gun for Hire* (1942), *The Glass Key* (1942), and *The Blue Dahlia*

(1946). In her heyday she hob-nobbed and courted with Howard Hughes and Aristotle Onassis, then married director Andre De Toth (*House of Wax,* 1953). Around 1952, after her divorce from De Toth, she took a long hiatus from the limelight, occasionally making a few headlines with public drunkenness. *Flesh Feast* was an integral part of her brief comeback, which also included a fascinating autobiography titled *Veronica.* Three years after this film was released she died of hepatitis. • For shots involving a multitude of maggots, the production staff utilized rice mixed in with the real squirmers.

The 4-D Man (1959; Universal) D: Irwin Yeaworth, Jr. P: Jack H. Harris, Irwin Yeaworth, Jr. S: Theodore Simonson, Cy Chermak. C: Theodore J. Pahle. Cast: Robert Lansing, Lee Meriwether, James Congdon, Robert Strauss, Edgar Stehli. A scientist discovers a way to break into the fourth dimension and pass through solid objects. Unfortunately, this alters him so that he now must periodically renew his life energy. When he touches a person, they rapidly age and die as he sucks their life force from them. He becomes unhinged and turns to crime. In the finale, after being shot by his former love, he walks into a wall of carbonite and is absorbed completely, with only his hand protruding outside. • In casting the lead, producer Jack H. Harris stated: "I picked up Robert Lansing from Broadway; I found myself choosing between him and Jason Robards. I thought Lansing had more of a romantic leading man look about him." • Actress Patty Duke, 14 at the time, played Marjorie Sutherland in her sixth film appearance. • Special effects man Barton Sloane provided the numerous 4-D sequences that took nearly nine months to complete. A process known as "rotoscope" was used in the scenes where Lansing was required to reach through a person. The technique required the combining of two negatives and the scraping away of film emulsion a little at a time to achieve the disappearing and reappearing of his hand. • Producer Jack H. Harris contacted Lloyds of London for a million dollar promotional guarantee to anyone who could duplicate the 4-D man's feats. No one ever tried.

4-Sided Triangle (1953; Hammer/Astor; U.K.) D: Terence Fisher. P: Alexander Paal. S: Paul Tabori, Terence Fisher. C: Reginald Wyer. Cast: Barbara Payton, Stephen Murray, John Van Eyssen, Percy Marmont, James Hayter. A pair of scientists in love with the same woman perform an equitable experiment by duplicating the beautiful Barbara Payton. Unfortunately for Stephen Murray, both the original and the duplicate fall in love with his rival because they are, in fact, identical. ¶ "He outdid Frankenstein, and held strange powers. Powers to duplicate anything on Earth. Power to create this beautiful woman. Power to satisfy his lust for passion!" — ad line. • The film is noteworthy in that it was director Terence Fisher's first foray into the fantasy/sci-fi genre. Of course, he went on to create some of Hammer studio's biggest hits, including *The Curse of Frankenstein* (1957), *Horror of Dracula* (1958), *The Mummy* (1959), and *Brides of Dracula* (1960).

From Beyond (1986) (see DEMONS AND DEVILS). A mad scientist named Dr. Praetorius invents a machine called a "resonator" which bridges the gap between our world and a dimension populated by hideous demon-like beings. The willing mad doctor is eventually transformed into a grotesque demon/monster himself. • The crazy doctor-turned-monster is named after the mad scientist from *Bride of Frankenstein* (1935) — "Dr. Praetorius").

Hand of Death (1962; 20th Century–Fox) D: Gene Nelson. P/S: Eugene Ling. C: Floyd Crosby. Cast: John Agar, Paula Raymond, Steve Dunne, Roy Gordon, John Alonzo, Butch Patrick. A researcher (John Agar) develops a paralyzing nerve gas for the military, then accidentally becomes contaminated after spilling it. The effects of the substance leave Agar with dark bloated features and a lethal touch (a *Hand of Death*). After killing a colleague, he is shot and killed by the police at the climax. • Instead of the usual stunt performer wearing the rubber mask and gloves, it was John Agar himself in the monster suit. • This was Gene Nelson's directorial debut. He had formerly been an accomplished dancer, working in numerous Warner Bros. films, including *Oklahoma* (1955). • The film was distributed by 20th Century–Fox on a double bill alongside *Cabinet of Dr. Caligari,* scripted by Robert Bloch.

The Hideous Sun Demon (1959; Pacific International) D/P: Robert Clarke. S: E. S. Seely, Jr., Duana Hoag. C: John Morrill, Vilis Lapenieks, Stan Follis. Cast: Robert Clarke, Patricia Manning, Nan Peterson, Patrick Whyte, Peter Similuk, Robert Garry. An accident at an atomic research laboratory turns scientist Gilbert McKenna (Robert Clarke) into a Jekyll and Hyde–like human reptile who transforms when exposed to the rays of the sun. Forced to go into hiding because of his strange affliction and his uncontrollable fury when in the reptile state, Clarke is eventually hunted down by a police dragnet and falls to his death off a gas storage tank. ¶ "His whole appearance has changed into something scaly, almost lizard like." • The Sun Demon mask cost $500 to make. Creature-maker Jack Kevan offered to do it for $2,000, which was too expensive, so they settled for Richard Cassarino's version. Robert Clarke, who wore the suit, said, "The suit was made on the base of a skin-diving wetsuit, and it was hotter than blue blazes!" • The film itself cost a little under $50,000 to make, and was shot exclusively on weekends (12 consecutive ones to be exact, which is why three cinematographers were employed). • Many prints of the film have been shown with one particularly tasteless scene edited out — the crushing of a rat in Robert Clarke's hand. Clarke said in Tom Weaver's book, *Interviews with B Science Fiction and Horror Movie Makers,* "We didn't hurt the rat — we put some ketchup or something on it and squeezed it so that the ketchup would come out between the fingers. Actually, we probably shouldn't have used it; it was not in good taste and I'm glad that it has been cut."

Horror Hospital (1973; Hallmark; U.K.) (also *Computer Killers; Dr. Bloodbath* [video title]). D: Anthony Balch. P: Richard Gordon. S: Anthony Balch, Alan Watson. C: David McDonald. Cast: Michael Gough, Robin Askwith, Vanessa Shaw, Ellen Pollock, Dennis Price, Skip Martin. A musician and his girlfriend visit a horrible hospital run by the demented (and disfigured) Michael Gough (who's experimenting with brain control techniques).

The House by the Cemetery (1981) (see ZOMBIES). A family moving into a new house is trapped and killed one by one by mad Dr. Freudstein, living in the hidden cellar. Freudstein was a scientist who discovered the means to turn himself into a walking zombie and keep himself "alive" for 150 years.

The Human Vapor (1960; Toho/Allied Artists; Japan) D: Inoshiro Honda. P: Tomoyuki Tanaka. S: Shinichi Sekizawa. C: Hajime Koizumi. Cast: Yoshio Tsuchiya, Kaoru Yachgusa, Tatsuya Mihashi, Keiko Sata, Bokuzen Hidari. A scientist gives a thief the ability to transform into gaseous vapor — very handy for breaking and entering.

The Hunchback of the Morgue (1972) (see FREAKS) (also *The Rue Morgue Massacre*). Goto, the hunchbacked employee of a hospital morgue (Paul Naschy), murders those students who intend to dissect the body of a girl that he loves (she died of tuberculosis). Goto is taken in by an unscrupulous mad scientist who promises to resurrect his lost love if Goto helps him in his nefarious plans. The scientist, however, is more interested in tending to a monstrous mass of protoplasm he has created than in aiding the poor hunchback.

I Was a Teenage Werewolf (1957) (see WEREWOLVES — OTHER LYCANTHROPES). A troubled teenager with an anger control problem falls prey to a mad doctor (Whit Bissell) who wants to transform him back into his primordial existence (as a werewolf).

The Incredible Two-Headed Transplant (1971) (see TWO-HEADED CREATURES). Bruce Dern is the mad scientist who transplants the head of a killer onto the body of a retarded giant.

The Indestructible Man (1956; Allied Artists) D/P: Jack Pollexfen. S: Vy Russell, Sue Bradford. C: John Russell, Jr. Cast: Lon Chaney, Jr., Marian Carr, Robert Shayne, Ross Elliott, Stuart Randall, Kenneth Terrell. The dead body of murderer Charles "Butcher" Benton is experimented on by a deranged scientist who subjects it to a 287,000 volt charge, restoring him to life. Benton then goes on a vengeance spree before being trapped and killed in the L.A. sewer system at the climax. • The credited screenwriters for the film were the wives of director/producer Jack Pollexfen's two favorite cameramen — Bill Bradford and John Russell. Mr. Russell photographed this venture. • Pollexfen said of his star, Lon Chaney, Jr., in Tom Weaver's book, *Interviews with B Science Fiction and Horror Movie Makers,* "I found him intelligent, probably more so than many actors. He warned me before we started shooting, 'Don't make any changes in dialogue, or add any new dialogue, after lunch!' — which he drank down rather liberally."

The Invisible Ray (1936; Universal) D: Lambert Hillyer. P: Edmund Grainger. S: John Colton. C: George Robinson. Cast: Boris Karloff, Bela Lugosi, Frances Drake, Frank Lawton, Walter Kingsford, Beulah Bondi, Violet Kemble Cooper. A scientist (Boris Karloff) recovers a substance known as "Radium X" from a meteor in Africa. He becomes contaminated, however, which causes him to glow and gives him a lethal touch. Insanity sets in along with his newfound abilities, and he sets out to take revenge on those he feels have wronged him.

The "manimal" creations of Dr. Moreau (Charles Laughton) revolt against their sadistic maker on the Island of Lost Souls (1933)

¶ "You're not used to people Janos, you never will be. Your experiments are your friends. Leave people alone"—his wise mother to Boris Karloff's mad scientist. • This film was the third teaming of Karloff and Lugosi. Its original title was to be *The Death Ray*. • *The Invisible Ray* contained this bold, forward-looking statement: "Every scientific fact accepted today once burned as a fantastic fire in the mind of someone called mad."

The Island of Dr. Moreau (1977; AIP) D: Don Taylor. P: John Temple-Smith, Skip Steloff. S: John Herman Shaner, Al Ramrus. C: Gerry Fisher. Cast: Burt Lancaster, Michael York, Nigel Davenport, Barbara Carrera, Richard Basehart, Nick Cravat. In this inferior remake of the 1933 classic, *Island of Lost Souls,* Burt Lancaster plays mad scientist Dr. Moreau who, in trying to speed up evolution, turns animals into beast-men (and vice-versa—men into animals). ¶ "No matter how far I take my creatures they begin to revert. They can't tell me what happens inside their bodies when that occurs, until now. You will do that for me. You will explore that inner battlefield, that war of the cells, and bring back the

knowledge, the ultimate knowledge to become an animal. To feel it inside your body and your brain what no man has ever known before." • Burt Lancaster takes over from Charles Laughton, while Richard Basehart assays the Bela Lugosi role from the original. • This "Island of Dr. Moreau" was located in the Virgin Islands (where it was filmed). • Makeup man John Chambers, who headed a 12-man team to create the startling "humanimal" visages here, also worked on the wonderful simian countenances from *Planet of the Apes* (1968).

Island of Lost Souls (1933; Paramount) D: Erle C. Kenton. S: Waldemar Young, Philip Wylie. C: Karl Struss. Cast: Charles Laughton, Richard Arlen, Kathleen Burke, Arthur Hohl, Leila Hyams, Stanley Fields. In this classic version of H. G. Wells' *The Island of Dr. Moreau,* Dr. Moreau (Charles Laughton) tampers with the laws of evolution by creating people out of various mammals. The unsatisfactory results leave his private island populated with a rebellious lot of half-men/half-beasts. Moreau then plots to mate a shipwreck victim (Richard Arlen) with his panther woman (Kathleen Burke). His plans are interrupted when the "manimal" law-sayer (Bela Lugosi) leads a vicious revolt against their creator at the film's conclusion. ¶ "Not to run on all fours, that is the law. Are we not men?!" • This is the first-ever adaptation of H. G. Wells' novel *The Island of Dr. Moreau,* and it is reported that the author did not think too highly of this film. • The cast of manimal monsters included some impressive newcomers like Randolph Scott and Alan Ladd. • The camera work for *Island* was credited to one of the all time greats, Karl Struss. The illustrious career of this fine cinematographer from New York City spanned four decades and included a bevy of hits like *Ben Hur* (1926), *Sunrise* (1927; for which he won an Academy Award), *Dr. Jekyll and Mr. Hyde* (1932), *The Great Dictator* (1940), *Rocketship XM* (1950), and *The Fly* (1958). • A publicity campaign focused on a nationwide search for the right actress to play the Panther Woman. The winner was Kathleen Burke, a former Chicago dental assistant.

Island of Terror (1967; Universal; U.K.) D: Terence Fisher. P: Tom Blakeley. S: Alan Ramsen, Edward Andrew Mann. C: Reg Wyer. Cast: Peter Cushing, Edward Judd, Carole Gray, Eddie Byrne, Sam Kydd, Niall MacGinnis. Scientific cancer research unleashes a tentacled turtle-like monster called a "Silicate" that sucks the bones from its victims. The living cancer cell creatures overrun an island and nearly destroy all of its inhabitants. ¶ "It's like nothing I've ever seen. There was no face, just a horrible mush, with eyes sitting in it."

Jungle Captive (1944) (see APES AND MONKEYS). A scientist resurrects the body of "Paula the Ape Woman" (again) in this second sequel to *Captive Wild Woman.*

Jungle Woman (1944) (see APES AND MONKEYS). In the first sequel to *Captive Wild Woman* (1943), mad scientist J. Carroll Naish brings "Paula the Ape Woman" back to life.

The Kindred (1987) (see FREAKS). Allen Brooks stars as a scientist who decides to organize his deceased mother's legacy of genetic research. With a team of scientists at her house, he discovers that his mom was harboring a genetic mutation (his "cloned" brother) which a less-than-sane scientist (Rod Steiger) wishes to study. The murderous freak goes on a rampage and is finally destroyed by fire along with the house.

Kiss Me Monster (1968; Aquila Film Enterprises; Spain) (also *Castle of the Doomed*). D/S: Jesus Franco. P: Pier A. Caminecci, Adrian Hoven. C: Jorge Her-

rero. Cast: Janine Reynard, Rossana Yanni, Adrian Hoven, Michel Lemoine, Chris Howland. A mad doctor on an isolated Caribbean island experiments on men and animals à la *Island of Lost Souls.*

The Lady and the Monster (1944) (see BRAINS—DISEMBODIED BRAINS). This first version of the Curt Siodmak novel, *Donovan's Brain,* follows an evil scientist (Erich von Stroheim) who keeps the brain of a corrupt millionaire alive, cultivating its mind-controlling powers.

Lady Death (1968; Mexico) Cast: John Carradine. Carradine plays a crazy scientist who wants blood from young women to produce a serum that can cure a disfigured girl.

Lifespan (1975; U.S./U.K./Belgium) D/P/S: Alexander Whitelaw. Cast: Hiram Keller, Klaus Kinski, Tina Aumont. A doctor working on a serum that can extend life uses subjects from a nursing home with some unfortunate results.

The Mad Doctor of Blood Island (1969; Hemisphere; Philippines/U.S.) (also *Tomb of the Living Dead*). D: Eddie Romero, Gerardo de Leon. P: Eddie Romero. S: Reuben Candy. C: Justo Paulino. Cast: John Ashley, Angelique Pettyjohn, Ronald Remy, Alicia Alonso, Bruno Punzalan. The mad scientist of Blood Island creates a hideous green-blooded monster with an experimental chlorophyll drug. ¶ "I will not give up the work of a lifetime simply because you think I am mad!" • Ronald Remy, who played the mad Dr. Lorca, and star John Ashley popped up again in 1970 in a sequel called *Beast of Blood.* • An unusual promotional gimmick tried in a few theaters involved the handing out of green blood (colored water) to patrons.

The Mad Doctor of Market Street (1942; Universal) D: Joseph H. Lewis. P: Paul Malvern. S: Al Martin. C: Jerome Ash. Cast: Lionel Atwill, Una Merkel, Nat Pendleton, Anne Nagel, Claire Dodd, Noble Johnson. Lionel Atwill is a mad doctor on the lam for murder who is shipwrecked on a remote South Sea island. After reviving an island princess from the dead, he is worshiped as the "God of Life" by the native tribe. He uses his new status to manipulate his fellow castaways and lay hands on the reluctant heroine. In the end, he fails to perform an encore performance on a drowned native, and is dispatched.

The Mad Monster (1942) (see WERE-WOLVES—OTHER LYCANTHROPES). George Zucco plays a mad doctor who transforms retarded handyman Glenn Strange into a

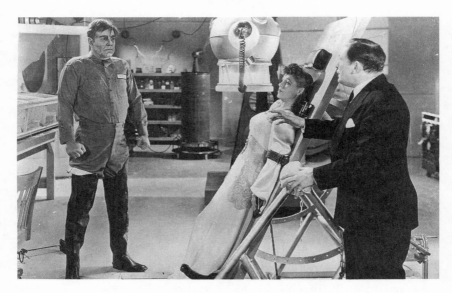

Mad scientist Lionel Atwill is unable to control his electrically charged Man Made Monster *(1941), played by Lon Chaney, Jr.*

werewolf by giving him injections of wolf's blood.

The Man in Half Moon Street (1944; Paramount) D: Ralph M. Murphy. P: Walter MacEwen. S: Charles Kenyon. C: Henry Sharp. Cast: Nils Asther, Helen Walker, Reinhold Schuenzel, Paul Cavanagh, Brandon Hurst, Edmund Breon. A man must commit murder once every six years in order to obtain the gland transplants which give him eternal life. At the climax he rapidly matures to the age of 80.

Man Made Monster (1941; Universal) (also *The Atomic Monster*). D: George Waggner. P: Jack Bernhard. S: Joseph West. C: Elwood Bredell. Cast: Lionel Atwill, Lon Chaney, Jr., Anne Nagel, Frank Albertson, Samuel S. Hinds, William Davidson, Ben Taggart. Mad scientist Dr. Rigas (Lionel Atwill) takes the sole survivor of a bus accident (Lon Chaney, Jr.) in which every other person was electrocuted and transforms him into a walking electrically-charged monster. ¶ "Of course I'm mad, but while you were fooling with conventions, I have conquered destiny!" • This film's scenario was originally written in 1936 as a vehicle for Karloff and Lugosi called *The Man in the Cab,* but was shelved and never made. Producer George Waggner dragged it out, dusted it off, did a script rewrite (using

the pseudonym Joseph West), and cast Lon Chaney, Jr., in the Karloff role and Lionel Atwill in the Lugosi part. • The heavily made-up Lon Chaney, Jr., had to wear a 70-pound rubber suit for the role. The film's pressbook stated that he lost 16 pounds during the production. • *Man Made Monster* carried a shooting title of *The Mysterious Dr. R.* • Soon after this film's success, Universal dropped the "Jr." from Lon Chaney, Jr.'s, name, a move opposed by the independent-minded Chaney. Just as in the 1920s, there was once again a "Lon Chaney" stalking the Universal lot. Chaney reflected upon his work in this film and upon his father, saying, "After witnessing the torture my father endured in his various makeups, I was more than ready to heed his advice about not doing that type of work. And yet, I suppose the fact that I'm here proves that some people just can't escape their destiny." • The Man Made Monster is destroyed at the end when his insulated suit is caught on barbed wire, which drains away his electrical power, and his life as well.

The Man They Could Not Hang (1939; Columbia) D: Nick Grinde. P: Wallace MacDonald. S: Karl Brown. C: Benjamin Kline. Cast: Boris Karloff, Lorna Gray, Robert Wilcox, Roger Pryor, Don Beddoe, Ann Doran, Charles Trowbridge. Experimentation with a mechanical heart goes awry when police interrupt Dr. Savaard's (Boris Karloff) task of bringing a live subject back from death. After an exhausting trial, Boris is condemned to death and then brought back to life (using Karloff's mechanical heart apparatus) by his assistant. He then traps his condemning judge and jurors at his house and begins to exact revenge on them one by one. ¶ "When those you love best lie dying, think back to this moment when you held their salvation in your hands and threw it away. Always remember that I offered you life and you gave me death!" • The film was inspired by actual experiments by a Dr. Cornish involving the supposed reanimation of dead dogs. • The idea of an artificial heart was unheard of at the time the film was made, but science has proven Karloff right.

The Man Who Could Cheat Death (1959; Hammer/Paramount; U.K.) D: Terence Fisher. P: Anthony Hinds. S: Jimmy Sangster. C: Jack Asher. Cast: Anton Diffring, Hazel Court, Christopher Lee, Arnold Marle, Delphi Lawrence, Francis DeWolfe. Anton Diffring discovers that gland transplants, together with a special potion, can keep one eternally young and impervious to disease. Every ten years Diffring must murder someone for new glands. At the finale, he reverts to his natural age and is burned to death when a lantern is tossed in his direction. ¶ "I shall become the inheritor of all my 104 years, of all the sickness I never had, of every pain, blemish, disease—a lifetime of illness in one moment." • Peter Cushing was originally slated for Anton Diffring's part but was unavailable at the time.

The Man Who Turned to Stone (1957; Columbia) D: Leslie Kardos. P: Sam Katzman. S: Raymond T. Marcus. C: Benjamin H. Kline. Cast: Victor Jory, Charlotte Austin, William Hudson, Frederick Ledebur, Ann Doran, Jean Willes, Paul Cavanagh. A group of 200-year-old scientists run a reform school for girls and occasionally borrow the life-force from one or two to rejuvenate themselves. If they go too long without their treatments, their skin hardens and they turn into human monoliths.

The Man with Nine Lives (1940; Columbia) D: Nick Grinde. S: Karl Brown. C: Benjamin Kline. Cast: Boris Karloff, Roger Pryor, Jo Ann Sayers, Stanley Brown, John Dilson, Hal Taliaferro, Byron Foulger, Charles Trowbridge, Ernie Adams. A well-meaning scientist, who is working on curing cancer ailments by freezing, is accidentally trapped inside an ice cave for ten years. A young doctor finds him and revives the scientist, proving the validity of his treatment. When his formula is thoughtlessly destroyed by one of his callous rescuers, however, he becomes unhinged and attempts to rediscover this medical miracle by using his rescuers as human guinea pigs. ¶ "I, for one, am resolved that no matter what sacrifices I may be forced to make—of myself or of others—I will not be stopped in my research for this secret so long as I shall live"—an excerpt from the noble but overzealous scientist's journal. • Columbia tried to add some bogus scientific dignity to the film's fantastical plot by opening with this written narration: "In research hospitals today, men and women are alive and breathing—their bodies encased in ice." • The screenplay stressed the nobility of this particular mad scientist, and Karloff played him in a very sympathetic (if misguided) light. The film's closing statement is delivered by the hero: "It's unfortunate Dr. Kravaal's intensity of purpose, his reaching for success, forced him beyond the limits of the law. He paid with his life, that we might have this, his parting gift to humanity."

Mansion of the Doomed (1976; Group 1) D: Michael Pataki. P: Charles Band. S: Frank Ray Perilli. C: Andrew Davis. Cast: Richard Basehart, Trish Stewart, Gloria Grahame, Lance Henriksen, Vic Tayback, Arthur Space. A distraught surgeon abducts a large number of people and removes their eyes in the hope of finding just the right ones that will restore sight to his daughter, blinded in a car accident. At the climax, the victims escape their underground prison and take revenge by tearing out the doctor's own eyes.

Master of the World (1961; AIP) D: William Witney. P: James H. Nicholson. S: Richard Matheson. C: Gil Warrenton. Cast: Vincent Price, Henry Hull, Charles Bronson, Mary Webster, David Frankham, Wally Campo. A mad inventor who abhors warfare of any kind sets out to destroy all the world's weaponry from his incredible flying airship, the "Albatross." • The film is based on the Jules Verne novel, *Clipper of the Clouds.*

Mesa of Lost Women (1953) (see BUG-PEOPLE). A demented scientist living on a Mexican mesa experiments with men, women, and spiders. He, his work, and his super-race of spider-women are all blown up at the climax. ¶ "No . . . No . . . You can't do these things! You're tampering with the work of the Creator! You're evil!" • Jackie Coogan joked about the making of the film saying, "There were a dozen beautiful women running around the set but I couldn't see any of them. As the mad scientist in the picture, part of my costume was a pair of fogged spectacles!" • Coogan was a tremendously popular "child" star in his youth, starring alongside Charlie Chaplin in *The Kid* (1921).

Mill of the Stone Women (1960; Parade; France/Italy) D/S: Giorgio Ferroni. P: Gianpaolo Bigazzi. S: Remigio Del Grosso, Ugo Liberatore, Giorgio Stegani. C: Pierludovico Pavoni. Cast: Pierre Brice, Scilla Gabel, Dany Carrel, Wolfgang Preiss, Herbert Boehme. A scientist draws the blood of young women for the purpose of keeping his daughter alive. The resulting effect turns the donors into statues.

The Monster Maker (1944) (see FREAKS). A mad scientist infects the father of the girl he covets with a disease (acromegaly) only he can cure.

The Most Dangerous Man Alive (1961; Columbia) D: Allan Dwan. P: Benedict Bogeans. S: James Leicester, Philip Rock. C: Carl Carvahal. Cast: Ron Randell, Debra Paget, Elaine Stewart, Anthony Caruso, Gregg Palmer, Morris Ankrum. More a tale of science-gone-mad than of mad scientists, framed gangster Ron Randell escapes and wanders onto the test site of a new type of cobalt bomb. The bomb detonates but he is not killed. Instead, Randell becomes a "man of steel"—his flesh absorbs steel. He takes his newfound talent and goes to find the gang who framed him. To their dismay, bullets will not stop him, electricity will not stop him, apparently nothing will stop him. He is finally cornered by a battalion of police and national guardsmen and fried with a flame-thrower. ¶ "I'm not human anymore.... All I can feel now is hate!" • Though filmed in 1958 (in Mexico), it was not released until three years later. • Actress Elaine Stewart was once chosen by magazine cover artists as "The Most Beautiful Cover Girl in America."

Murder by Television (1935; Imperial Pictures Corp.) D: Clifford Sanforth. P: William Pizor. S: Joseph O'Donnell. Cast: Bela Lugosi, June Collyer, Huntley Gordon, George Meeker, Henry Mowbray. A group of unscrupulous promoters plan to steal a television apparatus from a scientist. There follows a series of murders with the television as the tool of death. ¶ "The mad monarch of the laboratory waves his mighty hands and death-dealing rays strike down his hapless victims"—ad line. • Lugosi plays twin brothers in the film. (Doubtful) press-

book advances claimed that Bela created his own makeup for the film, using 43 different shades of grease paint on his face to get the desired look for this black and white production. • *Murder by Television* carried the shooting title of *The Houghland Murder Case.*

The Murder Clinic (1966; Europix; France/Italy) (also *Revenge of the Living Dead*). D: Michael Hamilton (Elio Scardamaglia), Domenico De Felice. P: Michael Hamilton. S: Julian Berry (Ernesto Gastaldi), Martin Hardy (Luciano Martino). C: Mark Lane (Marcello Masciocchi). Cast: William Berger, Françoise Prévost, Mary Young, Barbara Wilson, Delphine Maurin. A plastic surgeon performs skin graft operations on an old deformed woman while his wife dons a hood and goes out seeking the raw materials.

Murders in the Rue Morgue (1932) (see POE FILMS—EARLY POE). Bela Lugosi stars as Dr. Mirakle, a carnival barker (and mad scientist) who is killing young women in order to mix their blood with that of an ape.

Mutations (1972) (see FREAKS) (also *Freakmaker*). Donald Pleasence plays a mad doctor who crossbreeds humans with plants for some astonishing results, many of which are sent to a local sideshow.

My Son the Vampire (1952) (see ROBOTS) (also *Old Mother Riley Meets the Vampire; Vampire Over London*). Bela Lugosi is a mad doctor who lives in an old dark house and thinks he is a vampire. Old Mother Riley finally foils his nefarious plans involving an army of robots. ¶ "I believe we are dealing with a dangerous character, not for what he claims to be, but for what he is—a fanatical scientist with a stupid gang of men who have allowed themselves to be mesmerized by a legend."

Night of the Bloody Apes (1968) (see APES AND MONKEYS). A well-meaning but misguided scientist places the heart of a gorilla into the body of his dying son, with the unexpected result of him changing into an ape-man periodically. Plenty of footage from real open heart surgery was inserted to spice up the proceedings in this Mexican horror.

The Night Strangler (1973; TV movie) D/P: Dan Curtis. S: Richard Matheson. C: Robert B. Hauser. Cast: Darren McGavin, Jo Ann Pflug, Simon Oakland, Scott Brady, Wally Cox, Margaret Hamilton, John Carradine, Richard Anderson. Reporter Carl Kolchak encounters a mad scientist/alchemist living in underground Seattle, who possesses the secret of eternal life and surfaces every 21 years to go on a strangling spree. • Horror legend John Carradine plays a newspaper owner in this second feature film pilot of "The Night Stalker" TV series. • *The Night Strangler* was shot as *The Time Killer.*

Nightmare Castle (1965) (see GHOSTS). A scientist murders his unfaithful wife (Barbara Steele) and her lover, and uses his wife's blood to restore the youth of his aging mistress. The man then marries his wife's blonde cousin (Steele again, in a dual role), but is eventually brought to justice by the vengeful ghosts of his first wife and her paramour. ¶ Scientist: "It was possible for me to give you back your youth, but I could do nothing about your mind." Mistress: "It doesn't matter doctor, it's not my mind that is useful to you when you need it."

Nothing But the Night (1972; Cinema Systems; U.K.) D: Peter Sasdy. P: Anthony Nelson-Keys. S: Brian Hayles. C: Ken Talbot. Cast: Christopher Lee, Peter Cushing, Diana Dors, Georgia Brown, Gwynneth Strong, Keith Barron, John Robinson. Murderous orphaned children injected with a serum that contains memory genes of dead people are controlled by Gwynneth Strong. Both the children and their scientist controllers meet their demise by falling into the sea. • This film, never released theatrically in the U.S., was made by a production company set up by Anthony Nelson-Keys and Christopher Lee. The company's name was "Charlemagne," and its brief existence produced this lone film.

The Phantom Creeps (1939; Universal) D: Ford Beebe, Saul A. Goodkind. P: Henry MacRae. S: George Plympton, Basil Dickey, Mildred Barish. C: Jerome Ash, William Sickner. Cast: Bela Lugosi, Robert Kent, Dorothy Arnold, Regis Toomey, Edward Van Sloan, Roy Barcroft. In this condensed feature version of a 12-chapter serial, Bela Lugosi plays mad scientist Zorka, who is after world domination with the use of an eight-foot tall robot and an invisibility belt.

The Projected Man (1966; Universal; U.K.) D: Ian Curteis. P: John Croydon, Maurice Foster. S: John C. Cooper, Peter Bryan. C: Stanley Pavey. Cast: Bryant Haliday, Mary Peach, Norman Woolard, Tracey Crisp, Ronald Allen, Derek Farr. A matter transmitting device is sabotaged and transforms its inventor into a disfigured, electrically-charged monster whose touch can kill. ¶ "What I have achieved is the projection of an object in three dimensions — something that has weight, depth, and body — and without a receiver. Yesterday, I achieved my first projection of a living creature. Unfortunately, something went wrong and the subject died."

Real Genius (1985; Tri-Star Pictures) D: Martha Coolidge. P: Brian Grazer. S: Noel Israel, Pat Proft, Peter Torokvei. C: Vilmos Zsigmund. Cast: Val Kilmer, Gabe Jarret, Michelle Meyrink, William Atherton, Patti Darbanville, Robert Prescott. College students try to thwart a creepy professor who is using his students' scientific ability to complete his own government project — an extremely powerful laser machine that could be used as the next ultimate weapon. ¶ "Look at the facts — very high powered, portable, limited firing time, unlimited range. All you'd need is a tracking system and a large spinning mirror and you could vaporize a human target from space."

Re-Animator (1985) (see ZOMBIES). A brilliant, obsessive (and slightly deranged) young medical student named Herbert West develops a "reanimation" serum which restores life to dead bodies. Unfortunately, the reanimated bodies are wracked with pain and so become violent murdering monsters.

The Return of Dr. X (1939) (see ZOMBIES). Humphrey Bogart plays the title character, an evil doctor executed for murder who is brought back to life by a misguided scientist working on an artificial blood compound which can restore life to the dead. There is one hitch, though; the resurrected subject must have fresh blood periodically or he will die again (for good). ¶ "True, in the eyes of society he [Dr. X] was a murderer. He was also a medical genius. And I felt that he had been a martyr to science."

The Return of the Zombies (1939) (see ZOMBIES). A mad doctor steals bodies from the nearby cemetery and experiments on them, turning them into walking, obedient zombies who murder all those standing in the way of his experiments. He activates the corpses by "inserting a small capsule into the brain" which can "receive thought patterns."

Revenge in the House of Usher (1983; Eurocine) (also *Nevrosus*). D/P: A. M. Frank (Jesus Franco). S: H. L. Rostaine. C: Allan Hardy. Cast: Howard Vernon, Dan Villers, Jean Tolzac, Joan Virly, Françoise Blanchard, Oliver Mato. Though the credits claim it is "Based on 'The Fall of the House of Usher' by Edgar Allan Poe," this film shares nothing but the name with Poe's story. Dr. Eric Usher, an obsessed mad scientist, is attempting to revive his dead daughter by kidnapping young girls and using them as unwilling donors in his bizarre experiments. ¶

"Some things had better remain mysteries, lest the mind should snap under an awareness beyond its scope"—closing narration. • Footage from the rare Jesus Franco film, *The Awful Dr. Orloff* (1962), turns up here to pad out this movie's running time.

Revenge of the Zombies (1943) (see ZOM-BIES). John Carradine is a mad scientist creating an army of zombies for the Nazis in the Louisiana bayous. He goes so far as to use his own wife as a subject, turning her into a zombie to demonstrate the technique to his superiors. ¶ "I am prepared to supply my country with a new army—an army that will not need to be fed, that cannot be stopped by bullets, that is in fact invincible—an army of the living dead."

Satanik (1968; Rodiancines; Italy/Spain) D: Piero Vivarelli. P: Romano Mussolini. S: Eduardo M. Brochero. C: Silvano Ippoliti. Cast: Magda Konopka, Julio Peña, Armando Calvo, Umberto Raho, Luigi Montini, Mimma Ippoliti. A scientist is kiled by his ugly, deformed female assistant. She drinks a solution he had concocted which turns her into a seductive beauty, then commits more acts of murder until the police catch on to her scheme. She, of course, reverts back to her former self at the climax.

Scream and Scream Again (1970) (see ROBOTS). A mad scientist (Vincent Price) creates a new race of artificial beings, one of which is hunted by the police for several vampire-like killings. Price is part of an international organization bent on world domination and he himself is an android.

Screamers (1979) (see FISH-PEOPLE). Set in the nineteenth century, Joseph Cotten plays a scientist turning natives into fish-creatures on a remote Pacific island. It is the old advance-evolution-for-the-sake-of-mankind theory again.

Secret of the Telgian (1960; Toho; Japan) D: Jun Fukuda. P: Tomoyuki Tanaka. S: Shinichi Sekizawa. C: Kazuo Yamada. Cast: Koji Tsuruta, Akihiko Hirata, Yumi Shirakawa, Tadao Nakamura, Seizaburo Kawazu. A scientist invents a device during the war that can teleport a human being. A soldier who was left behind by his comrades uses the machine to exact his revenge.

She Demons (1958; Astor Pictures) D: Richard E. Cunha. P: Arthur A. Jacobs. S: Richard E. Cunha, H. E. Barrie. C: Meredith Nicholson. Cast: Irish McCalla, Tod Griffin, Victor Sen Yung, Rudolph Anders, Leni Tana, Gene Roth. A shipwrecked couple encounters a mad Nazi scientist who has created a host of hideously deformed women in an attempt to restore his wife's good looks. The scientist, his demons, and the island, all get drenched in lava at the climax. • *She Demons* cost under $70,000 to make and was shot at Paradise Cove and Griffith Park. • Director Richard Cunha said in Tom Weaver's book, *Interviews with B Science Fiction and Horror Movie Makers,* "I was trying to get even with the world at the time and just having a good time. These were really tongue in cheek films, and we enjoyed doing them a great deal and had as much fun as possible." • Richard Cunha's wife was the demon-masked stand-in for Leni Tana, who wore bandages almost exclusively throughout the film. When the bandages were to be removed, she did not want to wear the makeup so the director's wife did the dirty work. The other "She Demons" were played by the Diana Nellis Dancers, and they did wear their own makeup. • Irish McCalla, popularly known to fans as "Sheena, Queen of the Jungle," said of the change from TV to cinema: "It's a lot of fun to be rescued. In TV I usually am the one fording rivers and climbing high mountains to rescue some man in danger, but now I'm enjoying being swept to safety in strong masculine arms."

She Devil (1957; 20th Century–Fox) D/P: Kurt Neumann. S: Carroll Young, Kurt Neumann. C: Karl Struss. Cast: Mari Blanchard, Jack Kelly, Albert Dekker, John Archer, Fay Baker, Paul Cavanagh. A pair of scientists use a serum from fruit flies to cure a terminally ill patient (Mari Blanchard). The side effects that result include the ability to change hair color at will, and the ability to withstand any means of physical destruction. Blanchard uses these skills to murder those who get in her way, until the scientists manage to reverse the process, causing her to die from her former condition, tuberculosis. ¶ "Well, you created me and I'm your responsibility." • The film is based on a short story by Stanley G. Weinbaum (who wrote under the pseudonym John Jessel) called "The Adaptive Ultimate." • Cinematographer Karl Struss used filters (a technique which had proved so effective in the transformation sequences of his 1932 effort, *Dr. Jekyll and Mr. Hyde*), to create the illusion of Blanchard's hair changing color before our very eyes. • The role of an invalid receiving a miraculous cure is not new to Mari Blanchard. At the age of nine she was stricken with polio and paralyzed from the waist down. Doctors, who had predicted the worst, were astonished to see her walking normally at age 12. She went on to become an excellent dancer.

Of her role, Mari said, "My part in *She Devil* is not exactly sympathetic, but it gives me a chance to act and I consider it one of the best roles I've had yet."

Shock Treatment (1973; France/Italy) D/S: Alain Jessua. Cast: Alain Delon, Annie Giradot. Doctors kill youths for the blood needed to make a formula that will prevent aging.

The Sorcerers (1967) (see PSYCHIC ABILITY). Boris Karloff plays a scientist and former stage hypnotist who, along with his scheming wife, builds a machine which allows them to experience the thrills of youth by mentally controlling a young man.

SSSSSSS (1973) (see SNAKES). Strother Martin is a mad scientist attempting to transform people into snakes. One of his experimental failures ends up at the local sideshow, while his eventual success turns on him in a hissing and slithering fit of fury.

Teenage Zombies (1960) (see ZOMBIES). Katherine Victor plays a mad scientist who has discovered a gas which turns people into mindless zombies. She kidnaps four teenagers who stray onto her deserted island home and plans to use them as subjects.

The Terminal Man (1974) (see COMPUTERS). Doctors hoping to curb the violent tendencies of George Segal place a tiny computer into his brain. The device proves to be a disaster when it sparks his brain's pleasure center, inducing him to commit acts of violence in order to satisfy these impulses.

Terror Is a Man (1959) (see CAT-PEOPLE) (also *The Blood Creature*). Francis Lederer plays Dr. Durard, a mad scientist on a remote island who transforms a leopard into a hideous man-beast in this early U.S./Philippine co-production borrowing from H. G. Wells' *The Island of Dr. Moreau*. ¶ "What you're doing is so wrong; I hate it, all of it!" — Dr. Durard's worried wife. • Francis Lederer returned a decade later in a similar mad scientist role as the evil "Dr. Lorca" in another U.S./Philippine co-production for producer Eddie Romero — *Beast of Blood* (1970).

These Are the Damned (1961; Hammer/Columbia; U.K.) (also *The Damned*). D: Joseph Losey. P: Anthony Hinds. S: Evan Jones. C: Arthur Grant. Cast: MacDonald Carey, Shirley Anne Field, Viveca Lindfors, Alexander Knox, Oliver Reed. A cold-blooded scientist keeps a group of children in a cave, exposing them to radiation in an attempt to prepare them for survival in the post-holocaust world to come. ¶ "Damned! The diabolical mastermind! Damned! The wild ones! Damned! The beautiful decoy! Come at your own risk … if you come alone!" — ad line. • *These Are the Damned* won the Golden Asteroid award at the Trieste Film Festival in 1964. • Oliver Reed, a gang leader in this film, is a nephew of famous British director Carol Reed (*The Third Man*, 1949). Ollie was born in Wimbledon, London, in 1938 and left home at age 17 to become a night club bouncer and boxer. • The story is based on the H. L. Lawrence novel, *The Children of Light*. • Publicity gimmicks suggested by the studio included setting up a geiger counter inside the theater to test the radiation count of passersby.

They Came from Within (1975; Trans America; Canada) (also *The Parasite Murders*). D/S: David Cronenberg. P: Ivan Reitman. C: Robert Saad. Cast: Paul Hampton, Joe Silver, Lynn Lowry, Barbara Steele, Allan Migicovsky, Susan Petrie. A misguided physician implants parasites into the stomachs of patients and the four-inch creatures mix a hearty sexual appetite with some gruesome exits, wreaking havoc at an isolated apartment complex.

The Tingler (1959; Columbia) D/P: William Castle. S: Robb White. C: Wilfrid M. Cline. Cast: Vincent Price, Philip Coolidge, Judith Evelyn, Darryl Hickman, Pamela Lincoln, Patricia Cutts. Vincent Price is a doctor who believes that many people who have died from extreme fear were killed by a parasite that takes shape within one's vertebrae. The creature is usually stopped from materializing when the victim screams. However, if a person is not able to release this tension, the "tingler" takes shape and cracks the person's spine. Eventually Price finds the perfect subject, a paranoid deaf mute, and with a little unexpected help from the woman's husband, he manages to capture a live tingler. The spinal parasite gets loose in a theater, providing just the lead-in necessary for a William Castle gimmick known as "Percepto" (the theater seats were electrically wired to give mild "shocks" at opportune moments. The buzz came from small war surplus motors which, when turned on, caused a vibration on the bottom of the seat). ¶ "Ladies and gentlemen, just a word of warning: If any of you are not convinced you have a tingler of your own, the next time you're frightened … don't scream." • The film, photographed in black and white, contains a color sequence in some prints that shows a bathtub full of red blood. • Screenwriter Robb White said in an interview with Tom Weaver and John Brunas in *Filmfax* #18: "We didn't want to buy thousands of vibrators without knowing whether they would really work out, so we scouted around until we found a theater in the Valley that was running *The Nun's Story....* Just at the most tragic moments of *The Nun's Story,* somebody touched the master switch and the seats began vibrating in wave after wave. There was absolute pandemonium! The other problem was the kids. They came and unscrewed the motors, broke them off and stole the things. They cost a lot of money, too. So that gimmick didn't work very long." White's overall opinion of horror films? "I hated them. And for years I didn't see some of these movies that I made with Bill Castle. I mean, they're so dumb! God, there's not a worm in your backbone when you get scared!"

Torture Ship (1939; Producers Pictures Corporation) D: Victor Halperin. C: Jack Greenhaugh. Cast: Lyle Talbot, Irving Pichel, Jacqueline Wells, Sheila Bromley, Anthony Averill. A mad doctor conducts gland experiments on humans aboard his ocean-liner laboratory. ¶ "I know what you're thinking—Bob is my nephew. I've sacrificed everything to prove my theory. Bob is free from criminal taint, a perfect subject." • *Torture Ship* features "a screenplay suggested by the story 'A Thousand Deaths' by Jack London." • *Torture Ship* was only the second production of the fledgling independent film company called "Producers Pictures Corporation." After a few more films (and a further name change to "Producers Distributing"), the company finally evolved into PRC (Producers Releasing Corporation—or, in the eyes of the more acerbic critics, "Poverty Row Cinema"). A mainstay of "B" horror films in the 40s, PRC produced and or distributed such memorable low-budget fare as *The Devil Bat* (1941), *Strangler of the Swamp* (1945), and *The Brute Man* (1946). • Though an actor of some note, Irving Pichel (who plays the mad doctor) is best known for working behind the camera. Pichel directed or co-directed over three dozen features, including *The Most Dangerous Game* (1932; co-director), *She* (1935; co-director), and the 1950 George Pal landmark science fiction film, *Destination Moon.* By 1940 Pichel had stopped acting completely and concentrated purely on directing.

The Twilight People (1972; New World; Philippines) D: Eddie Romero. P: Eddie Romero, John Ashley. S: Eddie Romero, Jerome Small. Cast: John Ashley, Pam Grier. This ultra-cheap adaptation of H. G. Wells' novel *The Island of Dr. Moreau* features a mad scientist creating animal-people on a remote island. • This is actually Eddie Romero's second stab at the Moreau motif, as he made a similar film in 1959 called *Terror Is a Man.*

The Unearthly (1957; Republic) D/P: Brook L. Peters. S: Geoffrey Davis. C: Merle Connell. Cast: John Carradine, Allison Hayes, Myron Healy, Sally Todd, Tor Johnson, Arthur Batanides, Harry Fleer. A mad scientist, played by John Carradine, attempts to arrest the aging process with the aid of a newly discovered gland. His numerous test subjects don't fare so well as they all become disfigured freaks, whom Carradine keeps locked in a basement. ¶ "I have the secret of life, of growth, and the cause of death." • Allison Hayes, who many regard as the chief rival to Beverly Garland's title of "Queen of the B's," was the Washington entry in the 1949 Miss America contest. She also had a brief career in television, appearing as a regular on the "General Hospital" soap opera, and the short-lived series, "Acapulco." She will probably be best remembered for her numerous roles in 50s fantastique films, including the unforgettable *Attack of the 50 Foot Woman* (1958). In her earlier years she was a graduate of the National Law School in Washington, D.C. In an official reception for Chief Justice Warren at the capitol, the honorable judge suggested that she try for a motion picture career and later he took time out to write a few letters to some of the studios recommending they give her a screen test. Her real name was Mary Anne Hayes. • New York-born John Carradine's first Hollywood job was as a scenery painter for a Cecil B. De-Mille production. He also studied sculpture before turning to the stage. • *The Unearthly* was released on a double bill with the giant grasshopper film, *Beginning of the End.*

Unnatural ... the Fruit of Evil (1952; DCA; W. Germany) D: Arthur Maria Rabenhalt. P: Styria Carlton (company). S: Kurt Heuser. C: Friedel Behn-Grund. Cast: Hildegarde Neff, Erich von Stroheim, Karlheinz Böhm, Rolf Henninger, Harry Meyen, Harry Halm. A mad scientist (Erich von Stroheim) creates a human female in his laboratory by means of artificial insemination. The beautiful creature, called Alraune, was fathered by a criminal about to be hanged, and her mother was a streetwalker. Her wicked inner nature comes out as she plots to break the heart of every male she meets, then lead them to their death. Eventually she does fall in love with an assistant and is killed in the end by her jealous creator. ¶ "Born outside the laws of God and man!"— ad line. • Erich von Stroheim has gained more fame as a director, producer, and writer of films, than from his acting credentials. Stroheim was well-known for his directing extravagance and his insistence on authentic detail (which nearly drove Universal's Irving Thalberg crazy on the expensive film, *Foolish Wives,* 1921). Stroheim's greatest achievement was directing the MGM classic, *Greed* (1923). The initial print was a seven-hour, 42-reel epic, which was hailed as one of the cinema's best works by those critics who were able to see it. The studio eventually wrestled it away from Stroheim and cut it down to ten reels. The original 42-reel version is preserved in the MGM vaults. • The German born Hildegarde Neff (who played Alraune) studied in Berlin during the war. Her career got off to a rocky start when all her scenes from the first film she was in ended up on the editing room floor, and her second effort went up in flames when the studio was bombed.

The Vampire Bat (1933; Majestic) D: Frank Strayer. P: Phil Goldstone. S: Edward T. Lowe. C: Ira Morgan. Cast: Lionel Atwill, Fay Wray, Dwight Frye, Melvyn Douglas, George E. Stone, Maude Eburne. Vampire murder victims, drained of blood, merely turn out to be victims of a human mad scientist (Lionel Atwill) who needs the blood to keep his sponge-like artificially-created creature alive. Halfwit Dwight Frye is mistakenly staked by superstitious villagers. ¶ "I have lifted the veil! I have created life, wrested the secret of life from life." • The talented Dwight Frye, typecast by Hollywood as the perennial ghoulish assistant after films like *Dracula* (1931) and *Frankenstein* (1931), lamented his ignoble fate at the hands of unimaginative producers. He made this statement in the pressbook for *The Vampire Bat:* "If God is good, I will be able to play comedy in which I was featured on Broadway for eight seasons and in which no producer of motion pictures will give me a chance! And please, God, may it be before I go screwy playing idiots, halfwits, and lunatics on the talking screen!" • Dwight Frye was born in Salina, Kansas, on February 22, 1899. His film career started with *The Doorway to Hell, Man to Man,* and *Dracula,* all in the same year — really 1930. He died in 1943, at the age of 44 from a heart attack. • The low-budgeted *Vampire Bat* utilized many standing sets on the Universal lot, including the interiors from *The Old Dark House* (1932).

Voodoo Woman (1957) (see VOODOO). Tom Conway plays a mad scientist intent upon creating a perfect human. He gives native girls injections and has the local voodoo priest intone incantations over them. With this combination of science and voodoo, Conway turns a woman into a hideous scaly monster that he can control with his mind.

The Vulture (1966) (see BIRDS). An accident involving an atomic-powered matter transmitter turns a scientist and a dead vulture into a half-man, half-vulture monster. His transformation is thought to coincide with a family curse by Cornwall locals.

Watchers (1988; Universal) D: Jon Hess. P: Damian Lee, David Mitchell. S: Bill Freed, Damian Lee. C: Richard Leiterman. Cast: Corey Haim, Barbara Williams, Michael Ironside, Lala, Duncan Fraser, Dale Wilson, Blu Mankuma, Coleen Winton. A precocious teen teams up with a super-intelligent, genetically mutated golden retriever to try to outwit a genetically-bred killing machine dubbed "Oxcon" (the result of experiments-gone-haywire in a clandestine government lab). Michael Ironside plays a ruthless killer agent out hunting Oxcon — and the boy. ¶ "If this thing is as vicious as you say it is, what are we gonna do once we find it? Throw a net over it?" • Oxcon resembles a Bigfoot/werewolf-type creature, and likes to gouge out the eyes of his victims.

Watchers 2 (1990; Concorde/New Horizons) D: Thierry Notz. P: Roger Corman. S: Henry Dominic. C: Edward Pei. Cast: Marc Singer, Tracy Scoggins, Jonathan Farwell, Irene Miracle, Mary Woronov, Tom Poster. The super-intelligent golden retriver from the first film returns and befriends a marine. The dog and his new pal contact an animal psychologist at the original genetics lab, all the time dodging attacks by a hybrid monster sent out after them.

The Werewolf (1956) (see WEREWOLVES — OTHER LYCANTHROPES). Two scientists use a man found at a car accident as a human guinea pig for their experimental "wolf serum," intended to protect humans against atomic radiation(!). The serum has the unfortunate side effect of turning him into a werewolf whenever he becomes angry.

The Woman Eater (1959) (see PLANTS) (also *Womaneater*). A mad scientist brings back a carnivorous tree from the Amazon jungle to which he feeds buxom young women in order to extract from it a special serum he uses in an attempt to revive the dead.

X — The Man with the X-Ray Eyes (1963; AIP) D/P: Roger Corman. S: Robert Dillon, Robert Russell. C: Floyd Crosby. Cast: Ray Milland, Diana Van Der Vlis, Don Rickles, John Hoyt, Harold J. Stone, Lorie Summers, Vicki Lee. Dr. Xavier (Ray

Milland) uses a special eyedrop formula to give him X-ray vision. After increasing the dosage and nearly going insane, he accidentally kills a man, then goes into hiding at a carnival. The show's greedy owner uses Milland first as a spiritualist, then later as a medical miracle worker. Eventually he leaves the outfit and winds up at a religious tent revival where, with some zealous prompting, he tears out his own eyes. ¶ "If thine eye offend thee, pluck it out!" • Roger Corman said of the film in Mark McGee's book, *Fast* *and Furious:* "The picture was shot in three weeks on a medium low budget (approximately $300,000) and I felt we were not going to be able to photograph what Xavier could see, and that the audience would be cheated.... The effects just weren't there. We did the best we could." • Despite Corman's doubts, the film won the Best Film award at the Trieste Science Fiction Film Festival of 1963. • Popular comedian Don Rickles plays the sideshow owner trying to exploit *X — The Man with the X-Ray Eyes.*

Madmen

(*See also* Cannibals; Jack the Ripper; Phantoms; Poe Films; Wax Museums)

This is by far the largest of all the chapters in this book, covering well over 300 films. One can speculate as to why the theme of madness had proved so popular to movie-going audiences and filmmakers alike. Perhaps it is the innate need to learn more about ourselves, our own psychological makeup, that draws people to this theme. Or perhaps it is like the fascination of the freak show — the unusual, bizarre, and especially the dangerous is much more interesting than the "normal" and mundane. Or it may even be that films about madmen are just plain cheap and easy to make (involving everyday sets and minimal special effects to speak of), and so have been churned out with economical regularity by producers bankrupt of both money and fresh ideas (this last could be a verbatim definition of the recent slasher epidemic). Whatever the reasons, films about madmen (and madwomen) have been, and continue to be, quite popular. Because of the sheer volume of films covered here, the subject has been broken up into three sub-sections by time period, each with its own unique character.

The first madman of note was that original asylum inmate, Dr. Caligari, who spun the frightening tale of Cesare the Somnambulist in *The Cabinet of Dr. Caligari* (1919). It is interesting to note that this first ever full-length horror film (indeed, *Caligari* has been called the father of horror cinema) was told through the eyes of a madman.

The year 1932 was great for madness. Three classics of screen dementia were thrust upon an unsuspecting and thrill-hungry public that year. The sinister, lustful Count Zaroff, hunting humans for sport in *The Most Dangerous Game;* the sadistic Fu Manchu, murdering and torturing with abandon in *The Mask of Fu Manchu;* and the wonderfully eccentric (and dangerously mad) members of the Femm family encountered in *The Old Dark House,* all showed their cringing audiences what a good madman could really do.

The forties continued the psychopathic tradition. In 1944, John Carradine (playing a sensitive artist driven mad by love to kill repeatedly) created a classic portrayal of tortured madness in the low-budget near-classic, *Bluebeard.* In contrast, *Bedlam* (1946) showed us Boris Karloff as the sneering, sadistic, "sane" head of the Bethlehem Asylum, whose cruel actions spoke louder of a pathologic condition than the sympathetic charges in his care.

Over two score madmen had giggled and lunged across the screen before Alfred Hitchcock redefined screen insanity in 1960 with his introduction of the ultimate psychotic momma's boy, Norman Bates. *Psycho* broke all the rules (and a few box office records as well), creating a character so terrifying in his psychosis that an entire nation was afraid to take a shower. (Though this may be a slight exaggeration, the film's impact was so powerful that there are people who even today admit to being a bit uneasy about drawing that shower curtain every morning.) Up to this point, madmen had been defined by their actions — the awful deeds they perpetrated being enough to brand them as mad and leave it at that. *Psycho* changed all that, for it was the first noteworthy horror film to dig beneath the cracked surface and delve into the twisted psyche of madness. It got at the roots of madness and opened up a whole new ball of psychological wax that eager filmmakers rushed to take advantage of. Soon the screens were flooded with pseudo-psychiatric babble about repressed childhoods and domineering mothers. Madness and madmen were off in a whole new direction with copycat films like William Castle's *Homicidal* (1961) and Hammer's *Paranoiac* (1963). For a time it seemed as if everyone was jumping on the *Psycho*tic bandwagon, even low-budgeted Bert I. Gordon (Mr. B.I.G. himself, maker of "giant" films like *The Amazing Colossal Man,* 1957; *Beginning of the End,* 1957; *The Spider,* 1958; etc.) with his imitative *Picture Mommy Dead* (1966). *Psycho* popularized the madman, as evidenced by the sheer number of films produced in its wake: Over *nine times* as many madmen movies have been made in the three decades since *Psycho* than in the four decades before it.

Variations emerged, such as the "elderly psycho lady" trend started with *What Ever Happened to Baby Jane?* in 1962, a truly brilliant and disturbing film that revived the sagging careers of Bette Davis and Joan Crawford. Every aging actress in Hollywood seemingly rushed to play an elderly lunatic in the spate of films that followed. There was *Hush . . . Hush, Sweet Charlotte* (1964), again with Ms. Davis; *Die! Die! My Darling* with Tallulah Bankhead calling the psychotic shots; *The Nanny* (1965) and *The Anniversary* (1968), both with Bette Davis; Geraldine Page in *What Ever Happened to Aunt Alice?* (1969); and *Who Slew Auntie Roo?* (1971, with Shelley Winters giving Bette Davis a much deserved rest).

Then in 1978, John Carpenter made a low-budget psycho movie called *Halloween* and screen madmen were never the same again. This suspenseful, frightening tale of a seemingly unkillable madman stalking a group of teens created a whole new subgenre, the "Slasher" film. But THE SLICE 'N' DICE WAVE really crested two years later with Paramount's well-promoted release of *Friday the 13th* in 1980. Though *Halloween* preceded it by two years, it took this poorly-made, poorly-acted, ultra-successful movie to open the floodgates of Hollywood and let the sea of slasher cinema spray out. Blame *Friday the 13th* for the countless "slice 'n' dice," "stalk 'n' slash," "slay 'n' spray" teen-kill pictures that every producer without an original idea in his head suddenly rushed into production. Whether you love it or hate it, however, there is no denying the importance of *Friday the 13th* in genre history. The sheer number of imitations and variations which followed ensures this film and its far superior predecessor, *Halloween,* a place in cinema history. The fact that the slasher film as a sub-genre started dying out after only a few years (peaking in the early-to-mid 1980s), and was all but dead at the close of the decade speaks volumes on the quality of the product. To be fair, there *have* been a few well-done and entertaining variations, with the tense and truly surprising Canadian import, *My Bloody Valentine* (1981), and the suspenseful *Slumber Party Massacre* (1982) being two unusual examples.

Fortunately, some filmmakers have foregone the slice 'n' dice formula and have dealt with their madmen in a serious, intelligent fashion, making their study in psychosis much more realistic and all the more frightening. Four excellent examples of the future hope for madmen movies are: the intensely disturbing and realistic look at a psychotic serial killer in *Henry: Portrait of a Serial Killer* (1986); the superbly acted shocker *The Stepfather* (1987); David Cronenberg's harrowing look at obsession and madness in *Dead Ringers* (1988); and the powerful, gripping *Silence of the Lambs* (1991). With films like these, there is hope for madmen yet.

See also CANNIBALS, JACK THE RIPPER, PHANTOMS, POE FILMS, and WAX MUSEUMS for more movie madness.

Early Madmen (from The Cabinet of Dr. Caligari *to* Psycho: *1919–1960)*

The Beast with Five Fingers (1947) (see HANDS). Peter Lorre plays a demented astrologer haunted by the manifestation of his own guilt in the form of his deceased employer's disembodied hand. Though we see the mobile member moving about on its own on several occasions, at the end it is revealed to be only in Lorre's mind. Lorre is the real killer, using his *own* hand (which is still connected) to murder. • Peter Lorre played many madmen on the screen over the course of his career, beginning with the sick child murderer in *M* (1931) and including such early classic madmen movies as *Mad Love* (1935) and *Stranger on the Third Floor* (1940).

Bedlam (1946; RKO) D: Mark Robson. P: Val Lewton. S: Mark Robson, Carlos Keith (Val Lewton). C: Nicholas Musuraca. Cast: Boris Karloff, Anna Lee, Billy House, Richard Fraser, Glenn Vernon, Ian Wolfe, Jason Robards, Sr., Leland Hodgson, Joan Newton, Elizabeth Russell, Skelton Knaggs. Boris Karloff plays Master Sims, the sadistic keeper of the Bethlehem lunatic asylum, generally referred to as "Bedlam." When a young woman scorns him and his aristocratic master, Sims has her put away in his horrid asylum. But with the aid of a young Quaker and her courage and kindness towards the inmates, she is set free while Sims meets his deserved fate at the hands of the unfortunate inmates. ¶ "These people are not guilty under the law, not answerable for what they do. Why should I add to their burdens?" • *Bedlam* was inspired by a set of engravings by William Hogarth, and the artist's paintings are featured in the film. • In a bit of upscale economizing, heroine Anna Lee wears Vivien Leigh's best dress from *Gone with the Wind* (1939). • The asylum itself was the converted church set from the Bing Crosby vehicle *The Bells of St. Mary's* (1945).

The Black Castle (1952; Universal) D: Nathan Juran. P: William Alland. S: Jerry Sackheim. C: Irving Glassberg. Cast: Richard Greene, Boris Karloff, Stephen McNally, Paula Corday, Lon Chaney, Jr., John Hoyt, Michael Pate, Nancy Valentine, Tudor Owen, Henry Corden, Otto Waldis. Stephen McNally plays a mad eighteenth century count who is fond of torture and hunting, with humans as his favorite big game. A young adventurer journeys to the count's castle and learns that the madman had killed his two friends and plans to kill the heroine. Boris Karloff plays the count's doctor, who aids the young hero. ¶ "For five years I lived in a nightmare of hate, reliving the agony I suffered because of this. I found only one relief for that agony. The hope that someday, somehow, I'd find you."

The Black Room (1935; Columbia) D: Roy William Neill. P: Robert North. S: Henry Myers, Arthur Strawn. C: Al Seigler. Cast: Boris Karloff, Marian Marsh, Robert Allen, Thurston Hall, Katherine DeMille. Boris Karloff plays twin aristocratic brothers—Anton, the good and kindly brother, and Gregor, the evil and sadistic sibling. An ancient family curse states that the youngest twin shall slay the elder in the castle's dreaded "Black Room." Anton leaves the estate to avoid the curse, but years later Gregor summons him back when the countryside is up in arms over Gregor's sadism and debauchery. Gregor announces that he is abdicating his ruling position to his kindly brother, then kills Anton by pushing him into the pit in the Black Room. Gregor takes his place, impersonating his own brother. He is found out in the end, and the curse is completed when a mob chases Gregor to the Black Room and he falls into the pit, there to be impaled on his dead brother's knife. ¶ "The older brother killed by the younger brother's knife—the prophecy has been fulfilled."

Bloodlust (1959; Crown International) D/P/S: Ralph Brooke. C: Richard E. Cunha. Cast: Wilton Graff, Lilyan Chauvin, Robert Reed, June Kenny, Joan Lora. In this low-budget version of *The Most Dangerous Game* (1932), the mad Dr. Balleau hunts humans for sport and keeps their bodies preserved in his trophy room. ¶ "A lust, a lust for blood, a lust that has grown over the years and one that I've spent my entire life trying to satisfy." • Hero Robert Reed later became familiar to TV audiences as the friendly patriarch of "The Brady Bunch."

Bluebeard (1944; PRC) D: Edgar G. Ullmer. P: Leon Fromkess. S: Pierre Gendron. C: Jockey A. Feindel. Cast: John Carradine, Jean Parker, Nils Asther, Ludwig Stossel, George Pembroke, Teala Loring, Sonia Sorel, Henry Kolker, Emmett Lynn, Iris Adrian, Patti McCarty. John Carradine plays the charming but mad nineteenth century Parisian painter/puppeteer Gaston Morel, who is driven to kill the women he paints. ¶ "I thought that [killing her] would stop her defiling the image I created of her, stop her degrading my work, I thought that would be the end of what she could do to me. But it wasn't ... every girl I painted turned out to be Jeanette, and every time I painted her, I had to kill her again." • Director Edgar G. Ulmer had planned to film *Bluebeard* many years before it was finally made. When Ulmer was affiliated with Universal in the 1930s, that studio had originally intended Karloff to play the title role, with Ulmer directing. The project never got off the ground and Ulmer eventually went to the low-budget studio PRC with the idea. • In the supporting cast is actress Sonia Sorel as "Renee," one of Carradine's victims. Ms. Sorel and Mr. Carradine were living together at the time while Carradine waited for the divorce from his first wife to come through. Soon after, the two were married. • *Bluebeard,* along with *Strangler of the Swamp* (1945), is generally considered to be the prolific but cheap PRC studio's finest horror picture.

A Bucket of Blood (1959; AIP) D/P: Roger Corman. S: Charles B. Griffith. C: Jack Marquette. Cast: Dick Miller, Barboura Morris, Anthony Carbone, Julian Burton, Ed Nelson, John Brinkley, John Shaner, Judy Babmer, Myrtle Domerel, Bert Convy, Jean Burton. Walter Paisley, a slow-witted busboy at the local beatnik coffeehouse has aspirations of becoming a great artist. When he accidentally impales a cat with a knife, he panics and covers it up with clay. The "statue" is hailed as a product of genius by the beatnik patrons, and soon Paisley graduates from animal to people, murdering them and covering their bodies in clay to make his statues. When he is found out, he is chased back to his apartment. When the crowd breaks down the door they find him hanging by the neck and partially covered in clay, becoming his own final "masterpiece." ¶ "I suppose he would have called it 'Hanging Man,' his greatest work." • Low-budget Roger Corman beat his own record of a six-day shooting schedule with this picture; *A Bucket of Blood* was shot in only five days. This "experiment," as Corman has called it, is one of the first black comedies in the genre. He followed it up a year later with *The Little Shop of Horrors* (1960). • Star Dick Miller (who played Walter Paisley) thought very highly of the film. "*A Bucket of Blood* is still my favorite picture," stated the actor. "None of these are great pictures, understand. But I always thought if *A Bucket of Blood* had had another chunk of money in production it would have ranked with any of the top horror films. It's the best script Chuck [Griffith] ever wrote."

The Cabinet of Dr. Caligari (1919) (see HYPNOTISTS). Dr. Caligari is a carnival mesmerist who uses his hypnotic power to control a somnambulist called "Cesare." The demented Caligari sends Cesare out to murder on command. In the film's epilogue, it is revealed that the story is nothing more than the ravings of a lunatic locked away in an asylum. ¶ "Today he is a raving madman, chained to his cell."

The Cat and the Canary (1927; Universal) D: Paul Leni. P: Carl Laemmle. S: Robert F. Hill, Alfred A. Cohn. C: Gilbert Warrenton. Cast: Laura LaPlante, Creighton Hale, Lucien Littlefield, Flora Finch, Arthur Edmund Carewe, Tully Marshall. A group of greedy relatives gather at a spooky old house for the reading of a will. When a young girl is chosen as heiress, some of her unscrupulous relations set about trying to drive her insane, including staging a bit about an escaped lunatic who prowls about like a cat looking for a canary to kill. • This is the first of four film versions of the story: Two of the same title (1939 and 1978) and one called *The Cat Creeps* (1930). • *The Cat and the Canary* was brilliant German director Paul Leni's first American film. He went on to direct another classic of the silent era, *The Man Who Laughs* (1928). Tragically, Leni suffered a premature death from blood poisoning in 1929.

The Cat and the Canary (1939; Paramount) D: Elliot Nugent. P: Arthur Hornblow, Jr. S: Walter De Leon, Lynn Starling. C: Charles Lang. Cast: Bob Hope, Paulette Goddard, John Beal, Douglas Montgomery, Gale Sondergaard, George Zucco. Once again an estranged family gathers at an old mansion for the reading of a will. This time, Bob Hope plays the outwardly cowardly but inwardly courageous hero who must uncover the mysterious goings-on, including a supposed escaped maniac wandering about committing murder. ¶ "There are spirits all around you"—Gale Sondergaard. "Well, could you put some in a glass? I need it badly"—Bob Hope. • This successful remake is more an out-and-out comedy (thanks to the presence of the witty Bob Hope) than its two predecessors (*The Cat and the Canary*, 1927; and *The Cat Creeps*, 1930). It was popular enough to induce Paramount to rush out another (and even better) Hope/Goddard horror/comedy the following year, *The Ghost Breakers* (1940).

The Cat Creeps (1930; Universal) D: Rupert Julian. P: Carl Laemmle, Jr. S: Gladys Lehman, William Hurlbut. C: Jerry Ash, Hal Mohr. Cast: Helen Twelvetrees, Raymond Haskell, Neil Hamilton, Jean Hersholt, Montague Love. This first sound remake of *The Cat and the Canary* (1927) follows the original storyline quite closely, with Helen Twelvetrees as the imperiled heroine, and Neil Hamilton as the supposed escaped lunatic murderer known as "The Cat."

Chamber of Horrors (1941; Pathé/Monogram; U.K.) (also *The Door with Seven Locks*). D: Norman Lee. P: John Argyle. S: Norman Lee, Gilbert Gunn. C: Alex Bryce, Ernest Palmer. Cast: Leslie Banks, Lilli Palmer, Romilly Lunge, Gina Malo, Richard Bird, David Horne. A secret kept behind a door with seven locks is sought after by numerous unsavory characters. Foremost among them is Leslie Banks, a madman who employs his torture chamber to gruesome effect. ¶ "A woman's scream was music to his ears!"—according to the advertising. • Leslie Banks had endeared himself to horror fans nine years earlier when he played the sinister madman Count Zaroff, who liked to hunt *The Most Dangerous Game* in 1932.

The Face Behind the Mask (1941; Columbia) D: Robert Florey. P: Wallace Macdonald. S: Allen Vincent, Paul Jarrico. C: Franz Planer. Cast: Peter Lorre, Evelyn Keyes, Don Beddoe, George E. Stone, John Tyrrell, Stanley Brown, Al Seymour, James Seay, Warren Ashe, Charles Wilson, George McKay. Peter Lorre plays immigrant craftsman Janos Szabo, whose face is so horribly disfigured in a fire that he is unable to find work, forcing him into a life of crime. Hiding his face behind a mask made to resemble his original features, the now ruthless criminal falls in love with a blind girl, who cannot see his hideous countenance. When she is killed in an attempt upon his life by his own gang, Janos goes mad with revenge and flies his gang's plane into the middle of the desert, there to perish from heat and thirst. • Peter Lorre did not actually wear a mask for his role, his face was coated with heavy white makeup to *simulate* a mask.

A Game of Death (1945; RKO) D: Robert Wise. P: Herman Schlom. S: Norman Houston. C: J. Roy Hunt. Cast: John Loder, Audrey Long, Edgar Barrier, Russell Wade, Jason Robards, Noble Johnson. In this loose remake of *The Most Dangerous Game* (1932), Edgar Barrier plays a German madman who hunts humans for sport on his isolated Caribbean island. • Actor Noble Johnson appeared in both this and the earlier version. • Footage from RKO's earlier film turned up at the climax of this remake. • The screams of heroine Audrey Long are actually screams made by that ultimate screamer herself—Fay Wray—taken from an old soundtrack recording.

The Ghost Ship (1943; RKO) D: Mark Robson. P: Val Lewton. S: Donald Henderson Clarke. C: Nicholas Musuraca. Cast: Richard Dix, Russell Wade, Edith Barrett, Ben Bard, Edmund Glover. A sea captain (Richard Dix) is driven to homicidal madness by the weight of authority and his own fear. A young third officer sailing aboard his ship realizes that the captain is responsible for the deaths of several of the crew and must try to convince the men of the captain's madness. ¶ "The man is dead. With his death the waters of the sea are open to us. But there will be other deaths and the agony of dying before we come to land again." • This is the only one of the nine horror films producer Val Lewton made for RKO in the 1940s (including two other early madmen movies—*The Leopard Man*, 1943, and *Bedlam*, 1946) that has not had a significant release or showing on television. Apparently there were some legal problems regarding story rights which has kept this dark, stylish thriller under wraps.

The Haunted Strangler (1958; Anglo Amalgamated/MGM; U.K.) D: Robert Day.

P: John Croydon. S: Jan Read, John C. Cooper. C: Lionel Banes. Cast: Boris Karloff, Jean Kent, Elizabeth Allan, Anthony Dawson, Vera Day. Boris Karloff plays a criminologist investigating the infamous Haymarket Strangler case of 20 years ago, believing the police hanged the wrong man. He is correct, and it is revealed that Karloff himself is the notorious madman (without being aware of it), turning from kindly criminologist to maniacal killer whenever he handles the original murder weapon. ¶ "Perhaps he had a compulsion to kill. Afterwards, in his lucid moments, he might bitterly regret his actions. He might forget them altogether." • For his transformations into deformed killer, Karloff used very little makeup and instead relied on body language and facial movements to portray the psychotic madman.

Horrors of the Black Museum (1959; Anglo-Amalgamated/AIP; U.S./U.K.) D: Arthur Crabtree. P: Herman Cohen. S: Aben Kandell, Herman Cohen. C: Desmond Dickinson. Cast: Michael Gough, Graham Curnow, June Cunningham, Shirley Ann Field, Geoffrey Keen, Gerald Andersen, Beatrice Varley, Nora Gordon, John Warwick. Michael Gough plays a sadistic crime-reporter who hypnotizes his young assistant and sends him out to commit gruesome murders which Gough can then write about to titillate the public. Gough also keeps his own "black museum" in his basement, featuring all manner of horrible devices, including a pair of binoculars which contain spikes in the lenses to gouge out the eyes of unwary users. • Producer/co-screenwriter Herman Cohen came up with the idea for this film after he toured Scotland Yard's real "Black Museum" (and saw the infamous spiked binoculars — a real murder weapon). • This was the first color film for AIP — the most prolific independent film company making monster pictures in the 50s and 60s. Oddly enough, black and white prints of the film were often shown in theaters and later on TV (presumably because color negatives were much more expensive to produce in quantity). • Advertising from AIP ballyhooed a gimmick called "Hypnovista," claiming "you can't resist it!" on their posters. This turned out to be a 13-minute lecture on hypnotism tacked to the start of the film.

How to Make a Monster (1958; AIP) D: Herbert L. Strock. P: Herman Cohen. S: Kenneth Langtry, Herman Cohen. C: Maury Gertzman. Cast: Robert H. Harris, Paul Brinegar, Gary Conway, Gary Clarke, Walter Reed, Robert Shayne, Morris An-

krum, John Ashley. When a studio makeup man is fired, the unhinged artist uses a special drugged makeup base to control the actors wearing his monster makeup. He sends out a caveman, the "Teenage Frankenstein Monster," and the "Teenage Werewolf" to kill the studio heads who fired him. ¶ "I'll destroy them first, and I'll use the very monsters they mocked to bring them to an end." • The teen version of AIP's classic monsters were utilized: The Frankenstein Monster is from *I Was a Teenage Frankenstein* (1957; with actor Gary Conway repeating his earlier role) and the werewolf is from *I Was a Teenage Werewolf* (1957; with Gary Clarke filling in for Michael Landon). • Being the undisputed masters of film exploitation in the 1950s, AIP came up with a wonderfully lurid poster for *How to Make a Monster,* coupled with this classic camp ad line: *"It will scare the living* yell *out of you!"* • The mad makeup man keeps old monster masks on display in his home and you can spot AIP's own monsters from *Invasion of the Saucermen* (1957) and *The She-Creature* (1956). • *How to Make a Monster* was originally released on a teen-pleasing double bill with *Teenage Caveman.*

The Human Monster (1939; Pathé/Monogram; U.K.) (also *Dark Eyes of London*). D: Walter Summers. P: John Argyle. S: Patrick Kirwan, Walter Summers, J. F. Argyle. C: Ryan Langley. Cast: Bela Lugosi, Hugh Williams, Greta Gynt, Edmon [sic] Ryan, Wilfred Walter, Alexander Field. In this film, Bela Lugosi plays a dual role (as Dr. Orloff *and* Mr. Dearborn). As Dr. Orloff, he runs an insurance company and lends money against policies in which he is the beneficiary. As Mr. Dearborn, he runs a home for the blind and uses it and its unwitting occupants in his nefarious schemes, which include torture and murder. ¶ "He wanted to be a doctor but — 'brilliant but unbalanced,' — *that* was the verdict." • This was the first British film to receive the British censor's new "H" rating for "Horror" created in 1937. • Since Bela Lugosi's distinctive voice and accent would have immediately given away his identity as the kindly Mr. Dearborn, his voice was dubbed by British actor O. B. Clarence. Lugosi's own voice was used for his other persona — Dr. Orloff. • The story was remade in West Germany in 1961 as *Dead Eyes of London.*

The Invisible Ghost (1941; Monogram) D: Joseph H. Lewis. P: Sam Katzman. S: Helen Martin, Al Martin. C: Marcel Le Picard. Cast: Bela Lugosi, Polly Ann Young, John McGuire, Betty Compson,

Clarence Muse. Bela Lugosi plays the mild-mannered Dr. Kessler grieving for his dead wife. But his wife is not dead, and she periodically wanders around the house and grounds in a state of dazed amnesia. Whenever Lugosi catches sight of her, he goes temporarily insane and becomes a vicious homicidal maniac, choking any throat he can get his hands around. • The film went through several title changes before finally becoming *The Invisible Ghost,* including *Murder by the Stars* and *The Phantom Killer.* • Supposedly, the story was based on the real-life murder/suicide case of Walter Krivitsky, which involved various political machinations and Soviet spies (none of which made it into the film).

Island of Doomed Men (1940; Columbia) D: Charles Barton. P: Wallace Macdonald. S: Robert D. Andrews. C: Benjamin Kline. Cast: Peter Lorre, Rochelle Hudson, Robert Wilcox, Don Beddoe, George E. Stone, Kenneth MacDonald, Charles Middleton, Stanley Brown, Earl Gunn. The cruel and sadistic Stephen Danel (Peter Lorre) owns Dead Man's Isle, which he runs as a private penal colony, working and torturing the men to death while forcing himself on his unwilling wife. A Department of Justice agent is framed for murder and ends up on the madman's island, where he organizes a revolt against the repulsive "Fastidious connoisseur of human suffering" (as the film's publicity proclaimed him). ¶ From the poster: "Women shuddering at his cruel caress! Men dying under his torturing lash!"

The Leopard Man (1943; RKO) D: Jacques Tourneur. P: Val Lewton. S: Ardel Wray. C: Robert Grasse. Cast: Dennis O'Keefe, Margo, Jean Brooks, Isabell Jewell, James Bell, Abner Biberman, Tula Parma. A maniacal killer masquerades as an escaped leopard to commit his gruesome murders in this lesser Val Lewton effort.

M (1931; Paramount; Germany) D: Fritz Lang. P: Seymour Nebenzal. S: Thea von Harbou. C: Fritz Arno. Cast: Peter Lorre, Ellen Widmann, Inge Landgut, Gustaf Grundgens, Fritz Gnass, Fritz Odemar, Paul Kemp, Theo Lingen, Ernst Stahl-Nachbaur, Franz Stein, Otto Wernicke. Peter Lorre plays Hans Beckett, a sick child molester and murderer of little girls, whose crimes hold Berlin in a grip of panic. The police step up their raids against the underworld in an attempt to apprehend the madman, causing the beleaguered criminals to decide to find the murderer themselves in order to relieve the police pressure. They finally corner the killer and try him in a mock court held at an abandoned brewery. Just as the sentence of death is pronounced, the police arrive and take both the killer and his would-be executioners into custody. ¶ "You are all criminals because you want to be. But I . . . I do what I do because I can't help it!" • The film *M* is based on the real-life child murderer Peter Kurten, known as "The Vampire of Düsseldorf." • This was director Fritz Lang's first talkie. • It was also Peter Lorre's first film, and his critically acclaimed performance catapulted him into international stardom as well as type-casting him for life. • For the kangaroo court climax, in which Lorre is tried by a band of criminals, Lang recruited real-life criminals to add realism to the scene.

Macabre (1958; Allied Artists) D/P: William Castle. S: Robb White. C: Carl E. Guthrie. Cast: William Prince, Jim Backus, Jacqueline Scott, Christine White, Philip Tonge, Ellen Corby. A small-town doctor, who has just lost his wife and sister-in-law under mysterious circumstances, now finds his young daughter kidnapped and supposedly buried alive by a madman. Concerned parties frantically race against the clock to find the buried child, but it turns out to be a plot engineered by the doctor himself, who had murdered the two women and is now attempting to frighten his father-in-law to death in order to claim the family wealth. • William Castle, the "King of the Gimmicks," gained publicity for his film by offering free insurance, underwritten by Lloyds of London, to anyone that died of heart failure while viewing the movie. "Of course it would be an awful thing if somebody actually did die in the theater," Castle remarked, then added, "but the publicity would be terrific." This was prolific genre director William Castle's first horror movie. • Castle filmed *Macabre* in nine days for $90,000. Ballyhooed by its insurance gimmick, it grossed over $5,000,000. • The film is based on the book *The Marbel Forest,* a novel written chapter by chapter by 13 members of the Mystery Writers of America using a pseudonym.

Mad Love (1935) (see HANDS). This classic version of Maurice Renard's novel, *Les Mains d'Orlac (The Hands of Orlac),* features Colin Clive as concert pianist Stephen Orlac whose hands are horribly mutilated in a train accident. In desperation his wife Yvonne goes to the brilliant surgeon Dr. Gogol (Peter Lorre) for help. Gogol harbors a mad love for Yvonne, a stage actress, and agrees to operate. He grafts the hands of an executed murderer onto Stephen's arms. Gogol, now consumed with madness due to his unrequited love, sets about driving Stephen insane and frames him for murder, and then attempts to strangle the object of his insane desires with her own hair. ¶ "Each man kills the thing he loves." • In 1935, Charles Chaplin said of Lorre, "He is the greatest living actor."

The Man Who Reclaimed His Head (1934; Universal) D: Edward Ludwig. P: Carl Laemmle, Jr. S: Jean Bart (Marie Antoinette Sarlabous), Samuel Ornitz. C: Merritt Gerstad. Cast: Claude Rains, Joan Bennett, Lionel Atwill, Baby Jane, Henry O'Neill, Henry Armetta, Wallace Ford, Lawrence Grant, William B. Davidson. Though more of a melodrama than a horror film, *The Man Who Reclaimed His Head* was promoted as a horror picture by Universal and does contain some gruesomely horrific elements. Told in flashbacks, peaceloving French ghost-writer Paul Verin is taken advantage of by his greedy publisher Henri Dumont. Verin is betrayed by the ambitious Dumont, who uses his newfound influence to incite war. Dumont also arranges to have Verin sent to the front when he decides to go after Verin's lovely wife. Verin finally realizes what is happening, and returns just as Dumont is forcing himself on his wife. Verin goes temporarily insane and hacks off Dumont's head with his bayonet. • Jean Bart (along with Samuel Ornitz) adapted her own stageplay for the screen. The story was remade by Universal for one of their "Inner Sanctum" films starring Lon Chaney, Jr., as *Strange Confession* (1945). • Claude Rains reprised his New York stage role for the film. • Joan Bennett, who plays Rains' wife, was the highest paid cast member, earning $12,500, $2,000 more than Rains himself.

Maniac (1934; Hollywood Producers and Distributors) D/P: Dwain Esper. S: Hildegarde Stadie. C: William Thompson. Cast: Bill Woods, Horace Carpenter, Ted Edwards, Phyllis Diller (not the comedienne), Thea Ramsey, Jennie Dark. In this early grind-house exploitationer, a madman impersonates a doctor in order to commit rape and murder. He is finally discovered when the yowling of a cat (borrowing from Edgar Allan Poe's "The Black Cat") exposes to the authorities the place where he had hidden a body. • This early anomaly features partial nudity and scenes of grotesquery not found in films of this period. In one particularly daring (and distasteful) scene, the *Maniac* gouges out the eye of a cat and pops the eyeball into his mouth like a tasty snack. •

Screenwriter Hildegarde Stadie is the wife of producer/director Dwain Esper. The husband and wife filmmaking team also brought us *Marijuana, Weed with Roots in Hell* (1936) and *How to Undress in Front of Your Husband* (1937).

The Mask of Fu Manchu (1932; MGM) D: Charles Brabin. P: Irving Thalberg. S: Irene Kuhn, Edgar Allan Woolf, John Willard. C: Tony Gaudio. Cast: Boris Karloff, Lewis Stone, Karen Morley, Charles Starrett, Myrna Loy, Jean Hersholt, Lawrence Grant, David Torrence. That evil Oriental madman Fu Manchu (Boris Karloff) is after the mask and sword of Ghengis Khan, using all manner of torture and sadism to get them. But he will have to battle English archeologists and Scotland Yard before attaining the symbolic means of power to unite Asia against the West: "Should Fu Manchu put that mask across his wicked eyes, and take that scimitar into his bony cruel hands, all Asia arises." ¶ "I am a doctor of Philosophy from Edinburgh. I am a doctor of Laws from Christ's College. I am a doctor of Medicine from Harvard. My friends, out of courtesy, call me 'doctor'." • Myrna Loy, later achieving stardom in the "Thin Man" series, portrayed Fu Manchu's sadistic nymphomaniac daughter, whom that villain is willing to compromise if necessary. • Director Charles Brabin was actually a replacement for the original (first-time) director Charles Vidor, who was fired by MGM during production. Much of the existing footage was re-shot by the new director. • This is the first time Boris Karloff played an oriental character. He donned the false eyelids again for *West of Shanghai* (1937) and the five "Mr. Wong" films in which he plays a Chinese detective.

The Most Dangerous Game (1932; RKO) D: Ernest B. Schoedsack, Irving Pichel. P: Merian C. Cooper. S: James Ashmore Creelman. C: Henry Gerrard. Cast: Joel McCrea, Fay Wray, Leslie Banks, Robert Armstrong, Noble Johnson, Steve Clemento, William Davidson, Dutch Hendrian. Robert Rainsford, a big game hunter by profession, is stranded on an island in the Malay archipelago. There he encounters the island's owner, the sinister Count Zaroff, as well as several other stranded guests. It is soon revealed that the mad Zaroff, whose passion is hunting, likes to hunt "the most dangerous game"—man. Rainsford and a young woman must match wits and strength with Zaroff in his hunt of death. ¶ "Kill, then love! When you have known that you have known everything!" • *The Most Dangerous Game* is based on the Richard Connell short story of the same name. Two straight remakes (as well as several films which "borrowed" the concept) were filmed — *A Game of Death* (1945) and *Bloodlust* (1961). • This film was made by the same team who created *King Kong* (1933) — the director/producer team of Ernest B. Schoedsack and Merian C. Cooper, and screenwriter James Creelman. *The Most Dangerous Game* also utilized the jungle sets from *King Kong,* and though released before *Kong,* was actually filmed after the start of that classic ape movie (which took close to a year to complete, mostly due to the time consuming animation work). Several actors from *Kong* starred in this film as well: Fay Wray, Robert Armstrong, and Noble Johnson. • According to Fay Wray, the directing chores were split up between the two men with Ernest B. Schoedsack directing the action and Irving Pichel directing the dialogue. • Co-director Irving Pichel worked in front of as well as behind the camera. As an actor he created the unforgettable role of "Sandor," the evil, slimy, scheming servant of *Dracula's Daughter* in 1936.

Murders in the Zoo (1933; Paramount) D: Edward Sutherland. S: Philip Wylie, Seton I. Miller. C: Ernest Haller. Cast: Charlie Ruggles, Lionel Atwill, Randolph Scott, Gail Patrick, John Lodge, Kathleen Burke, Harry Beresford, Edward McWade. Lionel Atwill plays the sadistic and maniacally jealous Eric Gorman, a wealthy big game hunter and zoo patron, who uses the venom from the deadly green mamba snake and various zoo animals to kill off his wife's real and imagined lovers. • One of Atwill's snake-bite victims, lawyer-turned-actor John Lodge, retired from acting after World War II and turned to politics, eventually becoming governor of Connecticut in 1950. • Ironically, Paramount cast Kathleen Burke as Atwill's terrified wife, who is eaten by animals (crocodiles to be precise). She had played "Lota" the panther girl (who was created from an animal) in *Island of Lost Souls* earlier that same year. • At the time of its release, *Murders in the Zoo* was generally condemned for its excessiveness and bad taste (as was Paramount's other 1933 horror — *Island of Lost Souls*), though by today's standards it is tame indeed.

The Mystery of the Marie Celeste (Hammer; 1936; U.K.) (also *Phantom Ship*). D: Denison Clift. P: M. Fraser Passmore. S: Charles Larkworthy. C: Goeffrey Faithfull, Eric Cross. Cast: Bela Lugosi, Shirley Grey, Arthur Margetson, Edmund Willard, Dennis Hoey, George Mozart, Johnnie Scho-

field, Gunner Moir, Ben Weldon. Captain Briggs and his new bride set sail on the *Mary Celeste* (the correct name of the ship). Soon, crew members are found murdered or simply disappear from the ship. It is finally revealed that one of the sailors, a one-armed man who had lost his arm on a previous sailing of the *Mary Celeste,* has gone mad and committed the crimes. ¶ "When this ship sails, death sails upon her." • This film takes its inspiration from a true incident in 1872 in which a clipper ship, the *Mary Celeste,* was found adrift with no sign of the crew on board. It remains a mystery to this day. • Exteriors were shot on the English Channel in a rented schooner called the *Mary B. Mitchell.* • Hammer later revived the horror movie with its gothic remakes in the 1950s and 1960s, beginning with *The Curse of Frankenstein* (1957).

Night Must Fall (1937; MGM; U.K.) D: Richard Thorpe. P: Hunt Stromberg. S: John Van Druten. C: Ray June. Cast: Robert Montgomery, Rosalind Russell, Dame May Whitty, Alan Marshal, Kathleen Harrison, E. E. Clive, Beryl Mercer. Robert Montgomery plays a charming Cockney psychopath who carries a severed head around in a box while worming his way into the confidence of Dame May Witty. ¶ "You can kill me. I dare say you would have anyway. But at least now I know what you *are,* I know what you're like — mad, mad and *horrible!*" • The film was remade in 1964 by MGM and starred Albert Finney.

Night of Terror (1933; Columbia) D: Benjamin Stoloff. S: Beatrice Van, William Jacobs. C: Joseph A. Valentine. Cast: Bela Lugosi, Sally Blane, Wallace Ford, George Meeker, Tully Marshall, Edwin Maxwell, Bryant Washburn, Gertrude Michael, Mary Frey, Matt McHugh. This typical murder-in-an-old-house horror/mystery features a repulsive maniac (a man voluntarily buried alive to test his new revival serum) and Bela Lugosi as a turbaned swami whose wife goes into trances at inopportune moments. ¶ "I am the maniac!" • The film's original title was the lurid *He lived to kill.* The story was inspired by a European scientist who claimed to have discovered a drug which would revive a person buried alive for seven days. • In a bit of good-humored self-spoofing, the ending has the killer arise from the grave and threaten to haunt the audience if they reveal the plot. • Star Bela Lugosi was filming another movie concurrent with this one *(The Devil's in Love),* so all his scenes for *Night of Terror* were shot at night while he worked on the other film during the day.

The evil lord Fu Manchu (Boris Karloff) and his sensuous daughter (Myrna Loy) inspect their death ray device in The Mask of Fu Manchu *(1932).*

The Old Dark House (1932; Universal) D: James Whale. P: Carl Laemmle, Jr. S: Benn W. Levy. C: Arthur Edeson. Cast: Boris Karloff, Melvyn Douglas, Charles Laughton, Lilian Bond, Ernest Thesiger, Eva Moore, Raymond Massey, Gloria Stuart, John Dudgeon, Brember Wills. During a violent rainstorm in the Welsh mountains, a group of people are forced to take refuge in the "benighted household" of the eccentric and outright mad Femm family. They include the effeminate, disdainful Horace Femm; the pious and intolerant Rebecca Femm; the maniacal and dangerous Saul Femm; and the lecherous butler Morgan. ¶ "Morgan is an uncivilized brute. Sometimes

Boris Karloff plays the brutish butler Morgan, who attacks Gloria Stuart in The Old Dark House *(1932).*

he drinks heavily. A night like this will set him going and once he's drunk he's rather dangerous." • Playing the "savage brute" Morgan, this was Karloff's first horror film after *Frankenstein* (1931), and Universal was quick to play up their new horror star. The studio tacked on this caption at the film's beginning: "*Producer's Note:* Karloff, the mad butler in this production is the same Karloff who created the part of the mechanical monster in *Frankenstein.* We explain this to settle all disputes in advance, even though such disputes are a tribute to his great versatility." • This was the first film to give Karloff top star billing (he was billed fourth in *Frankenstein*). • The role of the 102-year-old family patriarch, Sir Roderick Femm, was actually played by a *woman,* an elderly stage actress named Elspeth Dudgeon (whose first name was changed to "John" in the film's credits). • This picture marked the American film debut of both Charles Laugh-ton and Raymond Massey. • Along with this classic James Whale also directed *Franken-stein* (1931), *The Invisible Man* (1933), and *Bride of Frankenstein* (1935), making him the most outstanding director in the Golden Age of Horror. • *The Old Dark House* was based on the J. B. Priestley novel *Be-nighted.* William Castle filmed an abysmal comic remake in 1963.

Pillow of Death (1945; Universal) D: Wallace Fox. P: Ben Pivar. S: George Bricker. C: Jerome Ash. Cast: Lon Chaney, Jr., Brenda Joyce, J. Edward Bromberg, Rosalind Evan, Clara Blandick, George Cleveland, Wilton Graff, Bernard B. Thomas. Lon Chaney plays a man seemingly haunted by the voice of his murdered wife, who was killed by suffocation. He is suspected by the police, and it appears as if he is being framed for her murder. Several more "pillow kill-ings" occur, and the heroine finally learns that it *is* Chaney after all; he is insane and

The mute butler Morgan (Boris Karloff) carries the body of Saul Femm (Brember Wills) inside The Old Dark House *(1932) while Charles Laughton and Raymond Massey look on.*

carries on imaginary conversations with his dead wife. Obedient to the end, he falls to his death when his wife's phantom voice tells him to leap out of a window. ¶ "At last she realizes that you are a psychopathic killer." • This was the last of Lon Chaney, Jr.'s, "Inner Sanctum" films at Universal, and was rushed into production mere days after the wrapping of the previous entry *Strange Confession* (1945). Six Inner Sanctum movies were made—two involving hypnotism, one centering on voodoo, and a straight mystery. One other dealt with madness and that was *Strange Confession*. • Supporting player Clara Blandick is best remembered as "Auntie Em" from *The Wizard of Oz* (1939).

Scared to Death (1947; Screen Guild) D: Christy Cabanne. P: William B. David. S: W. J. Abbott. C: Marcel Le Picard. Cast: Bela Lugosi, George Zucco, Nat Pendleton, Molly Lamont, Joyce Compton, Gladys Blake, Roland Varno, Douglas Fowley, Stanley Andrews, Angelo Rossitto, Lee Bennett, Stanley Price. This strange, convoluted $135,000 film follows the fears of

Molly Lamont as she begins to go mad and finally finds death at a sinister sanitarium populated by strange characters, including Bela Lugosi as a mysterious magician named "Leonide." ¶ "We're sending the report over. She was *scared to death*." • This low-budget Bela Lugosi vehicle featured the rather novel concept of being narrated by a corpse. It carried shooting titles of *The Autopsy* and *Accent on Horror*. • This was Bela Lugosi's first and only color film. "Photographed in *Natural Color*" claimed the credits, but it actually employed a cheap, garish-looking color process called "Cinecolor" which was discontinued entirely in 1955. • Lionel Atwill was originally to have played the George Zucco role, but was too ill to do the picture. He died of cancer the same month it was completed (April of 1946—the film was not released until over a year later).

The Strange Case of Dr. Rx (1942; Universal) D: William Nigh. P: Jack Bernhard. S: Clarence Upson Young. C: Woody Bredell. Cast: Patric Knowles, Lionel Atwill,

Anne Gwynne, Samuel S. Hinds, Mona Barrie, Shemp Howard, Paul Cavanagh, Edmund MacDonald. When a number of big-time crooks are acquitted, they are mysteriously murdered by a sinister "self-appointed angel of vengeance" calling himself Dr. Rx. A young detective is called in on the case, and after being nearly frightened to death by the madman in an attempt to warn him off, uncovers the unlikely identity of the "egomaniac psychopath." ¶ "For every crime there is a punishment. Men who sin must pay a just penalty." • Originally titled *Dr. Rx,* the film's moniker was changed before release, possibly to avoid confusion wtih Warner Bros.' *Dr. X* (1932). • Despite having received second billing and having his image dominate the poster art, horror stalwart Lionel Atwill has only a small role in the film (as "Dr. Fish"—a red herring). • Leading man Patric Knowles was on army furlough when *The Strange Case of Dr. Rx* was filmed. Both Knowles and co-star Anne Gwynne claimed that much of the dialogue was ad-libbed since they were forced to shoot with an incomplete script.

Strange Confession (1945; Universal) (also *The Missing Head*). D: John Hoffman. P: Ben Pivar. S: M. Coates Webster. C: Maury Gertsman. Cast: Lon Chaney, Jr., Brenda Joyce, J. Carrol Naish, Milburn Stone, Lloyd Bridges, Addison Richards, Mary Gordon, George Chandler, Gregory Muradian. Told in flashback, Lon Chaney, Jr., plays Jeff Carter, a brilliant young chemist who works for a greedy drug manufacturer named Graham. Carter is working on a cure for influenza, and Graham sends him to South America to perfect the new drug, while he sets his lecherous sights on Carter's beautiful wife. Unbeknownst to Carter, when an influenza epidemic breaks out, the callous Graham puts the drug on the market before it is perfected. Carter's young son Tommy contracts the disease and dies while his mother tries treating him with the ineffective drug. Enraged at Graham's lack of ethics, Carter returns home, finds his son is dead, and goes insane. He visits Graham at his home and hacks off his head with a South American knife. The police arrive to take him away, but the lawyer friend to whom he had told his story promises to do all he can for Carter. ¶ "I had the feeling that Graham was me, me—Jeff Carter. My mind was his, my brain was in his head, and I knew that I must have it back to make it mine again. Don't you see? That's why I killed him, just to get back something that belonged to me, that's all." •

This has been called the best of Lon Chaney's "Inner Sanctum" pictures made for Universal. He made a total of six unrelated films in the series based on the popular "Inner Sanctum" books and radio program, several of them belonging to the standard whodunnit school. Two others were released this same year—*The Frozen Ghost* and *Pillow of Death.* • *Strange Confession* is a remake of Universal's previous *The Man Who Reclaimed His Head* (1934) starring Claude Rains. Both were based on the play "The Man Who Reclaimed His Head" by Jean Bart (Marie Antoinette Sarlabous). • A young Lloyd Bridges has a supporting role as Chaney's down-to-earth assistant.

The Strange Door (1951; Universal) D: Joseph Pevney. P: Ted Richmond. S: Jerry Sackheim. C: Irving Glassberg. Cast: Charles Laughton, Boris Karloff, Sally Forrest, Richard Stapley, Michael Pate, Paul Cavanagh, Alan Napier, William Cottrell, Morgan Farley, Edwin Parker, Charles Horvath. A sadistic and debauched nobleman (Charles Laughton) plans to wed his niece to an irresponsible rogue in a plan to further exact revenge on his brother, who he has secretly tortured and imprisoned in the castle dungeons. He finally traps the couple in a cell along with his brother and plans to crush them to death with moving walls. His plan is foiled by his vengeful servant (Boris Karloff), who sends the mad nobleman to his own death within a huge spinning waterwheel. ¶ "You've perhaps heard of Cabriza, the torturer. In the Middle Ages he used this chateau for some of his favorite experiments." • Karloff had teamed with Laughton once before, at the very beginning of his stardom, in *The Old Dark House* (1932) (which was Laughton's American debut).

Stranger on the Third Floor (1940; RKO) D: Boris Ingster. P: Lee Marcus. S: Frank Partos. C: Nicholas Musuraca. Cast: Peter Lorre, John McGuire, Margaret Tallichet, Charles Waldron, Elisha Cook, Jr., Charles Halton, Ethel Griffies, Cliff Clark, Oscar O'Shea, Alec Craig, Otto Hoffman. A young reporter is apprehended for murder on circumstantial evidence, with only the description of a bizarre-looking stranger (Peter Lorre) seen lurking about that day as a lead for his defense. His fiancée searches for the sinister stranger and finally finds him, learning that he is an escaped lunatic who murders all those who learn the truth—including her. She is saved from death when the insane stranger is hit by a truck while chasing her through the streets. • *Stranger* *on the Third Floor* has achieved the distinction of being heralded as the first "film noir." • The story was originally a radio thriller before being turned into a film. • Though he appears onscreen for only a few minutes in the brief (but pivotal) role of the mad stranger, Peter Lorre was awarded top billing.

Terror in the Haunted House (1958; Howco International) (also *My World Dies Screaming*). D: Harold Daniels. P: William S. Edwards. S: Robert C. Dennis. C: Frederick E. West. Cast: Gerald Mohr, Cathy O'Donnell, William Ching, John Qualen, Barry Bernard. A newly married woman has a recurring nightmare about an old mansion, and her husband takes her off for a rest—to that very same mansion. She begins having hallucinations, centering around a series of axe killings, which culminates in the confrontation of a real-life maniac wielding an axe. • The film was shot using a process the filmmakers called "Psychorama." Psychorama was actually the subliminal flashing of pictures of skulls and gruesome faces superimposed on the screen, intending to induce more shudders in the audience. Right.

Tower of London (1939; Universal) D/P: Rowland V. Lee. S: Robert N. Lee. C: George Robinson. Cast: Basil Rathbone, Boris Karloff, Barbara O'Neil, Ian Hunter, Vincent Price, Nan Grey, Ernest Cossart, John Sutton, Leo G. Carroll. This embellished account of Richard III's murderous rise to power in fifteenth century England features Boris Karloff as Mord the Executioner and Chief Torturer, who carries out the evil bidding of his master Richard, a man driven by mad ambition. ¶ "I've never killed in *hot* blood. It must be different, more ... more exciting"—Karloff as Mord the Executioner. • Roger Corman remade *Tower of London* in 1962 but filmed along the lines of a ghost story rather than of an historical horror epic. Interestingly, Vincent Price, who here plays the Duke of Clarence, drowned by Richard and Mord in a vat of wine, graduated to the role of Richard himself in Corman's low-budget remake. • At the film's beginning, actor John Rodion falls under the blade of Mord's headsman's axe, providing top-billed Basil Rathbone with the dubious pleasure of watching the execution of his own offspring—John Rodion is Rathbone's real-life son. • The production of *Tower of London* was plagued with problems, finally wrapping ten days over schedule and $80,000 over budget (quite a bit over, considering the total budget was only $500,000). Director Rowland V. Lee had great difficulty in shooting the battle scenes. Three hundred extras were there ready for battle, only to have their cardboard helmets and shields disintegrate when the rain machines were turned on. Lee finally overcame these obstacles by shooting small bands of men fighting and transposing them against a background of battle scenes already shot to create a montage effect.

You'll Find Out (1940; RKO) D/P: David Butler. S: James V. Kern. C: Frank Redman. Cast: Kay Kyser, Boris Karloff, Peter Lorre, Helen Parrish, Dennis O'Keefe, Bela Lugosi, Alma Kruger, and Kay Kyser's Band. This musical comedy features the "Three Horror Men" (Boris Karloff, Peter Lorre, and Bela Lugosi) as villains conspiring to kill a rich heiress for her fortune. When a houseful of party guests, including Kay Kyser and his "Kollege of Musical Knowledge" Band, are trapped there on a stormy night, the three evil conspirators make several attempts on the life of the heroine before finally threatening to blow the whole place up and kill everyone. Of course it all turns out in the end, with band member Ish Kabibble's dog grabbing the explosives and blowing up the villains with their own dynamite.

Early Psychos (from Psycho *to* Halloween: *1960–1978)*

The Abominable Dr. Phibes (1971; AIP; U.K.) D: Robert Fuest. P: Louise M. Heyward, Ronald S. Dunas. S: James Whiton, William Goldstein. C: Norman Warwick. Cast: Vincent Price, Joseph Cotten, Hugh Griffith, Terry-Thomas, Virginia North, Audrey Woods, Susan Travers, Alex Scott, Edward Burnham, Peter Gilmore, Peter Jeffrey. The brilliant but mad (and hideously disfigured) Dr. Anton Phibes (his doctorate is in music and theology) takes revenge on the medical team which operated unsuccessfully on his wife, killing them off one by one by ingeniously employing the Old Testament's biblical curses—boils, bats, frogs, blood, hail, rats, beast, locusts, and death of the first born. ¶ "Nine killed you and nine shall die!" • This successful blending of bizarre art deco sets, campy black humor (carried over even into the ad campaign: "Love means never having to say you're ugly"), quirky characterizations, and grotesque deaths was so popular that it inspired a sequel, *Dr. Phibes Rises Again,* made the following year, and again starring Vincent Price as Phibes. • British beauty Caroline Munro portrayed Phibes' deceased wife, appearing first as a photograph in *The Abominable Dr. Phibes,* and then in person as a corpse in its sequel, *Dr. Phibes Rises Again* (1972). • *The Abominable Dr. Phibes* was publicized as Vincent Price's one hundredth feature film.

Alice, Sweet Alice (1976; Allied Artists) (also *Communion; Holy Terror*). D: Alfred Sole. P: Richard K. Rosenberg. S: Rosemary Ritvo, Alfred Sole. C: John Friberg, Chuck Hall. Cast: Linda Miller, Mildred Clinton, Paula Sheppard, Niles McMaster, Rudolph Willrich, Brooke Shields, Jane Lowry. A killer in a yellow raincoat and flesh-colored makeup stalks a Catholic family, committing gruesome murders, including that of an eight-year-old girl on the day of her first communion. • Popular child actress Brooke Shields made her screen debut as the eight-year-old victim of the knife-wielding maniac.

The Anniversary (1968; Hammer/20th Century–Fox; U.K.) D: Roy Ward Baker. P/S: Jimmy Sangster. C: Harry Waxman. Cast: Bette Davis, Sheila Hancock, Jack Hedley, James Cossins, Elaine Taylor, Christian Roberts, Timothy Bateson, Arnold Diamond. Bette Davis plays the mentally unbalanced Mrs. Taggart, a woman who dominates her three sons at the annual family reunions by employing unusual and oft-times grisly methods in this black comedy from Hammer.

Apartment on the Thirteenth Floor (1974; Atlas International; Spain) D/S: Eloy de la Iglesia. P: Joe Truchado. S: Raoul Artigot. Cast: Vincente Parra, Emma Cohen, Eusebio Poncela, Vicky Lagos, Ismael Merlo, Charlie Bravo, Rafael Hernandez, Lola Herrera, Valentin Tornos. A disturbed young man becomes flustered with a cabdriver and kills him. He then disposes of his fiancée, who objects to his rather hasty violent action. Next he must kill his brother, who discovers a corpse under his bed . . . and so on in this "video nasty" which was banned in Britain.

The Baby (1974; Scotia International) D: Ted Post. P: Milton Polsky, Abe Polsky. S: Abe Polsky. Cast: Anjanette Comer, Ruth Roman, Marianna Hill, David Manzy. A deranged, man-hating mother raises her full-grown son to act like an infant. The man-sized son crawls around in diapers and sleeps in a crib. He also has the strength to kill, as a young social worker attempting to rectify the perverted situation discovers.

Barn of the Naked Dead (1973; Twin World) (also *Terror Circus*). D: Alan Rudolph. P: Gerald Cormier. S: Roman Valenti. C: E. Lynn. Cast: Andrew Prine, Manuella Thiess, Sherry Alberoni, Gyle Roland. Madman Andrew Prine imagines himself to be a big-time animal trainer and keeps a group of women chained up in his barn to train as his "animal act." ¶ "I'm your trainer! You obey me and you'll be part of the greatest animal menagerie in history. But if you disobey, you will *suffer!*"

The Beast in the Cellar (1971; Tigon/Cannon; U.K.) (also *Are You Dying Young Man?*). D/S: James Kelly. P: Graham Harris. C: Harry Waxman. Cast: Beryl Reid, Flora Robson, Tessa Wyatt, John Hamill, T. P. McKenna, David Dodimead, Dafydd Havard. Two elderly spinsters imprison their brother during World War II so he cannot go off to fight. Thirty years later he is still locked in the cellar, but is now a homicidal maniac who periodically breaks out and goes on a killing spree. • The "beast" kept in the cellar is quite a disappointment when finally revealed. With his scrawny body and long matted hair, he looks more like a sickly derelict than a vicious madman.

Bell from Hell (1973; Avco Embassy; Spain/France) (also *The Bell of Hell*). D/P: Claudio Guerin Hill. S: Santiago Moncada. C: Manuel Rojas. Cast: Fenaud Verley, Viveca Lindfors, Alfredo Mayo, Maribel Martin, Nuria Gimeno. A man returns home from an asylum to take vengeance upon those greedy family members who had had him committed for his money. He terrorizes his relatives until he is finally locked in a bell tower with the bell rope tied around his neck. • Tragically, director/producer Claudio Guerin Hill fell to his death from the same bell tower on the last day of shooting.

Berserk (1968; Columbia; U.K.) D: Jim O'Conolly. P: Herman Cohen. S: Aben Kandel, Herman Cohen. C: Desmond Dickinson. Cast: Joan Crawford, Ty Hardin, Diana Dors, Michael Gough, Robert Hardy, Judy Geeson. Joan Crawford plays the domineering owner/ringmaster of a traveling circus, whose performers are dying in bizarre accidents — accidents staged by a maniacal killer with a familial grudge against Crawford, as revealed in the twist ending.

Beware the Brethren (1972; Cinerama; U.K.) (also *The Fiend*). D/P: Robert Hartford-Davies. S: Brian Comport. C: Desmond Dickinson. Cast: Ann Todd, Tony Beckley, Patrick Magee, Madeline Hinde, Percy Herbert, Suzannah Leigh. A young man, influenced by a reactionary religious sect, kills prostitutes in order to save them from sinning.

The Bird with the Crystal Plumage (1970; U.M. Distributors; Italy/W. Germany) (also *Phantom of Terror*). D/S: Dario Argento. P: Salvatore Argento. C: Vittorio Storaro. Cast: Tony Musante, Suzy Kendall, Eva Renzi, Umberto Raho, Mario Adorf, Enrico Maria Salerno, Renato Romano. A man witnesses a vicious slasher attack, and is then hounded by the knife-wielding maniac while more murders are committed. Finally, the man uncovers the surprise identity of the slasher in the twist ending. • This early psycho film was Italian horror maestro Dario Argento's first feature.

The Black Zoo (1963) (see CATS). Michael Gough plays the disturbed owner of a private zoo who sends out his big cats to murder his enemies. Gough also ushers the various lions and tigers into his living room periodically so he can play the organ for them.

Blood and Black Lace (1964; Woolner; Italy/France/W. Germany). D: Mario Bava. P: Massimo Patrizi, Alfred Mirabel, Lou Moss (English version). S: Mario Bava, Marcello Fondato, Giuseppe Barilla. C: Herman Tarzana (Ubaldo Terzano). Cast: Eva Bartok, Cameron Mitchell, Thomas Reiner, Ariana Gorini, Mary Arden, Lea Kruger, Claudia Dantes, Harriet White, Nadia Anty, Heidi Stroh. A masked madman with a metal-clawed glove stalks a fashion salon which is a front for a drug ring, violently killing the beautiful young models. • English and Italian versions of the movie were filmed simultaneously. • Star Cameron Mitchell gave high praise to Italian director Mario Bava. "I loved Mario Bava," the actor told Tom Weaver for *Fangoria* #103. "In many ways he might have been the best director—certainly the best one I've worked with in Europe, and maybe the best of them all.... He never had a really good script, but he could make a film out of anything."

Blood and Lace (1971; AIP) D: Philip Gilbert. P: Ed Carlin, Gil Lasky. S: Gil Lasky. C: Paul Hipp. Cast: Gloria Grahame, Melody Patterson, Milton Selzer, Len Lesser, Vic Tayback, Terri Messina, Ronald Taft, Dennis Christopher, Peter Armstrong, Maggie Corey. A teenage girl, the daughter of a murdered prostitute, is sent to an orphanage run by a sadistic woman and her homicidal handyman. The pair brutally murders all those kids who try to run away and stores their bodies in a meat locker. When the girl rebels, she is stalked by a hammer-wielding maniac wearing a hideous mask. ¶ From the ads: "*Shock* after *Shock* after *Shock* as Desire drives a bargain with *Murder!*"

The Bloody Pit of Horror (1965; Pacemaker; Italy) (also *The Crimson Executioner; The Red Hangman*). D: Max Hunter (Massimo Pupillo). P: Francesco Merli. S: Robert Christmas (Roberto Natale), Robert McLorin (Romano Migliorini). C: John Collins (Luciano Trasatti). Cast: Mickey Hargitay, Walter Brandt, Louise Barrett (Luisa Baratto), Ralph Zucker, Alfred Rice, Femi Martin (Femi Benussi), Rita Klein, Barbara Nelli, Moha Tahi, Nick Angel. Muscleman Mickey Hargitay (then-husband of Jayne Mansfield) is an unbalanced ex-actor who snaps when a group of photography models visits his castle. He goes mad and in his mind becomes the "Crimson Executioner," a sadistic medieval torturer. ¶ From the trailer: "Never before so much paralyzing terror as in this hair-raising orgy of sadism, influenced by the shocking writings of the evil, depraved Marquis de Sade."

Bluebeard (1972; Cinerama; Italy/Hungary) D: Edward Dmytryk. P: Alexander Salkind. S: Ennio De Concini, Edward Dmytryk, Maria Pia Fusco. C: Gabor Pogany. Cast: Richard Burton, Raquel Welch, Joey Heatherton, Virna Lisi, Nathalie Delon, Marilu Tolo, Karin Schubert, Agostina Belli, Sybil Danning, Mathieu Carrière. Richard Burton plays a wealthy admired aristocrat who marries women and then viciously kills them when his manhood is threatened, storing his ex-wives in a walk-in freezer. ¶ "I love you Anne, I really do, probably more than any other woman I've ever loved. But I have to kill you Anne, like all the others." • This exploitative (with plenty of nudity), dull, ineffectual version of the classic story is far inferior to the 1944 version of *Bluebeard,* and even to the lesser but entertaining film, *Bluebeard's Ten Honeymoons.*

Bluebeard's Ten Honeymoons (1960; Allied Artists; U.K.) D: W. Lee Wilder. P: Roy Parkinson. S: Myles Wilder. C: Stephen Dade. Cast: George Sanders, Corinne Calvet, Jean Kent, Patricia Roc, Greta Gynt, Maxine Audley, Ingrid Hafner. George

Sanders is Monsieur Landru, an antique furniture broker in Paris who discovers a much more lucrative way to make a living. He woos rich women, takes over their business affairs, and brutally murders them. In the end, the sister of one of his victims discovers his hideous crimes and he goes to the guillotine.

The Brides of Fu Manchu (1966; Anglo Amalgamated/Seven Arts; U.K./W. Germany) D: Don Sharp. P: Harry Alan Towers. S: Peter Welbeck (Harry Alan Towers). C: Ernest Steward. Cast: Christopher Lee, Douglas Wilmer, Howard Marion-Crawford, Marie Versini, Rupert Davies, Tsai Chin, Roger Hanin, Harold Leipnitz, Heinz Drache, Joseph Furst. Fu Manchu kidnaps 12 beautiful girls, all daughters of influential families or powerful government officials, and holds them hostage to insure their families' cooperation in his plans of world domination. He then builds a powerful ray gun with which to carry out his world-conquering ambitions. ¶ "You will hear from me again!" — Fu Manchu, in a line that proved repetitious in each succeeding Fu Manchu entry. • This is the second (of five) Fu Manchu films to star Christopher Lee. It follows up *Face of Fu Manchu* (1965). *The Vengeance of Fu Manchu* (1968) was next. • Advertising for this Fu Manchu installment centered around the publicity stunt of holding a contest to pick 12 girls, each from a different country, to appear in the film. • Star Christopher Lee was not overly pleased with the finished product, calling it "the first step down the slippery slope that leads to overexposure to a character in inadequate films." He also wondered why producer Harry Alan Towers chose to ignore all of Sax Rohmer's rich Fu Manchu stories, and create a new story of his own (Towers wrote the screenplay under the pseudonym Peter Welbeck).

The Cabinet of Caligari (1962; 20th Century-Fox) D/P: Roger Kay. S: Robert Bloch. C: John Russell. Cast: Dan O'Herlihy, Glynis Johns, Estelle Winwood, Vicki Trickett, J. Pat O'Malley. Glynis Johns plays a woman who is held prisoner in the home of the sinister Dr. Caligari. After numerous illusionary experiences, she finally realizes that she is actually a patient recovering at a mental hospital. • Though it shares the name, this version has very little to do with the 1919 silent classic *The Cabinet of Dr. Caligari,* nor does it possess any of the earlier's films merits. • Screenwriter Robert Bloch wrote the novel *Psycho,* upon which Hitchcock's 1960 classic is based.

The Castle of Fu Manchu (1968; International Cinema; Spain/Italy/W. Germany/U.K.) (also *Assignment Istanbul*). D: Jesus Franco. P: J. Balcazar, Harry Alan Towers. S: M. Barthel (Harry Alan Towers). C: Manuel Merino. Cast: Christopher Lee, Richard Greene, Tsai Chin, Rosalba Neri, Gunther Stoll, José Manuel Martin, Maria Perschy, H. Marion Crawford. Once again, the nefarious Fu Manchu is out to dominate the world, this time working out of a hidden fortress in Turkey. • This is the last (and some say worst) film in Christopher Lee's Fu Manchu series started with *The Face of Fu Manchu* (1965). Harry Alan Towers produced all five films and also wrote all five screenplays using the pseudonym Peter Welbeck (or in this instance M. Barthel).

Cauldron of Blood (1967; Cannon; Spain) (also *Blind Man's Bluff*). D: Edward Mann (Santos Alcocer). P: Robert D. Weinbach. S: John Nelson, Edward Mann. C: Francisco Sempere. Cast: Jean-Pierre Aumont, Boris Karloff, Viveca Lindfors, Jacqui Speed, Rosenda Monteros, Milo Quesada, Dianik Zurakowska, Ruben Rojo. Boris Karloff is a blind sculptor who unwittingly uses real human bones in his statues, supplied by his mad, murderous wife. ¶ "Don't you think we've killed enough people for your husband's *statues?*" • Claude Rains, the original Invisible Man, was scheduled to star in *Cauldron of Blood,* but became ill and was replaced by Boris Karloff. • Though filmed in 1967, the film was not released until 1971, nearly three years after Karloff's death.

The Chooper (1971; Program Releasing) (also *Blood Shack*). D: Wolfgang Schmidt (Ray Dennis Steckler). P: Carol Flynn. S: Christopher Edwards. C: Sven Christian (Ray Dennis Steckler) Cast: Carolyn Brandt, Ron Haydock, Jason Wayne, Laurel Spring, John Bates, Linda Steckler, Laura Steckler, Steve Edwards. A young woman inherits a large ranch in the desert along with an old house supposedly haunted by the murderous Indian spirit called "The Chooper." Of course, there is no "Chooper," simply a maniacal neighbor obsessed with buying the ranch and killing everyone who comes near the house. ¶ "They're not gonna tear this old house down ... so you just keep killin' all you want and I'll keep buryin' 'em. But they'll never knock this old house down." • No-budget filmmaker Ray Dennis Steckler directed the film using the pseudonym Wolfgang Schmidt, and photographed (and edited) it under the name Sven Christian. Lead actress Carolyn Brandt is Steckler's wife, and the two children in the film are his daughters. • Steckler claimed he made *The Chooper* in three days.

Circus of Horrors (1960; Anglo Amalgamated/AIP; U.K.) D: Sidney Hayers. P: Julian Wintle, Leslie Parkyn. S: George Baxt. C: Douglas Slocombe. Cast: Anton Diffring, Erika Remberg, Yvonne Monlaur, Donald Pleasence, Jane Hylton, Conrad Phillips, Kenneth Griffin, Vanda Hudson, Yvonne Romain, Colette Wilde. A sadistic plastic surgeon hides out from the police by running a small circus. He takes disfigured women into his circus, reconstructs their faces to make them beautiful, and then keeps them in his circus. When they disobey or try to leave, they meet with an "accident" — a knife-thrower's assistant receives a knife in the throat, an acrobat falls to her death, a lion-tamer is mauled, etc. • The circus facilities and some of the acts were furnished by Billy Smart's Circus.

Color Me Blood Red (1965; Box Office Spectaculars) D/S/C: Herschell Gordon Lewis. P: David F. Friedman. Cast: Don Joseph, Candi Conder, Scott H. Hall, Elyn Warner, Patricia Lee, Jerome Eden, Jim Jaekel. A mad painter finally achieves recognition when he uses a new type of paint on his canvases — blood. He turns to murder to obtain his precious pigments. ¶ "They say Gauguin was obnoxious too!" • This is Herschell Gordon Lewis' (The "Godfather of Gore") third gore film.

The Confessional (1976; Atlas; U.K.) (also *House of Mortal Sin*). D/P: Pete Walker. S: David McGillivray. C: Peter Jessop. Cast: Anthony Sharp, Susan Penhaligon, Stephanie Beacham, Sheila Keith, Norman Eshley, Hilda Barry, Stuart Bevan, Mervyn Johns. A maniacal Catholic priest tapes the confessions of young women for blackmail purposes and murders those who get in his way, using rosary beads to strangle a woman, or a flaming incense burner, or poison communion wafers, etc.

The Crazies (1973; Cambist) D/S: George A. Romero. P: Alvin C. Croft. C: S. William Hinzman. Cast: Lane Carroll, W. G. McMillan, Harold Wayne Jones, Lloyd Hollar, Richard Liberty, Lynn Lowry. A military plane carrying an experimental virus for bacteriological warfare crashes near Evans City, Pennsylvania, and infects the drinking water, transforming the town's citizens into crazed killers.

The Creature with the Blue Hand (1971; Rialto/New World; W. Germany) D: Alfred Vohrer. S: Alex Berg. C: Ernest Kalinke. Cast: Klaus Kinski, Diana Korner, Carl Lang, Ilse Page, Harald Leipnitz, Siegfried Schurnenberg. Klaus Kinski plays a man wrongly institutionalized for a murder he did not commit. He escapes the asylum and returns home to the mansion of his twin brother, intending to prove his innocence. His arrival coincides with a series of murders committed by a one-eyed hooded maniac known as the "Blue Hand," so named because of the vicious razor-clawed medieval gauntlet he uses to slice up his victims.

Crescendo (1969; Hammer/Warner Bros; U.K.) D: Alan Gibson. P: Michael Carreras. S: Jimmy Sangster. C: Paul Beeson. Cast: Stefanie Powers, James Olson, Margaretta Scott, Jane Lapotaire, Joss Ackland, Kirsten Betts. A young American woman becomes involved with a bizarre French family which includes a demented widow, her cripped drug-addicted son, and a murderous mad twin locked away in the attic.

Crucible of Horror (1971; Cannon; U.K.) (also *The Corpse; Velvet House*). D: Viktor Ritelis. P: Gabrielle Beaumont. S: Olaf Pooley. C: John Mackey. Cast: Michael Gough, Yvonne Mitchell, Sharon Gurney, Simon Gough, Olaf Pooley, David Butler, Mary Hignett, Nicholas Jones. A sadistic man (Michael Gough) is murdered by his wife and daughter, who can no longer live with his tyrannical treatment. He is not truly dead, however, for his "corpse" continues to pop up to terrorize his family, and he eventually re-takes his place as the head of the household with his wife gone quietly insane. • Screenwriter Olaf Pooley appears in the film as a nosy neighbor.

Crucible of Terror (1971; Scotia/Barber; U.K.) D: Ted Hooker. P: Tom Parkinson. S: Ted Hooker, Tom Parkinson. C: Peter Newbrook. Cast: Mike Raven, Mary Maude, James Bolam, Ronald Lacey, Betty Alberge, John Arnatt, Beth Morris, Judy Matheson, Melissa Stribling, Me Me Lay. Mike Raven plays a mad artist who kills his models and covers their bodies in molten bronze to make life-like statues. • Villain Mike Raven was a disc jockey for the BBC before turning to acting.

Dead Eyes of London (1961; Magna; W. Germany) D: Alfred Vohrer. P: Herbert Sennewald. S: Trygve Larsen. C: Karl Loeb. Cast: Joachim Fuchsberger, Karin Baal, Dieter Borsche, Klaus Kinski, Ady Berber, Wolfgang Lukschy. An evil reverend runs a home for the blind and uses his charges to murder wealthy insurance holders. • *The Dead Eyes of London* is a remake of the 1939 Bela Lugosi vehicle, *The Human*

Monster. Both versions are based on the Edgar Wallace story "The Testament of Gordon Stuart."

Dear Dead Delilah (1972; Avco Embassy) D/S: John Farris. P: Jack Clement. C: William R. Johnson. Cast: Agnes Moorehead, Will Geer, Michael Ansara, Patricia Carmichael, Dennis Patrick, Anne Meacham, Robert Gentry, Ruth Baker, Elizabeth Eis, Ann Gibbs. Agnes Moorehead plays the domineering, wheelchair-bound matriarch of a southern family. She tells her greedy relations that $600,000 is buried on the family estate and they commence a frantic search for the money. The search does not go well, however, as one by one they are picked off by a mysterious axe murderer. • *Dear Dead Delilah* was filmed in Nashville and produced by record producer Jack Clement, who has worked with country legends Johnny Cash and Charley Pride among others.

Deep Red (1976; Mahler; Italy) (also *The Hatchet Murders*). D: Dario Argento. P: Salvatore Argento. S: Giuseppe Bassan. C: Luigi Kuveiller. Cast: David Hemmings, Daria Nicolodi, Gabriele Lavia, Macha Meril, Clara Calamai, Glauco Mauri, Eros Pagni, Giuliana Calandria, Nicoletta Elmi. An Englishman in Rome witnesses a brutal murder and is drawn into an ever-tightening web of violence involving a psychotic pianist and his deranged mother. ¶ From the trailer: "*Deep Red*—it'll put you into deep shock." • Female lead Daria Nicolodi is the wife of director Dario Argento.

Dementia 13 (1963; AIP/Filmgroup) D/S: Francis Ford Coppola. P: Roger Corman. C: Charles Hannawalt. Cast: William Campbell, Luana Anders, Bart Patton, Mary Mitchell, Patrick Magee, Barbara Dowling. An eccentric family living at an Irish estate is steeped in tragedy, deceit, and murder, revolving around the drowning of a young child years earlier and an axe-murder by a demented family member. • Though this is often cited as Francis Ford Coppola's first film, it is not. But it *is* an early entry from the great director, and his first foray into the realm of the macabre.

Deranged (1974; AIP; Canada) D/S: Jeff Gillen, Alan Ormsby. P: Tom Karr. C: Jack McGowan. Cast: Roberts Blossom, Marion Waldman, Cosette Lee, Robert Warner, Marcia Diamond, Brian Sneage, Robert McHeady, Micki Moore, Pat Orr. Based on the real-life grave robber/murderer Ed Gein, dubbed "The Wisconsin Ghoul" by the press, Roberts Blossom plays a sexually-repressed momma's boy driven by loneliness and madness to unearth his mother's corpse

and then provide "companions" for her. ¶ "This is a true story. These events really happened"—opening narration. • Both *Psycho* (1960) and *The Texas Chainsaw Massacre* were said to be inspired by the Ed Gein case, but this film is the truest depiction of the hideous crimes of the "Wisconsin Ghoul." • In an interview with *HorrorFan* magazine, filmmaker Bob Clark claimed that it was *he* who produced the film. He removed his name, feeling its horror was just too real. "I decided to take my name off it," explained Clark. "It was too good. It was so real and so horrible as it was played.... That's where I had trouble with the film. You felt for him [the killer]. It's chilling, because when he kills and mutilates people, you do feel something for him. It was too much." • Clark went on to say that co-director "Alan [Ormsby] hated directing. Making *Deranged* for $200,000 was grueling work."

Die! Die! My Darling (1965; Hammer/Columbia; U.K.) (also *Fanatic*). D: Silvio Narizzano. P: Anthony Hinds. S: Richard Matheson. C: Arthur Ibbetson. Cast: Tallulah Bankhead, Stefanie Powers, Peter Vaughn, Maurice Kaufman, Yootha Joyce, Donald Sutherland. Tallulah Bankhead plays the mad religious fanatic Mrs. Trefoile who imprisons her dead son's ex-fiancee (Stefanie Powers) in the attic, intending to purify and then kill her so she can marry her deceased son in Heaven. • This was Ms. Bankhead's last film.

Dr. Phibes Rises Again (1972; AIP; U.K.) D: Robert Fuest. P: Louis M. Heyward. S: Robert Fuest, Robert Blees. C: Alex Thomson. Cast: Vincent Price, Robert Quarry, Valli Kemp, Fiona Lewis, Peter Cushing, Beryl Reid, Terry-Thomas, Hugh Griffith, Peter Jeffrey. Phibes is back, searching for the "River of Life" in his obsession to revive his dead wife. The search takes him to Egypt where he crosses paths with another man with the goal of attaining eternal life. Numerous inventive murders are committed before Phibes sails down the River of Life on a barge with his wife's coffin while "Somewhere Over the Rainbow" plays on the soundtrack. ¶ Inspector Trout: "Do you think you know where we are, sir?" Trout's superior: "I don't think, I know!" Inspector Trout: "I don't think you know either, sir." • Director Robert Fuest rose again for the sequel, as did Vincent Price as Phibes and Peter Jeffrey as Inspector Trout. • Plans were made to continue the series with a third Phibes movie, but this sequel didn't live up to their box office expectations and plans for further Phibes films were dropped.

Don't Look in the Basement (1973; Hall-mark) D/P: S. F. Brownrigg. S: Tim Pope. C: Robert Alcott. Cast: William Bill Mc-Ghee, Anne MacAdams, Rosie Holotik, Gene Ross, Jessie Lee Fulton, Camilla Carr, Harriet Warren. The director of an ex-perimental insane asylum is axed to death, and a female inmate takes his place, con-ducting bizarre and brutal "therapy" ses-sions. ¶ "Ripe strawberries are the color of blood!" • *Don't Look in the Basement* was filmed in 12 days for $100,000. It carried the shooting title of *The Forgotten.*

Drive-in Massacre (1976; New American) D/P: Stuart Segall. S: John Goff, Buck Flower. Cast: Jake Barnes, Adam Law-rence, Douglas Gudbye. A madman goes berserk at a drive-in and begins killing the patrons in various gruesome ways. ¶ "Not everyone comes to watch the movie"—ad line. • The film's ending features a gimmick worthy of a William Castle film—a voice (supposedly the manager) comes on and warns the audience that the killer is loose in the drive-in.

The Dungeon of Harrow (1964; Herts-Lion) D: Pat Boyette. P: Russ Harvey, Don Russell. S: Pat Boyette, Henry Garria. C: James Houston. Cast: Russ Harvey, Helen Logan, William McNutty, Michelle Bu-quor, Maurice Harris, Eunice Grey, Lee Morgan. In the nineteenth century, two men are shipwrecked and wash ashore on a presumably deserted island. They find a cas-tle and meet the five inhabitants, including the mad lord of the castle named Count Lorente de Sade and his leprous wife locked away in the dungeon. One man is tortured and killed, but the other falls in love with the only eligible female in the household and kills the evil count, but ironically suffers the same fate as the madman. He is now con-taminated with the hideous disease of leprosy and is doomed to live out the rest of his days on the island, taking the place of the mad count as he too slowly sinks into the madness of the horrible disease. ¶ "For another time, another place, I might have brought honor and glory to the house of Fallon, but instead I shall leave a legacy of decay and unspeakable horror." • This no-budget, semi-professional independent was filmed in San Antonio, Texas.

Eaten Alive (1976; New World) (also *Death Trap; Horror Hotel Massacre; Star-light Slaughter*). D: Tobe Hooper. P: Mardi Rustam. S: Alvin Fast, Mardi Rustam. C: Robert Caramico. Cast: Neville Brand, Mel Ferrer, Carolyn Jones, Marilyn Burns, William Finley, Stuart Whitman, Roberta Collins, Kyle Richards, Robert Englund. Neville Brand plays the proprietor of a run-down backwoods Louisiana hotel, a psycho who runs amok, killing his guests with a huge scythe and feeding them to an enor-mous crocodile. • This was director Tobe Hooper's second feature, his first being *The Texas Chainsaw Massacre* (1974). • Actress Marilyn Burns, who here is tied up and tormented by loony Neville Brand, was also tied up and tormented in *The Texas Chain-saw Massacre.* • Robert Englund appears as one of the unfortunate victims. He later went on to achieve horror stardom as the dreamkiller Freddy Krueger of the *Night-mare on Elm Street* series. • *Eaten Alive* is said to be inspired by the real-life Texas murderer Joe Ball, who fed his victims to his alligators.

Eyeball (1974; Italy/Spain) D/S: Um-berto Lenzi. P: José Maria Cinilles. Cast: John Richardson, Silvia Solar, Martha May. A maniac, whose eyes were plucked out as a teenager, roams the streets as an eyeless adult in search of replacement orbs in just the right shade of blue.

The Face of Fu Manchu (1965; Seven Arts; U.K./Ireland/W. Germany) D: Don Sharp. P: Harry Alan Towers, Oliver Unger. S: Peter Welbeck (Harry Alan Towers), Don Sharp. C: Ernest Steward. Cast: Christopher Lee, Nigel Green, Tsai Chin, Joachim Fuchsberger, Karin Dor, Howard Marion-Crawford, Walter Rilla, James Robertson Justice, Poulet Tu, Peter Mosbacher. The evil Fu Manchu concocts a gas from a rare Tibetan flower and wipes out an entire English village. The inscrutable madman plans to rule the world from his secret hideout below the River Thames in the heart of London itself. ¶ "The world has not heard the last of Fu Manchu." • And he was right, for this film kicked off a series of four more Fu Manchu pictures starring Christopher Lee: *The Brides of Fu Manchu* (1966), *The Vengeance of Fu Manchu* (1968), *Kiss and Kill* (1968), and *The Castle of Fu Manchu* (1968). • Lee apparently felt that the series began to deteriorate im-mediately, when he stated: "The first one should have been the last one, in my opin-ion, because it was the only real good one. It was the old, old story: when you get a popular type of picture, people do it to death—as with the *Dracula* films" (from *The Films of Christopher Lee,* by Pohle and Hart). • Out of all the monstrous characters he has played over the years—Dracula, Frank-enstein's Monster, The Mummy—Lee claims that the makeup for Fu Manchu was the most uncomfortable to wear. He had to endure two to three hours in the makeup chair just for the application of the Chinese eyefold alone.

Fear in the Night (1972; Hammer/International; U.K.) D/P: Jimmy Sangster. S: Jimmy Sangster, Michael Syson. C: Arthur Grant. Cast: Judy Geeson, Peter Cushing, Joan Collins, Ralph Bates, Gillian Lind, James Cossins, John Brown, Brian Grellis. A new teacher (Ralph Bates) takes an appointment at a private boys' school run by Peter Cushing, the mentally unbalanced headmaster. The teacher's wife is attacked and soon fears for her life. It turns out to be a plot hatched by the new teacher and Cushing's unfaithful wife (Joan Collins) to drive the young woman insane and goad her into murdering Cushing. • Joan Collins was pregnant during filming.

The Flesh and Blood Show (1973; Entertainment Ventures; U.K.) D/P: Pete Walker. S: Alfred Shaughnessy. C: Peter Jessop. Cast: Jenny Hanley, Ray Brooks, Luan Peters, Judy Matheson, Candace Glendinning, Robin Askwith, Tristan Rogers, Penny Meredith, Patrick Barr, Peter Walker. A troupe of actors arrive at a dilapidated seaside theater to rehearse a grand guignol play. They are stalked one by one by a hooded maniac who turns out to be an ex-actor consumed with hatred for the profession.

The Ghastly Ones (1969; JER) D/P/C: Andy Milligan. S: Andy Milligan, Hal Sherwood. Cast: Don Williams, Veronica Radburn, Maggie Rogers. Three couples visit their old family mansion to await the reading of a will. Soon, a series of grisly murders occurs, courtesy of a maniac who just loves to eat live rabbits. ¶ From the poster: "Mad creatures of the night existing only for sensual sadistic moments of *human slaughter!*" • One-man film crew Andy Milligan shot this no-budget gore film in 16mm on Staten Island. He remade it in 1978 as *Legacy of Blood.* • Milligan made this film as a period piece, set in the Victorian era. He later explained why: "Most things are retitled and sent out again and again. If you do a costume setting, it can be reissued and reissued and reissued and you can't tell what year it was made."

The Ghost (1963; Magna Pictures; Italy) D: Robert Hampton (Riccardo Freda). P: Louis Mann (Luigi Carpentieri, Ermanno Donati). S: Robert Davidson (Oreste Biancoli), Riccardo Freda. C: Donald Green (Raffaele Masciocchi). Cast: Barbara Steele, Peter Baldwin, Leonard Elliot (Elio Jotta),

Harriet White, Raoul H. Newman (Umberto Raho), Charles Kechler, Reginald Price, Carol Bennet. In this follow-up film to *The Horrible Dr. Hichcock* (1962), Dr. Hichcock is back as a cripple who is killed by his unfaithful wife (Barbara Steele) and her lover. The doctor is only faking his death however, and returns to drive his wife insane and exact revenge on her lover. • Star Barbara Steele told *Fangoria* #102 that *The Ghost* was made on a bet. "[Director Riccardo] Freda made a bet one day at lunch with a producer, Pietro Pupillo," reported the actress. "He said he could write a script *and* shoot a movie in a week. He wrote it in a day; we had a day of preproduction, and he shot it in three days. One night I slept on the set, because I knew we would be shooting again in four hours."

Goodbye Gemini (1970; Cinerama Releasing Corporation; U.K.) D: Alan Gibson. P: Peter Snell. S: Edmund Ward. C: Geoffrey Unsworth. Cast: Judy Geeson, Martin Potter, Michael Redgrave, Alexis Kanner, Mike Pratt, Freddie Jones, Peter Jeffrey. When a reclusive woman steps out and becomes involved with a man, her psychotically possessive twin brother drives her to murder her lover. He then kills his sister and himself.

The Gore Gore Girls (1972; Lewis Pictures) (also *Blood Orgy*). D/P: Herschell Gordon Lewis. S: Alan J. Dachman. C: Alex Ameri (Eskandar Ameripoor). Cast: Frank Kress, Amy Farrell, Hedda Lubin, Russ Badger, Nora Alexis, Phil Laurenson, Frank Rice, Ray Sager, Henny Youngman. Go-go girls in a nightclub are murdered in various gruesome ways. A private detective, with the aid of a female reporter, tries to solve the violent mystery. ¶."Face mutilated with a meat tenderizer, throat slit, and this one had her ass beat in." • This is Herschell Gordon Lewis' last horror movie (and last film as director as well). The "Godfather of Gore" outdid himself with this one when he included scenes of a woman's mutilated buttocks being rubbed with salt, and a girls' nipples being cut off—with one of them oozing *chocolate* milk! • In John McCarty's book *Splatter Movies,* Dan Krough, a former assistant to H. G. Lewis, had this to say about Lewis' attitude as a filmmaker: "I remember being in the screening room looking at the rushes of *The Gore Gore Girls* with him and him chuckling and saying, 'Well, that'll make 'em sick out in the drive-ins.' But it wasn't a malevolent attitude at all. He never *really* wanted to make anybody sick. Behind his films, there was always a very sly smile."

Gruesome Twosome (1967; Mayflower) D/P/C: Herschell Gordon Lewis. S: Louise Downe. Cast: Elizabeth Davis, Gretchen Welles, Chris Martell, Rodney Bedell. As filmmaker H. G. Lewis himself described the plot: "It's about a little old woman who runs a wig shop. And her idiot son who lives in the basement gives her the makings to make these wigs. On one side of the house she has rooms for rent and on the other side of the house she has wigs for sale. All these young girls, naturally, come in, rent a room, are promptly scalped by the idiot son, and the wigs are made." • When Lewis was through shooting the picture he learned that a terrible miscalculation had been made regarding the film's running time — it was ten minutes short. So he promptly shot a pre-credits sequence featuring talking manne-quin heads to fill the void.

Hands of a Stranger (1962) (see HANDS). In yet another adapation of Maurice Re-nard's French novel *The Hands of Orlac,* a pianist has the hands of a murdered man grafted onto his arms after an accident. Unlike in the first sound version, *Mad Love* (1935), the surgeon who performed the operation is not the madman, but instead is the romantic lead who falls in love with Orlac's sister. Orlac, in the meantime, goes mad himself because of his new hands' in-ability to play the piano, and resolves to kill all those associated with his misfortune.

Happy Mothers Day, Love George (1973; Cinema 5) D/P: Darren McGavin. S: Rob-ert Clouse. C: Walter Lassally. Cast: Pa-tricia Neal, Cloris Leachman, Bobby Darin, Tessa Dahl, Ron Howard, Kathi Browne, Joe Mascolo, Simon Oakland, Thayer David, Gale Garnett. A man returns to a small New England fishing village to try and uncover the identity of his father. Once there, a series of gruesome murders occur. • Actor Darren McGavin stepped behind the camera to make his directorial debut on this film. • Bobby Darin died shortly after filming, following open heart surgery. This was his last starring role.

Hatchet for a Honeymoon (1969; G.G.P. Pictures; Spain/Italy) D: Mario Bava. P: Manuel Cano Sanciriaco. S: Santiago Mon-cada, Mario Bava. C: Mario Bava, Antonio Rinaldi. Cast: Stephen Forsyth, Dagmar Lassander, Laura Betti, Jesus Puente, Femi Benussi, Antonia Mas, Alan Collins, Ger-ard Tichy, Fortunato Pasquale, Veronica Llimera. A psychotic fashion designer axes women in bridal gowns to make up for his impotency. He also keeps a room full of mannequins dressed as blushing brides.

Headless Eyes (1971) D: Kent Bateman. P: Ronald Sullivan. Cast: Bo Brundin, Gordon Ramon, Kelley Swartz, Mary Jane Early. Bo Brundin plays a burglar who loses one of his eyes during a robbery. This turns him into a maniacal killer who stalks women for their eyes, which he gouges out, takes home, and makes into mobiles or eyeball art. ¶ "I pray, I pray that those beady little eyes will catch sight of my work."

Homicidal (1961; Columbia) D/P: Wil-liam Castle. S: Robb White. C: Burnett Guffey. Cast: Glenn Corbett, Patricia Bres-lin, Jean Arless, Eugenie Leontovich, Rich-ard Rust. In this first of the many *Psycho* imitations, a young woman named Emily hires a man to marry her for a day, then stabs the justice of the peace. She goes to a mysterious mansion owned by a reclusive and troubled young man named Warren. Emily announces that she is Warren's wife, and more murders follow. It is finally revealed (though most everyone in the audience had already guessed) that Emily and Warren are one in the same. • This film is purportedly based on a real-life Scandi-navian murder case. • Gimmick-meister William Castle added a "Fright Break" just prior to the film's climax, in which any patron too timid to watch the ending could follow the yellow streak and slink off to the "coward's corner." • Castle not only copied plot elements from *Psycho*, but he also bor-rowed from Hitchcock's successful ad cam-paign: "Don't reveal the ending to your friends or they will kill you. If they don't, I will."

The Horrible Dr. Hichcock (1962; Sigma III; Italy) (also *The Terror of Dr. Hich-cock*). D: Robert Hampton (Riccardo Freda). S: Julyan Perry (Ernesto Gastaldi). P: Louis Mann (Luigi Carpentieri, Ermanno Do-nati). C: Donald Green (Raffaele Mascioc-chi). Cast: Barbara Steele, Robert Flemyng, Montgomery Glenn (Silvano Tranquilli), Teresa Fitzgerald (Maria Teresa Vianello), Harriet White, Spencer Williams, Al Chris-tianson, Evar Simpson, Nat Harley. In 1885 London, a necrophiliac doctor accidentally kills his wife when he gives her an overdose of anesthetic. He uses the anesthetic to make her appear dead so he can make lover to her. Grief stricken, he abandons his ancestral house, though he returns 12 years later with a new wife (Barbara Steele). She is terrorized first by the seeming specter of his first wife, and then by the doctor him-self, who wants to make a real corpse out of her. It is revealed that his first wife had not died after all, but was buried alive and is now completely mad, as is the doctor who still loves her. ¶ "You must be buried like I was buried, shut up alive down here! . . . It's you, you who must die!" • The American advertising played up the perversity in the film's subject matter with lines like: "His secret was a coffin named desire!" and "The candle of his lust burnt brightest in the shadow of the grave!" • The same directing/producing team made a sequel of sorts the following year titled *The Ghost,* again with Barbara Steele.

Horror House (1969; Tigon/AIP; U.K.) D: Michael Armstrong. S: Michael Armstrong, Peter Marcus. P: Louis M. Heyward. C: Jack Atcheler. Cast: Frankie Avalon, Jill Haworth, Dennis Price, Julian Barnes, Mark Wynter, Richard O'Sullivan, Gina Warwick, Robin Stewart, Carol Dilworth. Frankie Avalon, fresh from his California beach movies, plays a swinging hedonist in London, who goes with a group of thrill-seeking friends to visit a haunted house. After several murders, it turns out that one of the group has a psychopathic second personality.

House of Evil (1968) (see DOLLS). At a sinister family mansion a madman employs murderous toy automatons to kill off the members of the family one by one.

House of Psychotic Women (1975; Independent International; Spain) D: Carlos Aured. P: José Antonio Perez Giner. S: Jacinto Molina, Carlos Aured. C: Francisco Sanchez. Cast: Paul Naschy, Diana Lorys, Eduardo Calvo, Eva Leon, Maria Perschy, Ines Morales, Antonio Pica, Luis Ciges, Pilar Barden. An ex-con goes to work for three women living in an eerie mansion. One woman is a nymphomaniac, another has an artificial hand, and the third is a wheelchair-bound madwoman. Soon corpses of young blue-eyed blonde women begin to turn up, each with their eyes gouged out. • Star Paul Naschy co-wrote the script using his real name of Jacinto Molina.

The House That Screamed (1969; AIP; Spain) (also *The Boarding School*). D: Narciso Ibañez Serrador. P: Arturo Gonzalez. S: Luis Verna Penafiel. C: Manuel Berenguer. Cast: Lilli Palmer, Cristina Galbo, John Moulder Brown, Mary Maude, Candida Losada. At a French boarding school for girls, the mentally disturbed headmistress admonishes her psychopathic son to stay away from the "unclean girls." He takes it one step further and sets about murdering the girls and cutting off various body parts to construct a composite "perfect woman" in the basement. ¶ "Why do you

always watch the girls and follow them around?"

The House That Vanished (1974; AIP; U.K.) (also *Scream and Die*). D: Joseph Larraz. P: Diana Daubeney. S: Derek Ford. C: Trevor Wrenn. Cast: Andrea Allan, Karl Lanchbury, Maggie Walker, Peter Forbes-Robertson, Judy Matheson, Annabella Wood, Alex Leppard, Lawrence Keane, Daphne Lea. A young model witnesses a psycho-killer in a black coat and gloves commit murder at an old house, then later cannot seem to find the house. The killer turns out to be her own boyfriend, kept under the repressive influence of a demented aunt.

Hush . . . Hush, Sweet Charlotte (1964; 20th Century–Fox) D/P: Robert Aldrich. S: Henry Farrell, Lukas Heller. C: Joseph Biroc. Cast: Bette Davis, Olivia De Havilland, Joseph Cotten, Agnes Moorehead, Cecil Kellaway, Victor Buono, Mary Astor. Thirty-seven years afer a gruesome unsolved murder on a Louisiana plantation, an aging southern belle (Bette Davis) is being driven insane by grief, memories, and greedy relatives. ¶ "It's not often we have a homicide and can't find the victim's head or hands." • Joan Crawford was originally set to play the role of Bette Davis' cousin, but due to illness was replaced by Olivia De Havilland. • This follow-up film to the surprise hit *What Ever Happened to Baby Jane?* (1962) featured that earlier film's same producer/director and screenwriter team (Robert Aldrich and Lukas Heller).

Hysteria (1965; Hammer/MGM; U.K.) D: Freddie Francis. P/S: Jimmy Sangster. C: John Wilcox. Cast: Robert Webber, Lelia Goldoni, Anthony Newlands, Jennifer Jayne, Maurice Denham, Peter Woodthorpe, Sandra Boize, Sue Lloyd. An amnesiac American in London fears he is going insane when he experiences some frightening hallucinations . . . or are they truly all in his mind?

I Dismembered Mama (1972; Europix) (also *Poor Albert and Little Annie*). D: Paul Leder. P: Leon Roth. S: William Norton. C: William Swenning. Cast: Zooey Hall, Geri Reishl, Joanne Moore Jordan, Greg Mullavey, Marlene Tracy. An escaped mental patient sets out to take revenge on his mother, who had had him committed to the sanitarium. The deranged psycho also kills various "impure" women and falls in love with a nine-year-old girl. ¶ "What good is breeding if all it ever results in is a multiplication of worms?"

I Drink Your Blood (1971; Cinemation) D/S: David Durston. P: Jerry Gross. C:

Jacques Demarecaux. Cast: Bhaskar, Jadine Wong, Ronda Fultz, Elizabeth Marner-Brooks, George Patterson, Riley Mills, Iris Brooks, John Damon, Richard Bowler. This unpleasant low budget film follows a band of hippie/satanists who arrive in a small nowhere town and proceed to cause trouble for all the "decent" folks thereabouts, including attacking a young girl and feeding LSD to her grandfather. The girl's pre-teen brother retaliates by injecting rabies into the group's meat pies. Soon, the hippies start foaming at the mouth and commiting atrocities against each other and anyone else they can find. • *I Drink Your Blood* was released on a double bill with the re-titled *I Eat Your Skin.*

I Saw What You Did (1965; Universal) D/P: William Castle. S: William McGivern. C: Joseph Biroc. Cast: Joan Crawford, John Ireland, Leif Erickson, Patricia Breslin, Andi Garrett, Sharyl Locke, Sara Lane, John Archer. This tense William Castle shocker is about a pair of teenage girls who dial numbers at random and repeat the film's title. One number they dial happens to be that of John Ireland, who has just killed his wife in the shower, and now is forced to come after the girls. • Since William Castle had the reputation of "king of the gimmicks," some theaters installed seatbelts to keep their patrons in place during the shock scenes. • Castle was no stranger to the psycho-subject, having previously made *Homicidal* (1961), *The Old Dark House* (1963), and *Strait-Jacket* (1964).

I Spit on Your Grave (1977; Jerry Gross Organization) D/S: Meir Zarchi. P: Joseph Zbeda, Meir Zarchi. C: Yuri Haviv. Cast: Camille Keaton, Eron Tabor, Richard Pace, Anthony Nichols. A young female writer rents a house in the country and is brutally raped and beaten by four locals. She then proceeds to hang, axe, and castrate the lot of them. ¶ From the ads: "This woman has just cut, chopped, broken, and burned five men beyond recognition ... but no jury in America would ever convict her!" • This controversial rape/revenge film was originally released as *Day of the Woman* to poor box office, but then was retitled with the more exploitable *I Spit on Your Grave* and re-released to booming business. • Star Camille Keaton, who is brutally raped (repeatedly) in graphic detail in the film, is the grand-niece of Buster Keaton.

The Incredible Torture Show (1976; Rochelle) (also *Blood Sucking Freaks*). D/P/S: Joel M. Reed. C: Gerry Toll. Cast: Seamus O'Brien, Louie De Jesus, Niles McMaster, Viju Krim, Alan Dellay, Dan Fauci, Ernie Peysher, Lynette Sheldon. A deranged off-Broadway theater owner named Sardu stages grand guignol shows and fronts a white slavery ring on the side, indulging in all manner of torture when he feels the urge. • This crude and tacky gore film parody earned the wrath of the moralistic group "Women Against Pornography."

Island of the Damned (1976; AIP; Spain) D: Narciso Ibañez Serrador. P: Manuel Perez. S: Luis Penafiel (Narciso Ibañez Serrador). C: José Luis Alcaine. Cast: Lewis Fiander, Prunella Ransome, Maria Durille, Lourdes de la Camara, Roberto Nauta, Javier de la Camara, Luis Mateos, José Luis Romero. A couple of visiting tourists arrive on an island where inexplicably there are no adults, only children. They soon stumble upon various mutilated bodies and discover that the children have gone mad and killed everyone over the age of 16.

Kiss and Kill (1968; Warner–Seven Arts/ Commonwealth United Entertainment; Spain/W. Germany/U.S./U.K.) (also *The Blood of Fu Manchu; Fu Manchu and the Kiss of Death; Against All Odds*). D: Jesus Franco. P: Harry Alan Towers. S: Peter Welbeck (Harry Alan Towers). C: Manuel Merino. Cast: Christopher Lee, Richard Greene, Shirley Eaton, Tsai Chin, Maria Rohm, Howard Marion-Crawford, Gotz George, Ricardo Palacios. Fu Manchu sends ten beautiful girls loaded with deadly poison to kiss and kill top world officials. • This fourth installment in the Christopher Lee/Fu Manchu series was shot on location in Brazil by prolific Spanish director Jesus Franco. Next, and last, in line was *The Castle of Fu Manchu* (1968).

Lady in a Cage (1964; Paramount) D: Walter Grauman. P/S: Luther Davis. C: Lee Garmes. Cast: Olivia De Havilland, James Caan, Ann Sothern, Jeff Corey. Olivia De Havilland is a wealthy widow whose house is invaded by three psychos led by James Caan. They murder a wino and torment Olivia who is trapped in her mansion elevator. • Because of its violence, *Lady in a Cage* was banned in Great Britain.

Last House on the Left (1972; AIP/ Hallmark) D/S: Wes Craven. P: Sean S. Cunningham. C: Victor Hurwitz. Cast: David Hess, Lucy Grantheim, Sandra Cassel, Marc Sheffier, Jeramie Rain, Fred Lincoln, Gaylord St. James, Cynthia Carr, Ada Washington. Two young girls are kidnapped, terrorized, and raped by a band of four psycho thugs. When they try to escape, the girls are brutally murdered. In a bizarre plot twist, the killers' car breaks down, and they take refuge at the home of one of the murdered girls' parents. When the couple find out that they are entertaining their daughter's murderers, they wreak a terrible and brutal revenge on the four. ¶ "To avoid fainting keep repeating: It's only a movie ... only a movie...." — This effective ad campaign has been copied countless times to promote subsequent films. • Director Wes Craven claimed that this film "blew away all the clichés of handling violence. Before that violence had been neat and tidy — I made it painful and protracted and shocking and very human." It certainly caused a great deal of controversy and at the same time generated a great deal of box office revenue. • Producer Sean S. Cunningham (who had previously made porno movies) went on to produce/direct/write the sequel-spawning slice 'n' dice trendsetter *Friday the 13th* (1980). • A film titled *Last House on the Left Part 2* was released soon after this, but it has nothing to do with the original. Some American distributors made some cuts in a Mario Bava film called *Twitch of the Death Nerve* and retitled it to capitalize on the success and controversy generated by *Last House on the Left.*

Legacy of Blood (1973; Universal Entertainment) (also *Blood Legacy*). D/P: Carl Monson. S: Eric Norden. C: B. Rombouts, Jack Beckett. Cast: John Carradine, Faith Domergue, Merry Anders, Jeff Morrow, Richard Davalos, Roy Engel. The heirs of a deceased millionaire are forced to spend a week at his spooky mansion in order to claim their inheritance. One by one they are picked off by a mad killer. ¶ "I think we're loners in this *patchwork of insanity*." • The most notable thing about this mad killer film is that it's a near 20-year reunion for Faith Domergue and Jeff Morrow from *This Island Earth* (1955).

Legacy of Blood (1978; Ken Lane Films) D/P/S/C: Andy Milligan. This remake of Milligan's earlier *The Ghastly Ones* (1969) is about a group of people come to an old mansion seeking their inheritance. One by one they are murdered in various nasty ways by a maniac. (Though released in 1978, it was filmed *before Halloween*.)

The Little Girl Who Lives Down the Lane (1977; AIP; Canada) D: Nicolas Gessner. P: Zev Braun. S: Laird Koenig. C: Rene Verzier. Cast: Jodie Foster, Martin Sheen, Alexis Smith, Scott Jacoby, Mort Shuman, Dorothy Davis, Hubert Noel. Jodie Foster is a 13-year-old girl ostensibly living alone with her father, but actually living alone with the two corpses of her parents locked in the basement. She befriends a lonely crippled teenager and murders all those who discover her secret.

Love Butcher (1975; Mirror) D: Mikel Angel, Don Jones. P: Gary Williams, Mickey Belski. S: Don Jones, James Evergreen. C: Don Jones, Austin McKinney. Cast: Erik Stern, Kay Neer, Jeremiah Beecher, Edward Roehm, Robin Sherwood. A balding crippled gardener has constant abuse heaped upon him by his female suburban employers. To combat this, he transforms into his handsome alter-ego "brother" Lester, who seduces the offending women and murders them with garden tools. ¶ "I'm going to awaken you from this earthly nightmare ... awaken you to the sweet repose of ... death!" • Though filmed in 1975, *Love Butcher* was not released until 1982, at the height of the slasher craze.

Love Me Deadly (1972; Cinema National) D/S: Jacques La Certe. P: Buck Edwards. C: David Aaron. Cast: Mary Wilcox, Lyle Waggoner, Christopher Stone, Timothy Scott, I. William Quinn. Mary Wilcox plays a woman obsessed with images of her dead father, and strangely attracted to graveyards, funerals, and dead bodies. She falls in with a necrophiliac mortician who picks up prostitutes (of both sexes) and murders them, supplying bodies for his necrophilia club. ¶ "Doomed to love only the dead!" — trailer ad line.

Madhouse (1974; Amicus/AIP; U.K.) (also *The Revenge of Dr. Death*). D: Jim Clark. P: Max J. Rosenberg, Milton Subotsky. S: Greg Morrison, Ken Levinson. C: Ray Parslow. Cast: Vincent Price, Peter Cushing, Robert Quarry, Adrienne Corri, Natasha Pyne, Michael Parkinson, Linda Hayden, Harry Dennen. An actor is seemingly stalked by his own monstrous screen persona — "Dr. Death," which is responsible for a number of gruesome deaths. It turns out to be an elaborate revenge plot. • Star Vincent Price sang the movie's theme song over the end credits. • Makeup artist George Blackner discussed Price's makeup in *Famous Monsters* #109. "I felt the skull effect was really symbolic of Dr. Death. Vincent's face is very adaptable so there's no need to add anything artificial. I told Vincent he's the only man in the business walking around with his teeth painted onto his lips in luminous white makeup!"

Magic (1978; TCF) D: Richard Attenborough. P: Joseph E. Levine. S: William Goldman. C: Victor J. Kemper. Cast: Anthony Hopkins, Ann-Margret, Burgess Meredith, Ed Lauter, E. J. Andre, David Ogden Stiers. Anthony Hopkins plays an unbalanced ventriloquist who becomes obsessed with his dummy, eventually culminating in murder. Is he a maniac with a split personality? Or is he the victim of some evil force inside the doll? Only the screenwriter knows for sure. (Though released in 1978, *Magic* was filmed *before Halloween*.) • William Goldman adapted his own novel for the screen.

Maniac (1963; Hammer/Columbia; U.K.) D: Michael Carreras. P/S: Jimmy Sangster. C: Wilkie Cooper. Cast: Kerwin Mathews, Nadia Gray, Donald Houston, Liliane Brousse, Norman Bird, George Pastell, Jerold Wells, Arnold Diamond. An American artist becomes involved with a young French woman and her devious stepmother whose husband is imprisoned in an asylum for committing murder with an acetylene torch. Soon, more blow-torch murders start up until all is revealed in the final twist ending.

Massacre at Central High (1976; Evans Productions) D/S: Renee Daaler. P: Harold Sobel. C: Bert Van Munster. Cast: Derrel Maury, Andrew Stevens, Kimberly Beck, Robert Carradine, Ray Underwood, Steve Bond, Steve Sikes, Lani O'Grady, Damon Douglas, Rainbeaux Smith. When a new student at Central High defies the school bullies, they drop a car off its jack onto his legs, crippling him. He then sets out for revenge, killing them one by one. Now life at Central High is much more pleasant, but soon a group of previously downtrodden students begin to form their own clique and take control, which sets him off again on another murder spree.

The Nanny (1965; Hammer/20th Century–Fox; U.K.) D: Seth Holt. P/S: Jimmy Sangster. C: Harry Waxman. Cast: Bette Davis, Wendy Craig, Jill Bennett, James Villiers, William Dix, Pamela Franklin, Jack Watling, Maurice Denham, Alfred Burke. Bette Davis plays a prim and proper nanny who is actually a demented murderess. The family's ten-year-old boy is released from a home for disturbed children where he had been sent after he supposedly drowned his little sister. Of course it was the nanny that was responsible and now she is trying to kill the boy as well as the rest of the family. ¶ "I gave Master Joey his chance but he wouldn't take it. If something doesn't stop this chatter, one day someone will believe him. Then Nanny will have to go."

The Night Digger (1971; MGM; U.K.) (also *The Road Builder*). D: Alistair Reid. P: Alan D. Courtney, Norman S. Powell. S: Roald Dahl. C: Alex Thomson. Cast: Patricia Neal, Pamela Brown, Nicholas Clay, Jean Anderson, Yootha Joyce, Peter Sallis, Brigit Forsyth, Graham Crowden, Diana Patrick. A blind domineering old woman and her repressed daughter give haven to a psychotic handyman who rapes and kills women and buries their bodies in the path of a road to be paved. • Screenwriter Roald Dahl (author of *Charlie and the Chocolate Factory*) is married to actress Patricia Neal (who plays the spinster daughter).

Night Must Fall (1964; MGM; U.K.) D: Karel Reisz. P: Albert Finney, Karel Reisz. S: Clive Exton. C: Freddie Francis. Cast: Albert Finney, Mona Washbourne, Susan Hampshire, Sheila Hancock, Michael Medwin, Joe Gladwin, John Gill, Martin Wyldeck. Albert Finney plays an insane Welsh axe-murderer in this chilling remake of the 1937 film. He moves in with a wealthy widow to redecorate the house, seduces her daughter and the maid, and performs bizarre rituals with the severed head he keeps in a box.

Night of a Thousand Cats (1972) (see CATS). This south-of-the-border exploitation quickie features a wealthy sicko who brings women to his castle-like retreat, cuts their heads off, and feeds their bodies to his pit full of flesh-eating cats ... until, of course, the ferocious felines escape and give him his just dessert (or more precisley, make him *their* dessert).

Night of Bloody Horror (1969; Howco International) D/P: Joy N. Houck, Jr. S: Joy N. Houck, Jr., Robert A. Weaver. C: Robert A. Weaver. Cast: Gerald McRaney, Gaye Yellen, Evelyn Hendricks, Herbert Nelson, Lisa Dameron, Charlotte White, Nicholous R. Krieger, Michael Anthony, Burt Robert, Gordon Ogden. A young man is experiencing blackouts while his girlfriends are violently murdered. It is revealed that he had accidentally killed his brother as a child, and his now-demented mother is the one doing the gruesome killings. She also keeps the mummified body of her son and husband (who had committed suicide) in her basement (in an obvious nod to *Psycho*). ¶ "The producers strongly recommend this film for mature audiences only, for those who can take the supreme voyage into the realistic realm of sheer terror; the terror of beautiful women who meet sudden brutal horror at the hands of a blood psycho gone berserk"—promotional hype from the film's trailer. • The movie's advertising touted this early gore movie as being filmed in "Violent Vision," though it was actually shot in 16mm.

Nightmare (1963; Hammer/Universal; U.K.) D: Freddie Francis. P/S: Jimmy Sangster. C: John Wilcox. Cast: David Knight, Moira Redmond, Jennie Linden, Brenda Bruce, George A. Cooper, Irene Richmond. A young heiress is seeing frightening apparitions of murder and goes insane. The plot to drive her crazy backfires on the culprits in a twist ending.

Nightmare Hotel (1973; Vezafilms; Spain) (also *A Candle for the Devil; It Happened at Nightmare Inn*). D: Eugene Martin. P: José Lopez Moreno. S: Eugene Martin, Antonio Fos. C: José Fernandez Aguayo. Cast: Judy Geeson, Aurora Bautista, Esperanza Roy, Vic Winner, Lone Fleming, Blanca Estrada. Two sisters, one of whom is a sexually suppressed maniac, run the local hotel in a small Spanish village. The mad sibling kills all the guests whose moral conduct she finds objectable, cuts their bodies up into little pieces, and stores them in jars in the basement.

The Old Dark House (1963; Hammer/Universal; U.K.) D: William Castle. P: William Castle, Anthony Hinds. S: Robert Dillon. C: Arthur Grant. Cast: Tom Poston, Fenella Fielding, Janette Scott, Robert Morley, Joyce Grenfell, Mervyn Johns, Peter Bull, Danny Green. A confused salesman is stranded at the mansion of the mad Femm family, where murder is a family matter. • This lukewarm comical remake is a long way from the 1932 James Whale classic. • The background pictures for the film's credits were drawn by Charles Addams.

Paranoiac (1963; Hammer/Universal; U.K.) D: Freddie Francis. P: Anthony Hinds. S: Jimmy Sangster. C: Arthur Grant. Cast: Janette Scott, Oliver Reed, Alexander Davion, Sheila Burrell, Liliane Brousse, Maurice Denham. Oliver Reed plays a psycho who likes to sit and play the organ for the mummified corpse of the baby brother he murdered years ago. But the brother seems to show up alive, which causes Reed's sister to believe she is going mad. It all comes right in the end with the revelation that the now-grown brother is really an imposter out to corner the murderer. • Director Freddie Francis made two other early psycho films for Hammer — *Nightmare* (1963) and *Hysteria* (1965).

Peeping Tom (1960; Anglo Amalgamated/Astor; U.K.) D/P: Michael Powell.

S: Leo Marks. C: Otto Heller. Cast: Karl Boehm, Anna Massey, Maxine Audley, Moira Shearer, Esmond Knight, Shirley Anne Field, Jack Watson, Nigel Davenport, Miles Malleson. A disturbed and introverted cameraman (Karl Boehm) moonlights at night as a nudie photographer. As a child he was made the subject of his father's cruel experiments in fear, and now is obsessed with filming the reactions of fright. To this end he uses a stiletto hidden in his camera tripod to murder the models and record their terror on film. ¶ *"Warning! Don't see Peeping Tom unless you are prepared to see the screaming shock and raw terror in the faces of those marked for death! See it from the beginning!"* — ad line. • As a result of its critical and public outcry, this voyeuristic murder film effectively ruined the career of brilliant British director Michael Powell. Now it is considered something of a classic — a film way ahead of its time. • Michael Powell himself plays the murderer's sadistic psychologist father in the home-movie flashback sequences.

Picture Mommy Dead (1966; Embassy Pictures) D/P: Bert I. Gordon. S: Robert Sherman. C: Ellsworth Fredricks. Cast: Don Ameche, Martha Hyer, Susan Gordon, Zsa Zsa Gabor, Maxwell Reed, Wendell Corey, Signe Hasso. Mr. B.I.G. (Bert I. Gordon — maker of "giant" films like *The Amazing Colossal Man* [1957], *Beginning of the End* [1957], *The Spider* [1958], etc.) jumps on the psycho-horror bandwagon with this tale of a girl returning home after three years in an asylum recovering from being traumatized by the mysterious death of her mother. The girl's father has remarried, but her new "wicked stepmother" plots to have her recommitted and murders those who stand in her way. • Director/producer Bert I. Gordon cast his own daughter, Susan Gordon, in the role of the troubled girl.

Play Misty for Me (1971; Universal) D: Clint Eastwood. P: Robert Daley. S: Joe Heims. C: Bruce Surtees. Cast: Clint Eastwood, Jessica Walter, Donna Mills, John Larch, Jack Ging, Irene Hervey, James McEachin, Clarice Taylor, Donald Siegel. Clint Eastwood plays a Monterey disc jockey who makes the mistake of getting involved with a psychotically possessive fan whose manipulating behavior makes his life a living hell, and who eventually demonstrates how handy she is with a kitchen knife. ¶ "I hope he likes what he sees when he walks in here, because that's what he's taking to *hell* with him!" • Clint Eastwood's own fledgling film company, "Malpaso,"

Anthony Perkins as Norman Bates, the original Psycho *(1960), is horrified when he finds his alter ego's bloody handiwork in Janet Leigh's shower.*

financed the production, a kind of hip 70s version of *Fatal Attraction.* • Independent filmmaker John Carpenter said that he was offered *Fatal Attraction* but turned it down, claiming "Eastwood did it better, I'm not going to be able to top that."

Playgirl Killer (1970; Canada) (also *Decoy for Terror*). D: Enrick Santamaran. P: Max

A. Sendel. Cast: William Kerwin, Jean Christopher, Neil Sedaka, Andree Champagne, Mary Lou Collier. A psychotic artist finds the perfect way to force his models to stay in one pose — he kills them and freezes their bodies in a meat locker.

Psycho (1960; Paramount) D/P: Alfred Hitchcock. S: Joseph Stefano. C: John L.

Russell. Cast: Anthony Perkins, Janet Leigh, Vera Miles, John Gavin, Martin Balsam, John McIntyre. This groundbreaking psycho film following the bloody exploits of Norman Bates (the ultimate momma's boy) set the standard in psychological horror for the next two decades, as well as making an entire nation afraid to take a shower. ¶ "I hope they are watching, they'll see. They'll see and they'll know and they'll say, why, she wouldn't even harm a fly." • For *Psycho*'s advertising, Alfred Hitchcock jokingly implored: "Please don't give away the ending. It's the only one we have." • For the notorious shower scene, Hitchcock used chocolate syrup for blood, which photographed with just the right consistency in black and white. The sound effect of the knife penetrating Janet Leigh's body in this sequence was actually the sound of a knife slicing into a casaba melon. • Both actress Janet Leigh and dirctor Alfred Hitchcock were nominated for Academy Awards, but neither won. • Pat Hitchcock, Alfred Hitchcock's own daughter, played Janet Leigh's co-worker in the film (the flirting secretary).

The Psycho Lover (1970; Medford) (also *The Loving Touch; Psycho Killer*). D/P/S: Robert Vincent O'Neil. C: Bob Maxwell, Stan Rabjohn. Cast: Lawrence Montaigne, Joanne Meredith, Elizabeth Plumb, Frank Cuba, John Vincent. A mad psychiatrist brainwashes his mental patients and sends them out to try and kill his wife.

Psychomania (1963; Victoria Films) (also *Violent Midnight*). D: Richard Hilliard. P: Del Tenney. S: Robin Miller. C: Louis McMahon. Cast: Lee Philips, Shepperd Strudwick, Jean Hale, Lorraine Rogers, Margot Hartman, Kaye Elhardt, James Farentino, Dick Van Patten, Sylvia Miles. A war-hero turned artist is suspected of being the psycho-killer responsible for the brutal deaths of two women, so he conducts his own invetigation to clear himself. ¶ "No one but a trained professional can really help a *deeply* disturbed person."

The Psychopath (1966; Amicus/Paramount; U.K.) D: Freddie Francis. P: Max J. Rosenberg, Milton Subtosky. S: Robert Bloch. C: John Wilcox. Cast: Patrick Wymark, Margaret Johnson, John Standing, Alexander Knox, Judy Huxtable, Thorley Walters, Don Borisenko, Robert Crewdson, Colin Gordon. The investigation of a series of gruesome murders in which a doll in the likeness of each victim is found at the crime scene leads to a crazy old woman with a house full of dolls and her trod-upon neurotic son.

The Psychopath (1973; Brentwood) D/P/S: Larry Brown. Cast: Tom Basham. A children's TV host retaliates against those parents who beat and mistreat his young viewers by disposing of them in various nasty ways, including using a baseball bat and lawn mower in this no-budget amateurish production.

Repulsion (1965; Royal; U.K.) D: Roman Polanski. P: Gene Gutowski. S: Roman Polanski, Gerard Brach. C: Gilbert Taylor. Cast: Catherine Deneuve, Ian Hendry, John Fraser, Patrick Wymark, Yvonne Furneaux, James Villiers. Catherine Deneuve plays a disturbed, repressed young woman sharing a London flat with her sister. When her sister leaves on holiday with her boyfriend, Catherine sinks ever deeper into hallucination and psychosis, culminating in murder. • This hard-edged, frightening film is acclaimed Polish director Roman Polanski's (*Rosemary's Baby,* 1968; *The Tenant,* 1976; etc.) first English-language film.

The Sadist (1963; Fairway International) (also *The Profile of Terror*). D/S: James Landis. P: L. Steven Snyder. C: Vilmos Zsigmond. Cast: Arch Hall, Jr., Helen Hovey, Richard Alden, Marilyn Manning, Don Russell. Psycho-teen Arch Hall, Jr., shoots several teachers and policemen, and then terrorizes three motorists whose car has broken down. ¶ "To have complete mastery over another, to make him a helpless object, to humiliate him, to enslave, to inflict moral insanity on the innocent, *that* is his objective, his *twisted pleasure*" — opening narration.

Schizo (1977; Niles Entertainment; U.K.) (also *Amok; Blood of the Undead*). D/P: Pete Walker. S: David McGillivray. C: Peter Jessop. Cast: Lynne Frederick, John Leyton, Stephanie Beacham, John Fraser, Jack Watson, Queenie Watts, Trisha Mortimer, John McEnery, Victor Winding, David McGillivray. A woman is hounded by a maniac, though all is not as it would seem (as the title and posters so unsubtly suggest). ¶ "*Schizophrenia* ... When the left hand doesn't know who the right hand is killing!" — ad line. • Star Lynne Frederick was Peter Sellers' last wife.

Scream Baby Scream (1969; Westbury) D/P: Joseph Adler. S: Lawrence Robert Cohen. C: Julio Chavez. Cast: Ross Harris, Eugenie Wingate, Chris Martell, Suzanne Stuart, Larry Swanson, Jim Vance, Naomi Fink. A group of students visit the mansion of an artist in search of their friends who have mysteriously disappeared. It turns out the artist is a madman who kidnaps and surgically disfigures people so he can use them as models for his grotesque paintings.

Scream Bloody Murder (1972; Indepix) D/P/S: Robert J. Emery. Cast: Paul Vincent, Marlena Lustik, Nick Kleinholz III, Paul Ecenia, Nancy Whetmore. A psychotic young man murders his father with a tractor and loses his hand in the process. Years later he wears a hook in place of his hand, with which he murders his mother and stepfather before kidnapping a prostitute he's become infatuated with. ¶ From the ads: "Filmed in violent vision and gory color! So horrifying you need a blindfold to see it!"

Scream of Fear (1961; Hammer/Columbia; U.K.) (also *Taste of Fear*). D: Seth Holt. P/S: Jimmy Sangster. C: Douglas Slocombe. Cast: Susan Strasberg, Ronald Lewis, Ann Todd, Christopher Lee, Leonard Sachs, Anne Blake, John Serrett, Fred Johnson, Bernard Brown, Richard Klee. A crippled heiress goes to France to visit her father, but is told by her new stepmother that he is away on business. Soon she begins seeing her father's soaking corpse popping up in unlikely places and assumes her stepmother and a sinister doctor are trying to drive her mad. With a few neat twists at the end the guilty parties are revealed and justice is served. • This is the first of many early psycho films producer/screenwriter Jimmy Sangster made for Hammer. The others are: *Maniac* (1963), *Paranoiac* (1963; screenwriter only), *Nightmare* (1963), *Hysteria* (1965), *The Nanny* (1965), *The Anniversary* (1968), *Crescendo* (1969; screenwriter only), and *Fear in the Night* (1972; director as well). • Christopher Lee was very pleased with the result, calling this "the best film Hammer ever made," and praising Seth Holt as "one of the best directors Britain ever had" (from *The Films of Christopher Lee,* by Pohle and Hart). • Gary Cooper visited the set, which greatly impressed Christopher Lee: "I was so overcome by this, I just couldn't think of anything."

See No Evil (1971; Columbia; U.K.) (also *Blind Terror*). D: Richard Fleischer. P: Martin Ransohoff, Leslie Linder. S: Brian Clemens. Cast: Mia Farrow, Dorothy Alison, Robin Bailey, Diane Grayson, Lila Kaye. A blind girl (Mia Farrow) goes to stay at her uncle's mansion. While she is out, a madman slaughters her uncle's entire family, and when she returns she slowly comes to the realization that the maniac is still there, silently stalking her. • Screenwriter Brian Clemens cut his teeth on the popular British TV series "The Avengers."

The Severed Arm (1973; Media Cinema/ Media Trend) D: Thomas S. Alderman. P: Gary Adelman. S: Thomas S. Alderman, Darrel Presnell, Larry Alexander, Marc B. Rand. C: Bob Maxwell. Cast: Deborah Walley, Paul Carr, David G. Cannon, Vincent Martorano, Roy Dennis, Marvin Kaplan, John Crawford, Bob Guthrie, George Dann. Six amateur spelunkers are trapped in a cave for two weeks. They agree to draw lots to decide who will sacrifice an arm so that they might survive and not starve to death. With terrible timing, just as Dennis' (the loser) arm is amputated, help arrives. Years later, members of the group start meeting grisly deaths at the hands (or hand, actually) of a now mad and vengeful Dennis, or at least so it seems.

Shock Treatment (1964; 20th Century-Fox) D: Denis Sanders. P: Aaron Rosenberg. S: Sydney Boehm. C: Sam Leavitt. Cast: Lauren Bacall, Roddy McDowall, Stuart Whitman, Carol Lynley, Ossie Davis, Douglass Dumbrille. Lauren Bacall plays an unscrupulous asylum psychiatrist attempting to trick homicidal maniac patient Roddy McDowall into revealing the secret of a hidden fortune.

Silent Night, Bloody Night (1972; Cannon) (also *Death House; Night of the Dark Full Moon*). D: Theodore Gershuny. P: Ami Artzi, Jeffrey Konvitz. S: Theodore Gershuny, Jeffrey Konvitz, Ira Teller, Ami Artzi. C: Adam Giffard. Cast: Patrick O'Neal, John Carradine, Walter Abel, James Patterson, Mary Woronov, Astrid Herren, Candy Darling, Ondine, Tally Brown, Jack Smith. Patrick O'Neal is a lawyer hired to sell a decrepit mansion which used to be an insane asylum. He is murdered in the house and the former asylum's horrible history is revealed through flashbacks. ¶ From the trailer: "'Twas the night before Christmas and all through the house, not a creature was left . . . living." • *Silent Night, Bloody Night* was filmed at Oyster Bay, Long Island, and features many New York underground movie veterans.

Silent Night, Evil Night (1974; Warner Bros.; Canada) (also *Black Christmas; Stranger in the House*). D: Bob Clark. P: Bob Clark, Gerry Arbeid. S: Roy Moore. C: Reginald Morris. Cast: Olivia Hussey, Keir Dullea, Margot Kidder, Andrea Martin, John Saxon. Sorority sisters at a Canadian university are stalked by a maniac over the Christmas break. ¶ From the trailer: "If this movie doesn't make your skin crawl, it's on too tight!" • Keir Dullea plays the maniac; he's probably most recognized as the astronaut who embarked on *2001—A Space*

Odyssey (1969). One of his victims, Margot Kidder, later became Superman's girlfriend in the current series started with *Superman* (1978). • Director Bob Clark, in an interview with *HorrorFan* magazine, claimed to have written the script as well: "I didn't take credit but I actually did write it."

Sisters (1973) (see FREAKS). Margot Kidder is one half of a pair of Siamese-twins who were separated by an operation. When approached by a man, the repressed Kidder is taken over by the murderous personality of the twin who died during the separation.

Snuff (1976; Monarch Pictures; Argentina/U.S.) D: Michael Findlay, Roberta Findlay. P/S: Michael Findlay. C: Roberta Findlay. Cast: No cast credits were ever given in order to perpetuate the idea that this was a genuine "snuff" film. The exploitation filmmaking husband and wife team of Michael and Roberta Findlay went to Argentina to make a cheap gore film called *Slaughter* in 1971, which was made to cash in on the Manson murders: A group of female psychos follow their cult leader in massacring a pregnant actress and her friends. It was so bad that it sat on the shelf for five years until a four-minute sequence in which a woman is systematically tortured and disemboweled was tacked on. *Snuff* was then released amid a flurry of fake publicity and reaped quite a profit. ¶ "The film that could only be made in South America ... where Life is *Cheap!*"—ad line. • This notorious phony gore film promoted (to successful financial returns) the idea that it showed actual real-life killings and mutilation on screen (intimating in its advertising that it was an actual "snuff" film). • Michael Findlay was later killed in a bizarre gruesome accident atop the Pan Am Building in New York—he was decapitated by a helicopter blade. Roberta went on to continue her low-budget exploitation career.

So Sad About Gloria (1973; Centronics) D/P: Harry Thomason. S: Marshal Riggan. C: Jim Roberson. Cast: Loria Saunders, Bob Ginnaven, Dean Jagger, Lou Hoffman, Seymour Treitman, Linda Wyse. A psychopath commits a series of axe murders in another drive-the-woman-mad plot.

The Spectre of Edgar Allan Poe (1974; Cinerama) D/P/S: Mohy Quandour. C: Robert Birchall. Cast: Robert Walker, Mary Grover, Cesar Romero, Tom Drake, Carol Ohmart, Marsha Mae Jones, Frank Packard, Mario Milano, Karen Hartford, Dennis Fimple. Though not based on any of his works, this film features Edgar Allan Poe himself as a character. When Edgar's beloved Lenore is nearly buried alive, she goes mad. Poe takes her to a private asylum run by Cesar Romero. Romero is mad himself, conducting bizarre experiments on humans, and tortures Poe with a watery pit full of snakes. There is also a madwoman kept chained by Romero, who gets loose and terrorizes the household with an axe. ¶ From the closing theme song: "Without Lenore, life doesn't mean a thing/ Lord if you bring back Lenore I'll never ask for more."

Strait-Jacket (1964; Columbia) D/P: William Castle. S: Robert Bloch. C: Arthur Arling. Cast: Joan Crawford, Diane Baker, Leif Erickson, Anthony Hayes, Howard St. John, Rochelle Hudson, George Kennedy. Joan Crawford plays a woman coming home to live with her grown daughter after a 20-year stint at an insane asylum for axing her husband and his lover to death. She begins having hallucinations involving severed heads, and a new batch of axe murders starts up. Has Joan gone back to her old habits, or is there something even more diabolical afoot? ¶ "Warning! *Strait-Jacket* vividly depicts axe murders!"—from the less-than-subtle ads. • Leif Erickson, who welcomed home Joan Crawford from the insane asylum, is probably most known for starring in TV's "High Chapparal." • Robert Bloch, who scripted this film, can be considered a psycho-movie expert. He also wrote the novel *Psycho* upon which the Alfred Hitchcock classic was based.

Succubus (1968; Trans-American; W. Germany) D: Jesus Franco. P: Adrian Hoven. S: Pier A. Caminneci. C: Franz Lederle, Georg Herrero. Cast: Janine Reynaud, Howard Vernon, Jack Taylor, Michele Lemoine, Adrian Hoven. An S&M nightclub performer believes she is possessed by a demon and begins having difficulty distinguishing reality from fantasy. She begins killing her lovers. ¶ "She loved the games men played with death, when death must win."

Tales from the Crypt (1972) (see ANTHOLOGIES). The first story in this four-part omnibus, called "All Through the House," has Joan Collins murder her husband on Christmas Eve, only to be stalked herself by a maniac dressed in a Santa suit. She is undone when her little girl opens the door for the madman, thinking she is letting in the real Santa Claus. ¶ "A man described as a homicidal maniac has escaped from the Hospital for the Criminally Insane." • This film features the screen's first killer Santa (a topic that was later beaten to death in films like

Christmas Evil (1980) and *Silent Night, Deadly Night* parts 1 and 2; 1984 and 1987).

Targets (1968; Paramount) D/P/S: Peter Bogdanovich. C: Laszlo Kovacs. Cast: Boris Karloff, Tim O'Kelly, Nancy Hsueh, James Brown, Sandy Baron, Arthur Peterson, Peter Bogdanovich. Boris Karloff aptly plays Byron Orlock, an aging horror star who has become convinced that his brand of gothic horror does not scare anyone anymore in this modern world full of senseless violence. At the same time a seemingly all-American young man buys a new rifle, shoots his entire family, and begins sniping at passing cars from a water tower. The two storylines converge at a drive-in where Orlock is making his final personal appearance. The killer holes up inside the screen and begins shooting at people in their cars until finally cornered and cowed into submission by the old horror star himself. • The story goes that Roger Corman gave Peter Bogdanovich the use of Boris Karloff for five days, a few thousand dollars, and 20 minutes of footage from *The Terror* (1963) to make a new feature. *Targets* was the result. (*The Terror* is playing on the screen at the drive-in). • Released soon after Robert Kennedy's assassination, Paramount decided to tack a gun-control prologue onto the film. • The screenplay was inspired by the 1966 Whitman sniper killings in Texas. • During the film Boris Karloff watches himself in an actual 1931 Howard Hawks movie on TV—the classic prison movie *The Criminal Code.* • *Targets,* arguably Boris Karloff's best film in a decade, had a paltry budget of $130,000. • In order to save money, Peter Bogdanovich, the director of *Targets,* did double duty as an actor, playing the part of Sammy, Byron Orlock's director. So the film's director plays the film's director.

The Tenant (1976; Paramount; France) D: Roman Polanski. P: Andrew Braunsberg. S: Roman Polanski, Gerard Brach. C: Sven Nykvist. Cast: Roman Polanski, Isabelle Adjani, Melvyn Douglas, Jo Van Fleet, Shelley Winters, Bernard Fresson, Lila Kedrova, Claude Dauphin. Roman Polanski himself stars as a timid Polish file-clerk in Paris who moves into the apartment of a woman who jumped to her death from the window. The bizarre neighbors seem to be in a conspiracy to induce him to repeat her act, and he slips deeper and deeper into an obsessive psychosis, culminating in his dressing up in the dead woman's clothes and jumping not once, but twice, since the first time did not quite do the job.

The Texas Chainsaw Massacre (1974) (see CANNIBALS). No listing of early psycho movies would be complete without mentioning the seminal *Texas Chainsaw Massacre.* Five young people end up at the isolated house of a family of cannibals, which include the infamous "Leatherface"—a burly mute maniac who wears a mask of human skin and wields a nasty looking chain saw. ¶ "They're crazy! You gotta make 'em stop! Please!!!" • Despite its title, only one person is actually killed by chain saw, though others are bludgeoned to death with a hammer and stuck on huge hooks.

Theatre of Blood (1973; United Artists; U.K.) D: Douglas Hickox. P: John Kohn, Stanley Mann. S: Anthony Greville-Bell. C: Wolfgang Suschitzky. Cast: Vincent Price, Diana Rigg, Ian Hendry, Harry Andrews, Coral Browne, Robert Coote, Jack Hawkins, Michael Hordern, Arthur Lowe, Robert Morley, Dennis Price, Milo O'Shea, Eric Sykes. Vincent Price plays Edward Lionheart, a hamfisted Shakespearean actor who, with the aid of his beautiful daughter and a group of besotted derelicts, begins murdering his critics using methods outlined in the Bard's plays. ¶ Ad-line: "Vincent Price has reserved a seat for you in *Theatre of Blood.*" • His character of Edward Lionheart hit close to home for star Vincent Price. "*Theatre of Blood* was a dream to make, and very real to me," stated the actor. "I really understand the man who is doing his very best and yet is unrecognized." • Vincent Price later married one of his co-stars, Coral Browne (still his current wife). • Director Douglas Hickox accepted this assignment at the urging of a six-year-old boy. Hickox's son, Anthony, who grew up to direct horror movies himself (*Waxworks,* 1988), related this story in a *Fangoria* #78 interview: "I was about six years old. My dad mentioned something about a horror movie offer, and I begged him to do it. He claims he did it because I persuaded him to."

Theatre of Death (1967; Hemisphere; U.K.) (also *Blood Fiend*). D: Samuel Gallu. P: Michael Smedley Aston. S: Ellis Kadison, Roger Marshall. C: Gilbert Taylor. Cast: Christopher Lee, Lelia Goldoni, Jenny Till, Julian Glover, Ivor Dean, Evelyn Lane, Joseph Furst. Philippe Darvas (Christopher Lee) is the unpleasant, obsessive director of a Grand Guignol theater in Paris. When he mysteriously vanishes, he is suspected of being the blood-drinking murderer terrorizing the city. Actually, we learn that he himself is a victim of the maniac—

his own mistress and protégée, who was fed blood as an infant when trapped by a blizzard in the mountains. ¶ "He wanted to turn tragedy into comedy, comedy into tragedy."

The Thrill Killers (1965; Hollywood Stark) (also *The Maniacs Are Loose, The Monsters Are Loose*). D: Ray Steckler. P: George J. Morgan. S: Ray Steckler, Gene Pollock. C: Joseph V. Mascelli. Cast: Cash Flagg (Ray Steckler), Liz Renay, Brick Bardo, Gary Kent, Carolyn Brandt, Atlas King, Ron Haydock. No-budget filmmaker Ray Dennis Steckler stars (under the pseudonym "Cash Flagg") as "Mad Dog Glick," a maniac on a murder spree. At the same time three escapees from a mental hospital run around decapitating people.

Tomb of Torture (1965; Film Development Corporation; Italy/W. Germany) D: Anthony Kristye (Antonio Boccaci). P: Frank Campitelli. S: Anthony Kristye (Antonio Boccaci), Johnny Seemonell (Giorgio Simonelli). C: William Grace. Cast: Annie Albert, Thony Maky, Mark Marian (Marco Mariani), Elizabeth Queen, William Gray, Bernard Blay. A young woman has some mysterious link with a murdered countess. She returns to the countess' abandoned castle and runs afoul of a giggling madman with a hideously disfigured face who likes to torture and kill young girls. Aided by the ghost of the countess, she is able to thwart the madman and the evil woman controlling him.

Torso (1975; Joseph Brenner Associates; Italy) D: Sergio Martino. P: Antonio Cervi. S: Ernesto Gastaldi, Sergio Martino. C: Giancarlo Ferrando. Cast: Suzy Kendall, Tina Aumont, Luc Merenda, John Richardson, Angela Covello. A hooded maniac wielding a hacksaw goes about dismembering college girls.

Tower of Evil (1971; Fanfare; U.K.) (also *Horror on Snape Island*). D/S: Jim O'Connolly. P: Richard Gordon. C: Desmond Dickinson. Cast: Bryant Halliday, Jill Haworth, Anna Palk, Jack Watson, Mark Edwards, Derek Fowlds. A team of researchers travel to the remote and lonely Snape Island to investigate both the bizarre murders which recently occurred there, and the rumors of Phoenician treasure buried on the island. After several gory murders, the final revelation discloses a crazed madman living in a cave and guarding the treasure.

The Town That Dreaded Sundown (1977; AIP) D/P: Charles B. Pierce. S: Earl E. Smith. C: Jim Roberson. Cast: Ben Johnson, Andrew Prine, Dawn Wells, Jimmy Clem, Charles B. Pierce. Reportedly based on a true story, a hooded maniac who killed five people in 1946 returns to stalk the populace of Texarkana. • Female lead Dawn Wells is best remembered as "Mary Ann" from TV's "Gilligan's Island."

Twitch of the Death Nerve (1972; Hallmark; Italy) (also *Carnage; Last House on the Left Part 2*). D: Mario Bava. P: Giuseppe Zaccariello. S: Mario Bava, Carlo Reali. C: Mario Bava, Antonio Rinaldi. Cast: Claudine Auger, Luigi Pistilli, Claudio Volonté, Anna Maria Rosati, Laura Betti, Chris Avram, Brigitte Skay, Isa Miranda. Thirteen murders are carried out in various nasty ways by several different killers with the aim of possessing a prime piece of real estate. • This early body-count film created the infamous "two lovers skewered by a spear" sequence which was later copied in the *Friday the 13th* film series. • Upon entering the theater, patrons received a printed notice called "The Final Warning Station" which contained a series of warnings like, "Can you stand shock after incredible shock?"

The Vengeance of Fu Manchu (1968; Warner Bros.–Seven Arts; U.K./W. Germany/Hong Kong/Ireland) D: Jeremy Summers. P: Harry Alan Towers. S: Peter Welbeck (Harry Alan Towers). C: John von Kotze. Cast: Christopher Lee, Douglas Wilmer, Tony Ferrer, Tsai Chin, Howard Marion-Crawford, Horst Frank, Noel Trevarthen. The evil Fu Manchu substitutes a double for Nayland Smith, his nemesis, and has him convicted of murder. • *The Vengeance of Fu Manchu* is the third film in the series; preceded by *The Brides of Fu Manchu* (1966), and followed by *Kiss and Kill* (1968). • This is the first (and only) film in the series to be filmed in the Orient—Hong Kong, where it was shot in the Sir Run Run Shaw studios. • Christopher Lee relayed this disturbing anecdote in *The Films of Christopher Lee*, by Pohle and Hart: "One member of the Chinese crowd was always pushing himself forward to get into every shot. His colleagues got so angry they killed him. They chased him down the road toward Hong Kong and actually killed him."

What! (1963; Futuramic Releasing; France/Italy) (also *Night Is the Phantom; The Whip and the Body*). D: John M. Old (Mario Bava). S: Julian Berry (Ernesto Gastaldi), Robert Hugo, Martin Hardy. C: David Hamilton (Ubaldo Terzano). Cast: Daliah Lavi, Christopher Lee, Tony Kendall, Isli Oberon, Harriet White, Jacques Herlin, Alan Collins. Kurt, a cruel, sadistic prodigal son returns to the family castle after being banished for causing the suicide death of a servant's daughter. He attacks Nevenka, his brother's wife, who has a mental collapse. Kurt is found murdered and Nevenka goes mad, having hallucinations involving the dead man which culminate in her own death. ¶ "Kurt was here, alive. And his boots full of mud, as though he has climbed out of a grave."

What a Carve Up! (1961; Embassy; U.K.) (also *No Place Like Homicide*). D: Pat Jackson. P: Robert S. Baker, Monty Berman. S: Ray Cooney, Tony Hilton. C: Monty Berman. Cast: Kenneth Connor, Sidney James, Shirley Eaton, Donald Pleasence, Dennis Price, Michael Gough. This British horror spoof centers around a family living at Blackshaw Towers on the Yorkshire Moors. When the family patriarch dies it is time to read the will, and time for the masked killer to go to work. • *What a Carve Up!* is a comedy remake of the straight 1933 British horror film *The Ghoul,* starring Boris Karloff.

What Ever Happened to Aunt Alice? (1969; Cinerama) D: Lee H. Katzin. P: Robert Aldrich. S: Theodore Apstein. C: Joseph Biroc. Cast: Geraldine Page, Ruth Gordon, Rosemary Forsyth, Robert Fuller, Mildred Dunnock, Joan Huntington. Geraldine Page is a crazy widow left nothing but a stamp collection by her dead husband. To make ends meet she hires elderly housekeepers, kills them for their money, and buries their bodies in the garden. Ruth Gordon arrives to become her latest housekeeper/potential victim, but Ruth is wise to Ms. Page and is actually there searching for a missing friend (Page's former employee). • This is the third "elderly psycho lady" movie producer Robert Aldrich was involved with. He had earlier directed *What Ever Happened to Baby Jane?* (1962; and produced) and *Hush . . . Hush, Sweet Charlotte* (1964).

What Ever Happened to Baby Jane? (1962; Warner Bros.) D/P: Robert Aldrich. S: Lukas Heller. C: Ernest Haller. Cast: Bette Davis, Joan Crawford, Victor Buono, Marjorie Bennett, Anna Lee. Joan Crawford plays the wheelchair-bound former movie star at the mercy of her crazy sister (Bette Davis), the ex-child star Baby Jane Hudson. Jane wears grotesque little-girl makeup and plans a comeback with sleazy musician Victor Buono while tormenting her helpless sister. • This wonderfully macabre film started a whole new trend in madman movies, creating a new type of psycho—the "crazy grande dame." • This was the first time Bette Davis played the "crazy psycho lady" role—a role she was to repeat on several occasions: *Hush . . . Hush, Sweet Charlotte* (1964), *The Nanny* (1965), and *The Anniversary* (1968).

Who Slew Auntie Roo? (1971; AIP; U.S./U.K.) (also *Whoever Slew Auntie Roo?*). D: Curtis Harrington. P: Samuel Z. Arkoff, James H. Nicholson. S: Jimmy Sangster, Robert Blees, Gavin Lambert, C: Desmond Dickinson. Cast: Shelley Winters, Mark Lester, Chloe Franks, Ralph Richardson, Lionel Jeffries, Hugh Griffith. Shelley Winters plays a crazed American widow in England who keeps the mummified corpse of her dead daughter close at hand. She also kidnaps a young girl and her brother to take the place of her lost child.

Wicked, Wicked (1973; MGM) D/P/S: Richard L. Bare. C: Frederick Gately. Cast: David Bailey, Tiffany Bolling, Scott Brady, Edd Byrnes, Randolph Roberts, Diane McBain, Arthur O'Connell. A handyman dons a monster mask to murder and dismember blonde women at a seaside hotel. ¶ "See the hunter, see the hunted both at the same time"—ad line, referring to the film's split-screen gimmick. • The entire film was made using a split-screen technique dubbed "Duo-Vision" which showed two things happening at once.

The Slice 'n' Dice Wave (in the wake of Halloween: 1978–)

After Midnight (1989; MGM) D/S: Ken and Jim Wheat. P: Richard Arlook, Peter Greene, Ken and Jim Wheat. C: Phedon Papamichael. Cast: Judie Aronson, Marg Helgenberger, Marc McClure, Ed Monaghan, Alan Rosenberg, Monique Salcido, Pamela Segall, Penelope Sudrow, Nadine Van Der Velde, Tracy Wells, Ramy Zada, Jillian McWhirter. A bizarre psychology professor gathers some select students at his house to learn the "psychology of fear" by telling three terror tales of psychos and murder. The first involves a scary practical joke that backfires in a decapitation. The second is about a group of teenage girls who stumble upon a psychotic streetperson and his killer dogs. The third story is about a woman working at an all-night answering service who is plagued by a maniacal phone-caller. ¶ "It is my belief that to understand fear you have to experience fear." • Co-director Ken Wheat explained the concept behind *After Midnight* to *Fangoria* #90: "The whole idea behind this film was to do scary stories that were nonsupernatural—in other words, scary things that can really happen. If there's any point to this movie, it's that things that can really happen to you can be scarier than any kind of imagined monster."

Alone in the Dark (1982; New Line Cinema) D/S: Jack Sholder. P: Robert Shaye. C: Joseph Mangine. Cast: Jack Palance, Donald Pleasence, Martin Landau, Dwight Schultz, Erland Van Lidth, Deborah Hedwall. During a power blackout, a group of homicidal maniacs escape from a maximum security asylum and go on the rampage.

American Gothic (1988; Vidmar Entertainment) D: John Hough. P: John Quested, Christopher Harrop. S: Burt Wetanson, Michael Vines. C: Harvey Harrison. Cast: Rod Steiger, Yvonne De Carlo, Michael J. Pollard, Fiona Hutchinson, Sarah Torgov, Mark Lindsay Chapman. Rod Steiger plays the puritanical head of a reclusive family living on a remote island in the Pacific Northwest. A group of yuppies visit the island and become splatter-fodder for the various demented family members.

Anguish (1986) D/S: Bigas Luna. P: Pepon Coromina. C: J. M. Civit. Cast: Zelda Rubinstein, Michael Lerner, Talia Paul, Angel Jove, Clara Pastor, Isabel Guacia Lorca. A psychotic mother directs her grown son to kill and gouge out his victims' eyes, adding them to the gruesome family collection. But wait—this is only a movie being watched by an audience. In reality (relatively speaking) there is a maniac stalking the theater patrons, murdering them one by one. ¶ "The eyes of the city are mine."

April Fool's Day (1986; Paramount) D: Fred Walton. P: Frank Mancuso, Jr. S: Danilo Bach. C: Charles Minsky. Cast: Jay Baker, Deborah Foreman, Deborah Goodrich, Ken Olandt, Griffin O'Neal, Leah King Pinsent, Clayton Rohner, Amy Steel, Thomas F. Wilson. Muffy, a college-age girl with a history of mental illness, invites a bunch of her friends over to her family's old island mansion for an April Fool's Day weekend. On the ferry across, one of the ferrymen is dumped into the water, horribly mutilated, and assumed dead as a result of the gang's pranks. Once on the island, it appears as if a mad killer is at work as bodies and heads start turning up. Of course it all turns out to be an elaborate April Fool's joke. Ha ha. ¶ "But Muffy hasn't been in an institution for three years; she's been at Vassar!" • This five million dollar production was filmed on Vancouver Island in British Columbia, Canada.

Blood Hook (1987; Troma) D: James Mallon. P: David Herbert. S: Larry Edgerton, John Galligan. C: Marsha Kahm. Cast: Mark Jacobs, Don Cosgrove, Patrick Danz, Paul Drake, Dale Dunham, Donald Franke. In a small Wisconsin fishing town, a series of murders occurs during the "Muskie Madness" fishing contest. A maniac is wandering the woods and reeling in unsuspecting teens with a huge lure. • Includes the song "Fishing for Your Love."

Blood Salvage (1990; Paragon) (also *Mad Jake*). D: Tucker Johnston. P: Martin J. Fischer, Ken C. Sanders. S: Tucker Johnston, Ken C. Sanders. C: Michael Karp. Cast: Danny Nelson, Christian Hesler, Ralph Pruitt Vaughn, Lori Birdsong, Ray Walston, Laura White, John Saxon. In the Georgia backwoods, Jake and his two half-wit sons arrange road "accidents" and keep the victims alive on homemade life support systems while periodically removing their organs to sell to black market organ broker Mr. Stone. A young handicapped girl must fight for her life when she and her family fall into the clutches of the psychotic kinfolk. ¶ "Over 100 families a year get lost on vacation and never get found."

Blood Sisters (1987; Reeltime) D/S/C: Roberta Findlay. P: Walter E. Sear. Cast: Amy Brentano, Shannon McMahon, Dan Erickson, Maria Machart, Elizabeth Rose, Cjerste Thor, Patricia Finneran, Gretchen Kingsley, Brigette Cossu, Randall Walden. A group of sorority pledges must spend an evening in a supposedly haunted house—an old bordello. They are killed off one by one by a mysterious maniac wearing a prostitute's negligee. The madman turns out to be the transvestite son of a prostitute who was responsible for the bloody massacre which took place there years earlier.

Blood Song (1982; Allstate Film Company/Mountain High Enterprises) D: Alan J. Levi. P: Frank Avianca, Lenny Montana. S: James Fargo, Frank Avianca, Lenny Montana. C: Steve Posey. Cast: Donna Wilkes, Richard Jaeckel, Frankie Avalon, Antoinette Bower, Dane Clark, Lenny Montana. Frankie Avalon(!) plays an axe murderer on the loose and stalking the heroine, leaving corpses wherever he goes.

Bloody Birthday (1980; Judica Productions) D: Ed Hunt. P: Gerald T. Olson. S: Ed Hunt, Barry Pearson. C: Stephen Posey. Cast: Susan Strasberg, Jose Ferrer, Lori Lethin, Melinda Cordell, Julie Brown, Joe Penny, Billy Jacoby, Michael Dudikoff. This slice-and-dice film features not one but three killers, and ten-year-old *children* at that (the unrelated tykes were all born on the same day during a total eclipse — which supposedly is what gives them homicidal tendencies). As their tenth birthday approaches the three pre-pubescent psychos band together and set about decimating the local populace.

The Burning (1981; Filmways) D: Tony Maylam. P: Harvey Weinstein. S: Peter Lawrence, Bob Weinstein. C: Harvey Harrison. Cast: Brian Matthews, Leah Ayres, Brian Backer, Larry Joshua, Jason Alexander, Ned Eisenberg, Garrick Glenn, Carolyn Houlihan, Fisher Stevens, Lou David. This early *Friday the 13th* clone features a horribly disfigured camp counselor returning to kill and maim as many promiscuous teens as he can get his various murder weapons on. • Legendary makeup man Tom Savini provided the film's gore effects.

Butcher, Baker, Nightmare Maker (1982; International Film Marketing) (also *Night Warning; Nightmare Maker; Thrilled to Death*). D: William Asher. P: Stephen Breimer, Eugene Mazzola. S: Stephen Breimer, Alan Jay Glueckman, Boon Collins. Cast: Jimmy McNichol, Susan Tyrrell, Bo Svenson, Marcia Lewis, Julia Duffy, Britt Leach. After his parents die in a car accident, 17-year-old Jimmy McNichol goes to live with his crazy old aunt — a psychopathic killer who murders men she fails to seduce. • Star Jimmy McNichol is the brother and ex-singing partner of better-known Kristy McNichol.

Cheerleader Camp (1988; Atlantic Entertainment) (also *Bloody Pom Poms*). D: John Quinn. P: John Quinn, Jeff Prettyman. S: David Lee Fein, R. L. O'Keefe. C: Bryan England. Cast: Betsy Russell, Leif Garrett, Lucinda Dickey, Lorie Griffin, Buck Flower, Travis McKenna, Teri Weigel. Lindo Valley's cheerleading squad journeys to a camp for cheerleaders where they are systematically killed off by a cheerleader-hating maniac. ¶ "Give me a K. Give me an I. Give me an L. Give me another L." — catchy ad line.

Clownhouse (1989; Commercial Pictures)

D/S: Victor Salva. P: Michael Danty, Robin Mortarotti, Victor Salva. C: Robin Mortarotti. Cast: Nathan Forrest Winters, Brian McHugh, Sam Rockwell, Vileita Skillman, Timothy Enos, Karl Heinz-Teuber, Frank Diamonti, Tree. Three escaped mental patients murder a trio of clowns at the Jolly Bros. traveling circus and go on a murder spree dressed in clown outfits. It is up to three brothers, one of whom is deathly afraid of clowns, to battle the maniacal mirthmakers. ¶ "That's what I don't like about clowns, their faces are fake — big happy eyes, great big smiles, it's not real. You never know what they really are."

The Curse (1987) D: David Keith. P: Ovidio G. Assonitis. S: David Chaskin. C: Robert D. Forges. Cast: Wil Wheaton, Claude Akins, Malcolm Denare, Cooper Huckabee, John Schneider, Amy Wheaton, Steve Carlisle, Kathleen Jordon Gregory. A meteor lands in a midwestern farming community and transforms Wil Wheaton's family into grotesque homicidal maniacs. • A film titled *Curse 2: The Bite* was released in 1989, but it is a snake movie having absolutely nothing to do with this one.

Curtains (1982; Curtain Productions; Canada) D: Jonathan Striker (Richard Ciupka). P: Peter R. Simpson. S: Robert Guza, Jr. C: Robert Paynter. Cast: Samantha Eggar, John Vernon, Linda Thorson, Anne Ditchburn, Lynne Griffin, Sandra Warren. A casting session at a film director's isolated mansion turns into a bloodbath when one of the actresses turns out to be a homicidal maniac.

Dead Ringers (1988; Morgan Creek) D: David Cronenberg. P: David Cronenberg, Marc Boyman. S: David Cronenberg, Norman Snider. C: Peter Suschitzky. Cast: Jeremy Irons, Genevieve Bujold. This harrowing look into the psyches of two identical twins, both eminent gynecologists, shows how they are drawn deeper and deeper into madness by one's obsession with an unstable actress and the other's increasing dependence on drugs. • *Dead Ringers* is based on the 1977 novel *Twins*, which itself was based on the 1975 deaths of two New York gynecologists — identical twins — who died in an apparent suicide pact.

Death Valley (1982; Universal) D: Dick Richards. P: Elliot Kastner. S: Richard Rothstein. C: Stephen H. Burum. Cast: Paul Le Mat, Catherine Hicks, Stephen McHattie, A. Wilford Brimley, Peter Billingsley, Edward Herrman. A young boy goes to visit his mother in Phoenix and becomes the target of a murdering madman on the rampage in the area. Correction, make that two murdering madmen, since it turns out the gruesome deaths were caused by a pair of identical (and psychotic) twins.

Deranged (1987; Platinum Pictures) D/P: Chuck Vincent. S: Craig Horall. C: Larry Revene. Cast: Jane Hamilton (Veronica Hart), Paul Siederman, Jennifer Deolora, Jill Cumer, James Gillis, Gary Goldman, John Brett, Loretta Palma, Jessica Rose. Jane Hamilton plays a woman on the edge of a nervous breakdown. When her husband leaves town, an intruder breaks into her apartment. She manages to kill him, which pushes her over the edge, causing her to hallucinate about her abusive father and even imagine the intruder has returned to life. • Star Jane Hamilton is former porno actress Veronica Hart using her real name. James (Jamie) Gillis is also a porn star. Director/producer Chuck Vincent is a veteran hard core filmmaker.

Dr. Caligari (1989) (see MAD SCIENTISTS). The granddaughter of the original Dr. Caligari is performing mad experiments on her insane charges at the "Caligari Asylum" in this bizarre day-glow art film.

Don't Answer the Phone (1980; Manson International) (also *The Hollywood Strangler*). D/P: Robert Hammer. S: Robert Hammer, Michael Castle. C: James Carter. Cast: James Westmoreland, Flo Gerrish, Ben Frank, Nicholas Worth, Stan Haze. A sadistic madman rapes and kills women in a bizarre ritualistic manner, then calls a female psychologist on a radio advice program. Eventually he sets his sights on the psychologist as his next victim.

Don't Go in the House (1980; Film Venture) D: Joseph Ellison. P: Ellen Hammill. S: Joseph Ellison, Ellen Hammill, Joseph Masefield. C: Oliver Wood. Cast: Dan Grimaldi, Robert Osth, Ruth Dardick, Charlie Bonet, Bill Ricci. A maniac, tortured as a child by his mother who liked to hold his arms over open flames, kidnaps girls, incinerates them, and dresses the charred corpses in his mother's clothes.

Don't Open 'Til Christmas (1984; Spectacular Trading International; U.K.) D: Edmund Purdom. P: Steve Minasian, Dick Randall. S: Derek Ford. C: Alan Pudney. Cast: Edmund Purdom, Alan Lake, Belinda Mayne, Gerry Sundquist, Mark Jones, Caroline Munro. A newspaper reporter with less-than-fond memories of Christmas past goes about hacking and slaying every streetcorner Santa he can find. ¶ Ad slogan: "'Twas the night before Christmas/ and all through the house/ Not a creature was stir-ring ... they were all *dead!*" • Sadly, actor Alan Lake, who played the Santa-hating psycho, committed suicide shortly after this film's completion, following the death of his wife, actress Diana Dors.

Doom Asylum (1987; Film World Productions) D: Richard Friedman. P: Steve Menkin. S: Rick Marx. C: Larry Revene. Cast: Patty Mullen, Ruth Collins, Kristin Davis, William Hay, Kenny L. Price, Harrison White, Dawn Alvan, Michael Rogan. A man and his lover are in a terrible auto accident. They both appear to die, but during the autopsy the man awakens. Now horribly mutilated, he goes insane and kills the coroner. Ten years later the hospital has been abandoned. A group of teenagers visit the supposedly haunted hospital, and are killed one by one by the mad fiend using various autopsy tools. • The advertising played up the comedic aspects of this film with lines like: "It'll send shivers up your funny bone." • The ads also emphasized the fact that female lead Patty Mullen was the 1987 "Penthouse Pet of the Year," even listing her on the poster as "Patty Mullen 'Penthouse Pet'." • *Doom Asylum* was filmed in eight days for the ridiculously low sum of $90,000.

Dressed to Kill (1980; Filmways) D/S: Brian De Palma. P: George Litto. C: Ralf Bode. Cast: Michael Caine, Angie Dickinson, Nancy Allen, Keith Gordon, Dennis Franz. Michael Caine plays a psychiatrist whose patient seems to be having a gender crisis—he dresses up in women's clothing and uses a straight razor to slash to death any woman who excites him ... or is it a patient after all? The teenage son of one of his victims and a high-priced call girl who glimpsed the murderer team up to find out. • Heroine Nancy Allen, who played the imperiled prostitute, is director Brian De Palma's wife.

The Driller Killer (1979; Rochelle) D: Abel Ferrara. P: Rochelle Weisberg. S: Nicholas St. John. C: Ken Kelsch. Cast: Jimmy Lane (Abel Ferrara), Carolyn Marz, Harry Schultz, Baybi Day, Richard Howorth, Alan Wynroth. A demented painter journeys out into the back alleys of New York to murder derelicts with a power drill. ¶ "Several pints of blood will spill when teenage girls confront his drill!"—poetic ad line. • The psycho artist handy with a Black and Decker is played by the director.

Fade to Black (1980; Compass International) D/S: Vernon Zimmerman. P: George Braunstein, Roy Hamady. C: Alex Phillips, Jr. Cast: Dennis Christopher, Linda Kerridge,

Tim Thomerson, Morgan Paull, Marya Small. An obsessive movie fanatic takes revenge on real life by dressing up as his favorite movie villains and murdering his enemies, becoming dubbed by the local police as "the Celluloid Killer." ¶ "Eric Binford lives for the movies.... Sometimes he kills for them, too!"—ad line.

Final Exam (1981; Avco Embassy) D/S: Jimmy Huston. P: John L. Chambliss, Myron Meisel. Cast: Cecile Bagdadi, Joel S. Rice, Ralph Brown, Deanna Robbins, Sherry Willis-Burch. Set at a small college, a knife-wielding maniac stalks the students in yet another *Halloween* clone. ¶ From the ads— "Some may pass the test ... God help the rest."

The Final Terror (1981; Samuel Z. Arkoff) (also *Campsite Massacre*). D: Andrew Davis. P: Joe Roth. S: Jon George, Neill Hicks, Ronald Shusett. C: Andreas Davidescu. Cast: John Freidrich, Adrian Zmed, Daryl Hannah, Mark Metcalf, Ernest Harden, Jr., Rachel Ward, Akosua Busia, Joe Pantoliano. A group of ranger trainees and their girlfriends take a backwoods rafting trip, only to be set upon by a crazed maniac who picks them off one by one. • Stars-to-be Daryl Hannah and Rachel Ward put in brief appearances.

Friday the 13th (1980; Paramount) D/P: Sean Cunningham. S: Victor Miller. C: Barry Abrams. Cast: Betsy Palmer, Adrienne King, Jeannine Taylor, Robbi Morgan, Kevin Bacon, Harry Crosby, Laurie Bartram, Mark Nelson. A summer camp is reopened for the first time in years after a pair of brutal murders occurred there many years before. One by one the new teen counselors are gruesomely murdered, with the killer finally revealed to be the demented mother of a boy who had accidentally drowned there. ¶ "Did you know that a young boy drowned? ... His name was Jason." • Though *Halloween* (1978) preceded it by two years, it took this poorly-made, poorly-acted, incredibly successful film to let loose the flood of slice 'n' dice imitations that followed. • Though this one created the hockey-masked, unstoppable killer character of "Jason," he appears on screen for only five seconds in the film, and then simply as a deformed pre-teen. It was Jason's deranged mother who was the original killer, though each succeeding *Friday the 13th* entry focused on the grown Jason himself. • Actor Harry Crosby, who gets an arrow in the eye, is the son of Bing Crosby. • Makeup wizard Tom Savini provided the "Special Makeup Effects and Stunts."

Friday the 13th Part 2 (1981; Paramount) D/P: Steve Miner. S: Ron Kurz. C: Peter Stein. Cast: Amy Steel, John Furey, Adrienne King, Kirsten Baker, Stu Charno, Warrington Gillette, Walt Gorney, Marta Kober, Bill Randolph, Jack Marks. For the first time in the series, it is the hulking maniac Jason who is doing the slicing and dicing (picking up from his demented mother in the first film). He lurks in the woods around Camp Crystal Lake and selects his victims from a new batch of camp-counselors-in-training. • Producer/director Steve Miner served as executive producer on the original *Friday the 13th* (1980). Miner went on to direct *Part 3* as well.

Friday the 13th Part 3 (1982; Paramount) D: Steve Miner. P: Frank Mancuso, Jr. S: Martin Kitrosser, Carol Watson. C: Gerald Feil. Cast: Dana Kimmell, Paul Kratka, Tracie Savage, Jeffrey Rogers, Catherine Parks, Larry Zerner. A new batch of young victims goes in ignorance to the area around Camp Crystal Lake, where of course they encounter the deadly hockey-masked killer Jason and his assortment of death-dealing implements. • For the first time, Jason dons his signature hockey-mask. • This is the only entry in the long-running series to be filmed in 3-D.

Friday the 13th Part 4: The Final Chapter (1984; Paramount) D: Joseph Zito. P: Frank Mancuso, Jr. S: Barney Cohen. C: João Fernandes. Cast: Kimberly Beck, Peter Barton, Corey Feldman, E. Erich Anderson, Crispin Glover, Alan Hayes, Camilla More, Carey More. This one picks up right where number 3 left off, with Jason dead and his body brought to the morgue. Only Jason isn't quite so dead after all—he wakes up, kills a morgue attendant and a nurse, and makes his way back to Crystal Lake to take up his old habits with a new batch of teens. ¶ "I don't want to scare anyone, but I'm gonna give it to you straight about old Jason. His body was never recovered from the lake after he drowned. And if you listen to the old timers in town they'll tell you he's still out there." • A very young Corey Feldman plays the pre-teen hero, Tommy, who does in Jason with a machete.

Friday the 13th Part 5: A New Beginning (1985; Paramount) D: Danny Steinmann. P: Timothy Silver. S: Martin Kitrossef, David Cohen, Danny Steinmann. Cast: John Shepard, Melanie Kinnaman, Shavar Ross, Richard Young, Carol Lacatell. Fans of Jason felt cheated by this "new beginning," for it turns out that everyone's favorite killer is *not* behind the hockey-mask dealing death to a group of unwary teens after all, it is a hate-filled psycho ambulance attendant who simply borrowed Jason's mask and modus operandi.

Friday the 13th Part 6: Jason Lives (1986; Paramount) D/S: Tom McLoughlin. P: Don Behrns. C: Jon Kranhouse. Cast: Thom Mathews, Jennifer Cooke, David Kagan, Renee Jones, Kerry Noonan, Darcy Demoss, Tom Fridley. Jason lives all right—as a now-unkillable zombie-like maniac. A troubled teen digs up Jason's grave to make sure the object of his nightmares is truly dead. When he angrily stabs a pole into Jason's obviously dead, maggot-ridden corpse, lightning strikes (literally) and Jason is revived, ready to take care of the world's teen problem once again. ¶ "Jason belongs in Hell, and I'm gonna see he gets there."

Friday the 13th Part 7: The New Blood (1988; Paramount) D: John Carl Buechler. P: Iain Patterson. S: Daryl Haney, Manuel Fidello. C: Paul Elliott. Cast: Lar Park Lincoln, Terry Kiser, Susan Blu, Kevin Blair, Susan Jennifer Sullivan, Elizabeth Kaitan. An emotionally disturbed teenage girl with telekinetic powers travels to Crystal Lake with her mother and psychiatrist as part of her therapy, having indirectly caused the drowning death of her abusive father while vacationing there as a little girl. Her unconscious wish for her father's return unwittingly brings a waterlogged Jason (residing at the bottom of the lake) back to life, to once again go on the teen-slicing warpath.

Friday the 13th Part 8: Jason Takes Manhattan (1989; Paramount) D/S: Rob Hedden. P: Randolph Cheveldave. C: Bryan England. Cast: Jensen Daggett, Scott Reeves, Barbara Bingham, Peter Mark Richman, Martin Cummins, Gordon Currie, Alex Diakun, V. C. Dupree, Saffron Henderson, Kelly Hu, Sharlene Martin, Warren Munson, Kane Hodder. The now unkillable, zombie-like Jason is back, this time stowing away onboard a senior class cruise to pick off the teens one by one in his usual style. The ship finally ends up in New York Harbor, where Jason continues to follow and decimate the terrified teens. ¶ Teenage heroine: "You don't understand, there is a maniac trying to kill us!" Bored waitress: "Welcome to New York."

Funeral Home (1982; MPM/Wescon; Canada) D/P: William Fruet. S: Ida Nelson. C: Mark Irwin. Cast: Lesleh Donaldson, Kay Hawtry, Barry Morse, Dean Garbett, Stephen Miller. A young man investigates the mysterious disappearances which have been occurring at his grandmother's hotel—a converted funeral home, finally uncovering the terrible *Psycho*-like secret in the basement.

The Funhouse (1981; Universal) D: Tobe Hooper. P: Derek Powers, Steven Bernhardt. S: Larry Block. C: Andrew Laszlo. Cast: Elizabeth Berridge, Cooper Huckabee, Miles Chapin, Largo Woodruff, Sylvia Miles, William Finley, Kevin Conway. Two teenage couples sneak into a sleazy carnival funhouse for a night of fun, only to be stalked by a deformed maniac wearing a Frankenstein's Monster mask.

Graduation Day (1982; Bedford) D/P: Herb Freed. S: David Baughn, Herb Freed. C: Daniel Yarussi. Cast: Christopher George, Patch MacKenzie, E. Danny Murphy, E. J. Peaker. A high school track team is picked off one by one by a mad killer who likes to use track and field equipment as murder weapons, including a javelin spear and a bed of spikes placed in the pole vaulting pit. • The only unique aspect of this *Friday the 13th* clone is the fact that the gore effects were done by a woman, Jill Rockow.

Grandmother's House (1989; Omega Entertainment) D: Peter Rader. P: Nico Mastorakis. S/C: Peter Jensen. Cast: Eric Foster, Kim Valentine, Brinke Stevens, Ida Lee, Len Lesser, David Donham, Joan-Carol Bensen, Angela O'Neill, R. J. Walker, Furley Lumpkin. A teenage girl and her preteen brother come to live with their creepy grandparents when their father is killed in an accident. While the grandparents behave suspiciously, a maniacal woman, said to be the kids' real mother gone mad, shows up, murders several people, and plays a cat-and-mouse chase game with the kids.

Halloween (1978; Compass International) D: John Carpenter. P/S: John Carpenter, Debra Hill. C: Dean Cundey. Cast: Jamie Lee Curtis, Donald Pleasence, Nancy Loomis, P. J. Soles, Charles Cyphers, Kyle Richards. This prototype slasher film stands head and shoulders above all its subsequent imitators. It starts out with eight-year-old Michael Myers cold-bloodedly murdering his teenage sister with a butcher knife on Halloween night. Incarcerated for 15 years, he escapes and returns to his small home town, dons a white-faced Halloween mask, and begins picking off a group of local high-schoolers one by one. ¶ "I spent eight years trying to reach him and then another seven trying to keep him locked up because I realized that what was living behind that boy's eyes was purely and simply evil." •

That unstoppable slasher known as Jason is back from the dead (again) and wielding an axe in Friday the 13th Part 7: The New Blood *(1988).*

Director John Carpenter also wrote the film's musical score—one that, like the music for *Psycho* (1960), inspired numerous imitations and variations for Slasher films to follow. • The unstoppable killer is referred to simply as "The Shape" in the film's credits. This enduring character has starred in three sequels to date—*Halloween 2, 4,* and *5* (with *Halloween 3* being the exception—a sequel in name only). • Babysitting heroine Jamie Lee Curtis and her charges watch two sci-fi classics on TV before they are so rudely interrupted—*The Thing* (1951) and *Forbidden Planet* (1956). • The man behind Michael Myers' mask was Nick Castle, a fellow film-school student and friend of John Carpenter. Castle went on to become a respected director with films like *Tap; The Boy Who Could Fly;* and *The Last Starfighter.*

Halloween 2 (1981; Universal) D: Rick Rosenthal. P/S: Debra Hill, John Carpenter. C: Dean Cundey. Cast: Jamie Lee Curtis, Donald Pleasence, Charles Cyphers, Jeffrey Kramer, Lance Guest, Pamela Susan Shoop. Jamie Lee Curtis returns as the sole surviving teen from the original. It picks up with Curtis being admitted to the hospital after her ordeal, followed closely by "The Shape" who apparently escaped death.

There he murders various hospital personnel as he tries to get to Curtis. She finally learns that she is actually his sister before she blows him up. ¶ "All-New! *More* of The Night He Came Home"—poster ad line. • John Carpenter (who directed the original) handed over the directorial reigns to Rick Rosenthal and served as producer on this sequel. However, Rosenthal apparently did not live up to Carpenter's expectations, since Carpenter stepped in at the last minute to shoot additional scenes. • Dick Warlock wore two hats on this film, stunt coordinator and masked killer. The 5'9" stuntman turned actor to play the hulking masked madman, Michael Myers, wearing lifts in his shoes to give him the added height he needed.

Halloween 4: The Return of Michael Myers (1988; Trancas International) D: Dwight H. Little. P: Paul Freeman. S: Alan B. McElroy. C: Peter Lyons Collister. Cast: Donald Pleasence, Ellie Cornell, Danielle Harris, Michael Pataki, Beau Starr, Kathleen Kinmont, Sasha Jenson. Though psycho-killer Michael Myers (a.k.a. "The Shape") was blown up at the end of *Halloween 2,* he apparently didn't die and has spent the last ten years incarcerated in a maximum security asylum. While being transferred, he escapes and returns to Haddonfield, Illinois, on Halloween night to go on another killing spree while trying to get to and kill his niece (the daughter of Jamie Lee Curtis' character in the first two films). ¶ "We're not talking about any ordinary prisoner, Hoffman, we are talking about an *evil* on two legs." • John Carpenter (director of the original *Halloween*) was once again asked to do another sequel, but refused to be associated with the on-going series, calling it a "curse." • Donald Pleasence reprises his role of Dr. Loomis from the first two *Halloweens*. The filmmakers reportedly secured Pleasence's services by invoking Carpenter's name. "The producers told me that [John Carpenter] read the script," related Pleasence, "and thought it was the best of the *Halloween* series," (*Fangoria* #78). Of course, Carpenter had never even *seen* the script. • This entry was shot in and around Salt Lake City, Utah, on the modest budget of $5.5 million. • Intending this to be a "less gory and more suspenseful" sequel, director Dwight Lee realized after principal photography was completed that they had gone a little too far in attaining this goal, and that this slasher movie was too short on the "slash." So Little called up special effects expert John Buechler and asked him to add some gore effects sequences. As Buechler told *Gorezone* magazine: "[It] was not an R-rated horror film. They discovered after the fact that the picture was a little softer than anticipated. I was called in to give it more punch."

Halloween 5: The Revenge of Michael Myers (1990; Galaxy) D: Dominique Othenin Girard. P: Ramsey Thomas. S: Michael Jacobs, Dominique Othenin Girard. C: Robert Draper. Cast: Donald Pleasence, Danielle Harris, Ellie Cornell, Beau Starr, Wendy Kaplan, Tamara Glynn. Surprise! Michael Myers is not dead after all (despite being shot full of holes and falling down a mine shaft in Part 4). His nine-year-old niece now has a telepathic link with her slasher uncle, and Dr. Loomis (Donald Pleasence in his fourth Halloween appearance) hopes to use this link to track Michael down and put an end to his evil. ¶ "*You* haven't offered up your life to send him to hell, and then discovered that hell would not have him!" • Stuntman/actor Don Shanks shared his insights into playing the masked killer, Michael Myers, with *Fangoria* #88: "I was pretty much myself until the moment I put on the mask. When the mask went on, I just sort of clicked into the Myers personality. That's when the joking stopped, because when you've got a mask on and a knife in your hand, things just stop being funny."

Happy Birthday to Me (1981; Columbia; Canada) D: J. Lee Thompson. P: John Dunning, Andre Link. S: John Saxton, Peter Jobin, Timothy Bond. C: Miklos Lente. Cast: Glenn Ford, Melissa Sue Anderson, Lawrence Dane, Sharon Acker, Frances Hyland, Tracy Bregman. Melissa Sue Anderson is suffering guilt feelings over the accidental death of her mother. Meanwhile, her college friends are brutally murdered one by one, culminating in a macabre birthday celebration attended by the mutilated corpses of the victims. • Melissa Sue Anderson achieved fame on TV's wholesome "Little House on the Prairie."

He Knows You're Alone (1980; United Artists) D: Armand Mastroianni. P: George Manasse, Robert Di Milia, Nan Pearlman. S: Scott Parker. C: Gerald Feil. Cast: Don Scardino, Caitlin O'Heaney, Elizabeth Kemp, Tom Rolfing, Lewis Arlt, Patsy Pease, James Rebhorn, Tom Hanks, Joseph Leon, James Carroll. A knife-wielding maniac murders various bridesmaids and guests until finally getting around to chasing the bride-to-be herself. • Director Armand Mastroianni is the American cousin of Italian superstar actor Marcello Mastroianni.

Heathers (1989; New World) D: Michael Lehmann. P: Denise Di Novi. S: Daniel Waters. C: Francis Kenny. Cast: Winona Ryder, Christian Slater, Shannen Doherty, Lisanne Falk, Kim Walker, Penelope Milford, Glenn Shadix, Lance Fenton, Patrick Labyorteaux, Jeremy Applegate. This witty black comedy on the social ills of your typical high school follows a popular young girl named Veronica who leaves her powerful clique (headed by three girls—all named "Heather") and hooks up with J.D., the new guy in class who has some radical ideas—like murdering all the offensive jocks and stuck-up girls in the school. ¶ Veronica: "You think you're a rebel? You're not a rebel, you're fucking psychotic!" J.D.: "You say tomato, I say 'tom-*a*-to'."

Hell High (1989; DGS) D: Douglas Grossman. P: Douglas Grossman, David Steinman. S: Leo Evans, Douglas Grossman. C: Steven Fierberg. Cast: Christopher Stryker, Maureen Money, Christopher Cousins, Millie Prezioso, Jason Brill. Four high school students play a malicious prank on one of their teachers, but the plan backfires when the stunt pushes her over the edge, turning her into a knife-wielding madwoman. ¶ "You never should have hurt my dolly."

Hell Night (1981; Compass International) D: Tom DeSimone. P: Irwin Yablans, Bruce Cohn Curtis. S: Randolph Feldman. C: Mac Ahlberg. Cast: Linda Blair, Vincent Van Patten, Peter Barton, Kevin Brophy, Jenny Neumann, Suki Goodwin, Jimmy Sturtevant, Hal Ralston, Cary Fox, Ronald Gans. A pair of mutant marauders murder and mangle a group of sorority pledges undergoing their initiation by spending a night in a "haunted house."

Henry: Portrait of a Serial Killer (1986; Maljack Productions) D: John McNaughton. P: John McNaughton, Lisa Dedmond, Steven A. Jones. S: Richard Fire, John McNaughton. C: Charlie Lieberman. Cast: Michael Rooker, Tracy Arnold, Tom Towles. This intensely disturbing film follows the exploits of amoral serial killer, Henry, as he goes across the country brutally murdering all those who cross his path. ¶ "If you shoot somebody in the head with a 45 every time you kill somebody, it becomes like your fingerprint, see? But if you strangle one, stab another, one you cut up, one you don't, then the police don't know what to do. They'll think you're four different people." • This controversial movie received only a limited theatrical release due to the MPAA's slapping an "X" certificate on it. According to the film board the "X" was not due to any specific scenes of excess nudity or graphic violence, but to the very nature of the film itself, and no amount of scene cutting could gain it an "R" rating. *Henry* is now thought of as an innovation in filmmaking, and has received much critically favorable attention.

Hide and Go Shriek (1987; New Star Entertainment) D: Skip Schoolnik. P: Dimitri Villard. S: Michael Kelly. C: Eugene Shluglett. Cast: Brittain Frye, Donna Baltron, George Thomas, Rebunkah Jones. Eight teenagers decide to hold their all-night graduation party in a furniture store. But a game of hide-and-seek becomes a game of life-and-death when they're picked off one by one by a vicious maniac. ¶ From the ads: "Close your eyes. Count to ten. And run for your life." • Even almost ten years after the advent of the slasher film, producers were still trying to cash in on the slice 'n' dice wave, as evidenced by this film's advertising: "In the terrifying tradition of *Friday the 13th* and *Halloween.*"

The Hitcher (1986; HBO Pictures) D: Robert Harmon. P: Kip Ohman. S: Eric Red. C: John Seale. Cast: Rutger Hauer, C. Thomas Howell, Jeffrey DeMunn, Jennifer Jason Leigh. Rutger Hauer plays a psychotic hitchhiker out on a murder spree who dogs the path of a young man driving a car to California, leaving a trail of blood behind him which points to the innocent student as the mad killer. ¶ *"The Hitcher* will leave you so frightened you won't want to stop for the next red light"—*New York Post* review.

Home Sweet Home (1980; I.W.D.C.) D: Nettie Penn. P: Don Edmunds. S: Thomas Bush. Cast: Jake Steinfeld, Sallee Elyse, Peter dePaula, Collette Trugg, Vanessa Shaw. The Bradley family Thanksgiving is interrupted by an escaped homicidal maniac out to kill their entire family and visiting guests.

Honeymoon Horror (1982; Omega) D: Harry Preston. P: Nick Calpeno. S: L. L. (Jack) Carney. Cast: William F. Pecchi, Cheryl Black, Bob Wagner. Three newlywed couples are set upon by a disfigured maniac at a secluded honeymoon lodge.

Hospital Massacre (1982; Cannon) (also *X-Ray*). D: Boaz Davidson. P: Menahem Golem, Yoram Globus. S: Marc Behm. C: Nicholas Von Sternberg. Cast: Barbi Benton, Chip Lucia, Jon Van Ness, Den Surles, Gay Austin, John Warner Williams, Lanny Duncan, Gloria Morrison, Karyn Smith, Michael Frost. Former Playmate and girlfriend of Hugh Hefner, Barbi Benton, plays a woman who enters the hospital for a routine examination only to be terrorized by a madman she had spurned when they were children. The killer leaves a trail of mangled bodies as he searches for her, intending to cut her heart out for revenge.

House of Death (1981; ABA Productions) D: David Nelson. P: Chuck Ison, Ernest Bouskos. S: Paul C. Elliott. Cast: Susan Kiger, Jody Kay, Jennifer Chase, William T. Hicks, Martin Tucker. A deranged killer, ostracized from the small town festivities as a child, takes it out (with a machete) on a group of college students staging a party at an old abandoned house. ¶ "He wants their bodies . . . in pieces"—ad line.

House of the Long Shadows (1983; Cannon; U.K.) D: Pete Walker. P: Jenny Craven. S: Michael Armstrong. C: Norman Langley. Cast: Christopher Lee, Peter Cushing, Vincent Price, Desi Arnaz, Jr., John Carradine, Sheila Keith, Julie Peasgood, Richard Todd. An American writer makes a bet he can write a novel in 24 hours and goes to a remote old country mansion to prove it. Once there, he encounters an eccentric family whose members end up gruesomely murdered one by one. In a silly twist ending, it all turns out to be a hoax put over by his publisher. • More of an old-fashioned mystery movie (with a little gore) than a slasher film, this disappointing picture is remarkable solely for the fact that it is the only time these four masters of horror appeared together—Christopher Lee, Peter Cushing, Vincent Price, and John Carradine.

The House on Sorority Row (1982; VAE Productions) (also *House of Evil*). D/S: Mark Rosman. P: Mark Rosman, John G. Clark. C: Timothy Suhrstedt. Cast: Kathryn McNeil, Eileen Davidson, Lois Kelso Hunt, Christopher Lawrence, Janis Zido, Charles Serio. The members of a sorority house begin dying, killed off by the crazed, deformed son whose mother used to own the house.

Humongous (1981; Embassy; Canada) D: Paul Lunch. P: Anthony Kramreither. S: William Gray. C: Brian R. R. Hebb. Cast: Janet Julian, David Wallace, Janet Baldwin, John Wildman, Joy Boushel, Layne Coleman. A group of teenagers wreck their boat on an island inhabited by the seven-foot-tall mutant son of a woman raped there 36 years earlier ... and this resident madman does not take kindly to visitors.

The Initiation (1984; New World) D: Larry Stewart. P: Scott Winant. S: Charles Pratt, Jr. Cast: Vera Miles, Clu Gulager, James Read, Daphne Zuniga. Four sorority pledges are supposed to break into a department store and steal the security guard's uniform. Once they are locked inside the mall a maniac killer goes to work. ¶ "...the night new blood is pledged"—apt ad line.

The Invisible Maniac (1990) (see INVISIBILITY). In this slasher/mad scientist hybrid, a brilliant but unstable physicist goes insane and uses his newfound invisibility serum to spy on and kill a group of high school students in various gruesome ways.

Junior (1989) D: Jim Henley. P: Don Carmody. S: John Maxwell, Don Carmody. Cast: Suzanne Delaurentis, Linda Singer, Jeremy Ratchford, Michael McKeever. A madman with a chain saw and a mother complex goes after a couple of young girls.

Just Before Dawn (1980; Movielab) D: Jeff Lieberman. P: David Sheldon, Doro Vlado Hreljanovic. S: Mark Arywitz, Gregg Irving. C: Joel King, Dean King. Cast: George Kennedy, Mike Kellin, Chris Lemmon, Gregg Henry, Deborah Benson. Five overnight campers are stalked by a terrible team of twins brandishing meat cleavers. Exploitation stalwart George Kennedy plays a forest ranger.

Killer Party (1986; MGM) D: William Fruet. P: Michael Lepiner. S: Barney Cohen. Cast: Martin Hewitt, Ralph Seymour, Elaine Wilkes, Paul Bartel, Sherry Willis-Burch, Alicia Fleer. Three coeds are forced to spend the night in the abandoned Delta Sigma fraternity house, the site of an accidental hazing death 20 years ago. The girls soon learn they are not alone in the house, however, when a madman begins picking them off one by one.

Killer Workout (1987; Winters Group) (also *Aerobi-cide*). D/S: David A. Prior. P: Peter Yuval. C: Peter Bonilla. Cast: Marcia Karr, David James Campbell, Fritz Matthews, Ted Prior, Teresa Vander Woude, Richard Bravo, Dianne Copeland, Laurel Mock. A beautiful model is horribly burned in a freak tanning spa accident. Five years later she owns her own health club where her patrons start dying, murdered by a maniac wielding a giant safety pin. ¶ "I think it eats you up inside to look at all those beautiful young bodies, knowing that you have to spend a lifetime hiding yours, knowing that any man would get *sick* if he tried to make love to you!"—sensitive police detective.

Killer's Moon (1978; Rothernorth; U.K.) D/S: Alan Birkinshaw. P: Alan Birkinshaw, Gordon Keymer. C: Arthur Lavis. Cast: Anthony Forrest, Tom Marshall, Georgina Kean, Nigel Gregory, David Jackson, Paul Rattee. In Britain's lovely Lake District, four slobbering maniacs set upon a busload of schoolgirls and their boyfriends on a camping holiday, murdering them with expected regularity.

Lady Stay Dead (1982; Ryntare Productions; Australia) D/P/S: Terry Bourke. C: Ray Henman. Cast: Chard Hayward, Louise Howitt, Deborah Coulls, Roger Ward, Les Foxcroft, James Elliott. A psycho gardener rapes and murders the young women who hire him.

The Last Horror Film (1982; Twin Continental Films) D: David Winters. P: David Winters, Judd Hamilton. S: Judd Hamilton, David Winters, Tom Klassen. C: Tom DeNove. Cast: Caroline Munro, Joe Spinell, Judd Hamilton, Devin Goldenberg, David Winters, Stanley Susanne Beaton. Joe Spinell plays a deranged New York cabbie-cum-filmmaker who goes to the Cannes Film Festival to locate the object of his obsession—actress Caroline Munro. There follows a series of gruesome murders as Spinell dogs Munro and finally kidnaps her. • Caroline Munro's co-star, Judd Hamilton, is Munro's real-life husband. He also co-wrote and co-produced the film. • Joe Spinell's real-life mother, Mary Spinell, appears in the film . . . as his mother. Both Spinell and his mother won awards at the thirteenth annual Sitges Film Festival. "We were the only mother and son team in a movie to ever win an award in Europe, maybe in the world," claimed Spinell in an interview for *Psychotronic #2*.

Luther the Geek (1990; Quest Entertainment) D: Carlton J. Albright. P: David Platt. S: Whitey Styles. C: David Knox. Cast: Edward Terry, Joan Roth, J. Jerome Clarke, Tom Mills, Stacy Haiduk. A maniac "geek" (a man who bites the heads off live chickens in carnival sideshows) with metal teeth and a taste for human blood lays siege to a farmhouse and attempts to bite out the throats of its occupants. ¶ "But of all the bizarre acts, the strangest was the 'geek.' The geek was a man so down on his luck he'd do anything for a drink; but to earn that shot of cheap whiskey, he had to bite the head off a live chicken and drink its blood in front of a stunned audience. The geek, an American phenomenon" — opening narration. • Luther as a child is played by the director's own son.

Madhouse (1981; O. G. Assonitis; Italy/U.S.) D/P: Ovidio G. Assonitis. S: Ovidio G. Assonitis, Stephen Blakely, Peter Shepherd, Robert Gandus. C: Piazzoli. Cast: Trish Everley, Dennis Robertson, Michael Macrae, Morgan Hart, Richard Baker. The disfigured mad twin sister of a teacher at a school for the deaf escapes from the asylum and vows revenge on the sister who put her there. Corpses pile up in the basement until the twist ending, revealing the true identity of the demented killer.

Madman (1982; Jensen Farley) D/S: Joe Giannone. P: Gary Sales, Joe Giannone. C: James Momel. Cast: Alexis Dubin, Tony Fish, Harriet Bass, Seth Jones, Jan Claire, Alex Murphy. When an abandoned summer camp is reopened, the trainee counselors are told the story of the deranged farmer, aptly named "Madman Marz," who went on the killing spree that resulted in the original camp closure. Legend has it that if the madman's name is called three times he will return. Of course some wiseguy does just that, and farmer Marz comes out of the woods to wield his sharp implements once again.

Maniac (1980; Analysis. D: William Lustig. P: Andrew Garroni, William Lustig. S: Z. A. Rozenberg, Joe Spinell. C: Robert Lindsay. Cast: Joe Spinell, Caroline Munro, Gail Lawrence, Kelly Piper, Rita Montone, Hyla Marrow, Tom Savini. In this mean-spirited low-budget slasher movie, frequently reviled even by gore hounds, Joe Spinell stars as repulsive psycho killer Frank Zito, a man who murders young women, scalps them, and nails their bloody hair onto mannequins in his apartment. • *Maniac* was shot on 16mm with a budget of $35,000. • Makeup artist Tom Savini, who provided the film's gore effects, appears in the movie as a victim. He later regretted his involvement with it and denounced the film (along with big-time critics Siskel and Ebert and countless women's groups). • Director William Lustig is Jake LaMotta's nephew.

Maniac Cop (1988; Shapiro Glickenhaus Entertainment) D: William Lustig. P/S: Larry Cohen. C: Vincent J. Rabe. Cast: Tom Atkins, Bruce Campbell, Laurene Landon, Richard Roundtree, William Smith, Robert Z'dar, Sheree North. A hulking maniac in a police uniform is terrorizing the streets, murdering right and left. ¶ "You have the right to remain silent . . . Forever" — catchy ad line. • This $1.5 million film was shot in New York and L.A. Director Sam Raimi (the *Evil Dead* films) has a brief cameo in the film as a newscaster.

Mardi Gras Massacre (1978) D/P/S: Jack Weis. Cast: Curt Dawson, Gwen Arment, Wayne Mack, Ronald Tanet. In New Orleans, a few days before Mardi Gras, a maniac who believes he is an Aztec priest stalks prostitutes and cuts out their hearts. ¶ "Honey, I'm as evil as you can get."

Memorial Valley Massacre (1988; Motion Picture Corporation) D: Robert C. Hughes. P: Brad Krevoy, Steven Stabler. S: Robert C. Hughes, George Francis Skrow. C: James Mathers. Cast: William Smith, Cameron Mitchell, John Kerry, Mark Mears, Lesa Lee, John Caso. A greedy park developer opens up the Memorial Valley Campground only to have the campers killed off one by one by a half-wild maniac.

Misery (1990; Columbia) D: Rob Reiner. P: Andrew Scheinman, Rob Reiner. S: William Goldman. C: Barry Sonnenfeld. Cast: James Caan, Kathy Bates, Frances Sternhagen, Richard Farnsworth, Lauren Bacall. Writer Paul Sheldon (James Caan) drives his car off an icy road and ends up trapped at the home of a psychotic, possessive fan named Annie Wilkes, who alternately nurses and torments him. ¶ "I'm your number one fan." • Warren Beatty was originally set to play Paul Sheldon but dropped out for a variety of reasons, including his starring in *Dick Tracy,* and was replaced by James Caan. • *Misery* is based on the novel by Stephen King (the eighteenth film adaptation of a King story).

Director Rob Reiner claims that King was pleased with the movie, and "he said it's by far the best film that's ever been made out of any of his books" (*Fangoria* #101). • Co-star Kathy Bates won the Oscar for Best Actress for her powerful portrayal of psycho-fan Annie Wilkes.

Mortuary (1981; Movie Makers Co.) D: Howard Avedis. P/S: Howard Avedis, Marlene Schmidt. Cast: Mary McDonough, David Wallace, Bill Paxton, Lynda Day George, Christopher George. Ever since his father's mysterious death, Christie Parson is having terrible nightmares, while a hooded maniac lurking in the town mortuary turns out to be all too real. ¶ From the promotional trailer: "Before your funeral, and your coffin lid is closed . . . before you are buried, and your flesh turns cold . . . before you are covered with the last shovelful of dirt, be sure you are really *dead*."

Mother's Day (1981; United Film Distribution) D/P: Charles Kaufman. S: Charles Kaufman, Warren D. Leight. C: Joe Mangine. Cast: Nancy Hendrickson, Deborah Luce, Tania Pierce, Holden McGuire, Billy Ray McQuade, Rose Ross. A pair of psychotic hillbilly brothers live in a backwoods shack with their domineering mother. They have two hobbies—collecting "Sesame Street" and "Star Trek" paraphernalia, and kidnapping, torturing, and killing hikers and campers.

Mountaintop Motel Massacre (1986; New World) D: Jim McCullough. P: Jim McCullough, Jim McCullough, Jr. S: Jim McCullough, Jr. C: Joseph Wilcots. Cast: Bill Thurman, Anna Chappell, Will Mitchell, Virginia Loridans, Major Brock, Amy Hill, Marian Jones, Greg Brazzel, Jill King. (A crazy woman operates a run-down motel (à la Norman Bates) and either murders her guests with a sickle or throws snakes, bugs, and rats on them. ¶ "Six bodies in there? Sorry I was so late in getting here"—the tardy sheriff. • The single point of interest in this low-budget slasher copy is the film's amusing ad line: "Don't disturb Evelyn . . . she already is!" Checkout time cannot come soon enough for the viewers of this slice 'n' dice tripe. • Top billed Bill Thurman was a regular in Larry Buchanan's no-budget sci-fi remakes of the 1960s (*In the Year 2889; Zontar, the Thing from Venus;* etc.). • *Mountaintop Motel Massacre* was filmed in 1983 but shelved for three years by New World for fear it would be overshadowed by *Psycho 2.*

Movie House Massacre (1984) D: Alice Raley. Cast: Mary Woronov, Jonathan Blakely, Lynne Darcy. An old movie theater, the sight of a previous tragedy, is reopened only to have the patrons stalked and slashed by a mad killer.

The Mutilator (1984; OK Productions) D: Buddy Cooper, John Douglass. P/S: Buddy Cooper. C: Peter Schnall. Cast: Matt Mitler, Ruth Martinez, Bill Hitchcock, Connie Rogers, Frances Raines, Morey Lampley, Jack Chatham, Ben Moore. A college student and his friends spend their winter break at his father's beachfront condo, only to be axed, chopped, and mangled by a mad killer. The killer turns out to be the boy's own troubled father, who had quietly gone insane over his wife's accidental shooting death at the hands of his own son.

My Bloody Valentine (1981; Paramount; Canada) D: George Mihalka. P: John Dunning, Andre Link, Stephen Miller. S: John Beard. C: Rodney Gibbons. Cast: Paul Kelman, Lori Hallier, Neil Affleck, Keith Knight, Alf Humphreys, Cynthia Dale. Twenty years after a series of murders occurred in the mining town of Valentine's Bluff, they decide to restage the annual Valentine's Day dance, during which the tragic killings had taken place. Big mistake, for the killings start up again (with the crazed killer cutting out his victims' hearts with a pick-axe and sending them to the authorities in candy boxes), culminating in the masked killer crashing an illicit party held in the mine by the town's teens.

Nail Gun Massacre (1987; Reel Movies) D: Terry Lofton, Bill Leslie. P: Terry Lofton. S: Terry Lofton. C: Bill Leslie. Cast: Rocky Patterson, Michelle Meyer, Ron Queen, Beau Leland, Sebrina Lawless, Monica Lawless. A girl is raped by a group of construction workers. Years later, someone dressed in army fatigues and a black motorcycle helmet is going around killing a construction crew with a nail gun. Who is the mysterious maniac?

New Years Evil (1981; Cannon) D: Emmett Alston. P: Menahem Golan, Yoram Globus. S: Leonard Neubauer. C: Edward Thomas. Cast: Roz Kelly, Kip Niven, Chris Wallace, Grant Cramer, Louisa Moritz. A psychotic killer, calling himself "Evil," phones the host of a live New Year's Eve TV rock show and states he will murder one of her friends for every time midnight strikes in the different time zones across America, finally ending with her own murder. ¶ "On the one night they were celebrating New Year's Eve, he was out ending their lives"—promotional trailer.

New York Ripper (1982; Fulvia Film; Italy) D: Lucio Fulci. P: Fabrizio De Angelis. S: Gianfranco Clerici, Dardano Sacchetti, Vincenzo Mannino, Lucio Fulci. C: Luigi Kuveiller. Cast: Jack Hedley, Almanta Keller, Paolo Malco, Howard Ross (Renato Rossini), Alexandra Delli Colli, Andrew Painter. A knife-wielding maniac goes through the streets of New York slashing and slaughtering all those women he encounters that he deems sexually provocative.

Night of the Creeps (1986) (see ZOMBIES). This entertaining tale of zombies and sluglike creatures from outer space contains a flashback sequence in which a psycho escapee from a mental institution chops up the investigating cop's ex-girlfriend. Killed by the cop, the madman is resurrected 27 years later as an axe-wielding zombie. ¶ "I found her in the car . . . and on the road . . . and in the woods."

Night School (1981; Paramount) (also *Terror Eyes*). D: Ken Hughes. P: Larry Babb, Ruth Avergan. S: Ruth Avergan. C: Mark Irwin. Cast: Leonard Mann, Rachel Ward, Drew Snyder, Joseph R. Sicari. A mysterious killer likes to chop the heads off young students at Wendell College School for Girls. • *Night School* was directed by the same man who brought us *Chitty Chitty Bang Bang* (1968)!

The Night Stalker (1987; Almi Pictures) D: Max Kleven. P: Don Edmonds. S: John Goff, Don Edmonds. C: Don Burgess. Cast: Charles Napier, Michelle Reese, Katherine Kelly Lang, Gary Crosby, Robert Z'dar, Robert Viharo. A hulking psychopath likes to ritualistically kill prostitutes.

Nightbreed (1990) (see FREAKS). Director-turned-actor David Cronenberg plays a vicious serial killer who is after the secret of a hidden subterranean city called "Midian" inhabited by a host of freakish creatures. This cold killer is revealed to be much more monstrous than those "monstrosities" living in Midian.

Nightmare (1981; 21st Century) D/S: Romano Scavolini. P: John L. Watkins, William Milling. C: Gianni Fiore. Cast: Baird Stafford, Sharon Smith, C. J. Cooke, Mik Cribben, Danny Ronen. A psychopath undergoing drug therapy, who had murdered his parents with an axe for engaging in bondage games, snaps when he visits a sex shop. He resumes his murderous ways, conducting a deadly cat-and-mouse game with a single woman and her three children. • This gory film's posters and advertising played up the name of special effects wizard Tom Savini, even though Savini did not work on the movie! When Savini threatened to sue, the filmmakers had his name covered up on all the advertising.

Nightmare at Shadow Woods (1987; FCG) D: John W. Grissmer. P: Marianne Kanter. S: Richard Lamden. C: Richard E. Brooks. Cast: Louise Lasser, Mark Soper, Marianne Kanter, Julie Gordon, Jayne Bentzen, William Fuller. At a drive-in, a psychotic teenager viciously murders a man and pins the blame on his innocent twin brother. The twin is sent away to a prison for the criminally insane. Ten years later, the innocent twin escapes, which gives the evil twin an excuse to go on a machete-wielding rampage with the intent of blaming the carnage on his escaped brother. • Though filmed in 1984, it was not released (and then only briefly) until 1987.

Open House (1987; Intercontinental) D: Jag Mundhra. P: Sandy Cobe. S: David Mickey Evans. C: Robert Hayes, Gary Louzon. Cast: Joseph Bottoms, Adrienne Barbeau, Rudy Ramos, Mary Stavin, Scott Tompson Baker, Darwyn Swalve. In this bargain basement slasher film, Joseph Bottoms plays a radio talk show host who makes contact with a homicidal maniac named "Harry." Bottoms' girlfriend (Adrienne Barbeau) is a real estate agent who is targeted by the killer. The psycho turns out to be a monstrous homeless man who murders real estate agents in various gory ways, blaming them for the high cost of housing.

Pandemonium (1982; United Artists) D: Alfred Sole. P: Doug Chapin. S: Richard Whitler, Jamie Klein. C: Michel Hugo. Cast: Tom Smothers, Carol Kane, Miles Chapin, Debralee Scott, Marc McClure, Judge Reinhold, Teri Landrum, Candy Azzara. In 1963 a rash of bizarre murders causes a cheerleading camp to close. Years later it is reopened, and the expected rash of killings begins again in this unfunny parody of slasher movies. The killer is finally revealed to be a deranged football hero nursing a secret desire to be a cheerleader. ¶ "Even a man who is pure in heart and says his prayers at night may become a cheerleader when the pom poms bloom and the autumn moon is bright." • Before making it big as "Pee-Wee Herman," Paul Reubens appeared in this film as "Johnson," Royal Canadian Mountie Tom Smothers' assistant. • Actress Debralee Scott is recognizable by TV fans as "Hotsie-Totsie" from "Welcome Back Kotter."

Phobia (1980; Paramount; Canada) D:

John Huston. P: Zale Magder. S: Lew Lehman, Jimmy Sangster, Peter Bellwood. C: Reginald H. Morris. Cast: Paul Michael Glaser, John Colicos, Susan Hogan, Alexandra Stewart, David Bolt, Robert O'Ree, David Eisner, Lisa Langlois, Kenneth Welsh, Patricia Collins. Paul Michael Glaser (of TV's "Starsky and Hutch" fame) stars as a psychotherapist whose disturbed phobic patients are being killed off one by one by a madman employing the patients' own worst fears to murder them. • This is respected director John Huston's only horror film. Deemed unsuitable for a nationwide release, it only saw regional distribution before hitting cable and video.

Pieces (1981; Almena Films/Fort Fils; Spain/Puerto Rico). D/S: Juan Piquer Simon. P: Dick Randall, Steve Miniasian. C: Juan Marine. Cast: Christopher George, Edmund Purdom, Lynda Day George, Paul L. Smith, Frank Braña, Ian Sera, Jack Taylor, Gerard Tichy, Isabel Luque. The husband and wife team of Christopher and Lynda Day George star in this gory import about a sick psychopath who murders women for their choice body parts, which he intends to use in completing a grotesque human jigsaw puzzle. ¶ "You don't have to go to Texas for a chain saw massacre" — ad line.

Pledge Night (1988; S.G.E.) D: Paul Ziller. P/S: Joyce Snyder. Cast: Todd Eastland, Shannon McMahon, Joey Belladonna, Will Kempe. Twenty years ago, an initiation prank gone wrong immerses new pledge Sid in a vat of boiling acid. Now, the Phi Up fraternity is still plagued with occasional hazing "accidents," the handiwork of "Acid Sid" who enjoys killing off the local frat brats. • Joey Belladonna, who plays the murderous Acid Sid, is the lead singer of the heavy metal band "Anthrax."

Popcorn (1991; Studio Three) D: Mark Herrier. P: Torben Johnke, Gary Goch, Ashok Amritraj. S: Tod Hackett. C: Ronnie Taylor. Cast: Jill Schoelen, Tom Villard, Dee Wallace Stone, Derek Rydall, Elliott Hurst, Kelly Jo Minter, Malcolm Danare, Ray Walston, Tony Roberts. At a condemned theater, a college film class stages an old-time horror marathon, complete with 50s-style gimmicks and hype, in order to raise money. During the show, however, the students begin dying one by one, killed off by a twisted maniac with a grudge against the heroine. ¶ "Half an hour to midnight, I still have a little time . . . to kill." • The movie marathon of old "stinkers" includes a fictitious film called *Mosquito* (a take-off on big bug movies like *The Deadly Mantis,* 1957), and one called *Attack of the Amazing Electrified Man* (an homage to the 1956 Lon Chaney vehicle, *The Indestructible Man*). The students also reuse the gimmick of wiring theater seats to send mild electric shocks to select members of the audience, just like showmeister William Castle did for *The Tingler* (1959). Actual posters from both *The Tingler* and *The Deadly Mantis* can be seen in the dressed-up theater lobby. • Alan Ormsby (*Children Shouldn't Play with Dead Things,* 1972; *Deranged,* 1974; etc.) was the film's original director, but left in the middle of production due to "creative differences" with the film's backers and was replaced by first-time director Mark Herrier. • Though set in the fictional southern California town of "Oceanview," *Popcorn* was actually filmed entirely in and around Kingston, Jamaica.

Prom Night (1980; Avco Embassy) D: Paul Lynch. P: Pete Simpson. S: William Gray. C: Robert New. Cast: Leslie Nielsen, Jamie Lee Curtis, Casey Stevens, Antoinette Bower, Pita Oliver, Robert Silverman. At a prom dance, a hooded killer is stalking and slashing the four teens responsible for the death of Jamie Lee Curtis' little sister six years earlier. ¶ "If you're not back by midnight . . . you won't be coming home!" — ad line. • Jamie Lee Curtis, the reigning queen of slice 'n' dice: *Halloween* (1978), *Prom Night* (1980), *Halloween 2* (1981), *Terror Train* (1981). • A sequel, *Hello Mary Lou: Prom Night 2* was made in 1987, but it had nothing to do with the original, and was a supernatural ghost story rather than a slasher film.

The Prowler (1981; Sandhurst) (also *Rosemary's Killer*). D: Joseph Zito. P: Joseph Zito, David Streit. S: Glenn Leopold. C: Raul Lomas. Cast: Vicki Dawson, Christopher Goutman, Cindy Weintraub, Farley Granger, John Seitz, Lawrence Tierney. A World War II veteran murders his unfaithful girlfriend and her lover with a pitchfork, and 35 years later returns to pick up where he left off by mutilating a new batch of teenagers.

Psycho 2 (1983; Universal) D: Richard Franklin. P: Hilton A. Green. S: Tom Holland. C: Dean Cundey. Cast: Anthony Perkins, Vera Miles, Meg Tilly, Robert Loggia, Claudia Bryar, Dennis Franz. After 22 years in an asylum, Norman Bates is "cured" and released. He returns home, takes a job in a diner, acquires a girlfriend of sorts, and is plagued by a new series of murders; not to mention Norman's real mother revealing herself after all these years (though she turns out to be just as stiflingly possessive as the first woman, now revealed to be a foster mother). ¶ "You smell like the toasted cheese sandwiches my mother used to bring me."

Psycho 3 (1986; Universal) D: Anthony Perkins. P: Hilton A. Green. S: Charles Edward Pogue. C: Bruce Surtees. Cast: Anthony Perkins, Diana Scarwid, Jeff Fahey, Roberta Maxwell, Hugh Gillin, Lee Garlington, Robert Alan Browne. Norman has reopened the Bates Motel and hires a sleazy drifter to help run things. In the meantime, a former nun who has lost her faith ends up at the motel and befriends Norman. When his sexual feelings are aroused (feelings his mother would not have approved of), Norman squelches them with another round of murders. ¶ Heroine to Norman: "I'm afraid I did leave the bathroom in a mess." Norman's reply: "I've seen it worse." • Anthony Perkins only agreed to do another *Psycho* film if he could direct it, which he did here.

Psycho 4: The Beginning (1990; Cable TV movie) D: Mick Garris. P: George Zaloom, Les Mayfield. S: Joseph Stefano. C: Rodney Charters. Cast: Anthony Perkins, Olivia Hussey, Henry Thomas, C. C. H. Pounder, Warren Frost, Donna Mitchell, Thomas Schuster, Sharen Camille, Bobbi Evors. The middle-aged Norman is married now (to his former psychiatrist), and his wife is pregnant. Instead of being happy with his new, normal life, Norman is deathly afraid that his "evil seed" will continue, and he plans to kill her. In the meantime, he calls a radio talk-show program on matricide, and his early life and development into the original psycho is revealed in flashbacks. ¶ "[My mother] always has had and always will have a *strong* effect on my behavior."

Psychos in Love (1987; Bleecker-Infinity) D/P/C: Gorman Bechard. S: Carmine Capobianco, Gorman Bechard. Cast: Carmine Capobianco, Debi Thibeault, Frank Stewart, Cecilia Wilde, Donna Davidge. Two psychos meet, fall in love, and give up their murderous ways in this low-budget horror satire shot in 16mm. When they decide to go on the massacre bandwagon so to speak, they live out their murderous fantasies vicariously by watching slasher movies on videocassette. • Carmine Capobianco, who plays the male psycho, also wrote and performed the music, served as second assistant director, and helped with the special effects. Female lead Debi Thibeault served as the costumer and assistant editor.

Return to Horror High (1987; New World) D: Bill Froelich. P: Mark Lisson. S: Bill Froelich, Mark Lisson, Dana Escalante, Greg H. Sims. C: Roy Wagner. Cast: Lori Lethin, Brendan Hughes, Alex Rocco, Scott Jacoby, Andy Romano, Richard Brestoff, Al Fann, Pepper Martin, Maureen McCormick, Vince Edwards. A film crew comes to a small town high school to make a slasher movie based on a real life massacre that occurred there several years earlier. As expected, cast and crew members begin dying in various gruesome ways, killed by the maniac, until the big surprise at the "cheat" ending of this tongue-in-cheek slasher movie. • Maureen McCormick plays a policewoman who becomes sexually excited by the sight of blood. TV fans will be dismayed (or perhaps delighted) to remember her as "Marsha" from "The Brady Bunch." • *Return to Horror High* was filmed entirely at a deserted junior high school outside of Los Angeles.

Savage Weekend (1981; Upstate Murder Co.) (also *The Killer Behind the Mask; The Upstate Murders*). D/S: David Paulsen. P: David Paulsen, John Mason Kirby. C: Zoli Vidor. Cast: Christopher Allport, James Doerr, Marilyn Hamlin, Kathleen Heaney, David Gale. A group of friends spend the weekend at a large house in upstate New York, only to be picked off one by one by a masked maniac. • The film was made in 1976 as *The Killer Behind the Mask* but was not released until 1981 as *Savage Weekend,* predating the body-count slice 'n' dice wave by two years. (Its late release and its subject matter caused it to be included in this section.)

Schizoid (1980; Cannon) (also *Murder by Mail*). D/S: David Paulsen. P: Menahem Golan, Yoram Globus. Cast: Klaus Kinski, Marianna Hill, Craig Wasson, Donna Wilkes, Richard Herd, Christopher Lloyd. Psychiatrist Klaus Kinski appears to be murdering his group therapy patients with a pair of scissors . . . but of course there is a surprise ending.

Silence of the Lambs (1991; Orion) D: Jonathan Demme. P: Kenneth Utt, Edward Saxon, Ron Bozman. S: Ted Tally. C: Tak Fujimoto. Cast: Jodie Foster, Anthony Hopkins, Scott Glenn, Ted Levine, Brooke Smith, Roger Corman. An F.B.I. trainee (Jodie Foster) agrees to interview a dangerous killer (Anthony Hopkins) incarcerated in a maximum security institution with the hope of obtaining some new insight on a present serial killer case. The intelligent, vicious cannibal, Dr. Hannibal Lector (a former psychiatrist), provides the needed clues to help Foster track down the twisted killer known as "Buffalo Bill." At the end, Lector escapes after being transferred to a new holding facility, intent on resuming his own violent career. • Director Jonathan Demme and actors Jodie Foster and Scott Glenn all spent time at the F.B.I. training center in Quantico, Virginia, interviewing agents and researching case files and photos. Glenn said in *People Weekly* magazine April 1, 1991: "I lost a certain degree of innocence. To this day I find myself having unpleasant dreams about what I found out." • The film's killer, dubbed "Buffalo Bill," was actually a composite figure of three different real-life serial killers — Gary Heidnik, who imprisoned victims in his basement; Ted Bundy, who used the arm-in-a-cast trick to lure his victims into aiding him; and Ed Gein, the sadistic killer who wore the skins of his victims. Gein's reign of terror also inspired the 1974 Tobe Hooper horror classic, *Texas Chainsaw Massacre*. • Brooke Smith, who played the role of an abducted daughter, said the inspiration for her line, "I want my Mommy!" came from F.B.I. consultant John Douglas, who claimed that victims often revert back to their childhood in similar situations.

Silent Night, Deadly Night (1984; Slayride Inc.) D: Charles E. Sellier, Jr. P: Ira Richard Barmak. S: Michael Hickey. Cast: Lilyan Chauvin, Gilmer McCormick, Toni Nero, Robert Brian Wilson. As a young boy, Billy was emotionally scarred when he witnessed his parents' brutal murder at the hands of a maniac in a Santa suit. Now 18, Billy snaps when he is forced to don a Santa outfit himself at the department store where he works, and embarks on his own holiday murder spree. • This particular slasher flick, with its exploitative advertising showing a homicidal St. Nick wielding various death-dealing instruments, caused a furor among parental groups, eventually leading to the film's hasty withdrawal. Of course, all this negative publicity was enough to send video sales through the roof and open up the way for two sequels.

Silent Night, Deadly Night Part 2 (1987; Ascot Entertainment Group–Silent Night Releasing) D: Lee Harry. P: Lawrence Appelbaum. S: Lee Harry, Joseph H. Earle. C: Harvey Genkins. Cast: Eric Freeman, James L. Newman, Elizabeth Clayton, Jean Miller. This is more of a rehash of than a sequel to the original *Silent Night, Deadly Night,* about a boy whose parents were murdered by a man wearing a Santa suit, and now, years later, dons the red and white outfit

himself to commit his own atrocities. • Extensive footage from the original was used to pad out this sequel's running time.

Silent Night, Deadly Night 3: Better Watch Out! (1989; Quiet Films) D: Monte Hellman. P: Arthur H. Gorson. S: Carlos Laszlo. C: Josep M. Civit. Cast: Richard Beymer, Bill Moseley, Samantha Scully, Eric Dare, Laura Herring, Elizabeth Hoffman, Robert Culp. A young blind girl with ESP abilities becomes psychically linked to a long-term coma patient — the psychotic Santa Claus Killer from the earlier films. He revives and goes on another killing spree, following her to her grandmother's house for the holidays.

Silent Scream (1980; American Cinema Releasing) D: Denny Harris. P: Joan Harris, Denny Harris. S: Ken Wheat, Jim Wheat. C: Michael D. Murphy, David Shore. Cast: Rebecca Balding, Cameron Mitchell, Avery Schreiber, Barbara Steele, Steve Doubet. Unable to get regular college housing, a group of students take rooms at the Engels family mansion, home of an eccentric family with a terrible secret locked in the attic — a mute psychopathic daughter who periodically gets loose and murders the students.

Slaughter High (1987; Vestron) D/S: George Dugdale, Mark Ezra, Peter Litten. P: Steve Minasian, Dick Randall. C: Alain Pudney. Cast: Caroline Munro, Simon Scuddamore, Carmine Iannaccone, Donna Yaeger, Gary Hartman, Billy Martin. A group of cliquish high school students play an April Fools joke on the class nerd, but it backfires and he is horribly burned by acid. Years later, the students are invited back to the closed school for a reunion and the expected massacre begins.

Slaughterhouse (1987; American Artists) D/S: Rick Roessler. P: Ron Matonak. C: Richard Benda. Cast: Joe Barton, Sherry Bendorf, Don Barrett, William Houck. A hulking backwoods maniac named "Buddy" and his deranged dad stalk and slaughter a group of teens who sneak into their old disused slaughterhouse. ¶ "I'd never allow 30 percent fat! It's people like you who are clogging our young people's arteries!" — Lester Bacon, elder half of the father/son maniac team.

Sleepaway Camp (1983) D/P/S: Robert Hiltzik. Cast: Mike Kellin, Jonathan Tiersten, Felissa Rose, Paul De Angelo, Christopher Collet, Karen Fields, Katherine Kamhi, John E. Dunn. A crazed killer is after the teens at a summer camp in this obvious *Friday the 13th* ripoff. ¶ "A nice place for summer vacation. A perfect place to die" — ad line.

Sleepaway Camp 2: Unhappy Campers (1988; Double Helix Films) D: Michael A. Simpson. P: Jerry Silva, Michael A. Simpson. S: Fritz Gordon. C: Bill Mills. Cast: Pamela Springsteen, Brian Patrick Clarke, Renee Estevez, Walter Gotell, Susan Marie Snyder, Heather Binion. At Camp Rolling Hills, a female counselor named Angela goes berserk with chain saw and drill press in this first sequel to (or more likely *copy* of) the equally derivative *Sleepaway Camp.* • Star Pamela Springsteen is the sister of superstar rocker Bruce Springsteen. • Heroine Renee Estevez has a better-known brother named Emilio.

Sleepaway Camp 3: Teenage Wasteland (1989; Double Helix Films) D: Michael A. Simpson. P: Jerry Silva, Michael A. Simpson. S: Fritz Gordon. Cast: Pamela Springsteen, Tracy Griffith, Michael J. Pollard. The filmmakers of *Sleepaway Camp 2* are back and so is the murderous Angela, who sets upon a new batch of teens with knife, gun, and lawn mower(!). ¶ "She's back to *slash* last year's record" — ad slogan. • *Sleepaway Camp 3* was shot back to back with *Sleepaway Camp 2.*

The Slumber Party Massacre (1982; New World Pictures) P/D: Amy Jones. S: Rita Mae Brown. C: Steve Posey. Cast: Michele Michaels, Robin Stille, Michael Villella, Debra Deliso, Andree Honore, Gina Mari, Jennifer Meyers. An escaped mass murderer with a portable electric drill invades a small town to take out as many teens as he can get his Black and Decker on, culminating in the crashing of a sexy slumber party. ¶ "You're pretty. All of you are very pretty. I love you. It takes a lot of love for a person to do *this*" — psycho killer. • This is one of the few slasher films (or horror films for that matter) to be made by women — director/producer Amy Jones and screenwriter Rita Mae Brown (a devout feminist). • Director Amy Jones won this, her first, directing assignment in a rather ingenious manner. As Roger Corman, then-head of New World Pictures, told it in his autobiography, *How I Made a Hundred Movies in Hollywood and Never Lost a Dime,* Jones got a hold of New World's shooting script, then titled *Don't Open the Door,* and "went out with some UCLA students as actors, a crew of four, and a bunch of "short ends" — the cheap remnants of unused film on short rolls. She shot the first seven pages of the script, edited it on Joe Dante's moviola as he was finishing *The Howling,* and put some

music and sound on it. She showed it to Joe and he immediately called me.... I offered her $10,000 to direct and she was on her way."

Slumber Party Massacre 2 (1987) (see DREAMKILLERS). One of the surviving sisters from the original *Slumber Party Massacre* begins having dreams about a leatherjacketed singer with a drill at the end of his guitar. Her dream comes to life as the rock 'n' roll maniac begins offing her friends one by one.

Sorority House Massacre (1987; Concorde) D/S: Carol Frank. P: Ron Diamond. C: Marc Reshovsky. Cast: Angela O'Neill, Wendy Martel, Pamela Ross, Nicole Rio, John C. Russell, Marcus Vaughter, Vincent Bilanco, Joe Nassi. A troubled sorority sister is having dreams of a bloody massacre. Soon the maniac of her dreams shows up with a knife in hand, and commences to splatter all the sisters within blade reach.

Splatter University (1984; Troma) D/P: Richard Haines. C: Fred Cohen, Jim Grib. Cast: Francine Forbes, Cathy Lacommare, Dick Biel, Denise Texeira. A deranged psycho-killer stalks a co-ed campus in this bottom of the barrel splatter entry. ¶ "Where the school colors are blood red" — ad line.

The Stepfather (1987; New Century-Vista) D: Joseph Ruben. P: Jay Benson. S: Donald E. Weslake. C: John W. Lindley. Cast: Terry O'Quinn, Jill Schoelen, Shelley Hack, Charles Lanyer, Stephen Shellen, Stephen E. Miller, Robyn Stevan, Jeff Schultz. Terry O'Quinn plays a psycho in search of the American dream in this atypical, critically acclaimed, superior slasher film. He is genial, loving, and the perfect family man in search of the perfect readymade family. When he finds one, he happily settles down to a life of suburban bliss. But when his new family does not measure up to his Ward Cleaver standards, he slaughters them and goes looking for greener familial pastures. He finds recently widowed Shelley Hack and her teen daughter, but again reality intercedes and they must fight for their lives against this psychotic Ozzie Nelson. • A sequel, *Stepfather 2,* again starring Terry O'Quinn, was made in 1989.

Stepfather 2 (1989; ITC) D: Jeff Burr. P: Darin Scott, William Burr. S: John Auerbach. C: Jacek Laskus. Cast: Terry O'Quinn, Meg Foster, Caroline Williams, Jonathan Brandis, Henry Brown, Mitchell Laurance. *The Stepfather* (Terry O'Quinn) did not die in the original as thought. Having recovered from the knife wounds inflicted in the first film, he is now a patient at the Puget Sound Institute for the Criminally Insane. He escapes and goes to California, where he sets himself up as a family counselor, and begins looking for another ready-made family to commandeer. He sets his sights on a divorced woman and her son living across the street, and is forced to murder several people on the way to his marrying his intended. On the day of the wedding, circumstances reveal his true nature, and he is forced into a bloody confrontation with his bride-to-be and her young son. ¶ "What kind of man changes names like other people change their clothes and then marries into fatherless families? And how can such a man be a loving father, a devoted husband, right up until the time he decides to come and *wipe* that family off the face of this planet?"

Stripped to Kill (1987; Concorde) D: Katt Shea Ruben. P: Andy Ruben, Mark Byers, Matt Leipzig. S: Katt Shea Ruben, Andy Ruben. C: John Leblanc. Cast: Kay Lenz, Greg Evigan, Norman Fell, Tracy Crowder, Athena Worthey, Carlye Byron, Debbie Nassar, Luci Nagy Lexington, Michelle Foreman, Pia Kamakahi. The girls at a strip club are being systematically murdered. A female cop (Kay Lenz) goes undercover as a stripper to try and solve the murders. She sinks ever deeper into the seedy world of the strip joint before finally encountering the killer — one of the strippers. In a surprise twist, Lenz stabs the psychotic girl in the chest, only to have her peel off her false breasts, revealing that the murderer is actually a man — the deranged brother of the girl he is impersonating (having killed his sister in a fit of jealousy and taken her place). • Director/co-writer Katt Shea Ruben and co-producer/co-writer Andy Ruben are husband and wife.

Stripped to Kill 2: Live Girls (1989; Concorde) D/S: Katt Shea Ruben. P: Andy Ruben. C: Phedon Papamichael. Cast: Mario Ford, Ed Lottimer, Karen Mayo Chandler. A mad killer who conceals a razor blade in his (or her) teeth is brutally murdering the girls at a strip club. All evidence points to a new girl who is having blackouts and dreams of the killings, but a detective who's fallen in love with her believes otherwise. ¶ "In 1970 a bunch of New York hookers were busted. The arresting officers found out the hard way that the girls were carrying razor blades in their mouths. They used them to protect themselves against certain clients. Useful skill actually." • The husband and wife team of

Katt Shea Ruben and Andy Ruben returned from the first *Stripped to Kill* to make this sequel. • Roger Corman, head of Concorde Pictures, explained in a *Fangoria* #83 interview why they decided to make a sequel: "[*Stripped to Kill*] was only a moderate success at the box office. It was ok, nothing great, so we never would have thought of a sequel. But when it went to videocassette, it became an *incredible* success."

Student Bodies (1981; Paramount) (also *Thursday the 12th*). D/S: Mickey Ross. P: Allen Smithee. Cast: Kristen Riter, Matt Goldsby, Richard Brando. A crazed murderer known as "The Breather" terrorizes Lamba High, but the senior class decides to fight back against the maniac decimating their ranks in this splatter spoof.

Tenebrae (1982; Sigma Cinematographia; Italy) D: Dario Argento. P: Claudio Argento. S: George Kemp, Dario Argento. C: Luciano Tovoli. Cast: Anthony Franciosa, John Saxon, Giuliano Gemma, Daria Nicolodi, Christian Borromeo, John Steiner, Veronica Laric. An American novelist in Rome becomes embroiled in a series of vicious murders of young women which seem to follow the plot of his most recent book.

Terror Train (1980; 20th Century–Fox; Canada) D: Roger Spottiswoode. P: Harold Greenberg. S: Y. T. Drake. C: John Alcott. Cast: Ben Johnson, Jamie Lee Curtis, Hart Bochner, David Copperfield, Derek Mackinnon, D. D. Winters (Vanity). A fraternity hires a passenger train for an all-night New Year's Eve Party. The party is disrupted, however, by a former pledge who was the victim of a humiliating prank. He steals on board, dons various costumes, and viciously murders the students one by one. • The famous magician David Copperfield turned actor for this film (as well as performing some of his patented magic tricks).

Thou Shalt Not Kill ... Except (1987; Filmworld) D: Josh Becker. P: Scott Spiegel. S: Josh Becker, Scott Spiegel. Cast: Brian Schulz, John Manfredi, Robert Rickman, Tom Quill, Sam Raimi, Cheryl Hanson, Perry Mallette. A Manson-like cult leader and his family of psychotic hippies kidnaps the girlfriend of a recently returned Vietnam veteran in this independent gore film made in Detroit. It is up to the vet and his army buddies to track down the maniac cult and rescue the girl. • This $250,000 gore feature was filmed in and around Detroit on an on-again/off-again four-month shooting schedule. Though completed in 1985, it did not find a distributor until two years later. • Horror filmmaker Sam Raimi (*The Evil Dead* series) steps out as an actor in the role of the mad cult leader. • One scene features a group of marines taking on a group of bikers in a bar fight. The marines were actors but the bikers were members of a real biker gang. Producer Scott Spiegel said of them: "They were the greatest guys, but a little scary."

The Toolbox Murders (1978; Selected) D: Dennis Donnelly. P: Tony Didio. S: Robert Easter, Ann N. Kindberg. C: Gary Graver. Cast: Cameron Mitchell, Pamelyn Ferdin, Wesley Eure, Nicolas Beauvy, Tim Donnelly, Aneta Corseaut, Faith McSwain, Marcie Drake. Cameron Mitchell plays a psychotic apartment manager who blames the death of his daughter on the "evil" and "corruption" of those with "loose morals." So he goes about murdering "sinful" women with power drill, hammer, screwdriver, nail gun, etc. • Mitchell said of the film, "I don't like pictures like that. I won't see 'em. I make 'em, but can't stand seeing 'em" (*Fangoria* #103).

Trick or Treats (1982; Lone Star Pictures International) D/S/C: Gary Grover. P: Caruth C. Byrd, Lee Thornberg. Cast: Jackelyn Giroux, Peter Jason, Chris Graven, David Carradine, Carrie Snodgrass, Steve Railsback, Jillian Kesner. On Halloween night an escaped madman (sound familiar?) terrorizes a young prankster and his babysitter. ¶ Ad line: ". . . When Halloween night stopped being fun."

The Unseen (1981; World Northal) D: Peter Foleg. P: Anthony B. Unger. S: Michael L. Grace. C: Roberto Quezada. Cast: Barbara Bach, Sydney Lassick, Stephen Furst, Lelia Goldoni, Karen Lamm, Doug Barr, Lois Young. A TV reporter (Barbara Bach) spends the night at the old mansion owned by a sinister museum caretaker and his sister. Locked in the basement is a huge mentally deficient "baby," the product of the two occupants' incestuous relationship. The hulking maniac breaks out and kills two of Barbara's friends, with her next in line.

Vampire at Midnight (1988) (see HYPNOTISTS). A rash of "vampire killings" in which young women are found drained of their blood holds the city in a grip of fear. Dr. Victor Radkoff is a "hypno-therapist" who works with performing artists to bring out their true potential. He is also the "vampire killer," who hypnotizes his victims and then cuts their throats and drinks their blood. Though we are led to believe Radkoff is a real vampire, it is revealed that he is a human madman, though his deadly powers of hypnotism are very real.

Visiting Hours (1981; Filmplan International; Canada) D: Jean Claude Lord. P: Claude Heroux. S: Brian Taggert. C: Rene Verzier. Cast: Michael Ironside, Lee Grant, Linda Purl, William Shatner, Lenore Zann, Harvey Atkin. Michael Ironside plays a woman-hating psychopath who attacks a female TV journalist. She is taken to the hospital, but the demented killer follows and continues terrorizing and murdering until finally killed by the reporter herself.

When a Stranger Calls (1979; Columbia) D: Fred Walton. P: Doug Chapin, Steve Feke. S: Steve Feke, Fred Walton. Cast: Charles Durning, Tony Beckley, Carol Kane, Colleen Dewhurst, Rachael Roberts. A psychopathic phone caller keeps ringing up to sinisterly suggest babysitter Carol Kane check on the children. It turns out the maniac was phoning from an upstairs line and had indeed slaughtered the children. Seven years later he escapes from a mental institution and once again terrorizes Kane, who now has children and babysitters of her own. • The film is based on the director's 1978 short called "The Sitter."

Witchfire (1985; Panda) D: Vincent I. Privitera. P: James R. Orr. S: James R. Orr, Vincent J. Privitera. C: Michael Delahoussaye. Cast: Shelley Winters, Corinne Chateau, Francesca De Sapio, Peter Masterson, David Mendenhall, James Mendenhall, Paula Shaw, Al Shannon, Gary Swanson. When their beloved doctor dies in an automobile accident, psychotic Shelley Winters breaks out of the asylum with two of her fellow inmates. Winters believes she is a witch and intends to use her "powers" to bring back the dead doctor. The trio hide out at an abandoned house, where they mistake a passing hunter for their resurrected doctor and proceed to tie him up and torment him. ¶ "Walk on a crack, break your mother's back; concentrate on the dead, they'll end up in your bed."

You Better Watch Out (1980) (also *Christmas Evil; Terror in Toyland*). D/S: Lewis Jackson. P: Edward Prebbman. Cast: Brandon Maggart, Jeffrey DeMunn, Dianne Hull, Scott McKay, Joe Jamrog, Peter Friedman. A young boy sees momma having sex with Santa and grows up to be a puritanical psychopath who dons a Santa suit and delivers stolen toys to kids while delivering death to unsympathetic adults. ¶ "You better believe in Santa . . . or he'll slay you" — ad line.

Zero Boys (1986) D: Nico Mastorikis. Cast: Kelli Maroney, Daniel Hirsch, Tom Shell, Nicole Rio, Jared Moses, Joe Phelan.

A group of survival game players stop off at a secluded house which appears to be abandoned, only to be set upon by a psycho who plays for keeps.

Magicians

Magic, in its broadest definition, is a force used to control human actions or natural events. In its truest form, magic encompasses a wide range of talents and techniques, including fortune telling, astrology, spells and incantations, as well as magical objects such as swords, jewels, or what have you.

The appeal of magic is widespread. People throughout history have used magic as a form of insurance — that is, they believe in it because they feel the need to reduce anxiety about events. The belief in magic can give a feeling of control over the outcome of a situation.

This leads us to magicians. While "true" magic is of a supernatural origin, modern magicians are practitioners of illusion and showmanship rather than occult powers. This chapter is devoted to films dealing primarily with stage performers using some form of illusionary "magic" (though in the realm of fantasy films, this magic sometimes turns out to be real after all).

There are basically three branches or types of magicians. The first is composed of those who perform sleight-of-hand tricks and close-up magic acts, represented by real-life illusionists like Harry Blackstone, Harry Kellar, Thurston Howard, and their mentor, Frenchman Robert Houdin. The second type is the "mentalist" or "mind reader," such as "The Amazing Kreskin." And the final branch of magicians is made up of the escape artists, typified by the legendary Harry Houdini.

This section features a mixed bag of magicians performing feats of magic. The favorite motif of magician filmmakers is to show the mesmerist as a madman, utilizing his talents and abilities for evil purposes.

Other subjects loosely related to this subgenre are HYPNOTISTS, PSYCHIC ABILITY and DOLLS (which features mad puppeteers and ventriloquists). For "true" supernatural magic, look to the occult sections which include DEMONS AND DEVILS, SWORD AND SORCERY, VOODOO and WITCHES, WARLOCKS AND CULTS.

Chandu, the Magician (1932; 20th Century–Fox) D: Marcel Varnel, William Cameron Menzies. S: Phili Klein, Barry Conners. C: James Wong Howe. Cast: Bela Lugosi, Edmund Lowe, Irene Ware, Herbert Mundin, Henry B. Walthall. A great spiritualist/magician named Chandu takes on a madman armed with a death ray. The mad Roxor (Bela Lugosi) imprisons the ray's inventor, trying to pry loose the secret of its power. ¶ "Paris! New York! Imperial Rome! All shall be destroyed. Men shall return to savagery! Great dams shall burst, pouring their tons of water onto the countrysides, drowning the people like rats! They shall all know me, the supreme intelligence — me, Roxor!"

Curse of the Demon (1956) (see DEMONS AND DEVILS). Julian Karswell (Niall Mac-

Ginnis) is the leader of a devil cult who can bring forth fire demons to destroy his enemies. He also dabbles in stage magic on the side, entertaining children at his large estate.

Houdini (1953; Paramount) D: George Marshall. P: George Pal. S: Philip Yordan. C: Ernest Laszlo. Cast: Tony Curtis, Janet Leigh, Torin Thatcher, Angela Clarke, Sig Rumann. The life and exploits of famed magician Harry Houdini are brought to the screen, covering his beginnings as a part-time carny to his breathtaking feats as the world's foremost escape artist. The film also chronicles his failed attempts to discover the nature of dematerialization and his search for the truth about life after death.

The Mad Magician (1954; Columbia) D: John Brahm. P: Bryan Foy. S: Crane Wilbur. C: Bert Glennon. Cast: Vincent Price, Mary Murphy, Eva Gabor, John Emery, Patrick O'Neal. The clever inventor of magicians' tricks decides to murder his magician employer and take his place on the stage. ¶ "For years I've been inventing illusions for big-name magicians and watching them take all the bows. 'Til I finally caught the fever myself." • The picture was originally shown in 3-D.

The Magician (1926; MGM) D/P/S: Rex Ingram. C: John Seitz. Cast: Paul Wegener, Ivan Petrovitch, Alice Terry, Firmin Geier, Gladys Hamer. Paul Wegener plays a crazed magician/conjurer who is looking for blood from just the right virgin so he can finish his Frankenstein-like experiments. The girl's fiancé arrives just in time to save her.

The Mask of Diijon (1946; PRC) D: Lew Landers. P: Max Alexander, Alfred Stern. S: Arthur St. Claire, Griffin Jay. C: Jack Greenhalgh. Cast: Erich von Stroheim, Jeanne Bates, William Wright, Edward Van Sloan, Denise Vernac, Mauritz Hugo. A stage magician (Erich von Stroheim) uses hypnotism to compel his wife to kill the lover that she left him for. In the end von Stroheim is decapitated by a guillotine he uses in his own act. ¶ "You'd better play Hearts and Flowers, I'm going to kill you."

The Phantom of Paris (1931; MGM) D: John S. Robertson. S: Edwin Justus Mayer, John Meehan, Bess Meredyth. Cast: John Gilbert, Leila Hyams, Lewis Stone, Jean Hersholt, C. Aubrey Smith. A magician decides to confront a murderer and force a trick confession by having his face changed to resemble one of the victims. • The film is based upon the Gaston Leroux novel, *Cheri-Bibi*. Leroux also authored the original *Phantom of the Opera*.

Scared to Death (1947) (see MADMEN — EARLY MADMEN). This low-budget convoluted film follows the trials of Molly Lamont as she begins to go mad and finally finds death at a sinister sanitarium populated by strange characters, including Bela Lugosi in a red herring role as an apparently sinister magician named "Leonide."

The Seven Faces of Dr. Lao (1964; MGM) D/P: George Pal. S: Charles Beaumont. C: Robert Bronner. Cast: Tony Randall, Barbara Eden, John Ericson, Arthur O'Connell, Lee Patrick, Minerva Urecal, Noah Beery, Jr., Douglas Fowley. Tony Randall stars as the multi-dimensional Chinese mesmerist who brings a little magic (and understanding) to a Western town with his sideshow of mythical attractions. The sights seen include Merlin the Magician, the blind Apollonius, Medusa the Gorgon, Pan, the Abominable Snowman, an unusual snake, and a Loch Ness monster lookalike. ¶ "Mike, the whole world is a circus if you look at it the right way. Every time you pick up a handful of dust and see not the dust but a mystery, a marvel there in your hand — every time you stop and think, 'I'm alive and being alive is fantastic' — every time such a thing happens Mike, you're part of the Circus of Dr. Lao." • The metamorphosis of the sea serpent was done by moving the creature closer and closer to the camera between exposures, substituting different models in different stages. The background features, such as the troublemaking cowpokes, were rear projected into the shot while the circus foreground was later added with a static matte. • Tony Randall said in an interview appearing in Jeff Rovin's book, *The Fabulous Fantasy Films,* "I never wanted it to end, and that's the only time this has ever happened. Working on and developing the makeups was just so much fun. You see, an actor like me is freed by makeup." • The illusion of Medusa was achieved by a puppeteer who worked above the actor, moving the wired electro-magnetic plastic snakes by the use of a magnet — the snakes in Medusa's hair were controlled magnetically. • The film is based on the 1935 Charles Finney novel, *The Circus of Dr. Lao.*

Two on a Guillotine (1965; Warner Bros.) D/P: William Conrad. S: Henry Slesar, John Kneubuhl. C: Sam Leavitt. Cast: Connie Stevens, Dean Jones, Cesar Romero, Virginia Gregg, Parley Baer, Connie Gilchrist. A mad magician who accidentally decapitated his wife while performing a guillotine trick leaves a bizarre will for his daughter (Connie Stevens). In it, he states that she must spend the night alone in his house, and he is to be handcuffed. Cesar Romero plays the crazed magician who does indeed return, intending to try the guillotine trick a second time. • Connie Stevens plays a dual role in this feature as both the daughter and the mother who lost her head.

The Wizard of Gore (1970; Mayflower Pictures) D/P: Herschell Gordon Lewis. S: Allen Kahn, Herschell Gordon Lewis. C: Alex Ameri. Cast: Ray Sager, Judy Cler, Wayne Ratay, Phil Laurensen, Jim Rau, John Elliot, Don Alexander. This crude gore-fest centers around "Montag the Magician," a stage performer who performs wild mutilation tricks on women. The volunteers come out of it okay, but later on, after they have gone home, the illusion wears off

The Great Gallico (Vincent Price) guides Mary Murphy through her act as he imitates one of the magicians he had built illusions for in The Mad Magician *(1954).*

and the gory results kick in for real. In the bizarre finale, nothing is as it seems when illusion joins with reality to create an inescapable time loop (or some such thing). ¶ "What is real? Are you certain you know what reality is? How do you know at this second you aren't asleep in your bed, dreaming that you are here?" • This low-budget gore film was finished in 1968, but took two years to get a release date.

Mars

Only a mere 100,000,000 miles from Earth, the "angry red planet" has certainly made its mark in the Cinema of the Fantastique. Thomas Edison was the first to take *A Trip to Mars,* way back in 1910. Then, after a few more imaginative Martian epics, including a musical jaunt in *Just Imagine* (1930), the planet took a two-decade hiatus from the screen. Twenty years later, when the advent of sound had become commonplace, Lloyd Bridges and the *Rocketship XM* helped usher in the space boom of the 1950s when the title space rocket aimed at the Moon went off course and landed on Mars. From then on, until the mid–1960s, Mars enjoyed a newfound popularity.

In November, 1964, the U.S. spaceship Mariner 4 was launched from Cape Kennedy. Two hundred twenty-six days later, it reached its destination, eventually bringing back to Earth clear and concise photographs of Mars which laid to rest all of the fantastical theories and myths that the silver screen had perpetuated about the planet. No bug-eyed creatures, man-eating plants, alien invaders, or indestructible warships were discovered — just a relatively barren planet, uninhabited, devoid of oxygen, composed of rock and sand. With the mysterious Martian bubble now burst, the cinema was forced to take a more realistic approach to their movies about Mars. For instance, the $60 million-plus modern epic, *Total Recall* (1990), gave us a futuristic spy thriller with Arnold Schwarzenegger arriving on the colonized red planet and showing us a more "realistic" vision of the possibility of a community on Mars.

Abbott and Costello Go to Mars (1953) (see VENUS). The bumbling comedy duo lands on Venus instead of their planned destination of Mars.

Aelita (1924; Mezrapbom; Russia) (also *Aelita: the Revolt of the Robots*). D: Yakov Protazanov. S: Fedor Ozep, Aleksey Fajko. C: Yuri Zheliabovsky, Emil Schoenemann. Cast: Yulia Solntseva, Nikolai Batalov, Igor Illinski, Nikolai Tseretelli, Vera Orlova. A Russian engineer dreams about escaping to Mars after shooting his wife. While there, he falls in love with the Queen, and is sentenced to work in the slave caves. After instigating a revolution among the Martian proletariat, he is betrayed by Queen Aelita, then wakes up. • The film was quite popular in Russia, and many children who were born that year were given the name Aelita. The story is based upon a Leo Tolstoy novel. • The 1951 science fiction film *Flight to Mars* coincidentally(?) features a Martian Queen character with the name "Alita." In *Flight to Mars,* however, the Queen aids the space travelers.

The Airship (1917; Denmark) (also *Himmelskibet; The Sky Ship*). D: Holger Madsen. P: Ole Olsen. S: Ole Olsen, Sophus Michaelis. C: Louis Larsen, Frederik Fuglsang. Cast: Nicolai Neiiendam, Gunnar Tolnaes, Zanny Petersen, Alf Bluetecher, Frederick Jacobsen. A professor and his son fly a rocket to Mars where they encounter a utopian civilization. They bring back to Earth the daughter of a Martian leader who carries with her a message of peace and harmony.

Alien Contamination (1981) (see ALIENS — INVADERS ON EARTH: THE 80S AND BEYOND). The alien causing the contamination is from Mars.

The Angry Red Planet (1960; AIP) D: Ib Melchior. P: Sid Pink, Norman Maurer. S: Ib Melchior, Sid Pink. C: Stanley Cortez. Cast: Gerald Mohr, Nora Hayden, Les Tremayne, Jack Kruschen, J. Edward McKinley, Tom Daly. Four astronauts land on the red planet and encounter three-eyed Martians, a giant amoeba, and a huge bat-rat-spider monster. Only the team's woman commander (Nora Hayden) makes it back alive. ¶ "If we meet any more creatures like that last one, I'd hate to have to fight 'em in the dark." • Producers Sid Pink and Norman Maurer developed a color separation process, known as "solarization," for this film. Two different prints, a positive 35mm black and white, and a negative were joined onto a third piece of film which was then exposed to red, giving the image a pinkish tint. Pink coined the name "Cinemagic" for the process that blended actors, miniatures, drawings, or whatever was needed into a cohesive looking whole that has a cartoonlike effect. • The picture was filmed at the Hal Roach Studios on a budget of $190,000, and a ten-day shooting schedule. • The gigantic bat-rat-spider monster was in actuality only a two-foot marionette. The materials used to build it were so lightweight that the thing often bounced about when it was manipulated by wires. The amoeba was a three-foot model attached to an underwater track. Small air hoses were used to produce the bubbling water effect when the creature was about to surface. The three-eyed Martian was a built-up costume worn by midget Billy Curtis. • Co-producer Norman Maurer is the son-in-law of Moe Howard, leader of The Three Stooges.

Battle Beyond the Sun (1963; AIP) D/P: Thomas Colchart. S: Nicholas Colbert, Edwin Palmer. Cast: Edd Perry, Arla Powell, Andy Stewart, Bruce Hunter. A cold war race to Mars culminates with the American astronauts being rescued by the Russians, and a monster battle between two huge phallic-looking Martians. • This picture was the brainchild of Roger Corman and Francis Ford Coppola. The film relies heavily on stock footage from the Russian film, *Niebo Zowiet* (1959). Coppola, a UCLA student at the time, was hired for $250 to write an English version of the story. This film served as the stepping stone to Francis' *Dementia 13*. • Mark McGee reported in his book,

Fast and Furious, that when Coppola asked Corman what kind of monsters he was thinking about incorporating into the film, Corman replied, "Something phallic in concept. . . . Might make it interesting." Coppola then delegated the monster-creating task to some fellow UCLA students.

Conquest of Space (1955) (see SPACE TRAVEL). A spaceship is sabotaged on its exploratory mission to Mars. • Artist Chesley Bonestell, who worked on the 1950 George Pal film, *Destination Moon,* provides the colorful view of the planet Mars and its atmosphere.

The Day Mars Invaded the Earth (1963) (see ALIENS — INVADERS ON EARTH: THE 60S AND 70S). Martians attempt to stop expeditions to their planet by replicating key people involved in Earth's space program.

Devil Girl from Mars (1954) (see ALIENS — INVADERS ON EARTH:THE 50S). A female Martian and her powerful robot land near a hotel in the English countryside looking for a suitable mate (and intending to conquer the Earth).

Flight to Mars (1951; Monogram) D: Lesley Selander. P: Walter Mirisch. S: Arthur Strawn. C: Harry Neumann. Cast: Cameron Mitchell, Marguerite Chapman, Arthur Franz, Virginia Huston, John Litel, Morris Ankrum, Richard Gaines, Raymond Bond, Everett Glass. An expedition lands on Mars where they are met by human-like aliens who live underground and plot to take over our own world. ¶ "And when we finish with the ruins of their world, what then — a plan to conquer the universe, more rocketships, where is the end of it?" • The Martians' plan is to manufacture more rockets like the one our astronauts have brought. Their motive for the conquest of Earth is that their supply of Corium, a crucial Martian resource, is nearly depleted. • Star Cameron Mitchell truly believes there is life on other planets. He told Tom Weaver in a recent *Fangoria* #103 interview, "I saw a flying saucer 40 years ago, and I do believe in these things." • A sequel to *Flight to Mars* was announced (entitled *Voyage to Venus*) again starring Cameron Mitchell, but the film was never made.

Invaders from Mars (1953) (see ALIENS — INVADERS ON EARTH:THE 50S). Big, awkward Martian drones, controlled by a tentacled "head" Martian intelligence, land in a family's back yard and begin a widespread operation to control mankind. The plot is revealed in the climax to be only an imaginative dream of a small boy . . . or is it?

Invaders from Mars (1986) (see ALIENS —

INVADERS ON EARTH: THE 80S AND BEYOND). Martian invaders hide underground and implant devices into human victims to carry out their plans.

It! The Terror from Beyond Space (1958) (see ALIENS — ENCOUNTERS IN OUTER SPACE). Astronaut Marshall Thompson radios to Earth how some mysterious presence on Mars killed off his crew one by one. When he is rescued by a second expedition, one of the vicious Martian creatures stows away onboard the ship and the killings begin again. ¶ "Another name for Mars is Death." • All of the film's action takes place inside the spaceship returning to Earth, and the experiences on the planet Mars itself are only talked about by Thompson and not shown onscreen.

Just Imagine (1930) (see FUTURES ON EARTH — UTOPIAS AND DYSTOPIAS). A fickle New Yorker, hoping to prove himself worthy enough to marry Maureen O'Sullivan, flies an experimental spaceship to Mars, then proceeds to fall for a Martian woman. ¶ Hero: "I'm going to *Mars!*" Incredulous friend: "You've been drinking, you're going to *bed!*"

Mars Needs Women (1966) (see ALIENS — BENEVOLENT ALIENS). Martian Tommy Kirk comes to Earth to find some beautiful women to repopulate their home planet with.

A Martian in Paris (1961) (see ALIENS — BENEVOLENT ALIENS). The Martians send one of their members down to Earth to study the emotion of love, which they consider a disease.

Martians Go Home (1990) (see ALIENS — BENEVOLENT ALIENS). Green Martians with an overdeveloped sense of humor are lured to Earth by a musician where they drive everyone crazy with their constant joke-telling.

A Message from Mars (1913) (see ALIENS — BENEVOLENT ALIENS). A Martian reforms a sinner.

A Message from Mars (1921) (see ALIENS — BENEVOLENT ALIENS). This sci-fi-styled "A Christmas Carol" features a Martian who reforms a sinner by showing him the error of his ways. • This is a remake of the 1913 version.

Mission Mars (1968; Allied Artists) D: Nick Webster. P: Everett Rosenthal. S: Mike St. Clair. C: Cliff Poland. Cast: Darren McGavin, Nick Adams, George De Vries, Heather Hewitt, Michael De Beausset. Three American astronauts on a journey to Mars find the bodies of two dead Soviets. When they arrive on the planet, a third Russian, frozen alive, is revived, and the group then battles sphere-like Martian beings propelled by sun-powered polarites. • Director Nick Webster had made another low-budget Martian feature four years earlier, the infamous *Santa Claus Conquers the Martians*.

Queen of Blood (1966) (see ALIENS—ENCOUNTERS IN OUTER SPACE). The sole survivor of a wrecked spaceship on Mars turns out to be a blood-sucking vampiric alien.

Red Planet Mars (1952) (see ALIENS—BENEVOLENT ALIENS). Scientists bounce radio signals off the planet Mars and begin to receive messages of peace. At first the messages are revealed to be a fake, but at the climax, one last real communication (with biblical overtones) is heard.

Robinson Crusoe on Mars (1964; Paramount) D: Byron Haskin. P: Aubrey Schenck. S: Ib Melchior, John C. Higgins. C: Winton C. Hoch. Cast: Paul Mantee, Vic Lundin, Adam West. An astronaut crash lands on the desolate surface of Mars, where he struggles for survival and becomes desperately lonely for human company. Alien spaceships, armed with powerful rays, appear, looking for slaves. The astronaut befriends one of the escaped, human-looking slaves and begins a Robinson Crusoe/Friday–type relationship. • Adam West (TV's "Batman") played the doomed astronaut partner of Paul Mantee. Aside from his alien "Man-Friday," whom he rescues from alien slavers, Mantee is mostly kept company throughout the film by a monkey named Mona. • The alien spaceships are actually the recycled ships from another Martian film, *War of the Worlds* (1953).

Rocketship XM (1950; Lippert) D/P/S: Kurt Neumann. C: Karl Struss. Cast: Lloyd Bridges, Osa Massen, John Emery, Noah Beery, Jr., Hugh O'Brian, Morris Ankrum. A spaceship headed for the Moon gets sidetracked by a meteor shower and ends up on Mars. While exploring the planet, the astronauts discover highly radioactive ruins, leading them to deduce that the Martian civilization was destroyed by atomic warfare. Cave-dwelling mutant aliens then attack the party, killing their commander. Lloyd Bridges, Osa Massen, and Hugh O'Brian must make it back to their ship but unfortunately run out of fuel on their return flight and must face a dramatically fatal conclusion. ¶ "They are completely off their course, moving at an incredible velocity out into limitless space." • The original release prints of the film contained a red tinted image while on the planet Mars. • Morris Ankrum delivers this uplifting speech at the film's climax: "Every point of our rocket theory has been established. It is proven that interspace travel is not only possible, but practical, and it has supplied us with information which may well mean the salvation of our own world. No, gentlemen, the flight of the RXM is not a failure. Tomorrow we start construction of RXM 2."

Santa Claus Conquers the Martians (1964; Embassy) D: Nick Webster. P: Paul Jacobson. S: Glenville Mareth. C: David Quaid. Cast: John Cal, Leonard Hicks, Vincent Beck, Victor Stiles, Donna Conforti, Bill McCutcheon. Santa Claus tricks the Martians and escapes after being abducted for the purpose of satisfying the wants of the children of Mars.

Spaced Invaders (1990) (see ALIENS—BENEVOLENT ALIENS). Some wild and crazy little green men from Mars land in a small Midwest town on Halloween night with the mistaken idea that their spacefleet has invaded (from listening to a re-broadcast of Orson Welles' "War of the Worlds"). Once they realize their error, they must dodge the riled townsfolk, repair their damaged ship, and avoid a killer robot drone before they can escape back into the safety of space. ¶ "How could they not know we're Martians— we're little green men with antennas!"

The Three Stooges in Orbit (1962) (see ALIENS—INVADERS ON EARTH: THE 60s AND 70s). A Martian spy on Earth reports back to his superiors about the invention of a submarine-rocket which the aliens fear may be used to stop their invasion. Two big-headed Martians, named Og and Zog, are sent to settle the matter.

Total Recall (1990; Carolco) D: Paul Verhoeven. P: Buzz Feitshans, Ronald Shusett. S: Ronald Shusett, Dan O'Bannon, Gary Goldman. C: Jost Vacano. Cast: Arnold Schwarzenegger, Rachel Ticotin, Sharon Stone, Michael Ironside, Ronny Cox, Marshall Bell, Michael Champion, Mel Johnson, Jr. In the future, a secret agent from Mars has his past memories wiped clean as part of an interplanetary conspiracy. When he begins to experience brief glimpses of his past, he goes to a memory implantation business called "Recall." He then embarks on a thrilling mission to Mars to find his identity and uncover a corporate plot (organized by Ronny Cox) to withhold a device that would create a livable atmosphere for the colonized red planet. Dogging his every step is the company's hired killer (Michael Ironside) who has a personal score to settle. Whether all this slam-bang action is actually happening or is just a dream at Recall is left for the audience to ponder. ¶ "I'm sorry to tell you this Mr. Quaid, but you've suffered a schizoid embolism. We can't snap you out of your fantasy, and I've been sent to try to talk you down. . . . Think about it, your dream started in the middle of the implant procedure. Everything after that — the chases, the trip to Mars, the suite at the Hilton — are all elements of your Recall Holiday and ego trip. You paid to be a secret agent." • The film was inspired by the Phillip K. Dick short story, "We Can Remember It for You Wholesale." • It took 15 years for *Total Recall* to finally make it to the screen (with Dan O'Bannon [*Alien*] having written the first screenplay back in 1975). In 1984, David Cronenberg was set to direct, with Richard Dreyfuss to star. When that fell through, director Bruce Beresford took over, with Patrick Swayze cast in the lead. Due to the collapse of the De Laurentiis Entertainment Group, the project once again fell through until revived by Arnold Schwarzenegger, who induced Carolco to purchase the film rights for five million dollars.

A Trip to Mars (1910; Edison) A professor develops a powder which disrupts the law of gravity. He accidentally spills some of it on himself and off he goes until he lands on Mars. There he discovers giant trees and a gigantic Martian, whose breath freezes him. The surface pressure causes the frozen professor to grow and explode, catapulting him back to Earth.

War of the Worlds (1953) (see ALIENS — INVADERS ON EARTH: THE 50s). Martian warships disguised as meteors crash on the Earth, then proceed to attack and demolish everything in their path.

Warlords of Atlantis (1978) (see ATLANTIS). The *Warlords of Atlantis* are actually descended from Martian aliens.

A Witch Without a Broom (1966) (see WITCHES, WARLOCKS, AND CULTS). A professor falls in love with a blonde witch who accidentally transports him to the stone age, the sixteenth century, and finally to the planet Mars!

Wizard of Mars (1964) D/P/S: David Littlewitt. Cast: John Carradine, Roger Gentry, Vic McGee, Jerry Rannow, Eve Bernhardt. Four astronauts crash-land on Mars and encounter terrible aliens, an ancient city, and a super-intelligent wizard who will not allow them to leave.

Monkeys *see* **Apes and Monkeys**

The Moon

As it is the closest natural object in space to our own Earth, and we can see it every night during a clear sky, the Moon has become an important symbol — a milestone for humanity to ponder, write about, and eventually travel to.

In 1902, the science fiction film was born with George Méliès' *A Trip to the Moon*. Interestingly, the next big breakthrough film in science fiction, *Destination Moon* (1950), was also about a voyage to the lunar surface. Producer and guiding hand George Pal utilized new techniques that awed audiences of the time with its spectacle. *Destination Moon*'s overall impression did not last long, however, for the next year its memory faded in the wake of two classic alien epics — *The Day the Earth Stood Still* and *The Thing*. The success of these two films proved that just traveling to the Moon was not going to be enough, and the lunar films that followed usually featured some sort of alien action in their plots as well.

In 1990, a rare collection of NASA footage was released in a feature length documentary entitled *For All Mankind*, which is a breathtaking true-life recounting of space travel and Man's journey to the Moon. But this non-fiction film was overshadowed by the fantastic, and played only in the smaller "art house" theaters, demonstrating that the public's imaginations have far outdistanced reality and require something more. Recent Moon movies bear this out with *The Dark Side of the Moon* (1989) tying in the Bermuda Triangle mystery(!), and *Moontrap* (1989), which features an army of robots on the Moon waiting to conquer Earth.

Battle in Outer Space (1960) (see ALIENS— ENCOUNTERS IN OUTER SPACE). Earth space-ships sent to battle an alien armada land on the Moon, where they first meet their strange-looking adversaries. ¶ The Moon is captured—The Earth is next!"—ad line.

Cat Women of the Moon (1953; Astor Pictures) (also *Rocket to the Moon*). D: Arthur Hilton. P: Jack Rabin, Al Zimbalist. S: Roy Hamilton. C: William Whitley. Cast: Victor Jory, Sonny Tufts, Marie Windsor, Bill Phipps, Douglas Fowley, Carol Brewster. A space expedition to the dark side of the Moon encounters beautiful female cat-like Moon aliens living underground. After contacting the astronauts, the hypnotic aliens scheme to seize their ship but are thwarted when one of their own decides to help the Earthlings. ¶ "You're too smart for me baby, I like 'em stupid." • The cat-women, clad in black tights and sporting some heavy makeup, made for an interesting threat to the space program. They were billed in the credits as "The Hollywood Covergirls," and they prowled about the cave and danced to the musical score of Elmer Bernstein with some seductive flair. • This picture contains some of the best clunker lines of the 1950s: "Look Helen, I have a very high regard for you. You're smart, you have courage, and you're all woman, and if it hadn't been for Laird I'd have tried to make it you and me a long time ago," or "Every man a tiger, let's go!" and "Watch out for that first step, it's a pip." • The film also features two big hairy critters resembling eight-foot long spiders that bellow loudly when they are stabbed.

Countdown (1968) (see SPACE TRAVEL). An American astronaut (Robert Duvall) pilots a rocket to the Moon during a cold war space race.

The Dark Side of the Moon (1989; Wild Street Pictures) D: D. J. Webster. P: Keith Walley. S: Carey W. Hayes, Chad Hayes. C: Russ T. Alsobrook. Cast: Will Bledsoe, Alan Blumenfeld, John Diehl, Robert Sampson, Wendy MacDonald, Camilla More, Joe Turkel. The crew of Space Core One, on a routine Moon mission, encounters a mysterious force that "feeds on human souls" while exploring the lunar surface. • This film offers a novel explanation to the Bermuda Triangle mystery: The Bermuda Triangle displaces matter to a heretofore unknown location—the dark side of the Moon.

Destination Moon (1950; Eagle-Lion) D: Irving Pichel. P: George Pal. S: Robert A. Heinlein, Alford Van Ronkel, James O'Hanlon. C: Lionel Linden. Cast: John Archer, Dick Wesson, Warner Anderson, Tom Powers, Ted Warde. A powerful industrialist induces his fellow captains of industry to build a rocketship, targeted to land on the Moon. A crew is assembled, and off they go to encounter weightlessness, space sickness, a fuel shortage, and a walk on the hard, cracked lunar surface. ¶ "Tell them how we looked up and saw the Earth vulnerable, exposed forever, never setting in this lunar sky." • Star John Archer shows the industrial big-wigs a Woody Woodpecker cartoon to help demonstrate the plausibility of space rocket flight. • The Moonscape, colorful planets, and stars were brought to life by artist Chesley Bonestell and the Oscar-winning special effects team headed by Lee Zavitz. The effects were considered at the time to be as ground-breaking as the story, which is really one of the first serious pictures about space travel. The film's historic achievements were quickly forgotten, however, when *The Thing* and *The Day the Earth Stood Still* came out the following year.

First Men in the Moon (1964; Columbia) D: Nathan Juran. P: Charles Schneer. S: Nigel Kneale, Jan Read. C: Wilkie Cooper. Cast: Edward Judd, Martha Hyer, Lionel Jeffries, Miles Malleson, Norman Bird. This H. G. Wells–inspired epic (told in flashback) features an eccentric scientist who takes a young couple with him to the Moon. After landing, the trio encounters a huge caterpillar and a fascinating stratified society of insect-like aliens called "Selenites." ¶ "Poor Cavor, he did have such a terrible cold." • The cold which the aged Edward Judd was referring to in the above quote was the ironic means by which they accidentally destroyed the entire race of Selenites. They were "creatures completely without immunity." • The trip to the Moon was made in a sphere constructed by the scientist (Lionel Jeffries). He coated the sphere with a substance of his own invention (called "Cavorite"—after his own name, Cavor), which broke the field of gravity, enablng the object to fly upwards. • The story begins with the United States landing for the first time on the barren lunar surface. Once there, however, they find evidence that the Moon was once claimed for England in the name of Queen Victoria, 1899, by our trio of Victorian astronauts. • The special effects (dubbed "Dynamation" by stop-motion animator Ray Harryhausen) used miniature models, traveling mattes, split screen effects, and stop-motion animation. In addition to the stop-motion Selenites, Harryhausen also employed small children to wear the insect alien costumes in some scenes.

For All Mankind (1990) Incredible previously unseen NASA footage of past flights to the Moon, as well as breathtaking shots of astronauts on the surface is edited together in one masterful celebration of the space flight experience.

From the Earth to the Moon (1958) (see SPACE TRAVEL). Joseph Cotten develops an all-powerful substance known as "Power X" and uses it to propel a spacecraft to the Moon. A fanatical scientist, played by George Sanders (who believes that the substance is too dangerous for mankind), goes along for the ride and sabotages the venture.

H. G. Wells' The Shape of Things to Come (1979) (see ROBOTS) (also *The Shape of Things to Come*). After a series of nuclear and robotic wars, the final vestige of humanity is living on a Moon base. In need of a substance called RADIC-Q2, a group of adventurers is sent to Delta 3 where they must fight an evil dictator and his robot army to obtain the substance.

Invisible Invaders (1959) (see ALIENS—INVADERS ON EARTH:THE 50s). Invisible aliens leave their base on the Moon when they decide the time is right to conquer the Earth. Their plan involves inhabiting the bodies of dead humans in order to overrun the Earth. ¶ "More than 20,000 years ago, my planet invaded the Moon and destroyed the life that existed there. We have controlled the Moon since then and made it an impregnable base for our spaceships." • No spaceships or space footage is seen in this low-budget sci-fi potboiler. Nor for that matter, is any alien (since they're invisible)—just the pasty-faced humans who are supposedly reanimated corpses.

Jules Verne's Rocket to the Moon (1967) (see SPACE TRAVEL) (also *Those Fantastic Flying Fools*). Showman P. T. Barnum plans to have a midget shot to the Moon, but the rocketship misfires with saboteurs aboard, and they all end up in the Soviet Union.

Missile to the Moon (1958; Astor Pictures) D: Richard Cunha. P: Marc Frederic. S: H. E. Barrie, Vincent Fotre. C: Meredith Nicholson. Cast: Richard Travis, Tommy Cook, Cathy Downs, Gary Clarke, K. T. Stevens, Michael Wahalen, Nina Bara, Laurie Mitchell. This remake of *Cat Women of the Moon* features a private expedition (with a couple of stowaway youths onboard) that encounters a race of female aliens, rock creatures, and a big spider on and below the lunar surface. ¶ "I am Lido, high ruler of our humble domain. I am told you are intruders from an unknown origin." • *Cat Women of the Moon* used the "Hollywood Covergirls," but *Missile to the Moon* used several international beauty contest winners to play the parts of the Moon women. Director Richard Cunha discussed working with the young ladies in Tom Weaver's book, *Interviews with B Science Fiction and Horror Movie Makers:* "None of them were actresses as such, they were all beauty queens who couldn't hit marks and couldn't say lines. It was quite frustrating." • Cunha shot the film on a six-day schedule for under $80,000. Many of the cave sequences were filmed outside Los Angeles at a place called Red Rock Canyon. The giant spider used in the cave scenes was borrowed from Universal Pictures. Cunha talked about the poor souls who had to play the rock men. "We had one scene where we had to plaster them to the sides of giant rocks, for them to break out. And, you know it, it took a while for the plaster to dry with them in there! They'd be yelling, 'Get us out of here, get us out of here!' So yes, that was very, very difficult for them, but they were all good guys. We laughed over a beer about it later."

Mission Stardust (1968; Times Films; Spain/Italy/W. Germany) D: Primo Zeglio. P: E. Von Theumer. S: Karl H. Volgeman, Federico De Urritia. C: Riccardo Pallottini. Cast: Essy Persson, Lang Jeffries, John Karlsen, Pinkas Braun, Luis Davila. Perry Rhodan heads an expedition to the Moon and encounters two representatives of a highly advanced alien race looking for a cure to their people's blood disease. The Earth astronauts agree to help them in secret and they return home to seek the help of a famous blood specialist. • The film is a sequel to *Perry Rhodan—Sos Aus Dem Weltall* (1967). Both films are based on a series of novels written by Walter Enstine.

Moon 44 (1990; Centropolis Film Productions) D: Roland Emmerich. P: Dean Heyde, Roland Emmerich. S: Dean Heyde, Oliver Eberle. C: Karl Walter, Linden Laub. Cast:

Three astronauts leave their rocketship to explore the cracked and craggy lunar sur-face in Destination Moon *(1950).*

Michael Pare, Lisa Eichhorn, Malcolm McDowell, Brian Thompson, Dean Devlin, Stephan Geoffreys, Leon Rippy, Roscoe Lee Browne. The Earth of the future is under siege by rival multinational corporations fighting over valuable mining planets. Michael Pare is sent to the lunar colony of Moon 44 to discover who is leaking info to the enemy corporation known as Pirite.

Moon Zero Two (1969; Hammer/Warner Bros.; U.K.) D: Roy Ward Baker. P/S: Michael Carreras. C: Paul Beeson. Cast: James Olson, Catherina Von Schell, Warren Mitchell, Adrienne Corri, Bernard Bresslaw. In the future, a rocketship pilot is hired to tug a sapphire asteroid to another part of the Moon by a wealthy man named Hubbard. He eventually learns that Hubbard is responsible for the death of a girl's brother so he sets out to move the valuable asteroid to an area on the surface that the girl had inherited. ¶ "Ride a rocket Texas-style! Have a shoot-out in Moon City! Find a new frontier and a new kind of pioneer. But watch out for deadly Moon maidens.

It's the first Moon Western" — ad lines playing up the wild west angle. • Special effects man Les Bowie received an amusing memo from the studio brass asking, "Make us one moon similar to the one that has been in the news so much lately. Not quite so big, please." Bowie and his 12-man team then fashioned a fiberglass sphere in six weeks with handcarved valleys and mountains. The model was then lit against a jet black background. • "Moon Zero Two" refers to the hero's spaceship.

Moontrap (1989; Shapiro Glickenhaus Entertainment) D/P: Robert Dyke. S: Tex Ragsdale. Cast: Walter Koenig, Bruce Campbell, Leigh Lombardi. On a Moon mission, astronaut Jason Grant (Walter Koenig) battles an army of robots that have been waiting for 14,000 years to conquer Earth. • Hero Walter Koenig is best known as the popular Russian helmsman, Chekov, from the *Star Trek* series; while hero number two, Bruce Campbell, is most recognized as "Ash," the rather dim pro-tagonist of *The Evil Dead* series.

Mouse on the Moon (1963; United Artists; U.K.) D: Richard Lester. P: Walter Shenson. S: Michael Pertwee. C: Wilkie Cooper. Cast: Margaret Rutherford, Bernard Cribbins, Ron Moody, David Kossoff, Terry-Thomas. A wine-powered rocketship, sponsored by the Duchess of Fenwick, beats the Americans and Russians to the Moon, then rescues them when they become stranded upon arrival. • This light-hearted comedy is a sequel to *The Mouse That Roared* (1959).

Mutiny in Outer Space (1965; Allied Artists; U.S./Italy) D: Hugo Grimaldi. P: Hugo Grimaldi, Arthur C. Pierce. S: Arthur C. Pierce. C: Archie Dalzell. Cast: William Leslie, Dolores Faith, Pamela Curran, James Dobson, Richard Garland, Glen Langan. Astronauts exploring Moon caves bring back a strange fungus to their space station. Heat causes it to spread and destroy all in its path before it is stopped by placing frozen particles throughout the station.

Perry Rhodan — SOS Aus Dem Weltall (1967; Times Films; W. Germany/Italy/Spain) D: Primo Zeglio. P: E. Von Theumer. S: K. H. Scheer, Karl H. Vogelman. C: Riccardo Pallottini. Cast: Lang Jeffries, Essy Persson, Joachim Hansen, Ann Smyrner, Luis Dávila, Pinkas Braun, Daniele Martin. Astronaut Perry Rhodan returns from the Moon with a pair of extraterrestrials.

Project Moonbase (1953; Lippert) D: Richard Talmadge. P: Jack Seaman. S: Robert A. Heinlein, Jack Seaman. C: Willard Thompson. Cast: Donna Martell, Ross Ford, Hayden Rorke, James Craven, Larry Johns, Ernestine Barrier. A rocket pilot (Ross Ford), his loving second in command (Donna Martell), and a spy crash on the Moon. The spy is killed in the crash, but the lovers survive, only to be married on the Moon. ¶ "We've tried for two years to get an agent on that space station, but due to impregnable security precautions we have been unable to do so." • This feature was condensed from episodes of an unreleased TV series that was to be called "Ring Around the Moon." • The spy is discovered when he is unable to answer any questions about the famous Brooklyn Dodgers. Near the film's end, the President of the United States, a woman, gives the astronaut couple a promotion.

They Came from Beyond Space (1967) (see ALIENS — BENEVOLENT ALIENS). Aliens inhabit the bodies of humans for the purpose of repairing their wrecked space craft on the Moon. A couple travels to the Moon and strikes a compromise with the well-meaning but desperate aliens.

A Trip to the Moon (1902; France) P: George Méliès. Cast: George Méliès, Victor André, Bleuette Bernon, Ballerinas of the Théâtre du Chatelet, Acrobats of the Folies-Bergères. A missile carrying astronauts is shot into the eye of the Moon. The passengers, exploring a crater, encounter weird creatures known as the Selenites. • Though *A Trip to the Moon* is only a two-reel short, it is included here because of its historical importance as the first science fiction film. • The Moon creatures disintegrate in a puff of smoke when hit, and the astronauts eventually make it back to Earth and splash down in the ocean. • Méliès, who is regarded as the father of science fiction films, was born in Paris in 1861, and was quite an accomplished magician/illusionist. He began to experiment with a bioscope projector and camera, often learning the mechanics of trick photography by accident. *A Trip to the Moon* was a whopping 21 minutes long — a lifetime epic back in those fledgling days of cinema.

12 to the Moon (1960; Columbia) D: David Bradley. P: Fred Gebhardt. S: DeWitt Bodeen. C: John Alton. Cast: Ken Clark, Anthony Dexter, Francis X. Bushman, Tom Conway, Robert Montgomery, Jr., John Wengraf. A multi-national group of astronauts meet subterranean Moon men who threaten to freeze the Earth if humanity continues to make war. ¶ "We have learned that all your Earth emotions are not evil and warlike. Someday when you come back you will be welcome."

2001: A Space Odyssey (1968) (see SPACE TRAVEL). William Sylvester is sent to the Moon to study a mysterious obelisk uncovered on the surface.

Way ... Way Out (1966; 20th Century-Fox) D: Gordon Douglas. P: Malcolm Stuart. S: William Bowers, Laslo Vadnay. C: William H. Clothier. Cast: Jerry Lewis, Connie Stevens, Robert Morley, Dennis Weaver, Brian Keith, Dick Shawn, Anita Ekberg. This wacky futuristic comedy set on the Moon details Jerry Lewis' infatuation

Opposite top: The giant spider puppet which kills a Moon girl named Lambda (Laurie Mitchell) in Missile to the Moon *(1958) was originally designed for the Universal advertising campaign on* Tarantula *(1955). Bottom: Ross Ford and Larry Johns survey the landscape after making a forced landing in* Project Moonbase *(1953).*

with Connie Stevens. • Director Gordon Douglas dabbled in the genre only one other time, creating the classic big bug masterpiece, *Them,* in 1954.

Woman in the Moon (1929; UFA; Germany) (also *By Rocket to the Moon*). D/P: Fritz Lang. S: Thea von Harbou. C: Kurt Courant, Otto Kanturek, Oscar Fischinger. Cast: Gerda Maurus, Willy Fritsch, Fritz Rasp, Klaus Pohl, Gustav Von Wangenheim. This early silent science fiction film is about industry bigwigs who finance a rocketship to the Moon in search of gold. • The film has received a certain historical recognition for its depiction of the first recorded "countdown" ever seen in the movies.

The X from Outer Space (1967) (see JAPANESE MONSTERS — OTHER GIANT JAPANESE MONSTERS). A returning spaceship brings back an alien spore which grows into a giant man-in-a-monster suit. Somewhere in between all the footstomping is a trip to a moonbase.

Mummies

The time—1921; the place—a secret tomb in the Egyptian desert. Bramwell Fletcher translates the forbidden Scroll of Thoth, silently mouthing the words as he works. The camera moves from him to the still form of a mummy resting upright in its sarcophagus. After a moment of pregnant stillness, the mummy's eyes slowly open—ever so slowly. The camera pans down its torso and we see the arms, crossed on its chest, slowly slide down its body, breaking free of the rotted bandages that has held it for 3,700 years. We see Fletcher again, still engrossed in his translations, and the camera moves down to the scroll on the table. A hand enters the frame, a long, bony, dessicated hand which briefly touches the scroll, almost in a caress, before drawing it away. Fletcher looks up and gives a startled, hysterical yell and backs away. He begins to laugh, starting low but gaining in intensity until it becomes a horrible, uncontrollable laugh of madness. The camera pans to the floor and we see two trailing bandages being drawn out the door as Fletcher's mad laugh continues—the only sound punctuating an otherwise silent soundtrack. This subtle introduction of the monster menace known as *The Mummy* (1932), fraught with tension and terror, is truly one of the most memorable scenes of horror ever filmed, and a fitting beginning for one of the most unique creatures in horrordom.

Often when one thinks of "The Mummy" an image comes to mind of a bandaged monster sent out to do the evil bidding of a sinister high priest. The creature's face is wrinkled and blank as it slowly and inexorably limps toward the intended victim, its single good arm outstretched to strangle the life out of anyone who stands in its way. This is the mummy of Universal's four sequels made to the original Karloff vehicle, *The Mummy* (*The Mummy's Hand,* 1940; *The Mummy's Tomb,* 1942; *The Mummy's Ghost,* and *The Mummy's Curse,* both 1944). They are sequels in name only, for they create their own history (though not above borrowing the impressive flashback sequence from the original), and have very little to do with the original. Though entertaining in their own right, these "B" sequels don't even come close to the quality and power of *The Mummy* (1932). As so often happens in cinema, the first turned out to be the best.

Aside from the original Universal films, a second mummy series was produced (in Mexico), featuring the "Aztec Mummy." Four original Aztec Mummy films were made, as well as two other features which utilized the character and extensive footage from the first movies mixed in with new scenes (usually of people sitting around talking) shot by no-budget filmmaker Jerry Warren. This series followed the exploits of "Popoca," an Aztec warrior who was entombed alive for attempting to save his beloved from human sacrifice. Now he is an imposing desiccated corpse who arises from his tomb whenever the sacred Aztec treasure he guards is threatened. Among his adversaries are the master criminals known as "The Bat" and "The Dragon," and even a robot. Extremely cheap and poorly dubbed for American release, the Aztec Mummy films provide some good-natured fun for fans of south-of-the-border bad cinema.

Another two-score mummies have stalked across the screen, including several (unrelated) from Hammer. Their first, simply titled *The Mummy* (1959), features Christopher Lee as one of the screen's most energetic and imposing bandaged monsters. While mummies no longer seem to be a big draw for fright fans, they still manage to pop up as supporting players now and again, putting in impressive appearances in *The Outing* (1987), *Waxwork* (1988), and *Tales from the Darkside: The Movie* (1990).

The Universal Series

Abbott and Costello Meet the Mummy (1955; Universal) D: Charles Lamont. P: Howard Christie. S: John Grant. C: George Robinson. Cast: Bud Abbott, Lou Costello, Marie Windsor, Michael Ansara, Dan Seymour, Richard Deacon, Kurt Katch, Richard Karlan, Eddie Parker. In Egypt, Bud and Lou are caught between a group of crooks (who intend to steal the treasure of the recently discovered mummy of Klaris) and the religious followers of Klaris (who intend to return the mummy to its rightful tomb and kill the infidels). Of course the mummy returns to life to complicate matters even further and to create an opportunity for more unfunny sight gags from the fading comical team. ¶ "It has been said that a man's best friend is his mummy. In Egypt today, this theory has been in great dispute, for two bold adventurers are about to discover another kind of "mummy"— opening narration. • For this final comical end to Universal's Mummy, "Kharis" has now inexplicably become "Klaris." The poorly made-up, baggy-suited mummy is destroyed by dynamite in the end. • This is the last of the "meet the monsters" movies for Abbott and Costello, and the next to last film the team made together.

The Mummy (1932; Universal) D: Karl Freund. P: Carl Laemmle, Jr. S: John L. Balderston. C: Charles Stumar. Cast: Boris Karloff, Zita Johann, David Manners, Edward Van Sloan, Arthur Byron, Bramwell Fletcher, Noble Johnson, Henry Victor. A 1921 British expedition uncovers a secret tomb in the Egyptian desert, where they find the 3,700-year-old mummy of Im-Ho-Tep, who was buried alive when he attempted to use the Scroll of Thoth to revive his lover, Princess Anck-es-en-Amon. The mummy comes to life and disappears with the scroll (also found by the expedition). Eleven years later a strange man appears, looking dried and withered, and tells them where to dig to find the tomb of the Princess. The man calls himself Ardeth Bey, but in fact is the living mummy Im-Ho-Tep (without the bandages). Im-Ho-Tep attempts to restore the mummy of the Princess to life with the scroll, but he cannot, for the Princess' soul has been reincarnated as a woman named Helen Grosvenor. Im-Ho-Tep draws Helen to him, intending to sacrifice her body in order to make her a living mummy like himself. ¶ "You will not remember what I show you now. And yet I shall awaken memories of love and crime, and death"—Im-Ho-Tep to his reincarnated love. • This first Mummy, Im-Ho-Tep, is not the same one as in Universal's four serious sequels (in which the Mummy is called "Kharis"). Rather than the shambling, inarticulate bandaged creature of the sequels who strangles his victims with his one good hand, Karloff's mummy is an intelligent being of power—supernatural power—a master of the black arts. He does not kill through physical violence, but through mere exertion of his own will. • Karl Freund, making his directorial debut, brought *The Mummy* in *under* schedule and *under* budget. This after an incredibly rushed beginning (he received the final script on a Saturday, cast the film on Sunday, and began shooting on Monday). Freund was a brilliant cinematographer who filmed the classics *Metropolis* (1926) and *Dracula* (1931) among others. He also went on to direct the "Hand" classic, *Mad Love,* in 1935. • When the project was originally announced by executive producer Carl Laemmle, Jr., it was under the name *Cagliostro,* which was based on a nine-page treatment by Wilcox Putnam and Richard Schayer. The title of *The Mummy* wasn't finalized until halfway through production. The film was started under the title *Im-Ho-Tep.* • It took makeup man Jack Pierce eight hours to transform Boris Karloff into the Mummy. • Karloff, now one of Universal's biggest stars, was billed as "Karloff the Uncanny" in the film's advertising. • Screenwriter John L. Balderston had suggested Katherine Hepburn for the role of heroine Helen Grosvenor, but the actress was unavailable at the time.

The Mummy's Curse (1944; Universal) D: Leslie Goodwins. P: Ben Pivar. S: Bernard Schubert. C: Virgil Miller. Cast: Lon Chaney, Jr., Peter Coe, Virginia Christine, Kay Harding, Dennis Moore, Martin Kosleck, Kurt Katch. Princess Ananka, who had sunk into the swamp with her former lover Kharis in *The Mummy's Ghost,* rises from the mire after being uncovered by a bulldozer. Drawing power from the rays of the sun, she is transformed into a beautiful girl. The amnesiac Ananka is found wandering about in a daze by government workers sent to drain the swamp. Meanwhile, Martin Kosleck, another acolyte, is sent to the area to find and revive Kharis, sending him out to try and retrieve Ananka. ¶ "The Mummy's on the loose, and he's dancin' with the devil!" • This contemporized sequel (the last in the series—supposedly taking place 25 years after the events in *The Mummy's Ghost*) is set in the Louisiana bayous, though how the setting was changed from New England in the previous entry to southern Louisiana for this one is never explained. • Even *before* the release of *The Mummy's Ghost* (1944), Universal announced this next Mummy sequel, then titled *The Mummy's Return.* • *The Mummy's Curse* was shot on a very brief 12-day shooting schedule. • Lon Chaney, Jr., was paid the sum of $8,000 for his work in this last mummy movie (his third turn as the bandaged one). Reportedly, this was Chaney's least favorite monster role; he despised the makeup and uncomfortable bandages. Third-billed Virginia Christine (Princess Ananka) received less than one tenth of Chaney's salary, making less than $800. • *The Mummy's Curse* was released on a double

bill in support of Universal's monster rally, *House of Frankenstein.*

The Mummy's Ghost (1944; Universal) D: Reginald LeBorg. P: Ben Pivar. S: Griffin Jay, Henry Sucher, Brenda Weisberg. C: William Sickner. Cast: John Carradine, Lon Chaney, Jr., Robert Lowery, Ramsay Ames, Barton MacLane, George Zucco. In Universal's fourth Mummy movie, and third film in the "Kharis" series, high priest George Zucco is once again passing his mission on to a young acolyte (this time it is John Carradine, since Turhan Bey had failed so miserably in *The Mummy's Tomb,* 1942). Carradine is sent to Mapleton to find and retrieve Kharis and the mummy of Ananka (which is housed at the local Scripps museum). But the body of Ananka crumbles to dust when touched—her soul has been reincarnated in the woman Amina, girlfriend of hero Tom. Both Carradine and Kharis take a shine to Amina, and the Mummy turns on its master and carries the girl off toward the swamp. Amina begins to age until she too is nothing but a dried mummy and the pair of ancient lovers sink into the swamp together, reunited at last. ¶ Newspaper headline—"MUMMY BELIEVED TO BE BACK IN NEW ENGLAND. Mapleton Monster, Thought Destroyed, Is Blamed for New Atrocity." • No explanation is given as to how the Mummy escaped the flames in *The Mummy's Tomb* (1942), or what he has been doing in the interim. He simply walks out of the woods at the film's beginning, searching for tana leaves. • For no apparent reason, the High Priest of "Karnak" (from *The Mummy's Tomb*) has now become the High Priest of "Arkham." • *The Mummy's Ghost* is the first mummy picture to make use of the reincarnation theme since the 1932 original. • Acquanetta was originally to have starred as the female lead, but on the first day of shooting she fell and struck her head, resulting in a mild concussion. She was replaced by Ramsay Ames (a superior actress as it turned out). • This was prolific B-horror director Reginald LeBorg's first horror film. • Lon Chaney, Jr., donned the bandages again for this film. Even at this early stage in his career, Chaney's legendary drinking problem was affecting the actor. Director LeBorg changed his shooting strategy accordingly: "I tried to get everything in up to 2:00," he told Tom Weaver for his book, *Interviews with B Science Fiction and Horror Movie Makers,* "then he had his lunch and started on the bottle. He couldn't shake it." • According to LeBorg, Chaney sometimes got carried away on the set. In

Boris Karloff stars as the revived Egyptian mummy "Im-Ho-Tep" who is searching for his reincarnated princess in The Mummy *(1932).*

the scene in which he strangles Professor Norman (Frank Reicher), Chaney squeezed Reicher's throat so tightly that the elderly actor nearly fainted, complaining "He nearly *killed* me!" • Chaney also had a mishap of his own. For the scene in which the Mummy breaks into the museum, he was supposed to crash through a plate glass door. When it came time to shoot, they discovered that the prop department had

In the 1940 film The Mummy's Hand, *high priest George Zucco and the mummy "Kharis" (Tom Tyler) stand over heroine Peggy Moran lying on the altar within the redressed temple set from* Green Hell *(1940).*

failed to install breakaway glass. LeBorg told Chaney to just push the door open, but when it came time for the shot, the actor went right through the real glass anyway, cutting his hand in the process. Chaney explained to LeBorg, "I wanted to show you that I had the courage." • Though it has long been rumored that Chaney had a stand-in for much of the time, director LeBorg stated that Chaney never had a stand-in and did all the stunts himself. • Actor Robert Lowery, who plays hero Tom Hervey, is a direct descendant of Abraham Lincoln. Lowery also played the hero in Universal's *House of Horrors* (1946). • Next (and last) in line was *The Mummy's Curse* (1944).

The Mummy's Hand (1940; Universal) D: Christy Cabanne. P: Ben Pivar. S: Griffin Jay, Maxwell Shane. C: Elwood Bredell. Cast: Dick Foran, Peggy Moran, Wallace Ford, Eduardo Ciannelli, George Zucco, Cecil Kellaway, Tom Tyler, Charles Trowbridge. An expedition, led by Dick Foran, discovers the tomb of Princess Ananka, but instead of the princess, they find the unmarked sarcophagus of a man. George Zucco, protector of Ananka's tomb, brews the life-giving tana leaves and brings the mummy (Kharis) to life. Intending to lure Kharis to them, Zucco plants vials of the tana juice on his intended victims ("Kill, kill wherever you find the fluid"), and sends Kharis out to dispatch all those who seek to defile the sacred tomb. ¶ "If Kharis should obtain the rest of the tana fluid, he would become a monster such as the world has never known." • Cowboy actor Tom Tyler was reportedly chosen to play the Mummy in this belated first sequel to *The Mummy* (1932) because of his resemblance to Boris Karloff (though now the Mummy is called "Kharis," not "Im-Ho-Tep" as in the original, and is still fully wrapped, unlike Karloff's mummy). Universal lifted the flashback sequence from the original *The Mummy* for this film, but spliced in shots of Tyler for the close-ups. The life-giving "Scroll of Thoth" from the original has been replaced by the "forbidden tana leaves." • There seems to be some discrepancy, even among the priests of Karnac, about the name of the living mummy. Eduardo Ciannelli (as the High Priest) pronounces the name as "Kar-iss," whereas George Zucco (who takes over from Ciannelli) calls the mummy "Karrees." • At the film's end, Kharis is dis-

Lon Chaney, Jr., shows off his Jack Pierce makeover in this publicity pose from The Mummy's Tomb *(1942).*

patched by fire when hero Dick Foran upends a flaming brazier on the Mummy. • The spectacular temple set from James Whale's 1940 film *Green Hell* was used as the Temple of Karnak. • *The Mummy's Hand*, a slick B production, cost less than half the original ($84,000 for *The Mummy's Hand* vs. $196,000 for *The Mummy*—made eight years earlier!). The shooting schedule was extremely tight as well, often making it an arduous job for the performers, as star

Peggy Moran later revealed: "We would work sometimes from eight in the morning until four the next morning" (*Universal Horrors* by Brunas, Brunas, and Weaver). • *The Mummy's Tomb* was next.

The Mummy's Tomb (1942; Universal) D: Harold Young. P: Ben Pivar. S: Griffin Jay, Henry Sucher. C: George Robinson. Cast: Dick Foran, Lon Chaney, Jr., John Hubbard, Elyse Knox, George Zucco, Wallace Ford, Turhan Bey. In this second film in the

Kharis the Mummy series, 30 years have passed since the events of *The Mummy's Hand* (1940). High priest George Zucco (who, despite all indications otherwise, apparently survived the previous film) instructs acolyte Turhan Bey to take the Mummy to Mapleton, U.S.A., on a mission to destroy all members of the Banning family (it was Steve Banning [Dick Foran] who had led the expedition which uncovered the tomb of Ananka in the previous film). ¶ "Whether you believe it or not, the facts are here and we've got to face them. A creature that's been alive for over 3,000 years is in this town, and it's brought death with it." • This was Lon Chaney, Jr.'s, first turn behind the bandages as Kharis the Mummy. He played the creature in the remaining two entries (*The Mummy's Ghost* and *The Mummy's Curse*, both 1944) as well. Universal dropped the "Jr." from Chaney's name, much to that actor's irritation—he wanted to keep the distinction between his and his famous father's name. • Cost-conscious Universal inserted stock shots of angry villagers from *Frankenstein* (1931) for this film, as well as lifting flashback sequences from *The Mummy's Hand*. • Three actors returned from *The Mummy's Hand* to appear in this sequel—Dick Foran, Wallace Ford, and George Zucco. • Just as in the previous film, the Mummy is immolated by fire at the climax (though once again, this wasn't enough to keep him from returning for *The Mummy's Ghost*). • Actor John Hubbard, who was thrown down the stairs and landed on his torch, was actually burned in the filming of that scene.

The Aztec Mummy Series

Attack of the Mayan Mummy (1964; Medallion; Mexico/U.S.) D/P: Jerry Warren. S: Gilbert Solar, Alfred Salimar (Alfred Salazar). C: Richard Wallace. Cast: Nina Knight, Richard Webb, John Burton, Peter Mills, Steve Conte, Jorge Mondragon, Emma Roldan, George Mitchell, Chuck Niles, Bill White, Fred Hoffman. Under hypnosis, a woman reveals that she is the reincarnation of a Mayan princess who had an illicit affair with a warrior. She was killed and the warrior entombed alive. Now the warrior is a mummy who guards the treasure of the Mayans. He comes to life when a breastplate (which holds the secret to the treasure's whereabouts) is taken from his pyramid. The mummy is brought back to a research institute for study, but escapes and abducts the girl. Both are hit by a car(!) and are destroyed (the most ignoble and unexciting end to a mummy in the history of the cinema). ¶ "An embalmed creature whose age has been estimated at something near 2,000 years at the minimum had risen from somewhere in the darkness of the pyramid to crush the body of Dr. Redding." • Grade-Z filmmaker Jerry Warren took scenes from the Aztec Mummy series and shot some additional footage of American actors sitting around talking to create yet another Aztec Mummy feature (though referring to it as "Mayan" in this instance).

The Aztec Mummy (1957; Azteca; Mexico) D: Rafael Lopez Portillo. P: William Calderón Stell. S: Alfred Salazar. C: Enrique Wallace. Cast: Ramon Gay, Rosita Arenas, Crox Alvarado, Luis Aceves Casta-neda. In this first Aztec Mummy film, the mummy named Popoca guards the sacred breastplate and bracelet in his pyramid tomb, which holds the key to the Aztec treasure. • William Calderón Stell produced all four of the legitimate Aztec Mummy films, while director Rafael Portillo directed only the first three (Rene Cardona took over the helm for the fourth—*The Wrestling Women vs. the Aztec Mummy,* 1965). Next up for Popoca was *Curse of the Aztec Mummy* (1959).

Curse of the Aztec Mummy (1959; AIP-TV; Mexico) D: Rafael Portillo, Paul Nagel (English version). P: William Calderón Stell, K. Gordon Murray (English version). S: Alfred Salazar. C: Enrique Wallace. Cast: Ramon Gay, Rosita Arenas, Crox Alvarado, Luis Aceves Castaneda, Jorge Mondragon. The evil criminal mastermind known as "The Bat" is after the Aztec treasure guarded by the living mummy, Popoca. Popoca wears an ancient breastplate and bracelet which are the key to locating the Aztec treasure. The Bat tries to get to the mummy through the daughter of an eminent scientist, who is the reincarnation of Popoca's lost love. ¶ "In my opinion he'll probably find some place where mortals seldom tread, a spot where he can sleep his eternal sleep and keep watch over the objects that his forefathers entrusted to his care." • This is the second entry in the Aztec Mummy series. *The Robot vs. the Aztec Mummy* (1959) was next.

Face of the Screaming Werewolf (1964; ADP Productions) D/P: Jerry Warren. S:

Gilbert Solar, Alfred Salimar (Alfred Salazar). C: Richard Wallace. Cast: Landa Varle, Lon Chaney, Jr., Donald Barron, Raymond Gaylord, Steve Conte, Jorge Mondragon, Emma Roldan, George Mitchell, Chuck Niles, Bill White, Fred Hoffman. An expedition to an ancient pyramid on the Yucatan peninsula yields two bodies — that of an ancient mummy and that of a modern man in some sort of mummified condition. Both come back to life and the second body turns out to be a werewolf. ¶ "The other [body] is that of a modern man, placed in the pyramid only recently after an exchange of body fluids with the mummy in an effort to achieve an apparent state of death." • Jerry Warren once again cribbed shots from the Aztec Mummy series (many of the *same* shots he used in *Attack of the Mayan Mummy,* 1964) and spliced them together. He even reused some of the new footage he shot for that previous film. • Chaney's last turn under the werewolf whiskers (looking similar to his Universal appearances but a little shaggier) is a silent one — he has no dialogue. The mummy never meets the werewolf (since all the mummy footage is taken from other films), and in fact, except for the lone statement listed above, the two storylines are unconnected.

The Robot vs. the Aztec Mummy (1959; AIP-TV; Mexico) D: Rafael Portillo, Manuel San Fernando (English version). P: William Calderón Stell, K. Gordon Murray (English version). S: Alfred Salazar. C: Enrique Wallace. Cast: Ramon Gay, Rosita Arenas, Crox Alvarado, Luis Aceves Castaneda, Jorge Mondragon. That evil criminal scientist "The Bat" is back again, searching for the breastplate and bracelet guarded by the Aztec Mummy. He builds a destructive robot, which he sends out to battle the mummy. ¶ "I tortured many animals, with pleasure, to find the answers — the very answers of Man's existence!" — The Bat. • Following in the footsteps of the Universal series, the Aztec Mummy series also utilized extensive footage from the previous films as "flashback" sequences to save on production costs. For this third film in the series they went a bit overboard, however, since over 30 minutes of this movie is footage borrowed from the first two.

The Wrestling Women vs. the Aztec Mummy (1965; AIP-TV; Mexico) D: Rene Cardona, Manuel San Fernando (English version). P: William Calderón Stell, K. Gordon Murray (English version). S: Alfred Salazar. C: Ezequiel Carrasco. Cast: Lorena Velazquez, Armand Silvestre, Elizabeth Campbell, Eugenia Saint Martin, Chucho Salinas, Raymond Bugarini, Victor Velazquez. This entry features a new villain, the evil Asian gangster called "The Dragon," who (along with his two evil judo/wrestling sisters) is after the Aztec treasure guarded by the Aztec Mummy. A pair of wrestling heroines and their assorted boyfriends and sidekicks oppose the Dragon and get to the mummy first, only to realize that the sacred breastplate which holds the secret to the treasure should remain where it belongs — under the watchful eye of the mummy. ¶ "He who profanes the tomb of the Aztecs and finds the breastplate will be under the threat of death, until the breastplate is returned to the tomb." • This final entry changed several things about the Aztec Mummy. He is now a sorcerer who can transform himself into a bat or a tarantula (in the other films he has no such powers). And like a vampire, he only comes out at night, returning to his tomb to sleep through the daylight hours.

More Mummies

Assignment Terror (1970) (see ALIENS — INVADERS ON EARTH:THE 60s AND 70s). Michael Rennie plays an alien (a long way from *The Day the Earth Stood Still,* 1951) who plans to dominate the world by preying on Man's fears of the supernatural. To this end he revives Dracula, the Frankenstein Monster, the Wolf Man, and, of course, the Mummy. • For the first time in screen history, the Mummy battles another classical monster — the Wolf Man. The Mummy loses, however, when the Wolf Man cheats and sets him on fire with a torch.

The Awakening (1980; Warner Bros.) D: Mike Newell. P: Robert Solo. S: Allan Scott, Chris Bryant, Clive Exton. C: Jack Cardiff. Cast: Charlton Heston, Susannah York, Jill Townsend, Stephanie Zimbalist, Patrick Drury, Ian McDiarmid. Charlton Heston plays an archeologist who invades the tomb of Egyptian Queen Kara just as his infant daughter is born. Years later he becomes obsessed with a ritual that could bring the mummy back to life, and his obsession culminates with the soul of the Queen merging with his now-grown daughter. •

The film is (very loosely) based on Bram Stoker's story, "The Jewel of the Seven Stars."

Blood from the Mummy's Tomb (1972; Hammer/AIP; U.K.) D: Seth Holt, Michael Carreras. P: Howard Brandy. S: Christopher Wicking. C: Arthur Grant. Cast: Andrew Keir, Valerie Leon, James Villiers, Hugh Burden, George Coulouris, Mark Edwards. The mummy of the Egyptian queen Tara exerts a malevolent influence on the grown daughter of the man who discovered it. The evil Egyptian queen intends to possess the daughter and induce her to commit murder. • Like *The Awakening* (1980), this film is based on "The Jewel of the Seven Stars," by Bram Stoker (though the two pictures are quite different). • This is the fourth and last mummy movie (all unrelated) made by Hammer Studios, the first three being *The Mummy* (1959), *The Curse of the Mummy's Tomb* (1964), and *The Mummy's Shroud* (1967). • Director Seth Holt died during filming and Michael Carreras stepped in for the final week of production. Carreras was no stranger to the mummy theme, having produced and directed *The Curse of the Mummy's Tomb* in 1964. • In Britain, the film was released on a double bill with *Dr. Jekyll and Sister Hyde*.

Curse of the Faceless Man (1958; United Artists) D: Edward L. Cahn. P: Robert E. Kent. S: Jerome Bixby. C: Kenneth Peach. Cast: Richard Anderson, Elaine Edwards, Adele Mara, Luis Vann Rooten, Gar Moore. ¶ From the ads: "Stalking the Earth . . . *The Volcano Man* of 2,000 years ago!" A 2,000-year-old mummified man (a slave named Quintilius, buried in the eruption of Mount Vesuvius) is found at Pompeii and comes back to life to abduct Elaine Edwards, whom he believes to be the reincarnation of his lost love.

The Curse of the Mummy's Tomb (1964; Hammer/Columbia; U.K.) D/P: Michael Carreras. S: Henry Younger. C: Otto Heller. Cast: Terence Morgan, Fred Clark, Ronald Howard, Jeanne Roland, George Pastell, Jack Gwillim, Michael Ripper. A crass American showman uncovers the mummy of King Ra, intending to take it on a world tour. The mummy awakens from its long sleep and takes revenge on those who defiled its resting place. ¶ "Anybody that opens the Pharaoh's tomb is doomed to die horribly. There's thousands of dollars worth of free publicity in that, and don't think I'm not going to ballyhoo it in my campaign." • This is an unrelated follow-up to Hammer's *The Mummy* (1959). • Stuntman Dickie Owen plays the mummy in this entry. • Producer/director Michael Carreras also scripted the film using the pseudonym "Henry Younger."

Dawn of the Mummy (1981; Goldfarb; U.S./Italy/Egypt) D/P: Frank Agrama. S: Frank Agrama, Daria Price, Ronald Dobrin. C: Sergio Rubini. Cast: Brenda King, Barry Sattels, George Peck, John Salvo, Joan Levy, Diane Beatty. When a fashion photographer and his models disturb the tomb of an ancient Egyptian king, the mummy comes to life and summons its zombie slaves to kill those who desecrated his tomb. Then the mummy and its zombies go on a bloody rampage of violence and cannibalism in the nearby village. • This first (and only to date) mummy gore movie was filmed on location in Egypt.

The Monster Squad (1987) (see VAMPIRES — DRACULA AND FAMILY). The evil Dracula has summoned all the famous classic monsters together (the Creature from the Black Lagoon, Frankenstein's Monster, the Wolf Man, and the Mummy) in an attempt to gain possession of an occult amulet which would let the forces of darkness rule the earth. Their only opposition is a band of young kids and an old man. • The mummy, with its sunken face and emaciated form, is given a more historically authentic appearance here (relatively speaking) than in traditional mummy movies. The bandaged one, who is never given much to do in the film, is unceremoniously dispatched when the kids speedily unravel his wrappings, leaving nothing but a pile of dust and brittle bones.

The Mummy (1959; Hammer/Universal; U.K.) D: Terence Fisher. P: Michael Carreras. S: Jimmy Sangster. C: Jack Asher. Cast: Peter Cushing, Christopher Lee, Yvonne Furneaux, Eddie Byrne, Felix Aylmer, Raymond Huntley, George Pastell. Peter Cushing is among a British expedition that finds the tomb of Princess Ananka in Egypt. Cushing's father, the expedition leader, reads the scroll of life found in the tomb and unknowingly brings the hidden mummy of Kharis, Ananka's forbidden lover, to life. Three years later, a follower of the god Karnak brings the living mummy to England on a mission of vengeance against all those who desecrated the tomb. Cushing is spared this fate when Kharis is stopped by the sight of Cushing's wife, who happens to resemble the dead Princess. Eventually the mummy carries her off into the swamp, and while she uses her influence to free herself from him, the creature sinks into the mire. ¶ "After 4,000 years, the words of the scroll brought it to life again. It hates us, John. It hates us for desecrating the tomb of its Princess. It will kill us! It will kill us — all of us!" • Hammer's update of the Universal series is more of a synthesis of *The Mummy's Hand* (1940) and *The Mummy's Tomb* (1942) than a remake of *The Mummy* (1932). The names are the same, "Kharis" and "Ananka," as in these later Universal films. • Star Christopher Lee tried to downplay the monstrousness of his part, saying, "I only kill three people, and not in a ghastly way — I just break their necks." • Lee severely strained his back and neck muscles during filming from carrying his victims about, and claims this was the most physically arduous role of his career. • In a *Famous Monsters of Filmland* #88 interview, Christopher Lee discussed some of the film's special effects. "The spear sequence in *The Mummy* was done with split-cutting photography. When he was speared, the front was already protruding from the back. The bullet holes were caused by inserting plates on the bandages on which were laid small charges of gunpowder. These were detonated electronically at specific moments to synchronize with the shots, and as each charge exploded it blew away pieces of the wrappings and made the holes."

The Mummy and the Curse of the Jackals (1969/85; Vega International) D: Oliver Drake. P/S: William C. Edwards. C: William Trolano. Cast: Anthony Eisley, John Carradine, Robert Allen Browne, Marliza Pons, Maurine Dawson, Saul Goldsmith, William Whitton. Anthony Eisley plays an archeologist who unearths two mummies — one is a beautiful princess (still stunningly preserved) and the other is a male mummy in the Lon Chaney mold ("Serac," guardian of the princess). When the princess' case is opened, Eisley falls under a curse which transforms him into a sort of "werejackal." The princess revives and Eisley falls in love with her. After both the werejackal and the mummy wander around the Vegas strip, they end up battling in a lake while the princess crumbles to dust. ¶ "We can't stand by and let a 4,000-year-old mummy and a jackal-man take over the city!" • Scott Brady was originally going to play the part of the werejackal while Anthony Eisley was cast in the role of his well-meaning friend. But Brady dropped out of the project, and Eisley became the jackal-man, with Robert Allen Browne stepping in as the friend. • This inept feature was never even released (and according to star Anthony Eisley, was never finished) until it was patched together

and released on video in 1985. Eisley told Tom Weaver for his book, *Interviews with B Science Fiction and Horror Movie Makers,* "I don't mean this disrespectfully, but the director was quite senile at the time."

Mummy's Boys (1936; RKO) D: Fred Guiol. P: Samuel J. Briskin, Lee Marcus. S: J. Townley, Philip G. Epstein, Charles Roberts. C: Jack McKenzie. Cast: Bert Wheeler, Robert Woolsey, Barbara Pepper, Moroni Olsen, Willie Best. An Egyptian curse seemingly kills ten people, but it turns out to be a fake mummy.

The Mummy's Revenge (1973; Lotus Films/Sara Films; Spain) (also *The Vengeance of the Mummy*). C: Carlos Aured. S: Jacinto Molina. C: Francisco Sanchez. Cast: Paul Naschy, Jack Taylor, Maria Silva, Helga Line, Eduardo Calvo, Luis Dávila, Luis Gaspar, Celia Cruz, Rina Ottolina. In this nearly unwatchable Spanish version of the Mummy theme, a sadistic Pharaoh is mummified alive for his cruel crimes. Three thousand years later, an Egyptologist uncovers the mummy, who revives and goes on a bloody rampage before going up in flames at the hands of the hero. • Spanish horror star Paul Naschy, after having played the werewolf (in numerous films), Dracula (in *Dracula's Greatest Love,* 1972), and even a Jekyll/Hyde character (*Dr. Jekyll and the Wolfman,* 1971) dons the bandages of the Mummy to add it to his repertoire of classic monsters. Naschy also wrote the script (as he does for many of his movies) under his real name of Jacinto Molina. • Oddly enough, much of the advertising for this film utilized artwork picturing the Mexican monster "Popoca," better known as *The Aztec Mummy.*

The Mummy's Shroud (1967; Hammer-Seven Arts/20th Century-Fox; U.K.) D/S: John Gilling. P: Anthony Nelson Keys. C: Arthur Grant. Cast: Andre Morell, John Phillips, David Buck, Elizabeth Sellars, Maggie Kimberly, Michael Ripper. Yet another mummy (named "Prem" this time) is found and transported to a museum, only to rise up and take revenge upon those who have disturbed his resting place. Finally a young archeologist discovers a scroll inscribed with the proper sacred incantation which will cause the bandaged monster to crumble to dust. ¶ "Beware the beat of the cloth-wrapped feet" — rhythmic ad slogan. • This is Hammer's third mummy film (all unrelated). • Peter Cushing serves as narrator for *The Mummy's Shroud.* Cushing starred in Hammer's first foray into the subject, *The Mummy* (1959).

The National Mummy (1981; Spain) D: José Ramón Larraz. P: José Frade. S: José Ramón Larraz, Juan Alonso Millan. C: Raul Perez Cubero. Cast: Paco Algora, Azucena Hernandez, Quique Camoiras, José Jaime Espinosa, Lili Murati. This imported horror/comedy centers around the mummy of an Egyptian princess who, when unwrapped, becomes a beautiful predatory woman, intent on seducing all the men she meets.

Orgy of the Dead (1965) (see ZOMBIES). A horror writer and his girlfriend visit a cemetery after dark and are taken captive by the "Master of the Dead" and the "Princess of Darkness." They are forced to watch various women called up from the dead to dance topless to please the Master. Two supernatural servants aid the Master—a werewolf and a mummy, and both talk.

The Outing (1987) (see GENIES). An evil genie kills off a group of teenagers who have snuck into a museum and inadvertently released him from his lamp. At one point, the demonic djinn uses his powers to reanimate a dessicated mummy, which sits up and rips out the throat of one of the teens.

The Pharaoh's Curse (1957; Bel-Air/United Artists) D: Lee Sholem. P: Howard W. Koch. S: Richard Landau. C: William Margulies. Cast: Mark Dana, Ziva Rodann, Diane Brewster, Terence De Marney, George Neise, Kurt Katch, Ralph Clanton. This nearly forgotten mummy movie centers on a desecrated tomb protected by the soul of a high priest. Among the archeological party is an Egyptian guide who, upon the opening of the tomb, falls ill only to rise as a horribly aged mummy-like *thing,* wreaking vengeance on the defilers by draining their blood. ¶ "The flesh of my flesh shall crawl into thy body and feed on the flesh of thy soul"—the Pharaoh's Curse. • The makeup is excellent, with the monster's hideous visage looking like a dried-up eviscerated skull covered in parchment-like skin and with teeth all blackened and rotted. • The exteriors were all shot in Death Valley in one day(!) and stand in quite well for the Egyptian desert.

Tales from the Darkside: The Movie (1990) (see ANTHOLOGIES). In the "Lot 247" episode, a brilliant young student takes revenge on those who have wronged him by reading the sacred scroll which brings the mummy in Lot 247 to murderous life. ¶ "Who in their right mind would really believe that a 3,000-year-old mummy had come back to life?" • This episode is based on a short story by Sir Arthur Conan Doyle.

Time Walker (1982) (see ALIENS — BENEVOLENT ALIENS). A mummy named "Ank Fen Haris" who, unbeknownst to archeologist Ben Murphy, is actually an *alien* from another world, is embalmed alive in ancient Egypt. Murphy finds him in King Tut's tomb and brings him back to the United States. The mummy revives when his sarcophagus is x-rayed, and he sets out to retrieve his stolen crystals that will allow him to "phone home." Murphy finally confronts the walking mummy only to have him change into a benign alien (à la *Close Encounters...*) right before his eyes. ¶ "It's a slow night—you drink a little beer, steal a mummy."

Voodoo Black Exorcist (1975; U.S./Spain) D: M. Cano. P: Rosgard of Miami, Mingyar of Madrid. S: S. Monkada. C: Robert Ochoa. Cast: Aldo Sambrell, Tanyeka Stadle, Alexander Abrahan, Fernando Sancho. In this obscure imported oddity, the 1,000-year-old mummy of an African voodoo priest is revived and sets about finding the reincarnation of the girl he loves. ¶ "Heads decapitated, sarcophaguses, mummies, voodoo rites, lying scientists ... I don't like this"—disgruntled police inspector. • This particular mummy has the ability to regain (through sorcery) his normal appearance as a man for certain periods of time, but then ultimately he reverts back to a hideous mummified corpse.

Waxwork (1988) (see WAX MUSEUMS). David Warner runs a small, sinister, and very special wax museum. Anyone who gets too close to the various exhibits is sucked into that wax figure's world and meets a gruesome death at the hands of the evil creature. One character stumbles into the exhibit for The Mummy and is entombed alive by the bandaged one. ¶ "Those who desecrate the tomb of Raoul will be condemned to a painful death at the hands of ... good heavens, it's the mummy!"

We Want Our Mummy (1939; Columbia) D: Del Lord. P: Jules White. S: Elwood Ullman, Searle Kramer. C: Allen G. Siegler. Cast: The Three Stooges (Jerry "Curly" Howard, Moe Howard, Larry Fine), Bud Jamison, James C. Morton, Robert Williams, Dick Curtis. Only fake mummies this time, but they scare the life out of the Three Stooges.

Mythology
(*See also* Genies; Sinbad; Sword and Sorcery)

Using the strictest definition of mythology allows a wide variety of fantasy films to be encompassed under that subject heading. A myth is a story usually involving some kind of supernatural being, event, or action which embodies the culture of a people or community and is to some extent an imaginative explanation of some part of a society's ideology. With that in mind, we could list several thousand films in this section, including numerous vampire movies, werewolf films, etc. When most western filmgoers hear the word "mythology," however, they usually think of the classical Greek mythology (and to a lesser extent, the Roman offshoot). Therefore, in this chapter we are staying close to the mythological roots of the Greeks and Romans.

The most frequently appearing mythological character in films is the legendary Hercules, son of Zeus. His cinematic output probably makes Hercules one of Italy's leading exports. Steve Reeves was the screen's first (and many say best) *Hercules* in 1959, but throughout the 1960s (Hercules' most popular decade) this mythological hero was played multiple times by various actors, including Alan Steel, Kirk Morris, Reg Park, and Dan Vadis.

Other chapters with mythological leanings would be GENIES and SINBAD (both of which contain Arabian-style legends), and SWORD AND SORCERY.

Atlas Against the Cyclops (1961; Medallion; Italy) (also *Atlas in the Land of the Cyclops*). D: Antonio Leonviola. P: Ermanno Donati, Luigi Carpentieri. S: Oreste Biancoli, Gino Mangini. C: Riccardo Pallottini. Cast: Gordon Mitchell, Chelo Alonso, Vira Silenti. An Italian strongman battles the mythological Cyclops, and runs up against an evil queen.

Clash of the Titans (1981; MGM) D: Desmond Davis. P: Charles Schneer, Ray Harryhausen. S: Beverley Cross. C: Ted Moore. Cast: Laurence Olivier, Claire Bloom, Harry Hamlin, Maggie Smith, Ursula Andress, Burgess Meredith, Judy Bowker, Jack Gwyllim, Freda Jackson. Perseus (Harry Hamlin of TV's "L.A. Law") must battle a myriad of mythological creatures in his effort to win the hand of Princess Andromeda. • Among the creatures encountered are a snake-haired gorgon, a two-headed wolf dog, and the monstrous underwater terror known as the Kraken. Perseus is aided by the winged horse Pegasus.

Devil Woman (1970; Philippines) D/S: José Flores Sibal. C: Steve Perez. Cast: Divina Valencia, Roger Calvin, Perla Bautista, Eddie Garcia. This picture features the Filipino version of the gorgon, who can send out cobras to do her bidding.

The Fury of Hercules (1961; Italy) D: Gianfranco Parolini. S: P. Parloni, Giorgio C. Simonelli, C. Madison. C: Francesco Izzarelli. Cast: Brad Harris, Brigitte Corey, Alan Steel. Brad Harris plays the muscle bound hero this time out.

The Giants of Thessaly (1960; Medallion; Italy/France) (also *Jason and the Golden Fleece*). D: Riccardo Freda. P: Virgilio De Blasi. S: Giuseppe Masini, Mario Rossetti, Riccardo Freda, Ennio De Concini. C: Vaclav Vich, Raffaele Masciocchi. Cast: Roland Carey, Ziva Rodann, Massimo Girotti, Alberto Farnese. Jason and Orpheus encounter witches and monsters during their search for the mythological golden fleece.

The Golden Voyage of Sinbad (1973) (see SINBAD). Sinbad encounters some unusual mythological creatures, including a winged griffin, a centaur, a tiny homunculus, and a six-armed statue of the goddess Kali.

Goliath and the Dragon (1960; American International; Italy/France) (also *Vengeance of Hercules*). D: Vittorio Cottafavi. P: Achille Piazzi, Gianni Fuchs. S: Mario Piccolo, Archibald Zounds, Jr. C: Mario Montuori. Cast: Mark Forest, Broderick Crawford, Leonora Ruffo, Gaby Andre. Replacing Steve Reeves is the skinnier Mark Forest as Goliath, who comes up against several mythological monstrosities, including the three-headed dog from Hell named "Cerberus," a centaur, and a dragon. • Famous *King Kong* (1933) model-maker

Marcel Delgado teamed up with Jim Danforth (*When Dinosaurs Ruled the Earth*, 1970) to build the dragon model used in this picture. A full scale head was built for the menacing closeups.

The Gorgon (1964; Hammer; U.K.) D: Terence Fisher. P: Anthony Nelson Keys. S: John Gilling. C: Michael Reed. Cast: Peter Cushing, Christopher Lee, Richard Pasco, Barbara Shelley, Michael Goodlife, Patrick Troughton. A German village is being terrorized by the snake-headed gorgon named "Megara," whom Peter Cushing is protecting, and Christopher Lee is trying to expose and destroy. ¶ "It is said that when mortals looked upon her face they were turned to stone." • British horror actress Barbara Shelley landed the role of the gorgon, but only in its human-looking state as "Carla." The actress under the ghostly snake makeup of Roy Ashton was Prudence Hyam. • Lurid ad lines for *The Gorgon* read: "A Monster with the Power to Turn Living Screaming Flesh into Silent Stone."

Hercules (1959; Embassy/Warner Bros.; Italy) D: Pietro Francisci. P: Federico Teti. S: Ennio De Concini, Pietro Francisci, Gaio Frattini. C: Mario Bava. Cast: Steve Reeves, Sylvia Koscina, Gianna Maria Canale, Fabrizio Mione, Ivo Garrani, Arturo Dominici. The mythological strongman helps Jason find the golden fleece that was stolen from his ship, the *Argo,* and along the way beats off soldiers, bests a Nemean lion, bullies the Cretan bull, routes an army of apemen, deals with a dragon, and topples a palace. ¶ "Prove to me your head isn't just a mass of muscle up there." • Producer Joseph E. Levine bought the rights to this film for $10,000 and sold it to Warner Bros., whose promotion helped make it such a tremendous success that the screens were deluged with sequels. The film grossed over five million dollars in America alone. • Steve Reeves was born in Glasgow, Montana, and held the bodybuilding titles of Mr. America, Mr. World, and Mr. Universe before turning to acting. • The dragon which Hercules and his comrades encounter looks just like a "Tyrannosaurus Rex" and bellows like Godzilla. In fact, it *is* the sound effects from the original *Godzilla* (1954) that were used on the soundtrack.

Hercules (1983) D/S: Lewis Coates. P: Menahem Golan, Yoram Globus. Cast: Lou Ferrigno, Brad Harris, Sybil Danning, William Berger, Rossana Podesta, Ingrid Anderson, Mirella D'Angelo. This updated version has Zeus's favorite son, Hercules, called upon to fight the forces of darkness led by the evil King Minos and his daughter Arianna. The Goddess Hera assists Hercules as he matches skills against snakes, mechanical monsters, and deadly laser rays. ¶ "You're too reliant on your strength, my hero. You look musclebound, but you're pretty agile, aren't you?"

Hercules Against Rome (1964; AIP-TV; France/Italy) D: Piero Pierotti. S: Arpad De Riso, Nino Scolaro. C: Augusto Tiezzi. Cast: Alan Steel, Wandisa Guida, Domenico Palmara, Daniele Vargas. Muscleman Alan Steel takes over from Steve Reeves in this sword and sandal story about Hercules rescuing a kidnapped princess and battling the legions of Rome. • Alan Steel's real name is Sergio Ciani.

Hercules Against the Barbarians (1960; Alta Vista Productions; Italy) D: Domenico Paolella, Robert Spafford (American version). P: Jacopo Comin, Ferdinando Felicioni. S: Domenico Paolella, Luciano Martino, A. Ferrau. C: Raffaele Masciocchi. Cast: Mark Forest, José Greci, Ken Clarke, Gloria Milland, Renato Rossini, Mirko Ellis, Roldano Lupi. Hercules confronts the forces of Ghengis Khan to save a lovely Asian princess. ¶ "Anyone who breaks into the house of Ghengis Khan must die!"

Hercules Against the Moon Men (1965; Governor; Italy/France) D: Giacomo Gentilomo. P: Luigi Mondello. S: Arpad De Riso, Nino Scolaro, Giacomo Gentilomo, Angelo Sangarmano. C: Oberdan Trojani. Cast: Alan Steel, Jany Clair, Annamaria Polani, Nando Tamberlani. Hercules battles stone-like robots, magical moon men, and encounters their Queen who is in need of blood to revive her from sleep. ¶ "The supernatural and the real clash in a world of *horror!*"—promotional trailer.

Hercules Against the Sons of the Sun (1964; Wonder; Italy/Spain) D/P: Osvaldo Civirani. S: Osvaldo Civirani, Franco Tannuzzini. C: Julio Ortas Plaza. Cast: Mark Forest, Anna Maria Pace, Giuliano Gemma, Angela Rhu, Ricardo Valle. Hercules is shipwrecked on the land of the Incan civilization. There he bonds with a band of rebel mountain men who want to overthrow the current despicable ruler. ¶ "Thank you Hercules. The good will in your heart is like the strength in your body." • Richard McNamara directed the English language version.

Hercules and the Captive Women (1963; Woolner Brothers/SPA Cinematografica; Italy/France) (also *Hercules and the Haunted Women; Hercules Conquers Atlantis*). D: Vittorio Cottafavi. P: Achille Piazzi. S: Alessandro Continenza, Vittorio Cottafavi,

Duccio Tessari. C: Carlo Carlini. Cast: Reg Park, Fay Spain, Ettore Manni, Luciano Marin, Laura Allan. Hercules is shipwrecked on a living island with an appetite for humans. While there he battles a monster which can change form (ball of fire, snake, lion, eagle, etc.) and then meets a girl from Atlantis. After taking her back home, he locks horns with their evil Queen, knocks off an albino army and punches a hole near the Temple of Uranus which causes the continent to sink. ¶ "Could she subdue this giant of a man with her sorcery?" — ad line.

Hercules and the Tyrants of Babylon (1964; AIP-TV; Italy) D: Domenico Paolella. S: Luciano Martino, Domenico Paolella. C: Augusto Tiezzi. Cast: Rock Stevens, Helga Line, Mario Petri, Annamaria Polani, Livio Lorenzon. Hercules takes on a malevolent sorceress.

Hercules in New York (1970; United Films) (also *Hercules: The Movie*). D: Arthur A. Seidelman. P/S: Aubrey Wisberg. Cast: Arnold Strong, Arnold Stang. Hercules is sent to modern day New York after bothering Zeus up on Mount Olympus. His trip to Manhattan includes a chariot ride up Broadway, and tangling with an escaped bear. • Hercules actor Arnold Strong later changed his name to Arnold Schwarzenegger and now commands seven-figure salaries.

Hercules in the Haunted World (1964; Woolner Brothers; Italy) D: Mario Bava. P: Achille Piazzi. S: Alessandro Continenza, Mario Bava, Duccio Tessari, Franco Prosperi. C: Mario Bava, Ubaldo Terzano. Cast: Reg Park, Christopher Lee, Eleonora Ruffo, Giorgio Ardisson, Franco Giacobini, Marisa Belli. Hercules and his buddy Theseus enter Hell to find the means to break the spell that has been placed upon a princess. While there, they face a bizarre rock monster and a demonic agent (played by Christopher Lee) and his vampiric hordes. ¶ "Hercules in a haunted world, an unearthly world of eternal darkness, ghostly kingdom of the undead *demons of death*."

Hercules in the Vale of Woe (1962; Avco Embassy–TV; Italy) (also *Maciste Against Hercules in the Vale of Woe*). P: Ignazio Luceri. S: Vittorio Metz, Marcello Marchesi. Cast: Kirk Morris, Frank Gordon, Bice Valori, Liana Orfei, Franco Franchi. Hercules (Frank Gordon) and Maciste (Kirk Morris) are visited by a pair of contemporary con artists via a time machine, who want to promote a fight between the two.

Hercules of the Desert (1964; Cineluxor; Italy) D: Tanio Boccia. S: Mario Moroni, Tanio Boccia, Alberto De Rossi. C: Aldo

Giordano. Cast: Kirk Morris, Hélène Chanel, Alberto Farnese, Furio Meniconi. Hercules takes on a group of powerful men with the magical ability to start avalanches.

Hercules, Prisoner of Evil (1967; AIP-TV; Italy) D: Anthony Dawson (Antonio Margheriti). P: Adelpho Ambrosiano. Cast: Reg Park, Mireille Granelli, Ettore Manni, Maria Teresa Orsini, Furio Meniconi. Hercules tackles a witch and her werewolves.

Hercules, Samson, and Ulysses (1965; MGM; Italy) D/S: Pietro Francisci. P: Joseph Fryd. C: Silvano Ippoliti. Cast: Kirk Morris, Richard Lloyd, Enzo Cerusico, Liana Orfei, Fulvia Franco. The pumped-up trio (Morris as Hercules, Lloyd as Samson, and Cerusico as Ulysses) takes on a sea monster in this entry, and at the climax Samson and Hercules topple a palace. ¶ "But in all Judea can there exist another giant like this, who, without a weapon, can kill a lion with his bare hands?"

Hercules the Invincible (1963; Metheus; Italy) D/P: Alfredo Mancori. S: Kirk Mayor, Pat Klein, Alfredo Mancori. C: Claude Haroy. Cast: Dan Vadis, Spela Rozin, Carla Calo, Ken Clark, Jon Simons. Hercules battles a dragon and brings destruction to a terrible underground city by starting a volcanic eruption.

Hercules Unchained (1960; Embassy/ Warner Bros.; Italy/France) D: Pietro Francisci. P: Bruno Vailati. S: Pietro Francisci, Ennio De Concini. C: Mario Bava. Cast: Steve Reeves, Sylva Koscina, Primo Carnera, Sylvia Lopez, Sergio Fantoni. After drinking from the waters of forgetfulness, Hercules loses his memory and falls in with a wicked queen who likes to have the men in her life stuffed. After some friends jog his memory, Hercules takes on the Son of the Earth (Primo Carnera). In the battle, every time Carnera is thrown down he gains new strength (when he touches the ground he marshals the Earth forces), so Hercules drops him off a cliff into a lake. ¶ "Hercules, that ceremony you went through, the bonds of matrimony, now you're married so drive carefully." • The actress who played Queen Lydia, Sylvia Lopez, died of leukemia soon after the movie was filmed. • Primo Carnera was a former heavyweight boxing champion of the world. He was no match for Hercules unchained, however.

Jason and the Argonauts (1963; Columbia; U.K.) D: Don Chaffey. P: Charles Schneer. S: Jan Read, Beverley Cross. C: Wilkie Cooper. Cast: Todd Armstrong, Nancy Kovack, Gary Raymond, Laurence Naismith, Niall MacGinnis, Michael Gwynn,

Sorcery raises up a horde of skeletal warriors to battle Jason (Todd Armstrong) in Jason and the Argonauts *(1963). Armstrong, the only American in the principally British cast, had his voice dubbed by an English actor.*

Honor Blackman, Nigel Green, Jack Gwillim, John Crawford. This bold mythological adventure centers around Jason's quest for the golden fleece, and how the Greek gods on Mount Olympus play out their little games of fate with mortals. On his journey, Jason and his crew of "Argonauts" encounter a giant bronze titan named Talos, Phineas the blind man and his tormenting harpies, Neptune, god of the sea, a monstrous hydra with seven serpent heads, and an army of living skeletons. ¶ "The gods of Greece are cruel. In time all men shall learn to do without them!" • One of Charles Schneer and Ray Harryhausen's most lavish productions, *Jason,* filmed in Italy, took over two years to complete and cost over three and a half million dollars to make, which at that time made it one of the most expensive fantasy films ever made. • Ray Harryhausen said in Jeff Rovin's book, *From the Land Beyond,* "I've been able to put on the screen some of the most unusual and, I think, dynamic situations, and it seems to be taken for granted! ... Charles

and I have more in one of our pictures, like *Jason and the Argonauts,* than you see in about six pictures of ordinary calibre.... That's why I really believe that *Jason* could have and should have made as much money as *Jaws.*" • The ship, named the *Argo,* was actually a dressed-up fishing barge over 90 feet long, costing $250,000 to construct. • There were a total of 11 stop-motion figures to animate, the most difficult being the seven-headed Hydra. The most time consuming was the skeleton sequence which took over five months to complete, though it lasts only a few minutes on screen. • There were some additional scenes which were scrapped due to time constraints. One involved Jason journeying to Hell and encountering the three-headed dog "Cerberus." • The film was to be called *Jason and the Golden Fleece,* but the title was changed when they realized an Italian 1960 film, *The Giants of Thessaly,* already had used that alternate title for its European release.

The Legend of Doom House (1972; Artistes Associes; France/Belgium/W. Germany) D: Harry Kuemel. P: Paul Laffargue, Rita Laffargue. S: Jean Ferry. C: Gerry Fisher. Cast: Orson Welles, Mathieu Carrière, Susan Hampshire, Jean-Pierre Cassel, Charles Janssens, Walter Rilla. This weird tale features several mythological creatures (including a gorgon and three furies) disguised as humans, who are trapped by Orson Welles and Charles Janssens in an old dark house.

The Loves of Hercules (1960; Contact; Italy/France) (also *Hercules and the Hydra; Hercules vs. the Hydra*). D: Carlo Ludovico Bragaglia. P: Alberto Manca. S: Allesandro Continenza, Luciano Doria. C: Enzo Serafin. Cast: Jayne Mansfield, Mickey Hargitay, Massimo Serato, Tina Gloriani, Rosella Como, Moira Orfei. Among the monsters encountered by the bearded Hercules are a three-headed dragon, a cyclops, a bull, and a tree-man. ¶ "Hercules will never surrender himself to you, there is another woman in possession of his heart." • Jayne Mansfield plays two roles in the film. First, the Queen, whom Hercules rescues, and then the part of a red-haired Amazon. Jayne was the real-life wife of Mickey Hargitay (who played Hercules).

Medusa vs. the Son of Hercules (1962; Copercines; Italy/Spain) D: Alberto de Martino. P: José Antonio, Emo Bistolfi. S: Luciano Martino, Mario Guerra, José Mallorqui. C: Dario Di Palma, Eloy Mella. Cast: Richard Harrison, Anna Ranalli, Leo Anchóriz, Arturo Dominici. Perseus (the son of Hercules) rescues a princess from a dragon and takes on Medusa, who has the power to turn men into stone.

The Minotaur (1961; United Artists; Italy) D: Silvio Amadio. P: Dino Mordini. Giorgio Agliani, Rudolphe Solmsen. S: Alessandro Continenza, Paolo Callegari, Daniel Mainwaring. C: Aldo Giordani. Cast: Bob Mathias, Rosanna Schiaffino, Alberto Lupo, Rik Battaglia, Nico Pepe, Carlo Tamberlani, Susanne Loret. Some clouded Greek politics and assassination attempts are overshadowed when Theseus is given a magical sword by Amphitrite, goddess of the sea. After spurning her advances, he uses his new magical weapon to slay the giant half-man, half-bull Minotaur that lives within a Cretan labyrinth. ¶ "Stalking out of a time of unbridled passion and terror it comes . . . the half-man, half-beast that made a civilization bow down before it and feed its gargantuan lusts!" — ad line. • Theseus was played by 6'4" Bob Mathias, a two-time winner of the Olympic Decathlon. Many of his Olympic skills were put to test on this film. "I had to make a broken field run of about

100 yards, and it's a long time since my football days at Stanford. I swam under water, galloped off on a horse without a saddle, and finally topped the whole thing off with a bloody battle against a ten-foot monster," Mathias stated, adding, "You'd think that would be a day's work, but then I had to fight this big stale bull! That Minotaur never got tired." • Although many historical sites in Italy were used in the film, such as the fountains at Tivoli, most of the battle sequences were shot in Yugoslavia.

The Seven Faces of Dr. Lao (1964) (see MAGICIANS). Tony Randall stars as the oriental magician Dr. Lao, whose traveling sideshow exhibits some mythological figures, including the demi-god Pan and a gorgon (Medusa). All of the characters are revealed to be a part of Lao himself.

Thief of Bagdad (1960; MGM; France/Italy) D: Arthur Lubin. P: Bruno Vailati. S: Agusto Frassinetti, Filippo Sanjust, Bruno Vailati. C: Tonino Delli Colli. Cast: Steve Reeves, Georgia Moll, Edy Vessel, Arturo Dominici, Daniele Vargas. Muscleman Steve Reeves is a rogue in love with a princess, and uses the mythological winged horse Pegasus in his search for a fabled blue rose.

The Three Stooges Meet Hercules (1962; Columbia) D: Edward Bernds. P: Norman Maurer. S: Elwood Ullman. Cast: Moe Howard, Larry Fine, Curly Joe De Rita, Emil Sitka, Gene Roth, Samson Burke. The Stooges accompany a scientist and his girlfriend on a trip back in time to where Hercules, Achilles, and Ulysses live. While there, they face a myriad of mythic-type creatures which include a siamese cyclops, and an (off-screen) hydra.

Time Bandits (1981) (see TIME TRAVEL). In one sequence, Sean Connery, playing the legendary Agamemnon, is seen battling a minotaur (half-man, half-bull).

Triumph of Hercules (1964; Cinematografica/Castle Hill; Italy/France) (also *Hercules vs. the Giant Warriors*). D: Alberto De Martino. P: Alberto Chimenz, Vico Pavoni. S: Roberto Gianviti, Allessandro Ferrau. C: Pier Ludovico Pavoni. Cast: Dan Vadis, Pierre Cressoy, Marilu Tolo, Piero Lulli, Enzo Fiermonte, Renato Rossini, Moira Orfei. Hercules is called upon to help avenge the death of a king, who was assassinated by his treacherous nephew. The evil lad is aided by a witch, who lends him a dagger with the capability to call forth invincible bronze-headed soldiers. Hercules is stripped of his strength by Zeus who returns it when his boy must face the ten bronze warriors. ¶ "Our arrows and swords bounced

right off their bodies, or they broke in pieces. There's nothing you can do. Any weapon is useless against those monsters."
Ulysses (1955; Paramount; Italy) D: Mario Camerini. P: Dino De Laurentiis, Carlo Ponti. S: Franco Brusati, Mario Camerini, Ennio De Concini, Hugh Gray, Ben Hecht, Ivo Perilli, Irwin Shaw. C: Harold Rosson. Cast: Kirk Douglas, Silvana Mangano, Anthony Quinn, Rossana Podestà, Daniel Ivernel. The mythic escapades of Ulysses are depicted as he washes ashore with amnesia, then finally regains the memories of his heroic deeds via a series of flashbacks. Among his adventures are a fierce battle with Neptune's cyclopian son, a near fatal encounter with a group of Sirens, and a run-in with a sorceress. After his memory is regained, he returns to his house to attack the unwelcome suitors who have attempted to move in on his faithful wife and son. ¶ "Bye Polyphemus, you drunken son of Neptune, enjoy your wine, and remember the stringy Greeks, and the dance they danced in your cave ... roar on you sightless drunkard, roar on!" • Ulysses ("How do you prefer me master? Roasted, boiled, spiced, raw?") disposes of the Cyclops by getting him drunk on wine, and stabbing him in the eye with the sharpened end of his own giant club. Douglas goads the giant into drink by declaring that he will need something good to wash down the Greek sailors he wants to eat. "These Greeks are tough, uuughh, with stringy meat."
Ulysses Against the Son of Hercules (1963; Embassy; Italy/France) D: Mario Caiano. P: G. Pasquale, A. Fantechi. S: Mario Caiano, Andre Tabet. C: Alvaro Mancori. Cast: Georges Marchal, Michael Lane, Alessandra Panaro, Gianni Santuccio. Hercules is sent by the gods, Jupiter and Neptune, to dispose of Ulysses, but the two heroes are both captured by a society of bird-people. After a few more adventures, which include a fight with a band of Troglodytes, the two become friends.
Venus Against the Son of Hercules (1962; Embassy; Italy) D: Marcello Baldi. S: Marcello Baldi, Alessandro Continenza. C: Marcello Masciocchi. Cast: Massimo Serato, Roger Browne, Jackie Lane, Dante Di Paolo, Linda Sini. Man-eating plants and a magic spell are featured in this Hercules entry.
Warrior Empress (1961; Columbia; Italy) D: Pietro Francisci. P: Gianni Hecht Lucari. S: Pietro Francisci, Ennio De Concini, Luciano Martino. C: Carlo Carlini. Cast: Tina Louise, Kerwin Mathews, Riccardo Garrone, Alberto Farnese. Sirens, Aphrodite and the underwater kingdom of Poseidon are all featured in this mythological adventure starring Kerwin Mathews (*The Seventh Voyage of Sinbad,* 1958) and Tina Louise (of "Gilligan's Island" fame).

Nuclear Holocaust *see* Futures on Earth

Phantoms

In the truest sense of the word, a phantom is an illusion—something that can be seen but is really not there, such as a ghostly manifestation. In horror films, however, "phantom" carries the connotation of a mysterious dark figure (often hooded or masked) creeping about, bent on some kind of murder or mayhem. In this section, we have included those films that fit this classic "phantom" description. The Phantom of the Opera is generally considered to be the archetypal phantom figure, and the character against which all other phantoms are measured. Aside from the five "straight" adaptations of Gaston Leroux's novel, there are a handful of other pictures cast from this "phantom" mold, most owing at least their inspiration to the original 1925 Lon Chaney classic. More often than not, screen phantoms inspire pathos as well as terror. These poor, blighted individuals, unjustly having to live in seclusion and loneliness, frequently strike out and commit horrible acts. However, their life is not entirely of their own making, and their actions often not without a sense of justice.

Creature with the Blue Hand (1971; New World; W. Germany) D: Alex Berg. P: Horst Wendlandt, Preben Philipsen. S: Alfred Vohrer. Cast: Klaus Kinski, Diana Korner, Harold Lepnvitz. A cloaked phantom lurks within a castle asylum.

The Curse of the Living Corpse (1963; 20th Century–Fox) D/P/S: Del Tenney. C: Richard L. Hilliard. Cast: Helen Waren, Roy Scheider, Margot Hartman, Robert Milli, Hugh Franklin, Candace Hilligoss. A millionaire deathly afraid of premature burial vows vengeance on his family if he is buried alive. Upon his death and interment, his greedy relations gather at the estate. Sure enough, his tomb turns up empty, and a cloaked, hooded figure is stalking the grounds, killing relatives one by one, employing the method of death that each fears most. • Roy Scheider made his film debut here as one of the money-hungry relatives. • *The Curse of the Living Corpse* was released on a double bill with *Horror of Party Beach,* another Del Tenney independent.

Darkman (1990) (see MAD SCIENTISTS). The disfigured, cloaked "Darkman" uses his scientific knowledge to change his appearance and come out at night to wreak vengeance. ¶ "I'm everywhere and no one. I'm everywhere and nowhere. Call me Darkman!"

Horror Island (1941; Universal) D: George Waggner. P: Ben Pivar. S: Maurice Tombragel, Victor McLeod. C: Elwood Bredell. Cast: Dick Foran, Peggy Moran, Fuzzy Knight, Leo Carrillo, John Eldredge, Lewis Howard, Hobart Cavanaugh, Walter Catlett. A pair of seafaring fortune hunters one step ahead of their creditors join a peg-legged sailor and put on a treasure hunt adventure trip to the supposedly haunted island of Morgan the pirate. Their money-making scheme gets a jolt when a mysterious cloaked figure known as "The Phantom" tries to drive them away so he can uncover the "real" hidden treasure. Peggy Moran plays the rich love interest in this horror who-done-it featuring some stunning gothic atmospheric locations designed by Oscar-winning set builder Russel A. Gausman. ¶ "Riches, ghosts, a haunted castle on a deserted island!" • Dick Foran, who plays the hero, starred in numerous genre features, including *The Mummy's Hand* (1940; also with Peggy Moran), *The Mummy's Tomb* (1942), and *The Atomic Submarine* (1959).

House of Wax (1953) (see WAX MUSEUMS). A cloaked disfigured character, which turns out to be a burned-up Vincent Price, stalks the streets and back alleys looking for just the right model for his wax sculptures.

Man of a Thousand Faces (1957; Universal) D: Joseph Pevney. P: Robert Arthur. S: Ivan Goff, R. Wright Campbell, Ben Roberts. C: Russell Metty. Cast: James Cagney, Dorothy Malone, Robert Evans, Roger Smith, Jim Backus, Marjorie Rambeau, Jane Greer. This standard Hollywood biopic about the life of Lon Chaney stars James Cagney in the title role. The film includes some interesting sequences about the making of his 1925 film, *Phantom of the Opera.* ¶ "He caught me fooling around in his makeup box. Copying one of his faces, he's got a thousand of 'em." • *Man of a Thousand Faces* received an Academy Award nomination for its screenplay. • Lon Chaney, Sr.'s, mother in the film was played by Peter Lorre's wife, Celia Lovsky.

Mystery of the Wax Museum (1933) (see WAX MUSEUMS). A horribly charred character, cloaked in black, stalks the streets looking for bodies and fresh victims to be used as wax figures.

Phantom of Crestwood (1932; RKO) D: J. Walter Ruben. P: David O. Selznick. S: J. Walter Ruben, Bartlett Cormack. C: Henry Gerrard. Cast: Ricardo Cortez, H. B. Warner, Anita Louise, Karen Morley, Pauline Frederick. A blackmailing woman assembles her victims in a spooky old house, haunted by a phantom killer.

The Phantom of Hollywood (1974; TV movie) D/P: Gene Levitt. S: Robert Thom, George Shenk. Cast: Jack Cassidy, Broderick Crawford, Jackie Coogan, Peter Lawford, Kent Taylor, Regis Toomey, John Ireland. An actor, disfigured from a stunt accident, haunts backlot #2 of Worldwide Studios, using a bow and arrow to discourage those trying to demolish the lot. • Skye Aubrey, daughter of a former MGM studio president, appeared in this movie.

Phantom of Soho (1963; CCC Productions/Producers Releasing Company; W. Germany) D: Franz Josef Gottlieb. P: Artur Brauner. S: Ladislas Fodor. C: Richard Angst. Cast: Dieter Borsche, Barbara Ruetting, Hans Sohnker, Elisabeth Flickenschildt, Peter Vogel. A hooded Jack the Ripper–style killer wearing a skull mask is loose in the Soho district of London.

Phantom of the Mall: Eric's Revenge (1988; Fries Entertainment) D: Richard Friedman. P: Tom Fries. S: Scott J. Schneid, Tony Michelman, Robert King. C: Harry Mathias. Cast: Derek Rydall, Jonathan Goldsmith, Rob Estes, Pauly Shore, Kari Whitman, Morgan Fairchild. Eric is a high school student whose house happens to sit right in the middle of the proposed site for a shopping mall. The greedy developer burns down the house, with Eric inside. Thought dead, the now-hideously disfigured Eric stalks through the mall's subterranean passageways seeking revenge and the girl-friend he is still obsessed with. • This two million dollar production was filmed at the Sherman Oaks Galleria, the same complex at which *Chopping Mall* was lensed.

Phantom of the Opera (1925; Universal) D: Rupert Julian. P: Carl Laemmle. S: Raymond Schrock, Elliot J. Clawson. C: Virgil Miller. Cast: Lon Chaney, Mary Philbin, Norman Kerry, Gibson Gowland, Snitz Edwards, John Sainpolis. A man possessing a hideous skull face haunts the Paris Opera House where he secretly tutors a young singer who believes him to be the spirit of music sent from above. He is all-too-human, however, when he kidnaps the would-be opera star and carries her off to his dungeon retreat below the opera house. ¶ "Feast your eyes — glut your soul — on my accursed ugliness!" • This same film, with additional sequences and sound added, was released again in 1930. The new sound segments were directed by Ernst Laemmle, and the audible dialogue was written by Frank McCormack. The parts played by John Sainpolis, and John Miljan were deleted, and a new cast member, Edward Martindel, was edited in. • Lon Chaney's legendary makeup was described in the film as follows: "His face is like leprous parchment, yellow skin stretched drum tight over protruding bones!" Chaney's eyes were said to have been dilated by chemicals. A device was placed in his nose to flare the nostrils, the corners of his mouth were drawn back by the use of small prongs, and celluloid disks were put inside his mouth to distort the cheekbones. The final appearance has been called by many fans and film critics the most frightening visage ever seen in the cinema. Stories have been told about how in the theaters of that time, men used to cover the faces of their dates with their hands, shielding them from "the naked face of horror." Lon Chaney died at the tragically early age of 44. • Director Rupert Julian was replaced by Edward Sedgwick before the film was finished after Julian had a major disagreement over the character played by Chaney. • The film was budgeted at over one million dollars, which, in 1925, was an unheard of amount.

Phantom of the Opera (1943; Universal) D: Arthur Lubin. P: George Waggner. S: Eric Taylor, Samuel Hoffenstein, John Jacobs (adaptation). C: Hal Mohr, W. Howard Greene. Cast: Nelson Eddy, Susanna

Foster, Claude Rains, Edgar Barrier, Leo Carrillo, Miles Mander. An ex-violinist's concerto is taken without his consent, and in the subsequent fight the wronged musician is disfigured by acid. He retreats into the Opera's underground byways, and his mysterious presence gives rise to tales of ghosts and phantoms. He then murders a rival opera star so that his singing protégée, Kristine (whom he has been secretly financing) can take the lead role in the upcoming performance. At the climax the singer unmasks the "Phantom of the Opera," and a misfired shot brings down the underground walls, crushing the Phantom. ¶ "He was a kind and inoffensive man, until he thought Pleyal was robbing him of his life's work. Then something snapped, and he became a homicidal maniac. In his state he may commit other murders. It's urgent that we capture him as soon as possible." • The production cost approximately $1.5 million, and the opera stage, with its auditorium, boxes, and orchestra pit, was the same set built for the 1925 version. • Director Arthur Lubin commented on star Claude Rains in Gregory Mank's book, *The Hollywood Hissables:* "Claude was a brilliant actor. For the scenes with the violin, he studied a week with a tutor; he studied a week or two so he could play a small portion of the piano concert; he was an astute actor." Lubin also commented on the toned-down (and disappointing) makeup: "However, he didn't want the public to see him when the mask was pulled off, because he felt it might ruin his status as a romantic leading man. He didn't want it to be horrible. We compromised, and cut it down to that one brief moment." • Leo Carrillo, who played Susanna Foster's singing instructor, was a former vaudeville and stage performer, and popular character actor who had a special gift for playing Latin comedy relief parts. He also co-starred in another "phantom" film, *Horror Island* (1941), as a peg-legged pirate searching for "Morgan's gold." • This celebrated remake received Academy Award nominations for Sound Recording, Musical Score, and won Oscars for Color Cinematography, and Color Art Direction. • This version of *Phantom of the Opera* featured a screen appearance by Fritz Leiber, Sr., whose son wrote the novel, *Conjure Wife,* which was the basis for the "Inner Sanctum" feature *Weird Woman* (1944), starring Lon Chaney, Jr.

Phantom of the Opera (1962; Hammer/ Universal; U.K.) D: Terence Fisher. P: Anthony Hinds. S: John Elder (Anthony

Lon Chaney, Sr., in all his ghastly glory, poses by a statue of Beethoven. Chaney employed some painful makeup tricks for his role as the Phantom of the Opera *(1925), including inserting celluloid disks inside his mouth to exaggerate his skull-like appearance with distended cheekbones.*

Hinds). C: Arthur Grant. Cast: Edward De Souza, Heather Sears, Herbert Lom, Michael Gough, Thorley Walters, Miles Malleson, Michael Ripper, Martin Miller. A small opera house is haunted by a phantom and his murderous assistant. Heather Sears plays the young singer the Phantom kidnaps and attempts to tutor. Herbert Lom plays the disfigured Phantom who was once a poor composer whose music was stolen by the opera's tyrannical director, Ambrose Darcy. In the end, the sympathetic Phantom is killed by a falling chandelier while rescuing Sears on stage. ¶ "When you sing, it will be only for me." • This version, the most romantic retelling of the famous story, was originally written for Cary Grant! "Cary Grant came to us and said he wanted to make a horror film," claimed producer/screenwriter Anthony Hinds in a *Fangoria* #74 interview. "The only thing we could think of was *Phantom of the Opera.* I knew he'd never make it, but he was insistent, so I wrote the thing for him. He was on vacation, and I knew that once he got back to the States his agent would tell him he couldn't make it. And that's what happened."

Phantom of the Opera (1983; TV movie) D: Robert Markowitz. P: Robet Halmi, Sr. S: Sherman Yellen. C: Larry Pizer. Cast: Maximilian Schell, Jane Seymour, Michael York, Jeremy Kemp, Diana Quick, Philip Stone, Paul Brooke. Maximilian Schell plays the mysterious Phantom obsessed with taking revenge on those who drove his young opera singer wife to suicide. He is distracted from his diabolical goal by an up-and-coming singer who resembles his dead wife. • This fourth version of the classic novel slighted author Gaston Leroux by giving him no credit for his timeless story. It was filmed on location in Budapest, Hungary.

Phantom of the Opera (1989; 21st Century Film Corp.) D: Dwight H. Little. P: Harry Alan Towers. S: Duke Sandefur. Cast: Robert Englund, Jill Schoelen, Alex Hyde-White, Bill Nighy, Terence Harvey, Stephanie Lawrence. Freddie (Robert Englund) goes to the Opera in this updated version of the Gaston Leroux story about a mutilated composer who destroys all obstacles in the path of a singer's rise to the top (including murdering her competition). • Director Dwight Little was no fan of the previous screen adaptations. "The only one with any appeal is the Lon Chaney version," he told *Fangoria* #88, "because of the sophistication of its film language for its time and the makeup effects that Chaney was able to achieve. But even that version is very long and dull in many places, so I'm not all that excited by any of the movie versions, although Chaney's Phantom was memorable." • Just like the previous Phantom film (the 1983 TV movie), this version was shot on location in Hungary. • This *Phantom* bombed at the box office. Star Robert Englund had a contract with 21st Century Film Corp. to do a sequel (titled *Phantom of Manhattan*). When this first film lost money, rather than make a sequel to an unsuccessful film, they created a whole new story and renamed it *Terror of Manhattan.* Chairman of the Board Menahem Golan explained in *Fangoria* #103, "Since *Phantom* didn't do too well at the box office theatrically, we decided not to do a sequel but to use the contract we had with Robert Englund and make a different picture. It's also the first horror picture to be shot in Russia." (*Terror of Manhattan* is as yet unreleased at presstime.)

Phantom of the Paradise (1974; 20th Century–Fox) D/S: Brian De Palma. P: Edward R. Pressman. C: Larry Pizer. Cast: Paul Williams, William Finley, Jessica Harper, George Memmoli, Gerrit Graham. This horror/comedy rock opera has a mysterious phantom haunting the nightclub called "The Paradise." • Paul Williams (who also starred in the film) received an Academy Award nomination for Best Original Song. • Director Brian De Palma (*Sisters,* 1972; *Carrie,* 1976; *The Fury,* 1978) said of this film, "I was trying to find a new way to enter the horror world. I felt the rock world was so stylized and expressionistic to begin with that it would be a perfect environment in which to tell old horror tales." • The company representing the rock group "Led Zeppelin" sued the makers of this picture because of their references to Swan Song Records. • *Phantom of the Paradise* paid homage to some of the great horror classics with references to films like *Frankenstein, The Picture of Dorian Gray,* and *The Cabinet of Dr. Caligari.*

Phantom of the Red House (1954; Chapultepec; Mexico) D: Miguel M. Delgado. S: R.Pl Pelaez. C: Raul Martinez Solares. Cast: Alma Rosa Aguirre, Raul Martinez, Che Reyes, Anthony Espino. A group of heirs kill each other off for the fortune hidden inside a spooky mansion. A masked villain is behind all the knifings.

Planet of the Apes Series

In 1968, one of the most popular science fiction features ever made was released by 20th Century–Fox. *Planet of the Apes,* in which astronaut Charlton Heston and companions journey to a planet where apes are the dominant species and humans are just mute animals, was much more than an exciting high tech space trek to a world-gone-mad. It brought a new evolutionary slant to cinematic sci-fi and added several painful twists to the cold approach taken by the scientific community towards animal behavioral research. Film audiences were afforded the opportunity to view a turning of the tables on mankind, and given a more humble perspective on how we fit into the ecosystem.

Along with its anthropological sensibilities, the picture touched on some popular themes of the time, such as the issues of personal liberty and freedom of speech. By depicting the established planetary hierarchy as being rigid, unyielding, and attempting to stifle new ideas and new thinking, the film struck a chord with the disgruntled youth of 1968. The right wing regressive old generation, personified by the character of Dr. Zaius, used ritualistic tradition to cloud the society's judgment by breeding fear and suspicion over what modern technology could (and as it turns out, *did*) do to the face of civilization.

This point was driven home at the powerful climax in which the Ape Planet is revealed to be our own Earth in the distant future. Here we realize that Heston's space expedition had broken not only the boundaries of space, but of time, opening the door to a whole new series of questions.

The open-ended possibilities of how Earth evolved to this state and the prospects of time travel ignited an imaginative fuse which led to the production of four sequels retracing the roots of the Planet of the Apes. The first sequel, far and away the best, added a new wrinkle by showing us what was left of the intelligent human race — a pitiful handful of mutants living in a sick society huddled *Beneath the Planet of the Apes*. James Franciscus followed the footsteps of Charlton Heston in a film which expanded upon the original by exposing how the decimated remnants of Earth's human society have come to worship that very thing which brought about their fall — the nuclear bomb.

Each subsequent sequel then began where the previous film left off. In the next three entries, the paradox of time travel was explored as Cornelius and Zira made their *Escape from the Planet of the Apes* to journey back in time to contemporary Earth. Their attempts to find peace and correct the destructive fate of man only brought about a quickened reoccurrence of the evolutionary cycle (in *Conquest of the Planet of the Apes*) and led to the final (unexciting) *Battle for the Planet of the Apes*.

Battle for the Planet of the Apes (1973; 20th Century-Fox) D: J. Lee Thompson. P: Arthur P. Jacobs. S: John William Corrington, Joyce Hooper Corrington. C: Richard H. Kline. Cast: Roddy McDowall, Claude Akins, Natalie Trundy, Severn Darden, Lew Ayres, John Huston. The fifth and final film in the series is actually a prequel to the original, telling the story of how after the nuclear holocaust the apes defeated man and became the dominant species. • The famous director (and sometimes actor) John Huston played an orangutan in this entry. • Lew Ayres (of *Donovan's Brain* fame) and singer/actor Paul Williams are also made to look like monkeys in this film. • Once again the star is Roddy McDowall, the only actor to participate in all five

"Planet of the Apes" entries. • This film was producer Arthur P. Jacobs's last film before he died. • John Landis, popular director and star of the ape film *Schlock* (1972), appeared as a human in this film. He said of his experience, "Before I was through with my part, though, I was thinking nostalgically of the days when I was portraying a Schlockthropus." He also said of the battle sequences, "When I got mixed up with the rebel gorillas, my scenes got pretty violent. They were jumping on me, stomping me, grabbing me by my long hair, and that was just in the rehearsals!"

Beneath the Planet of the Apes (1969; 20th Century-Fox) D: Ted Post. P: Arthur P. Jacobs. S: Paul Dehn, Mort Abrahams. C: Milton Krasner. Cast: James Franciscus,

Charlton Heston, Kim Hunter, Victor Buono, Maurice Evans, Jeff Corey, Roddy McDowall (voice only). Picking up where *Planet of the Apes* left off, this first sequel follows the wandering Charlton Heston's encounters with mutant humans who worship a doomsday bomb. James Franciscus is a fellow astronaut sent to rescue Heston and companions, who encounters the same time warp and lands on the "monkey planet." ¶ "The only good human is a dead human." • This entry was predominantly shot at a studio located at the Fox movie ranch in Malibu, while the desert sequences were filmed in Utah and Arizona. • John Chambers's makeup budget topped the one million dollar mark because of the large numbers of apemen and mutant humans. Chambers said, "We thought it would be easier the second time around, but there were new problems and situations no one anticipated." The acting conditions were terrible on location, with temperatures soaring over 100 degrees. The makeup for the gorilla actors had to be frequently taken off. "That desert heat is deadly to someone not wearing makeup! Imagine how you'd feel with another face on top of your own!" quipped Chambers. • Chambers said of the mutant makeup, "We had to determine what the appearance might be of a human being 2,000 years hence, centuries after the nuclear destruction of their ancestors' civilization, along with the effects of radiation fallout on intervening generations." • Gregory Sierra plays the friendly ape Cornelius this time, the part assayed by Roddy McDowall in the original. Roddy was busy directing another film *(Devil's Widow)* and so could not appear. However, he did lend his voice to the production, which was later dubbed over Sierra's. • Co-scripter Paul Dehn went on to write (on his own) the next two films in the series, *Escape...* and *Conquest....*

Conquest of the Planet of the Apes (1972; 20th Century–Fox) D: J. Lee Thompson. P: Arthur P. Jacobs. S: Paul Dehn. C: Bruce Surtees. Cast: Roddy McDowall, Don Murray, Natalie Trundy, Ricardo Montalban, Hari Rhodes, Severn Darden. In this fourth entry in the series, the talking ape Caesar (son of Zira and Cornelius of the previous film) leads the domesticated apes in a revolt against the humans. • Set in the near future, apes have replaced dogs and cats as pets (who were all wiped out by disease). • Roddy McDowall played the ape Cornelius in *Escape from the Planet of the Apes* and then played Caesar, Cornelius' son, in this film. • Actress Natalie Trundy is

the real-life wife of producer Arthur P. Jacobs.

Escape from the Planet of the Apes (1971; 20th Century–Fox) D: Don Taylor. P: Arthur P. Jacobs. S: Paul Dehn. C: Joseph Biroc. Cast: Roddy McDowall, Kim Hunter, Ricardo Montalban, Bradford Dillman, Eric Braeden, Natalie Trundy. In this third film in the series, Zira and Cornelius (the two friendly apes from the first two films) travel back through the time warp to present day, there to be met with suspicion and hostility, and ultimately their death ... but not before a son is born to carry on in *Conquest of the Planet of the Apes*. • *Escape* marks actor Sal Mineo's *(Rebel Without a Cause*, etc.) final film performance before his brutal murder in 1976. • Female lead Kim Hunter's real name is Janet Cole, and she appeared in Val Lewton's subtly effective devil-cult film, *The Seventh Victim* (1943). • Ricardo Montalban (of TV's "Fantasy Island" and "Cordoba" commercials fame) plays a sympathetic circus owner who helps the two fugitive apes.

Planet of the Apes (1968; 20th Century–Fox) D: Franklin J. Schaffner. P: Arthur P. Jacobs. S: Michael Wilson, Rod Serling. C: Leon Shamroy. Cast: Charlton Heston, Roddy McDowall, Kim Hunter, Maurice Evans, James Whitmore, James Daly, Linda Harrison, Lou Wagner, Woodrow Parfrey, Buck Kartalian, Robert Gunner, Jeff Burton, Norman Burton, Wright King, Paul Lambert. Astronauts travel to another planet where apes have evolved as the dominant species and humans are merely mute animals (of course, in the now-famous powerful final scene it is revealed that this planet is actually Earth in the future). ¶ "Man has no understanding. He can be taught a few simple tricks, nothing more." • The film is based on the novel, *The Monkey Planet* by Pierre Boulle (who also wrote *Bridge on the River Kwai*). • The script was co-written by six-time Emmy winner Rod Serling, of "Twilight Zone" fame. Serling, who was born on Christmas day, 1924, died at the age of 50 from a heart attack. • *Planet of the Apes* received two Academy Award nominations, for Best Original Score and Costume Design. • This film was so popular it spawned four sequels and a short-lived TV series (again starring Roddy McDowall). • Arthur P. Jacobs produced all five films in the series. • *Planet of the Apes* was shot mostly in and around the national parks of Utah and Arizona.

Earth astronaut Taylor (Charlton Heston) and his mute mate, Nova (Linda Harrison), are captured by a society of intelligent simians ruling the Planet of the Apes *(1968).*

Plants

Perhaps the most unlikely menace to be featured in a monster movie would be the vegetation which inhabits this planet. Our general perception of this vital life resource is that it consumes, grows, and dies without really knowing what it is doing.

We certainly don't view plants as thinking life forms. Yet a series of special features in the 1950s perked the public's interest in plants of an unusual nature (including the venus flytrap, which attracts, then devours, small insects), and the public's perception of plants began to perceptibly alter. The fantastique cinema first utilized this fright potential in 1946, when Gale Sondergaard fed the blood of victims to a hungry plant in *The Spider Woman Strikes Back*. Next came the appearance of an intelligent vegetable alien (jokingly referred to as a "super-carrot" in the film) menacing the world in *The Thing* (1951). There followed a flurry of fiendish foliage in the fifties, including the absurdly entertaining *From Hell It Came* (1957), *The* (sudsy) *Unknown Terror* (1957), and the offbeat British import, *The Woman Eater* (1959). Then in 1960, Roger Corman brought to the screen a horror satire which insured carnivorous plants a place in cinema posterity. *The Little Shop of Horrors* (a three-day wonder) fostered a whole forest of man-eating plant features (as well as an insipid musical remake in 1986), including the sobering 1963 near-classic, *Day of the Triffids* — arguably the best serious killer plant film to date.

Not all plant pictures followed the pattern set forth by the carnivorous man-eaters. Normally harmless tomatoes menaced mankind in *Attack of the Killer Tomatoes* (1978), while creeping vines went on a strangling spree in *Dr. Terror's House of Horrors* (1965). Then there are the mutated blendings of plants and people, such as *From Hell It Came* (1957) featuring the infamous "Tabonga," and *Mutations* (1972) which showed us the world's first venus flytrap–man. The atmospheric Japanese cult film, *Attack of the Mushroom People* (1963) saw shipwrecked survivors transformed into giant fungi; and in 1982, the plant kingdom spawned its own comic book super hero with *Swamp Thing*.

It would seem that most of the plant formulas have already sprouted and been fully harvested by movie makers, but so long as there are filmmakers willing to explore new possibilities, there is bound to be more promising plant pictures.

The Angry Red Planet (1960) (see MARS). A voyage to Mars reveals a three-eyed Martian, a bat-rat-spider monster, a giant blob, *and* a tendriled, carnivorous Martian plant.

Attack of the Killer Tomatoes (1978; NAI Entertainment D: John DeBello. P: Steve Peace, John De Bello. S: Costa Dillon. C: John K. Culley. Cast: David Miller, George Wilson, Sharon Taylor, Jack Riley, Rock Peace. In this weak sci-fi spoof, mutant tomatoes of all sizes take on a life of their own and attack San Diego. • The scene involving a helicopter crash (the only striking effect in the whole production) was unplanned — it was a real accident. • It took ten years for people to recover enough to stomach a sequel, *Return of the Killer Tomatoes* (1988).

Attack of the Mushroom People (1963; Toho; Japan) (also *Matango*). D: Inoshiro Honda, Eiji Tsuburaya. P: Tomoyuki Tanaka. S: Takeshi Kimura. C: Hajime Koizumi. Cast: Akira Kubo, Yoshio Tsuchiya, Kenji Sahara, Hiroshi Koizumi, Kumi Mizuno, Miki Yashiro, Hiroshi Tachikawa. The lone survivor from a stranded group of sailing vacationers tells the story of their

incredible experiences on an island laden with radioactive mushrooms. When eaten, these mushrooms transform people into walking fungus-monsters. ¶ "Matango, according to your understanding, means a person no longer human." • The woes of selfishness, greed, and temptation are explored in the story's theme, as we watch the dissenting crew gradually succumb to the weakness of the flesh and consume the dangerous mushrooms. • Director Inoshiro Honda is the same man who unleashed *Godzilla* (1954) and numerous seuqels on an unsuspecting movie-going population. • The grotesque mushroom monsters depicted in various stages of growth were furnished by effects man and co-director Eiji Tsuburaya.

Blood (1973; Bryanston Kent) D/S/C: Andy Milligan. P: Walter Kent. Cast: Allen Berendt, Hope Stansbury, Eve Crosby, Patti Gaul, Pamela Adams. The Wolf Man's son and Dracula's daughter marry and move to America to begin experimenting with carnivorous plants. • That one-man filmmaker from Staten Island, Andy Milligan, does it again, this time with a bigger budget than usual — the princely sum of $20,000.

One of the carnivorous plant monsters from The Day of the Triffids *(1963) gets a few finishing touches in this behind the scenes photo.*

Burnt Offerings (1976) (see WITCHES, WARLOCKS, AND CULTS). At one point, the beleaguered family tries to leave the evil house in which they are trapped by supernatural forces, but their exit is closed off by the vines and plants of the surrounding woods which seem to possess their own form of evil sentient life.

Creepshow (1982) (see ANTHOLOGIES). In the film's second segment, "The Lonesome Death of Jordie Verrell," a backwoods farmer cracks open a meteorite and as a result is transformed into a fungus/grass monster. • Screenwriter and famous horror author Stephen King stars as Jordie Verrell.

The Day of the Triffids (1963; Security

Paul Blaisdell is inside the absurd yet imaginative "Tabonga" tree-monster suit he built for From Hell It Came *(1957). In this scene, the avenging Tabonga tosses a native girl into the local quicksand pool, its favorite victim disposal site.*

Pictures/Allied Artists; U.K.) D: Steve Sekely. P: George Pitcher. S: Philip Yordan. C: Ted Moore. Cast: Howard Keel, Nicole Maurey, Janette Scott, Kieron Moore, Mervyn Johns, Alison Leggatt, Ewan Roberts, Janina Faye. A meteor shower blinds most of the Earth's population. The meteors also bring with them a plant spore which develops into huge deadly mobile plants (called "triffids") which move about, stinging people to death. ¶ "All plants move. [But] they don't usually pull themselves out of the ground and chase you!" • What is left of the human race is saved when it is discovered that the unstoppable triffids are attracted to sound and melt in salt water. • Star Howard Keel was so dissatisfied with Philip Yordan's script that he re-wrote most of his own dialogue. • Actors Janette Scott and Kieron Moore teamed up again for the world-threatening saga *Crack in the World* in 1965. • *The Day of the Triffids* is based on the novel of the same name by John Wyndham. • In the 1980s, *The Day of the Triffids* was remade into an engrossing, intelligent BBC television miniseries.

Dr. Terror's House of Horrors (1965) (see ANTHOLOGIES). In the "Creeping Vine" story, a man's house is engulfed by strangling vines which kill a colleague and the family dog.

The Evil Dead (1982) (see DEMONS AND DEVILS). During one particularly shocking scene, a woman trying to flee through the woods is raped by the possessed trees and vines around her.

From Hell It Came (1957; Allied Artists) D: Dan Milner. P: Jack Milner. S: Richard Bernstein. C: Brydon Baker. Cast: Tod Andrews, Tina Carver, Suzan Ridgway, Gregg Palmer, Robert Swan, Baynes Barron, Linda Watkins, John McNamara. On a Pacific island, nuclear scientists encounter a tree-monster lumbering about the island dropping the natives into quicksand. ¶ "I know, why don't we psychoanalyze the monster. Maybe its mother was scared by an oak tree." • Audiences were stumped as to the tree monster's origin. Radiation effects are alluded to, as are island superstitions. As legend has it, a warrior who is treacherously murdered may turn into a tree and avenge itself if buried upright in the hollow of a tree trunk. • The wooden acting of the "tabonga" (the titular tree monster) is credited to master makeup-effects man Paul Blaisdell, who also designed the monster suit. • Hero Tod ("If you people feel like chopping wood I don't mind a little exercise") Andrews stopped the lurching log when he shoots at the handle of a protruding dagger, driving it deep into the creature's heart and causing the terrible twig to topple backwards into the quicksand.

The Guardian (1990; Universal) D: William Friedkin. P: Joe Wizen. S: Stephen Volk, Dan Greenburg, William Friedkin. C: John A. Alonzo. Cast: Jenny Seagrove, Dwier Brown, Carey Lowell, Brad Hall, Miguel Ferrer, Natalia Nogulich, Pamela Brull, Gary Swanson. A professional babysitter turns out to be more than a yuppie family bargained for when she is revealed to be the human manifestation of an ancient druidic tree monster. She uses her powers to abduct newborn children in her charge and sacrifice them to the tree-creature in the forest. At the climax, while the wife battles the powerful tree-woman, the husband tackles the ancient tree itself with (what else) a chain saw. ¶ "For thousands of years, a religious order known as the Druids worshiped trees, sometimes even sacrificing human beings to them. To these worshipers, every tree has its guardian spirit. Most are aligned with goodness and life, but some embody powers of darkness and evil"—opening narration. • The huge tree-monster absorbs the souls of the infants to sustain its eternal life. Instead of sap, it contains blood, and it defends itself by decapitating and impaling people with its huge ambulatory limbs. • This is director/co-screenwriter William Friedkin's first horror movie in 17 years (since his film, *The Exorcist,* set a new standard for horror in 1973). • Author Dan Greenburg helped adapt his own story, "The Nanny," for the screenplay.

Konga (1961) (see APE GIANTS). Michael Gough experiments with a growth formula and inadvertently creates "Konga," a King Kong clone. He also experiments with plants and keeps a greenhouse full of the giant carnivorous variety, including a large venus flytrap which ends up grabbing and presumably (since we're never shown her fate) devouring the young heroine.

The Land Unknown (1957) (see DINOSAURS—LOST WORLDS). Hero Jock Mahoney must save heroine Shawn Smith from the clutches of a man-eating (or make that "woman-eating") prehistoric plant.

The Little Shop of Horrors (1960; Film-group) D/P: Roger Corman. S: Charles B. Griffith. C: Archie Dalzell. Cast: Jonathan Haze, Jackie Joseph, Mel Welles, Dick Miller, Myrtle Vail, Jack Nicholson. This black comedy features Jonathan Haze as a skid row errand boy named Seymour Krelboin, who must satisfy the bloodlust of his ever growing, ever hungry man-eating plant, dubbed "Audrey, Jr." ¶ "Feeeeeed Meeeee!"—Audrey, Jr. • The voice behind the hungry Audrey was none other than scriptwriter Charles B. Griffith, who appeared briefly as a dental patient as well. • Mel Welles, the actor who portrayed Mr. Mushnik, the flower shop owner, turned director for another killer plant movie, *Man-Eater of Hydra* (1966). • Oscar-winning Jack Nicholson (early in his career) had the small but amusing part of the masochistic Wilbur Folce, who just adores dental appointments. "Please, no novocaine, it dulls the senses." • "King of the quickies," Roger Corman, shot the film in only two days and one night. At the time, Jonathan Haze was said to have had a great deal of influence with Roger concerning actors and writers—as Jonathan put it—"because he didn't know anything." • *The Passionate People Eater* was the film's original title.

The Little Shop of Horrors (1986; The Geffen Co.) D: Frank Oz. P: David Geffen. S: Howard Ashman. Cast: Rick Moranis, Ellen Greene, Vincent Gardenia, Steve Martin, James Belushi, John Candy, Christopher Guest, Bill Murray. In this musical remake of Roger Corman's 1960 low-budget comedy classic, a flower-shop flunky finds a one-of-a-kind plant that grows to enormous size, talks (and sings), and eats people. • This version was based on the off-Broadway musical (which in turn was based on the Roger Corman film). Female lead Ellen Greene reprises her role from the play. • This time, instead of the aggressive man-eating plant being named "Audrey, Jr.," as in the first film, the vociferous plant is named "Audrey 2" (in a nod to today's sequelitis numbering system?). • Levi Stubbs, former singer for The Four Tops, was the voice of Audrey 2. • *The Little Shop of Horrors* was nominated for two Academy Awards—Best Visual Effects and Best Original Song ("Mean Green Mother from Outer Space"). It didn't win in either category.

The Lost Continent (1968) (see CRABS AND CRUSTACEANS). A cargo ship drifts into uncharted waters inhabited by Spanish conquistadores, giant prehistoric crabs, and killer seaweed (which holds the ship fast and menaces the passengers).

Man-Eater of Hydra (1966; Allied Artists; Spain/W. Germany) (also *Island of the Doomed*). D: Ernest Von Theumer (Mel Welles). P: George Ferrer. S: Stephen Schmidt, Ira Meltcher. C: Cecilio Paniagua. Cast: Cameron Mitchell, Elisa Montes, George Martin, Kay Fisher, Rolf V. Naukoff, Matilde Munoz. On his own private island, Cameron Mitchell creates new species of plant life, including a large tree which wraps its tendrils around its victims and sucks out their blood. • The vampiric tree was a mechanical construction costing a whopping $30,000. "And then it didn't work," complained director Mel Welles. "So we wound up using the old-fashioned trick of pulling the branches with wires" (*Fangoria* #58). • Actor/filmmaker Mel Welles directed using the pseudonym "Ernest Von Theumer" because of "government technicalities." The name was actually that of the film's German associate producer.

Mutations (1972) (see FREAKS) (also *Freakmaker*). Donald Pleasence is a mad scientist experimenting on combining plant life with humans. He succeeds — sort of — and we have the world's first venus flytrap–man.

The Navy vs. the Night Monsters (1965; Standard Club of California/Realart) (also *Monsters of the Night*). D/S: Michael Hoey. P: George Edwards. C: Stanley Cortez. Cast: Mamie Van Doren, Anthony Eisley, Pamela Mason, Bill Gray, Bobby Van, Walter Sande. Primitive man-eating plants are found in Antarctica and shipped to a U.S. naval base on Gow Island in the South Seas. There they flourish and go on a rampage, moving about to eat as many cast members as they can lay their tendrils on. ¶ "Gow Island, in the past virtually unknown to the rest of the world, today a famous landmark in Man's struggle with the unknown, another step forward in the march of science"—narrator. • *The Night Crawlers* was the film's shooting title. It was released as *Monsters of the Night* in the United Kingdom. • Blonde bombshell Mamie Van Doren, a low-budget Marilyn Monroe, stars as the imperiled heroine everyone wants to save. • According to actor Anthony Eisley, the film was ruined by some severe tampering which took place after principal photography was completed. "The producer recut that picture after it was made," Eisley told Tom Weaver in a *Fangoria* #66 interview, "and he totally destroyed any validity it might have had. Months after the picture was shut down, the producer put in this stupid stock footage of bombers blowing up the island at the end and shot these monoto-

nous talking scenes of generals on the telephone that were not at all germane to the original story." • *The Navy vs. the Night Monsters* is based on the novel *The Earth's End*, by Murray Leinster.

Please Don't Eat My Mother (1972; Boxoffice International) (also *Please Not My Mother*). D/P: Carl Monson. S: Eric Norden, Dee Drew. C: Jack Beckett. Cast: Rene Bond, Buck Kartalian, Flora Wisel, Alicia Friedland, David Curtis, Adam Blari, Lyn Lundgren. In this truly abysmal adults-only uncredited remake of Roger Corman's horror/comedy, *The Little Shop of Horrors* (1960), a peeping tom finds a strange carnivorous plant which grows to gigantic proportions and develops a taste for human flesh. ¶ "Frogs dear boy. Oh Henry, Henry hit me, hit me with one, c'mon baby!"—Henry is a hungry "female" plant.

Poltergeist (1982) (see GHOSTS). Among the many frightening supernatural happenings, a young boy is grabbed and nearly eaten by the large tree outside his bedroom window.

Return of Swamp Thing (1989; Light Years Entertainment) D: Jim Wynorski. P: Michael E. Uslow. S: Derek Spencer, Grant Morris. C: Zoran Hochstatter. Cast: Louis Jourdan, Heather Locklear, Sarah Douglas, Dick Durock. In this sequel to *Swamp Thing,* the big plant-man hero is back to fight the evil Louis Jourdan again and save heroine Heather Locklear. ¶ "When I look at you, you know what I see? The soul of a beautiful human being." • In an interview for *HorrorFan* #2, director Jim Wynorski applied this amusing analogy to his movie: "This kind of film is like a Twinkie. You can eat one just about any time of the day or night. It doesn't sit in your stomach and it's real enjoyable while you're downing it." (Of course he failed to mention that a Twinkie is actually just bad junk food.)

Return of the Killer Tomatoes (1988; New World) D: John DeBello. P: J. Stephen Peace. S: Constantine Dillon, J. Stephen Peace. C: Steven Kent Welch. Cast: Anthony Starke, George Clooney, Karen Mistal, Steve Lindquist, Charlie Jones, John Astin. In this superior follow-up to *Attack of the Killer Tomatoes* (1978), mad scientist John Astin transforms innocent tomatoes into zombie commandos and sends them out to conquer the world. ¶ "Tomatoes are evil! A good tomato is a *squashed* tomato!" • "They were out for blood and rotten to the core. Now they're back ... the Vegetables of Doom!" This ad slogan set the tone for the entire film. • Director John DeBello and producer J. Stephen Peace were responsible for the first film as well. • John Astin, the head of TV's "The Addams Family," played Professor Gangrene, the man behind the *Return of the Killer Tomatoes.*

The Revenge of the Teenage Vixens from Outer Space (1985) (see ALIENS — INVADERS ON EARTH: THE 80s AND BEYOND). In this no-budget sci-fi comedy, a group of attractive alien invaders use their zap guns to turn the local male teen population into giant vegetables (carrot, pickles, etc.) when the youths prove inadequate for their needs.

Seeds of Evil (1974; KKI Films) (also *The Gardener*). D/S: Jim Kay. P: Tony Belletier. C: Michael Zingale. Cast: Katharine Houghton, Joe Dallesandro, Rita Gam, James Congdon, Theodorina Bello. Joe Dallesandro plays a gardener cultivating killer plants who eventually turns into a tree himself. ¶ "Garden of *Love* . . . Garden of *Death* . . . He plants the *Seeds of Evil*" — poster ad line. • Ex-Warhol actor Joe Dallesandro starred in both *Andy Warhol's Dracula* and *Andy Warhol's Frankenstein* earlier this same year. • Heroine Katharine Houghton is best remembered as Sidney Poitier's love interest (and Katharine Hepburn and Spencer Tracy's daughter) in *Guess Who's Coming to Dinner* (1967).

The Spider Woman Strikes Back (1946; Universal) D: Arthur Lubin. P: Howard Welsch. S: Eric Taylor. C: Paul Ivano. Cast: Gale Sondergaard, Brenda Joyce, Kirby Grant, Rondo Hatton, Milburn Stone, Hobart Cavanaugh, Tom Daly. Despite the title, the focus is not on spiders but on carnivorous plants grown by the evil Gale Sondergaard, to which she feeds the blood of young girls. ¶ "With your own strength you've made it strong. You're going to die, Jean, like the others. But it won't really be dying, because you'll live on in this beautiful plant." • Gale Sondergaard played the title villainess in the Sherlock Holmes film *The Spider Woman* (1944), and Universal decided to capitalize on that film's success by using the same name and the same actress, while foregoing the continuity of the character. They had intended to create a series of Spider Woman pictures with Sondergaard, but no others ever materialized. • Sondergaard's assistant was played by Rondo Hatton, whose distorted visage was the result of the real-life disease, acromegaly. Hatton was also fresh from a Sherlock Holmes film — *The Pearl of Death* (1944), in which he played the "Hoxton Creeper." • The basement lab set is the same one used in *Werewolf of London* (1935).

Swamp Thing (1982; Embassy) D/S: Wes Craven. P: Benjamin Melniker, Michael E. Uslan. C: Robin Goodwin. Cast: Louis Jourdan, Adrienne Barbeau, Ray Wise, Dick Durock, David Hess. A scientist's formula changes him into a half-man, half-plant monster who heals with his touch and fights bad buys. • Adrienne Barbeau, director John Carpenter's (*Halloween,* 1978) wife, plays a government agent, while stunt-man Dick Durock takes over for actor Ray Wise after he is transformed into the powerful Swamp Thing.

Tales That Witness Madness (1973) (see ANTHOLOGIES). In the segment titled "Mel," Joan Collins must battle a living tree for the love of her husband.

The Twilight People (1972) (see MAD SCIENTISTS). On a remote island, a mad scientist creates various animal-monsters, and one very strange looking tree-woman.

The Unknown Terror (1957; Lippert) D: Charles Marquis Warren. P: Robert Stabler. S: Kenneth Higgins. C: Joseph Biroc. Cast: John Howard, Mala Powers, Paul Richards, May Wynn, Gerald Milton, Duane Gray. A jungle expedition encounters a mysterious cave occupied by a deadly living fungus cultivated by mad scientist Dr. Ramsey. Ramsey transforms the local natives into fungus monsters. ¶ "We can't let it out. We've got to seal it in this cave, otherwise it'll destroy the world." • The horrible fungus monsters are simply actors covered with unconvincing soap suds. • *The Unknown Terror* features a calypso singer named Sir Lancelot who performs his own song. Sir Lancelot had previously appeared in two Val Lewton classics of the 1940s — *I Walked with a Zombie* and *Curse of the Cat People.*

Untamed Women (1952) (see DINOSAURS — LOST WORLDS). A pilot is rescued by Naval authorities and tells of his lost world adventure on an island inhabited by a tribe of "untamed" beauties, savage "hairy men," and dinosaurs. In addition to the woolly mammoths, giant armadillos, and dressed-up lizards which menace the cast, they run across a variety of man-eating plants.

Voodoo Island (1957) (see VOODOO). On a remote island lorded over by a tribe of voodoo practitioners, Boris Karloff and party encounter several varieties of man-eating plants. ¶ "What are we supposed to do, wait around till it gets to be their meal time?"

The Woman Eater (1959; Columbia; U.K.) (also *Womaneater*). D: Charles Saunders. P: Guido Coen. S: Brandon Fleming.

C: Ernest Palmer. Cast: George Coulouris, Vera Day, Peter Wayn, Joyce Gregg, Joy Webster, Jimmy Vaughan, Sara Leighton, Maxwell Foster, Marpessa Dawn. A scientist brings back a carnivorous tree from the Amazon jungle which eats only buxom young women (or at least that's all mad scientist George Coulouris feeds it). This tree then excretes a special serum which Coulouris hopes to use to revive the dead. ¶ "She'll become part of the plant. And from it I'll get the serum to bring the dead back to life. She won't have died in vain." • In Britain they shortened the two-word title to just one word — *Womaneater.*

Poe Films

Edgar Allan Poe, the foremost author of the macabre, has held a deep fascination for filmmakers throughout the years. The themes of madness, torture, and death which permeate his work lend themselves well to horror cinema, and producers were quick to exploit this.

Unfortunately, Poe's nineteenth century literary style, coupled with the often sketchy plot lines of his short stories, made his work difficult to adapt into a full-length feature film. Therefore, screenwriters often had to invent their own storylines while trying to retain the essence of Poe's work. One of the earliest and best examples is Universal's classic 1934 version of *The Black Cat,* starring Boris Karloff and Bela Lugosi (the first time these "Two Titans of Terror" were united on the screen). Though the film had little to do with Poe's wonderful story, it follows the spirit of Poe admirably.

Other Poe adaptations did not come off as well, with the filmmakers sometimes taking nothing but the title from Poe in an attempt to cash in on his still bankable name (the tepid 1941 version of *The Black Cat,* again by Universal, being a prime example).

Over the first 30 years of sound cinema, there were scarcely more than a half dozen films produced based on Poe's works. Still, this was fairly respectable for an author who had been dead for nearly 100 years. But then in 1960 Roger Corman broke out of his "B" movie mold and produced/directed *House of Usher* in living color for AIP. The lurid color, star Vincent Price's understated portrayal of madness, and Corman's fluid direction, coupled with Poe's classic themes (madness, premature burial, and decay) struck a chord with critics and moviegoers alike. The movie's success caused Corman to make a string of Poe films for AIP, utilizing and building upon many of Poe's classic stories.

The last 30 years have yielded still more Poe adaptations which have cropped up at regular intervals, though more often than not producers have simply borrowed Poe's name and skipped the stories. There have even been several films that have featured Edgar Allan Poe himself as a character (*Castle of Blood,* 1964; *The Spectre of Edgar Allan Poe,* 1974; etc.).

Recently, there seems to be a Poe renaissance looming upon the celluloid horizon, with a remake of *Masque of the Red Death* (1989), the "Poe-inspired" *Buried Alive* (1989), and the upcoming Poe features in progress — *Two Evil Eyes* (by two of the modern masters of horror, George Romero and Dario Argento), Stuart *(Re-Animator)* Gordon's remake of *The Pit and the Pendulum,* and producer Harry Alan Towers's remake of *House of Usher.*

Early Poe

The Black Cat (1934; Universal) (also *The Vanishing Body*). D: Edgar G. Ulmer. P: E. M. Asher. S: Peter Ruric. C: John J. Mescall. Cast: Boris Karloff, Bela Lugosi, David Manners, Jacqueline Wells, Lucille Lund, Egon Brecher, Harry Cording, Henry Armetta, Albert Conti. In the wake of a road accident a honeymooning couple end up at the fortress-like home of satanist Hjalmar Poelzig (Boris Karloff). With them is Dr. Vitus Werdegast, a long-standing enemy who has come seeking revenge on Poelzig. Poelzig had sold Fort Marmorus to the Russians toward the end of World War I and as a result, Werdegast was taken prisoner and his wife and daughter were taken by Poelzig. Poelzig holds a black mass ceremony at the "dark of the moon" and plans to offer up the young bride as a human sacrifice. The two adversaries face off against each other in a deadly cat and mouse game, with the innocent couple caught in the middle. ¶ "You say your soul was killed, that you have been dead all these years. And what of me? Did we not both die here in Marmorus fifteen years ago? Are we any the less victims of the war than those whose bodies were torn asunder? Are we not *both* the living dead?" • Though "suggested by the immortal Edgar Allan Poe classic" the story is far from the letter of Poe, but the film's mood and brooding intensity are close to the *spirit* of Poe. To nominally justify the title, Karloff keeps a black cat on hand ("the symbol of evil") and Lugosi is intensely afraid of cats. • This is the first teaming of those two titans of terror—Boris Karloff and Bela Lugosi (they appeared jointly in a total of seven films). • For the first time in his career, Boris Karloff was given the ultimate honor of being billed by surname alone—simply as *Karloff*. As well as being top billed, Karloff earned nearly twice the salary of Lugosi, $1,850 per week for Karloff vs. $1,000 per week for Lugosi. • Bela Lugosi, whose character has an "intense and all-consuming horror of cats" in the film, shared his character's fear in real life. According to Hope Lugosi, his fifth wife, "he was afraid of cats. He hated them." • The character of Hjalmar Poelzig was fashioned by Edgar Ulmer (who shared story credit with Peter Ruric) after the infamous Aleister Crowley, a real-life satanist labeled by the sensational press of the day as "the Wickedest Man in the World." • Among the crowd of devil-worshipers who gather at Poelzig's house is John Peter Richmond, later known as John Carradine (he plays the organ). • In the United Kingdom, the film's title was changed to *The House of Doom*.

The Black Cat (1941; Universal) D: Albert S. Rogell. P: Burt Kelly. S: Robert Lees, Frederic I. Rinaldo, Eric Taylor, Robert Neville. C: Stanley Cortez. Cast: Basil Rathbone, Hugh Herbert, Broderick Crawford, Bela Lugosi, Gale Sondergaard, Anne Gwynne, Gladys Cooper, Cecilia Loftus, Claire Dodd, John Eldredge, Alan Ladd. An eccentric spinster who loves cats is taken ill and her greedy relatives gather at her death bed. She recovers, however, but is promptly murdered in this mystery thriller that has little to do with Poe and nothing to do with Universal's earlier film, *The Black Cat* (1934). • The one nod to Poe comes at the climax, in which the whereabouts of the endangered heroine is given away by the wailing of a black cat (just as the dead body is revealed in Poe's original story). • Richard Carlson, later to become popular in 50s sci-fi hits like *Creature from the Black Lagoon* (1954), was originally to have played the romantic lead (a role which ultimately went to Broderick Crawford). • Bela Lugosi, wasted here in the small red-herring role of "Eduardo" the gardener, starred in two previous Poe pictures— *Murders in the Rue Morgue* (1932) and Universal's earlier like-titled film, *The Black Cat* (1934). • Marlene Dietrich appears in *The Black Cat* (or at least her back does). According to Universal historian Michael Fitzgerald, Dietrich, who was dating Broderick Crawford at the time, was a frequent set visitor to *The Black Cat*. For one non-dialogue scene, Dietrich, with her back to the camera, stood in for Claire Dodd, who had already left for the day.

The Crime of Dr. Crespi (1935; Republic) D/P: John H. Auer. S: Lewis Graham, Edwin Olmstead. C: Larry Williams. Cast: Erich von Stroheim, Harriet Russell, Dwight Frye, Paul Guilfoyle, John Bohn, Geraldine Kay, Jeanne Kelly, Patsy Berlin, Joe Verdi, Dean Raymond, Edward Van Sloan. Erich von Stroheim plays a surgeon who is mad for vengeance against the man who married the woman he loves. When the man needs an operation, von Stroheim administers a drug which causes him to appear dead. Buried alive, the man is rescued by two colleagues and wanders the hospital as a ghostly figure, eventually driving von Stroheim to commit suicide. ¶ "Your eyes open and you can see, you can hear everything. And here you lie,

Hjalmar Poelzig (Boris Karloff), high priest of a satanic cult, sits upon the neo-expressionistic sets developed by Charles Hall and director Edgar G. Ulmer for The Black Cat *(1934).*

helpless, paralyzed, unable to shield yourself. And you wonder why." • The credits read: "Suggested by Edgar Allen Poe's 'The Premature Burial.'" Republic misspelled the famous author's name here—it should be Allan. • This was Erich von Stroheim's first horror film, and he was generally well-received by the critics. The *Hollywood Reporter* said that he "out-Karloffs Karloff without a makeup," and gives "such a cruel, cold, malignant and malevolent portrayal of a fiend in human flesh, that one gets an insane urge to up and let him have it."

The Fall of the House of Usher (1928; Jean Epstein Films; France) D/P/S: Jean Epstein. C: Georges Lucas, Jean Lucas. Cast: Margaret Gance, Jean Debucourt, Charles Lamy, Abel Gance. In this early French version of the classic Poe story, Roderick and Madeline Usher are not brother and sister as in Poe's tales, but husband and wife. He is painting a portrait of his wife — who weakens as the work progresses. Finally she dies, only to come back just in time to rescue Roderick from the fiery destruction of the house.

The Fall of the House of Usher (1948; G.I.B. Productions; U.K.) D/C: Ivan Barnett. P: L. Barry Bernard, Arthur Manson. S: Dorothy Cat, Kenneth Thompson. Cast: Gwendoline Watford, Kaye Tendeter, Irving Steen. This slow, stodgy, yet at times gruesome adaptation of Poe's story of the doomed House of Usher centers around Roderick and Madeline Usher, brother and sister, who live under a curse. The curse was placed upon them by their mother's secret lover, who was found out and decapitated years earlier by their father. Their mother, driven mad by this horrible event, now stands guard over her lover's head at an old temple on the edge of the estate. The only way to break the curse (that the two siblings shall not reach the age of 30) is to burn the head. After an attempt fails, Madeline dies, though she returns from the tomb, apparently buried alive ... or is her appearance simply all in the now-mad mind of the tormented Roderick? ¶ "She's alive I tell you! We have put her living in the tomb! I tell you I heard her first feeble movements in the hollow coffin many hours ago!"

The Living Dead (1932; Roto Film; Germany) (also *Extraordinary Tales*). D: Richard Oswald. P: Gabriel Pascal. S: Heinz Goldbert, Eugen Szatmari. C: Heinrich Gaertner. Cast: Paul Wegener, Harald Paulsen, Bert Reisfeld, Roma Bahn, Mary Parker. In this early German anthology film, five comedic tales are told, including one amusing story derived from combining the two Poe stories, "The System of Dr. Tarr and Professor Fether" and "The Black Cat." • This is a comedic remake of director Richard Oswald's own silent film, *Tales of the Uncanny* (1919). • Star Paul Wegener is best remembered as the man behind the makeup of *The Golem* (both the 1917 and 1921 versions).

Maniac (1934) (see MADMEN — EARLY MADMEN). This early grind-house exploitationer about a madman who impersonates a doctor in order to commit rape and murder takes its ending (without giving credit) from Poe's "The Black Cat." After gouging out the eye of a black cat (just as in Poe's story — though the film makes it even more distasteful by having him pop the eyeball into his mouth and eat it!), the madman walls up a victim and inadvertently walls up the cat with it, whose yowling eventually gives the crime away.

Murders in the Rue Morgue (1932; Universal) D: Robert Florey. P: Carl Laemmle, Jr. S: Tom Reed, Dale Van Every. C: Karl Freund. Cast: Sidney Fox, Bela Lugosi, Leon Waycoff, Bert Roach, Betsy Ross Clarke, Brandon Hurst, D'Arcy Corrigan, Noble Johnson, Arlene Francis. Bela Lugosi plays Dr. Mirakle, a side-show exhibitor and mad scientist who injects women with ape blood in order to prove some pet theory of evolution (there is also the implication of an unholy mating of the two species as well). To this end he sends Erik the ape out to kidnap the heroine, only to have the beast turn on him in the end. ¶ "Only Poe dared imagine it! Only people who can stand excitement and shock should dare to see it!" — advertising trailer. • *Murders in the Rue Morgue* was the consolation prize Universal awarded director Robert Florey when James Whale took *Frankenstein* away from him. Florey had been set to direct *Frankenstein*, and had even done his own script and storyboards for the project. • When the picture's budget was cut from $130,000 to a mere $90,000, Florey stalked off the picture. He soon returned, however, and the film eventually came in with a budget of $186,000. • Robert Florey said of Bela Lugosi: "It was at times difficult to control his tendency to chew the scenery." • Leon Ames made his film debut under his real name of Leon Waycoff. He later talked about his debut (in the fan magazine *Famous Monsters of Filmland*), calling it "a perfectly awful film which still pops up on TV to haunt me!" • John Huston, later to become famous as one of America's leading directors, received an "Additional Dialogue" credit on this film. • Statuesque black actor Noble Johnson (*King Kong; Son of Kong*, both 1933) appears in the film (wearing white-face) as the sadistic servant Janos. • Bette Davis was considered, but dropped, for the female lead.

The Raven (1935; Universal) D: Louis Friedlander (later Lew Landers). P: David

A disfigured, unwilling servant (Boris Karloff) turns the tables on his mad, Poe-obsessed master (Bela Lugosi) during The Raven *(1935). There is a swinging razor-sharp pendulum suspended above the table to which Lugosi is strapped.*

Diamond. S: David Boehm. C: Charles Stumar. Cast: Boris Karloff, Bela Lugosi, Irene Ware, Lester Matthews, Samuel S. Hinds, Inez Courtney, Ian Wolfe, Spencer Charters, Maidel Turner, Arthur Hoyt. "When a man of genius is denied of his great love he goes mad. His brain, instead of being clear to do his work, is tortured. So he begins to *think* of torture." This is the basic plot of *The Raven*. Lugosi plays the brilliant Dr. Vollin, a man obsessed with Poe. His masterful surgery saves the life of a young dancer, whom he subsequently falls madly in love with. When the girl and her father spurn him, Vollin blackmails an escaped criminal named Edward Bateman (Karloff) into helping him torture those who stand in his way. ¶ "What torture, what a delicious torture, Bateman. Greater than Poe! Poe only conceived it, I have *done* it, Bateman. Poe, you are avenged!"—a raving Bela Lugosi. • *The Raven* is suggested by the poem "The Raven" and the tale "The Pit and the Pendulum" by Edgar Allan Poe. Vollin has created a torture chamber in his basement, building many of the devices from Poe's stories, including the deadly Pendulum. • With its themes of lust, sadism, and torture, *The Raven* was a major con-tributor to the banning of horror films in England (which contributed to a cessation of horror production in Hollywood for two years!). • Though Lugosi has the starring role and almost double the screen time of Karloff, Karloff was given top billing and twice the salary ($5,000 for Lugosi, $10,000 for Karloff). • In a curiously careless error, Universal mistakenly switched the names of two actors in the film's credits. The tall, gaunt Ian Wolfe played "Geoffrey" in the film, whereas the short, corpulent actor Spencer Charters played "Colonel Bertram Grant." The credits, however, listed Wolfe as "Colonel Grant" and Charters as "Geoffrey."

Tales of the Uncanny (1919; Richard Oswald Film; Germany) D/P: Richard Oswald. S: Richard Oswald, Robert Leibman. C: Carl Hoffman. Cast: Conrad Veidt, Anita Berber, Reinhold Schuenzel, Georg John, Hugo Doeblin. This anthology film features one "tale of mystery and horror" by Edgar Allan Poe—a story which combines "The Black Cat" with "The System of Dr. Tarr and Professor Fether." • Richard Oswald remade the same film with sound (and with a comedic bent) in 1932 as *The Living Dead*.

The Corman Cycle

The Haunted Palace (1963) (see WITCHES, WARLOCKS, AND CULTS). Vincent Price plays Charles Dexter Ward, the great-great grandson of warlock Joseph Curwen. Price returns to his ancestral village and is taken over by the spirit of his evil ancestor. The possessed Price uses his dark powers to take revenge on the descendants of the villagers who had burned him at the stake over 100 years before. • Though touted by AIP as another entry in Corman's "Poe" cycle, the film is actually based on an H. P. Lovecraft story, "The Case of Charles Dexter Ward." The studio erroneously claimed that *The Haunted Palace* is based on a story by Poe. The title (and nothing else) is actually taken from one of Poe's *poems*.

House of Usher (1960; AIP) D/P: Roger Corman. S: Richard Matheson. C: Floyd Crosby. Cast: Vincent Price, Mark Damon, Myrna Fahey, Harry Ellerbe, Bill Borzage, Mike Jordon, Nadajan, Ruth Oklander, George Paul, David Andar. A young man arrives unexpectedly at the Usher estate to see his fiancée, Madeline Usher. There he finds Roderick Usher, Madeline's brother, who tells him his beloved is dying, tainted with madness. Madeline dies and is placed in the family tomb. But Madeline was only in a cataleptic trance, and she escapes her coffin. Now completely mad, she attacks her brother and they both go up in flames as the house burns to the ground while her suitor looks on in horror. ¶ "The house lives! The house breathes!" • This was the first of the Corman Poe films and was a great critical and financial success (bringing in over $1,000,000 initially with only $270,000 in production costs). Its success led to the follow-up film, *The Pit and the Pendulum* (1961), and their successors. • In Roger Corman's autobiography, *How I Made a Hundred Movies in Hollywood and Never Lost a Dime,* he reveals how he achieved the decayed and burned-out look for his exterior shots of the landscape. "As 'luck' would have it, there was a forest fire in the Hollywood Hills just as we were going into production.... The next day I went out to the hills with a skeleton crew, the second male lead, Mark Damon, and a horse. It was great. The ground was gray with ash; the trees were charred and black. And we threw a little fog in to add some effect.... This was a great instance of being fast on your feet — a forest fire that had wrecked people's homes and the hills had provided a wonderful opening sequence." • Corman also revealed how he got the wonderful conflagration at the film's end when the house goes up in flames: "Just by chance, we located an old barn out in Orange County that was going to be demolished by developers. We asked the owner: 'Instead of demolishing it, how would you like to burn it down? But burn it down at night and I'll be out there with $50 and two cameras rolling.'" Corman re-used the impressive shots of burning rafters he took that night in several other of his Poe films as well.

The Masque of the Red Death (1964; AIP) D/P: Roger Corman. S: Charles Beaumont, R. Wright Campbell. C: Nicholas Roeg. Cast: Vincent Price, Hazel Court, Jane Asher, David Weston, Patrick Magee, Nigel Green, Skip Martin, John Westbrook, Gay Brown, Julian Burton, Verina Greenlaw. Prince Prospero, a cruel devil-worshiping prince, locks himself and his guests inside his castle to avoid a plague — the dreaded "Red Death." For entertainment he humiliates his guests and attempts to corrupt an innocent village girl. When he holds a masked ball, a mysterious figure dressed all in red arrives — it is the Red Death himself. ¶ "Each man creates his own heaven and his own hell." • A subplot involving a dwarf who takes murderous revenge on a nobleman is derived from another Poe story, "Hop Toad." • Roger Corman himself has called this "the biggest and best-looking of the Poe films" (in *The Films of Roger Corman,* by Ed Naha). It is generally considered to be the pinnacle of the series. • *The Masque of the Red Death* is star Vincent Price's personal favorite of all his Poe films. He starred in seven of the eight entries in Corman's series. • Nicholas Roeg's striking cinematography has often garnered critical acclaim. Roeg went on to become a respected director on such films as *Don't Look Now* (1973) and *The Man Who Fell to Earth* (1976). • For *Masque,* Corman went to England to shoot, and was able to utilize some of the standing sets from the big-budgeted film, *Becket* (1964), to give his movie a grander scale. • Paul McCartney paid a visit to *Masque.* He was currently dating Corman's leading lady, Jane Asher, and she brought him to the set one day, since he had never been on a movie set before.

The Pit and the Pendulum (1961; AIP) D/P: Roger Corman. S: Richard Matheson. C: Floyd Crosby. Cast: Vincent Price, John Kerr, Barbara Steele, Luana Anders, Antony Carbone, Patrick Westwood, Lynne

Bernay, Larry Turner, Mary Menzies, Charles Victor. In sixteenth century Spain, Vincent Price plays a man tormented by the manifestations of the wife (Barbara Steele) he thought he had accidentally buried alive. She is not dead, however, and plots with her lover to drive Price over the edge of sanity. The plot works all too well when the once kindly Price takes on the persona of his sadistic father, a grand inquisitor, and puts to use the implements of torture in the castle dungeon (including the dreaded pit . . . and the horrific pendulum). ¶ "Do you know where you are, Bartholome? I will tell you where you are. You are about to enter *Hell,* Bartholome — the netherworld, the infernal regions, the abode of the damned, the place of torment, Pandemonium, Shabbat, Gahen, Narakka, the *Pit!* . . . and the pendulum." • This is the second film in Corman's Poe series and was even more successful at the box office than its predecessor, *House of Usher* (1960). *Pit* cleared over two million in film rentals with a production cost of only $200,000. • Critically, it was a success as well. For example, Howard Thompson of *The New York Times* called it "Hollywood's most effective Poe-style horror flavoring to date."

The Premature Burial (1962; AIP) D/P: Roger Corman. S: Charles Beaumont, Ray Russell. C: Floyd Crosby. Cast: Ray Milland, Hazel Court, Richard Ney, Heather Angel, Alan Napier, John Dierkes, Richard Miller, Brendan Dillon. Ray Milland plays a man deathly afraid of being buried alive. In anticipation of this he builds a special mausoleum equipped with all manner of escape devices. When Milland is confronted with his father's skeleton and realizes his own father was buried alive, he succumbs to a heart attack. His new wife buries him not in the special vault but in an ordinary grave. Milland is not dead, however, and when two graverobbers dig him up, they find a dangerous *living* corpse. Unhinged, Milland seeks vengeance on those who buried him. ¶ From the lurid British poster: *"It's going to happen! You are there in sudden darkness when the heartbeat starts . . . will you be the first to crack?"* • This third Poe film by Corman is the only one *not* to star Vincent Price (Ray Milland plays the lead).

The Raven (1963; AIP) D/P: Roger Corman. S: Richard Matheson. C: Floyd Crosby. Cast: Vincent Price, Peter Lorre, Boris Karloff, Hazel Court, Olive Sturgess, Jack Nicholson, Connie Wallace, William Baskin, Aaron Saxon. This light-hearted comedy features Vincent Price, Peter Lorre, and

Boris Karloff as sixteenth century magicians who face off against one another, with Price's scheming wife Lenore, thought dead, inciting all the magical machinations. To justify the title, *The Raven* starts out with Price reciting passages of the famous poem only to be interrupted by the bird itself. The bird is actually Peter Lorre, whom Karloff had transformed into a raven in a fit of magician's pique. ¶ Vincent Price: "Are you some dark winged messenger from beyond? Answer me monster, shall I ever hold again that radiant maiden whom the angels call Lenore?" Raven: "How the hell should I know?" • Corman explained his reasons for turning Poe into comedy in Ed Naha's book, *The Films of Roger Corman:* "We had to play *The Raven* for laughs because both Richard Matheson, our writer, and I were getting tired of the stock Poe pictures. As it turned out, this film was the most fun we ever had on a Poe picture." • This was the first time these three horror legends — Boris Karloff, Vincent Price, and Peter Lorre — had all appeared together in the same film. • Oscar-winning actor Jack Nicholson (early in his career) played Peter Lorre's bumbling son. Nicholson had great respect and admiration for these three elder horror stars, especially Lorre, saying, "I loved those guys. I sat around with Peter all the time." Nicholson had less-than-fond memories of the real raven used in the film: "The raven that we used shit endlessly over everybody and everything. It just shit endlessly. My whole right shoulder was constantly covered with raven shit" (from Roger Corman's autobiography, *How I Made a Hundred Movies in Hollywood and Never Lost a Dime*). • *The Raven* was the biggest box office success thus far in the already successful Poe series. It was Corman's fifth Poe film.

Tales of Terror (1962; AIP) D/P: Roger Corman. S: Richard Matheson. C: Floyd Crosby. Cast: Vincent Price, Maggie Pierce, Leona Gage, Peter Lorre, Joyce Jameson, Basil Rathbone, Debra Paget, David Frankham. This anthology film features three tales culled from four Poe stories — "Morella," "The Black Cat" and "The Cask of Amontillado" (combined in the second segment), and "The Facts in the Case of M. Valdemar." Vincent Price stars in all three tales (as different characters). ¶ "I have been asleep, but now I am *dead*" — Vincent Price as M. Valdemar in the final segment. • The middle story was Corman's first stab at Poe humor, a trend later expanded to feature length for *The Raven* (1963), Corman's next

Vincent Price clutches at Elizabeth Shepherd in a dramatic moment from The Tomb of Ligea *(1964).*

Poe film. • This is the only movie to date to feature Poe's oft-overlooked story of "Morella."

The Tomb of Ligea (1964; AIP) D: Roger Corman. P: Pat Green, Roger Corman. S: Robert Towne. C: Arthur Grant. Cast: Vincent Price, Elizabeth Shepherd, John Westbrook, Oliver Johnson, Derek Francis, Richard Vernon, Ronald Adam, Frank Thornton, Denis Gilmore, Penelope Lee. Verdon Fell (Vincent Price) is a man deep in mourning over the death of his wife, Ligea. Eventually he remarries, but is horrified when his new wife goes into a trance and speaks in Ligea's voice. A friend exhumes Ligea's body and finds that it is a wax dummy — Fell has ensconced Ligea's corpse in a secret room which he visits periodically, apparently under the hypnotic power of his dead wife, reaching out to him from beyond the grave. ¶ "She will not rest because she is not dead! ... to me." • *The Tomb of Ligea* was Corman's last Poe picture ("I stopped because I was tired of doing them," he stated). It was shot under the title *The House at the End of the World.* • The romantic leading role of Verden Fell was originally written for Richard Chamberlain, but was played by Vincent Price at AIP's insistence. • Vincent Price discussed his "Poe" work in *Famous Monsters* #109, saying, "I'm a great admirer of Poe, for the last 15 years I have been going out as a lecturer, trying to bring him to life for young people."

Modern Poe

The Black Cat (1966; Hemisphere) D/S: Harold Hoffman. P: Patrick Sims. C: Walter Schenk. Cast: Robert Frost, Robyn Baker, Sadie French, Scotty McKay, George R. Russell. This updating of Edgar Allan Poe's classic short story is about a disturbed man who becomes morbidly obsessed with the black cat given him by his wife as an anniversary present. He maims it (by gouging out its eye), then kills it, but this (or another) cat comes back. The psychotic husband nearly gets away with murdering his wife and walling her up in the basement until the wailing of the cat, which he had accidentally walled up with her body, gives the crime away to police. ¶ From the ads: "What force drives him to commit acts *against nature*...? to terrify ... to torture and torment...!!"

The Blood Demon (1967; Hemisphere; W. Germany) (also *The Torture Chamber of Dr. Sadism*). D: Harald Reinl. P: Wolfgang Kuhnlenz. S: Manfred R. Kohler. C: Ernst W. Kalinke, Dieter Liphardt. Cast: Lex Barker, Karin Dor, Christopher Lee, Karl Lange, Vladimir Medar, Christiane Rucker, Dieter Eppler. Though officially based on Poe's "The Pit and the Pendulum," the bizarre storyline is far from its acknowledged source. Christopher Lee plays Count Regula, who must sacrifice his thirteenth victim in order to achieve immortality. There is a pit, at the bottom of which is a plethora of poisonous snakes, and there is a swinging pendulum, which is used to torture the hero (Lex Barker). • Heroine Karin Dor is wife of director Harald Reinl. • Lex Barker is best remembered for playing "Tarzan" in five films between 1949 and 1953.

Buried Alive (1989; 21st Century Film Corporation; U.S./South Africa) D: Gerald Kikoine. P: Harry Alan Towers. S: Jake Clesi, Stuart Lee. C: Gerald Loubeau. Cast: Robert Vaughn, Donald Pleasence, Karen Witter, John Carradine, Nai Long, Ginger Allen. Robert Vaughn plays a progressive psychologist who runs Ravenscroft Hall, a former insane asylum, now a school for difficult girls. Vaughn is not in his right mind, however (having been the victim of his cruel father and his own insanity), and he uses his own special techniques to cure those particularly troublesome girls—he walls them up alive in the basement. ¶ "He thought I was crazy, but I cured myself—right here. He didn't know what it felt like to be totally confined in a small dark place all alone, with hardly any air to breathe. He found out, and you will too." • Calling itself "Edgar Allen Poe's *Buried Alive*," this film blatantly uses Poe's name without using any of his work or inspiration (aside from the common theme of being buried alive). Note that the filmmakers did not even bother to spell his name correctly on the film prints (it should be Edgar Allan Poe). • Hoping to jazz up a tepid screenplay, the filmmakers throw in a totally incongruous supernatural element by having Vaughn's dead father break out of the wall and attack him at the end. This obvious desperation ploy makes little sense in the context of the rest of the film. • John Carradine fans will be disappointed with this, his final film appearance (he was on his way home from the South African location when he died in Milan, Italy). Though billed fourth in the credits, Carradine only has two scenes in the picture, and is onscreen for no more than a minute.

Castle of Blood (1964) (see GHOSTS) (also *Castle of Terror*). Though not based on one of his stories, this film features Edgar Allan Poe as a character. Poe challenges a man to spend a night in a haunted castle on All Souls' Eve. The man accepts the challenge and witnesses several ghosts reenact their murders, even falling in love with one of the specters.

The Conqueror Worm (1968) (see WITCHES, WARLOCKS, AND CULTS) (also *The Witchfinder General*). This British film has nothing to do with the Edgar Allan Poe poem it is said to be based upon. After their successful Corman Poe series, AIP decided that the author's name was still bankable, and changed the title for the American distribution. To justify the Poe tie-in, they added a voiceover narration at the film's end with Vincent Price reciting Poe's poem. The story features Price as Matthew Hopkins, a notorious seventeenth century witchhunter who travels from town to town, using his powers of fate and death to satisfy his personal lusts for power, money, and women. ¶ "Out, out are the lights, out all. And over each quivering form the curtain, a funeral pall, comes down with the rush of a storm while the angels, all pallid and wan, uprising, unveiling, affirm that the play is the tragedy 'Man' ... and its hero the Conqueror Worm"—closing narration (the last stanza of Poe's poem).

Dr. Tarr's Torture Dungeon (1972; Group 1; Mexico) D: Juan Lopez Moctezuma. P: Roberto Viskin. S: Juan Lopez Moctezuma, Carlos Illescas. C: Rafael Corkidi. Cast: Claudio Brook, Stuart Hansel, Ellen Sherman, Martin LaSalle. Loosely based on Poe's story, "The System of Doctor Tarr and Professor Fether," a journalist visits an asylum only to gradually discover that the inmates have taken over, led by an articulate madman impersonating the rightful head of the institution. ¶ "Guards and patients traded roles, and the lunatics were set free and their keepers locked up in rotten dungeons."

An Evening of Edgar Allan Poe (1970;

AIP-TV) D/P: Ken Johnson. S: David Welch, Ken Johnson. Cast: Vincent Price. In this made-for-TV production, Vincent Price, the only cast member, performs faithful recitations of four Poe stories: "The Tell-Tale Heart," "The Sphinx," "The Cask of Amontillado," and "The Pit and the Pendulum." Each recitation takes place on an appropriate and realistic set, ranging from nineteenth century drawing room to spacious dining hall to rat-infested dungeon. The marvelous sets are matched by equally striking costumes for Price.

The Fall of the House of Usher (1982; TV movie) D/P: James L. Conway. S: Stephen Lord. C: Paul Hipp. Cast: Martin Landau, Robert Hays, Charlene Tilton, Dimitra Arliss, Ray Walston, Peg Stewart. This "Classics Illustrated" TV adaptation of Poe's story of the disintegrating Usher family stars Martin Landau as Roderick Usher. • Though filmed in 1978, it wasn't aired until four years later.

The Fall of the House of Usher (1983; Elite Films; Spain) D/P/S/C: Jesus Franco. Cast: Howard Vernon, Lina Romay, Robert Foster. Howard Vernon plays Roderick Usher who murders his young wife in a fit of unfounded jealousy. She returns as a ghost to torment him. When a doctor finally burns his wife's corpse, Roderick suffers a fatal heart attack and the house begins to crumble with his death.

Legend of Horror (1972; General Film Corporation) D: Bill Davies. P: Ricky Torres Tudela. Cast: Karin Field. In this little-seen version of Poe's "The Tell-Tale Heart," a mad murderer believes the beating of his dead victim's heart will give him away.

Masque of the Red Death (1989; Concorde/New Horizons) D: Larry Brand. P: Roger Corman. S: Daryl Haney, Larry Brand. C: Edward Pei. Cast: Patrick Mac-Nee, Clare Hoak, Jeff Osterhage, Tracey Reiner, Kelly Ann Sebatsso, Maria Ford, Adrian Paul. Set in the Middle Ages, a mysterious man on horseback rides across the countryside, leaving a ravaging plague wherever he goes. Meanwhile, the debauched young Prince Prospero locks himself and his fellow nobles within the safe confines of his castle, while setting his lecherous sights on corrupting an innocent peasant girl. But no one can escape his fate at the hands of the Red Death. • Roger Corman himself produced this remake of his classic 1964 version for his newly-formed Concorde film company. From the disappointing result, one can only wish he had directed it as well. • Second female lead Tracey Reiner, who plays

Prince Prospero's lascivious half-sister, is the daughter of Rob Reiner and Penny Marshall.

Master of Horror (1960; U.S. Films; Argentina) D: Enrique Carreras. P: Nicolas Carreras. S: Louis Penafiel. C: Amerigo Hoss. Cast: Narciso Menta, Inez Moreno. This Argentinian omnibus film features two stories, both adaptations of Poe tales — "The Facts in the Cast of M. Valdemar" and "The Cask of Amontillado" (two stories also featured in Corman's Poe anthology, *Tales of Terror,* made two years later). • A third segment, "The Tell-Tale Heart," was deleted from the dubbed American release by exhibitor Jack H. Harris.

Murders in the Rue Morgue (1971; AIP) D: Gordon Hessler. P: Louis M. Heyward. S: Christopher Wicking, Henry Slesar. C: Manuel Berenguer. Cast: Jason Robards, Herbert Lom, Christine Kaufmann, Adolfo Celi, Lilli Palmer, Maria Perschy, Michael Dunn, José Calvo, Peter Arne, Werner Umberg. In nineteenth century France, a killer stalks a Grand Guignol theater which is presenting Poe's "Murders in the Rue Morgue." The murderous phantom is a horribly scarred actor out for revenge. ¶ "Marot was buried, but he was buried alive.... It took hours, hours of terror, but somehow Marot found the strength to lift the lid of the coffin. It was the strength of a madman because by now Marot was completely insane." • Director Gordon Hessler had this to say about his film's radical departure from Poe's story: "The problem was that the original Poe story, which is a mystery where the *monkey* did it, was not the kind of story you could do anymore." • This particular version, though an American production, was filmed in Spain.

The Murders in the Rue Morgue (1986; TV movie) D: Jeannot Szwarc. P: Robert Halmi. S: David Epstein. C: Bruno de Keyzer. Cast: George C. Scott, Rebecca De Mornay, Ian McShane, Neil Dickson, Val Kilmer. This, the most faithful adaptation of Poe's story to date, follows the workings of literature's first detective, Monsieur C. Auguste Dupin, as he uses logic and deductive reasoning (over 40 years before Sir Arthur Conan Doyle put pen to paper to create Sherlock Holmes) to solve the case of the Rue Morgue murders — and discover the killer is an enraged ape.

The Oblong Box (1969; AIP; U.S./U.K.) D/P: Gordon Hessler. S: Lawrence Huntington, Christopher Wicking. C: John Coquillon. Cast: Vincent Price, Christopher Lee, Rupert Davies, Uta Levka, Sally Geeson,

Peter Arne, Alastair Williamson, Hilary Dwyer, Maxwell Shaw, Carl Rigg, John Barrie. The brother of Vincent Price is hideously disfigured by voodoo magic while in Africa. Back in England, Price keeps him locked away in a room of their mansion. His brother escapes when he feigns death, but is buried alive. Two grave robbers dig him up and deliver his coffin to a Dr. Neuhart (Christopher Lee), whom the brother blackmails into sheltering him while he carries out his plan of revenge against the family. ¶ "Buried? Yes. Waking up in that horrible oblong box, no air to breathe, trapped and no escape, the earth raining down on the lid, every shovelful burying you more *deeper*!" • Though borrowing the name of Poe's story, "The Oblong Box," this film is closer to "The Premature Burial"; though again, the similarities are tenuous at best. • Director Michael Reeves began *The Oblong Box,* but died (an apparent suicide) early on, and was replaced by Gordon Hessler.

Phantom of the Rue Morgue (1954; Warner Bros.) D: Roy Del Ruth. P: Henry Blanke. S: Harold Medford, James E. Webb. C: Peverell Marley. Cast: Karl Malden, Claude Dauphin, Patricia Medina, Steve Forrest, Allyn McLerie, Charles Gemora. This loose adaptation of Poe's "Murders in the Rue Morgue" follows Karl Malden as a mad zoologist who trains a gorilla to attack and kill when it hears the tinkling of bells. • *Phantom in the Rue Morgue* was filmed in 3-D (following up Warner's 3-D hit *House of Wax,* 1953) making it the only 3-D adaptation of a Poe story to date. • Charles Gemora wore the ape suit in this picture. He also played the ape 22 years earlier in the 1932 adaptation of *Murders in the Rue Morgue.*

Revenge in the House of Usher (1983) (see MAD SCIENTISTS). Though the credits claim it is "Based on 'The Fall of the House of Usher' by Edgar Allan Poe," this film shares nothing but the name with Poe's story. Dr. Eric Usher, an obsessed mad scientist, is attempting to revive his dead daughter by kidnapping young girls and using them as unwilling donors in his bizarre experiments.

The Spectre of Edgar Allan Poe (1974) (see MADMEN — EARLY PSYCHOS). Though not based on any of his works, this film features Edgar Allan Poe as a character. When Edgar's beloved Lenore is nearly buried alive, she goes mad. Poe takes her to a private asylum headed by Cesar Romero. Romero is mad himself, and tortures Poe with a watery pit full of snakes.

Spirits of the Dead (1968; AIP; France/ Italy) D: Roger Vadim, Louis Malle, Federico Fellini. S: Roger Vadim, Pascal Cousin, Louis Male, Federico Fellini, Bernardino Zapponi. C: Claude Renoir, Tonino Delli Colli, Giuseppe Rotunno. Cast: Jane Fonda, Peter Fonda, Alain Delon, Brigitte Bardot, Terence Stamp. Three tales of Poe are presented by three European directors. In an adaptation of Poe's story "Metzengerstein" (directed by Roger Vadim), a dead lover's spirit returns in the form of a huge black stallion. "William Wilson" (directed by Louis Malle) follows a man whose sadism is challenged by a mysterious double — his other self. Finally, in "Never Bet the Devil Your Head" (directed by Federico Fellini), a troubled film star is haunted by the vision of a mysterious child, leading to his decapitation in a car accident. • In a bit of perverse casting, Jane and Peter Fonda, brother and sister, play the two would-be lovers in "Metzengerstein." Director Roger Vadim was married to Jane Fonda at the time. • Though many of Poe's stories have been adapted for the screen on numerous occasions, this is the only filming to date of "Metzengerstein." • Orson Welles was originally approached to direct one of the episodes, but dropped out before filming began and was replaced by Federico Fellini. • For the English-language version, Vincent Price served as narrator.

The Tell-Tale Heart (1960; The Danzigers; U.K.) D: Ernest Morris. P: Brian Taylor. S: Brian Clemens, Elden Howard. C: Jimmy Wilson. Cast: Laurence Payne, Adrienne Corri, Dermot Walsh, Selma Vaz Diaz, John Scott, John Martin, Annette Carell, Rosemary Rotheray, Suzanne Fuller, Yvonne Buckingham. Edgar Allan Poe is encouraged by his friend to make an acquaintance of the pretty girl living across the street. Edgar falls in love with her, but when he discovers she is in love with his friend rather than himself, he flies into a murderous rage and kills his friend. As in Poe's story, he places the body under the floorboards, and is haunted by the beating of the dead man's heart. ¶ "Your attention please! To those who are squeamish or react nervously to shock, we suggest that when you hear this sound [the beating of a heart] . . . close your eyes and do not look at the screen again until it stops" — introductory narration.

Torture Garden (1967) (see ANTHOLOGIES). In the final episode of this omnibus, titled "The Man Who Collected Poe," Jack Palance is an avid Poe collector who covets the collection of Poe memorabilia owned by Peter

Cushing. He murders Cushing, only to discover that Cushing has somehow resurrected Edgar Allan Poe himself, keeping him locked in a basement room to continue his writing. At the end, both Poe and Palance go up in flames.

War Gods of the Deep (1965) (see FISH-PEOPLE) (also *City Under the Sea*). Claimed to be based on Poe's poem, "City Beneath the Sea," the film has nothing to do with the author's romantic poem. Vincent Price plays the ruler of a sunken city which is populated by gill-men.

Web of the Spider (1972) (see GHOSTS). This remake of *Castle of Blood* (1964) again features Edgar Allan Poe as a character. A man is challenged by Poe to spend a night in a haunted castle. He accepts the challenge and is beset by ghosts reenacting their own murders, until he too finally falls victim to the evil castle's influence and joins their ranks.

Psychic Ability

This subgenre, which is loosely titled PSYCHIC ABILITY, contains films about people who possess mental powers or skills which go beyond the realm of the five natural senses. This includes a variety of mental phenomena and abilities, including clairvoyance, E.S.P., precognition, telekinesis, and telepathy.

In 1935, Claude Rains starred in one of the first mentalist pictures, entitled *The Clairvoyant*. In that film, Rains played a phony mind reader who came to believe he had the ability to predict disasters. Back in those days, however, psychic ability was primarily associated with spiritualism and therefore generally regarded as supernatural mumbo jumbo. It wasn't until the 1960s that E.S.P. and the like really became a serious area of scientific research. The 1968 film *The Power* was one of the first movies to (semi) seriously depict a group of scientists studying this phenomenon. No doubt that film helped spark two later sci-fi hits involving governmental intervention in psychic research — *The Fury* (1978) and *Scanners* (1980). Both of these films dealt with the harnessing and exploitation of individuals' telekinetic powers for an organization's own geo-political purposes. These features also capitalized on the post–Watergate mood, exploiting the public's general distrust of secretive government agencies.

The single greatest influence on the cinema of psychic ability has been the 1976 Stephen King shocker, *Carrie*. In it, a young Sissy Spacek plays a painfully naive and repressed teenage girl who rebels against her domineering, religiously fanatical mother and callous high school classmates by unleasing a terrifying onslaught of telekinetic power. The film caught on big with movie audiences (and critics) everywhere, and (like many innovative and successful films) inspired a slew of inferior imitations.

Modern films continue to exploit the public's fascination with psychic abilities, though often including them merely as a sidelight. More recently, those with psychic "gifts" have encountered aliens (*Biohazard*, 1984), demons (*Cameron's Closet*, 1989), ghosts (*The First Power*, 1990), maniacs (*Friday the 13th Part 7: The New Blood*, 1988), and even zombies (*Kiss Daddy Goodbye*, 1981).

The Asphyx (1973; Glendale; U.K.) D: Peter Newbrook. P: John Brittany. S: Brian Comfort. C: Freddie Young. Cast: Robert Stephens, Robert Powell, Jane Lapotaire, Alex Scott, Fiona Walker, Ralph Arless. A man seeking immortality plots to trap his "asphyx" (his own personal spirit of death) with an experimental beam while slowly electrocuting himself. With his asphyx safely contained, he is now immortal. His daughter tries the technique but something goes wrong and she dies. Her lover then commits suicide, leaving the father alone with his grief for all eternity. ¶ "My researches into psychic phenomena show me that in Greek mythology they refer to the spirit of death — they called it the 'asphyx.' It manifests itself only in times of danger, having existed in eternal agony. It seeks out the dying, or the damned, for only by possessing those about to die is it at last released from unspeakable torment."

Biohazard (1984) (see ALIENS — INVADERS ON EARTH: THE 80S AND BEYOND). The use of an experimental drug gives a woman psychic powers. When enhanced by scientific machinery in a materialization experiment, she opens up a doorway to another dimension which allows a vicious lizard-like alien to appear and go on a killing spree. ¶ "While I'm sure Miss Martin doesn't view herself as any sort of 'freak,' she does possess keen psychic impulses of an extraordinary manner."

Cameron's Closet (1989) (see DEMONS AND DEVILS). Professor Owen uses his son Cameron in a series of experiments to tap into the "vast unused powers of the mind." Cameron unwittingly uses his newfound telekinetic abilities to summon up an evil demon, which gathers its strength in his closet until its malevolent will becomes strong enough for it to break out and commit horrible murders. ¶ "I'm a frightened old drunk who made the mistake of prying into a little boy's mind."

Carrie (1976; MGM/United Artists) D: Brian De Palma. P: Paul Monash. S: Lawrence D. Gordon. C: Mario Tosi. Cast: Sissy Spacek, William Katt, Amy Irving, Piper Laurie, Nancy Allen, John Travolta, P. J. Soles. A repressed teenage girl, out of touch with herself and the world around her (thanks to her fanatical bible-thumping mother), struggles with her classmates and her own adolescence. She possesses tremendous telekinetic abilities, which she reveals to her shocked mother when mom unwisely forbids Carrie to go to the prom. At the dance she is made the butt of a vicious practical joke, and unleashes her fury on everyone in the building. • Carrie, filmed for only $1.8 million, grossed over $15 million at the box office. • Sissy Spacek (playing the title role) was nominated for Best Actress and Piper Laurie (in the role of Carrie's domineering psychotically religious mother) received a Best Supporting Actress nomination. • The screenplay was adapted from Stephen King's first published novel. • It was King himself who suggested Brian De Palma direct, based upon the director's work on *Sisters* (1973).

The Clairvoyant (1935; Gainsborough;

U.K.) (also *The Evil Mind*). D: Maurice Elvey. P: Michael Balcon. S: Charles Bennett, Bryan Edgar Wallace. C: Glen MacWilliams. Cast: Claude Rains, Fay Wray, Jane Baxter, Mary Clare, Athole Stewart, Ben Field. A fraudulent mindreader is shocked when one of his predictions about an impending disaster actually comes true.

The Crawling Eye (1958) (see ALIENS — INVADERS ON EARTH: THE 50S). Forrest Tucker meets two sisters on his way to Trollenberg, Switzerland. One of the girls (Janet Munro) is telepathic and she becomes the target of attack by invading alien eyeball-creatures and their zombie-like slaves. She aids the protagonists by sensing the alien presence and locating lost climbers in the snow.

Creepers (1985) (see BUGS) (also *Phenomena*). A deformed killer stalks a girl who can communicate telepathically with insects.

Dead of Night (1945) (see ANTHOLOGIES). The wraparound story of this classic anthology involves an architect with precognitive feelings about visiting a country house. He relates his deja vu–like predictions to the guests at the estate, who in turn relate a series of macabre stories from their own experiences. At the climax, after being driven to murder, the audience is shown that the man is caught up in a cyclical nightmare.

The Dead Zone (1983; Paramount) D: David Cronenberg. P: Debra Hill. S: Jeffrey Boam. C: Mark Irwin. Cast: Christopher Walken, Brooke Adams, Tom Skerritt, Herbert Lom, Martin Sheen, Anthony Zerbe, Colleen Dewhurst. A teacher (Christopher Walken) awakens from a five-year coma with the ability to see visions of a person's past and future by simply touching that person. One such vision — that of a presidential candidate who will eventually go crazy and lead the nation into nuclear warfare — creates a deadly moral dilemma for Walken. ¶ "Yes John, that is your 'Dead Zone,' — the possibility of altering the outcome of your ... your premonitions." • This psychic melodrama is based upon the popular Stephen King novel of the same name. King had written his own screenplay adaptation, but it was rejected by executive producer Dino De Laurentiis. • Star Christopher Walken is an Oscar winner (for his supporting performance in *The Deer Hunter*, 1978).

Destiny (1944; Universal) D: Reginald LeBorg, Julian Duvivier. P: Howard Benedict, Roy William Neill. S: Roy Chanslor, Ernest Pascal. C: George Robinson, Paul Ivano. Cast: Alan Curtis, Gloria Jean,

Frank Craven, Grace McDonald. An escaped convict takes refuge on a farm, then kills the owner and attacks his blind daughter. What he doesn't know is that the girl possesses telekinetic abilities which make the forces of nature her allies. The criminal is attacked by the dog, menaced by trees and frightened by a storm. • The film is actually an episode that was cut from the anthology film *Flesh and Fantasy* and expanded to feature length.

The Devil Commands (1941) (see MAD SCIENTISTS). Boris Karloff's attempt to contact his dead wife involves the use of electrical equipment and a psychic, played by Anne Revere. In the film, she acts as a medium and even conducts a séance.

Dr. Terror's House of Horrors (1965) (see ANTHOLOGIES). Peter Cushing stars as Dr. Terror, a fortune teller who foretells the supernatural destinies of five train passengers with a deck of tarot cards. ¶ "I don't know, a gypsy once told me that I was going to get an unexpected gift, and that very day I walked under a pigeon."

The Eyes of Laura Mars (1978; Columbia) D: Irvin Kershner. P: Jack H. Harris. S: John Carpenter, David Zelag Goodman. C: Victor J. Kemper. Cast: Faye Dunaway, Tommy Lee Jones, René Auberjonois, Raul Julia, Brad Dourif, Frank Adonis. A famous fashion photographer has the ability to see visions through the eyes of a killer. She then has her models pose in the position of the killer's victims. Her ultimate nightmare is eventually realized when she sees herself as the next target.

Fear (1990; Vestron) D/S: Rockne S. O'Bannon. P: Richard Kobritz. C: Robert Stevens. Cast: Ally Sheedy, Michael O'Keefe, Stan Shaw, Dina Merrill, Dean Goodman, Keone Young. A clairvoyant woman (Ally Sheedy) helps the police track a sadistic serial killer who also possesses psychic abilities (as well as a penchant for human fear).

Firestarter (1984; Universal) D: Mark L. Lester. P: Frank Capra, Jr. S: Stanley Mann. Cast: David Keith, Drew Barrymore, Freddie Jones, Heather Locklear, Martin Sheen, George C. Scott, Art Carney, Louise Fletcher. A government organization known as "The Shop" tries to harness and exploit the psychic powers of a young girl who can start fires with a glance. • This $15 million film is based on the novel by Stephen King. • Despite being paid one million dollars for the movie rights, Stephen King called this adaptation of his work "the worst of the bunch."

The First Power (1990) (see GHOSTS). An L.A. cop (Lou Diamond Phillips) is aided by an attractive young psychic in tracking down the spirit of an executed killer who has returned to possess the bodies of the living and continue his murder spree.

Flesh and Fantasy (1943) (see ANTHOLOGIES). Two stories in this macabre trilogy directed by Julien Duvivier involve unique mental abilities. The first features Edward G. Robinson as a man whose life changes when he meets a fortune teller. The second stars Charles Boyer as a circus star with E.S.P. whose premonitions revolve around his own doom.

Friday the 13th Part 7: The New Blood (1988) (see MADMEN — THE SLICE 'N' DICE WAVE). Tina, the teen heroine who must battle the unstoppable Jason, uses her talent for telekinesis to finally kill the hockey-masked killer (at least until the next installment).

The Fury (1978; 20th Century–Fox) D: Brian De Palma. P: Ron Preissman. S: John Farris. C: Richard H. Kline. Cast: Kirk Douglas, Andrew Stevens, Amy Irving, John Cassavetes, Charles Durning, Carrie Snodgrass, Fiona Lewis. The scheming head of a government agency hopes to exploit those with telekinetic powers. He attempts to kill a former colleague (Kirk Douglas), and kidnaps his son who possesses these extraordinary abilities. Douglas, aided by a young girl (Amy Irving) who also possesses the power, tries to rescue his son. In the end, Douglas discovers that his boy has been corrupted by the agency, while the fiendish government chief (played by John Cassavetes) literally loses his head over an angry Amy Irving. ¶ "Those films of his father's death have unleashed an incredible emotional force. Why, he's developing the power of an atomic reactor." • Tall, blonde star-to-be Daryl Hannah made an early career appearance as a girl named Pam in this film.

Harlequin (1980; Ace Theatres; Australia) D: Simon Wincer. P: Antony I. Ginnane. S: Everett De Roche. C: Gary Hansen. Cast: Robert Powell, David Hemmings, Carmen Duncan, Broderick Crawford, Alison Best, Gus Mercurio. A faith healer with psychic powers cures the son of a political figure (David Hemmings) and then locks horns with a powerful industrialist.

I Bury the Living (1957; United Artists) D: Albert Band. P: Albert Band, Louis Garfinkle. S: Louis Garfinkle. C: Frederick Gately. Cast: Richard Boone, Theodore Bikel, Peggy Maurer, Howard Smith, Herbert

Anderson, Robert Osterloh. A cemetery chairman believes he possesses the ability to kill people by simply sticking a black pin into a cemetery map, hitting the pre-purchased cemetery plot with the victims' name on it. ¶ "It's possible for some people to have things inside them that make other things happen. Nothing is impossible for a man like that if he thinks about it hard enough." • The film was first titled *Killer on the Wall* before acquiring its final moniker. • The "happy" ending was a result of pressure applied by the distributor, United Artists. "Originally," explained director Albert Band in a *Fangoria* #68 interview, "the dead people came out of their graves and went after Dick Boone, who had barricaded himself inside that little cabin. When they appeared at the window, he dropped dead of a heart attack." Boone survives the final released version. No "dead people" appear, and the supernatural or psychic proceedings are even explained away as the work of a murderous caretaker.

Initiation of Sarah (1978; TV movie) D: Robert Day. P: Jay Benson. S: Don Ingalls, Carol Caraceno, Kenette Gfeller. Cast: Kay Lenz, Shelley Winters, Tony Bill, Kathryn Crosby, Morgan Fairchild. An introverted college student is forced to join an unpopular sorority and learns to use her psychic powers for revenge.

Jack the Ripper (1958) (see ANTHOLOGIES). Two stories in this anthology film feature psychic phenomena. In one, a man sees a murder three days before it happens and then helps bring the killer to justice. In the other, a psychic helps the police track Jack the Ripper in nineteenth-century London.

Jennifer (1978) (see SNAKES). A girl with psychic abilities is bullied at a girls' school until she uses her mind-power to call up a variety of snakes which she uses to exact revenge.

Kiss Daddy Goodbye (1981) (see ZOMBIES). Two young children use their psychic abilities to raise their father from the dead and send him out as a walking corpse to get the bikers that had killed him. ¶ "You're very special, Michael. Do you want strangers to find out about it? Do you want them to come and put you in a room with all sorts of machinery and stick needles into your head? Then you can't use the power when anyone else can see" — the protective father before he becomes a zombie.

Kiss of the Tarantula (1976) (see BUGS) (also *Shudder*). A young girl lashes out at her enemies via her ability to communicate with tarantulas.

The Last Wave (1977; United Artists; Australia) D: Peter Weir. P: Hal and Jim McElroy. S: Peter Weir, Tony Morphett, Petru Popescu. C: Russell Boyd. Cast: Richard Chamberlain, Olivia Hamnett, Fred Parslow. An aborigine prophecy of world disaster by flood is confirmed by a lawyer's clairvoyant dreams.

Making Contact (1985; New World Pictures) D: Roland Emmerich. P: Klaus Dittrich. S: Roland Emmerich, Hans J. Haller, Thomas Lechner. Cast: Joshua Morell. When Joey's dad passes away, strange things begin to happen in the neighborhood. Toys come to life, a kindly spirit talks to him on his little red phone, and an evil force is embodied within a dummy. Joey himself begins to realize that he has kinetic powers of his own and when these dark demons from another dimension begin to threaten his family and friends, Joey enters a magical door to combat the supernatural.

The Medusa Touch (1978; Citeca; U.K./France) D: Jack Gold. P: Arnon Milchan, Elliott Kastner. S: John Briley. C: Arthur Ibbetson. Cast: Richard Burton, Lee Remick, Lino Ventura, Harry Andrews, Jeremy Brett, Alan Badel. A writer comes to the realization that he possesses the power to cause disasters at will. ¶ "Most paranoiacs think the world is too much for them, but Mr. Morlar thinks he is too much for the world."

The Misadventures of Merlin Jones (1963; Buena Vista) D: Robert Stevenson. P: Walt Disney. S: Tom August, Helen August. Cast: Tommy Kirk, Annette Funicello, Leon Ames. A college student invents an electronic helmet which gives him the power to read minds. He uses it to expose a crooked judge.

Night Monster (1942; Universal) D/P: Ford Beebe. S: Clarence Upson Young. C: Charles Van Enger. Cast: Bela Lugosi, Lionel Atwill, Leif Erikson (this is the way it appeared in the credits, not correctly as Erickson), Irene Hervey, Ralph Morgan, Don Porter, Nils Asther, Fay Helm, Frank Reicher, Doris Lloyd, Francis Pierlot, Robert Homans, Janet Shaw, Eddy Waller, Cyril Delevanti. A rich man with no legs is taught by an Eastern swami how to regenerate his limbs through a mystical force of the mind. He gathers the medical men responsible for his unfortunate condition at his gloomy mansion and murders them one by one. ¶ "A little knowledge of the occult is dangerous. Unless it is used for good, disaster will follow in its wake. That is cosmic law." • The Universal head office was so pleased with producer/director Ford Beebe's performance on this film that they assigned him the bigger scoped *Son of Dracula* to produce.

Pandemonium (1982) (see MADMEN – THE SLICE'N' DICE WAVE). This absurb spoof of slasher films features a heroine with telekinetic abilities (à la *Carrie*), who eventually uses them to dispatch the mad killer (by running him over with a statue she animates).

Patrick (1978; Filmways; Australia) D: Richard Franklin. P: Anthony I. Ginnane, Richard Franklin. S: Everett De Roche. C: Don McAlpine. Cast: Robert Thompson, Susan Penhaligon, Robert Helpmann, Rod Mullinar, Bruce Barry. A man in a coma begins to use his telekinetic powers to disrupt his hospital home. • The film features music by Brian May (who also provided the score for *The Road Warrior,* 1980). • Screenwriter Everett De Roche also acts in the film.

Poltergeist (1982) (see GHOSTS). Parapsychological researchers and a midget psychic (Zelda Robenstein) aid a family terrorized by restless spirits.

Poltergeist 2: The Other Side (1986) (see GHOSTS). The midget psychic (Zelda Rubenstein) from the first film is back, once again aiding the beleaguered family who is haunted by the ghost of an evil preacher named Kane.

The Power (1968; MGM) D: Byron Haskin. P: George Pal. S: John Gay. C: Ellsworth Fredericks. Cast: George Hamilton, Michael Rennie, Gary Merrill, Arthur O'Connell, Suzanne Pleshette, Nehemiah Persoff, Earl Holliman, Aldo Ray, Barbara Nichols, Richard Carlson, Yvonne De Carlo. One member of a group of scientists exploring the limits of human endurance has harnessed his telekinetic ability for murder. • Producer George Pal made a brief appearance in the picture, but during the final editing stages the movie was running too long and his scenes ended up on the cutting room floor.

The Premonition (1976; Avco Embassy) D/P: Robert Allen Schnitzer. S: Anthony Mahon, Robert Allen Schnitzer. C: Victor C. Milt. Cast: Sharon Farrell, Jeff Corey, Edward Bell, Chitra Neogy, Richard Lynch, Ellen Barber, Danielle Brisebois. A couple uses clairvoyance and E.S.P. to locate their adopted daughter who has been kidnapped by her real mom returned from the grave.

The Psychic (1977; Group 1; Italy) D: Lucio Fulci. P: Franco Cuccu. S: Roberto Gianviti, Lucio Fulci, Dardano Sacchetti.

C: Sergio Salvati. Cast: Jennifer O'Neill, Gabriele Ferzetti, Marc Porel, Gianni Garko, Jenny Tamburi. Jennifer O'Neill experiences precognitive visions of other people's deaths, and eventually, her own.

The Psychic Killer (1976; Avco Embassy) D: Ray Danton. P: Mardi Rustam. S: Greydon Clark, Ray Danton, Mike Angel. Cast: Jim Hutton, Julie Adams, Neville Brand, Paul Burke, Whit Bissell, Rod Cameron, Aldo Ray, Nehemiah Persoff, Della Reese. A psychiatrist mistakenly helps a mental patient (who has learned the technique of astral projection) obtain a discharge. The freed patient then uses his ability to destroy all those who had crossed him in the past.

The Psychotronic Man (1980; International Harmony) D: Jack M. Sell. P: Peter Spelson. S: Peter Spelson, Jack M. Sell. Cast: Peter Spelson. A barber with strange psychic abilities can kill or make people commit suicide with the powers of his mind.

Resurrection (1981; Universal) D: Daniel Petrie. P: Renee Missel, Howard Rosenman. S: Lewis John Carlino. C: Mario Tosi. Cast: Ellen Burstyn, Eva Le Gallienne, Sam Shepard, Richard Farnsworth, Roberts Blossom, Clifford David. A woman involved in a car accident has a life after death experience, then discovers that after the incident she has the ability to heal others. At one point in the film she goes to a psychic research facility which tests her ability to direct forces. At the climax, she is killed by her fanatical boyfriend who shoots her in an attempt to prove that she is Christ returned. ¶ "If this were the work of the Holy Spirit you'd be speaking his name!" • Ellen Burstyn received an Academy Award nomination for Best Acgress, and Eva Le Gallienne was nominated for Best Supporting Actress.

Scanners (1980; Filmplan International; Canada) D/S: David Cronenberg. P: Claude Heroux. C: Mark Irwin. Cast: Jennifer O'Neill, Stephan Lack, Patrick McGoohan, Michael Ironside, Lawrence Dane. Scanners are a small group of people with the ability to telepathically scan another person's thoughts and in so doing, control or destroy them at will. One such powerful scanner (Michael Ironside) goes berserk and plans to induce every scanner to join him on a murderous crusade. If they refuse to join, he kills them. A secret government branch counters Ironside and his allies with their own scanner (Stephen Lack). ¶ "I'm going to suck your brain dry!" • Legendary makeup man Dick Smith (*The Fly*, 1958, many others) served as a special effects consultant on the film.

The Sender (1982; Paramount) D: Roger Christian. P: Edward S. Feldman. S: Thomas Baum. C: Roger Pratt. Cast: Kathryn Harrold, Zeljko Ivanek, Shirley Knight, Paul Freeman, Sean Hewitt. A young amnesiac with uncanny telepathic abilities is able to transmit his nightmares to a psychiatrist and to the patients residing in a mental hospital. The resulting hallucinations are quite horrific and wreak a great deal of havoc at the hospital. The spirit of the young man's mother decides to lend a hand in this psychic affair as well.

The Shining (1980) (see GHOSTS). Jack Nicholson stars as a writer who takes his family with him when he accepts a job as winter caretaker at a plush, completely isolated resort hotel. Affected by cabin fever and the hotel's ghostly manifestations, Nicholson goes mad and attempts to murder his wife and telepathic boy. His son learns of his psychic ability (referred to in the film as "the shine") when he communicates with Scatman Crothers (who also possesses "the shine") without speaking aloud.

The Shout (1978; Rank; U.K.) D: Jerzy Skolimovsky. P: Jeremy Thomas. S: Michael Austin, Jerzy Skolimovsky. C: Mike Molloy. Cast: Alan Bates, Susannah York, John Hurt, Robert Stephens, Tim Curry. A man possesses the unusual (and deadly) ability to kill with a tremendous shout of his voice. His special gift is said to have originated from the Australian aborigines.

Silent Night, Deadly Night 3: Better Watch Out (1989) (see MADMEN — THE SLICE 'N' DICE WAVE). A young blind girl with E.S.P. abilities is a subject in some dream experiments. The doctor conducting the experiments causes her to become psychically linked to a long-term coma patient — who just happens to be the psychotic Santa Claus killer from the earlier films. The psycho revives and goes on another killing spree. ¶ "I don't want to see the future, or the past, or anything weird. I just want to be normal."

Something Weird (1966) (see WITCHES, WARLOCKS, AND CULTS). A man is involved in an electrical accident which leaves him both hideously disfigured *and* the possessor of extrasensory powers. An old witch strikes a bargain with him to restore his face. He goes on to become a famous psychic and helps police solve murder cases before fate catches up with him.

The Sorcerers (1967; Tigon/Global; U.K.) D: Michael Reeves. P: Arnold L. Miller, Patrick Curtis, Tony Tenser. S: Michael Reeves, Tom Baker. C: Stanley Long. Cast: Boris Karloff, Catherine Lacey, Ian Ogilvy, Susan George, Elisabeth Ercy, Victor Henry. An old couple devise a system whereby they can telepathically control a young man and experience his sensations. When the young man dies in a fiery car wreck at the climax, the elderly couple burns up with him.

Spontaneous Combustion (1990) D: Tobe Hooper. P: Jim Rogers. S: Tobe Hooper, Howard Goldberg. C: Levie Isaacks. Cast: Brad Dourif, Cynthia Bain, Jon Cypher, William Prince, Dey Young, Melinda Dillon. Brad Dourif (the offspring of two subjects in a government experiment) develops the latent ability (which he cannot control) to start fires, both in himself and in others. • In an interview made shortly after the completion of the film, director Tobe Hooper revealed, "What I did a lot of on this film was shoot until I got the pieces I needed. I did not need perfect takes, if takes three and four were prints, but weren't perfect, I was able to cut and paste to get what I needed. I wasn't concerned with making good dailies as I was with making a good movie." (Unfortunately, he failed, and this film was panned by critics and moviegoers alike.) • Filmmaker John Landis, a friend of Tobe Hooper's, puts in a cameo appearance as an obnoxious technician.

Stigma (1981; Yantra Cinematografica; Italy/Spain) D/S: José Ramón Larraz. P: Jesus Balcazar. C: Giuseppe Bernardini. Cast: Christian Borromeo, Alexandra Bastedo, Helga Line, Emilio Gutierrez Caba, Irene Gutierrez Caba. A young adolescent, who can kill by force of will, murders his brother and his girlfriend before committing suicide.

The Thing That Couldn't Die (1958) (see BRAINS — LIVING HEADS). A girl with E.S.P. powers uses a divining rod to uncover a chest containing the disembodied living head of a warlock. Once it is removed, the head uses its Satanic powers to control a dimwitted handyman in an attempt to find and reunite with its body.

Tourist Trap (1978; Compass) D: David Schmoeller. P: J. Larry Carroll. S: David Schmoeller, J. Larry Carroll. C: Nicholas von Sternberg. Cast: Chuck Connors, Tanya Roberts, Keith McDermott, Dawn Jeffory, Jon Van Ness, Jocelyn Jones. A man with incredible telekinetic powers traps four teen tourists in his mannequin-filled museum, then lets loose with his psychic powers.

Twilight Zone: The Movie (1983) (see ANTHOLOGIES). One of the segments features a small boy who is able to project his will on other objects and living beings. Consequently, his family has become imprisoned in their own home, where they are forced to cater to his slightest whim for fear of death.

Vibes (1988) D: Ken Kwapis. P: John Bailey. Cast: Jeff Goldblum, Cyndi Lauper, Peter Falk. A pair of hapless New York psychics (possessing the ability of astral projection) are conned by Peter Falk into using their respective skills in locating a lost Incan city in Ecuador. The secret hamlet is hidden high in the mountains and houses a mysterious glowing structure of immeasurable power. A paranormal researcher, who earlier had tested the psychic couple, follows them in the hope of gaining the stone's unusual energy. • Ron Howard *(Splash)* served as the film's executive producer. • This was pop rock singer Cyndi Lauper's film debut.

Zapped (1982) D: Robert J. Rosenthal. P: Jeffrey D. Apple. Cast: Scott Baio, Willy Aames, Scatman Crothers, Roger Bowen, Sue Ane Langdon. A lab explosion accidentally gives a high school student telekinetic powers, which he puts to such noble uses as looking under girls' dresses.

Psychos *see* Madmen

Rats

Gene Wilder summed up our feelings on this subject when he "comforted" Teri Garr in *Young Frankenstein* (1974): "Don't be frightened dear, it's just a rat — a *filthy, slimy* rat!" Rats possess a vicious cannibalistic nature, they carry plague and pestilence, and are generally associated with disease and death. Many people find these little fur-bearing rodents to be one of the most foul and disgusting members of the animal kingdom. It is no wonder, then, that rats have carved (or chewed) out their own niche in horror cinema.

The first rat picture (aside from the comical mouse-man seen in *Abbott and Costello Meet Dr. Jekyll and Mr. Hyde,* 1953) was *Willard* (1971). This popular entry in the worm-turns mold was the prototype rat attack film. Following its sequel, *Ben,* released the next year, killer rat movies have enjoyed a steadily increasing popularity. Even the rats themselves grew bigger and fiercer, after rats devoured the *Food of the Gods* in 1976 and grew to the size of Saint Bernards. Whether they be of normal size or gargantuan, rats have proved to be a formidable foe for mankind.

Perhaps the most effective film to date on the rodent subject is *Of Unknown Origin* (1983). In it, a single rat manages to drive Peter Weller to the point of obsessive madness, stripping him of his home, his friends, and his job, proving that even one rat can be one rat too many.

Abbott and Costello Meet Dr. Jekyll and Mr. Hyde (1953) (zee DR. JEKYLL AND FAMILY). At one point in the film, Costello drinks a potion (which is supposed to bring out one's true nature) in Jekyll's lab and turns into a giant mouse. ¶ "How do you like that Dr. Jekyll, he turned me into a mouse — the rat!"

The Abominable Dr. Phibes (1971) (see MADMEN — EARLY PSYCHOS). The mad Dr. Phibes employs the ten biblical curses from the Old Testament, including rats, to dispatch those he feels wronged him.

Ben (1972; Bing Crosby Productions) D: Phil Karlson. P: Mort Briskin. S: Gilbert A. Ralston. C: Russell Metty. Cast: Lee Harcourt Montgomery, Arthur O'Connell, Joseph Campanella, Rosemary Murphy, Meredith Baxter, Kaz Garas, Paul Carr, Kenneth Tobey, Norman Alden, Richard Van Fleet. *Ben,* a sequel to *Willard* (1971), is again a rats-run-rampant film. • Ben, the super-intelligent lead rat, is a survivor from the first film (*Willard*) and again escapes death in this one (presumably to chew another day, though that day has yet to arrive since no further sequels were made). • The film's musical theme, "Ben's Song," was sung by a young Michael Jackson and became a hit single. • As a promotional gimmick in many cities, the first 500 lucky theater patrons received a free photo of Ben, "signed" by the star—the corner of the photo was punctured by tiny teeth marks. • The makers of *Willard* generally were disappointed with this hasty sequel. "I didn't think much of *Ben,*" actor Bruce Davison (star of *Willard*) told *Fangoria* #56. "It went for schmaltz rather than a story." Screenwriter Gilbert Ralston called *Ben* "typical Hollywood scare fare, and not nearly as sensitive as the first one." Even rat-handler Moe DiSesso, returning from the first film, complained that they were just "making another Japanese monster movie.... They ruined it."

Deadly Eyes (1982; Filmtrust) D: Robert Clouse. P: Jeffrey Schechtman, Paul Kahnert. S: Lonon Smith. Cast: Sam Groom, Sara Botsford, Scatman Crothers, Lisa Langlois, Cec Linder, Lesleh Donaldson. Giant mutant rats grow to the size of dogs and begin gnawing people to death. ¶ Ad line: "Tonight they will rise from the darkness beneath the cities ... to feed." • *Deadly Eyes* is based on the novel by noted author James Herbert (*Dune* and sequels). • Director Robert Clouse is most noted for directing Bruce Lee's kung-fu opus, *Enter the Dragon.*

Food of the Gods (1976) (see ANIMAL GIANTS). A mysterious substance bubbling out of the ground turns animals and insects into giants. Marjoe Gortner and friends must battle giant rats among other things. • The rats in this film were only eight inches long in reality, but made to look gigantic with the use of trick photography. They came from Northern California and were accompanied by some U.C.L.A. students who trained them. After the film was completed they were sold to school classrooms for science lessons on rat behavior. The effects team on the film also constructed a huge life size model for close-ups.

Food of the Gods Part 2 (1989; Carolco;

Canada) D: Damian Lee. P: Damian Lee, David Mitchell. S: Richard Bennett, E. Kim Brewster. C: Curtis Petersen. Cast: Paul Coufos, Lisa Schrage, Michael Copeman, Colin Fox, Frank Pellegrino, Jackie Burroughs. An experimental growth hormone is accidentally exposed to a group of rats in a college laboratory. They escape, grow to the size of Saint Bernards, and eat everyone they encounter until trapped in a building courtyard and blown away by a police SWAT team. ¶ "I've seen a lot of rats in my time, some big, some very very small. But that was the Loch Ness Monster of rats." • Though a sequel in name to the original *Food of the Gods* (1976), this film makes no reference at all to the original. In the first film, the growth substance was a natural one that bubbled up out of the ground. In this movie, it is a man-made concoction of growth hormones which does the trick. None of the same people who worked on *Food of the Gods* were involved with this film. • In the original we had all manner of giant animals, from mosquitos to chickens, as well as rats. Here, it is strictly rats (except for one subplot involving an eight-year-old child who becomes a giant). • Bert I. Gordon (who wrote, produced, and directed the original *Food of the Gods* in 1976) was originally approached by Carolco Productions with the idea of writing a script and providing the special effects for this sequel, but left the project early on due to "creative differences" according to the production unit publicist.

Graveyard Shift (1990; Paramount) D: Ralph S. Singleton. P: William J. Dunn, Ralph S. Singleton. S: John Esposito. Cast: Brad Dourif, Stephen Macht, David Andrews, Kelly Wolf, Andrew Divoff, Vic Polizos. A sub-basement of a rat-infested woolen mill is discovered and a clean-up crew is sent down there by the sadistic foreman. The workers are trapped, killed, and eaten one by one by a giant rat-bat mutant creature who has made his lair in the nearby graveyard, and tunnels under the mill looking for fresh prey. • The film is based on the short story, "Graveyard Shift," by Stephen King (the seventeenth film adaptation of a King story). • In an industry in-joke, the mill is called the "Bachman Mill." "Bachman" is the name used as a pseudonym by Stephen King on several books.

Mountaintop Motel Massacre (1986) (see MADMEN – THE SLICE 'N' DICE WAVE). A crazy woman running the Mountaintop Motel either slices her guests with a sickle or sets snakes and rats on them. • Top-billed semi-professional actor Bill Thurman, who is done-in by rats, is most noted for his appearances in the no-budget Larry Buchanan movies of the 1960s (*In the Year 2889, It's Alive!,* and *Zontar — The Thing from Venus;* all from 1968).

Nightmares (1983) (see ANTHOLOGIES). In the "Night of the Rat" segment, a family must defend themselves against a giant demon-rat. ¶ "It translates into 'The Devil Rodent.' It's a legend about huge malevolent rodents with unbelievable cunning and strength that terrorized certain villainous individuals in seventeenth century Europe."

Nosferatu the Vampyre (1979) (see VAMPIRES — DRACULA AND FAMILY). The title character is preceded wherever he goes by a veritable army of plague-carrying rats.

Of Unknown Origin (1983; Warner Bros.; Canada) D: George Pan Cosmatos. P: Claude Heroux. S: Brian Taggert. C: René Verzier. Cast: Peter Weller, Jennifer Dale, Lawrence Dane, Kenneth Welsh, Louis Del Grande, Maury Chakin, Keith Knight, Shannon Tweed. Peter Weller is a successful yuppie who has just renovated his New York brownstone. A vicious, cunning rat infests his house and disrupts his life to the point that it becomes an obsession, ending in an all-out war with the repulsive rodent. ¶ "You know what's the matter with you? You don't realize that maybe you're spending, oh, 20 percent of your time thinking about him, but he's spending 100 percent of his time figuring out ways of how to outsmart you. He's a rat, he's got nothing better to do." • *Of Unknown Origin* is based on the novel by Chauncey G. Parker III. • This was Peter Weller's first starring role. He later became famous with films like *The Adventures of Buckaroo Banzai, Robocop, Leviathan,* and *Robocop 2.*

Ratboy (1987) (see FREAKS). A young boy with the face of a rat is exploited by various people.

Rats: Night of Terror (1983; Beatrice Films/IMP. EX. Cl.; Italy/France) (also *Rats*). D: Vincent Dawn. P: Beatrice Films. Cast: Richard Raymond, Alex McBride, Richard Cross, Janna Ryann. In the postholocaust year of 2225, a surviving band of humans discovers a town with uncontaminated food and water. Unfortunately this town is infested by an army of rats with a taste for human flesh. ¶ "How's your appetite today, eh? I must try and remember mom's old recipes. Baked mouse, rat pie, fried rat tails. No, really, if you cook them in vinegar, they're fine."

The Rats Are Coming! The Werewolves Are Here! (1972) (see WEREWOLVES — OTHER LYCANTHROPES). This film about a family of werewolves features a (totally unrelated) subplot about a girl who raises man-eating rats. ¶ "Remarkable creatures, rats. They can be very friendly if they want to be. On the other hand they can be very destructive if they get mad. I lost my arm to them, you know." • Producer William Mishkin took director Andy Milligan's film *Curse of the Full Moon,* which only ran 67 minutes long, and inserted the rat scenes to cash in on the success of *Willard* (1971). • These rat scenes were shot on Staten Island (where Milligan films most of his no-budget movies).

Willard (1971; Bing Crosby Productions) D: Daniel Mann. P: Mort Briskin. S: Gilbert A. Ralston. C: Robert B. Hauser. Cast: Bruce Davison, Ernest Borgnine, Elsa Lanchester, Sandra Locke, Michael Dante, J. Pat O'Malley. Willard, a lonely, pushedaround office boy, befriends two superintelligent rats who lead their rat hordes out to put the bite on Willard's enemies. ¶ "Tear him up!" — Willard commanding his rats. • The film was a box office smash, much to the chagrin of actor Ernest Borgnine, who was given a payment choice of straight salary or profit percentage before the film was completed. He said, "I exercised my usual fine judgment, and took the salary. Who'd ever want to see a cast of rats?" • In order to put the cast and crew at ease about the 600 live rats used in the film, animal trainer Moe DiSesso arranged a demonstration. He had his whole body covered in peanut butter (the rats' favorite food) and laid down to let the rats swarm all over him. After the rats had licked him clean, he stood up to show the amazed onlookers that he was unharmed, without even a scratch. • Sondra Locke, former long-time girlfriend of Clint Eastwood, played *Willard*'s love-interest. • Elsa Lanchester, the original *Bride of Frankenstein* (1935) herself, played Willard's nagging mother. • *Willard* was based on the novel *Ratman's Notebooks,* by Stephen Gilbert. • The film was successful enough to produce a sequel, *Ben* (though this time, the film isn't named after the rats' human counterpart, but after the lead rat himself).

The Willies (1990) (see ANTHOLOGIES). In one of the film's pre-credit gross-out vignettes, a rotund woman buys a big bucket of chicken at the "Tennessee Frickasee" restaurant. As she hungrily bites into her first piece with relish, she lets out a scream when she sees it is not a chicken leg she is eating, but a whole fried rat. ¶ "It was a big old rat — extra crispy."

Reincarnation

Transmigration, or reincarnation as we have generally come to call it, is primarily a doctrine of East Indian religious beliefs. Deeply rooted in Buddhism and Hinduism, the ideology proposes that when a person dies, their spirit can be re-born into another living person or thing. Since our country is far more influenced by Christianity, western films have only had a sporadic association with reincarnation, often tossing it in merely as a subplot in the shadow of the movie's main theme. Despite the outspokenness of a few notable celebrities, such as Shirley MacLaine or General George Patton (who believed himself to be the reincarnation of Alexander the Great), we generally regard the topic as fanciful rather than factual. Because of our cultural heritage, it is no wonder that filmmakers have used reincarnation only sparingly in cinema. It certainly is not a doctrine of wide belief in the West, and the money-spending film audiences are far more interested in witches and mummies (two film subjects which occasionally include reincarnation as a subplot). The first movie to deal with the theme of reincarnation was the stodgy 1935 version of *She*. Then in the 1950s, the topical "Bridey Murphy" reincarnation case sparked the public's interest, and exploitation filmmakers were quick to capitalize (with the "fishy" tale of *The She-Creature* and the dull "exposé" *The Search for Bridey Murphy* (both 1956) taking advantage of the short lived fervor generated by the *In Search of Bridey Murphy* novel). The 1970s, with its "New Age" sensibilities, saw a reincarnation revival of sorts with the release of three "big" productions — *On a Clear Day You Can See Forever* (1970), *The Reincarnation of Peter Proud* (1975), and *Audrey Rose* (1977). Despite these respectable features, and a handful of other more or less sensationalistic stabs at the subject, reincarnation has remained a low-key player in the cinema of the fantastic.

Attack of the Mayan Mummy (1964) (see MUMMIES — THE AZTEC MUMMY SERIES). Under hypnosis a woman reveals that she is the reincarnation of a Mayan princess who had an illicit affair with a warrior. She was killed and the warrior entombed alive. Now the warrior is a living mummy who guards the treasure of the Mayans.

Audrey Rose (1977; United Artists) D: Robert Wise. P: Frank de Felitta, Joe Wizan. S: Frank de Felitta. C: Victor J. Kemper. Cast: Anthony Hopkins, Marsha Mason, Susan Swift, John Beck, John Hillerman, Norman Lloyd. A couple's daughter turns out to be the reincarnation of a girl (Audrey Rose) who burned to death in a car accident. Audrey's grieving father, played by Anthony Hopkins, uses hypnosis at the climax to free the girl of his daughter's agony.

The Aztec Mummy (1957) (see MUMMIES — THE AZTEC MUMMY SERIES). In this first Aztec Mummy film, the mummy named Popoca guards the sacred breastplate and bracelet in his pyramid tomb which holds the key to the Aztec treasure. A woman, the reincarnation of his long lost love, leads a group of scientists and treasure-seekers to the sacred objects.

The Bride and the Beast (1958) (see APES AND MONKEYS). Big-game hunter Lance Fuller learns that his new bride is actually a reincarnated gorilla with an urge to return to the jungle. At the climax, she spurns her human husband and sets up house with an ape. ¶ "Dan, the night we hypnotized her, she displayed some very unusual animal tendencies. That she had been a gorilla in a past life seems rather positive. I believe she's gone now, gone back where she came from."

Chances Are (1989; Tri-Star) D: Emile Ardolino. P: Mike Lobell. S: Perry Howze, Randy Howze. C: William A. Fraker. Cast: Cybill Shepherd, Robert Downey, Jr., Ryan O'Neal, Mary Stuart Masterson, Christopher McDonald, Josef Sommer, Joe Grifasi. Robert Downey, Jr., begins to remember the experiences of his past life. He realizes that his girlfriend is actually his daughter from his previous existence, and her mother was his wife.

Creature of Destruction (1967) (see FISH-PEOPLE). This no-budget remake of AIP's

The She-Creature centers around a hypnotist who sends a woman back to her prehuman existence as a sea creature.

The Crimson Cult (1968) (see WITCHES, WARLOCKS, AND CULTS) (also *The Curse of the Crimson Altar; The Crimson Altar*). Christopher Lee plays the modern reincarnation of the seventeenth century witch named "Lavinia."

Curse of the Aztec Mummy (1959) (see MUMMIES—THE AZTEC MUMMY SERIES). This entry in the Aztec Mummy series features the evil criminal mastermind known as "The Bat," who is after the Aztec treasure guarded over by the living mummy, Popoca. The Bat tries to get to the treasure through the daughter of an eminent scientist, who is the reincarnation of Popoca's lost love.

Curse of the Faceless Man (1958) (see MUMMIES—MORE MUMMIES). A 2,000-year-old mummified man (a slave named Quintilius, buried in the eruption of Mount Vesuvius) is found at Pompeii and comes back to life to abduct Elaine Edwards, whom he believes to be the reincarnation of his lost love.

Fright (1957; Allied Artists) (also *Spell of the Hypnotist*). D/P: W. Lee Wilder. S: Myles Wilder. Cast: Nancy Malone, Eric Fleming, Frank Marth, Humphrey Davis, Dean Almquist. A psychiatrist uses hypnotism to prevent a suicide and accidentally awakens memories of a former life in the woman—the mistress of a nineteenth century German ruler. ¶ "One murder committed twice—a century apart!"—ad slogan.

Hold That Hypnotist (1957; Allied Artists) D: Austen Jewell. P: Ben Schwalb. S: Dan Pepper. Cast: Huntz Hall, Leo Gorcey, Mel Welles, Stanley Clements. Huntz Hall gets his hands on Blackbeard's map after regressing back to the seventeenth century.

I Was a Teenage Werewolf (1957) (see WEREWOLVES—OTHER LYCANTHROPES). A mad doctor manages to bring out a troubled teen's past wolf-self with the aid of a serum and hypnosis.

I've Lived Before (1956; Universal) D: Richard Bartlett. P: Howard Christie. S: Norman Jolley, William Talman. C: Maury Gertsman. Cast: Jock Mahoney, Leigh Snowden, Ann Harding, John McIntire, Raymond Bailey. After his plane crashes, Jock Mahoney believes he is a reincarnated World War I fighter pilot. • Mahoney also crash-landed a year later in the prehistoric lost world film, *The Land Unknown* (1957). His co-star, Leigh Snowden, was busy the same year being protected by the gill-man in *The Creature Walks Among Us* (1956).

Let's Live Again (1948; 20th Century–Fox) D: Herbert I. Leeds. P: Frank N. Seltzer. S: Rodney Carlisle, Robert Smalley. C: Mack Stengler. Cast: John Emmery, Hillary Brooke, Taylor Holmes, Diana Douglas, James Millican. The brother of an atomic scientist is reincarnated as a dog.

The Mummy (1932) (see MUMMIES—THE UNIVERSAL SERIES). The soul of an Egyptian princess has been reincarnated as a modern woman named Helen Grovesnor. Imhotep, the forbidden lover of her previous incarnation, revives as a 3,700-year-old mummy and intends to sacrifice her body in order to make her a living mummy like himself.

The Mummy's Ghost (1944) (see MUMMIES—THE UNIVERSAL SERIES). In Universal's fourth Mummy movie, and third film in the "Kharis" series, acolyte John Carradine is sent to America to find and retrieve Kharis and the mummy of Ananka (which is housed at the local museum). But the body of Ananka crumbles to dust when touched—her soul has been reincarnated in the woman Amina, girlfriend of hero Tom. At the climax, the Mummy carries the girl off towards the swamp. Amina begins to age until she too is nothing but a dried mummy and the pair of ancient lovers sink into the swamp together, reunited at last.

Necropolis (1987) (see WITCHES, WARLOCKS, AND CULTS). A 300-year-old witch searches contemporary New York for the reincarnated souls of those who stopped her virgin sacrifice attempt back in 1685.

On a Clear Day You Can See Forever (1970; Paramount) D: Vincente Minnelli. P: Howard Koch. S: Alan Jay Lerner. C: Harry Stradling. Cast: Barbra Streisand, Bob Newhart, Yves Montand, Jack Nicholson, Larry Blyden, Simon Oakland. A psychiatrist learns that a woman is the reincarnation of many people. He falls in love with one of Daisy Gamble's former selves, an eighteenth century woman named Melinda. • Director Vincente Minnelli married actress Judy Garland in 1945, a union which resulted in the birth of another talented singer/actress, Liza Minnelli. He was a prolific director of musicals and won Oscars for his films, *Gigi* (1958) and *The Band Wagon* (1953).

The Reincarnate (1971; Meridian; Canada) D: Don Haldane. P/S: Seelig Lester. Cast: Jack Creley, Jay Reynolds, Trudy Young. A young sculptor agrees to a satanic ritual whereby he would receive the spirit of a dying lawyer. To complete the transfer, a young virgin must be sacrificed, and, unfortunately for the sculptor, the victim is reincarnated as his newborn baby. ¶ "No one ever dies," claimed the ads.

The Reincarnation of Peter Proud (1975; Cinerama) D: J. Lee Thompson. P: Frank P. Rosenberg. S: Max Ehrlich. C: Victor J. Kemper. Cast: Michael Sarrazin, Jennifer O'Neill, Margot Kidder, Cornelia Sharpe, Paul Hecht. Michael Sarrazin believes himself to be the reincarnation of a murder victim, so he journeys to the man's home town to meet the family. There, Sarrazin's former self begins to dominate his personality and fate repeats itself. • This horror yarn about drownings, murder, and possession was made by the production conglomerate headed by Bing Crosby.

The Robot vs. the Aztec Mummy (1959) (see MUMMIES—THE AZTEC MUMMY SERIES). That evil criminal scientist "The Bat" is back again, searching for the breastplate and bracelet guarded by the Aztec Mummy. He builds a destructive robot, which he sends out to battle the mummy. This entry in the series once again features a woman who is the reincarnation of the Mummy's long lost love.

The Search for Bridey Murphy (1956; Paramount) D/S: Noel Langley. P: Pat Duggan. C: John F. Warren. Cast: Louis Hayward, Teresa Wright, Kenneth Tobey, Nancy Gates, Richard Anderson. A housewife under hypnosis is revealed to be the reincarnation of a nineteenth century Irish woman. • The film is based upon a supposedly true account of reincarnation which made the best seller list as a novel in the 1950s, written by the hypnotist, Morey Bernstein.

She (1935; RKO) D: Irving Pichel, Lansing C. Holden. P: Merian C. Cooper. S: Ruth Rose. C: J. Roy Hunt. Cast: Helen Gahagan, Randolph Scott, Nigel Bruce, Helen Mack, Gustav von Seyffertitz, Samuel Hinds, Jim Thorpe, Noble Johnson. A Cambridge professor leads an expedition to a lost city in the Himalayas where they encounter their immortal Queen who believes Randolph Scott to be a reincarnated former lover. Scott does not go along with her plans and she steps into a magical fire, causing her to age rapidly. • Co-star Nigel Bruce later became *the* Dr. Watson, the bumbling friend of Basil Rathbone's Sherlock Holmes in 14 films. • Director Irving Pichel also co-directed *The Most Dangerous Game* (1932) with Ernest B. Schoedsack *(King Kong)*. In 1950, he was chosen to direct George Pal's breakthrough space epic, *Destination Moon*.

She (1965; Hammer-Seven Arts/MGM; U.K.) D: Robert Day. P: Michael Carreras.

S: David T. Chantler. C: Harry Waxman. Cast: Ursula Andress, Peter Cushing, John Richardson, Bernard Cribbins, Christopher Lee, Andre Morell, Rosenda Monteros. This updated version of the 1935 film is set in Africa. John Richardson plays the reincarnation of the former lover of "She Who Must Be Obeyed." Unlike Randolph Scott in the original, Richardson gains immortality in the end (while She rapidly ages and dies) and remains in the lost city. • Director Robert Day began his film career as a cameraman. His other horror credits include *The Haunted Strangler* (1958), *First Man into Space* (1959), and *Corridors of Blood* (1962).

The She-Creature (1956) (see FISH-PEOPLE). A mad hypnotist brings forth a woman's past alter ego—that of a prehistoric amphibious creature—to carry out his murderous predictions. ¶ "Ladies and gentlemen, I shall give you living proof of reincarnation, of perpetual life itself." • The film is (reportedly) based upon the true life story of Ruth Simmons, who with the help of a hypnotist, discovered that she apparently was the reincarnation of a nineteenth century woman named Bridey Murphy. The weird tale was made into a novel by the hypnotist, Morey Bernstein.

Stigma (1981) (see PSYCHIC ABILITY). A young lad with tremendous destructive mental abilities discovers that he is the reincarnation of a boy who massacred his family—and follows suit.

The Undead (1956) (see WITCHES, WARLOCKS, AND CULTS). A young woman visits a psychiatrist who discovers she is the reincarnation of a woman who was executed for witchcraft several centuries ago. Via hypnosis, he takes her back to her former life to confront a coven of real witches. When an attempt to kill a witch fails, the doctor forfeits his own existence at the fateful climax. • This feature was another Bridey Murphy–inspired reincarnation story originally designed to be a horror comedy. When the Murphy phenomenon died down, director Roger Corman had the script sobered up, and gave more emphasis to the witchcraft aspect of the plot.

The Vengeance of She (1968; Hammer-Seven Arts/20th Century-Fox; U.K.) D: Cliff Owen. P: Aida Young. S: Peter O'Donnell. C: Wolfgang Suschitzky. Cast: John Richardson, Olinka Berova, Edward Judd, Colin Blakely, Andre Morell, Derek Godfrey, Noel William. This direct sequel to *She* (1965) features Olinka Berova as the reincarnation of Ursula Andress in the first film.

John Richardson, who achieved immortality while Andress died in the original, continues the cycle by "calling" her to his lost city. When she refuses to be his new queen, Richardson fulfills his destiny and steps into the fire and dies. In the end, the city blows up, and Olinka escapes. ¶ Ad line: "*She*— The ultimate female who used her beauty and her body to bring kingdoms to their downfall and men to their knees!"

Voodoo Black Exorcist (1975) (see MUMMIES — MORE MUMMIES). In this obscure imported oddity, the 1,000-year-old mummy of an African voodoo priest is revived and sets about finding the reincarnation of his long lost love.

You Never Can Tell (1951; Universal) D: Lou Breslow. P: Leonard Goldstein. S: Lou Breslow, David Chandler. C: Maury Gertsman. Cast: Dick Powell, Peggy Dow, Charles Drake, Joyce Holden, Albert Sharpe. A dog is killed and enters animal heaven before being sent back to earth as a man to expose the killer. He is assisted by his comedic female companion, a reincarnated horse. ¶ "He's an old Army buddy of mine.... We were in the canine corps together." • Dick Powell is the dog-in-man's-clothing with a penchant for munching doggy snacks, and his female companion (the reincarnated horse) turns heads with her ability to run down speeding cars.

Robots

(*See also* Computers; Machines)

According to the dictionary, a robot is "a machine in the form of a human being that performs the mechanical functions of a human being but lacks sensitivity." Made in the image of humans, the robot was assembled with the intention of lessening the human's work load. Their creators built them without the capacity for human emotion so they would be able to perform their tasks objectively and with more efficiency. At least that was the idea according to most cinematic examples, but something always seems to go wrong.

From out of this invention of modern technology came two themes which filmmakers have latched onto in their robot epics. The first is the very real fear people have of being replaced in society by a faster, more efficient machine. Springing from this uneasiness, we have plotlines that depict technology overrunning our lives to such an extent that we lose control of our own destiny and purpose (as in the machine-controlled world of *The Terminator,* 1984). The second theme would be the malfunctioning of, or out-and-out loss of control over, the machines themselves. The latter premise has certainly fit in well with many of the genre films depicting robots. In *Metropolis* (1926), we saw how the scheme of a greedy corporate head backfired and nearly destroyed an entire city. His robot double of Maria (symbolic leader of the working class) could not be controlled, and, acting on its own, managed to incite a destructive revolution that nearly doomed them all. In *Westworld* (1973), the robots which populated the fantasy lands of Delos turned on their makers and the park's patrons with a brutal vengeance. And of course, we can only wonder what might have happened if Patricia Neal had forgotten the words which halted Gort's reign of destruction in *The Day the Earth Stood Still* (1951).

According to their definition, robots "lack sensitivity"—lack human feelings. Ironically, many of the robots depicted in the cinema have been full of emotions and have even grappled with weighty moral dilemmas. The screen's most endearing robot—Robby the Robot from *Forbidden Planet* (1956)—was very personable for a machine. He was articulate, eager to please, and he had a built-in directive that forbade him from harming human life forms. Children loved him, and it was this kind of natural affection which prompted MGM to bring his character back again one year later for *The Invisible Boy*. In that story, the beloved Robby became a deadly tool of an ominous computer, and was ordered to kill the young son of a scientist. As you might imagine, Robby's humanistic qualities were too strong, and in the end he finally broke through the mechanical spell (often to a loud round of audience applause).

Falling within our broad definition of "robots" are not only the metallic machines like Robby and *Gog* (1954), but the "android" (or cyborg). An android is an artificial being or machine with a coating of synthetic (or natural) skin on the outside which gives him or her a human appearance. Androids are not like the monstrous, cumbersome, unthinking robots in *Target Earth* (1954) or *Devil Girl from Mars* (1954). They are generally endowed with that little spark of humanity which their makers consider imperative for instilling the necessary morals which guide their behavior. This humanistic factor, which is designed to make them more versatile than ordinary robots, often leads to a budding free will or an inquisitive spirit. The androids in Ridley Scott's *Blade Runner* (1982), for instance, were savagely hunted down because they were showing signs of an increased self-awareness which their creators deemed dangerous. A clever juxtaposition of attitudes began to take shape as the androids became more human and the humans became more "robotic." The machines wanted to live their lives freely and in peace, and desired strongly to know who and why they were. The Blade Runner character (Harrison Ford), on the other hand, had submerged his emotions in order to carry out his assigned task. The climactic irony of the story was that the fugitive android proved that he loved life more than his human enemy did by saving Ford from death, just as his own life had run out. It is these kinds of stories which makes the robot figure so attractive to audiences. Today, the robot subgenre is enjoying a successful resurgence with hard-hitting films like *The Terminator* (1984), and new heroes like *Robocop* (1987).

These man-like machines are often portrayed as naive, innocent characters who serve as a reflection of our own lives and ideals, and hopefully prompt us to examine our humanity just a little closer.

Alien (1979) (see ALIENS — ENCOUNTERS IN OUTER SPACE). A spaceship crew has to deal not only with an unstoppable killer alien, but a treacherous crew member who turns out to be an android carrying out the secretive orders of their unscrupulous employers.

Aliens (1986) (see ALIENS — ENCOUNTERS IN OUTER SPACE). Lance Henriksen plays an android hero who literally gets ripped in half by the Alien queen.

Android (1982; New World) D: Aaron Lipstadt. P: Mary Ann Fisher. S: James Reigle, Don Opper. C: Tim Suhrstedt. Cast: Don Opper, Klaus Kinski, Brie Howard, Norbert Weisser, Crofton Hardester, Kendra Kirchner. Klaus Kinski creates an emotional humanoid robot, named Max 404, who longs to learn about relations between human men and women. The story, which takes place on a space station, concerns itself with Max coming to grips with sexual-ity and his impending scheduled termination. ¶ "An android is a robot that possesses all the physical characteristics of a human being down to the smallest detail." • At one point Max is seen viewing the Frank Capra classic, *It's a Wonderful Life* (1946) aboard the station.

The Black Hole (1979) (see SPACE TRAVEL). A crazed scientist uses robots to guard his ship, which is drifting near a Black Hole in space. • The evil robot guarding his master's ship is named Maximilian. Ironically, it is the same name as the actor playing his mad-scientist creator — Maximilian Schell.

Blade Runner (1982; Warner Bros.) D: Ridley Scott. P: Michael Deeley. S: Hampton Fancher, David Peoples. C: Jordan Cronenworth. Cast: Harrison Ford, Rutger Hauer, Sean Young, Edward James Olmos, Daryl Hannah, M. Emmet Walsh, William Sanderson, Brion James, Joe Turkel. In the near future, Harrison Ford is assigned the task of hunting down and "retiring" (executing) a series of A.W.O.L. robots known as replicants, who wish only to live out their lives in peace. ¶ "I don't know why he saved my life. Maybe in those last moments he loved life more than he ever had before. Not just his life. Anybody's life. My life. All they wanted were the same answers as the rest of us want. Where do I come from, where am I going, how long have I got? All I could do was sit there and watch him die." • Brion James, who co-stars as the replicant "Leon," stated that *Blade Runner* was the favorite of all his films, calling it "one of the classic science fiction movies ever made," in a *Fangoria* #82 interview.

The Bowery Boys Meet the Monsters (1954) (see MAD SCIENTISTS). The Bowery boys encounter a robot named Gorog who eventually helps them to escape a spooky old house beset with monsters. In the end the robot takes to the sport of baseball to relieve the pressure of mad scientists and everyday life.

Castle of Evil (1966; United Pictures) D: Francis D. Lyon. P: Earle Lyon. S: Charles A. Wallace. C: Brick Marquard. Cast: Scott Brady, Virginia Mayo, Lisa Gaye, Hugh Marlowe, David Brian, William Thourlby. A group of people arrive at a disfigured scientist's island for the reading of his will. His real motive is to kill the one responsible for his bad looks with the aid of a powerful robot which looks just like him. One of the heirs has some plans of his own and manages to re-program the robot, beginning a killing spree. ¶ "Furthermore, every one of you six people had the opportunity on that day and date to commit my murder. All six of you had a motive." • Scott Brady finally does in the rampaging robot (played by William Thourlby) with a laser gun.

Cherry 2000 (1986) (see FUTURES ON EARTH—UTOPIAS AND DYSTOPIAS). In the near future, Melanie Griffith drives a souped-up Mustang and is looking to retrieve another model of a rare female robot for a guy who accidentally short circuited his in the kitchen. • Two famous screen robots—"Gort" from *The Day the Earth Stood Still* (1951) and "Robby the Robot" from *Forbidden Planet* (1956)—are seen as you pass through a robot factory early on in the film.

Chopping Mall (1986; Concorde) (also *Killbots*). D: Jim Wynorski. P: Julie Corman. S: Jim Wynorski, Steve Mitchell. C: Tom Richmond. Cast: Kelli Maroney, Tony O'Dell, John Terlesky, Russell Todd, Karrie Emerson, Barbara Crampton, Suzee Slater, Nick Segal. Three high-tech security robots

at a shopping mall malfunction and turn into killing machines, menacing a group of teenagers who have snuck into the mall for some after-hours fun. ¶ "They remind me of your mother—it's the laser eyes." • The most interesting thing about this film are the few cameo appearances/in-jokes. Paul Bartel and Mary Woronov appear briefly in the film's beginning as Mr. and Mrs. Bland (from *Eating Raoul,* 1982). Dick Miller also appears as Walter Paisley (his flower-eating character from *The Little Shop of Horrors,* 1960). • Look for a clip from Roger Corman's *Attack of the Crab Monsters* (1957). • *Chopping Mall*'s producer, Julie Corman, is Roger's wife.

The Colossus of New York (1958; Paramount) D: Eugene Lourie. P: William Alland. S: Thelma Schnee. C: John F. Warren. Cast: John Baragrey, Ross Martin, Otto Kruger, Mala Powers, Charles Herbert, Ed Wolff, Robert Hutton. An internationally acclaimed scientist (Ross Martin) dies in a car accident and his father, who cannot bear to see his son's life wasted, decides to transplant his son's brain into the body of a robot so he can carry on with his work. The experiment works, but Martin is driven mad by his mechanical condition and goes on a climactic killing spree at the United Nations building. The robot, in a moment of regained humanity, asks his own son Billy to turn off his life support switch at the end, and thus end his uncontrolled reign of terror. ¶ "Billy, I want you to stop me." • Ross Martin was popularly known as Robert Conrad's partner, Artemus Gordon, in the TV series, "The Wild Wild West." In an interview with Al Taylor and David Everitt, appearing in *Filmfax* #16, Ross Martin discussed his role. "The script said that he was to be played as 'intellectually brilliant.' But that was not my major concern. Instead I played him as a warm human being, one who cared about the people around him, as well as his work. Then his death would matter all the more. That's what I was reaching for." Martin also relayed a humorous anecdote about the filming of his character's memorial service—Martin (playing the corpse) fell asleep in the casket and began snoring, which fouled up the scene. • The 160-pound Colossus costume was worn by a giant of an actor named Ed Wolff. He was 7'4" and weighed about 320 pounds. In his early years, he had a small part in the 1925 classic, *Phantom of the Opera,* with Lon Chaney, Sr. • Promotional materials for the film included the gimmicky idea of putting on a "tall man" contest for free tickets into the theater. Ads read: "Attention men! Do you consider yourself a colossus? If you are 6'5" tall, or more, you qualify to be a guest of the _____ theater."

Crash and Burn (1990) (see FUTURES ON EARTH—UTOPIAS AND DYSTOPIAS). At the climax of this futuristic film, the young, technically-talented heroine reactivates a scrapped 80-foot robot machine to dispatch a vicious killer android called a "synthoid." ¶ "Any 'synth' can kill you if you override its programming with a crash and burn virus."

Creation of the Humanoids (1962; Emerson Film Enterprises) D: Wesley E. Barry. P: Wesley E. Barry, Edward J. Kay. S: Jay Simmons. C: Hal Mohr. Cast: Don Megowan, Frances McCann, Erica Elliot, Don Dolittle, Dudley Manlove. Humanoid robots called "clickers" desire equality with humans. Don Megowan plays a scientist giving the robots blood transfusions in order to make them fertile.

Cyborg (1989) (see FUTURES ON EARTH—UTOPIAS AND DYSTOPIAS). A female cyborg with the secret cure for the radiation sickness plaguing the devastated world is rescued by a powerful mercenary.

Cyborg 2087 (1966; Feature Film Corp.) D: Franklin Adreon. P: Earle Lyon. S: Arthur C. Pierce. Cast: Michael Rennie, Karen Steele, Wendell Corey, Warren Stevens, Eduard Franz, Harry Carey, Jr. A cyborg (Michael Rennie) travels back in time to stop a scientist from producing a machine that will set the world on a future course of mind control and repression. ¶ "As you can see, my transmitting equipment is built in. [It] is one of numerous mechanical and electronic devices I carry in my body." • Michael (*The Day the Earth Stood Still,* 1951) Rennie also appeared in two episodes of the popular "Batman" TV series as a character named "The Sandman." He died in England in 1971.

D.A.R.Y.L. (1985; Paramount) D: Simon Wincer. P: John Heyman. S: David Ambrose, Allan Scott, Jeffrey Ellis. C: Frank Watts. Cast: Mary Beth Hurt, Michael McKean, Barett Oliver, Kathryn Walker, Josef Sommer, Colleen Camp. A robot boy is taken into a foster home until his real parents find him. • The acronym stands for "Data Analyzing Robot Youth Lifeform."

The Day the Earth Stood Still (1951) (see ALIENS—BENEVOLENT ALIENS). Lock Martin plays a huge peace-keeping robot named Gort which emerges from a flying saucer operated by Michael Rennie. ¶ "In matters of aggression we have given them absolute power over us. This power cannot be re-

voked. At the first signs of violence they act automatically against the aggressor. The penalty for provoking their action is too terrible to risk." • Gort possesses a disintegrator ray, which he uses to destroy military weapons. He also has the power to bring life to Klaatu's dead body.

Deadly Friend (1986) D: Wes Craven. P: Robert M. Sherman. S: Bruce Joe Rubin. Cast: Mathew Laborteaux, Kristy Swanson, Michael Sharrett, Anne Twomey. A boy genius comes to a small-town university to study artificial intelligence. He builds a cute robot named "BeeBee" and falls for the girl next door. When she is accidentally killed (the result of abuse from her father), the whiz kid steals her body, implants a robot circuit in her brain, and brings her back to life. Unfortunately, she has more robot than human now and goes on a killing spree, dispatching all those who wronged her. • Starring in *Deadly Friend* gave 16-year-old actress Kristy Swanson nightmares. "It was really weird," she told *Fangoria* #60. "They began when I started doing *Deadly Friend* and I would have them about two or three times a week during the entire shooting schedule. When we finished the film, the nightmares stopped." • The film is based on the novel *Friend,* by Diana Henstell.

Devil Girl from Mars (1954) (see ALIENS—INVADERS ON EARTH: THE 50s). A large square-shaped robot named "Chani" helps the invading Devil Girl conquer (a small part of) Britain. ¶ "Chani is a mechanical man, a robot with many of the characteristics of a human, but improved by an electronic brain."

Dr. Coppelius (1966; Childhood Productions; Spain/U.S.) D/S: Ted Kneeland. P: Frank J. Hale. C: Cecilo Paniagua. Cast: Walter Slezak, Claudia Corday, Eileen Elliott, Caj Selling, Carman Rojas. Complications arise when a scientist's beautiful dancing robot creation draws the attention of another man.

Dr. Goldfoot and the Bikini Machine (1965; AIP) D: Norman Taurog. P: James H. Nicholson, Samuel Z. Arkoff. S: Elwood Ullman, Robert Kaufman. C: Sam Leavitt. Cast: Vincent Price, Frankie Avalon, Susan Hart, Dwayne Hickman, Fred Clark, Harvey Lembeck. Bikini-wearing female robots are created by the nefarious Dr. Goldfoot in a plot to conquer the world. • Dwayne Hickman (TV's "Doby Gillis") and Frankie Avalon and Harvey Lembeck (from AIP's beach movies) all appear in this teenage sci-fi spoof. Watch for Annette Funicello also!

Dr. Goldfoot and the Girl Bombs (1966; AIP: Italy/U.S.) D: Mario Bava. P: Louis M. Heyward, Fulvio Luciano. S: Louis M. Heyward, Robert Kaufman, Castellano & Pippolo. C: A. Rinaldi. Cast: Vincent Price, Fabian, Franco Franchi, Ciccio Ingrassia, Laura Antonelli. This sequel to *Dr. Goldfoot and the Bikini Machine* has Goldfoot (Vincent Price) plotting to start a war between the United States and the Soviet Union by sending sexy female robots out to kill NATO generals. ¶ Outlandish ad lines: "The most Titillating time-bombs you were ever tempted to trigger! Don't touch — She's a booby-bomb . . . with a delicate relaxivity fuse! . . . The girls with thermo-nuclear navels!" • Rock 'n' roll teen idol, Fabian, plays the agent who foils the plans of Dr. Goldfoot. Goldfoot receives his backing from China in the film, and the robot girls are equipped with exploding navels.

The Earth Dies Screaming (1964; 20th Century–Fox) D: Terence Fisher. P: Robert L. Lippert, Jack Parsons. S: Henry Cross. C: Len Harris. Cast: Virginia Field, Dennis Price, Thorley Walters, Vanda Godsell, David Spenser, Anna Polk. An alien sends robots to attack our Earth and resurrect zombie corpses. An American pilot lands in a devastated England with robots and zombies running amok.

Egghead's Robot (1970; Children's Film Foundation; U.K.) D: Milo Lewis. P: Cecil Musk. S: Leif Saxon. C: Johnny Coquillon. Cast: Keith Chegwin, Jeffrey Chegwin, Kathryn Dawe, Roy Kinnear, Richard Wattis. This British Disney-like feature is about a father who makes a robot double of his son to keep the boy's tormentors at bay. • Keith Chegwin plays the boy, and his real life twin brother, Jeffrey, plays the robot double.

Eliminators (1986) (see TIME TRAVEL). A "mandroid" (part man, part machine) rebels against his mad scientist creator with the help of some tough friends.

Eve of Destruction (1991; Orion) D: Duncan Gibbins. P: David Madden. S: Duncan Gibbins, Yale Udoff. C: Alan Hume. Cast: Gregory Hines, Renee Soutendijk. A female military robot runs amok. ¶ "Its creator made it in her own image. The military made it deadly. Now, only one man can stop her!" — ad line.

First Spaceship on Venus (1962) (see VENUS). The spaceship crew traveling to Venus is accompanied by a chess-playing robot.

Forbidden Planet (1956) (see ALIENS — ENCOUNTERS IN OUTER SPACE). Dr. Morbius (Walter Pidgeon) has built a super-robot which was designed to perform numerous tasks, including the manufacturing of synthetic foods, helping with experiments, and protection for both him and his daughter. • This is the first appearance of the screen's most famous robot — Robby the Robot.

Frankenstein Meets the Space Monster (1965) (see ALIENS — INVADERS ON EARTH: THE 60S AND 70S) (also *Duel of the Space Monsters*). The "Frankenstein" mentioned in the title is actually a robot space pilot who is horribly disfigured in a crash. The haywire android turns murderous, but finally regains his senses in time to battle a group of invading aliens and their mutant monster. ¶ "We have here, for all practical purposes, a normal human being created out of normal parts, transplanted, except for his synthetic skin and the electronic sensory control system of course . . . we can learn all we need to know about extended space travel without the loss of one man."

Future World (1976; AIP) D: Richard T. Heffron. P: Paul N. Lazarus III, James T. Aubrey. S: Mayo Simon, George Schenck. C: Howard Schwartz, Gene Polito. Cast: Peter Fonda, Blythe Danner, Arthur Hill, Yul Brynner, Harry Margolin, John Ryan. Peter Fonda plays a reporter attempting to uncover a robot takeover scheme in the reopened amusement park called Delos. • This film is a direct sequel to *Westworld* (1973), wherein the robot fantasy community goes berserk and begins killing the tourists. Yul Brynner reprises his role as the relentless robot gunslinger from the first film. • It turns out at the film's climax that the new head of Delos is a robot trying to replace world leaders with automated clones. Fonda and Danner escape Futureworld when they overcome the robot counterparts who have been sent to kill and replace them. Fonda flips off one of the Delos administrators as he leaves the complex, demonstrating that their plot has and will indeed fail. • The new Delos amusement park seen in this film features four different worlds — Romanworld and Medievalworld (which were also in the original), along with Futureworld and Spa World.

Galaxina (1980; Crown International) D/S: William Sachs. P: Marilyn J. Tenser. C: Dean Cundey. Cast: Dorothy Stratten, Stephen Macht, James David Hinton, Avery Schreiber. Galaxina is the robot navigator of the space cruiser "Infinity" whose mission is to recover the powerful Blue Star from the planet Altar 1. Though a robot, she has emotions, and one of the ship's crew members falls in love with her. ¶ "It's forbidden for space police to fraternize with machines — you may go blind." • Former Playboy playmate Dorothy Stratten (Galaxina) was murdered by her estranged husband just as the film was released.

Gog (1954; United Artists) D: Herbert L. Strock. P: Ivan Tors. S: Tom Taggart. C: Lothrop B. Worth. Cast: Richard Egan, Constance Dowling, Herbert Marshall, John Wengraf, Philip Van Zandt, Michael Fox, William Schallert, Tom Daly. Mysterious deaths and sabotage occur at an underground complex in New Mexico that is developing components for a planned space station. It turns out that a high flying jet is controlling their central computer which in turn uses the installation's two robots (Gog and Magog) to go after the scientists. Once the plane is destroyed, order is restored. ¶ "One day, Dr. Sheppard, my robots will pilot our rocket into space." • The picture was originally released in 3-D.

H. G. Wells' The Shape of Things to Come (1979; Film Ventures; Canada) (also *The Shape of Things to Come*). D: George McGowan. P: William Davison. S: Martin Lager. C: Reginald Morris. Cast: Jack Palance, Carol Lynley, Barry Morse, Nicholas Campbell, John Ireland. After a series of nuclear and robotic wars, the final vestige of humanity is on a Moon base. In need of a substance called RADIC-Q2, a group of adventurers (one of whom is a wise-cracking robot) are sent to Delta 3 where they must fight an evil dictator and his robot army to obtain the vital substance.

Hardware (1990; Millimeter Films; U.K.) D/S: Richard Stanley. P: Paul Trybits, Jo Anne Sellar. C: Steven Chivers. Cast: Dylan McDermott, Stacey Travis, John Lynch, William Hootkins, Iggy Pop. In the overcrowded, squalid, radiation-plagued future, a space jockey finds a cyborg head and brings it home to his girlfriend who sculpts art out of scrap. The robot, however, turns out to be an experimental military model called Mark 13, designed solely to kill. It reactivates and rebuilds itself using her tools and scrap parts. Trapped in her apartment, they are forced into close-quarters combat with the mechanical monster. ¶ "They're lyin' if they think that thing is gonna kill the enemy. It doesn't care who it kills!" • *Hardware* is based on an original story by Steve MacManus and Kevin O'Neill titled "SHOK!" which appeared in Fleetway Comics' "2,000 AD." Director/writer Richard Stanley claimed he never saw the comic book, and was inspired instead by the 1980 robot film, *Saturn*

3. The incredible similarities between the "SHOK" story, first published in 1980, and the *Hardware* script, however, led to a lawsuit which was settled out of court for an undisclosed five-figure amount and a hastily added screen credit. • Rock musician Iggy Pop plays "Angry Bob," a futuristic disc jockey. Though given good billing, he never appears in the film — just his voice is heard.

Heartbeeps (1981; Universal) D: Allan Arkush. P: Michael Phillips. S: John Hill. C: Charles Rosher, Jr. Cast: Andy Kaufman, Bernadette Peters, Randy Quaid, Kenneth McMillan, Christopher Guest, Melanie Mayron. A pair of domestic robots take off to explore the world around them and build a family.

The Human Duplicators (1965) (see ALIENS — INVADERS ON EARTH: THE 60s AND 70s). An alien creates a race of androids with which he can imitate and replace high ranking officials. ¶ Secretary: "Would you know an android if you saw one?" Secret Agent: "Well I … I don't believe I would." • Bullets can't stop these androids, but their heads will crack open like a porcelain doll when they fall (showing us that their heads contain nothing more than a bunch of loose blue lincoln logs and silver nuts and bolts!) • George Nader, who also appeared in another "robot" picture — *Robot Monster* (1953), is the hero in this film.

The Invisible Boy (1957; MGM) D: Herman Hoffman. P: Nicholas Nayfack. S: Cyril Hume. C: Harold Wellman. Cast: Richard Eyer, Philip Abbott, Diane Brewster, Harold J. Stone, Robert H. Harris. Robby the Robot from *Forbidden Planet* (1956) pops up in this Disney-like comedy/thriller about a power-hungry computer that wants to break a secret code enabling it to operate freely. The supercomputer uses Robby to abduct the son of a scientist in the hope of extorting the code from the scientist, but good old Robby just cannot hurt the boy, and eventually the computer's control device is switched off. A comedic side plot in the film involves Robby giving the little boy a potion which makes him invisible. • Robby's appearance in the film is explained by the boy's father as a time traveling endeavor by a deceased colleague who apparently retrieved the robot from our future. • In addition to controlling Robby, the computer also has the ability to control some high ranking officials.

Looker (1981; Warner Bros.) D/S: Michael Crichton. P: Howard Jeffry. C: Paul Lohmann. Cast: Albert Finney, James Coburn, Susan Dey, Leigh Taylor-Young, Darryl

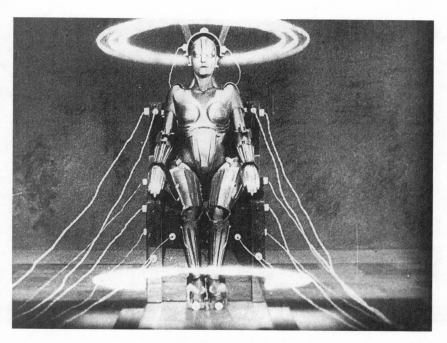

The "robotrix" comes to life via the electrical machinery of the evil scientist Rotwang, and nearly causes the destruction of the city of Metropolis (1926). The robot suit was constructed without a back, and so was filmed solely from the front.

Hickman, Dorian Harewood. James Coburn, who heads a TV commercial company, has found a way to replicate beautiful models and use them in his ads. One problem though, he must have the human counterparts murdered. Plastic surgeon Albert Finney, who is suspected of the crimes, looks into the affair. • *Looker* stands for Light Ocular Oriented Kinetic Energetic Responsers. • Former "Partridge Family" member, Susan Dey, plays the heroine.

Loss of Feeling (1935; Mezrapbom; U.S.S.R.) D: Aleksander Andreievsky. S: G. Grebner. C: M. Magidson. Cast: S. Vecheslov, V. Gardin, M. Volgina, A. Chekulaeva, V. Orlov. An inventor manufactures robots to do the work of people.

Making Mr. Right (1987; Orion) D: Susan Seidelman. P: Mike Wise, Joel Tuber. S: Floyd Byars, Laurie Frank. C: Edward Lachman. Cast: John Malkovich, Ann Magnuson, Glenne Headly, Ben Masters, Laurie Metcalf, Polly Bergen. A liberated female publicist goes out with a scientist (John Malkovich) who has created an an-

droid double of himself. The girl falls for the sensitive android instead of the cold scientist. • The android's name is Ulysses.

Master of the World (1934; Ariel Film; Germany) D: Harry Piel. S: George Muehlen-Schulte. C: Ewald Daub. Cast: Walter Janssen, Sybille Schmitz, Siegfried Schuerenberg, Walter Franck, Klaus Pohl. A mad scientist creates a robot army.

Metropolis (1926) (see FUTURES ON EARTH— UTOPIAS AND DYSTOPIAS). The evil scientist Rotwang creates a robot in the image of Maria (Brigitte Helm), a pure and saintly woman whom the workers of Metropolis all love. The robot double then incites a revolt that nearly brings destruction to everyone. • The robot Maria costume was only a front view shell, and was never photographed from the rear—because it had no backside.

Moontrap (1989) (see THE MOON). Two astronauts face an army of robots that have been waiting on the Moon for 14,000 years, formulating a plan to conquer Earth. ¶ "We don't take no shit from a machine."

Mutant Hunt (1987; Entertainment Concepts/Wizard Video) D/S: Tim Kincaid. P: Cynthia DePaula. C: Thomas Murphy. Cast: Rick Gianasi, Mary Fahey, Ron Reynaldi, Taunie Vrenon, Bill Peterson, Mark Umile, Stormy Spill. In the future, an evil corporate chairman uses a drug called Euphoron on his army of cyborgs, turning them into homicidal hedonists. They are eventually stopped by a martial arts expert and his buddies who are asked to help by the sister of the cyborg's original inventor, now held captive. ¶ "Don't get me steamed, cyborg!" • *Mutant Hunt* carried a shooting title of *Matt Riker: Mutant Hunt*. • This movie is the third in a trio of films made for Empire Pictures by Tycin Entertainment. The first two were *Breeders* and *Robot Holocaust*.

My Son, the Vampire (1952; Blue Chip Productions; U.K.) (also *Old Mother Riley Meets the Vampire; Vampire Over London*). D/P: John Gilling. S: Val Valentine. C: Dudley Lovell. Cast: Bela Lugosi, Arthur Lucan, Kitty McShane, Dora Bryan, Hattie Jacques, Dandy Nichols, Charles Lloyd Pack. A robot, created by a mad scientist who imagines himelf to be a vampire, kidnaps Mother Riley. The old woman must use her "wits" to foil the mad doctor's plans for world domination using an army of robots. ¶ "I have done the impossible! I have created a robot with a living brain! It can think for itself!"

The Mysterians (1959) (see ALIENS—INVADERS ON EARTH: THE 50s). Invading aliens deposit a giant death-ray-shooting, bird-like robot on Earth in this Japanese monster movie.

984 Prisoner of the Future (1984) (see FUTURES ON EARTH—UTOPIAS AND DYSTOPIAS) (also *Tomorrow Man*). A man without a name is imprisoned in a futuristic nightmare world full of robots.

The Phantom Creeps (1939) (see MAD SCIENTISTS). Mad scientist Zorka uses invisibility, a deadly gas, and an eight-foot robot in his quest to conquer the world.

Programmed to Kill (1987; Trans World Entertainment) (also *The Retaliator*). D: Allan Holzman, Robert Short. P: Don Stern. S: Robert Short. C: Nitcho Lion Nissim, Ernest Holzman. Cast: Robert Ginty, Sandahl Bergman, James Booth, Alex Courtney, Paul W. Walker, Arnon Tzador. A beautiful P.L.O. assassin (Sandahl Bergman) is captured by a tough mercenary soldier and brought back to the C.I.A. After placing some computer chips in her skull (giving her tremendous abilities) she is programmed to infiltrate the terrorist team she used to side with. Unfortunately, her programming goes awry and she turns on the C.I.A., killing a number of Americans before meeting the mercenary warrior again in the final confrontation of superior fighters. ¶ "She's a Barbie-Rambo killing machine."

Revenge of the Stepford Wives (1980; TV movie) D: Robert Fuest. P: Scott Rudin. S: David Wiltse. C: Ric Waite. Cast: Sharon Glass, Julie Kavner, Audra Lindley, Don Johnson, Mason Adams, Arthur Hill. This sequel of sorts to *The Stepford Wives* has a TV reporter stumble onto the secret of a small New England town in which the women are being "reprogrammed" to act as perfect domestic automatons for their husbands.

Robocop (1987; Orion) D: Paul Verhoeven. P: Arne Schmidt. S: Edward Neumeier, Michael Miner. C: Jost Vacano. Cast: Peter Weller, Nancy Allen, Daniel O'Herlihy, Ronny Cox, Kurtwood Smith, Miguel Ferrer. In near-future Detroit, patrolman Murphy (Peter Weller) is made into a programmable man-machine after he is obliterated by a dangerous group of criminals. Their leader (played by Kurtwood Smith) is in with corporate executive Ronny Cox, who is one of the chief administrators for a business which builds automated defense weapons. One of his rival executives (Miguel Ferrer) initiates the Robocop experiment when Cox's own version of a mechanized peacekeeper (ED 209) goes haywire. Cox then enlists the aid of his criminal accomplice (Smith) to get rid of Ferrer, but Robocop has the last word. ¶ "It gives me great pleasure to introduce to you the future of law enforcement—Ed 209." • Nancy Allen, who plays Robocop's partner, Lewis, is known for her connections both on and off the screen with director Brian De Palma. • The picture was made on a $13 million budget, and during its initial screening, was given an X rating by the MPAA. The X was appealed and finally lowered to an R rating. • An elementary school that Robocop visits is named after famous car company president, Lee Iacocca.

Robocop 2 (1990; Orion) D: Irvin Kershner. P: Jon Davison. S: Frank Miller, Waylon Green. C: Mark Irwin. Cast: Peter Weller, Nancy Allen, Daniel O'Herlihy, Tom Noonan, Belinda Bauer, Gabriel Damon. Picking up where *Robocop* left off, Detroit, a city under criminal siege, is in the middle of a police strike. A new designer drug called "nuke" is at the bottom of widespread corruption which involves three unscrupulous factions—a drug gang, City Hall, and O.C.P., the makers of Robocop. Peter Weller again plays Robocop, a cyborg having difficulty in differentiating between the good guys and the bad. Eventually, O.C.P. unleashes "Robocop 2," a huge cyborg which possesses the brain of a "nuke"-addicted psychopath. Running amok, it's up to Robocop to put a stop to the mayhem. ¶ "And now we take a quantum leap forward—state of the art destructive capabilities, commended by a unique combination of software and organic systems. In every way an improvement over the original. It gives me great pleasure to introduce to you Robocop 2." • A third installment is currently in production (without Peter Weller this time).

Robot Holocaust (1987; Tycin Entertainment/Wizard Video) D/S: Tim Kincaid. P: Cynthia DePaula. C: Arthur D. Marks. Cast: Norris Culf, Nadine Hart, Joel Von Ornsteiner, Jennifer Delora, Andrew Howarth. Set in a future where robot revolts have brought about a devastated world, a scientist discovers a means for humans to breathe the poisonous air which a mysterious power known as "The Dark One" uses to keep the humans in line. The scientist is captured by the Dark One's robot henchman, but his daughter organizes a rescue team. In the end, they eventually break through all defense barriers, and shut off the Dark One's power station. Sadly, her father, who has been turned into something monstrous, must be killed.

Robot Jox (1990; Empire Pictures) D: Stuart Gordon. P: Albert Band. S: Joe Haldeman. C: Mac Ahlberg. Cast: Gary Graham, Anne-Marie Johnson, Paul Koslo, Robert Sampson, Danny Kamekona, Hilary Mason, Michael Alldredge. In the year 2050, the world is divided into two warring countries. But instead of conventional warfare, these superpowers settle all disputes through the battling of gigantic transformer-like robots controlled by highly trained fighters called Robot Jox. • This troubled production was begun in 1987, but filming was shut down for more than year when the financing fell through.

Robot Monster (1953) (see ALIENS—INVADERS ON EARTH: THE 50s). An alien wearing an ape suit and diving helmet passes himself off as a robot monster from space attempting to conquer Earth. ¶ "I cannot, yet I must. How do you calculate that? At what point on the graph do must and cannot meet? Yet I must, but I cannot!" • Though he claims to have no emotions, and refers to himself as a "Ro-Man," there is no evidence that he is actually a mechanical being.

The Robot vs. the Aztec Mummy (1959) (see MUMMIES—THE AZTEC MUMMY SERIES). The famous Aztec Mummy battles a destructive robot, controlled by the evil scientist/villain known as "The Bat."

Runaway (1984) (see MACHINES). A cop assigned to stop malfunctioning "runaway" robots and machines unravels the mystery behind numerous deaths attributed to their destructive domestic devices.

Saturn 3 (1980; Transcontinental; U.K.) D/P: Stanley Donen. S: Martin Amis. C: Billy Williams. Cast: Kirk Douglas, Farrah Fawcett, Harvey Keitel, Ed Bishop. A mad scientist builds a huge robot on a space station, which develops devious designs on Farrah Fawcett. • The eight-foot-tall murderous robot is named Hector. Hector was built by FX expert Colin Chilvers, who based the design on a drawing by famous fifteenth century Italian artist/inventor, Leonardo Da Vinci.

Scream and Scream Again (1970; AIP) D: Gordon Hessler. P: Max J. Rosenberg, Milton Subotsky. S: Christopher Wicking. C: John Coquillon. Cast: Vincent Price, Christopher Lee, Peter Cushing, Alfred Marks, Christopher Mathews, Judy Huxtable, Michael Gothard. A series of vampire-style killings can be traced back to the work of a mad scientist (Vincent Price), who is making an army of androids created from both human and artificial parts. At the climax, Price is revealed to be a "composite" himself, but his plans are foiled when a communist android comrade decides that Price and his work should be destroyed for the good of the organization. Price wins his personal battle with the Eastern Bloc android, but commits suicide when confronted by police chief Christopher Lee, who might even be one himself. ¶ "In 20 years time, we will be in positions of power, then we'll be ready to act for the good of humanity." • The film is based on the novel, "The Disoriented Man," by Peter Saxon. • Coincidentally, stars Vincent Price and Christopher Lee (who don't have any scenes together in the film) share the same birthday, May 27. Peter Cushing's is May 26.

Short Circuit (1986; Tri-Star) D: John Badham. P: David Foster, Lawrence Turman. S: S. S. Wilson, Brent Maddock. C: Nick McLean. Cast: Ally Sheedy, Steve Guttenberg, Fisher Stevens, Austin Pendleton, G. W. Bailey. Computer genius Steve Guttenberg creates a robot named "Number 5" which is brought to life by a lightning

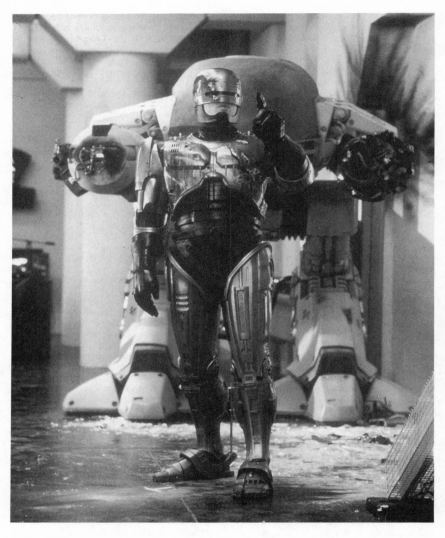

Peter Weller makes his point against crime lords and evil doers in the futuristic robot-cop film, Robocop *(1987). Standing behind him is an ED 209 unit, which he must battle to the (mechanized) death.*

bolt. ¶ "Whatever it takes to put that stupid contraption out of commission, gentlemen, you do."

Silent Running (1971) (see SPACE TRAVEL). Bruce Dern is ordered to destroy his ecological space platform which contains some of the last vestiges of Earth's vegetation. He rebels, and sets off into space on his own with his precious plant cargo, accompanied by three robot drones—his only companions. • The names of the three robots are Huey, Dewey, and Louie. They were played by a group of legless actors.

Sins of the Fleshapoids (1965; Film Makers)

Robots

475

D/P/S/C: Mike Kuchar. Cast: Bob Cowan, Donna Kerness, George Kuchar, Maren Thomas, Julius Mittleman, Gina Zuckerman. Humanoid robots called "fleshapoids" are used by post-war survivors of the future to perform all domestic tasks. One of them (called Zar) decides to start a family of his own when he begins to feel a yearning for human emotion.

Spaced Invaders (1990) (see ALIENS — BENEVOLENT ALIENS). Some wild and crazy little green men from Mars mistakenly land in a small midwestern town where they must dodge the riled townsfolk, repair their damaged ship, and avoid a killer robot drone which is programmed to terminate them if they do not complete their mission of a full scale invasion. Of course there is no invasion; the flying, spider-like death robot just *thinks* there is after hearing a rebroadcast of Orson Welles' "War of the Worlds."

Spy with My Face (1966; MGM) D: John Newland. P: Sam Rolfe. S: Clyde Ware, Joseph Cavelli. C: Fred Koenekamp. Cast: Robert Vaughn, David McCallum, Senta Berger, Leo G. Carroll, Michael Evans, Sharon Farrell, Paula Raymond, Harold Gould. This "Man from U.N.C.L.E." feature film involves a robot lookalike of superspy Napoleon Solo.

The Stepford Wives (1974; Palomar) D: Bryan Forbes. P: Edgar J. Scherick. S: William Goldman. C: Owen Roizman. Cast: Katharine Ross, Paula Prentiss, Nanette Newman, Peter Masterson, Patrick O'Neal, Tina Louise. Wives in a small Connecticut community are being replaced by robot doubles made by scientist Patrick O'Neal. Katharine Ross plays a new wife in the area who discovers the secret just a little too late. • Tina Louise (of "Gilligan's Island" fame) played one of the Stepford wives. • A made-for-TV sequel, *Revenge of the Stepford Wives,* was released in 1980.

Target Earth (1954) (see ALIENS — INVADERS ON EARTH: THE 50s). A few residents wake up to find that their city, which is now nearly completely devoid of people, is under siege by alien robots shooting death rays.

The Terminator (1984; Orion) D: James Cameron. P: Gale Ann Hurd. S: James Cameron, Gale Ann Hurd. C: Adam Greenburg. Cast: Arnold Schwarzenegger, Michael Biehn, Linda Hamilton, Paul Winfield, Lance Henriksen, Bess Mota. An unstoppable humanoid robot from the machine-controlled future of 2029 is sent back in time to kill the mother of their chief adversary, rebel John Connor, thus preventing his

birth. Hero Michael Biehn follows the terminator back through time to our present to rescue Sarah Conner. ¶ "That Terminator is out there. It can't be bargained with, it can't be reasoned with, it doesn't feel pity or remorse or fear, and it absolutely will not stop, ever! — until you are dead!" • In a perplexing twist of destiny, Biehn, who has come from the future to the present, turns out to be the father of John Connor, his hero in the future. • Director James Cameron originally saw Arnold Schwarzenegger as the *hero* (in the role that eventually went to Michael Biehn), with Jurgen Prochnow or Lance Henriksen as the unstoppable Terminator. • Leading lady Linda Hamilton (playing Sarah Connor) broke her ankle three weeks before filming and was almost let go due to the injury. • *A Bucket of Blood* (1959) star Dick Miller plays a gunshop owner who gets blown away by the vicious robot. • The Terminator is described by hero Michael Biehn as a cyborg — a cybernetic organism with a hyper-alloy combat chassis that is controlled by a micro processor. On the outside is living tissue. • *Terminator 2* has been released (with a reported budget of $85 million!). Schwarzenegger returns, but as a good guy this time (reportedly at the actor's request). Arnold was paid $14 million for this sequel.

Terrornauts (1967) (see ALIENS — ENCOUNTERS IN OUTER SPACE). Scientists are taken by a robot in an alien spaceship to an uninhabited asteroid. They learn that the robot is a relic from a civilization destroyed by an enemy planet, and that the asteroid is designed to send out warning signals.

THX 1138 (1971) (see FUTURES ON EARTH — UTOPIAS AND DYSTOPIAS). Johnny Weissmuller, Jr., the son of the famous "Tarzan" actor, plays a robot in this film about a sterile society of the future.

The Time Travelers (1964) (see TIME TRAVEL). The earth of the future has been totally devastated by atomic warfare and its survivors are protected from surface mutants by dome-topped robots.

Tobor the Great (1954; Republic) D: Lee Sholem. P: Richard Goldstone. S: Philip MacDonald. C: John L. Russell. Cast: Billy Chapin, Taylor Holmes, Charles Drake, Lew Smith, Karin Booth, William Schallert, Robert Shayne. Two scientists unveil a powerful but benign robot named Tobor, who befriends a small boy and foils the plans of communist spies. ¶ "A little childish joke on my part — Tobor is robot spelled backwards." • Tobor is telepathic, and he was billed as a "Man Made Monster with

Every Human Emotion!" • Director Lee Sholem's nickname is "Roll'em Sholem," because of his get-it-out-fast reputation.

Torture Garden (1967) (see ANTHOLOGIES). The second tale in this anthology film, "Terror over Hollywood," features an up-and-coming actress who learns that the stars she idolizes are really androids.

The Troublesome Double (1971; Interfilm; U.K.) D: Milo Lewis. P: Cecil Musk. S: Leif Saxon. C: Alfred Hicks. Cast: Keith Chegwin, Julie Collins, Tracy Collins, Richard Wattis, Josephine Tewson. An inventor creates a robot double for his sister, who would like to win an important swimming race. • The picture is a semi-sequel to the Milo Lewis film, *Egghead's Robot* (1970), which also starred Keith Chegwin and Richard Wattis. In the former film, Keith Chegwin and his twin brother Jeffrey played a boy and his duplicate robot. Here the same scenario is played by the Collins twins, Julie and Tracy.

War of the Robots (1978; Italy) D: Al Bradley. S: Al Bradley, Alan Rowton, Michael Salter, Adrienne Bell. Cast: Antonio Sabàto, Yanti Sommer, Melissa Long, Patricia Gore, James R. Bradley. An Earthship journeys to the planet Anthor, and fights with humanoid robots who serve the Anthorian race as slaves.

Westworld (1973; MGM) D/S: Michael Crichton. P: Paul N. Lazarus III. C: Gene Polito. Cast: Richard Benjamin, James Brolin, Yul Brynner, Norman Bartold, Alan Oppenheimer. Delos is the ultimate amusement park, a place where people can take part in an authentic recreation of past eras—ancient Rome, medieval times, or the Old West. The three "worlds" are populated by robots which look and act exactly as expected. Chaos ensues, however, when the robots malfunction and begin killing the tourists. ¶ "We are sure you will enjoy your stay in Western World. When you are there please do whatever you want. There are no rules, and you should feel free to indulge your every whim. Do not be afraid of hurting anything or of hurting yourself. Nothing can go wrong." • The Delos complex is made up of three separate parks—Westworld, Romanworld, and Medievalworld. The cost to visit Delos is $1,000 a day. • The only way to tell robots in Westworld apart from humans is by looking at their hands (which they haven't perfected yet). • Richard Benjamin, who plays the lone human survivor stalked by a robot gunslinger (Yul Brynner), kills the robot gunfighter a total of three times in the film—the last for keeps. The robot is patterned after a popular role created by Brynner back in 1960—the gunfighter named Chris, leader of *The Magnificent Seven.*

Sasquatch *see* Bigfoot

Satan *see* Demons and Devils

Sea Monsters

(*See also* Crabs and Crustaceans; Fish; Fish-People)

Sea monsters, such as the Biblical "Leviathan," the mythical "Kraken," and even the Loch Ness Monster, have spawned countless stories and legends down through the ages. It is only natural that some of these watery terrors made it into the movies. One of the screen's earliest sea serpents was revealed as *The Secret of the Loch* in 1934 (a rather dull variation on the Loch Ness Monster. It was not until the early 1950s, though, that the sea monster really found a home on theater screens (alongside every other kind of monster imaginable). In 1953, special effects man Ray Harryhausen brought us "The Sea's Master Beast of the Ages" (as its poster called it) in the form of *The Beast from 20,000 Fathoms,* and two years later he followed it up with the giant squid epic, *It Came from Beneath the Sea.* Our definition of a "sea monster" is not limited solely to the sea serpent or squid variety. Generally speaking, a "sea monster" is an aquatic creature that lives and or stalks in and around bodies of water.

This broad definition entails a variety of creatures besides squids, octopi, and serpent-like animals. Strange, unidentifiable aquatic things like the monsters of *Blood Beach* (1981) and *The Phantom from 10,000 Leagues* (1956) are also included as sea monsters. The carnivorous bacteria-like creatures in *The Flesh Eaters* (1964), the giant underwater mollusks of *The Monster That Challenged the World* (1957), and the man-sized bloodsucking swamp creatures found in *The Giant Leeches* (1959) also fit into this watery subgenre.

Sharks, barracuda, piranha, and other killer fish, however, will be found in their own FISH chapter, due to their abundance and similarity to one another. Also, prehistoric animals that live under the sea are only cross-referenced in this section, since, if they are clearly of dinosaur origin, their main entries will be found in the DINOSAURS chapter.

The future looks fairly bright for the dark terrors of the deep. Two aquatic hits of 1989 — *Deep Star Six* and *Leviathan* — make it a safe bet that more damp denizens of the deep are on their way.

The Abyss (1989) (see ALIENS — BENEVOLENT ALIENS). Friendly aquatic aliens (resembling transparent manta rays) from the bottom of the sea come to the aid of a team of underwater oil drillers. The closest thing to a sea monster in the film is the organic-looking undersea alien spacecraft itself.

Around the World Under the Sea (1966; MGM) D/P: Andrew Marton. S: Arthur Weiss, Art Arthur. C: Clifford Poland. Cast: Lloyd Bridges, Shirley Eaton, Brian Kelly, David McCallum, Keenan Wynn, Marshall Thompson, Gary Merrill. A technically advanced submarine on a mission to plant sensing devices on the ocean floor to detect volcanic activity is menaced by a giant eel. • The man who wore the *Creature from the Black Lagoon* (1954) suit, Ricou Browning, directed the underwater sequences.

Atragon (1963) (see JAPANESE GIANT MONSTERS — OTHER GIANT JAPANESE MONSTERS). The underwater empire of Mu, and their gigantic eel-serpent called Wenda, is stopped by Atragon, the flying super-sub.

The Beast from 20,000 Fathoms (1953) (see DINOSAURS — DINOSAURS ON THE LOOSE). A sea-dwelling "Rhedosaurus" terrorizes the waters off the North Atlantic coast. ¶ "If all the items of seamen reporting monsters were placed end on end they'd reach to the Moon, my boy."

Blood Beach (1981; Jerry Gross Organization) D/S: Jeffrey Bloom. P: Steven Nalevansky. C: Steve Poster. Cast: David Huffman, Marianna Hill, John Saxon, Otis Young, Stefan Gierasch, Burt Young. People start disappearing at a popular L.A. beach, sucked under the sand and devoured by a grotesque monster. ¶ "Just when you thought it was safe to go back into the water, you can't get across the beach." • Actor John Saxon (whose real name is Carmen Orrico) was a male model before breaking into films in the 1950s.

Blood Tide (1981; Athon; U.K.) D: Richard Jefferies. P: Nico Mastorakis, Donald Langdon. S: Richard Jefferies, Nico Mastorakis, Donald Langdon. C: Ari Stavrou. Cast: James Earl Jones, Jose Ferrer, Deborah Shelton, Lila Kedrova, Mary Louise Weller. A sea-god monster prowls the waters off Greece after explosions set off by a treasure seeker free it from the ocean depths. • *Blood Tide* was shot on location in Greece.

Bride of the Monster (1956) (see MAD SCIENTISTS) (also *Bride of the Atom*). Bela Lugosi creates (among other things) an atomic octopus monster that he keeps in a swampy pond near his isolated laboratory. The creature finally proves to be Bela's undoing. • In an article by Ted Okuda in *Filmfax* #6, actor David Ward explained how director Ed Wood "acquired" the octopus: "They had this prop octopus which he claimed had been used in *Wake of the Red Witch* (1948). According to Ed, he knew where it was being stored, so he just snuck in and walked out with it. It was a deflated octopus and he had no way of inflating it or making it move, so it was an awful looking thing."

Captain Nemo and the Underwater City (1969; Omina; U.K.) D: James Hill. P: Bertram Oster. S: Pip and Jane Baker, R. Wright Campbell. C: Alan Hume. Cast:

Robert Ryan, Chuck Connors, Nanette Newman, John Turner, Luciana Paluzzi. Captain Nemo and his followers have built a huge domed city named "Templemere" under the sea. A handful of people, including an American senator (Chuck Connors), are saved from a shipwreck and taken to Templemere by Nemo. The scourge of Templemere is a monstrous manta ray named "Mobula" which periodically attacks the undersea city.

Clash of the Titans (1981) (see MYTHOLOGY). Harry Hamlin stars as Perseus, who at the film's climax uses the severed head of Medusa to turn the dreaded giant sea beast known as the Kraken to stone.

The Crater Lake Monster (1977) (see DINOSAURS — DINOSAURS ON THE LOOSE). A prehistoric plesiosaurus wreaks havoc at the famous Oregon volcanic lake.

Creature from the Haunted Sea (1961; Filmgroup) D/P: Roger Corman. S: Charles B. Griffith. C: Jack Marquette. Cast: Antony Carbone, Betsy Jones-Moreland, Robert Towne, Edmundo Rivera, Beach Dickerson. This low-budget comedy-horror film has smugglers, counter-revolutionaries, gangsters, and a government agent (XK150) encountering a sea monster off the coast of Cuba. The creature resembles a waterlogged "Michelin Man" with ping pong balls for eyes. ¶ "The big cheese was Renzo Capeto, alias Coppo Rizetto, alias Ratto Pizetti, alias Zeppo Staccato, alias Shirley LaMore. At 15 he served his first stretch for rolling a drunk in the lobby of the Waldorf Astoria on New Year's Eve, 1934. In 1940, he was involved in an unsuccessful attempt to nominate Benito Mussolini for the Republican ticket." • This picture was an afterthought by Corman, who was shooting two films *(The Last Woman on Earth* and *Battle of Blood)* on location in Puerto Rico. He decided to maximize his time there and shoot a third film. The script was written in one week. • Roger Corman was to have originally played the part of Happy Jack, an emotionally disturbed gunman in Renzo Capeto's gang. However, after realizing how complex the character was (and how insecure he was about his acting abilities), he decided to promote his boom man, Bobby Beam, to play the role instead.

Dagora the Space Monster (1964) (see GIANT JAPANESE MONSTERS — OTHER GIANT JAPANESE MONSTERS). Dagora is actually a giant radioactive octopus/jellyfish monster that possesses the ability to fly.

Deepstar Six (1989; Tri-Star Pictures) D: Sean S. Cunningham. P: Sean S. Cunningham, Patrick Markey. S: Lewis Abernathy, Geof Miller. Cast: Greg Evigan, Nancy Everhard, Nia Peeples, Taurean Blacque, Miguel Ferrer, Matt McCoy, Marius Weyers, Cindy Pickett. The crew of a military research lab on the ocean floor is menaced by a giant deep sea creature released from an undersea cave by the project's excavations. ¶ From the trailer: "Save your last breath ... to scream!" • The film's poster sent some misguided signals with the ad line, "Not all aliens are from space." The underwater sea creature turned out to be a form of cave dwelling arthropod, not an alien monster. • Producer/director Sean S. Cunningham was the man responsible for starting the seemingly endless *Friday the 13th* series.

The Flesh Eaters (1964; Vulcan) D: Jack Curtis. P: Jack Curtis, Terry Curtis, Arnold Drake. S: Arnold Drake. C: Carson Davidson. Cast: Martin Kosleck, Byron Sanders, Rita Morley, Ray Tudor, Barbara Wilkin. Members of a crash-landed passenger plane encounter tiny carnivorous bacteria-creatures from the sea that swarm over and consume people in seconds. They were created by mad scientist Martin Kosleck. ¶ "Face facts professor, we've stumbled upon a living horror!"

Frogs (1972; AIP) D: George McCowan. P: George Edwards, Peter Thomas. S: Robert Hutchison, Robert Blees. C: Mario Tosi. Cast: Ray Milland, Sam Elliott, Joan Van Ark, Lynn Borden, Adam Roarke, Judy Pace. Ray Milland and family are menaced by assorted nasty reptiles and insects, seemingly led by the ferocious frogs that have surrounded and overwhelmed their island home, rebelling against the thoughtlessly polluting humans. ¶ "Millions of slimy bodies squirming everywhere — millions of gaping mouths!" — advertisement for *Frogs*. • Believe it or not, one cast member is even done in with the aid of a snapping turtle! • This was one of the earliest, and most influential "nature-strikes-back" films of the environmentally conscious 70s and spawned numerous imitations.

The Giant Leeches (1959; AIP) (also *Attack of the Giant Leeches*). D: Bernard L. Kowalski. P: Gene Corman. S: Leo Gordon. C: John M. Nickolaus. Cast: Ken Clark, Yvette Vickers, Jan Shepard, Bruno Ve Sota, Tyler McVey, Michael Emmet. Huge bloodsuckers the size of a man feed off some locals in the swamps near Cape Canaveral. ¶ "Like I was saying, I put five slugs into that critter before it went under. Doggonedest thing I ever seen. Had regular

A giant octopus, courtesy of master film animator Ray Harryhausen, surfaces at the San Fancisco dockyards in the sea monster epic It Came from Beneath the Sea *(1955).*

arms on it like a man, it was sort of different lookin', had, had suckers on 'im, like one of them, like one of them octopus things." • These swamp monsters were billed on the posters as the "Crawling horror ... Rising from the depths of Hell ... to kill and conquer!" (though in actuality the only "conquering" they did was to kill a few backwoods locals). • The leeches were actors in converted rubber raincoat costumes. One of the actors, Ross Sturlin, had played another monster for the directing/producing team of Bernard Kowalski and Gene Corman — the alien in *Night of the Blood Beast* (1958). • *The Giant Leeches* was filmed in eight days for approximately $70,000. The swamp shots were taken at the Pasadena Arboretum; interiors were filmed at Chaplin Studios. The underwater footage was shot at a swimming pool in a private home.

It Came from Beneath the Sea (1955; Columbia) D: Robert Gordon. P: Charles H. Schneer. S: George Worthing Yates, Hal Smith. C: Henry Freulich. Cast: Kenneth Tobey, Faith Domergue, Donald Curtis, Ian Keith, Dean Maddox, Jr., Harry Lauter. A giant radioactive octopus breaks through naval defenses and settles in San Francisco Bay for a round of bridge-wrecking and general waterfront mayhem. At the climax, Ken Tobey and Donald Curtis send the cephalopod to Davey Jones' locker with a submarine torpedo. ¶ "H-bombs have been blamed for every freak accident that's happened since, up to, and including, marine monsters being disturbed." • This picture marks the debut of the successful partnership of producer Charles H. Schneer and special effects wizard Ray Harryhausen. • Ray Harryhausen talked about the difficulties of integrating emotion into his giant octopus in Jeff Rovin's book, *From the Land Beyond Beyond.* "You had to put emotion, if I may say so, in a tentacle." The octopus was actually a "quintopus" — it had only five tentacles. "Not only did it save money in the building of the model," explained Charles Schneer, "but it gave Ray several limbs less to animate, thus reducing the length of the production schedule." • Harryhausen coated his monstrous cephalopod with glycerin to achieve the realistic "wet look" of its skin texture. • Charles Schneer originally wanted to shoot the movie in 3-D, but abandoned the idea when he learned that the special effects shooting schedule would have to be tripled to accommodate the special process. • The filmmakers were denied permission to officially shoot on the Golden Gate Bridge (but they went ahead and did it anyways). The city officials apparently were concerned that it would undermine public confidence in the bridge.

Leviathan (1989; MGM) D: George Pan Cosmatos. P: Luigi De Laurentiis, Aurelio De Laurentiis. S: David Peoples, Jeb Stuart. C: Alex Thompson. Cast: Peter Weller, Richard Crenna, Amanda Pays, Daniel Stern, Ernie Hudson, Michael Carmine, Meg Foster, Hector Elizondo. A lethal gene-altering bacteria is found aboard a sunken Russian sub and inadvertently creates a nasty genetic sea-mutation monster which absorbs the people it consumes. ¶ "It has all the characteristics of deep sea marine life—scales, gills, regeneration, even a period of dormancy." • The dozen deep water diving suits built by the film's FX team reportedly cost a cool half-million dollars. • This film reunites director George Cosmatos and star Peter Weller from the 1983 rat epic, *Of Unknown Origin.* • *Leviathan* was shot in Italy and financed by Dino De Laurentiis's cousins, Luigi De Larentiis and Aurelio De Laurentiis.

Lords of the Deep (1989) (see ALIENS—BENEVOLENT ALIENS). This low-budget copy of *The Abyss* (1989) centers around a group of benign aliens living at the bottom of the ocean who eventually save a group of humans working down there. Despite its setting, no sea monsters appear.

The Lost Continent (1968) (see CRABS AND CRUSTACEANS). The passengers and crew of a freighter encounter living seaweed and a tentacled aqua-monster in the Sargasso Sea.

Monster from the Ocean Floor (1954; Lippert) D: Wyott Ordung. P: Roger Corman. S: William Danch. C: Floyd Crosby. Cast: Anne Kimbell, Stuart Wade, Dick Pinner, Wyott Ordung, Jack Hayes. Anne Kimbell and a pair of Stanford biologists discover a giant tentacled one-eyed protozoa monster terrorizing a superstitious coastal community. In the finale, the hero rams his mini sub directly into its vulnerable glowing eye. ¶ "Whatever you do, don't head for the surface, he'll snap off your legs like ripe bananas." • This low-budget film was reportedly shot in six days for the paltry sum of $12,000. The production was so cheap

that producer Roger Corman drove his own trucks until told otherwise by the Teamsters union. It was originally to be titled *It Stalked the Ocean Floor,* but the distribution big wigs thought the title was too "cerebral" and changed it. • This was Roger Corman's producing debut, and the picture brought in over $100,000 for Robert Lippert's company. Corman took the profits he earned and used them to start his next picture, *The Fast and the Furious.* • According to Mark McGee in his book, *Fast and Furious,* during the film's preview screening, one viewer commented that the monster looked like his wife's diaphragm. So Corman contacted puppet-maker Bob Baker to devise a new tentacled creature (which appears in the film's final version). • Roger Corman induced Aerojet General to loan them a mini-sub for free, claiming the film could bring in some good publicity for them. Unfortunately the sub never appears to be under control or even riding straight, and is often seen swerving and rolling. You may notice that the sub is never seen for more than about six seconds without cutting away to the next shot.

The Monster That Challenged the World (1957; United Artists) D: Arnold Laven. P: Jules V. Levy, Arthur Gardner. S: Patricia Fielder. C: Lester White, Charles Welborn (underwater sequences). Cast: Tim Holt, Audrey Dalton, Hans Conried, Marjorie Stapp, Harlan Warde, Casey Adams, Barbara Darrow, Gordon Jones, Mimi Gibson, Jody McCrea, Eileen Harley. Several giant mollusks (possibly the result of radiation) are released from the bottom of the Saltan Sea by an earthquake. All the caterpillar-like aquatic snails with vicious pincer-jaws are finally tracked down and destroyed by a naval commander (Tim Holt)—except one, which menaces Audrey Dalton and her young daughter at a naval base lab. The terrified Tim Holt manages to hold it off with a steam hose long enough for the girls to escape, and for reinforcements to come and cut it down in a hail of bullets. ¶ "Can you imagine an army of these things descending upon one of our cities?" • Actor Tim Holt retired from acting shortly after this film was released and managed a radio station in Oklahoma up until his death in 1973. He is best remembered for his role of "Curtin" alongside Humphrey Bogart in *Treasure of the Sierra Madre* (1948). His father, Jack Holt, a prolific actor in the silent era of filmmaking on up to the early 50s, worked with his son on *Treasure of the Sierra Madre* (along with a second father/son team— John and Walter Huston).

Mysterious Island (1961; Columbia; U.S./ U.K.) D: Cy Endfield. P: Charles H. Schneer. S: John Prebble, Daniel Ullman, Crane Wilbur. C: Wilkie Cooper. Cast: Michael Craig, Gary Merrill, Michael Callan, Percy Herbert, Herbert Lom, Joan Greenwood, Beth Rogan, Dan Jackson. This grand spectacle, based on Jules Verne's novel, *L'Ile Mystérieuse,* follows a group of Civil War soldiers who escape from a prison camp by balloon. They end up on an island inhabited by gigantic animals (courtesy of Captain Nemo). This film is highlighted by an underwater battle with a monstrous squid at the climax. ¶ "Why don't we turn this island into a democracy and elect a leader—one who won't keep escaping to places which need escaping *from?*" • Ray Harryhausen provides the animated monster thrills which include a gigantic crab, bird, bee, and of course, squid. • Harryhausen stated (in *Keep Watching the Skies!* by Bill Warren), "If I remember correctly, the script went through a number of changes, one of which involved prehistoric animals and the sunken Atlantis. However, the final script dropped many of these ideas, including the green man sequence. Part of the Atlantis idea was left in the underwater sequence." According to Harryhausen, actor Nigel Green was to have played the part of the "green man"— Thomas Ayerton, whose bones were found by the soldiers. Ayerton was called the green man because he ate a certain variety of mushrooms that made his skin green, but also made his body distasteful to the island's carnivorous plants. This subplot was never filmed, however, because the producers felt it would have made the film too long. • Bernard Herrmann, a multiple Academy Award winner, composed many other film scores for Harryhausen movies in addition to this one. The two also combined efforts on *The Seventh Voyage of Sinbad* (1958), *The Three Worlds of Gulliver* (1960), and *Jason and the Argonauts* (1963).

The Neptune Disaster (1973; 20th Century–Fox; Canada) (also *The Neptune Factor*). D: Daniel Petrie. P: Sanford Howard. S: Jack DeWitt. C: Harry Makin. Cast: Ben Gazzara, Walter Pidgeon, Yvette Mimieux, Ernest Borgnine. A deep-sea sub, looking for a lost underwater lab, encounters an underwater grotto populated by sea monsters. • The sea monsters are actually just aquarium fish photographically enhanced with a macro lens.

The Phantom from 10,000 Leagues (1956; American Releasing Corp.) D: Dan Milner. P: Jack Milner. S: Lou Rusoff. C: Brydon Baker. Cast: Kent Taylor, Kathy Downs, Michael Whalen, Helene Stanton, Philip Pine. A mysterious sea-beast, created by radioactivity, begins to kill beachcombers and local fishermen. An oceanographic scout and a government agent begin to suspect that a local scientist is involved, and eventually discover the professor's secret underwater uranium deposit. After a passing ship explodes due to the uranium's rays, the mad professor, who created the mutant "phantom," decides to blow up the works. Both the scientist and the sea monster are killed in the explosion. ¶ "Nature has many secrets that man must not disturb. This was one of them." • The title creature resembles a Chinese dragon, with scaly arms and legs and a huge papier mâché-looking head mounted on a thick, awkward neck. In an embarrassing moment for Jack and Dan Milner, the cumbersome sea monster is seen floating up towards a boat, bumping its head on the bottom. Obviously because of the costume's size, visibility was a problem, and most of the monster's intended victims tended to *drift* into its hulking arms rather than being grabbed by the hungry beast. • This Milner Brothers production was one of the first double bill formulas of the AIP-styled sci-fi films aimed at the teenage audience. Its more successful partner was *Day the World Ended,* a Roger Corman post-nuclear war movie. • Kent Taylor was the popular "Boston Blackie" of the television series. His real name is Louis Weiss.

The Saga of the Viking Women and Their Voyage to the Waters of the Great Sea Serpent (1957; AIP) (also *The Viking Women and the Sea Serpent*). D/P: Roger Corman. S: Louis Goldman. C: Monroe P. Askins. Cast: Abby Dalton, Susan Cabot, Jonathan Haze, Brad Jackson, June Kenney, Richard Devon, Betsy Jones-Moreland, Gary Conway. A group of Viking women (and one young male stowaway) set sail to find their lost husbands and eventually land on an island of Grimault warriors who have enslaved their lovers. After rescuing their mates, they head back out to sea with the Grimaults in hot pursuit. When the ships reach the legendary whirlpool "Vortex," the bad guys are eaten by the sea serpent who resides there. ¶ "Get your filthy hands off her, you big slobbering dog!" • According to Roger Corman, the movie was conceived as sketches drawn up by Jack Rabin (who served as the special effects supervisor on the film). When they had difficulty thinking up a name for their movie they decided to make an outlandish title that would prove to be

This suggestive poster artwork is the most interesting aspect of The Phantom from 10,000 Leagues *(1956).*

the longest in film history. They came up with *The Saga of the Viking Women and Their Voyage to the Waters of the Great Sea Serpent*. The distributor elected to play it safe and shortened the title on all the advertising because exhibitors could not fit the name on their marquees. • Filming was beset by a myriad of unusual mishaps which included effects man Irving Block being nearly electrocuted, riders on horseback almost falling off a cliff, "killer hunting dogs" that were so loveable they had to be thrown on the actresses, and the leading lady calling in sick the first day of shooting. Abby Dalton got the call to replace her and everyone else was bumped up a notch. Another crazy incident occurred when the viking girls' ship filled up with water and sank. Most of the actresses couldn't swim very well so they had to wave down two surfers to take them in to shore. • The picture, shot primarily at an ocean inlet known as Crystal Cove, was another quickly made project, taking up about ten days and a $100,000 budget.

The Secret of the Loch (1934; Associated British Film Distributors; U.K.) D: Milton Rosemer. P: Bray Wyndham. S: Julie Bristow, Charles Bennett. C: James Wilson, Eric Cross (underwater photography). Cast: Seymour Hicks, Nancy O'Neil, Gibson Gowland, Frederick Peisley, Eric Hales, Rosamund John, Ben Field, Rob Wilton, Hubert Harben, F. Llewellyn. A professor is scoffed at when he claims that there is a recently-hatched aquatic dinosaur living in Loch Ness. A young London reporter is almost eaten when he lends an unwanted hand in proving that indeed there is a sea serpent residing in a secluded cave deep beneath the lake's dark waters. ¶ "The monster which is haunting the waters of Loch Ness is nothing more or less than a reptilian survivor of prehistoric ages, a giant dinosaur — 'diplodocus'." • This "giant dinosaur" turns out to be nothing more than a photographically enlarged iguana! No evidence or confirmation is given, apart from the professor's one statement, that this sea monster truly is a dinosaur.

The Seven Faces of Dr. Lao (1964) (see MAGICIANS). A small fish grows into a gigantic sea serpent when it is removed from its water bowl. Fortunately, it is transformed back into a tiny guppy-like thing when Dr. Lao creates a rainstorm.

Tentacles (1976; AIP; Italy) D: Oliver Hellman. P: Ovidio Asonitis, E. F. Doris, S: Jerome Max, Tito Carpi, Steve Carabatsos, Sonia Molteni. C: Roberto D'Ettorre Piazzoli. Cast: Shelley Winters, John Huston, Bo Hopkins, Henry Fonda, Claude Akins, Cesare Danova, Delia Boccardo. A giant octopus menaces the California coast, snatching anyone it can get its tentacles on and leaving only their skeletons. ¶ "This one's very special, this one has tasted blood." • *Tentacles* is killed at the climax by Bo Hopkins' pet killer whale. Actually there were two whales—named Summer and Winter. • Nestor Ungaro directed and coordinated the marine and underwater sequences.

20,000 Leagues Under the Sea (1954; Buena Vista/Walt Disney) D: Richard Fleischer. P: Walt Disney. S: Earl Felton. C: Franz Planer, Till Gabbani. Cast: James Mason, Kirk Douglas, Peter Lorre, Paul Lukas, Robert J. Wilke. Captain Nemo rescues three passengers and takes them aboard his amazing underwater submarine, the Nautilus. Nemo plans to destroy all warships in an attempt to force the world into peace. The highlight of the film is a tremendous battle with a giant squid. ¶ "We'll be fighting at close quarters with the most tenacious of all sea beasts. Stay clear of the tentacles, they'll seize anything within reach and hang on 'til the death. The only vital spot is directly between the eyes." • This five million dollar project, based on the Jules Verne novel, was filmed in cinemascope and featured a life-size monster squid model operated by 50 prop and engineering people. • The underwater stuntwork was provided by Ricou Browning, who is best known as the man inside the *Creature from the Black Lagoon* (1954) suit. • At the time the film was being cast, Peter Lorre had just gone through a serious illness which had caused him to gain over 100 pounds. • *20,000 Leagues Under the Sea* was nominated for an Academy Award in Editing, and won Oscars for Art Direction and Special Effects.

Voyage to the Bottom of the Sea (1961; 20th Century–Fox) D/P: Irwin Allen. S: Irwin Allen, Charles Bennett. C: Winton Hoch. Cast: Walter Pidgeon, Robert Sterling, Frankie Avalon, Michael Ansara, Peter Lorre, Joan Fontaine, Barbara Eden, Henry Daniell. A giant octopus attacks the submarine called the *Seaview* during its mission to save the Earth (and stop the imminent destruction of our planet when the Van Allen Radiation Belt surrounding Earth catches on fire). ¶ "We hope to see sights never before seen by man, and by seeing, solve some of the mysteries of the deep." • The tremendous submarine cost over $400,000 to build. It was used again by Irwin Allen in the popular television series of the same name. • Only two actors from the original movie appeared in the TV series. Delbert Monroe was one and Mark Slade was a regular during the first season.

Sharks *see* Fish

Shrinkage

Altering the human condition, an idea explored in the early 1933 classic, *The Invisible man,* certainly opened up imaginative possibilities for film audiences. Wouldn't it be interesting to be able to go out about our world unnoticed, undetected? Director Tod Browning went off in a different direction from invisibility when he shot *The Devil Doll* (1936), a film in which people can move about unseen not because they are invisible, but because they are only six inches tall. The movie's special effects were breathtaking for the time, but Browning focused more on the emotions and plight of the story's normal-sized characters than on the film's two shrunken people (portrayed as nothing more than mindless automatons under

Dr. Thorkel (Albert Dekker), a.k.a. Dr. Cyclops *(1940), holds one of his miniaturized colleagues (Mary Robinson), whom he's shrunk down by harnessing the radioactive powers of uranium deep in the Amazon jungle.*

the control of vengeance-seeking Lionel Barrymore). In 1940, Ernest B. Schoedsack (who also made *King Kong,* 1933) made the first feature to focus on the plight of otherwise normal people shrunk down to a smaller size. In this successful picture, the tiny protagonists must overcome a variety of perils, including *Dr. Cyclops* himself.

Due to the tremendous problems associated with making a film of this type (working with huge props and specialized photographic techniques), there have only been a handful of filmmakers who were willing to attempt putting their gigantic vision on the screen. After the public had been awed with the likes of *The Devil Doll* and *Dr. Cyclops,* two hard acts to follow, the subject literally shrunk from view for the next decade.

Not until 1957 did anyone consider trying it again. Jack Arnold, another genius of science fiction, with an intelligent and sensitive script by Richard Matheson, directed *The Incredible Shrinking Man* (the pinnacle of the shrinkage cinema). It explored all the possible emotions — paranoia, fear, desperation, despondency — that would be experienced by a person losing total control of himself and his world. The picture was not only an exciting special effects extravaganza, it was a tremendous testament to the human spirit — of a man watching his personal control literally shrinking from view, having to adapt to a new, frightening, alien world while still maintaining some semblance of his humanity.

Though a small subset of the cinema of the fantastic, SHRINKAGE still holds some fascination for filmmakers and audiences alike, as evidenced by two recent hits — *Innerspace* (1987) and *Honey I Shrunk the Kids* (1989). It is interesting to note that the three most recent shrinkage movies (these two and *The Incredible Shrinking Woman,* 1981) were all *comedies.* Perhaps the public is not willing to take tiny terrors seriously anymore, or perhaps recent filmmakers just are not willing to risk another serious effort on the subject, opting instead for the more surefire route of parody and "cute" comedy.

Attack of the Puppet People (1958; AIP) D/P: Bert I. Gordon. S: George Worthington Yates. C: Ernest Laszlo. Cast: John Hoyt, John Agar, June Kenny, Jack Kosslyn, Michael Mark, Marlene Willis, Laurie Mitchell, Ken Miller, Scott Peters, June Jocelyn, Hank Patterson, Jean Moorehead. A mad, lonely doll-maker uses a high frequency vibration ray to miniaturize the people he grows fond of, keeping the foot-tall subjects in a state of suspended animation until he takes them out to keep him company. ¶ "I love my dolls and I'm quite sure they'll never leave me." • Before he is shrunk down to size, hero John Agar takes his girlfriend to a drive-in that is showing *The Amazing Colossal Man,* another Bert Gordon film. Ironically, it is about a man who cannot stop *growing.* When asked by the girl why he chose this particular film, Agar replies, "I get tired of the same thing all the time." • Bert I. Gordon said of this picture, "I made *Attack of the Puppet People* a tongue-in-cheek production aimed at teenagers, with light and humorous elements included to offset some of its more terrifying aspects." • John Hoyt (who plays the mad doll-maker) is no stranger to 50s science fiction — he played the crippled money baron, Sidney Stanton, in *When Worlds Collide* (1951), and appeared in numerous others including *Lost Continent* (1951), *The Black Castle* (1952), and *Curse of the Undead* (1959). • The part of Agnes, the little girl

who is enchanted by the miniaturized cat, was played by Bert Gordon's daughter, Susan Gordon.

The Devil Doll (1936; MGM) D: Tod Browning. P: E. J. Mannix. S: Garrett Fort, Guy Endore, Erich Von Stroheim, Tod Browning. C: Leonard Smith. Cast: Lionel Barrymore, Maureen O'Sullivan, Frank Lawton, Rafaela Ottiano, Henry B. Walthall, Grace Ford, Arthur Hohl. Lionel Barrymore escapes from Devil's Island along with a scientist who has discovered the means to shrink and control people. After his elderly friend dies, Barrymore disguises himself as an old woman and uses the "living dolls" to take revenge on those who framed him for a crime he did not commit. He also uses his masquerade to seek out and befriend his embittered daughter, who has grown to hate him over the years. ¶ "We'll make the whole world *small!*"

Dr. Cyclops (1940; Paramount) D: Ernest B. Schoedsack. P: Dale Van Every. S: Tom Kilptrick. C. Henry Sharp, Winton Hoch. Cast: Albert Dekker, Thomas Coley, Janice Logan, Charles Halton, Victor Kilian, Frank Reicher, Paul Fix, Frank Yaconelli. Up in the Amazonian wilds, biologist Dr. Thorkel (Albert Dekker) harnesses the radioactive powers of uranium to shrink a group of visiting scientists. ¶ "I can hear Dr. Bullfinch saying 'Impossible!' when he awakens to find himself dressed in a pocket handkerchief."

The Incredible Shrinking Man *(1957), played by Grant Williams, fends off a spider with a needle and thread. Williams was matted in alongside a Panamanian tarantula with exceptional results.*

Fantastic Voyage (1966; 20th Century–Fox) D: Richard Fleischer. P: Saul David. S: Harry Kleiner. C: Ernest Laszlo. Cast: Stephen Boyd, Raquel Welch, Donald Pleasence, Arthur Kennedy, Edmond O'Brien, Arthur O'Connell. A small submarine and its crew is miniaturized and injected via hypodermic needle into the bloodstream of a dying scientist in an attempt to dislodge a blood clot in his brain which is preventing him from relaying some vital information. ¶ "They can only keep things miniaturized for exactly 60 minutes, after that everything starts to grow back to its original size." • Director Richard Fleischer related one of the reasons why he made this film: "What also attracted me was the possibility of being able to inspire young people to some understanding of the incredible complexity of the human body and sheer *wonder* of it." • The largest working model of the human heart ever built — measuring 30 by 40 feet — was constructed for this film.

Honey, I Shrunk the Kids (1988; Walt Dis-

ney) D: Joe Johnston. P: Penny Frankilman Cox. S: Ed Naha, Tom Schulman. C: Hiro Narita. Cast: Rick Moranis, Matt Frewer, Marcia Strassman, Kristine Sutherland, Thomas Brown, Jared Rushton, Amy O'Neill, Robert Oliveri. The children of an eccentric scientist accidentally activate his experimental shrinking ray, which shrinks them down to the size of insects. They end up in their own back yard, now an alien jungle, and must make their way back to the house, encountering a variety of friendly and dangerous giant insects along the way.

The Incredible Shrinking Man (1957; Universal) D: Jack Arnold. P: Albert Zugsmith. S: Richard Matheson. C: Ellis Carter. Cast: Grant Williams, Randy Stuart, April Kent, Paul Langton, William Schallert, Raymond Baily, Billy Curtis. A radioactive mist causes Grant Williams to slowly and inexorably shrink. At first he must deal with being a media freak, but soon his plight turns into one of life or death when he falls into the basement after being chased by his now-gigantic pet cat. Assumed dead, and with no one to help him, he explores and eventually masters his new world by defeating the cellar's previous occupant — a gigantic black spider. ¶ "Yes, smaller than the smallest, I meant something too. To God there is no zero, I still exist." • The photography and special effects, spearheaded by Clifford Stine and Ellis Carter, utilized numerous mattes, rear projection trickery, and image overlays to present a realistic picture of this "basement universe." Grant Williams was sometimes shot from as far away as 250 feet to make him look smaller in perspective, and then added to other pieces of film to create the proper illusion. • Jack Arnold found a unique solution to the technical problem of how to make gigantic drops of water look realistic — he used condoms filled with water which kept the giant water drops from dissipating before they splashed. • A Panamanian tarantula was the giant spider which menaced Grant Williams, helped along with tiny jets of air to prod it into "acting" in the right direction.

The Incredible Shrinking Woman (1981; Universal) D: Joel Schumacher. P: Hank Moonjean. S: Jane Wagner. C: Bruce Logan. Cast: Lily Tomlin, Charles Grodin, Ned Beatty, Henry Gibson, Elizabeth Wilson. This comedic venture follows the misadventures of the shrinking wife of an advertising man who is captured by whacko scientists plotting to duplicate the phenomenon and take over the world. • This film reunites two "Laugh-in" regulars — Lily Tomlin and Henry Gibson. • Universal had originally planned to have John Landis write and direct the film but eventually scrapped the idea (along with most of its budget). • Makeup man Rick Baker plays a gorilla (that aids Tomlin) in a suit he designed himself.

Innerspace (1987; Warner Bros.) D: Joe Dante. P: Michael Finell, Chip Proser. S: Jeffrey Boam, Chip Proser. C: Andrew Laszlo. Cast: Dennis Quaid, Martin Short, Meg Ryan, Kevin McCarthy, Fiona Lewis, Vernon Wells, Robert Picardo, Wendy Schaal, Harold Sylvester, William Schallert, Henry Gibson. A hotshot pilot (Dennis Quaid) agrees to participate in a top secret experiment in which he will be shrunk down to microscopic size and injected into the body of a rabbit. The bad guys break in, however, steal a crucial piece of hardware, and Quaid is accidentally injected into the body of Martin Short, a hypochondriac grocery clerk. The two of them must find the evil agents before it is too late and Quaid's oxygen supply runs out. ¶ "You just digested the bad guy." • Joe Dante, a fan-turned-filmmaker, filled his movie with genre veterans. There is William Schallert, player in many 50s features; Kevin McCarthy, star of *Invasion of the Body Snatchers* (1956); Dick Miller (a former Corman regular); and Ken Tobey, star of *The Thing* (1951).

The Phantom Planet (1961) (see ALIENS — ENCOUNTERS IN OUTER SPACE). An astronaut lands on a planetoid where the inhabitants are only six inches tall. When he breathes the atmosphere, he too shrinks to their diminutive height.

The Seventh Voyage of Sinbad (1958) (see SINBAD). Sinbad's betrothed is miniaturized by a curse from an evil sorcerer, and Sinbad must journey to the monster-infested island of Colossus to break the spell. The petite princess is so small she can slide into a magic lamp which houses a genie.

Sinbad

The origin of the legendary character known as Sinbad the Sailor (which should be spelled "Sindbad," though most film versions drop the "d") is based in the collection of popular stories known as *A Thousand and One Nights*. This compilation, also called *The Arabian Nights,* is steeped in mystery — research has been unable to turn up the exact date they were written, or even who the author or authors were. With the exception of the *Koran,* these stories (which also introduced the characters of Aladdin and his magic lamp, and Ali Baba and his 40 thieves) are perhaps the greatest Arabian literary contribution to the Western world.

The adventures of Sinbad are romantic, exotic tales of sailing across uncharted waters to mythical lands harboring fantastical creatures and fabulous treasures.

The film roots of Sinbad go as far back as 1919, with Norman Dawn's silent depiction of the dream voyages of Sinbad. But it was not until nearly three decades later that the first popular Sinbad film was released (in 1947). Who better to play the part of *Sinbad the Sailor* than Douglas Fairbanks, Jr., who managed to capture the devil-may-care zeal and love of adventure that the role so fervently needed. In this story of Sinbad's search for the treasure of Alexander, the thrust of the plot remains firmly fixed upon the character's zest for life, rather than on any elements of the fantastic. This "oversight" was rectified a decade later, however, when stop-motion animation genius Ray Harryhausen decided to exploit the numerous mythical monsters associated with the Sinbad legend (and adding a few of his own making, as well). In 1958, he brought to the screen *The Seventh Voyage of Sinbad,* which remains to this day the quintessential Sinbad film. Its popularity was tremendous, eventually demanding further editions of the story (in the form of *The Golden Voyage of Sinbad,* 1973; and *Sinbad and the Eye of the tiger,* 1977). In these pictures, the excitement was not necessarily generated by Sinbad himself, but by the incredible array of monsters that he faced (brought to vibrant life by Mr. Harryhausen). Because the films' focus was more on the monsters than on Sinbad, the later movies were not hurt by the casting of different "Sinbad" actors. Sinbad features eventually did, however, grow less and less appealing to the public's ever-more-sophisticated palate. This little subgenre of fantasy films will more than likely never again be able to match the brief moment of fervor that was generated by *The Seventh Voyage of Sinbad.*

See GENIES for another *Arabian Nights*– related subject.

Adventures of Sinbad (1962; Toei; Japan) D: Taiji Yabushita. S: Osamu Tezuka, Morio Kita. This is a Japanese version of the Sinbad legend.

Arabian Nights (1942; Universal) D: John Rawlins. P: Walter Wanger. S: Michael Hogan. C: Milton Krasner. Cast: Maria Montez, Jon Hall, Sabu, Billy Gilbert, Shemp Howard, Leif Ericksen, Turhan Bey, Acquanetta. Shemp Howard (one of The Three Stooges) plays Sinbad in this Arabian adventure story.

Captain Sinbad (1963; MGM) D: Byron Haskin. P: Frank King, Herman King. S: Samuel B. West, Harry Relis. C: Gunter Senffleben, Eugen Shutfan. Cast: Guy Williams, Heidi Bruhl, Pedro Armendariz, John Crawford, Abraham Sofaer. Guy "Zorro" Williams plays Sinbad, who must face a dragon, an invisible giant, boulder-dropping vultures, bird-men, a hydra, and a heartless caliph and his evil sorcerer, in order to rescue a beautiful princess. ¶ "You're Sinbad—one moment a great captain and the next minute, shark food!"

The Golden Voyage of Sinbad (1973; Columbia) D: Gordon Hessler. P: Charles H. Schneer, Ray Harryhausen. S: Brian Clemens. C: Ted Moore. Cast: John Phillip Law, Caroline Munro, Tom Baker, Douglas Wilmer, Martin Shaw, Gregoire Aslan, Kurt Christian, Takis Emmanuel, John D. Garfield, Aldo Sambrell. Sinbad and his mask-wearing comrade, the Grand Vizier, face repeated attacks by Koura the magician who is after an amulet of unthinkable power. Their journey to find all three of the amulet's scattered pieces eventually leads them to the Isle of Lemuria, home to the Fountain of Destiny. Within the fountain lies the crown of Marabia, which at the climax restores the Vizier's disfigured face. ¶ "I follow an old proverb: Trust in Allah, but tie up your camel"—Sinbad. • The mythological monsters encountered by Sinbad and his crew include a miniature winged homunculus (an extension of the evil sorcerer's eyes and ears), a ship's wooden figurehead come to murderous life, a six-armed sword-wielding bronze statue of Kali (from East Indian mythology), a one-eyed centaur, and a winged griffin. • In Ray Harryhausen's *Film Fantasy Scrapbook,* he mentioned that "I personally found *The Golden Voyage of Sinbad* an exciting and most pleasant film to work on. We had an international crew and cast with the actors under the able direction of Gordon Hessler. The fine cooperation of everyone concerned along with the Spanish production team and craftsmen, made the project a most interesting and exciting experience." • Producer Charles Schneer commented in Jeff Rovin's book, *From the Land Beyond Beyond:* "Ray and I made quite

Sinbad (John Phillip Law) plunges his sword into the throat of a centaur while the beguiling Caroline Munro looks on in The Golden Voyage of Sinbad *(1973).*

a few films, and I would never permit us to repeat ourselves. When you're making a picture about the Arabian Nights, there are certain things that you're going to have that are repetitious, like a sword and a turban. But as far as incidents, plot structure, characterization, and monsters are concerned, we hope that they are widely divergent. And we think we've succeeded there."

The Lost World of Sinbad (1965; Toho/AIP; Japan) D: Senkichi Taniguchi. P: Yuko Tanaka. S: Takeshi Kimura. C: Shinichi Sekizawa. Cast: Toshiro Mifune, Makoto Satoh, Jun Fanado, Ichiro Arishima. A Japanese sailor encounters a witch with the ability to turn people to stone simply by looking at them. Only in English versions of this film is the sailor called Sinbad. In Japan, the title was [translated] *Daitozoku: Samurai Pirate.* • This film won the Italian "Five Continents" trophy as the best specialized film of 1963.

Magic Voyage of Sinbad (1953; Filmgroup; U.S.S.R.) D: Alexander Ptushko. S: K. Isayer. C: Fedor Provorov. Cast: Edward Stolar, Anne Larion. This Russian adventure features Sinbad searching for the Bird of Happiness with the aid of an un-

derwater princess. • A dubbed version of the film was released in 1961 by Roger Corman.

The Seventh Voyage of Sinbad (1958; Columbia) D: Nathan Juran. P: Charles H. Schneer. S: Kenneth Kolb. C: Wilkie Cooper. Cast: Kerwin Mathews, Kathryn Grant, Torin Thatcher, Richard Eyer, Alec Mango. Sinbad (Kerwin Mathews) is pitted against a powerful magician named Sokurah (Torin Thatcher), who has used a potion to shrink Sinbad's beloved princess down to the size of a mouse. To find the cure and prevent war between her father's kingdom and his own, Sinbad must journey to the Isle of Colossa, a dangerous place ruled over by the giant cyclops. Once there, he faces not only the cyclops, but a hostile crew bent on mutiny, Sokurah's huge dragon, and a skeleton come to life. Fortunately, Sinbad is assisted by a friendly boy genie (whom Sokurah desperately wants to possess) which our hero frees at the film's end. ¶ "From the land beyond beyond, from the world past hope and fear, I bid you genie now appear." • Ray Harryhausen discussed the genesis of *The Seventh Voyage of Sinbad* in Jeff Rovin's book, *From the Land Beyond Beyond:* "On the animals, it hits me during the drawing stage. What we're striving for is the unusual, and we try to get bizarre situations that still have a thread of credibility to them. As for the story, it's not something that forms itself at once, it evolves from the innumerable story conferences that Charles, myself, and the writer have." • The fantastic monsters brought to the screen by Harryhausen included a giant two-headed bird called a "Roc," a writhing snake-woman, a living skeleton, a cloven-hoofed cyclops, and a fire-breathing dragon. There was also to be a sequence involving harpy sirens attacking Sinbad's ship but budget constraints prevented its inclusion. • Harryhausen's cyclops underwent many conceptual changes. For instance, it began with no horns, then two, and finally settled on one. • Harryhausen took up fencing to better understand the movements required during the swordfight sequence between Sinbad and the skeleton. Kerwin Mathews himself trained with an Olympic-caliber fencing instructor. The biggest problem Mathews had in performing his "shadow fencing" for this scene was to keep his eye on his imaginary opponent and stop his heavy sword in mid swing when it was supposed to have struck something. • The picture was a tremendous success at the box office, and Harryhausen felt the film should have won the Academy Award for its special effects, which were far superior to anything else released that year. • *The Seventh Voyage of Sinbad* was one of the first Harryhausen ventures filmed in color, and he had to adapt his effects to this new variable. The picture was filmed in Spain (on the Costa Brava, Granada, Majorca, and the outskirts of Madrid).

Sinbad Against the Seven Saracens (1964; Avis; Italy) D/S: Erminio Salvi. C: Mario Parapetti. Cast: Bella Cortez, Dan Harrison, Gordon Mitchell. This Arabian Nights adventure pits Sinbad against seven nomadic Moslem warriors.

Sinbad, Ali Baba, and Aladdin (1963; India) D/P: P. N. Nrora. Cast: Pradeep Kumar, Sayeeda Khan, Agha, Bhagwan, Rajan Haksar, S. Banerjee. Sinbad (armed with a magic sword), Ali Baba (possessing his famed magic carpet), and Aladdin (aided by his genie of the lamp) team up to face a fire-breathing dragon.

Sinbad and the Eye of the Tiger (1977; Columbia) D: Sam Wanamaker. P: Charles H. Schneer, Ray Harryhausen. S: Beverly Cross. Cast: Patrick Wayne, Taryn Power, Jane Seymour, Margaret Whiting. Sinbad aids the brother of his beloved princess, who

has been turned into a baboon by the wicked female sorceress, Zenobia. Together with a magician of their own, named Melanthius, the foursome sails to the Valley at World's End to battle Zenobia and her monsters, and restore the brother who is to be the new caliph. ¶ "Within the passing of seven moons, if Kasseem is not crowned Caliph he will lose his right forever, that is the law." • Among Ray Harryhausen's animated creations are the baboon brother, a huge troglodyte, a gigantic walrus, a giant sabertoothed tiger, and the bronze man-bull called "Minaton." The Minaton was both an animated model and, in some sequences, a man in a large Minaton costume. • Actress Taryn Power is the daughter of famous actor Tyrone Power, and actor Patrick Wayne (Sinbad) is the son of John Wayne. • The picture's original shooting title was *Sinbad at the End of the World*.

Sinbad of the Seven Seas (1989; Cannon International; Italy) D/P: Enzo G. Castellari. S: Tito Carpi, Enzo G. Castellari, Ian Danby. C: Blasko Giurato. Cast: Lou Ferrigno, John Steiner, Leo Gullotta, Teagan, Haruhiko Yamanouchi, Stefania Girolami, Melonee Rodgers. Bodybuilder Lou Ferrigno plays a hulking Sinbad who must recover some sacred gems in order to vanquish a spell that has fallen over the great city of Bazrah. ¶ "They'll take care of the soldiers, you'll take care of the monster, and I'll take care of Jiffar!" • *Sinbad of the Seven Seas* is said to be based upon an Edgar Allan Poe fable entitled, "The Thousand and Second Tale of Scheherazade," published in 1845 in a periodical called "Lady's Book."

Sinbad the Sailor (1919; Universal) D: Norman Dawn. This early dream tale about the voyages of Sinbad features a cast of children.

Sinbad the Sailor (1947; RKO) D: Richard Wallace. P: Stephen Ames. S: John Twist. C: George Barnes. Cast: Douglas Fairbanks, Jr., Maureen O'Hara, Anthony Quinn, Walter Slezak, Jane Greer, Sheldon Leonard, Alan Napier. Douglas Fairbanks, Jr., makes the role of Sinbad his own in this tongue-in-cheek swashbuckler. No fantastical element is present, however. ¶ "Oh masters, Oh noble persons, Oh brothers, know you that in the time of the Caliph Harun Al Rashid there lived on the golden shore of Persia a man of adventure called Sinbad the Sailor. Strange and wondrous were the tales told of him and his voyages." • This picture marked Douglas Fairbanks, Jr.'s, return to the silver screen after a stint in the U.S. Navy.

Son of Sinbad (1955; RKO) D: Ted Tetzlaff. P: Robert Sparks. S: Aubrey Wisberg, Jack Pollexfen. C: William Snyder. Cast: Dale Robertson, Sally Forrest, Vincent Price, Mari Blanchard. The secret of the "Greek Fire" is used to help Sinbad and Omar Khayyam escape an evil caliph. • As well as Sinbad, this picture also features Ali Baba's 40 thieves, only here they are all women. • Film producer and millionaire recluse Howard Hughes helped finance and back the picture, which was originally shot in 3-D, but released theatrically in the standard flat format.

The Thief of Damascus (1952; Columbia) D: Will Jason. P: Sam Katzman. S: Robert E. Kent. C: Ellis W. Carter. Cast: Paul Henreid, John Sutton, Jeff Donnell, Lon Chaney, Jr., Elena Verdugo. This costume spectacular fatures Aladdin (without his lamp), Ali Baba, and Sinbad opposing an evil Damascus ruler. Nothing in the film (apart from the garish costumes and the presence of Lon Chaney, Jr.) is of a fantastical nature. • Star Paul Henreid is best known for his role of Victor in the Bogart/Bergman classic, *Casablanca* (1943). Discovered in 1933 by Otto Preminger, Henreid eventually tried his hand at directing films as well.

Slasher Movies *see* Madmen — The Slice 'n' Dice Wave

Snakes

These repulsive reptiles, which good old St. Patrick drove out of Ireland, have plagued mankind for centuries. Actually, any good zoologist will tell you that they are wonderful animals and very necessary to the ecosystem. Natural benefits aside, these scaly, squirmy creatures make for a perfect monster menace, and are hated and feared by many, often to the point of phobia. With no arms or legs, these cold-blooded reptiles can seem more alien to us than aliens from outer space.

Though you may disagree with this bias, you would have to admit that the snake's blackened reputation (which can be traced back even to the Bible) has not been improved any by the horror cinema. In films, snakes have frequently been utilized as emissaries of death by their mad caretakers, as in *Stanley* (1972) or *Fangs* (1974). Sometimes, they simply go wild of their own volition and rebel against humans on their own, as witnessed in the nature-strikes-back film, *Frogs* (1972). Then there are the snake-people, like those seen in *Cult of the Cobra* (1955) and *The Lair of the White Worm* (1988), as well as the oversized snake mutations inflicting *Curse 2: The Bite* (1989) and *Spasms* (1983). It makes one wonder how producers could find actors and actresses not too squeamish to allow themselves to be attacked by these reptiles. Lionel Atwill, who starred in one of the first horror films ever to use a snake as a screen menace, was one actor who didn't mind working with snakes. The film was *Murders in the Zoo* (1933), and during the shooting of the climax, Atwill (the villain in the picture) was strangled by a huge python. Apparently during the making of the film he became more than a little attached to his slender co-star, and after the picture was completed, he bought the big snake and took it home.

The Brides of Fu Manchu (1966) (see MADMEN — EARLY PSYCHOS). The insidious Fu Manchu (Christopher Lee) frequently employs a snake pit as a method of torture.

Cobra Woman (1944; Universal) D: Robert Siodmak. P: George Waggner. S: Gene Lewis, Richard Brooks. C: George Robinson, W. Howard Greene. Maria

Montez plays the dual role of twin islanders—one sweet and innocent, the other the evil ruler and high priestess of "Cobra Island." The island natives worship snakes and engage in a plethora of writhing snake-dancing. • John (*The Invisible Man,* 1933) P. Fulton is credited with the special effects for his picture.

Conan the Barbarian (1982) (see SWORD AND SORCERY). James Earl Jones plays the priest of a snake cult with the ability to transform himself into a giant python. He also has the ability to turn smaller snakes into lethal arrows, which he uses to kill Conan's love interest.

Creatures the World Forgot (1971) (see CAVEPEOPLE). While two primitive Homo sapiens are busy fighting over the heroine (Julie Ege), she is attacked by a large python.

Cult of the Cobra (1955; Universal) D: Francis D. Lyon. P: Howard Pine. S: Cecil Maiden, Richard Collins. C: Russell Metty. Cast: Richard Long, Faith Domergue, Marshall Thompson, Kathleen Hughes, David Janssen, Jack Kelly. While in India, some soldiers witness a secret snake cult ceremony. The cult's cobra-woman goddess (Faith Domergue) follows them back home to administer the penalty for their desecration. ¶ "This very night there is a meeting. For a hundred dollars of your money, I will show you she-that-is-a-snake-and-yet-a-woman." • Art director Alexander Golitzen worked on over ten fantasy films of the 50s, including *This Island Earth* (1955), and *The Monolith Monsters* (1957).

Curse 2: The Bite (1989; Viva Entertainment/Town Productions) D: Fred Goodwin. P: Stephano Priori. S: Susan Zelouf, Federico Prosperi. C: Roberto D'Ettorre Piazzoli. Cast: Jill Schoelen, J. Eddie Peck, Jamie Farr, Savina Gersak, Bo Svenson. A couple traveling through the desert run across an abandoned nuclear test site where the man is bitten on the arm by a mutant snake. His arm transforms into a huge, uncontrollable snake head(!) and eventually his whole body is turned into a grotesque snake-monster. ¶ "The first bite is the deadliest"—ad line. • Though labeled a sequel to *The Curse* (1987), this film has absolutely nothing to do with the first film, which was about a meteor landing in a farming community, causing people to mutate into ugly homicidal maniacs. • The hero here, the man who ends up shooting the snake-monster, is none other than "Klinger" from TV's M*A*S*H (actor Jamie Farr).

The Cyclops (1957) (see HUMAN GIANTS).

The title creature is a normal man, though horribly mutilated (with only one good eye—thus the title), who has grown to a height of 25 feet due to radiation. Other creatures that live in the same radioactive valley are a giant iguana, a giant lizard, and a giant boa constrictor (which the cyclops wrestles).

Day of the Animals (1977) (see BEARS) (also *Something Is Out There*). The depletion of the ozone layer has affected the animal kingdom, causing them to become aggressive killers. At one point a group of rattlesnakes viciously attack a man (Jon Cedar).

Deadly Blessing (1981) (see DEMONS AND DEVILS). A woman unknowingly takes a bubble bath with a snake.

Death Curse of Tartu (1967) (see WITCHES, WARLOCKS, AND CULTS). In the Florida Everglades, a Seminole witch doctor's spirit materializes as various reptiles, including a snake, to wreak vengeance upon those who disturbed his resting place.

Devil Woman (1970) (see MYTHOLOGY). Superstitious villagers antagonize a local gorgon, who sends out cobras to wreak vengeance upon them.

Devil's Partner (1958) (see WITCHES, WARLOCKS, AND CULTS). A man with satanic powers is able to transform himself into various creatures, including a deadly snake, to carry out his diabolical plans.

Dr. Phibes Rises Again (1972) (see MADMEN—EARLY PSYCHOS). The fiendishly clever Dr. Phibes employs both a mechanical and a live snake to commit a murder.

Dreamscape (1984) (see DREAMKILLERS). Dennis Quaid plays a young man with telepathic ability who, "with a little help from science, can psychically project himself into another person's dream," and thereby help that person overcome the demons of their subconscious. Quaid enters the dream of a little boy troubled by horrifying nightmares, and there confronts the hideous "snake-man," helping the boy defeat his object of terror.

Fangs (1974; Holy Wednesday Productions) D: Arthur A. Names. P/S: Arthur A. Names, John T. Wilson. C: George E. Mather. Cast: Les Tremayne, Janet Wood, Bebe Kelly, Marvin Kaplan, Alice Nunn. A Texas snake handler uses his charges to eradicate his enemies.

Frogs (1972) (see SEA MONSTERS). A group of people on an island estate are set upon by all manner of rebellious reptiles—including snakes.

House of Fright (1960) (see DR. JEKYLL AND FAMILY). As Mr. Hyde, an enraged Dr.

An Indian snake-worshipper performs a seductive reptilian dance ritual for the Cult of the Cobra *(1955) before their ceremony is disrupted by a group of overly curious American GIs.*

Jekyll locks his unfaithful wife's lover in a closet with a snake dancer's python, there to be crushed to death.

Jaws of Satan (1983) D: Bob Claver. S: Gerry Holland. Cast: Fritz Weaver, Gretchen Corbett, Jon Korkes. A demon serpent in the form of a king cobra is sent to terrorize priest Fritz Weaver. The cobra also commands a legion of deadly snakes (asps, cottonmouths, rattlers, water moccasins, etc.).

Jennifer (1978; AIP) D: Brice Mack. P: Steve Krantz. S: Kay Cousins. Cast: Lisa Pelikan, Jeff Corey, Nina Foch, John Gavin, Bert Convy. In this reptilian version of *Carrie,* the titular troubled teen has the ability to call forth all manner of slithery snakes to take vengeance on her tormentors. • Actress Nina Foch had not appeared in a horror film in 34 years (since she had played the queen of the werewolves in 1944's *Cry of the Werewolf*). Genre fans will also remember Ms. Foch from *Return of the Vampire* (1943), in which she played opposite Bela Lugosi.

King Kong (1933) (see APE GIANTS). Kong battles a giant snake-creature on his island home.

King Kong (1976) (see APE GIANTS). Once again Kong fights and defeats a giant snake (this time an ordinary oversized boa constrictor).

The Lair of the White Worm (1988; Vestron Pictures) D/P/S: Ken Russell. C: Dick Bush. Cast: Amanda Donohoe, Hugh Grant, Catherine Oxenberg, Peter Capaldi, Sammi Davis, Stratford Johns. Vampiric snake people, led by Amanda Donohoe, worship and offer up human sacrifices to a legendary giant snake creature living in a cave in northern England. • The highly independent filmmaker, Ken Russell, shot this picture in England with a total budget of only $1.3 million—a remarkable achievement when one considers the copious (and effective) special effects. • Russell's films are customarily reviled and banned by the Catholic Film Board (his *The Devils* [1971] was judged by that critical body to be one of the most sacrilegious films ever made), and *The Lair of the White Worm* is no exception. *Lair* abounds in less-than-reverent imagery, including scenes of Christ on the cross with a huge snake wrapped about him, and the raping and impaling of nuns. • *The Lair of* *the White Worm* is based on the short story by Bram Stoker, author of *Dracula*.

Mountaintop Motel Massacre (1986) (see MADMEN — THE SLICE 'N' DICE WAVE). A crazy woman murders guests at her Mountaintop Motel by either carving them up with a sickle or utilizing various forms of wildlife, including a poisonous snake.

Murders in the Zoo (1933) (see MADMEN — EARLY MADMEN). Lionel Atwill, a wealthy hunter and zoo patron, uses animals (and particularly the venom from the poisonous green mamba) to dispose of his wife's real and imagined lovers. At the climax, Atwill himself is crushed to death by a python. ¶ "Oh my goodness, here it is time for me to meet the boat and I find myself whiling away the hours with snakes." • The 20-foot python that puts the stranglehold on Atwill at film's end was named "Elsie." Fascinated by the creature, Atwill refused a stunt double (over the objections of director Edward Sutherland), and so it is the actor himself who is seen wrapped in the giant snake's smothering coils. Atwill was so taken with Elsie that he actually bought the snake and took it home with him after the film wrapped.

Night of the Cobra Woman (1972; New World; Philippines/U.S.) D: Andrew Meyer. P: Kerry Magness, Harvey Marks. S: Kerry Magness, Andrew Meyer. C: Nonong Rasca. Cast: Joy Bang, Marlene Clark, Roger Garrett, Slash Marks. In the jungles of the Philippines, a woman uses a combination of snake venom and sex to attain eternal youth. The side effect is that she periodically transforms into a cobra. ¶ From the ads: "She sucks the very life from the bodies of men." • *Night of the Cobra Woman* was filmed in "slitherama" (according to the ads). • The cast list contains a most unusual (and telling) name — "Slash Marks."

The Outing (1987) (see GENIES). A group of teens are trapped in a museum with a malevolent genie brought forth from an ancient lamp (naturally). At one point, the demonic genie restores life to an assortment of snakes in preservation jars, and sets the pickled reptiles on a girl in a bathtub.

Phobia (1980) (see MADMEN — THE SLICE 'N' DICE WAVE). A psychotherapist conducts intense therapy with a group of phobics who mysteriously die via their own particular phobias — including the fear of snakes. • This is revered director John Huston's only foray into the cinema of the macabre as a director.

Rattlers (1976; Boxoffice International) D/P: John McCauley. S: Jerry Golding. Cast: Sam Chew, Elisabeth Chauvet, Dan Priest, Ron Gold, Tony Ballen. In the Mojave Desert, snakes are exposed to a leaky canister of experimental nerve gas, turning them into wanton killers (even by reptilian standards). ¶ "What a horrible way to die" — poster ad-line set above a drawing of a naked woman screaming in a bathtub infested with writhing snakes.

The Reptile (1966; Hammer–Seven Arts; U.K.) D: John Gilling. P: Anthony Nelson Keys. S: John Elder. C: Arthur Grant. Cast: Noel Willman, Jennifer Daniel, Ray Barrett, Jacqueline Pearce, Michael Ripper, John Laurie, Marne Maitland, David Baron, Charles Lloyd Pack, Harold Goldblatt, George Woodbridge. A series of bizarre murders plague a small English village, the result of a Malayan curse which periodically transforms the local landowner's daughter (Jacqueline Pearce) into a murderous snake woman. ¶ "The dreaded curse of the Ourang Sancto turned her into a slithering snake!" — ad line. • The fascinating snake-woman effects were created by Hammer makeup regular, Roy Ashton. • *The Reptile* was released on a double bill with *The Plague of the Zombies,* and both films were shot back to back in Cornwall, utilizing many of the same sets.

The Serpent and the Rainbow (1988) (see VOODOO). Snakes are featured prominently in this set-in-Haiti tale of voodoo and zombies. The most striking scene involves a voodoo-induced hallucination sequence in which the hero is confronted with the withered corpse of a voodoo priestess, out of whose decayed mouth leaps a python to latch onto his face.

The Snake People (1968) (see VOODOO). The story centers around a snake-worshiping voodoo cult, with plenty of writhing pythons and snake ceremony.

The Snake Woman (1961; United Artists; U.K.) D: Sidney J. Furie. P: George Fowler. S: Orville H. Hampton. C: Stephen Dade. Cast: John McCarthy, Susan Travers, Geoffrey Danton, Arnold Marle, Elsie Wagstaff. A man injects venom into his pregnant wife to save her from going mad. The wife dies while giving birth to a daughter who now has the ability to turn herself into a cobra. After her father dies she sets out to avenge the deaths of her parents.

Spasms (1983; National Trust; Canada) (also *Death Bite*). D: William Fruet. P: John G. Pozhke, Maurice Smith. S: Don Enright. C: Mark Swain. Cast: Peter Fonda, Oliver Reed, Kerrie Keane, Al Waxman,

Miguel Fernandes. Oliver Reed captures a demonic snake and brings it to America. Snake cult members free the oversized serpent which goes on a killing spree. The "spasms" referred to in the title are the grotesque (special) effects associated with being bitten by the snake. • The demon snake was called "N'Gana Sunbu" by its followers. • It finally took an all-out machine gun assault to kill this mutant snake-monster.

The Spectre of Edgar Allan Poe (1974) (see POE FILMS — MODERN POE). Edgar Allan Poe visits a private asylum, only to be tortured by being strapped down in a watery pit full of snakes. (Though Poe himself escapes, the snakes end up claiming another victim.) • Cesar Romero is the unhinged doctor running the slithery torture pit.

SSSSSSS (1973; Universal) D: Bernard L. Kowalski. P: Dan Striepeke. S: Hal Dresner. C: Gerald Perry Finnerman. Cast: Strother Martin, Dirk Benedict, Heather Menzies, Richard B. Shull, Tim O'Connor. Mad scientist Strother Martin transforms his assistant into a "cobra man," who ends up as an exhibit in a freak show. Working a bit harder, he perfects his mad technique and finally turns Dirk Benedict into a full king cobra. Martin also employs various snakes to slither out and slay his enemies. ¶ "Don't say it, hiss it" — ad line for *SSSSSSS*. ¶ John Chambers (*Planet of the Apes,* 1968) provided the makeup along with Nick Marcellino. Actor Dirk Benedict, who played the part of the snake man, was required at times to undergo seven hours of makeup applications for the transformation scenes. In his final mutated form, he had to be carried onto the set on a stretcher.

Stanley (1972; Crown International) D/P: William Grefe. S: Gary Cruther. C: Cliff Poland. Cast: Chris Robinson, Alex Rocco, Steve Alaimo, Susan Carroll, Gary Crutcher. A Vietnam vet uses rattlesnakes to carry out acts of vengeance. ¶ Ad slogan: "Tim has a pet rattlesnake, when Tim gets mad — Stanley gets deadly!"

Venom (1982; Paramount) D: Piers Haggard. P: Martin Bregman. S: Robert Carrington. Cast: Klaus Kinski, Oliver Reed, Susan George, Sarah Miles, Michael Gough, Cornelia Sharpe, Sterling Hayden, Nicol Williamson. A deadly black mamba terrorizes a group of kidnappers. • Tobe Hooper (*The Texas Chainsaw Massacre,* 1974; *Poltergeist,* 1982; etc.) started as director on this film but was replaced early on with Piers Haggard. • Actor Oliver Reed was back the next year to face another killer snake in *Spasms* (1983).

Space Travel

(*See also* Aliens — Encounters in Outer Space; Mars; The Moon; Venus)

This chapter features films which focus on humans in space who do *not* encounter aliens. Rather than featuring extraterrestrial activity, these "space flight" movies depict man's journey into space and his struggle to expand and survive in the greater universe. One of the earliest influential space travel films is 1950's *Destination Moon,* which set the screen on fire with its breathtaking special effects that were, at the time, far ahead of anything done before. The film also signaled the beginning of the 50s space craze, which to this day has not lost its momentum. A year after *Destination Moon* was released, however, it was quickly forgotten when *The Day the Earth Stood Still* and *The Thing* triumphed at the box office. Audiences found aliens from space far more interesting than just plain humans in space, and from that point onward, with a rare few exceptions (*When Worlds Collide,* 1951; *Conquest of Space,* 1955; and a few other lesser efforts) the space travel film was grounded as a popular cinema subject. Not until travel into outer space became a reality did the humans-in-space type of film catch on again in the late 1960s, exploring the conflicts of man living and traveling through the airless void.

The prototype, of course, is Stanley Kubrick's epic, *2001: A Space Odyssey*

(1968), which used space travel as a setting for the conflict between man and technology. Though a difficult act to follow (as evidenced by the disappointing, simplistic sequel — *2010*), many films jumped on the space travel bandwagon, often simply transferring various Earth-bound dramas into space.

See also ALIENS — ENCOUNTERS IN OUTER SPACE for more films which feature humans in space.

Android (1982) (see ROBOTS). Fugitives from justice travel to a space station run by a mad scientist and his inquisitive android, Max.

Around a Star (1906; Pathé; France) D: Gaston Velle. An astronomer travels to a star in a soap bubble.

Assignment Outerspace (1961; AIP; Italy) D: Antonio Margheriti. S: Vassily Petrov. C: Marcello Masciocchi. Cast: Rik Van Nutter, Gabriella Farinon, Dave Montresor, Archie Savage, Alain Dijon. A reporter at a space station manages to detonate a runaway missile, saving the day.

The Bamboo Saucer (1968; World Entertainment) D/S: Frank Telford. P: Jerry Fairbanks. C: Hal Mohr. Cast: Dan Duryea, John Ericson, Lois Nettleton, Bob Hastings, Bernard Fox. Two Americans and one Russian enter a flying saucer found in Red China and head into outer space at the climax.

The Black Hole (1979; Walt Disney) D: Gary Nelson. P: Ron Miller. S: Jeb Rosebrook, Gerry Day. C: Frank Phillips. Cast: Maximilian Schell, Robert Forster, Anthony Perkins, Joseph Bottoms, Yvette Mimieux, Ernest Borgnine. Researchers in space come upon Maximilian Schell's robot-controlled ship. Schell is planning to do the impossible and travel through a Black Hole. ¶ Ads boasted that "Nearly 14 months of simultaneous and post-production filming and processing will be required for the creation of this amazing screen venture!" • Winston Hibler carried this film through its pre-production stages until he died in 1976. The project was then taken over by special effects man Peter Ellenshaw, who had wanted to call the picture *Space Probe*. Ellenshaw is also responsible for many of the effects seen in the Disney films *20,000 Leagues Under the Sea* (1954) and *Mary Poppins* (1964; for which he won an Oscar). Ellenshaw's own son worked on *The Black Hole*'s matte effects. • This feature, riding the wake of success initiated by *Star Wars*, boasted a tremendous (for the time) $20 million budget. • Actress Yvette Mimieux, former star of *The Time Machine* (1960), joked, "After all, if a fragile little Eloi like me could fight off the cannibalistic Morlocks of the far distant future, and I could fall in love with the Grim Reaper himself in *Death Takes a Holiday*, I guess I can cope with a Black Hole."

Capricorn One (1978; Lew Grade) D/S: Peter Hyams. P: Paul Lazarus III. C: Bill Butler. Cast: Elliott Gould, James Brolin, Sam Waterston, Brenda Vaccaro, O. J. Simpson, Hal Holbrook, Telly Savalas, Karen Black, David Huddleston. A mission to Mars turns out to be faked, and the astronauts then become the target of killers hired by the space program to keep them quiet.

Conquest of Space (1955; Paramount) D: Byron Haskin. P: George Pal. S: George O'Hanlon. C: Lionel Lindon. Cast: Walter Brooke, Eric Fleming, Mickey Shaughnessy, Phil Foster, Benson Fong, Ross Martin, William Hopper, Michael Fox. A ship launched from a space station travels to Mars. The commander goes crazy and plots to crash the ship, but his son (Eric Fleming) intervenes. During their exploration, the son is forced to kill his father when he tries to deplete the water supply. ¶ "This is the story of tomorrow, or the day after tomorrow — in the last and greatest adventure of mankind, a plunge toward the *Conquest of Space*" — opening narration. • The picture underwent numerous rewrites before finally settling on a script pieced together by George O'Hanlon. Others who tried their hand at it but were rejected included Barre Lyndon, Philip Yordan, and George Worthington Yates. • Producer George Pal hired John P. Fulton (creator of *The Invisible Man*, 1933) to do the film's special effects. • According to the film's pressbook, Eric Fleming bowed out as a regular member of the Broadway production of *My Three Angels* to accept the role offered him by Pal and Haskin.

Countdown (1968; Warner Bros.) D: Robert Altman. P: William Conrad. S: Loring Mandel. C: William W. Spencer. Cast: Robert Duvall, James Caan, Barbara Baxley, Joanna Moore, Charles Aidman, Steve Ihnat. This Cold War espionage film includes some brief rocket exploits. • After the film was completed, director Robert Altman was reportedly very discouraged when Warner Bros. took great liberties in editing his original conception.

The Crawling Hand (1963) (see HANDS). An astronaut's ship blows up in mid-flight, and his severed hand falls back to Earth, inhabited by some strange space organism.

Dark Star (1974; Jack H. Harris Productions) D/P: John Carpenter. S: John Carpenter, Dan O'Bannon. C: Douglas Knapp. Cast: Brian Narelle, Drew Pahich, Cal Kuniholm, Dan O'Bannon, Joe Saunders, Miles Watkins. The space-weary crew of the Dark Star are on a prolonged mission to seek out and destroy unstable planets. The beleaguered crew must deal with fatigue, boredom, a dead captain kept in a cryogenic freezer, and a pessimistic talking bomb which keeps threatening to detonate prematurely. ¶ "When you hit the atmosphere, you'll start to burn. What a beautiful way to die—as a falling star." • *Dark Star* is veteran horror director John Carpenter's film debut. It began as a U.S.C. film project and was turned into a feature film over a three-year period for the laughably low price tag of $60,000. • Screenwriter Dan O'Bannon also starred in the film *and* provided the special effects.

The Day the Sky Exploded (1961; Exelsior; Italy/France) D: Paolo Heusch. P: Guido Giambartolomei. S: Marcello Coscia, Alessandro Continenza. C: Mario Bava. Cast: Paul Hubschmid, Madeleine Fischer, Fiorella Mari, Ivo Garrani. An international rocket collides with the Sun, causing a shower of deadly asteroids to come hurtling towards the Earth. The countries of the world unite to stop the destructive debris with atomic bombs.

Doomsday Machine (1967; First Leisure) (also *Escape from Planet Earth*). D: Lee Sholem, Harry Hope. P: Harry Hope. S: Stuart James Byrne. C: Stanley Cortez. Cast: Bobby Van, Ruta Lee, Mala Powers, James Craig, Grant Williams, Henry Wilcoxon, Casey Kasem. The Chinese set off a "doomsday device," destroying most of the Earth after an exploratory spaceship blasts off for Venus. When they arrive at their destination they come across a Russian craft, then encounter a collective intelligence which refuses to allow the two ships to land on Venus. After destroying what is left of the human race, the omnipotent presence sends the ships off on an "even greater journey." • In an interview in Tom Weaver's book, *Interviews with B Science Fiction and Horror Movie Makers,* Lee Sholem stated, "They called me in to see if I could make anything out of it. Everything was just a hodgepodge—I don't know why they let the director carry on as long as they did. They had nowhere to go, they didn't know what

to do. They knew they had nothing, the cutter was proving that—they couldn't even cut what they had! It was a monstrous job—it was a patch job more than anything." It was five years before the film was released. • Scenes of the spaceship in flight were lifted from the 1956 film, *Warning from Space.* • *Doomsday Machine* sports quite a cast: Grant Williams (*The Incredible Shrinking Man,* 1957; *The Monolith Monsters,* 1958) plays a cowardly crew member while Mike Farrell ("M*A*S*H") and "Top 40" deejay Casey Kasem appear in bit parts, not to mention the appearance of shapely Mala Powers, who had been menaced by *The Unknown Terror* (1957).

Earth 2 (1971; MGM) D: Tom Gries. P/S: William Read Woodfield, Allan Balter. C: Michel Hugo. Cast: Gary Lockwood, Scott Hylands, Tony Franciosa, Mariette Hartley, Hari Rhodes, Gary Merrill, Lew Ayres. This space station drama features American astronauts detonating a bomb. • Producers Woodfield and Balter supervised the popular TV series, "Mission Impossible."

First Man into Space (1959; Anglo Amalgamated/MGM; U.K.) D: Robert Day. P: John Croydon, Charles F. Vetter, Jr. S: John C. Cooper, Lance Z. Hargreaves. C: Geoffrey Faithfull. Cast: Marshall Thompson, Marla Landi, Robert Ayres, Bill Edwards, Bill Nagy, Carl Jaffe. An astronaut (Bill Edwards) returns to Earth covered in a strange "space-crust" as a result of flying through meteor dust. The man/monster now needs blood to survive and goes on a killing spree while his brother and fellow astronaut (Marshall Thompson) tries to track him down. • According to executive producer Richard Gordon (in an interview with the author), *First Man into Space* was originally filmed as a co-feature for the Boris Karloff vehicle *Corridors of Blood,* but due to a sudden public interest in the space program it was decided that the two should be released separately. *First Man into Space* did quite well on its own, whereas *Corridors of Blood* was a dismal failure financially.

For All Mankind (1990) (see MOON). Previously unseen NASA footage of their trips to the Moon is edited together in this cinematic celebration of Man's conquest of space.

From the Earth to the Moon (1958; Warner Bros.) D: Byron Haskin. P: Benedict Bogeaus. S: Robert Blees, James Leicester. C: Edwin B. DuPar, Jorge Stahl, Jr. Cast: Joseph Cotten, George Sanders, Debra Paget, Don Dubbins, Patric Knowles,

Henry Daniell, Morris Ankrum. Nineteenth century inventor Victor Barbicane (Joseph Cotten) develops a substance with incredible explosive power, using it to propel a rocket to the Moon. His fanatical companion (George Sanders) sabotages the ship, endangering their lives and the life of his stowaway daughter. ¶ "The world cannot be trusted with such a force, the human race isn't ready for it, not for power X." • The film is based upon the Jules Verne novels, *From the Earth to the Moon* and *A Trip Around It*. Jules Verne is featured as a character in the film (played by Carl Esmond). • Joseph Cotten, who was boosted into the business by Orson Welles's Mercury Theatre troupe, starred in numerous screen classics, including *Citizen Kane* (1941), *Shadow of a Doubt* (1943) and *The Third Man* (1949). He married actress Patricia Medina in 1960, who was in *Phantom of the Rue Morgue* (1954) and *The Beast of Hollow Mountain* (1956). • Prolific 50s supporting actor Morris Ankrum appears as former President Ulysses S. Grant, who talks Barbicane out of selling his dangerous product to the world.

Gorath (1963; Toho/Columbia; Japan) D: Inoshiro Honda. P: Tomoyuki Tanaka. S: Takeshi Kimura. C: Hajime Koizumi. Cast: Ryo Ikebe, Akihko Hirata, Jun Tazaki, Yumi Shirakawa, Takashi Shimura, Kumi Mizuno. A spaceship observing a magnetic meteor dubbed "Gorath" is nearly drawn into the fiery mass and destroyed. Scientists decide to move the Earth away from its present orbit with the use of jets of hydrogen gas to avoid a tremendous collision with the asteroid. Meanwhile, Gorath's gravitational pull creates devastating problems on Earth, including earthquakes, torrential rains, and tidal waves. ¶ "See! Astronauts, satellites and spaceships operating from South Polar base!" • The Japanese version of the film includes a monstrous walrus unleashed by the earthquakes. These sequences were excised from the American release print.

Jules Verne's Rocket to the Moon (1967) (also *Those Fantastic Flying Fools*). D: Don Sharp. P: Harry Alan Towers. S: Dave Freeman. C: Reg Wyer. Cast: Burl Ives, Troy Donahue, Gert Frobe, Terry-Thomas, Lionel Jeffries, Hermione Gingold, Daliah Lavi, Dennis Price, Edward De Souza, Klaus Kinski. P. T. Barnum (Burl Ives) plans to launch a circus midget to the moon but sabotage sends the rocket to Russia.

Just Imagine (1930) (see FUTURES ON EARTH—UTOPIAS AND DYSTOPIAS). A space voyage to Mars is depicted.

Man in the Moon (1961; Allied Filmmakers; U.K.) D: Basil Dearden. P: Michael Relph. S: Michael Relph, Bryan Forbes. C: Harry Waxman. Cast: Kenneth More, Shirley Anne Field, Norman Bird, Michael Hordern, John Glyn-Jones, John Phillips. This space spoof features a space flight ending up in Australia instead of Mars.

Marooned (1969; Columbia) D: John Sturges. P: M. J. Frankovich. S: Mayo Simon. C: Daniel Fapp. Cast: Gregory Peck, Richard Crenna, David Janssen, James Franciscus, Gene Hackman, Lee Grant, Nancy Kovack, Mariette Hartley, Scott Brady. During a joint American/Soviet expedition, three American astronauts marooned in Earth's orbit are rescued. • Richard Crenna plays an astronaut who commits suicide to buy his companions more time when their air supply begins to dwindle. • John Sturges (*The Magnificent Seven,* 1960) directed this Mayo Simon script based on a novel by Martin Caidin.

Mouse on the Moon (1963) (see MOON). A tiny country sends a rocket to the Moon. The one-of-a-kind spacecraft is powered by wine.

Outland (1981; U.K.) D/S: Peter Hyams. P: Richard A. Roth. C: Stephen Goldblatt. Cast: Sean Connery, Peter Boyle, Frances Sternhagen, Kika Markham, Clarke Peters. A space marshal (Sean Connery) uncovers a plot by Peter Boyle to drug workers in order to increase their efficiency at a mining colony located on one of Jupiter's moons. At the climax, Connery faces (*High Noon*-style) space age hit men armed with special weaponry. ¶ "It's an amphetamine, strongest thing you ever saw. It makes you feel wonderful, you do 14 hours of work in six hours, that kind of nonsense. Especially manual labor, makes you work like a horse. The army tested it a few years ago. It made everybody work all right, then it made them psychotic. It takes a while, ten, maybe eleven months, then it fries your brains."

Project Moonbase (1953) (see MOON). Members of an orbiting space station travel to the Moon to look for a good location in which to build a base.

The Reluctant Astronaut (1967; Universal) D/P: Edward J. Montagne. S: Jim Fritzell, Everett Greenbaum. C: Rexford Wimpy. Cast: Don Knotts, Arthur O'Connell, Leslie Nielsen, Joan Freeman, Jeanette Nolan, Jesse White. In this astronaut farce, comedian Don Knotts deceives his family into believing that he is training to be an astronaut when he is actually just a floor sweeper. Space program heads decide that they would like to test their rocket's capabilities by putting a buffoon in the rocket (and Knotts is their choice candidate). ¶ "He might be suffering from hallucinatory regression as a result of cosmic bombardment, or it's possible he's inhaled some helium and it affected his vocal chords — or, he's had a baby."

Riders to the Stars (1954; United Artists) D: Richard Carlson. P: Ivan Tors. S: Curt Siodmak. C: Stanley Cortez. Cast: William Lundigan, Herbert Marshall, Richard Carlson, Martha Hyer, Dawn Addams, King Donovan, Michael Fox, James K. Best. Three astronauts head out into space in three different rockets to capture and bring back a meteor to Earth. Only one man lives to tell about it. ¶ "Man, during his brief existence on the Earth, has met every challenge but one, the void of outer space. Having explored the world he lives in, he has turned his gaze upon the heavens, has focused his attention on the timeless lure of the universe. Now a rocket probes high above the Earth, travels through a region of deadly radiation, agonizing heat and cold. What story will it have to tell, what message will it bring back?" • The space suit worn by William Lundigan was reported as one of the single most expensive costumes ever made (at that time), coming in at $1,800. • The *Riders to the Stars* theme song was one of the most insipid offerings to date. Sample: "Riders to the stars, that is what we are, every time we kiss in the night/ Jupiter and Mars aren't very far, anytime you're holding me tight."

Satellite in the Sky (1956; Warner Bros.) D: Paul Dickson. P: Edward J. Danziger, Harry Lee Danziger. S: John Mather, J. T. McIntosh, Edith Dell. C: Denys Coop. Cast: Kieron Moore, Lois Maxwell, Donald Wolfit, Bryan Forbes, Jimmy Hanley. A rocketship and crew are stranded in space with a bomb from which they cannot escape.

Saturn 3 (1980) (see ROBOTS). Harvey Keitel builds robots in outer space.

Silent Running (1971; Universal) D: Douglas Trumbull. P: Michael Gruskoff. S: Deric Washburn, Mike Cimino, Steve Bochco. C: Charles F. Wheeler. Cast: Bruce Dern, Cliff Potts, Ron Rifkin, Jesse Vint, Mark Persons. Bruce Dern plays a botanist/astronaut in the year 2001, who is in charge of the Earth's last greenery — contained in three domed platforms orbiting the planet. Dern rebels when the controlling corporations deem this preservation too expensive and order the domes destroyed. • The historic name of the spaceship is the "Valley Forge."

Slave Girls from Beyond Infinity (1988; Urban Classics D/S: Ken Dixon. P: Ken Dixon, John Eng, Mark Wolf. C: Ken Wiatrak. Cast: Elizabeth Cayton, Cindy Beal, Brinke Stevens, Don Scribner, Carl Horner, Kirk Graves. This low-budget retelling of "The Most Dangerous Game" in outer space has three beautiful girls escape a slave ship only to crash-land on a remote planet where they are hunted for sport by their charming but deadly host armed with high tech weaponry. ¶ Ad line: "Big Movie. Big Production. Big Girls." (Of course, only the last part is accurate.) • The picture was released on a double bill with *Creepazoids*.

Space Mutiny (1989; AIP Distribution, Inc.) D/P: David Winters. S: Maria Dante. C: Vincent G. Cox. Cast: Reb Brown, James Ryan, John Phillip Law, Cameron Mitchell, Cissy Cameron. An evil man named Kalgan incites a mutiny aboard the "Southern Sun" spacecraft in order to scrap the ship and sell the passengers off as slaves. Only Reb Brown and a few followers armed with laser cannons and neutron grenades are there to stop him.

Space Rage (1985; Vestron) D: Conrad E. Palmisano, Peter McCarthy. P: Morton Reed, Eric Barrett. S: Jim Lenahan. C: Tim Suhrstedt. Cast: Richard Farnsworth, Michael Pare, Lee Purcell, William Windom, John Laughlin. Set on a prison planet, a bounty hunter comes out of retirement to save the colony singlehandedly from a group of prison bad buys and their ruthless leader, played by Michael Pare. • The film underwent numerous title changes during production. Some of those suggested included *A Dollar a Day, Trackers, Trackers: 2081,* and *The Last Frontier.*

Spaceflight 1C (1965; Lippert/20th Century-Fox; U.K.) D: Bernard Knowles. P: Robert L. Lippert, Jack Parsons. S: Harry Spalding. C: Geoffrey Faithfull. Cast: Bill Williams, Norma West, John Cairney, Linda Marlowe, Jeremy Longhurst. A mutiny occurs aboard a ship traveling through space on a mission to find a habitable planet.

Spaceways (1953; Lippert/Hammer; U.K.) D: Terence Fisher. P: Michael Carreras. S: Paul Tabori, Richard Landau. C: Reginald Wyer. Cast: Howard Duff, Eva Bartok, Alan Wheatley, Philip Leaver, Michael Medwin. This soap opera space story features a rocket scientist who is accused of killing his wife and her supposed lover, and placing their bodies inside a satellite he sends into orbit. The scientist (Howard Duff) decides to prove his innocence by going up in a second rocket, and then falls for a female crew member. ¶ "We believe that we can send a rocket into an elliptical orbit to become the first artificial satellite of our globe, that circles the Earth for an eternity." • Pressbook stories emphasized the film's real-life plausibility with articles like this: "As written by Landau and Paul Tabori, the new film is first to concern itself with the establishment of space stations 1,075 miles above the Earth. Just a few days after the movie's subject matter was revealed, a prominent public figure, in a Los Angeles speech, advocated the immediate planning of U.S. space islands — at 1,075 mile altitude!" • Heroine Eva Bartok was born in Hungary and made her stage debut at the age of 16 in Budapest. Her first American role was with Burt Lancaster in *The Crimson Pirate* (1952).

Star Slammer: The Escape (1988) (also *Prison Ship*). D: Fred Olen Ray. P: Jack H. Harris, Fred Olen Ray. S: Michael D. Sonye. C: Paul Elliot. Cast: Ross Hagen, Sandy Brooke, Susan Stokey, Marya Grant, Dawn Wildsmith, Michael Sonye, Aldo Ray, John Carradine. This is low-budget filmmaker Fred Olen Ray's answer to the women-in-prison genre, only this time the prison is a spaceship some time in the far-distant future. The film features plenty of cell block "cat-fights" and an all-hell-breaks-loose prison breakout at the climax. ¶ "Remember, it's *your* universe, keep it clean." • Producer Jack H. Harris is the same man who produced *The Blob* in 1958. He is featured in *Star Slammer* as the voice of the intercom announcer: "Attention, tonight's movie is *Jailhouse Rocket*." • Low-budget director Fred Olen Ray borrowed from previous films to give his production a bigger look than he could afford. For example, all the spaceships seen in the film are from previous movies — *Dark Star* (1974), *Buck Rogers in the 25th Century* (1979), and *Battle Beyond the Stars* (1980).

Starflight One (1982; Orion) D: Jerry Jameson. P: Peter Nelson, Arnold Orgolini. S: Robert Malcolm Young. C: Hector Figueroa. Cast: Lee Majors, Hal Linden, Lauren Hutton, Ray Milland, Robert Webber. The space shuttle Columbia rescues a rocket-powered plane gone awry.

Things to Come (1936) (SEE FUTURES ON EARTH — UTOPIAS AND DYSTOPIAS). At the uplifting climax, a brother and sister team is sent to explore space in a giant rocket called a "space gun."

2001: A Space Odyssey (1968; MGM) D/P: Stanley Kubrick. S: Stanley Kubrick, Arthur C. Clarke. C: Geoffrey Unsworth.

Cast: Keir Dullea, Gary Lockwood, William Sylvester, Daniel Richter, Leonard Rossiter. Stanley Kubrick's science fiction spectacle chronicles the strange role of a mysterious monolith which is somehow connected with the dawn of mankind. After depicting the human race's primitive beginnings, the story cuts away to the technical sophistication of space travel in Earth's future. When another obelisk appears on the Moon, and its signal extends to Jupiter, a spaceship is sent to investigate what is located at the other end of the communication. Astronauts Keir Dullea and Gary Lockwood are led on their journey by "the brain and central nervous system of the ship" — a computer named HAL. Confused by conflicting directives, HAL runs amok and kills everyone on board except Dullea, who manages to disconnect him. The final confrontation with the third obelisk of unknown origin sends Dullea (and the audience) on a cosmic tour through a new dimension of time and space. ¶ "I know I've never completely freed myself from the suspicion that there are some very odd things about this mission." • This was the first science fiction film to break the $10 million budget barrier, and quickly made back double the investment soon after the movie's release. • The picture won an Oscar for its groundbreaking special visual effects (which carried through on its advertising promise of being "The Ultimate Trip"). The film also garnered nominations for Best Director, Screenwriting, and Art Direction as well. • Douglas Rain was the smooth, reassuring voice of HAL, who calmly stated, "This mission is too important for me to allow you to jeopardize it." • The film is based on the original short story, "The Sentinel," by Arthur C. Clarke. Clarke and Kubrick's screenplay features a blending of the profound with the practical. For instance, this is the first movie to feature the daunting "Zero Gravity Toilet."

2010 (1984; MGM/United Artists) D/P/S/C: Peter Hyams. Cast: Roy Scheider, Helen Mirren, Keir Dullea, John Lithgow, Bob Balaban. This sequel to *2001: A Space Odyssey* details a joint U.S./Soviet space mission in orbit around Jupiter. After seeing strange manifestations of the only returning cast member from the first film (Keir Dullea), the team is faced with the prospect of a world war between their respective countries. ¶ "It's going to be wonderful!"

Voyage to the End of the Universe (1964; AIP; Czechoslovakia). D: Jack Pollack (Jindrich Polak). P: Rudolph Wohl. S: Pavel

Juracek, Jindrich Polak. C: Jan Kalis. Cast: Zdenek Stepanek, Rodney Lucas (Radovan Lakavsy), Dana Meredith (Dana Medricka), Francis Smolen, Irene Kova, Otto Lack. A spaceship searching for new worlds to inhabit encounters tremendous hardships in space, which include a highly radio-active dark star. The ship and crew eventually land on a planet inhabited by intelligent beings. The planet is Earth – or is it a second Earth?

When Worlds Collide (1951; Paramount) D: Rudolph Mate. P: George Pal. S: Sydney Boehm. C: John F. Seitz, W. Howard Greene. Cast: Richard Derr, Barbara Rush, Peter Hanson, Larry Keating, John Hoyt, Stephen Chase, Hayden Rorke, Judith Ames. Scientists attempt to build a rocketship before two astral masses collide with Earth and destroy the planet. They end up flying their space age Noah's Ark to one of the new planets, Zyra, as it passes, there to begin a new life for mankind. ¶ "Needles in a heavenly haystack. There are more stars in the heavens than there are human beings on Earth." • The rich and cynical cripple, Sydney Stanton (John Hoyt), accurately predicts that when they finish building the rocket he has helped finance, the people who lose out on the lottery selection process will revolt. At the climax, Larry Keating decides to prevent Stanton from going on the flight by holding his wheelchair back. Stanton miraculously walks, but to no avail. • The film was originally to be titled *The End of the World,* with a suggested cast including Ronald Colman, Susan Hayward, Charles Bickford, David Wayne, Thelma Ritter, and Douglas Fairbanks, Jr. • *When Worlds Collide,* which won an Oscar for its special effects, was made for slightly under one million dollars. • The infamous painted "sunrise" landscape on the new planet that appeared at the film's climax was a matte painting by Chesley Bonestell. Originally, George Pal wanted a realistic miniature set built for the last shot, but Paramount was hot on getting the film out on the market, so they opted for the (quicker) surrealistic painting. • The film is based on the novel of the same title by Philip Wylie and Edwin Balmer.

Woman in the Moon (1929) (see MOON) (also *By Rocket to the Moon),* this early, silent, science fiction film, about wealthy industrialists financing a rocketship to the Moon in search of gold, features the first recorded "countdown" ever seen in the movies.

Statues Come to Life

Most of us at one time or another have seen a statue or monument of some historical figure close up. While gazing intently at its features it is not hard to imagine the person alive, and sometimes – with a little imaginative coaxing – you can almost see the motionless monument begin to move. Fantasy filmmakers have taken this fanciful idea one step further by having a statue (a representation of life) literally uproot itself and take on a life of its own. Within this section you will find films featuring statues or figures made from various materials (stone, marble, clay, wood, metal, etc.), which at some point in the movie come to life.

The most significant walking statue in film history is the Golem of Jewish folklore. Medieval legends arose during the oppression of the Jews that told of wooden or clay images brought to life by saints to protect their masters. Films about the Golem legend have been made in Germany, France, Poland, England and the United States. The most popular version (1920; Germany) starred Paul Wegener as the powerful man of clay, whose wave of destruction is stopped at the climax by an innocent little girl.

Ray Harryhausen has also made his mark on the subject by using stop-motion animation monoliths to terrorize Sinbad in *The Golden Voyage of Sinbad* (1973) and *Sinbad and the Eye of the Tiger* (1977), and Jason (of the Golden Fleece fame) in *Jason and the Argonauts.*

The Japanese even developed their own statuesque monster called "Majin" (*Majin, Monster of Terror; Majin Strikes Again;* and *The Return of Giant Majin,* all 1966). This gigantic stone samurai, like Godzilla in later films, was transformed through the course of its three-film career into a monster hero with a special fondness for children.

Burn Witch Burn (1962) (see VOODOO). A large statue of a hawk is brought to life by a voodoo-practicing woman intent on destroying the career of a college professor.

Creepshow 2 (1987) (see ANTHOLOGIES). One of this anthology's stories, "Old Chief Wood'nhead," involves a cigar store wooden Indian come to life to exact tribal revenge.

Curse of the Faceless Man (1958) (see MUMMIES). A victim of the Pompeii volcanic eruption (now a petrified man of stone) returns to life and begins searching for his long-lost love.

Ghostbusters 2 (1989) (see GHOSTS). At the climax of this comedy sequel, the Ghostbusters utilize supernatural "slime" energy to cause the Statue of Liberty to leave its island and carry them into battle against the spirit of an evil Moldavian prince.

The Golden Voyage of Sinbad (1973) (see SINBAD). A sorceress brings a ship's wooden masthead to life to retrieve an amulet and menace Sinbad. The film also features an animated six-armed sword-wielding bronze statue of Kali (from East Indian mythology).

The Golem (1914; Germany) D/S: Paul Wegener. Cast: Paul Wegener. Workers digging a well in a synagogue uncover a clay statue, which is sold to an antiques dealer. With the help of sorcery and a magical formula, he manages to bring the statue to life and force it to be his servant. The Golem falls in love with the dealer's daughter, who is afraid of him. Spurned, the Golem destroys everything in his path as he follows the girl. At the climax he falls from a tower and shatters. • This film was presumed lost for many years until, in 1958, a European film collector named Paul Sauerlaender found a print in a toy shop. The owner had been cutting up old movie reels and giving them away to patrons who bought his machines. Sauerlaender managed to salvage the pieces and the film was saved.

The Golem (1920; Paramount; Germany) D: Paul Wegener, Carl Boese. S: Paul Wegener, Henrik Galeen. C: Karl Freund. Cast: Paul Wegener, Albert Steinrueck, Ernst Deutsch, Lyda Salmonova, Otto Gebuehr, Hanns Sturm, Loni Nest, Greta Schroeder, Max Kronert. This prequel to the first *Golem* film told how the man of clay came into the world. In the fifteenth century, a time of magic and witchcraft, an astrologer sees a terrible vision in the stars for the Jews. A rabbi then finds a statue, the Golem, and brings it to life with the use of sorcery and a magic word. His scheming assistant then puts it to use performing dastardly deeds. After running amok, the clay man is eventually stopped by a little girl who pulls the amulet from his chest, turning him back into a statue again. ¶ "Call all the elders together to pray. The stars predict disaster." • "Aemaer" is the magic word that brought life to the Golem. The word was folded and placed inside the amulet on his chest. • Two French versions of the story were also made as well—in 1937 and 1966, though only the first has been released in English. There is also a Polish version of the Golem, made in 1979. • Paul Wegener (who played the title role in the 1914 version as well as in this one) also appeared in *The Golem and the Dancer* (1917), in which he wears a Golem costume to impress a dancer. • Henrik Galeen, the film's co-writer, wrote the screenplay for *Nosferatu* (1922).

The Golem (1937; Metropolis; France/Czechoslovakia). D: Julien Duvivier. P: Charles Philippe. S: Julien Duvivier, André Paul Antoine. C: Vaclav Vich, Jan Stallich. Cast: Harry Baur, Germaine Dussey, Roger Karl, Ferdinand Hard, Jany Holt, Charles Dorat. A paranoid Emperor commits acts of mayhem, forever fearing the Golem which awaits him in the city's ghetto district. ¶ "Like me, you're half-man and half-specter. Just make a small sign and I'll know you're my friend."

It (1967; Goldstar–Seven Arts/Warner Bros; U.K./U.S.) D/P/S: Herbert J. Leger. C: David Bolton. Cast: Roddy McDowall, Jill Haworth, Paul Maxwell, Aubrey Richards, Ernest Clark. A museum curator (Roddy McDowall) invokes life to a Golem-like stone statue and sends it on a murderous rampage. • Not even an atomic bomb blast could kill *It*, though it did destroy its master, Roddy McDowall.

Jason and the Argonauts (1963) (see MYTHOLOGY). The gigantic bronze statue of the mythical titan called "Talos" comes to life when Hercules and Hylas remove something from the treasure trove in the statue's base.

Majin, Monster of Terror (1966; Daiei/AIP-TV; Japan) (also *Majin*). D: Kimiyoshi Yasuda, Yoshiyuki Kuroda. P: Masaichi

Nagata. S: Tetsuo Yoshida. C: Fujio Morita. Cast: Miwa Takada, Yoshihiko Aoyama, Jun Fujimaki, Ryutaro Gomi, Tatsuo Endo. The giant Japanese statue of a samurai warrior awakens to put an end to a tyrant who has enslaved the people of an assassinated lord. Majin punctuates his point by driving a gigantic spike through the body of the evil usurper at the climax.

Majin Strikes Again (1966; Daiei; Japan) D: Issei Mori. P: Masaichi Nagata. S: Tetsuo Yoshida. C: Fujio Morita, Hiroshi Imai. Cast: Hidecki Ninomiya, Masahide Kuzuka, Shinji Hori, Shiei Iizuka. In this third episode of the Majin trilogy, the giant samurai statue rescues some children from a tyrant.

The Mummy (1932) (see MUMMIES — THE UNIVERSAL SERIES). At the climax, the statue of Isis raises its arm and fires a ray of supernatural force which leaves the Mummy a pile of dust.

The Return of Giant Majin (1966; Daiei; Japan) (also *The Return of Majin*). D: Kenji Misumi. P: Masaichi Nagata. S: Tetsuo Yoshida. C: Fujio Morita. Cast: Kojiro Hongo, Shiho Fujimura, Tara Fujimura, Taro Murui, Jutaro Hojo, Takashi Kanda. Majin comes to life after some ungratefuls desecrate his sacred image. When a courageous woman cries into a lake from which he came, the stone idol ceases his rampage and returns to the lake.

Sinbad and the Eye of the Tiger (1977) (see SINBAD). The huge bull-like statue of a minotaur is brought to life by a witch.

Sword and Sorcery

(*See also* Mythology; Sinbad)

Though in film the Sword and Sorcery subgenre is a modern phenomenon, its historical roots go back to the time of King Arthur. One would think that legends of valiant warriors fighting evil sorcerers possessing strange powers in lands where dragons roam would have been thoroughly explored (and exploited) by now, but this is not the case. Imaginative, popular films like *Dragonslayer* (1981), *Conan the Barbarian* (1982), and *Sword and the Sorcerer* (1982) have sparked a modern film trend, with no end in sight. Apart from their mythological brethren (found in the MYTHOLOGY section), over 80 percent of all Sword and Sorcery films have been made in the last decade, making it a true 80s phenomenon. Sword and Sorcery pictures are the ultimate escapist movies. They are pictures of pure fantasy, set in ancient, fictional lands where magic and wizardry is commonplace and anything can happen. Not only is this free range of imagination appealing to audiences, it is advantageous for the filmmakers as well. Since this subgenre's audience is already programmed to expect the unexpected, filmmakers have less of a struggle achieving audience believability. By the very nature of the Sword and Sorcery film, this willing suspension of disbelief is built right in, giving free reign (budget allowing) to the filmmakers' fantastical visions.

See also MYTHOLOGY for additional features filled with swordfights and sorcery.

Amazons (1987; Concorde-Aries) D: Alex Sessa. P: Hector Olivera. S: Charles Saunders. C: Leonard Solis. Cast: Windsor Taylor Randolph, Penelope Reed, Joseph Whipp, Danitza Kingsley, Wolfram Hoechst, Annie Larronde. The evil Lord Alungo and his Pegash army are out to conquer an Amazon city. The Emerald Queen, however, sends her two best warriors out to retrieve the invincible Sword of Azundati. Along the way, the pair must battle a Kalungo female warrior who can transform into a lion. The Amazonian heroine, Dyala, prevails, and returns just in time to behead the usurping lord. • Roger Corman served as the film's associate producer.

Ator the Fighting Eagle (1983; Filmirage) D/S: David Hills. P: Patrick Murphy. C:

Fred Slonisco. Cast: Miles O'Keeffe, Sabrina Siani, Warren Hillman, Ritza Brown, Edmund Purdom. The Grand Priest of the Spider sets out to kill the first born of Thorn. After learning that he is adopted, Thorn's son, Ator, falls for his sister Sunya, and gains approval to be married. On their wedding night, the black knights of the evil priest kidnap Sunya, and take her back to the Temple of the Spider. Ator, with the help of a martial arts expert named Roon, sets out to retrieve his love. When he arrives at the temple he must face the wicked monster known as "the Spider." ¶ "The Earth trembles like a virgin being drawn to the nuptial bed."

Barbarian Queen (1984; Vestron) D: Hector Olivera. Cast: Lana Clarkson, Dawn Dunlap, Susana Traverso, Victor Bo. A beautiful buxom Queen and her female comrades avenge the death of an innocent tribe by slaughtering the savage gang that destroyed them. ¶ "You are much too beautiful a girl to let yourself be broken into food for the royal dogs."

The Barbarians (1987; Cannon International; U.S./Italy) D: Ruggero Deodato. P: John Thompson. S: James R. Silke. C: Gianlorenzo Battaglia. Cast: Peter Paul, David Paul, Richard Lynch, Eva LaRue, Michael Berryman, Virginia Bryant. Identical twins named Gore and Kutchek are kidnapped and raised to be tremendous gladiators. Later, after escaping their tyrannical master, they decide to set their country straight by rescuing a Queen, killing the dreaded Bog Dragon, and recovering the magical Ruby of Life. • Peter and David Paul both stand six feet tall, and weigh in at 260 pounds. The brothers also appeared in the films *D.C. Cab* (with Mr. T) and *The Flamingo Kid* (with Matt Dillon).

The Beastmaster (1982; MGM/United Artists) D: Don Coscarelli. P: Paul Pepperman, Sylvio Tabet. S: Don Coscarelli, Paul Pepperman. C: John Alcott. Cast: Marc Singer, Tanya Roberts, Rip Torn, John Amos. The sole survivor of a massacre vows to take revenge. He uses his magical ability to communicate with animals to aid him in his quest. Among the perils he must face is a witch, a legion of bat-men, and a fiendish cult. ¶ "You will die at the hands of Zed's unborn son."

The Blade Master (1984; Heron) D/S: David Hills. P: Chris Trainor. Cast: Miles O'Keeffe, Lisa Foster. The mythical blademaster named Ator leads a group of warriors in defending the Castle of Knowledge from the forces of evil.

The Challenge (1982; CBS Inc.) D: John Frankenheimer. P: Robert L. Rosen, Ron Beckman. S: Richard Maxwell, John Sayles. Cast: Scott Glenn, Toshiro Mifune, Donna Kei Benz. This contemporary sword and sorcery samurai film features an American drifter drawn into a personal battle between two brothers and their family swords which possess magical properties.

Conan the Barbarian (1982; Universal) D: John Milius. P: Buzz Feitshans, Rafaella De Laurentiis. S: John Milius, Oliver Stone. C: Duke Callaghan. Cast: Arnold Schwarzenegger, Sandahl Bergman, Gerry Lopez, James Earl Jones, Ben Davidson, William Smith, Mako, Cassandra Caviola, Max Von Sydow. The epic life and times of Conan are depicted here, beginning with his birth and the hardships of his youth. After growing up in slavery he learns how to handle a sword and fight like a mighty warrior. When he eventually gains his freedom, he bands together with a thief, a magician, and the beautiful Sandahl Bergman to steal a treasure from a horrible snake cult. Soon he realizes that the leader of the cult was the one responsible for massacring his people and selling him into slavery, so he sets out to take his revenge. ¶ "The secret of steel has always carried with it a mystery. You must learn its riddle, Conan, you must put out its discipline. For no one, no one in this world can you trust. Not men, not women, not beasts. This you can trust." • Writer Oliver Stone went on to become one of the industry's best film directors, with Academy Award–winning hits like *Wall Street, Platoon, Born on the Fourth of July, The Doors* and *JFK*.

Conan the Destroyer (1984; Universal) D: Richard Fleischer. P: Rafaela De Laurentiis. S: Stanley Mann. C: Jack Cardiff. Cast: Arnold Schwarzenegger, Grace Jones, Wilt Chamberlain, Mako, Tracey Walter, Sarah Douglas, Olivia D'Abo. Conan accompanies a princess on a quest to find a magical treasure. If they are successful, Queen Taramis will bring his old girlfriend (from the original *Conan*), Valeria, back to life. The Queen's real intention, however, is to have both the princess and Conan killed. After picking up a band of misfit warriors along the way, Conan eventually squares off against a god-like creature called Dagotti at the climax. • Dagotti was constructed by the same man who brought the lovable alien, E.T., to life—Carlo Rambaldi.

Conquest (1984; Heron International; Italy/Spain) D: Lucio Fulci. P: Giovanni Di Clemente. S: Gino Capone, José Antonio de

la Loma, Carlos Vasallo. Cast: George
Rivero, Andrew Occhipinti, Conrado Sanmartin, Violeta Cela, José Gras Palau,
Maria Scola, Sabrina Sellas. The land of
Cronos is under siege by a demonic sorceress called Ocron, who controls the life-
giving Sun. Two young warriors named Ilias
and Matz take her on.

The Dark Crystal (1983; Universal) D:
Jim Henson, Frank Oz. P: Jim Henson,
Gary Kurtz. S: David Odell. C: Oswald
Morris. Cast: Voices of Billie Whitelaw,
Stephen Garlick, Lisa Maxwell. In a far-off
world, an elf named Jen is given the prophetic task by his mystical master to retrieve
the missing crystal shard of the all-powerful
"Dark Crystal," making it whole again so it
can bring light into the world. • Jim Henson, the creator of the popular "Muppets,"
worked on this project for over five years.

Deathstalker (1983; Palo Alto) D: John
Watson. P: James Sbardellati. S: Howard
R. Cohen. Cast: Richard Hill, Barbi Benton, Richard Brooker, Lana Clarkson. The
powerful warrior known only as "Deathstalker" heads for a tournament to win the
throne of a wizard, attain mystical powers,
and receive the hand of Princess Codille. •
Love-interest Barbi Benton is a former
Playboy playmate of the year and girlfriend
of Hugh Hefner.

Deathstalker 2 (1987; Concorde Pictures)
D: Jim Wynorski. P: Frank Isaacs, Jr. S:
Neil Rutterberg. Cast: John Terlesky, Monique Gabrielle, John Lazar, Toni Naples,
Maria Socas. This semi-sequel (featuring a
new cast) has Deathstalker saving a kingdom from an evil wizard named Jerak and
his Queen, Sultana. The terrible twosome
have taken over the kingdom by replicating
the Princess Evie, and the real Evie joins up
with Deathstalker to battle pirates, amazons, and zombies before matching the
wizard and the queen in the final confrontation. ¶ "Stalker, is that your sword or are
you just happy to see me?"

Dragonslayer (1981; Paramount/Walt
Disney) D: Mathew Robbins. P: Hal Barwood. S: Mathew Robbins, Hal Barwood.
C: Derek Vanunt. Cast: Peter MacNicol,
Caitlin Clark, Ralph Richardson, John
Hallum, Peter Eyre, Albert Salmi, Sydney
Bromley. A sorcerer's apprentice and a
courageous young girl take it upon themselves to rid the land of a flying dragon with
the aid of a magical amulet. At the climax,
the old sorcerer (played by Ralph Richardson), who was killed earlier in the film, reappears to aid the imperiled youths. ¶ "If it
weren't for sorcerers there wouldn't be any

dragons. Once, the skies were dotted with
them — magnificent horned backs, leathered
wings, soaring in their hot breath wind." •
Star Peter McNichol is the brother of
popular television actress, Kristy McNichol.
He turned in a wonderful performance in
the Oscar-winning Meryl Streep vehicle,
Sophie's Choice (1982). • The picture was
filmed on location in Scotland and northern
Wales, as well as London's Pinewood
studios.

The Dungeonmaster (1983; Empire Pic-
tures/Ragewar Productions) D: Rosemarie
Turko. P: Charles Band. S: Allen Actor. C:
Mac Ahlberg. Cast: Richard Moll, Jeffrey
Byron, Leslie Wing, Blackie Lawless, Danny
Dick. Sword and sorcery meets up with the
computer age in this tale of a programmer
who is coerced by a warlord named Mes-
terna (Richard Moll) into playing a deadly
life and death dungeons and dragons–styled
game devised by a galaxy-wandering wizard. Jeffrey Byron must face zombies and
stone creatures in this game of death to save
his kidnapped girlfriend.

Excalibur (1981; Warner Bros.) D/P:
John Boorman. S: John Boorman, Rospo
Pallenberg. C: Alex Thomson. Cast: Nigel
Terry, Nicol Williamson, Helen Mirren,
Nicholas Clay, Cherie Lunghi, Paul Geoffrey. This retelling of the King Arthur
legend features magic swords, wizardry, the
Holy Grail, and the Lady of the Lake. ¶
"Hereafter, so that we remember our bonds,
we shall always come together in a circle to
hear and tell of deeds good and brave. I will
build a round table where this fellowship
shall meet. And a hole about the table, and
a cursal about the hole, and I will marry,
and the land will have an heir to wicld Excalibur. Knights of the Round Table!"

Goliath Against the Giants (1962; Medallion; Italy/Spain) D: Guido Malatesta. P:
Cesare Seccia, Manuel Perez. S: Cesare Seccia, Gianfranco Parolini, Giovanni Simonelli, Arpad De Riso, Sergio Sollima. Cast:
Brad Harris, Gloria Milland, Fernando
Rey, Barbara Carrol, José Rubio. The
muscleman known as Goliath faces a sea
monster, Amazon women, and a valley
loaded with giants.

Goliath and the Vampires (1964; American International; Italy) (also *The Vampires*). D: Giacomo Gentilomo, Sergio Corbucci. P: Paolo Moffa. S: Sergio Corbucci,
Duccio Tessari. C: Alvaro Mancori. Cast:
Gordon Scott, Jacques Sernas, Gianna
Maria Canale, Eleanora Ruffo, Guido Ce-
lano. Goliath (Gordon Scott) engages in a
battle with a vampire sorcerer who can

change into different people. Under the vampire's command is an army of human robots, which he uses to watch over the human sacrifice carried out in his underground world. ¶ "And from a serpent, born in the depths of the Kingdom of Evil, sprang the monster that nourishes itself on human blood." • At the climax, Goliath takes on the vampire, rips off his face, and then does battle with the muscular monster underneath. The actor in the monster costume is none other than Steve "Hercules" Reeves.

Gor (1987; Cannon International) D: Fritz Kiersch. P: Harry Alan Towers, Avi Lerner. S: Rick Marx. C: Hans Khule. Cast: Urbano Barberini, Rebecca Ferratii, Jack Palance, Paul L. Smith, Oliver Reed, Larry Taylor, Graham Clarke. • Tarl is a meek New Hampshire college professor who is transported across time and space (by a magic ring) to a sword and sorcery world where he becomes a hero. ¶ Warrior: "You've come to a land called 'Gor'." Tarl: "Appropriate name." • The film is based on the novel, *Tarnsman of Gor,* by John Norman.

Hawk the Slayer (1980; Chips Productions; U.K.) D: Terry Marcel. P: Harry Robertson. S: Terry Marcel, Harry Robertson. Cast: Jack Palance, John Terry, Shane Briant, Patrick Magee, Ferdy Mayne, Harry Andrews, Roy Kinnear. Two brothers— Hawk, the strong and good one, and Voltan, the elder evil one—wage war against each other at the Weir Forest and in the Abbey of Caddonbury.

Hearts and Armour (1983; Warner Bros.) D: Giacomo Battiato. P: Nicola Carraro. S: Franco Cristaldi, Nicola Carraro. C: Dante Spinotti. Cast: Tanya Roberts, Rick Edwards, Barbara De Rossi, Ron Moss, Leigh McCloskey. Noble sword-fighting warriors possessing high ideals, and practicing codes of conflict from the Middle Ages, battle to the death. Tanya Roberts plays a Moorish princess in love with a Christian warrior.

Highlander (1986; Cannon) D: Russell Mulcahy. P: Peter Davis, William Panzer. S: Gregory Widen, Peter Bellwood, Larry Ferguson. Cast: Christopher Lambert, Roxanne Hart, Clancy Brown, Sean Connery. A pair of immortal warriors from the year 1536 face off in contemporary New York. They can only be destroyed by decapitation.

Iron Warrior (1987; Trans World Ent.; Italy) D: Al Bradley. P: Sam Sill. S: Steven Luotto, Al Bradley. C: Wally Gentleman. Cast: Miles O'Keeffe, Savina Gersak, Iris Peynado, Elisabeth Kaza, Tim Lane. Ator the barbarian goes up against an evil sorceress named Kaza and her iron skull-masked warrior, who just happens to be Ator's twin brother, kidnapped at birth. • The picture was filmed on location in Malta and Gozo.

Jack the Giant Killer (1962; United Artists) D: Nathan Juran. P: Edward Small. S: Orville H. Hampton, Nathan Juran. C: David S. Horsley. Cast: Kerwin Mathews, Judi Meredith, Torin Thatcher, Walter Burke, Rober Mobley, Don Beddoe. After killing a giant who had kidnapped a princess, the King rewards a young farmer/hero (named Jack) by appointing him his daughter's bodyguard. The wizard Pendragon, who sent the giant, manages to recapture the princess. Jack, a cabin boy, a Viking fisherman, and a leprechaun then journey to the wizard's castle to face various monsters and rescue the girl. ¶ "It's nothing, I kill a giant every morning before breakfast—starts my day right." • Some of the terrible foes faced by Jack include an army of demons, giant zombie warriors, a two-headed ogre, and a winged dragon. • Pendragon's castle is filled with candelabra held by disembodied arms (borrowing from Jean Cocteau's *Beauty and the Beast,* 1946), and the fortress's major domo is a being with the body of a man and the head of an animal. • The film's producer, Edward Small, once turned down Ray Harryhausen and his fabulous sketches which eventually became the popular *The Seventh Voyage of Sinbad* (1957). Coming to regret this decision, Small made this film, which starred two of *Seventh Voyage*'s best actors—Kerwin Mathews and Torin Thatcher (playing nearly identical roles as they did in the Sinbad movie). In the absence of Harryhausen, Small hired Jim Danforth to do the (passable but inferior) stop-motion animation effects. • There are two versions of this feature. One is a straight fantasy aimed at the young adult audience, while the other is a cloying musical intended to soften the film's frightening aspects for the children. The footage is basically the same in both, but the musical version dubs "cute" songs over the dialogue.

Krull (1983; Columbia) D: Peter Yates. P: Ron Silverman. S: Stanford Sherman. C: Peter Suschitzky. Cast: Ken Marshall, Lysette Anthony, Freddie Jones, Francesca Annis, Alun Armstrong. A distant planet features a sword and sorcery–like civilization.

Labyrinth (1986; Tri-Star Pictures) D: Jim Henson. P: Eric Rattray. S: Terry Jones, Jim Henson. C: Alex Thomson. Cast: David Bowie, Jennifer Connelly, David

Goelz, Toby Froud, Shelley Thompson, Steve Whitmire, Karen Prell. A girl who wishes that her bothersome brother would disappear is shocked to discover that a Goblin King from another world has followed up on her request by taking the boy to his castle. The girl, Sarah, comes to the rescue but must first pass through the labyrinth of mazes and mystical creatures that lies between her and the castle. • Muppet-maker Jim Henson, who tragically died in 1990, co-wrote the screenplay as well as designing and operating the numerous puppet-like creatures.

Ladyhawke (1985; Warner Bros.) D: Richard Donner. P: Richard Donner, Lauren Shuler. S: Edward Khmara, Michael Thomas, Tom Mankiewicz. C: Vittorio Storaro. Mathew Broderick, Rutger Hauer, Michelle Pfeiffer, Leo McKern, John Wood. A warrior and his lover are cursed by an evil bishop who lords over the infamous prison fortress of Aquila. The terrible spell has left them in a tragic condition in which they can never truly be together. By day the warrior (Rutger Hauer) is himself, but at night he turns into a wolf. Conversely, his lady love (Michelle Pfeiffer) is normal at night but is transformed into a hawk during the day. With the aid of a young thief (Mathew Broderick), they break into the impregnable fortress in order to confront the evil bishop and break the cruel curse.

Legend (1986; Universal) D: Ridley Scott. P: Arnon Milchan. S: William Hjortsberg. C: Alex Thomson. Cast: Tom Cruise, Mia Sara, Tim Curry, David Bennent, Billy Barty. Tom Cruise, who lives in a mythical forest populated by goblins, fairies, and a unicorn, must face the Lord of Darkness (Tim Curry) and stop his plan of bringing another ice age to the world. • Makeup artists Rob Bottin and Peter Robb-King were nominated for an Academy Award for their work on this picture.

Lionheart (1990; Warner Bros.) D: Franklin J. Schaffner. P: Stanley O'Toole, Talia Shire. S: Menno Meyjes, Richard Outten. C: Alec Mills. Cast: Eric Stoltz, Gabriel Byrne, Nicola Cowper, Dexter Fletcher, Deborah Barrymore. Eric Stoltz plays a knight in the time of King Richard (the Lionheart) who champions the young victims of a cruel warlord slaver. The brave knight must not only face the warlord, but the magic of wizards and an underground city populated by stone monsters.

The Magic Sword (1962; United Artists) D/P: Bert I. Gordon. S: Bernard Schoenfeld. C: Paul Vogel. Cast: Gary Lockwood, Basil Rathbone, Estelle Winwood, Anne Helm, Liam Sullivan, Jack Kosslyn, Angelo Rossitto, Vampira, Richard Kiel. This story, set in fourth century England, is about a young man's quest to save the daughter of a king and win her hand in marriage. After receiving a lightning-fast horse and magic sword from his witch mother, George assembles six brave knights (called up from stone) and heads off to an evil sorcerer's castle to free the princess. Along the way he must face each of the wizard's seven curses sent to stop him. ¶ "Seven deadly curses await would-be rescuers on the way to my castle!" • George's sword is called "Ascalon," and his white horse, "Bayard," is the fastest horse in the world. • The seven curses are as follows: One—a 25-foot-tall Ogre; two—a terrible Moor; three—a grotesque looking vampire hag (played by Vampira); four—an onslaught of fire-balls; five—a cave of fire devils; the sixth curse is met at Lodac's castle and includes a variety of the sorcerer's creations, including a two-headed dragon; the seventh and last curse is Lodac himself, who begins to conjure up all his powers, but by this time George's mother has arrived and she snatches Lodac's power ring before turning into a panther and killing him. • Over five months of special effects work (with a strong emphasis on black light projection) was required to complete the project. Bert I. Gordon called his processes "Super-Percepto-Vision." He said of the effects, "In bringing the effects to life on the screen it is essential that the same concept envisioned in the writing of the original story, and in experimenting with the special effects, be carried forward and brought to the screen."

Masters of the Universe (1987; Cannon) D: Gary Goddard. P: Menahem Golan, Yoram Globus. S: David Odell. C: Hanania Baer. Cast: Dolph Lundgren, Frank Langella, Meg Foster, Billy Barty, Courteney Cox. He-Man and his furry dwarf fights Skeletor and his cronies for possession of a magical key which can open up the secrets of the universe. The battle takes place on contemporary Earth, and He-Man is aided by teenager Julie, who is rewarded in the end with a trip through space. ¶ "I must possess all or I possess nothing." • This $15 million sword and sorcery film, starring *Rocky*'s Russian opponent (Dolph Lundgren), is ironically the first feature length film to be inspired by a toy (instead of the other way around).

Merlin and the Sword (1982; Comworld) D: Clive Donner. P: Martin Poll. S: J. David

Wyler. Cast: Malcolm McDowell, Candice Bergen, Edward Woodward, Dyan Cannon. A time-traveling tourist is sent back in time to Camelot, where he meets all the legendary characters including King Arthur, Guinevere, the sorcerer Morgan Lefay, and of course, the Knights of the Round Table.

The Neverending Story (1984; Warner Bros.; W. Germany) D: Wolfgang Petersen. P: Bernd Eichinger, Dieter Geissler. S: Wolfgang Petersen, Herman Weigel. Cast: Noah Hathaway, Barret Oliver, Tami Stronach, Patricia Hayes, Moses Gunn. A boy enters the magical world of imagination through the pages of a book, and encounters a land filled with magical creatures, including a racing snail, a hang-glider bat, a wise tortoise, a flying "Luckdragon," elves, a terrible Rock Biter, and a swirling energy force known as "The Nothing" (which is about to engulf this mystical universe). • Some of the magical regions explored in the film include the Howling Forest, the Ivory Tower, the Swamps of Sadness, the Magic Minor Gate, and the Sea of Possibilities. • Giorgio Moroder provided the film's musical score. He is the man responsible for bringing *Metropolis* (1926) to the screen again in the 1980s with a contemporary rock music score.

Neverending Story 2: The Next Chapter (1991; Warner Bros.) D: George Miller. P: Dieter Geissler. S: Karin Howard. C: Dave Connell. Cast: Jonathan Brandis, Kenny Morrison, Clarissa Burt, John Wesley Shipp, Martin Umbach. A meek young boy uses the magical storybook to enter the mystical world of "Fantasia." There he must rescue a childlike empress and face a wicked sorceress who attempts to stop his mission by draining away his memories. ¶ "Begin an all new adventure as a young boy returns to a world of wonder on the wings of his own imagination"—ad line. • This sequel to *The Neverending Story* includes many of the fantasy characters introduced in the original, including the gigantic Rock Biter and the friendly Luckdragon. The new creatures encountered include a "Lavaman" and a "Mudwart."

The Princess Bride (1987; 20th Century–Fox) D: Rob Reiner. P: Arnold Scheinman, Rob Reiner. S: William Goldman. C: Adrian Biddle. Cast: Cary Elwes, Robin Wright, Mandy Patinkin, Chris Sarandon, Fred Savage, Peter Falk, Andre the Giant, Wallace Shawn, Billy Crystal, Christopher Guest, Carol Kane, Peter Cook. This tongue-in-cheek swashbuckler set in a fantasy world involves a romance broken up by an evil prince. The young hero is nearly killed, but with the help of his two oddball associates, they are able to storm the castle and retrieve his love. ¶ "My name is Inigo Montoya. You killed my father. Prepare to die!" • Screenwriter William Goldman (a former Oscar winner with *Butch Cassidy and the Sundance Kid,* 1969) adapted the story from his own novel. • Rob Reiner, who made the picture on a $17-million budget and pushed hard to get the idea onto film, has stated that he would like "The Princess Bride" to be on his tombstone. • The picture was shot on location in England, Ireland, and Shepperton Studios.

Prisoners of the Lost Universe (1983). D: Terry Marcle. Cast: Richard Hatch, Kay Lenz, John Saxon, Peter O'Farrell, Ray Charleson. Richard Hatch and Kay Lenz drop into a medieval world after entering a new dimension in time.

Quest for the Mighty Sword (1989; Filmirage) D: David Hills. C: Federico Slonisco. Cast: Eric Allen Kramer, Margaret Lenzey, Donal O'Brien, Dina Marrone, Chris Murphy. In the days of sorcery, dragons, trolls, and two-headed swordsmen, Ator and his sacred sword of Graal must face a wicked god-like being known as Thorn.

Red Sonja (1985; MGM/United Artists) D: Richard Fleischer. P: Christian Ferry. S: Clive Exton, George MacDonald Fraser. Cast: Brigitte Nielsen, Arnold Schwarzenegger, Sandahl Bergman, Paul Smith, Ronald Lacey. The ultimate female warrior joins forces with her male counterpart to avenge the murder of her family by Queen Gedren, who has a magical talisman at her disposal. ¶ "I will tell the future in your entrails, red woman!" • This film reunites Arnold Schwarzenegger and Sandahl Bergman from *Conan the Barbarian* (1982).

She (1985; American Distributors, Inc.) D: Avi Nesher. P: Renato Dandi. S: Avi Nesher. C: Sandro Mancori. Cast: Sandahl Bergman, Quin Kessler, David Goss, Harrison Muller, Gordon Mitchell. In a post-nuclear world of sword and sorcery, a woman warrior takes on the evil mutants known as the Norks.

Siegfried (1924; UFA; Germany) D: Fritz Lang. S: Fritz Lang, Thea von Harbou. C: Carl Hoffman, Gunther Rittau, Walter Ruttmann. Cast: Paul Richter, Margarete Schon, Theodor Loos, Bernhard Goetzke, Hanna Ralph, Hans Adalbert von Schlettow. Siegfried slays a great dragon and bathes in its blood, making him invulnerable except for one small portion covered by a leaf. After winning the hand of a King's sister, treachery and deceit from the Queen rears up in the form of a henchman's arrow, which hits the fatal spot and kills the valiant dragon slayer. Siegfried's wife then marries Attila the Hun, lures the old King, Queen, and warrior henchman to her camp and has them annihilated. Remorse over this act causes Attila to slay his own wife, putting an end to this tragic story of fate and atonement.

Sorceress (1982; New World Pictures) D: Brian Stuart. P: Jack Hill. S: Jim Wynorski. Cast: Leigh Harris, Lynette Harris, Bob Nelson. A sorcerer's wife runs away from her spouse with their twin girls in order to keep them safe from being sacrificed. She finally manages to kill the sorcerer, but in 20 years time he comes back from the dead to send warriors out to retrieve the twins. By sacrificing the girls, the sorcerer will be able to attain a new level of supernatural power, but in those 20 years the girls have learned to call upon the forces of light to act in their defense.

Sword and the Dragon (1956; Valiant: U.S.S.R.) D/P: Alexander Ptushko. S: V. Kotochnev, Mikhail Kochnev. C: Jasha Kuhn, F. Provorov. Cast: Boris Andreyev, Andrei Abrikosov, Natalie Medvedeva, Alexei Shvorin. Cast: A Russian mythical hero with magical sword takes on a giant, a wind demon, and a three-headed dragon. ¶ "The seven wonders of the motion picture world! Four years in the making! Cast of 106,000 . . . 11,000 horses! On the screen at the same time!"—ad line hype.

Sword and the Sorcerer (1982; Universal) D: Albert Pyun. P: Brandon Chase, Marianne Chase. S: Tom Karnowski. C: Joseph Magine. Cast: Lee Horsley, Kathleen Beller, Simon MacCorkindale, George Maharis, Richard Lynch, Robert Tessier, Anthony DeLongis, Richard Moll. Evil King Cromwell enlists the aid of a sorcerer to conquer the kingdom of Eh Dan. Handsome Prince Talon escapes, and 11 years later organizes a group of mercenaries to help a girl rescue her brother from Cromwell's clutches. Eventually Talon confronts and destroys both the evil sorcerer and Cromwell with his great strength and three-bladed sword. • Richard Lynch, playing the unscrupulous King Cromwell, won the year's Best Actor award from the Academy of Science Fiction, Fantasy, and Horror.

Sword of the Barbarians (1983; Italy) D: Michael E. Lemick. Cast: Peter MacCoy, Sabrina Siani, Margarethe Christian, Yvonne Fraschetti. The son of Ator travels to the Ark of the Templars to obtain a special crossbow which he uses against the members of a fanatical religious order that had murdered his wife.

Sword of the Valiant (1984; Cannon Group Inc.) D: Stephen Weeks. P: Menahem Golan, Yoram Globus. S: Stephen Weeks, Howard C. Pen, Philip M. Breen. C: Freddie Young, Peter Hurst. Cast: Miles O'Keeffe, Cyrielle Claire, Leigh Lawson, Sean Connery, Trevor Howard, Peter Cushing, Ronald Lacey. The medieval legend of Sir Gawain and the Green Knight is retold in this sword and sorcery outing. ¶ "Oh come, the sport is simple, a cut for a cut, and yours to be the first. Who's going to deal me my blow? Who's the jolly gambler to play my game? Who shall lay his pride, his prowess, his courage, on the line of my neck?"

The Thief of Bagdad (1924; United Artists). D: Raoul Walsh. P: Douglas Fairbanks. S: Lotta Woods. C: Arthur Edeson. Cast: Douglas Fairbanks, Snitz Edwards, Charles Belcher, Julianne Johnson, Anna May Wong, Noble Johnson. A thief (Douglas Fairbanks), in love with a caliph's daughter, tackles a series of incredible foes in order to secure the rights to marry the girl. • Among his adventures are battles with a terrible spider, a dragon, a giant bat, and a tree monster to name just a few. He also acquires a magic carpet, which comes in handy when fighting a band of Mongols. • The fabulous magic carpet was actually a platform suspended by steel piano wires, and moved over the city set at the rate of 25 mph. The final illusion was brought about by speeding up the shot with the camera and a projector.

Thor the Conqueror (1982; Italy) D: T. Ricci. Cast: Conrad Nichols, Malisa Lang. Inhabitants of a strange fantasy world vie for a magic sword.

War of the Zombies (1963) (see ZOMBIES). (also *Night Star, Goddess of Electra*). Set in the time of the Roman Empire, John Barrymore plays a sorcerer planning to revive the corpses of Roman soldiers and create an army of zombies to use against the power of Rome.

The Warrior and the Sorceress (1984; New Horizons) D/S: John Broderick. P: Frank K. Isaac, Jr. Cast: David Carradine, Luke Askew, Maria Socas, Anthony DeLongis, Harry Townes. David Carradine basically adapts his role from the TV series "Kung Fu" to a futuristic sword and sorcery setting. Carradine's character (called Kain) is a mighty warrior/priest on the mystical world of Ura, who becomes involved in a village

war and meets up with a sorceress whose destiny he feels is intertwined with his own.
• *The Warrior and the Sorceress* was originally set to be a science fiction rather than straight sword and sorcery film, according to star David Carradine. "It was conceived as a science fiction samurai movie called *Kain of Dark Planet*," the actor told *Fangoria* #59. "I wanted to have glimpses of wrecked technology, ruined spacecraft and things like that. But because of exigencies in the budget, you never notice that it's happening on another planet. So, it becomes fantasy."

Willow (1988; MGM) D: Ron Howard. P: Nigel Wooll. S: Bob Dolman. C: Adrian Biddle. Cast: Val Kilmer, Joanne Whalley, Warwick Davis, Patricia Hayes, Gavan O'Herlihy, Phil Pondacaro, Pat Roach, Jean Marsh. Set in "a time of dread," this sword and sorcery story tells the legend of a child savior, protected by "Willow" the dwarf and a handsome warrior (Val Kilmer), who will one day stop the powerful Queen Bavmorda. Bavmorda is trying to alter the legend's prophecy by capturing all the pregnant women and destroying their children at birth. ¶ "Now you will watch me draw upon the power of the universe to send that child into the netherworld!"

The Witch's Curse (1963; Medallion; Italy) (also *Maciste in Hell*). D: Riccardo Freda. P: Ermanno Donati, Luigi Carpentieri. S: Eddy H. Given, Oreste Biancoli, Piero Pierotti. C: Ricardo Pallottini. Cast: Kirk Morris, Hélène Chanel, Angelo Zanolli, Andrea Bosic, Vira Silenti. Maciste journeys to seventeenth century Scotland and faces demons from hell to rid a village of its curse.

Wizards of the Lost Kingdom (1985; Concorde Pictures) D: Hector Olivera. P: Frank Isaac, Alex Sessa. S: Tom Edwards. Cast: Bo Svenson, Vidal Peterson, Thom Christopher, Barbara Stock. A young apprentice wizard battles an evil sorcerer and assorted monsters with the help of Kor the warrior (Bo Svenson).

The Wonderful World of the Brothers Grimm (1962) (see ANTHOLOGIES). One of the segments, entitled "The Singing Bone," tells about a dragon slayer who is murdered by his unscrupulous master. When a flute is made out of bones of the dead man, the song that is played reveals the treachery and brings the wronged man back to life.

Yor, the Hunter from the Future (1983) (see TIME TRAVEL). Reb Brown journeys in time to a variety of sword and sorcery worlds.

Telekinesis *see* Psychic Ability

Telepathy *see* Psychic Ability

Time Travel

Time travel has always been a popular concept to filmmakers. It can open up so many doors to different plot developments and ideas, giving us imaginative glimpses into our past and into our future as well as exploring all the intriguing paradoxical concepts inherent in traveling through time. With so much latitude in story lines and diverse cinematic possibilities, time travel films will never lose their audience appeal. It certainly is not a quick-buck subgenre, however (as evidenced by the abysmal results of cut-rate time travel attempts like *The Yesterday Machine,* 1965; and *Journey to the Center of Time,* 1967), since (effectively) depicting worlds of the past and future onscreen usually requires a fair amount of expensive art direction.

Traveling through time is a good science fiction tool, since Einstein's theory of relativity leaves just enough room to make it a theoretically plausible concept. Time traveling is not exclusively a "scientific" idea, however, according to the cinema.

Sometimes supernatural events or objects cause the transference in time (such as the magical ring in *Gor,* 1987; or the genie in *The Boy and the Pirates,* 1960).

The means to time travel are as varied as the films themselves. Time machines or devices are some of the most popular. Films like H. G. Wells' *The Time Machine* (1960), *Dr. Who and the Daleks* (1965), and *Time After Time* (1979) all used scientifically created machines to send their protagonists backwards and or forwards in time. Sometimes less scientifically controlled forces are the cause of time trauma. A bullet fired from a gun sent *The Atomic Man* (1956) seven seconds forward in time. A Bermuda Triangle–like storm hurled a ship toward *The Final Countdown* (1980). A quartet of youngsters made a *Journey to the Beginning of Time* (1955/66) by simply floating down a river. *The Time Bandits* (1981) utilized a time portal to drop in and out of the lives of historical figures. *The Fiddlers Three* (1950) went whirling back to the Roman Empire after being struck by lightning. Robert Clarke simply flew his jet *Beyond the Time Barrier* (1960). And *Hu-Man* (1976) even went time traveling with the power generated by television audiences.

One of the more common themes of these films is the possible havoc wreaked by time travel (explored in movies like the *Back to the Future* series and *Millennium,* 1989). Even small changes in the past may have grave effects on the future. As a questioning sailor observed in *The Final Countdown* (1980), "I'm talking about the classic paradox in time. Imagine for example I go back in time to meet my own grandfather, long before he got married, before he had children. We have an argument and I kill him. Now if that happens, how am I ever going to be born? And if I can never be born, how can I go back in history and meet my very own grandfather?"

Time travel films can be broken up into two basic categories involving the juxtaposition of settings. The first has people from the future traveling to the present or the past, while the second type has those from the present heading into the past or future. The third possibility in time travel — people from the past traveling to the present or future — has been left largely unexplored by filmmakers. Interestingly enough, the two exceptions — *The Time Machine* (1960) and *Time After Time* (1979) — turned out to be two of the best time travel films ever made.

The Atomic Man (1956; United Artists) (also *Timeslip*). D: Ken Hughes. P: Alec C. Snowden. S: Charles Eric Maine. C: A. T. Dinsdale. Cast: Gene Nelson, Faith Domergue, Joseph Tomelty, Peter Arne, Vic Perry, Donald Gray, Launce Maraschal. A man surviving a gunshot wound and a life-saving operation awakens with his mind set seven and a half seconds ahead in the future. ¶ "You said that he was clinically dead for seven to eight seconds, right? I just timed him — his answers come back exactly seven and a half seconds ahead of the questions."

Back to the Future (1985; Universal) D: Robert Zemeckis. P: Neil Canton, Bob Gale. S: Robert Zemeckis, Bob Gale. C: Dean Cundey. Cast: Michael J. Fox, Christopher Lloyd, Lea Thompson, Crispin Glover, Claudia Wells, Thomas F. Wilson. Michael J. Fox accidentally goes back in time three decades by way of his scientist friend's (Christopher Lloyd) De Lorean time machine in this comedy blockbuster. There he inadvertently alters his own future by changing the conditions under which his (then teenage) parents meet. ¶ "If my calculations are correct, when this baby hits eighty-eight mph, you're going to see some serious shit." • At the film's climax, Christopher Lloyd travels briefly into the future, then comes back uttering the sequel-inspiring statement, "Where we're going we don't need roads."

Back to the Future Part 2 (1989; Universal) D: Robert Zemeckis. P: Bob Gale, Neil Canton. S: Bob Gale. C: Dean Cundey. Cast: Michael J. Fox, Christopher Lloyd, Lea Thompson, Thomas F. Wilson. Marty McFly and Doc travel to the year 2015 to resolve more complications with the McFly family future. When they return home, they find their tampering has resulted in a nightmarish society which requires a return to 1955 to undo the mess.

Back to the Future Part 3 (1990; Universal) D: Robert Zemeckis. P: Bob Gale, Neil Canton. S: Bob Gale. C: Dean Cundey. Cast: Michael J. Fox, Christopher Lloyd, Mary Steenburgen, Thomas F. Wilson, Lea Thompson. Marty travels back to the wild wild west of 1885 where he and Doc deal with Indian attacks and various bad guys. ¶ "It's a very interesting story, future boy." • *Part 3* was shot back to back with *Part 2,* and was strategically released a year later.

Beneath the Planet of the Apes (1969) (see PLANET OF THE APES SERIES). James Franciscus inadvertently breaks through the same time barrier that his colleague, Charlton Heston, encountered in the first *Planet of the Apes* film.

Berkeley Square (1933; 20th Century–Fox) D: Frank Lloyd. P: Jesse L. Lasky. S: Sonya Levien, John Balderston. C: Ernest Palmer. Cast: Leslie Howard, Heather Angel, Valerie Taylor, Irene Brown, Beryl Mercer, Alan Mowbray. A time traveler (Leslie Howard) finds himself discussing matters with a group of eighteenth century residents at a London house. • The film was remade in 1951 as *I'll Never Forget You.*

Beyond the Time Barrier (1960; American International) D: Edgar G. Ulmer. P: Robert Clarke. S: Arthur C. Pierce. C: Meredith M. Nicholson. Cast: Robert Clarke, Darlene Tompkins, Vladimir Sokoloff, Red Morgan, Arianne Arden, Stephen Bekassy. Robert Clarke plays a test pilot passing through a time warp to the year 2024. There he finds our desolate Earth (made so by a cosmic radiation plague) inhabited by mostly sterile (and occasionally telepathic) underground humans and surface mutants. ¶ "You—will rocket through the fifth dimension! You—will see sights to stagger the imagination! You—are there in the underground cities of 2024 A.D.!"—ad lines. • The movie was filmed by Miller Consolidated Pictures in Texas at the old 1936 Centennial Fairgrounds, and at Forth Worth's Carswell Field, a B-52 air base. The budget came in at about $125,000, and the shooting schedule lasted ten days. • Writer Arthur C. Pierce has a brief cameo in the film as a mutant. • Star Robert Clarke was married to Alyce King, one of the four King Sisters of the Alvino Rey band. • Arianne Arden, who played the femme fatale "Markova" in the film, is director Edgar Ulmer's daughter.

Bill and Ted's Excellent Adventure (1989; Orion) D: Stephen Herek. P: Scott Kroopt, Michael S. Murphey, Joel Soisson. S: Chris Matheson, Ed Solomon. C: Timothy Suhrstedt. Cast: Keanu Reeves, Alex Winte,

Robert Barron, George Carlin, Terry Camilleri, Clifford David, Al Leong, Rod Loomis, Dan Shor. A couple of "excellent dudes" travel back in time via a phone booth/time machine to bring back historical figures (Napoleon, Billy the Kid, Genghis Khan, Joan of Arc, Abraham Lincoln, etc.) for their oral class project in History. It turns out that Bill and Ted will become historical figures themselves with their rock 'n' roll ventures in the future according to time traveler George Carlin. ¶ "We're in danger of flunking most heinously, Ted!"

The Boy and the Pirates (1960) (see GENIES). A genie grants a boy's wish by sending him back in time to the period in which Blackbeard the pirate lived.

Cavegirl (1985) (see CAVEPEOPLE). A time continuum test sends a teen back into the prehistoric past.

Cyborg 2087 (1966) (see ROBOTS). A cyborg (Michael Rennie) from the future steals a time machine and returns to the year 1966 to persuade Eduard Franz not to build a mind-controlling device. Apparently, in the years to come, the mind control machine is used to establish a totalitarian state, monitored by cyborgs. Rennie, a cyborg believer in free society, wants to alter this bleak future, even at the risk of negating his own existence. ¶ "You also do not understand the significance of the professor's discoveries, nor does he. You'd be terrified if you knew the importance of radio telepathy in the world a hundred years from today."

Daleks: Invasion Earth 2150 A.D. (1966) (see ALIENS—INVADERS ON EARTH: THE 60s AND 70s). A London policeman accidentally touches off a time machine (called "Tardis") and sends himself, Dr. Who (Peter Cushing), and a pair of nieces into the future. There, they discover that a race of invading aliens called Daleks are controlling the Earth.

The Day Time Ended (1978; Manson International) D: John "Bud" Cardos. P: Wayne Schmidt, Steve Neill. S: Wayne Schmidt, J. Larry Carroll, David Schmoeller. C: John Morrill. Cast: Jim Davis, Chris Mitchum, Dorothy Malone, Marcy Lafferty, Scott Kolden, Natasha Ryan. A family living in a solar powered home in the southern California desert encounters life forms from the future while trapped within a time/space warp. ¶ "Time exists in a continuum ... words spoken thousands of years ago are still around somewhere in the vast infinity of space. The future as we call it, that too is with us now. Past, present and future are constantly in conflict in a finite world." • Some of the futuristic sights the family sees include a glowing obelisk, two giant ugly humanoid creatures, numerous alien ships of varied shapes and sizes, and a Peter Pan–like alien.

Dr. Who and the Daleks (1965) (see ALIENS — ENCOUNTERS IN OUTER SPACE). A bumbling assistant of Dr. Who transports himself, the Doctor, and a pair of girls through time to a futuristic planet by switching on a small time machine called the Tardis. ¶ "Young man, do you know what you have just done? You have transferred us into time and space and I haven't even set the controls. Now I don't know where we are. We could be anywhere in the universe, and at any time. Rather exciting isn't it!"

Eliminators (1986; Empire Pictures) D: Peter Manbogian. P: Charles Band. S: Paul Demeo, Danny Bilson. C: Mac Ahlberg. Cast: Andrew Prine, Roy Dotrice, Denise Crosby, Pat Reynolds, Conan Lee. A time-traveling scientist is bent on ruling the world, but is stopped by his own "mandroid" creation accompanied by battle-tested friends.

Escape from the Planet of the Apes (1971) (see PLANET OF THE APES SERIES). In this, the third episode of the "Ape" saga, the sympathetic chimpanzees Zira and Cornelius journey through the time warp which had brought Charlton Heston and James Franciscus to the Planet of the Apes, and end up back on contemporary Earth. While there, the complexities of altering the future are explored as they are first welcomed, then hunted because of the possible consequences of their arrival.

The Fiddlers Three (1950; Ealing; U.K.) D: Harry Watt. P: Robert Hamer. S: Diana Morgan, Angus Macphail. C: Wilkie Cooper. Cast: Frances Day, Francis L. Sullivan, Tommy Trinder, Sonnie Hale, Ernest Milton, Diana Decker, Elizabeth Welch. This comedy follows the adventures of two sailors and a girl who are struck by lightning while touring Stonehenge, and are then transported back in time to the Roman Empire.

The Final Countdown (1980; United Artists) D: Don Taylor. P: Peter Vincent Douglas. S: David Ambrose, Gerry Davis, Thomas Hunter, Peter Powell. C: Victor J. Kemper. Cast: Kirk Douglas, Martin Sheen, Katherine Ross, James Farentino, Charles Durning, Ron O'Neal. The U.S.S. *Nimitz* is transported back to the year 1941 (just prior to the attack on Pearl Harbor) after being engulfed by a mysterious storm. ¶ "I'm talking about the classic paradox in time. Imagine for example I go back in time to meet my own grandfather, long before he got married, before he had children. We have an argument and I kill him. Now if that happens, how am I ever going to be born? And if I can never be born, how can I go back in history and meet my very own grandfather?" • The filming actually took place on board the *Nimitz,* the world's largest aircraft carrier. In the story, the *Nimitz* eventually returns to the present through another time warp.

Frankenstein Unbound (1990) (see FRANKENSTEIN'S MONSTER — FURTHER FRANKENSTEINS). John Hurt plays a scientist in the future of 2031 whose implosion research leads to the creation of a "time slip," which hurls him back to the shores of Lake Geneva in 1817, Switzerland. There he encounters not only Mary Shelley, soon-to-be author of *Frankenstein,* but also the real Dr. Victor Frankenstein (Raul Julia) and his hideous creature. In the end, Hurt manages to send himself, Frankenstein, and his creation into the barren uncertainty of the far distant future. ¶ "It is the gateway to another world. I made it, came through it, fractured the core of time and space. I wanted to do the world a favor, but like Victor Frankenstein, I created a monster."

Gor (1987) (see SWORD AND SORCERY). A meek college professor possesses a magical ring which transports him to another time and another dimension, dropping him right in the middle of a mini-war in the land of "Gor." He is taught to fight, becomes a champion, and eventually sets out to free the people from the tyrannical slavery of the overlord (played by Oliver Reed).

Hercules in the Vale of Woe (1962) (see MYTHOLOGY) (also *Maciste Against Hercules in the Vale of Woe*). A pair of contemporary con artists use a time machine to journey back to the days of Hercules, intending to stage a fight between Hercules and another legendary hero, Maciste.

Hu-Man (1976; France) D/S: Jerome Laperrousaz. Cast: Terence Stamp, Jeanne Moreau. An actor can be propelled into the past and the future by the emotional force generated by television audiences watching him act in dangerous situations.

I'll Never Forget You (1951) (also *House on the Square*). D: Roy Baker. Cast: Tyrone Power, Ann Blyth, Michael Rennie, Dennis Price. This remake of *Berkeley Square* (1933) concerns a man who travels back in time to the eighteenth century and falls in love.

Je T'aime, Je T'aime (1968; France) D: Alain Resnais. A time traveler gets lost within a time continuum.

The Jetty (1962; Arcturus Films; France) (also *The Pier*). D/S: Chris Marker. C: Jean Chiabaud. Cast: Hélène Chatelain, Jacques Ledoux, Davos Hanich, André Heinrich, Jacques Branchu. Scientists send a man back in time to a period before World War III erupts, but he only worsens the situation by his own actions, and is hunted down by additional time travelers.

Journey to the Beginning of Time (1955/ 66) (see DINOSAURS—TIME OF THE DINOSAUR). Four boys floating down an underground river are carried backwards in time, passing through the ice age, the dawn of mammals, and finally, the time of the dinosaurs.

Journey to the Center of Time (1967; Republic) D: David L. Hewitt. P: Ray Dorn, David L. Hewitt. S: David Prentiss. C: Robert Laramico. Cast: Scott Brady, Gigi Perreau, Anthony Eisley, Abraham Sofaer, Poupee Gamin, Lyle Waggoner, Austin Green. A group of scientists go backwards and forwards in time via time machine. Their voyages take them into the future (where they encounter aliens and mutants), and to the prehistoric past (where they battle dinosaurs). ¶ "Time, from creation to now, tugs toward all yesterdays almost as strongly as the unborn tomorrows that stretch toward all eternity." • Early on in the film, the bat-rat-spider monster from *The Angry Red Planet* (1960) makes a brief appearance on one of the time capsule's viewing screens.

Jubilee (1978; Whaley-Malin; U.K.) D/S: Derek Jarman. C: Peter Middleton. Cast: Jenny Runacre, Little Nell, Toyah Willcox, Jordan, Hermine Demoriane. Queen Elizabeth I is transported into the future by her astrologer, and is shocked by the urban society she encounters.

Merlin and the Sword (1982) (see SWORD AND SORCERY). A tourist visiting Stonehenge is sent back in time to the age of King Arthur and Camelot.

Millennium (1989; 20th Century–Fox) D: Michael Anderson. P: Douglas Leiterman. S: John Varley. C: Rene Ohashi. Cast: Kris Kristofferson, Cheryl Ladd, Daniel J. Travanti, Robert Joy, Al Waxman, Lloyd Bochner. Time travelers from our polluted future abduct people from the past who are doomed to die. On one such occasion, a female traveler leaves behind a stun gun which can move people from the past to the future. When she goes back to retrieve the object, she inadvertently creates a paradox with the potential to destroy the future. ¶ "This is the hard part about looking for time

travelers. They don't want to be found. You must look for them in places where no one is, or where there are people no one will ever see again." • A paradox occurs when something is altered in the past which can change the future. The lady time traveler is played by model Cheryl Ladd, and she falls in love with a plane crash investigator (Kris Kristofferson) whom she meets twice in his lifetime—first as an adult, and a second time when he is a boy. At the climax, Kristofferson and Ladd head out into the distant future together through a time traveling gateway. Robert Joy plays a futuristic man/robot who declares in the film's final moments, "This is not the end. This is not the beginning of the end, it is the end of the beginning."

My Science Project (1985; Touchstone Films) D/S: Jonathan Betuel. P: Jonathan Taplin. C: David M. Walsh. Cast: John Stockwell, Dennis Hopper, Danielle von Zerneck, Fisher Stevens, Raphael Sbarge, Barry Corbin. A pair of high school boys manage to build a time machine out of junkyard materials. Their treks through time take them all the way back to the prehistoric era, and also to World War II.

Peggy Sue Got Married (1986; Tri-Star Pictures) D: Francis Coppola. P: Paul R. Gurian. S: Jerry Leichtling, Arlene Sarner. C: Jordan Cronenweth. Cast: Kathleen Turner, Nicolas Cage, Barry Miller, Catherine Hicks, Don Murray, Barbara Harris, Will Shriner, Maureen O'Sullivan, Leon Ames, John Carradine. While at her high school reunion, the middle-aged Peggy Sue falls unconscious and travels back in time to her high school days. There she learns to see her (future) husband, family, and friends in a new light. ¶ "Right now, you're just browsing through time. Choose the things you'll be proud of, things that last."

The Philadelphia Experiment (1984; New World Pictures) D: Stewart Raffill. P: Joel B. Michaels, Douglas Curtis. S: William Gray, Michael Janover. C: Dick Bush. Cast: Michael Pare, Nancy Allen, Bobby Di Cicco, Michael Currie, Louise Latham. An experiment to cloak warships from radar creates a time warp which transports sailors from 1943 to the present. • Co-star Nancy Allen's character (who shares the same name with popular 50s genre actress Allison Hayes), is the person responsible for taking care of the bewildered sailors and acclimating them to our culture.

Planet of the Apes (1968) (see PLANET OF THE APES SERIES). Charlton Heston and his crew inadvertently travel through a time warp in space which catapults them to the monkey planet of our Earth's future.

Repeat Performance (1947; Eagle Lion) D: Alfred L. Werker. P: Aubrey Schenck. S: Walter Bullock. C: Lew O'Connell. Cast: Louis Hayward, Joan Leslie, Tom Conway, Richard Basehart, Virginia Field. A woman who commits a crime discovers she can be sent back in time to repeat the year over.

Slaughterhouse 5 (1972; Universal) D: George Roy Hill. P: Paul Monash. S: Stephen Geller. C: Miroslav Ondricek. Cast: Michael Sacks, Ron Leibman, Valerie Perrine, Eugene Roche, Sharon Gans, Roberts Blossom. A man caught in a time continuum re-experiences events in his past and future, including the bombing of Dresden and becoming an alien specimen living under a glass dome on the planet Tralfamador. ¶ "Oh you can't see us Mr. Pilgrim, we live in the fourth dimension." • The aliens decide to furnish him with some company in the form of naked adult film star, Montana Wildhack (played by Valerie Perrine). • The film is based on the best-selling novel by Kurt Vonnegut.

Somewhere in Time (1980; Universal) D: Jeannot Szwarc. P: Stephen Deutsch. S: Richard Matheson. C: Isidore Mankofsky. Cast: Christopher Reeve, Christopher Plummer, Jane Seymour, Teresa Wright, Bill Erwin, George Voskovec. Christopher Reeve is a romantic playwright who travels back in time to Michigan's Mackinac Island to meet and fall in love with Jane Seymour, an actress from days gone by. • Richard Matheson adapted the screenplay from his own novel, *Bid Time Return*.

Star Trek 4: The Voyage Home (1986) (see ALIENS — ENCOUNTERS IN OUTER SPACE). Kirk and his crew travel back in time to twentieth century San Francisco to bring back two humpback whales and avert global disaster instigated by a dangerous, omnipotent space probe.

Tales That Witness Madness (1973) (see ANTHOLOGIES). The second story of this British anthology film, titled "Penny Farthing," features an old-style bicycle which propels a man into the past.

The Terminator (1984) (see ROBOTS). A man from our machine-dominated future follows a robot "terminator" back to our present, intent on stopping the killer machine from murdering the mother of a yet-to-be-born resistance leader.

Terror from the Year 5000 (1958; AIP) (also *Cage of Doom*). D/P/S: Robert J. Gurney, Jr. C: Arthur Florman. Cast: Ward Costello, Joyce Holden, John Stratton, Frederic Downs, Salome Jens, Fred Herrick. Scientists on an island in Florida create a time machine that can retrieve objects from the future. On one occasion, a mutant female (in spangled tights) with homicidal tendencies is brought back. She then assumes the identity of a nurse, and plots to take back one of the men with her to introduce new, mutation-free stock into the gene pool. ¶ "The future is what we make of it. Whether there will be creatures like her depends on us — on all of us, on mankind — on what we do today, in the present." • The mutant woman, who peels off the face of the nurse she murdered, possesses hypnotic fingernails and a burning radioactive touch. Her hideously disfigured face is the result of the ever increasing amounts of radiation in the future. "By the year 5000," she says, "every fifth child born was a mutant. Unable to cure these freaks, our rulers put them in special isolated colonies. It was one of these colonies that your apparatus probed." • Two other objects retrieved from the future include an odd looking statue, and a four-eyed mutant cat.

The Thirty Foot Bride of Candy Rock (1959) (see HUMAN GIANTS). Lou Costello uses his computerized talking time machine (dubbed "Max") to transform the Army, which is in pursuit of his Thirty Foot Bride, into increasingly primitive forces from the past. Their final state is that of cavemen throwing rocks.

The Three Stooges Meet Hercules (1962) (see MYTHOLOGY). A scientist, his girlfriend, and the Three Stooges are transported back into mythological times via time machine. During their stay they meet Ulysses, Hercules, a Siamese cyclops, and an evil ruler named "Odius."

Time After Time (1979; Orion) D/S: Nicholas Meyer. P: Herb Jaffe. C: Paul Lohmann. Cast: Malcolm McDowell, David Warner, Mary Steenburgen, Charles Cioffi, Kent Williams, Andonia Katsaros. Jack the Ripper eludes police by escaping in a time machine built by nineteenth century author/inventor H. G. Wells. Wells pursues the murdering fiend into the future of twentieth century San Francisco. ¶ "Every age is the same. It's only love that makes any of them bearable."

Time Bandits (1981; HandMade Films; U.K.) D/P: Terry Gilliam. S: Terry Gilliam, Michael Palin. C: Peter Biziou. Cast: David Rappaport, Kenny Baker, John Cleese, Sean Connery, Ian Holm, Ralph Richardson, David Warner, Shelley Duvall, Katherine Helmond, Michael Palin. A motley group of dwarves accompanies an English schoolboy as he journeys through a time portal, meeting various legendary and historical figures. • Some of the characters encountered include Robin Hood (John Cleese), Agamemnon (Sean Connery), Napoleon (Ian Holm), a supreme evil being (David Warner), and a deity (Ralph Richardson). • The Monty Python comedy group is well represented here by Terry Gilliam, John Cleese, and Michael Palin. All three starred in the troupe's comedy hits *Monty Python and the Holy Grail* (1975) and *Monty Python's Life of Brian* (1979).

Time Flies (1944; Gainsborough; U.K.) D: Walter Forde. P: Edward Black. S: J. O. C. Orton, Ted Kavanaugh, Howard Irving Young. C: Basil Emmott. Cast: Tommy Handley, Felix Aylmer, Evelyn Dall, George Moon, Graham Moffatt, Moore Marriott. A professor takes his assistant and two businessmen back to the Elizabethan period of Queen Bess in his time machine.

The Time Machine (1960; MGM) D/P: George Pal. S: David Duncan. C: Paul C. Vogel. Cast: Rod Taylor, Yvette Mimieux, Alan Young, Sebastian Cabot, Tom Helmore, Whit Bissell, Doris Lloyd, Paul Frees. Rod Taylor plays George, a young inventor who develops a time machine. Leaving London in the year 1899, he goes ever further ahead in time (through several World Wars—including number three) until finally stopping in the far-distant future of 802,701. Earth now houses two societies— the passive, apathetic Elois who live in a garden paradise above ground, and the hideous mutated cannibalistic Morlocks, who live below ground and harvest the Elois like cattle. ¶ "So this was the destiny of the Eloi, they were being bred by the Morlocks, who had degenerated into the lowest form of human life—cannibalism." • At the climax, George returns from the future for a brief moment to take three books back with him to rebuild the future. The film ends with his friend asking the thought-provoking question: "Which three books would you take?" • *The Time Machine* project was kept as secret as possible by George Pal and screenwriter David Duncan, who didn't want quick-buck imitators to beat them to the punch in their story of time travel. • Distinguished British actor Paul Schofield, who won an Oscar for his role in *A Man for All Seasons* (1966), was Pal's first choice to play George (a role that eventually went to Rod Taylor). • This was 21-year-old Yvette Mimieux's second movie; she made her screen debut earlier that same year in *Platinum*

High School. Here she plays the innocent "Weena," with whom Rod Taylor falls in love. • When asked by Tom Weaver, the author of *Interviews with B Science Fiction and Horror Movie Makers,* about his favorite film, screenwriter David Duncan replied, "*The Time Machine,* by a huge margin. The Wells novel is a classic of science fiction. I first read it when I was about 15 years old and it has always been one of my favorite stories. So it was a challenge to turn it into a film without degrading the quality. I hope I did so."

Time Trackers (1989; Concorde) D/S: Howard R. Cohen. P: Roger Corman. C: Ronn Schmidt. Cast: Wil Shriner, Ned Beatty, Kathleen Beller, Lee Bergere, Alex Hyde-White, Parley Baer, Robert Cornthwaite, Bridget Hoffman. A group of scientists working on a time machine in 2025 must chase one of their evil members back in time first to 1991, then to 1146, to try and prevent him from altering history and wiping them all out of existence. ¶ "I understand it now. The past never changes. No matter how many times we replayed it, Zandor would *always* go back." • Actor Robert Cornthwaite, who plays the time travel project's head scientist and father of the heroine, is best remembered for his role of Professor Carrington, the scientist who unsuccessfully tried to reason with *The Thing* (1951).

The Time Travelers (1964; AIP) D/S: Ib Melchior. P: William Redlin. C: William Zsigmond. Cast: Preston Foster, Merry Anders, John Hoyt, Dennis Patrick, Carol White, Philip Carey. Survivors of a nuclear-devastated Earth (whose surface is populated by wandering mutants and robots) encounter a group of scientists who created a time portal in 1964, and are now stuck in the future. They are able to return to the present at the end of the film, but are unable to alter future events. • Director/writer Ib Melchior was born and educated in Denmark. He worked in the theater as an actor, stage manager, and even as a set designer at the Radio City Music Hall. After his service in World War II, he directed a number of television shows in New York before hooking up with producer Sidney Pink to film *The Angry Red Planet* in 1960.

Time Warp (1981) D: Allan Sandler, Robert Emenegger. Cast: Adam West, Gretchen Corbett, Chip Johnson, Kirk Alyn. A time paradox wreaks havoc on an astronaut traveling to Jupiter.

Timerider: The Adventures of Lyle Swan (1983; Zoomo) D: William Dear. P: Harry Gites. S: Michael Nesmith, William Dear.

A gang of cannibalistic "Morlocks" in our distant future are looking for trouble in George Pal's The Time Machine *(1960).*

C: Larry Pizer. Cast: Fred Ward, Belinda Bauer, Peter Coyote, Richard Masur, Ed Lauter, L. Q. Jones. A motorcyclist riding in the Baja 500 enters a time portal in the desert.

Trancers (1984) (also *Future Cop*). D/P: Charles Band. S: Danny Bilson, Paul De Meo. C: David Boyd. Cast: Tim Thomerson, Helen Hunt, Michael Stefani, Art LaFleur, Telma Hopkins. Tim Thomerson stars as a cop from the future who travels to 1985 Los Angeles to stop a time-traveling mystic and his band of zombie-like killers called "Trancers." • The future cop's name is Jack Deth, and he is a resident of Angel City (what's left of L.A. in the year 2247). His mission is to stop the mystic from killing the ancestors of council members from the future. • Before going into acting, Tim Thomerson was a popular night club comedian with his own unique brand of macho-satire.

The Two Worlds of Jennie Logan (1979; TV movie) D/S: Frank de Felitta. P: Paul Radin. C: Al Francis. Cast: Lindsay Wagner, Marc Singer, Henry Wilcoxon, Alan Feinstein, Linda Gray, Joan Darling. Lindsay Wagner plays a woman living in her Victorian home who attempts to change her fate after being caught in a time continuum.

Unidentified Flying Oddball (1979; Walt Disney) D: Russ Mayberry. S: Don Tait. Cast: Dennis Dugan, Jim Dale, Ron Moody, Kenneth More, John Le Mesurier. King Arthur's court gets an amusing visit from a time-traveling space engineer and his robot.

A Witch Without a Broom (1966) (see WITCHES, WARLOCKS, AND CULTS). A professor falls in love with a blonde witch who accidentally transports him back in time first to the stone age and then to the sixteenth century.

World Without End (1956; Allied Artists) D/S: Edward Bernds. P: Richard Heermance. C: Ellsworth Frederick. Cast: Hugh Marlowe, Nancy Gates, Nelson Leigh, Rod Taylor, Shawn Smith, Lisa Montell, Christopher Dark, Booth Colman, Everett Glass. Astronauts break through the time barrier and land on the nuclear-devasted Earth of the future. The planet is inhabited by surface mutants, gigantic spiders, and an ever-

Astronauts inadvertently travel through time and return to the Earth of our future, facing primitive mutant surface beasts, among other things, in World Without End *(1956).*

weakening underground human society. ¶ "While we were blacked-out for what seemed like minutes to us, the slow centuries were passing on Earth." • This is the first American picture to incorporate Einstein's postulate that if you can attain enough speed, time will eventually stand still. It is also one of the first pictures to depict astronauts landing on Earth of the future. • The closing sequence was shot at the historic Iverson ranch. Director Edward Bernds intended to include scenes at the film's end which would show the reconstruction of the world, but it was not in the film's budget. • The giant spider used in this film was also utilized in another Edward Bernds feature— *Queen of Outer Space* (1958), as well as being seen in *Valley of the Dragons* (1961). • Now-famous filmmaker Sam Peckinpah served as dialogue director on this movie. • Ed Bernds's first choice for the lead of John Borden was Sterling Hayden, not Hugh Marlowe. Frank Lovejoy was also considered for the part as well. • Rod Taylor, who plays good-humored astronaut Herbert Ellis, was cast in another (more famous)

time travel adventure, George Pal's *The Time Machine* (1960). • The picture was filmed in cinemascope and technicolor.

The Yesterday Machine (1965) D/P/S: Russ Marker. C: Ralph K. Johnson. Cast: Tim Holt, James Britton, Ann Pelegrino, Jack Herman. Two college kids on their way to a football game encounter a pair of Confederate soldiers in the woods. The boy is shot but escapes and the girl disappears. A hard-bitten reporter (James Britton) pairs up with the missing girl's sister to crack the case. They discover a time machine, run by a crazed Nazi scientist whose ultimate goal is to use the device to raise up Hitler and see the Third Reich rule the world. ¶ "Yesterday should be left alone because today we have enough problems trying to make sure there will be a tomorrow." • Tim Holt (from *The Monster That Challenged the World,* 1958) is top billed but puts in only a brief appearance. Actor Bill Thurman, who has a small part as a police detective, became a regular in Larry Buchanan movies (*In the Year 2889,* 1966; *It's Alive,* 1968, etc.).

Yor, the Hunter from the Future (1983;

Italy/U.S.) D: Anthony M. Dawson. P: Michele Marsala. S: Anthony M. Dawson, Robert Bailey. C: Marcello Masciocchi. Cast: Reb Brown, Corinne Cléry, John Steiner. The muscular warrior named Yor (Reb Brown) is propelled through time by his magic medallion. The first half of the film takes place in an ancient time of sword and sorcery, while the latter is set in the nuclear-devastated Earth of the future, ruled by an alien overlord and his army of robots. • Though a predominantly Italian production, *Yor* included some location shooting in Turkey.

Trees *see* Plants

Two-Headed Creatures

This section includes films that feature animals, humans, and monsters with two heads. Many mythological creatures have two or more heads, but until Ray Harryhausen brought his tremendous stop-motion animation skills to bear on the subject, there had been no two-headed attempts on the silver screen. Harryhausen's first dual-domed monster was a gigantic bird, a "Roc," found on the island of Colossus during *The Seventh Voyage of Sinbad* (1958). The penchant of moviegoers for weird creatures enticed Harryhausen and other special effects–oriented filmmakers to further explore mythical legends and monsters (including those of the two-headed variety).

As far as two-headed humans are concerned, the 1962 Japanese production of *The Manster* was the pioneer (and the best of the bunch). In the early 1970s, a pair of exploitation films were made involving the transplanting of a second head onto the body of another person. Both films, *The Incredible Two-Headed Transplant* (1971) and *The Thing with Two Heads* (1972), were low-budget drive-in oriented features which played up the comical angle of what a shock it would be to wake up in the morning to discover you have got a second head on your shoulders. Both films featured a crude irony in their situation (*The Incredible Two-Headed Transplant* has the head of a highly intelligent killer grafted onto the body of a gentle halfwit; *The Thing with Two Heads* has the had of a white bigot transplanted onto the body of a black man).

The two-headed topic is generally not a seller by itself (as evidenced by the poor showing of both of these later films) which accounts for the fact that so few films on the subject have been made. Apparently two heads are *not* better than one.

Clash of the Titans (1981) (see MYTHOLOGY). This mythical fantasy adventure features a variety of creatures, including a two-headed wolf-dog.

The Incredible Two-Headed Transplant (1971; AIP) D: Anthony M. Lanza. P: John Lawrence. S: James Gordon White, John Lawrence. C: Jack Steely, Glen Cano, Paul Hipp. Cast: Bruce Dern, Pat Priest, Casey Kasem, Albert Cole, John Bloom, Berry Kroeger. The head of a maniacal killer is grafted onto the body of a retarded man. ¶ "You know, sometimes too much imagina-tion can destroy a man." • The film's immortal song, "Incredible," was sung by Bobbie Boyle and included the telling passage, "It's incredible how many things we seem to hide, all the real things we can't admit because of pride." • Pop music broadcaster and countdown king Casey Kasem co-stars in the film. • The caretaker character known as Andrew was played by popular horror movie host Larry Vincent, better known to his fans as "Seymour."

Jack the Giant Killer (1962) (see SWORD AND SORCERY). Jack encounters and slays a giant two-headed ogre (Galligantua) with horns and long vampire-like fangs.

The Magic Sword (1962) (see SWORD AND SORCERY). Gary Lockwood stars as young George, who must face the seven curses of an evil sorcerer (Basil Rathbone), including a two-headed dragon.

The Manster (1962; Lopert Pictures Corp.; U.S./Japan) D: Kenneth G. Crane, George Breakston. P: George Breakston. S: Walt Sheldon. C: David Mason. Cast: Peter Dyneley, Jame Hylton, Satoshi Nakamura, Terri Zimmern, Van Hawley, Jerry Ito. An American correspondent visits a mad Japanese scientist experimenting on the secrets of evolution. While there, he is drugged and injected with a serum which causes him to grow a second hairy head, and gives him homicidal tendencies. At the climax, the reporter literally splits in two, separating from his evil second self. ¶ "He might separate completely, split into two human beings. But Tara, what will they be?" • The script was adapted from an original story called "Nightmare," by George Breakston, who served as the film's producer and co-director. Breakston was also an actor when he was young, starring as Pip in *Great Expectations* (1934). • Satoshi Nakamura, who played mad doctor Suzuki, was Frank Sinatra's dialogue coach on the World War II picture, *None But the Brave* (1965). • *The Manster* was shot in Japan.

The Seventh Voyage of Sinbad (1958) (see SINBAD). Sinbad and his crew feel the wrath of a giant two-headed bird, called a Roc, after they kill its oversized baby chick. The shell from this creature's egg is an ingredient needed to make the potion which will restore Sinbad's shrunken fiancée back to her normal size.

The Thing with Two Heads (1972; AIP) D: Lee Frost. P: Wes Bishop. S: Lee Frost, Wes Bishop, James Gordon White. C: Jack Steely. Cast: Ray Milland, Rosey Grier, Don Marshall, Roger Perry, Kathy Bauman. A terminally ill, racist doctor (Ray Milland) plans to have his head transplanted onto the healthy body of a convict. But he experiences the ultimate irony when he awakens to find he is stuck on the body of a black man—whose head is still there. • Former pro football star Rosey Grier, famous as an L.A. Rams defensive lineman with a penchant for needlepoint, stars as the black convict. • Director Lee Frost and producer Wes Bishop both have brief roles in the movie. • James Gordon White and Jack Steely also worked on another two-headed project a year earlier—*The Incredible Two-Headed Transplant*.

The Three Stooges Meet Hercules (1962) (see MYTHOLOGY). The stooges are asked to rid the countryside of various monsters, including a terrible two-headed cyclops, which the boys drug.

Willow (1988) (see SWORD AND SORCERY). In this fantasy feature, a valiant hero decapitates one-half of a two-headed monster.

Underground Worlds

Very few places on the surface of the Earth are as yet unexplored. Technological advancements have even engineered the means to travel both to outer space and deep under the sea. The world which lies beneath our feet, however, is still something of a mystery.

Geological studies and seismic waves have given science sound evidence as to the nature of the Earth's interior. Within the Earth are layers identified as the crust, the mantle, the outer core, and the inner core. Because of its great depth, however, theories concerning the makeup of the inner core remain speculative. This uncertainty has given rise to the imaginative ponderings on the possible existence of an inner world deep beneath the Earth's surface which might be inhabitable, or even . . . inhabited.

The ancient tales of Gilgamesh, which surfaced circa 640 B.C., told of an underground civilization (aspects of which were adapted into the 1956 film, *The Mole People*). Along with the Biblical notion of a netherworld known as Hades, or Hell, these tales have served to spark many legends and myths concerning the makeup and exploration of the Earth's underground.

The cinema has exploited this mystery with a variety of fantastical visions of underground worlds. Many consider the definitive film on the subject to be the 1959 Jules Verne epic, *Journey to the Center of the Earth*. This feature (with the unlikely team of James Mason and Pat Boone) effectively captured the awe and inspiration of human endeavor to investigate the world beneath us. The film blended scientific fact and fantasy together with the depiction of an underground sea, remnants of the lost city of Atlantis, and the presence of prehistoric dinosaurs.

While many underground world films feature hidden treasures and fantastic monsters, there are some which stay within more serious (and mundane) boundaries, merely focusing on the exploration itself (*Unknown World*, 1951; and *Crack in the World*, 1965). Those underground features which do not contain fantastical elements, however, are usually buried at the box office. Prospects for future films dealing with underground worlds or monsters rising from the interior will surely "see the light" for years to come.

Adventure to the Center of the Earth (1965; Mexico) A young man gets lost while on an underground cave tour, then goes insane after seeing a weird creature. An expedition sets out to check his story, and they too encounter weird monsters far beneath the Earth's surface.

Alien from L.A. (1988) (see ATLANTIS). A California "valley girl," searching for her missing father, discovers the secret underground world of the lost city of Atlantis, which is planning a war against the surface. ¶ "I went to Africa and fell down this bottomless pit to the center of the Earth and ended up in this city called Atlantis." • In an obvious nod to Jules Verne's *Journey to the Center of the Earth*, the heroine's name is Wanda *Saknussemm*.

Allan Quatermain and the Lost City of Gold (1987; Cannon) D: Gary Nelson, Newt Arnold. P: Menahem Golan, Yoram Globus. S: Gene Quintano, Lee Reynolds. C: Alex Phillips, Frederick Elmes. Cast: Richard Chamberlain, Sharon Stone, James Earl Jones, Henry Silva, Robert Donner. Quatermain and his African party journey to the center of the Earth in search of the Golden City and encounter blood-thirsty warriors and deadly earthworms. • The film was actually made in 1985 along with the first contemporary Quatermain movie, *King Solomon's Mines*. The producers then shelved the picture for two years, hoping to give the first film's box office failure a chance to fade in the minds of moviegoers. Despite this delay, the second film did not fare much better.

At the Earth's Core (1976; Amicus; U.K.) D: Kevin Connor. P: John Dark. S: Milton Subotsky. C: Alan Hume. Cast: Doug McClure, Peter Cushing, Caroline Munro, Cy Grant, Keith Barron. This juvenile Edgar Rice Burroughs adaptation follows a pair of scientists who travel to the underground world of Pellucidar. ¶ "Yes, it is a somewhat aggressive-looking creature." • Some of the dangers encountered include a race of pterodactyl-people called "Mahars," and a hippo-like dinosaur called a "rhinosaur." • *At the Earth's Core* is a part of the Burroughs's film trilogy which includes *The Land That Time Forgot* (1974) and *The People That Time Forgot* (1977)—all starring Doug McClure.

Battle Beneath the Earth (1968; MGM; U.K.) D: Montgomery Tully. P: Charles Reynolds. S: L. Z. Hargreaves. C: Kenneth Talbot. Cast: Kerwin Mathews, Viviane Ventura, Robert Ayres, Martin Benson, Peter Arne. The Chinese use lasers to tunnel their way to America.

Crack in the World (1965; Paramount) D: Andrew Morton. P: Bernard Glasser, Lester A. Sansom. S: Jon Manchip White, Julian Halevy. C: Manuel Berenguer. Cast: Dana Andrews, Janette Scott, Kieron Moore, Alexander Knox, Peter Damon. Underground testing creates tidal waves and an earthquake which starts an ever-growing crack in the Earth's crust.

Goonies (1985; Warner Bros.) D: Richard Donner. P: Richard Donner, Harvey Bernhard. S: Chris Columbus. Cast: Sean Astin, Josh Brolin, Jeff Cohen, Corey Feldman. A group of young misfits find a seventeenth century pirate map which leads them to an incredible subterranean world full of caverns, skeletons, and a pirate ship. They also encounter a huge pig-eared monster played by former defensive lineman John Matuszak.

The Incredible Petrified World (1960; Governor Films) D/P: Jerry Warren. S: John W. Sterner. C: Victor Fisher, Mel Fisher. Cast: Robert Clarke, Phyllis Coates,

Several of The Mole People *(1956) claw and dig through the earth in the ancient underground world of Sumeria. The set on which the stunt actors worked was built around a waterless pool with a rubber sheet stretched across it. Piled on top were mounds of burnt cork to represent the dirt. The holes through which the monsters popped in and out were slits cut into the rubber layering.*

Allen Windsor, John Carradine, Sheila Noonan. A diving bell crashes into the ocean bottom and the crew emerges to explore the underground caverns, which are filled with air pockets containing "forgotten men, monsters, earthquakes, and boiling volcanoes" (according to the ads). ¶ "Room to breathe—you know, I never thought about it much, but there's nothing greater." • This no-budget picture was shot in Colossal Cave in New Mexico with a minimal crew (a cameraman, a sound man, and director Jerry Warren). It was released on a double bill with *Teenage Zombies,* another Jerry Warren film. • Robert Clarke detailed his experiences making the film in Tom Weaver's book, *Interviews with B Horror and Science Fiction Movie Makers.* "We drove over there in cars and stayed in some sleazy little motel, and it was hard—very hard work. Jerry would feed us hamburgers for dinner and hamburgers for lunch—and maybe for breakfast, too! And I remember when we

got over there I was astonished that the crew consisted of a cameraman, who did his own lighting, and a sound man. When one of us wasn't in the scene, we would hold the boom!"

Journey Beneath the Desert (1961) (see ATLANTIS). Three lost pilots discover a tunnel at a desert atomic test site, which takes them to the lost city of Atlantis.

Journey to the Center of the Earth (1959; 20th Century–Fox) D: Henry Levin. P: Charles Brackett. S: Charles Brackett, Walter Reisch. C: Leo Tover. Cast: James Mason, Pat Boone, Arlene Dahl, Peter Ronson, Thayer David, Diane Baker. James Mason leads an expedition to Iceland where they descend into a crater (called Snuffels Youcol) which leads them to the fabled center of the Earth. There they find the ruins of the lost city of Atlantis and several giant lizards passed off as dinosaurs. ¶ "Don't you see what's at stake here—the ultimate aim of all science, to penetrate the unknown. Do you realize we know less about the Earth we live on than about the stars or the galaxies of outer space? The greatest mystery is right here! Right under our own feet!" • Noted Christian singer, Pat Boone, sang a number of songs in the film. The musical score was provided by Bernard Herrmann, who also worked on *The Day the Earth Stood Still* (1951) and *The Birds* (1963).

Journey to the Center of the Earth (1989) (see ATLANTIS). A nanny and two teen brothers are caught in a cave-in while exploring a cavern underneath a Hawaiian volcano. They end up in Atlantis and encounter some bizarre inhabitants.

The Mole People (1956; Universal) D: Virgil Vogel. P: William Alland. S: Laszlo Gorog. C: Ellis Carter. Cast: John Agar, Hugh Beaumont, Cynthia Patrick, Alan Napier, Nestor Paiva. Archeologists discover an underground world inhabited by the lost people of Sumeria and their monstrous slave mutants, the mole people. ¶ "Archeologists are underpaid publicity agents for deceased royalty." • Climbing footage of Sir Edmund Hillary's tour of Everest was used in the picture. • Jack Kevan created the mole monsters, filling the humps on their backs with newspapers. During the energetic mole people battle scene, the papers began to fly out of their shirts, necessitating the entire sequence being re-shot. • Director Virgil Vogel was less than pleased with female lead Cynthia Patrick and resorted to some drastic measures to induce her "cooperation." "Cynthia Patrick, being quite inexperienced at the time, was a bit of a trial," the director told *Fangoria* #73. "You remember that in the picture, the mole monsters pull their victims down into the ground? We had very stiff rubber across the top of a swimming pool.... We slit the rubber and covered it up with ground cork.... As we were ready to shoot that, she came up to me and said, 'I'm not going down through that hole.' I said (sweetly), 'Well, of course not, darling, a stuntwoman will do that. All I need you to do is run across there.' She said she would do that. Then I went to Al, the stuntman playing the monster, and I said, 'Al, when she hits that goddamned hole, you grab her legs and pull!' So he did it. (laughs) She screamed and yelled as she went down, but it was probably the best acting she did in the picture."

The Slime People (1963; Hansen Enterprises) D: Robert Hutton. P: Joseph F. Robertson. S: Vance Skarstedt. C: William Troiano. Cast: Robert Hutton, Les Tre-

mayne, Robert Burton, Judee Morton, Susan Hart, John Close. Large prehistoric man-monsters covered with scales and slime rise from their underground world to kill and conquer, lowering the temperature above ground with a ring of solidified fog. ¶ "The report of large monstrous creatures roaming about the fog of our city and committing mass murder has been confirmed." • The spear-wielding slime people are presumed to have left their subterranean homes because of underground nuclear testing. • Director/star Robert Hutton filmed *The Slime People* for an incredibly low $56,000. "We could only afford to have two outfits made for the Slime People, and they were supposed to take over the world in the movie!" recalled Hutton in a *Fangoria* #87 interview. The Slime People suits cost $3,000 to $4,000 each. • The butcher's shop in which the protagonists hole up against the Slime People belonged to Hutton's father-in-law.

Transatlantic Tunnel (1935; Gaumont; U.K.) (also *The Tunnel*). D: Maurice Elvey. P: Micheal Balcon. S: L. Du Garde Peach, Clemence Dane. C: G. Krampf. Cast: Richard Dix, Leslie Banks, Madge Evans, Walter Huston, George Arliss, Helen Vinson. A tremendous tunnel is built with the use of a radium drill, which links the United States and the United Kingdom.

Tremors (1989; Universal) D: Ron Underwood. P/S: Brent Maddock, S. S. Wilson. C: Alexander Gruszynski. Cast: Kevin Bacon, Fred Ward, Finn Carter, Michael Gross, Reba McEntire, Victor Wong, Bobby Jacoby, Ariana Richards. Gigantic burrowing worm-like creatures come up from underground and terrorize the locals in the small desert community named "Perfection." ¶ "They're under the ground, *under — the — ground!* They can dig like a sonofabitch! Big monsters, underground!" • Michael Gross (from TV's "Family Ties") plays the part of an enthusiastic survivalist. Country western star Reba McEntire plays his equally gung-ho wife. McEntire also sings the song played over the closing credits.

Unknown World (1951; Lippert) D: Terrel O. Morse. P: Jack Rabin, Irving Block. S: Millard Kaufman. C: Allen G. Siegler, Henry Freulich. Cast: Victor Kilian, Bruce Kellogg, Otto Waldis, Jim Bannon, Tom Handley, Dick Cogan. A "cyclotram" burrows deep into the Earth to discover an underground fallout shelter, but instead it creates a volcanic eruption. ¶ "And so my colleagues and I believe that humanity can escape annihilation, can find a temporary haven, a promise of hope that come what may, life can be sustained deep within the Earth itself. Far below the surface we shall seek a natural, a geological, shelter." • The producers, Rabin and Block, were more popularly known in the industry as a special effects team. They provided the trick work for this film as well. • The picture was filmed in the vast pits of Carlsbad Caverns in New Mexico, at depths of 700 feet below the surface.

What Waits Below (1983) D: Don Sharp. P: Sandy Howard. Cast: Robert Powell, Timothy Bottoms, Anne Heywood, Richard Johnson, Lisa Blount. A soldier heads down into a military-created underground cavern and encounters a group of rock monsters and an albino race known as the Lemurians.

Where Time Began (1977; Almena; Spain) (also *Journey to the Center of the Earth*). D/P: Juan Piquer. S: John Melson, Carlos Piquer, Juan Piquer. Cast: Kenneth More, Ivonne Sentis, Frank Brana, Pep Munne, Jack Taylor. Kenneth More plays Oliver Lindenbrook, the leader of an underground exploration team that encounters live volcanoes, earthquakes, sea serpents, and dinosaurs in this low-budget remake of *Journey to the Center of the Earth* (1959).

Underwater Monsters *see* Sea Monsters

Utopias *see* Futures on Earth

Vampires

Of all the classic monsters in the movies, the vampire is without a doubt the most popular and prolific (with nearly 200 vampire films produced to date). The appeal of the vampire can be traced to two things — sex and death. The classic bloodsucker is often an attractive figure, possessing charm and charisma irresistible to members of the opposite sex. They also live forever (barring the wooden stake or a walk in the sun). Thus, the vampire is the supernatural embodiment of eroticism and immortality, two of humanity's greatest concerns.

Of course, the King of the Undead, the ultimate vampire, is Dracula. Though not the first literary appearance of a vampire (*Varney the Vampire,* by Thomas Preskett Prest and *Carmilla,* by Sheridan Le Fanu preceded it by 50 and 25 years, respectively), Bram Stoker's *Dracula* (first published in 1897) is the father of all screen bloodsuckers. Vampires and Dracula arrived on the silver screen together, since the first vampire film was an unauthorized adaptation of Stoker's novel. *Nosferatu* (1922) is a classic of the vampire cinema (and a favorite of a latter-day Dracula, Christopher Lee). Since then, Dracula has appeared onscreen in over 50 films, but none having more impact than the 1931 Universal adaptation which skyrocketed an unknown Hungarian stage actor named Bela Lugosi to stardom (and typecasting purgatory). Every horror film made since then owes an enormous debt to *Dracula* (1931), for it was this immensely popular film which gave birth to the horror genre in America (assisted by Universal's follow-up feature made later the same year — *Frankenstein*).

In 1958, the British Hammer Film Company injected new blood into the tired veins of the gothic vampire cinema with their remake of *Dracula* (titled *Horror of Dracula* in the United States). Christopher Lee played the role of the Count in a manner unlike Lugosi or anyone before him. His ferocious, noble, unpredictable, and sexually appealing vampire set a new standard for the undead (and created a new horror star — some even hail Lee as the definitive Dracula, rather than Lugosi). Hammer produced a string of Dracula pictures as well as branching off into other vampire films (including the loosely related Karnstein trilogy). These Hammer productions all shared common characteristics — deep rich color, wonderful period sets, a good sense of pacing, and effective professional acting. Hammer made 15 vampire films in all — more than any one film company in the history of cinema (including Universal).

Largely thanks to Hammer, vampire films have continued to flourish throughout each successive decade. More recently, filmmakers have taken vampires in a variety of new and exciting directions — a few of the more notable being the sophisticated urban vampires of *The Hunger* (1983); the new age outlaws roaming the southern states in Winnebagoes in *Near Dark* (1987); and the modern update of the suave vampire image in the witty homage, *Fright Night* (1985).

Dracula and Family

Abbott and Costello Meet Frankenstein (1948; Universal) D: Charles T. Barton. P: Robert Arthur. S: Robert Lees, Frederic I. Rinaldo, John Grant. C: Charles Van Enger. Cast: Bud Abbott, Lou Costello, Lon Chaney, Bela Lugosi, Glenn Strange, Lenore Aubert. Count Dracula (played by Bela Lugosi) enlists the aid of a female mad scientist in a plan to transplant Costello's brain into the body of the Frankenstein monster. ¶ "What we need today is young blood and brains" — Dracula. • At the climax, Dracula is dispatched when he is grabbed in bat form by the Wolf Man who then plunges over a cliff with the vampire/bat clutched in his talons. • For this one, Dracula uses the alias "Dr. Lahos." • This was only the second (and last) time Lugosi played Dracula on the silver screen. He appeared in several other films as a vampire, but never as the undead Count himself. • Lugosi was 65 years old, and makeup man Bud Westmore applied a heavy coating of makeup to disguise the actor's age. • This is the only film in which Bela Lugosi changes from a man to a bat *on screen*.

Andy Warhol's Dracula (1974; Bryanston; Italy/France) (also *Andy Warhol's Young Dracula; Blood for Dracula*). D/S: Paul Morrissey. P: Andrew Braunsberg. C: Luigi Kuveiller. Cast: Joe Dallesandro, Udo Kier, Vittorio De Sica, Maxime McKendry, Arno Juerging, Milena Vukotic, Dominique Darel, Stefania Casini, Silvia Dionisio. In this gory/sexy/satirical version of Dracula, the vampiric Count is experiencing a shortage of virgin blood in his homeland (only virgin blood will do — he retches uncontrollably every time he drinks the blood of a girl who was not a "wirgin"). Led by his psy-

chotic henchman, Dracula packs up his coffin and goes to Italy, where he stays with an impoverished nobleman, his four daughters, and their communist handyman, who saves the day by deflowering the daughters. ¶ "You must have the blood of a virgin, or in a few weeks you will be dead." • Prolific Italian director Antonio Margheriti (who often goes by the pseudonym Anthony Dawson) is credited as director in Italian sources; Paul Morrisey is given credit on all other prints. • The three male leads, Udo Kier, Joe Dallesandro, and Arno Juerging all returned for *Andy Warhol's Frankenstein* the same year. • Famed director Roman Polanski appears in a wonderful cameo as a surly villager winning a game of "You can't do what I do." • *Andy Warhol's Dracula* was slapped with an "X" rating in the United States, though undoubtedly it would be awarded an "R" by today's standards.

Assignment Terror (1970) (see ALIENS — INVADERS ON EARTH: THE 60s AND 70s). An alien comes to Earth and revives the Wolf Man, the Frankenstein Monster, the Mummy, and yes, Dracula, in a plot to conquer the world by using Man's fear of these supernatural monsters.

Billy the Kid vs. Dracula (1966; Embassy Pictures) D: William Beaudine. P: Carroll Case. S: Carl K. Hittleman. C: Lothrop Worth. Cast: John Carradine, Chuck Courtney, Melinda Plowman, Virginia Christine. Dracula invades the Old West when he poses as the uncle of a pretty ranch owner, whose foreman (and sweetheart) just happens to be a reformed Billy the Kid. ¶ "Eighteen and beautiful — yes, I *would* like to see her" — Dracula. • *Billy the Kid vs. Dracula* was released on a double bill with *Jesse James*

Meets Frankenstein's Daughter to create the oddest western double feature (or monster double feature for that matter) ever produced. Both films were directed by William "One Shot" Beaudine. • These two features were director Beaudine's last. He directed over 150 movies in his 44-year career behind the camera. • John Carradine plays Dracula for the first time in over 20 years (1945's *House of Dracula* being his last go-round as the Count). Carradine was 60 years old. • Carradine often cites this as his worst film. Taking into account some of his later appearances, it has plenty of worthy competition. "It was a bad film," Carradine said. "I don't even remember it. I was absolutely numb!"

Blacula (1972) (see OTHER VAMPIRES, this section). An African prince visits Europe with the aim of enlisting Count Dracula's aid in halting the slave trade (not knowing that the politically powerful Count is one of the undead). Dracula laughs at the prince and turns him into a vampire for his troubles. • Dracula was played by Charles Macaulay, who bites the proud Prince named "Mamuwalde" and christens him with the name "Blacula."

Blood (1973) (see PLANTS). Dracula's daughter and the son of the Wolf Man marry and grow killer plants in this low, low-budget one-man production from director/screenwriter/cinematographer Andy Milligan.

Blood of Dracula (1957) (see OTHER VAMPIRES, this section). No Dracula appears in *Blood of Dracula*, just a sinister chemistry teacher who hypnotizes a young girl with an occult amulet and transforms her into a vampiric fiend.

Blood of Dracula's Castle (1967; Paragon Pictures) (also *Dracula's Castle*). D: Jean Hewitt, Al Adamson. P: Al Adamson, Rex Carlton. S: Rex Carlton. C: Laszlo Kovacs. Cast: John Carradine, Paula Raymond, Alex D'Arcy, Robert Dix, Ray Young, Vicki Volante, Kent Osborne, John Cardos, Lon Chaney, Jr. Count Dracula and his wife, using the alias "Townsend," have moved to America where they keep women chained up in their basement to supply them with blood cocktails and provide the occasional sacrifice to the god "Luna." • In this case, "Dracula's Castle" was the Manson ranch. The film was shot at the former home of cult leader/mass murderer Charles Manson and his fanatical "Family." • Paula Raymond, former star of *The Beast from 20,000 Fathoms* (1953), played Countess Dracula, a role originally set for Jayne Mansfield. •

Disappointingly, that distinguished former Dracula — John Carradine — did not play a vampire in this film; he was given the subordinate role of a dim-witted handyman. • Co-producer/co-director Al Adamson, famous for his no-budget inept cheapies, made another Dracula film, *Dracula vs. Frankenstein*, in 1971. It was definitely *not* a step up from this one.

The Brides of Dracula (1960) (see HAMMER'S UNDEAD, this section). This well-thought-of Hammer entry does not actually feature Dracula himself. The film focuses on one of "Dracula's disciples," a Baron Meinster.

Count Dracula (1970; Fenix-Filmar/Cinematografica-Korona/Towers of London/Tigon; Spain/Italy/W. Germany/U.K./Liechtenstein) (also *Bram Stoker's Count Dracula*). D: Jesus Franco. P: Harry Alan Towers. S: Peter Welbeck, Jesus Franco, Augusto Finocchi, Carlo Fadda, M. G. Cuccia. C: Manuel Merino. Cast: Christopher Lee, Herbert Lom, Klaus Kinski, Maria Rohm, Frederick Williams, Soledad Miranda, Jack Taylor, Paul Müller. In the most faithful big-screen adaptation of Bram Stoker's novel to date, Christopher Lee plays Dracula as a white-haired mustachioed aristocrat who grows increasingly younger with the imbibing of blood. • According to star Christopher Lee, this film "is the only time ... that Stoker's character has been presented authentically, as he described him, on the screen." • Lee, of course, had played Dracula five times before in the successful film series from Hammer Studios. Here his interpretation of the infamous vampire is quite different from those previous outings. • During the planning stages, it was announced that Vincent Price would play the role of Van Helsing, but the part eventually went to Herbert Lom. • German actor Klaus Kinski (father of Nastassia Kinski) is often cited for his brilliant portrayal of the tortured "Renfield." Kinski later graduated to a full-fledged vampire role when he played the title role in the 1979 remake of *Nosferatu* — itself based on *Dracula*. • Co-scriptwriter "Peter Welbeck" is actually producer Harry Alan Towers working under a pseudonym.

Count Dracula (1977; BBC-TV; U.K.) D: Philip Saville. P: Morris Barry. S: Gerald Savory. C: Peter Hall. Cast: Louis Jourdan, Frank Finlay, Susan Penhaligon, Judi Bowder, Jack Shepherd, Mark Burns, Bosco Hogan, Richard Barnes. This British television adaptation of Bram Stoker's novel follows the book very closely in telling the tale of Dracula and his journey to England in search of fresh blood. ¶ "Listen to them, the children of the night; what music they make." • The BBC originally broadcast *Count Dracula* in three parts. The telefilm is nearly three hours long.

Countess Dracula (1970) (see BATHORY, ELIZABETH: THE BLOODY COUNTESS). The only "Dracula" that appears in this tale of Elizabeth Bathory is in the film's title, which employs the name merely as an attention-getter.

Deafula (1975; Signscope) D/S: Peter Wechsberg. P: Gary R. Holmstrom. Cast: Peter Wechsberg, James Randall, Dudley Helstreet, Lee Darrel, Gary R. Holmstrom. A child infected by Dracula grows up to become a theology student who periodically grows fangs and a thirst for blood. • *Deafula* is unique in the annals of horror films, for it was filmed entirely in sign language. It does carry a voice-over narration, however, for the uninitiated.

Dracula (1931; Universal) D: Tod Browning. P: Carl Laemmle, Jr. S: Garrett Fort. C: Karl Freund. Cast: Bela Lugosi, Helen Chandler, David Manners, Dwight Frye, Edward Van Sloan, Herbert Bunston, Frances Dade. In this first "official" (see *Nosferatu,* 1922) and most famous version of Bram Stoker's novel, Bela Lugosi plays the undead Count who leaves his homeland in search of fresh blood in England. ¶ "To die! To be really dead! That must be glorious!"—Bela Lugosi as Dracula. • Though based on the book *Dracula* by Bram Stoker, the film more closely follows the stage play adaptation by Hamilton Deane and John L. Balderston. The characters are Stoker's, but their actions are the playwrights'. • *Dracula* was released on February 14, 1931, Valentine's Day. Universal's publicity department, trying to play up the romantic angle, dubbed it "The Story of the Strangest Passion the World Has Ever Known." • Universal's first choice as Dracula was *not* Bela Lugosi, but Conrad Veidt. When Veidt bowed out and returned to Germany (ironically due to his poor grasp of English—a handicap shared by Lugosi; though Veidt later overcame this while Lugosi never did), Universal next chose Lon Chaney, Sr., the "Man of a Thousand Faces" and the first true horror star. Unfortunately, Chaney died of throat cancer, and the studio considered various actors, including Ian Keith and Paul Muni(!), before eventually choosing (at the last minute) Bela Lugosi. Lugosi had starred in the hit Broadway stageplay and had been energetically lobbying for the

part all along. Film historians often maintain that the studio's choice was predominantly a financial rather than creative decision, for they knew they could get Lugosi quite cheaply, and wound up paying him a pitiful $500 a week (while tepid leading man David Manners earned four times that sum at $2,000 weekly!). • Dwight Frye's portrayal of Renfield, Dracula's pitiful slave, was so effective (with his mad pleadings like, "I'll be loyal master ... you'll see that I get lives? Not human lives, but small ones, with blood in them....") that Hollywood typecast him in similar roles for the remainder of his career, despite his coming from a successful stage career on Broadway and possessing an affinity for comedy. • This was Canadian-born leading man David Manners's first role in a horror film, and he played similar parts in two later classics, *The Mummy* (1932), and *The Black Cat* (1934). • Lugosi was not the only veteran from the Broadway play to appear in the film version; stage actor Edward Van Sloan also repeated his role of Professor Van Helsing for the movie. • A Spanish version of *Dracula* was filmed simultaneously with the English version, using the same sets but a different cast and crew. The English version was shot during the day, with the Spanish crew working at night. Those who have seen it (including this author) maintain that cinematically speaking, the Spanish version is superior to the English one. • In 1938 *Dracula* was re-released on a double bill with *Frankenstein* and was so successful that it triggered Hollywood's second "golden age" of horror (after a dry spell of nearly two years in which no horror film was produced in America). • *Dracula* is considered a flawed classic, often cited by critics as having a wonderful beginning but slowing down to a stagy crawl in the middle and winding up with an anti-climactic ending (with the Count disappointingly slain off-screen).

Dracula (1974; TV movie/Universal) D/P: Dan Curtis. S: Richard Matheson. C: Oswald Morris. Cast: Jack Palance, Simon Ward, Nigel Davenport, Fiona Lewis, Pamela Brown, Penelope Horner, Virginia Wetherell. Jack Palance plays an unattractive Dracula in love with an English woman in this retelling of Stoker's classic story. • This particular version was produced as a TV movie but was released theatrically in Europe. • During its initial TV broadcast, *Dracula*'s start time was delayed by then-president Nixon announcing the resignation of vice-president Spiro Agnew. • Producer/director Dan Curtis wins the crown of "King

Bela Lugosi as Dracula *(1931) recoils from a cross held in the unknowing hand of Renfield (Dwight Frye), soon to become Dracula's pitiful slave.*

of TV Horror," for in addition to *Dracula,* he has produced TV versions of nearly all the classics: *The Strange Case of Dr. Jekyll and Mr. Hyde* (1968), *Frankenstein* (1973), *The Picture of Dorian Gray* (1973), and *The Turn of the Screw* (1974). • Curtis was no stranger to vampirism, having created and produced the popular daytime soap opera "Dark Shadows," featuring Barnabas Collins—a vampire—as a main character.

Dracula (1979; Universal) D: John Badham. P: Walter Mirisch. S: W. D. Richter. C: Gilbert Taylor. Cast: Frank Langella, Laurence Olivier, Donald Pleasence, Kate Nelligan, Trevor Eve, Tony Haygarth. This particular *Dracula* is a big-budgeted update starring Frank Langella as the screen's most alluring vampire. • As was the original *Dracula* (1931), this version is based on the Hamilton Deane and John L. Balderston stage adaptation of Bram Stoker's novel.

Dracula Against Frankenstein (1972; Fenix/Comptoir Français du Film; Spain/France) (also *Dracula vs. Dr. Frankenstein; The Screaming Dead* [video title]). D/S: Jesus Franco. P: Robert de Nesle, Arturo

Marcos. C: Jose Climent. Cast: Dennis Price, Howard Vernon, Alberto Dalbes, Britt Nichols, Anne Libert, Fernando Bilbao, Brandy. Count Dracula (Howard Vernon) and his wife initiate a new wave of vampirism in the Carpathian Mountains, while Dr. Frankenstein creates a monster to combat Dracula. • Prolific director Jess (or Jesus) Franco had previously made the film often cited as being the version closest to Stoker's novel, *Count Dracula* (1970).

Dracula and Son (1979) (see OTHER VAMPIRES, this section). A vampire Count (*not* Dracula) and his worthless son flee their homeland when a communist government takes control in this vampire black comedy. • This is another case of filmmakers thoughtlessly plundering Dracula's literary name. About the title, star Christopher Lee later told authors Robert W. Pohle, Jr., and Douglas C. Hart for their book *The Films of Christopher Lee:* "By no stretch of the imagination was it a Dracula film. I told them, 'You can't put the title *Dracula* on that film.'"

Dracula Blows His Cool (1979; Lisa

Film/Barthonia Film; W. Germany) D: Carlo Ombra. P: Martin Friedman. S: Gruenbach and Rosenthal. C: Heinz Hoelscher. Cast: Gianni Garko, Betty Verges, Linda Grondier, Ralf Wolter, Giacomo Rizzo. A young fashion photographer returns to his ancestral castle with a bevy of beautiful models to shoot a layout. There he finds his undead grandfather and vampire mistress, and ends up turning the castle into a hotel/disco bar called "Hotel Dracula," with the resident vampires serving as a draw for tourists. • Obviously a farcical treatment of the vampire legend with plenty of nudity and soft-core sex thrown in. The U.S. distributors originally intended to title the film *Dracula Sucks,* before they learned of a hardcore film which had already used that title.

Dracula Sucks (1978; First International Pictures) (also *Lust at First Bite*). D: Philip Marshak. P: Darryl A. Marshak. S: Darryl A. Marshak, David J. Kern. C: Tanania Baer. Cast: Jamie Gillis, Annette Haven, John Leslie, Sereno, Detlef Van Berg (Reggie Nalder), Kay Parker, John Holmes, Mike Ranger, Paul Thomas, Richard Bulik, Seka. In this crude, rude, and inept retelling of the Dracula legend, the Count is living near Dr. Seward's asylum where he sees and falls in love with the beautiful Mina. ¶ "But don't lose your head over me because I am Count Dracula, and Dracula sucks!" — refrain from the theme song. • Originally filmed as a hard-core porno movie, it was edited down to a soft-core version for wider distribution (much as the better-known *Flesh Gordon* was). • Actor Reggie Nalder was not overly proud of his participation in this film (he played Dracula's nemesis, Dr. Van Helsing), and so used a pseudonum — "Detlef Van Berg." The actor later told *Fangoria* #82: "I didn't want them to use my name. It was terrible. One day to another, they'd write the script." Nalder had appeared in *Dracula's Dog* this same year and he played the vampire in *Salem's Lot* the following year. For both these films he *did* use his own name. • Though populated primarily with porno actors, the performance of "straight" actor Richard Bulik as Renfield stands out. He does an uncannily accurate impersonation of Dwight Frye's Renfield from the original *Dracula* (1931).

Dracula, the Dirty Old Man (1969; Whit Boyd Productions) D/P/S: William Edwards. C: William Troiam. Cast: Vince Kelly, Ann Hollis, Bunny Boud, Adarinne. This obscure vampire sex/comedy has Count Alucard (again!) kidnapping young virgins.

Dracula vs. Frankenstein (1972; Independent International) D: Al Adamson. P: Al Adamson, John Van Horne. S: William Pugsley, Samuel M. Sherman. C: Gary Graver, Paul Glickman. Cast: J. Carrol Naish, Lon Chaney, Regina Carrol, Angelo Rossitto, Zandor Vorkov, Anthony Eisley, Russ Tamblyn, Jim Davis, John Bloom. Dracula takes the dormant body of the Frankenstein Monster to Dr. Frankenstein, currently hiding under the alias Dr. Durea, and convinces him to revive the Monster. Dracula hopes to use a blood serum that the doctor has been working on to allow him to endure sunlight. The Monster is employed to procure victims for their experiments, but alas, all does not go as planned and the expected confrontation between Dracula and the Frankenstein Monster occurs at the climax. ¶ *"Yesterday* they were *cold and dead — Today* they're *hot and bothered"* — exploitative ad line. • As originally shot in 1971, the film was called *The Blood Seekers* and did not feature either Dracula *or* Frankenstein. When *The Blood Seekers* was deemed too short and incomprehensible by Sam Sherman at Independent International, the characters of Dracula and Frankenstein were added, new scenes shot, and a movie was made (more or less). The reason why J. Carrol Naish is called Dr. Durea throughout the film when he's supposed to be Dr. Frankenstein, is because his was a character from the original version, whose name was changed to Frankenstein after the fact. • According to Donald F. Glut in his *The Dracula Book,* it was Forrest J Ackerman, editor of *Famous Monsters of Filmland,* who came up with the name of "Zandor Vorkov" right on the set, which was taken as a stage name by the curly-headed actor playing Count Dracula. Ackerman also has a cameo in the film as Dr. Beaumont, the Monster's first victim. • The monster was played by 7'4" John Bloom, who also appeared in *The Incredible Two-Headed Transplant* (1971). • This was the last film of both J. Carrol Naish and Lon Chaney, Jr. Chaney had played the famous Count once before, in *Son of Dracula* (1943), but was reduced here to playing a mindless mute servant. • The film is said to have utilized some of the voltage machines used in the original trio of Frankenstein films, which were built by Ken Strickfaden.

Dracula's Daughter (1936; Universal) D: Lambert Hillyer. P: E. M. Asher. S: Garrett Fort. C: George Robinson. Cast: Otto Kruger, Gloria Holden, Marguerite Churchill, Edward Van Sloan, Irving Pichel, Nan Gray, Gilbert Emery, Hedda Hopper, E. E.

As shown by this rare pre-production publicity herald, Universal "Ace" James Whale was originally set to direct Dracula's Daughter *(1936). Lambert Hillyer eventually helmed the project. Note the superimposed likeness of Bela Lugosi to the left. Lugosi was originally signed to reprise his role of* Dracula *in this sequel to the 1931 classic, but the part was ultimately dropped from the film during early script revisions. Bound by a contract, Universal was obliged to pay Lugosi $4,000 anyway, even though the actor never appeared in the film. (Courtesy of Lynn Naron.)*

Clive. Taking up right where the original *Dracula* (1931) left off, it is revealed that Dracula has a daughter. She comes to America, burns her father's corpse, and attempts to free herself from the vampire curse. She cannot escape her blood heritage however, and reverts to her vampiric ways. ¶ "She was beautiful when she died ... a hundred years ago." • This was the last film produced by a floundering Universal under the Laemmle regime. It came in terribly over-budget and over-schedule, and was released two months after the studio changed hands. • During the planning stages, Bela Lugosi was signed to reprise his role of Dracula. When the script was changed and the character of Dracula was dropped, Universal was still obligated to Lugosi and was forced to pay him $4,000, even though he never appeared in the picture. • Though the credits claim that the film is based on the Bram Stoker short story "Dracula's Guest," there is little resemblance to it in the final film. • Irving Pichel, who plays the vampiress's sinister servant was a director as well as an actor. Among his directorial credits are *The Most Dangerous Game* (1932; as co-director), *She* (1935), and *Destination Moon* (1950).

Dracula's Dog (1978; Crown International) (also *Zoltan, Hound of Dracula*). D: Albert Band. P: Charles Band, Frank Ray Perilli. S: Frank Ray Perilli. C: Bruce Logan. Cast: Michael Pataki, Reggie Nalder, Jose Ferrer, Jan Shutan, Libbie Chase. Dracula's vampiric dog is revived and travels to America with Dracula's former servant in search of a new master. The pair set their sights on a man named Michael Drake, a mortal who is the last descendant of Dracula. • In a new twist on vampire lore, Dracula's former servant, while not a vampire himself, is an undead being called a "fractional lamia." He does not have a craving for blood and can move about in the daytime. • The actor who played this undead servant, Reggie Nalder, went on the play a vampire himself the following year in *Salem's Lot* (1979). • Director Albert Band told *Fangoria* #68 why he chose to do this project (aside from the fact that his son Charles was producing it): "The idea of doing a canine Bela Lugosi appealed to me. And I thought it came out rather well."

Dracula's Great Love (1972; Cinema Shares; Spain) (also *Cemetery Girls; Dracula's Virgin Lovers*). D: Javier Aguirre. P: Francisco Lara Polop. S: Jacinto Molina,

Alberto Insua. C: Raul Perez Cubero. Cast: Paul Naschy, Haydee Politoff, Rossana Yanni, Mirta Miller, Vic Winner, Ingrid Garbo, Julio Peña. Count Dracula vampirizes a group of travelers staying at his castle. He falls in love with one of them though, and cannot bring himself to take her blood. When she rejects him, he drives a stake into his own heart. • Star Paul Naschy, who plays the role of Count Dracula, also co-wrote the script under his real name of Jacinto Molina. Naschy is most recognized for his Waldemar Daninski/Wolfman character which he has played in ten different films.

Dracula's Widow (1988; De Laurentiis Entertainment Group) D: Christopher Coppola. P: Stephen Traxler. S: Kathryn Ann Thomas, Christopher Coppola. C: Giuseppe Macari. Cast: Sylvia Kristel, Josef Sommer, Lenny Von Dohlen, Rachael Jones, Stefan Schnabel. Vanessa, the wife of Dracula, is revived in modern-day America and begins her own reign of vampiric terror. ¶ "Then it's true, I'm a widow?" • Director Christopher Coppola is the nephew of famed filmmaker Francis Ford Coppola.

The Empire of Dracula (1966; Filmica Vergara; Mexico) D: Federico Curiel. P: Luis Enrique Vergara. S: Ramón Obon, Jr. C: Alfredo Uribe. Cast: Eric del Castillo, Cesar del Campo, Lucha Villa, Ethel Carrillo, Rebecca Inturbide. At "Castle Draculstein," the sinister Igor kills a woman and uses her blood to raise up the Count from his ashes. Dracula then commences vampirizing all those who come within biting distance. • *The Empire of Dracula* has the distinction of being the first Mexican horror film shot in color. • The resurrection of Dracula in this film is very similar to a sequence in Hammer's *Dracula, Prince of Darkness* made the previous year.

The Evil of Dracula (1975; Toho; Japan) D: Michio Yamamoto. P: Fumio Tanaka. S: Ei Ogawa, Masaru Takasue. C: Katsumi Hara. Cast: Toshio Kurosawa, Mariko Mochizuki, Shin Kishida, Hunie Tanaka, Katsuhiko Sasaki. Two descendants of Dracula run a boarding school for girls, occasionally choosing a victim from among the students. • Director Michio Yamamoto made two other vampire films for Toho Studios — *The Night of the Vampire* (1970) and *Lake of Dracula* (1972).

Guess What Happened to Count Dracula (1970; Merrick International) D/S: Laurence Merrick. P: Leo Rivers. C: Bob Caramico. Cast: Des Roberts, Claudia Barron, John Londen, Robert Branche, Frank Donato, Sharon Beverly, Damu King. Dracula is now going under the name of Count Adrian and frequenting a mod discotheque called "Dracula's Castle." • Actor Des Roberts, who plays Dracula, also composed the music for the film and conducted the orchestra as well.

Horror of Dracula (1958) (see HAMMER'S UNDEAD, this section) (also *Dracula*).

House of Dracula (1945; Universal) D: Erle C. Kenton. P: Paul Malvern. S: Edward T. Lowe. C: George Robinson. Cast: Lon Chaney, Jr., John Carradine, Martha O'Driscoll, Lionel Atwill, Onslow Stevens, Jane Adams, Ludwig Stossel, Glenn Strange. Dracula shows up at the house of renowned scientist Dr. Edelmann, asking for a cure for his vampiric condition. Likewise, Larry Talbot (the Wolf Man) arrives begging the doctor to help *him*. The Frankenstein Monster is found and this monster rally follow-up to *House of Frankenstein* is complete. ¶ "That's why I've come to you, to seek release from a curse of misery and horror" — John Carradine as Count Dracula. • Halfway through the curative process, Dracula changes his mind and decides he wishes to remain a vampire after all when he meets Dr. Edlemann's attractive assistant, whom he promptly sets out to vampirize. Dracula also spitefully mixes his vampiric blood with that of Dr. Edelmann, turning the altruistic doctor into a Jekyll and Hyde–type fiend. • When the project was first announced by Universal, it was under the name of *The Wolf Man vs. Dracula*. Presumably, drastic changes were made because, disappointingly, Dracula never comes in contact with the Wolf Man (or the Frankenstein Monster for that matter). • Further along in production the film went under the title *Destiny*. • In an odd mixing of genres, Universal released *House of Dracula* on a double bill with *The Daltons Ride Again,* a western(!) which also starred Lon Chaney, Jr., and Martha O'Driscoll.

House of Frankenstein (1944; Universal) D: Erle C. Kenton. P: Paul Malvern. S: Edward T. Lowe. C: George Robinson. Cast: Boris Karloff, Lon Chaney, Jr., John Carradine, J. Carrol Naish, Anne Gwynne, Peter Coe, Lionel Atwill, George Zucco, Elena Verdugo. *"Frankenstein's Monster! Wolf Man! Dracula! Hunchback! Mad Doctor!"* screamed the ads for this plot by Universal to unite as many of their classic monsters as could fit onto one screen. Dr. Niemann (Boris Karloff) finds Dracula's skeleton, pulls the stake from its chest, and agrees to protect his resting place if the vampire serves him. Dracula agrees and kills one of Niemann's enemies, but is found out and perishes in the sun when an ungrateful Niemann pushes Dracula's coffin out into the cold light of dawn. The film continues, with the traveling Niemann later encountering the Wolf Man and the Frankenstein Monster. ¶ "When I look at it [Dracula's ring] I see glimpses of a strange world, a world of people who are dead ... and yet alive." • One Hollywood story has it that a then-struggling Bela Lugosi asked Universal for the role of Dracula but was passed over for John Carradine. Another version claims that Universal *wanted* Lugosi but the actor was unavailable due to other commitments. • This was John Carradine's first appearance as Dracula. He reprised the role for the next film in Universal's monster series, *House of Dracula,* but no explanation was given for this miraculous resurrection (having been transformed into a bleached skeleton by the rays of the sun in this film). • Years later, Carradine told *Fangoria* about his intent in playing the Count: "When they asked me to play Dracula, I said yes, if you let me make him up and play him the way Bram Stoker described him—as an elderly, distinguished gentleman with a drooping mustache. [Universal] didn't like a big mustache, so I had to trim it and make it a very clipped, British mustache. It wasn't really in character." • Those wishing to see Dracula fight one of the other famous monsters in the film went away disappointed. Dracula appears at the film's beginning and is already dead by the time the Wolf Man and the Frankenstein Monster put in appearances. • For this film, Dracula chose to use the alias "Baron Latos."

Lake of Dracula (1972) (see OTHER VAMPIRES, this section). Despite the title, there is no Dracula, just a Japanese vampire living in a castle by a lake.

Last Rites (1980; New Empire Features/Cannon) (also *Dracula's Last Rites*). D/C: Domonic Paris. P: Kelly Van Horn. S: Ben Donnelly, Domonic Paris. Cast: Patricia Lee Hammond, Gerald Fielding, Victor Jorge, Michael Lally. In a small New York town, the local mortician named "Lucard" (spell it backwards) is a vampire living off the blood of accident victims. • This is an incredibly cheap attempt to update the vampire legend. With the production values of a threadbare soap opera, microphones dip into camera range and the tops of sets are often visible throughout the film.

The Legend of the Seven Golden Vampires (1974) (see HAMMER'S UNDEAD, this section) (also *The Seven Brothers Meet Dracula*).

Lemora, the Lady Dracula (1974) (see OTHER VAMPIRES, this section). The female vampire, Lemora, is no relation to the famous count.

Love at First Bite (1979; AIP) D: Stan Dragoti. P: Joel Freeman. S: Robert Kaufman. C: Edward Rosson. Cast: George Hamilton, Susan Saint James, Richard Benjamin, Dick Shawn, Arte Johnson. In this comic spoof of the Dracula legend, George Hamilton is the suave Dracula who must leave his ancestral home when the communist government commandeers his castle for use as a gymnasium. Dracula comes to New York with his faithful bug-eating servant Renfield, and falls in love with a fashion model (Susan Saint James). ¶ "Children of the night ... shut up!" • Director Stan Dragoti was married to supermodel Cheryl Tiegs at the time. On the way to the Cannes Film Festival to promote the film, Dragoti was arrested for cocaine possession. • A sequel was announced but never materialized. It was to be called *Love at Second Bite.*

Mama Dracula (1980) (see BATHORY, ELIZABETH: THE BLOODY COUNTESS). Louise Fletcher actually plays an Elizabeth Bathory–type named Countess Dracula who bathes in the blood of virgins to stay young. She has twin sons, however, who *do* display traditional vampiric tendencies (such as sprouting fangs and sucking blood).

Men of Action Meet Women of Drakula (1969; Philippines) D: Artemio Marquez. P: Victoria Villanueva. Cast: Dante Varona, Eddie Torrente, Ruben Obligacion, Norman Henson, Ernesto Beren, Angelito Marquez. A group of tumbler/wrestlers battle a band of vampire women headed by Dracula himself.

The Monster Squad (1987; Tri-Star) D: Fred Dekker. P: Jonathan A. Zimbert. S: Shane Black, Fred Dekker. C: Bradford May. Cast: Andre Cower, Robby Kiger, Stephen Macht, Duncan Regehr, Mary Ellen Trainor, Leonardo Cimino, Tom Noonan. The evil Dracula has summoned all the famous classical monsters together (the Creature from the Black Lagoon, Frankenstein's Monster, the Mummy, and the Wolf Man) in an attempt to gain possession of an occult amulet which would let the forces of darkness rule the earth. Their only opposition is a band of young kids and an old man.

Nocturna, Granddaughter of Dracula (1979; Compass International) D/S: Harry Tampa. P: Vernon Becker. C: Mac Ahlberg. Cast: John Carradine, Nai Bonet, Yvonne

De Carlo, Brother Theodore. Count Dracula follows his rebellious granddaughter to New York. Various comedic episodes follow, including a visit to a disco. ¶ "As long as there is death there's hope!" • This is John Carradine's fourth screen appearance as Count Dracula, the previous three being *House of Frankenstein* (1944), *House of Dracula* (1945), and *Billy the Kid vs. Dracula* (1966). • According to Michael Weldon in his *Psychotronic Encyclopedia of Film,* this feature was financed by ex-actor/embezzler William Callahan, who was slain gangland style two years later.

Nosferatu (1922; Prana Film; Germany) D: Friedrich Wilhelm Murnau. S: Henrik Galeen. C: Fritz Arno Wagner. Cast: Alexander Granach, Max Schreck, Gustav von Wangenheim, Greta Schroeder, John Gottowt, Ruth Landshoff, G. H. Schnell, Gustav Botz. In this pirated version of Bram Stoker's novel *Dracula,* the Count's name has been changed to Orlock, and the setting of London has been replaced with the German city of Bremen. The basic story remains the same however. ¶ "Is this your wife? What a beautiful neck!" • This is the first-ever film adaptation of *Dracula* (though no credit was given to its source). • Two months after its release, Bram Stoker's widow sued the Prana Film Company for copyright infringement. A court decision in 1925 ordered all prints destroyed, but fortunately some copies survived. • German actor Max Schreck played the role of Count Orlock (Dracula). His last name literally means "terror" in German. • In 1979, Werner Herzog remade *Nosferatu* with Klaus Kinski as the vampire Count. Herzog has called the original, "The most important film in the entire history of German cinema."

Nosferatu the Vampyre (1979; Gaumont/ 20th Century–Fox; W. Germany/France) D/P/S: Werner Herzog. C: Joerg Schmidt-Reitwein. Cast: Klaus Kinski, Isabelle Adjani, Bruno Ganz, Roland Topor, Walter Ladengast. In this remake of Murnau's silent classic, the characters are no longer disguised under false names, and Count Orlock is now Count Dracula. ¶ "Can you imagine centuries enduring the same futilities?"—a world-weary Dracula. • Herzog filmed two versions, one in English and one in German. Since very few of his actors understood English, that version apparently did not come off too well and was never released. Instead, the German version was presented with subtitles.

Old Dracula (1973; World Film Services/ AIP; U.K.) (also *Vampira*). D: Clive Donner. P: Jack H. Wiener. S: Jeremy Lloyd. C: Tony Richmond. Cast: David Niven, Peter Bayliss, Teresa Graves, Nicky Henson, Jennie Linden, Bernard Bresslaw, Linda Hayden, Veronica Carlson, Freddie Jones. In another Dracula farce, David Niven plays the Count who comes to England in search of a rare blood type in order to revive his wife, Vampira. • In a sight gag bordering on racial bad taste, Vampira is revived with the blood of a black woman and turns black herself. At the end, Dracula also turns black when Vampira bites him, presumably to live happily ever after in a now-racially stable relationship. • Actress Veronica Carlson encountered Dracula once before, in *Dracula Has Risen from the Grave* (1968).

The Return of Dracula (1958; United Artists) (also *The Curse of Dracula*). D: Paul Landres. P: Jules V. Levy, Arthur Gardner. S: Pat Fielder. C: Jack McKenzie. Cast: Francis Lederer, Norma Eberhardt, Ray Stricklyn, Jimmie Baird, John Wengraf, Virginia Vincent. Dracula escapes his enemies and comes to America. There he masquerades as an artistic cousin from the Old Country named "Belac," and insinuates himself into the midst of a typical southern California family. ¶ "You must listen to me! You are bound to me! You shall die as you are predestined to die!"

The Saga of the Draculas (1972; Profilmes; Spain) (also *The Dracula Saga; Dracula, the Bloodline Continues* [video title]). D: Leon Klimovsky. P: José Antonio Perez Giner. S: Lazarus Kaplan. C: Francisco Sanchez. Cast: Tina Saenz, Tony Isbert, Helga Line, Narciso Ibañez-Menta, Maria Kost, Christiana Suriani. A young man (a descendant of Dracula) and his pregnant wife return to the castle of his grandfather (the Count). Due to inbreeding the Dracula line is in danger of dying out and the unborn vampire in the wife's womb is the family's greatest hope.

Son of Dracula (1943; Universal) D: Robert Siodmak. P: Ford Beebe. S: Eric Taylor. C: George Robinson. Cast: Lon Chaney, Jr., Louise Albritton, Robert Paige, Evelyn Ankers, Frank Craven, J. Edward Blomberg, Samuel S. Hinds, Adeline de Walt Reynolds. Dracula (the Count himself, *not* his son) comes to Louisiana under the name of Count Alucard. There he marries a morbid young woman who embraces his vampirism and plots to destroy the Count and make her current human fiancé into a vampire like herself so they can

Max Schreck stars as the ghoulish vampire known as Nosferatu *(1922). Though the title character is named Count Orlock, the film is a thinly disguised version of Bram Stoker's* Dracula *(and in fact was the cause of a lengthy lawsuit brought by Stoker's widow).*

share eternal life together. ¶ "I am here because this is a young and virile race, not dry and decadent like ours. You have what I want, what I need, what I must have!" • This was the first time that over-used alias "Alucard" ("Dracula" spelled backwards) was employed. • This was also the first film to feature a mustachioed vampire. • Screenwriter and novelist Curt Siodmak was originally set to write the script, but when his brother, director Robert Siodmak, came on board the project, Curt was promptly fired by his own brother. According to Curt, "We had a sibling rivalry. He only wanted one Siodmak around." • Lon Chaney, Jr., played Dracula, and this was his only appearance as a vampire, though he played the Wolf Man, the Mummy, and even Frankenstein's Monster multiple times.

Son of Dracula (1974; Cinemation; U.K.) D: Freddie Francis. P: Ringo Starr. S: Jay Fairbanks. Cast: Harry Nilsson, Ringo Starr, Dennis Price. Dracula's son is named Count Down and plays with a rock band in the castle basement in this failed horror/comedy/musical. • Singer Harry Nilsson plays the title role and supplied much of the music for the film from his tie-in albums, "Nilsson Schmilsson" and "Son of Schmilsson" (the latter pictured him on the album cover dressed in a Dracula cape). • Producer and ex–Beatle Ringo Starr plays "Merlin the Magician" in the film. • Also featured in the cast were rock musicians Keith Moon, John Bonham, and Peter Frampton. • British director Freddie Francis had previously directed two other Dracula films—*Dracula Has Risen from the Grave* (1968) and *The Vampire Happening* (1971).

A Taste of Blood (1967; Ajay Films) (also *The Secret of Dr. Alucard*). D/P: Herschell Gordon Lewis. S: Donald Stanford. C: Andy Romanoff. Cast: Bill Rogers, Elizabeth Wilkinson, Thomas Wood, Otto Schlesinger, Eleanor Vaill, Lawrence Tobin, H. G. Lewis. An American descendant of Dracula receives a mysterious bottle of Slivovitz in the mail, and upon drinking it is transformed into a vampire with the aim of wreaking vengeance upon those who had slain his ancestor. ¶ From the ads: "A ghastly tale drenched with gouts of blood spurting from the writhing victims of a madman's lust!" • *A Taste of Blood* was filmed in Miami by the "Godfather of Gore," Herschell Gordon Lewis, a filmmaker some say is *without* taste. • Lewis considers this film his "epic." It has much less gore than his other pictures, and he called it "a step into the mainstream—and a big mistake." • Lewis himself appears in the film as a cockney sailor (only because, he claims, no one else could do a cockney accent—though he freely admits neither could he).

To Die For (1988; Arrowhead Entertainment/Lee Caplin) D: Deran Sarafian. P: Barin Kumar. S: Leslie King. C: Jacques Haitkin. Cast: Brendan Hughes, Sydney Walsh, Amanda Wyss, Scott Jacoby, Micah Grant, Duane Jones, Steve Bond. A vampire named Vlad Teppes (a.k.a. Dracula) moves to Los Angeles and falls in love with a young real estate agent. Tom, an old vampire nemesis of Vlad, seeks revenge on his noble enemy by setting his sights on the girl. The two struggle in a battle of wills, one for pure love, the other for vampiric revenge. • Straining for some historical/literary accuracy, Dracula is named Vlad Teppes in this movie, the same name as the fifteenth century Wallachian Prince Bram Stoker based his character of Dracula upon.

The Vampire Happening (1971; Acquila Films; W. Germany) D: Freddie Francis. P: Pier A. Caminnecci. S: August Rieger. C: Gerard Vandenberg. Cast: Pia Degermark, Thomas Hunter, Ingrid van Bergen, Ferdy Mayne, Lyvia Bauer, Joachim Kemmer, Daria Damer, Yvor Murillo. A movie star goes back to her ancestral castle where she encounters Dracula and a vampire relative who looks exactly like herself in this European vampire comedy. • Unlike most Dracula movies, the Count escapes in the end. He flies off to safety not with bat wings, however, but with the more modern convenience of a helicopter. • Ferdy Mayne, who plays Dracula, was no stranger to vampire roles, having been the lead bloodsucker in Roman Polanski's *The Fearless Vampire Killers* (1967). • Leading lady Pia Degermark is producer Pier A. Caminnecci's wife.

Vampyres, Daughters of Dracula (1975) (see OTHER VAMPIRES, this section). The two beautiful female vampires featured in this film are daughters of Dracula in a metaphorical sense only.

Hammer's Undead

The Brides of Dracula (1960; Hammer/Universal; U.K.) D: Terence Fisher. P: Anthony Hinds. S: Jimmy Sangster, Peter Bryan, Edward Percy. C: Jack Asher. Cast:

Peter Cushing, David Peel, Martita Hunt, Yvonne Monlaur, Miles Malleson, Mona Washbourne, Michael Ripper, Henry Oscar, Andree Melly. Hammer's first follow-up to *Horror of Dracula* (1958) is actually a "cheat" sequel since it is without Dracula. Baron Meinster, a "disciple of Dracula," is kept locked up by his mother, who occasionally brings him young girls to feed on. A young schoolteacher, unaware of his condition, takes pity on him and sets him free, with the result of her almost becoming one of the titular "brides." ¶ "Count Dracula, monarch of all vampires, is dead, but his disciples live on to spread the cult and corrupt the world" — opening narration. • Despite the fact that Dracula never appeared, *Brides of Dracula* was originally to be called *Dracula 2,* with its poster claiming: "The most evil *Dracula* of all!" • During the course of the film, that unflappable vampire hunter, Dr. Van Helsing (Peter Cushing returning from *Horror of Dracula*), is bitten by the vampire and must purge the unholy taint from his body by burning the vampire's mark from his own neck with a hot iron. • Actor David Peel, who played the boyish blond vampire, Baron Meinster, was actually 40 years old, though he looked to be in his twenties. His only other appearance in a horror film was a brief bit as an airplane pilot in the 1961 version of *The Hands of Orlac.* • *Brides of Dracula* features a totally unique method of killing a vampire. At the climax, Dr. Van Helsing swings the blades of a windmill to make a giant shadow of the cross in the moonlight, which disintegrates the vampire caught within the holy shadow.

Captain Kronos, Vampire Hunter (1973; Hammer/Paramount; U.K.) D/S: Brian Clemens. P: Albert Fennell, Brian Clemens. C: Ian Wilson. Cast: Horst Janson, John Carson, Shane Briant, Caroline Munro, John Cater, Lois Daine, Ian Hendry, Wanda Ventham. The swashbuckling Captain Kronos and his hunchbacked assistant Professor Grost are professional vampire hunters come to rid the countryside of a type of vampire which draws the life force from its victims. ¶ "There are as many species of vampire as there are beasts of prey. Their methods and their motive for attack can vary in a hundred different ways." • The vampires here do not draw blood from their victims but instead drain their youth, causing them to die of old age in a few seconds. They also have no difficulty walking about in the daytime. • Instead of the usual stake, Kronos slays the vampires with a sword fashioned out of blessed metal taken from a cross. • Director Brian Clemens is most associated with British television (he often wrote for "The Avengers" TV series). • *Captain Kronos* was released on a double bill with *Frankenstein and the Monster from Hell,* and despite a novel approach and a good sense of humor, was not successful.

Countess Dracula (1970) (see BATHORY, ELIZABETH: THE BLOODY COUNTESS). The title character's name is actually Bathory, not Dracula, and rather than drinking blood she bathes in it to stay young.

Dracula A.D. 1972 (1972; Hammer/Warner Bros.; U.K.) (also *Dracula Today*). D: Alan Gibson. P: Josephine Douglas. S: Don Houghton. C: Dick Bush. Cast: Christopher Lee, Peter Cushing, Stephanie Beacham, Christopher Neame, Michael Coles, William Ellis, Janet Key, Michael Kitchen, Caroline Munro. In a brief prologue, Dracula is killed by Dr. Van Helsing. Jumping ahead 100 years to 1972, Dracula is resurrected in an occult ceremony by a group of "swinging" youths looking for kicks. He then goes on a rampage of revenge against the descendants of his old nemesis, Van Helsing. ¶ "I have returned to destroy the house of Van Helsing forever, the old through the young." • Both *Dracula, Chelsea '72* and *Dracula Chases the Mini Girls* were considered as titles but (thankfully) discarded. • This was the first film in Hammer's Dracula series to be set in modern times. • Peter Cushing appears as *both* Dracula's nemesis Prof. Van Helsing (in the film's nineteenth century prologue) *and* his equally intrepid grandson (in modern day). • At the close of the prologue Count Dracula is killed when a broken spoke of a coach's wheel pierces his heart. • Dracula's modern vampiric disciple carried the not so subtle name of "Johnny *Alucard*" (read it backwards). • Screenwriter Don Houghton also penned *The Legend of the Seven Golden Vampires* (1974), Hammer's last Dracula film. • Audiences were dared to take part in the "Horroritual" which was a prologue added to American prints. In it, TV vampire Barry Atwater would rise from a coffin and have viewers swear to be "good Draculas." Another bit of promotional gimmickry involved honorary membership cards reading "I've been to a Horroritual with Dracula" given away free at the box office booths. • Christopher Lee was a little skeptical of this film's merit, saying, "I have very grave doubts about the mixing of the styles, and great reservations." • In *Famous Monsters of Filmland* #97, Lee explained how they achieved Dracula's startling blood-red eye effect (as well as expounding upon the perils of playing an undead fiend): "I hate to tell you this, it's giving away the secrets of the trade. Contact lenses. And very uncomfortable they are. I can't see a thing. They cover the whole eye. And it is rather unnerving if you're running up and down staircases and leaping over tables, I may tell you, when you come crashing into them."

Dracula Has Risen from the Grave (1968; Hammer/Warner-Seven Arts; U.K.) (also *Dracula's Revenge*). D: Freddie Francis. P: Aida Young. S: John Elder. C: Arthur Grant. Cast: Christopher Lee, Rupert Davies, Veronica Carlson, Barbara Ewing, Barry Andrews, Ewan Hooper, Michael Ripper, George A. Cooper, Marion Mathie. A weak-willed priest accidentally revives the undead Count and becomes his unwilling servant in a plot of revenge. ¶ "The flowers of garlic should be placed on either side of the head of the one to be protected, no more than a handspread away from the throat." • Dracula is revived by the blood of a wounded priest trickling onto his lips through a crack in the frozen ice he is encased in. The vampire was trapped in the ice at the conclusion of Hammer's previous Dracula film — *Dracula, Prince of Darkness* (1966). • Though not a comedy in any shape or form, Hammer's advertising for the film took a decidedly humorous turn with such lines as "Boy, does he give a hickey!" and "You just can't keep a good man down!" Apparently this strategy worked, for *Dracula Has Risen from the Grave* was the most successful Dracula film for Hammer to date. • *Dracula Has Risen from the Grave* made several departures from traditional vampire movie lore. For one, when Dracula is first introduced, we are shown his *reflection* in a pool of water. For another, at one pint the Count is staked but is able to pull the stake from his heart because the hero fails to say the appropriate prayer. • Star Christopher Lee had this to say about these deviations in *The Films of Christopher Lee*, by Poole and Hart: "In my opinion, an enormous error was committed in terms of Vampire Law, when a stake was driven into Dracula's body while he lay in his coffin, without the inevitable result. The excuse they used for the fact that he did not die was that this ritual was ineffective without the aid of prayer. Apparently, the young man was an atheist and unable to pray. This struck me as quite ludicrous, but apparently the scene made a tremendous impact on the screen." • For this film, Christopher Lee wore an exact duplicate of Bela Lugosi's original Dracula

ring (given to him by Forrest J Ackerman). • The Queen of England herself visited the set of *Dracula Has Risen from the Grave*. • Screenwriter "John Elder" is actually Anthony Hinds using a pseudonym. Hinds was a frequent producer for Hammer; his credits include *Horror of Dracula* (1958) and *The Brides of Dracula* (1960). Hinds (again using the name John Elder) also wrote Hammer's next two Dracula films, *Scars of Dracula* and *Taste the Blood of Dracula* (both 1970).

Dracula, Prince of Darkness (1966; Hammer-Seven Arts/20th Century-Fox; U.K.) (also *Revenge of Dracula; Blood for Dracula*). D: Terence Fisher. P: Anthony Nelson Keys. S: John Sansom. C: Michael Reed. Cast: Christopher Lee, Barbara Shelley, Andrew Keir, Francis Matthews, Suzan Farmer, Charles Tingwell, Thorley Walters, Philip Latham, Joyce Henson. Two vacationing couples wind up at Castle Dracula where a loyal servant of the undead Count uses the blood of one of them to raise his master from the ashes. Dracula then vampirizes one of the women and must face the wrath of a local no-nonsense vampire-killing priest. ¶ "My master's hospitality is renowned." — Dracula's loyal servant, "Klove." • Though *The Brides of Dracula* (1960) was the first "official" sequel to *Horror of Dracula, Dracula Prince of Darkness* (the third film in the series) is the first sequel to include the Count himself. The film's shooting title was *Dracula 3*. • Christopher Lee, returning for the first time to the role of Dracula which he had established in *Horror of Dracula* (1958), was given absolutely *no* dialogue in this film. He later commented (in *The Films of Christopher Lee* by Pohle and Hart): "This was the only Dracula film in which I didn't say a word. The reason? May have been that they had no idea of what to give me to say. There was a great deal of dialogue originally, but it was so bad that I refused to deliver it. I finally said, 'For God's sake, give me some of Stoker's lines.'" Obviously they decided not to heed Lee's plea and Dracula remains speechless in the film. • Screenwriter "John Sansom" was actually Jimmy Sangster (screenwriter for the two previous Dracula films — *Horror of Dracula,* 1958, and *The Brides of Dracula,* 1960). He was so dissatisfied with the final product that he had his real name removed from the credits and this pseudonym substituted. • At the film's climax, Dracula is dispatched when he is trapped on the frozen moat of his castle. The priest shoots the ice around him, causing it to crack and break, trapping the vampire until he finally sinks into the water (running water is deadly to vampires). This scene was achieved with real blocks of ice in a swimming pool layered with wax to make it look frozen over. The piece of ice that Dracula teetered on before falling in was a plaster block mounted on pivots. • The contact lenses worn by Christopher Lee to produce those bloodshot eyes created so many difficulties in vision that at one point he accidentally ran into co-star Barbara Shelley in one scene and actually knocked her down.

Horror of Dracula (1958; Hammer/Universal; U.K.) (also *Dracula*). D: Terence Fisher. P: Anthony Hinds. S: Jimmy Sangster. C: Jack Asher. Cast: Peter Cushing, Christopher Lee, Michael Gough, Melissa Stribling, Carol Marsh, John Van Eyssen, Valerie Gaunt. In one of the best vampire films ever made, Christopher Lee totally "revamped" the image of the famous Count Dracula, creating a very different character than the one found in Bela Lugosi's portrayal in the 1931 version of *Dracula*. ¶ "It only remains for me now to await the daylight hour when, with God's help, I will forever end this man's reign of terror." • Christopher Lee later said of his landmark interpretation of Dracula: "I always tried when playing Dracula to impress on the audience the majesty and dignity of this immortal character as well as the savagery, ferocity, and above all, great sadness." He went on to elaborate on the character: "This is truly a heroic figure; a man with great qualities of leadership, of intellect, with an enormous appeal for women; a man envied by other men for all these qualities — and above all, a human being" (from *The Films of Christopher Lee,* by Pohle and Hart). • This was Christopher Lee's first starring role (he had played the monster in *The Curse of Frankenstein,* 1957, but the role was a subordinate one and he was only fourth billed). Much like Bela Lugosi, it type-cast him as a horror star. Unlike Lugosi however, Lee was eventually able to shake this stigma and work in a diverse array of films. Incidentally, Lee was upstaged in billing by his friend and frequent co-star Peter Cushing, who was billed first. • *Dracula*'s startling blood-red eyes were achieved by using rose-tinted contact lenses with tiny red lines etched on the surface, making vision next to impossible for Christopher Lee. • During the scene in which Dracula throws the heroine into a grave-like hole, Lee, in an early take, dropped her body into the hole and then promptly lost his balance and fell in on top of her. Fortunately, neither was injured.

• The picture received some harsh criticism during its initial release as the media bandied about phrases like "cheap blood and gore." Lee (who had not seen the original Bela Lugosi *Dracula,* 1931) defended its realistic approach saying, "I was convinced that it was essential for the public to believe in what they saw. We were attempting to create the realistic and believable out of the improbable and the incredible." • Hammer big-wig Michael Carreras said in a *Famous Monsters of Filmland* #123 interview that, "Dracula had equally spectacular box office results (in comparison to *Curse of Frankenstein,* 1957). Christopher Lee emerged from monster makeup to chill audiences as the yellow-eyed Count Dracula. Again in color, the film was far more explicit than the original Bela Lugosi version with Dracula's victims actually enjoying rather than resisting his neck biting advances." • *Horror of Dracula* was Hammer's first Dracula picture, and it spawned a whole series of sequels (eight to be exact). Christopher Lee has stated that this film is far and away his favorite of the Hammer series: "Undoubtedly my favorite Dracula picture of those I made was the first one, for obvious reasons. It did follow the book. Since then I think the writers have problems trying to think up something new."

Kiss of the Vampire (1963; Hammer/Universal; U.K.) (also *Kiss of Evil*). D: Don Sharpe. P: Anthony Hinds. S: John Elder. C: Alan Hume. Cast: Clifford Evans, Edward De Souza, Noel Willman, Jennifer Daniel, Barry Warren, Brian Oulton, Noel Howlett, Jacquie Wallis. A honeymooning couple accept an invitation at the castle of Dr. Ravenna, the leader of a vampire cult. The wife falls under his vampiric spell and the husband enlists the aid of Professor Zimmer to rescue her and rid the land of the vampires' evil influence. ¶ "When the devil attacks a man or woman with this foul disease of the vampire, the unfortunate human being can do one of two things — either he can seek God through the church and pray for absolution, or he can persuade himself that his filthy perversion is some kind of new and wonderful experience to be shared by the favored few." • These vampires can move about during the daylight hours but still fear direct sunlight, since the sun is "the one thing they can't tolerate." • At the film's climax, Professor Zimmer uses magic to summon up a horde of vampire bats which attack and kill the vampires. In a unique and ironic twist on vampire lore, the vampires are slain by bats! The bat

Christopher Lee looks proudly on in this closeup from Dracula, Prince of Darkness *(1966), his second outing as the dreaded Count.*

rampage was orchestrated by special effects artist Les Bowie, who used rubber bats on wires plus a few model bats moved with nylon cords to create the effective bat attack on the vampire guests of Dr. Ravenna. • *Kiss of the Vampire* was significantly altered for the American television version, with many scenes deleted and several new ones inserted in their place. The climactic bat attack, for instance, was completely excised for this version (which was retitled *Kiss of Evil*). • Screenwriter John Elder is actually producer Anthony Hinds (using his *nom de plume*).

The Legend of the Seven Golden Vampires (1974; Hammer/Shaw Brothers; U.K./ Hong Kong) (also *The Seven Brothers Meet Dracula*). D: Roy Ward Baker. P: Don Houghton, Vee King Shaw. S: Don Houghton. C: John Wilcox, Roy Ford. Cast: Peter Cushing, David Chiang, Julie Ege, Shih Szu, Robin Stewart, Robert Hanna, John

Forbes-Robertson, Chan Shen, James Ma. Dracula possesses the body of a Chinese magician and aids the dreaded seven golden vampires in terrorizing the Chinese countryside. Professor Van Helsing and a family of six brothers and one sister (all martial arts experts) do battle with the vampires and their zombie slaves. ¶ "In Europe the vampire walks in dread of the crucifix, but here it would be the image of the Lord Buddha." • This is the world's *first* kung fu/vampire movie, and also the *last* vampire movie produced by Hammer Films. • Peter Cushing plays Professor Van Helsing for the sixth and final time in his career. • Dracula is initially played by John Forbes-Robertson before the vampire transforms into the Chinese version.

Lust for a Vampire (1971; Hammer/Continental; U.K.) (also *To Love a Vampire*). D: Jimmy Sangster. P: Harry Fine, Michael Style. S: Tudor Gates. C: David Muir. Cast: Ralph Bates, Barbara Jefford, Suzanna Leigh, Michael Johnson, Yutte Stensgaard, Helen Christie, Pippa Steel, David Healy, Harvey Hall, Mike Raven. In this sequel to *The Vampire Lovers,* a vampire named Mircalla Karnstein enrolls at a girls' finishing school where she seduces and vampirizes students and teachers alike. ¶ "They prey on young virgins, put a spell on them. Sometimes they woo them, slowly sucking their life away. Sometimes they kill quickly, one feast, one bite of their fangs!" • This is the second film in the "Carmilla" trilogy produced by Hammer, with the third being *Twins of Evil*. These films are ostensibly based on the vampire story *Carmilla,* by Sheridan Le Fanu. • "Mircalla" is actually an anagram for "Carmilla." *Lust for a Vampire* relies more heavily on nudity and sex than on horror, though this strategy backfires in one particularly inept scene in which Mircalla seduces a victim to the strains of a silly song titled "Strange Love." • Top-billed Ralph Bates considers this his worst film. Bates replaced Peter Cushing (in the role of the doomed schoolmaster) at the last moment when Cushing's wife fell ill. • Screenwriter-turned-director Jimmy Sangster had written both *Horror of Dracula* (1958) and *The Brides of Dracula* (1960), among many others for Hammer. • Screenwriter Tudor Gates penned both the other films in this series, *The Vampire Lovers* (1970) and *Twins of Evil* (1971).

The Satanic Rites of Dracula (1973; Hammer/Dynamite Entertainment; U.K.) (also *Count Dracula and His Vampiric Bride*). D: Alan Gibson. P: Roy Skeggs. S: Don Houghton. C: Brian Probyn. Cast: Christopher Lee, Peter Cushing, Michael Coles, William Franklyn, Freddie Jones, Joanna Lumley. Dracula takes on the cover persona of a reclusive billionaire named D. D. Denham (which star Christopher Lee described as "a combination of Dr. No and Howard Hughes") in a plot to unleash a new virulent strain of bubonic plague throughout the world. Peter Cushing plays a descendant of Dr. Van Helsing who thwarts the vampire's destructive plans. • *Dracula is Dead and Well and Living in London* was the film's shooting title. • *The Satanic Rites of Dracula* was screened for Warner Bros. in 1975 but they failed to pick it up and the film was not shown in the United States until three years later when Dynamite Entertainment released it under the title *Count Dracula and His Vampire Bride*. • Dracula is finally killed by becoming entangled in a hawthorn bush, whose holy thorns prick the vampire to death (Christ's crown of thorns was made from a hawthorn bush). • This was the seventh and last Hammer film to feature Christopher Lee as Dracula. After it was completed, Lee swore he would never play the part of Count Dracula again.

Scars of Dracula (1970; Hammer-EMI/American Continental; U.K.) D: Roy Ward Baker. P: Aida Young. S: John Elder (Anthony Hinds). C: Moray Grant. Cast: Christopher Lee, Dennis Waterman, Jenny Hanley, Christopher Matthews, Patrick Troughton, Michael Gwynn, Michael Ripper, Wendy Hamilton, Anoushka Hempel. A young rake stumbles into Dracula's castle and pays the price. The young man's brother and fiancée come searcing for him and find a hospitable host in the form of Count Dracula. Soon, however, the count reveals his true nature. ¶ "What we shall be facing in a few hours is not a man. He is evil, he is the embodiment of all that is evil, he is the very Devil himself." • At the climax, Dracula is struck by lightning and sent toppling off the castle parapets in flames just as he's about to hurl a metal spear at the hero (divine intervention perhaps?). • Harking back to Bram Stoker's original novel, one striking scene has Dracula crawling down the sheer outer wall of his castle face downward, like a huge lizard. • Christopher Lee, in *The Films of Christopher Lee,* by Pohle and Hart, called this "the weakest and most unconvincing of the 'Dracula' stories. Probably the poorest of the whole lot." • Lee, the most prolific screen Dracula of all time, surpassed even himself by playing

This closeup of Christopher Lee from Taste the Blood of Dracula *(1970) reveals the (by all accounts, painful) contacts lenses worn to create Dracula's chilling blood-red eyes.*

Dracula in *three* different films in *one* year (a record)—in this film, *Taste the Blood of Dracula* (another Hammer entry), and *Count Dracula.* • *Scars of Dracula,* the fifth Lee/Dracula movie from Hammer, is the follow-up film to *Taste the Blood of Dracula.* Next in the series is *Dracula A.D. 1972.*

Taste the Blood of Dracula (1970; Hammer/Warner–Seven Arts; U.K.) D: Peter: Sasdy. P: Aida Young. S: John Elder (An-

thony Hinds). C: Arthur Grant. Cast: Christopher Lee, Geoffrey Keen, Peter Sallis, John Carson, Linda Hayden, Isla Blair, Martin Jarvis, Ralph Bates, Martha Hargood. Four Victorian "gentlemen" out looking for a good time find more than they bargained for when one of them invokes a ritual to revive Count Dracula. Terrified by these proceedings, the other three beat the man to death, and Dracula vows vengeance upon them. The count proceeds to vampirize their daughters, and commands the girls to kill their own fathers. • Production on *Taste the Blood of Dracula* began while *The Private Life of Sherlock Holmes* was still finishing up, making it a bit hectic for star Christopher Lee who played Sherlock's brother (Mycroft Holmes) in the latter. • This was Peter Sasdy's directorial debut. He went on to direct *Countess Dracula* (1970), a film that, despite its title, is neither a Dracula film nor even a vampire film, but a re-telling of the Elizabeth Bathory legend.

Twins of Evil (1971; Hammer/Universal; U.K.) D: John Hough. P: Harry Fine, Michael Style. S: Tudor Gates. C: Dick Bush. Cast: Peter Cushing, Dennis Price, Mary Collinson, Madeleine Collinson, Isobel Black, Kathleen Byron, Damien Thomas, David Warbeck. Count Karnstein vampirizes one of two beautiful twins, who then changes places with her angelic sister to avoid being burned at the stake. ¶ "We are the undead. We walk the Earth, but we exist only in *hell*." • This is the third and final entry in Hammer's "Carmilla Karnstein" series; the first two being *The Vampire Lovers* (1970) and *Lust for a Vampire* (1971). • Peter Cushing, while not exactly his usual Van Helsing character, again plays the steadfast opponent of the undead in the form of the puritanical witchhunting uncle of the twins. Cushing also played the vampire killer in the first film of this series, *The Vampire Lovers*. • The title twins were played by *Playboy* magazine's first twin playmates, Mary and Madeline Collinson. • *Twins of Evil* was originally to be called *Virgin Vampires* before the title was changed to the current (and less exploitative) one.

Vampire Circus (1972; Hammer/20th Century-Fox; U.K.) D: Robert Young. P: Wilbur Stark. S: Judson Kinberg. C: Moray Grant. Cast: Adrienne Corri, Thorley Walters, John Moulder-Brown, Anthony Corlan, Lawrence Payne, Lynne Frederick, Richard Owens, Domini Blythe, Elisabeth Seal. The mysterious "Circus of the Night" comes to a small Serbian village, the site of a vampire slaying many years ago. The visiting circus is run by vampires, relations of the slain bloodsucker, who have come seeking revenge on the villagers and intend to resurrect their slain brethren. ¶ "One lust feeds the other"—a line indicative of Hammer's inceasing mixing of sex with their blood. • *Vampire Circus* features a vampire that can turn not only into a bat, but a panther as well (a very handy talent in a circus). • *Vampire Circus* was originally released on a double bill with *Countess Dracula*. • David Prowse, who plays the circus strong man and human servant to the vampires, is best known for playing Darth Vader in the *Star Wars* trilogy.

The Vampire Lovers (1970; Hammer/AIP; U.K.) D: Roy Ward Baker. P: Harry Fine, Michael Style. S: Tudor Gates. C: Moray Grant. Cast: Ingrid Pitt, Pippa Steele, Madeline Smith, Peter Cushing, George Cole, Dawn Addams, Kate O'Mara, Douglas Wilmer, Ferdy Mayne, Harvey Hall. A beautiful vampiress named Carmilla Karnstein invades the homes of noble families in order to seduce and drain their daughters. ¶ "This ruined castle, where I lay in wait, had once been the home of the Karnstein family. And at certain times their evil spirits thrust out from their mouldering tombs and took a kind of human shape to roam the countryside and seek the victims to satisfy their need, their *passion,* their thirst ... for *blood.*" • This is the first film in Hammer's "Karnstein" trilogy derived from Sheridan Le Fanu's vampire tale *Carmilla.* The subsequent entries are *Lust for a Vampire* and *Twins of Evil* (both 1971). The producing team of Harry Fine and Michael Style produced all three films. • The lead bloodsucker, a lesbian vampire, goes by three different aliases over the course of the film—Mircalla, Carmilla, and Marcella. • This was Hammer's first horror film containing nudity, starting a trend that continued throughout the company's remaining productions. • Vampiress Ingrid Pitt encountered plenty of blood in another Hammer film, *Countess Dracula,* made later the same year. As the title character (though her name was not really Countess Dracula, it was Countess Bathory), she wasn't a vampire in the traditional sense; instead of drinking the blood of young girls, she bathed in it to achieve eternal youth.

Other Vampires

Atom Age Vampire (1961) (see MAD SCIENTISTS). A doctor attempts to restore the scarred face of the woman he loves by killing women to remove their glands. He uses a serum which transforms him into a pasty-faced monster, allowing him to acquire his "materials" without being recognized. Despite the title, no vampires appear.

Beast of Morocco (1966; Associated British Pathé/Schoenfeld Films; U.K.) (also *The Hand of Night*). D: Frederic Goode. P: Harry Field. S: Bruce Stewart. C: William Jordan. Cast: William Sylvester, Diane Clare, William Dexter, Alizia Gur, Edward Underdown, Terence de Marney. In Northern Africa, an architect running away from his tragic memories is pursued by a mysterious young woman, a fourteenth century princess who was buried alive and now stalks the world as a vampire. She attempts to seduce the troubled man into her world of darkness. ¶ "The choice is still as I told you in the beginning—between light and darkness—each must choose." • Actress Diane Clare, who plays the part of the hero's imperiled girlfriend, is said to be the great granddaughter of Buffalo Bill. Clare has also appeared in *Witchcraft* (1964) and *The Plague of the Zombies* (1966).

Beverly Hills Vamp (1988; American Independent/Austin Enterprises) D: Fred Olen Ray. P: Grant Austin Walden, Fred Olen Ray. S: Ernest D. Farino. C: Stephen Ashley Blake. Cast: Eddie Deezen, Tim Conway, Jr., Jay Richardson, Britt Ekland, Michelle Bauer, Robert Quarry, Dawn Wildsmith. In this broad vampire parody, Britt Ekland runs a Beverly Hills bordello populated by vampires. Three nerdish aspiring filmmakers come to Hollywood to seek their fortune and run afoul of this nest of vampire beauties. ¶ "Just remember, my son, a man hath no greater friend than one who's willing to jam a wooden stake through his heart ... really!" • Prolific low-budget director Fred Olen Ray (he has been called "the Roger Corman of the 80s") made an earlier vampire-type film, *The Tomb* (1985), which also featured actress Michelle Bauer as a bloodsucker. • Actress Dawn Wildsmith, cast as a producer's secretary who falls victim to the vampires, is Fred Olen Ray's ex-wife. • Robert Quarry, here playing a hip, script-writing priest on the side of good, was on the other side of the fangs nearly two decades earlier as *Count Yorga, Vampire* (1970).

Black Sabbath (1964) (see ANTHOLOGIES). In this film's last and best segment, titled "The Wurdulak," Boris Karloff plays a Balkan patriarch who becomes a vampire and must prey upon his own family. ¶ "They only drink the blood of those they love the best." • This is the only time Boris Karloff, the screen's consumate bogeyman, played a vampire.

Black Sunday (1960) (see WITCHES, WARLOCKS, AND CULTS) (also *Revenge of the Vampire*). Princess Asa is condemned to death as a witch. Two centuries later she and her servant rise from the dead and try to possess her descendant. In addition to being witches, they are also vampires. ¶ The body of Asa the witch is placed in the tomb of her ancestors, forevermore to be called by that foulest of names—*vampire.*" • Asa is resurrected by a few drops of blood falling upon her corpse.

Blacula (1972; AIP) D: William Crain. P: Joseph T. Naar. S: Joan Torres, Raymond Koenig. C: John M. Stevens. Cast: William Marshall, Denise Nichols, Vonetta McGee, Gordon Pinset, Thalmus Rasulala, Emily Yancy, Lance Taylor, Sr., Kitty Lester, Charles Macaulay. The African Prince Mamuwalde travels to Transylvania to meet with Count Dracula in an effort to halt the slave trade. Dracula turns him into a vampire, christens him "Blacula," and imprisons him in a tomb. Two centuries later, Blacula's coffin ends up in Los Angeles where the vampire finally gets to quench his thirst. ¶ "I curse you with my name. You will be ... Blacula, a vampire like myself! A living fiend!"—Count Dracula. • Though promoted as the first black horror film, *Blacula* was not even close—*Drums 'o' Voodoo* beat it by 38 years! *Blacula* did, however, feature the screen's first black vampire.

Blood and Roses (1960; Paramount; France/Italy) D: Roger Vadim. P: Raymond Eger. S: Roger Vadim, Claude Brule, Claude Martin, Roger Vailland. C: Claude Renoir. Cast: Mel Ferrer, Elsa Martinelli, Annette Vadim, Jacques-René Chauffard, Marc Allegret. A mysterious woman named Carmilla (a beautiful vampire) enters the lives of a well-to-do family in Rome and sets her sights on the bride-to-be. • *Blood and Roses* is based on Sheridan Le Fanu's novella, *Carmilla.* • Annette Vadim, who played the object of Carmilla's vampiric attention, was the wife of director Roger Vadim at the time.

Blood Bath (1966; AIP) (also *Track of the Vampire*). D: Jack Hill, Stephanie Rothman. P/S: Jack Hill. C: Alfred Taylor. Cast: William Campbell, Marissa Mathes, Lori Saunders, Sandra Knight, Jonathan Haze. An unstable artist living in modern-day Venice believes he is the reincarnation of his fifteenth century ancestor, a vampire who was burned at the stake. His dementia leads him to kill his models and paint portraits of their corpses. • Executive producer Roger Corman fired director Jack Hill halfway through the picture and replaced him with Stephanie Rothman, who was then given footage from a Yugoslavian vampire film and told to use it along with Hill's footage. • Gary Kurtz, who served as sound man on this film, later went on to bigger and better things, including producing the *Star Wars* trilogy.

The Blood Drinkers (1966; Hemisphere; Philippines) (also *The Vampire People*). D: Gerardo de Leon. P: Danilo Santiago. S: Cesar Amigo. C: Felip Sacdalan. Cast: Amalia Fuentes, Ronald Remy, Eddie Fernandez, Eva Montez, Celia Rodriguez. Marco is an aristocratic vampire whose lover is dying. He goes to her village to obtain the healthy heart of her twin sister. There he lords over the village with the help of his two assistants, a beautiful woman and a dwarf, until the local priest and villagers band together against him. ¶ From the ads: "The *Blood Drinkers* will sink their teeth into *anything* that *moves!*" • Gerardo de Leon also directed the small-scale but effective *Terror Is a Man* (1959), a reworking of *The Island of Dr. Moreau.* • As a promotional gimmick, audiences were given free packets of "Green Blood" (which usually ended up on the theater seats and floors).

Blood of Dracula (1957; AIP) D: Herbert L. Strock. P: Herman Cohen. S: Ralph Thornton. C: Monroe P. Askins. Cast: Sandra Harrison, Louise Lewis, Gail Ganley, Jerry Blaine, Malcolm Atterbury, Thomas B. Henry, Richard Devon. An unpopular bobbysoxer at a boarding school is transformed into a vampire by the sinister chemistry teacher. The transformations are achieved through the use of hypnotism and an amulet with occult powers. ¶ "I can release a destructive power in a human being that would make the split atom seem like a blessing." • Subtle promo: "In her eyes—desire! In her veins—the blood of a monster!" • *Blood of Dracula* completed producer Herman Cohen's "teenage trilogy" started with *I Was a Teenage Werewolf* and *I Was a Teenage Frankenstein* (both 1957). Perhaps a better title for this film would have been *I Was a Teenage Vampire.* • Actor Jerry Blaine sang the song "Puppy Love" (which he also wrote) before being attacked by the vampire.

The Blood of Nostradamus (1960; Estudios America/AIP-TV; Mexico) D: Frederick Curiel. P: Victor Parra. S: Charles Taboada, Alfred Ruanova, Frederick Curiel. C: Fernando Alvarez Garces. Cast: German Robles, Julio Aleman, Domingo Soler, Aurora Alvarado, Manuel Vergara. A vampire is the descendant of the great prophet Nostradamus in this south-of-the-border

cheapie culled from a 12-part serial. • Four features were created from this same serial and sold to American television. The other three are (in order): *The Curse of Nostradamus, Monster Demolisher,* and *Genii of Darkness* (all 1960). *The Blood of Nostradamus* is the fourth and final film in the series. • German Robles, who plays the vampire, is Mexico's answer to Bela Lugosi and Christopher Lee. Robles played aristocratic vampires in numerous features, including *The Vampire's Coffin* (1957), *The Castle of the Monsters* (1957), and the other three companion features to this one.

The Blood of the Vampire (1958; Tempean/Universal; U.K.) D: Henry Cass. P: Robert S. Baker, Monty Berman. S: Jimmy Sangster. C: Geoffrey Seaholm. Cast: Donald Wolfit, Vincent Ball, Barbara Shelley, Victor Maddern, William Devlin, Andrew Faulds, Bryan Coleman, John Le Mesurier, Milton Reid. The anemic Dr. Callistratus is a scientific vampire who runs an insane asylum. There he finds all the fresh blood he needs to keep himself rejuvenated. ¶ "Once a man sets foot in this place, he never leaves." • The team of Robert S. Baker and Monty Berman also produced *The Crawling Eye* (1958), *Jack the Ripper* (1959), and *Mania* (1960).

The Blood Spattered Bride (1974; Europix; Spain) (also *Bloody Fiancée*). D/S: Vincent Aranda. P: Antonio Perez Olea. C: Fernando Arribas. Cast: Simon Andreu, Maribel Martin, Alexandra Bastedo, Dean Selmier, Monserrat Julio, Angel Lombarte, Maria Rosa Rodriguez. In this unpleasant variation on Sheridan Le Fanu's *Camilla,* the story centers around a 200-year-old vampire-like murderess who ensnares and seduces a young bride. The vampire turns the newlywed against her husband and induces her to commit several gruesome murders of her own. • In the film's most striking scene, the vampire is given one of the strangest introductions in cinema history when the husband finds her on the beach, her body completely buried in the sand with only her breasts and a diving mask exposed. • At the film's climax, the husband finds his wife and the vampiress sleeping together in a coffin for two, which he promptly riddles with bullets. He then proceeds to cut out their hearts.

The Bloodsuckers (1971; Titan International/Chevron; U.K.) (also *Doctors Wear Scarlet; Incense for the Damned*). D: Michael Burrowes (Robert Hartford-Davies). P: Graham Harris. S: Julian More. C: Desmond Dickinson. Cast: Patrick Mower, Peter

Cushing, Patrick MacNee, Imogen Hassall, Alex Davion, Johnny Sekka, Madeline Hinde, Edward Woodward, David Lodge. An Oxford student is swept into the world of vampiric perversion when he falls under the spell of a Greek woman who practices vampirism as a sexual outlet. • *The Bloodsuckers* is based on the novel *Doctors Wear Scarlet* by Simone Raven. • Edward Woodward, featured in a supporting role here, later achieved fame in America by starring in the popular TV series "The Equalizer."

The Bloody Vampire (1961; AIP-TV; Mexico) D/S: Michael Morata. P: Rafael Perez Grouas. C: Raul Martinez Solares. Cast: Carlos Agosti, Begona Palacios, Erna Bauman, Raul Farrell, Bertha Moss, Antonio Raxel, Enrique Lucero. A Van Helsing-type named Count Cagliostro goes head to head with a vampire named Count Frankenhausen(!). • At one point, the professor claims that he has invented a new method for killing vampires, but we never get to see it used and nothing else is ever said about it. • This vampire transforms into a bat possessing the largest, funniest rabbit-like ears in cinema history. • Count Frankenhausen escapes in the end, only to turn up again in *Invasion of the Vampires* (1961).

The Body Beneath (1971; Nova International) D/P/S/C: Andy Milligan. Cast: Gavin Reed, Jackie Skarvellis, Richmond Ross, Berwick Kaler, Emma Jones, Susan Heard, Colin Gordon. One-man production crew, Andy Milligan, filmed this no-budget, muddled tale of Reverend Ford, the head of a vampire cult in modern England which dates back to 98 B.C. The evil vampires, who all reside at Highgate cemetery, are planning an exodus to America to obtain fresh blood and a new start. ¶ "We never drink ... wine at this hour—religious reasons." • The head vampire, Reverend Ford, makes it possible for himself to move about in the daylight by taking daily injections of blood intravenously (*why* this odd mixing of science and supernatural works is never explained). • Milligan fills in his movie with many homages to (and plagarisms of) the original *Dracula* (1931), including naming their home "Carfax Abbey," and giving the head fiend three vampire women to do his bidding, reminiscent of Dracula's three wives. In one scene, the hero discovers Ford is a vampire by seeing that he casts no reflection in his mirrored cigarette case—a scene lifted straight out of the original.

The Bowery Boys Meet the Monster (1954; Allied Artists) D: Edward Bernds. P: Ben Schwalb. S: Elwood Ulman, Edward

Bernds. C: Harry Neumann. Cast: Leo Gorcey, Huntz Hall, Lloyd Corrigan, Ellen Corby, John Dehner, Laura Mason. In another one of their juvenile features, the "boys" run afoul of a bizarre family which includes a female vampire (Laura Mason).

Caged Virgins (1971; Les Films ABC; France) (also *Crazed Vampire; Requiem for a Vampire; Virgins and Vampires*). D/S: Jean Rollin. P: Jean Rollin, Sam Selsky. C: Renan Polles. Cast: Marie-Pierre Castel, Mireille Dargent, Louise Dhour, Philippe Gaste, Dominique. Two women criminals running from the law end up at an old castle inhabited by vampires. ¶ Two young girls ... trapped with no escape! Their innocence violated beyond description—in an endless nightmare of terror"—lurid poster ad line. • This was low-budget director Jean Rollin's fourth erotic vampire film, the first three being *Queen of the Vampires* (1967), *The Nude Vampire* (1969), and *Sex and the Vampire* (1970). • Rollin went on to make many other horror films, often increasing the sexual content to include hard core sex scenes. Most were never released in the United States.

The Case of the Full Moon Murders (1971; Newport) (also *The Case of the Smiling Stiffs*). D/P: Sean Cunningham. S: But Talbot, Jerry Hayling. C: Gus Graham. Cast: Fred Lincoln, Ron Browne, Cathy Walker, Harry Reems, Shelia Stuart. A beautiful vampire who kills by oral sex is tracked down by two Dragnet-style detectives. • Originally, this was released as a hard-core feature (Harry Reems is an early porno star). • Producer/director Sean Cunningham later went on to direct the notorious *The Last House on the Left* (1972) and the series-starting *Friday the 13th* (1980).

Castle of the Monsters (1957; Producciones Sotomayor; Mexico) D: Julian Soler. P: Jesus Sotomayor. S: Fernando Galiana, Carlos Orellana. C: Victor Herrera. Cast: Antonio Espino, Evangelina Elizondo, German Robles, Carlos Orellana, Guillermo Orea. In a south-of-the-border version of an Abbott and Costello routine, two newlyweds run afoul of various monsters, including a vampire played by German Robles.

Cave of the Living Dead (1964; Trans-Lux; Yugoslavia/W. Germany) D: Akos von Ratony. P: Akos von Ratony, Richard Gordon (English version). S: C. von Rock. C: Hrvoj Saric. Cast: Adrian Hoven, Carl Moehner, Erika Remberg, Karin Field, Wolfgang Preiss, Emmerich Schrenck, John Kitzmiller, Vida Juvan, Stane Sever. An inspector comes to a small village to investigate the disappearance of seven girls. He discovers that the local professor is really a vampire who has turned the girls into the living dead and keeps them in a cave under his castle. • Male lead Adrian Hoven later went behind the camera to produce the sadistic exploitation films *Mark of the Devil* (1970) and *Mark of the Devil 2* (1972).

Condemned to Live (1935; Invincible Pictures Corp.) D: Frank R. Strayer. P: Maury M. Cohen. S: Karen DeWolfe. C: M. A. Anderson. Cast: Ralph Morgan, Pedro de Cordoba, Maxine Doyle, Russell Gleason, Mischa Auer, Lucy Beaumont, Carl Stockdale, Barbara Bedford. Unknown to all but his faithful servant, saintly Professor Paul Kristan (Ralph Morgan) becomes a vampire-like fiend at night, ripping out the throats of young girls and draining their blood. ¶ "These hideous monsters swoop down upon their victims in the night and fasten themselves to the throat and drink the blood." • The explanation given for his unholy condition is that his mother was attacked by a vampire bat while pregnant with him in Africa: "A monstrous bat had fastened to your mother's throat. They beat it off but the harm was already done. *You were born that night Paul — condemned to live.*" • The vampiric transformation is triggered by darkness. • When the benign professor learns the horrible truth about himself, he commits suicide by jumping off a cliff.

Count Yorga, Vampire (1970; AIP) D/S: Robert Kelljan. P: Michael Macready. C: Arch Archambault. Cast: Robert Quarry, Roger Perry, Donna Anders, Judith Lang, Michael Murphy, Michael Macready, Edward Walsh, Julie Conner, Paul Hansen, Marsha Jordan. In modern day Los Angeles, Count Yorga, a vampire, charms the local ladies and turns them into his devoted followers. • Originally planned as a sexploitation film, the filmmakers changed their minds at the last minute and *Count Yorga, Vampire* was turned into a PG-rated straight horror movie. It was quite successful and spawned a sequel the following year, *The Return of Count Yorga.* • Producer Michael Macready plays one of the two heroes in the film. Macready also enticed his veteran actor father, George Macready, into doing the film's narration. • The film was shot for a mere $64,000. By his own account, star Robert Quarry was paid only $1,229 (plus a $350 bonus when the movie became a financial hit).

Creatures of Evil (1970; Hemisphere; U.S./Philippines) (also *Curse of the Vam-*

pires). D: Gerardo de Leon. P: Amalia Muhlach. S: Ben Fello, Pierre L. Salas. C: Mike Accion. Cast: Amalia Fuentes, Eddie Garcia, Romeo Vasques, Mary Walter, Johnny Monteiro. A brother and sister return home to find their mother locked in the basement because she is a vampire. The brother is vampirized and spreads the evil throughout the family. • This is Gerardo de Leon's follow-up to *The Blood Drinkers* (1966).

Crypt of the Living Dead (1973; Coast Industries; U.S./Spain) (also *Hannah, Queen of the Vampires*). D: Ray Danton. P/S: Lou Shaw. C: Juan Gelpi. Cast: Andrew Prine, Mark Damon, Patty Sheppard, Teresa Gimpera, Ihsan Genik. An archeologist uncovers the tomb of "Gimpera," an undead woman buried alive in the thirteenth century, at a place appropriately called "Vampire Island." ¶ Advertising slogan: "She's 700 years old and still going strong!" • Actor-turned-director Ray Danton had previously directed another little-known vampire film, *The Deathmaster,* in 1972.

The Curse of Nostradamus (1960; Estudios America/AIP-TV; Mexico) D: Frederick Curiel. P: Victor Parra. S: Charles Taboada, Alfred Ruanova, Frederick Curiel. C: Fernando Alvarez Garces. Cast: German Robles, Julio Aleman, Domingo Soler, Aurora Alvarado, Manuel Vergara. The son of Nostradamus is a vampire who plans to build a cult dedicated to glorifying his father. To this end he attempts to blackmail a prominent professor into acknowledging the presence of vampires by committing a series of impossible crimes. ¶ "I don't think I've ever met anyone so completely strange" — the hero after meeting the vampire. • At the film's climax, the hero chases the vampire through the catacombs with a pistol loaded with *platinum* bullets (apparently silver wasn't good enough). • This is the first of four features made from a 12-part serial. The others are: *The Monster Demolisher, Genii of Darkness,* and *The Blood of Nostradamus* (all 1960).

The Curse of the Crying Woman (1961) (see WITCHES, WARLOCKS, AND CULTS). This tale of a family held under the curse of "the Wailing Witch," features a sorceress who exhibits several vampiric tendencies: She casts no reflection in mirrors; she has an affinity with bats; and she has a need to drink human blood. ¶ "You'll need blood to feed your new body, it's a strong craving you can't resist!"

Curse of the Undead (1959; Universal) D: Edward Dein. P: Joseph Gershenson. S:

Edward Dein, Mildred Dein. C: Ellis Carter. Cast: Eric Fleming, Michael Pate, Kathleen Crowley, John Hoyt, Bruce Gordon, Edward Binns. Set in the old west, a vampire gunslinger named Don Drago Robles comes to town and sets his fangs on the beautiful local ranch owner. • The vampire finally meets his end when he faces the local minister in a shootout. The vampire is impervious to ordinary lead bullets, but the minister cleverly carves a cross on his. • This was the screen's first vampire western.

Dance of the Damned (1988; Concorde/ New Horizons) D: Katt Shea Ruben. P: Andy Ruben. S: Katt Shea Ruben, Andy Ruben. Cast: Starr Andreeff, Cyril O'Reilly. A suicidal exotic dancer attracts a vampire. She strikes a bargain to expose him to the pleasures of fleshly love if in exchange, he will end her life. But her mood changes and they lock in a struggle of the living vs. the undead. ¶ Dancer: "Are you gay?" Vampire: "I'm not even human."

Dead Men Walk (1943; PRC) D: Sam Newfield. P: Sigmund Neufeld. S: Fred Myton. C: Jack Greenhalgh. Cast: George Zucco, Mary Carlisle, Nedrick Young, Dwight Frye, Fern Emmett, Robert Strange. George Zucco plays identical twins — one good, and the other an evil occultist. The good twin murders the bad to rid the world of his evil. Unfortunately, the matter does not end there, for the evil twin comes back as a vampire, seeking revenge on his brother and his brother's daughter. ¶ "You'll know that I am no intangible fiend from your imagination when you feel the weight of my hatred. Your life will be a torment. I'll strip you of everything you hold dear." • This was Dwight Frye's last horror film (he died the same year). Here, Frye once again is cast in the role of crazed henchman just as he was in *Dracula* (1931).

The Deathmaster (1972; AIP) D: Ray Danton. P: Fred Sadoff. S: R. L. Grove. C: Wilmer C. Butler. Cast: Robert Quarry, Bill Ewing, Brenda Dickson, John Fiedler, Betty Ann Rees. A vampire's coffin washes up on the shores of California and he becomes the undead Manson-like leader of a hippie cult. ¶ Ad-line: "Eyes like hot coals ... Fangs like Razors! The Deathmaster has escaped from his Grave!" • The vampire is played by Robert Quarry, fresh from his appearance as Count Yorga in *Count Yorga, Vampire* (1970) and *The Return of Count Yorga* (1971).

The Devil's Wedding Night (1973) (see BATHORY, ELIZABETH: THE BLOODY COUNTESS). A countess bathes in the blood of

young girls to stay young. She also has a servant who is your standard fanged vampire; and for some inexplicable reason, the countess herself is shown turning into a giant bat while making love.

Devils of Darkness (1965; Planet; U.K.) D: Lance Comfort. P: Tom Blakeley. S: Lyn Fairhurst. C: Reg Wyer. Cast: William Sylvester, Hubert Noel, Carole Gray, Tracey Reed, Diana Decker, Rona Anderson. A 380-year-old vampire named Count Sinistre heads up a devil cult which preys upon British vacationers at a small French village in Brittany. ¶ "I, Sinistre, leader of the living dead, summon you and others who follow, both near and afar, to pledge allegiance to the Devil of Darkness." • This is the first British vampire film with a contemporary setting (pre-dating Hammer's attempt to update vampirism to the twentieth century with *Dracula A.D. 1972* by seven years). • Hero William Sylvester (best remembered as Dr. Floyd in *2001: A Space Odyssey,* 1968) encountered another bloodsucker the following year in *Beast of Morocco* (1966).

Dinner with a Vampire (1988; Dania Films; Italy) D: Lamberto Bava. S: Dardano Sacchetti, Lamberto Bava. C: Gianfranco Transunto. Cast: George Hilton, Patrizia Pellegrino, Riccardo Rossi, Valeria Milillo, Yvonne Scio, Danielle Aldrovandi, Igor Zalewski, Roberto Pedicini, Letizia Ziaco, Stefano Sabelli, Isabel Russinova. Four young actors and actresses are chosen from an audition to spend a weekend at the castle of Karl Urich, a "world famous horror director." Urich is actually a 4,000-year-old vampire who is seeking a release from his ageless non-life. However, his vampiric nature will not allow him to take his own life ("his human part wants to die, but his vampiric instinct does not agree") so he brings the four to his castle, wanting them to kill him (or be killed *by* him in the process). ¶ "Kill me. Please kill me — before the night is over, before dawn. Otherwise I'll have to drink your blood and turn you into horrible undead monsters." • This vampire is unaffected by garlic, stakes through the heart, or crosses (he even wears a crucifix around his own neck — "for luck"). He also has strange supernatural powers which allow him, among other things, to cause a person's heart to burst from his body and fly into his outstretched hand. The only way to kill this undead fiend is to destroy a reel of film which was taken when a film crew accidentally released him from his tomb in the 1920s. ("The film ... is like the portrait of Dorian Gray — it represents the soul of Urich.")

Dr. Terror's Gallery of Horrors (1966) (see ANTHOLOGIES) (also *Return from the Past*). In one of the five segments of this no-budget anthology, Mitch Evans plays "Count Alucard," a vampire who ends up battling a werewolf.

Dr. Terror's House of Horrors (1965) (see ANTHOLOGIES). In the fourth story, Donald Sutherland brings a new wife home from France, only to discover that he has married a vampire. With the aid of his fellow doctor, he is able to dispatch his undead spouse. In a twist ending, it is revealed that his doctor friend is himself a vampire, and he lets Sutherland be led away by the police, charged with murdering his wife. ¶ "There's not room enough in this town for two doctors ... or two vampires!"

Dracula and Son (1979; Gaumont International/Universal; France) D: Eduard Molinaro. P: Alan Poire. S: Eduard Molinaro, Alan Godard, Jean-Marie Poire. C: Alan Levent. Cast: Christopher Lee, Bernard Menez, Marie-Hélène Breillat, Catherine Breillat, Jack Boudet, Geoffrey Carey, Robert Dalban, Mustapha Dali, Anna Gaël. An aristocratic vampire (*not* Dracula) and his foppish son are forced to flee their homeland when the communist government takes control of their ancestral castle. They wind up in Paris where they engage in all manner of comical misadventures. ¶ "According to a recent survey, one in three people is a vampire. Think of it, think of three of your closest friends; if they seem all right to you then *you're* the one"—introductory narration. • Though filmed in 1975, *Dracula and Son* was not released in the United States until four years later. • *Dracula and Son* was filmed in French and Christopher Lee, who can speak several languages fluently, spoke his own dialogue. In fact he later boasted, "I am almost the only non–French actor the French will accept in a French film without dubbing the voice." • When the movie was finally dubbed into English, it was mercilessly butchered and much of Christopher Lee's own English dialogue (which the actor had initially dubbed himself) was dubbed over by another actor doing an atrocious Bela Lugosi impersonation.

Erotikill (1973; General Films/Eurocine; France/Belgium) (also *The Loves of Irena; Jacula, the Bare-Breasted Countess*). D: J. P. Johnson (Jesus Franco). P: Marius Lesoeur, Pierre Querut. S: P. Belair (Jesus Franco), Gerard Brissaud. C: Joan Vincent. Cast: Lina Romay, Jack Taylor, Alice Arno, Monica Swin, Jess Franck (Jesus Franco), Luis BarBoo. Countess Irina Karl-stein, a mute vampire who drains her victims sexually as well as bloodily, falls in love with a young poet. He gives himself freely to her, and in the end she commits suicide in a bathtub. ¶ "He was killed by a mouth. He was bitten, in the middle of an orgasm, and the vampire sucked his semen and his life away." • Jesus Franco made three different versions of this film—as a straight horror film titled *La Comtesse Noire* (unreleased in English in this version), as a horror/sex film titled *Erotikill,* and as a hardcore version which downplays the horror element titled *Les Avaleuses* (retitled *The Loves of Irena* for the English language release). • As well as directing, Franco also appears in the film as a doctor who uncovers the truth about the vampire. • Lina Romay, who plays the sexually active vampire, is Franco's wife.

Face of Marble (1946) (see MAD SCIENTISTS). A scientist devises a way to revive a person from the dead. The only problem is that the person can occasionally walk through walls and sometimes drinks blood. Scientist John Carradine first applies the technique to his dog, then to his wife, with tragic results in both cases. • The vampire aspect is played down in the film, and the blood-drinking is tossed out just as an aside.

Fangs of the Living Dead (1968; Europix; Spain/Italy) (also *Malenka, the Vampire*). D/S: Armando de Ossorio. P: Aubrey Ambert, Rossana Yanni. C: Fulvio Testi. Cast: Anita Ekberg, Julian Ugarte, John Hamilton, Diana Lorys, Audrey Ambert, Maria Luisa de Benedictus, Rossana Yanni, Carlos Casaravilla, Paul Müller. Anita Ekberg plays a young woman who inherits a castle, complete with vampiric uncle. He tries to convince her that she is the reincarnation of her ancestor who was burned as a witch. It is finally revealed that her uncle staged the vampiric killings and is simply trying to drive her mad. But at the film's end, the vampire turns to bones with the rays of the sun, so his true nature remains ambiguous.

The Fearless Vampire Killers (1967; MGM; U.K.) (also *Dance of the Vampires*). D: Roman Polanski. P: Gene Gutowski. S: Gerald Brach, Roman Polanski. C: Douglas Slocombe. Cast: Jack MacGowran, Roman Polanski, Sharon Tate, Alfie Bass, Jessie Robins, Ferdy Mayne, Ian Quarrier, Terry Downes, Fiona Lewis, Ronald Lacey. Professor Ambrosius and his bumbling student Alfred are on a mission to seek out and destroy the plague of the undead. They discover Count von Krolock and his vampire followers and narrowly escape with their lives ... or do they? ¶ From the preview trailer: "Two men on a vampire hunt. Simple? *They* certainly are!" • This well-liked parody carries a two-part title: *The Fearless Vampire Killers ... or Pardon Me But Your Teeth Are in My Neck.* • The *Fearless Vampire Killers* features two screen firsts—a Jewish vampire and a homosexual vampire. • As well as directing, Roman Polanski starred in the film as Alfred, the timid assistant vampire hunter. • Female lead Sharon Tate was married to director Roman Polanski at the time. Tragically, two years after the film's completion she was brutally murdered by the Manson Family. • When the production arrived in the Italian Alps to shoot the film's snowy castle scenes, they discovered that all the snow had melted away and so had to return to London and construct their castle set on an MGM lot at Boreham Wood. The resulting complication shifted the shooting schedule from three to seven months. • In the film's credits, Ludwig von Krankheit was credited for the fangs. Krankheit is German for "sickness."

The Female Butcher (1972) (see BATHORY, ELIZABETH: THE BLOODY COUNTESS). A Countess bathes in the blood of virgins to keep eternally young, aided by her husband, a vampire.

Fright Night (1985; Columbia) D/S: Tom Holland. P: Herb Jaffe. C: Jan Kiesser. Cast: Chris Sarandon, William Ragsdale, Amanda Bearse, Roddy McDowall, Stephen Geoffreys, Jonathan Stark, Dorothy Rielding, Art J. Evans. Charlie is your typical high school student. Peter Vincent is your typical hammy has-been horror actor (now relegated to hosting a local station's late-night horror program called "Fright Night"). Stylish, contemporary Jerry Dandridge is *not* your typical vampire. He moves in next door to Charlie, who enlists the reluctant aid of former movie vampire-killer Peter Vincent in a battle against the deadly vampire. ¶ "Welcome to 'Fright Night'—for *real.*" • Chris Sarandon plays the charming vampire with a sense of humor, one who is fond of whistling "Strangers in the Night" for example. Though sprinkled with humor, this film is *not* a comedy, and takes its subject matter seriously. • Though vampires are often shown changing into bats, this is one of the few vampire films to take advantage of, and show fully, a vampire's ability to transform into a wolf. • An inferior sequel, *Fright Night Part 2,* was made in 1988.

Fright Night Part 2 (1988; The Vista Organization) D: Tommy Lee Wallace. P: Herb Jaffe, Mort Engelberg. S: Tim Metcalfe, Miguel Tejada-Flores, Tommy Lee Wallace. Cast: Roddy McDowall, William Ragsdale, Traci Lin, Julie Carmen. Regine Dandridge, sister of vampire Jerry Dandridge from the original *Fright Night* and herself a vampire, shows up to take revenge upon her brother's killers—college student Charlie Brewster and horror-movie host Peter Vincent. ¶ "The suckers are back"—ad line. • Roddy McDowall as Peter Vincent and William Ragsdale as Charlie Brewster both reprise their roles from the first film. • Stephen Geoffreys was originally scheduled to continue his role of "Evil Ed" from the original, but bowed out at the last minute to star in *976-Evil* (1989). • Inside the hero's home can be seen a variety of B-movie posters including one from Roger Corman's 1958 movie, *Teenage Caveman.*

Ganja and Hess (1973; Kelly Jordan Enterprises) (also *Blood Couple; Double Possession*). D/S: Bill Gunn. P: Chiz Schultz. C: James E. Hinton. Cast: Duane Jones, Marlene Clark, Bill Gunn, Sam Waymon, Leonard Jackson. An anthropologist studying an ancient African cult is stabbed with a ceremonial dagger and infected with a form of vampirism in this, the screen's second black vampire film (*Blacula* being the first). • Lead actor Duane Jones is more popularly known as the black zombie-killing hero in the cult classic *Night of the Living Dead* (1968).

Genii of Darkness (1960; Estudios America/AIP-TV; Mexico) D: Frederick Curiel. P: Victor Parra. S: Charles Taboada, Alfred Ruanova, Frederick Curiel. C: Fernando Alvarez Garces. Cast: German Robles, Julio Aleman, Domingo Soler, Aurora Alvarado, Manuel Vergara. In this third installment in the "Son of Nostradamus" series generated from a 12-part Mexican serial, the vampiric ancestor of Nostradamus falls in love.

Goliath and the Vampires (1964) (see SWORD AND SORCERY) (also *The Vampires*). In this Italian sword and sorcery flick, the hero Maciste (dubbed Goliath in English prints) must face off against a vampire and his army of human robots.

Grave of the Vampire (1972; Entertainment Pyramid) (also *Seed of Terror*). D: John Hayes. P: Daniel Cady. S: John Hayes, David Chase. C: Paul Hipp. Cast: William Smith, Michael Pataki, Kitty Vallacher, Lyn Peters, Duane Holden. A vampire rapes a woman in a cemetery. She gives birth to a sickly baby who drinks blood as well as milk. Eventually the mother dies from loss of blood and the baby grows up

The young vampire "Evil Ed" (Stephen Geoffreys) sports a burn mark on his forehead, the result of a run-in with a cross in Fright Night *(1985).*

apparently normal. Now a man, he sets out to find and kill his vampire father, but blood is thicker than water, and his vampiric urges win out. • Michael Pataki, who plays the vampiric father, was on the other end of the stake when he faced *Dracula's Dog* in 1978.

Graveyard Shift (1986; Cinema Ventures; Canada) D/S: Gerard Ciccoritti. P: Michael Bockner. C: Robert Bergman. Cast: Silvio Oliviero, Helen Papas, Cliff Stoker. A vampire works a night job (naturally) driving a cab for the Black Cat Cab Company. It is also a great way to meet potential victims. He eventually bites and falls in love with a woman who is dying of an incurable disease, and soon it becomes a struggle between a vampire hunter and the vampire horde over the soul of the heroine. ¶ "Lots of people work the graveyard shift — cops, firemen, waitresses, cab drivers . . . and vampires"— ad line. • Writer/director Gerard Ciccoritti related the genesis of *Graveyard Shift* in a *Fangoria* #69 interview: "There was a Bruce Springsteen video on, and while the clip was playing, my mind just wandered. I had an image of a down-home, middle- American guy wearing a checkered shirt with the sleeves rolled up, nailing something together. And as this song ended, in my daydream I had a zoom out, and I saw what he was building: a coffin. It was his own coffin, and he was a vampire. So the thought struck me — how about a vampire as a working stiff?" • When shown in Paris, the film carried the title of *Central Park Driver* (perhaps revealing the French perception of American drivers?). • *Graveyard Shift* was filmed on the streets of Toronto, Canada. • A sequel was made in 1988 called *The Understudy: Graveyard Shift 2,* again written and directed by Gerard Ciccoritti.

The Horrible Sexy Vampire (1973; Cinefilms/Paragon; Spain) D/S: Jim Delavena (José Luis Madrid). P: Al Peppard (Edmondo Amanti). C: Francis Madur (Francisco Madurga). Waldemar Wohlfahrt, Patricia Loran, Luis Induñi, Adela Tauler, Joe Camroy. A young man and his lover return to the family estate to claim his inheritance, only to encounter a vampire ancestor who likes to prey on naked women in this horror nudie from Spain.

House of Dark Shadows (1970; MGM) D/P: Dan Curtis. S: Sam Hall, Gordon Russell. C: Arthur Ornitz. Cast: Jonathan Frid, Joan Bennett, Roger Davis, Grayson Hall, Kathryn Leigh Scott, Nancy Barrett, John Karlen, Thayer David, Louis Edmonds, Donald Brice. Barnabas Collins, a 150-year-old vampire, is released from his coffin. Posing as his own descendant, he insinuates himself into the powerful Collins family. • This is a feature version of the popular daytime soap opera "Dark Shadows" which ran from 1966 to 1970. Much of that series' plot is condensed into this 90-minute movie, and many of the same actors reprise their roles. • At the film's end, the vampire is shot with a crossbow — the first time such a weapon had been used against the undead. One would have expected that the numerous vampire hunters throughout film history would have thought of using this effective weapon sooner than this. • Producer/director Dan Curtis was the TV series' creator and directed many of

the early TV episodes. • A second "Dark Shadows" film was made the following year, though it dealt with ghosts (another plot line from the TV series) rather than vampires.

The House That Dripped Blood (1971) (see ANTHOLOGIES). In the final story, a rather whimsical one entitled "The Cloak," Jon Pertwee plays a horror actor who dons a special cape which transforms him into a real vampire. • Actress Ingrid Pitt is also turned into a vampire during this segment, a role she was well versed in from starring in *The Vampire Lovers* the previous year.

The Hunger (1983; MGM/United Artists) D: Tony Scott. P: Richard A. Shepard. S: Ivan Davis, Michael Thomas. C: Stephen Goldblatt, Tom Mangravite. Cast: Catherine Deneuve, Susan Sarandon, David Bowie, Cliff de Young, Beth Ehlers, Dan Hedaya, Ann Magnusson, Rufus Collins, Suzanne Bertish, James Aubrey. Catherine Deneuve plays a vampire from ancient Egypt in modern-day New York whose paramour (David Bowie) suddenly begins to age rapidly. Susan Sarandon is an age researcher who is drawn into the vampires' web of blood and death and immortality. ¶ "You'll be back. When the hunger hurts so much it knows no reason, *then* you'll have to feed." • These thoroughly contemporary vampires are very comfortable in today's society. They procure their victims from night clubs and bars. They are not affected by sunlight and they do not possess fangs. Instead, they slash their victims with a small ceremonial knife and then drink their blood from the open wound. They also "sleep six hours out of 24 and feed one day in seven." • Director Tony Scott is brother of Ridley Scott (the director of *Alien,* 1979).

Invasion of the Vampires (1961; Tele Talia Films/K. Gordon Murray Productions; Mexico) D/S: Miguel Morayta. P: Rafael Perez Grovas. C: Raul Martinez. Cast: Erna Martha Bauman, Rafael del Rio, Carlos Agosti, Tito Junco, Fernando Soto, Berta Moss, David Reynoso, Enrique Garcia Alvarez. A professor of the occult faces off against a vampire named Count "Frankenhausen"(!) and his vampiric hordes. • In an original twist, the professor distills an acid from black garlic, and uses it to combat the vampires. • Count Frankenhausen was also featured in *The Bloody Vampire,* released earlier this same year. At the close of *Invasion of the Vampires,* the count is killed when he is pinned to the wall in bat form.

Isle of the Dead (1945; RKO) D: Mark Robson. P: Val Lewton. S: Ardel Wray, Jesef Mischel. C: Jack MacKenzie. Cast:

Boris Karloff, Ellen Drew, Marc Cramer, Katherine Emery, Helene Thimig, Alan Napier, Jason Robards, Sr. During the Balkan War, a group of people are isolated on a Greek island by plague. As they are struck down one by one, a belief starts that it is the work of a "vorvoloka," a type of vampire that sucks the life force from its victims. • During the 1940s, while Universal was turning out their action-oriented monster rallies, producer Val Lewton took a different approach and made a series of low-key intelligent horror films like this one. His other films include *Cat People* (1942), *I Walked with a Zombie* (1943), and *The Body Snatcher* (1945). • During production, increasing back problems caused star Boris Karloff to be confined to a wheelchair between takes. Finally, it forced him to enter the hospital and production had to be shut down while Karloff recuperated, not to be resumed again for four months. • Director Mark Robson also directed *Ghost Ship* (1943) and *Bedlam* (1946; again with Karloff) for producer Val Lewton.

The Jitters (1989; Skouras Pictures) D/P: John M. Fasano. S: Jeff McKay, Sonoko Kondo. C: Paul Mitchnick. Cast: Sal Viviano, Marilyn Tokuda, James Hong, Frank Dietz, Handy Atmadja, John Quincy Lee, Doug Silberstein. In Chinatown, a series of mysterious deaths are the result of Chinese vampires called "Gyonsi." • These nearly mindless vampires have pointy ears and hop about like some bizarre bloodthirsty jackrabbit. To combat them, a piece of paper with sacred Chinese characters written on it must be pasted to their forehead, making them inactive.

Jonathan (1970; Iduna Film/New Yorker; W. Germany) D/S: Hans W. Geissendoerfer. P: Ullrich Steffen. C: Robbi Mueller. Cast: Juergen Jung, Paul Albert Krumm, Hertha von Walter, Oscar von Schab, Hansdieter Jendreyko, Eleonore Schminke. A decadent Count feeds off the local peasants at his seaside castle. Jonathan is sent to rouse the inhabitants against the vampires in this political allegory against fascism. • After initial screenings, additional scenes of sex and violence were added to the film to make it more marketable.

The Lair of the White Worm (1988) (see SNAKES). In northern England, vampiric snake-people worship and offer up human sacrifices to a legendary giant snake-creature. ¶ "When the venom attacks the nervous system, the victim appears to be afflicted with a form of vampirism." • When aroused, these reptilian vampires sprout snake-like fangs, whose bite transforms the victim into a creature like themselves. Also, their saliva causes hallucinations when touched. • At one point, the Scottish hero uses the bagpipes to charm the vampire/snake-people, just as a snake charmer would use his flute.

Lake of Dracula (1972; Toho; Japan) (also *Bloodthirsty Eyes; Lake of Death; Japula*). D: Michio Yamamoto. P: Fumio Tanaka. S: Ei Ogawa, Katsu Takeura. C: Rokuro Nishigaki. Cast: Mori Kishida, Midori Fujita, Osahide Takahashi, Sanae Emi. A concealed castle on the shores of a lake deep in a forest houses a vampire—*not* Dracula however. The undead creature breaks free of his chained coffin and terrorizes the surrounding countryside. ¶ "I know I am going to die soon. The vampire sucks my blood every night and I do not have much strength left.... The worst thing about this is the sad fact that my *son* is the vampire." • This was the first full-fledged vampire movie produced in Japan. • Though filmed in 1971, it was not released in the United States until 1972.

The Last Man on Earth (1964) (see ZOMBIES). Due to a plague, almost the entire population of the Earth is transformed into near-mindless ghouls who possess certain vampiric characteristics. • Though they cannot stand sunlight, garlic, or their own reflection, these creatures are not true vampires, for they do not drink blood; they merely possess a mindless instinct to kill. The hero does employ the traditional stake through the heart to dispatch them, however.

Lemora, the Lady Dracula (1974; Media Cinema) (also *The Legendary Curse of Lemora; Lemora, a Child's Tale of the Supernatural*). D: Richard Blackburn. P: Robert Fern. S: Richard Blackburn, Robert Fern. C: Robert Caramico. Cast: Lesley Gilb, Cheryl Smith, William Whitton, Steve Johnson, Hy Pyke, Maxine Ballantyne. In Georgia in the 1920s, a female vampire tricks a young girl into coming to her home, with the intention of initiating her into the ways of vampirism. ¶ "She was holy and divine and I wish that girl was mine/ Her eyes they were the bluest of them all/ But on that dark black day when she left and walked away/ I knew she was a headin' for a fall"— the film's country-western theme song. • Director/co-screenwriter Richard Blackburn appears in the film as a preacher. • *Lemora* was condemned by the Catholic Film Board.

Leonor (1975; Goya Films/Arcadie Productions/Transeuropa Films; Spain/France/

Italy) D: Juan Buñuel. S: Juan Buñuel, Roberto Bodegas, Bernardino Zapponi. C: Luciano Tovoli. Cast: Michel Piccoli, Liv Ullmann, Ornella Muti, Antonio Ferrandis, José Ma Prada, Angel de Pozo. A fourteenth century knight, grieving over the death of his wife, makes a pact with the devil to bring her back to life. She comes back, but as a vampire who also carries the plague. • Director/co-writer Juan Buñuel is the son of famous filmmaker Luis Buñuel.

Let's Scare Jessica to Death (1971; Paramount) D: John Hancock. P: Charles B. Moss, Jr., William Badalto. S: Norman Jonas, Ralph Rose. C: Bob Baldwin. Cast: Zohra Lampert, Barton Heyman, Kevin O'Connor, Gretchen Corbett, Alan Manson, Mariclare Costello. A woman, just released from a mental hospital, moves to a farm in Connecticut. A female vampire arrives and soon the unhinged woman must face an entire countryside seemingly full of the undead. • These are not your typical vampires, for they can walk about in the daylight and do not seem to have any further supernatural powers. They do, however, still drink blood.

Lifeforce (1985) (see ALIENS — INVADERS ON EARTH: THE 80s AND BEYOND). Humanoid aliens are discovered in the tail of Halley's Comet by exploratory astronauts. Brought back to Earth, the three vampiric aliens live by draining the life force from their victims, leaving them a dried-up husk (which, incidentally, rises a few hours later as a mindless zombie).

London After Midnight (1927) D/P: Tod Browning. S: Waldemar Young. C: Merritt B. Gerstad. Cast: Lon Chaney, Marceline Day, Henry B. Walthall, Percy Williams, Conrad Nagel, Polly Moran, Edna Tichenor, Claude King. This "lost film" (no prints seem to have survived the ravages of time) stars Lon Chaney as an inspector who poses as a vampire to catch a murderer. ¶ "This is the crowning indignity! I think that hereafter I shall be invisible, it's really less complicated that way." • All that is apparently left of the film are some (admittedly mouthwatering) stills, particularly of Chaney in vampire makeup wearing a top hat and sporting a wicked set of sharp teeth. • Browning remade his own film in 1935 as *Mark of the Vampire.* The single Chaney role in the original seems to have been split into two parts for the remake — that of the inspector (Lionel Barrymore) and the part of an actor playing the vampire (Bela Lugosi). In *London,* Chaney, Sr., plays both Dr. Yates and the "vampire."

The Lost Boys (1987; Warner Bros.) D: Joel Schumacher. P: Harvey Bernhard. S: Janice Fischer, James Jeremias. C: Michael Chapman. Cast: Corey Feldman, Jami Gertz, Corey Haim, Edward Herrmann, Barnard Hughes, Jason Patrick, Kiefer Sutherland, Dianne Wiest. In the small town of Santa Carla, two brothers are drawn into the world of the young vampires living on the fringe of this California community. ¶ "One thing about livin' in Santa Carla I never could stomach — all the damn vampires." • In a particularly novel vampire death scene, an arrow is shot through a vampire and pierces some hi-fi equipment behind him, causing him to explode ("death by stereo," as the adolescent hero puts it). • Richard Donner was originally set to direct, but was offered *Lethal Weapon* and chose to pursue that instead.

The Magic Sword (1962) (see SWORD AND SORCERY). A group of intrepid knights set out to rescue a princess from the evil wizard Lodac. Along the way they must face Lodac's "Seven Challenges," one of which is an enticing maiden who suddenly transforms into a hideous vampire hag and puts the bite on one of the knights.

Mama Dracula (1980) (see BATHORY, ELIZABETH: THE BLOODY COUNTESS). Louise Fletcher plays "Countess Dracula" — not a vampire, but a woman who bathes in the blood of virgins to stay young. She has twin sons, however, who display vampiric tendencies (such as sprouting fangs and sucking blood). They seem unaffected by any of the other trappings of vampirism, however.

Mark of the Vampire (1935; MGM) D: Tod Browning. P: E. J. Mannix. S: Guy Endore, Bernard Schubert. C: James Wong Howe. Cast: Bela Lugosi, Lionel Barrymore, Elizabeth Allan, Jean Hersholt, Lionel Atwill, Carol Borland, Donald Meek. An inspector investigating a mysterious murder uncovers what appears to be a pair of vampires (Bela Lugosi and Carol Borland). It turns out that the vampires are merely actors hired by the inspector to flush out the murderer. ¶ "Did you watch me, I was greater than any *real* vampire!" — Bela Lugosi at the film's end. • Bela Lugosi, playing a vampire (sort of) for the first time since *Dracula* (1931), was given no dialogue (except for a few gag lines at the end like the one cited above). • Curiously, instead of the traditional garlic, a fictitious herb called "bat thorn" was used as protection against vampires. • Actress Carol Borland had appeared with Bela Lugosi in the stage production of *Dracula* as his victim before co-starring as his accomplice in the film. • This was director Tod Browning's "comeback" film, after the violent outrage generated over his *Freaks* (1932) had quieted down. • *Mark of the Vampire* was originally to be titled *Vampires of Prague.*

The Mark of the Wolfman (1968) (see WEREWOLVES—SPAIN'S "WALDEMAR DANINSKY" SERIES) (also *Frankenstein's Bloody Terror*). A werewolf goes to a pair of occult specialists seeking a cure for his lycanthropy, but the couple turn out to be vampires, whom the werewolf eventually destroys. Incidentally, no Frankensteins appear. ¶ "We have only a few hours in which to search. When night falls the vampires begin their search for blood again."

Martin (1977; Braddock Associates/Libra) D/S: George A. Romero. P: Richard Rubinstein. C: Michael Gornick. Cast: John Amplas, Lincoln Maazel, Christine Forrest, Elyane Nadeau, Tom Savini, Fran Middleton. Martin is a sexually troubled teenage "vampire" who slashes his victims with a razor and drinks their blood. He comes to live with his elderly cousin in Pittsburgh, and the old man, thinking him a traditional "nosferatu," attempts the usual vampire exorcisms without success. ¶ "Do you believe the whole world runs by the few laws of science we have been able to discover? There is more, much more. But people are satisfied. They know so much, they think they know it all." • It is never made clear whether Martin is truly an age-old vampire or merely a psychotic teen. There are several flashback sequences which allude to the former, though again, these may just be the fantasies of Martin's troubled mind. • Famous makeup man Tom Savini appears in the film as the fiancé of Martin's young female cousin. • Director George Romero also appears in the film as an ineffectual priest.

Mary, Mary, Bloody Mary (1975; Translor Films/Proa Films; U.S./Mexico) D: Juan Moctezuma. P: Robert Yamin, Henri Bollinger. S: Malcolm Marmorstein. C: Miguel Garzon. Cast: Christina Ferrare, John Carradine, David Young, Helena Rojo, Arturo Hansel, Enrique Lucero, Susan Kamini. Christina Ferrare plays a bisexual vampire who stabs her lovers in the neck and drinks their blood. Her father (John Carradine), also a vampire, comes looking for her in order to kill her and release her from the vampiric curse. • Christina Ferrare, once a model, achieved her brightest moment of fame as the wife of notorious cocaine dealer John DeLorean. • John Carradine left before the film was

completed, so some scenes feature a rather unconvincing double.

The Monster Club (1980) (see ANTHOLOGIES). In the wraparound sequence of this tongue-in-cheek anthology, vampire Vincent Price spares a potential victim (John Carradine) and invites him to "The Monster Club"—a disco where monsters hang out. Once there, the vampire regales the human with a variety of stories about monsters. • This was Vincent Price's first film after a five-year hiatus. It was also the first (and only) time Price played a vampire.

Monster Demolisher (1960; Estudios America/AIP-TV; Mexico) D: Frederick Curiel. P: Victor Parra. S: Charles Taboada, Alfred Ruanova, Frederick Curiel. C: Fernando Alvarez Garces. Cast: German Robles, Julio Aleman, Domingo Soler, Aurora Alvarado, Manuel Vergara. Once again the vampire son of Nostradamus is on the loose, this time enslaving a notorious criminal to do his bidding. • This is the second of four features created from a 12-part serial. The first is *The Curse of Nostradamus* (1960). • The professor, arch-enemy of the vampire, uses a machine which emits soundwaves harmful to bats to defend himself against the undead creature.

My Best Friend Is a Vampire (1988; Kings Road Entertainment) D: Jimmy Huston. P: Dennis Murphey. S: Tab Murphey. C: James Bartle. Cast: Robert Sean Leonard, Lee Anne Locken, Cheryl Pollak, Cecilia Peck, Fannie Flagg, David Warner. This vampire teen comedy follows high school student Jeremy Capello who receives a "love bite" while on a hot date with a mysterious woman. Soon he finds his reflection has vanished and he has developed a craving for raw steak. Vampire hunter Professor McCarthy shows up to further complicate Jeremy's altered life.

My Son the Vampire (1952) (see ROBOTS) (also *Old Mother Riley Meets the Vampire; Vampire Over London*). Bela Lugosi plays a mad scientist who believes he is a vampire. He dresses and acts the part, going so far as to sleep in a coffin wearing a full suit of evening clothes. He sends his robot out to kidnap Old Mother Riley (British comedian Arthur Lucan in drag), who ends up foiling his plans. ¶ "He is a descendant of Baron von Husen, who legend immortalized as a vampire. For reasons of his own, von Husen claims to be an earthly reproduction of his notorious ancestor, owing his continual existence to the consumption of human blood." • Bela Lugosi was paid a mere $5,000 to star in this low-brow British comedy.

Near Dark (1987; Film Entertainment) D: Kathryn Bigelow. P: Steven Charles Jaffe, Eric Red. S: Eric Red, Kathryn Bigelow. C: Adam Greenberg. Cast: Adrian Pasoar, Jenny Wright, Lance Henriksen, Bill Paxton, Jenette Goldstein, Tim Thomerson. In the rural Southwest, a young man is drawn into a gang of violent vampires who travel about living the style of *new* West outlaws (taveling in vans and Winnebagoes instead of riding horses, etc.). ¶ "Those people back there, that wasn't normal; normal folks don't *spit out* bullets when you shoot 'em, no sir." • Though these vampires do not sleep in coffins or sport pointy fangs, they drink (and spill) plenty of blood. They also sizzle, burn, and finally explode when exposed to the rays of the sun. • In most vampire movies, in order to turn someone into a vampire the victim must die from a vampire's bite. In this unique and innovative vampire film, the victim is transformed if bitten and left alive (when you're "bit but not bled" as they so colorfully put it).

Night of the Devils (1971; Filmes Cinematografica/Due Cinematografica; Italy) D: Giorgio Ferroni. P: Luigi Mariani. S: Romano Migliorini, Giambattista Mussetto, Eduardo M. Brochero C: Manuel Berenguer. Cast: Gianni Garko, Agostina Belli, Mark Roberts, Cinzia de Carlos, Teresa Gimpera. A young man learns that his fiancée's family is tainted with vampirism.

Night of the Sorcerers (1973) (see VOO-DOO). An expedition in the African jungle encounters a group of voodoo witches-turned-vampires who wear leopard skin bikinis and kill anyone who ventures into their territory.

The Night of the Vampire (1970; Toho; Japan) D: Michio Yamamoto. P: Tomoyuki Tanaka, Fumio Tanaka. S: Ei Ogawa, Hiroshi Nagano. C: Kazutami Hara. Cast: Kayo Matsuo, Akira Nakao, Yukiko Kobayashi, Atsuo Nakamura, Junya Usami. A distraught mother makes a pact with the devil to save her daughter after an accident. The daughter does survive, but she is transformed into a vampire. • Director Michio Yamamoto went on to direct two more vampire films, the more traditional, full-blooded *Lake of Dracula* (1971), and *The Evil of Dracula* (1975).

The Night Stalker (1971; TV movie) D: John Moxley. P: Dan Curtis. S: Richard Matheson. C: Michel Hugo. Cast: Darren McGavin, Carol Lynley, Simon Oakland, Ralph Meeker, Claude Akins, Charles McGraw, Kent Smith, Barry Atwater, Larry Linville, Jordan Rhodes. A wise-cracking reporter uncovers the truth about the recent rash of bizarre murders plaguing Las Vegas — they are being committed by a vampire. ¶ "So when you have finished this bizarre account, judge for yourself its believability, and then try to tell yourself, wherever you may be, it couldn't happen here." • *The Night Stalker* was the pilot film for the short-lived TV series of the same name, in which Darren McGavin encountered everything from werewolves to ancient Aztec gods. • Robert Quarry (*Count Yorga* himself) claimed that he was offered the role of the vampire but had to turn it down due to commitments to AIP.

Nightmare in Blood (1978; PFE) D: John Stanley. P/S: John Stanley, Ken Davis. C: Charles Rudnick, Ken Davis. Cast: Jerry Walter, Dan Caldwell, Barrie Youngfellow, John H. Cochran, Kerwin Mathews, Ray K. Goman, Hy Pike, Irving Israel, Justine Bishop. This low-budget horror film, seated firmly in the world of comic book shops and horror conventions, is about a horror star who turns out to be a real vampire. • Director/co-producer/co-writer John Stanley is a former TV horror host (of the Oakland based "Creature Features" program), and author of *The Creature Features Movie Guide*. • Kerwin Mathews, though given good billing, only appears in the film's three-minute prologue.

Nosferatu (1922) (see DRACULA AND FAMILY, this section). Though the vampire is named Count Orlock instead of Dracula, this is a thinly veiled adaptation of the Bram Stoker novel.

Not of This Earth (1956) (see ALIENS — INVADERS ON EARTH: THE 50s). Humanoid aliens from a dying planet come to Earth in an attempt to save themselves from a degenerate blood disease. These vampiric aliens must periodically receive blood transfusions in order to stay alive, and are not above murder to get their precious blood. ¶ "This killer is a fiend of the most diabolical kind, interested in only one thing — blood."

Not of This Earth (1988) (see ALIENS — INVADERS ON EARTH: THE 80s AND BEYOND). In this campy remake of the 1956 Roger Corman film, alien invaders need a constant supply of blood to survive; they have a degenerate blood disease (the result of too much radiation on their warring home planet).

The Nude Vampire (1969; Les Films ABC; France) D/P: Jean Rollin. S: Jean Rollin, S. H. Mosti. C: Jean-Jacques Remon. Cast: Oliver Martin, Maurice Lemaitre,

Portrait of the "New West" vampires from Near Dark *(1987) — Lance Henriksen, Jenette Goldstein, Bill Paxton.*

Caroline Cartier, Ly Letrong, Bernard Musson. A young man is led by a mysterious woman to a castle inhabited by vampires. • French filmmaker Jean Rollin made many low-budget erotic horror film in the 1970s, including two more vampire movies — *Sex and the Vampire* (1970), and *Caged Virgins* (1971).

Once Bitten (1985; Samuel Goldwyn Company) D: Howard Storm. P: Dimitri Villard, Robby Wald, Frank E. Hildebrand. S: David Hines, Jeffrey Hause, Jonathan Roberts. C: Adam Greenberg. Cast: Lauren Hutton, Jim Carrey, Karen Kopins, Cleavon Little, Thomas Ballatore, Skip Lackey, Richard Schaal, Peggy Pope, Peter Elbling. A beautiful female vampire (Lauren Hutton) must find the blood of a virgin before Halloween in order to keep her youth (not an easy task in 1989 L.A.). She sets her fangs on a wholesome high school student and must contend with his possessive but pure girlfriend. ¶ "Being a vampire in the twentieth century is a nightmare!"

Planet of the Vampires (1965) (see ALIENS —

ENCOUNTERS IN OUTER SPACE). Vampires in name only, this Italian sci-fi film features astronauts landing on a strange planet and being possessed by alien beings intent on conquering Earth. • Director Mario Bava did in fact direct two other true vampire tales — *Black Sunday* (1960) and *Black Sabbath* (1964; an anthology film which featured Boris Karloff as a vampire).

The Playgirls and the Vampire (1960; Nord Film Italiana/Fanfare; Italy) D/S: Piero Regnoli. P: Tiziano Longo. C: Ugo Brunelli. Cast: Walter Brandt, Lyla Rocco, Maria Giovannini, Tilde Damiani, Corinne Fontaine, Erika Di Centa, Marisa Quattrini, Alfredo Rizzo. A busload of chorus girls ends up at the castle of Count Kernassy. The count's lookalike ancestor, a vampire, lurks below in the castle catacombs, waiting to claim the scantily clad lovelies. • Walter Brandt, who plays both the count and his vampiric ancestor, appeared as another vampire in *The Vampire and the Ballerina* this same year.

A Polish Vampire in Burbank (1983;

Paromount Studios [*not* Paramount]) D/ P/S: Mark Pirro. C: Craig Bassuk. Cast: Mark Pirro, Lori Sutton, Bobbi Dorsch, Hugh O. Fields, Mayra Gant, Eddie Deezen. This tacky, amateurish, no-budget comedy deals with an immigrant vampire family whose young son is having trouble losing his sanguinary virginity so to speak.

Queen of Blood (1966) (see ALIENS— ENCOUNTERS IN OUTER SPACE). Earth receives an alien distress call from Mars. A rescue rocket is launched and the crew finds one female alien alive. She turns out to be a sort of alien vampire, for on the way back she systematically murders the crew by draining their blood—she lives on blood.

Queen of the Vampires (1967; Les Films ABC/Sam Selsky; France) (also *Vampire Women*). D/S: Jean Rollin. P: Jean Rollin, Sam Selsky. C: Guy Leblond. Cast: Bernard Letrou, Solange Pradel, Ursule Pauly, Nicole Romain, Catherine Devil. With a very disjointed narrative, the plot revolves around a vampire queen and her horde of vampire girls, and an attempt to lift a vampire's curse from two girls. • This was prolific French horror director Jean Rollin's first full-length feature. It was made with little money and utilized mostly non-actor friends of the director. Rollin later went on to direct a whole string of erotic vampire films, including *Sex and the Vampire* (1970) and *Caged Virgins* (1971).

Red Blooded American Girl (1990; Prism) D: David Blyth. P: Nicolas Stiliadis. S: Alan Moyle. C: Ludek Bogner. Cast: Andrew Stevens, Heather Thomas, Christopher Plummer, Kim Coates, Lydie Denier. Andrew Stevens plays a viral scientist who is recruited by the sinister Christopher Plummer and his mysterious research organization. Stevens eventually learns that Plummer and his cohorts are infected with a "vampire virus" which causes an intense craving for human blood (as well as eventual death from the breakdown of their own corpuscles). ¶ "Vampirism exists. It's not just a mythology, it's an actual virus."

The Return of Count Yorga (1971; AIP) D: Bob Kelljan. P: Michael Macready. S: Bob Kelljan, Yvonne Wilder. C: Bill Butler. Cast: Robert Quarry, Mariette Hartley, Roger Perry, Yvonne Wilder, Tom Toner, Rudy de Luca, Walter Brooks, Craig Nelson, Karen Huston, Paul Hansen. Count Yorga is back (without explanation though, since he was staked at the climax of *Count Yorga, Vampire*) and lurking about a San Francisco orphanage. Yorga sets his sights on the heroine and has his horde of female vampires slaughter her entire family before her fiancé finally tracks the undead fiend to his mansion home and dispatches him. ¶ Catchy ad line: "Beware the stare! These are the eyes that paralyze!" • Bob Kelljan went on to direct another vampire sequel, *Scream Blacula Scream*, in 1973. • Producer Michael Macready's more famous dad, George, appears in a cameo as a professor. It was his last film.

Return of the Vampire (1944; Columbia) D: Lew Landers. P: Sam White. S: Griffith Jay. C: John Stumar, L. W. O'Connell. Cast: Bela Lugosi, Frieda Inescort, Nina Foch, Matt Willis, Roland Varno, Miles Mander, Ottola Nesmith, Gilbert Emery. Bela Lugosi is Armand Tesla, a vampire revived during the London blitz of World War II. With the reluctant help of his servant, a werewolf(!), the vampire begins a reign of terror on the local high-society crowd. ¶ "Even the power of evil cannot stand against the power of faith." • *Return of the Vampire* carried a shooting title of *Vampires of London*. • *Return of the Vampire* began in a very topical way for a war-torn America: The vampire is revived when a German bomb uncovers his tomb in London and a local constable removes the iron stake from his body thinking it was a piece of shrapnel. • This was the first real vampire role for Lugosi since *Dracula* (1931). The actor was paid $3,500 for his work. • The rather gruesome climactic scene of the vampire's face melting under the rays of the sun was removed from all British prints because it was deemed too horrific by the censors.

The Return of the Wolfman (1980) (see WEREWOLVES—SPAIN'S "WALDEMAR DANINSKY" SERIES) (also *The Craving* [video title]). In this ninth film in the series, Waldemar Daninsky and his master—an evil vampiric countess—are executed in the sixteenth century. Both the countess and the werewolf are revived in modern times, with Waldemar rebelling against the evil vampire woman. The two creatures go at each other, and the werewolf is victorious when he rips out the throat of the vampiress.

A Return to Salem's Lot (1987; Warner Bros.) D: Larry Cohen. P: Paul Kurta. S: Larry Cohen, James Dixon. C: Daniel Pearl. Cast: Michael Moriarty, Samuel Fuller, Andrew Duggan, Ricky Addison Reed, June Havoc, Evelyn Keyes. A writer and his young son return to the town of his boyhood, only to find it populated by vampires leading everyday vampiric lives. They breed cattle for blood and only sample the occasional human. ¶ "I must confess I

Vampire Armand Tesla (Bela Lugosi) is assisted from his coffin by his werewolfian slave Andreas (Matt Willis) in Return of the Vampire *(1944).*

prefer human blood. Axle says I have a drinking problem." • These vampires cast reflections and can eat garlic. They still, however, sleep in coffins and come out only at night. They have human helpers they refer to as "drones" to work for them during the daylight hours. • Larry Cohen shot *A Return to Salem's Lot* virtually back to back with *It's Alive 3: Island of the Alive.* • Larry Cohen explained how this sequel is a sequel in name only in *Fangoria* #67: "I told Warner Bros. I didn't want to handle the same material Tobe Hooper worked with [in *Salem's Lot*]. I suggested using just the title and the basic premise of vampires in New England, and making up my own stories and characters." • Cohen cast his friend, the legendary director Sam Fuller, in the role of the feisty Jewish vampire hunter.

Rockula (1990; Pathé) D: Luca Bercovici. P: Jeffry Levy. S: Luca Bercovici, Jeffry Levy, Christopher Verwiel. C: John Schwartzman. Cast: Dean Cameron, Tawny Fere, Susan Tyrell, Bo Diddley, Thomas Dolby, Toni Basil. A teenage vampire named Ralph is out to break a curse involving his would-be girlfriend Mona with the help of his new rock 'n' roll band "Rockula" in this horror/teen/comedy.

Salem's Lot (1979; TV movie) D: Tobe Hooper. P: Richard Kobritz. S: Paul Monash. C: Jules Brenner. Cast: David Soul, James Mason, Lance Kerwin, Bonnie Bedelia, Reggie Nalder, Lew Ayres, Julie Cobb, Elisha Cook, George Dzundza, Ed Flanders, Clarissa Kaye, Geoffrey Lewis, Barney McFadden, Kenneth McMillan, Fred Willard, Marie Windsor. The mysterious Mr. Straker comes to a small New England town with his unseen partner Mr. Barlow, and people begin dying. Barlow is a vampire, and soon there are more vampires in the town than people. It is left to a troubled writer and an orphaned youth to take a stand against the undead. • Originally produced as a three-hour TV movie, *Salem's Lot* was given a theatrical release in Europe in a shortened, more violent version. • Barlow, the head vampire in *Salem's Lot*, resembles the undead *Nosferatu* of the 1922 classic more than the Bela Lugosi or Christopher Lee–type vampires. With a bald head, dagger-like fingernails, a pasty cadaverous face, and two sharp incisors, he is a hideous monster rather than a suave seducer. Curiously, this bloodsucker lacks the power of speech, something its vampire progeny does not. • This Nosferatu-like appearance was conceived by film auteur Larry Cohen, who had written an early adaptation of Stephen King's book for Warner Bros. "I patterned the vampire after the Max Schreck character in F. W. Murnau's *Nosferatu*," admitted Cohen in *Fangoria* #67. Though ultimately not involved with this project, Cohen went on to direct a sequel (in name anyway)—*A Return to Salem's Lot* (1987). • James Mason's real-life wife, Clarissa Kaye, ends up as a female vampire in the movie. • Director Tobe Hooper made his strong horror debut five years earlier when he unleashed *The Texas Chainsaw Massacre* in 1974.

Scream and Scream Again (1970) (see ROBOTS). Mad scientist Vincent Price is creating a race of artificial humans. One specimen escapes and terrorizes the surrounding countryside. There is a problem with this particular creature—it attacks women and drinks their blood.

Scream Blacula Scream (1973; American International) D: Bob Kelljan. P: Joseph T. Naar. S: Joan Torres, Raymond Koenig, Maurice Jules. C: Isidore Mankofsky. Cast: William Marshall, Don Mitchell, Pam Grier, Michael Conrad, Richard Lawson, Janee Michelle, Lynn Moody, Barbara Rhoades, Bernie Hamilton. In this inferior sequel to *Blacula,* the titular bloodsucker goes up against a voodoo priestess. ¶ "I mean I don't mind bein' a vampire and all that shit, but this really ain't hip. I mean a man has *got* to see his face"—a new vampire acolyte when he finds he cannot see himself in a mirror. • Believe it or not, *Blacula Is Beautiful* was a title under consideration before the filmmakers decided upon the present moniker.

Sex and the Vampire (1970; Les Films ABC/Films Modernes; France) (also *Vampire Thrills*). D/P/S: Jean Rollin. C: Jean-Jacques Renon. Cast: Sandra Julien, Dominique, Nicole Nancel, Michel Delahaye, Jacques Robiolles, Marie Pierre Tricot. A honeymooning couple stumble upon a castle of vampires and fall prey to their various lusts in this low-budget erotic vampire tale from the prolific filmmaker Jean Rollin (*The Nude Vampire,* 1969; *Caged Virgins,* 1971; etc.).

The Slaughter of the Vampires (1962; Pacemaker; Italy) (also *Curse of the Blood-Ghouls*). D/S: Roberto Mauri. P: Dino Sant'Ambrogio. C: Ugo Brunelli. Cast: Walter Brandt, Dieter Eppler, Graziella Granata, Paolo Solvay, Gena Gimmy, Alfredo Rizzo, Edda Ferronao, Maretta Procaccini. A vampire hunter attacks the wife of a doctor, who enlists the aid of a Van Helsing–type vampire hunter to destroy the undead threat. • At the climax, the husband eschews the old wooden stake trick and instead drives the spikes of an iron gate into the vampire's chest.

Terror in the Crypt (1964) (see WITCHES, WARLOCKS, AND CULTS) (also *Crypt of Horror; The Curse of the Karnsteins*). A family is plagued by a witch who is raised from the dead. The witch is also a vampire, though her vampiric tendencies are kept in the background.

Theatre of Death (1967) (see MADMEN—EARLY PSYCHOS). A blood-drinking murderer terrorizes the city of Paris. It turns out to be a human rather than supernatural fiend who is perpetrating these vampire-like killings — a woman who was fed blood as an infant when trapped by a blizzard in the mountains.

Thirst (1979; New Line Cinema; Australia) D: Ron Hardy. P: Antony I. Ginnane. S: S: John Pinkney. C: Vincent Monton. Cast: Chantal Contouri, David Hemmings, Henry Silva, Max Phipps, Shirley Cameron, Rod Mullinar, Robert Thompson, Walter Pym, Lulu Pinkus. A woman is kidnapped and brought to a bizarre compound run by the "Hyma Brotherhood." They are an elite group of men and women who believe that drinking blood bestows great power upon them. They harvest the blood of captives and distribute it in milk cartons to their brethren around the world.

The Tomb (1985) (see DEMONS AND DEVILS). "Nefratis" is an ancient but beautiful Egyptian vampire/demon who is seeking vengeance against those who desecrated her tomb and stole her magic amulets. As well as having demonic powers, she sports fangs and does not mind the occasional drop of blood.

Uncle Was a Vampire (1959; Embassy; Italy) D: Stefano Steno. P: Mario Cecchi Gori. S: Edoardo Anton, Dino Verde, Alessandro Continenza. C: Marco Scarpelli. Cast: Renato Rascel, Sylva Koscina, Christopher Lee, Lia Zoppelli, Kay Fischer. Christopher Lee plays Baron Rodrigo, an old-style vampire who passes on his vampirism to his bumbling nephew. Due to financial troubles, the nephew is forced to turn the ancestral castle into a hotel, where the vampires become a leading tourist attraction for the excited guests. • Christopher Lee, fresh from his success as the count in *Horror of Dracula* (1958), spoofs his own Dracula performance in this film.

The Understudy: Graveyard Shift 2 (1988; Cinema Ventures; Canada) D/S: Gerard Ciccoritti. P: Stephen R. Flaks, Arnold H. Bruck. C: Barry Stone. Cast: Wendy Gazelle, Mark Soper, Silvio Oliviero, Ilse von Glatz, Tim Kelleher, Leslie Kelly, Paul Amato, Carl Alacchi. In this quick sequel, a man shows up at a film production just when they are looking for an actor to play the part of a vampire. The mysterious stranger fits the role perfectly because he really is a vampire. The undead actor sets his sights on the leading lady. ¶ "For this leading man, acting is in the blood" — ad line.

Valley of the Zombies (1946; Republic) D: Philip Ford. P/S: Dorrell McGowan, Stuart McGowan. C: Reggie Lanning. Cast: Robert Livingston, Adrian Booth, Ian Keith, Thomas Jackson, Charles Trowbridge, Earle

Hodgins. Ian Keith plays an undertaker who returns from the dead needing periodic transfusions of fresh blood to sustain his undead existence. • Ian Keith was one of the actors originally considered for the role of *Dracula* in 1931 before Universal settled on Bela Lugosi.

Vamp (1986; New World Pictures) D: Richard Wenk. P: Donald P. Borchers. S: Richard Wenk. C: Elliot Davis. Cast: Chris Makepeace, Sandy Baron, Robert Rusler, Dedee Pfeiffer, Gedde Watanabe, Grace Jones, Billy Drago, Brad Logan, Lisa Lyon. Three fraternity pledges journey to the big city in search of "entertainment" for their upcoming party and instead find a strip joint full of vampires (appropriately named the "After Dark Club"). • The role of Katrina, queen of the vampires, was originally written with Tina Turner in mind, but when the singer-turned-actress declined, the role was given to model-turned-actress Grace Jones.

The Vampire (1957; United Artists) (also *Mark of the Vampire*). D: Paul Landres. P: Jules V. Levy, Arthur Gardner. S: Pat Fielder. C: Jack McKenzie. Cast: John Beal, Coleen Gray, Kenneth Tobey, Lydia Reed, Dabbs Greer. A doctor mistakenly takes some pills belonging to a professor doing research on bats. The pills are habit forming and they transform him into a crusty-faced vampire with a thirst for human blood. ¶ "A new kind of killer to stalk the screen," promised the poster while the movie delivered your standard ugly vampire, albeit a scientific rather than supernatural one.

The Vampire (1957; Cinematografica ABSA/K. Gordon Murray; Mexico) D: Fernando Mendez. P: Abel Salazar. S: Ramón Obon. C: Rosalio Solano. Cast: German Robles, Abel Salazar, Ariadna Welter, Carmen Montego, José Luis Jimeniz, Mercedes Soler. Not to be confused with the science-oriented American film of the same name released the same year, the Mexican *The Vampire* harkens back to the Universal classics to tell an atmospheric tale of Count Lavud, a Hungarian vampire come to Mexico to purchase an estate and spread his vampirism. • Count Lavud returns again in *The Vampire's Coffin* (1958), again played by German Robles. • Producer Abel Salazar stars as the hero.

Vampire (1979; TV movie) D: E. W. Swackhammer. P: Gregory Hoblit. S: Steve Bochco, Michael Kozell. C: Dennis Dalzell. Cast: Jason Miller, Richard Lynch, E. G. Marshall, Kathryn Harrold, Barrie Youngfellow, Michael Tucker, Jonelle Allen,

Jessica Walter. David Lynch is a vampire in modern San Francisco, with E. G. Marshall and Jason Miller as two modern-day vampire hunters hot on his trail. • "I'll drain them drop by drop. No love, no bonds, no sanctuary, to live isolated until you begin feeding upon each other like rats." • This TV movie was originally projected as a pilot for a TV series which never materialized. The vampire gets away in the end. • Jason Miller is most recognized for battling a different kind of supernatural terror in *The Exorcist* (1973).

The Vampire and the Ballerina (1960; Consorzio Italiano Films/United Artists; Italy) (also *The Vampire's Lover*). D: Renato Polselli. P: Bruna Bolognesi. S: Renato Polselli, Ernesto Gastaldi, Guiseppe Pellegrini. C: Angelo Balstrocchi. Cast: Hélène Remy, Tina Gloriani, Maria Luisa Rolando, Walter Brandt, Isarco Ravaioli, John Turner. Two ballet dancers stumble across a castle while lost in the woods. The castle belongs to a vampire countess who, with her ugly vampire servant, terrorizes the dancers.

Vampire at Midnight (1988) (see HYPNOTISTS). A rash of "vampire killings" in which young women are found drained of their blood holds the city in a grip of fear. Dr. Victor Radkoff is a "hypno-therapist" who works with performing artists to bring out their true potential, using his powers of hypnotism to release their inner talents. He is also the "vampire killer" who hypnotizes his victims and then cuts their throats to drink their blood. • Throughout the film the audience is led to believe that Radkoff is a real vampire (he sleeps during the day, he shies away from crosses, and he even sports a set of fangs when he kills). It turns out, however, that he is a decidedly human killer (with false fangs), though his deadly powers of hypnotism are real enough.

The Vampire Bat (1933) (see MAD SCIENTISTS). A mad doctor sends his hypnotized servant out to kill villagers and drain their blood which he feeds to his sponge-like lump of artificial flesh. No real vampires are present.

Vampire Hookers (1979; Capricorn Three; Philippines) (also *Graveyard Tramps; Sensuous Vampires; Vampire Playgirls*). D: Cirio H. Santiago. P: Robert E. Waters. S: Howard R. Cohen. C: Carding Remias, John Araojo. Cast: John Carradine, Bruce Fairbairn, Trey Wilson, Vic Diaz, Leo Martinez, Kern Stride, Lenka Novak, Katie Dolan. John Carradine plays a venerable vampire in the Philippines whose three female acolytes like to "kiss and tease but always please" (as the ads put it) before putting the bite on their male victims. Two American sailors stumble across their cemetery lair and put an end to their nightly romps. ¶ From the "Vampire Hooker Theme Song": "So if you need a hooker, and she seems so sweet and kind/ Be careful if you date her, your life may be on the line/ They're beautiful and sultry, but they're not what you expect/ You'll be begging them for mercy, as they bite you in the neck/ Because they're Vampire Hookers, yeah they're Vampire Hookers...." • Carradine is a far cry from his Universal Dracula portrayals of the 1940s in this sophomoric sex farce. He is given little to do but dress in a white suit and cape and spout Shakespearean dialogue.

Vampire Men of the Lost Planet (1970) (see ALIENS — ENCOUNTERS IN OUTER SPACE) (also *Horror of the Blood Monsters*). An expedition is sent to another planet where they encounter a primitive tribe of Filipino(!) vampire people. • The footage of the vampire tribe was taken from a black and white Filipino film and then tinted in an attempt to match the new color footage.

The Vampire of the Opera (1964; NIF; Italy) (also *The Monster of the Opera* D/S: Renato Polselli. Cast: John MacDouglas (Giuseppe Addobbati), Vittoria Prado, Marc Marian (Marco Mariani), Barbara Howard, Catla Cavelli. A combination of *Dracula* and *Phantom of the Opera,* this film tells the story of a vampire living deep below an abandoned opera house who enslaves women and spreads his vampiric disease. • Director Renato Polselli was no stranger to vampire films, having made *The Vampire and the Ballerina* in 1960. • *The Vampire and the Opera* was started soon after Polselli's completion of *The Vampire and the Ballerina,* but was not finished or released until four years later, in 1964.

The Vampire's Coffin (1958; Cinematografica ABSA/K. Gordon Murray; Mexico) D: Fernando Mendez. P: Abel Salazar. S: Ramón Obon, Javier Mateos. C: Victor Herrera. Cast: German Robles, Abel Salazar, Ariadna Welter, Yerye Beirute, Alicia Montoya, Guillermo Orea, Carlos Ancira. A curious doctor has the body of vampire Count Lavud disinterred. When the stake is removed from his heart, the vampire is once again loose upon the world. ¶ Now look, a vampire is a horrible beast that needs to be captured. Try and find it." • In this sequel to *The Vampire* (1957), German Robles (Count Lavud), Abel Salazar (the hero — and incidentally the film's producer), and Ariadna

Welter (the imperiled heroine) all return from the first film. • In one of the film's highlights, the hero tracks the fleeing vampire by following his shadow on the wall. Of course, according to traditional vampire lore, the undead cast no reflection and therefore cast no shadows as well.

The Vampire's Ghost (1945; Republic) D: Lesley Selander. P: Armand Schaefer. S: Leigh Brackett, John K. Butler. C: Bud Thackery, Robert Pittack. Cast: John Abbott, Peggy Stewart, Roy Barcroft, Charles Gordon, Grant Withers, Adele Mara. John Abbott plays a vampire who runs a criminal empire on the west coast of Africa. • Though claimed to be based on John Polidori's novella, *The Vampyre,* in truth this poverty-row film bears little relation to the story.

The Vampire's Night Orgy (1973; International Amusen Corp.; Spain) (also *Orgy of the Vampires*). D: Leon Klimowski. P: José Frade Almoke. S: Gabriel Antonio. C: Antonio Balleste. Cast: Jack Taylor, Dianik Zurakowska, José Guardiola, Char Soriano, Helga Line. A busload of tourists ends up in a village populated by vampires, lorded over by a beautiful countess. The visitors are fed human flesh (unknown to them) and vampirized one by one.

Vampyr (1931; Carl Theodor Dreyer Filmproduktion/Klang Film; Germany/ France) (also *Castle of Doom; The Strange Adventure of David Gray*). D/P: Carl Theodor Dreyer. S: Carl Theodor Dreyer, Christian Jul. C: Rudolf Mate. Cast: Julian West (Nicolas de Gunzburg), Sibylle Schmitz, Henriette Gerard, Jan Hieronimko, Maurice Schutz, Rena Mandel, Albert Bras, N. Babanini. In this first ever (loose) adaptation of Sheridan Le Fanu's *Carmilla,* a traveler named David Gray becomes involved with two sisters who have fallen under the spell of a vampire. ¶ "There exist certain beings whose very lives seem bound by invisible chains to the supernatural ... their imagination is so developed that their vision reaches beyond that of most men. David Gray's personality was thus mysterious"—opening written narration. • *Vampyr* is often regarded as an art house classic today, though it did not do well upon its initial release. With a cryptic storyline and meandering narrative, it is often difficult to follow, but it is filled with beautiful and often surreal images (such as when a man sits down on a bench and his shadow suddenly detaches itself from him to walk off by itself). • The vampire in question is not a suave aristocrat like Dracula, it takes the form of an ugly old woman—cinema's first female vampire. • *Vampyr* was financed by Dutch aristocrat Nicolas de Gunzburg, who played the male lead under the alias Julian West. • With the exception of lead actress Sibylle Schmitz, the entire cast was made up of non-professional actors, friends of director Carl Dreyer. • Danish director Carl Theodor Dreyer filmed *Vampyr* silently in France, then later added a soundtrack in Berlin (though there is very little dialogue in the film, and much of the movie is still silent). • To achieve a hazy, dreamlike look, Dreyer filmed his exteriors only during dawn and dusk. • Austrian cinematographer Rudolf Mate later turned director, eventually helming the sci-fi classic, *When Worlds Collide* in 1951.

Vampyres, Daughters of Dracula (1975; Essay Films/Cambist; U.K.) (also *Daughters of Darkness*). D: Joseph Larraz. P: Brian Smedley-Aston. S: Diana Daubeney. C: Harry Waxman. Cast: Marianne Morris, Anulka, Murray Brown, Brian Deacon, Sally Faulkner, Bessie Love, Michael Byrne, Carl Lanchberry, Elliot Sullivan. Two beautiful female vampires lure travelers into their crumbling old mansion for sex and blood. One of their victims survives the night and falls in love with his bloodthirsty paramour. • Anulka, who played one of the vampires, was a *Playboy* Playmate of the Month in 1973.

The Vault of Horror (1973) (see ANTHOLOGIES). In the "Midnight Mess" story, a man goes in search of his sister and winds up in a restaurant catering strictly to vampires, serving such delicacies as "bloodclot soup." • The brother and sister were played by Daniel and Anna Massey—brother and sister.

The Velvet Vampire (1971; New World) D: Stephanie Rothman. P: Charles S. Swartz. S: Maurice Jules, Charles S. Swartz, Stephanie Rothman. C: Daniel Lacambre. Cast: Sherry Miles, Michael Blodgett, Celeste Yarnall, Paul Prokop, Gene Shane, Jerry Daniels, Sandy Ward, Bob Tessier, Chris Woodley. A bisexual female vampire lives in the California desert and entices potential victims to her luxurious home. There she seduces them and either drains their blood or initiates them into the rites of vampirism..¶ From the ads: "Climax after climax of terror and desire ... where the living change places with the dead." • This particular vampire has no difficulty with sunlight—she has a habit of riding around in a dune buggy in the daytime. She does, however, still fear crosses, which is what leads to her eventual demise. • One of the few women directors in the horror field, Stephanie Rothman also co-directed *Blood Bath* in 1966, another tale of perverted vampirism.

Voodoo Heartbeat (1972) (see VOODOO). Voodoo ceremonies turn a man into a vampire-like creature with a thirst for blood.

Waxwork (1988) (see WAX MUSEUMS). A mysterious wax museum houses exhibits which come to life when entered. One includes a vampire and his minions.

The Werewolf vs. the Vampire Women (1970) (see WEREWOLVES—SPAIN'S "WALDE-MAR DANINSKY" SERIES) (also *Blood Moon* [video title]). A man who becomes a werewolf when the moon is full falls in love with one of two female students on holiday who stumble upon his castle. The other girl finds an ancient crypt and releases a female vampire. The two monsters—werewolf and vampire—end up locked in a life and (un)death struggle.

The World of the Vampires (1960; Cinematografica Calderón/AIP-TV) D: Alfonso Corona Blake. P: Abel Salazar. S: Paul Zenteno, Ramón Obon. C: Jack Draper. Cast: Guillermo Murray, Mauricio Garces, Erna Martha Bauman, Silvia Fournier, Jose Baviera, Mari Carmen Vela, Wally Barron, Alicia Moreno, Carlos Nieto. A vampire, with the aid of his female horde, seeks vengeance upon a professor and his family. The vampire controls his followers through music played on his organ made of human bones. • In an odd twist on vampire lore, the professor explains that vampires are susceptible to certain sound waves. He puts this theory into practice when he destroys the undead by playing a special tune on an organ.

Zombie Brigade (1988) (see ZOMBIES). In this low-budget Australian import, a small Australian Outback town is besieged by zombies when the development-hungry mayor has the local Vietnam Veterans monument blown up. That night, a horde of zombie soldiers crawl up out of the rubble and go on a rampage through the town, killing and drinking the blood of everyone they can get their undead hands on. These zombies exhibit many vampiric characteristics: They shun the sun, they drink blood, they must be killed by a stake through the chest, and they even sport fangs. Crosses however, have no effect on them, as the local priest learns much to his regret.

Venus

The 1950s and 60s were the prime years in which the planet Venus was utilized as a science fiction setting in the cinema. Though life on (or from) Mars has always been a popular topic, Venus (with its impenetrable cloud cover) has remained for the most part a complete mystery. Fairly close to our Earth, yet relatively unknown, Venus made for a more exotic alternative to Mars as a place where alien creatures might exist or originate. The wildest and certainly most notorious picture ever made about Venus was *Queen of Outer Space* (1958). This half-baked Ed Bernds feature depicted a world run by a race of domineering females who had it out for our Earth, and especially Earth males. Their Queen wore a mask which hid her terribly disfigured face but did not mask her hatred for men. The film contained some of the most outlandishly chauvinistic dialogue ever heard on the screen. While the story placed women in nontraditional (dominant) roles, in the end it only served to reinforce the general stereotypes of the time (with the rebellious group of women who overthrow the male-hating Queen swooning in the arms of the Earthmen at film's end). Naming the planet after the Roman Goddess of Love turned out to be very apt indeed.

In addition to Zsa Zsa Gabor (in *Queen of Outer Space*), some of the strangest monsters ever seen on the screen originated from the planet Venus. Who can forget Ray Harryhausen's giant Ymir that came *Twenty Million Miles to Earth* (1957), or the crazy cucumber creature with the massive underbite seen in *It Conquered the World* (1956)? Not only did weird creatures travel from Venus to Earth, but some pretty weird comedy teams (by Venusian standards) made the journey from Earth to Venus as well. The Three Stooges (*Have Rocket Will Travel,* 1959) and Abbott and Costello (*Abbott and Costello Go to Mars,* 1953) all managed to travel off course and make an unintended excursion to this far-out planet. The Stooges ran up against a huge spider on their trip while Bud and Lou met up with a group of love-starved women (relatives of the *Queen of Outer Space?*).

Abbott and Costello Go to Mars (1953; Universal) D: Charles Lamont. P: Howard Christie. S: D. D. Beauchamp, John Grant. C: Clifford Stine. Cast: Bud Abbott, Lou Costello, Mari Blanchard, Horace Mc-Mahon, Jack Kruschen, Robert Paige, Martha Hyer, Anita Ekberg. Bud and Lou accidentally take off in a rocket for Mars but end up at a Mardi Gras in New Orleans, thinking that the costume-wearing people are Martians. They blast off again, this time into outer space (and accompanied by two bank robbers on the lam) and eventually land on Venus. There they encounter a female race of Venusians, and their queen falls for Lou, but later has them chased off the planet when his fancy proves too fickle.

Doomsday Machine (1967) (see SPACE TRAVEL) (also *Escape from Planet Earth*). The Chinese set off a "doomsday device," destroying the Earth after a space ship heads for Venus. When they arrive at their destination along with a Russian ship, a collective intelligence emanating from Venus does not permit them to land and sends the ships off on an "even greater journey."

First Spaceship on Venus (1962; Crown International; E. Germany/Poland) D: Kurt Maetzig. S: Jan Fethke, Wolfgang Kohlaase, Guenther Reisch, Guenther Ruecker, Alexander Graf Stenbock-Fermor. C: Joachim Hasler. Cast: Yoko Tani, Oldrich Lukes, Ignacy Machowski, Julius Ongewe, Michail Postnikow. A communication from Venus is received which indicates an attack on Earth is imminent. An international expedition is launched, accompanied by a robot, to journey to the planet to investigate. On Venus they find a civilization completely destroyed by warfare. ¶ "We still have a grave task before us. We must use our knowledge to explore other planets. We'll fly further and further—mankind's destiny." • This Soviet Bloc film features a black astronaut, something unheard of in American cinema of the 1960s.

Have Rocket Will Travel (1959; Columbia) D: David Lowell Rich. P: Harry Romm. S: Raphael Hayes. C: Ray Cory. Cast: Moe Howard, Larry Fine, Joe De Rita, Jerome Cowan, Anna-Lisa. The Three Stooges take off in a rocket and land on Venus. After encountering a giant spider, a talking unicorn, and a crazy computer, the Stooges are shrunken then duplicated. • The Stooges had a falling out with producer Harry Romm involving payment. Romm apparently used clips of Stooges short-reelers and built them into a feature-length film without their permission. The trio sued, won an out-of-court settlement, then had him fired.

The Illustrated Man (1969) (see ANTHOLOGIES). In the second tale (titled "The Long Rains") of this Ray Bradbury–inspired anthology, a rocket crew crashlands on Venus, where the planet's unrelenting rainstorm drives them mad.

It Conquered the World (1956) (see ALIENS—INVADERS ON EARTH: THE 50s). A Venusian creature, resembling a cross between a giant turnip and a cucumber with fangs, journeys to Earth on board a satellite with the intention of conquering mankind.

Queen of Outer Space (1958; Allied Artists) D: Edward Bernds. P: Ben Schwalb. S: Charles Beaumont. C: William Whitley. Cast: Zsa Zsa Gabor, Eric Fleming, Laurie Mitchell, Paul Birch, Patrick Waltz, Dave Willock. A rocket arrives at a space station only to see it destroyed by a powerful ray. Caught in this ray, the ship is propelled to Venus. While exploring the planet, the crew, headed by Eric Fleming, is captured by a masked Queen (disfigured by radiation burns) and her army of female beauties. Fortunately for the astronauts, Zsa Zsa Gabor has initiated an underground movement to oust the Queen, and with Zsa Zsa's help the crew is able to thwart the plan to destroy the Earth. ¶ "Oh come off it, how can a bunch of women invent a gizmo like that . . . sure, and even if they invented it, how could they aim it? You know how women drivers are." • The story for *Queen of Outer Space* was submitted to director Edward Bernds by Walter Wanger. Wanger had just been released from prison for shooting an agent in the crotch after having an affair with his wife. Twenty-eight-year-old writer Charles Beaumont took the story and adapted it into a screenplay which was later juiced up with more satirical elements by Bernds, Ben Schwalb (the film's producer),

Eric Fleming and his companions disarm the hateful Queen of Outer Space *(1958), played by Laurie Mitchell wearing disfiguring makeup by Emile LaVigne.*

and Elwood Ullman. Beaumont died nine years later in 1967 at the young age of 37. • Bernds used stock rocket footage from a previous film of his, *World Without End* (1956), and he also borrowed the big spider prop from that movie as well. • Director Ed Bernds discussed his experiences with Zsa Zsa Gabor in a Tom Weaver interview appearing in *Filmfax* #17. "She's a beautiful woman, no doubt about it, but she was not very young, even in 1958," confided Bernds. "We had some of the most beautiful women we could find, any number of beauty queens, and I think the competition was a little steep for her. She was not thoroughly professional, she didn't have her lines well prepared, she had a kind of giddy attitude toward things.... Ben went to the hospital with ulcers halfway through, and I was left to cope with her alone. And she damn near gave me ulcers! It bothered me that here on this planet Venus, she was the only one who spoke with a foreign accent.... If the picture's shown on TV I won't watch it, because Zsa Zsa Gabor still gives me a swift pain." • Pressbook advances claimed that, "before going before the cameras, [Zsa Zsa's] hair and body were sprayed with a gold paint, and her gowns were fashioned from gold cloth. Her gowns featured a split, designed to show her shapely legs." • Promotional

materials played up the Gabor reputation by saying, "A Gabor is an expensively reared woman who collects diamonds and other gems like the average American woman collects coupons at the supermarket. A Gabor is also one who can have three widely different men, a Turkish prince, an American hotel tycoon, a world famous actor, see each of them dissolved by divorce. And not collect a penny of alimony!" • Many of the girls appearing in the film were former beauty contest winners. Marilyn Buferd was a former Miss America winner, and Mary Ford won the title of Miss Minnesota. • Art director David Milton said of his fantastical sets, "They may give a hint as to what might be found on Venus in the not too distant future. At least, they mirror my ideas, and who can say I'm wrong!"

Stranger from Venus (1955) (see ALIENS — BENEVOLENT ALIENS) (also *Immediate Disaster*). A Venusian comes to Earth to warn humanity that they must stop making war.

Twenty Million Miles to Earth (1957) (see ALIENS — INVADERS ON EARTH: THE 50s). A creature from Venus is brought back via rocketship, then grows to enormous size and menaces Italy.

Voyage to the Planet of Prehistoric Women (1966; Filmgroup) D: Peter Bogdanovich. P: Norman D. Wells. S: Henry

Ney. Cast: Mamie Van Doren, Mary Mark, Paige Lee. Astronauts landing on the planet Venus encounter carnivorous plants, lizard men, and a telepathic prehistoric female tribe who worships a pterodactyl as a god. • One-time B-movie sex goddess, Mamie Van Doren, plays the leader of the telepathic female tribe. • Famous director Peter Bogdanovich made his debut on this Roger Corman project, which lifted most of its effects from the 1962 Soviet film, *Planeta Burg*. Bogdanovich used the pseudonym "Derek Thomas" in the credits. He also narrates the film.

Zontar, the Thing from Venus (1966) (see ALIENS—INVADERS ON EARTH: THE 60S AND 70S). This Larry Buchanan uncredited remake of *It Conquered the World* follows the world-conquering exploits of an invading creature from Venus.

Voodoo
(*See also* Witches, Warlocks, and Cults)

What differentiates voodoo movies from their witchcraft brethren is more than just the idea that voodoo practitioners derive their supernatural powers from voodoo gods like "Damballah," whereas the more traditional western witch is a follower of Satan. Voodoo films possess their own unique flavor. Often filled with exotic rituals, frenzied sensuous dancing, tropical locales, and sometimes featuring bizarre creatures like zombies, voodoo movies appeal to the western audience's thrill of the exotic, the strange, the foreign. While there are plenty of Satan worshipers right here at home (at least if your home is anywhere near L.A.), voodoo is a more foreign, mysterious, and intriguing presence.

Voodoo films often cross over into zombie territory, since zombies originally owed their existence solely to voodoo magic in the early days of cinema (before science began churning out their own version of the walking dead). While many voodoo movies contain zombies, and many zombie movies contain voodoo, we placed each film according to what we felt was its main focus.

White Zombie (1932), though primarily a zombie film, was the first Hollywood horror movie to deal with the shadowy subject of voodoo. It was inspired by William Seabrook's novel, *The Magic Island*, which described the author's experiences with voodoo magic on the island of Haiti. Bela Lugosi played voodoo practitioner and zombie-master "Murder Legendre" in such a brooding, powerful style that he lived up to, and even surpassed, his character's unlikely name.

The only other voodoo movies to be made during the first decade of Hollywood's "Golden Age of Horror" were a string of all-black curiosities produced within the confines of the so-called Negro Film Industry (as it was referred to at the time)—*Drums o' Voodoo* (1934), *Drums of the Jungle* (1935), and *Pocomania* (1939).

The 1940s brought us the Val Lewton classic, *I Walked with a Zombie* (1943; though predominantly a zombie movie, it contained a heavy dose of voodoo ambience and some impressive scenes of voodoo ritual). *Weird Woman,* the best of Universal's "Inner Sanctum" series, was made a year later, as was Monogram's bottom-of-the-barrel, unintentionally amusing *Voodoo Man*.

Voodoo took off in the 1950s and 60s, with many films exploiting the exotic (and often erotic) appeal of the subject by including at least an element of the mysterious voodoo in their pictures. This period also produced one of the finest voodoo films to date—*Burn, Witch, Burn* (1962).

Voodoo has recently returned to the big screen in a flurry of films like the scattered misfire, *The Believers* (1987), the intriguing *Angel Heart* (1987), the low-budget plodder, *Scared Stiff* (1988), and the nightmarish, underrated attempt at updating and authenticating voodoo in the modern world (within the parameters of a horror movie of course), *The Serpent and the Rainbow* (1988).

See also ZOMBIES for more voodoo hoo-doo, and WITCHES, WARLOCKS, AND CULTS for further supernatural magic.

Angel Heart (1987; Tri-Star) D/S: Alan Parker. P: Alan Marshall, Elliott Kastner. C: Michael Seresin. Cast: Mickey Rourke, Robert De Niro, Lisa Bonet, Charlotte Rampling, Stocker Fontelieu, Brownie McGhee, Michael Higgins, Elizabeth Whitcraft. Private eye Harry Angel is hired by the mysterious "Mr. Cyphre" to track down a missing singer, and becomes involved in murder, voodoo, and his own inevitable fate. • *Angel Heart* is based on the novel *Fallen Angel* by William Hjortsberg. • Robert Redford originally bought the book's movie rights, but could not see himself in the role of Harry Angel. • Writer/director Alan Parker considered Marlon Brando for the role of Louis Cyphre (a.k.a. Lucifer) before deciding on Robert De Niro. • Lisa Bonet, one of the Cosby kids from TV's "The Cosby Show," stepped out to do a nude love scene in *Angel Heart*. Parker had never seen "The Cosby Show" when he cast Bonet. • For the voodoo dance sequences, actual Haitian ceremonial dance music was played in the background and choreographer Louis *(Fame)* Falco worked in parts of genuine voodoo rites in the dance arrangements. • Ironically, the slate number of Lisa Bonet's voodoo dance scene just happened to be 666.

The Believers (1987; Orion) D/P: John Schlesinger. S: Mark Frost. C: Robby Muller. Cast: Martin Sheen, Helen Shaver, Robert Loggia, Richard Massur, Harley Cross. Martin Sheen plays a skeptical psychologist who comes up against the evil magic of "Brujeria" voodoo when his son is marked for human sacrifice. He must turn to the more balanced magic of the "Santeria" religion for help. • *The Believers* is based on Nicholas Conde's novel, *The Religion.*

Bride of the Gorilla (1951) (see APES AND MONKEYS). Raymond Burr murders his boss and marries the widow, only to run afoul of a voodoo priestess who curses him by turning him into a gorilla (or at least making him *think* he turns into a gorilla).

Burn, Witch, Burn (1962; Anglo Amalgamated/AIP; U.K.) (also *Night of the Eagle* [original British title]). D: Sidney Hayers. P: Albert Fennell. S: Charlie Beaumont, Richard Matheson, George Baxt. C:

Reginald Wyver. Cast: Peter Wyngarde, Janet Blair, Margaret Johnston, Anthony Nicholls, Colin Gordon, Kathleen Byron, Reginald Beckwith, Norman Bird, Judith Scott. A skeptical college professor marries a young woman who practices voodoo in order to aid and protect her husband. He discovers her magical "help" and forces her to dispose of all her superstitious charms and protections. Soon his life is turned upside down by forces beyond his control and he must finally accept the truth and rescue his wife from an evil voodoo spell. ¶ "I tell you Norman, I will not be responsible for what happens to us if you make me give up my protection." • This is the second film based on Fritz Leiber's novel, *Conjure Wife,* the first being *Weird Woman* (1944). • As a publicity gimmick, American theater patrons were given a packet of salt along with an ancient incantation to ward against evil. • *Burn, Witch, Burn* was placed on the bottom half of a double bill with AIP's Roger Corman Poe film, *Tales of Terror.* While not a financial success, *Burn, Witch, Burn* scored high marks with the critics.

Child's Play (1988) (see DOLLS). A mortally wounded killer uses the powers of voodoo to transfer his evil soul into the plastic body of a child's doll. The animated doll then goes on a killing spree, searching for the right person into which he can transfer his soul so that he does not have to spend the rest of his life as a toy.

Creepshow (1982) (see ANTHOLOGIES). In the wraparound segment, a boy uses a mail-order voodoo doll purchased through an ad in the back of his comic book (called "Creepshow" of course) to take care of his abusive father.

Curse of the Doll People (1960) (see DOLLS). A man steals a sacred idol from a voodoo cult and is stalked by the voodoo witch doctor and his killer dolls.

Curse of the Voodoo (1965; Allied Artists; U.K./U.S.) (also *Curse of Simba*). D: Lindsay Shonteff. P: Kenneth Rive. S: Tony O'Grady, Leigh Vance. C: Gerald Gibbs. Cast: Bryant Halliday, Dennis Price, Lisa Daniely, Mary Kerridge, Ronald Leigh Hunt, Jean Lodge. A big game hunter slays a sacred lion in Africa. A witch doctor places a voodoo curse upon the offender, causing fever, hallucinations, and various forms of mental anguish. The hunter eventually returns to Africa to kill the witch doctor and end the curse.

Dead and Buried (1981) (see ZOMBIES). Jack Albertson (in his last film role) plays the town mortician in Potter's Bluff, who uses a combination of voodoo and science to transform the citizens into zombies. ¶ "Call it black magic, call it a medical breakthrough. I'll take my secret to the grave."

The Dead One (1961) (see ZOMBIES). A woman afraid of losing her inheritance uses voodoo to bring her dead brother back to life as a zombie in this obscure cheapie.

The Devil's Hand (1959; Crown International) (also *The Naked Goddess; Live to Love*). D: William J. Hole, Jr. P: Alvin K. Bubis. S: Jo Heims. C: Meredith Nicholson. Cast: Linda Christian, Robert Alda, Neil Hamilton, Adriana Welter, Gene Craft. A man dreams about a beautiful woman only to discover that she is not just a dream after all when she suddenly appears and takes control of his life. Exercising some strange power, she draws him into a modern-day voodoo cult which practices human sacrifice. • Star Robert Alda is the father of actor/writer/director Alan Alda of TV's "M*A*S*H" fame. • Neil Hamilton, who plays the voodoo high priest, is best remembered by TV viewers as Commissioner Gordon on "Batman."

The Devil's Own (1966) (see WITCHES, WARLOCKS, AND CULTS) (also *The Witches*). Joan Fontaine plays a woman traumatized by voodoo in Africa. Returning to England, she falls prey to a modern-day witch cult.

The Disembodied (1957; Allied Artists) D: Walter Grauman. P: Ben Schwalb. S: Jack Townley. C: Harry Neumann. Cast: Paul Burke, Allison Hayes, John E. Weingraf, Eugenia Paul, Joel Marston. Allison Hayes is "Tonda the Voodoo Queen," a white woman living in the jungle with her husband, a research doctor. Tonda uses her voodoo powers to seduce men and lord it over the natives. • *The Disembodied* was paired with *From Hell It Came*, a movie about a walking tree stump monster, to complete a silly-yet-entertaining double bill. • Sultry Allison Hayes was a staple of B horror and science fiction movies in the 1950s. She even played the title role in the cult favorite, *Attack of the 50 Foot Woman,* made the same year.

Dr. Terror's House of Horrors (1965) (see ANTHOLOGIES). In this anthology film's more musical segment, a hip London jazz musician travels to the West Indies where he hears a forbidden voodoo melody. He incorporates the sacred tune into his music and consequently incurs the wrath of the voodoo god "Damballah."

Drums o' Voodoo (1934; Sack Amusement Enterprises) (also *Louisiana*). D: Arthur Hoerl. P: Louis Weiss. S: L. Augustus Smith. C: Walter Strenge, J. Burgi Contner. Cast: Laura Bowman, Edna Barr, Lionel Monagan, J. Augustus Smith, Morris McKennon, A. B. Comathich, Alberta Perkins, Fred Bonny, Paul Johnson, Trixie Smith, Carrie Huff. In this rare, early all-black horror film, a Louisiana black community is plagued by the evil vices of Tom Cat, a greedy juke-joint owner who is blackmailing the town preacher and attempting to corrupt the innocent heroine. The community, led by the local aged voodoo priestess, uses its ancient voodoo magic to take care of the vile Tom Cat. ¶ "Beat dem drums.... Beat dem drums.... Beat dem drums.... The ancient god Voodoo commands you ... Beat ... Beat ... Beat ... Beat!"

Drums of the Jungle (1935; Terwilliger) (also *Oanga*). D/P/S: George Terwilliger. C: Carl Berger. Cast: Fred Washington, Sheldon Leonard, Philip Brandon, Marie Paxton, Winifred Harris. A voodoo priestess uses her powers in an attempt to ensnare the man she loves, but when this fails she kidnaps his fiancée, intending to use her as a human sacrifice. • Director/producer/ writer George Terwilliger was once a screenwriter for the famed D. W. Griffith. • Terwilliger originally planned to shoot this all-black horror film in Haiti to heighten the film's authenticity, but that country's political upheaval, coupled with a real-life voodoo threat, caused him to relocate to Jamaica.

The Four Skulls of Jonathan Drake (1959; United Artists) D: Edward L. Cahn. P: Robert E. Kent. S: Orville H. Hampton. C: Maury Gertsman. Cast: Eduard Franz, Valerie French, Henry Daniell, Grant Richards, Paul Cavanagh, Paul Wexler. A family curse involving decapitation and headshrinking is enforced by a 200-year-old voodoo witch doctor with the head of a white man sewn onto his body. ¶ "When the head of a strong valiant enemy is properly taken, the possessor acquires the spirit, the soul, the vital spark that kept his enemy alive—a degree of immortality!"

The House That Dripped Blood (1971) (see ANTHOLOGIES). The third tale of this Robert Bloch–scripted anthology, titled "Sweets to the Sweet," stars Christphoer Lee as a man bedeviled by family voodoo.

Peter Wyngarde is cornered in his own college classroom by a demonic stone eagle brought to life by voodoo in Burn, Witch, Burn *(1962). On the blackboard behind the previously skeptical Wyngarde, the phrase "I do not believe" has been slightly altered to read "I do believe."*

I Walked with a Zombie (1943) (see ZOM-BIES). A nurse travels to the West Indies to care for the wife of a troubled plantation owner. The wife apparently has been turned into a zombie through a voodoo curse, and the nurse, in desperation, attempts to cure her through the local voodoo practitioners.

The Leech Woman (1960; Universal) D: Edward Dein. P: Joseph Gerschenson. S: David Duncan. C: Francis Rosenwald. Cast: Coleen Gray, Grant Williams, Philip Terry, Gloria Talbot, John Van Dreelen, Estelle Hemsley. A scientist and his aging, neglected wife travel to darkest Africa where they find a voodoo-practicing tribe which has discovered the secret of eternal youth—the male pineal gland. So the wife kills her husband, steals a voodoo ring, and goes on a pineal-hunting spree. ¶ From the ads: "Her evil, jungle-born secret of eternal youth . . . drained the love life from every man she trapped!" • This was director Edward Dein's last feature. This prolific poverty-row filmmaker started out as a

writer on such movies as the hackneyed sequel, *Jungle Woman,* and the subtly sinister *Soul of a Monster* (both 1944). • Co-star Gloria Talbott, in a *Fangoria* #65 interview, gave a unique reason for appearing in this film: "I've got to admit, I made that picture because I wanted to buy a horse for my son, and *The Leech Woman* got him a really nice horse and saddle."

Macumba Love (1960; United Artists) D/P: Douglas Fowley. S: Norman Graham. C: Rudolfo Icsey. Cast: Walter Reed, Ziva Rodann, William Wellman, Jr., June Wilkinson, Ruth de Souza. A writer, his daughter, and his son-in-law journey to an island off the coast of South America to write an exposé book on voodoo. There they run afoul of the local voodoo queen named Mama Rataloy, who threatens them with her voodoo magic. She casts evil spells and kidnaps the young couple with the intention of sacrificing them in a voodoo ritual. ¶ From the ads: "Blood-Lust of the *Voodoo Queen!* Weird, Shocking, Savagery in Native

Jungle Haunts ... It's Happening Today!"
• According to the film's pressbook, beautiful Israeli-born Ziva Rodann, who plays the hero's love interest, is "the world's most glamorous army veteran," having served for a year in the Israeli army. • *Macumba Love* was shot on location in Brazil.

Night of the Sorcerers (1973; Avco Embassy; Spain) D/S: Armando de Ossorio. P: José Antonio Perez Giner, Luis Laso Moreno. C: Francisco Sanchez. Cast: Jack Taylor, Simon Andreu, Lorena Tower, Maria Kosti, Kali Hansa, Joseph Thelman, Barbara King. An expedition in the African jungle comes across a group of voodoo witches/vampires wearing leopard-skin bikinis who appear at night to kill anyone who ventures into their territory. • Male lead Jack Taylor is a regular in the films of prolific Spanish director Jesus Franco.

The Oblong Box (1969) (see POE FILMS— MODERN POE). While in Africa, the brother of Vincent Price is horribly afflicted by voodoo magic as a result of Price's careless killing of a black child. Back in England, Price keeps his disfigured brother Edward locked in a room, until he inadvertently buries him alive. The coffin is dug up by graverobbers and Edward proceeds to exact his revenge. ¶ "A man turned inside out through sorcery by a handful of powders and obscure drugs—my mind's been unhinged, my face destroyed."

The Offspring (1987) (see ANTHOLOGIES) (also *From a Whisper to a Scream*). The third story in this gory omnibus takes place at a rundown carnival owned by a voodoo priestess. Using her voodoo magic, she gives a young man the power to eat glass. When he disobeys her, she takes the power away, with painfully gruesome results.

The Plague of the Zombies (1966) (see ZOMBIES). A voodoo-practicing squire in Cornwall raids the local cemetery for corpses he can turn into walking zombies to work in his tin mine. ¶ "I find all kinds of witchcraft slightly nauseating, and this I find absolutely *disgusting*."

Pocomania (1939; Lenwal) (also *The Devil's Daughter*). D/P: Arthur Leonard. S: George Terwilliger. Cast: Nina Mae McKinney, Jack Carter, Ida James, Hamtree Harrington. A woman uses voodoo to terrify her sister in this early all-black horror obscurity. • Screenwriter George Terwilliger had filmed his own all-black voodoo movie four years earlier (*Drums of the Jungle*, 1935).

Scared Stiff (1988; Mansion International) D: Richard Friedman. P: Daniel F. Bacaner. S: Mark Frost, Daniel F. Bacaner, Richard Friedman. C: Yuri Denysenko. Cast: Andrew Stevens, Mary Page Keller, David Ramsey, Josh Sega. A thirty-something female rock star, her seven-year-old son, and her new psychiatrist husband all move into an old house once owned by a notorious slave trader named Masterson. A flashback sequence reveals that a voodoo curse was placed on him by his mistreated slaves which transformed him into a hideous monster. Masterson comes back, induces hallucinations in the mom, and possesses the psychiatrist. • *Scared Stiff* was lensed in Florida on a low $1.3 million budget. Director Richard Friedman left the project a few days before completion of principal photography, and the feature was finished by producer Dan Bacaner. • The only memorable aspect of this forgettable cheapie is the monster makeup, by which Masterson's head is transformed into a living African death mask.

Scream Blacula Scream (1973) (see VAMPIRES—OTHER VAMPIRES). In this sequel to the black vampire movie, *Blacula* (1972), the titular bloodsucker runs afoul of a voodoo priestess (blaxploitation actress Pam Grier). • In a screen first, a vampire is killed by voodoo—the priestess drives a tiny stake into the chest of a voodoo doll, causing Blacula's death.

The Serpent and the Rainbow (1988; Universal) D: Wes Craven. P: David Ladd, Doug Claybourne. S: Richard Maxwell, A. R. Simoun. C: John Lindley. Cast: Bill Pullman, Cathy Tyson, Zakes Mokae, Paul Winfield, Brent Jennings, Conrad Roberts, Michael Gough, Theresa Merritt. A young investigator goes to Haiti to check on the reported existence of zombies. He wants to find the secret behind the "zombie drug" which causes the victim to appear dead, intending to adapt it for use in the field of medicine. Once there, he finds more than he bargained for when he encounters an evil voodoo sorcerer who uses this special "zombie powder" in combination with diabolical voodoo magic to steal the souls of his victims and control their bodies. ¶ "Don't let them bury me. I'm not dead!" • Much of *The Serpent and the Rainbow* was shot on location in the politically unstable country of Haiti. Director Wes Craven and producer David Ladd traveled to Haiti before the start of production to secure "protection" for their cast and crew. "David [Ladd] and I attended real voodoo ceremonies and talked with real voodoo priests," Craven told *Fangoria* #71. "We told them we wanted to do a movie about voodoo and that we

Henry Daniell and his voodoo Indian assistant, Zutai (Paul Wexler), practice the art of head shrinking in the 1959 film, The Four Skulls of Jonathan Drake.

wanted to treat the subject fairly. And to prove how serious we were, we asked that we be given protection, through a voodoo ceremony, before filming actually started." • Despite this magical protection, the production was plagued with problems that often took on a nightmarish quality. "Nearly three-fourths of the cast and crew had come down with something," related Craven, "and just about everybody was suffering from nausea, vomiting or dizziness." And there were a number of experiences involving supernatural visions. "One person came out of a voodoo ceremony, turned around and immediately hallucinated about seeing an animal with eyes like television screens staring back at him." In another incident, "an actor was exploring the remains of an old fortress when he saw the ghost of a Haitian general on horseback." And even worse, "one staff member went completely insane after being in the country for only four days." (Fortunately, the person recovered completely after only a few days back in the States.) • The film is based on the nonfiction book *The Serpent and the Rainbow* by Wade Davis.

The Snake People (1968; Filmica Vergara/Columbia; Mexico/U.S.) D: Juan Ibañez, Jack Hill. P: Henry Verg (Enrique Vergara). S: Henry Verg, Jack Hill. C: Raul Dominguez, Austin McKinney. Cast: Boris Karloff, Julissa, Charles East, Ralph Bertan, Tongolele, Quintin Bulnes, Santanoni, July Marichael. Boris Karloff plays a plantation owner on the island of Kulabai whose natives are being terrorized by a voodoo snake cult presided over by a mysterious figure named "Damballah." It is revealed that the evil voodoo priest Damballah is none other than Karloff himself. • This is one in a series of four pictures Karloff made for producer Enrique Vergara—the last films Karloff made before his death. • Though predominantly a Mexican production, all of Karloff's scenes were shot in Hollywood in four weeks (*all* of his scenes for *all four* films). The footage was then shipped to Mexico for integration into the film. • Reportedly, financial difficulties coupled with the premature death of producer Vergara caused extensive changes in the films — so much so that they were no longer the same movies Karloff had agreed to make.

Sugar Hill (1974) (see ZOMBIES) (also *Zombies of Sugar Hill; Voodoo Girl*). A woman named Sugar Hill makes a pact with a voodoo priest to raise a horde of zombies in order to kill the white racketeers who murdered her boyfriend.

The Vault of Horror (1973) (see ANTHOLOGIES). An embittered artist finds that voodoo magic will make everything he paints come true. He uses this supernatural talent to paint the demise of his enemies until it finally catches up with him on his own self-portrait.

Voodoo Black Exorcist (1975) (see MUMMIES). The mummy of a 1000-year-old African voodoo priest comes to life and seeks out the reincarnation of his lost love.

Voodoo Heartbeat (1972; TWI) D/S: Charles Nizet. P: Ray Molina. Cast: Ray Molina, Philip Ahn, Ern Dugo, Forrest Duke, Ebby Rhodes, Mike Zapata, Ray Molina, Jr., Stan Mason, Mary Martinez, Mike Meyers. Voodoo turns a man into a hairy, blood-drinking monster (with long sideburns no less!) in this ultra-cheap voodoo fest filmed in Las Vegas. • Producer Ray Molina stars as the hairy horror.

Voodoo Island (1957; United Artists) D: Reginald LeBorg. P: Howard W. Koch. S: Richard Landau. C: William Margulies. Cast: Boris Karloff, Beverly Tyler, Murvyn Vye, Elisha Cook, Rhodes Reason, Jean Engstrom, Frederick Ledebur, Glenn Dixon, Owen Cunningham, Herbert Patterson, Jerome Frank. Boris Karloff plays a professional skeptic hired by a rich hotel builder to investigate the title island. There Karloff and his party encounter man-eating plants, zombies, and voodoo dolls before being captured by the voodoo-practicing natives. Finally, the white intruders are set free when Karloff agrees to keep their powerful secrets and leave their island untouched by the outside world. • *Voodoo Island* was filmed on the "garden island" of Kauai in Hawaii.

Voodoo Man (1944; Monogram) D: William Beaudine. P: Sam Katzman. S: Robert Charles. C: Marcel le Picard. Cast: Bela Lugosi, John Carradine, George Zucco, Michael Ames, Wanda McKay, Ellen Hall, Louise Currie. In this poverty-row quickie, Bela Lugosi plays Dr. Marlowe, who abducts girls in the hope of finding one on the "same mental plane" as his zombiefied wife. With the help of hypnotism, voodoo, and the "great god Ramboona," he attempts to transfer the life force of these girls into his undead wife. His numerous failures end up in the basement as zombies themselves. ¶ "The failures we've had were due to the subjects, they were not the right ones. But remember, Ramboona is all-powerful." • Genre vets John Carradine and George Zucco were wasted in demeaning roles as Lugosi's helpers. Zucco plays a gas station attendant who directs the girls to Lugosi's house, then dons a feathery headdress and mutters voodoo gibberish during the soul-transference ceremony. Carradine plays a halfwit handyman who beats out a rhythm on a tom tom and says things like, "She's not here. She must be somewhere else." • The film ends on a humorous note, one which is pure vintage Hollywood: The hero (a Hollywood scenario writer) delivers a script to his producer based on the events he just lived through, and he calls it "Voodoo Man." When asked who he had in mind to play the title role he replies, "Say, why don't you get that actor — Bela Lugosi. It's right up his alley."

Voodoo Woman (1957; AIP) D: Edward L. Cahn. P: Alex Gordon. S: Russel Bender, V. I. Voss. C: Frederick E. West. Cast: Marla English, Tom Conway, Touch Connors, Mary Ellen Kaye, Lance Fuller, Paul Blaisdell. Tom Conway plays a mad scientist intent upon creating a perfect human. To this end he gives native girls injections and has the local voodoo priest intone incantations over the girl. With this combination of science and voodoo, Conway turns a woman into a hideous scaly monster that he can mentally control. ¶ "We're doing it Chaka, white man's science and black voodoo. You know what they said about me in the States? That I was a man of science trying to outrage the laws of nature. That life forms couldn't change. We're proving them wrong." • Tom Conway, brother of the better-known George Sanders, ran into voodoo trouble 14 years earlier in *I Walked with a Zombie* (1943), though at that time he was the hero rather than the villain. • The title creature was played by monster-maker Paul Blaisdell. In a reflection of the film's no-frills budget, Blaisdell simply re-used his monster suit from *The She-Creature* (1956) and topped it with a dime store rubber skull mask and wig. In a move which may have shown great prudence, this pitiful looking monster is never shown very clearly in the film. We just see shots of her back, arm, leg, etc.; and the photography gets mysteriously foggy whenever she is shown in long shot.

Tom Conway stands to the right of his monstrous female creation known as the
Voodoo Woman *(1957), a product of science and voodoo combined. Inside the*
monster suit is creature-creator Paul Blaisdell, who reused the body suit he built for
The She-Creature *(1956) and topped it with a new (cheap) mask.*

Weird Woman (1944; Universal) D: Reginald LeBorg. P: Oliver Drake. S: Brenda Weisberg. C: Virgil Miller. Cast: Lon Chaney, Jr., Anne Gwynne, Evelyn Ankers, Ralph Morgan, Elisabeth Risdon, Lois Collier, Elizabeth Russell, Harry Hayden, Phil Brown, Jackie Lou Harding. Lon Chaney, Jr., is cast as a college professor whose wife dabbles in voodoo to protect him and advance his career. When the skeptical Chaney forces her to destroy all her voodoo paraphernalia, everything begins to go wrong, including Chaney being accused of murder. • *Weird Woman* was one of six films in Universal's "Inner Sanctum" series, which borrowed its name and some of its stories from the popular radio program. They all starred Lon Chaney, Jr. • The two female leads, Anne Gwynne and Evelyn Ankers, played mortal enemies in the film though they were best friends in real life. According to director Reginald LeBorg, this caused some problems on the shoot: "When Ankers had a scene with Gwynne that was rather

macabre, she *couldn't* do it very well because she loved Gwynne so much; she *couldn't* be mean to her. I gave her a few pointers and after three or four takes, she did it very well" (from *Universal Horrors,* by Brunas, Brunas, and Weaver). • Phil Brown, who in this film plays the insanely jealous David Jennings and makes two attempts on Chaney's life, later appeared as Luke Skywalker's kindly uncle in *Star Wars* (1977). • This is the first adaptation of Fritz Leiber's novel, *Conjure Wife.* It was filmed again in 1962 as *Burn, Witch, Burn,* the definitive version.

White Zombie (1932) (see ZOMBIES). Bela Lugosi plays a voodoo sorcerer who creates zombies to work in his sugar mill.

Zombie Nightmare (1987) (see ZOMBIES). A man is killed in a hit-and-run accident. The man's widow has a mysterious Haitian woman perform a voodoo rite to bring his body back to life. She uses her zombie husband to take vengeance on those who had gang-raped her years before.

Wax Museums

A wax museum has always been an intriguing place to visit, and it is not surprising that filmmakers have utilized it as a setting for tales of mystery and horror. With all the motionless figures (often of a horrific nature) who are so still yet so lifelike, the wax museum is a natural for inducing thrills and chills (and the perfect place for a madman to haunt or hide).

The first and foremost feature centering on a wax museum was Paul Leni's masterful *Waxworks* (1924), wherein a poet dreams of the wax figures in a museum. The wild and imaginative set designs orchestrated by Leni and Max Reinhardt make this classic of slient cinema one of the most visually intriguing films of all time.

Michael Curtiz's *Mystery of the Wax Museum* (1933) and its enjoyable 3-D remake, *House of Wax* (1953) began an interesting trend by putting forth the notion that perhaps those lifeless figures are not just wax after all, but actually real bodies encased in a molten tomb. Both these films featured an excellent actor (Lionel Atwill and Vincent Price, respectively) in the role of the disfigured mad wax sculptor who uses real bodies as foundations upon which to build his creations.

This is another small subgenre, one which often works best as a period thriller set in the last century (in which the museums really had their heyday). With it being such a natural setting for shocks to occur, it is rather surprising that the wax museum has not been utilized more often than it has.

Abbott and Costello Meet Frankenstein (1948) (see FRANKENSTEIN'S MONSTER — UNIVERSAL SERIES). McDougal's "House of Horrors" wax museum is where Lou Costello first encounters Dracula (Bela Lugosi) and the Frankenstein Monster (Glenn Strange).

Chamber of Horrors (1966; Warner Bros.) D/P: Hy Averback. S: Stephen Kandel. C: Richard Kline. Cast: Patrick O'Neal, Cesare Danova, Wilfrid Hyde-White, Laura Devon, Patrice Wymore, Suzy Parker, Marie Windsor, Jeanette Nolan, Tony Curtis. A pair of suave wax museum owners (who moonlight as sleuths) attempt to solve the murders of Jason Cravatte, a demented killer who once chopped off his own hand to affect an escape. The stump is now custom-made to fit various slashing instruments like hooks, knives, and cleavers. At the climax, Cravatte is impaled upon the knife held by his own wax image at the museum. ¶ "And thus the Butcher of Baltimore earned double immortality by dying exactly as you see him now, on his own wax image. And that, ladies and gentlemen, concludes tonight's final tour of the House of Wax." • *Chamber of Horrors* was originally made as a pilot for a projected TV series but was deemed too gruesome to air, and was released theatrically instead. • A William Castle–styled warning precedes the picture saying, "The management has instituted visual and audible warnings at the beginning of each of the Four Supreme Fright Points." These warnings included the "Fear Flasher" and the "Horror Horn." Audiences were instructed to "Turn away when you see the 'Fear Flasher,'" and "Close your eyes when you hear the 'Horror Horn'."

The Frozen Ghost (1945) (see HYPNOTISTS). Lon Chaney, Jr., is "Gregor the Great," a stage hypnotist. When a man dies while under Gregor's hypnotic spell, the remorseful mesmerist withdraws to the wax museum owned by a woman friend. The resident wax sculptor and Gregory's business manager conspire to drive Gregor mad by making him think he is responsible for another death. At one point, they disguise the body of the murdered owner as a wax figure and finally dispose of it in the basement furnace. Using his powers of hypnosis, Gregor finally uncovers the truth in time to save yet another victim from a fiery death. • This is Universal's only horror film set at a wax museum.

The House of Exorcism (1975) (see DEMONS AND DEVILS) (also *Lisa and the Devil*). Elke Sommer plays a possessed young woman who sees a wax figure of herself in an hallucination.

House of Wax (1953; Warner Bros.) D: Andre de Toth. P: Bryan Foy. S: Crane Wilbur. C: Bert Glennon, J. Peverell Marley.

The wheelchair-bound wax museum proprietor, Lionel Atwill, confers with his two sculpting assistants, Arthur Edmund Carewe (left) and Allen Vincent (right), in Mystery of the Wax Museum *(1933).*

Cast: Vincent price, Frank Lovejoy, Phyllis Kirk, Carolyn Jones, Paul Picerni, Charles Bronson. This successful 3-D remake of *Mystery of the Wax Museum* (1933) stars Vincent Price as a mad disfigured sculptor who uses human victims as the base for his wax figures. ¶ "To you they are wax, but to me, their creator, they live and breathe." • Vincent Price said of his experiences on this film, "The *House of Wax* was very demanding, as I had to get to the studio every morning at 5:30 A.M. to put that makeup on. It took three hours to put on and it was agony, absolute agony." • Because the film was photographed in 3-D, Price was required to perform all his own stunts in the film. In *Little Shop of Horrors* #3, Price described the sequence in which the museum burns down: "The most difficult stunt was at the very beginning, when the fire starts in the museum, and I run under this balcony that's in flames just before it falls. I actually did that. We figured out a course for me to take around these burning figures so I could get

into a little tiny closet when this 3,000 pounds of burning balcony fell. It was scary." • Ironically, the film's director, Andre de Toth, could not appreciate the film's 3-D effects. De Toth had only one eye, and two are required to see the 3-D effect.

The House That Dripped Blood (1971) (see ANTHOLOGIES). One of the four segments, entitled "Waxworks," features Peter Cushing as a man obsessed with the wax figure of Salome. At the climax, he loses his head over her, literally, when the museum owner cuts it off and serves it up on a platter to the waxen figure.

Mystery of the Wax Museum (1933; Warner Bros.) D: Michael Curtiz. S: Don Mullaly, Carl Erickson. C: Ray Rennahan. Cast: Lionel Atwill, Fay Wray, Glenda Farrell, Frank McHugh, Allen Vincent, Gavin Gordon, Edwin Maxwell, Holmes Herbert. Lionel Atwill plays a New York wax sculptor who is burned to death when his unscrupulous partner decides to set fire to the museum for the insurance. Years later, a disfigured phantom kills the partner and lurches about the museum at night where Atwill's twin brother has now taken over. The deranged brother (actually the original sculptor thought dead) uses real bodies for his wax figures. In the end, his face too is revealed to be made of wax after heroine Fay Wray shatters Atwill's wax visage to reveal the disfigured countenance beneath. ¶ "I don't know what he was, but he made Frankenstein look like a lilly." • *Mystery of the Wax Museum,* like *Doctor X,* was one of the first horror films ever made with a color process (utilizing the inferior three-strip technicolor process). In 1954, the last known print of the film was destroyed, placing the picture among the "lost film" ranks for years until a 35mm color print was discovered in Jack Warner's personal vault. • The grotesque makeup used for the fire-scorched Atwill was created by Perc Westmore, whose famous brother Bud became the Head of Makeup at Universal studios in 1947. Perc was one of six sons who went into the makeup business (along with one sister). • Lionel Atwill said of his role, "I'd been practicing before a mirror for weeks, learning how to keep my face as stiff as a board and just wiggle my jaws in talking, eyes set and staring, a grand effect, but then in the finished picture I looked so much like a stone image that they had to cut all those close-ups out for fear of giving away the fact that my face was supposed to be a wax mask" (from the *Famous Monsters of Filmland* yearbook, 1971). • Fay Wray has said that during the scene in which she hammers away at Atwill's face, finally revealing his horrible visage underneath, the actress herself had not seen the hideous makeup beforehand. Her initial reaction was one of true terror as she literally froze up on the set and was unable to continue with the scene. • Glenda Farrell, who created the prototype of the cynical, wise-cracking blonde reporter for this film, used her role in this picture as a pattern for her "Torchy Blane" reporter film series produced by Warner Bros. in the late 1930s. Farrell appeared in seven of the nine movies (which began with *Smart Blonde,* 1936) that were usually directed by either William Beaudine or Frank McDonald. • In 1953, a 3-D remake, called *House of Wax* and starring Vincent Price in the Lionel Atwill role, made its way into movie houses. The film used Baltimore instead of New York for its setting.

Nightmare in Wax (1969; Crown International) (also *Crimes in the Wax Museum*). D: Bud Townsend. P: Martin B. Cohen. S:

R. Carlton. C: Glen Smith. Cast: Cameron Mitchell, Scott Brady, Anne Helm, Berry Kroeger, Victoria Carrol. A deranged makeup artist takes his vengenace on the movie business by abducting and waxing various members of the film community.

Samson in the Wax Museum (1964; Azteca; Mexico) (also *Santo in the Wax Museum*). D: Alfonso Corona Blake. P: Alberto Lopez. S: Fernando Galiana, Julio Porter. C: José Ortiz Ramos. Cast: Santo, Claudio Brook, Ruben Rojo, Norma Mora, Ruxana Bellini, José Luis Jiminez. The masked Mexican wrestler matches strength with a mad scientist and his wax museum monsters.

Terror in the Wax Museum (1973, Cinerama) D: George Fenady. P: Andrew J. Fenady. S: Jameson Brewer. C: William Jurgensen. Cast: Ray Milland, Elsa Lanchester, Broderick Crawford, Maurice Evans, Louis Hayward, Mark Edwards, Nicole Shelby, John Carradine, Patric Knowles, Shani Wallis. A London wax museum, filled with notorious figures from history, is the site of a murderous plot to keep the exhibits (which seemingly come to life) from being moved to America. The Jack the Ripper-style killer turns out to be a pub owner (*not* the wax figure come to life) who is after the dead owner's fortune hidden somewhere inside the museum. ¶ "In these aisles, ladies and gentlemen, you will meet some of the most fiendish monsters in all history. You'll meet vampires, cannibals, poisoners, stranglers, stabbers and rippers."

Waxwork (1988; Vestron Pictures) D/S: Anthony Hickox. P: Staffan Ahrenberg. C: Gerry Lively. Cast: Zach Galligan, Deborah Foreman, Michelle Johnson, Dana Ashbrook, Miles O'Keeffe, Charles McCaughan, J. Kenneth Campbell, John Rhys Davies, Patrick MacNee, David Warner. David Warner runs a small, sinister, and very special wax museum. Anyone who gets too close to the various exhibits is sucked into the wax figure's world and meets gruesome deaths at the hands of the evil characters. The figures include a vampire, werewolf, mummy, zombies, the Marquis de Sade, etc. ¶ "There is nowhere to run. If even one of these gets out, the world will be contaminated within a few days!"

Waxworks (1924; Viking; Germany) (also *Three Wax Men*). D: Paul Leni. S: Henrik Galeen. C: Halmar Lerski. Cast: Emil Jannings, Conrad Veidt, Werner Krauss, John Gottowt, William Dieterle. After visiting a wax museum, a poet first writes about, then dreams of, Harun al-Rashid, Ivan the Terrible, and Jack the Ripper. • Brilliant German director Paul Leni was also a master art director and painter. The critical success of *Waxworks* caught the eye of producer Carl Laemmle, and he invited Leni over to Hollywood for a short, but celebrated, stint at Universal. Among his credits are *The Man Who Laughs* (1928) and the renown silent cinema classic, *The Cat and the Canary* (1927). His sudden tragic death from blood poisoning in 1929, at the age of 44, cut his promising career far too short. • Paul Leni described his philosophy concerning set design in a 1924 issue of *Kinematograph,* saying, "For my film *Waxworks* I have tried to create sets so stylized that they evince no idea of reality. My fairground is sketched in with an indescribable fluidity of light, moving shapes, shadows, lines, and curves. It is not extreme reality that the camera perceives, but the reality of the inner event, which is more profound, effective and moving than what we see through everyday eyes, and I equally believe that the cinema can reproduce this truth, heightened effectively." • Future director William Dieterle (*The Hunchback of Notre Dame,* 1939) played four roles in this film.

Werewolves

The popular concept of the werewolf (or lycanthrope) has entered the public consciousness not through great works of literature as so many other monsters have (Dracula, the Frankenstein Monster, Jekyll and Hyde), but instead leapt straight from the pen of Hollywood screenwriters. Though the folklore of many cultures embraces the legend of the werewolf, Hollywood generally bypassed the old, often conflicting, folk tales and created their own set of lycanthropic lore. The cinema werewolf was born in 1935 with Universal's rather stodgy first stab at a werewolf film, *Werewolf of London* (1935). Six years later, the lycanthrope really came into his own with Universal's second (and much more successful) attempt—the classic *The Wolf Man* (1941). This film introduced an entirely new set of rules for werewolves, including the idea that only silver can kill one. *The Wolf Man* also introduced one of horrordom's favorite characters, the tragic Lawrence Talbot, providing the rather limited horror star Lon Chaney, Jr., with his most enduring (and only original) monster/character. Talbot/Chaney appeared together in four other Universal horrors, though each time the Wolf Man was paired with another monster from the Universal stables, until he too was one that "met" the boys in *Abbott and Costello Meet Frankenstein* (1948).

A few updates on werewolfery followed: Everything from science-induced lycanthropy in the sci-fi dominated 1950s (*The Werewolf,* 1956, and *I Was a Teenage Werewolf,* 1957) to the gothic reworkings of Hammer's *The Curse of the Werewolf* (1961). Then in 1968, the ex-wrestler/architect/circus performer Jacinto Molina changed his name to Paul Naschy for the screen and created a European sensation with his portrayal of the doomed Waldemar Daninsky in *The Mark of the Wolfman.* The success of this picture in Europe led to nine sequels and turned Naschy into Spain's Vincent Price, Peter Cushing, and Christopher Lee all rolled into one. Curiously, the Daninsky series stayed a European phenomenon, with the films given only limited exposure in the United States. While Naschy's low-budget efforts are not always the most coherent (often poorly re-edited and suffering from bad dubbing) they are at least lively and deserve to be seen by werewolf fans everywhere.

A werewolf revival of sorts occurred in the 1980s, beginning with Joe Dante's witty and entertaining *The Howling* (1981), a film which paid homage to its predecessors while at the same time opening up new ground in werewolf effects and

The Frankenstein Monster (Bela Lugosi) gains the upper hand against the Wolf Man (Lon Chaney, Jr.) in this publicity pose for Frankenstein Meets the Wolf Man *(1943).*

makeup. Unfortunately, this shining example has been somewhat tarnished by the glut of poorly made sequels that followed (four to date, with no end in sight). Another worthy addition to the lycanthropic legions was John Landis's *An American Werewolf in London* (1981), a movie that successfully mixed humor with straight horror, helping to pave the way for the now-common horror/comedy. *An American Werewolf* also earned special effects man Rick Baker the first ever Academy Award for Best Makeup Effects.

Werewolves continue to be popular creatures; their inherent pathos and tortured personalities continue to fascinate. And let's not forget that the werewolf film brought us one of horrordom's most amusing movie titles — 1961's *Werewolf in a Girls' Dormitory.*

Universal's "Larry Talbot" Series

Abbott and Costello Meet Frankenstein (1948; Universal) D: Charles T. Barton. P: Robert Arthur. S: Robert Lees, Frederic I. Rinaldo, John Grant. C: Charles Van Enger. Cast: Bud Abbott, Lou Costello, Lon Chaney, Jr., Bela Lugosi, Glenn Strange, Lenore Aubert. Lon Chaney, Jr., appears for the fifth and final time as Larry Talbot, the Wolf Man. In this comic entry, he attempts to warn Bud and Lou that Dracula is scheming to revive the Frankenstein monster. ¶ Chaney: "I know you think I'm crazy, but in a half an hour the Moon will rise and I'll turn into a wolf." Costello: "You and twenty million other guys." • At the climax, the Wolf Man gets the better of Dracula when he grabs the vampire in bat form and plunges over a cliff with the vampire/bat clutched in his talons. • Besides the Wolf Man, Chaney played another monster in the film. Glenn Strange (playing Frankenstein's Monster) broke his foot during the production, and had to complete the film wearing a foot cast. At one point Chaney wore the Frankenstein Monster makeup to fill in for the injured Strange. Chaney was an old hand at playing the monster, having previously done the role in *The Ghost of Frankenstein* (1942). • Lon Chaney, Jr., was not overly fond of the horror spoof, claiming, "Abbott and Costello ruined the horror films; they made buffoons out of the monsters."

Frankenstein Meets the Wolf Man (1943; Universal) D: Roy William Neill. P: George Waggner. S: Curt Siodmak. C: George Robinson. Cast: Ilona Massey, Patric Knowles, Lon Chaney, Lionel Atwill, Bela Lugosi, Maria Ouspenskaya, Dennis Hoey. When graverobbers disturb his crypt during the full moon, Lawrence Talbot revives as the Wolf Man. Accompanied by the Gypsy woman Maleva, he travels to the region where Dr. Frankenstein worked to search for Frankenstein's diaries, from which he hopes to discover a way to truly die and thus end his tormented existence. Once there,

Talbot finds the monster, whom he eventually battles in the spectacular climax. ¶ "If I can find Dr. Frankenstein's diary, I can break this curse and find peace in death." • This was Universal's first film utilizing their desperation strategy of "more is better," by combining their box office monsters. Ostensibly, this is the fifth film in the "Frankenstein" series, but more accurately it is the first sequel to *The Wolf Man* (1941), since most of the film focuses on Lawrence Talbot (the Frankenstein monster does not appear until the second half of the picture, and even then he is given a subordinate role to Talbot). • This is the first film in which Lon Chaney, Jr., changed from a man to a wolf before our very eyes (he only transformed from wolf to man in *The Wolf Man*).

House of Dracula (1945; Universal) D: Erle C. Kenton. P: Paul Malvern. S: Edward T. Lowe. C: George Robinson. Cast: Lon Chaney, Jr., John Carradine, Martha O'Driscoll, Lionel Atwill, Onslow Stevens, Jane Adams, Ludwig Stossel, Glenn Strange. Larry Talbot, a.k.a. the Wolf Man, shows up at the house of renowned scientist Dr. Edelmann, begging for help with his lycanthropic condition. Likewise, Dracula arrives asking the doctor to help *him*. Also, the Frankenstein Monster is found in some caves underneath the doctor's house, carried there by the mud and quicksand he had sunk into at the climax of *House of Frankenstein*. Dr. Edelmann is tricked by Dracula and is contaminated by the vampire's blood. This causes a Jekyll and Hyde condition in him, and he sets about reviving the Frankenstein Monster. Larry Talbot (after being cured by the doctor) shoots the now-mad Edelmann and topples a shelf of chemicals which burst into flame and consume the monster. • This fourth appearance of Lawrence Talbot as the Wolf Man makes no attempt to explain how the lycanthrope recovered from the fatal shooting in *House of Frankenstein* (1944). Talbot simply shows up at Dr.

Edelmann's home, asking for help. • Screenwriter Edward T. Lowe offered a more scientific explanation for the Wolf Man's condition: Dr. Edelmann explains that lycanthropy (the affliction that causes Larry Talbot to change into a werewolf) is caused by "a crowding of the brain because the cranial cavity failed to enlarge sufficiently." • Fans of Lawrence Talbot were heartened to find the tragic character finally experiencing a happy ending when the Wolf Man is *cured* in this picture. (Apparently the cure did not take, however, since he was back in werewolf form again (without explanation) for *Abbott and Costello Meet Frankenstein,* 1948). • When the project was first announced by Universal, it was under the name of *The Wolf Man vs. Dracula.* Presumably drastic changes were made since, disappointingly, the Wolf Man never comes in contact with Dracula. • In an odd mixing of genres, Universal released *House of Dracula* on a double bill with *The Daltons Ride Again,* a western(!) which also starred Lon Chaney, Jr., and Martha O'Driscoll. • Shortly after the completion of *House of Dracula,* Universal dropped Lon Chaney, Jr.'s, contract.

House of Frankenstein (1944; Universal) D: Erle C. Kenton. P: Paul Malvern. S: Edward T. Lowe. C: George Robinson. Cast: Boris Karloff, Lon Chaney, Jr., John Carradine, J. Carrol Naish, Anne Gwynne, Peter Coe, Lionel Atwill, George Zucco, Elena Verdugo. After making use of (and then disposing of) Dracula, Dr. Niemann, a criminal scientist wishing to follow in Dr. Frankenstein's footsteps, heads to the ruins of Castle Frankenstein. There he finds the bodies of the Wolf Man and Frankenstein's Monster and revives them both. Niemann promises to cure the Wolf Man (Larry Talbot) if he aids him in his experiments. But Niemann hems and haws until it is too late and Talbot, now in wolf form, is shot and killed (with a silver bullet of course) by a Gypsy girl who has fallen in love with him. Meanwhile, the villagers storm the castle and chase the Frankenstein Monster into the swamps, where he sinks into the quicksand with his beloved Dr. Niemann. ¶ "Why have you freed me from the ice that imprisoned the beast that lived within me?" • This is the third outing for the doomed Lawrence Talbot. He appears next (without explanation) in *House of Dracula* (1945). • At one point in the film, mad scientist Boris Karloff planned to transfer the brain of Frankenstein's Monster into the body of the Wolf Man (Karloff's Dr. Niemann had a penchant

for playing "musical brains" throughout the picture). • *House of Frankenstein* was shot under the title of *The Devil's Brood.* • Initially, the Mummy was also scheduled to appear in *House of Frankenstein* but was eventually dropped from the roster.

The Wolf Man (1941; Universal) D/P: George Waggner. S: Curt Siodmak. C: Joseph Valentine. Cast: Lon Chaney, Jr., Claude Rains, Evelyn Ankers, Ralph Bellamy, Maria Ouspenskaya, Bela Lugosi, Patric Knowles, Fay Helm, Warren William. Larry Talbot returns from America to greet his estranged father at his ancestral home in Wales. After a local Gypsy carnival, Talbot is bitten by a werewolf, killing the beast in the process. Now, during a full moon he transforms into a werewolf himself and terrorizes the countryside, with no memory afterwards. Finally, the locals organize a hunt and it is Talbot's own father who is forced to kill his son with a heavy silver-handled cane. ¶ "Even a man who is pure in heart, and says his prayers by night, may become a wolf when the wolfbane blooms, and the Autumn moon is bright." • Initially called *The Wolf Man,* the title was changed over the course of the project to *Destiny,* before finally going back to the original title again for the release. • Though this was Universal's second werewolf venture (*Werewolf of London* was produced six years earlier, in 1935), this was the picture that introduced the tragic character of Lawrence Talbot as the Wolf Man, and created the now-standard folklore governing cinema werewolves. • Though Lon Chaney, Jr., played the title character, Claude Rains was given top billing in *The Wolf Man.* Chaney is the *only* actor to ever play Lawrence Talbot/the Wolf Man (returning four more times as the doomed lycanthrope). • Consummate character actor Claude Rains, playing Lawrence Talbot's father, was a little overzealous in the final tragic scene in which he beats the creature to death with a silver-tipped cane. Rains, ever throwing himself into his role, threw a bit too much force into his blows and hit Chaney in the eye with the cane, necessitating Universal sending the actor home until the swelling had gone down. • The ill-fated Gypsy who bites Lon Chaney, Jr., and passes on the curse of the werewolf to him was played by Bela Lugosi. Bela's character's name was, appropriately enough, "Bela." • During the course of production, Chaney, Jr., was filmed on the same set upon which his illustrious father walked for *The Hunchback of Notre Dame* (1923). • Universal's makeup wizard Jack Pierce created the Wolf Man out of *yak* hairs. Chaney had to endure four hours in the makeup chair to be transformed into the hairy one. • Though considered a classic, *The Wolf Man* is not above the occasional continuity problem. One scene shows Chaney ripping off his teeshirt during the transformation process, but in the next scene we see him as a werewolf wearing a long-sleeve shirt (and it seems unlikely that the savage Wolf Man would stop and don a fresh shirt before going out to commit his lycanthropic mayhem). • During the production, a 600-pound bear (used in scenes of the Gypsy camp ultimately cut from the release print) got loose, causing most of the cast and crew to flee. The bear even chased leading lady Evelyn Ankers up a ladder before being subdued by its trainer.

Spain's "Waldemar Daninsky" Series

Assignment Terror (1970) (see ALIENS — INVADERS ON EARTH: THE 60s AND 70s). Michael Rennie plays an alien who plans to dominate the world by preying on Man's fears of the supernatural. To this end he revives Dracula, the Frankenstein Monster, the Mummy, and of course, the Wolfman — none other than Waldemar Daninsky (Paul Naschy in his third screen appearance as the tragic character). • Previous to this film, a werewolf had battled Frankenstein's Monster (*Frankenstein Meets the Wolf Man,* 1943) and Dracula (*Abbott and Costello Meet Frankenstein,* 1948), but this is the first (and only) time in screen history a werewolf has battled a mummy. The Wolfman is the victor (though it is a cheat — he sets the Mummy on fire with a torch. Every *child* knows that no self-respecting werewolf would ever go near fire while in wolf form). • *The Werewolf vs. the Vampire Women* (1970) was next.

The Beast and the Magic Sword (1983; Aconito Films/Amachi; Spain/Japan) D/ P/S: Jacinto Molina (Paul Naschy). C: Julio Burgos. Cast: Paul Naschy, Shigeru Amachi, Beatriz Escudero, Junko Asahina, Violeta Cela, Yoko Fuji. This tenth (and last to date) outing for Paul Naschy as Waldemar Daninsky the Wolfman is set in sixteenth century Japan where a holy man unsuccessfully tries to lift the werewolf curse from him. Waldemar continues to go on killing sprees under the influence of the full moon until a Japanese woman who loves him ends his misery with a silver sword. • In a screen first, the Wolfman wrestles a tiger. The werewolf wins, ripping out the big cat's throat. • Paul Naschy produced, directed, and wrote the screenplay (using his real name of Jacinto Molina) as well as starred in this picture. Though he wrote every film in the series, this is the first time as producer and only his second time as director.

Curse of the Devil (1973; Goldstone; Spain/Mexico) D: Charles Avred (Carlos Aured). P: Luis Mendez. S: Jack Moll (Jacinto Molina). C: Frank Sanchez. Cast: Paul Naschy, Faye Falcon, Vinc Molina, May Oliver, Maira Silva, Ana Farra, Eduardo Calvo, Patty Shepard, Santiago Rivero, Ines Morales. In this seventh outing featuring Waldemar Daninsky as the Wolfman, the centuries old family curse is reactivated when a beautiful woman seduces him and infects him with the werewolf virus. He goes on a fanged rampage during the course of the full moon until his lover plunges a silver dagger into his heart, ending the curse and his life. • *Night of the Howling Beast* (1976) was next up for Waldemar.

Dr. Jekyll and the Wolfman (1971; International Cinema Films; Spain) D: Leon Kaminsky. P: José Frade. S: Jacinto Molina. C: Francisco Fraile. Cast: Paul Naschy, Shirley Corrigan, Jack Taylor, Marta Miller, Barta Barri, Luis Induñi. A descendant of Dr. Jekyll attempts to cure Waldemar of his lycanthropy by using his great grandfather's infamous "personality changing" serum — with the expected disastrous results. Now instead of two personalities, the poor wretch has three to deal with — Waldemar, the Wolfman, and Mr. Hyde. ¶ "The only way he can be killed and put out of his misery is by the hand of a woman who loves him enough to pierce his heart with a silver weapon, a silver bullet for instance." • This is the sixth entry in the series, followed by *Curse of the Devil* (1973).

The Fury of the Wolfman (1970; Avco Embassy; Spain) D: José Maria Zabalza. P: Plata Films. S: Jacinto Molina. C: Leopoldo Villaseñor. Cast: Paul Naschy, Perla Cristal, Veronica Lujan, Mark Stevens, Michel Rivers. Count Waldemar Daninsky, in his fifth appearance, once again seeks help from science for his condition (just as he did in *Night of the Werewolf,* 1968). This time he goes to a female scientist whom he had earlier spurned for another woman. Out of spiteful revenge, she induces him to bite and infect his current lover before all meet their various fates. ¶ "When the heliotrope starts growing among rough rocks, and the full moon shines at night, in a certain area of the Earth a man turns into a wolf"— opening narration (and the Spanish version of the Universal ditty, "Even a man who is pure in heart..."?). • For his next appearance, Waldemar meets the great grandson of Dr. Jekyll in *Dr. Jekyll and the Wolfman* (1971).

The Mark of the Wolfman (1968; Independent International; Spain) (also *Frankenstein's Bloody Terror*). D: Henry Egan (Enrique L. Equiluz). S: Jacinto Molina. C: Emilio Foriscot. Cast: Paul Naschy, Diane Konopka, Julian Ugarte, Rossana Yanni, Michael Manz, Joseph Morton, Carl Casara, Anita Avery, Gilbert Granger, Victoriano Lopez. The first film to introduce Count Waldemar Daninsky (Paul Naschy) as the Wolfman has him slaying a revived werewolf and in the process becoming infected himself. In desperation, he sends for a strange couple, experts in the occult, for help. They turn out to be vampires, and he kills the undead creatures before succumbing to a silver bullet shot by a woman who loves him. ¶ "Now, the most frightening Frankenstein story of all, as the ancient werewolf curse brands the family of monster-makers as 'Wolfstein.' Wolfstein—the inhuman clan of blood-hungry wolf-monsters"—tacked-on opening narration (the only mention of any "Frankenstein"). • Star Paul Naschy wrote the screenplay as well, using his real name of Jacinto Molina. Naschy/Molina wrote or co-wrote all ten films in the series. Naschy did not originally intend to star as the Wolfman, but after the producers had difficulty in casting the role, they asked Naschy to play it. • *The Mark of the Wolfman* was released in 3-D in Spain, but only adulterated flat prints made it to U.S. theaters (with the totally misleading title change of *Frankenstein's Bloody Terror*). • *Night of the Werewolf* (1968) was the next stop for Count Daninsky.

Night of the Howling Beast (1976; Independent International; Spain) (also *The Werewolf and the Yeti*). D: M. I. Bonns. P: Profilms. S: Jacinto Molina. C: Tomas Pladevall. Cast: Paul Naschy, Grace Mills, Silvia Solar, Gil Vidal, Luis Induñi. In this eighth picture in the series, Waldemar travels to Tibet with an expedition searching for the elusive Yeti. While in the mountains he enters a cave and encounters two beautiful demonic women who seduce and then infect him with the werewolf virus. He encounters bandits, black magic, and finally the Yeti himself, which he battles in werewolf form—a first in horror history. (The werewolf wins when he rips out the Yeti's throat.) ¶ "The full moon has always filled me with fear. But now, with all my strength, I wish it would come so I could destroy you." • Taking its cue from *Werewolf of London* (1935), this film also postulates that the only cure for lycanthropy is a rare Tibetan flower. "There exists a magic plant, with red flowers on it. When its petals are mixed with the blood of a young girl, it can cure those like you," claims a wise Tibetan monk. Unlike the 1935 film, this one has a happy ending, with Waldemar being cured by the plant. • Waldemar returned for the aptly-titled *Return of the Wolfman* in 1980.

Night of the Werewolf (1968; Kin Films; Spain/France) D: René Govar. S: Jacinto Molina, Carlos Belario, René Govar. Cast: Paul Naschy, Monique Brainville, Hélène Vatelle, Peter Beaumont. This first sequel to *The Mark of the Wolfman,* and second film in the series, has Waldemar seek the help of a scientist to cure him of his condition. The evil doctor, however, merely wants to use the Wolfman to get rid of his competitive colleagues. • This quick follow-up film never made it to American shores, and appears to be a lost film, even in Europe.

The Return of the Wolfman (1980; Dalmata Films; Spain) (also *The Craving* [video title]). D/S: Jack (Jacinto) Molina. P: Dalmata Films. C: Alejandro Ulloa. Cast: Paul Naschy (Jacinto Molina), Jully Saly, Silvia Aguilar, Narciso Ibañez Menta, Azucena Hernandez, Beatriz Elorietta, Pilar Alcon, Pepe Ruiz. In his ninth appearance, Waldemar Daninsky and an evil vampiric countess are executed in the sixteenth century. Grave robbers remove the silver cross embedded in Waldemar's heart, and the countess is revived by three young students. The two creatures go at each other, and the werewolf is victorious when he rips out the throat of the vampiress. Finally, a woman who loves him lays Waldemar to rest with that same silver cross. ¶ "Waldemar Daninsky, this high tribunal condemns you because of your despicable and evil crimes. It has been proven that on the nights of the full moon you become a wolf, devouring hundreds of poor, innocent people." • Star Paul Naschy stepped behind the camera to direct this picture as well as script it, using his real-life name of Jacinto Molina. • Unfortunately for director/screenwriter/star Paul Naschy, this ninth film in the series was a box office flop and threatened his newly-formed production company with bankruptcy. He next took his werewolf to Japan for *The Beast and the Magic Sword* (1983).

The Werewolf vs. the Vampire Women (1970; Ellman Enterprises; Spain/W. Germany) (also *Blood Moon* [video title]). D: Leon Klimowsky. P: Salvadore Romero. S: Jacinto Molina, Hans Munkel. C: Leopoldo Villaseñor. Cast: Paul Naschy, Patty Shepard, Gaby Fuchs, Barbara Capell, Andrew Reese, Julio Peña, Yelena Samarina, José Marco, Barta Barri. In this fourth entry, Waldemar the Werewolf is revived when doctors remove the silver bullets from his heart during an autopsy. He returns to his ancestral home and falls in love with one of two female students on holiday who stumble upon his castle. The other girl finds an ancient crypt and releases a female vampire. The two monsters — werewolf and vampire — end up locked in a life and death struggle. ¶ "I'm going to take out those two silver bullets, and I can assure you our Mr. Daninsky will be as dead as ever" — a coroner about to make the biggest mistake of his career. • The tragic character next experienced *The Fury of the Wolfman* in 1970.

Other Lycanthropes

An American Werewolf in London (1981; Universal) D/S: John Landis. P: George Folsey, Jr. C: Robert Paynter. Cast: David Naughton, Jenny Agutter, Griffin Dunne, Brian Glover, John Woodvine, Lila Kaye, Frank Oz, Don McKillop, Colin Fernandes, Paul Kember. Two Americans traveling in northern England are attacked on the moors by a werewolf. Jack is killed, but David survives. Now Jack appears to David periodically, though each time more decayed, to try and convince David to kill himself and thereby sever the werewolf's bloodline ... because David is now a werewolf himself. ¶ "I'm sure if there was a monster roaming around northern England we'd have seen it on the telly." • Humor is liberally laced in with the truly horrific shocks in this werewolf update. The humor often comes from David's dead friend Jack, who says things like, "You'll kill and make others like me. I'm not having a nice time here," and "Have you ever talked to a corpse? It's boring!" • *An American Werewolf in London* aptly opened with the Marcels' song "Blue Moon." • For his incredible prosthetics and groundbreaking transformation scenes, Rick Baker won the first ever Academy Award for Best Makeup.

The Beast Must Die (1974; Amicus/Cinerama; U.K.) (also *Black Werewolf*). D: Paul Annett. P: Max J. Rosenberg, Milton Subotsky. S: Michael Winder. C: Jack Hildyard. Cast: Calvin Lockhart, Peter Cushing, Marlene Clark, Charles Gray, Anton Diffring, Ciaran Madden, Tom Chadbon, Michael Gambon. Calvin Lockhart is a millionaire with a passion for hunting who wants to hunt the biggest game of all — a werewolf. To this end he invites a group of people to his estate, one of which he knows is a werewolf. ¶ "Tonight is my last chance, the last night of the full moon. Tonight, the beast must die, and will." • This film features the unique gimmick of a 30-second "Werewolf Break" towards the end of the picture in which a narrator invites the audience to try and figure out the identity of the werewolf. • Rather than the Lon Chaney, Jr., look, the "werewolf" here is a large dog dressed up with a furry mane. • Peter Cushing played Dr. Lundgren, the resident expert on lycanthropy, who told us how *The Beast Must Die*. He faced another werewolf the following year in *Legend of the Werewolf* (1975).

Blood (1973) (see PLANTS). The son of the Wolf Man and the daughter of Dracula marry and move to America to begin experimenting with carnivorous plants. • This is grade-Z filmmaker Andy Milligan's second film to touch on the werewolf theme, the first being *The Rats Are Coming! The Werewolves Are Here!* (1972).

The Boy Who Cried Werewolf (1973; Universal) D: Nathan Juran. P: Aaron Rosenberg. S: Bob Homel. C: Michael P. Joyce. Cast: Kerwin Mathews, Elaine Devry, Scott Sealey, Robert J. Wilke, Bob Homel. A 12-year-old boy sees a werewolf but can get no one to believe him. His father fends off the attacker but is bitten, and now transforms into a werewolf himself during the full moon.

The Company of Wolves (1984; Palace Pictures; U.K.) D: Neil Jordan. P: Stephen Wolley, Nik Powell. S: Neil Jordan, Angela Carter. C: Bryan Loftus. Cast: Angela Lansbury, Sarah Patterson, David Warner, Graham Crowden, Brian Glover, Kathryn Pogson, Stephen Rea, Russe Silberg, Micha Bergese, Georgia Slowe. This convoluted, almost surreal adult fantasy in the vein of "Little Red Riding Hood" follows a young girl and her fantastical adventures in a forested land populated by wise old grandmothers and "wolves in men's clothing."

Cry of the Banshee (1970) (see WITCHES, WARLOCKS, AND CULTS). In the sixteenth century, an English magistrate (Vincent Price) persecutes a seemingly peaceful witch cult headed by a druidic high priestess who vows vengeance before she dies. She sends an emissary of evil (in the form of a young man who changes into a werewolf-like creature) to punish the cruel and misguided magistrate.

Cry of the Werewolf (1944; Columbia) D: Henry Levin. P: Wallace MacDonald. S: Griffin Jay, Charles O'Neal. C: L. W. O'Connell. Cast: Nina Foch, Stephen Crane, Osa Massen, Barton MacLane, Fritz Leiber. Nina Foch plays Celeste La Tour, Queen of the Gypsies, who inherits not only the title from her mother, but the taint of lycanthropy as well. ¶ "The tradition of werewolves and vampires dates back almost to the world's earliest recorded history. Of the two, the werewolf is perhaps the most horrible of the ghosts. The instinct for evil is so strong that they willingly and cunningly assume the shape of a beast in order to kill." • Columbia tried to keep the horror element low-key, even having all transformation scenes take place off-screen. Celeste is not a "wolf woman" but a true "werewolf" — she transforms into a full-blooded wolf, not a half-man, half-wolf (as in *The Wolf Man*, 1941). • Star Nina Foch had this to say about the film (in *Filmfax* #26): "I'll tell you the best thing about playing a werewolf — you get to rest while the wolf works." Ms. Foch does *not* consider this or her other horror film, *Return of the Vampire* (1943), to be career highlights. "I'm not amused by horror pictures," she stated.

The Curse of the Werewolf (1961; Hammer/Universal; U.K.) D: Terence Fisher. P: Anthony Hinds. S: John Elder. C: Arthur Grant. Cast: Oliver Reed, Clifford Evans, Hira Talfrey, Catherine Feller, Yvonne Romain, Anthony Dawson, Richard ·Wordsworth, Warren Mitchell. A servant girl is raped by a bestial beggar kept in the castle dungeon, and dies giving birth to a boy named Leon. Upon reaching adulthood, Leon begins to turn into a werewolf during the full moon. The only thing that can save him from the transformations is the love he has found with a young woman, but when he is denied that love by the actions of others, he again transforms into a snarling beast and must be killed by a silver bullet. ¶ "A silver bullet from a crucifix, the only bullet that will kill a werewolf." • Following in the footsteps (or more accurately — paw marks) of Universal's original *The Wolf Man* (1941), the werewolf is once again killed by his own father. • The film is based on the Guy Endore novel, *Werewolf of Paris*. Screenwriter John Elder is actually producer Anthony Hinds writing under his pen name. This was Hinds's first produced screenplay. "I wrote it," claimed Hinds in a *Fangoria* #74 interview, "because the budget I was given as a producer wasn't enough to include a writer." He went on to pen a number of screenplays for Hammer, including *Kiss of the Vampire* (1963), *The Evil of Frankenstein* (1964), and *Scars of Dracula* (1970). • Since it is based on a book called *Werewolf of Paris,* the film was naturally set in France. The setting, however, was changed from France to Spain. Screenwriter/producer Anthony Hinds explained why: "[Studio head Michael Carreras] was setting up a picture about the Spanish Inquisition. We had already built the sets when we got a tip that the Catholic Church would ban the picture. So he pulled out and I was left with these sets. That's why it was set in Spain. I had to change all the names."

Daughter of Dr. Jekyll (1957) (see JEKYLL, DR., AND FAMILY). Gloria Talbott plays the daughter of Dr. Jekyll who comes to England to claim her father's inheritance. Mysterious murders occur and suspicion falls on her. The crimes are eventually revealed to be the work of her former guardian (Arthur Shields) who has discovered Jekyll's secrets and periodically transforms into a werewolf-like creature.

Deadtime Stories (1987) (see ANTHOLOGIES). In the film's second story, "Little Red Runninghood," a nubile young girl stops by a pharmacy to pick up some medicine for her grandmother. The pharmacist mistakenly gives her the medication intended for a young man as a treatment for lycanthropy. The young man goes to her house to try and get his medication back but it is too late and he turns into a wolf, forcing Red to drive a silver cake knife through his neck.

Devil Wolf of Shadow Mountain (1964; Prin Productions) D: Gary Kent. P: Robert Dietz. S: Gene Pollock. Cast: Johnny Cardoz, Gene Pollock. Set in the Old West, a man drinks from a wolf track and turns into a werewolf.

Dr. Terror's Gallery of Horrors (1966) (see ANTHOLOGIES). In one of the five segments of this amateurish cheapie, Mitch Evans plays "Count Alucard," a vampire who ends up battling a werewolf.

Dr. Terror's House of Horrors (1965) (see ANTHOLOGIES). In the first segment, Neil McCallum uncovers evidence of lycanthropy in the basement crypt. The surprise ending sees him confronting a (rare) female werewolf.

Dracula Against Frankenstein (see VAMPIRES—DRACULA AND FAMILY) (also *Dracula vs. Dr. Frankenstein; The Screaming Dead* [video title]). In a narrative nightmare, Dr. Frankenstein creates a creature to battle Dracula. At one point the creature is aided by a werewolf in the fight against Dracula. It all makes very little sense.

Face of the Screaming Werewolf (1964; ADP Productions) D/P: Jerry Warren. S: Gilbert Solar, Alfred Salimar (Abel Salazar). C: Richard Wallace. Cast: Landa Varle, Lon Chaney, Donald Barron, Raymond Gaylord, Steve Conte, Jorge Mondragon, Emma Roldan, George Mitchell, Chuck Niles, Bill White, Fred Hoffman. An expedition to an ancient pyramid on the Yucatan peninsula yields two bodies, that of an ancient mummy and that of a modern man in some sort of mummified condition. Both come back to life and the second body turns out to be a werewolf. ¶ "The other [body] is that of a modern man, placed in the pyramid only recently after an exchange of body fluids with the mummy in an effort to achieve an apparent state of death." • This no-budget pastiche features more shots cribbed from the Aztec Mummy film series spliced together with film of Lon Chaney, Jr., as a werewolf by grade-Z hack Jerry Warren. Of course, since the mummy scenes are stolen from a completely different film, the two monsters never meet. • Lon Chaney, Jr.'s, last turn under the werewolf whiskers (looking similar to his Universal appearances but a big shaggier) is a silent one—he has no dialogue.

Full Moon High (1982; Filmways) D/P/S: Larry Cohen. Cast: Adam Arkin, Roz Kelly, Ed McMahon, Elizabeth Hartman, Alan Arkin, Bill Kirchenbauer, Joanne Nail. In 1960, high school student Adam Arkin (the son of Alan Arkin) visits Romania and is bitten by a werewolf. Doomed to roam the Earth as a werewolf himself, he finally returns to his home town 20 years later, only to have trouble adjusting to the changes in his friends and surroundings. • Auteur Larry Cohen had this to say about this little-seen lycanthropic spoof: "It's more than a comedy. It has some interesting ideas about how life has changed sexually and politically since the early sixties.... And whereas he changes into a werewolf all of the time, his friends change into middle-aged people while he is gone, with different values and different ideas."

Hercules, Prisoner of Evil (1967) (see MYTHOLOGY). Hercules (Reg Park) must battle an evil witch and her faithful werewolves.

House of the Black Death (1964) (see WITCHES, WARLOCKS, AND CULTS). This obscure low-budget tale of witchcraft and satanism features a bizarre subplot about werewolves. The evil warlock Belial Desard (Lon Chaney, Jr.) leads his coven in placing a curse on a young member of the Desard family returning to his ancestral home—the curse of the werewolf. ¶ "I could feel the fangs slide into the flesh, the blood flow, and the bone crack." • The film's budget was so low that it did not include any werewolf makeup. We simply see his back as he escapes the room he has been imprisoned in, and then his normal human face again after he has been killed.

House on Bare Mountain (1962; Olympic International) D: Lee Frost. P: Bob Cresse, David Andrew, Wesdon Bishop. S: Denver Scott. C: Greg Sandor. Cast: Bob Cresse, Laura Eden, Angela Webster, Ann Meyers, Hugh Cannon, Warren Ames, Jeffrey Smithers. This obscure early nudie has three classic monsters crashing a party at a girls' school—Dracula, Frankenstein's Monster, and a werewolf. Dracula and Frankenstein's Monster are fakes, but the werewolf turns out to be real. ¶ From the ads: "20 terrified teen lovelies tastefully unattired."

How to Make a Monster (1958) (see MADMEN). When a studio makeup man is fired, he uses a special hypnotic makeup base to control the actors wearing his monster outfits. He sends out a caveman, a "Teenage Frankenstein Monster," and the "Teenage Werewolf" (seen in *I Was a Teenage Werewolf*, 1957) to kill the studio heads who fired him.

The Howling (1981; Avco Embassy) D: Joe Dante. P: Michael Finnell, Jack Conrad. S: John Sayles, Terence H. Winkless. C: John Hora. Cast: Dee Wallace, Patrick MacNee, Dennis Dugan, Belinda Balaski, Kevin McCarthy, John Carradine, Slim Pickens, Charlie Barton, Dick Miller. A psychiatric retreat called "The Colony" turns out to be a haven for modern-day werewolves, headed by the non-violent Patrick MacNee. After experiencing a trauma, a young TV reporter and her husband visit The Colony. The husband is seduced into their lycanthropic ranks, leaving the woman to discover the truth and fight the beasts. ¶ "Humans are our prey!

We should feed on them like we always done. Screw all this 'channel our energies' crap." • Director Joe Dante, a self-professed monster movie fan, filled *The Howling* with references and in-jokes to previous werewolf movies, even in the naming of the characters. For instance, one is called "Jack Molina" (a reference to Jacinto Molina, which is Paul Naschy's — star of Spain's "Waldemar Daninsky" werewolf series — real name), and Patrick MacNee's character is named "Dr. George Waggner." It was George Waggner who produced and directed *The Wolf Man* in 1941. • Though he has played many murderers, mad scientists, and vampires, this is the first and only time John Carradine has played a werewolf in his long career. His character is named "Erle Kenton." Erle C. Kenton directed both *House of Frankenstein* (1944) and *House of Dracula* (1945) — both featuring Lawrence Talbot as the Wolf Man. • That legendary low-budget monster movie producer/director, Roger Corman, made a silent cameo appearance as the man in the phone booth in *The Howling* (1980). • Makeup effects creator Rob Bottin also served as associate producer on the film. • *The Howling* was successful enough to inspire four (generally unrelated) sequels to date.

Howling 2: Your Sister Is a Werewolf (1986; Helmdale) (also *Howling 2: Stirba, Werewolf Bitch* [video title]). D: Philippe Mora. P: Steven Lane. S: Robert Sarno, Gary Brandner. C: Geoffrey Stephenson. Cast: Christopher Lee, Annie McEnroe, Reb Brown, Marsha A. Hunt, Sybil Danning, Judd Omen, Ferdinand Mayne. The brother of the TV reporter heroine from *The Howling* teams up with an occult expert (Christopher Lee) to journey to Czechoslovakia to eradicate the source of the werewolf line, the Queen of Werewolves herself. ¶ "Even now there are great numbers of werewolves living secretly among us." • Building on the usual werewolf lore, this film maintains that the most powerful werewolves are immune to silver bullets, and only *titanium* can kill them. • *Howling 2* was filmed on location in Czechoslovakia, with a generally native crew. Director Philippe Mora later complained about the language barrier: "It was difficult enough filming orgy scenes where the constant grappling caused the hair of the wolf suits to fly everywhere, without trying to explain to the crew what was the matter!" (*Cinefantastique* Vol. 18, no. 2). • Despite the rather humorous tag-line, *Howling 2* is serious (and some would say "humorless"). It is based on the novel *Howling 2* by Gary Brandner. • In spite of this muddled sequel's critical and financial drubbing, director Philippe Mora was allowed to direct (and write) the third "Howling" picture. • Sybil Danning, who plays the werewolf queen, is shown during one scene to be covered from head to toe in hair. It took eight hours to apply this hair and makeup to create the full-bodied werewolf effect. "It was not a suit," the actress stated, "they put it all on like eyelashes." • At one point in the film Sybil Danning rips her top off in a moment of passion, exposing her breasts. In a tasteless and exploitative move, the filmmakers repeat this one-second scene over and over and over again during the closing credits sequence. Co-screenwriter Gary Brandner claimed that when Miss Danning saw this at the film's premier, she burst into tears and left the theater. Her agent, however, denies this ever happened, but undoubtedly she was less than pleased by this turn of events.

Howling 3: The Marsupials (1987; Square Pictures; Australia) D/S: Philippe Mora. P: Charles Waterstreet, Philippe Mora. C: Louis Irving. Cast: Barry Otto, Imogen Annesley, Dasha Blahova, Max Fairchild, Ralph Cotterill, Leigh Biolos, Frank Thring, Michael Pate. This third installment (and lowest budgeted) in the "Howling" series is related to the other two in name only. A race of werewolves has evolved along the same lines as humans, and in Australia they evolved from marsupial wolves. A beautiful young woman tries to run away from her marsupial destiny but is drawn back into the world of Australian lycanthropes. • The town which is home to the colony of werewolves is named "Flow" ("wolf" spelled backwards).

Howling 4: The Original Nightmare (1988; Allied Artists) D: John Hough. P: Harry Alan Towers. S: Clive Turner, Freddie Rowe. C: Godfrey Godar. Cast: Romy Windsor, Michael T. Weiss, Antony Hamilton, Susanne Severeid, Lamya Derval. A beautiful young mystery writer, troubled by recurring hallucinations, takes a country vacation to the remote small town of "Drago," which just happens to be populated by werewolves. • Though subtitled *The Original Nightmare,* there is nothing original in *Howling 4,* nor is it in any way related to the other films in the series.

Howling 5: The Rebirth (1989; Allied Vision) D: Neal Sundstrom. P: Clive Turner. S: Clive Turner, Freddie Rowe. C: Arledge Armenaki. Cast: Philip Davis, Victoria

Gary Clarke dons the whiskers and letterman's jacket to play the "Teenage Werewolf" in How to Make a Monster *(1958), taking over for Michael Landon from* I Was a Teenage Werewolf *(1957).*

Catlin, Elisabeth Shue, Ben Cole, William Shockley, Mark Sivertsen, Stephanie Faulkner, Mary Stavin. A disparate group of foreign tourists are invited to and then stranded at an old Romanian castle, there to be stalked one by one by the resident werewolf.

I Was a Teenage Werewolf (1957; AIP) D: Gene Fowler, Jr. P: Herman Cohen. S: Ralph Thornton. C: Joseph LaShelle. Cast: Michael Landon, Yvonne Lime, Whit Bissell, Tony Marshall, Dawn Richard, Barney Phillips, Ken Miller, John Launer, Guy Williams, Vladimir Sokoloff, Louise Lewis. Michael Landon, in his first film role, plays a troubled teen who goes to see Dr. Brandon (Whit Bissell), seeking help for his violent temper. The unscrupulous psychiatrist uses a special formula and hypnosis to send him back to his primitive beginnings, and turns him into a werewolf! ¶ "Do you remember how it felt to run over the hills in the moonlight, to hide by the stream and wait in silence.... Remember how wonderful it was when you sprang suddenly and dug in with your fangs—soft throat, the gush of warm blood." • Dr. Brandon uses a combination of hypnosis and a drug called "Scopolamine" to transform Michael Landon into the teen werewolf. • Michael Landon, who gives an intense, effective performance as the titular troubled teen, went on to star in the popular TV western series, "Bonanza," and later, "Little House on the Prairie." • At the time of its release, *I Was a Teenage Werewolf* sparked a lot of controversy with its provocative advertising campaign. Even a Senate subcommittee discussed the film, which cost $125,000 to make, was shot in seven days, and earned over two million dollars before the year was out. Its tremendous cult appeal and success encouraged AIP to churn out dozens of other "teen" monster movies in the years to come. • According to director Gene Fowler, Jr., screenwriter Ralph Thornton is actually novelist Abe Kandel writing under a pseudonym.

Kiss of the Beast (1990; Full Moon Entertainment) (also *Meridian*). D: Charles Band. P: Charles Band, Debra Dion. S: Dennis Paoli. C: Mac Ahlberg. Cast: Sherilyn Fenn, Malcolm Jamieson, Hilary Mason, Charlie, Alex Daniels, Phil Fondacaro. Sherilyn Fenn plays a young heiress returning to her family estate in Italy. When a small touring carnival performs on her land, she invites the players to dine at the castle. She soon becomes embroiled with the two identical brothers who lead the troup — Lawrence (the evil brother) and Oliver (the good and noble brother). Oliver is cursed, however, and when amorous feelings are aroused he is transformed into a werewolf-like beast. The 400-year-old curse can only be ended by the lady of the castle and she must love the man/beast. ¶ "You kill me. Kill the beast. Save my human soul from this eternal torment." • The story borrows more from *Beauty and the Beast* than it does from *The Wolf Man,* but the creature is quite impressive, with a huge hairy body and beastly features, and there is an effective transformation scene. • Star Sherilyn Fenn became famous this same year for her role as the seductive Audrey on the offbeat hit TV series, "Twin Peaks."

Ladyhawke (1985) (see SWORD AND SORCERY). This medieval sword and sorcery tale tells the story of a brave knight and his maiden fair who are cursed most horribly by an evil bishop. During the day the knight's lady transforms into a hawk, while at nightfall, when she becomes human again, the knight himself is turned into a wolf — so that they can never truly be together.

Legend of the Werewolf (1975; Tyburn; U.K.) D: Freddie Francis. P: Kevin Francis. S: John Elder. C: John Wilcox. Cast: Peter Cushing, Ron Moody, Hugh Griffith, Roy Castle, David Rintoul, David Bailie, Lynn Dalby, Stefan Gryff, Renee Houston, Norman Mitchell, Mark Weavers. A family fleeing persecution in Europe is attacked and killed by wolves. But the newborn baby is cared for and raised by the animals until he is taken in by a traveling showman and displayed as "the Wolf Boy." As he grows, he develops into a werewolf. He goes to Paris and takes a job at a small zoo, where he can be near his beloved animals. When he falls in love with a prostitute, his animal nature gets the best of him and he stalks the clients of the brothel, until he is finally cornered in the sewers by the police and shot with a silver bullet. ¶ "Help me . . . please" — the only words spoken by the hunted werewolf, who apparently still had the power of speech while in wolf form. • Producer Kevin Francis is the son of director Freddie Francis. The elder Francis is a cinematographer who turned director for Hammer and helmed many of their later entries. • Screenwriter John Elder is actually producer/writer Anthony Hinds. Hinds also wrote the superior *Curse of the Werewolf* for Hammer in 1961.

Legend of the Wolfwoman (1977; Dimension; Italy) (also *She Wolf* [video title]). D: Rino Di Silvestro. P: Diego Alchimede. S: Rino Di Silvestro, Howard Ross. C: Mario Capriotti. Cast: Annik Borel, Frederick Stafford, Dagmar Lassander, Howard Ross, Tino Carraro, Osvaldo Ruggieri, Felicita Fanny. Daniela (Annik Borel) is a woman who was sexually traumatized as a child. She also happens to have a lookalike ancestor who was burned alive as a werewolf. So now, when amorous feelings are aroused, Daniela ends up biting her victims and murderng them (*without* turning into a werewolf). ¶ "She's suffering from ancestral complexes." • We are only shown the titular wolfman once, at the film's opening, when the story of the ancestor is told.

The Mad Monster (1942; PRC) D: Sam Newfield. P: Sigmund Neufeld. S: Fred Myton. C: Jack Greenhalgh. Cast: Johnny Downs, Anne Nagel, George Zucco, Glenn Strange, Mae Busch. George Zucco plays a mad doctor who injects retarded handyman Glenn Strange with wolf's blood, thereby turning him into a poor-man's version of the Wolf Man. ¶ "It don't seem fair to lock a man up — like an animal." • In this PRC version of *The Wolf Man,* the werewolf is burned alive at the end when a providential bolt of lightning starts a fire in the house. • Glenn Strange is best known as Universal's fourth Frankenstein Monster, playing the part in *House of Frankenstein* (1944), *House of Dracula* (1945), and *Abbott and Costello Meet Frankenstein* (1948).

Monster Dog (1985; Trans World Entertainment) D: Clyde Anderson. P: Clark Tyrrel. S: C. Fracasso. Cast: Alice Cooper, Victoria Vera. Alice Cooper is a rock star whose band returns to his old family mansion to shoot a music video. It seems that Alice's father had been a werewolf, and now the locals want to make sure Alice does not follow in his father's footsteps. • The famous "Bad Boy of Rock," Alice Cooper, had his voice dubbed(!) for this obscure werewolf entry.

The Monster Squad (1987) (see VAMPIRES — DRACULA AND FAMILY). The evil Dracula has summoned all the famous classical monsters together (the Creature from the Black Lagoon, Frankenstein's Monster, the Mummy, and the Wolf Man) in an attempt to gain possession of an occult amulet which would let the forces of darkness rule the earth. Their only opposition is a band of young kids and an old man. ¶ "I kicked the Wolf Man in the nards!"

Moon of the Wolf (1972; TV movie) D: Daniel Petrie. P: Everett Chambers, Peter Thomas. S: Alvin Sapinsley. C: Richard C. Glouner. Cast: David Janssen, Barbara Rush, Bradford Dillman, John Beradino, Geoffrey Lewis, Royal Dano. David Janssen plays a Louisiana sheriff who hunts for the "loup garou" responsible for a series of local murders. • *Moon of the Wolf* is based on the novel by Leslie H. Whitten.

The Mummy and the Curse of the Jackals (1969/85) (see MUMMIES — MORE MUMMIES). Anthony Eisley plays an archeologist who falls under the "Curse of the Jackals" when he unearths the mummy of a beautiful Egyptian princess (still stunningly preserved). When the princess's case is opened, the curse turns Eisley into a sort of "werejackal." The princess revives and Eisley falls in love with her. Eventually, this Jackal Man kills a few people, wanders around the Vegas strip, and ends up battling a living mummy (in the Lon Chaney mold) in a lake while the princess finally crumbles to dust. • Star Anthony Eisley commented on the Jackal Man makeup in Tom Weaver's book *Interviews with B Science Fiction and Horror Movie Makers:* "Early in production they shot a transformation scene where I was lying on a table; they were putting one layer of makeup on at a time, shooting a few frames of film at a time, and that took all day. Well, as I said, the director was sort of losing his faculties, and I realized after a few days that he really didn't know what the hell was going on at all times. They had a second mask — just a quick pull-over thing, for my stunt double to use — so, to be very honest, the stunt double and I got to be friends, somewhere along the line I realized the director would never know, and I never put that makeup on again! Every time I became the Jackal Man, it was the stunt double. And the director never knew it! That took the curse off of that picture." • Eisley called his Jackal Man "just a rip off of the Wolf Man."

My Mom's a Werewolf (1989; Crown International) D: Michael Fischa. P: Steven J. Wolfe. S: Mark Pirro. C: Bryan England. Cast: Susan Blakely, John Saxon, Katrina Caspary, Diana Barrows, Ruth Buzzi. John Saxon plays "Harry Thropen," an amorous lycanthrope who bites suburban mom Susan Blakely and transforms her into a werewolf, much to the chagrin of her husband and teenage daughter. ¶ "Look, a singing werewolf. You don't see many of them these days." • This film plays around a bit with the werewolf legend. Here, "werewolves have the power to hypnotize people into thinking they're friends." • Whatever happened to Marcia Wallace, who played Carol, Bob's secretary, on the original "Bob Newhart Show"? She appears as a hairdresser in *My Mom's a Werewolf.*

Orgy of the Dead (1965) (see ZOMBIES). A horror writer and his girlfriend visit a cemetery after dark and are taken captive by the "Master of the Dead" and the "Princess of Darkness." They are forced to watch various women called up from the dead to dance topless to please the Master. Two supernatural servants aid the Master — a mummy and a werewolf, and both talk.

The Rats Are Coming! The Werewolves Are Here! (1972; William Mishkin Motion Pictures) D/S/C: Andy Milligan. P: William Mishkin. Cast: Hope Stansbury, Jackie Skarvelis, Noel Collins, Joan Ogden, Douglas Phair, Ian Innes, Berwick Kaler, Chris Shores, George Clark, Lillian Frith. A young woman brings her new husband home to her family estate. The various eccentric family members are living under a curse — during the full moon they change into werewolves. At the film's end, they all transform and kill each other off. ¶ "He's not normal. He's always howled like that when the moon was becoming full." • Producer William Mishkin took director Andy Milligan's film *Curse of the Full Moon,* which ran only 67 minutes long, and inserted scenes about a girl who raises man-eating rats to cash in on the success of *Willard* (1971).

Return of the Vampire (1944) (see VAMPIRES — OTHER VAMPIRES). The werewolfian slave in the thrall of vampire Armand Tesla eventually finds his faith at the climax and ends his master's reign of terror. ¶ "Poor Andreas, he found his soul after all. May he have peace forever." • The werewolf creature is called Andreas, and he can talk while in werewolf form. He is played by actor Matt Willis.

She Wolf of London (1946; Universal) D: Jean Yarbrough. P: Ben Pivar. S: George Bricker. C: Maury Gertsman. Cast: June Lockhart, Don Porter, Sara Haden, Jan Wiley, Dennis Hoey, Martin Kosleck. A young girl (June Lockhart) lives in fear of a family curse involving werewolves. A rash of murders, coupled with her waking up streaked with mud and blood convinces her that she is the "she-wolf" sought by Scotland Yard for the vicious mutilation murders. In the end, it is all revealed to be a plot to get the young heiress's inheritance, and the she-wolf is actually an unbalanced servant with a garden trowel. • *She Wolf of London* was released on a double bill with *The Cat Creeps,* a more straightforward mystery.

Silver Bullet (1985; Paramount) D: Daniel Attias. P: Martha Schumacher. S: Stephen King. C: Armand Nannuzzi. Cast: Gary Busey, Everett McGill, Corey Haim, Megan Follows, Terry O'Quinn, Bill Smitrovich, Robin Groves, Lawrence Tierney, Kent Broadhurst. A young handicapped boy learns that their small town reverend is actually a werewolf. With the aid of his older sister and his garrulous "Uncle Red," the determined boy faces off against the evil beast painting his town (blood) red. ¶ "I'm a little too old to play 'The Hardy Boys Meet Reverend Werewolf'."

Teen Wolf (1985; Atlantic Releasing Corporation) D: Rod Daniel. P: Mark Levinson, Scott Rosenfelt. S: Joseph Loeb III, Matthew Weisman. C: Tim Suhrstedt. Cast: Michael J. Fox, James Hampton, Scott Paulin, Susan Ursitti, Jerry Levine, Jim MacKrell, Lorie Griffin, Mark Arnold, Matt Adler, Mark Holton, Jay Tarses. Michael J. Fox plays your normal, everyday high school basketball player with one exception—he comes from a family of werewolves. At first he is taken aback by his transformations, but soon revels in "The Wolf's" newfound sports prowess and popularity ... until it gets out of hand. ¶ "You're just some kind of animal!" • Unlike his vicious supernatural forefathers, there is nothing dangerous about this werewolf—he is polite, well-groomed, and still in possession of his human faculties. He also can transform back and forth at will. • This surprise hit comedy inspired the inevitable tepid sequel—*Teen Wolf Too* (1987), in which the presence of the likable Michael J. Fox was sorely missed.

Teen Wolf Too (1987; Atlantic Releasing Corporation) D: Christopher Leitch. P: Kent Bateman. S: R. Timothy Kring. C: Jules Brenner. Cast: Jason Bateman, Kim Darby, John Astin, Paul Sand, Mark Holton, James Hampton, Estee Chandler, Stuart Fratkin. This charmless sequel to the popular Michael J. Fox vehicle, *Teen Wolf,* follows the exploits of Fox's cousin as he goes away to college. Nothing more than a weak rehash of the original, he discovers his wolfish qualities, uses them to his own advantages (including winning at boxing—which stands in for the basketball of the original film), and eventually realizes it is his true self that is important, not "The Wolf." • Makeup sessions for the application of the werewolf face lasted over three hours (though judging from the end result some might say it was time wasted). • Producer Kent Bateman is the father of star Jason Bateman. Jason's sister is Justine Bateman from TV's "Family Ties."

The Undying Monster (1942; 20th Century-Fox). D: John Brahm. P: Bryan Foy. S: Lillie Hayward, Michel Jacoby. C: Lucien Ballard. Cast: James Ellison, Heather Angel, John Howard, Bramwell Fletcher, Heather Thatcher. The Hammond family (primarily a brother and sister) seems to be haunted by the "Hammond Monster," a werewolf-like fiend who likes to stalk and attack the locals. The creature abducts the sister and is finally shot. Reverting to human form, we see it is the visage of the brother. ¶ "Hammond Hall at the turn of the century—when the age old mystery of the Hammond Monster was at last revealed to all England. That mystery, which although by 1900 had become a legend, was indeed a real tragedy and constant threat to the lives of all the seemingly doomed members of the House of Hammond"—opening narration. • This was 20th Century-Fox's failed attempt to cash in on the success of *The Wolf Man* of the previous year. • In a bizarre sidelight that seems to be as far removed from werewolf lore as one can get, the local doctor had been attempting to cure the brother of his lycanthropic condition with injections of cobra venom(!). • At the film's conclusion, the script attempts to negate the supernatural element of lycanthropy when one of the characters explains it away as a *medical* condition in which the sufferer merely *thinks* he's a wolf. Never mind the fact that the werewolf in question physically changed before our very eyes at the climax. By the way, we only see the werewolf in one brief scene at the film's end.

Waxwork (1988) (see WAX MUSEUMS). Anyone who gets too close to the various exhibits of this bizarre wax museum is sucked into the wax figure's world and meets gruesome deaths at the hands of the evil characters. One of the exhibits is of a woodsman who transforms into a werewolf.

The Werewolf (1956; Columbia) D: Fred F. Sears. P: Sam Katzman. S: Robert E. Kent, James B. Gordon. C: Edwin Linden. Cast: Steven Ritch, Don Megowan, Joyce

Steven Ritch plays the science-created titular lycanthrope in The Werewolf *(1956).*

Holden, John Launer, Eleanor Tanin. Two scientists find a man after a car wreck and use him to test out their experimental wolf serum. This has the unfortunate side effect of turning him into a werewolf whenever he becomes angry. He escapes and ends up in a small town, where the killings begin. Tracking him by his murders, the two scientists show up to kill him, but he gets the upper paw. Despite the pleadings of the man's wife and child, he is hunted down by a posse and destroyed. ¶ "Atom age scientists turn man into a deadly snarling beast"—promotional trailer. • No supernatural trappings here, just a scientific "wolf serum" which the two mad doctors hope to use to combat the effects of atomic radiation. Right. Consequently, silver bullets are not necessary for this creature, ordinary bullets do the job. • Producer Sam Katzman said of *The Werewolf* in *Famous Monsters* #106: "What does count is that the picture moves pretty fast, it's interesting at times and will serve its purpose of providing pretty fair entertainment."

Werewolf in a Girls' Dormitory (1961; MGM; Italy/Austria) D: Richard Benson (Paolo Heusch). P: Jack Forrest (Guido Giambartolomei). S: Julian Berry (Ernesto Gastaldi). C: George Patrick. Cast: Barbara Lass, Carl Schell, Curt Lowens, Maurice Marsac, Mary McNeeran, Grace Neame. A private school for wayward girls is plagued by a series of vicious murders. A dishonored doctor comes to the school as a teacher and must solve the case of the mysterious murders, finally discovering that the superintendent suffers from the disease of lycanthropy—he is a werewolf. ¶ "It's not fair to treat a lycanthropus like a murderer." • The much ballyhooed (in the ads) and often talked-about theme song of this imported obscurity, titled "The Ghoul in School," lasts for exactly ten seconds at the film's opening and then is never heard again. It is just long enough for a woman's voice to sing, "There's a ghoul in school," with a musical chorus, and then it ends. • A movie pressbook can be an amazing thing. For instance, this film's pressbook contained the following publicity "article": "A lovely 17-year-old student at an exclusive girls' school outside Turin, Italy, was found pregnant during a routine physical examination. Upon questioning, she revealed that eight weeks before, under the light of the full

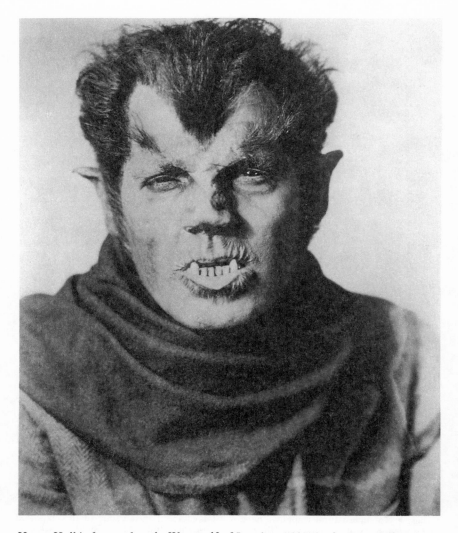

Henry Hull is featured as the Werewolf of London *(1935) in the screen's first werewolf film. Jack P. Pierce designed the rather sparse makeup (the result of Hull's antipathy toward the long makeup sessions).*

moon, a werewolf entered her room in the girls' dormitory. Upon further questioning, she claimed that the werewolf had a long, hairy face and drooled at the lips. Local authorities are skeptical of her story, pointing out that the girl might have been influenced by the recent location shooting of the startling new horror film, *Werewolf in a Girls' Dormitory* in and near the city. However, the mayor has decided to adopt a 'wait and see' attitude for the next eight months."

Werewolf of London (1935; Universal) D: Stuart Walker. P: Stanley Bergerman. S: John Colton, Robert Harris. C: Charles Stumar. Cast: Henry Hull, Warner Oland,

Valerie Hobson, Lester Mathews, Spring Byington, Lawrence Grant. A British botanist (Henry Hull) travels to the mountains of Tibet in search of a rare flower which blooms only in the moonlight. There he is attacked and bitten by a werewolf. Returning home with his precious flower, he is contacted by a Dr. Yogami (Warner Oland) who informs him that the flower is the only known antidote for lycanthropy. Of course, Yogami is the werewolf who attacked Hull, who is now a werewolf as well. The two lycanthropes fight over the curse-relieving plant and Yogami is killed, but Hull, now in werewolf form, is shot down as well. ¶ "A werewolf instinctively seeks to kill the thing it loves best." • This first-ever werewolf film made up its own set of rules on lycanthropy. First of all, the only cure to lycanthropy is a rare flower called "Marifasa lupina" which blooms only in the moonlight. As one character says, "That flower is the only known antidote to werewolfery." Secondly, silver was not an issue: "Thanks . . . thanks for the bullet. It was the only way. In a few moments now I'll know why all this had to be," claims the dying Henry Hull as he returns to human form—shot by an ordinary *lead* bullet. Also, this werewolf could talk. • Valerie Hobson, here playing the wife of a man-turned-monster, played the wife of a man-who-created-a-monster earlier this same year in *Bride of Frankenstein*. • Hobson revealed to *Famous Monsters* readers in the #86 issue, "I knew Mr. Hull was supposed to look horrible, but I had no idea he would look like that. I took one look at him and then started to scream. I couldn't stop. He thought I was joking so he ran towards me and let out an unearthly yell while he reached out a hairy hand as though to grasp my throat. Suddenly he and director Stuart Walker discovered I was in the middle of a fit of hysterics. They rushed me to the studio hospital where they gave me a sedative. When I quieted down I was so weak I could

not walk. I had to go home for the remainder of the day." • Jack Pierce's werewolf makeup for Henry Hull was originally much like the makeup he later used for Lon Chaney, Jr., in *The Wolf Man* (1941). Actor Henry Hull reportedly balked at the lengthy sessions in the makeup chair and so Pierce streamlined the makeup into the more austere wolf man we see in this film.

Werewolf of Washington (1973; Diplomat D/S: Milton Moses Ginsberg. P: Nina Schulman. C: Bob Baldwin. Cast: Dean Stockwell, Biff McGuire, Clifton James, Jane House, Beeson Carroll, Michael Dunn. A White House press secretary is bitten by a werewolf while on a visit to Hungary. Back in Washington he goes on the typical rampage and endangers the political future of the president as well in this political horror satire. ¶ "Will you please not bark at me!"

Werewolves on Wheels (1971; Fanfare) D: Michel Levesque. P: Paul Lewis. S: Michel Levesque, David M. Kaufman. C: Isadore Mankovsky. Cast: Stephen Oliver, Severn Darden, D. J. Anderson, Deuce Berry, William Gray, Gary Johnson, Owen Orr, Anna Lynn Brown, Leonard Rogel. A band of bikers rough up a group of devil-worshipers, who place a curse on one of them, turning him into a werewolf. The lycanthropic biker picks off his fellow gang members one by one in the night. • This is the only film to date which offers the dubious sight of a full-fledged werewolf riding a Harley.

Wolfman (1979; E. D. Corp.) D/S: Worth Keeter. P: Earl Owensby. C: Darrell Catheart. Cast: Earl Owensby, Kristina Reynolds, Sid Rancer, Edward Grady. Set in 1910 Georgia, Earl Owensby plays a rich man who becomes a werewolf. • Producer Earl Owensby is a drive-in movie mogul whose pictures (usually starring himself—though he is not much of an actor) play strictly on the Southern drive-in circuits.

Witches, Warlocks, and Cults

(*See also* Voodoo)

Witches are the human embodiment of supernatural evil. They are the Devil's disciples, the children of Satan. They also present the clearest picture of our fascination with, and attraction to, evil. What could be better than to have the power to smash your enemies and succeed in whatever you wished? A witch is granted this power for his or her own gain, and so (in psychological terms) is given supernatural aid in the release and gratification of their id. Of course, witches usually have to sell their souls to attain this, but when love or money or power is the issue, a soul can often become a trivial factor.

Witches, satanists, and cult members come in many shapes and forms, from the traditional ugly fairy tale creatures found in *The Witches* (1990), to the outwardly normal homey busybodies watching over *Rosemary's Baby* (1968), to the sophisticated Manhattan socialites choosing *The Seventh Victim* (1943).

Apart from the traditional satanic witches and cults represented in the cinema (with the notable likes of *Horror Hotel,* 1960; *The Devil's Bride,* 1968; and *Rosemary's Baby,* 1968 leading the devilish pack), there are also several distinct offshoots of witchcraft and cultism. For instance, there are the Druid films — the muddled *Cry of the Banshee* (1970), the inept *Invasion of the Blood Farmers* (1972), the non-sequel *Halloween 3: Season of the Witch* (1982), and the recent interesting failure, *The Guardian* (1990). By far the best film to deal with the old pagan religion, however, is the lyrical *The Wicker Man* (1972). This multi-layered, poetic shocker explores the conflict between the old and the new gods, between the ancient pagan religion and the relative newcomer, Christianity.

Another type of witchcraft film is the "Witchhunter" movie — period pieces which deal with the horrendous witch trials of centuries gone by. More often than not, however, producers simply exploited rather than explored this rich subject matter, using the historically documented beatings, burnings, and tortures as an excuse to show in graphic detail all of the sadistic acts one human could inflict on another. Films like *Mark of the Devil* (parts 1 and 2, 1970 and 1972), Paul Naschy's *Inquisition* (1976), and even *Night of the Blood Monster* (1971; starring the generally more prudent Christopher Lee) typify the bottom end of this movie type. Fortunately, a few filmmakers with a modicum of style decided to tackle this emotional subject, like Ken Russell with his controversial and thought-provoking *The Devils* (1971), and Michael Reeves with his grim, engrossing *The Conqueror Worm* (1968).

There are "Indian Witchcraft" movies, such as *Death Curse of Tartu* (1967), *Hex* (1973), and *The Manitou* (1978), in which medicine men conjure up their own type of evil magic. There are even "Asian Sorcerer" films, focusing on Asian warlocks employing their unique Eastern powers for evil (*Revenge of the Zombies,* 1981; *Big Trouble in Little China,* 1986; and *The Vineyard,* 1989).

There are also many films about the spirit of a witch returning to possess a living person (*The She Beast,* 1965; *Witchboard,* 1986; etc). As a general rule of thumb, if the film's main focus is on the satanic powers and witch-like nature of the spirit (e.g., *The She Beast*), then its main entry will be listed here, under WITCHES, WARLOCKS, AND CULTS. If, however, the main thrust is on its ghostly nature, with the spirit's status as a witch taking a subordinate role to its status as a specter (e.g., *Witchboard*), then the film's main entry will be found under GHOSTS.

See also VOODOO for West Indies–flavored witchery, and SWORD AND SORCERY for more mythological magic.

The Alchemist (1981; Ideal Films) D: Charles Band. P: Lawrence Appelbaum. S: Alan J. Adler. C: Andrew W. Friend. Cast: Robert Ginty, Lucinda Dooling, John Sanderford, Viola Kate Simpson, Robert Glaudini. An evil alchemist places a curse on a man, promoting a battle of wills over the man's soul, eventually ending with a portal to Hell opening and disgorging a horde of demons. ¶ "The single way to release the soul accursed be to curse another."

Alucarda (1975; Films 75/Yuma Films; Mexico) D: Juan Lopez Moctezuma. P: Eduardo Moreno, Max Guefen. S: Juan Lopez Moctezuma, Yolanda L. Moctezuma, Alexis T. Arroyo. C: Xavier Cruz. Cast: Tian Romero, Susana Kamini, Claudio Brook, David Silva, Martin Lasalle. At a monastery, an evil female witch named Alucarda corrupts a young innocent named Justine, and the monks must battle the forces of evil for her soul.

Asylum of Satan (1972; Studio One) D/S: William Girdler. P: J. Patrick Kelly III. C: William L. Asman. Cast: Charles Kissinger, Carla Borelli, Nick Jolly, Sherry Stein. A satanist named Dr. Spectre runs an insane asylum and offers up a young girl as a virgin sacrifice to his master. It is revealed that the girl is not a virgin, however, and Satan, disappointed and unwilling to go away empty handed, claims Dr. Spectre instead. • First time director William Girdler went on to helm the bigger-budgeted Indian witchcraft movie, *The Manitou,* in 1978. Tragically, Girdler died while scouting Philippine locations for an upcoming film in 1978.

Back from the Dead (1957) (see GHOSTS). The spirit of Arthur Franz's first wife comes back to possess his new bride. The evil ghost was a satanist when alive, and is now aided by a family of black magic practitioners who plan to make the possession permanent.

Beyond Evil (1980) (see GHOSTS). Lynda Day George is possessed by the ghost of a witch. With the aid of a local healer, husband John Saxon uses his love to fight the satanic spirit.

Big Trouble in Little China (1986; 20th Century–Fox) D: John Carpenter. P: Larry J. Franco. S: Gary Goldman, David Z. Weinstein, W. D. Richter. C: Dean Cundey. Cast: Kurt Russell, Kim Cattrall, Dennis Dun, James Hong, Victor Wong, Kate Burton, Donald Li, Carter Wong, Peter Kwong, James Pax. An evil 2000-year-old Chinese wizard needs a particular girl with green eyes to retain his eternal life. Truck-driving hero Kurt Russell and various Asian allies (including a practitioner of white magic) oppose the demonic wizard. • Director John Carpenter also co-wrote the film's musical score.

The Black Cat (1934) (see POE FILMS—EARLY POE). A honeymooning couple end up at the fortress-like home of satanist Hjalmar Poelzig, who is engaged in a cat and mouse game with a long-standing enemy. Poelzig holds a black mass ceremony at the "dark of the moon" and plans to offer up the young bride as a human sacrifice.

Black Sunday (1960; AIP; Italy) (also *Revenge of the Vampire*). D: Mario Bava. P: Massimo Derita. S: Ennio De Concini, Mario Bava, Marcello Coscia, Mario Seranore. C: Mario Bava, Ubaldo Terzano. Cast: Barbara Steele, John Richardson, Ivo Garrani, Andrea Checchi, Arturo Dominici, Enrico Olivieri, Clara Bindi, Antonio Pierfederici, Tino Bianchi, Germana Dominici. Princess Asa is condemned as a witch along with her vampiric servant, and a spiked mask is driven into her face. Two hundred years later, the witch is revived when blood is spilled on her dessicated corpse. She summons her servant and attempts to possess her lookalike descendant, Princess Katia. ¶ "One day in each century it is said that Satan walks among us. To the God-fearing this day is known as Black Sunday"—opening narration. • Mario Bava, a talented cinematographer-turned-director, made his solo directorial debut on this film. He has developed something of a cult following, and many consider this first picture to be his best. • This was scream queen Barbara Steele's first horror film. She soon made a name for herself playing seductive witches and ghosts in a string of Italian, British, and American features in the 1960s. • Theater managers gave out free index-sized cards with the word "Spell" printed on it to chant when they were frightened.

The Blood on Satan's Claw (1970; Tigon/Cannon; U.K.) (also *Satan's Skin*). D: Piers Haggard. P: Peter L. Andrews, Malcolm B. Heyworth. S: Robert Wynne-Simmons, Piers Haggard. C: Dick Bush. Cast: Patrick Wymark, Linda Hayden, Barry Andrews, Michele Dotrice, James Hayter. In a small seventeenth century English village, a young girl leads the local children in worshiping Satan, committing murder, and engaging in orgiastic rituals. The local magistrate is called in, and must face the devil himself, finally impaling the Prince of Darkness on a blessed sword. ¶ "Doctor, witchcraft is dead, and discredited. Are you bent on reviving forgotten horrors?!"

Blood Orgy of the She-Devils (1973; Gemini) D/P/S: T. V. Mikels. C: Anthony Salinas. Cast: Lila Zaborin, Tom Pace, Leslie McRae, Victor Izay, William Bagdad. Mara, Queen of the Witches, leads a satanic coven of beautiful women in California, contacting evil spirits and sacrificing young men to Satan.

Bloodbath at the House of Death (1983; Wildwood Productions; U.K.) D/P: Ray

Cameron. S: Ray Cameron, Barry Cryer. C: Brian West, Dusty Miller. Cast: Kenny Everett, Pamela Stephenson, Vincent Price, Gareth Hut, Don Warrington, John Fortune, Sheila Steafel, John Stephen Hill, Cleo Rocos, Graham Stark. A group of scientists visit Headstone Manor to investigate strange occurrences there, including a night in which 18 people were murdered. They are set upon by a group of devil-worshiping monks, who disguise themselves to look like the various investigators and kill them in inventive and gruesome ways. ¶ "Some say the monks are extraterrestrial visitors from an alien planet, emissaries of Lucifer, the Prince of Darkness, who used the manor as an instrument for their evil powers on earth." • The first half of the film is strictly weak parody, but once the murders begin it gets right to the heart of the gruesome matter. • In an incongruous blending of the subjects of satanism and aliens, the devil-worshiping monks finally dispatch all the investigators, enter the house, and blast off in what seems to be a spaceship (with the above quote the only word of explanation given).

Brotherhood of Satan (1971; Columbia) D: Bernard McEveety. P: L. Q. Jones, Alvy Moore. S: William Welch. C: John Arthur Morrell. Cast: Strother Martin, L. Q. Jones, Charles Bateman, Ahna Capri, Charles Robinson, Alvy Moore. Strother Martin is the head of a modern devil cult whose elderly members plan to transfer their souls from their old bodies into the bodies of children they have kidnapped, thus regaining their youth. ¶ "Aw, c'mon Jack. Twenty-six people slaughtered in a little over seventy-two hours, six families wiped out, all those kids missing, Perkins family slashed up like a threshing machine was run through the bedroom, the Vermers pulverized ... and those families he found, suffocated and crushed, three more kids missin'. Now what's *supernatural* about that, boy?!" • *The Brotherhood of Satan* gave unsavory-character actor Strother Martin his first starring role. • Among the powers wielded by the satanists is the ability to turn children's toys into instruments of destruction, including a child's toy tank which grows to life size proportions and crushes a station wagon and its occupants. • This is the second witchcraft film to feature actor Alvy Moore (best recognized from TV's "Green Acres"). Moore starred in *The Witchmaker* in 1969 before acting in and producing this one. • Patrons were given a free packet of "blood flower" seeds which, when planted,

could foretell the future (though the packets warned that the flowers might not sprout).

Burn, Witch, Burn (1962) (see VOODOO). Despite the use of the world "witch" in the title, the story does not involve a satanic brand of magic, but rather deals with voodoo.

Burnt Offerings (1976; United Artists) D/P: Dan Curtis. S: William F. Nolan, Dan Curtis. C: Jacques Marquette. Cast: Oliver Reed, Karen Black, Bette Davis, Lee Montgomery, Burgess Meredith, Eileen Heckart, Dub Taylor, Anthony James, Orin Cannon. A family rents an old house for the summer, not knowing that it is possessed by evil forces. There is a sinister witch-like "mother" locked away in an upstairs room who exerts an evil influence on the new family. • Dan Curtis is best known for his many television adaptations of horror classics (*Frankenstein,* 1973; *Dracula,* 1973; etc.) as well as creating the horror soap opera, "Dark Shadows."

The Conqueror Worm (1968; Tigon/AIP; U.K.) (also *The Witchfinder General*). D: Michael Reeves. P: Lewis M. Heyward, Philip Waddilove, Arnold Miller. S: Tom Baker, Michael Reeves. C: John Coquillon. Cast: Vincent Price, Ian Ogilvy, Rupert Davies, Robert Russell, Nicky Henson, Hilary Dwyer, Patrick Wymark, Wilfred Brambell. Vincent Price plays a notorious seventeenth century witchhunter who travels from town to town using his powers of life and death to satisfy his personal lusts for power, money, and women. ¶ "In a time where the superstitions of country folk are still a powerful factor, Matthew Hopkins preys upon them, torturing and killing in a supposed drive to eliminate witchcraft from the country, and doing so with the full blessing of what law there is" — opening narration. • *The Conqueror Worm* has nothing to do with the Edgar Allan Poe poem it is said to be based upon. The decision was made by AIP that another Poe film was needed, so they changed the original title of this British production for American distribution and added a voice-over narration at the film's end of Vincent Price reciting Poe's poem. • Price's character, Matthew Hopkins, is based on an actual historical figure — a witchhunter who plied his trade in England during the 1640s. • *The Conqueror Worm* is far superior to the few other films of its type, including the exploitative *Night of the Blood Monster* (1971) and the unpalatable *Mark of the Devil* (1970) and *Mark of the Devil 2* (1972). • Promising young British director Michael Reeves died soon after the film's completion, an apparent victim of suicide at the age of 25. Reeves also directed *The She Beast* in 1965, which featured a *real* witch.

Craze (1974; Warner Bros.; U.K.) (also *The Infernal Idol*). D: Freddie Francis. P: Herman Cohen. S: Aben Kandel (Kenneth Langtree), Herman Cohen. C: John Wilcox. Cast: Jack Palance, Diana Dors, Julie Ege, Edith Evans, Hugh Griffith, Trevor Howard, Michael Jayston, Suzy Kendall, Martin Potter. Jack Palance plays an antiques dealer who practices witchcraft by offering human sacrifices to an idol he keeps in his basement.

The Crimson Cult (1968; Tigon/AIP; U.K.) (also *The Curse of the Crimson Altar; The Crimson Altar*). D: Vernon Sewell. P: Louis M. Heyward. S: Mervyn Haisman, Henry Lincoln, Gerry Levy. C: Johnny Coquillon. Cast: Boris Karloff, Christopher Lee, Mark Eden, Barbara Steele, Michael Gough, Virginia Wetherell, Rupert Davies, Rosemarie Reede, Derek Tansley, Michael Warren. A man comes to the mysterious Greymarsh Lodge in search of his missing brother. There he encounters a male descendant of a notorious seventeenth century witch named Lavinia. The man starts having what he believes are dreams of the sadistic but beautiful witch (played by Barbara Steele), and discovers that her descendant is also a practicing witch. The evil sorcerer is intent upon avenging the death of Lavinia by killing the descendants of all those who burned her alive two centuries earlier. ¶ When told, "It's a bit like one of those old houses in horror films," the hero (Mark Eden) responds with, "Yeah, I know what you mean, as though Boris Karloff is going to pop up at any minute." Karloff did indeed pop up later in the film, playing an expert on witchcraft. • This was Boris Karloff's last English-language film (he made four more films before he died but they were Mexican productions). It is rumored that the wheelchair-bound actor caught a respiratory cold during production which later developed into pneumonia and ultimately contributed to his death. • This was the first time these three horror stars—Boris Karloff, Christopher Lee, and Barbara Steele—ever appeared together (though Karloff and Lee had played opposite one another once before, ten years earlier, in *Corridors of Blood*). This is primarily what *The Crimson Cult* is known for, since many fans and critics were disappointed with the film and feel that it wasted the talents of their favorite stars. Chris Lee later stated (in *The*

Films of Christopher Lee, by Pohle and Hart): "I did this film simply to be with [Boris Karloff], before he left us." • The film is based on the H. P. Lovecraft story, "Dreams in the Witch House," though it is uncredited. • *The Crimson Cult* was shot in the actual house of W. S. Gilbert (of Gilbert and Sullivan fame), which has a longstanding reputation of being haunted.

Cry of the Banshee (1970; AIP; U.K.) D/P: Gordon Hessler. S: Jim Kelly, Christopher Wicking. C: John Coquillon. Cast: Vincent Price, Elisabeth Bergner, Hilary Dwyer, Essy Persson, Patrick Mower, Sally Geeson, Pamela Fairbrother, Hugh Griffith, Marshall Jones, Michael Elphick, Robert Hutton. In the sixteenth century, an English magistrate (Vincent Price) persecutes a seemingly peaceful witch cult, headed by a druidic high priestess who vows vengeance before she dies. She sends an emissary of evil (in the form of a young man who changes into a werewolf-like creature) to punish the cruel and misguided magistrate. ¶ "Who spurs the beast the corpse will ride, who cries the cry that kills? When Satan questioned, who replied. Whence blows this wind that chills? Who wanders 'mongst these empty graves and seeks a place to lie? 'Tis something God had ne'er planned. A thing that ne'er had learned to die"—ad line. • Actress Hilary Dwyer, here playing Vincent Price's beloved daughter, was the *victim* of Vincent Price two years earlier in *The Conqueror Worm* (1968). • This is the third witchcraft film for cinematographer John Coquillon. He also lensed *The Conqueror Worm* and *The Crimson Cult* (both 1968).

The Curse of the Crying Woman (1961; AIP-TV; Mexico) D: Raphael Baledon, Stim Segar (English language version). P: Abel Salazar, K. Gordon Murray (English language version). S: Raphael Baledon. C: Joseph Oritiz Ramos. Cast: Rosita Arenas, Abel Salazar, Rita Macedo, Carlos Lopes Moctezuma, Henry Lucero, Mario Sevilla, Julissa del Llano, Roy Fletcher. A sinister woman summons her estranged niece to her isolated mansion, revealing that she is a descendant and follower of "the Wailing Witch." She intends to use her young niece in a plan to resurrect the powerful witch and thus cement her own diabolical powers and immortality. ¶ "In exchange for her eternal existence, she was to become a part of the forces of evil. She was to do harm to all others as payment for her franchise. . . . She employed black magic and witchcraft, efficient instruments with which she dominated other people's souls." • Producer Abel Salazar also stars as the hero (brave husband to the imperiled niece).

Curse of the Demon (1956) (see DEMONS AND DEVILS). Dana Andrews plays a doubting psychologist who denounces the leader of a devil cult as a fraud, only to find that the powers of Satan are all-too-real when faced with a fire demon from Hell.

Dark Intruder (1965; Universal) D: Harvey Hart. P: Jack Laird. S: Barre Lyndon. C: John F. Warren. Cast: Leslie Nielsen, Mark Richman, Judi Meredith, Gilbert Green, Charles Bolender, Werner Klemperer. At the turn of the century, an expert on the occult (Leslie Nielsen) is called in to help the police investigate a series of gruesome murders apparently committed by some beast or demon. Finally, the perpetrator is revealed to be a horribly malformed man who employs the ancient black arts of Sumerian witchcraft. He intends to transfer his soul into the body of a normal man—but not just any man as the film's final twist illuminates. ¶ From the ads: "*He killed* with the *power of demons* a million years old!" • *Dark Intruder* was originally made as a pilot for the unsold TV series "Black Cloak" but eventually was released as a theatrical feature. • Star Leslie Nielsen was quite pleased with the finished product, as he stated in a 1981 interview for *Cinemacabre*: "There aren't that many films that are made for television that can be released as a theatrical film. It just was well done." That's Werner Klemperer—Colonel Klink from TV's "Hogan's Heroes"—under the gruesome makeup.

Daughters of Satan (1972; United Artists; Philippines) D: Hollingsworth Morse. P: Aubrey Schenk. S: John C. Higgins. C: Nonong Rasca. Cast: Tom Selleck, Barra Grant, Toni Phelps, Guthrie Paraluman, Vic Silayan, Vic Diaz, Gina Laforteza, Paquito Salcedo. Tom Selleck, the descendant of a witch hunter, buys a painting of three witches being burned at the stake. Oddly, his wife resembles one of the witches in the picture, and soon it is revealed that she *is* the witch. With the aid of two other reincarnated witches, she attempts to kill her husband and avenge her previous death. • Star Tom Selleck later made it big on TV as "Magnum P.I.," and on the silver screen with films like *Three Men and a Baby*.

Day of Wrath (1943; Palladium; Denmark) D/P: Carl Dreyer. S: Carl Dreyer, Poul Knudsen, Mogens Skot-Hansen. C: Carl Andersson. Cast: Thorkild Roose, Lisbeth Movin, Sigrid Neiiendam, Preben Lerdoff Rye, Anna Svierkier. In a seventeenth century village, an elderly cleric condemns an old woman to be burned alive as a witch, and in turn is cursed by her with his own impending death. His new wife, much younger than he, is secretly the daughter of a supposed witch herself. When the cleric's grown son returns home, the two young people fall in love and the young wife wishes her older husband dead—and it comes to pass. The unfaithful witch/wife finally confesses to the corpse that, "I killed you with the Evil One's help." ¶ "If she wished someone dead, he died!" • This slow-moving but engrossing tragedy is based on the play "Anna Pedersdotter," by Hans Wiers Jenssen.

The Day the Earth Froze (1959; AIP; Finland/U.S.S.R.) D: Aleksandr Ptushko, Julius Strandberg. P: Gregg Sebelious. A witch steals the sun and causes the Earth to freeze in this Nordic fantasy. Eventually the sound of a sacred harp is used to vanquish the witch and turn her to stone.

Deadtime Stories (1987) (see ANTHOLOGIES). In this anthology's first story, a young lad is sold into slavery to two hideous old witches who intend to bring back to life their deceased third sister.

Death Curse of Tartu (1967; Thunderbird International) D/S: William Grefe. P: Joseph Fink, Juan Hidalgo-Gato. C: Julio Chavez. Cast: Fred Pinero, Babette Sherril, Mayra Christine, Sherman Hayes, Doug Hobart. In the Florida Everglades, the resting place of an Indian witchdoctor is disturbed by four archeology students. He rises from the dead and uses his magic to transform into a shark, snake, alligator, and Indian brave to stalk the desecrators of his grave. ¶ "My grandfather and the elder members of my tribe say that 400 years ago a witchdoctor named Tartu had power to turn himself into a wild creature. When he died he swore if anyone would disturb the burial ground he would change himself into a wild beast and kill him." • See also *The Manitou* for more Indian witchdoctors.

The Demon Lover (1976) (see DEMONS AND DEVILS). This low-budget independent devil-worship film is about the leader of a devil cult who punishes his unfaithful followers by conjuring up an ugly horned demon to dispatch them.

Demon Witch Child (1974; Coliseum; Spain) D/S: Armando de Ossorio. C: Vicente Minaya. Cast: Julian Mateos, Marian Salgado, Lone Fleming, Maria Kosti, Fernando Sancho, Angel del Pozo, Tota Alba. An ancient witch possesses a nine-year-old girl. The little girl periodically turns into an old hag and conducts satanic rituals before finally being rescued by a priest in a climactic battle between good and evil. • Director/screenwriter Armando de Ossorio is best known for his four "Blind Dead" zombie films, beginning with *The Blind Dead* (1972).

Demoniacs (1973; Les Films ABC/Nordia Films/General Films; France/Belgium) D/S: Jean Rollin. P: Lionel Wallman. C: Jean-Jacques Renon. Cast: Joelle Coeur, Patricia Hermenier, Lieva Burr, John Rico, Isabell Copejans, Mireille Dargent, Louise Dhour, Paul Biscaglia, Misha Zimovir. In a rugged coastal village, two shipwrecked women are brutally attacked and raped by a gang who prey on shipwreck victims. The two girls survive, make a pact with the devil, and use their newfound supernatural powers to take revenge upon their attackers. • This is another low-budget film from prolific French director Jean Rollin, who made a string of vampire/sex films in the 1970s. His movies are usually long on nudity and short on narrative, though occasionally they show flashes of an almost surrealistic quality which makes them nearly palatable.

Demonoid (1979) (see HANDS). A young couple working a silver mine uncover an ancient mummified hand which was once the symbol of power used by a devil cult. The hand possesses various people and forces them to commit murder and self-mutilation.

The Demons (1972; Interfilme/Comptoir Français du Film; France/Portugal) D/S: Clifford Brown (Jesus Franco). P: Victor De Costa. C: Raoul Artigot. Cast: Anne Libert, Britt Nichols, Howard Vernon, Alberto Dalbes, Karin Field, John Foster, Luis Bar-Boo, Doris Thomas. A corrupt witch hunter called Judge Jeffreys is cursed by a witch he burns alive. The witch's two daughters, who are sequestered in a nunnery (which they thoroughly corrupt), eventually enact the witch's vengeance by delivering a kiss of death to the judge (one kiss from them and their partner becomes a skeleton). • This is the second film Franco made using the character of Judge Jeffreys ("The Bloody Judge"). His first film on the subject was *Night of the Blood Monster* (1971), starring Christopher Lee. • Franco adapted the story from his own novel which he wrote under his pen name, David Kuhne.

The Devils (1971; Warner Bros.; U.K.) D/S: Ken Russell. P: Robert H. Solo, Ken Russell. C: David Watkins. Cast: Oliver Reed, Vanessa Redgrave, Dudley Sutton, Max Adrian, Gemma Jones, Murray Melvin, Michael Gothard, Georgina Hale, Christopher Logue, Andrew Faulds. Oliver Reed plays "Grandier," a strong-willed priest doomed by the political machinations of seventeenth century France. Vanessa Redgrave is a sexually repressed Mother Superior who whips her nuns up into an hysterical frenzy, believing themselves to be witches. A sadistic witch-finder is brought in, and Grandier is caught in the middle of the torture and burnings, eventually being burnt alive at the stake as a witch himself.

The Devil's Bride (1968; Hammer–Seven Arts/20th Century–Fox; U.K.) (also *The Devil Rides Out*). D: Terence Fisher. P: Anthony Nelson Keys. S: Richard Matheson. C: Arthur Grant. Cast: Christopher Lee, Charles Gray, Nike Arrighi, Leon Greene, Patrick Mower, Gwen Frangcon-Davies, Sarah Lawson, Paul Eddington, Rosalyn Landor, Russell Waters. The Duc de Richleau, an expert on the occult, tries to save his young friend from the clutches of a modern-day devil cult headed by the powerful Mocata. Mocata sends all manner of evils to silence Richleau, including a black "Angel of Death" riding on horseback. ¶ "The Power of Darkness is more than just a superstition, it is a living force which can be tapped at any given moment of the night." • Star Christopher Lee, who owns quite an extensive collection of occult books, intoned a genuine black magic chant (a real Sussamma ritual of exorcism) in the scene where he faces the Angel of Death. • In *The Films of Christopher Lee,* the actor told authors Pohle and Hart that, "the reason the film is called *The Devil's Bride* in the U.S. is apparently because some executive genius decided that the American public, when informed of the original title [*The Devil Rides Out*], would believe that this film could only be a Western." • *The Devil's Bride* is based on Dennis Wheatley's best-selling novel, *The Devil Rides Out.*

The Devil's Mistress (1966; WGW Pictures) D/S: Orville Wanzer. P: Wes Moreland. C: Teddy Gregory. Cast: Joan Stapleton, Robert Gregory, Forrest Westmoreland, Douglas Warren, Oren Williams, Arthur Resley. Four cowboys traveling through a hostile mountain range come upon an isolated cabin in the middle of nowhere, inhabited by a strange man and his mute woman who "came from Salem many years before" to escape religious persecution. Two of the cowpokes shoot the man, rape the woman, and then bring her along when they leave. Soon they begin dying mysteriously — one with the life drained out of him, another by snakebite, and yet another by hanging. The woman is a witch, with the ability to control animals and suck the life out of men. At the end, her dead husband returns and gathers her back into the fold of his cloak as he recites the following curse. ¶ "They shall be burned with hunger and devoured with passion and bitter destruction. I will also send the poison of the serpent and the mouth of the beast upon them."

Devils of Darkness (1965) (see VAMPIRES — OTHER VAMPIRES). A vampire leads a devil cult in offering up human sacrifices in modern-day Brittany and England. ¶ "In the name of our Lord Satan, do you acknowledge the Powers of Darkness?!"

The Devil's Own (1966; Hammer/20th Century–Fox; U.K.) (also *The Witches*). D: Cyril Frankel. P: Anthony Nelson Keys. S: Nigel Kneale. C: Arthur Grant. Cast: Joan Fontaine, Kay Walsh, Alec McCowan, Ingrid Brett, Martin Stephens, Duncan Lamont, Gwen Frangcon-Davies, Leonard Rossiter, Michele Dotrice, Viola Keats. Joan Fontaine plays a woman who escapes the horror of voodoo in Africa only to encounter a modern-day devil cult back in England. She is finally forced to kill the head witch in order to save a young girl from becoming a virgin sacrifice. • *The Devil's Own* was not a box office success, and Joan Fontaine decided to retire from the screen.

Devil's Partner (1958; Filmgroup) D: Charles R. Rondeau. P: Hugh M. Hooker. S: Stanley Clements, Laura J. Mathews. C: Edward Cronjager. Cast: Ed Nelson, Edgar Buchanan, Jean Allison, Richard Crane, Spencer Carlisle, Byron Foulger, Claire Carleton, Brian O'Hara, Harry Fleer, Joe Hooker. An old man who practices black magic seems to die, but he returns as a young man claiming to be his own nephew. He uses his satanic powers (including the ability to transform into a demonic horse and poisonous snake) to try and control a woman he wants and do away with the man who stands in his way. ¶ "From all indications, our young friend Nick Richards seems to have a tremendous power, power to such an extent that he's capable of turning himself into anything he wants."

The Devil's Rain (1975; Bryanston) D: Robert Fuest. P: James V. Cullen, Michael S. Glick. S: Gabe Essoe, James Ashton, Gerald Hopman. C: Alex Phillips. Cast: Ernest Borgnine, Eddie Albert, Ida Lupino, William Shatner, Keenan Wynn, Tom Skerritt. William Shatner is in possession of an ancient book which is desperately sought

after by a modern-day devil cult and its demonic leader (the reincarnation of a seventeenth century warlock). At the film's end, a bottle containing all the souls of the warlock's victims is broken, causing a rainstorm which reduces his followers to oozing puddles of slimy goo. • Soon-to-be superstar John Travolta appeared in a tiny role as one of the melting devil-worshipers. • Actor Ernest Borgnine, playing the cult leader, said of his role, "I had to go through a lot of changes playing Corbis, including at one point getting transformed into a goat-like image of the Devil, the hottest, most difficult makeup I've ever had to wear!" (from *Famous Monsters of Filmland* #120).

The Devonsville Terror (1983) D/P/C: Ulli Lommel. S: Ulli Lommel, George T. Lindsey, Suzanna Love. Cast: Suzanna Love, Robert Walker, Paul Willson, Donald Pleasence. In 1683, members of the town of Devonsville tortured and murdered three young women as witches. Three hundred years later, the descendants of those townspeople responsible for that heinous act commit a new series of crimes which set in motion the 300-year-old curse. A young schoolteacher arrives in Devonsville and uses supernatural powers to exact retribution from the guilty descendants.

Dr. Death, Seeker of Souls (1972; Cinerama Releasing) D/P: Eddie Saeta. S: Sal Ponti. C: Kent Wakeford, Emil Oster. Cast: John Considine, Barry Coe, Cheryl Miller, Stewart Moss, Leon Askin, Jo Morrow. A man whose wife has been killed in a car accident goes to the mysterious "Dr. Death" who claims to have the power to restore his wife to life again via soul transference. Dr. Death has apparently survived centuries through the use of this power. • This was the last film of 77-year-old Moe Howard (of "The Three Stooges" fame).

The Dunwich Horror (1969; AIP) D: Daniel Haller. P: James H. Nicholson, Samuel Z. Arkoff. S: Curtis Lee Hanson, Henry Rosenbaum, Ronald Silkosky. C: Richard C. Glouner. Cast: Sandra Dee, Dean Stockwell, Ed Begley, Sam Jaffe, Lloyd Bochner. Dean Stockwell plays a man who steals an evil tome called the "Necronomicon" with the intent of using it to restore the Evil One's dominion on Earth. To this end he intends to sacrifice the lovely Sandra Dee in a bizarre fertility rite. • *The Dunwich Horror* is based on the H. P. Lovecraft story of the same name. • Director Daniel Haller had delved into Lovecraft territory once before with *Die Monster Die* (1965). • Talia Shire, who has a small part in the film, is Francis Ford Coppola's younger sister.

Elvira, Mistress of the Dark (1988; New World Pictures) D: James Signorelli. P: Eric Gardner, Mark Pierson. S: Sam Egan, John Paragon, Cassandra Peterson. C: Hanania Baer. Cast: Cassandra Peterson, Edie Mc-Clurg, Jeff Conaway, W. Morgan Sheppard, Daniel Greene, Susan Kellerman. Elvira quits the horror hostess business and journeys to Fallwell, Massachusetts, to claim her inheritance left by her great-aunt. It turns out Elvira is really a witch descended from a long line of witches, and she must battle an evil warlock who is after a powerful book of spells. ¶ "I'm never going to work for that sleazeball again! I'll just have to find *another* sleazeball." • Elvira is the stage name and horror-hostess persona of Cassandra Peterson, who co-wrote the script. • Elvira's deceased Aunt Morganna (a witch) shared the same last name with *The Wolf Man*—Talbot.

Eye of the Devil (1966; MGM; U.K.) D: J. Lee Thompson. P: John Calley, Martin Ransohoft. S: Robin Estridge, Dennis Murphy. C: Erwin Hillier. Cast: Deborah Kerr, David Niven, Donald Pleasence, Flora Robson, Emlyn Williams, Sharon Tate, David Hemmings, John Le Mesurier, Edward Mulhare. David Niven plays a wealthy vineyard owner (and coven member) in France whose crops are failing. As the head of the family, it is his duty to sacrifice himself in an occult ritual in order to improve the harvest. • Sharon Tate, of *The Fearless Vampire Killers* (1967) fame (and later a victim of the infamous Manson Family murders), appears in the film as a witch.

Eyes of Fire (1984) (see DEMONS AND DEVILS). In 1750, a small group of settlers on the American frontier stumble into a haunted valley inhabited by a black-faced demon. The evil creature captures people's souls and stores them in the trees. A young girl, whose mother was burned as a witch, possesses a strange magical power which is the settlers' only hope in fighting the demon and saving their souls.

Ghoulies (1984) (see DEMONS AND DEVILS). The son of a sorcerer follows in his father's satanic footsteps and unwittingly unleashes a horde of diminutive demons whose specialty is mischief and murder.

Goremet, Zombie Chef from Hell (1986) (see CANNIBALS). This ultra-cheap semi-professional gore film features a 600-year-old sorcerer named Goza who has been cursed with eternal life by the "Righteous Brother-hood," so that he must continually consume human flesh or his body will decay.

The Guardian (1990) (see PLANTS). A professional babysitter turns out to be more than a yuppie family bargained for when she is revealed to be the human manifestation of an ancient druidic tree monster, to whom she offers the souls of newborn children. With her witch-like powers she commands wolves and can fly through the air.

Halloween 3: Season of the Witch (1982; Universal) D/S: Tommy Lee Wallace. P: Debra Hill, John Carpenter. C: Dean Cundey. Cast: Tom Atkins, Stacey Nelkin, Dan O'Herlihy, Ralph Strait, Michael Currie. A mad Irish toymaker, a descendant of the Druid cult, creates three Halloween masks which, when worn by the children while viewing a hypnotic TV commercial, causes them to explode in a mass of bugs and snakes. By doing this he intends to restore Halloween to its devilish roots. • The deadly Halloween masks gain their diabolical properties from a microchip containing a piece of Stonehenge. • Though in name this is a sequel to John Carpenter's *Halloween* (1978), it has nothing to do with the unstoppable slasher-maniac, Michael Meyers. John Carpenter (who directed the original) served as co-producer for *Halloween 3*.

The Haunted Palace (1963; AIP) D/P: Roger Corman. S: Charles Beaumont. C: Floyd Crosby. Cast: Vincent Price, Debra Paget, Lon Chaney, Frank Maxwell, Leo Gordon, Elisha Cook, Jr. Charles Dexter Ward (Vincent Price), the great-great-grandson of evil Warlock Joseph Curwen, whom the villagers burned at the stake over 100 years ago, returns to the village of his family and is slowly taken over by the spirit of his evil ancestor. He then sets about using his dark powers to take revenge on the descendants of those who had killed him. ¶ "Ah yes, Torquemada spent many a happy hour here a few centuries ago"—Vincent Price walking through his basement torture chamber. • Though touted by AIP as another film in Corman's "Poe" series, this is actually based on the story "The Case of Charles Dexter Ward," by H. P. Lovecraft. The studio claimed *The Haunted Palace* was based on a "story" by Edgar Allan Poe, though the title (and nothing else) is from one of Poe's *poems*. Corman was not pleased with the deception, later stating, "I fought against that title change," in *The Films of Roger Corman*, by Ed Naha.

Hex (1973; 20th Century-Fox) (also *The Shrieking* [video title]). D: Leo Garen. P:

Clark Paylow. S: Leo Garen, Steve Katz. C: Charles Rosher, Jr. Cast: Keith Carradine, Scott Glenn, Hilarie Thompson, Gary Busey, Robert Walker, Mike Combs, Doria Cook, Tina Herazo, Dan Haggerty. In 1919, an early version of a motorcycle gang is run out of the small town of Bingo, Nebraska. The bikers take refuge on the isolated farm of two young sisters, daughters of an Indian shaman and his white wife. When the bikers get out of hand, the eldest daughter uses her powers of Indian witchcraft to torment and kill the offenders. ¶ "Something awful funny is goin' on here; it ain't natural!" • *Hex* was filmed on location at the Cheyenne River Sioux Indian Reservation in South Dakota.

Hollywood Chainsaw Hookers (1988; Camp Motion Pictures/American Independent) D/S: Fred Olen Ray. P: Dr. S. Carver, B. J. Nestles, Fred Olen Ray, T. L. Lankford. C: Scott Ressler. Cast: Gunnar Hansen, Linnea Quigley, Jay Richardson, Dawn Wildsmith, Michelle McLellan, Dennis Mooney, Jerry Fox, Esther Alise, Tricia Burns, Jimmy Williams, Dukey Flyswatter. This tongue-in-cheek low-budget oddity is about a bizarre cult in L.A. made up of prostitutes who sacrifice their "johns" to the beloved 'saw. ¶ "We, your humble slaves, offer you the Virgin Dance of the Double Chainsaws." • The double-edged ad line: "They charge an arm and a leg." • Gunnar Hansen, appearing here as "the Master" of the chainsaw cult, was no stranger to the old Black and Decker. He had previously played *the* chainsaw-wielding maniac from *The Texas Chainsaw Massacre* (1974). • This low-budget, tongue-in-cheek wonder was filmed over the course of two weekends.

Horror Hotel (1960; Trans-Lux; U.K.) (also *The City of the Dead*). D: John Moxey. P: Donald Taylor. S: George Baxt. C: Desmond Dickinson. Cast: Dennis Lotis, Christopher Lee, Betta St. John, Patricia Jessel, Venetia Stevenson, Tom Naylor, Valentine Dyall, Ann Beach. A college professor who specializes in the occult (Christopher Lee) is also the leader of a witch coven in the mysterious village of Whitewood, Massachusetts. He sends his students there for "research" but uses them as sacrificial victims. ¶ Poster ad line: "Just ring for doom service!" • British horror star Christopher Lee used an American accent for his part (an admirable achievement for a British actor), since he was supposed to be an American warlock.

Horror Rises from the Tomb (1972; Avco Embassy; Spain) D: Carlos Aured. P: Ricardo Muñez Suay, José Antonio, Perez Giner. S: Jacinto Molina. C: Manuel Merino. Cast: Paul Naschy, Emma Cohen, Vic Winner (Victor Alcazar), Helga Line, Betsabe Ruiz, Luis Ciges, Julio Peña, Cristina Suriani. Spanish horror star Paul Naschy plays a fifteenth century knight beheaded for witchcraft. His modern-day descendant returns with some friends to his ancestral estate where his severed head is unearthed. When head and body are rejoined, the evil warlock wreaks havoc, using his black arts to murder them one by one in order to eat their hearts. He plans to cement his power via a black magic ceremony on the seventh night of the full moon. ¶ "Our bodies may be destroyed, but our vengeful spirits will persecute you forever!" • Star Paul Naschy wrote the script (as he does with many of his films) under his real name of Jacinto Molina.

House of the Black Death (1964; Medallion/Taurus) D: Harold Daniels. P: William White, Richard Shotwell. S: Rich Mahoney. C: Murray De Atley. Cast: John Carradine, Andrea King, Tom Drake, Delores Faith, Lon Chaney, Jr., Sabrina. Lon Chaney, Jr., and John Carradine play two brothers who are rival warlocks. Carradine is the good warlock and Chaney is the evil one, and they engage in a satanic struggle for control of their ancestral home. ¶ "To be born a Desard is to be born under a curse; you will pay the price unto Satan's purse." • Low-budget schlockmeister Jerry Warren has stated that it was he who actually finished this film (without taking credit). In *Interviews with B Science Fiction and Horror Movie Makers,* he told Tom Weaver: "They had a terrible mishmash of a movie—it *wasn't* a movie, it was a bunch of film. Somebody took over the project, contacted me and asked if I could make a movie out of it.... The whole thing was laid in my lap and I functioned as *everything*—as producer, as director, as editor, putting music in it, the whole works. It came out *bad* but it came out playable, too, and it did pull out some money for the people who backed it.".

Hungry Wives (1972; Latent Image) (also *Jack's Wife; Season of the Witch*). D/S/C: George A. Romero. P: Nancy M. Romero. Cast: Jan White, Ray Laine, Anne Muffly, Joedda McClain, Bill Thunhurst, Neil Fisher, Esther Lapidus, Dan Mallinger, Ken Peters, Virginia Greenwald. A bored and unstable housewife is drawn into the world of a modern-day witch cult. She completes her initiation by inadvertently murdering her husband. • This was George Romero's third film and his follow-up horror movie to the ultra-successful *Night of the Living*

Christopher Lee (second from right) and his fellow coven members look on in terror as two of their own go up in flames after being exposed to the shadow of a cross in Horror Hotel *(1960).*

Dead (1968). *Hungry Wives* was not a success, however, either financially or critically (though Romero cites it as his personal favorite among his first four films). • The distributor trimmed 40 minutes off its original 130-minute running time before release.

Inferno (1980; 20th Century–Fox; Italy) D/S: Dario Argento. P: Claudio Argento. C: Romano Albani. Cast: Irene Miracle, Leigh McCloskey, Daria Nicolodi, Eleonora Giorgi, Alida Valli, Sacha Pitoeff, Feodor Chaliapin, Veronica Lazar, Gabriele Lavia. A New York apartment building houses a coven of witches presided over by one of the "Three Mothers." A woman living in the building is murdered and her brother returns from Italy to investigate, only to confront the demonic witch herself. • This was Argento's follow-up to *Suspiria* (1976), yet another film short on narrative but long on imagery.

Inquisition (1976; Ancla Anubis; Spain) D/S: Jacinto Molina. C: Miguel Mila. Cast: Paul Naschy, Ricardo Merino, Toni Osbert,

Monica Randall, La Pocha, Julia Saly, Tota Alba, Antonio Iranzo, Maria Salerno, Antonio Casas. In the sixteenth century, three judges set out to rid the countryside of all witchcraft. Their brand of lethal hysteria backfires, however, when one of the judges is tempted by a so-called witch and ends up being burnt at the stake himself. • Spanish horror star Paul Naschy made his directorial debut on this film, as well as writing the screenplay under his real name of Jacinto Molina.

Invasion of the Blood Farmers (1972; NMO Distributing) D/P: Ed Adlum. S: Ed Adlum, Ed Kelleher. C: Frederick Douglass. Cast: Norman Kelly, Tanna Hunter, Bruce Detrick, Paul Craig Jennings, Jack Neubeck, Richard Erickson. A modern-day Druid cult (called the "Sangroid" druids) goes to the backwoods of Jefferson Valley to search for the right victim needed to resurrect their queen and allow their race to continue. ¶ "They were the Druids, the secret people, the 'Sangroid Blood Eaters.' Midnight was their sacred hour and blood sacrifice under the full moon their religion" — opening narration. • This shoddy grade-Z gore film was shot for a mere $40,000 in upstate New York. • The tasteless but amusing advertising: *"We Warn You!* Don't eat before you see this show and you'll have nothing to lose!!"

Kill Baby Kill (1966) (see GHOSTS) (also *Curse of the Living Dead*). The ghost of a little girl who died due to the negligence of some villagers comes back to take revenge. A local witch uses her powers to fight the evil force and free the village from the curse.

The Kiss (1988; Tri-Star; U.S./Canada) D: Pen Densham. P; Pen Densham, John Watson. S: Stephen Volk, Tom Ropelewski. C: François Protat. Cast: Joanna Pacula, Meredith Salenger, Mimi Kuzyk, Nicholas Kilbertus, Jan Rubes. After a woman is killed in a tragic accident, the woman's estranged sister comes to visit her grieving husband and teenage daughter. Using her diabolical magic, the evil sister seduces the husband and sets her sights on her niece, whom she wants to possess, intending to transfer her soul into the younger body via a demonic parasite-like creature living inside her. • Tri-Star changed the title twice, to *The Host* and *Kissed,* before finally settling on the present moniker.

Kiss Me, Kill Me (1973; 14 Luglio Cinematografica/Productions Simone Allouche; Italy/France) (also *Baba Yaga*). D/S: Corrado Farina. P: Simone Allouche. C: Ajace Parolin. Cast: Carroll Baker, Isabelle de Funes, George Eastman, Ely Galleani, Daniela Balzaretti. A female fashion photographer is drawn into the sado-masochistic world of a modern-day witch, who uses her dark powers to entice the woman into her world of whips and torture and sensuality. ¶ "We're all whores of various species. The only difference is that I'm a whore and admit it while the majority are whores and play at being sane."

Lady Terminator (1989; Philippines/ U.S.) D: Jalil Jackson. P: Ram Soraya. S: Karr Kruinowz. C: Chuchu Suteja. Cast: Barbara Anne Constable, Christopher J. Hart, Audia Angelique Rademaker, Joseph P. McGlynn, Adam Stardust, Ikang Fawzi. The husband of an evil witch called "The South Sea Queen" betrays her and steals her power. Walking into the sea, the malevolent witch swears to take revenge on his descendants. One hundred years after her death, the witch's spirit returns and possesses the body of a woman. She then goes on a killing spree trying to find her husband's descendant (a female rock singer) to exact her revenge. Just like the robot in *The Terminator,* she cannot be stopped by bullets or even by fire, and shoots everyone who stands in her way, including an entire police station full of cops (borrowing from the original). ¶ "The struggle within our souls is never ending, the life of Man short and brutal. Torn between good and evil, of the eternity around us we know nothing" — closing narration. • This (unauthorized) supernatural version of *The Terminator* (1984) steals heavily from its model, even down to copying the scene in which Schwarzenegger operates on his own eye, not to mention having her destroyed in a fire only to have her rise up and keep coming as a skeletal monster (though she is a flesh-and-blood rather than a robot skeleton this time). The climax is even set in a deserted factory just like in the original. • Star Barbara Anne Constable also did the makeup chores for the film.

Land of the Minotaur (1976; Crown International) (also *The Devil's People*). D: Costas Carayiannis. P: Frizos Constantine. S: Arthur Rowe. C: Aris Stavrou. Cast: Donald Pleasence, Peter Cushing, Luan Peters, Nikos Verlakis, Costas Skouras, Vanna Revilli, Anna Mentgosrani, Jane Lyle, Bob Behling, Fernando Bislani. Peter Cushing leads a local cult in worshiping the image of the minotaur and making periodic human sacrifices to it.

The Legacy (1979; Universal) (also *The Legacy of Maggie Walsh*). D: Richard Marquand. P: David Foster. S: Jimmy Sangster, Patrick Tilley, Paul Wheeler. C: Dick Bush, Alan Hume. Cast: Katherine Ross, Sam Elliot, John Standing, Ian Hogg, Charles Gray, Margaret Tyzack, Roger Daltrey, Lee Montague, Hildegard Neil, Marianne Broome. A group of people reluctantly gather at the old house of a dying satanist, who is to choose an heir and pass along his satanic powers before he succumbs. Those guests not worthy of the diabolical honor are killed in various gruesome ways. • Roger Daltrey, lead singer for "The Who," plays one of the not-so-lucky hopefuls.

Look What's Happened to Rosemary's Baby (1976) (see DEMONS AND DEVILS) (also *Rosemary's Baby 2*). This TV sequel to the critically acclaimed blockbuster, *Rosemary's Baby* (1968), follows the demonic awakenings of the now-grown Son of Satan, surrounded by the obligatory devil cult (including Ruth Gordon from the first film), making sure he grows up with the proper influence.

Love at Stake (1988; Helmdale; Canada)

D: John Moffitt. P: Michael Gruskoff. S: Terry Sweeney, Lanier Laney. C: Mark Irwin. Cast: Patrick Cassidy, Kelly Preston, Bud Cort, David Graf, Stuart Pankin, Dave Thomas, Barbara Carrera. In 1692 Salem, Massachusetts, the lecherous mayor and corrupt judge hatch a scheme to promote witch hysteria and confiscate the land and property of the innocent citizens. A real witch enters the picture in the alluring form of Barbara Carrera, who uses her devilish powers to humiliate the hypocrites and finally expose the fraud in this rather sophomoric comedy misfire. ¶ *"This* is Mrs. Elizabeth Goodbody, an innocent young woman who was demonically transformed into a piece of *granite!* I ask you Parson, is this to be the fate of the people of our community? Do you want to go down in history as the man who let Salem turn into a *quarry!?"*

The Manitou (1978; Avco Embassy) D/P: William Girdler. S: William Girdler, Jon Cedar. C: Michael Hugo. Cast: Tony Curtis, Michael Ansara, Susan Strasberg, Stella Stevens, Jon Cedar, Ann Sothern, Burgess Meredith, Paul Mantee, Jeanette Nolan, Lurene Tuttle. In modern-day San Francisco, a young woman develops a tumor on her back which turns out to be the fetus of an ancient Indian witchdoctor seeking to be reincarnated. The evil witchdoctor is "born" and wreaks mystical havoc in the hospital. He is opposed by the woman's boyfriend and a modern "good" medicine man. • The film's title is derived from the Indian word for the spirit or soul that is contained in all things — trees, rocks, even computers. It is not only people that have manitous, but all things in existence. • The good Indian medicine finally summons the spiritual manitou of the hospital's huge supercomputer to try and combat the diabolical witchdoctor.

Manos, the Hands of Fate (1966; Emerson) D/P/S: Hal P. Warren. Cast: Tom Neyman, John Reynolds, Diane Mahree. A vacationing family stumbles into a house populated by satanists, complete with a backyard temple and revived "master" named Manos. • Director/producer/screenwriter Hal P. Warren's real job is fertilizer salesman in El Paso, Texas.

Mark of the Devil (1970; Hallmark; W. Germany/U.K.) D: Michael Armstrong. P: Adrian Hoven. S: Sergio Cassner, Percy Parker (Adrian Hoven). C: Ernst W. Kalinke. Cast: Herbert Lom, Udo Kier, Olivera Vuco, Reginald Nalder, Herbert Fuchs, Michael Maien, Ingeborg Schoener, Gaby Fuchs, Dorothea Carrera, Adrian Hoven. In eighteenth century Austria, a sadistic witchhunter and his apprentice roam the countryside torturing and burning witches. The apprentice balks at the abuse of power his mentor is employing and rebels. But it is too late, for the local populace, finally up in arms over the cruelties and injustices they have suffered at the hands of the witchhunters, capture the apprentice and kill him, while the evil witchfinder gets away. ¶ Ad line: "Guaranteed to upset your stomach!" • Udo Kier, a German actor known for his association with Andy Warhol films, played the doomed hero. • This tasteless, exploitative gore film played up its unpleasantness in the film's advertising. "Vomit bags" were handed out to theater patrons and ads claimed it was "rated V for violence." It was successful enough for the filmmakers to make a sequel, *Mark of the Devil Part 2,* two years later.

Mark of the Devil Part 2 (1972; AIP; W. Germany/U.K.) D/P: Adrian Hoven. S: Adrian Hoven, Fred Denger. C: Ernst W. Kalinke. Cast: Erica Blanc, Anton Diffring, Percy Hoven, Reggie Nalder, Lukas Ammann, Jean-Pierre Zola, Astrid Kilian, Ellen Umlauf, Rosy-Rosy, Harry Hardt, Dietrich Kerky, Johannes Buzalski. A sadistic witchfinder attempts to gain control of an aristocrat's fortune by torturing his widow as a witch. ¶ "Between the fourteenth and eighteenth centuries the lives of approximately eight million men, women and children were destroyed due to the religious and fanatical mania against the belief in witchcraft.... This film shows the story of the young Countess von Solmenau. It is bassed [sic] upon fact and not fiction" — opening written narration. (*Note:* The misspelling of the word "based" in the last line is not a typo, but how it appears on the screen — the filmmakers misspelled it on their film.) • Producer Adrian Hoven followed up his successful (and equally exploitative) *Mark of the Devil* with this film, co-writing as well as directing this time. Hoven also appears in the film as the murdered husband of the countess. • *Part 2* is not a true sequel (since there is no continuity of characters), but basically more of the same from the original (i.e., nudity, torture, and mutilation). Reggie Nalder once again plays a witchfinder's sadistic assistant (just as he did in the first *Mark of the Devil,* though with a different name). • The exploitative advertising claimed this film contained, "10 scenes that you will *positively* not be able to stomach." • Reggie Nalder claimed that a *Part 3* was planned, but director/producer Adrian Hoven died before the project could get off the ground.

Mark of the Witch (1970; Favorite Films) D: T. Moore. P: Mary Moore. Cast: Robert Elston, Anitra Walsh, Darryl Wells, Marie Santell. An evil 300-year-old witch terrorizes a college town.

The Masque of the Red Death (1964) (see POE FILMS — THE CORMAN CYCLE). The satan-worshiping Prince Prospero invites a group of nobles into his castle as protection against the plague of Red Death scouring the countryside. He also takes in a young innocent whom he plans to corrupt with his evil satanic influence. ¶ "But because of me, through my mediation with my master, the Lord of Flies, you, all of you, will be safe from the Red Death ... unless, of course, you incur my displeasure."

The Mephisto Waltz (1971; 20th Century–Fox) D: Paul Wendkos. P: Quinn Martin. S: Ben Maddow. C: William W. Spencer. Cast: Alan Alda, Jacqueline Bisset, Barbara Parkins, Bradford Dillman, Curt Jurgens, William Windom. A dying pianist uses his satanic powers to transfer his soul into a young, healthy musician. ¶ "People should be born at 70, and live their lives backward. The present arrangement simply doesn't make sense."

Midnight (1980; Independent International). D/S: John A. Russo. P: Donald M. Redinger. C: Paul McCollough. Cast: Lawrence Tierney, Melanie Verlin, John Amplas, Greg Besnak, John Hall, Charles Jackson, David Marchick, Robin Walsh. A young girl fleeing her unhappy home falls into the clutches of a family of psychotic backwoods satanists who plan to offer her up as a human sacrifice on Easter Sunday. ¶ "There are times when evil will triumph and nothing can overcome it. Evil is more powerful than good." • Director/screenwriter John Russo is best known for writing the zombie classic, *Night of the Living Dead* (1968).

The Naked Witch (1964; Mishkin) (also *The Naked Temptress*). D/C: Andy Milligan. P: William Mishkin. S: Clay Guss. Cast: Beth Porter, Robert Burgos, Lee Forbes. A student finds the body of a nineteenth century witch. When he removes the stake from her heart, she is restored to life and promptly puts him under her spell. • This is prolific grade-Z filmmaker Andy Milligan's first horror film. It was shot in New Jersey on a minuscule budget of $7,500. Though filmed in 1961, it was not released until three years later.

Necromancy (1972; Cinerama) (also *The Witching*). D/P/S: Bert I. Gordon. C: Winton Hoch. Cast: Orson Welles, Pamela Franklin, Michael Ontkean, Lee Purcell, Harvey Jason, Lisa James, Sue Bernard, Terry Quinn. Recovering from a personal tragedy, a couple comes to a small town named Lilith where the husband has found a job working for the local toy manufacturer, Mr. Cato. Besides running the factory, Mr. Cato also runs a local devil cult and uses his factory to produce occult objects. He also has his sights set on the man's wife, whom he plans to sacrifice in a ceremony to bring his dead son back to life. ¶ "Life to the child, life to the child oh Horned One." • This was one of filmmaker Bert I. Gordon's (Mr. B.I.G.) few "normal-sized" movies. He is best remembered as the man who brought us hordes of giant creatures in films like *The Amazing Colossal Man* (1957), *Village of the Giants* (1965), and *The Food of the Gods* (1976).

Necropolis (1987; Empire) D/S: Bruce Hickey. P: Cynthia DePaula, Tim Kincaid. C: Arthur D. Marks. Cast: LeeAnne Baker, Jacquie Fitz, Michael Conte, William K. Reed, Paul Ruben, Andrew Bausili, Gy Mirano, Letnam Yekim. A 300-year-old witch sets out to complete a ceremonial virgin sacrifice designed to endow her with eternal life which was interrupted back in 1685. In the meantime she sucks the "life force" out of various New Yorkers and searches for the reincarnations of those who spoiled her ceremony centuries before.

Night of Dark Shadows (1971) (see GHOSTS). In this second (and last) "Dark Shadows" film, Quentin Collins inherits an estate and becomes possessed by the ghost of his ancestor. There is also a female ghost — an evil witch who is trying to return to the land of the living.

Night of the Blood Monster (1971; AIP; Spain/Portugal/Italy/W. Germany) (also *The Bloody Judge*). D: Jess Frank (Jesus Franco). P: Harry Alan Towers. S: Jesus Franco, E. Colombo, Peter Welbeck (Harry Alan Towers). C: Manuel Merino. Cast: Christopher Lee, Maria Schell, Leo Genn, Hans Hass, Maria Rohm, Margaret Lee, Werner Abrolat, Howard Vernon. Christopher Lee plays historical figure Judge Jeffreys, Lord Chief Justice of England, who conducted notorious witch trials in seventeenth century Britain. The sadistic Jeffreys uses his power to torture and rape until William of Orange's victory finally ends his perverted reign of terror. • Reportedly, the many scenes of gruesome torture were added after star Christopher Lee completed his portion of the shoot. Lee ranks this as one of his best performances.

Night of the Witches (1970; Medford) D/S: Keith Erik Burt. P: Keith Erik Burt, Vincent Forte. C: Herb V. Theiss. Cast: Keith Erik Burt, Randy Stafford, Ron Taft, Kathryn Loder, Leon Charles, Ernest L. Rossi. A rapist disguised as a preacher gets his comeuppance when he falls in with a coven of California witches in search of a sacrifice.

One Dark Night (1982) (see ZOMBIES). Karl Raymar, an evil practitioner of the black arts, dies and is interred in a mausoleum. A group of teens enter that very mausoleum as part of an initiation. Raymar uses his evil powers from beyond the grave to transform the mausoleum's occupants into walking zombies, which dispatch the teens one by one.

Prime Evil (1988; Reeltime Distributing) D/C: Roberta Findlay. P: Walter E. Sear. S: Ed Kelleher, Harriette Vidal. Cast: William Beckwith, Christine Moore, Mavis Harris, Max Jacobs, Tim Gail, George Krause. In the plague-ravaged fourteenth century, a group of monks break away from the church and turn to Satan. Now in the present day, cult members must sacrifice a blood relation every 13 years in order to retain their eternal youth and keep the powers of darkness given them by their Dark Lord. A nun infiltrates the cult in order to save their next intended victim and bring down the evil organization. ¶ "There was a great turbulence within the church. The fallen angel Lucifer seized this opportunity. He chose a leader who would create a following and administer his Prime Evil throughout the Earth." • This dull, unwatchable, low-budget mess was churned out by former exploitation and porno filmmaker Roberta Findlay (who served as her own cinematographer).

Psychomania (1972) (see ZOMBIES) (also *The Death Wheelers*). The leader of a British motorcycle gang learns the secret of immortality from his devil-worshiping mother and commits suicide. He returns to life as an unstoppable zombie and induces the rest of his gang to do the same.

Pumpkinhead (1988) (see DEMONS AND DEVILS). In this tale of demonic revenge, a man whose little boy has just been accidentally killed goes to an old crone, a backwoods witch, seeking vengeance. She aids him in summoning up a demon to take revenge on those involved.

The Pyx (1973; Cinerama; Canada) D: Harvey Hart. P: Maxine Samuels, Julian Roffman. S: Robert Schlitt. C: Rene Verzier. Cast: Christopher Plummer, Karen Black, Jean-Louis Roux, Donald Pilon, Yvette Brind'Amour, Jacques Godin. Two detectives investigating the mysterious death of a prostitute uncover black magic rituals involving human sacrifice. • The film's title derives from the name given to the container used to hold the sacred host during mass.

Race with the Devil (1975; 20th Century-Fox) D: Jack Starrett. P: Wes Bishop. S: Lee Frost, Wes Bishop. C: Robert Jessup. Cast: Peter Fonda, Warren Oates, Loretta Swit, Lara Parker, R. G. Armstrong. Two couples traveling across Texas in a motor home witness a group of devil-worshipers kill a young girl as a human sacrifice. Soon they are racing for their lives with the far-flung members of the cult in murderous pursuit. • Loretta Swit is best remembered as "Hotlips" on TV's "M*A*S*H."

The Raven (1963) (see POE FILMS—THE CORMAN CYCLE). In this comical addition to Roger Corman's Poe gallery, Vincent Price, Peter Lorre, and Boris Karloff play rival sorcerers who must fight a duel of magic to see who will be the head magician. The title is justified when Lorre is turned into a raven by piqued warlock Karloff.

Revenge (1986; United Entertainment Pictures) D/S: Christopher Lewis. P: Linda Lewis. C: Steve McWilliams. Cast: Patrick Wayne, John Carradine, Bennie Lee McGowan, Josef Hardt, Stephanie Knopke, Fred Graves, Charles Ellis. In a small Oklahoma town, "many prominent citizens have fallen under the influence of the blood sacrifice cult of Caninis—the god of death, resurrection, and worldly advancement." These cult members murder people to take their body parts for a hideous ritual of sacrifice. ¶ "Those men and women you call degenerates, abominations, they are the true believers. Through the glory of Caninis they can fulfill desires no other god would allow." • This low-budget stinker was shot in 16mm in 14 days on a budget of $150,000. • John Carradine claimed this to be his five hundredth film.

Revenge of the Zombies (1981) (see ZOMBIES) (also *Black Magic 2*). A black magic sorcerer in Hong Kong casts spells and revives zombies to do his bidding. To maintain his youth, the evil magician drinks human milk. ¶ "When I cast a spell, I must borrow a spirit from Hell to help carry it out. That spirit must be paid for. It costs five years of my life every time."

Rosemary's Baby (1968; Paramount) D/S: Roman Polanski. P: William Castle.

C: William Fraker. Cast: Mia Farrow, John Cassavetes, Ruth Gordon, Sidney Blackmer, Maurice Evans, Ralph Bellamy. A young couple move into a new apartment building and are immediately inundated with nosy, eccentric neighbors. The wife dreams she is raped by a demon and soon becomes pregnant. It is revealed that the neighbors are a modern-day coven of witches, and the wife has been chosen to bear the Son of Satan himself. ¶ "Satan is his father, not Guy. He came up from Hell and begat a son of mortal woman." • Ruth Gordon (playing the part of the nosy neighbor/witch) won an Oscar for Best Supporting Actress. • This is arguably the best and most prestigious picture filmmaker William Castle ever worked on. Castle is generally known as the "King of the Gimmicks" from the 1950s and 60s, with his successful showmanship films like *The Tingler* (1959), *House on Haunted Hill* (1959), and *Strait-Jacket* (1964). Castle makes a cameo appearance in this film as a man in a phone booth. • The production was plagued by several tragedies, including the sudden death of the film's 35-year-old musical composer, and the poisoning and nervous breakdown suffered by the producer, William Castle. Castle said in John Brosnan's book, *The Horror People*, "I do believe that the film, which I lived through and almost died through, was controlled by some unexplainable force which was rather frightening.... After all the peculiar things that had happened I just fell apart. I was recuperating in San Francisco when I saw the headlines about the Sharon Tate murders. That was all I needed. I drove right down to Los Angeles, went to Paramount where Roman was and just fell apart again. Roman is a strange man. He believes in nothing except what he sees, whereas I believe in the occult and evil forces. After we finished the picture there was an interview with him in the *New York Times* and he was asked whether it was due to the occult and to evil forces at work during *Rosemary's Baby* that there were a lot of mishaps and that I became ill. He said, 'No, the only thing it was due to was that Castle couldn't stand success, and it was all the success and the making of so much money that went to his head.'" • Szandor LaVey, founder of the Church of Satan, served as technical advisor on the film.

Satan's Cheerleaders (1977; World Amusements) D: Greydon Clark. P: Alvin L. Fast. S: Greydon Clark, Alvin L. Fast. C: Dean Cundey. Cast: John Ireland, Yvonne De Carlo, Jack Kruschen, John Carradine, Sidney Chaplin, Jacqulin Cole, Kerry Sherman, Hillary Horan, Alisa Powell, Sherry Marks. Four cheerleaders are kidnapped by a group of backwoods satanists. One of the girls turns out to be a real witch and they dispatch their captors. It ends with the girls using the powers of darkness to aid their football team. ¶ "Some townspeople feel the Prince of Darkness might desire that the blood of a maiden flow tonight."

Satan's Slave (1976; Crown International) D: Norman J. Warren. P: Les Young, Richard Crafter. S: David McGillivray. Cast: Candace Glendenning, Michael Gough, Martin Potter, Barbara Kellerman, Michael Craze, James Bree, Gloria Walker, Celia Hewitt. A young woman visits her uncle at his country mansion. He heads a devil cult and plans to use her body in a ceremony to resurrect an ancient witch.

The Seventh Victim (1943; RKO) D: Mark Robson. P: Val Lewton. S: DeWitt Bodeen, Charles O'Neal. C: Nicholas Musuraca. Cast: Tom Conway, Kim Hunter, Jean Brooks, Isabel Jewell, Elizabeth Russell, Evelyn Brent, Hugh Beaumont. A girl goes off to New York to find her sister who has mysteriously disappeared. She discovers her sister has joined an elite set of devil-worshipers. She has betrayed the satanists, and now they are searching for her as well, intent on forcing her to commit suicide as price for her betrayal. ¶ "I runne to death and death meets me fast/ and all my pleasures are like yesterday" — opening epigraph. • Scriptwriter DeWitt Bodeen attended an actual devil-worshipers meeting on New York's west side while preparing the story for *The Seventh Victim*. His co-writer, Charles "Blackey" O'Neal, is Ryan O'Neal's father. • One aspect of the script that was eventually omitted explained how every member of the cult had an emotional, mental, or physical defect (one character had only one arm for instance), and explored why they were attracted to the cult. • Tom Conway plays Dr. Louis Judd, the same unsavory character who was killed off in a previous Val Lewton film, *Cat People* (1942). No explanation is given as to how the character came back from the dead to appear in this picture. • This film was Mark Robson's directing debut. He was formerly a respected editor who helped organize Orson Welles's *Citizen Kane* (1941), though he didn't receive any film credit on that effort. • This was Kim Hunter's first role.

The She Beast (1965; Europix; Italy) (also *Revenge of the Blood Beast; Sister of Satan*). D: Michael Reeves. P: Paul Maslansky. S: Michael Byron (Michael Reeves). C: G. Gengarelli. Cast: Barbara Steele, Ian Ogilvy, John Karlsen, Mel Welles, Jay Riley, Richard Watson, Ed Randolph. A newlywed couple vacationing in Transylvania have an auto accident, running their car into a lake. Two hundred years earlier, a hideous witch named Vardella was drowned by the villagers in that same lake. When the wife emerges from the water, she is possessed by the spirit of the vengeful witch, causing her to take on the visage of an ugly old crone and go on a murder spree. ¶ "The powers of evil shall make manifestation of themselves, using for a fusing agent the person and spirit of an innocent." • This was director Michael Reeves's first feature; he was 21 years old. Reeves went on to direct *The Sorceress* (1967), and another witch film, *The Conqueror Worm* (1968) before a premature death at the age of 25 — an apparent suicide. • Barbara Steele fans are often disappointed with her limited screen time (she is only onscreen for about 15 minutes, despite her star billing). The budget was so low for the film that the producers could only afford her for four days of shooting (at a fee of $5,000).

Simon, King of the Witches (1971; Fanfare) D: Bruce Kessler. P: David Hammond. S: Robert Phippeny. C: David Butler. Cast: Andrew Prine, Brenda Scott, George Paulsin, Norman Burton, Gerald York, Ultra Violet, Michael C. Ford, Lee J. Lambert, Angus Duncan. Andrew Prine is a modern-day warlock conducting satanic rituals in the sewers of Los Angeles. ¶ From the lurid poster: "*The Black Mass . . . The Spells . . . The Incantations . . . The Curses . . . The Ceremonial Sex. . . .*"

Slime City (1989; Camp Motion Pictures) D/S: Gregory Lamberson. P: Gregory Lamberson, Peter J. Clark, Marc Makowski. C: Peter J. Clark. Cast: Robert C. Sabin, Mary Huner, T. J. Merrick, Dennis Embry, Dick Biel. A college student moves into a new apartment building where he is possessed by the soul of a satanist who had committed suicide there along with his coven. The other tenants in the building are already possessed by coven members and they feed him "ectoplasm" slime and a special elixir which prepares him for full possession by their master. Once possessed, the youth periodically begins to melt(!) into a slimy goo and must kill to regain normal form. ¶ "I had to kill him or the slime would have consumed me." • This ultra low-budget independent was shot in New York City on a budget of $100,000.

Something Weird (1966; Mayflower) D/C: Herschell Gordon Lewis. P/S: James F. Hurley. Cast: Tony McCabe, Elizabeth Lee, William Brooker. A handsome man's face is horribly scarred in a high-tension-wire accident. After the accident he gains extrasensory powers. An ugly witch agrees to restore his face if he becomes her lover, which he does, only to fall prey to an ESP investigator who has become obsessed with the now-beautiful witch.

Something Wicked This Way Comes (1982; Walt Disney) D: Jack Clayton. P: Peter Vincent Douglas. S: Ray Bradbury. C: Stephen H. Burum. Cast: Jason Robards, Jonathan Pryce, Diane Ladd, Pam Grier, Royal Dano, Vidal Peterson, Shawn Carson. A nightmarish carnival comes to a small town, headed by the sinister Mr. Dark and his beautiful but deadly witch. The carnival promises to make the townspeoples' dreams come true but in the end delivers only misery and pain. A young boy and his elderly father must stop the evil, armed with nothing but the weapon of laughter. • Noted author Ray Bradbury adapted his own lyrical novel for the screenplay.

Spellbinder (1988; MGM) D: Janet Greek. P: Joe Wizan, Brian Russell. S: Tracy Torme. C: Adam Greenberg. Cast: Timothy Daly, Kelly Preston, Rick Rossovich, Audra Lindley, Anthony Crivello, Diana Bellamy, Cary-Hiroyuki Tagawa. A yuppie lawyer rescues a beautiful girl from her dangerous-looking boyfriend only to find himself trapped in the tightening web of a modern-day devil cult who wants her back. • The "surprise" ending is lifted right out of the superior film, *The Wicker Man* (1972).

Spiritism (1961; Young America Productions; Mexico) D: Benito Alazraki, Manuel San Fernando (English version). P: William Calderón Stell, K. Gordon Murray (English version). S: Rafael Garcia Travesi. C: Henry (Enrique) Wallace. Cast: Joseph L. Jimenez, Nora Veryan, Beatriz Aguirre, Alice Caro, Carmelita Gonzalez, Anthony Bravo, George Mondragon, August Benedico, William Zetina, George Russek, Maria Eugenia San Martin, Rene Cardona, Jr. A middle-aged couple become involved with a benevolent group of spiritualists, who contact the dead in order to help them pass on to their next stage. When the couple's finances fail due to the inept business dealings of their son, the wife calls upon the evil forces of witchcraft to help her. Satan himself appears and gives her "Pandora's Box" to open if she chooses. Desperately in need of money, she opens the box and finds a severed hand, upon which she makes her wish. The wish comes true, but at the cost of her son's life. She makes another wish — for the return of her son — and it also comes true, to her ultimate horror. ¶ "You are invoking the villainous spirits to help you. They represent forces so sinister and powerful that you'll be a toy in their hands, and later they will bring destruction." • Though uncredited in English language prints, this film is based on the classic short story, "The Monkey's Paw." • The filmmakers include this bogus warning in the closing narration: "The incidents you have just seen could have been true, or false — lunacy, or witchcraft. There are many who are helplessly driven by a desire to explore forbidden phenomena. If, with this picture, we are able to quelch that unhealthy curiosity in some, we will consider *our* job well done."

Superstition (1982; Almi Pictures) D: James Roberson. P: Ed Carlin. S: Donald G. Thompson. Cast: James Houghton, Albert Salmi, Lynn Carlin, Larry Pennell. In 1874, Elondra Sharack is crucified as a witch. Her satanic soul lurks in nearby Black Pond and 200 years later rises from the depths for vengeance — directed at Reverend Thompson and his family who have just moved to the area. ¶ "Also, one of the girls was microwaved."

Suspiria (1976; International Classics; Italy) D: Dario Argento. P: Claudio Argento. S: Dario Argento, Daria Nicolodi. C: Luciano Tovoli. Cast: Jessica Harper, Stefania Casini, Udo Kier, Alida Valli, Joan Bennett, Flavio Bucci, Miguel Bosé, Rudolf Schuendler, Barbara Magnolfi. A new student at a ballet school is imperiled by the "Black Widow," a witch whose coven makes its home there. ¶ "Magic is all around us." • "Dark Shadows" fans will recognize actress Joan Bennett as the owner of the ballet school and leader of the coven. • In 1980, Dario Argento made a follow-up witchcraft film to *Suspiria*, called *Inferno*.

The Tempter (1974; Avco Embassy; Italy) D: Alberto De Martino. P: Edmondo Amati. S: Alberto De Martino, Vincenzo Mannino. C: Aristide Massaccesi. Cast: George Coulouris, Mel Ferrer, Carla Gravina, Arthur Kennedy, Alida Valli, Umberto Orsini, Anita Strindberg, Mario Scaccia, Ernesto Colli, Remo Girone. A young girl is possessed by the evil spirit of her ancestor, a witch, who makes her do all manner of terrible things like kill her father, seduce her brother, and perform *Exorcist*-like tricks (including levitation and spitting up green vomit).

Terror in the Crypt (1964; AIP; Italy/Spain) (also *Crypt of Horror; The Curse of the Karnsteins*). D: Thomas Miller (Camillo Mastrocinque), Robert Spafford (American version). P: William Mulligan. S: Julian Berry (Ernesto Gastaldi), Robert Bohr (Bruno Valeri), José L. Monter, Maria Del Carmen, Martinex Roman. C: Julio Ortas, Giuseppe Aquari. Cast: Christopher Lee, Audrey Amber (Adriana Ambessi), Ursula Davis, José Campos, Vera Valmont, Nela Conjiu. Christopher Lee plays Count Karnstein, whose ancestor was a witch. Before she was executed, the witch placed a curse on all her female descendants. The Count, fearing for the safety of his daughter, commissions a young historian to find the witch's tomb. He does, but the count's housekeeper, with the aid of a mysterious friend visiting his daughter, raises up the spirit of the evil witch, and soon the murders begin.

The Thing That Couldn't Die (1958) (see BRAINS — LIVING HEADS). A young woman with ESP powers uncovers a chest containing the head of a devil-worshiper executed by Sir Francis Drake in the sixteenth century. The head is still alive and exerts its influence over a slow-witted handyman, ordering him to find its body. When the head and body are finally reunited, the now-powerful satanist plans to destroy all the protagonists. He is stopped only when an old talisman turns him to dust.

To the Devil ... a Daughter (1976; Hammer/Cine Artists; U.K./W. Germany) D: Peter Sykes. P: Roy Skeggs. S: Chris Wicking. C: David Watkin. Cast: Richard Widmark, Christopher Lee, Nastassia Kinski, Honor Blackman, Michael Goodliffe, Anthony Valentine, Denholm Elliott, Eva Maria Meineke. Christopher Lee plays a satan-worshiper posing as a priest who intends to use the body and soul of a young innocent (Nastassia Kinski) in his diabolical plans. He is opposed by an occult expert in the form of Richard Widmark. • This was the last theatrical feature made by that British horror institution, Hammer Films. • Star Christopher Lee was not happy with the ending of this picture, asking, "How do you kill the Devil by hitting him on the head with a rock? A ludicrous ending" (from *The Films of Christopher Lee,* by Pohle and Hart).

The Touch of Satan (1971; Futurama) (also *Night of the Demon; The Curse of Melissa; The Touch of Melissa*). D: Don Henderson. P: George E. Carey. S: James E. McLarty. Cast: Michael Berry, Emby

Mellay, Lee Amber, Yvonne Winslow, Jeanne Gerson. A young man stumbles upon a farm owned by two sisters, both witches. One is young and beautiful (though 127 years old), while the other looks her age. Occasionally the ugly sister (who is kept locked in the attic) gets out and embarks on a killing spree.

The Undead (1956; AIP) D/P: Roger Corman. S: Charles Griffith, Mark Hanna. C: William Sickner. Cast: Pamela Duncan, Richard Garland, Allison Hayes, Val Dufour, Dorothy Neuman, Billy Barty, Bruno Ve Sota, Richard Devon, Mel Welles. A young prostitute visits a psychiatrist who, through hypnotism, discovers that she is the reincarnation of a girl who lived three centuries earlier. While in a trance, she journeys back to her previous life where she is wrongly accused of being a witch. The psychiatrist travels back with her to try and stop her premature execution, and must battle a coven of real witches while walking a thin tightrope of events so as not to drastically alter the future by changing the past. ¶ "Sing a song of graveyards/ An acre full of germs/ Four and twenty landlords/ Dinner for the worms/ And when the box was planted/ The worms began to sing/ Wasn't that a dainty dish to set before the 'Thing'"—the mad but jolly grave digger. • Corman shot the picture in ten days on a budget of $70,000. Though many exteriors were featured in the film, it was totally studiobound. A fake forest was constructed inside a re-converted supermarket. • Actor Richard Devon, who played Satan himself in the film, related this revealing anecdote about Roger Corman's attitude towards lowbudget filmmaking: "Someone had left one of my speeches out of the script, so naturally I couldn't learn what wasn't there. And [Corman] was not just upset, he was *maniacal*. Anything that cost a penny over his minuscule budget turned him into a monster." Devon went on to say how the problem was handled: "So one of the prop guys wrote it out on a little cardboard box and I read it. We did it in one take, and that was it. Roger *never* did another take unless it was absolutely impossible to get around a mistake." • Allison Hayes, who plays the leader of the witch cult, is best remembered for her "big" role in *Attack of the 50 Foot Woman* (1957).

The Vineyard (1989; Northstar Entertainment) D: Bill Rice, James Hong. P: Harry Mok. S: James Hong, Douglas Kondo, James Marlowe. C: John Dirlam. Cast: James Hong, Karne Witter, Michael Wong.

An evil Asian sorcerer poses as a film director to lure a group of unsuspecting young people to his island home, intending to sacrifice them in black magic rituals. ¶ "An island of death fueled by the blood of its victims"—ad line.

Virgin Witch (1970; Tigon/Joseph Brenner Associates; U.K.) D: Ray Austin. P: Ralph Solomons. S: Klaus Vogel. C: Gerald Moss. Cast: Anne Michelle, Vicky Michelle, Keith Buckley, Patricia Haines, James Chase, Paula Wright, Christopher Strain, Neil Hallett, Esme Smythe, Garth Watkins. Two young women are introduced to the head of a modeling agency who uses her manor house as the base for a coven of modern-day witches. The coven attempts to initiate the two girls with sex and black magic ceremonies. • The two young women are played by Anne and Vicky Michelle, real-life sisters.

Warlock (1991; Trimark Pictures) D/P: Steve Miner. S: D. T. Twohy. C: David Eggby. Cast: Julian Sands, Lori Singer, Richard E. Grant. An evil warlock (well-played by respected British actor Julian Sands) escapes the gallows in 1691 and ends up in modern-day L.A., closely followed by the witchhunter who had originally tracked him down. The warlock intends to find the three parts of the "Grand Grimoire," the bible of black magic which has the power to "thwart creation itself" and destroy all life. Aided by a ditzy "California girl," the seventeenth century hero must face the warlock's terrifying powers to save all of creation. ¶ "You mean the warlock—the guy who fingerpaints with body fluids?!" • This film plays up several bits of witchcraft folklore to good effect: Witches cannot set foot on consecrated ground; and witches cannot stand salt (in fact, the diabetic heroine jabs the warlock with two syringes full of insulin contained in a saline solution, causing his fiery meltdown and death at the climax).

Warlock Moon (1973) (see CANNIBALS). At the old Soda Springs Spa, abandoned since 1930, a group of cannibals plan to sacrifice a young girl in some bizarre ritualistic ceremony (for no very clear reason).

Werewolves on Wheels (1971) (see WERE-WOLVES — OTHER LYCANTHROPES). A band of bikers run across a mysterious coven of black-robed satanists. The satanists drug the bikers and attempt to use one of their "ladies" in a black magic ceremony. The bikers wake up and rough up the devil worshipers, who place a curse on one of them, turning him into a werewolf.

The Wicker Man (1972; Warner Bros.;

Paganism and Christianity clash on a remote Scottish isle, culminating in a meeting with The Wicker Man *(1972).*

U.K.) D: Robin Hardy. P: Peter Snell. S: Anthony Shaffer. C: Harry Waxman. Cast: Edward Woodward, Britt Ekland, Diane Cilento, Ingrid Pitt, Christopher Lee, Roy Boyd, Walter Carr, Lindsay Kemp. Sergeant Howie, an upright Christian police officer, journeys to a small Scottish isle to investigate the disappearance of a young girl. His religious sensibilities are shocked to find the inhabitants worshiping the old pagan gods, led by Lord Summerisle (Christopher Lee) as their pagan priest. Things are not as they seem when he finally uncovers the truth about the island, involving a human sacrifice and the mysterious "Wicker Man." • Christopher Lee summed up the essence of the film when he called it, "the story of the conflict between two different beliefs—paganism and Christianity" (from *The Films of Christopher Lee,* by Pohle and Hart). Lee also called it, "the most exciting film of my career," and, "the best performance I have given." • Lee, an amateur opera singer, is given the chance to exercise his resonant voice in the film, though most of his songs ended up on the cutting room floor. (Reportedly, almost two hours of footage was cut from the final print.) • Edward Woodlock, who plays Sergeant Howie, later became TV's "The Equalizer." • *The Wicker Man,* given only spotty distribution, won the Grand Prize at the Festival of Fantastic Films in Paris in 1973. It is now considered by many to be a classic cult film.

The Witch (1952; Sonney; Finland) (also *The Witch Returns to Life*). D: Roland Af Hallstrom. S: Mika Waltari. C: Esko Toyri. Cast: Mirja Mane, Tiovo Makela, Hillevi Lagerstam, Aku Korhonen, Sakari Jurkka, Helge Herala. An archeologist and his wife find a skeleton with a wooden stake through its heart. He removes the stake and revives a 300-year-old witch.

The Witch (1966; G. G. Productions; Italy) D: Damiano Damiani. P: Alfredo Bini. S: Damiano Damiani, Ugo Liberatore. C: Leonida Barboni. Cast: Rosanna Schiaffino, Richard Johnson, Sarah Ferrati, Gian Maria Volonté, Margherita Guzzinati. An historian falls in love with a beautiful woman who incites him to murder a rival, only to discover that she is really an old witch.

A Witch Without a Broom (1966; Producers Releasing Organization; Spain/U.S.) D: José Elorrieta. P: Sid Pink. S: José Luis Navarro Basso, Howard Berk. C: Alfonso Nieva. Cast: Jeffrey Hunter, Maria Perschy, Gustavo Rojo, Perla Cristal, Reginald Gilliam, Al Mulock. A professor (Jeffrey Hunter) becomes involved with a blonde witch who accidentally transports him to the stone age, the sixteenth century, and even to the planet Mars. • Jeffrey Hunter tragically died three years later at the age of 43 following brain surgery after a fall. He was married briefly to actress Barbara Rush when she made *It Came from Outer Space* in 1953.

Witchboard (1986) (see GHOSTS). A young woman playing with a ouija board inadvertently makes contact with a spirit. Thinking it the spirit of a young child, she continues to use the board until she becomes obsessed with it. The spirit then reveals its *true* self—an evil warlock intent on possessing the woman.

Witchcraft (1964; 20th Century–Fox) D: Don Sharp. P: Robert L. Lippert. S: Harry Spalding. C: Arthur Lavis. Cast: Jack Hedley, Jill Dixon, Marie Ney, David Weston, Lon Chaney, Jr., Diane Clare, Viola Keats, Yvette Rees. Lon Chaney, Jr., plays the leader of the Whitlocks—a family of witches. When developers (led by the head of a rival family) bulldoze the Whitlock family cemetery, the witches employ the black arts to take revenge upon them. • At the stirring climax, the coven of witches is finally destroyed by being doused with burning hot oil. • The film's pressbook publicity made the preposterous claim that "In view of the reported rise in witchcraft and black magic practices, the film is useful in that it explains much about these centuries-old rites."

Witchcraft Through the Ages (1922; Biograph; Sweden) (also *Haxan*). D/S: Benjamin Christensen. P: Antony Balch (English sound version). C: Johan Ankerstjerne. Cast: Maren Pedersen, Clara Pontoppidan, Elith Pio, Oscar Stribolt, Tora Teje, Johs Andersen, Benjamin Christensen. This early fictionalized documentary-style account of "witchcraft through the ages" is based on witchcraft trials of the fifteenth and sixteenth centuries. It features scenes of torture, witches' ceremonies, the black mass, possession, and Satan himself. ¶ "The practice of witchcraft has plagued Man on this planet since he first used words." • The director himself (Benjamin Christensen) plays Satan. • The most popular version of this film is a 1966 re-release print with a voice-over narration by William Burroughs added.

Witchery (1989; Filmirage) (also *Witchcraft*). D: Martin Newlin. C: John Wynn. Cast: Linda Blair, David Hasselhoff, Catherine Hickland, Annie Ross, Hildegard Knef, Leslie Cumming, Bob Champagne, Rick Farnsworth, Michael Manchies. A group of people visit an old abandoned hotel on an island off Massachusetts. Stranded there, they are sucked into another dimension by an evil witch who tortures and kills them one by one. ¶ "There are three doors to the dark side—lust, avarice, and ire."

The Witches (1990; Warner Bros.; U.K.) D: Nicholas Roeg. P: Mark Shivas. S: Allan Scott. C: Harvey Harrison. Cast: Angelica Huston, Mai Zetterling, Bill Paterson, Brenda Blethyn, Rowan Atkinson, Jasen Fisher. A young boy is turned into a mouse by the "Grand High Witch" (Angelica Huston), conducting a witches' convention at an English seaside resort. She plans to turn every child in England into a mouse using her diabolical "Formula 86." With the aid of his cigar-smoking grandmother, the boy/ mouse must foil the plans of the witches and save the children of Britain. ¶ "Witches spend their time plotting to kill children, stalking the wretched child like a hunter stalks the bird of the forest." • According to this film, all witches share several physical traits by which they can be spotted by those who know what to look for. "Real witches have no toes, just square ends." They have a purple tinge to their eyes and are also bald (so they are often seen scratching their heads since they must constantly wear an itchy wig). They also "have a highly developed sense of smell," so that children smell like "dog do-do" to them. • Much of this wonderfully dark fantasy film was shot at Bray Studios, the former home of Hammer Films.

Witches' Mountain (1972; Avco-Embassy; Spain) D/P/S: Raoul Artigot. C: Ramón Sempere. Cast: Patty Shepard, John Caffari, Monica Randall. A photographer and his girlfriend trek into the mountains to do a report on witches. They find more than they bargained for when they visit a gloomy castle inhabited by an active coven of witches, who earmark the girl as their next human sacrifice. • Director/producer/screenwriter Raoul Artigot is a former cinematographer who worked steadily for prolific director Jesus Franco.

The Witches of Eastwicke (1987; Warner Bros.) D: George Miller. P: Neil Canton, Peter Gruber, Jon Peters. S: Michael Cristofer. C: Vilmos Zsigmond. Cast: Jack Nicholson, Cher, Susan Sarandon, Michelle Pfeiffer, Veronica Cartwright, Richard Jenkins, Keith Jochim, Carel Struzik, Becca Lish. Demonic Jack Nicholson is attracted to the sleepy little town of Eastwicke by the untapped feminine powers of three women who live there. This "unusual man" changes their lives and releases the hidden powers and supressed passions locked deep inside them, creating three witches who ultimately prove to be his undoing. ¶ "I'm just your average horny little devil."

Witchfire (1985) (see MADMEN — THE SLICE 'N' DICE WAVE). Shelley Winters thinks she is a witch, but she is just psychotic. When her beloved doctor is killed in a car crash she breaks out of the asylum with two other inmates, intending to use her "witch powers" to bring the dead doctor back to life. The trio latch onto a passing hunter, insisting that he is the resurrected doctor,

and proceed to tie him up and torment him.

The Witchmaker (1969; Excelsior) (also *Legend of Witch Hollow*). D/P/S: William O. Brown. C: John Arthur Morill. Cast: Anthony Eisley, Thordis Brandt, Alvy Moore, John Lodge, Shelby Grant, Tony Benson, Robyn Millan, Warrene Ott, Helene Winston. An investigative team goes to the Louisiana swampland to investigate the deaths of eight women. They find a warlock named "Luther the Berserk" running a coven of witches who kidnap and kill women to supply blood for their 200-year-old witch leader. ¶ "Yes sir, some towns is famous for their rhubarb, we was famous for our witches." • *The Witchmaker* was shot on location in Marksville, Louisiana.

The Witch's Curse (1963) (see SWORD AND SORCERY) (also *Maciste in Hell*). The Italian hero Maciste travels to Hell to find the witch who has put a curse on her descendant.

The Witch's Mirror (1960; Trans-International Films/AIP-TV; Mexico) D: Chano Urueta, Paul Nagle (English version). P: Abel Salazar, K. Gordon Murray (English version). S: Alfredo Ruanova, Carlos E. Taboada. C: Jorge Stahl, Jr. Cast: Rosita Arenas, Armando Calvo, Isabela Corona, Dian de Marco, Carlos Nieto, Alfredo W. Barron. A famous surgeon poisons his wife. His housekeeper, a black magic witch, vows revenge since the wife was her god-daughter. Later, the doctor remarries, but the housekeeper uses her witch's mirror to summon up the ghost of his first wife who torments and finally disfigures the new bride. The doctor commits murder to obtain corpses in order to restore his new wife's beauty, but the vengeful spirit intervenes and the doctor finally meets his just fate. ¶ "But only those that have reached the highest category, the witches that possess a limitless and profound knowledge of the hermetical sciences, have the necessary tools with which to make use of that ultimate object that contains infinite powers and properties and was invented by a great magician of old Persia — the *mirror*" — the end of the narrator's opening diatribe on witchcraft and witches.

Witchtrap (1989) (see GHOSTS). A group of psychic investigators are hired to check out a haunted house. They are terrorized and murdered one by one by the spirit of the house's former owner, an evil satanist. • This is the second witchcraft/ghost film made by director/screenwriter Kevin S. Tenney. He directed and wrote the screenplay for *Witchboard* in 1986.

The Wizard of Oz (1939; MGM) D: Victor

Fleming. P: Mervyn Le Roy. S: Noel Langley, Florence Ryerson, Edgar Allan Wolfe. C: Harold Rosson. Cast: Judy Garland, Ray Bolger, Jack Haley, Frank Morgan, Bert Lahr, Margaret Hamilton, Billie Burke, Charley Grapewin, Clara Blandick. A Kansas farm girl is hurled (in her own mind and imagination) into a magical world called Oz after a fall during a tornado. While in the colorful world of her subconscious she is aided by a good witch, and then runs afoul of a very wicked one which is scheming to get her hands on Dorothy's ruby red shoes. ¶ "There's no place like home."

The Woman Who Came Back (1945;

Republic) D/P: Walter Colmes. S: Dennis Cooper, Lee Willis. C: Henry Sharp. Cast: Nancy Kelly, John Loder, Otto Kruger, Ruth Ford, J. Farrell MacDonald. A young woman imagines she is becoming possessed by the spirit of a witch burned at the stake 300 years before. Seemingly supernatural events surround her presence and the superstitious townspeople turn against her. • Rather than play up the terrifying aspects of satanism, this film chose to present an intelligent treatment of witch-hunting hysteria and its devastating effects on people. It is finally revealed that she is *not* a witch after all, and the "supernatural" events were simply a set of unfortunate circumstances.

Yeti *see* The Abominable Snowman

Zombie Flesh Eaters

(*See also* Zombies)

Zombie Flesh Eaters were born in 1968, when first-time filmmaker George Romero made one of the most terrifying and influential horror pictures ever produced (particularly on the paltry sum of $114,000) — *Night of the Living Dead.* With its claustrophobic atmosphere, its nowhere-to-run terror, and its scenes of decaying zombies devouring the flesh of the living, *NOTLD* created a sensation and a new subgenre which to this day has not abated.

We have made the distinction between "zombies" and "zombie flesh eaters" because they are two unique types of creatures who behave quite differently. For instance, traditional non-hungry zombies are often controlled by their makers (whether by magic or science), who send these mindless walking corpses out to do their nefarious bidding. Flesh-eating ghouls, on the other hand, are interested solely in one thing — to eat the flesh of the living. They obey no master but their own undead stomachs, and so are much more chaotic in their actions.

The first decade following *Night of the Living Dead* saw only a handful of imitators reach the screen (*Garden of the Dead,* 1972; Italy's *Don't Open the Window,* 1974; and French horror director Jean Rollin's obscure entry, *Pesticide,* 1978). While all were inferior to their source, this early round of flesh-eaters did include a few worthy entries like *Children Shouldn't Play with Dead Things* (1972) and *The Child* (1977).

Then in 1979, Romero returned to his walking dead roots with the full-color gore-fest, *Dawn of the Dead. Dawn,* retitled *Zombie* for European release, took that continent by storm, and inspired a flood of Italian and Spanish zombie gutcruncher pictures (led by Lucio Fulci's unofficial "sequel" entitled *Zombie 2,* which was released as just plain *Zombie* in the United States).

George Romero further cemented his title of King of the Zombies by filming the third feature in his zombie trilogy, *Day of the Dead* (1985; the least of the trio), and also writing the script for Tom Savini's 1990 remake of *Night of the Living Dead,* a powerful updating of the original, laced with 90s sensibilities. Meanwhile, Italian gore-meister Lucio Fulci claimed the zombie crown of Europe with *Zombie* (1980), *The Gates of Hell* (1980), *Seven Doors of Death* (1981), and the more recent *Zombie 3* (1988) (not to mention his non-hungry zombie gore film — *The House by the Cemetery,* 1981).

In the post–*Night of the Living Dead* era, filmmakers abandoned the more traditional voodoo origins of the zombie and instead gave a variety of reasons for the reanimation of their flesh-eaters. The only flesh-eating zombies to be associated with voodoo were the hungry dead in Lucio Fulci's gory Italian import, *Zombie* (1980). Even Fulci's own sequel, *Zombie 3* (1988), bypassed voodoo in favor of a more scientific explanation (out-of-control government research). Filmmakers often linked science-gone-bad with their hungry undead, as in *Don't Open the Window* (1974) and *Chopper Chicks in Zombie Town* (1989). Other origins include psychic ability (*The Child,* 1977), some kind of military snafu (*Return of the Living Dead,* 1985), or even more traditional western occult origins (satanism rather than voodoo — e.g., *The Gates of Hell,* 1980).

While modern big-budget movie makers generally shy away from the subject, flesh-eating zombies are being kept alive by low-budget independent filmmakers who aim these pictures at the drive-in crowd (which , for all intents and purposes, has been replaced by the VCR crowd). Led by the blackly funny *Return of the Living Dead* (1985), the recent hungry dead have often taken a satirical (and even outright comical) turn. Films like the amateurish *Redneck Zombies* (1987), the puerile non-sequel *C.H.U.D. 2: Bud the Chud* (1989), and the genuinely witty *Chopper Chicks in Zombie Town* (1989) demonstrate that even a flesh-eating corpse can have a sense of humor.

Alien Dead (1979; Firebird International) (also *It Fell from the Sky*). D/P: Fred Olen Ray. S: Fred Olen Ray, Allan Nicholas. Cast: Buster Crabbe, Linda Lewis. An alien force lands on Earth via meteorite and transforms people into hungry walking corpses. • Prolific movie fan turned low-budget filmmaker Fred Olen Ray made his directorial debut on this ultra-cheap zombie feature. Ray explained his approach to no-budget filmmaking in a *Fangoria* #71 interview: "We started *Alien Dead* with a monster mask and $40. We had no insurance, no permits, and everyone worked on a deferred payment plan. We had that film in the can for less than $5,000, and Buster Crabbe got most of that." • Sadly, this was to be Buster Crabbe's last film.

Bloodsuckers from Outer Space (1987; Reel Movies International) D/S: Glen Coburn. P: Carl Boyd Latham. C: Chad D. Smith. Cast: Thom Meyers, Laura Ellis, Dennis Letts, Chris Heldman, Robert Bradeen, Billie Keller, John Webb, Rick Garlington. An airborne virus from outer space transforms the inhabitants of a small Texas town into a group of bloodsucking zombies in this low, low, low budget horror/comedy. A group of young people try to escape the zombie carnage while the military only wants to nuke the entire area.

Burial Ground (1980; Esteban Cinematografica; Italy) D: Andrea Bianchi. P: Gabriele Crisanti. S: Piero Regnoli. C: Gianfranco Maioletti. Cast: Karin Weil, Maria Angela Giordan, Gian Luigi Chirizzi, Peter Bark, Simone Mattioli. In yet another Italian zombie gut-cruncher, a group of guests weekending at an estate stumble upon an Etruscan tomb which disgorges a shambling horde of flesh-eating rotted corpses.

The Child (1977; Valiant International) (also *Kill and Go Hide*). D: Robert Voskanian. P: Robert Dadashian. S: Ralph Lucas. C: Mori Alavi. Cast: Laurel Barnett, Rosalie Cole, Frank Janson, Richard Hanners, Ruth Ballan, Blosson Bing Jong, Rod Medigovich, Wendell Hudiberg. A little girl lives alone with her older brother and father in seclusion. The girl has supernatural powers and is able to summon up flesh-eating zombies from the local cemetery to take revenge on those she feels were responsible for her mother's death.

Children Shouldn't Play with Dead Things (1972; Brandywine-Motionarts/Geneni) D:

Benjamin Clark. P: Gary Goch, Benjamin Clark. S: Benjamin Clark, Alan Ormark (Alan Ormsby). C: Jack McGowan. Cast: Valerie Mamcher, Alan Ormsby, Anya Ormsby, Jeffrey Gillen, Jane Daly, Paul Cronin. The director of a theater troupe induces his actors to journey to an island cemetery in the dead of night with the aim of performing a satanic ritual to raise the dead (all in fun of course). The invocation works, much to their dismay, and the group is besieged by a horde of flesh-hungry zombies. • This often-startling movie was filmed over the course of 11 nights with amateur actors and the unbelievably low budget of $50,000. • Star Alan Ormsby, who plays the egomaniac director, also co-wrote the script and did the zombie makeup himself (using the slightly altered name of "Alan Ormark"). His real-life wife, Anya Ormsby, co-stars with him.

Chopper Chicks in Zombie Town (1989; Chelsea Partners) D/S: Dan Hoskins. P: Maria Snyder. C: Tom Fraser. Cast: Jamie Rose, Catherine Carlen, Lycia Naff, Vicki Frederick, Kristina Loggia, Gretchen Palmer, Nina Petersen, Don Calfa. A gang of women motorcyclists called the "Cycle Sluts" cruise into the secluded town of Zariah, a desert community with a mysteriously high mortality rate. It seems the local mortician has been killing off the townspeople and turning them into walking zombies to mine radioactive materials. In a nod to *The Magnificent Seven* (there are even seven women in the gang), the "Sluts" have to save the town from the escaped flesh-eating ghouls. ¶ "You're the *'Sluts,'* try and act like it!"—leader of the "Cycle Sluts." • The way to kill this particular batch of zombies is to remove the special battery implanted in their dead brain by the mad mortician—basically, knock their block off.

C.H.U.D. 2: Bud the Chud (1989; Vestron) D: David Irving. P: Jonathan D. Krane. S: M. Kane Jeeves. C: Arnie Sirlin. Cast: Brian Robbins, Bill Calvert, Tricia Leigh Fisher, Gerrit Graham, Larry Cedar, Bianca Jagger, Larry Linville, Judd Omen, Robert Vaughn. The government C.H.U.D. research program, intended to perfect a type of soldier which would go on fighting even after he was dead, is discontinued, but not before their subject escapes and infects a small town with the cannibalistic zombie virus in this low-brow horror/comedy. ¶ "Steve, you have a live dead guy lying in your bathroom." • This is a sequel in name only, having nothing to do with the original *CHUD*, which was about homeless people

turned into cannibalistic mutants by radioactive waste. The first film was serious horror, this one played for broad (and none-too-effective) comedy. • Screenwriter M. Kane Jeeves is actually author/screenwriter/former magazine editor Ed Naha; the name is a nod to W. C. Fields, who, on occasion, used the pseudonym "Mahatma Kane Jeeves."

City of the Walking Dead (1980; Dialchi Film/Lotus Film International; Italy/Spain) (also *Nightmare City*). D: Umberto Lenzi. P: Diego Alchimede, Luis Mendez. S: Antonio Corti, Piero Regnoli. C: Hans Burman. Cast: Hugo Stiglitz, Laura Trotter, Mel Ferrer, Francisco Rabal, Maria Rosaria Omaggio, Sonia Viviani, Eduardo Fajardo, Manolo Zarzo, Alejandro de Enciso. A radiation leak turns a planeload of passengers into bloodthirsty ghouls. It lands and disgorges the zombies into the city where their numbers multiply and take over the world.

Dawn of the Dead (1979; Laurel Group Productions–Dawn Associates/United Film Distributors) (also *Zombie* [European title]). D/S: George Romero. C: Michael Gornick. Cast: David Emge, Ken Foree, Scott H. Reiningre, Gaylen Ross, David Crawford, David Early. In this first sequel to *Night of the Living Dead* (1968), four people escaping the nationwide zombie chaos commandeer a helicopter and land at a shopping mall. There they barricade themselves in against the zombies until a roving motorcycle gang breaks into their little consumerist microcosm and allows the flesh-eating ghouls to overrun the mall. ¶ "Every dead body that is not exterminated becomes one of them! It gets up and kills. The people it kills get up and kill.... They kill for food!" • "When there's no more room in *Hell,* the dead will walk the *Earth,*" was the chilling advertising slogan for this zombie sequel. • Makeup man Tom Savini, responsible for the numerous gruesome zombie faces and gore effects, appears in the film as the vicious leader of the biker gang. • Romero followed up this sequel with another in 1985, titled *Day of the Dead*.

Dawn of the Mummy (1981) (see MUMMIES—MORE MUMMIES). This first-ever mummy gore movie features a group of fashion models disturbing the burial place of an ancient Egyptian king. The dead king returns to life as a mummy and summons up his eight zombie slaves. In one of the film's gruesome highlights, the zombie servants interrupt a wedding feast and make their own feast out of the guests.

Day of the Dead (1985; Laurel Productions) D/S: George Romero. P: Richard P. Rubinstein. C: Michael Gornick. Cast: Lori Cardille, Terry Alexander, Joseph Pilato, Jarlath Conroy, Antone DiLeo, Jr., Richard Liberty, Howard Sherman. In this third (and last to date) film in Romero's "Living Dead" series, the zombies have overrun the country. A handful of volatile personnel are holed up in an underground research complex, where a rather eccentric doctor conducts experiments in domesticating the flesh-eating ghouls. ¶ "Look, it's a miracle! He doesn't see us as lunch!" • Director/screenwriter George Romero originally planned to wrap up his trilogy with a story about an elite group that trains zombies to fight other zombies, but it was deemed too costly and the present smaller-scale story was filmed.

Dead People (1974; VM Productions/Bedford Enterprises) (also *Messiah of Evil; Return of the Living Dead; Revenge of the Screaming Dead*). D: Willard Huyck. P: Gloria Katz. S: Willard Huyck, Gloria Katz. C: Stephen Katz. Cast: Michael Greer, Marianna Hall, Joy Bang, Anitra Ford, Royal Dano, Elisha Cook, Jr. A woman goes to a small California town to search for her missing father and encounters a group of flesh-eating zombies. • When the film was re-released in the early 1980s it carried the ad line: "When there is no more room in hell, the dead will walk the earth." This is the same slogan used by *Dawn of the Dead* in 1979, and *Dead People*'s distributors were sued over it.

Dead Pit (1989; Imperial Entertainment) D: Brett Leonard. P: Gimel Everett. S: Brett Leonard, Gimel Everett. C: Marty Collins. Cast: Jeremy Slate, Danny Gochnauer, Steffen Gregory Foster, Cheryl Lawson, Geha Getz, Joan Bechtel, Mara Everett, Randy Fontana, Michael Jacobs. Twenty years ago, Dr. Colin Ramsey conducted inhuman experiments in a hidden basement laboratory/dungeon beneath the "State Institution for the Mentally Ill." A colleague discovered his secret and was forced to kill him and seal up the unholy place. Now in the present day, an earthquake opens up the secret lab and the now-zombified doctor is back at work again, turning patients and staff alike into brain-hungry zombies. ¶ "For dead people, they sure are smart." • Oddly enough, even though these zombies were ostensibly created by science, it takes holy water(!) to destroy them.

Don't Open the Window (1974; Hallmark; Italy) (also *Breakfast at the Manchester Morgue; The Living Dead at the Manchester Morgue*). D: Jorge Grau. P: Edmondo Amati. S: Sandro Continenza, Marcello Coscia. C: Francisco Sempere. Cast: Ray Lovelock, Cristina Galbo, Arthur Kennedy, Aldo Massasso, Giorgio Trestini. An experimental agricultural machine designed to kill insects with "ultrasonic radiation" has the unpleasant side effect of reviving the dead as flesh-hungry zombies. ¶ "You talk about the dead walkin', about cannibalism, it's unscientific man!" • These zombies have a strange way of spreading their condition: "They transmit life to each other through the blood of the living, like a plague." They do this by touching their blood-soaked fingers to the eyelids of other corpses, causing them to rise as the walking dead.

Garden of the Dead (1972; Millennium Productions) (also *Tomb of the Undead*). D/S: John Hayes. P: H. A. Milton. C: Phil Kenneally. Cast: Duncan McLeod, John Dennis, John Dullaghan, Lee Frost, Lewis Sterling, Marland Procktor, Susan Charney. When formaldehyde is spilled on the graves of some prison inmates killed in an escape attempt, the corpses rise from the dead and attack.

The Gates of Hell (1980; Dania Film/Medusa/International Cinematografica; Italy) (also *City of the Living Dead*). D: Lucio Fulci. P: Giovanni Masini. S: Lucio Fulci, Dardano Sacchetti. C: Sergio Salvati. Cast: Christopher George, Janet Agren, Katriona MacColl, Carlo De Mejo, Antonella Interlenghi, Giovanni Lombardo Radice. A priest commits suicide in the town of Dunwich which triggers the opening of the gates of hell, allowing a horde of moldering corpses to rise up and eat the living. • This was Italian director Lucio Fulci's gory follow-up to his equally gory *Zombie* (1980). *The Gates of Hell* features such "highlights" as a woman regurgitating her own intestines and a man having a power drill shoved completely through his head.

Mutant (1983; Film Ventures). D: John "Bud" Cardos. P: Ed Montoro, Igo Kantor. Cast: Wings Hauser, Bo Hopkins, Jennifer Warren, Jody Medford. Toxic waste turns the residents of the town of Goodland into bloodthirsty undead zombies in this three million dollar "epic" from the director of *Kingdom of the Spiders* (1977). • John Cardos replaced director Mark Rosman a few days into the shoot when Rosman was deemed too slow by the producers.

Night of the Living Dead (1968; Image Ten) D/C: George A. Romero. P: Russell Streiner, Karl Hardman. S: John A. Russo. Cast: Judith O'Dea, Duane Jones, Karl

A group of flesh-eating zombies gather to look for their next meal during the ground-breaking cult classic, Night of the Living Dead *(1968).*

Hardman, Keith Wayne, Judith Ridley, Marilyn Eastman. For some reason never fully explained (though possible radiation from a Venus probe is alluded to), the dead are coming back to life as flesh-eating zombies. A disparate group of people hole up in a farmhouse to fight off the relentless onslaught of walking corpses. ¶ "If you have a gun, shoot 'em in the head, that's a sure way to kill 'em. If you don't grab yourself a club or a torch – beat 'em or burn 'em, they go up pretty easy." • This is it, the one that opened the floodgates for hungry zombies everywhere – the first (and many say best) "zombie flesh eater" movie. • This film set the ground rules for many imitations to come: The dead can only be killed by being shot or stabbed in the head (destroying the brain); all those bitten or killed by the walking corpses will soon rise as zombies themselves. • *The Night of Anubis* was the movie's original title, but was changed shortly before its release. • *Night of the Living Dead,* frequently hailed as a classic of modern horror, was shot in and around the environs of Pittsburgh, Pennsylvania (George Romero's home town), on a budget of $114,000 (by Romero's own estimation). A print of the film is now kept in the archives of the New York Museum of Modern Art. • Producers Russell Streiner and Carl Hardman both had substantial parts in the picture. Streiner played Johnny, the brother and ghoul-to-be of catatonic heroine Barbara (Judith O'Dea). Hardman played the obstinate and ultimately dangerous Mr. Cooper.

Night of the Living Dead (1990; Columbia) D: Tom Savini. P: John A. Russo, Russ Streiner. S: George A. Romero. C: Frank Prinzi. Cast: Tony Todd, Patricia Tallman, Tom Towles, William Butler, McKee Anderson. This well-done update of the classic 1968 flesh-eating zombie film follows the plot of the original quite closely, with a few deviations. This time the heroine, Barbara, is not the whimpering near-catatonic mess as in the original, but a tough fighter who takes out more than her fair share of zombies. A few twists have been tacked onto the bleak ending of the original as well, which makes it a bit more palatable to modern audiences weaned on Spielberg sensibilities (though the film's overall tone is still quite grim). ¶ "This is hell on Earth. This is pure hell on Earth." • Tom Savini made his big-screen directorial debut on this remake, which he dubs "more of a retelling than a remake." Savini is the master makeup artist who worked on both *Dawn of the Dead* (1979) and *Day of the Dead* (1985) for George Romero. • Romero, who wrote the screenplay for this version, directed the original *Night of the Living Dead* in 1968. • This film's producers (John Russo and Russ Streiner) were both involved in the original as well—Russo as screenwriter and Streiner as co-producer and actor.

Night of the Zombies (1981; N.M.D.) (also *Gamma 693*). D/S: Joel M. Reed. P: Lorin E. Price. Cast: Jamie Gillis, Joel M. Reed. An ex–Nazi creates zombies out of World War II soldiers and trains them to fight in this low-budget New York–based zombie feature. ¶ From the ads: "The dead are hungry, and they're coming to eat you alive!" • Lead actor Jamie Gillis works mostly in porno movies. • Director Joel M. Reed stars as the evil Nazi behind the zombies.

Night of the Zombies (1983; Beatrice/ Dana; Italy/Spain) D: Vincent Dawn. S: Claudio Fragasso, J. M. Cunilles. C: John Carrera. Cast: Birgit Evelyn Newton, Frank Garfield, Selan Karay, Robert O'Neil, Gaby Renom, Luis Fonoll. An experimental project goes haywire on the island of New Guinea, releasing a poisonous gas which transforms people into cannibalistic ghouls and causes the dead to rise up as flesh-eating zombies. A pair of television reporters hook up with a swat team to try and survive the zombie onslaught of this inept, gory, derivative import. ¶ "Look at that, they're eatin' him like pigs!"

Oasis of the Zombies (1982; Eurocine; Spain) D: A. M. Frank (Jesus Franco). S: A. L. Mariaux. C: Max Monteillet. Cast: Manuel Gelin, France Jordan, Jeff Montgomery, Myriam Landson, Eric Saint-Just, Caroline Audret, Henry Lambert. A group of young people travel to an accursed oasis in North Africa in search of six million dollars in Nazi gold lost there in 1943. They do not find the gold, but they do find the walking corpses of the soldiers who died there and now rise up out of the sand to guard their treasure and eat all the intruders. ¶ "The sand, they came out of the sand—the dead!"

Pesticide (1978; Les Films ABC/Rush Productions; France) (also *Grapes of the Dead*). D: Jean Rollin. P: Claude Guedj. S: Jean Rollin, Jean-Pierre Bouyxou, Christian Meunier. C: Claude Becognee. Cast: Marie-Georges Pascall, Serge Marquand,

Patricia Cartier, Felix Marten, Mirella Rancelot. A woman vacationing in the south of France comes across a village seemingly populated by walking corpses. The local vineyards have been sprayed with a pesticide which turns whomever drinks the wine into zombie flesh-eaters.

Redneck Zombies (1987; Full Moon/ TWE) D: Pericles Lewnes. S: Fester Smellman. P: Edward Bishop, George Scott, Pericles Lewnes. C: Ken Davis. Cast: Lisa M. DeHaven, William E. Benson, P. Floyd Piranha, William-Livingston Dekkar, Zoofeet, James H. Housely, Anthony Burlington-Smith, Martin J. Wolfman, Boo Teasedale, Darla Deans, Tyrone Taylor, Frank Lantz, Bucky Santini. This low-budget shot-on-video gore-fest is about a group of campers besieged by some backwoods rednecks who have been turned into flesh-eating zombies by a batch of moonshine contaminated with toxic waste. The only way to stop these flesh-hungry ghouls (other than dismemberment) is to spray underarm deodorant on them—the chemicals in it makes them melt. ¶ From the trailer: "But what happens when these simple down-to-earth folk accidentally drink a barrel of nuclear waste? Swillin' toxic moonshine they become flesh-eatin' bloodthirsty kinfolk from hell—they become *Redneck Zombies!* Redneck zombies, tobacco chewin', gut chompin' creatures of the night." • That is the director himself, Pericles Lewnes, as the sexually confused zombie-to-be Billy Bob/Ellie Mae. • *Redneck Zombies* was "filmed in gorgeous entrail-vision" (consisting of a few cheap video optical effects). It was shot entirely on location in the state of Maryland.

Return of the Living Dead (1985; Helmdale/Fox) D/S: Dan O'Bannon. P: Tom Fox, Graham Henderson. C: Jules Brenner. Cast: Clu Gulager, James Karen, Don Calfa, Thom Mathews, Miguel Nuñez, Brian Peck, John Philbin, Linnea Quigley, Beverly Randolph, Jewel Shepard, Mark Venturini. In this semi-sequel to *Night of the Living Dead* (1968), the army loses a shipment of zombie cylinders which mistakenly end up at the "Uneeda Medical Supplies" company in Louisville, Kentucky. When one of the cylinders is breached, it releases a gas which revives the dead in the local cemetery, where a group of punk rockers are having a party. Soon the area is overrun with brain-eating walking corpses. ¶ "Tina, I love you and you've got to let me eat your braaaaains"—boyfriend turned hungry zombie. • The evolution of this horror/comedy hit was a long and complicated

Zombie Flesh Eaters

621

process. John Russo, co-author of *Night of the Living Dead* split with partner George Romero and kept the rights to use the words "Living Dead," while Romero kept the rights to use the word "Dead" (which he did in his two direct sequels — *Dawn of the Dead,* 1979, and *Day of the Dead,* 1985). Russo, along with his partners, wrote a screenplay titled *Return of the Living Dead* but it sat on the shelf for many years before finally being purchased and totally revamped into the present version by screenwriter Dan O'Bannon (*Dark Star,* 1974; *Alien,* 1979; *Dead and Buried,* 1981). Story credit is given to Rudy Ricci, John Russo, and Russell Streiner. • Dan O'Bannon made his directorial debut on this film, an auspicious beginning. • Early on in the project, Tobe Hooper (*The Texas Chainsaw Massacre,* 1974; *Poltergeist,* 1982) was set to direct, but dropped out due to his commitment to *Lifeforce* (1985). • The tone of *Return of the Living Dead* is very different from its father film. Liberally laced with black humor, it successfully balanced suspense, comedy, and gore into a box office hit. • The zombies here do not quite follow the rules set down in *Night of the Living Dead.* They are able to talk (often to comic effect), they do not eat just any old flesh (they want strictly brains), and they no longer are so easily stopped (shooting or bashing in their heads does not seem to work anymore). When a flustered James Karen yells, "Well it worked in the movie," after bashing in the skull of a zombie with no effect, he of course was referring to the movie *Night of the Living Dead,* which he had previously explained was based on a real incident covered up by the military. • A sequel was filmed in 1987, predictably titled *Return of the Living Dead Part 2,* but was much less successful both artistically and financially.

Return of the Living Dead Part 2 (1987; Greenfox/Lorimar) D/S: Ken Wiederhorn. P: Tom Fox. C: Robert Elswit. Cast: James Karen, Thom Mathews, Dana Ashbrook, Marsha Dietelein, Suzanne Snyder, Philip Bruns, Michael Kenworthy. Once again the army loses one of its zombie-containers which ends up in a sleepy suburban community. The cylinder is breached and soon the brain-eating corpses are on the march. It is left to a 12-year-old boy, his sister, his sister's would-be boyfriend, and an eccentric doddering doctor to find a way to stop the living dead onslaught. ¶ "They seem to like brains so maybe they'll leave *you* alone." • Writer/director Ken Wiederhorn thought of this sequel as "the *Police Academy* of horror films," emphasizing the humor over the horror to an even greater extent than the original. This is Wiederhorn's second foray into zombie territory; he directed *Shock Waves* (a superior non–flesh eaters entry) ten years earlier, in 1977. • James Karen and Thom Mathews return from the first film, though as different (but similar) characters since they were transformed into zombies themselves in the original.

Seven Doors of Death (1981; Fulvia Film/ Aquarius Productions; Italy) (also *And You'll Live in Terror! The Beyond; The Beyond*). D: Louis Fuller (Lucio Fulci). P: Terry Levene (Fabrizio De Angelis). S: Roy Corchoran (Lucio Fulci, Giorgio Mariuzzo, Dardano Sacchetti). C: Glenn Kimbell (Sergio Salvati). Cast: Katherine MacColl, David Warbeck, Sarah Keller, Tony Saint John, Veronica Lazar. A young woman inherits an abandoned hotel in the Louisiana swampland with plans to renovate it. Unbeknownst to her, the hotel rests on one of the seven gateways to hell. Workers break through a wall and open the diabolical gateway, releasing flesh-eating zombies. ¶ "The seven dreaded gateways are concealed in seven cursed places. Woe be unto him who ventures near without knowledge." • This is Italian filmmaker Lucio Fulci's third cannibal zombie film, beginning with *Zombie* (1980) and *The Gates of Hell* (1980). • Thinking that U.S. audiences would not look favorably upon another Italian import, most of the production crew were given anglicized pseudonyms in the credits for its American release.

Toxic Zombies (1984; CM Productions) (also *Bloodeaters*). D/P/S: Charles McCrann. C: David Sperling. Cast: Charles Austin, Beverly Shapiro, Dennis Helfend, John Amplas. An experimental herbicide turns a group of marijuana growers into flesh-eating ghouls.

Waxwork (1988) (see WAX MUSEUMS). In a sinister wax museum where the exhibits come alive in their own little worlds, a boy stumbles into the zombie exhibit and is attacked by the flesh-hungry ghouls.

Zombie (1980; Variety Film/Jerry Gross Organization; Italy) (also *Zombie Flesh Eaters; Zombie 2*). D: Lucio Fulci. P: Ugo Tucci, Fabrizio De Angelis. S: Elisa Briganti. C: Sergio Salvati. Cast: Tisa Farrow, Ian McCulloch, Richard Johnson, Auretta Gay, Olga Karlatos, Al Cliver. Two couples visit an island in the West Indies where voodoo causes the dead to rise and devour the living. ¶ From the ads: "We are going to eat you!"

• Italian exploitation filmmaker Lucio Fulci rushed out this stomach-turning movie as an unofficial sequel to George Romero's *Dawn of the Dead* (1979), which was a huge hit in Europe under the title *Zombie*. Consequently the European title for Fulci's film was (confusingly) *Zombie 2;* and it was released in the United States simply as *Zombie*. • This gut-munching Italian zombie movie features such sights as a nine-inch splinter slowly piercing a human eyeball and a zombie overcoming and devouring an attacking shark underwater. • Male lead Ian McCulloch revealed this little-known fact in a *Fangoria* #52 interview: "Several people who've seen the film have remarked to me that many of the zombies look alike. Well, that's partly due to the makeup; under all that rotted flesh, it's difficult to make out fetaures, but all the zombies who were shot or set on fire were the Romano kids, seven boys and a girl who were European circus acrobats before becoming a film stunt team. They all look amazingly alike and under the zombie makeup, you couldn't tell one from the other." • Fulci went on to make three more zombie gut-wrenchers — *The Gates of Hell* (1980), *Seven Doors of Death* (1981), and *Zombie 3* (1988; this film's sequel, in name anyway).

Zombie 3 (1988; Flora Film Productions; Italy) D: Lucio Fulci. P: Franco Gaudenzi. S: Claudio Fragasso. C: Riccardo Grassetti.

Cast: Deran Sarafian, Beatrice Ring, Richard Raymond, Alex McBride. A government research lab develops a virus called "Death-1 Compound" which causes people to become flesh-hungry zombies. The virus is stolen and accidentally released, causing a countryside to become overrun with the walking dead. Three off-duty soldiers and a trio of young women must fight for their lives against the shambling horde. • Lucio Fulci made an unauthorized sequel to George Romero's *Dawn of the Dead* (1979) in 1980 called *Zombie 2* (released as just plain *Zombie* in the United States). This is Fulci's follow-up to *Zombie* (but since he knew it as *Zombie 2,* Fulci titled this one *Zombie 3,* and the U.S. distributor did not bother to change it to *Zombie 2*. Perhaps *Bride of the Zombie* would have been simpler). • To make things even more confusing, even though this is a sequel to *Zombie* (1980), it does not really have anything to do with the previous film, which dealt with voodoo-created zombies on a tropical island. • These particular flesh-eating zombies differ from the norm in that they can be killed in normal fashion; they do *not* have to be shot in the head — anywhere will do. In addition, some can talk, an unusual trait in flesh-eating ghouls. • Lucio Fulci reportedly was forced to leave the production due to ill health, and the film was completed by Bruno Mattei.

Zombies
(*See also* Zombie Flesh Eaters)

Often when one thinks of zombies today, an image comes to mind of a rotting corpse staggering out of the dark to clutch a living person and tear out chunks of flesh to feast upon. While this is the predominant concept of a "zombie" in the post–*Night of the Living Dead* film world, the less hungry walking dead had a rich history before (and even after) this groundbreaking 1968 film.

A "zombie" can broadly be defined as a walking or reanimated corpse. There are two distinct categories of zombies, which we have divided into two separate sections. The first (and the original) is the traditional dead body brought back to a kind of half-life by voodoo (though science and satanism soon gave voodoo a run for its money in the zombie business). This is the type of walking dead covered in this section. The second zombie-type is the "flesh-eating ghoul," which first appeared in the 1968 low-budget terror classic, *Night of the Living Dead*. These ambulatory corpses are featured in the preceding section, entitled ZOMBIE FLESH EATERS.

Zombies began their march across the silver screen with the release of the 1932 Bela Lugosi near-classic, *White Zombie*. Based on William Seabrook's novel, *The*

Magic Island, the film told the story of zombie-master Murder Legendre who reanimates the corpses of his enemies to work in the fields and sugar mills. These walking cadavers possessed all the characteristics of what is considered a "traditional" zombie—blank staring eyes, a slow, faltering gait, and mindless obedience to its master. Other films to feature these traditional members of the walking dead family include the thoughtful, atmospheric Val Lewton classic, *I Walked with a Zombie* (1943), the poverty-row potboiler, *Revenge of the Zombies* (1943), the abysmal comedy, *Zombies on Broadway* (1945), and the cheap, amusing *Zombies of Mora Tau* (1957). All these zombies were a product of voodoo, but filmmakers soon explored alternative origins for their walking dead.

As early as 1936, science created its first zombie (using the term loosely here) in the aptly-named Boris Karloff classic, *The Walking Dead.* More scientific zombies followed, with *The Return of Dr. X* (1939), *Revenge of the Zombies* (1943), *Creature with the Atom Brain* (1955), *Teenage Zombies* (1960), *The Astro-Zombies* (1968), and even the gore-filled *House by the Cemetery* (1981).

Then we come to *Night of the Living Dead,* as all discussions of zombies (flesh-eaters or not) must eventually return to this seminal classic. This film changed the face (literally) of zombies forever, with the old classical image of the zombie giving way to the more visceral creature featured in *NOTLD.* After *NOTLD,* even those non-flesh eaters were changed from the rather normal-looking clean-cut corpses of tradition into the hideously decayed, blood and pus cadavers of today. (Though Hammer's *The Plague of the Zombies* [1966] preceded it by two years by showing in full detail the gruesome nature of a walking corpse, it was *NOTLD* that created this impact.) Though unique and innovative films like *The Blind Dead* series (Spain's best), the shocking, socially conscious *Deathdream* (1972), and the deliriously bizarre modern zombie classic, *Re-Animator* (1985) feature the less-hungry variety of zombie, each owes a substantial debt to *Night of the Living Dead.*

The Astro-Zombies (1968; Geneni Film Distributors) (also *Space Vampires* [video title]). D/P: Ted V. Mikels. S: Ted V. Mikels, Wayne Rogers. C: Robert Maxwell. Cast: Wendell Corey, John Carradine, Tom Pace, Joan Patrick, Tura Satana, Rafael Campos. John Carradine plays the sinister Dr. DeMarco, a mad scientist who is trying to build a race of artificial men by creating zombies in his basement lab. The zombies look exactly like what they are—actors wearing dime store skull masks. ¶ "'Quasiman'? well you mean a sort of a *zombie?*" • This bottom-of-the-barrel zombie movie was so cheap that the skull-faced scientifically-created "zombies" held ordinary *flashlights* up to their foreheads in order to "recharge" themselves. • Wayne Rogers (of TV's "M*A*S*H") co-wrote the script and served as executive producer.

The Blind Dead (1972; Plata Films–Interfilme/Hallmark; Spain) (also *Crypt of the Blind Dead; Night of the Blind Dead; Tombs of the Blind Dead*). D/S: Armando de Ossorio. P: Salvador Romero. C: Pablo Ripoll. Cast: Oscar Burner, Lone Fleming, Maria Silva, José Telman, Helen Hay, Veronica Limera, Juan Cortes, Rufino Ingles. In the thirteenth century, the devil-worshiping order called The Knights Templar are executed and their corpses left for the crows to pick out the eyes. Now the Templars rise from their graves as mummified, blood-drinking corpses in search of new victims. A group of young people wander into the old abandoned monastery which houses the Templars' graves and fall prey to the walking blind corpses. ¶ From the ads: "They're the Blind Dead, but that will be no handicap for they can still *hear* their victims." • These zombies have no eyes, and so rely on sound to locate their victims. They also chase down their victims on horseback (though where the horses come from is anybody's guess). • Director/screenwriter Armando de Ossorio designed the effective zombie makeup himself (as applied by makeup man Jose Luis Campos), and supervised the special effects as well. The zombies' appearance is unique and quite striking—they appear as dessicated, mummified corpses shrouded in moldering hooded robes reaching out with claw-like bony hands. • This film was so successful in Europe that it spawned three sequels—*Return of the Blind Dead* (1973), *Horror of the Zombies* (1974), and *The Night of the Seagulls* (1975). All of them were directed and scripted by de Ossorio. • In a rare interview (granted to *Deep Red* #4), de Ossorio talked about what made these films successful: "One of the key elements that makes suspense build in the films is because they [the zombies] move so slowly and the tension mounts a step at a time. Viewers know the Templars are coming, but they have to wait and wait and wait. This makes the films all the more frightening because suspense and mounting tension is the secret to making a horror film frightening."

Bowery at Midnight (1942; Astor Pictures Corporation/Monogram) D: Wallace Fox. P: Sam Katzman, Jack Dietz. S: Gerald Schnitzer. C: Mark Stengler. Cast: Bela Lugosi, John Archer, Wanda McKay, Tom Neal, Vince Barnett, Anna Hope, John Berkes, J. Farrell MacDonald, Dave O'Brien, Lucille Vance, Lew Kelly, Wheeler Oakman, Ray Miller. Bela Lugosi is a prominent professor by day and a notorious criminal ringleader by night, working out of the Bowery mission he oversees. Lugosi kills his enemies and buries them in the cellar. At the film's climax, a disgruntled doctor revives the corpses which tear Lugosi to shreds. ¶ "I will save you Stratton, save you from the dead. Then you will belong to me."

Bride of Re-Animator (1990; Wildstreet Pictures) D/P: Brian Yuzna. S: Woody Keith, Rick Fry. C: Rick Fichter. Cast: Bruce Abbott, Claude Earl Jones, Fabiana Udenio, David Gale, Kathleen Kinmont, Mel Stewart, Jeffrey Combs. In this gory, tongue-in-cheek sequel to *Re-Animator* (1985), Herbert West is back with his reluctant partner Dan, working at a hospital during the day and experimenting with stolen body parts at night. They decide to create a new life out of body parts, building around the heart of Dan's deceased girlfriend (who died at the end of the first film). They succeed, to Dan's eventual horror, but are besieged by several reanimated zombies left over from the first movie, who have escaped from the psychiatric unit at the hospital and are led by the reanimated disembodied head of Dr. Hill (again from the original film). ¶ "This is no longer about just reanimating the dead. We will create new life!" • Brian Yuzna, who produced the first *Re-Animator* (1985), took on the directing chores as well for this sequel. • Though *Re-Animator* was based on the works of H. P. Lovecraft,

Yuzna stated (in the MTV special, "This Is Horror") that "*Bride of Re-Animator* is more influenced by Mary Shelley—and perhaps a little by James Whale and the Bride herself—than Lovecraft."

Cape Canaveral Monsters (1960) (see ALIENS—INVADERS ON EARTH: THE 60S AND 70S). Two aliens (appearing as bright pinpoints of light) come to Earth, cause a couple's car to crash, and then inhabit their dead, reanimated bodies. Their mission is to sabotage the local rocket program. The locals, led by a pair of young science students, foil their plans. • The male half of this alien zombie couple has trouble with his arm—it keeps falling off, supplying the audience with a large dose of unintentional humor. • *Cape Canaveral Monsters* is from the same man (Phil Tucker) who brought us *Robot Monster* in 1953, which goes a long way in explaining the frequent unintentional laughs found in this film.

The Children (1980; World Northal) D: Max Kalmanowicz. P: Max Kalmanowicz, Carlton J. Albright. S: Carlton J. Albright, Edward Terry. Cast: Martin Shakar, Gale Garnett, Gil Rogers, Jesse Abrams, Tracy Griswold, Joy Glacum. A busload of school children travels through a radioactive cloud leaking from the local nuclear power plant. The kids are transformed into atomic zombies with black fingernails who kill with a touch. ¶ "Cut off their hands! Cut off their hands!" • In this unique "Night-of-the-Living-Dead-Meets Mr. Rogers" movie, the only way to kill these zombie-tykes is to cut off their hands(!). • Gale Garnett, the country singer who scored a hit with "We'll Sing in the Sunshine," plays one of the concerned parents.

Creature of the Walking Dead (1965; A.D.P. Productions; Mexico) D: Frederic Corte (Fernando Cortes). P: Alfred Ripstein, Jerry Warren (English version). S: Alfredo Varela, Jr., Fernando Cortes, Joseph Unsain (English version). C: Richard Wallace. Cast: Rock Madison, Ann Wells, George Todd, Katherine Victor, Bruno Ve Sota. A mad doctor discovers how to retain his youth by extracting a special fluid from young girls. He is found out and hanged. But many years later his descendant, who happens to look exactly like him, digs him up and brings him back to life. Soon the evil zombie ancestor imprisons his well-meaning descendant and menaces his fiancée. ¶ "Is the world real, or thought essentially a true reflection or merely an illusion brought about by a mind separate from the ultimate reality? This is the question of man"—opening narration. • Producer Jerry Warren bought the Mexican film and added additional scenes (which often relate to the plot only indirectly) with Katherine Victor and Bruno Ve Sota to make a "new" feature. These new scenes are of people sitting around talking about things only vaguely connected to the story, resulting in a boring, incoherent mess of a movie. • Warren, a no-budget independent producer who frequently directed his features as well (simply because he could not afford to hire a director—his own admission), made a career out of rearranging foreign films with additional footage (*Invasion of the Animal People,* 1962; *Attack of the Mayan Mummy,* 1963, etc.).

Creature with the Atom Brain (1955; Columbia) D: Edward L. Cahn. P: Sam Katzman. S: Curt Siodmak. C: Fred Jackman, Jr. Cast: Richard Denning, Angela Stevens, John Launer, Michael Granger, Gregory Gay, Karl Davis. A mad scientist uses atomic energy to create robot-like zombies. The gangster who financed the work sends these "remote-controlled creatures, their brains powered by atomic energy" out to kill his rivals. ¶ "According to the evidence, Hennisey was murdered by a creature with atom rays of super human strength, and a creature that cannot be killed by bullets." • Screenwriter Curt Siodmak had written a previous (and far superior) zombie script—*I Walked with a Zombie* (1943; though in this first film the zombies were the result of voodoo rather than mad science).

Creepshow (1982) (see ANTHOLOGIES). This anthology contains two segments featuring zombies. The first is about a murdered patriarch who climbs from his grave as a rotted corpse in search of the birthday cake he did not get a chance to eat seven years ago (he was murdered on his birthday). The second episode deals with a jealous husband who buries his wife and her lover up to their necks in the sand and then watches as the tide comes in. The two waterlogged corpses come back to supply their watery brand of poetic justice.

Creepshow 2 (1987) (see ANTHOLOGIES). A spoiled rich woman accidentally runs over a hitchhiker, who then keeps popping up as an increasingly disgusting corpse in this anthology's final story.

Dead and Buried (1981; Avco Embassy) D: Gary A. Sherman. P: Ronald Shusett, Robert Fentress. S: Ronald Shusett, Dan O'Bannon. S: Steve Poster. Cast: James Farentino, Melody Anderson, Jack Albert-son, Dennis Redfield, Nancy Locke Hauser. The residents of Potters Bluff are turned into walking, talking zombies by the town's "official coroner/mortician." The local sheriff (James Farentino) must crack the veneer of normalcy in the town to uncover the rotten flesh below. ¶ "When people are dead, they don't get sick, they don't age. After I've worked on them they look so good, so healthy, I can't bear to bury them. They look even more beautiful than the living." • These zombies look and act normal—except that they murder people to supply their undertaker master with fresh corpses. They also need to return to the mortician for weekly touch-ups when they begin to decay. • In order to control his zombies, the mad mortician must cut out their hearts and keep them hidden in a safe place. • This is Jack Albertson's last film (he plays the zombie-making mortician). • Robert Englund appears as Harry, one of the undead townspeople. Englund went on to horror stardom as Freddy Krueger in the *Nightmare on Elm Street* series.

The Dead Don't Die (1975; TV movie) D: Curtis Harrington. P: Henry Coleman. S: Robert Bloch. C: James Crabe. Cast: George Hamilton, Ray Milland, Linda Cristal, Ralph Meeker, James McEachin, Joan Blondell, Reggie Nalder, Milton Parsons, William O'Connell, Yvette Vickers. In Chicago, a group of West Indians plan to rule the world by creating an army of zombies.

Dead Heat (1988; New World) D: Mark Goldblatt. P: Michael Meltzer, David Helpern. S: Terry Black. C: Robert D. Yeoman. Cast: Treat Williams, Joe Piscopo, Lindsay Frost, Darren McGavin, Clare Kirkconnell, Vincent Price. Treat Williams and Joe Piscopo are police detectives and best friends who are trying to find out why a recent rash of crimes are being committed by dead people in this buddy/cop/zombie/horror/comedy. They discover a "resurrection machine" at a local chemical and drug company and Williams is murdered. The machine revives him but he now has only 12 hours to live (and solve the case) before he decomposes into a puddle of zombie ooze. ¶ "You can't keep a good cop dead"—ad slogan. • Not only do we have zombie humans, but zombie animals as well. In one scene an entire butcher shop comes to life (including a complete cow carcass) to do battle with the two heroes.

The Dead One (1961; Favorite Films) D/P/S: Barry Mahon. C: Mark Dennes. Cast: Monica Davis, John McKay, Linda Or-mond, Clyde Kelley, Darlene Myrick. In New Orleans, a woman afraid of losing her inheritance when her cousin marries uses voodoo to reanimate the body of her dead brother, and sends the zombie out to murder her cousin's new wife. • At the climax, the zombie disintegrates when exposed to the rays of the sun. • Filmmaker Barry Mahon made a string of "nudie" flicks in the 1960s. He was formerly Errol Flynn's agent before turning to sexploitation filmmaking.

Deadly Friend (1986) (see ROBOTS). When the girlfriend of a boy genius/robotics wiz is accidentally killed, he steals her body, implants a robot circuit in her brain, and brings her back to life as a robot/zombie. Unfortunately, she is more robot than human now and goes on a killing spree, dispatching all those who wronged her.

Death Warmed Up (1984; Skouras Pictures; New Zealand) (also *Death Warmed Over*). D: David Blythe. P: Murray Newey. S: Michael Heath, David Blyth. C: Jame Bartle. Cast: Michael Hurst, Margaret Umbers, Norelle Scott, William Upjohn, David Letch, Gary Day, Bruno Lawrence. The mad neurosurgeon Dr. Archer Howell uses science to create zombies at his isolated Trans-Cranial Applications Hospital. Two teenage couples stumble into his complex and must fight for their lives against his undead hordes. ¶ "Our salvation belongs to medical engineering. *We* are the new messiahs." • *Death Warmed Up* won the Golden Unicorn prize at the Paris Horror Festival.

Deathdream (1972; Europix; Canada) (also *Dead of Night; The Night Andy Came Home*). D/P: Bob Clark. S: Alan Ormsby. C: Jack McGowan. Cast: John Marley, Lynn Carlin, Richard Backus, Henderson Forsyth, Anya Ormsby, Jane Daly, Michael Mazes. In this modern variation on "The Monkey's Paw," a mother wishes so hard for the return of her son from Vietnam that he does return—as a living zombie who needs fresh blood periodically to keep from decaying. ¶ "I died for you, Doc, now why shouldn't you return the favor?" • *Deathdream* was originally to be called *The Veteran,* but was renamed at the behest of the investors. It was shot in three weeks in Brooksville, Florida, for $250,000. • Screenwriter Alan Ormsby also did the zombie makeup, with the now-legendary Tom Savini helping out as an assistant. • Producer/ director Bob Clark made a second zombie movie this same year called *Children Shouldn't Play with Dead Things*—a more traditional "zombie flesh eater" picture.

Alan Ormsby co-wrote that feature (and starred in it as well). Clark went on to bigger (though not necessarily better) things with the successful mainstream comedy, *Porky's.*

Disciple of Death (1972; Avco Embassy; U.K.) D: Tom Parkinson. P/S: Tom Parkinson, Chuston Fairman. C: William Brayne. Cast: Mike Raven, Marguerite Hardiman, Stephen Bradley, Ronald Lacey, Virginia Wetherell, Nicholas Amer. Two lovers accidentally raise up a living-dead zombie (Mike Raven) when a drop of blood is spilled on his grave. The undead creature goes about the task of finding a virgin ready to sacrifice herself willingly to him.

Dr. Blood's Coffin (1961) (see MAD SCIENTISTS). Kieron Moore plays a young mad scientist who brings the long-dead corpse of Hazel Court's husband back to life by a heart transplant (much to the regret of all concerned). • The zombie theme is only a minimal part of this talky film, which instead focuses on the mad doctor angle, saving all zombie activity for the last five minutes.

Dr. Butcher M.D. (1979; Aquarius; Italy) (also *Queen of the Cannibals*). D/S: Frank Martin (Marino Girolami). P: Terry Levene (Gianfranco Couyoumdjian, Fabrizio De Angelis). C: Fausto Zuccoli. Cast: Ian McCulloch, Alexandra Cole (Alessandra Delli Colli), Sherry Buchanan, Peter O'Neal, Donald O'Brian. Four investigators journey to a remote Indonesian island where they encounter a tribe of cannibals and a mad doctor who is turning the natives into zombies. The mad medico accomplishes this by transplanting the brains of the living into the bodies of the dead. ¶ "Tomorrow morning I will transplant your brain into one of the cadavers you saw in the other room. You will die, only to live again in a younger body. Then you can tell me if the operation is a success—what it's like to pass from life to death, and death to life." • The film was released in America with a new pre-title sequence from an unreleased NYU film tacked on. It featured (amateurish) shots of zombies rising up from their graves (which has absolutely nothing to do with the film itself, since "Dr. Butcher's" zombies are created by science and were never buried to begin with). • The film's promotion included a traveling "Butchermobile" which ballyhooed the film in the New York City area.

The Earth Dies Screaming (1964) (see ROBOTS). Alien invaders send their robots out to kill the populace and then revive them as mindless, eyeless zombies.

Friday the 13th Part 6: Jason Lives (1986) (see MADMEN — THE SLICE 'N' DICE WAVE). Jason lives all right — as an unkillable zombie-like maniac. A troubled teen digs up Jason's grave to make sure the object of his nightmares is truly dead. When he angrily stabs a pole into Jason's obviously dead, maggot-ridden corpse, lightning strikes (literally) and Jason is revived, ready to do battle with the world's immoral teens once again.

The Ghost Breakers (1940) (see GHOSTS). Bob Hope and his manservant travel to Cuba to aid a young woman who is just inherited a remote island and its spooky castle. Once on the island, they encounter thieves, a real ghost, and a zombie — the son of the woman who lives on the island. ¶ Richard Carlson: "It's worse than horrible because a zombie has no will of his own. You see them sometimes, walking around blindly with dead eyes, following orders, not knowing what they do, not caring." Bob Hope: "You mean like democrats?" • With a bald head and grotesque makeup distorting his features, Noble Johnson cuts an impressive figure as the zombie. Johnson is best remembered by fans as the Native Chief in *King Kong* (1933).

The Ghoul (1933; Gaumont; U.K.) D: T. Hayes Hunter. S: Roland Pertwee, John Hastings Turner, Rupert Downing. C: Guenther Krampf. Cast: Boris Karloff, Cedric Hardwicke, Ernest Thesiger, Dorothy Hyson, Anthony Bushell, Kathleen Harrison, Harold Huth, D. A. Clarke-Smith, Ralph Richardson, Jack Raine. Boris Karloff plays a prominent Egyptologist who believes in the power of the old gods. He "acquires" the valuable jewel called "The Eternal Light," which will supposedly ensure his immortality. On his deathbed he instructs his servant to bury the jewel with him when he dies, warning that if this is not done, he will return from the grave and seek vengeance. He is buried with the jewel, but the servant sneaks into the crypt and steals it. True to his word, Karloff comes back as a hollow-eyed zombie to carry out his vengeance while seeking the jewel. ¶ "And on the night of the full moon, at the first star I will make my offering of The Eternal Light to Anubis, opener of the ways. If I have done well in his sight, those fingers will close over the jewel and he will open to me the gates of immortality." • Karloff, a British actor, returned to his homeland for the first time since coming to North America 24 years earlier, to film *The Ghoul*. • This was Britain's first attempt to cash in on the "hor-ror craze" started in the United States with *Dracula* in 1931. • Ralph Richardson, a respected British actor, made his screen debut in *The Ghoul*. • The film was lost for many years until a print was discovered in the Czechoslovakian film archives.

Graveyard Disturbance (1988; Dania Film; Italy) D: Lamberto Bava. P: Dania Film. S: Dardano Sacchetti, Lamberto Bava. C: Gianlorenzo Battaglia. Cast: Gregory Lech Thaddeus, Lea Martino, Beatrice Ring, Gianmarco Tognazzi, Karl Zinny, Lino Salemme, Giampaolo Saccarola. A group of teenagers out looking for kicks end up stranded at an old graveyard where they find a strange tavern inhabited by bizarre people. Underneath the tavern is a maze of crypts and catacombs, said to be cursed. The teens take up a standing bet that they cannot spend the night in the catacombs, and end up running and running and running (interminably) from the various zombie corpses which rise up out of their coffins. At the end it is intimated that they are all dead (killed in a car crash) and in Hell, but this theory is blown off when one of them stabs the creature that claims to be the Grim Reaper and escapes back into the real world and police custody. ¶ "Y'know, anything can happen in a cemetery." • Lamberto Bava, who directed and co-wrote this tedious, bloodless, semi-comic mishmash, is the son of famed director Mario Bava.

The Hanging Woman (1972; Prodimex Film/Petruka Films; Spain) (also *Beyond the Living Dead* [video title]; *Dracula, the Terror of the Living Dead; House of Terror* [video title]; *Orgy of the Dead; The Return of the Zombies*). D: John Richardson (José Luis Merino). P: Ramón Plana. S: José Luis Merino, Enrico Columbo. C: Modesto Rizzolo. Cast: Stan Cooper (Stelvio Rosi), Maria Pia Conte, Dianik Zorakowska, Pasquale Pasir, Gerard Tick, Charles Quine, Isarco Ravaioli, Paul Naschy. A mad doctor steals bodies from the nearby cemetery and experiments on them, turning them into walking, obedient zombies who murder all those standing in the way of his experiments. He activates the corpses by "inserting a small capsule into the brain" which can "receive thought patterns." ¶ "It's well known you can induce a *living* person to behave contrary to his own will. It's logical to assume you can do the same with a dead person." • Paul Naschy, Spain's number one horror star, plays Igor, the gravedigger.

Horror Express (1972) (see ALIENS — INVADERS ON EARTH: THE 60s AND 70s). An alien force which has the ability to inhabit the bodies of humans winds up on the Trans-Siberian railway. With a glance this alien can "boil the brains" of people and assimilate their knowledge. This process leaves the person a white-eyed zombie which the alien can then control.

Horror of the Zombies (1974; Independent International; Spain) D/S: Armando de Ossorio. P: J. L. Bermuder de Castro. C: Raul Artigot. Cast: Maria Perschy, Jack Taylor, Carlos Lemos, Blanca Estrada, Barbara Rey, Manuel de Blas, Margarita Merino. In this second sequel to *The Blind Dead* (1972), a group of fashion models and their friends run across a strange ship in a fog. When they board it they find the dessicated zombies of the Templars, who proceed to kill them one by one. These zombies are blind and move very slowly. They do not consume their victims, but they do have a penchant for blood. ¶ From the misleading ads: "Living dead men — existing on the flesh of the young and beautiful." (No flesh is eaten.) • Director Armando de Ossorio followed up this third "Blind Dead" film with one more — *The Night of the Seagulls* (1975).

Horror Rises from the Tomb (1972) (see WITCHES, WARLOCKS, AND CULTS). Spanish horror star Paul Naschy plays a fifteenth century knight who is beheaded for witchcraft. When his head is reunited with his body by his modern-day descendant, the warlock uses his black powers to, among other things, summon up four zombies (the recent victims of the warlock), causing the corpses to rise up from the lake they had been dumped in and attack the hero and heroine. The protagonists fight off these walking dead with fire (that tried and true zombie repellent).

The House by the Cemetery (1981; Fulvia Film; Italy) D: Lucio Fulci. P: Fabrizio De Angelis. S: Lucio Fulci, Dardano Sacchetti, Giorgio Mariuzzo. C: Sergio Salvati. Cast: Katherine MacColl, Giovanni De Nava, Dagmar Lassander, Anja Pieroni, Giovanni Frezza, Silvia Collatina, Daniele Doria, Carlo De Mejo. A family moves into an old house with a sinister reputation. The reputation is justified when they are trapped and killed by Dr. Freudstein, a hideous being who secretly lives in the hidden cellar. Freudstein was a doctor who discovered the means to turn himself into a walking zombie in order to keep himself "alive" for the past 150 years. • Director Lucio Fulci went even deeper into zombie territory with the zombie splatter-fest, *The Gates of Hell* (1980).

House of the Seven Corpses (1974; TCA Productions) D: Paul Harrison. P: Paul Harrison, Paul Lewis. S: Paul Harrison, Thomas J. Kelly. C: Don Jones. Cast: John Ireland, John Carradine, Faith Domergue, Charles Macauley, Carol Wells, Jerry Strickler. A film crew chooses a haunted house as the location in which to shoot their horror movie. One of the actresses reads from the Tibetan *Book of the Dead* which causes the dead to rise and attack the living.

House 2: The Second Story (1987) (see GHOSTS). One of the characters in this comical sequel to *House* is the hero's kindly zombie grandfather named "Jesse." This talking zombie does not look too healthy but at least he is friendly.

I Eat Your Skin (1964/71; Cinemation) (also *Zombies*). D/P/S: Del Tenney. C: Francois Farkas. Cast: William Joyce, Heather Hewitt, Betty Hyatt Linton, Dan Stephenson, Walter Coy, Robert Stanton. On a tropical island, mad scientist Dr. Biladeau creates an army of zombies with which he intends to conquer the world. No skin (or any other part of the anatomy for that matter) is eaten. • In 1971, producer Jerry Gross needed a co-feature for his *I Drink Your Blood,* so he bought a seven-year-old unreleased film titled *Voodoo Blood Bath* and renamed it *I Eat Your Skin* to match his first feature. The two were released on a double bill that was advertised as: "Two great blood horrors to rip out your guts!" • Low-budget independent filmmaker Del Tenney is best known for his *Horror of Party Beach* (1964), now a cult favorite.

I Walked with a Zombie (1943; RKO) D: Jacques Tourneur. P: Val Lewton. S: Curt Siodmak, Ardel Wray. C: J. Roy Hunt. Cast: James Ellison, Frances Dee, Tom Conway, Edith Barrett, James Bell, Christine Gordon, Teresa Harris, Sir Lancelot, Darby Jones. A young nurse is hired to come to the island of San Sebastian to care for the wife of a plantation owner. The wife is in some mysterious mindless state, and it is revealed that a voodoo curse has transformed her into a zombie. ¶ "I walked with a zombie. It does seem an odd thing to say." • *I Walked with a Zombie* was inspired by a series of non-fiction articles written by Inez Wallace about Haitian voodoo • Hero Tom Conway is the real-life brother of George Sanders. • Editor Mark Robson was promoted to director later this same year by producer Val Lewton, going on to direct four of Lewton's classic horror films — *The Seventh Victim* and *The Ghost Ship* (both 1943); *Isle of the Dead* (1945); and *Bedlam* (1946).

I Was a Teenage Zombie (1987; Horizon) D: John Elias Mechalakis. P: Richard Hirsh, John Elias Mechalakis. S: James Martin. C: Pete Leanes. Cast: Michael Ruben, George Seminara, Steve McCoy, Peter Bush, Kevin Nagle, Cassie Madden, Allen Rickman, Robert C. Sabin, Clive St. John. Radioactivity leaking into the local river turns anyone who swims in it into a vicious zombie in this ultra-low budget hybrid of the 50s and the 80s. It is up to a group of over-aged teens to stem the tide of these walking dead, including battling a particularly nasty zombie drug dealer. • *I Was a Teenage Zombie* was shot in 16mm and then blown up to 35mm for its brief tour of the New York City midnight circuit.

The Incredibly Strange Creatures Who Stopped Living and Became Mixed-Up Zombies (1964; Fairway International) (also *Teenage Psycho Meets Bloody Mary*). D/P: Ray Dennis Steckler. S: Gene Pollock, Robert Silliphant. C: Joseph V. Mascelli. Cast: Cash Flagg, Brett O'Hara, Carolyn Brandt, Atlas King, Sharon Walsh, Madison Clarke, Erina Enyo, Jack Brady, Toni Camel, Neil Stillman. At a visiting carnival, a gypsy fortune-teller named Madame Estrella throws acid in the faces of her patrons, locks them in a cage, and hypnotizes them. She then sends these "crazy mixed-up zombies" out to commit mayhem. • *The Incredibly Strange Creatures...* was billed as "The first monster musical!" • Hero "Cash Flagg" is actually director Ray Dennis Steckler, and the female lead, Carolyn Brandt, is his wife. • This is the best known film (possibly due to the title alone) from no-budget producer/director Ray Dennis Steckler. It was made for a mere $38,000.

Invasion of the Zombies (1961; Azteca; Mexico) D/S: Benito Alazraki. P: Fernando Oses. C: José O. Ramos. Cast: Santo, Lorena Valazquez, Armando Silvestre, Jaime Fernandez, Irma Serrano. A silver-masked wrestling hero must battle a mad scientist and his army of zombies intent upon conquering the world in this south-of-the-border wrestle/ monster fest.

Invisible Invaders (1959) (see ALIENS — INVADERS ON EARTH: THE 50s). Invisible aliens invade the Earth and inhabit reanimated corpses. John Agar is a military man who must hole up and protect a group of scientists trying to discover a way to stop the undead army of alien zombies. ¶ "My people will come to your planet and inhabit the bodies of other dead Earthmen. The dead will kill the living and the people on Earth will cease to exist."

J'Accuse (1939; Arthur Mayer & Joseph Burstyn, Inc.; France) (also *That They May Live*). D: Abel Gance. S: Abel Gance, Steve Passeur. C: Roger Hubert. Cast: Victor Francen, Line Noro, Marie Lou, Renée Devillers, Georges Saillard, Paul Amiot Rollin, André Nox. The lone survivor of the last patrol wiped out at the end of World War I makes a heartfelt promise to his fallen comrades that there will never be another war. An inventor, he develops a formula for steel glass. When he learns that his invention is to be used as a weapon in another war, he calls upon all the dead of World War I, "forgotten for 20 years," to rise up and prevent a repetition of the horrors of two decades earlier. • Director/screenwriter Abel Gance had filmed this story 20 years earlier as a silent short. • For this strikingly photographed, exquisitely acted anti-war film (made on the eve of the outbreak of World War II), Gance used real World War I veterans, disfigured in the war, as the walking dead.

King of the Zombies (1941; Monogram) D: Jean Yarbrough. P: Lindsley Parsons. S: Edmund Kelso. C: Mack Stengler. Cast: Dick Purcell, Joan Woodbury, Henry Victor, Mantan Moreland, John Archer. Henry Victor plays a madman on an island turning the natives into an army of zombies for a foreign power. • Henry Victor is most recognized as Hercules the Strong Man in *Freaks* (1932).

Kiss Daddy Goodbye (1981; Bandwagon Films Ltd.) (also *Revenge of the Zombie* [video title]; *Vengeance of the Dead* [video]). D: Patrick Regan. P: Alain Silver. S: Alain Silver, Patrick Regan, Ron Abraham, Mary Steward, C: George Bakken. Cast: Fabian Forte, Marilyn Burns, Jon Cedar, Marvin Miller, Chester Grimes, Jed Mills, Gay French, Robert Dryer, Bill Randal. Two children use their powers of telekinesis to raise up their father from the dead and send him out as a walking zombie to take revenge on the bikers who had killed him. ¶ "Why? Why did you make Daddy into a weird thing — a zombie?" • The strange storyline of this grade-Z oddity is a macabre variation on every child's fantasy — to be able to make your parents do whatever you want them to do. These two gifted tykes not only use their zombie Daddy to get the bad guys, they also have him do things like drive them to the beach so that they can make sand castles. • Former rock 'n' roll performer and teenage heartthrob Fabian Forte plays the local deputy sheriff investigating the weird goings-on. • Marilyn Burns, here playing a

Francis Dee, leading the titular zombie (Christine Gordon) on an eerie midnight walk through the cane fields, gazes up at a hanging goat, part of a ritualistic voodoo sacrifice in I Walked with a Zombie *(1943).*

sympathetic Board of Education worker caught in the middle of the macabre proceedings, is best known to fans as the screaming sole survivor of *The Texas Chainsaw Massacre* (1974).

The Last Man on Earth (1964; AIP; Italy/U.S.) D: Ubaldo Ragona, Sidney Salkow (U.S. version). P: Robert L. Lippert. S: Logan Swanson, William P. Leicester. C: Franco Delli Colli. Cast: Vincent Price, Franca Bettoia, Emma Danieli, Giacomo Rossi-Stuart, Umberto Rau. Vincent Price plays the lone survivor of a plague which first kills its victims and then brings them back to life as pasty-faced zombies. Price encounters a group of people who have escaped the plague by taking special injections, but are still not quite cured. Because he has inadvertently destroyed many of their number on his zombie-hunts, they fear him and ultimately kill The Last Man on Earth. ¶ From the ads: "By night they leave their graves, crawling, shambling through empty streets whimpering, pleading, begging for his blood!" • *The Last Man on Earth* is the first of two film adaptations of Richard Matheson's novel, *I Am Legend*—the second being *The Omega Man* (1971; though with a total lack of zombies). • Matheson originally wrote a screenplay for *The Last Man on Earth* in 1957 for Hammer Films, but they sold the project and it was eventually rewritten into its present form. Matheson was so unhappy with it that he had his name replaced with the pseudonym "Logan Swanson" for the credits.

The Legend of the Seven Golden Vampires (1974) (see VAMPIRES — HAMMER'S UNDEAD) (also *The Seven Brothers Meet Dracula*). Dracula leads the dreaded Seven Golden Vampires in terrorizing the Chinese countryside in this first-ever kung fu/vampire film. The vampires also have the power to call up the corpses of their victims as an army of zombies to do their bidding.

Lifeforce (1985) (see ALIENS — INVADERS ON EARTH: THE 80s AND BEYOND). Three space vampires are found and brought back to Earth. There they suck the life force from people, leaving them a dried-up husk. Two

David Bruce in the effective Jack P. Pierce zombie makeup for The Mad Ghoul *(1943).*

hours later, the desiccated corpses rise up as mindless zombies.

Loves of the Living Dead (1986) (see GHOSTS). This little-seen Hong Kong horror/comedy centers around the ghosts of a stripper named "Pinkish Red" and all the patrons who died in the fire that killed her coming back for revenge. One of the protagonists is a bumbling practitioner of the paranormal. He conducts an experiment in a graveyard with a "spirit machine" and accidentally raises up a horde of zombies, including a young woman zombie in a white gown who takes a shine to the bumbler and keeps chasing him in order to get a kiss. ¶ "Let me kiss you!" • These Chinese zombies don't lurch or stagger around like the typical Western walking dead, they move by taking short little hops! The power of a magic symbol is what finally stops them.

The Mad Ghoul (1943; Universal) D: James Hogan. P: Ben Pivar. S: Brenda Weisberg, Paul Gangelin. C: Milton Krasner. Cast: David Bruce, Evelyn Ankers,

George Zucco, Turhan Bey, Robert Armstrong, Milburn Stone, Rose Hobart, Charles McGraw. George Zucco plays a professor who discovers the secret of a deadly ancient Mayan gas which turns those exposed to it into the living dead (inducing a "state of death in life" as Zucco describes it). The victim needs fresh human hearts to restore him to normalcy. Zucco is in love with his assistant's fiancée and so uses the gas to turn his assistant into a walking ghoul which he can then control. ¶ "What am I? Alive or dead? Man or beast? What have you done to me?!" • Heroine Evelyn Ankers plays a successful concert singer in *The Mad Ghoul* and is shown singing in several scenes. Ankers had a wonderful singing voice and Universal originally had planned to allow the actress to record the songs in her own voice, but at the last moment opted to dub in the voice of professional singer Lillian Cornell instead. • Universal makeup ace Jack Pierce described how he was approached for the project: "All they told me was that they wanted [actor David] Bruce to look like a reasonably fresh cadaver. I said, 'How fresh?' They said a couple or three weeks buried. This was not much to go on but I did my best. They seemed satisfied" (from *Universal Horrors* by Brunas, Brunas, and Weaver). Pierce's effective makeup is one of the film's horrific highlights. • Tragically, director James Hogan never saw his film released, for he died of a heart attack just one week before its national premier. • *The Mad Ghoul* was released as a second feature to *Son of Dracula*.

Necropolis (1987) (see WITCHES, WARLOCKS, AND CULTS). A 300-year-old witch is intent upon completing a virgin sacrifice which will bestow eternal life upon her. She has six zombie followers whom she sends out in their monks' robes to aid her in her quest. • In one bizarre scene, the witch opens up her robe to reveal six breasts at which the zombies suckle to obtain their life force.

Neither the Sand Nor the Sea (1972; Tigon; U.K.) D: Fred Burnley. P: Jack Smith, Peter Fetterman. S: Gordon Honeycombe, Rosemary Davies. C: David Muir. Cast: Susan Hampshire, Frank Finlay, Michael Petrovitch, Jack Lambert, Michael Craze, David Garth. A woman has an extramarital affair but her lover soon dies. He comes back from the grave, however, and engineers the husband's death, and the two lovers walk off into the sea together. • *Neither the Sand Nor the Sea* was adapted by TV newsreader Gordon Honeycombe from his own novel.

Night Life (1990; Creative Movie Marketing) D: David Acomba. P: Charles Lippincott. S: Keith Critchlow. C: Roger Tonry. Cast: Scott Grimes, Cheryl Pollak, Anthony Geary, Alan Blumenfeld, Kenneth Ian Davis, Darcy DeMoss, Lisa Fuller, Mark Pellegrino, Phil Proctor, John Astin. A likable teneage mortuary assistant (Scott Grimes) is tormented by a pair of jocks and their snobbish girlfriends. When the quartet dies in a car accident, their bodies end up at the funeral home. A freak bolt of lightning revives them, and the now-zombiefied teens continue their harassment of Grimes, though now they're out for blood, not sport. • *Night Life* features a screen first — zombie sex (in a discreetly-shot scene).

Night of the Comet (1984; Atlantic 9000) D/S: Thom Eberhardt. P: Andrew Lane, Wayne Crawford. C: Arthur Albert. Cast: Robert Beltran, Catherine Mary Stewart, Kelli Maroney, Sharon Farrell, Mary Woronov, Geoffrey Lewis. The light of a passing comet either disintegrates those exposed to it or turns them into killer zombies. A group of L.A. teenagers attempts to rebuild civilization while battling the walking dead.

Night of the Creeps (1986; Tri-Star) D/S: Fred Dekker. P: Charles Gordon. C: Robert C. Nen. Cast: Jason Lively, Steve Marshall, Jill Whitlow, Tom Atkins, Wally Taylor, Bruce Solomon. Slug creatures from outer space (the escaped results of an alien experiment) land on Earth. The slimy creatures rush into people's mouths, transforming them into homicidal walking zombies while they lay their eggs in the brain. This creates a lot of zombie mayhem for Greek Row during pledge week. ¶ Detective: "I got good news and bad news, girls. The good news is, your dates are here." Sorority girl: "What's the bad news?" Detective: "The bad news is, they're dead." • The film was simply titled *Creeps* initially, and then *Kreeps,* before becoming *Night of the Creeps.* Writer/director Fred Dekker wrote the screenplay in one week. • Dekker called his film a "boy-meets-girl, boy-has-to-kill-zombies-from-outer-space-to-get-girl, boy-gets-girl story" (*Fangoria* #61). • After Dekker turned in his final cut, Tri-Star insisted that he add more blood. "I disown the last five or six seconds of *Night of the Creeps.* That's Tri-Star's," stated the disgruntled director. • References to horror and sci-fi movie history abound, including naming the college "Corman University" (for the prolific Roger Corman), and showing a clip from an early zombie/alien movie, the notorious *Plan Nine from Outer Space* (1959).

Night of the Ghouls (1959; Crown International) D/P/S: Edward D. Wood, Jr. C: William C. Thompson. Cast: Keene Duncan, "Duke" Moore, Valda Hansen, Tor Johnson, John Carpenter, Paul Marco, Criswell. A phony medium named Dr. Acula swindles people by pretending to contact lost loved ones. Unfortunately for the devious doctor, he apparently has some real occult power, for he actually succeeds in reviving some corpses and the zombies proceed to bury him alive. ¶ "Now I tell you a tale of the threshold people, so astounding that some of you may faint. This is the story of those in the twilight time; once human, now monsters, in a world between the living and the dead, monsters to be pitied, monsters to be despised" — narration lifted from Ed Wood's previous picture, *Plan Nine from Outer Space* (1959). • This was the infamous inept filmmaker Ed Wood, Jr.'s, second to last film as director, and his last horror movie. (His final film was *Sinister Urge* in 1961.) Wood is famous for such fondly remembered atrocities as *Bride of the Monster* (1956) and the above-mentioned *Plan Nine from Outer Space* (1959; another film which featured the walking dead).

The Night of the Seagulls (1975; Profilmes–Ancla Century/Big Apple; Spain) (also *Night of the Death Cult* [video title]; *Terror Beach* [video title]). D/S: Armando de Ossorio. P: José Angel Santos. C: Francisco Sanchez. Cast: Victor Petit, Maria Kosti, Sandra Mozarosky, Julie James, Julia Saly, José Antonio Calvo. This fourth and last "Blind Dead" film begun with *The Blind Dead* (1972) features frightened coastal villagers who make periodic sacrifices of their young girls to the blood-drinking zombie Templars. A new doctor and his wife come to the village and discover the horrible secret it harbors. ¶ "Corpses rise out of the sea, take away the pretty maidens, one each night for seven nights." • The title is derived from the strange flock of seagulls flying at night which herald the zombies' appearance. As one character explains: "The pretty girls, when they die they become the seagulls that scream and cry. They are the damned spirits of the sacrificed girls." • At the climax, the doctor discovers the lair of the Templars and destroys the idol of their unholy god, causing the mummified zombies to gush blood and crumble into dust. • Once again director/writer Armando de Ossorio supervised the makeup and special effects chores himself, as he did on all four films.

One Dark Night (1982) D: Tom McLoughlin. P: Michael Schroeder. S: Tom Mc-Loughlin, Michael Hawes. C: Hal Trussel. Cast: Meg Tilly, Melissa Newman, Robin Evans, Ronald Hotton, Adam West. A young girl must spend a night in a mausoleum as part of an initiation. Unfortunately for her and the group of pranksters who have followed her in, a practitioner of the black arts named Karl Raymar was interred in that very mausoleum that very day. He uses his evil powers from beyond the grave to reanimate a legion of corpses, which dispatch the teens one by one. • These zombies do not commit the usual acts of zombie violence — strangling, dismembering, chewing, etc. Instead, a group of the corpses simply fall on their intended victims and smother them to death.

Orgy of the Dead (1965; F.O.G. Distributors) D/P: A. C. Stephen. S: Ed Wood, Jr. C: Robert Caramico. Cast: "Criswell," Pat Berringer, Fawn Silver, William Bates, Louis Ojena, John Andrews, and "A Bevy of Gorgeous Girls!" (according to the ads). A horror writer and his girlfriend visit a cemetery after dark and are taken captive by the "Master of the Dead" and the "Princess of Darkness." They are forced to watch various zombie women called up from the dead who dance topless to please the Master. ¶ Opening narration: "I am Criswell! For years I have told the almost unbelievable, related the unreal and showed it to be more than a fact. Now I tell the tale of the threshold people, so astounding that some of you may faint!" • The notorious Ed Wood, Jr., who has been labeled as the worst filmmaker of all time (*Plan Nine from Outer Space,* 1959; etc.), wrote the screenplay for this atrocious nudie with very little plot to get in the way of the numerous strippers performing their acts on the graveyard soundstage. The above introductory quote is cribbed almost word for word from his earlier zombie movie, *Night of the Ghouls* (1959).

Pet Sematary (1989; Paramount) D: Mary Lambert. P: Richard P. Rubenstein. S: Stephen King. C: Peter Stein. Cast: Dale Midkiff, Fred Gwynne, Denise Crosby, Brad Greenquist, Michael Lombard, Mike Hughes, Blaze Berdahl. A young doctor and his family move to a new house near the local pet cemetery. When his little girl's cat is run over, rustic neighbor Fred Gwynne takes the doctor to an ancient Indian burial ground beyond the pet cemetery, which has the power to revive the dead. The only thing is, those revived are not quite the same. When the doctor's toddler son is tragically hit by a truck, the medico snaps and buries his son in the forbidden burial ground. The little tyke comes back all right, but as a fiendish homicidal zombie, and the horrifying events escalate from there. ¶ "Sometimes dead is better." • Shot for nine million dollars (on location in Stephen King's home state — Maine) it earned over $26 million at the box office. • Stephen King adapted his own novel for the screen. King appears briefly in the film as the minister presiding over the little boy's funeral. • King was not pleased with the casting: "I think Dale Midkiff is *stiff* in places," the author/screenwriter told *Cinefantastique* (Feb., 1991). "I think Denise Crosby comes across cold in places." He went on to praise director Mary Lambert however; "She went in and she didn't flinch." Still, the author rates *Pet Sematary* among his favorite adaptations (along with *Cujo* and *Stand by Me*). (After all, King *did* write the screenplay on this one.)

Phantasm (1979; Avco Embassy) D/S/C: Don Coscarelli. P: D. A. Coscarelli, Paul Pepperman. Cast: Michael Baldwin, Bill Thornbury, Reggie Bannister, Angus Scrimm, Kathy Lester, Terrie Kalbus, Ken Jones. The indestructible "Tall Man" steals bodies from a mortuary, compresses them down and turns them into hideous dwarf zombies, sending the diminutive creatures to another dimension as slave labor. • Filmmaker Don Coscarelli filmed a sequel in 1988 to this surprise low-budget horror/sci-fi hit.

Phantasm 2 (1988; Universal) D/S: Don Coscarelli. P: Roberto A. Quezada. C: Daryn Okada. Cast: James Lee Gros, Reggie Bannister, Angus Scrimm, Paula Irvine, Samantha Phillips, Kennet Tigar. The "Tall Man" is back, now moving from town to town and mortuary to mortuary, raiding their cemeteries and morgues for fresh corpses to compress down into dwarf zombies and transport to another dimension as slave labor. In hot pursuit of this otherdimensional zombie-maker are Mike and Reggie, the two survivors from the first film. ¶ "Now does it strike you as a little strange, Reg, that every single corpse in this entire graveyard is *missing?!*" • This sequel features footage from the original as well as two returning cast members, Reggie Bannister as "Reggie" and Angus Scrimm as "The Tall Man." It also (disappointingly) features a nearly carbon copy ending of the original. • Director Don Coscarelli, who wrote and directed the original, waited nine years to make a sequel because he "didn't want to be stereotyped as a horror filmmaker," and felt he "should make a big-

budget picture" (though he never did) (*Fangoria* #75).

The Plague of the Zombies (1966; Hammer/20th Century–Fox; U.K.) D: John Gilling. P: Anthony Nelson Keys. S: Peter Bryan. C: Arthur Grant. Cast: Andre Morrell, Diane Clare, John Carson, Alex Davion, Jacqueline Pearce, Brook Williams, Michael Ripper, Marcus Hammond. A voodoo-practicing squire in Cornwall raids the local cemetery for corpses that he can turn into walking zombies to work in his tin mine. ¶ "Didn't I bury him myself? But I saw him, in his shroud, standing, staring at me!" • Lead actress Diane Clare, playing the heroine imperiled by the evil squire and his zombies, is reputed to be Buffalo Bill's great granddaughter. • *Plague* was released on a double bill with *Dracula, Prince of Darkness*. In a promotional gimmick for fans attending this dynamic duo, the women were given "Zombie Eyes" and the men received "Dracula Fangs."

Plan Nine from Outer Space (1959) (see ALIENS — INVADERS ON EARTH: THE 50s). Aliens seek to conquer the Earth by turning the dead into murderous zombies. ¶ "This is the story of those in the twilight time — once human, now monsters — in a world between the living and the dead; monsters to be pitied, monsters to be despised!" — narration by "Criswell." • This unintentionally funny film is often touted as the worst movie of all time, with its cardboard sets, hubcap flying saucers, and laughably bad dialogue. The zombies are few (three to be exact), but ex-wrestler Tor Johnson cuts an impressive undead figure.

Planet of the Vampires (1965) (see ALIENS — ENCOUNTERS IN OUTER SPACE). Astronauts land on a mysterious planet and, influenced by an unseen alien presence, begin to fight amongst themselves. When some of them are killed, the alien force invades the bloody corpses and makes them rise up as murderous space zombies.

Psychomania (1972; Scotia International; U.K.) (also *The Death Wheelers*). D: Don Sharp. P: Andrew Donally. S: Julian Halevy. C: Ted Moore. Cast: George Sanders, Beryl Reid, Nicky Henson, Mary Larkin, Roy Holder, Robert Hardy, Patrick Holt. The leader of a British motorcycle gang learns the secret of immortality from his devil-worshiping mother and commits suicide, only to return as an unstoppable zombie. He convinces the rest of his gang (aptly called "The Living Dead") to do the same and soon there is a whole group of motorcycle-riding zombies terrorizing the populace. • This cheap but engaging feature was George Sanders's last film. The respected actor committed suicide later this same year.

Raiders of the Living Dead (1985; Independent International) D: Samuel S. Sherman. P: Dan Q. Kennis. S: Samuel S. Sherman, Brett Piper. C: Douglas Meltzer. Cast: Scott Schwartz, Robert Deveau, Doanna Asali, Bob Allen, Bob Sacchetti, Zita Johann, Corri Burt, Leonard Corman, Christine Farish, Nino Rigali, Barbara Patterson. In this nearly incomprehensible no-budget movie, an ex–prison doctor turned local coroner creates (for no particular reason) an army of zombies at the old abandoned prison. An investigative reporter, his girlfriend, and two kids and their grandpa arm themselves with homemade laser guns to fight the shambling horde of corpses and their mad creator. ¶ Opening theme song: "I saw something that I shouldn't see/ Now the zombies are coming after me/ I can't escape them, the dead are everywhere/ The evil is rising, does anybody care?" • These zombies, with their bald head and skull-like features, resemble a bargain basement version of *The Abominable Dr. Phibes* (1971). • *Raiders* was shot in three weeks for $250,000. • Actress Zita Johann (heroine of *The Mummy,* 1932) came out of a 50-year retirement to play the part of a librarian in this film.

Re-Animator (1985; Empire Pictures) D: Stuart Gordon. P: Brian Yuzna. S: Dennis Paoli, William J. Norris, Stuart Gordon. C: Mac Ahlberg. Cast: Bruce Abbott, Barbara Crampton, David Gale, Robert Sampson, Jeffrey Combs, Carolyn Purdy-Gordon, Peter Kent, Gerry Black. A brilliant (and slightly deranged) young medical student named Herbert West develops a "reanimation" serum which restores life to dead bodies. Unfortunately, the reanimated bodies are wracked with pain and so become violent murdering monsters. West talks another promising medical student into helping him with his experiments until a scheming doctor attempts to steal the formula, ending in a grisly climactic free-for-all at the morgue. ¶ "I'm sorry honey, but your dead father's been lobotomized." • *Re-Animator,* hailed by fans as a modern classic of horror, was filmed on a tight 22-day shooting schedule and a low budget of $800,000. • The zombies in *Re-Animator* behave very differently from the slow, methodical walking dead in most other pictures. Director Stuart Gordon explained his version of the zombie on the 1989 British TV program, "The Incredibly Strange Film

Show": "I wanted to depart from the Romero approach, to have the zombies be like speed freaks. They were completely charged up, like they'd just gotten voltage shot through them, which is what I'd tell the actors playing the zombies—pretend like you'd just stuck your finger in a light socket, and that all of your nerves are firing and you can't stop moving." • Aside from first-time director Stuart Gordon, there was also a first-time cameraman, Robert Ebinger. Part-way through production, Ebinger was replaced by experienced cinematographer Mac Ahlberg. "Having two people as green as we were was felt not to be the best way to proceed," explained Stuart Gordon in *Fangoria* #59. "We needed to have someone on set who had experience, who could get down to what was really important, which is where Mac Ahlberg fit in." "But," added Gordon, "the footage the original cameraman shot was all used. He got a credit and his work's terrific." • *Re-Animator* was originally released to the theaters unrated. Now both the unrated and a cut R-rated version of the film can be found on video. • A sequel was made in 1990 called (what else) *Bride of Re-Animator.*

The Return of Dr. X (1939; Warner Bros.) D: Vincent Sherman. P: Bryan Foy. S: Lee Katz. C: Sid Hickox. Cast: Wayne Morris, Rosemary Lane, Humphrey Bogart, Dennis Morgan, John Litel, Lya Lys, Huntz Hall, William Hopper, Creighton Hale, Glenn Langan. Humphrey Bogart plays Caine (a.k.a. Dr. Xavier), a murdering scientist brought back to life as a pasty-faced living-dead zombie needing periodic fixes of fresh blood. ¶ "Caine will continue to kill until he's destroyed. My experiments have turned into madness. I've created a monster." • Rumor has it that Bogart was being punished by the Warner Bros. front office for refusing too many assignments, and so was placed in this "B" movie thriller. He reportedly hated the role. • Besides Humphrey Bogart (in his only horror appearance), *The Return of Dr. X* featured a variety of interesting cast members. Female lead Rosemary Lane was one of the popular "Lane Sisters." Huntz Hall (one of the "Dead End Kids"), Glenn Langan (destined to stand tall as *The Amazing Colossal Man* in 1957), William Hopper (husband of famous Hollywood gossip columnist Hedda Hopper), and George "Superman" Reeves all appear in supporting roles or bit parts.

Return of the Blind Dead (1973; Ancla Century Films; Spain) (also *Return of the Evil Dead* [video title]). D/S: Armando (de)

Ossorio. P: Ramon Plana. C: Miguel F. Mila. Cast: Tony Kendall, Fernando Sancho, Esther Ray, Frank Blake. In this first sequel to *The Blind Dead* (1972), a village celebrating the ancient massacre of the evil Knights Templar is besieged by the blind, moldering corpses of the Templars riding on ghostly horses. ¶ "What do you mean, dead people on horses?! You mean you called me in the middle of the night to tell me some stupid fairy tale?!" • Since they have no eyes, these zombies must locate their victims by sound, and this film features a nail-biting climax in which the characters must move through a courtyard filled with zombies without making a sound. Just as it looks hopeless, the first rays of the sun catch the undead Templars and they crumble into dust. • The next film in the series is titled *Horror of the Zombies* (1974).

The Return of the Zombies (see *The Hanging Woman,* this section). • The title on the film reads *The Return of the Zombis*, forgetting the "e."

Revenge of the Dead (1984; Motion Picture Marketing; Italy) (also *Zeder*). D: Pupi Avati. P: Gianni Minervini, Antonio Avati. S: Pupi Avati, Maurizio Costanzo, Antonio Avati. C: Franco Delli Colli. Cast: Gabriele Lavia, Anne Canovas, Paola Tanziani, Cesare Barbetti, Bob Tonelli, Ferdinando Orlandi. A young writer and his wife stumble upon a mystery involving a dead ex-priest and something called "K zones"—certain places where the dead can rise up and walk. When the writer's wife is killed he buries her in the K zone, only to find that she returns as an unholy, loathsome thing (in a finale lifted from Stephen King's novel, *Pet Sematary*). ¶ "There are these special areas, called "K zones," that are suspended in a time lock, and where it's possible to bring those buried there back—back from beyond."

Revenge of the Zombies (1943; Monogram) D: Steve Sekely. P: Linsley Parsons. S: Edmund Kelso, Van Norcross. C: Mack Stengler. Cast: John Carradine, Robert Lowery, Veda Ann Borg, Gale Storm, Mantan Moreland, Bob Steele. John Carradine is a mad scientist creating an army of zombies for the Nazis in the Louisiana bayous. His own zombiefied wife finally leads the walking dead in a revolt against their master. ¶ "Against an army of zombies no army could stand. Why, even blown half to bits, undaunted by fire and gas, zombies would fight on so long as the brain cells which receive and execute commands still remained intact." • Carradine helped create

zombies again a year later in *Voodoo Man* (1944; again for Monogram), though in that film he was relegated to the role of halfwit assistant (to Bela Lugosi) rather than head zombie maker. • Black actor Mantan Moreland was once again the comic relief, playing a role nearly identical to one he created two years earlier in *King of the Zombies* (1941).

Revenge of the Zombies (1981; WW Entertainment; Hong Kong) (also *Black Magic 2*). D: Ho Meng-Hua. P: Run Run Shaw. S: I Kuang. C: Tsao Hui-Chi. Cast: Ti Lung, Tanny, Lo Lien, Liu Hui-Ju, Lily Li, Lin Wei-Tu. Set in Hong Kong, a black magic sorcerer who drinks human milk to stay eternally young places spells on people and makes use of zombies he keeps in the basement. A skeptical doctor, aided by a white-magic sorcerer, must fight his horde of ugly zombies to save the doctor's fiancée from the evil magician. ¶ "I always drink human milk, and that milk keeps my body young. Margaret, I shall drink your milk every day, understand?" • In a bizarre twist, the sorcerer animates his zombies by driving a spike into the top of their heads. When the spike is removed, the zombies either become inanimate or simply dissolve into goo.

Revolt of the Zombies (1936; Academy) D: Victor Halperin. P: Edward Halperin. S: Howard Higgins, Rollo Lloyd, Victor Halperin. C: J. Arthur Feindel. Cast: Dorothy Stone, Dean Jagger, Roy D'Arcy, Robert Noland, George Cleveland. A very young Dean Jagger plays a member of an expedition searching for a Tibetan formula that can create zombies. He finds it, but decides to use it to further his own selfish ends in a romantic triangle. • These particular "zombies" are not reanimated corpses, but simply living people placed under the hypnotic will of the "zombie-maker." At the film's end, Jagger finally realizes that what he has done is wrong and releases his hypnotic hold on the zombies, whereupon they return to normal and promptly shoot him. • This was the Halperin brothers' follow-up zombie movie to their earlier hit, *White Zombie* (1932)—Hollywood's *first* zombie film. *Revolt of the Zombies* was nowhere near their original effort in terms of either artistic or financial success, however. • For effect, the Halperins included shots of Bela Lugosi's eyes from *White Zombie,* even though the actor does not appear in the present film.

Scarecrows (1988) (see DEMONS AND DEVILS). A paramilitary unit steals three and a half million dollars from a military base. They hijack a plane and land near a remote abandoned farm. There they are killed off one by one by three hideous demon-scarecrows. Some of the victims are transformed into murderous zombies and attack their comrades.

Scared Stiff (1953) (see GHOSTS). Jerry Lewis and Dean Martin remade the Bob Hope vehicle *The Ghost Breakers* (1940) about a haunted castle in Cuba which just happens to include a zombie guard. • The rather normal-looking zombie in this version is nowhere near as impressive as the menacing Noble Johnson was in *The Ghost Breakers*.

The Serpent and the Rainbow (1988) (see VOODOO). A young investigator goes to Haiti to try and establish the existence of, and find the answer to, zombies. There he encounters a voodoo sorcerer who uses a special "zombie powder" in combination with voodoo magic to steal the souls of his victims and control their bodies. • The zombies in this film are not dead people brought back to a semblance of life by magic as in most zombie movies, they are living human beings who are made to appear dead and then resurrected by a powder. Voodoo magic does, however, allow the zombie master to control them.

Shanks (1974; Paramount) D: William Castle. P: Steven North. S: Ronald Graham. C: Joseph Biroc. Cast: Marcel Marceau, Tsilla Chelton, Philippe Clay, Cindy Eilbacher, Larry Bishop, Don Calfa, Giff Manard. A deaf-mute puppeteer works for a scientist who discovers how to reanimate dead animals with electricity. When the scientist dies, the puppeteer finds the process works with human cadavers as well. He revives various corpses to take revenge upon those who have wronged him. • Famous French mime Marcel Marceau plays the dual role of puppeteer and scientist. • The film's musical score by composer Alex North (who incidentally is the father of producer Steven North) was nominated for an Oscar. • This is the last film directed by William Castle (the "King of the Gimmicks" in the 1950s and 60s—*House on Haunted Hill*, 1958; *The Tingler*, 1959; *Homicidal*, 1961; etc.).

Shock Waves (1977; Cinema Shares) (also *Death Corps*). D: Ken Wiederhorn. P/C: Reuben Trane. S: John Harrison, Ken Wiederhorn. Cast: Peter Cushing, John Carradine, Brooke Adams, Fed Buch, Jack Davidson, Luke Halpin. A group of shipwrecked tourists wind up on a Caribbean island inhabited by Nazi zombies who live underwater, the result of a Nazi experiment implemented towards the end of World War II to create a zombie "Death Corps." ¶ "We called them "Der Toten Korps," the Death Corps, creatures more horrible than any you can imagine. Not dead, and not alive, but somewhere in between." • The only way to defeat these zombies is to remove their dark, protective eye goggles. • Alan Ormsby provided the zombie makeup, just as he did for *Children Shouldn't Play with Dead Things* and *Deathdream* (both 1972).

Sugar Hill (1974; AIP) (also *Zombies of Sugar Hill; Voodoo Girl*). D: Paul Maslansky. P: Elliot Schick. S: Tim Kelley, Alvin Kazak, Maurice Jules. C: Bob Jessup. Cast: Marki Bey, Robert Quarry, Don Pedro Colley, Richard Lawson, Betty Ann Rees. Sugar Hill goes to a voodoo priest seeking vengeance against the white racketeers who killed her boyfriend. The witch doctor creates a horde of zombies which he sends out to dispatch the guilty parties. ¶ "The mob didn't expect Sugar Hill and her zombie hit men"—ad line.

The Supernaturals (1987; Republic Entertainment International) D: Armand Mastroianni. P/S: Michael S. Murphey, Joel Soisson. C: Peter Collister. Cast: Maxwell Caulfield, Nichelle Nichols, Talia Balsam, Bradford Bancroft, LeVar Burton, Bobby Di Cicco, Margaret Shendal, Patrick Davis. A platoon of new Army recruits on a survival mission in the backwoods of Alabama begin dying mysteriously one by one. Finally it is revealed that they are being killed by the walking dead zombies of murdered confederate soldiers. • Director Armand Mastroianni (cousin of European superstar Marcello Mastroianni) commented on the film's chaotic production in a *Fangoria* interview: "They basically built a film around the *poster* design that everybody seemed to like. During filming, new pages of the script would be driven to the set daily, often moments before that scene was to be shot." • The tough-talking platoon leader is played by Nichelle Nichols, best known as "Lt. Uhura" from the *Star Trek* television series and films.

Tales from the Crypt (1972) (see ANTHOLOGIES). Three stories from this anthology film feature the walking dead. In the first, "Reflection of Death," an unfaithful husband is in a serious car wreck but is somehow able to make it back to his house, only to find it is two years later and he is actually a dying cadaver. The second tale has Peter Cushing rise from his grave to administer some "Poetic Justice" (the story's title); and the third is a variation on "The Monkey's Paw."

Teenage Zombies (1960; Governor) D/P: Jerry Warren. S: Jacques Lecotier. C: Allen Chandler. Cast: Don Sullivan, Katherine Victor, Steve Conte, J. L. D. Morrison, Bri Murphy, Paul Pepper, Mitzi Alpertson, Jay Hawk, Mike Concannon, Nan Green, Don Neeley. Four water-skiing teenagers are taken captive on a deserted island by a mad scientist and her zombie assistant. The female mad doctor has discovered a gas which turns people into mindless zombies who are easy to control, and she plans to use the teenagers as demonstration subjects for some foreign agents interested in her discovery. • Shot in 1957, this abysmal no-budget feature from filmmaker Jerry Warren (who is usually satisfied with buying bad foreign films and adding scenes in order to make a "new" feature) was not released until 1960. • Teen hero Don Sullivan played another teen hero in *The Giant Gila Monster* (1959).

Terror Creatures from the Grave (1965; Pacemaker; Italy) D: Ralph Zuker (Massimo Pupillo). P: Frank Merle. S: Roberto Natale, Romano Migliorini. C: Charles Brown (Carlo Di Palma). Cast: Barbara Steele, Walter Brandt, Marilyn Mitchell, Alfred Rice, Richard Garret. Set in Europe at the turn of the century, Barbara Steele plays a woman who has her huband murdered. Her husband, an expert in the occult, summons a horde of zombies from beyond the grave to avenge his death. • The zombies here are supposedly the bodies of plague victims. They are finally destroyed by ordinary rainwater—when the rain hits them they disintegrate. • This rather striking film was Massimo Pupillo's directorial debut. He also directed the sadistic (and silly) *Bloody Pit of Horror* later this same year.

Valley of the Zombies (1946) (see VAMPIRES—OTHER VAMPIRES). Ian Keith plays a man who returns from the dead as a type of vampire needing fresh human blood. He exhibits more vampiric tendencies than those of the typical zombie (title notwithstanding).

Vengeance of the Zombies (1972; Profilmes/Promofilms; Spain/Portugal) (also *Revolt of the Dead Ones; Walk of the Dead*). D: Leon Klimowsky. P: José Antonio Perez Giner. S: Jacinto Molina. C: Francisco Sanchez. Cast: Paul Naschy, Vic Winner, Romy, Mirta Miller, Maria Kosti, Aurora de Alba, Antonio Pica. A woman plagued by a violent family curse turns to a Krishna-like cult for help, only to find that an army of zombies, controlled by the cult leader's brother, is responsible for the violent deaths attributed to the curse. •

Scriptwriter Jacinto Molina is actually star Paul Naschy writing under his real name (something he did often for his films).

The Video Dead (1987; Manson International) D/P/S: Robert Scott. C: Greg Becker. Cast: Roxanna Augeson, Rocky Duvall, Vicky Bastel, Sam David McClelland, Michael St. Michaels, Jennifer Miro, Thaddeus Gogas, Cliff Watts, Al Millan, Patrick Treadway. An evil television set has the ability to turn itself on and run a film called *Zombie Blood Nightmare*. The zombies in the film break forth from the TV set and go on a bloody rampage. ¶ "When a living person shows fear, it all comes home again that they're different. All they wanna do is kill the only thing they can never be—the living." • The Video Dead can be trapped by mirrors since "the dead can't stand to look at themselves."

The Vineyard (1989) (see WITCHES, WARLOCKS, AND CULTS). An Asian sorcerer lures some unsuspecting young people to his island home, intending to sacrifice them to his black magic. He also keeps a horde of killer zombies on hand, though he occasionally has difficulty controlling them.

Voodoo Island (1957) (see VOODOO). Boris Karloff plays a professional skeptic who ventures to the title island only to have his personal opinions on voodoo and magic drastically changed. At one point, a member of his expedition is turned into a staring, catatonic zombie.

Voodoo Man (1944) (see VOODOO). Dr. Marlowe (Bela Lugosi) is searching for a cure for his zombie wife. He uses voodoo to try and transfer the life force from living women into his undead wife, with little success—the basement is full of zombie failures. • These zombie girls snap back to normal once Marlowe is killed at film's end. But his wife is a true zombie, and remains dead.

The Walking Dead (1936; Warner Bros.) D: Michael Curtiz. P: Lou Edelman. S: Ewart Adamson, Peter Milne, Robert Andrews, Lillie Hayward. C: Hal Mohr. Cast: Boris Karloff, Ricardo Cortez, Edmund Gwenn, Marguerite Churchill, Warren Hull, Barton MacLane, Henry O'Neill, Joseph King, Addison Richards, Paul Harvey, Robert Strange, Joseph Sawyer. Boris Karloff plays an ex-con framed by a group of racketeers for a murder he did not commit. He is executed but brought back to life by a kindly doctor using a new experimental technique. Karloff is in a zombie-like state most of the time, but occasionally he seems to gain a power and knowledge not granted

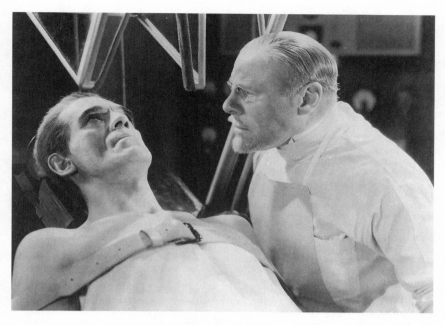

Edmund Gwenn (right) wonders what knowledge his zombie subject (Boris Karloff) brought back with him from beyond the veil of death in Michael Curtiz's The Walking Dead *(1936).*

to the living, and proceeds to confront the guilty parties, leading them to their own deaths. ¶ "Leave the dead to Our Maker. The Lord our God is a jealous god." • Director Michael Curtiz made over 100 films for Warner Bros., including *Mystery of the Wax Museum* (1933) and the highly acclaimed classic, *Casablanca* (1942; for which he won an Oscar).

War of the Zombies (1963; AIP; Italy) (also *Night Star, Goddess of Electra*). D: Giuseppe Vari. P: Ferrucio De Martino, Massimo De Rita. S: Piero Pierotti, Marcello Sartarelli. C: Gabor Pogany. Cast: John Drew Barrymore, Susy Andersen, Ettore Manni, Ida Galli, Mino Doro, Philippe Hersent, Matilde Calnan. Set in the time of the Roman Empire, John Barrymore plays a sorcerer who (with the aid of a mysterious goddess) revives the corpses of Roman soldiers to create an army of zombies to use against the power of Rome. ¶ "The Goddess will lead and protect us, will resurrect our dead enemies from the earth, transform them into mute and invincible allies." • In the end, the hero stabs the eye of the god-

dess's giant idol which blinds the sorcerer and causes the army of corpses to vanish. • Star John Drew Barrymore is the son of famed actor John Barrymore, of *Dr. Jekyll and Mr. Hyde* (1920) fame.

White Zombie (1932; Amusement Securities/United Artists) D: Victor Halperin. P: Edward Halperin. S: Garnett Weston. C: Arthur Martinelli. Cast: Bela Lugosi, Madge Bellamy, Joseph Cawthorne, Robert Frazer, John Harron, Clarence Muse, Brandon Hurst, Dan Crimmins, John Peters, George Burr McAnnan. Bela Lugosi plays Murder Legendre, a Haitian voodoo sorcerer who uses zombies to work in his sugar mill. A young couple becomes embroiled in his evil magic, and the woman is transformed into the "white zombie" of the title. ¶ "They are dead bodies—zombies, the living dead, corpses taken from their graves who are made to work in sugar mills and the fields at night." • *White Zombie* is the very first zombie film, and is now regarded by many as a minor classic. The Halperin brothers tried to repeat their success and returned to the zombie theme in 1936 with *Revolt of the*

Zombies, but it turned out to be vastly inferior to this first effort. • Makeup wizard Jack Pierce was borrowed from Universal to create the zombie faces, as well as Lugosi's diabolical countenance. • Lugosi played the part for a flat fee of $800. The film scored eight million at the box office. • The picture is based on the William Seabrook book, *The Magic Island.*

Zombie Brigade (1988; Smart Egg Cinema; Australia) D/P/S: Carmelo Musca, Barrie Pattison. C: Alex McPhee. Cast: John Moore, Khym Lam, Geoff Gibbs, Leslie Wright, Bob Faggetter, Adam A. Wong. When the greedy mayor of a small Australian Outback town tries to convince Japanese investors to build a "Robotman" theme park near their town, he has the local Vietnam Veterans monument blown up (it was in the way). That night, a horde of zombie soldiers crawl up out of the rubble and go on a rampage through the town, killing and drinking the blood of everyone they can get their undead hands on. Finally, the local aboriginal witch doctor uses tribal magic to call up the spirits of the town's World War II veterans to do battle with the Vietnam zombie soldiers. ¶ "Dead fellas come outta that cemetery thing, fellas that was killed in the war come back again." • It turns out the zombie soldiers were the result of a contagion released by the Vietcong—a combination of bacteriological warfare and folklore magic. The government, not knowing what to do with their now-uncontrollable soldiers, had them sealed up in a concrete bunker hidden under the memorial monument. • These zombies exhibit a lot of vampiric qualities. They shun the sun, they drink blood, and they even sport fangs. However, crosses do not have any effect, as the local priest discovers . . . a bit too late.

Zombie High (1987; Cinema Group) D: Ron Link. P: Marc Toberoff, Aziz Ghazal. S: Tim Doyle, Elizabeth Passerelli, Aziz Ghazal. C: David Lux, Brian Coyne. Cast: Virginia Madsen, Richard Cox, Kay Kuter, James Wilder, Sherilynn Fenn, Paul Feig, T. Scott Coffey, Paul Williams, Henry Sutton, Clare Carey. The teachers at an exclusive prep school are lobotomizing the students and replacing their missing brain tissue with a special quartz crystal that is activated by the classical music being pumped through the school, allowing the teachers to easily control the zombiefied students.

Zombie Lake (1980; Eurocine; Spain/France) (also *Lake of the Living Dead*). D: J. A. Lazer (Jean Rollin). P: Daniel Lasoeur. S: A. L. Mariaux. C: Max Mon-

teillet. Cast: Howard Vernon, Robert Foster, Pierre Escourrou, Marcia Sharif, Anouchka, Nadine Pascal, Julian Atienza. Dead soldiers from a Nazi platoon, drowned by villagers in World War II, rise up from the lake and attack the locals. Finally, the villagers trap the Nazi zombies in a barn and set it on fire. • Prolific Spanish director Jesus Franco was scheduled to direct this picture, but French producer Daniel Lasoeur handed it over to his fellow countryman, Jean Rollin, at the last minute. Franco told this version of the story in a *Fangoria* #90 interview: "*Zombie Lake* was offered to me, but it was too small. It was impossible to do anything different. I had accepted the idea and had worked on the film awhile. I wanted to shoot in a valley in Switzerland with a fantastic lake. It was perfect. But they told me it was too far, too expensive. Everything was going down and down and down. I said, 'I won't do it.'"

Zombie Nightmare (1987; Gold-Gems) D: John Bravman. P: Pierre Grise. S: David Wellington. C: Robert Racine. Cast: Adam West, Jon-Mikl Thor, Tia Carrere, Manuska Rigaud, Frank Dietz, Linda Singer, Francesca Bonacorsa, Linda Smith, John Fasano. A man is killed in a hit-and-run accident. The man's widow has a mysterious Haitian woman perform a voodoo rite to bring his body back to life. She uses her zombie husband to take vengeance on those who had gang-raped her years before. Since she was raped by members of a baseball team, the zombie beats them to death with a baseball bat.

Zombies of Mora Tau (1957; Columbia) D: Edward L. Cahn. P: Sam Katzman. S: Raymond T. Marcus. C: Benjamin H. Kline. Cast: Gregg Palmer, Allison Hayes, Autumn Russell, Joel Ashley, Morris Ankrum, Gene Roth. On the island of Mora Tau off the African coast, a group of fortune hunters searching for a treasure of diamonds run afoul of the zombies guarding it. The zombies are the walking corpses of the pirates who brought the treasure to the island and then died there. ¶ "They're dead. They have no morality!" • Producer Sam Katzman had dealt with zombies 13 years earlier when he produced *Voodoo Man* in 1944.

Zombies on Broadway (1945; RKO) D: Gordon Douglas. P: Ben Stoloff. S: Lawrence Kimble. C: Jack MacKenzie. Cast: Bela Lugosi, Wally Brown, Alan Carney, Anne Jeffreys, Sheldon Leonard, Darby Jones, Sir Lancelot. In the screen's first zombie comedy, the team of Brown and

Carney play bumbling publicity agents who travel to the Caribbean in search of a real zombie to be used in the opening of a new nightclub. They find Dr. Renault, who can create zombies with a special injection, and end up as their own attraction. • The ex-vaudeville team of Wally Brown and Alan Carney were groomed by RKO as an answer to Abbott and Costello. Though they made eight films, they never came close to the popularity of their rivals. • As Dr. Renault, this was Lugosi's third turn at zombie-maker (the first two being *White Zombie,* 1932, and *Voodoo Man,* 1944; not to mention becoming a zombie *victim* in *Bowery at Midnight,* 1942). • Darby Jones reprises his role as a cadaverous zombie from *I Walked with a Zombie* (1943); and Sir Lancelot sings calypso just as he did in that earlier zombie classic.

Appendix A: Blaxploitation

"Blaxploitation" refers to those films which feature an all-black or mostly-black cast and are aimed at black audiences. Below is a listing of horror, science fiction, and fantasy films that fall into this category.

Abby (1974)
Blackenstein (1973) (also *Black Frankenstein*)
Blacula (1972)
Def by Temptation (1990)
Dr. Black and Mr. Hyde (1975)
Drums 'o' Voodoo (1934) (also *Louisiana*)
Ganja and Hess (1973) (also *Blood Couple; Double Possession*)
J. D.'s Revenge (1976)
Pocomania (1939) (also *The Devil's Daughter*)
Scream Blacula Scream (1973)
Son of Ingagi (1940)
Sugar Hill (1974) (also *Zombies of Sugar Hill; Voodoo Girl*)
The Thing with Two Heads (1972)
Voodoo Black Exorcist (1975)

Appendix B: 3-D

The following films were released to theaters at one time or another in a 3-D format.

Amityville 3-D (1983)
Andy Warhol's Frankenstein (1974)
A*P*E (1976)
Cat Women of the Moon (1953)
Creature from the Black Lagoon (1954)
Friday the 13th Part 3 (1982)
Gog (1954)
Gorilla at Large (1954)
House of Wax (1953)
Hyperspace (1987)
It Came from Outer Space (1953)
Jaws 3-D (1983)
The Mad Magician (1954)
The Mark of the Wolfman (1968) (3-D in Europe only; it was released flat in the United States) (also *Frankenstein's Bloody Terror*)
The Mask (1961)
The Maze (1953)
Metalstorm: The Destruction of Jared-Syn (1983)
Phantom of the Rue Morgue (1954)
Parasite (1982)
Revenge of the Creature (1955)
Robot Monster (1953)
Space Hunter: Adventures in the Forbidden Zone (1983)

Appendix C: Westerns

The following films are set (at least in part) in the Old West.

Back to the Future Part 3 (1990)
Billy the Kid vs. Dracula (1966)
Curse of the Undead (1959)
Devil Wolf of Shadow Mountain (1964)
The Devil's Mistress (1966)
Ghost Town (1988)
Jesse James Meets Frankenstein's Daughter (1965)
The Seven Faces of Dr. Lao (1964)
Teenage Monster (1957) (also *Meteor Monster*)
Westworld (1973) (predominantly set at an amusement park *reproduction* of the
  Old West)

Title Index

The page number of the film's main entry is listed first, followed by secondary locations. Numbers in **boldface** refer to pages with photographs.

Nineteen hundred and eight of these titles have a numerical rating in brackets following their year. Each film is critically rated on a scale of 1 to 10 with 10 being the highest. A few select zeros were awarded those films we feel lack any redeeming qualities whatsoever.

A

Abbott and Costello Go to Mars (1953 [3]) 564; 29, 403
Abbott and Costello Meet Dr. Jekyll and Mr. Hyde (1953 [4]) 320; 459
Abbott and Costello Meet Frankenstein (1948 [7]) 525; 210, 106, 303, 574, 579
Abbott and Costello Meet the Invisible Man (1951 [4]) 303
Abbott and Costello Meet the Killer, Boris Karloff (1949 [3]) 297
Abbott and Costello Meet the Mummy (1955 [2]) 413
Abby (1974) 158
The Abominable Dr. Phibes (1971 [7]) 361; 88, 121, 459
The Abominable Snowman see The Abominable Snowman of the Himalayas
The Abominable Snowman of the Himalayas (1957 [7]) 173
The Abyss (1989 [8])42; 477
Adventure to the Center of the Earth (1965) 521
The Adventures of Buck-

aroo Banzai Across the Eighth Dimension (1984 [5]) 23
Adventures of Sinbad (1962) 488
Aelita (1924) 403; 29
Aelita: The Revolt of the Robots see Aelita
Aerobi-cide see Killer Workout
After Midnight (1989 [2]) 381; 58, 189
After the Fall of New York (1984) 239
Against All Odds see Kiss and Kill
The Airship (1917) 403; 29
Aladdin (1986 [0]) 257
Aladdin and His Lamp (1951) 257
The Alchemist (1981 [2]) 594; 158
Alice, Sweet Alice (1976) 362
Alien (1979 [9]) 29; 466
Alien Contamination (1981 [3]) 23; 403
Alien Dead (1979 [1]) 616; 17
Alien Encounter see Starship Invasions
The Alien Factor (1979) 18
Alien from L.A. (1988 [2]) 83; 23, 521
Alien High (1987 [2]) 23
Alien Nation (1988 [6]) 42, **43**

Alien Predator (1987 [2]) 23
Alien Seed (1989) 24
Alien Terror see The Incredible Invasion
Alien Warrior (1985) 24
Alien Women see Zeta One
Aliens (1986 [7]) 29; 466
Allan Quatermain and the Lost City of Gold (1987 [3]) 521
Alligator (1981 [5]) 53; 55
The Alligator People (1959 [4]) 54; **53**
Alone in the Dark (1982) 382
Alphaville (1965 [6]) 153
Altered States (1980 [6]) 142
Alucarda (1975) 595
The Amazing Colossal Man (1957 [5]) 291; **292**
The Amazing Transparent Man (1960 [1]) 303
Amazon Women on the Moon (1987) 3
Amazons (1987) 503
America 3000 (1986) 239
American Gothic (1988 [3]) 382
An American Werewolf in London (1981 [6]) 583
The Amityville Horror (1979 [4]) 158
Amityville 4: The Evil Escapes (1989) 159

649